ISBELL SCHOOL

PRENTICE HALL
LITERATURE

BRONZE

Annotated Teacher's Edition
Teaching Portfolio
Novel Study Guides

SILVER

Annotated Teacher's Edition
Teaching Portfolio
Novel Study Guides

GOLD

Annotated Teacher's Edition
Teaching Portfolio
Novel Study Guides

PLATINUM

Annotated Teacher's Edition
Teaching Portfolio
Novel Study Guides

THE AMERICAN EXPERIENCE

Annotated Teacher's Edition
Teaching Portfolio
Novel Study Guides

THE ENGLISH TRADITION

Annotated Teacher's Edition
Teaching Portfolio
Novel Study Guides

PRENTICE HALL
LITERATURE
BRONZE

PRENTICE HALL, Englewood Cliffs, New Jersey 07632

ISBN 0-13-698499-1

10 9 8 7 6 5 4

Art credits begin on page 881.

COVER AND TITLE PAGE: RAINY DAY, 1906, Frank Weston Benson, The Art Institute of Chicago

PRENTICE HALL
A Division of Simon & Schuster
Englewood Cliffs, New Jersey 07632

ACKNOWLEDGMENTS

Grateful acknowledgment is made to the following for permission to reprint copyrighted material:

Teresa Palomo Acosta
"My Mother Pieced Quilts" by Teresa Palomo Acosta.

T.D. Allen
"Grandfather" by Shirley Crawford. Copyright 1970. Used by permission of T. D. Allen.

Isaac Asimov
"Hallucination" by Isaac Asimov, published in *Boy's Life*. Copyright © 1985 by the Boy Scouts of America.

Atheneum Publishers, an imprint of Macmillan Publishing Co.
"Construction" copyright © 1965 by Patricia Hubbell, from *8 A.M. Shadows*. Andrew A. Rooney, "Letter Writing" from *And More By Andy Rooney*. Copyright © 1982 Essay Productions, Inc. Reprinted with the permission of Atheneum Publishers, an imprint of Macmillan Publishing Co.

Elizabeth Barnett, Literary Executor of the Estate of Norma Millay Ellis
"The Courage That My Mother Had" by Edna St. Vincent Millay. From *Collected Poems*, Harper & Row. Copyright © 1954 by Norma Millay Ellis. Reprinted by permission.

Gwendolyn Brooks
"Home" and "Pete at the Zoo" from *The World of Gwendolyn Brooks*, Harper & Row. Reprinted by permission of the author.

Clarion Books/Ticknor & Fields, a Houghton Mifflin Company, and The Bodley Head, Ltd.
"The Pointing Finger" from *Sweet and Sour: Tales from China* by Carol Kendall and Yao-wen Li. Copyright © 1980 by Carol Kendall and Yao-wen Li. Reprinted by permission.

Don Congdon Associates, Inc.
"All Summer in a Day" by Ray Bradbury. Copyright © 1954 by Ray Bradbury; renewed 1982 by Ray Bradbury. "The Third Level" by Jack Finney. Copyright © 1950 by *Collier's*; renewed 1977 by Jack Finney. Reprinted by permission of Don Congdon Associates, Inc.

Congdon & Weed, Inc.
"No Gumption" from *Growing Up* by Russell Baker. Copyright © 1982 by Russell Baker. Reprinted by permission of Congdon & Weed, Inc.

Harold Courlander
"All Stories are Anansi's" from *The Hat-Shaking Dance and Other Ashanti Tales from Ghana* by Harold Courlander with Albert Kofi Prempeh, Harcourt Brace Jovanovich, Inc. Copyright © 1957, 1985 by Harold Courlander.

Current History, Inc.
"A puppy whose hair was so flowing" by Oliver Herford. From *The Century Magazine*, copyright 1912. Reprinted by permission of Current History, Inc.

The Curtis Publishing Company
"Luke Baldwin's Vow" by Morley Callaghan. Reprinted from *The Saturday Evening Post*, copyright 1947, The Curtis Publishing Company.

(continued of page 878)

CONTENTS

SHORT STORIES

DRAMA

NONFICTION

POETRY

vii

PUTTING IT TOGETHER 530

MODEL

FOCUS ON READING: Making Inferences 534
YOU THE WRITER 536
YOU THE CRITIC 537

FABLES, MYTHS, AND LEGENDS

READING ACTIVELY 540

THE NOVEL

PRENTICE HALL
LITERATURE
BRONZE

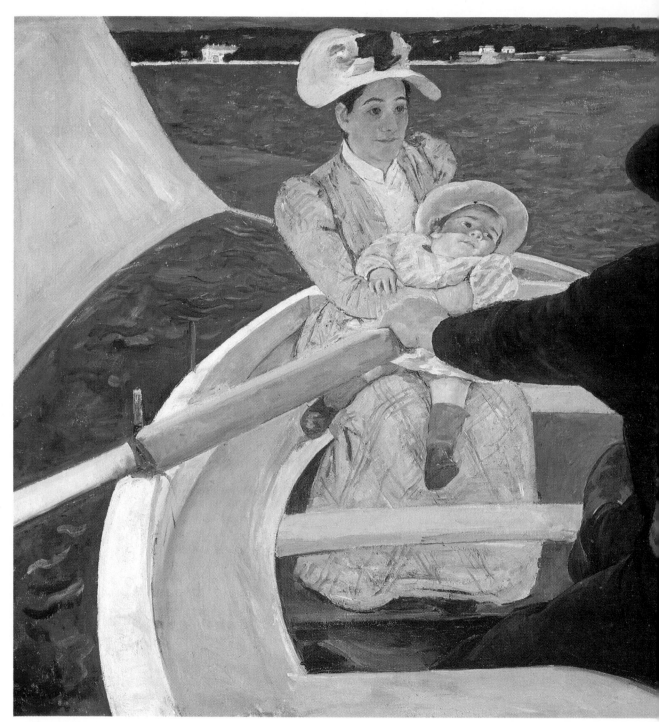

THE BOATING PARTY
Mary Cassatt
The National Gallery of Art, Washington

SHORT STORIES

One of the best loved forms of literature is the short story. It is a brief work of fiction containing made-up characters and events. Because short stories are brief, they do not take long to read. Usually you can start and finish one in a single sitting. Short stories are fun to read, presenting us with an endless variety of characters, places, and situations. In addition, they often reveal truths about life and so deepen our understanding of the human condition.

The basic meaning of the word *fiction* is "anything made up." Because short stories are made up from a writer's imagination, they are not just reports of events that actually happened. However, they are "made up" in another sense, too. They are put together from several basic elements: plot, characters, setting, and theme. The plot is the sequence of events in the story. The characters are, of course, the people, or sometimes the animals, that take part in the events. The setting is the time and place of the story. The theme is the central idea or insight into life that is revealed through the events of the story.

You will be learning more about these elements as you read the stories in this unit. As your understanding of these elements grows, so will the pleasure you gain from reading good fiction.

The Short Story

To read a short story successfully, you must become actively involved. You do this by thinking about the story as you read. In other words, you bring ideas to mind by stopping to ask questions and to predict what will happen. You occasionally pause to answer your questions and check your predictions and to summarize what has happened so far.

Use the following strategies to help you read actively. These strategies will help you "figure out" what is important in a story and what makes the story effective.

Question

Before you begin, think about what you expect to happen in the story. What does the title suggest to you? As you read, you might ask yourself questions about what is happening. What causes the events to occur as they do? What are the characters like? Is the setting, or place of the story, important? Why does the author include certain information? Then look for the answers to your questions as you read on.

Predict

Bring your own experience to the story. Consider what you already know about similar situations or people in your own life. Use your knowledge of how stories work. Then try to predict what will happen based on what you already know. As you read on, you will find out if your predictions are correct.

Clarify

When something in the story is not clear or does not seem to make sense, stop and try to clarify the confusion. Look for the answers to your questions, and check your predictions. By continually clarifying in these ways, you will be able to get meaning from a story.

Summarize

Occasionally pause to review what has happened so far. Identify what seems important, and try to determine how that piece of information works with everything else in terms of how the story is developing.

Pull It Together

Try to determine the central idea or point of the story. What did the story say to you? How do you feel about the story?

Using these strategies will help you to be a more effective reader. You will better be able to recall details from the story, interpret what you have read to find meaning, and apply this meaning to your world.

On the following pages is a model of how an active reader might read a story.

The Third Wish

Joan Aiken

Questions: Will this story be about three wishes? Why does the title mention only the third wish?

Once there was a man who was driving in his car at dusk on a spring evening through part of the forest of Savernake. His name was Mr. Peters. The primroses were just beginning but the trees were still bare, and it was cold; the birds had stopped singing an hour ago.

As Mr. Peters entered a straight, empty stretch of road he seemed to hear a faint crying, and a struggling and thrashing, as if somebody was in trouble far away in the trees. He left his car and climbed the mossy bank beside the road. Beyond the bank was an open slope of beech trees leading down to thorn bushes through which he saw the gleam of water. He stood a moment waiting to try and discover where the noise was coming from, and presently heard a rustling and some strange cries in a voice which was almost human—and yet there was something too hoarse about it at one time and too clear and sweet at another. Mr. Peters ran down the hill and as he neared the bushes he saw something white among them which was trying to extricate itself: coming closer he found that it was a swan that had become entangled in the thorns growing on the bank of the canal.

Question: Who is in trouble?

Prediction: Mr. Peters will help this person.

Clarification: The thing in trouble is not a person but a swan.

The bird struggled all the more frantically as he approached, looking at him with hate in its yellow eyes, and when he took hold of it to free it, it hissed at him, pecked him, and thrashed dangerously with its wings which were powerful enough to break his arm. Nevertheless he managed to release it from the thorns, and carrying it tightly with one arm, holding the snaky head well away with the other hand (for he did not wish his eyes pecked out), he took it to the verge of the canal and dropped it in.

Clarification: Mr. Peters does help this creature.

The swan instantly assumed great dignity and sailed out to the middle of the water, where it put itself to rights with much dabbling and preening, smoothing its feathers with little showers of drops. Mr. Peters waited, to make sure that it was all right and had suffered no damage in its struggles. Presently the swan, when it was satisfied with its appearance, floated in to the bank once more, and in a moment, instead of the great white bird, there was a little man all in green with a golden crown and long beard, standing by the water. He had fierce glittering eyes and looked by no means friendly.

"Well, Sir," he said threateningly, "I see you are presumptuous enough to know some of the laws of magic. You think that because you have rescued—by pure good fortune—the King of the Forest from a difficulty, you should have some fabulous reward."

Clarification: So this story *is* about three wishes.

"I expect three wishes, no more and no less," answered Mr. Peters, looking at him steadily and with composure.

"Three wishes, he wants, the clever man! Well, I have yet to hear of the human being who made any good use of his three wishes—they mostly end up worse off than they started. Take your three wishes then"—he flung three dead leaves in the air—"don't blame me if you spend the last wish in undoing the work of the other two."

Summary: Mr. Peters saves the King of the Forest from a difficulty and is granted three wishes.

Mr. Peters caught the leaves and put two of them carefully in his briefcase. When he looked up, the swan was sailing about in the middle of the water again, flicking the drops angrily down its long neck.

Question: How will Mr. Peters use his three wishes?

Mr. Peters stood for some minutes reflecting on how he should use his reward. He knew very well that the gift of three magic wishes was one which brought trouble more often than not, and he had no intention of being like the forester who first wished by mistake for a sausage, and then in a rage wished it on the end of his wife's nose, and then had to use his last wish in getting it off again. Mr. Peters had most of the things which he wanted and was very content with his life. The only thing that troubled him was that he was a little lonely, and had no companion for his old age. He decided to use his first wish and to keep the other two in case of an emergency. Taking a thorn he pricked his tongue with it, to remind himself not to utter rash wishes aloud.

Prediction: Mr. Peters seems a practical person. Perhaps he will not regret his wishes.

Then holding the third leaf and gazing round him at the dusky undergrowth, the primroses, great beeches and the blue-green water of the canal, he said:

Question: What happens to the leaf after he makes his wish?

"I wish I had a wife as beautiful as the forest."

A tremendous quacking and splashing broke out on the surface of the water. He thought that it was the swan laughing at him. Taking no notice he made his way through the darkening woods to his car, wrapped himself up in the rug and went to sleep.

BOUQUET WITH FLYING LOVERS, c. 1934–47
Marc Chagall
The Tate Gallery

When he awoke it was morning and the birds were beginning to call. Coming along the track towards him was the most beautiful creature he had ever seen, with eyes as blue-green as the canal, hair as dusky as the bushes, and skin as white as the feathers of swans.

"Are you the wife that I wished for?" asked Mr. Peters.

"Yes, I am," she replied. "My name is Leita."

She stepped into the car beside him and they drove off to the church on the outskirts of the forest, where they were married. Then he took her to his house in a remote and lovely valley and showed her all his treasures—the bees in their white hives, the Jersey cows, the hyacinths, the silver candlesticks, the blue cups and the luster bowl for putting primroses in. She admired everything, but what pleased her most was the river which ran by the foot of his garden.

"Do swans come up there?" she asked.

"Yes, I have often seen swans there on the river," he told her, and she smiled.

Leita made him a good wife. But as time went by Mr. Peters began to feel that she was not happy. She seemed restless, wandered much in the garden, and sometimes when he came back from the fields he would find the house empty and she would only return after half an hour or so with no explanation of where she had been. On these occasions she was always especially tender and would put out his slippers to warm and cook his favorite dish—Welsh rarebit[1] with wild strawberries—for supper.

One evening he was returning home along the river path when he saw Leita in front of him, down by the water. A swan had sailed up to the verge and she had her arms round its neck and the swan's head rested against her cheek. She was weeping, and as he came nearer he saw that tears were rolling, too, from the swan's eyes.

"Leita, what is it?" he asked, very troubled.

"This is my sister," she answered. "I can't bear being separated from her."

Now he understood that Leita was really a swan from the forest, and this made him very sad because when a human being marries a bird it always leads to sorrow.

---

1. Welsh rarebit: A dish of melted cheese served on crackers or toast.

Questions: Who is she? Where does she come from?

Question: Why is she so interested in swans?

Question: Where does she go?

Question: Who is this swan? Why is Leita weeping?

Clarification: Leita is really a swan, and this swan is her sister. So this is how the King of the Forest grants his wishes.

"I could use my second wish to give your sister human shape, so that she could be a companion to you," he suggested.

"No, no," she cried, "I couldn't ask that of her."

"Is it so very hard to be a human being?" asked Mr. Peters sadly.

"Very, very hard," she answered.

"Don't you love me at all, Leita?"

"Yes, I do, I do love you," she said, and there were tears in her eyes again. "But I missed the old life in the forest, the cool grass and the mist rising off the river at sunrise and the feel of the water sliding over my feathers as my sister and I drifted along the stream."

"Then shall I use my second wish to turn you back into a swan again?" he asked, and his tongue pricked to remind him of the old King's words, and his heart swelled with grief inside him.

"Who will take care of you?"

"I'd do it myself as I did before I married you," he said, trying to sound cheerful.

She shook her head. "No, I could not be as unkind to you as that. I am partly a swan, but I am also partly a human being now. I will stay with you."

Poor Mr. Peters was very distressed on his wife's account and did his best to make her life happier, taking her for drives in the car, finding beautiful music for her to listen to on the radio, buying clothes for her and even suggesting a trip round the world. But she said no to that; she would prefer to stay in their own house near the river.

He noticed that she spent more and more time baking wonderful cakes—jam puffs, petits fours, eclairs and meringues. One day he saw her take a basketful down to the river and he guessed that she was giving them to her sister.

He built a seat for her by the river, and the two sisters spent hours together there, communicating in some wordless manner. For a time he thought that all would be well, but then he saw how thin and pale she was growing.

One night when he had been late doing the account he came up to bed and found her weeping in her sleep and calling:

"Rhea! Rhea! I can't understand what you say! Oh, wait for me, take me with you!"

Summary: Mr. Peters uses his first wish to ask for a wife. She turns out to be a swan. Mr. Peters offers to use his second wish to turn Leita's sister into a human or to turn Leita back into a swan. Leita will have none of this and instead decides to bear her loneliness and stay with Mr. Peters.

Prediction: There seems to be no good solution to this problem. Perhaps the King of the Forest's words will prove to be true and Mr. Peters will wind up worse off than when he started.

Clarification: Rhea must be Leita's sister.

GLASS MOSAIC WALL MURAL: LANDSCAPE—BASE AND FOUNTAIN, c. 1905–1915 (detail)
Tiffany Studios
The Metropolitan Museum of Art

Clarification: So this is how Mr. Peters uses his second wish. He turns Leita back into a swan. This explains what happens to the leaf when he uses his wish. He blows it away.

Then he knew that it was hopeless and she would never be happy as a human. He stooped down and kissed her goodbye, then took another leaf from his notecase, blew it out of the window, and used up his second wish.

Next moment instead of Leita there was a sleeping swan lying across the bed with its head under its wing. He carried it out of the house and down to the brink of the river, and then he said, "Leita! Leita!" to waken her, and gently put her into the water. She gazed round her in astonishment for a moment, and then came up to him and rested her head lightly against his hand; next instant she was flying away over the trees towards the heart of the forest.

He heard a harsh laugh behind him, and turning round saw the old King looking at him with a malicious expression.

Questions: Will Mr. Peters use his third wish? I still don't know why this story is called "The *Third* Wish."

"Well, my friend! You don't seem to have managed so wonderfully with your first two wishes, do you? What will you do with the last? Turn yourself into a swan? Or turn Leita back into a girl?"

"I shall do neither," said Mr. Peters calmly. "Human beings and swans are better in their own shapes."

But for all that he looked sadly over towards the forest

where Leita had flown, and walked slowly back to his house.

Next day he saw two swans swimming at the bottom of the garden, and one of them wore the gold chain he had given Leita after their marriage; she came up and rubbed her head against his hand.

Mr. Peters and his two swans came to be well known in that part of the country; people used to say that he talked to swans and they understood him as well as his neighbors. Many people were a little frightened of him. There was a story that once when thieves tried to break into his house they were set upon by two huge white birds which carried them off bodily and dropped them in the river.

As Mr. Peters grew old everyone wondered at his contentment. Even when he was bent with rheumatism[2] he would not think of moving to a drier spot, but went slowly about his work, with the two swans always somewhere close at hand.

Sometimes people who knew his story would say to him:

"Mr. Peters, why don't you wish for another wife?"

"Not likely," he would answer serenely. "Two wishes were enough for me, I reckon. I've learned that even if your wishes are granted they don't always better you. I'll stay faithful to Leita."

One autumn night, passers-by along the road heard the mournful sound of two swans singing. All night the song went on, sweet and harsh, sharp and clear. In the morning Mr. Peters was found peacefully dead in his bed with a smile of great happiness on his face. In his hands, which lay clasped on his breast, were a withered leaf and a white feather.

Clarification: Mr. Peters dies without using his third wish. I know this because he still has the third leaf. This leaf seems to symbolize his victory over the King of the Forest.

Putting It Together: Mr. Peters did gain his first wish, which was really for a companion for his old age. Thus, he had no need to use his third wish to undo the first two.

---

2. rheumatism (r$\overline{oo}$′ mə tĭz m) *n.* Pain and stiffness of the joints and muscles.

Joan Aiken (1924–   ), the daughter of the American poet Conrad Aiken, always planned to be a writer. She has written several novels, as well as stories and plays for young people. She lives part of the year in England, which is the setting of "The Third Wish." Many of her stories deal with fantastic or mysterious events. In fact, her approach to writing can best be summed up by the title of the book from which "The Third Wish" was taken—*Not What You Expected.*

THINKING ABOUT THE SELECTION

Recalling

1. How does Mr. Peters gain his three wishes?
2. What is his first wish?
3. How is his first wish granted?
4. What is Mr. Peters' second wish?
5. Briefly describe his life after his second wish.

Interpreting

6. What does Mr. Peters' turning his wife back into a swan show about him?
7. Mr. Peters wished for a wife so that he would not be lonely in his old age. In what way is this wish fulfilled, despite the intentions of the King of the Forest?
8. Why does Mr. Peters die with a look of happiness on his face?
9. Explain why Mr. Peters is found with "a withered leaf and a white feather."

Applying

10. If you were Mr. Peters, would you have used your third wish? Why or why not?

ANALYZING LITERATURE

Understanding the Title

The **title** of a story gives you a hint about the work. An author might choose a title to call attention to a character or to suggest something about the plot. Often the title gives you a clue to a story's central idea, or the theme that the writer wishes to present. This is the case in "The Third Wish."

1. Why does the author call this story "The Third Wish" instead of, for example, "The Three Wishes"?
2. Would you have chosen another title for this story? If so, what would it be? Explain your answer.
3. The Third Wish" is taken from a collection of short stories called *Not What You Expected*. How is the ending of this story "not what you expected"?

CRITICAL THINKING AND READING

Finding Fantastic and Realistic Details

Fantastic details are strange and unusual. They are based on imagination rather than real life. In "The Third Wish," for example, the King of the Forest is a fantastic character. **Realistic details,** however, show life as we know it. Mr. Peters in this story is presented in a true-to-life fashion. A story based on fantasy often uses both realistic and fantastic details.

Find three realistic details in this selection and three fantastic details.

UNDERSTANDING LANGUAGE

Finding Word Origins

The word *fantasy* comes from the Greek word *phantasia,* which means "the appearance of a thing." In English, *fantasy* has come to mean the appearance of something imagined or dreamed as opposed to something real.

Many other words come from this same Greek word. Look up each word below in a dictionary and write its meaning. Note how each of these words relates to the idea of something dreamed or imagined. Then use each word in a sentence.

1. fantasize
2. fantasia
3. phantom
4. phantasmagoria

THINKING AND WRITING

Writing a Fantasy

Write your own story about the gift of three wishes. First brainstorm to decide what those three wishes will be. Remembering that the gift of three magic wishes can be more trouble than not, consider the complications that can be caused by each wish. Choose your characters with care, and make the person who grants the wishes a fantastic creature like the King of the Forest. Then prepare the first draft of your story. Read over this draft and make any necessary changes. Finally, proofread your story and share it with your classmates.

Plot

THE CALLERS
Walter Ufer
Smithsonian Institution

GUIDE FOR READING

Rikki-tikki-tavi

Rudyard Kipling (1865–1936) was born in India, to British parents. While still a young man, he became famous for his stirring accounts of adventure and courage. In 1907 he received a major award, the Nobel Prize for Literature, for his novels, short stories, and poetry. "Rikki-tikki-tavi" comes from one of Kipling's most popular collections of short stories, *The Jungle Book*. Notice how Kipling makes "the great war" between the animal characters in this story seem just as important as a human conflict.

Plot

The **plot** is the sequence of events in a short story. In many stories the events follow a pattern you can recognize. First, the writer describes a **conflict,** which is a struggle between opposing sides or forces. As the story develops, this struggle becomes more and more intense. Then the story reaches a **climax,** the point at which the conflict is greatest. After the climax you learn the **resolution,** or outcome of the conflict, before the story ends. You will be able to see this sequence of events as you read "Rikki-tikki-tavi."

Look For

As you read this action-packed story about a mongoose in India, look for the pattern beneath the surface. Can you identify the three most important elements of the plot: the conflict, the climax, and the resolution?

Writing

Recall an exciting movie or television drama you have seen. Briefly summarize the plot in this movie or program. Then freewrite about why you enjoyed this show.

Vocabulary

Knowing the following words will help you as you read "Rikki-tikki-tavi."

draggled (drag'ld) *adj.*: Wet and dirty (p. 13)
flinched (flinch't) *v.*: Moved back, as if away from a blow (p. 16)
mourning (morn' iŋ) *v.*: Feeling sorrow for the death of a loved one (p. 19)

consolation (kän' sə lā' shən) *n.*: Something that makes you feel better (p. 20)
cunningly (kun' iŋ lē) *adv.*: Cleverly (p. 20)

Rikki-tikki-tavi

Rudyard Kipling

This is the story of the great war that Rikki-tikki-tavi fought single-handed, through the bathrooms of the big bungalow in Segowlee cantonment.[1] Darzee, the tailor-bird, helped him, and Chuchundra,[2] the muskrat, who never comes out into the middle of the floor, but always creeps round by the wall, gave him advice; but Rikki-tikki did the real fighting.

He was a mongoose, rather like a little cat in his fur and his tail, but quite like a weasel in his head and his habits. His eyes and the end of his restless nose were pink; he could scratch himself anywhere he pleased, with any leg, front or back, that he chose to use; he could fluff up his tail till it looked like a bottle brush, and his war cry as he scuttled through the long grass, was: "*Rikk-tikk-tikki-tikki-tchk!*"

One day, a high summer flood washed him out of the burrow where he lived with his father and mother, and carried him, kicking and clucking, down a roadside ditch. He found a little wisp of grass floating there, and clung to it till he lost his senses. When he revived, he was lying in the hot sun on the middle of a garden path, very draggled indeed, and a small boy was saying: "Here's a dead mongoose. Let's have a funeral."

"No," said his mother; "let's take him in and dry him. Perhaps he isn't really dead."

They took him into the house, and a big man picked him up between his finger and thumb and said he was not dead but half choked; so they wrapped him in cotton wool, and warmed him, and he opened his eyes and sneezed.

"Now," said the big man (he was an Englishman who had just moved into the bungalow); "don't frighten him, and we'll see what he'll do."

It is the hardest thing in the world to frighten a mongoose, because he is eaten up from nose to tail with curiosity. The motto of all the mongoose family is, "Run and find out"; and Rikki-tikki was a true mongoose. He looked at the cotton wool, decided that it

---

1. Segowlee cantonment (sē gou′ lē kan tän′ mənt), *n.*: The living quarters for British troops in Segowlee, India.

2. Chuchundra (chōō chun′ drə)

was not good to eat, ran all round the table, sat up and put his fur in order, scratched himself, and jumped on the small boy's shoulder.

"Don't be frightened, Teddy," said his father. "That's his way of making friends."

"Ouch! He's tickling under my chin," said Teddy.

Rikki-tikki looked down between the boy's collar and neck, snuffed at his ear, and climbed down to the floor, where he sat rubbing his nose.

"Good gracious," said Teddy's mother, "and that's a wild creature! I suppose he's so tame because we've been kind to him."

"All mongooses are like that," said her husband. "If Teddy doesn't pick him up by the tail, or try to put him in a cage, he'll run in and out of the house all day long. Let's give him something to eat."

They gave him a little piece of raw meat. Rikki-tikki liked it immensely, and when it was finished he went out into the veranda and sat in the sunshine and fluffed up his fur to make it dry to the roots. Then he felt better.

"There are more things to find out about in this house," he said to himself, "than all my family could find out in all their lives. I shall certainly stay and find out."

He spent all that day roaming over the house. He nearly drowned himself in the bathtubs, put his nose into the ink on a writing table, and burned it on the end of the big man's cigar, for he climbed up in the big man's lap to see how writing was done. At nightfall he ran into Teddy's nursery to watch how kerosene lamps were lighted, and when Teddy went to bed Rikki-tikki climbed up too; but he was a restless companion, because he had to get up and attend to every noise all through the night, and find out what made it. Teddy's mother and father came in, the last thing, to look at their boy, and Rikki-tikki was awake on the pillow. "I

don't like that," said Teddy's mother; "he may bite the child." "He'll do no such thing," said the father. "Teddy's safer with that little beast than if he had a bloodhound to watch him. If a snake came into the nursery now—"

But Teddy's mother wouldn't think of anything so awful.

Early in the morning Rikki-tikki came to early breakfast in the veranda riding on Teddy's shoulder, and they gave him banana and some boiled egg; and he sat on all their laps one after the other, because every well-brought-up mongoose always hopes to be a house mongoose some day and have rooms to run about in, and Rikki-tikki's mother (she used to live in the General's house at Segowlee) had carefully told Rikki what to do if ever he came across Englishmen.

Then Rikki-tikki went out into the garden to see what was to be seen. It was a large garden, only half cultivated, with bushes as big as summer houses of Marshal Niel roses, lime and orange trees, clumps of bamboos, and thickets of high grass. Rikki-tikki licked his lips. "This is a splendid hunting ground," he said, and his tail grew bottle-brushy at the thought of it, and he scuttled up and down the garden, snuffing here and there till he heard very sorrowful voices in a thornbush.

It was Darzee, the tailorbird, and his wife. They had made a beautiful nest by pulling two big leaves together and stitching them up the edges with fibers, and had filled the hollow with cotton and downy fluff. The nest swayed to and fro, as they sat on the rim and cried.

"What is the matter?" asked Rikki-tikki.

"We are very miserable," said Darzee. "One of our babies fell out of the nest yesterday and Nag[3] ate him."

"H'm!" said Rikki-tikki, "that is very sad—but I am a stranger here. Who is Nag?"

_____

3. **Nag** (Näg).

Darzee and his wife only cowered down in the nest without answering, for from the thick grass at the foot of the bush there came a low hiss—a horrid cold sound that made Rikki-tikki jump back two clear feet. Then inch by inch out of the grass rose up the head and spread hood of Nag, the big black cobra, and he was five feet long from tongue to tail. When he had lifted one third of himself clear of the ground, he stayed balancing to and fro exactly as a dandelion tuft balances in the wind, and he looked at Rikki-tikki with the wicked snake's eyes that never change their expression, whatever the snake may be thinking of.

"Who is Nag?" he said. "*I am Nag*. The great god Brahm[4] put his mark upon all our people when the first cobra spread his hood to keep the sun off Brahm as he slept. Look, and be afraid!"

He spread out his hood more than ever, and Rikki-tikki saw the spectacle mark on the back of it that looks exactly like the eye part of a hook-and-eye fastening. He was afraid for the minute; but it is impossible for a mongoose to stay frightened for any length of time, and though Rikki-tikki had never met a live cobra before, his mother had fed him on dead ones, and he knew that all a grown mongoose's business in life was to fight and eat snakes. Nag knew that too, and at the bottom of his cold heart he was afraid.

"Well," said Rikki-tikki, and his tail began to fluff up again, "marks or no marks, do you think it is right for you to eat fledglings out of a nest?"

Nag was thinking to himself, and watching the least little movement in the grass behind Rikki-tikki. He knew that mongooses in the garden meant death sooner or later for him and his family; but he wanted to get

Rikki-tikki off his guard. So he dropped his head a little, and put it on one side.

"Let us talk," he said, "You eat eggs. Why should not I eat birds?"

"Behind you! Look behind you!" sang Darzee.

Rikki-tikki knew better than to waste time in staring. He jumped up in the air as high as he could go, and just under him whizzed by the head of Nagaina,[5] Nag's wicked wife. She had crept up behind him as he was talking, to make an end of him; and he heard her savage hiss as the stroke missed. He came down almost across her back, and if he had been an old mongoose he would have known that then was the time to break her back with one bite; but he was afraid of the terrible lashing return stroke of the cobra. He bit, indeed, but did not bite long enough, and he jumped

---

4. Brahm (bräm): An abbreviation of Brahma, the name of the chief god in the Hindu religion.

5. Nagaina (nə gī nə)

clear of the whisking tail, leaving Nagaina torn and angry.

"Wicked, wicked Darzee!" said Nag, lashing up as high as he could reach toward the nest in the thornbush; but Darzee had built it out of reach of snakes; and it only swayed to and fro.

Rikki-tikki felt his eyes growing red and hot (when a mongoose's eyes grow red, he is angry), and he sat back on his tail and hind legs like a little kangaroo, and looked all around him, and chattered with rage. But Nag and Nagaina had disappeared into the grass. When a snake misses its stroke, it never says anything or gives any sign of what it means to do next. Rikki-tikki did not care to follow them, for he did not feel sure that he could manage two snakes at once. So he trotted off to the gravel path near the house, and sat down to think. It was a serious matter for him.

If you read the old books of natural history, you will find they say that when the mongoose fights the snake and happens to get bitten, he runs off and eats some herb that cures him. That is not true. The victory is only a matter of quickness of eye and quickness of foot—snake's blow against mongoose's jump—and as no eye can follow the motion of a snake's head when it strikes, that makes things much more wonderful than any magic herb. Rikki-tikki knew he was a young mongoose, and it made him all the more pleased to think that he had managed to escape a blow from behind. It gave him confidence in himself, and when Teddy came running down the path, Rikki-tikki was ready to be petted.

But just as Teddy was stooping, something flinched a little in the dust, and a tiny voice said: "Be careful. I am death!" It was Karait,[6] the dusty brown snakeling that lies for choice on the dusty earth; and his bite is

as dangerous as the cobra's. But he is so small that nobody thinks of him, and so he does the more harm to people.

Rikki-tikki's eyes grew red again, and he danced up to Karait with the peculiar rocking, swaying motion that he had inherited from his family. It looks very funny, but it is so perfectly balanced a gait that you can fly off from it at any angle you please; and in dealing with snakes this is an advantage. If Rikki-tikki had only known, he was doing a much more dangerous thing than fighting Nag, for Karait is so small, and can turn so quickly, that unless Rikki bit him close to the back of the head, he would get the return stroke in his eye or lip. But Rikki did not know: his eyes were all red, and he rocked back and forth, looking for a good place to hold. Karait struck out. Rikki jumped sideways and tried to run in, but the wicked little dusty gray head lashed within a fraction of his shoulder, and he had to jump over the body, and the head followed his heels close.

Teddy shouted to the house: "Oh, look here! Our mongoose is killing a snake"; and Rikki-tikki heard a scream from Teddy's mother. His father ran out with a stick, but by the time he came up, Karait had lunged out once too far, and Rikki-tikki had sprung, jumped on the snake's back, dropped his head far between his fore legs, bitten as high up the back as he could get hold, and rolled away. That bite paralyzed Karait, and Rikki-tikki was just going to eat him up from the tail, after the custom of his family at dinner, when he remembered that a full meal makes a slow mongoose, and if he wanted all his strength and quickness ready, he must keep himself thin.

He went away for a dust bath under the castor-oil bushes, while Teddy's father beat the dead Karait. "What is the use of that?" thought Rikki-tikki. "I have settled it all"; and then Teddy's mother picked him up from the dust and hugged him, crying that

---

6. Karait (kə rīt′)

he had saved Teddy from death, and Teddy's father said that he was a providence,[7] and Teddy looked on with big scared eyes. Rikki-tikki was rather amused at all the fuss, which, of course, he did not understand. Teddy's mother might just as well have petted Teddy for playing in the dust. Rikki was thoroughly enjoying himself.

That night, at dinner, walking to and fro among the wineglasses on the table, he could have stuffed himself three times over with nice things; but he remembered Nag and Nagaina, and though it was very pleasant to be patted and petted by Teddy's mother, and to sit on Teddy's shoulder, his eyes would get red from time to time, and he would go off into his long war cry of "*Rikk-tikk-tikki-tikki-tchk!*"

Teddy carried him off to bed, and insisted on Rikki-tikki sleeping under his chin. Rikki-tikki was too well bred to bite or scratch, but as soon as Teddy was asleep he went off for his nightly walk round the house, and in the dark he ran up against Chuchundra, the muskrat, creeping round by the wall. Chuchundra is a brokenhearted little beast. He whimpers and cheeps all the night, trying to make up his mind to run into the middle of the room, but he never gets there.

"Don't kill me," said Chuchundra, almost weeping. "Rikki-tikki don't kill me."

"Do you think a snake-killer kills muskrats?" said Rikki-tikki scornfully.

"Those who kill snakes get killed by snakes," said Chuchundra, more sorrowfully than ever. "And how am I to be sure that Nag won't mistake me for you some dark night?"

"There's not the least danger," said Rikki-tikki; "but Nag is in the garden, and I know you don't go there."

"My cousin Chua, the rat, told me—" said Chuchundra, and then he stopped.

"Told you what?"

"H'sh! Nag is everywhere, Rikki-tikki. You should have talked to Chua in the garden."

"I didn't—so you must tell me. Quick, Chuchundra, or I'll bite you!"

Chuchundra sat down and cried till the tears rolled off his whiskers. "I am a very poor man," he sobbed. "I never had spirit enough to run out into the middle of the room. H'sh! I mustn't tell you anything. Can't you *hear*, Rikki-tikki?"

Rikki-tikki listened. The house was as still as still, but he thought he could just catch the faintest *scratch-scratch* in the world—a noise as faint as that of a wasp walking on a windowpane—the dry scratch of a snake's scales on brickwork.

"That's Nag or Nagaina," he said to himself; "and he is crawling into the bathroom sluice. You're right, Chuchundra; I should have talked to Chua."

He stole off to Teddy's bathroom, but there was nothing there, and then to Teddy's mother's bathroom. At the bottom of the smooth plaster wall there was a brick pulled out to make a sluice for the bath water, and as Rikki-tikki stole in by the masonry curb where the bath is put, he heard Nag and Nagaina whispering together outside in the moonlight.

"When the house is emptied of people," said Nagaina to her husband, "*he* will have to go away, and then the garden will be our own again. Go in quietly, and remember that the big man who killed Karait is the first one to bite. Then come out and tell me, and we will hunt for Rikki-tikki together."

"But are you sure that there is anything to be gained by killing the people?" said Nag.

"Everything. When there were no people in the bungalow, did we have any mongoose in the garden? So long as the bungalow is

---

7. a providence (präv′ ə dəns): A godsend; a valuable gift.

empty, we are king and queen of the garden; and remember that as soon as our eggs in the melon bed hatch (as they may tomorrow), our children will need room and quiet."

"I had not thought of that," said Nag. "I will go, but there is no need that we should hunt for Rikki-tikki afterward. I will kill the big man and his wife, and the child if I can, and come away quietly. Then the bungalow will be empty, and Rikki-tikki will go."

Rikki-tikki tingled all over with rage and hatred at this, and then Nag's head came through the sluice, and his five feet of cold body followed it. Angry as he was, Rikki-tikki was very frightened as he saw the size of the big cobra. Nag coiled himself up, raised his head, and looked into the bathroom in the dark, and Rikki could see his eyes glitter.

"Now, if I kill him here, Nagaina will know;—and if I fight him on the open floor, the odds are in his favor. What am I to do?" said Rikki-tikki-tavi.

Nag waved to and fro, and then Rikki-tikki heard him drinking from the biggest water jar that was used to fill the bath. "That is good," said the snake. "Now, when Karait was killed, the big man had a stick. He may have that stick still, but when he comes in to bathe in the morning he will not have a stick. I shall wait here till he comes. Nagaina—do you hear me?—I shall wait here in the cool till daytime."

There was no answer from outside, so Rikki-tikki knew Nagaina had gone away. Nag coiled himself down, coil by coil, round the bulge at the bottom of the waterjar, and Rikki-tikki stayed still as death. After an hour he began to move, muscle by muscle, toward the jar. Nag was asleep, and Rikki-tikki looked at his big back, wondering which would be the best place for a good hold. "If I don't break his back at the first jump," said Rikki, "he can still fight; and if he fights—O Rikki!" He looked at the thickness of the neck below the hood, but that was too much for him; and a bite near the tail would only make Nag savage.

"It must be the head," he said at last; "the head above the hood; and, when I am once there, I must not let go."

Then he jumped. The head was lying a little clear of the water jar, under the curve of it; and, as his teeth met, Rikki braced his back against the bulge of the red earthenware to hold down the head. This gave him just one second's purchase,[8] and he made the most of it. Then he was battered to and fro as a rat is shaken by a dog—to and fro on the floor, up and down, and round in great circles; but his eyes were red, and he held on as the body cartwhipped over the floor, upsetting the tin dipper and the soap dish and the fleshbrush, and banged against the tin side of the bath. As he held he closed his jaws tighter and tighter, for he made sure he would be banged to death, and, for the honor of his family, he preferred to be found with his teeth locked. He was dizzy, aching, and felt shaken to pieces when something went off like a thunderclap just behind him; a hot wind knocked him senseless and red fire singed his fur. The big man had been wakened by the noise, and had fired both barrels of a shotgun into Nag just behind the hood.

Rikki-tikki held on with his eyes shut, for now he was quite sure he was dead; but the head did not move, and the big man picked him up and said: "It's the mongoose again, Alice; the little chap has saved *our* lives now." Then Teddy's mother came in with a very white face, and saw what was left of Nag, and Rikki-tikki dragged himself to Teddy's bedroom and spent half the rest of the night shaking himself tenderly to find out whether he really was broken into forty pieces, as he fancied.

---

8. purchase (pur' chəs): In this case, a good hold on something.

When morning came he was very stiff, but well pleased with his doings. "Now I have Nagaina to settle with, and she will be worse than five Nags, and there's no knowing when the eggs she spoke of will hatch. Goodness! I must go and see Darzee," he said.

Without waiting for breakfast, Rikki-tikki ran to the thornbush where Darzee was singing a song of triumph at the top of his voice. The news of Nag's death was all over the garden, for the sweeper had thrown the body on the rubbish heap.

"Oh, you stupid tuft of feathers!" said Rikki-tikki, angrily. "Is this the time to sing?"

"Nag is dead—is dead—is dead!" sang Darzee. "The valiant Rikki-tikki caught him by the head and held fast. The big man brought the bang-stick and Nag fell in two pieces! He will never eat my babies again."

"All that's true enough; but where's Nagaina?" said Rikki-tikki, looking carefully round him.

"Nagaina came to the bathroom sluice and called for Nag," Darzee went on; "and Nag came out on the end of a stick—the sweeper picked him up on the end of a stick and threw him upon the rubbish heap. Let us sing about the great, the red-eyed Rikki-tikki!" and Darzee filled his throat and sang.

"If I could get up to your nest, I'd roll all your babies out!" said Rikki-tikki. "You don't know when to do the right thing at the right time. You're safe enough in your nest there, but it's war for me down here. Stop singing a minute, Darzee."

"For the great, the beautiful Rikki-tikki's sake, I will stop," said Darzee. "What is it, O Killer of the terrible Nag!"

"Where is Nagaina, for the third time?"

"On the rubbish heap by the stables, mourning for Nag. Great is Rikki-tikki with the white teeth."

"Bother my white teeth! Have you ever heard where she keeps her eggs?"

"In the melon bed, on the end nearest the wall, where the sun strikes nearly all day. She had them there weeks ago."

"And you never thought it worthwhile to tell me? The end nearest the wall, you said?"

"Rikki-tikki, you are not going to eat her eggs?"

"Not eat exactly; no. Darzee, if you have a grain of sense you will fly off to the stables and pretend that your wing is broken, and let Nagaina chase you away to this bush! I must get to the melon bed, and if I went there now she'd see me."

Darzee was a featherbrained little fellow who could never hold more than one idea at a time in his head; and just because he knew that Nagaina's children were born in eggs like his own, he didn't think at first that it was fair to kill them. But his wife was a sensible bird, and she knew that cobra's eggs meant young cobras later on; so she flew off from the nest, and left Darzee to keep the babies warm, and continue his song about the death of Nag. Darzee was very like a man in some ways.

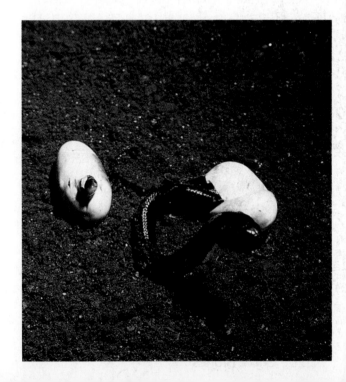

She fluttered in front of Nagaina by the rubbish heap, and cried out, "Oh, my wing is broken! The boy in the house threw a stone at me and broke it." Then she fluttered more desperately than ever.

Nagaina lifted up her head and hissed, "You warned Rikki-tikki when I would have killed him. Indeed and truly, you've chosen a bad place to be lame in." And she moved toward Darzee's wife, slipping along over the dust.

"The boy broke it with a stone!" shrieked Darzee's wife.

"Well! It may be some consolation to you when you're dead to know that I shall settle accounts with the boy. My husband lies on the rubbish heap this morning, but before night the boy in the house will lie very still. What is the use of running away? I am sure to catch you. Little fool, look at me!"

Darzee's wife knew better than to do *that*, for a bird who looks at a snake's eyes gets so frightened that she cannot move. Darzee's wife fluttered on, piping sorrowfully, and never leaving the ground, and Nagaina quickened her pace.

Rikki-tikki heard them going up the path from the stables, and he raced for the end of the melon patch near the wall. There, in the warm litter about the melons, very cunningly hidden, he found twenty-five eggs, about the size of a bantam's[9] eggs, but with whitish skin instead of shell.

"I was not a day too soon," he said; for he could see the baby cobras curled up inside the skin, and he knew that the minute they were hatched they could each kill a man or a mongoose. He bit off the tops of the eggs as fast as he could, taking care to crush the young cobras, and turned over the litter from time to time to see whether he had missed any. At last there were only three eggs left, and Rikki-tikki began to chuckle to himself, when he heard Darzee's wife screaming:

"Rikki-tikki, I led Nagaina toward the house, and she has gone into the veranda, and—oh, come quickly—she means killing!"

Rikki-tikki smashed two eggs, and tumbled backward down the melon bed with the third egg in his mouth, and scuttled to the veranda as hard as he could put foot to the ground. Teddy and his mother and father were there at early breakfast; but Rikki-tikki saw that they were not eating anything. They sat stone-still, and their faces were white. Nagaina was coiled up on the matting by Teddy's chair, within easy striking distance of Teddy's bare leg, and she was swaying to and fro singing a song of triumph.

"Son of the big man that killed Nag," she hissed, "stay still. I am not ready yet. Wait a little. Keep very still, all you three. If you move I strike, and if you do not move I strike. Oh, foolish people, who killed my Nag!"

Teddy's eyes were fixed on his father, and all his father could do was to whisper, "Sit still, Teddy. You mustn't move. Teddy, keep still."

Then Rikki-tikki came up and cried: "Turn round, Nagaina; turn and fight!"

"All in good time," said she, without moving her eyes. "I will settle my account with *you* presently. Look at your friends, Rikki-tikki. They are still and white; they are afraid. They dare not move, and if you come a step nearer I strike."

"Look at your eggs," said Rikki-tikki, "in the melon bed near the wall. Go and look, Nagaina."

The big snake turned half round, and saw the egg on the veranda. "Ah-h! Give it to me," she said.

Rikki-tikki put his paws one on each side of the egg, and his eyes were blood-red. "What price for a snake's egg? For a young

---

9. bantam's : A small chicken's.

cobra? For a young king cobra? For the last—the very last of the brood? The ants are eating all the others down by the melon bed."

Nagaina spun clear round, forgetting everything for the sake of the one egg; and Rikki-tikki saw Teddy's father shoot out a big hand, catch Teddy by the shoulder, and drag him across the little table with the teacups, safe and out of reach of Nagaina.

"Tricked! Tricked! Tricked! *Rikk-tck-tck*!" chuckled Rikki-tikki. "The boy is safe, and it was I—I—I that caught Nag by the hood last night in the bathroom." Then he began to jump up and down, all four feet together, his head close to the floor. "He threw me to and fro, but he could not shake me off. He was dead before the big man blew him in two. I did it. *Rikki-tikki-tck-tck*! Come then, Nagaina. Come and fight with me. You shall not be a widow long."

Nagaina saw that she had lost her chance of killing Teddy, and the egg lay between Rikki-tikki's paws. "Give me the egg,

Rikki-tikki. Give me the last of my eggs, and I will go away and never come back," she said, lowering her hood.

"Yes, you will go away, and you will never come back; for you will go to the rubbish heap with Nag. Fight, widow! The big man has gone for his gun! Fight!"

Rikki-tikki was bounding all round Nagaina, keeping just out of reach of her stroke, his little eyes like hot coals. Nagaina gathered herself together, and flung out at him. Rikki-tikki jumped up and backward. Again and again and again she struck, and each time her head came with a whack on the matting of the veranda and she gathered herself together like a watchspring. Then Rikki-tikki danced in a circle to get behind her, and Nagaina spun round to keep her head to his head, so that the rustle of her tail on the matting sounded like dry leaves blown along by the wind.

He had forgotten the egg. It still lay on the veranda, and Nagaina came nearer and nearer to it, till at last, while Rikki-tikki was drawing breath, she caught it in her mouth, turned to the veranda steps, and flew like an arrow down the path, with Rikki-tikki behind her. When the cobra runs for her life, she goes like a whiplash flicked across a horse's neck.

Rikki-tikki knew that he must catch her, or all the trouble would begin again. She headed straight for the long grass by the thornbush, and as he was running Rikki-tikki heard Darzee still singing his foolish little song of triumph. But Darzee's wife was wiser. She flew off her nest as Nagaina came along, and flapped her wings about Nagaina's head. If Darzee had helped they might have turned her; but Nagaina only lowered her hood and went on. Still, the instant's delay brought Rikki-tikki up to her, and as she plunged into the rat hole where she and Nag used to live, his little white teeth were clenched on her tail, and he went down with her—and very few mongooses, however wise and old they may be, care to follow a cobra into its hole. It was dark in the hole; and Rikki-tikki never knew when it might open out and give Nagaina room to turn and strike at him. He held on savagely, and struck out his feet to act as brakes on the dark slope of the hot, moist earth.

Then the grass by the mouth of the hole stopped waving, and Darzee said: "It is all over with Rikki-tikki! We must sing his death song. Valiant Rikki-tikki is dead! For Nagaina will surely kill him underground."

So he sang a very mournful song that he made up all on the spur of the minute, and just as he got to the most touching part the grass quivered again, and Rikki-tikki, covered with dirt, dragged himself out of the hole leg by leg, licking his whiskers. Darzee stopped with a little shout. Rikki-tikki shook some of the dust out of his fur and sneezed. "It is all over," he said. "The widow will never come out again." And the red ants that live between the grass stems heard him, and be-

gan to troop down one after another to see if he had spoken the truth.

Rikki-tikki curled himself up in the grass and slept where he was—slept and slept till it was late in the afternoon, for he had done a hard day's work.

"Now," he said, when he awoke, "I will go back to the house. Tell the Coppersmith, Darzee, and he will tell the garden that Nagaina is dead."

The Coppersmith is a bird who makes a noise exactly like the beating of a little hammer on a copper pot; and the reason he is always making it is because he is the town crier to every Indian garden, and tells all the news to everybody who cares to listen. As Rikki-tikki went up the path, he heard his "attention" notes like a tiny dinner gong; and then the steady "Ding-dong-tock! Nag is dead—dong! Nagaina is dead! Ding-dong-tock!" That set all the birds in the garden singing, and the frogs croaking; for Nag and Nagaina used to eat frogs as well as little birds.

When Rikki got to the house, Teddy and Teddy's mother and Teddy's father came out and almost cried over him; and that night he ate all that was given him till he could eat no more, and went to bed on Teddy's shoulder, where Teddy's mother saw him when she came to look late at night.

"He saved our lives and Teddy's life," she said to her husband. "Just think, he saved all our lives."

Rikki-tikki woke up with a jump, for all the mongooses are light sleepers.

"Oh, it's you," said he. "What are you bothering for? All the cobras are dead; and if they weren't, I'm here."

Rikki-tikki had a right to be proud of himself; but he did not grow too proud, and he kept that garden as a mongoose should keep it, with tooth and jump and spring and bite, till never a cobra dared show its head inside the walls.

Recalling

1. What kinds of behavior are typical of mongooses?
2. When does Rikki first meet the cobras?
3. What is Nag and Nagaina's plan to get control of the bungalow?
4. How does Rikki protect Teddy's father and then Teddy from the cobras?
5. What happens to Nagaina at the end of the story?

Interpreting

6. How does each of these animals resemble humans?
7. Compare and contrast the personalities of Rikki and the two cobras.
8. How is "the great war" in this story a battle between good and evil?

Applying

9. Why would Rikki's approach to problems in life work better than Darzee's?

ANALYZING LITERATURE

Understanding Plot

Plot is the sequence of events in a story. These events usually involve a **conflict,** or struggle between opposing sides. This struggle becomes the most intense at the **climax,** the point just before the conflict is resolved. The rest of the story is devoted to the **resolution,** or solving of the conflict.

The conflict in "Rikki-tikki-tavi" occurs between Rikki and the two cobras.

1. How does the first meeting between Rikki and the cobras make you want to read further?
2. Which battle occurs at the climax?
3. How is the conflict resolved?

CRITICAL THINKING AND READING

Putting Events in Chronological Order

In "Rikki-tikki-tavi" the events take place in **chronological order.** This means that they follow one another as time goes forward.

1. List the main events of the story in the order they occur.
2. About how much time passes between the first event in the story and the last?

UNDERSTANDING LANGUAGE

Using Context Clues

The **context** of a word consists of the words that surround it. When you see an unfamiliar word as you read, you can sometimes figure out its meaning by looking at its context. In the third paragraph of the story, for example, Rikki is described as being *draggled*. Since Rikki has just been in a flood, you can deduce that *draggled* means "wet and dirty."

Use context clues to figure out the meaning of the following *italicized* words from the story. Then check your answer in the glossary.

1. ". . . he *scuttled* up and down the garden, snuffing here and there. . . ."
2. "At the bottom of the smooth plaster wall there was a brick pulled out to make a *sluice* for the bath water. . . ."

THINKING AND WRITING

Writing a Story with a Strong Plot

In a story with a strong plot like "Rikki-tikki-tavi," the conflict rises to a climax and is then resolved. Imagine that a movie director has asked you to write such a story to serve as the basis for her next film. Brainstorm to think of a good idea for a conflict. Then use this idea to write a story with a strong plot. As you revise it, check to see that it has a climax and a resolution.

GUIDE FOR READING

The Confidence Game

Pat Carr (1932–   ), who was born in Grass Creek, Wyoming, is a writer of both fiction and nonfiction. A number of her stories for young people have been published in magazines, and she has won awards from the Iowa School of Letters and the Texas Institute of Letters. She writes on a variety of topics, particularly about the outdoors and about athletes. Many of her stories, like "The Confidence Game," deal with conflicts and emotions arising from competitive or challenging situations.

Conflict

A **conflict** is a struggle between opposing sides or forces. A conflict in a story may occur between one person and another or between a person and a force of nature. These are **external** conflicts. Another type of conflict may be **internal,** one that occurs between opposing ideas or feelings within a character. In an internal conflict, one side of a person seems to be warring against another side. Tobi, the main character in "The Confidence Game," experiences both an external conflict and an internal conflict.

Look For

As you read "The Confidence Game," notice the external conflict that confronts Tobi. The external conflict causes her to behave in a way that produces an internal conflict. How does she resolve both?

Writing

Discuss with your classmates what it means to be a "good sport." Then list the ways that you think a person demonstrates good sportsmanship.

Vocabulary

Knowing the following words will help you as you read "The Confidence Game."

quipped (kwipt) *v.*: Made a witty remark (p. 26)
milling (mil'iŋ) *v.*: Moving in a circular or random motion (p. 27)

postings (post' iŋz) *n.*: Notices of the racing time of each swimmer (p. 28)
ecstatic (ek stat'ik) *adj.*: Delighted (p. 30)

The Confidence Game

Pat Carr

My confidence started draining out my toes the day Angela Brady showed up at the pool for workout. I even started to chew the inside of my cheek, a nervous habit I usually reserve for fighting the fear that clutches at me just before a race. In a way, I guess I knew it *was* a race between Angela and me for the backstroke position on our team relay for National Championship.

I hadn't even seen her swim yet, but the whole team knew she had been swimming for a famous club in California. We were just a small city team, only two years old. But we had a coach whose middle name was motivation. He'd motivated me into swimming a grueling three miles a day, and now I was actually in the running to compete at the Nationals. Or I was until Angela showed up.

"Okay, swim freaks, hit the water for an 800 meter freestyle warm-up[1]!" barked Coach. Then he added in a more human voice, "Angela, why don't you try lane four today?"

Lane four was the fast lane, my lane. I'd had to earn my place in that lane by swimming 400 meters in less than five minutes. Now all Angela had to do was jump in. It wasn't fair.

I didn't think I could pretend friendliness, so I started the 800 before Angela hit

the water. But I didn't even have time to settle into my pace when I felt the water agitating behind me. I stroked harder, but I could still feel the churning water of someone closing in on me. I soon felt a light touch on my foot.

In swim workouts, it's one of the rules that when a teammate taps your foot, you move to the right to let that swimmer go ahead of you. I knew that, and I also knew that I was interfering with Angela's pace by not letting her pass me. My conscience told me to move over, but something stubborn kept my body in the middle of the lane.

At the end of the 800, I glanced up and saw Coach staring at me. Realizing that he had seen me refuse to let Angela pass, I took a deep breath and ducked underwater.

When the workout was over, everyone crowded around Angela, asking her if she knew any Olympic swimmers and stuff like that. Finding a quiet corner for myself, I slipped on my warm-up suit, draped a towel over my head and hurried toward my bike.

"Hey, Tobi! Where are you going?" someone shouted.

I didn't answer, just hopped on my bike and pedalled fast.

It was like that for the next two weeks. At every workout Angela was the star of the show; I was an invisible stagehand. Even worse, during time trials she beat me in all four strokes and took my place as lane leader.

---

1. freestyle warm-up: Preparation for a race in which swimmers may use any stroke.

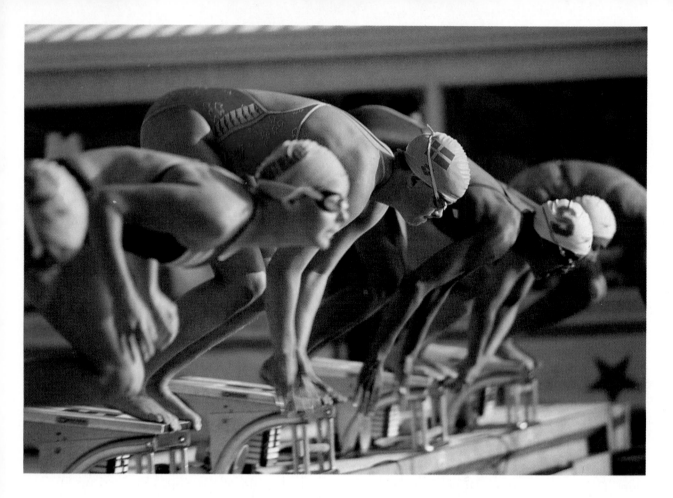

I was miserable. And I was scared, too; scared that Angela was taking away my chance at the Nationals, a chance I had earned by a lot of hard work.

I started to show up late to workouts so that I wouldn't have to talk to anyone. I even walked on the bottom of the pool and faked my stroke, a swimmer's cheating trick I'd never used before. It was easy to catch up to Angela that way. And I always managed to be underwater when she gave our lane instructions.

I'll admit I wasn't very happy with my actions. But my jealous feelings were like a current I couldn't swim against.

The day before the Riverdale Meet, Coach called me over. At that moment I would rather have tried to talk to King Kong.

"Tobi, I want to talk to you about sportsmanship," he began.

"Sportswomanship, in this case, Coach," I quipped, hoping to distract him.

"Okay, sportswomanship," he said, taking me seriously. "Or whatever you want to call it when one athlete accepts a better athlete in a spirit of friendly competition."

"Maybe the so-called better athlete is not as good as everyone thinks," I mumbled.

Coach left a big silence for my statement to fall into. I started to chew the inside of my cheek again.

"Let's stop talking about this athlete and that athlete," he said softly, "and talk instead about Tobi and Angela. She has made better time than you, Tobi. And that is an objective fact, not something everyone thinks."

He paused. I stared at my toes, which were curling under my feet as if trying to hide.

"The worst of it. Tobi, is that your attitude is hurting your performance. Do you know that your times have become worse in the last two weeks? Maybe showing up late and walking on the bottom have something to do with that," he said. My face felt as if it had been splashed with hot pink paint.

"Do you have anything you want to say?" he asked. I shook my head. "That's all then, Tobi. I'll see you tomorrow at the Riverdale Meet."

The next morning I was too nervous to eat my special breakfast of steak and eggs. This meet would decide who was going to Nationals.

The early skies were still gray when I arrived at the Riverdale pool for the warm-up session. The other swimmers were screeching greetings at each other like a flock of gulls. I jumped into the water to cut off the sound and mechanically began my stroke.

Half an hour later, I shuddered as the public address system squealed. The meet was about to start. After climbing out of the pool, I quickly searched the heat sheet[2] for my name. Disappointed, I saw that I had just missed making it into the last, and fastest, qualifying heat.[3] Angela's name, of course, was there. She'd taken my place just as she had at the trials.

Better not to think about Angela at all. I told myself, recalling Coach's words. Better to concentrate on my own race. Carefully, I went over Coach's instructions in my mind, shutting out the milling crowd around me, swimming my race perfectly, over and over again in my head, always perfectly.

"Would you like an orange?"

Without looking, I knew whose voice it was. "It's good for quick energy," continued Angela, holding the orange out to me.

"No thanks," I said. "I've got all I need." I saw that she was about to sit down next to me, so I added, "I don't like to talk before a race."

She nodded sympathetically. "I get uptight, too. The butterflies are free," she said with a nervous laugh.

For a moment I felt a little better toward her, knowing that she had the jitters, too. Then I remembered that she didn't have to worry.

"You'll be an easy winner," I said.

"You never know," she replied uncertainly.

My heat was called. Up on the blocks,[4] I willed my muscles into obedience, alert for the starter's commands. At the gun, I cut into the top of the water smoothly.

I swam exactly as I had been imagining it before the race, acting out the pictures in my mind. I felt the water stream past me, smooth, steady and swift. When I finished, I was certain I had done my best in that heat.

Overwhelmed by exhaustion, I sat on the deck for several minutes, eyes closed, totally spent. I knew I was missing Angela's heat, but I was too tired to care.

The sound of the announcer's voice was like a crackling firecracker of hope bursting through my fatigue. Then I heard my name. I'd made it!

I also heard Angela's name, but it was several minutes before I realized that my name had been called last. That meant my time had been better. Figuring there must have been a mistake I checked the official

---

2. heat sheet: A list of swimmers who will compete in the next heat, or preliminary round.
3. qualifying heat: A preliminary round: the winners are qualified to compete in the final round.

4. blocks *n.*: Small platforms from which the racers start.

postings, but there were our times with mine four seconds faster.

Heading for the gym, where all the swimmers rest and wait for the heats to be called, I saw Angela sitting with her back against the wall alone. Her shoulders were rounded in a slump.

It could be me, I whispered to myself, remembering what it feels like to mess up a race. There's no worse anger than the kind you feel toward yourself when you've ruined something you care about. I knew how she felt, and I also knew there was no way I could

make up for the way I had acted. But I just had to try.

"I don't talk before races, but I do talk after them. Sometimes it helps," I said, knowing Angela had every right to tell me to go drown myself.

"Talk if you want to," she murmured.

"Well, I will, but I was hoping you'd talk, too."

She hesitated, and I saw her trying to swallow. "I will as soon as I'm sure I'm not going to cry," she whispered.

So I babbled on for a few minutes about

the meet, some of the other swimmers, the team standings, anything. I knew it didn't matter what I said as long as I kept talking.

All at once, Angela interrupted my opinion of the snack bar's hamburgers, "I do this all the time," she burst out. "I do great at workouts, then comes a meet, and something happens; I just can't do it."

"Maybe you don't know how to play the confidence game," I said. She looked at me suspiciously, but I went on. "How do you psych yourself up for a race?"

"I don't exactly." She was twisting the ends of the towel into tiny corkscrews. "I just try to block it out, not think about it."

"What about during a race?"

"I concentrate on not making mistakes."

"Very negative methods," I commented.

"What do you mean?"

"Well, take my positive approach. First, I think about all the good things I've done in previous races. Then I plan my upcoming race carefully, going over each detail in my mind, picturing myself the perfect swimmer. Then when I'm in the water, I tell myself to do it again, only this time for real."

"And you win," Angela added with a smile. Now I really felt badly, remembering how I had acted when Angela had done better than I in workouts.

"Listen, I have an idea," I said. Maybe I *could* make it up to her. "You swim faster than me, right?" Angela looked doubtful.

"Yes, you do, that's an objective fact," I insisted. "Now my idea is that you use me as a pacer[5] in the backstroke final this afternoon.

At first Angela wasn't sure, but I soon had her convinced, and we were planning our strategy when Coach showed up.

"What's going on here?" He gave me an accusing look.

"We've got it all settled," Angela spoke up. "Tobi and I are going to be a team from now on."

"All right!" he said, giving us a smile usually reserved for winners.

As Angela and I sat together on the ready bench,[6] I had conflicting thoughts about helping her. What was I doing anyway? Handing her my relay position on a silver platter, that's what.

I hadn't time to get worked up over it, though, because the whistle blew, and we stepped up to the blocks. At the sound of the gun I was into the water with barely a splash, skimming the surface like a water bug.

As I reached the wall, I pretended all my strength was in my legs as I flipped and pushed off. Pull hard, hard, hard, I told myself, muscles aching from the effort. Then on the last lap, I concentrated on a single word. Win! I shot through the water and strained for the finish.

Immediately, I looked to Angela's lane. She was there, but it was too close to tell who had won. She gave me the thumbs up sign, and I returned it.

I stared at the electronic scoreboard. Usually it didn't take long for the times to appear, but now it remained blank for so long I was beginning to worry that a fuse had blown.

Please, please let me be the winner, I whispered over and over. Finally, the winning times flashed on. I blinked away the chlorine haze, or maybe tears. Angela had won. I managed to give her a congratulatory hug.

---

5. pacer *n*.: One who sets the pace for others in a race.

6. ready bench: The bench on which swimmers sit just before a race.

"I couldn't have done it without you, Tobi," she bubbled.

"You did it, girls!" Coach couldn't keep himself from shouting. he was so excited. "You've just raced yourself to the Nationals!"

I had never felt so left out, so disappointed in my whole life. "Well, at least Angela has," I said, struggling to smile.

Coach looked startled. "And you did, too, Tobi."

What was he talking about? "I saw that Angela won the place on our relay team."

"That's right, but you missed something. You both swam so fast that you made qualifying times[7] for the *individual* backstroke event!"

---

7. qualifying times: The racing time that makes a swimmer qualified to compete in the final round.

I was stunned. I had concentrated so hard on the relay place I hadn't even thought about the individual events.

"So you'll both go to the Nationals!" Coach couldn't resist doing a couple of dance steps, and I was so ecstatic, I joined him. But a wet concrete swim deck is not an ideal dance floor.

"Look out!" yelled Angela, as we just missed falling into the water. "I don't want my partner to break a leg. We've got a long way to go before the 1980 Olympics."

"What?" I gasped.

"Just doing some positive mental rehearsing," she grinned.

"A little confidence sure goes a long way," I retorted.

Still, maybe that *is* something to think about!

THINKING ABOUT THE SELECTION

Recalling

1. For what are Tobi and Angela competing?
2. Name three ways that Tobi shows poor sportsmanship.
3. What causes Tobi to change her behavior?
4. At the end of the story, who wins the race?

Interpreting

5. Why does Angela swim poorly during the meet?
6. How is Tobi's method of getting ready for a race different from Angela's?
7. What is "the confidence game"?

Applying

8. At one point Tobi says, "There's no worse anger than the kind you feel toward yourself when you've ruined something you care about." Explain how this is true in many situations.
9. Tobi's coach says sportsmanship (or sportswomanship) is shown "when one athlete accepts a better athlete in a spirit of friendly competition." What is your definition of sportsmanship?
10. Work with a group of your classmates to draw up a list of athletes you would cite for good sportsmanship.

ANALYZING LITERATURE

Understanding Conflict

A **conflict** is a struggle between opposing forces. In "The Confidence Game" Tobi experiences both an external conflict and an internal conflict. The external conflict occurs when Angela becomes a part of the swim team. The internal conflict is shown through Tobi's thoughts about the way she responds to the competition from Angela.

1. What threat does Angela pose to Tobi?
2. What opposing feelings does Tobi feel?
3. How does Tobi resolve her external conflict?
4. How does she resolve her internal conflict?
5. Do you think the resolution of these conflicts is realistic? Why or why not?

CRITICAL THINKING AND READING

Making Inferences

An **inference** is a reasonable conclusion that you draw based on evidence. When you read, you make inferences to gain more from a story than the author tells you directly. Sometimes you make small inferences to fill in gaps in the information given, and sometimes you make large inferences about how the information in the story works together to give you meaning. You make many inferences automatically while summarizing, predicting, or clarifying.

For example, you can infer that the coach is disappointed in Tobi's behavior early in "The Confidence Game." The author does not tell you this directly, but you can infer it from the coach's actions and his words: He calls Tobi aside to speak to her about sportsmanship, and he tells her that her attitude is hurting her performance.

What inference can you draw about Tobi's feelings from the following details?
a. She chews the inside of her cheek.
b. Her toes curl under her feet when the coach is talking to her.
c. Her face feels as if it has been "splashed with hot pink paint" when the coach mentions her recent behavior.

THINKING AND WRITING

Writing About Confidence

In this story Tobi teaches Angela how to play the confidence game. Discuss with your classmates whether you agree with her advice. Then imagine that you have a friend who is facing a challenging situation—tryouts for the softball team or auditions for the class play, for example. Consider what you would tell this person about confidence. Write a letter to your friend explaining how to play the confidence game. After you have drafted your letter, read it over to make sure you have expressed yourself as clearly as possible. Then proofread your letter and prepare a final draft.

GUIDE FOR READING

A Day's Wait

Ernest Hemingway (1899–1961), who was born in Oak Park, Illinois, is one of America's most famous writers. He received the Nobel Prize for his novels and short stories. Hemingway lived an adventurous life, participating in both World War I and World War II and spending much time hunting and fishing. Many of his books, like *The Old Man and the Sea,* are based on such experiences. "A Day's Wait" is not about adventures like these, but it does deal with a favorite Hemingway theme—courage.

Internal Conflict

An **internal conflict** is a struggle that occurs within a person's mind. Such a conflict may involve two opposing beliefs, feelings, or loyalties. For example, if you have two friends who are quarreling, you will probably experience a conflict. Your loyalty to each will result in a feeling of being divided.

Sometimes an internal conflict causes a person to take dramatic action, while in other cases the struggle goes on quietly inside. "A Day's Wait" is an example of a quiet internal conflict.

Look For

As you read, look for which character in "A Day's Wait" is experiencing a painful and secret internal conflict. At what moment is the conflict resolved?

Writing

Suppose that you were taking care of someone who was ill. Describe what you would say and do to make that person feel better.

Vocabulary

Knowing the following words will help you as you read "A Day's Wait."

epidemic (ep'ə dem' ik) *n.*: Outbreak of a contagious disease (p. 33)

prescribed (pri skrībd') *adj.*: Advised as a medicine by a doctor (p. 34)

slithered (sli*th*' ərd) *v.*: Slid (p. 34)

flushed (flusht) *v.*: Drove from hiding (p. 34)

poised (poizd) *v.*: Balanced (p. 34)

commenced (kə menst') *v.*: Began (p. 34)

kilometer (ki läm' ə tər) *n.*: 1,000 meters or about 5/8 of a mile (p. 34)

A Day's Wait

Ernest Hemingway

He came into the room to shut the windows while we were still in bed and I saw he looked ill. He was shivering, his face was white, and he walked slowly as though it ached to move.

"What's the matter, Schatz?"[1]

"I've got a headache."

"You better go back to bed."

"No. I'm all right."

"You go to bed. I'll see you when I'm dressed."

But when I came downstairs he was dressed, sitting by the fire, looking a very sick and miserable boy of nine years. When I put my hand on his forehead I knew he had a fever.

"You go up to bed," I said, "you're sick."

"I'm all right," he said.

When the doctor came he took the boy's temperature.

"What is it?" I asked him.

"One hundred and two."

Downstairs, the doctor left three different medicines in different colored capsules with instructions for giving them. One was to bring down the fever, another a purgative, the third to overcome an acid condition. The germs of influenza can only exist in an acid condition, he explained. He seemed to know all about influenza and said there was noth-

ing to worry about if the fever did not go above one hundred and four degrees. This was a light epidemic of flu and there was no danger if you avoided pneumonia.

Back in the room I wrote the boy's temperature down and made a note of the time to give the various capsules.

"Do you want me to read to you?"

"All right. If you want to," said the boy. His face was very white and there were dark areas under his eyes. He lay still in the bed and seemed very detached from what was going on.

I read aloud from Howard Pyle's *Book of Pirates*; but I could see he was not following what I was reading.

"How do you feel, Schatz?" I asked him.

"Just the same, so far," he said.

I sat at the foot of the bed and read to myself while I waited for it to be time to give another capsule. It would have been natural for him to go to sleep, but when I looked up he was looking at the foot of the bed, looking very strangely.

"Why don't you try to go to sleep? I'll wake you up for the medicine."

"I'd rather stay awake."

After a while he said to me, "You don't have to stay in here with me, Papa, if it bothers you."

"It doesn't bother me."

"No, I mean you don't have to stay if it's going to bother you."

I thought perhaps he was a little light-

---

1. Schatz (shäts): A German term of affection, used here as a loving nickname.

headed and after giving him the prescribed capsules at eleven o'clock I went out for a while. It was a bright, cold day, the ground covered with a sleet that had frozen so that it seemed as if all the bare trees, the bushes, the cut brush and all the grass and the bare ground had been varnished with ice. I took the young Irish setter for a little walk up the road and along a frozen creek, but it was difficult to stand or walk on the glassy surface and the red dog slipped and slithered and I fell twice, hard, once dropping my gun and having it slide away over the ice.

We flushed a covey[2] of quail under a high clay bank with overhanging brush and I killed two as they went out of sight over the top of the bank. Some of the covey lit in trees but most of them scattered into brush piles and it was necessary to jump on the ice-coated mounds of brush several times before they would flush. Coming out while you were poised unsteadily on the icy, springy brush they made difficult shooting, and I killed two, missed five, and started back pleased to have found a covey close to the house and happy there were so many left to find on another day.

At the house they said the boy had refused to let anyone come into the room.

"You can't come in," he said. "You mustn't get what I have."

I went up to him and found him in exactly the position I had left him, white-faced, but with the tops of his cheeks flushed by the fever, staring still, as he had stared at the foot of the bed.

I took his temperature.

"What is it?"

"Something like a hundred," I said. It was one hundred and two and four tenths.

"It was a hundred and two," he said.

"Who said so?"

"The doctor."

---

2. **covey** (kuv' ē) *n.*: A small flock of birds.

"Your temperature is all right," I said. "It's nothing to worry about."

"I don't worry," he said, "but I can't keep from thinking."

"Don't think," I said. "Just take it easy."

"I'm taking it easy," he said and looked straight ahead. He was evidently holding tight on to himself about something.

"Take this with water."

"Do you think it will do any good?"

"Of course it will."

I sat down and opened the *Pirate* book and commenced to read, but I could see he was not following, so I stopped.

"About what time do you think I'm going to die?" he asked.

"What?"

"About how long will it be before I die?"

"You aren't going to die. What's the matter with you?"

"Oh, yes, I am. I heard him say a hundred and two."

"People don't die with a fever of one hundred and two. That's a silly way to talk."

"I know they do. At school in France the boys told me you can't live with forty-four degrees. I've got a hundred and two."

He had been waiting to die all day, ever since nine o'clock in the morning.

"You poor Schatz," I said. "Poor old Schatz. It's like miles and kilometers. You aren't going to die. That's a different thermometer. On that thermometer thirty-seven is normal. On this kind it's ninety-eight."

"Are you sure?"

"Absolutely," I said. "It's like miles and kilometers. You know, like how many kilometers we make when we do seventy miles in the car?"

"Oh," he said.

But his gaze at the foot of the bed relaxed slowly. The hold over himself relaxed too, finally, and the next day it was very slack and he cried very easily at little things that were of no importance.

THINKING ABOUT THE SELECTION

Recalling

1. Why does the boy think he will die?
2. Why does the boy's father not correct this mistake until the end of the story?
3. How does the father explain the mistake to his son?

Interpreting

4. What is the meaning of the story's title?
5. Describe two ways in which the boy shows courage or concern for others.
6. Why does the boy cry "very easily at little things" the next day?

Applying

7. In this story the boy shows a kind of quiet courage. What other characters in literature can you name who have shown quiet courage?

ANALYZING LITERATURE

Understanding Internal Conflict

An **internal conflict** is a struggle within a character's mind. Usually an internal conflict makes a character feel troubled and divided until the conflict is resolved at the end of the story. In "A Day's Wait" the boy experiences such a conflict.

1. Which conflicting feelings are struggling within the boy's mind?
2. When does this internal conflict begin?
3. How is the conflict resolved?

CRITICAL THINKING AND READING

Making Inferences about Conflict

Since the conflict in "A Day's Wait" occurs in the boy's mind, you do not learn about it directly. Instead, you learn about it by making inferences based on clues in what the boy says and does.

The trick of finding clues to the boy's conflict is to search for statements and actions that seem out of place. Such unusual behavior indicates that the boy is responding to an inner conflict rather than to the actual situation around him. For example, one clue to the conflict is that the boy seems "very detached."

1. Find two other examples of unusual actions (not words) that indicate the boy is experiencing a conflict.
2. Find two examples of unusual statements that point to the boy's internal conflict.

UNDERSTANDING LANGUAGE

Recognizing the Greek Root *demos*

A **root** is the core of a word to which suffixes and prefixes can be added. Many English words have Greek roots. The word *epidemic,* for example, is made up of a Greek prefix (*epi-*) meaning "among" and a Greek root (*demos*) meaning "people."

Find the same root in the following words. Then look up each word in a dictionary. Finally, use it in a sentence.

1. democracy   2. democrat   3. pandemic

THINKING AND WRITING

Planning a Television Program

Imagine that your class is producing a program based on this story. As director, you have to write a memo telling the camera person how to show the boy's internal conflict. Brainstorm to think of different camera shots that would reveal the boy's inner struggle. Then use these ideas to write a one-page memo. Explain why each shot you have chosen would be effective. As you revise your memo, make sure that the camera person will be able to follow your directions.

GUIDE FOR READING

A Boy and a Man

James Ramsey Ullman (1907–1971) was born in New York City, but his interest in mountain climbing made him "more familiar with Tibet than with Times Square." His work as a reporter, playwright, and play producer did not prevent him from traveling in pursuit of adventure. Though too ill to climb Mount Everest in Tibet himself, he assisted the American expedition that conquered this mountain in 1963. "A Boy and a Man" captures Ullman's love of climbing.

Suspense

Suspense is the quality of a story that makes you want to keep reading until you learn how the events turn out. The word *suspense* comes from a Latin word meaning "suspended" or "uncertain," and uncertainty is an important part of suspense. You keep reading because the story is like a fascinating puzzle that fits together only at the end. Danger is another key ingredient in creating suspense. In many tales of suspense, the outcome is a matter of life or death. However, the danger in a suspenseful story does not have to be a physical threat. It can involve, for example, the possibility of losing a friend or failing a test.

The writer of "A Man and a Boy" wastes no time in creating suspense. As soon as the story opens, you are faced with a situation that is both uncertain and dangerous.

Look For

As you read "A Boy and a Man," a story about a mountain rescue in the Alps, look for the ways that the writer uses uncertainty and danger to create suspense. Which parts of the story keep you sitting on the edge of your seat?

Writing

Describe an episode from a suspenseful movie or television program you have seen. Explain why this show kept you sitting at the edge of your seat.

Vocabulary

Knowing the following words will help you as you read "A Boy and a Man."

crevasse (kri vas') *n.*: Deep crack (p. 37)
glacier (glā' shər) *n.*: Large mass of ice and snow (p. 37)
despair (di sper') *n.*: Loss of hope (p. 37)
prone (prōn) *adj.*: Lying face downward (p. 38)
taut (tôt) *adj.*: Tightly stretched (p. 39)
pummeled (pum' ld) *v.*: Beat (p. 39)
reconnoiter (rē' kə noit' ər) *v.*: Look around (p. 41)

A Boy and a Man

from *Banner in the Sky*

James Ramsey Ullman

The crevasse was about six feet wide at the top and narrowed gradually as it went down. But how deep it was Rudi could not tell. After a few feet the blue walls of ice curved away at a sharp slant, and what was below the curve was hidden from sight.

"Hello!" Rudi called.

"Hello—" A voice answered from the depths.

"How far down are you?"

"I'm not sure. About twenty feet, I'd guess."

"On the bottom?"

"No. I can't even see the bottom. I was lucky and hit a ledge."

The voice spoke in German, but with a strange accent. Whoever was down there, Rudi knew, it was not one of the men of the valley.

"Are you hurt?" he called.

"Nothing broken—no," said the voice. "Just shaken up some. And cold."

"How long have you been there?"

"About three hours."

Rudi looked up and down the crevasse. He was thinking desperately of what he could do.

"Do you have a rope?" asked the voice.

"No."

"How many of you are there?"

"Only me."

There was a silence. When the voice spoke again, it was still quiet and under strict control. "Then you'll have to get help," it said.

Rudi didn't answer. To get down to Kurtal would take at least two hours, and for a party to climb back up would take three. By that time it would be night, and the man would have been in the crevasse for eight hours. He would be frozen to death.

"No," said Rudi, "it would take too long."

"What else is there to do?"

Rudi's eyes moved over the ice-walls: almost vertical, smooth as glass. "Have you an ax?" he asked.

"No. I lost it when I fell. It dropped to the bottom."

"Have you tried to climb?"

"Yes. But I can't get a hold."

There was another silence. Rudi's lips tightened, and when he spoke again his voice was strained. "I'll think of something," he cried. "I'll think of *something!*"

"Don't lose your head," the voice said. "The only way is to go down for help."

"But you'll—"

"Maybe. And maybe not. That's a chance we'll have to take."

The voice was as quiet as ever. And, hearing it, Rudi was suddenly ashamed. Here was he, safe on the glacier's surface, showing fear and despair, while the one below, facing almost certain death, remained calm and controlled. Whoever it was down there, it was a real man. A brave man.

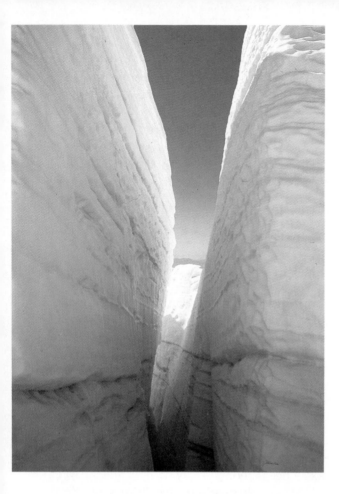

Rudi drew in a long, slow breath. With his climbing-staff he felt down along the smooth surface of the ice walls.

"Are you still there?" said the voice.

"Yes," he said.

"You had better go."

"Wait—"

Lying flat on the glacier, he leaned over the rim of the crevasse and lowered the staff as far as it would go. Its end came almost to the curve in the walls.

"Can you see it?" he asked.

"See what?" said the man.

Obviously he couldn't. Standing up, Rudi removed his jacket and tied it by one sleeve to the curved end of the staff. Then, holding the other end, he again lay prone and lowered his staff and jacket.

"Can you see it now?" he asked.

"Yes," said the man.

"How far above you is it?"

"About ten feet."

Again the staff came up. Rudi took off his shirt and tied one of its sleeves to the dangling sleeve of the jacket. This time, as he lay down, the ice bit, cold and rough, into his bare chest; but he scarcely noticed it. With his arms extended, all the shirt and half the jacket were out of sight beneath the curve in the crevasse.

"How near are you now?" he called.

"Not far," said the voice.

"Can you reach it?"

"I'm trying."

There was the sound of scraping boot-nails; of labored breathing. But no pull on the shirtsleeve down below.

"I can't make it," said the voice. It was fainter than before.

"Wait," said Rudi.

For the third time he raised the staff. He took off his trousers. He tied a trouser-leg to the loose sleeve of the shirt. Then he pulled, one by one, at all the knots he had made: between staff and jacket, jacket and shirt, shirt and trousers. He pulled until the blood pounded in his head and the knots were as tight as his strength could make them. This done, he stepped back from the crevasse to the point where his toes had rested when he lay flat. With feet and hands he kicked and scraped the ice until he had made two holes. Then, lying down as before, he dug his toes deep into them. He was naked now, except for his shoes, stockings and underpants. The cold rose from the ice into his blood and bones. He lowered the staff and knotted clothes like a sort of crazy fishing line.

The trousers, the shirt and half of the jacket passed out of sight. He was leaning over as far as he could.

"Can you reach it now?" he called.

"Yes," the voice answered.

"All right. Come on."

"You won't be able to hold me. I'll pull you in."

"No you won't."

He braced himself. The pull came. His toes went taut in their ice-holds and his hands tightened on the staff until the knuckles showed white. Again he could hear a scraping sound below, and he knew that the man was clawing his boots against the ice-wall, trying both to lever himself up and to take as much weight as possible off the improvised lifeline. But the wall obviously offered little help. Almost all his weight was on the lifeline. Suddenly there was a jerk, as one of the knots in the clothing slipped, and the staff was almost wrenched from Rudi's hands. But the knot held. And his hands held. He tried to call down, "All right?" but he had no breath for words. From below, the only sound was the scraping of boots on ice.

How long it went on Rudi could never have said. Perhaps only for a minute or so. But it seemed like hours. And then at last—at last—it happened. A hand came into view around the curve of the crevasse wall: a hand gripping the twisted fabric of his jacket, and then a second hand rising slowly above it. A head appeared. A pair of shoulders. A face was raised for an instant and then lowered. Again one hand moved slowly up past the other.

But Rudi no longer saw it, for now his eyes were shut tight with the strain. His teeth were clamped, the cords of his neck bulged, the muscles of his arm felt as if he were being drawn one by one from the bones that held them. He began to lose his toe-holds. He was being dragged forward. Desperately, frantically, he dug in with his feet, pressed his whole body down, as if he could make it part of the glacier. Though all but naked on the ice, he was pouring with sweat. Somehow he stopped the slipping. Somehow he held on. But now suddenly the strain was even worse, for the man had

reached the lower end of the staff. The slight "give" of the stretched clothing was gone, and in its place, was rigid deadweight on a length of wood. The climber was close now. But heavy. Indescribably heavy. Rudi's hands ached and burned, as if it were a rod of hot lead that they clung to. It was not a mere man he was holding, but a giant; or a block of granite. The pull was unendurable. The pain unendurable. He could hold on no longer. His hands were opening. It was all over.

And then it *was* over. The weight was gone. There was a scraping sound close beneath him; a hand on the rim of ice; a figure pulling itself up onto the lip of the crevasse. The man was beside Rudi, turning to him, staring at him.

"Why—you're just a boy!" he said in astonishment.

Rudi was too numb to move or speak. Taking the staff from him, the man pulled up the line of clothes, untied the knots and shook them out.

"Come on now. Quickly!" he said.

Pulling the boy to his feet, he helped him dress. Then he rubbed and pummeled him until at last Rudi felt the warmth of returning circulation.

"Better?" the man asked, smiling.

Rudi nodded. And finally he was able to speak again. "And you, sir," he said, "you are all right?"

The man nodded. He was warming himself now: flapping his arms and kicking his feet together. "A few minutes of sun and I'll be as good as new."

Nearby, a black boulder lay embedded in the glacial ice, and, going over to it, they sat down. The sunlight poured over them like a warm bath. Rudi slowly flexed his aching fingers and saw that the man was doing the same. And then the man had raised his eyes and was looking at him.

"It's a miracle how you did it," he said. "A boy of your size. All alone."

"It was nothing," Rudi murmured.

"Nothing?"

"I—I only—"

"Only saved my life," said the man.

For the first time, now, Rudi was really seeing him. He was a man of perhaps thirty, very tall and thin, and his face, too, was thin, with a big hawklike nose and a strong jutting chin. His weather-browned cheeks were clean-shaven, his hair black, his eyes deep-set and gray. And when he spoke, his voice was still almost as quiet as when it had been muffled by the ice-walls of the crevasse. He is—what?—Rudi thought. Not Swiss, he knew. Not French or German. English, perhaps? Yes, English. . . . And then suddenly a deep excitement filled him, for he knew who the man was.

"You are Captain Winter?" he murmured.

"That's right."

"And I—I have saved—I mean—"

Rudi stopped in confusion, and the Englishman grinned. "You've saved," he said, smiling, "one of the worst imbeciles that ever walked on a glacier. An imbecile who was so busy looking up at a mountain that he couldn't even see what was at his feet."

Rudi was wordless—almost stunned. He looked at the man, and then away in embarrassment, and he could scarcely believe what had happened. The name of Captain John Winter was known through the length and breadth of the Alps. He was the foremost mountaineer of his day, and during the past ten years had made more first ascents of great peaks than any other man alive. Rudi had heard that he had come to Kurtal a few days before. He had hoped that at least he would see him in the hotel or walking by in the street. But actually to meet him—and in this way! To pull him from a crevasse—save him. . . . It was incredible!

Captain Winter was watching him. "And you, son," he asked. "What is your name?"

Somehow the boy got his voice back. "Rudi," he said. "Rudi Matt."

"Matt?" Now it was the man's turn to be impressed. "Not of the family of the great Josef Matt?"

"He was my father," Rudi said.

Captain Winter studied him with his gray eyes. Then he smiled again. "I should have known," he said. "A boy who could do what you've done—"

"Did you know my father, sir?"

"No, unfortunately I didn't. He was before my day. But ever since I was a boy I have heard of him. In twenty years no one has come to the Alps and not heard of the great guide, Josef Matt."

Rudi's heart swelled. He looked away. His eyes fixed on the vast mountain that rose before them, and then he saw that Captain Winter was watching it too.

Unconsciously the Englishman spoke his thoughts. "Your father was—" He caught himself and stopped.

"Yes," said Rudi softly, "he was killed on the Citadel."

There was a silence. Captain Winter reached into a pocket and brought out an unbroken bar of chocolate. "Lucky I fell on the other side," he grinned.

He broke the bar in two and handed half to Rudi.

"Oh, no, sir, thank you. I couldn't."

"When I meet a boy your age who can't eat chocolate," said Winter, "I'll be glad to stay in a crevasse for good."

Rudi took it, and they sat munching. The sun was warm on their thawing bodies. Far above, it struck the cliffs and snowfields of the Citadel, so brightly that they had to squint against the glare.

Then there was Winter's quiet voice again. "What do you think, Rudi?"

"Think, sir?"

"Can it be climbed?"

"Climbed? The Citadel?"

"Your father thought so. Alone among all the guides of Switzerland, he thought so." There was another pause. "And I think so too," said Captain Winter.

The boy was peering again at the shining heights. And suddenly his heart was pounding so hard that he was sure the Englishman must be able to hear it. "Is—is that why you have come here, sir?" he asked. "To try to climb the Citadel?"

"Well, now—" Winter smiled. "It's not so simple, you know. For one thing, there's not a guide in the valley who would go with me."

"I have an uncle, sir. He is—"

"Yes, I know your uncle. Franz Lerner. He is the best in Kurtal, and I've spoken to him. But he would not go. Anything but that, he said. Any other peak, any route, any venture. But not *that*, he said. Not the Citadel."

"He remembers my father—"

"Yes, he remembers your father. They all remember him. And while they love and respect his memory, they all think he was crazy." Winter chuckled softly. "Now they think *I'm* crazy," he added. "And maybe they're right too," he said.

"What will you do, sir?" asked Rudi. "Not try it alone?"

"No, that crazy I'm not." Winter slowly stroked his long jaw. "I'm not certain what I'll do," he went on. "Perhaps I'll go over to the next valley. To Broli. I've been told there is a guide there—a man called Saxo. Do you know him?"

"Yes—Emil Saxo. I have never met him, but I have heard of him. They say he is a very great guide."

"Well, I thought perhaps I'd go and talk with him. After a while. But first I must rec-

onnoiter some more. Make my plans. Pick the route. If there *is* a route."

"Yes, there is! Of course there is!"

Rudi had not thought the words. They simply burst out from him. And now again he was embarrassed as the man looked at him curiously.

"So?" said Captain Winter. "That is interesting, Rudi. Tell me why you think so."

"I have studied the Citadel many times, sir."

"Why?"

"Because—because—" He stopped. He couldn't say it.

"Because you want to climb it yourself?"

"I am not yet a grown man, sir. I know I cannot expect—"

"I wasn't a grown man either," said the Captain, "when I first saw the Citadel. I was younger than you—only twelve—and my parents had brought me here for a summer holiday. But I can still remember how I felt when I looked up at it, and the promise I made myself that some day I was going to climb it." He paused. His eyes moved slowly upward. "Youth is the time for dreams, boy," he murmured. "The trick is, when you get older, not to forget them."

Rudi listened, spellbound. He had never heard anyone speak like that. He had not known a grown man could think and feel like that.

Then Winter asked:

"This east face, Rudi—what do you think of it?"

"Think of it, sir?"

"Could it be climbed?"

Rudi shook his head. "No, it is no good. The long chimney[1] there—you see. It looks all right; it could be done. And to the left, the

---

1. chimney (chim′ nē) *n*.: In mountain climbing, this word means a deep, narrow crack in a cliff face.

ledges"—he pointed—"they could be done too. But higher up, no. They stop. The chimney stops, and there is only smooth rock."

"What about the northeast ridge?"

"That is not good either."

"It's not so steep."

"No, it is not so steep," said Rudi. "But the rocks are bad. They slope out, with few places for holds."

"And the north face?"

Rudi talked on. About the north face, the west ridge, the southwest ridge. He talked quietly and thoughtfully, but with deep inner excitement, for this was the first time in his life that he had been able to speak to anyone of these things which he had thought and studied for so long. . . . And then suddenly he stopped, for he realized what he was doing. He, Rudi Matt, a boy of sixteen who worked in the kitchen of the Beau Site Hotel, was presuming to give his opinions to one of the greatest climbers in the world.

But Captain Winter had been listening intently. Sometimes he nodded. "Go on," he said now, as Rudi paused.

"But I am only—"

"Go on."

And Rudi went on . . .

"That doesn't leave much," said the captain a little later.

"No, sir," said the boy.

"Only the southeast ridge."

"Yes, sir."

"That was the way your father tried, wasn't it?"

"Yes, sir."

"And you believe it's the *only* way?"

"Yes, sir."

Captain Winter rubbed his jaw for a moment before speaking again. Then—"That also is very interesting to me, Rudi," he said quietly, "because it is what I believe too."

Later, they threaded their way down the Blue Glacier. For a while they moved in silence. Then Captain Winter asked:

"What do you do, Rudi?"

"Do, sir?"

"Are you an apprentice guide? A porter?"

Rudi swallowed. "No sir."

"What then?"

He could hardly say it. "A—dishwasher."

"A dishwasher?"

"In the Beau Site Hotel. It is my mother, sir. Since my father died, you see, she is afraid—she does not want—" Rudi swallowed again. "I am to go into the hotel business," he murmured.

"Oh."

Again they moved on without speaking. It was now late afternoon, and behind them the stillness was broken by a great roaring, as sun-loosened rock and ice broke off from the heights of the Citadel.

When they reached the path Rudi spoke again, hesitantly. "Will you please do me a favor, sir," he asked.

"Of course," said Winter.

"Before we come to the town we will separate. And you will please not tell anyone that I have been up here today?"

The Englishman looked at him in astonishment. "Not tell anyone? You save my life, boy, and you want me to keep it a secret?"

"It was nothing, sir. Truly. And if you say that I have been in the mountains, my mother and uncle will hear, and I will be in trouble." Rudi's voice took on a note of urgency. "You will not do it, sir? You will promise—please?"

Winter put a hand on his shoulder. "Don't worry," he said. "I won't get you in trouble." Then he smiled and added: "Master Rudi Matt–dishwasher."

They walked down the path. The sun sank. Behind them, the mountain roared.

THINKING ABOUT THE SELECTION

Recalling

1. Why doesn't Rudi go to Kurtal for help?
2. How does Rudi make a lifeline?
3. Why is Rudi "almost stunned" when he learns the identity of the man he has saved?
4. How did Rudi's father die?

Interpreting

5. Captain Winter says, "Youth is the time for dreams." What is Rudi's secret dream?
6. Why has Rudi been unable to fulfill his dream?
7. Why do you think this story is called "A Boy and a Man"?

Applying

8. Why do people sometimes keep secret their dreams and plans?

ANALYZING LITERATURE

Understanding Suspense

Writers create **suspense** by describing situations that are both uncertain and dangerous. Such dangers can be either physical or emotional. Many readers enjoy suspenseful stories because they want to discover what happens in the end and whether the characters avoid the dangers that face them. "A Boy and a Man" is a story that is filled with suspense.

1. How is Captain Winter's situation at the start of the story uncertain and dangerous?
2. How do Rudi's repeated attempts to rescue Captain Winter increase the suspense?
3. What future dangers are hinted at in the conversation between Rudi and the Captain?

CRITICAL THINKING AND READING

Identifying Details that Create Suspense

A writer creates suspense through details that increase the uncertainty and danger. Notice the details in the following description of Rudi's fourth attempt to make a lifeline for Captain Winter.

"He tied a trouser-leg to the loose sleeve of the shirt. Then he pulled, one by one, at all the knots he had made: between staff and jacket, jacket and shirt, shirt and trousers."

As you read, you wonder whether these knots will hold.

1. Find the paragraph that begins "He braced himself . . ." (page 39). Point out the details in this and the next few paragraphs that help create suspense.
2. Which specific words and phrases make you feel this suspense?

UNDERSTANDING LANGUAGE

Using Context Clues

The **context** of a word consists of the words that surround it. If you do not know a word's meaning, you can look for clues in the context. For example, from the description of a *crevasse* at the beginning of the story (p. 37), you could guess that the word *crevasse* means "a deep crack."

1. Find the reference to Rudi's "improvised lifeline" (p. 39). How does the description of the lifeline give you a clue to the meaning of the word *improvised*?
2. What does *improvised* mean?

THINKING AND WRITING

Writing About Suspense

Imagine that a magazine for teenagers is planning a special issue containing suspenseful stories. Think of stories you have read that would keep readers on the edge of their seats. Then choose the best one and write a letter to the editors of the magazine persuading them to use your story. (You may, of course, recommend "A Boy and a Man.") When revising your letter, make sure you have explained how your story contains the key ingredients of suspense: uncertainty and danger.

GUIDE FOR READING

A Secret for Two

Quentin Reynolds (1902–1965), born in Brooklyn, New York, was active as a newspaper reporter, a sportswriter, and an author of short stories. One of his best-selling books, *The Wounded Don't Cry,* is about the courage of the English people during World War II. He covered the war for a popular magazine, writing fast-moving reports from combat areas. His reporting won high praise from England's prime minister, Winston Churchill. Reynolds also found bravery in ordinary life, as you will see in "A Secret for Two."

A Hidden Problem

The **problem,** or conflict, on which a story is based is not always clearly indicated. Sometimes a writer will disguise the problem until the story is nearly over. Only at that point do you understand that something important has been going on under the surface of the action. In fact, you may be quite surprised to learn what a writer has been keeping back.

In "A Secret for Two," the writer includes clues to the "secret," but does not reveal the problem until the end.

Look For

As you read "A Secret for Two," look for clues that point to the story's hidden problem. When is the hidden problem finally revealed?

Writing

The "secret" of this story is shared by a man and a horse who feel affection for each other. Write a description of a "friendship" you have had with a pet or one you have seen between another person and his or her pet.

Vocabulary

Knowing the following words will help you as you read "A Secret for Two."
henceforth (hens fôrth′) *adv.:*
From this time on (p. 45)
sheen (shēn) *n.:* Brightness;
shininess (p. 45)
stalk (stôk) *v.:* Walk slowly and
stiffly (p. 45)

A Secret for Two

Quentin Reynolds

Montreal is a very large city, but, like all large cities, it has some very small streets. Streets, for instance, like Prince Edward Street, which is only four blocks long, ending in a cul-de-sac.[1] No one knew Prince Edward Street as well as did Pierre Dupin, for Pierre had delivered milk to the families on the street for thirty years now.

During the past fifteen years the horse which drew the milk wagon used by Pierre was a large white horse named Joseph. In Montreal, especially in that part of Montreal which is very French, the animals, like children, are often given the names of saints. When the big white horse first came to the Provincale Milk Company, he didn't have a name. They told Pierre that he could use the white horse henceforth. Pierre stroked the softness of the horse's neck; he stroked the sheen of its splendid belly, and he looked into the eyes of the horse.

"This is a kind horse, a gentle and a faithful horse," Pierre said, "and I can see a beautiful spirit shining out of the eyes of the horse. I will name him after good St. Joseph, who was also kind and gentle and faithful and a beautiful spirit."

Within a year Joseph knew the milk route as well as Pierre. Pierre used to boast that he didn't need reins—he never touched them. Each morning Pierre arrived at the stables of the Provincale Milk Company at five o'clock. The wagon would be loaded and Joseph hitched to it. Pierre would call "*Bon jour, vieille ami,*"[2] as he climbed into his seat and Joseph would turn his head and the other drivers would smile and say that the horse would smile at Pierre. Then Jacques, the foreman, would say, "All right, Pierre, go on," and Pierre would call softly to Joseph, "*Avance, mon ami,*"[3] and this splendid combination would stalk proudly down the street.

The wagon, without any direction from Pierre, would roll three blocks down St. Catherine Street, then turn right two blocks along Roslyn Avenue; then left, for that was Prince Edward Street. The horse would stop at the first house, allow Pierre perhaps thirty seconds to get down from his seat and put a bottle of milk at the front door and would then go on, skipping two houses and stopping at the third. So down the length of the street. Then Joseph, still without any direction from Pierre, would turn around and come back along the other side. Yes, Joseph was a smart horse.

Pierre would boast at the stable of Joseph's skill. "I never touch the reins. He knows just where to stop. Why, a blind man could handle my route with Joseph pulling the wagon."

---

1. cul-de-sac (kul′ də sak′) *n.*: A blind alley; a dead-end street.

2. *Bon jour, vieille ami* (bôn zhōōr′ vē ā′ äm ē′): French for "Hello, old friend."

3. *Avance, mon ami* (ä väns′ môn äm ē′): French for "Go forward, my friend."

So it went on for years—always the same. Pierre and Joseph both grew old together, but gradually, not suddenly. Pierre's huge walrus mustache was pure white now and Joseph didn't lift his knees so high or raise his head quite as much. Jacques, the foreman of the stables, never noticed that they were both getting old until Pierre appeared one day carrying a heavy walking stick.

"Hey, Pierre," Jacques laughed. "Maybe you got the gout,[4] hey?"

"*Mais oui*,[5] Jacques," Pierre said uncertainly. "One grows old. One's legs get tired."

"You should teach the horse to carry the milk to the front door for you," Jacques told him. "He does everything else."

He knew every one of the forty families he served on Prince Edward Street. The cooks knew that Pierre could neither read nor write, so instead of following the usual custom of leaving a note in an empty bottle if an additional quart of milk was needed they would sing out when they heard the rumble of his wagon wheels over the cobbled street, "Bring an extra quart this morning, Pierre."

"So you have company for dinner tonight," he would call back gaily.

Pierre had a remarkable memory. When he arrived at the stable he'd always remember to tell Jacques, "The Paquins took an extra quart this morning; the Lemoines bought a pint of cream."

Jacques would note these things in a little book he always carried. Most of the drivers had to make out the weekly bills and collect the money, but Jacques, liking Pierre, had always excused him from this task. All Pierre had to do was to arrive at five in the morning, walk to his wagon, which was always in the same spot at the curb, and deliver his milk. He returned some two hours later, got stiffly from his seat, called a cheery "*Au 'voir*"[6] to Jacques and then limped slowly down the street.

One morning the president of the Provincale Milk Company came to inspect the early morning deliveries. Jacques pointed Pierre out to him and said, "Watch how he talks to that horse. See how the horse listens and how he turns his head toward Pierre? See the look in that horse's eyes? You know, I think those two share a secret. I have often noticed it. It is as though they both sometimes chuckle at us as they go off on their route. Pierre is a good man, Monsieur[7] President, but he gets old. Would it be too bold for me to suggest that he be retired and be given perhaps a small pension?" he added anxiously.

---

6. au 'voir (ō vwär'): French for "until we meet again"; "goodbye."
7. monsieur (mə syur') *n.*: French for "mister" or "sir."

---

4. gout (gowt) *n.*: a disease characterized by swelling and pain in the hands and feet.
5. mais oui (mā wē): French for "but yes."

"But of course," the president laughed. "I know his record. He has been on this route now for thirty years and never once has there been a complaint. Tell him it is time he rested. His salary will go on just the same."

But Pierre refused to retire. He was panic-stricken at the thought of not driving Joseph every day. "We are two old men," he said to Jacques. "Let us wear out together. When Joseph is ready to retire—then I, too, will quit."

Jacques, who was a kind man, understood. There was something about Pierre and Joseph which made a man smile tenderly. It was as though each drew some hidden strength from the other. When Pierre was sitting in his seat, and when Joseph was hitched to the wagon, neither seemed old. But when they finished their work, then Pierre would limp down the street slowly, seeming very old indeed, and the horse's head would drop and he would walk very wearily to his stall.

Then one morning Jacques had dreadful news for Pierre when he arrived. It was a cold morning and still pitch-dark. The air was like iced wine that morning and the snow which had fallen during the night glistened like a million diamonds piled together.

Jacques said, "Pierre, your horse, Joseph, did not wake this morning. He was very old, Pierre, he was twenty-five, and that is like seventy-five for a man."

"Yes," Pierre said, slowly, "Yes. I am seventy-five. And I cannot see Joseph again."

"Of course you can," Jacques soothed. "He is over in his stall, looking very peaceful. Go over and see him."

Pierre took one step forward then turned. "No . . . no . . . you don't understand, Jacques."

Jacques clapped him on the shoulder. "We'll find another horse just as good as Joseph. Why, in a month you'll teach him to know your route as well as Joseph did. We'll . . ."

The look in Pierre's eyes stopped him. For years Pierre had worn a heavy cap, the peak of which came low over his eyes, keeping the bitter morning wind out of them. Now Jacques looked into Pierre's eyes and he saw something which startled him. He saw a dead, lifeless look in them. The eyes were mirroring the grief that was in Pierre's heart and his soul. It was as though his heart and soul had died.

"Take today off, Pierre," Jacques said, but already Pierre was hobbling off down the street, and had one been near one would have seen tears streaming down his cheeks and have heard half-smothered sobs. Pierre walked to the corner and stepped into the street. There was a warning yell from the driver of a huge truck that was coming fast and there was a scream of brakes, but Pierre apparently heard neither.

Five minutes later an ambulance driver said, "He's dead. Was killed instantly."

Jacques and several of the milk-wagon drivers had arrived and they looked down at the still figure.

"I couldn't help it." the driver of the truck protested, "he walked right into my truck. He never saw it, I guess. Why, he walked into it as though he was blind."

The ambulance doctor bent down. "Blind? Of course the man was blind. See those cataracts?[8] This man has been blind for five years." He turned to Jacques, "You say he worked for you? Didn't you know he was blind?"

"No . . . no . . ." Jacques said softly. "None of us knew. Only one knew—a friend of his named Joseph. . . . It was a secret, I think, just between those two."

---

8. cataracts (kat′ə rakts′) n.: An eye disease in which the lens becomes clouded over, causing partial or total blindness.

THINKING ABOUT THE SELECTION

Recalling

1. What does Pierre do on his job?
2. What is the "dreadful news" Jacques has for Pierre one morning?
3. How does Pierre die?
4. How do we learn Pierre's "secret"?

Interpreting

5. Why do Pierre and Joseph not seem old when they are together?
6. What makes Pierre keep his blindness a secret?

Applying

7. How is the friendship between Pierre and Joseph like a friendship between two people?

ANALYZING LITERATURE

Recognizing a Hidden Problem

In "A Secret for Two," the problem is hidden until the very end. Events continue, but you are not aware of an important fact that would explain the action. Going back over the story, however, you can find clues to the secret.

1. What is the hidden problem in "A Secret for Two"?
2. How might the story be different if the writer revealed the hidden problem sooner?
3. What is the meaning of the story's title?

CRITICAL THINKING AND READING

Finding Clues to a Hidden Problem

In "A Secret for Two," the writer gives you hints about the hidden problem. You can find these clues by looking for statements by the characters that seem exaggerated or unusual.

1. How does Pierre's boast about Joseph's skill give you a clue to the "secret"?
2. How does Jacques's unusual remark that Pierre and Joseph seem to "share a secret" hint at the hidden problem?

UNDERSTANDING LANGUAGE

Finding the Origins of English Words

Many English words have their origins, or beginnings, in other languages. Usually, a dictionary will tell you the language from which a word comes. For example, when you look up *cataract*, you will see the letters *Gr.* in brackets to indicate the origin of this word. The abbreviation *Gr.* stands for Greek. Other common abbreviations are *L.* for Latin, *Fr.* for French and *It.* for Italian.

Look up the following words from the story and identify the language or languages from which they come.

1. gout
2. ambulance
3. mustache
4. stable

THINKING AND WRITING

Writing a Short Story

You have just read a short story in which the main character faced a hidden problem. Now write a short story of your own in which a character has a secret difficulty. Get together with two or three classmates to think of ideas for this type of story. Remember that the problem does not have to be as serious as Pierre's. It can relate to an argument with a friend or a situation in school. Choose the idea you like best and develop it into a story. When you revise your story, make sure you have not revealed the hidden problem until the end.

GUIDE FOR READING

Zoo

Edward D. Hoch (1930–   ), whose last name rhymes with "poke," was born in Rochester, New York. After graduating from the University of Rochester, he worked as a researcher for the Rochester Public Library and as a copy writer for an advertising company. Hoch has written many stories and novels in the mystery and science fiction fields. In 1967, he won an award from the Mystery Writers of America for his short story "The Oblong Room." As you will see in "Zoo," Hoch has a lively imagination and a good sense of humor.

Plot and Point of View

Point of view refers to the angle or position from which a writer tells a story. By choosing to look through the eyes of a particular character or group, a writer gives you a certain impression of the sequence of events. In "Zoo," the writer views the events from two different angles. He tells the first part of the story from the point of view of the Earth people. Then he lets you look through the eyes of the horse-spider people of Kaan. This change in point of view affects the way you understand the events of the story.

Look For

Be alert to the change in point of view as you read about the "strange creatures" that Professor Hugo brings in his great silver spaceship. How would the sequence of events seem different if the writer let you see it from only one angle?

Writing

Remember a time when you cheered for a team at a sports event. Write a description of this event. Then imagine that you were a fan supporting the other team and tell about the contest from the opposite point of view. By doing so, you will be thinking about the same event from two perspectives.

Vocabulary

Knowing the following words will help you as you read "Zoo."
interplanetary (in′tər plan′ə ter′ē) *adj.*: Between planets (p. 51)
wonderment (wun′dər mənt) *n.*: Astonishment (p. 51)
awe (ô) *n.*: A mixed feeling of fear and wonder (p. 51)

Zoo

Edward D. Hoch

The children were always good during the month of August, especially when it began to get near the twenty-third. It was on this day that the great silver spaceship carrying Professor Hugo's Interplanetary Zoo settled down for its annual six-hour visit to the Chicago area.

Before daybreak the crowds would form, long lines of children and adults both, each one clutching his or her dollar, and waiting with wonderment to see what race of strange creatures the Professor had brought this year.

In the past they had sometimes been treated to three-legged creatures from Venus, or tall, thin men from Mars, or even snakelike horrors from somewhere more distant. This year, as the great round ship settled slowly to earth in the huge tri-city parking area just outside of Chicago, they watched with awe as the sides slowly slid up to reveal the familiar barred cages. In them were some wild breed of nightmare—small, horse-like animals that moved with quick, jerking motions and constantly chattered in a high-pitched tongue. The citizens of Earth clustered around as Professor Hugo's crew quickly collected the waiting dollars, and soon the good Professor himself made an appearance, wearing his many-colored rainbow cape and top hat. "Peoples of Earth," he called into his microphone.

The crowd's noise died down and he continued. "Peoples of Earth, this year you see a real treat for your single dollar—the little-known horse-spider people of Kaan—brought to you across a million miles of

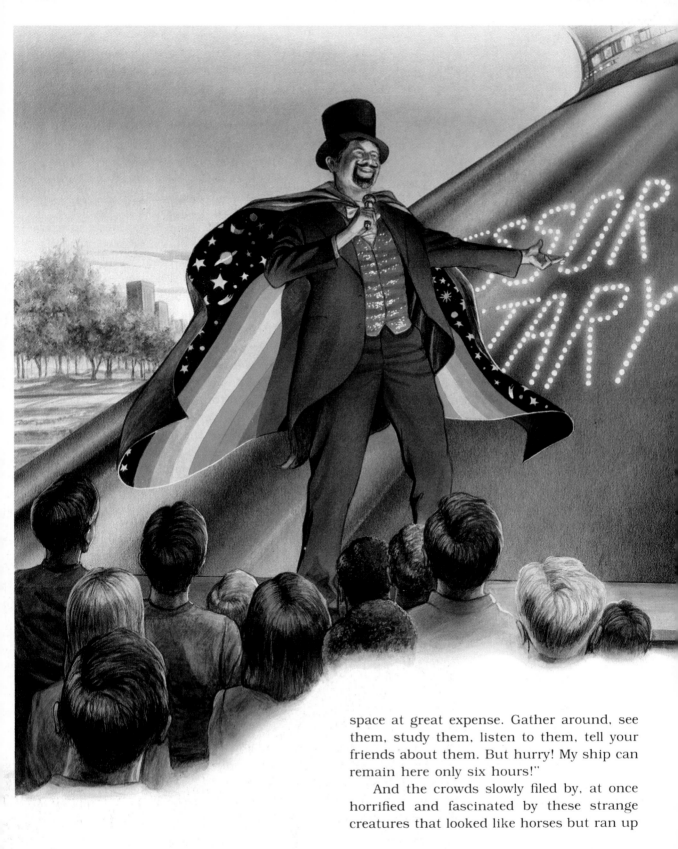

space at great expense. Gather around, see them, study them, listen to them, tell your friends about them. But hurry! My ship can remain here only six hours!"

And the crowds slowly filed by, at once horrified and fascinated by these strange creatures that looked like horses but ran up

Then, as the six-hour limit ran out, Professor Hugo once more took the microphone in hand. "We must go now, but we will return next year on this date. And if you enjoyed our zoo this year, telephone your friends in other cities about it. We will land in New York tomorrow, and next week on to London, Paris, Rome, Hong Kong, and Tokyo. Then on to other worlds!"

He waved farewell to them, and as the ship rose from the ground, the Earth peoples agreed that this had been the very best Zoo yet. . . .

Some two months and three planets later, the silver ship of Professor Hugo settled at last onto the familiar jagged rocks of Kaan, and the odd horse-spider creatures filed quickly out of their cages. Professor Hugo was there to say a few parting words, and then they scurried away in a hundred different directions, seeking their homes among the rocks.

In one house, the she-creature was happy to see the return of her mate and offspring. She babbled a greeting in the strange tongue and hurried to embrace them. "It was a long time you were gone. Was it good?"

And the he-creature nodded. "The little one enjoyed it especially. We visited eight worlds and saw many things."

The little one ran up the wall of the cave. "On the place called Earth it was the best. The creatures there wear garments over their skins, and they walk on two legs."

"But isn't it dangerous?" asked the she-creature.

"No," her mate answered. "There are bars to protect us from them. We remain right in the ship. Next time you must come with us. It is well worth the nineteen commocs it costs."

And the little one nodded. "It was the very best Zoo ever. . . ."

the walls of their cages like spiders. "This is certainly worth a dollar," one man remarked, hurrying away. "I'm going home to get the wife."

All day long it went like that, until ten thousand people had filed by the barred cages set into the side of the spaceship.

THINKING ABOUT THE SELECTION

Recalling

1. Why is there great excitement in Chicago?
2. What impression do Earthlings have of the people from Kaan?
3. How do the Kaanians describe humans?

Interpreting

4. Compare and contrast the ways in which Earthlings and Kaanians view each other.
5. What does the way Professor Hugo runs his zoo suggest about him?

Applying

6. Why is it easier to understand a situation if you see it from more than one angle?

ANALYZING LITERATURE

Understanding Plot and Point of View

Point of view is the position from which a writer tells a story. Often a writer will describe the sequence of events as they are seen by a particular person or group. In "Zoo," however, the writer treats point of view in an unusual way. He allows you to see the events from two different angles.

1. Identify the place in the story where the point of view changes.
2. How would the story have been different if it were told only from the Earthlings' point of view?
3. How does the change in point of view make the story effective?

CRITICAL THINKING AND READING

Considering Other Points of View

In "Zoo," the Earthlings think of the Kaanians as "small, horse-like animals" that are best viewed in a zoo. The Kaanians think of themselves as nor-

mal but regard the Earthlings as possibly dangerous "creatures." Neither group considers the other group's point of view. When studying people whose ideas or customs appear strange, you can keep an open mind by imagining what they think of *your* customs and ideas.

1. Imagine that you are a visitor to Earth from a planet where people travel by rockets. Describe your first impression of cars.
2. Describe your reaction to humans if on your planet people had eyes in the front *and* back of their heads.

UNDERSTANDING LANGUAGE

Appreciating Vivid Verbs

Writers use vivid, specific verbs so that you can picture what they are describing. A general word like *walk,* for example, can sometimes be effective. However, words that describe specific ways of walking—like *stumble, trudge, strut,* or even *tiptoe*—can make a description more lively.

Find the meaning of the vivid verbs printed in *italics* in the following descriptions from "Zoo."

1. ". . . the odd horse-spider creatures *filed* quickly out of their cages."
2. ". . . then they *scurried* away in a hundred different directions. . . ."

THINKING AND WRITING

Writing from Another Point of View

You have learned how the Earthlings and the Kaanians view the events of this story. However, Professor Hugo also must have a point of view. Imagine that the professor has kept a diary giving *his* impression of the story's events. List the type of entries the professor would make in his diary. Then use this list to write two diary pages indicating what the professor feels and thinks at each point of the story. When you revise these entries, make sure that the professor refers to himself as "I."

Character

FOUR GIRLS
August Macke
Three Lions

GUIDE FOR READING

Last Cover

Paul Annixter (1894–   ) was born Howard Allison Sturtzel in Minneapolis, Minnesota. While working a timber claim in northern Minnesota, Annixter began writing. He published more than five hundred stories and worked with his wife writing novels for young people. He said, "Our stories deal with some phase of human and animal interrelation, which offers to our minds a different and deeper sort of heart interest." "Last Cover" deals with this special relationship between a boy and a fox.

Character Traits

Character traits are the qualities that make a person an individual. For example, one person may appear to be calm, another excitable. One person may be musical, another athletic. Writers give their characters qualities that make them seem like real people. It is these character traits that determine how each character behaves and interacts with others.

Look For

At one point in this story, the narrator, Stan, says of his brother Colin: "It was a rare moment in which I really 'met' my brother, when something of his essence flowed into me. . . ." As you read the story, try to discover Colin's essence, or nature, for yourself, by looking for the character traits that make him special.

Writing

What is talent? How is it different from the type of learning we gain from books? Freewrite, exploring your answer.

Vocabulary

Knowing the following words will help you as you read "Last Cover."

abetting (ə bet′iŋ) v.: Helping or encouraging (p. 59)

passive (pas′iv) adj.: Inactive (p. 59)

vixen (vik′s′n) n.: A female fox (p. 59)

confound (kən found′) v.: Confuse (p. 61)

sanction (saŋk′shən) v.: Support (p. 62)

crafty (kraf′tē) adj.: Sly, cunning (p. 62)

wily (wī′lē) adj.: Sly (p. 64)

sanctuary (saŋk′choo wer′ē) n.: A place of protection (p. 64)

Last Cover

Paul Annixter

I'm not sure I can tell you what you want to know about my brother; but everything about the pet fox is important, so I'll tell all that from the beginning.

It goes back to a winter afternoon after I'd hunted the woods all day for a sign of our lost pet. I remember the way my mother looked up as I came into the kitchen. Without my speaking, she knew what had happened. For six hours I had walked, reading signs, looking for a delicate print in the damp soil or even a hair that might have told of a red fox passing that way—but I had found nothing.

"Did you go up in the foothills?" Mom asked.

I nodded. My face was stiff from held-back tears. My brother, Colin, who was going on twelve, got it all from one look at me and went into a heartbroken, almost silent, crying.

Three weeks before, Bandit, the pet fox Colin and I had raised from a tiny kit, had disappeared, and not even a rumor had been heard of him since.

"He'd have to go off soon anyway," Mom comforted. "A big, lolloping[1] fellow like him,

---

1. **lolloping** (läl′ əp iŋ) *adj.*: Moving in a clumsy or relaxed way, bobbing up and down or from side to side.

he's got to live his life same as us. But he may come back. That fox set a lot of store by you boys in spite of his wild ways."

"He set a lot of store by our food, anyway," Father said. He sat in a chair by the kitchen window mending a piece of harness. "We'll be seeing a lot more of that fellow, never fear. That fox learned to pine for table scraps and young chickens. He was getting to be an egg thief, too, and he's not likely to forget that."

"That was only pranking when he was little," Colin said desperately.

From the first, the tame fox had made tension in the family. It was Father who said we'd better name him Bandit, after he'd made away with his first young chicken.

"Maybe you know," Father said shortly. "But when an animal turns to egg sucking he's usually incurable. He'd better not come pranking around my chicken run again."

It was late February, and I remember the bleak, dead cold that had set in, cold that was a rare thing for our Carolina hills. Flocks of sparrows and snowbirds had appeared to peck hungrily at all that the pigs and chickens didn't eat.

"This one's a killer," Father would say of a morning, looking out at the whitened barn roof. "This one will make the shoats[2] squeal."

A fire snapped all day in our cookstove and another in the stone fireplace in the living room, but still the farmhouse was never warm. The leafless woods were bleak and empty, and I spoke of that to Father when I came back from my search.

"It's always a sad time in the woods when the seven sleepers are under cover," he said.

"What sleepers are they?" I asked. Father was full of woods lore.

"Why, all the animals that have got sense enough to hole up and stay hid in weather like this. Let's see, how was it the old rhyme named them?

Surly bear and sooty bat,
Brown chuck and masked coon,
Chippy-munk and sly skunk,
And all the mouses
'Cept in men's houses.

"And man would have joined them and made it eight, Granther Yeary always said, if he'd had a little more sense."

"I was wondering if the red fox mightn't make it eight," Mom said.

Father shook his head. "Late winter's a high time for foxes. Time when they're out deviling, not sleeping."

My chest felt hollow. I wanted to cry like Colin over our lost fox, but at fourteen a boy doesn't cry. Colin had squatted down on the floor and got out his small hammer and nails to start another new frame for a new picture. Maybe then he'd make a drawing for the frame and be able to forget his misery. It had been that way with him since he was five.

I thought of the new dress Mom had brought home a few days before in a heavy cardboard box. That box cover would be fine for Colin to draw on. I spoke of it, and Mom's glance thanked me as she went to get it. She and I worried a lot about Colin. He was small for his age, delicate and blond, his hair much lighter and softer then mine, his eyes deep and wide and blue. He was often sick, and I knew the fear Mom had that he might be predestined.[3] I'm just ordinary, like Father. I'm the sort of stuff that can take it— tough and strong—but Colin was always sort of special.

---

2. shoats (shōts) *n.*: Young hogs.

3. predestined (prē des' tind) *adj.*: In this case, marked to die early.

Mom lighted the lamp. Colin began cutting his white cardboard carefully, fitting it into his frame. Father's sharp glance turned on him now and again.

"There goes the boy making another frame before there's a picture for it," he said. "It's too much like cutting out a man's suit for a fellow that's, say, twelve years old. Who knows whether he'll grow into it?"

Mom was into him then, quick. "Not a single frame of Colin's has ever gone to waste. The boy has real talent, Sumter, and it's time you realized it."

"Of course he has," Father said. "All kids have 'em. But they get over 'em."

"It isn't the pox[4] we're talking of," Mom sniffed.

"In a way it is. Ever since you started talking up Colin's art, I've had an invalid for help around the place."

Father wasn't as hard as he made out, I knew, but he had to hold a balance against all Mom's frothing.[5] For him the thing was the land and all that pertained to it. I was following in Father's footsteps, true to form, but Colin threatened to break the family tradition with his leaning toward art, with Mom "aiding and abetting him," as Father liked to put it. For the past two years she had had dreams of my brother becoming a real artist and going away to the city to study.

It wasn't that Father had no understanding of such things. I could remember, through the years, Colin lying on his stomach in the front room making pencil sketches, and how a good drawing would catch Father's eye halfway across the room, and how he would sometimes gather up two or three of them to study, frowning and mut-

tering, one hand in his beard, while a great pride rose in Colin, and in me too. Most of Colin's drawings were of the woods and wild things, and there Father was a master critic. He made out to scorn what seemed to him a passive "white-livered" interpretation of nature through brush and pencil instead of rod and rifle.

At supper that night Colin could scarcely eat. Ever since he'd been able to walk, my brother had had a growing love of wild things, but Bandit had been like his very own, a gift of the woods. One afternoon a year and a half before, Father and Laban Small had been running a vixen through the hills with their dogs. With the last of her strength the she-fox had made for her den, not far from our house. The dogs had overtaken her and killed her just before she reached it. When father and Laban came up, they'd found Colin crouched nearby holding her cub in his arms.

Father had been for killing the cub, which was still too young to shift for itself, but Colin's grief had brought Mom into it. We'd taken the young fox into the kitchen, all of us, except Father, gone a bit silly over the little thing. Colin had held it in his arms and fed it warm milk from a spoon.

"Watch out with all your soft ways," Father had warned, standing in the doorway. "You'll make too much of him. Remember, you can't make a dog out of a fox. Half of that little critter has to love, but the other half is a wild hunter. You boys will mean a whole lot to him while he's kit, but there'll come a day when you won't mean a thing to him and he'll leave you shorn."

For two weeks after that Colin had nursed the cub, weaning it from milk to bits of meat. For a year they were always together. The cub grew fast. It was soon following Colin and me about the barnyard. It turned out to be a patch fox, with a saddle of darker fur across its shoulders.

---

4. the pox (päks): Any of a variety of diseases—like smallpox or chicken pox—that cause a rash on the skin.

5. frothing (frôth′ iŋ) vb.: Here, speaking angrily.

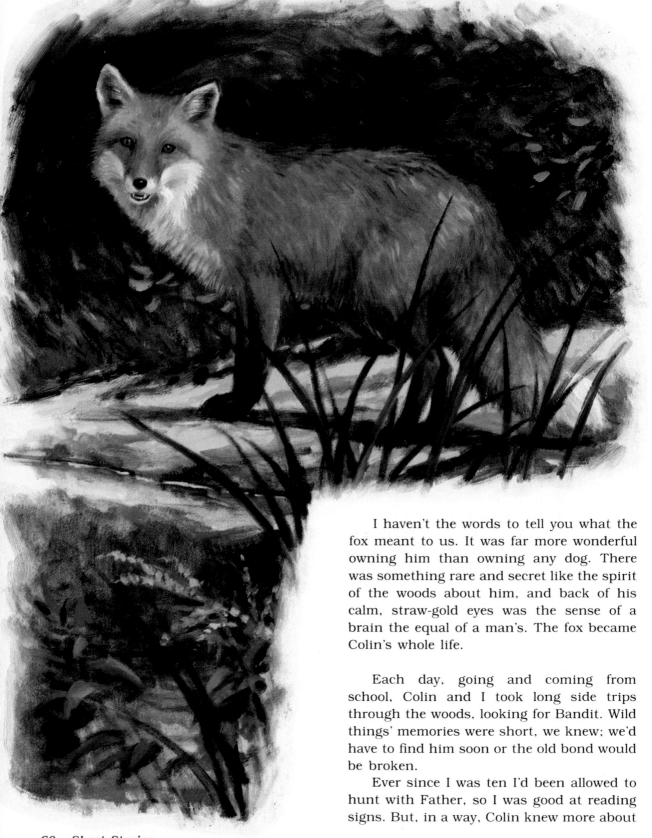

I haven't the words to tell you what the fox meant to us. It was far more wonderful owning him than owning any dog. There was something rare and secret like the spirit of the woods about him, and back of his calm, straw-gold eyes was the sense of a brain the equal of a man's. The fox became Colin's whole life.

Each day, going and coming from school, Colin and I took long side trips through the woods, looking for Bandit. Wild things' memories were short, we knew; we'd have to find him soon or the old bond would be broken.

Ever since I was ten I'd been allowed to hunt with Father, so I was good at reading signs. But, in a way, Colin knew more about the woods and wild things than Father or me. What came to me from long observation, Colin seemed to know by instinct.

It was Colin who felt out, like an Indian, the stretch of woods where Bandit had his den, who found the first slim, small fox-print in the damp earth. And then, on an afternoon in March, we saw him. I remember the day well, the racing clouds, the wind rattling the tops of the pine trees and swaying the Spanish moss. Bandit had just come out of a clump of laurel; in the maze of leaves behind him we caught a glimpse of a slim red vixen, so we knew he had found a mate. She melted from sight like a shadow, but Bandit turned to watch us, his mouth open, his tongue lolling as he smiled his old foxy smile. On his thin chops, I saw a telltale chicken feather.

Colin moved silently forward, his movements so quiet and casual he seemed to be standing still. He called Bandit's name, and the fox held his ground, drawn to us with all his senses. For a few moments he let Colin actually put an arm about him. It was then I knew that he loved us still, for all of Father's warnings. He really loved us back, with a fierce, secret love no tame thing ever gave. But the urge of his life just then was toward his new mate. Suddenly, he whirled about and disappeared in the laurels.

Colin looked at me with glowing eyes. "We haven't really lost him, Stan. When he gets through with his spring sparking[6] he may come back. But we've got to show ourselves to him a lot, so he won't forget."

"It's a go," I said.

"Promise not to say a word to Father," Colin said, and I agreed. For I knew by the chicken feather that Bandit had been up to no good.

A week later the woods were budding and the thickets were rustling with all manner of wild things scurrying on the love scent. Colin managed to get a glimpse of Bandit every few days. He couldn't get close though, for the spring running was a lot more important to a fox than any human beings were.

Every now and then Colin got out his framed box cover and looked at it, but he never drew anything on it; he never even picked up his pencil. I remember wondering if what Father had said about framing a picture before you had one had spoiled something for him.

I was helping Father with the planting now, but Colin managed to be in the woods every day. By degrees he learned Bandit's range, where he drank and rested and where he was likely to be according to the time of day. One day he told me how he had petted Bandit again, and how they had walked together a long way in the woods. All this time we had kept his secret from Father.

As summer came on, Bandit began to live up to the prediction Father had made. Accustomed to human beings he moved without fear about the scattered farms of the region, raiding barns and hen runs that other foxes wouldn't have dared go near. And he taught his wild mate to do the same. Almost every night they got into some poultry house, and by late June Bandit was not only killing chickens and ducks but feeding on eggs and young chicks whenever he got the chance.

Stories of his doings came to us from many sources, for he was still easily recognized by the dark patch on his shoulders. Many a farmer took a shot at him as he fled and some of them set out on his trail with dogs, but they always returned home without even sighting him. Bandit was familiar with all the dogs in the region, and he knew a hundred tricks to confound them. He got a reputation that year beyond that of any fox

---

6. sparking (spär' kiŋ) *n.*: An old-fashioned term for courting.

our hills had known. His confidence grew, and he gave up wild hunting altogether and lived entirely off the poultry farmers. By September the hill farmers banded together to hunt him down.

It was father who brought home that news one night. All time-honored rules of the fox chase were to be broken in this hunt; if the dogs couldn't bring Bandit down, he was to be shot on sight. I was stricken and furious. I remember the misery of Colin's face in the lamplight. Father, who took pride in all the ritual of the hunt, had refused to be a party to such an affair, though in justice he could do nothing but sanction any sort of hunt, for Bandit, as old Sam Wetherwax put it, had been "purely getting in the Lord's hair."

The hunt began next morning, and it was the biggest turnout our hills had known. There were at least twenty mounted men in the party and as many dogs. Father and I were working in the lower field as they passed along the river road. Most of the hunters carried rifles, and they looked ugly.

Twice during the morning I went up to the house to find Colin, but he was nowhere around. As we worked, Father and I could follow the progress of the hunt by the distant hound music on the breeze. We could tell just where the hunters first caught sight of the fox and where Bandit was leading the dogs during the first hour. We knew as well as if we'd seen it how Bandit roused another fox along Turkey Branch and forced it to run for him, and how the dogs swept after it for twenty minutes before they sensed their mistake.

Noon came, and Colin had not come in to eat. After dinner Father didn't go back to the field. He moped about, listening to the hound talk. He didn't like what was on any more than I did, and now and again I caught his smile of satisfaction when we heard the broken, angry notes of the hunting horn, telling that the dogs had lost the trail or had run another fox.

I was restless, and I went up into the hills in midafternoon. I ranged the woods for miles, thinking all the time of Colin. Time lost all meaning for me, and the short day was nearing an end, when I heard the horn talking again, telling that the fox had put over another trick. All day he had deviled the dogs and mocked the hunters. This new trick and the coming night would work to save him. I was wildly glad, as I moved down toward Turkey Branch and stood listening for a time by the deep, shaded pool where for years we boys had gone swimming, sailed boats, and dreamed summer dreams.

Suddenly, out of the corner of my eye, I saw the sharp ears and thin, pointed mask of a fox—in the water almost beneath me. It was Bandit, craftily submerged there, all but his head, resting in the cool water of the pool and the shadow of the two big beeches that spread above it. He must have run forty miles or more since morning. And he must have hidden in this place before. His knowing, crafty mask blended perfectly with the shadows and a mass of drift and branches that had collected by the bank of the pool. He

was so still that a pair of thrushes flew up from the spot as I came up, not knowing he was there.

Bandit's bright, harried eyes were looking right at me. But I did not look at him direct. Some woods instinct, swifter than thought, kept me from it. So he and I met as in another world, indirectly, with feeling but without sign or greeting.

Suddenly I saw that Colin was standing almost beside me. Silently as a water snake, he had come out of the bushes and stood there. Our eyes met, and a quick and secret smile passed between us. It was a rare moment in which I really "met" my brother, when something of his essence flowed into me and I knew all of him. I've never lost it since.

My eyes still turned from the fox, my heart pounding. I moved quietly away, and Colin moved with me. We whistled softly as we went, pretending to busy ourselves along the bank of the stream. There was magic in it, as if by will we wove a web of protection about the fox, a ring-pass-not that none might penetrate. It was so, too, we felt, in the brain of Bandit, and that doubled the charm. To us he was still our little pet that we had carried about in our arms on countless summer afternoons.

Two hundred yards upstream, we stopped beside slim, fresh tracks in the mud where Bandit had entered the branch. The tracks angled upstream. But in the water the wily creature had turned down.

We climbed the far bank to wait, and Colin told me how Bandit's secret had been his secret ever since an afternoon three months before, when he'd watched the fox swim downstream to hide in the deep pool. Today he'd waited on the bank, feeling that Bandit, hard pressed by the dogs, might again seek the pool for sanctuary.

We looked back once as we turned homeward. He still had not moved. We didn't know until later that he was killed that same night by a chance hunter, as he crept out from his hiding place.

That evening Colin worked a long time on his framed box cover that had lain about the house untouched all summer. He kept at it all the next day too. I had never seen him work so hard. I seemed to sense in the air the feeling he was putting into it, how he was *believing* his picture into being. It was evening before he finished it. Without a word he handed it to Father. Mom and I went and looked over his shoulder.

It was a delicate and intricate pencil drawing of the deep branch pool, and there was Bandit's head and watching, fear-filled eyes hiding there amid the leaves and shadows, woven craftily into the maze of twigs and branches, as if by nature's art itself. Hardly a fox there at all, but the place where he was—or should have been. I recognized it instantly, but Mom gave a sort of incredulous sniff.

"I'll declare," she said, "It's mazy as a puzzle. It just looks like a lot of sticks and leaves to me."

Long minutes of study passed before Father's eye picked out the picture's secret, as few men's could have done. I laid that to Father's being a born hunter. That was a picture that might have been done especially for him. In fact, I guess it was.

Finally he turned to Colin with his deep, slow smile. "So that's how Bandit fooled them all," he said. He sat holding the picture with a sort of tenderness for a long time, while we glowed in the warmth of the shared secret. That was Colin's moment. Colin's art stopped being a pox[7] to Father right there. And later, when the time came for Colin to go to art school, it was Father who was his solid backer.

---

7. pox (päks) *n.*: In this case, a bother or trouble.

THINKING ABOUT THE SELECTION

Recalling

1. Why does the father name the fox Bandit?
2. How does Colin's art cause tension in the family?
3. What do the farmers do when Bandit continues to attack their animals?
4. How does Bandit elude the farmers?
5. How does Colin use his art to explain this trick to his father?

Interpreting

6. The father has mixed feelings about Colin and his art. What are they?
7. How are the mother's and the father's attitudes about Colin's art changed at the end of the story when Colin shows them his picture?
8. In the next to the last paragraph, Stan says, "That was a picture that might have been done especially for him. In fact, I guess it was." Explain what Stan means.
9. What are two possible meanings of the title "Last Cover"?

Applying

10. Much of the communication in this story is done nonverbally—that is, without words. Give two examples of nonverbal communication in daily life.

ANALYZING LITERATURE

Understanding Character Traits

Character traits are the qualities that make a person an individual. There are many aspects of Colin's personality that make him special. As the story unfolds, Colin reveals these special traits in what he says and what he does.

1. Which of Colin's character traits make his mother and Stan worry about him?
2. Which of Colin's traits does his father at first not appreciate?
3. Which character traits allow Colin to find Bandit when no one else can?

CRITICAL THINKING AND READING

Comparing and Contrasting Characters

You can understand more about characters if you compare and contrast them. When you **compare** characters, you look at ways in which they are alike. When you **contrast** them, you look at ways in which they are different.

1. Name two character traits that Colin and Stan share.
2. Stan describes himself as "tough and strong." How does Colin differ?
3. Stan says, "Colin knew more about the woods and wild things than Father or me." While Stan learns of the woods through observation, how does Colin seem to know?

UNDERSTANDING LANGUAGE

Using Vivid Words

Vivid words present a lively and sharp picture. Words are usually more vivid when they are specific. For example, *clutch* is a more specific and more vivid word than *hold*. Authors use vivid words and expressions to make you see and feel a scene or action more clearly.

Find the paragraph on page 58 that begins "It was late February . . ." Point out three vivid words in it that help create a strong picture.

THINKING AND WRITING

Writing a Character Sketch

Think of a person you know well. Write a character sketch describing this person to someone who does not know him or her at all. First list all the traits that make this person special. Then write your first draft. As you revise your sketch, be sure you have included enough details to make this person come alive for your reader. Replace any tired words with more vivid words. Finally, correct all spelling and punctuation mistakes and prepare a final draft.

GUIDE FOR READING

The Sneaker Crisis

Shirley Jackson (1919–1965) wrote two kinds of stories. On the one hand she wrote stories, like her novel *We Have Always Lived in the Castle,* which are laced with horror and mystery. On the other hand, she wrote books like *Life Among the Savages* and *Raising Demons,* which build on events in the hectic family life she shared with her husband and four children. "The Sneaker Crisis," from *Raising Demons,* is a comical story about family life from the humorous side of Shirley Jackson.

Humorous Characters

Like real people, characters in stories may have a variety of traits, like honesty, strength, or dependability. In order to make a story amusing or funny, an author may choose to emphasize certain traits in a character, like forgetfulness or sloppiness, that lead to humorous situations. The characters display these traits in situations that become comical as small details are built up or overstated.

Look For

As you read "The Sneaker Crisis," notice the traits the author emphasizes in order to make the characters and situations seem humorous. Also notice how the author blows small details out of proportion so that a lost sneaker becomes a crisis.

Writing

The story you are about to read involves a search for a lost sneaker. Have you had the experience of searching for a lost item? What went through your mind as you searched? Freewrite about your experience, noting especially if there was anything funny in the situation.

Vocabulary

Knowing the following words will help you as you read "The Sneaker Crisis."

buffet (bə fāʹ) *n.*: A piece of furniture with drawers and cupboards for dishes, table linen, and so on (p. 67)

incredulously (in krejʹoo ləs lē) *adv.*: In a disbelieving manner (p. 68)

resignedly (ri zīnʹid lē) *adj.*: In a yielding and uncomplaining manner (p. 69)

ominously (ämʹə nəs lē) *adv.*: In a threatening manner (p. 69)

triumphant (trī umʹfənt) *adj.*: Rejoicing for victory; exulting in success (p. 70)

rigorously (rigʹər əs lē) *adv.*: In a strict, thorough way (p. 71)

The Sneaker Crisis

Shirley Jackson

Day after day after day I went around my house picking things up. I picked up books and shoes and toys and socks and shirts and gloves and boots and hats and handkerchiefs and puzzle pieces and pennies and pencils and stuffed rabbits and bones the dogs had left under the living room chairs. I also picked up tin soldiers and plastic cars and baseball gloves and sweaters and children's pocketbooks with nickels inside and little pieces of lint off the floor.

Every time I picked up something I put it down again somewhere else where it belonged better than it did in the place I found it. Nine times out of ten I did not notice what I was picking up or where I put it until sometime later when someone in the family needed it; then, when Sally said where were her crayons I could answer at once: kitchen windowsill, left. If Barry wanted his cowboy hat I could reply: playroom, far end of bookcase. If Jannie wanted her arithmetic homework, I could tell her it was under the ashtray on the dining room buffet.

I could locate the little nut that came off Laurie's bike wheel, and the directions for winding the living room clock. I could find the recipe for the turkey cutlets Sally admired and the top to my husband's fountain pen; I could even find, ordinarily, the little celluloid strips which went inside the collar of his nylon shirt.

That was, of course, entirely automatic, like still remembering the home telephone number of my college roommate and being able to recite "Oh, what is so rare as a day in June." If I could not respond at once, identifying object and location in unhesitating answer to the question, the article was very apt to remain permanently lost. Like Jannie's pink Easter-egg hat, which disappeared—let me see—it was the day Laurie got into the fight with the Haynes boys, and the porch rocker got broken—make it the end of October.

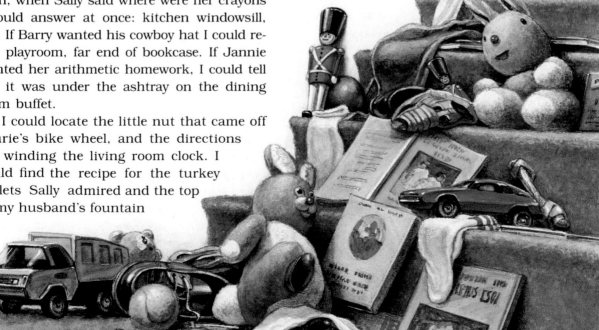

We had many small places in our big house where an Easter-egg hat could get itself hopelessly hidden, so when Jannie asked one night at dinner, the end of October, "Who took my Easter-egg hat?" and I found myself without an immediate answer, it was clear that the hat had taken itself off, and although we searched halfheartedly, Jannie had to wear a scarf around her head until the weather got cold enough to wear her long-tailed knitted cap.

Laurie's sneaker was of considerably more moment, since, of course, he could not play basketball with a scarf tied around his left foot. He came to the top of the back stairs of a Saturday morning and inquired gently who had stolen his sneaker. I opened my mouth to answer, found my mind blank, and closed my mouth again. Laurie came halfway down the stairs and bawled, "Mooooooom, where'd my *sneaker* get to?" and I still could not answer. "I neeeeeed my *sneaker*," Laurie howled, "I got to play baaaaaaasketball."

"I don't know," I called.

"But I need it," Laurie said. He crashed down the stairs and into the study, where I sat reading the morning paper and drinking a cup of coffee. "I got to play basketball, so I need my sneakers. I can't play on the basketball court without sneakers. So I need—"

"Have you looked? In your room? Under your bed?"

"Yeah, sure." He thought. "It's not there, though."

"Outdoors?"

"Now what would my sneaker be doing outdoors, I ask you? You think I get dressed and undressed out on the lawn, maybe, for the neighbors?"

"Well," I said helplessly, "you had it last Saturday."

"I *know* I had it last Saturday, you think I'm foolish or something?"

"Wait." I went and stood at the foot of the back stairs and called, "Jannie?"

There was a pause and then Jannie said, sniffling, "Yes?"

"Good heavens," I said, "are you reading *Little Women*[1] again?"

Jannie sniffled. "Just the part where Beth dies."

"Look," I said, "the sun is shining and the sky is blue and—"

"You seen my sneaker?" Laurie yelled from in back of me.

"No."

"You *sure*?"

Jannie came to the top of the stairs, wiping her eyes with her hand. "Hey," she said, "maybe some girl took it. For a keepsake."

"Wha?" said Laurie incredulously. "Took my *sneaker*? Who?"

"Like Mr. Brooke did Meg's glove, in *Little Women*, because he was in love with her and they got married."

"*Wha*?" For a minute Laurie stared at her, and then he turned deliberately and went back to the door of the study. "My sister," he announced formally to his father, "has snapped her twigs."

"That so?" said his father.

"I ask you." Laurie gestured. "Junk from books," he said.

"Well, he did," Jannie insisted, coming down the stairs. "He took it and hid it for ever so long and when Jo found out she—"

"Sally, Barry," I was calling from the back door. "Has either of you seen Laurie's sneaker?"

Sally and Barry were dancing on the lawn, turning and flickering among the last fallen leaves; when I called they circled and came toward the house, going "cheep-cheep." "We're little birds," Sally explained, coming closer. "Cheep-cheep."

"Have you seen Laurie's sneaker?"

---

1. *Little Women*: A novel by Louisa May Alcott about four sisters, Meg, Jo, Beth, and Amy, growing up in New England during the Civil War.

"Cheep-cheep."

"Well?"

Barry thought. "I have unseen it," he remarked. "I did unsee Laurie's sneaker a day and a day and a day and a day and *many* mornings ago."

"Splendid," I said. "Sally?"

"No. But don't worry. I shall get it back for dear Laurie, dear Mommy."

"If you mean magic you better not let your father hear you, young lady. No," I said over my shoulder to Laurie, "they haven't."

"But I will find it, Laurie dear, never fear, Laurie dear, I will find your sneaker find for you."

"Yeah. So what'm I gonna do?" he asked me. "Play basketball in my socks or something?"

"Are you *sure* you looked under your bed?"

He looked at me in the manner his favorite television detective reserves for ladies who double-talk the cops. "Yeah," he said. "Yeah, lady. I'm sure."

"Daddy won't notice," Sally said busily to Barry. "All this will take is just a little bit of golden magic and Daddy will never notice and there will be dear Laurie's sneaker just right here."

"Can I do magic too?"

"You can be my dear helper and you can carry the shovel."

I went into the study and sat down and Laurie followed me. "And he kept it for weeks and weeks next to his heart," Jannie was explaining to her father, "and she was looking for it just like Laurie but Mr. Brooke had it all the time."

"How about that little dark-haired girl?" my husband asked Laurie. "The one who keeps calling you so much?"

"Nah," Laurie said. "She's tipped, anyhow. Besides, how could she get my sneaker?" He slapped his forehead. "A veritable madhouse," he said. "Lose a sneaker

and they start criticizing your friends and trying to make out she stole it. Bah."

He flung himself violently into one of our good plastic leather chairs, which slid back across the floor and into the bookcase. "Bah," said Laurie. He threw his arms dramatically into the air and let them fall resignedly. "Never *find* anything around here, that's the *big* trouble," he explained. "Nothing's ever where you put it. If *she*—"

"If by *she* you mean *me*—" I began ominously.

"Always coming and picking things up and putting them away where a person can't find them. Always—"

"If you'd put things away neatly when you take them off instead of just throwing everything under your bed—" I stopped to think. "Have you looked under your bed?" I asked.

Laurie stood up and threw his arms wide. "Why was I ever born?" he demanded.

Jannie nodded. "In *Beverley Lee, Girl Detective,*" she pointed out, "when the secret plans for the old armory get lost, Beverley Lee and her girlfriend Piggy, *they* look for clues."

"A broken shoelace?" my husband suggested.

"Well, when did you see them last?" I asked reasonably. "Seems to me if you could remember when you had them last, you might remember where you put them then."

"Yeah. Well," Laurie said, scowling, "I *know* I had them last Saturday. But then I took them off and I remember they were on my bookcase because I had to remember to make that map for geography and that was for Wednesday when we had gym—say!" He opened his eyes and his mouth wide. "Gym. I wore them Wednesday to school for gym. So I had them on Wednesday."

"And Wednesday," I put in, "was the day you were so late getting home from school because you were hanging around Joe's with that pack of juvenile delinquents and—"

"I told you six times already, those girls just happened to come by there by *accident*, how'd *I* know they'd be around Joe's? And anyway you got no right to go calling my friends—"

"And you never got your chores done and I kept dinner till six-thirty."

"That girl called, too," my husband put in.

"And I must of had my sneakers on all that time, because I never had time because *she* made me do my chores and then I had to rush through dinner because—because—"

"You were going to the dance," Jannie said, triumphant. "You got all dressed up, so *naturally* you put on shoes."

"Hey!" Laurie swung around and gestured wildly. "I got dressed—"

"You took a shower," I said. "I remember because—"

He shuddered. "I took a shower because *she* wouldn't let me have my good blue pants from the cleaners *unless* I took a shower.'

"No gentleman escorts a lady to a public function unless he has bathed and dressed himself in completely clean clothes," my husband said.

"So I undressed in the bathroom because I always do and then when I went out I had this towel around me and I was carrying my clothes and the sneaker and I—"

"I saw it," I said suddenly. "I did see it after all. I came upstairs to get two aspirin after you had finally gone to the dance and I remember the way the bathroom looked; the floor was sopping and dirty towels all over and the soap and—"

"The sneaker," Laurie said impatiently, "keep on the subject. The sneaker, the sneaker."

I meditated. "It was lying just inside the door and one wet towel was half on top of it.

And I . . . and I . . . " I thought. "What *did* I do?"

"Think, think, think." Laurie stood over me flapping his hands.

"Look," I said. "I go around this house and I go around this house and I *go* around this house and I pick up shoes and socks and shirts and hats and gloves and handkerchiefs and books and toys and I always put them down again, someplace where they belong. Now when I went upstairs and saw that mess of a bathroom I had to clean up, I would have taken the soap and put it in the soapdish. And I would have taken the bathmat and put it over the edge of the tub. And I would have taken the towels—"

"And put them in the hamper," Laurie said impatiently. "We know."

"You do? Because I have often wondered what happens all the times I say to you to put the towels—"

"Yeah, so next time I'll remember, sure. What about the *sneaker*?"

"Anyway they were wet so I couldn't put them in the hamper. I would have hung them over the shower rail to dry so *then* I could put them in the hamper. And then I would have picked up the sneaker—"

"Laurie's sneaker is weaker and creaker and cleaker and breaker and fleaker and greaker . . . " Sally wound through the study, eyes shut, chanting. Barry came behind her, doing an odd little two-step. Sally had a pail of sand and a shovel and she was making scattering motions.

"Now *wait* a minute here," my husband began.

"It's all right," Sally said, opening one eye. "I'm just pretending. This is only sand."

"We're just untending," Barry explained reassuringly. "Bleaker and sneaker and weaker and deaker."

They filed out. My husband studied the floor morosely. "That certainly looked like magic to *me* ," he said. "and I don't *like* it. Going to have footwear popping up all over, right through the floor, probably wreck the foundations."

"Reconstruct the scene of the crime," Jannie said suddenly. "Because Beverley Lee Girl Detective and her girlfriend Piggy, that's what they did. In *The Mystery of the Broken Candle*, when they had to find the missing will. They reconstructed the scene of the crime. They got everybody there and put everything the way it was—"

"Say!" Laurie looked at her admiringly. "You're charged, girl. Come on," he said, making for the stairs, and stopped in the doorway to look compellingly at me. "Come *on*," he said.

"And creaker and beaker and leaker and veaker."

"Gangway, birdbait," Laurie said. He stopped to pat his younger sister on the head. "You keep sprinkling that there magic, Perfessor. Size six-and-a-half, white."

"Kindly do not poke the Sally," said Sally, drawing away stiffly.

"Unpoke, unpoke," Barry said.

"Come *on*," Laurie said to me. He called ahead to Jannie, "You get the towels wet and throw them on the floor. I'll get the other sneaker and when she comes we'll have it all ready."

"You might as well take two more aspirin," my husband said.

"I might as well," I said.

Wearily, I headed up the stairs, sand grinding underfoot. The bathroom is at the head of the stairs, and by the time I was near the top I could see that everything was prepared. Rigorously, I put my mind back three days. It is eight-thirty in the evening, I told myself. I am coming upstairs to get myself two aspirin. Laurie has just gone to the dance, I have just told him goodbye, get home early, behave yourself, be careful, do you have a clean handkerchief? Jannie is reading. Sally and Barry are asleep. It is eight-thirty Wednesday evening, I am coming to get two aspirin.

I came to the top of the stairs, and sighed. The bathroom floor was sopping, the bathmat was soaked and crumpled, wet towels lay on the floor. In the corner, half under a wet towel, was one white sneaker. I asked myself through my teeth how old people had to get before they learned to pick up after themselves and after all our efforts to raise our children in a decent and clean house here they still behaved like pigs and the sooner Laurie grew up and got married and had a wife to pick up after him the better off I would be and maybe I would just take his allowance and hire a full-time nursemaid for him.

I picked up the bathmat and hung it over the edge of the tub. I put the soap in the soap dish and hung the towels over the shower rail. I picked up the sneaker and resisted the temptation to slam it into the wastebasket. Then, with the sneaker in my hand, I went to the other side of the hall to the linen closet to get clean towels and a dry bathmat and Laurie and Jannie burst out of the guest room shouting, "You see? You see?"

Jannie said excitedly, "Just like Beverley Lee and it turned out it *was* the caretaker all the time."

"Look, look," Laurie said, pointing. I had the door of the linen closet open and I reached up onto the towel shelf and took down Jannie's Easter-egg hat.

"What?" I said, surprised.

"That's my hat," Jannie said.

"Why would I want to put your hat in the linen closet?" I demanded. "Don't be silly."

"My nice pink Easter-egg hat," Jannie said, pleased.

"Craazy," Laurie remarked. "Opens the closet and there's the hat. Craazy." He pushed past me and began to paw through the towels.

"Ridiculous," I said. "I *never* put hats in linen closets. Linen closets are where I keep towels and sheets and extra blankets, not hats."

"Not sneakers, either." Laurie stood back and dusted his hands.

"You pick up every one of those towels," I said, annoyed. "And then you and your sister can get right in there and clean up that bathroom. And the next time I find that pink hat lying around I am going to burn it. And you can tell Beverley Lee Girl Detective—"

"Any luck?" my husband called from the foot of the stairs.

"Certainly not." I started down. "Of all the idiotic notions and now it's too late in the year *any*way for a little hat like that."

"Sneaker, sneaker, sneaker!" It was Sally and Barry, in glory. Laurie raced past me down the stairs. "Got it? Sal," he yelled, "you *got* it?"

Proudly the little procession wound around to the front hall. Sally was still scattering sand but Barry was bearing the sneaker on high. "Gee," Laurie said. "Hey, kids, thanks. Where was it?"

"Under your bed," Sally said. "We did a lot of —" she glanced at her father "—blagic," she said. "And then we went up and looked. Very good, Barry." "Very good, Sally," Barry said. "Gosh." Laurie was pleased. He turned

and gave me an affectionate pat on the head. "Boy," he said, "are *you* ever a tippy old lady." Then, in a burst of gratitude, he added, "I'm going to go down right now on my bike and get you kids each a popsicle."

"Well, me, too, I should *think*," Jannie said indignantly. "After all, it was me thought of reconstructing the crime, and in *Elsie Dinsmore*[2] when Elsie—"

"What is this crime talk?" I said. "Anyone would think that instead of spending all my time picking up and putting away—"

"The sneaker," Laurie said to me, gesturing. "The other sneaker. I got to get down and get those popsicles, so let's have it."

---

2. *Elsie Dinsmore*: A series of twenty-six novels by Martha F. Finley (1828–1909).

"What?" I said.

"The sneaker, dear. The one you just had upstairs, for heaven's sake."

Uncomfortably, I looked down at my empty hands. "Now let's see," I said. "I had it just a minute ago. . . ."

THINKING ABOUT THE SELECTION

Recalling

1. Who does most of the picking up in this family?
2. What advice does Jannie give to help find the missing sneaker?
3. How do the younger children help to find the sneaker?
4. Where is the missing sneaker finally found?
5. At the end of the story, what other object is missing?

Interpreting

6. Although the family members all react differently to the missing sneaker, in what way is their behavior alike?
7. What does the title indicate about this family's handling of their everyday problems?

Applying

8. What advice might you give this family to prevent another "crisis" like this one?

ANALYZING LITERATURE

Understanding Humorous Characters

A writer may create humor in a story by emphasizing character traits that lead to unexpected or humorous situations. For example, Shirley Jackson builds this episode of the family's searching for a lost sneaker on Laurie's sloppiness and on the mother's forgetfulness.

1. How does Laurie's sloppiness contribute to the humor in this story?
2. The mother's forgetting where she puts two items causes the events of this story to happen. What are the two items?
3. What traits of the younger children contribute to making this story humorous?

CRITICAL THINKING AND READING

Recognizing Humorous Situations

Humor depends largely on the unexpected. An author creates a humorous situation by presenting a series of events that lead you to expect a certain outcome. Instead, something amusingly different from what you expect happens.

1. Imagine that the family had looked in the linen closet and found nothing but linens there. Would this situation have been as humorous as their finding the Easter-egg hat there? Why?
2. Once the sneaker is found at the end of the story, you expect that the "sneaker crisis" is solved. What unexpected event occurs then?

UNDERSTANDING LANGUAGE

Recognizing Slang

The way a character speaks can make him or her seem humorous. The author of "The Sneaker Crisis" has Laurie speak using **slang** to imitate the casual language of many teenagers.

Find three slang expressions in the story and explain what they mean. Why is each humorous?

THINKING AND WRITING

Writing About a Humorous Incident

Think of a time when you looked for a lost object or helped someone else find a lost item. Write about the incident, making it seem humorous. Perhaps you might exaggerate the importance of the lost item or emphasize what you learned about the way the other person thinks and acts under the circumstances. As you revise, consider adding or emphasizing details to make your story funny.

GUIDE FOR READING

The Luckiest Time of All

Lucille Clifton (1936–   ) was born in Depew, New York. She has written about the strength of the courageous black women who raised their families with dignity during the harsh period of slavery and its aftermath. In addition to several books of poetry, she has written a book called *Generations,* which contains anecdotes that celebrate the lives of her father and mother. "The Luckiest Time of All" deals with a theme common in her work: the importance of a strong black woman in handing on a family's traditions to a new generation.

Major and Minor Characters

A **major character** is the one on whom a story focuses. It is the character who plays the most important role. Because a major character shows several character traits, you learn the most about this character as you read a story. In contrast, a **minor character** plays only a small part in a story. Therefore, you learn only a little about each minor character.

Look For

As you read "The Luckiest Time of All," you will meet several characters. Identify the major and minor characters by noticing which character plays the most important role and which characters play less important parts. Why does the author include both major and minor characters?

Writing

In the story you are about to read, the great-grandmother tells about her "luckiest time of all." Make a list of lucky incidents that have happened to you or to someone you know. Then briefly describe one of these incidents, telling what happened and what made it a lucky time.

Vocabulary

In "The Luckiest Time of All" some words, particularly verbs, are spelled the way they are pronounced by the characters, such as *dancin* for *dancing* or *twirlin* for *twirling*. These spelling changes reflect spoken language. Since many people, particularly the characters in this story, drop the final *g* when they speak, these spellings reflect the way the words sound. You will be able to recognize these words from their context when you see them.

The Luckiest Time of All

from *The Lucky Stone*

Lucille Clifton

Mrs. Elzie F. Pickens was rocking slowly on the porch one afternoon when her Great-granddaughter, Tee, brought her a big bunch of dogwood blooms, and that was the beginning of a story.

"Ahhh, now that dogwood reminds me of the day I met your Great-granddaddy, Mr. Pickens, Sweet Tee.

"It was just this time, spring of the year, and me and my best friend Ovella Wilson, who is now gone, was goin to join the Silas Greene. Usta be a kinda show went all through the South, called it the Silas Greene show. Somethin like the circus. Me and Ovella wanted to join that thing and see the world. Nothin wrong at home or nothin, we just wanted to travel and see new things and have high times. Didn't say nothin to no-body but one another. Just up and decided to do it.

"Well, this day we plaited our hair and put a dress and some things in a crokasack[1] and started out to the show. Spring day like this.

"We got there after a good little walk and it was the world, Baby, such music and won-ders as we never had seen! They had every-thing there, or seemed like it.

"Me and Ovella thought we'd walk around for a while and see the show before goin to the office to sign up and join.

"While we was viewin it all we come up

MOM AND DAD
William H. Johnson
National Museum of American Art

---

1. **crokasack,** usually spelled *croker sack* (krō′ kər sak) *n.*: A bag made of burlap or similar material.

on this dancin dog. Cutest one thing in the world next to you, Sweet Tee, dippin and movin and head bowin to that music. Had a little ruffly skirt on itself and up on two back legs twistin and movin to the music. Dancin dancin dancin till people started throwin pennies out of they pockets.

"Me and Ovella was caught up too and laughin so. She took a penny out of her pocket and threw it to the ground where that dog was dancin, and I took two pennies and threw 'em both.

"The music was faster and faster and that dog was turnin and turnin. Ovella reached in her sack and threw out a little pin she had won from never being late at Sunday school. And me, laughin and all excited, reached in my bag and threw out my lucky stone!

"Well, I knew right off what I had done. Soon as it left my hand it seemed like I reached back out for it to take it back. But the stone was gone from my hand and Lord, it hit that dancin dog right on his nose!

"Well, he lit out after me, poor thing. He lit out after me and I flew! Round and round the Silas Greene we run, through every place me and Ovella had walked before, but now that dancin dog was a runnin dog and all the people was laughin at the new show, which was us!

"I felt myself slowin down after a while and I thought I would turn around a little bit to see how much gain that cute little dog was makin on me. When I did I got such a surprise! Right behind me was the dancin dog and right behind him was the finest fast runnin hero in the bottoms of Virginia.

"And that was Mr. Pickens when he was still a boy! He had a length of twine in his hand and he was twirlin it around in the air just like the cowboy at the Silas Greene and grinnin fit to bust.

"While I was watchin how the sun shined on him and made him look like an angel come to help a poor sinner girl, why, he twirled that twine one extra fancy twirl and looped it right around one hind leg of that dancin dog and brought him low.

"I stopped then and walked slow and shy to where he had picked up that poor dog to see if he was hurt, cradlin him and talkin to him soft and sweet. That showed me how kind and gentle he was, and when we walked back to the dancin dog's place in the show he let the dog loose and helped me to find my stone. I told him how shiny black it was and how it had the letter *A* scratched on one side. We searched and searched and at last he spied it!

"Ovella and me lost heart for shows then and we walked on home. And a good little way, the one who was gonna be your Great-granddaddy was walkin on behind. Seein us safe. Us walkin kind of slow. Him seein us safe. Yes." Mrs. Pickens' voice trailed off softly and Tee noticed she had a little smile on her face.

"Grandmama, that stone almost got you bit by a dog that time. It wasn't so lucky that time, was it?"

Tee's Great-grandmother shook her head and laughed out loud.

"That was the luckiest time of all, Tee Baby. It got me acquainted with Mr. Amos Pickens, and if that ain't luck, what could it be! Yes, it was luckier for me than for anybody, I think. Least mostly I think it."

Tee laughed with her Great-grandmother though she didn't exactly know why.

"I hope I have that kind of good stone luck one day," she said.

"Maybe you will someday," her Great-grandmother said.

And they rocked a little longer and smiled together.

THINKING ABOUT THE SELECTION

Recalling

1. "The Luckiest Time of All" is a story within a story. Who tells the story about the lucky stone and the Silas Greene Show?
2. Why do the people at the Silas Greene Show start throwing pennies?
3. What is Great-grandmother's reason for believing that the stone was lucky for her?

Interpreting

4. What was Mr. Pickens's real intention in saving Great-grandmother from being bitten by the dog and in following her home?
5. What evidence does the story provide to show that Great-grandmother and Mr. Pickens had a happy life?

Applying

6. Which do you think brings success more, hard work or luck? Give reasons for your answer.

ANALYZING LITERATURE

Identifying Major and Minor Characters

The **major character** in a story is the one on whom the story focuses and thus the one you learn the most about. **Minor characters** play small roles in the development of a story.

1. Who is the major character in "The Luckiest Time of All"?
2. Point out three facts you learn about the major character.
3. Name one minor character.
4. What do you learn about this minor character?

CRITICAL THINKING AND READING

Making Inferences About Characters

An **inference** is a conclusion that you make based on the information given. An author does not always tell you everything there is to know about a character. Sometimes you must make inferences about the character's personality traits based on what the character says and does.

1. What inference can you make about Mr. Pickens based on the following facts?
   a. He cradles the dog and speaks softly to it.
   b. He sees the young women safely home.
2. Find two details in the story that support the inference that Great-grandmother is a happy, good-natured person.

UNDERSTANDING LANGUAGE

Appreciating Vivid Action Verbs

Writers use strong action verbs to create clear pictures. For example, when Lucille Clifton writes ". . . he *twirled* that twine one extra fancy twirl and *looped* it right around one hind leg of that dancin dog . . . ," you see Mr. Pickens's actions very clearly.

1. Find three other examples of vivid action verbs in "The Luckiest Time of All."
2. Tell which is the more vivid verb in each of the following pairs:
   a. talk, chatter   c. wash, scrub
   b. try, struggle   d. shine, glitter

THINKING AND WRITING

Writing About Luck

Think about a person you know who is successful. Make notes about how much of this person's success is due to luck and how much is due to hard work. Then prepare the first draft of a composition to present before your class telling whether you think luck or hard work is more important to success. Begin with a topic sentence that summarizes your opinion. Then give examples to support your opinion. When you revise, be sure you have given enough examples to convince your classmates of your opinion.

GUIDE FOR READING

Amigo Brothers

Piri Thomas (1928–   ) grew up in the Spanish Harlem section of New York City. While serving time in jail as a young man, he began to write about his life. Later he published an autobiography called *Down These Mean Streets,* which describes his experiences in some of the city's toughest neighborhoods. Like Thomas himself, the two major characters in "Amigo Brothers" have a dream that helps them overcome the problems they encounter in their environment.

More Than One Major Character

Many stories tell about the experiences of just one major character. Sometimes, however, a story contains two or more major characters. Each of them may have a variety of character traits, or ways of acting and looking at the world. The focus of this type of story is often on the relationship between the major characters.

"Amigo Brothers" has two major characters. During the story, the friendship between them is put to a difficult test.

Look For

In "Amigo Brothers" the two major characters are Antonio and Felix. As you read, notice what character traits they share. Also pay attention to how the two boys differ from each other. Why are they such good friends?

Writing

In "Amigo Brothers" two friends compete against each other. Think of a time when you have competed against a close friend in the classroom, at an athletic event, or in a social situation. If you prefer, make up a situation. Then freewrite about the event.

Vocabulary

Knowing the following words will help you as you read "Amigo Brothers."

barrage (bə räzh′) *n.*: A heavy attack (p. 80)

gnawing (nô′ iŋ) *adj.*: Tormenting; bothering (p. 82)

perpetual (pər pech′oo wəl) *adj.*: Never stopping (p. 82)

dignitaries (dig′nə ter′ ēz) *n.*: People holding high positions or offices (p. 83)

interwoven (in′tər wōv′ən) *v.*: Mixed together (p. 83)

nimble (nim′b'l) *adj.*: Moving quickly and lightly (p. 84)

dispelled (dis peld′) *v.*: Driven away (p. 85)

feinted (fānt′ əd) *v.*: Pretended to make an attack (p. 85)

Amigo[1] Brothers

Piri Thomas

Antonio Cruz and Felix Varga were both seventeen years old. They were so together in friendship that they felt themselves to be brothers. They had known each other since childhood, growing up on the lower east side of Manhattan in the same tenement building on Fifth Street between Avenue A and Avenue B.

Antonio was fair, lean, and lanky, while Felix was dark, short, and husky. Antonio's hair was always falling over his eyes, while Felix wore his black hair in a natural Afro style.

Each youngster had a dream of someday becoming lightweight champion of the world. Every chance they had the boys worked out, sometimes at the Boys Club on 10th Street and Avenue A and sometimes at the pro's gym on 14th Street. Early morning sunrises would find them running along the East River Drive, wrapped in sweat shirts, short towels around their necks, and handkerchiefs Apache style around their foreheads.

While some youngsters were into street negatives, Antonio and Felix slept, ate, rapped,[2] and dreamt positive. Between them, they had a collection of *Fight* magazines second to none, plus a scrapbook filled with torn tickets to every boxing match they had ever attended, and some clippings of their own. If asked a question about any given fighter, they would immediately zip out from their memory banks divisions, weights, records of fights, knock-outs, technical knock-outs,[3] and draws or losses.

Each had fought many bouts representing their community and had won two gold-plated medals plus a silver and bronze medallion. The difference was in their style. Antonio's lean form and long reach made him the better boxer, while Felix's short and muscular frame made him the better slugger.[4] Whenever they had met in the ring for sparring sessions, it had always been hot and heavy.

Now, after a series of elimination bouts,[5] they had been informed that they were to meet each other in the division finals that were scheduled for the seventh of August, two weeks away—the winner to represent the Boys Club in the Golden Gloves Championship Tournament.

The two boys continued to run together along the East River Drive. But even when joking with each other, they both sensed a wall rising between them.

One morning less than a week before their bout, they met as usual for their daily work-out. They fooled around with a few jabs at the air, slapped skin, and then took off, running lightly along the dirty East River's edge.

---

1. amigo (ə mē′ gō) *adj.*: Spanish for "friend" (usually a noun).
2. rapped (rapt) *v.*: A slang term meaning "talked."

3. technical knock-outs: Occasions when a fight is stopped because one of the fighters is too hurt to continue, even though he is on his feet.
4. slugger (slug′ ər) *n.*: A boxer who relies more on the power of his punches than on his grace and form.
5. elimination bouts: A series of matches in which only the winners go on to fight in other matches.

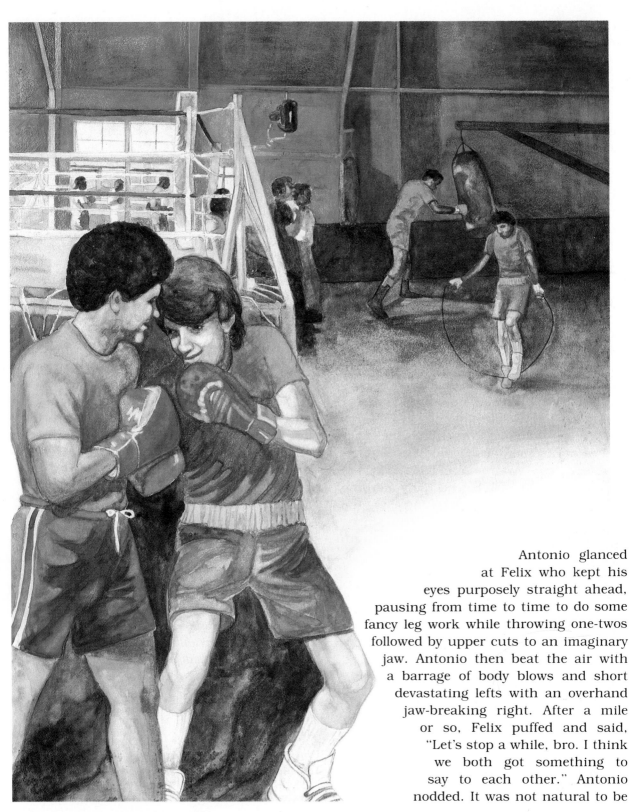

Antonio glanced at Felix who kept his eyes purposely straight ahead, pausing from time to time to do some fancy leg work while throwing one-twos followed by upper cuts to an imaginary jaw. Antonio then beat the air with a barrage of body blows and short devastating lefts with an overhand jaw-breaking right. After a mile or so, Felix puffed and said, "Let's stop a while, bro. I think we both got something to say to each other." Antonio nodded. It was not natural to be acting as though nothing unusual was happening when two ace-boon buddies were going to be blasting each other within a few short days.

They rested their elbows on the railing separating them from the river. Antonio wiped his face with his short towel. The sunrise was now creating day.

Felix leaned heavily on the river's railing and stared across to the shores of Brooklyn. Finally, he broke the silence.

"Man, I don't know how to come out with it."

Antonio helped. "It's about our fight, right?"

"Yeah, right." Felix's eyes squinted at the rising orange sun.

"I've been thinking about it too, *panín*.[6] In fact, since we found out it was going to be me and you, I've been awake at night, pulling punches on you, trying not to hurt you."

"Same here. It ain't natural not to think about the fight. I mean, we both are *cheverote*[7] fighters and we both want to win. But only one of us can win. There ain't no draws in the eliminations."

Felix tapped Antonio gently on the shoulder. "I don't mean to sound like I'm bragging, bro. But I wanna win, fair and square."

Antonio nodded quietly. "Yeah. We both know that in the ring the better man wins. Friend or no friend, brother or no . . . "

Felix finished it for him. "Brother. Tony, let's promise something right here. Okay?"

"If it's fair, *hermano*,[8] I'm for it." Antonio admired the courage of a tugboat pulling a barge five times its welterweight size.

"It's fair, Tony. When we get into the ring, it's gotta be like we never met. We gotta be like two heavy strangers that want the same thing and only one can have it. You understand, don'tcha?"

"Sí, I know." Tony smiled. "No pulling punches. We go all the way."

"Yeah, that's right. Listen, Tony. Don't you think it's a good idea if we don't see each other until the day of the fight? I'm going to stay with my Aunt Lucy in the Bronx. I can use Gleason's Gym for working out. My manager says he got some sparring partners with more or less your style."

Tony scratched his nose pensively. "Yeah, it would be better for our heads." He held out his hand, palm upward. "Deal?"

"Deal." Felix lightly slapped open skin.

"Ready for some more running?" Tony asked lamely.

"Naw, bro. Let's cut it here. You go on. I kinda like to get things together in my head."

"You ain't worried, are you?" Tony asked.

"No way, man." Felix laughed out loud. "I got too much smarts for that. I just think it's cooler if we split right here. After the fight, we can get it together again like nothing ever happened."

The amigo brothers were not ashamed to hug each other tightly.

"Guess you're right. Watch yourself, Felix. I hear there's some pretty heavy dudes up in the Bronx. *Suavecito*,[9] okay?"

"Okay. You watch yourself too, *sabe*?"[10]

Tony jogged away. Felix watched his friend disappear from view, throwing rights and lefts. Both fighters had a lot of psyching up[11] to do before the big fight.

The days in training passed much too slowly. Although they kept out of each other's way, they were aware of each other's progress via the ghetto grapevine.

The evening before the big fight, Tony made his way to the roof of his tenement. In

---

6. panín (pä nēn'): Spanish for "pal."
7. cheverote (che ve rô' tā): Spanish for "great."
8. hermano (er mä' nô): Spanish for "brother."

9. suavecito (swä vä sē' tô): Spanish for "take it easy."
10. sabe (sä' bā): Spanish for "understand?"
11. psyching (sīk iŋ) **up:** A slang term meaning "getting themselves mentally ready."

the quiet early dark, he peered over the ledge. Six stories below the lights of the city blinked and the sounds of cars mingled with the curses and the laughter of children in the street. He tried not to think of Felix, feeling he had succeeded in psyching his mind. But only in the ring would he really know. To spare Felix hurt, he would have to knock him out, early and quick.

Up in the South Bronx, Felix decided to take in a movie in an effort to keep Antonio's face away from his fists. The flick was *The Champion* with Kirk Douglas, the third time Felix was seeing it.

The champion was getting hit hard. He was saved only by the sound of the bell.

Felix became the champ and Tony the challenger.

The movie audience was going out of its head. The challenger, confident that he had the championship in the bag, threw a left. The champ countered with a dynamite right.

Felix's right arm felt the shock. Antonio's face, superimposed on the screen, was hit by the awesome blow. Felix saw himself in the ring, blasting Antonio against the ropes. The challenger fell to the canvas.

When Felix finally left the theatre, he had figured out how to psyche himself for tomorrow's fight. It was Felix the Champion vs. Antonio the Challenger.

He walked up some dark streets, deserted except for small pockets of wary-looking kids wearing gang colors. Despite the fact that he was Puerto Rican like them, they eyed him as a stranger to their turf.[12] Felix did a fast shuffle, bobbing and weaving, while letting loose a torrent of blows that would demolish whatever got in its way. It seemed to impress the brothers, who went about their own business.

Finding no takers, Felix decided to split

to his aunt's. Walking the streets had not relaxed him, neither had the fight flick. All it had done was to stir him up. He let himself quietly into his Aunt Lucy's apartment and went straight to bed, falling into a fitful sleep with sounds of the gong for Round One.

Antonio was passing some heavy time on his rooftop. How would the fight tomorrow affect his relationship with Felix? After all, fighting was like any other profession. Friendship had nothing to do with it. A gnawing doubt crept in. He cut negative thinking real quick by doing some speedy fancy dance steps, bobbing and weaving like mercury.[13] The night air was blurred with perpetual motions of left hooks and right crosses. Felix, his *amigo* brother, was not going to be Felix at all in the ring. Just an opponent with another face. Antonio went to sleep, hearing the opening bell for the first round. Like his friend in the South Bronx, he prayed for victory, via a quick clean knock-out in the first round.

Large posters plastered all over the walls of local shops announced the fight between Antonio Cruz and Felix Vargas as the main bout.

The fight had created great interest in the neighborhood. Antonio and Felix were well liked and respected. Each had his own loyal following. Antonio's fans counted on his boxing skills. On the other side, Felix's admirers trusted in his dynamite-packed fists.

Felix had returned to his apartment early in the morning of August 7th and stayed there, hoping to avoid seeing Antonio. He turned the radio on to *salsa* music[14] sounds

---

12. turf (turf): A slang term meaning "a gang's territory."

13. mercury (mur′ kyoo rē): The element mercury, also known as quicksilver because it is so quick and fluid. This element was named after the Roman god Mercury, who because of his quick thinking and speed served as the messenger of the gods.

14. salsa (säl′ sə) **music:** Latin American dance music.

and then tried to read while waiting for word from his manager.

The fight was scheduled to take place in Tompkins Square Park. It had been decided that the gymnasium of the Boys Club was not large enough to hold all the people who were sure to attend. In Tompkins Square Park, everyone who wanted could view the fight, whether from ringside or window fire escapes or tenement rooftops.

The morning of the fight Tompkins Square was a beehive of activity with numerous workers setting up the ring, the seats, and the guest speakers' stand. The scheduled bouts began shortly after noon and the park had begun filling up even earlier.

The local junior high school across from Tompkins Square Park served as the dressing room for all the fighters. Each was given a separate classroom with desk tops, covered with mats, serving as resting tables. Antonio thought he caught a glimpse of Felix waving to him from a room at the far end of the corridor. He waved back just in case it had been him.

The fighters changed from their street clothes into fighting gear. Antonio wore white trunks, black socks, and black shoes. Felix wore sky blue trunks, red socks, and white boxing shoes. Each had dressing gowns to match their fighting trunks with their names neatly stitched on the back.

The loudspeakers blared into the open windows of the school. There were speeches by dignitaries, community leaders, and great boxers of yesteryear. Some were well prepared, some improvised on the spot. They all carried the same message of great pleasure and honor at being part of such a historic event. This great day was in the tradition of champions emerging from the streets of the lower east side.

Interwoven with the speeches were the sounds of the other boxing events. After the sixth bout, Felix was much relieved when his trainer Charlie said, "Time change. Quick knock-out. This is it. We're on."

Waiting time was over. Felix was escorted from the classroom by a dozen fans in white T-shirts with the word FELIX across their fronts.

Antonio was escorted down a different stairwell and guided through a roped-off path.

As the two climbed into the ring, the crowd exploded with a roar. Antonio and Felix both bowed gracefully and then raised their arms in acknowledgment.

Antonio tried to be cool, but even as the roar was in its first birth, he turned slowly to meet Felix's eyes looking directly into his. Felix nodded his head and Antonio responded. And both as one, just as quickly, turned away to face his own corner.

Bong—bong—bong. The roar turned to stillness.

"Ladies and Gentlemen, *Señores y Señoras.*"[15]

The announcer spoke slowly, pleased at his bilingual efforts.

"Now the moment we have all been waiting for—the main event between two fine young Puerto Rican fighters, products of our lower east side. In this corner, weighing 134 pounds, Felix Vargas. And in this corner, weighing 133 pounds, Antonio Cruz. The winner will represent the Boys Club in the tournament of champions, the Golden Gloves. There will be no draw. May the best man win."

The cheering of the crowd shook the window panes of the old buildings surrounding Tompkins Square Park. At the center of the ring, the referee was giving instructions to the youngsters.

"Keep your punches up. No low blows. No punching on the back of the head. Keep

---

15. señores y señoras (se nyô räs ē se nyô räs): Spanish for "Gentlemen and Ladies."

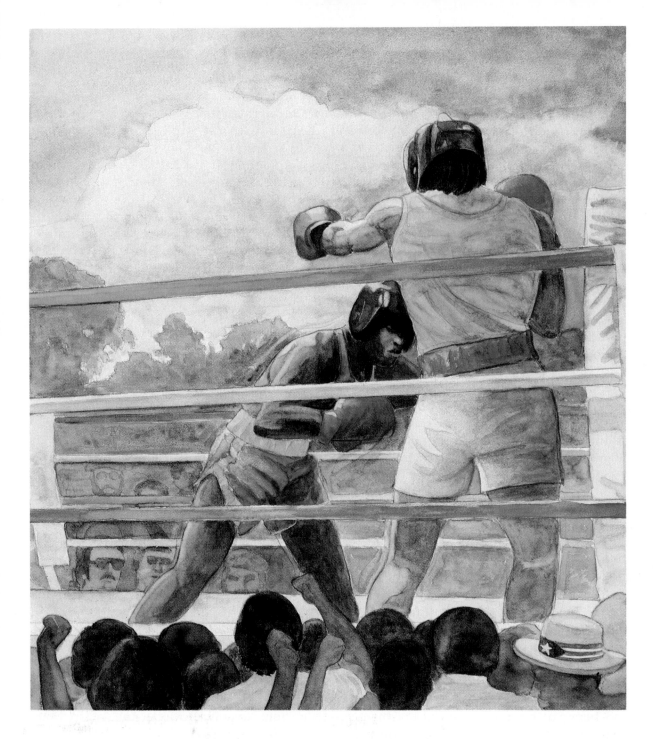

your heads up. Understand. Let's have a clean fight. Now shake hands and come out fighting."

Both youngsters touched gloves and nodded. They turned and danced quickly to their corners. Their head towels and dressing gowns were lifted neatly from their shoulders by their trainers' nimble fingers. Antonio crossed himself. Felix did the same.

BONG! BONG! ROUND ONE. Felix and

Antonio turned and faced each other squarely in a fighting pose. Felix wasted no time. He came in fast, head low, half hunched toward his right shoulder, and lashed out with a straight left. He missed a right cross as Antonio slipped the punch and countered with one-two-three lefts that snapped Felix's head back, sending a mild shock coursing through him. If Felix had any small doubt about their friendship affecting their fight, it was being neatly dispelled.

Antonio danced, a joy to behold. His left hand was like a piston pumping jabs one right after another with seeming ease. Felix bobbed and weaved and never stopped boring in. He knew that at long range he was at a disadvantage. Antonio had too much reach on him. Only by coming in close could Felix hope to achieve the dreamed-of knockout.

Antonio knew the dynamite that was stored in his *amigo* brother's fist. He ducked a short right and missed a left hook. Felix trapped him against the ropes just long enough to pour some punishing rights and lefts to Antonio's hard midsection. Antonio slipped away from Felix, crashing two lefts to his head, which set Felix's right ear to ringing.

Bong! Both *amigos* froze a punch well on its way, sending up a roar of approval for good sportsmanship.

Felix walked briskly back to his corner. His right ear had not stopped ringing. Antonio gracefully danced his way toward his stool none the worse, except for glowing glove burns, showing angry red against the whiteness of his midribs.

"Watch that right, Tony." His trainer talked into his ear. "Remember Felix always goes to the body. He'll want you to drop your hands for his overhand left or right. Got it?"

Antonio nodded, spraying water out between his teeth. He felt better as his sore midsection was being firmly rubbed.

Felix's corner was also busy.

"You gotta get in there, fella." Felix's trainer poured water over his curly Afro locks. "Get in there or he's gonna chop you up from way back."

Bong! Bong! Round two. Felix was off his stool and rushed Antonio like a bull, sending a hard right to his head. Beads of water exploded from Antonio's long hair.

Antonio, hurt, sent back a blurring barrage of lefts and rights that only meant pain to Felix, who returned with a short left to the head followed by a looping right to the body. Antonio countered with his own flurry, forcing Felix to give ground. But not for long.

Felix bobbed and weaved, bobbed and weaved, occasionally punching his two gloves together.

Antonio waited for the rush that was sure to come. Felix closed in and feinted with his left shoulder and threw his right instead. Lights suddenly exploded inside Felix's head as Antonio slipped the blow and hit him with a pistonlike left catching him flush on the point of his chin.

Bedlam broke loose as Felix's legs momentarily buckled. He fought off a series of rights and lefts and came back with a strong right that taught Antonio respect.

Antonio danced in carefully. He knew Felix had the habit of playing possum when hurt, to sucker an opponent within reach of the powerful bombs he carried in each fist.

A right to the head slowed Antonio's pretty dancing. He answered with his own left at Felix's right eye that began puffing up within three seconds.

Antonio, a bit too eager, moved in too close and Felix had him entangled into a rip-roaring, punching toe-to-toe slugfest that brought the whole Tompkins Square Park screaming to its feet.

Rights to the body. Lefts to the head. Neither fighter was giving an inch. Suddenly a short right caught Antonio squarely on the chin. His long legs turned to jelly and his arms flailed out desperately. Felix, grunting like a bull, threw wild punches from every direction. Antonio, groggy, bobbed and weaved, evading most of the blows. Suddenly his head cleared. His left flashed out hard and straight catching Felix on the bridge of his nose.

Felix lashed back with a haymaker,[16] right off the ghetto streets. At the same instant, his eye caught another left hook from Antonio. Felix swung out trying to clear the pain. Only the frenzied screaming of those along ringside let him know that he had dropped Antonio. Fighting off the growing haze, Antonio struggled to his feet, got up, ducked, and threw a smashing right that dropped Felix flat on his back.

Felix got up as fast as he could in his own corner, groggy but still game. He didn't even hear the count. In a fog, he heard the roaring of the crowd, who seemed to have gone insane. His head cleared to hear the bell sound at the end of the round. He was very glad. His trainer sat him down on the stool.

In his corner, Antonio was doing what all fighters do when they are hurt. They sit and smile at everyone.

The referee signaled the ring doctor to check the fighters out. He did so and then gave his okay. The cold water sponges brought clarity to both *amigo* brothers. They were rubbed until their circulation ran free.

Bong! Round three—the final round. Up to now it had been tic-tac-toe, pretty much even. But everyone knew there could be no draw and that this round would decide the winner.

This time, to Felix's surprise, it was Antonio who came out fast, charging across the ring. Felix braced himself but couldn't ward off the barrage of punches. Antonio drove Felix hard against the ropes.

The crowd ate it up. Thus far the two had fought with *mucho corazón*.[17] Felix tapped his gloves and commenced his attack anew. Antonio, throwing boxer's caution to the winds, jumped in to meet him.

Both pounded away. Neither gave an inch and neither fell to the canvas. Felix's left eye was tightly closed. Claret red[18] blood poured from Antonio's nose. They fought toe-to-toe.

The sounds of their blows were loud in contrast to the silence of a crowd gone completely mute. The referee was stunned by their savagery.

Bong! Bong! Bong! The bell sounded over and over again. Felix and Antonio were past hearing. Their blows continued to pound on each other like hailstones.

Finally the referee and the two trainers pried Felix and Antonio apart. Cold water was poured over them to bring them back to their senses.

They looked around and then rushed toward each other. A cry of alarm surged through Tompkins Square Park. Was this a fight to the death instead of a boxing match?

The fear soon gave way to wave upon wave of cheering as the two *amigos* embraced.

No matter what the decision, they knew they would always be champions to each other.

BONG! BONG! BONG! "Ladies and Gentlemen. *Señores* and *Señoras*. The winner and representative to the Golden Gloves Tournament of Champions is . . ."

The announcer turned to point to the winner and found himself alone. Arm in arm the champions had already left the ring.

---

16. haymaker: A punch thrown with full force.

17. mucho corazón (moo͞ɔ′ chŏ kô rä sôn′): Spanish for "much courage."

18. claret (klar′ it) **red:** Purplish red.

THINKING ABOUT THE SELECTION

Recalling

1. How do Antonio and Felix differ in appearance?
2. What dream do the boys share?
3. What event creates a wall between them?
4. What agreement do they make while jogging?
5. Describe the way the boys leave the ring at the end of the fight.

Interpreting

6. Why is boxing so important to Antonio and Felix?
7. Why do the boys decide not to see each other until the fight?
8. What do the boys discover they value as much as or more than winning?
9. *Amigo* means "friend." Why is "Amigo Brothers" an appropriate title for this story?

Applying

10. Why can it be hard for friends to compete?

ANALYZING LITERATURE

Considering Two Major Characters

Some stories deal with more than one major character. In "Amigo Brothers," both Antonio and Felix are fully developed and have a variety of character traits. The writer gives them equal attention. You learn about these two characters as you watch the dream they share become the barrier that divides them.

1. Explain how the boys' relationship is tested in this story.
2. Show how the boys' friendship is stronger or weaker as a result of this test.

CRITICAL THINKING AND READING

Comparing and Contrasting Characters

When you **compare** two characters you show how they are similar. When you **contrast** them, you show how they are different. Often, you can better understand stories with more than one major character by comparing and contrasting the characters. In "Amigo Brothers," for example, Antonio and Felix are different in height but similar in their love of boxing.

1. List three other ways in which the boys are similar.
2. Now list three ways in which they are different.
3. Which of these similarities and differences may have brought them together as friends?

UNDERSTANDING LANGUAGE

Using Words in Comparisons

Certain words are very helpful when you compare and contrast characters. Some words that express similarities are *like, identical to, the same as,* and *similar to.* For example, you could say: *Like* Felix, Antonio loves boxing. Words that express differences include *however, unlike, different from, while,* and *nevertheless.* For example, you could say: Felix and Antonio are both boxers; *nevertheless* (or *however*), Antonio is tall *while* Felix is short.

1. Express a similarity between Felix and Antonio using one of the words or phrases mentioned above.
2. Now express a difference between the two boys using one of the preceding words or phrases.

THINKING AND WRITING

Writing a Comparison and Contrast

Compare and contrast Antonio and Felix. As you brainstorm for ideas, recall your lists of the ways that the boys are similar and different. Also, remember to use some of the key words that show similarities and differences. When you have finished, revise your work to make sure it is clear.

GUIDE FOR READING

Stolen Day

Sherwood Anderson (1876–1941) was born in Camden, Ohio. Although Anderson had almost no formal education, he became a successful businessman, the manager of a paint factory. Then one day, surprisingly, he walked out of his job and went off to Chicago to become a writer. His most successful works were based on his boyhood, and many of his stories are about growing up. "Stolen Day" deals with a boy who has an experience that might help him to grow up.

Motivation

In stories as in life, people do things because they have reasons, or motives, for doing them. **Motivation** refers to the reasons behind actions. The word *motivation* contains the root *mot,* meaning "to move." Motivation moves a person forward, causing him or her to do something, to pursue some goal. Another word with the root *mot* is *emotion.* A powerful emotion, which causes a person to behave in certain ways, can be a strong motivation.

Look For

Motivation may be unconscious. For example, in "Stolen Day" the boy does not fully realize the reasons why he acts as he does. As you read "Stolen Day," look for the motivation behind the boy's behavior.

Writing

Has a beautiful spring day ever made you feel like stealing a day from a chore that had to be done? Freewrite, explaining the reasons you might give for taking a day off.

Vocabulary

Knowing the following words will help you as you read "Stolen Day."
inflammatory (in flam′ə tôr′ē) *adj.*: Characterized by pain and swelling (p. 89)
rheumatism (ro͞o′mə tiz′m) *n.*: A painful condition of the joints and muscles (p. 89)
solemn (säl′əm) *adj.*: Serious, somber (p. 90)
carp (kärp) *n.*: A fresh-water fish living in a pond or other quiet water (p. 92)

Stolen Day

Sherwood Anderson

It must be that all children are actors. The whole thing started with a boy on our street named Walter, who had inflammatory rheumatism. That's what they called it. He didn't have to go to school.

Still he could walk about. He could go fishing in the creek or the waterworks pond. There was a place up at the pond where in the spring the water came tumbling over the dam and formed a deep pool. It was a good place. Sometimes you could get some good big ones there.

I went down that way on my way to school one spring morning. It was out of my way but I wanted to see if Walter was there.

He was, inflammatory rheumatism and all. There he was, sitting with a fish pole in his hand. He had been able to walk down there all right.

It was then that my own legs began to hurt. My back too. I went on to school but, at the recess time, I began to cry. I did it when the teacher, Sarah Suggett, had come out into the schoolhouse yard.

She came right over to me.

"I ache all over," I said. I did, too.

I kept on crying and it worked all right.

"You'd better go on home," she said.

So I went. I limped painfully away. I kept on limping until I got out of the schoolhouse street.

Then I felt better. I still had inflammatory rheumatism pretty bad but I could get along better.

I must have done some thinking on the way home.

"I'd better not say I have inflammatory rheumatism." I decided. "Maybe if you've got that you swell up."

A COUNTRY LAD, 1873
Winslow Homer
Cooper-Hewitt Museum

I thought I'd better go around to where Walter was and ask him about that, so I did—but he wasn't there.

"They must not be biting today," I thought.

I had a feeling that, if I said I had inflammatory rheumatism, Mother or my brothers and my sister Stella might laugh. They did laugh at me pretty often and I didn't like it at all.

"Just the same," I said to myself, "I have got it." I began to hurt and ache again.

I went home and sat on the front steps of our house. I sat there a long time. There wasn't anyone at home but Mother and the two little ones. Ray would have been four or five then and Earl might have been three.

It was Earl who saw me there. I had got tired sitting and was lying on the porch. Earl was always a quiet, solemn little fellow.

He must have said something to Mother for presently she came.

"What's the matter with you? Why aren't you in school?" she asked.

I came pretty near telling her right out that I had inflammatory rheumatism but I thought I'd better not. Mother and Father had been speaking of Walter's case at the table just the day before. "It affects the heart," Father had said. That frightened me when I thought of it. "I might die," I thought. "I might just suddenly die right here; my heart might stop beating."

On the day before I had been running a race with my brother Irve. We were up at the fairgrounds after school and there was a half-mile track.

"I'll bet you can't run a half-mile," he said. "I bet you I could beat you running clear around the track."

And so we did it and I beat him, but afterwards my heart did seem to beat pretty hard. I remembered that lying there on the porch. "It's a wonder, with my inflammatory rheumatism and all, I didn't just drop down dead," I thought. The thought frightened me a lot. I ached worse than ever.

"I ache, Ma," I said. "I just ache."

She made me go in the house and upstairs and get into bed.

It wasn't so good. It was spring. I was up there for perhaps an hour, maybe two, and then I felt better.

I got up and went downstairs. "I feel better, Ma," I said.

Mother said she was glad. She was pretty busy that day and hadn't paid much attention to me. She had made me get into bed upstairs and then hadn't even come up to see how I was.

I didn't think much of that when I was up there but when I got downstairs where she was, and when, after I had said I felt better and she only said she was glad and went right on with her work, I began to ache again.

I thought, "I'll bet I die of it. I bet I do."

I went out to the front porch and sat down. I was pretty sore at Mother.

"If she really knew the truth, that I have the inflammatory rheumatism and I may just drop down dead any time, I'll bet she wouldn't care about that either," I thought.

I was getting more and more angry the more thinking I did.

"I know what I'm going to do," I thought; "I'm going to go fishing."

I thought that, feeling the way I did, I might be sitting on the high bank just above the deep pool where the water went over the dam, and suddenly my heart would stop beating.

And then, of course, I'd pitch forward, over the bank into the pool and, if I wasn't dead when I hit the water, I'd drown sure.

They would all come home to supper and they'd miss me.

"But where is he?"

Then Mother would remember that I'd come home from school aching.

She'd go upstairs and I wouldn't be there. One day during the year before, there was a child got drowned in a spring. It was one of the Wyatt children.

Right down at the end of the street there was a spring under a birch tree and there had been a barrel sunk in the ground.

Everyone had always been saying the spring ought to be kept covered, but it wasn't.

So the Wyatt child went down there, playing around alone, and fell in and got drowned.

Mother was the one who had found the drowned child. She had gone to get a pail of water and there the child was, drowned and dead.

This had been in the evening when we were all at home, and Mother had come run-

YOUNG FISHERMAN, 1889
Louis Michel Eilshemius
Hirshhorn Museum and Sculpture Garden

ning up the street with the dead, dripping child in her arms. She was making for the Wyatt house as hard as she could run, and she was pale.

She had a terrible look on her face. I remembered then.

"So," I thought, "they'll miss me and there'll be a search made. Very likely there'll be someone who has seen me sitting by the pond fishing, and there'll be a big alarm and all the town will turn out and they'll drag the pond."

I was having a grand time, having died. Maybe, after they found me and had got me out of the deep pool, Mother would grab me up in her arms and run home with me as she had run with the Wyatt child.

I got up from the porch and went around the house. I got my fishing pole and lit out for the pool below the dam. Mother was busy—she always was—and didn't see me go. When I got there I thought I'd better not sit too near the edge of the high bank.

By this time I didn't ache hardly at all, but I thought.

"With inflammatory rheumatism you can't tell," I thought.

"It probably comes and goes," I thought.

"Walter has it and he goes fishing," I thought.

I had got my line into the pool and suddenly I got a bite. It was a regular whopper. I knew that. I'd never had a bite like that.

I knew what it was. It was one of Mr. Fenn's big carp.

Mr. Fenn was a man who had a big pond of his own. He sold ice in the summer and the pond was to make the ice. He had bought some big carp and put them into his pond and then, earlier in the spring when there was a freshet, his dam had gone out.

So the carp had got into our creek and

one or two big ones had been caught—but none of them by a boy like me.

The carp was pulling and I was pulling and I was afraid he'd break my line, so I just tumbled down the high bank holding onto the line and got right into the pool. We had it out, there in the pool. We struggled. We wrestled. Then I got a hand under his gills and got him out.

He was a big one all right. He was nearly half as big as I was myself. I had him on the bank and I kept one hand under his gills and I ran.

I never ran so hard in my life. He was slippery, and now and then he wriggled out of my arms; once I stumbled and fell on him, but I got him home.

So there it was. I was a big hero that day. Mother got a washtub and filled it with water. She put the fish in it and all the neighbors came to look. I got into dry clothes and went down to supper—and then I made a break that spoiled my day.

There we were, all of us, at the table, and suddenly Father asked what had been the matter with me at school. He had met the teacher, Sarah Suggett, on the street and she had told him how I had become ill.

"What was the matter with you?" Father asked, and before I thought what I was saying I let it out.

"I had the inflammatory rheumatism," I said—and a shout went up. It made me sick to hear them, the way they all laughed.

It brought back all the aching again, and like a fool I began to cry.

"Well, I *have* got it—I *have*, I *have*," I cried, and I got up from the table and ran upstairs.

I stayed there until Mother came up. I knew it would be a long time before I heard the last of the inflammatory rheumatism. I was sick all right, but the aching I now had wasn't in my legs or in my back.

THINKING ABOUT THE SELECTION

Recalling

1. What happens to the boy in school?
2. How does the father find out that his son left school that day?
3. How do the members of the boy's family respond when he tells them he has inflammatory rheumatism?

Interpreting

4. Why does the boy stop limping once he gets away from the schoolhouse street?
5. What does the boy mean when he says, "I was having a grand time, having died."?
6. Why does he say this?
7. At the end of the story, the boy says, "I was sick all right, but the aching I now had wasn't in my legs or in my back." What do these words indicate?

Applying

8. To *justify* means "to provide good grounds or reasons for something." Why do people sometimes try to justify their behavior, even when they know that what they have done is wrong?

ANALYZING LITERATURE

Understanding Motivation

Motivation is the cause for characters' actions. It moves them to do what they do, to pursue their goals. Often, a powerful emotion can be a strong motivation. Understanding a character's motives gives you deeper insight into a story.

1. Why does the boy think he is ill?
2. Why does the boy at first not tell his family that he has inflammatory rheumatism?
3. Do you think the boy is fully conscious of his motives? Why or why not?

CRITICAL THINKING AND READING

Making Inferences About Motivation

Sometimes a character's motives are not directly stated. You must use the information avail-

able in the story to make an **inference,** or draw a reasonable conclusion, about them. For example, you can infer that the narrator would like to be able to go fishing on this spring day. The author does not tell you that directly, but you can infer it from the following information: The narrator goes by the pond on his way to school to see if Walter is there; and he feels that Walter can go fishing despite having inflammatory rheumatism.

What inference can you make about the narrator's motivation from the following sentences?

a. "Mother . . . hadn't paid much attention to me. She had made me get into bed upstairs and then hadn't even come up to see how I was."
b. "Maybe . . . Mother would grab me up in her arms and run home with me as she had run in with the Wyatt child."

UNDERSTANDING LANGUAGE

Using the Root *flam*

A **root** of a word is the part from which others grow. For example, the root in *inflammatory* is *flam,* meaning "flame." Knowing word roots can help you figure out the meaning of new words.

In a dictionary, find the definition of each of the following words. Show how it comes from the meaning of *flam.* Then use each word in a sentence.

1. inflame
2. flammable
3. flamboyant

THINKING AND WRITING

Writing a Diary Entry

Imagine that you are the narrator of this story. Write a diary entry in which you explain your behavior on this day. Include why you left school, why you got out of bed and went fishing, and what you imagined might happen if you fell in the pool. As you revise, check that what you have written explains your motivation.

Luke Baldwin's Vow

Morley Callaghan (1903–   ) was born in Toronto, Ontario, Canada. While working as a reporter for the *Toronto Star,* he published his first short stories. Callaghan is a dedicated writer, whose aim, in one critic's words, is "simply to write well and to go on writing well." Like many of Callaghan's stories, "Luke Baldwin's Vow" deals with the conflict between the sometimes hard demands of the "practical" world and a character's spiritual and emotional needs.

Direct and Indirect Characterization

Characterization is the art of making people in a story real. Authors can present characters in a direct or an indirect way. When they present characters directly, they tell you what they want you to know about a character. For example, Uncle Henry is described as ". . . so wonderfully practical. He takes care of everything in a sensible, easy way." When authors develop characters indirectly, they let the characters show their personalities through what they say or do.

Look For

As you read "Luke Baldwin's Vow,"look for what the author tells you directly in the second paragraph about the kind of man Uncle Henry is. Find details that support this judgment of him. Toward the end of the story, notice what Uncle Henry says or does that tells you more about him.

Writing

In the story you are about to read, Luke Baldwin grows up when he learns to take responsibility. Freewrite about a situation, real or imagined, in which a young person takes responsibility to improve an unsatisfactory situation.

Vocabulary

Knowing the following words will help you as you read "Luke Baldwin's Vow."

burly (bur′lē) *adj.*: Heavy and muscular (p. 95)

straightforward (strāt′for′wərd) *adj.*: Direct, frank, honest (p. 95)

amber (am′bər) *n.*: A brownish-yellow substance; *adj.*: Of a brownish-yellow color (p. 96)

sentimental (sen′tə men′t'l) *adj.*: Acting from feeling rather than from practical motives (p. 99)

resourceful (ri sôrs′fəl) *adj.*: Able to deal effectively with problems (p. 100)

competent (käm′pə tənt) *adj.*: Capable (p. 100)

exultation (eg′zəl tā′shən) *n.*: Rejoicing (p. 101)

apprehensively (ap′rə hen′ siv lē) *adv.*: Anxiously, fearfully (p. 103)

falter (fôl′tər) *v.*: Show uncertainty, act hesitantly (p. 103)

Luke Baldwin's Vow

Morley Callaghan

That summer when twelve-year-old Luke Baldwin came to live with his Uncle Henry in the house on the stream by the sawmill, he did not forget that he had promised his dying father he would try to learn things from his uncle; so he used to watch him very carefully.

Uncle Henry, who was the manager of the sawmill, was a big, burly man weighing more than two hundred and thirty pounds, and he had a rough-skinned, brick-colored face. He looked like a powerful man, but his health was not good. He had aches and pains in his back and shoulders which puzzled the doctor. The first thing Luke learned about Uncle Henry was that everybody had great respect for him. The four men he employed in the sawmill were always polite and attentive when he spoke to them. His wife, Luke's Aunt Helen, a kindly, plump, straightforward woman, never argued with him. "You should try and be like your Uncle Henry," she would say to Luke. "He's so wonderfully practical. He takes care of everything in a sensible, easy way."

Luke used to trail around the sawmill after Uncle Henry not only because he liked the fresh clean smell of the newly cut wood and the big piles of sawdust, but because he was impressed by his uncle's precise, firm tone when he spoke to the men.

Sometimes Uncle Henry would stop and explain to Luke something about a piece of timber. "Always try and learn the essential facts, son," he would say. "If you've got the facts, you know what's useful and what isn't useful, and no one can fool you."

He showed Luke that nothing of value was ever wasted around the mill. Luke used to listen, and wonder if there was another man in the world who knew so well what was needed and what ought to be thrown away. Uncle Henry had known at once that Luke needed a bicycle to ride to his school, which was two miles away in town, and he bought him a good one. He knew that Luke needed good, serviceable clothes. He also knew exactly how much Aunt Helen needed to run the house, the price of everything, and how much a woman should be paid for doing the family washing. In the evenings Luke used to sit in the living room watching his uncle making notations in a black notebook which he always carried in his vest pocket, and he knew that he was assessing the value of the smallest transaction that had taken place during the day.

Luke promised himself that when he grew up he, too, would be admired for his good, sound judgment. But, of course, he couldn't always be watching and learning from his Uncle Henry, for too often when he watched him he thought of his own father; then he was lonely. So he began to build up another secret life for himself around the sawmill, and his companion was the eleven-year-old collie, Dan, a dog blind in one eye and with a slight limp in his left hind leg. Dan was a fat slow-moving old dog. He was very affectionate and his eye was the color of amber. His fur was amber too. When Luke left for school in the morning, the old dog followed him for half a mile down the road, and when he returned in the afternoon, there was Dan waiting at the gate.

Sometimes they would play around the millpond or by the dam, or go down the stream to the lake. Luke was never lonely when the dog was with him. There was an old rowboat that they used as a pirate ship in the stream, and they would be pirates together, with Luke shouting instructions to Captain Dan and with the dog seeming to understand and wagging his tail enthusiastically. Its amber eye was alert, intelligent and approving. Then they would plunge into the brush on the other side of the stream, pretending they were hunting tigers. Of course, the old dog was no longer much good for hunting; he was too slow and too lazy. Uncle Henry no longer used him for hunting rabbits or anything else.

When they came out of the brush, they would lie together on the cool, grassy bank being affectionate with each other, with Luke talking earnestly, while the collie, as Luke believed, smiled with the good eye. Lying in the grass, Luke would say things to Dan he could not say to his uncle or his aunt. Not that what he said was important; it was just stuff about himself that he might have told to his own father or mother if they had been alive. Then they would go back to the house for dinner, and after dinner Dan would follow him down the road to Mr. Kemp's house, where they would ask old Mr. Kemp if they could go with him to round up his four cows. The old man was always glad to see them. He seemed to like watching Luke and the collie running around the cows, pretending they were riding on a vast range in the foothills of the Rockies.

Uncle Henry no longer paid much atten-

tion to the collie, though once when he tripped over him on the veranda, he shook his head and said thoughtfully, "Poor old fellow, he's through. Can't use him for anything. He just eats and sleeps and gets in the way."

One Sunday during Luke's summer holidays when they had returned from church and had had their lunch, they had all moved out to the veranda where the collie was sleeping. Luke sat down on the steps, his back against the veranda post, Uncle Henry took the rocking chair, and Aunt Helen stretched stopped, hearing Luke coming after him. All he needed was the touch of Luke's hand. Then he began to lick the hand methodically, as if apologizing.

"Luke," Uncle Henry called sharply, "bring that dog here."

When Luke led the collie back to the veranda, Uncle Henry nodded and said, "Thanks, Luke." Then he took out a cigar, lit it, put his big hands on his knees and began to rock in the chair while he frowned and eyed the dog steadily. Obviously he was making some kind of an important decision about the collie.

"What's the matter, Uncle Henry?" Luke asked nervously.

"That dog can't see any more," Uncle Henry said.

"Oh, yes, he can," Luke said quickly. "His bad eye got turned to the chair, that's all, Uncle Henry."

"And his teeth are gone, too," Uncle Henry went on, paying no attention to what Luke had said. Turning to the hammock, he called, "Helen, sit up a minute, will you?"

When she got up and stood beside him, he went on, "I was thinking about this old dog the other day, Helen. It's not only that he's just about blind, but did you notice that when we drove up after church he didn't even bark?"

"It's a fact he didn't, Henry."

"No, not much good even as a watchdog now."

"Poor old fellow. It's a pity, isn't it?"

"And no good for hunting either. And he eats a lot, I suppose."

"About as much as he ever did, Henry."

"The plain fact is the old dog isn't worth his keep any more. It's time we got rid of him."

"It's always so hard to know how to get rid of a dog, Henry."

herself out in the hammock, sighing contentedly. Then Luke, eying the collie, tapped the step with the palm of his hand, giving three little taps like a signal and the old collie, lifting his head, got up stiffly with a slow wagging of the tail as an acknowledgment that the signal had been heard, and began to cross the veranda to Luke. But the dog was sleepy; his bad eye was turned to the rocking chair; in passing, his left front paw went under the rocker. With a frantic yelp, the dog went bounding down the steps and hobbled around the corner of the house, where he

"I was thinking about it the other day. Some people think it's best to shoot a dog. I haven't had any shells for that shotgun for over a year. Poisoning is a hard death for a dog. Maybe drowning is the easiest and quickest way. Well, I'll speak to one of the mill hands and have him look after it."

Crouching on the ground, his arms around the old collie's neck, Luke cried out, "Uncle Henry, Dan's a wonderful dog! You don't know how wonderful he is!"

"He's just a very old dog, son," Uncle Henry said calmly. "The time comes when you have to get rid of any old dog. We've got to be practical about it. I'll get you a pup, son. A smart little dog that'll be worth its keep. A pup that will grow up with you."

"I don't want a pup!" Luke cried, turning his face away. Circling around him, the dog began to bark, then flick his long pink tongue at the back of Luke's neck.

Aunt Helen, catching her husband's eye, put her finger on her lips, warning him not to go on talking in front of the boy. "An old dog like that often wanders off into the brush and sort of picks a place to die when the time comes. Isn't that so, Henry?"

"Oh sure," he agreed quickly. "In fact, when Dan didn't show up yesterday, I was sure that was what had happened." Then he yawned and seemed to forget about the dog.

But Luke was frightened, for he knew what his uncle was like. He knew that if his uncle had decided that the dog was useless and that it was sane and sensible to get rid of it, he would be ashamed of himself if he were diverted by any sentimental considerations. Luke knew in his heart that he couldn't move his uncle. All he could do, he thought, was keep the dog away from his uncle, keep him out of the house, feed him when Uncle Henry wasn't around.

Next day at noontime Luke saw his uncle walking from the mill toward the house with old Sam Carter, a mill hand. Sam Carter was a dull, stooped, slow-witted man of sixty with an iron-gray beard, who was wearing blue overalls and a blue shirt. He hardly ever spoke to anybody. Watching from the veranda, Luke noticed that his uncle suddenly gave Sam Carter a cigar, which Sam put in his pocket. Luke had never seen his uncle give Sam a cigar or pay much attention to him.

Then, after lunch, Uncle Henry said lazily that he would like Luke to take his bicycle and go into town and get him some cigars.

"I'll take Dan," Luke said.

"Better not, son," Uncle Henry said. "It'll take you all afternoon. I want those cigars. Get going, Luke."

His uncle's tone was so casual that Luke tried to believe they were not merely getting rid of him. Of course he had to do what he was told. He had never dared to refuse to obey an order from his uncle. But when he had taken his bicycle and had ridden down the path that followed the stream to the town road and had got about a quarter of a mile along the road, he found that all he could think of was his uncle handing old Sam Carter the cigar.

Slowing down, sick with worry now, he got off the bike and stood uncertainly on the sunlit road. Sam Carter was a gruff, aloof old man who would have no feeling for a dog. Then suddenly Luke could go no farther without getting some assurance that the collie would not be harmed while he was away. Across the fields he could see the house.

Leaving the bike in the ditch, he started to cross the field, intending to get close enough to the house so Dan could hear him if he whistled softly. He got about fifty yards away from the house and whistled and waited, but there was no sign of the dog, which might be asleep at the front of the house, he knew, or over at the sawmill. With the saws whining, the dog couldn't hear the soft whistle. For a few minutes Luke couldn't make up his mind what to do, then he decided to go back to the road, get on his bike and go back the way he had come until he got to the place where the river path joined the road. There he could leave his bike, go up the path, then into the tall grass and get close to the front of the house and the sawmill without being seen.

He had followed the river path for about a hundred yards, and when he came to the place where the river began to bend sharply toward the house his heart fluttered and his legs felt paralyzed, for he saw the old rowboat in the one place where the river was deep, and in the rowboat was Sam Carter with the collie.

The bearded man in the blue overalls was smoking the cigar; the dog, with a rope around its neck, sat contentedly beside him, its tongue going out in a friendly lick at the hand holding the rope. It was all like a crazy dream picture to Luke; all wrong because it looked so lazy and friendly, even the curling smoke from Sam Carter's cigar. But as Luke cried out, "Dan, Dan! Come on, boy!" and the dog jumped at the water, he saw that Sam Carter's left hand was hanging deep in the water, holding a foot of rope with a heavy stone at the end. As Luke cried out wildly, "Don't! Please don't!" Carter dropped the stone, for the cry came too late; it was blurred by the screech of the big saws at the mill. But Carter was startled, and he stared stupidly at the riverbank, then he ducked his head and began to row quickly to the bank.

But Luke was watching the collie take what looked like a long, shallow dive, except that the hind legs suddenly kicked up above the surface, then shot down, and while he watched, Luke sobbed and trembled, for it was as if the happy secret part of his life around the sawmill was being torn away from him. But even while he watched, he seemed to be following a plan without knowing it, for he was already fumbling in his pocket for his jackknife, jerking the blade open, pulling off his pants, kicking his shoes off while he muttered fiercely and prayed that Sam Carter would get out of sight.

It hardly took the mill hand a minute to reach the bank and go slinking furtively around the bend as if he felt that the boy was following him. But Luke hadn't taken his eyes off the exact spot in the water where Dan had disappeared. As soon as the mill hand was out of sight, Luke slid down the bank and took a leap at the water, the sun glistening on his slender body, his eyes wild with eagerness as he ran out to the deep place, then arched his back and dived, swimming under water, his open eyes getting used to the greenish-gray haze of the water, the sandy bottom and the imbedded rocks.

His lungs began to ache, then he saw the shadow of the collie floating at the end of the taut rope, rock-held in the sand. He slashed at the rope with his knife. He couldn't get much strength in his arm because of the resistance of the water. He grabbed the rope with his left hand, hacking with his knife. The collie suddenly drifted up slowly, like a water-soaked log. Then his own head shot above the surface, and while he was sucking in the air he was drawing in the rope, pull-ing the collie toward him and treading water. In a few strokes he was away from the deep place and his feet touched the bottom.

Hoisting the collie out of the water, he scrambled toward the bank, lurching and stumbling in fright because the collie felt like a dead weight.

He went on up the bank and across the path to the tall grass, where he fell flat, hugging the dog and trying to warm him with his own body. But the collie didn't stir, the good amber eye remained closed. Then suddenly Luke wanted to act like a resourceful, competent man. Getting up on his knees, he stretched the dog out on its belly, drew him between his knees, felt with trembling hands for the soft places on the flanks just above the hipbones, and rocked back and forth, pressing with all his weight, then relaxing the pressure as he straightened up. He hoped that he was working the dog's lungs like a bellows. He had read that men who had been thought drowned had been saved in this way.

"Come on, Dan. Come on, old boy," he pleaded softly. As a little water came from the collie's mouth, Luke's heart jumped, and he muttered over and over, "You can't be dead, Dan! You can't, you can't! I won't let you die, Dan!" He rocked back and forth tirelessly, applying the pressure to the flanks. More water dribbled from the mouth. In the collie's body he felt a faint tremor. "Oh gee, Dan, you're alive," he whispered. "Come on, boy. Keep it up."

With a cough the collie suddenly jerked his head back, the amber eye opened, and there they were looking at each other. Then the collie, thrusting his legs out stiffly, tried to hoist himself up, staggered, tried again, then stood there in a stupor. Then he shook himself like any other wet dog, turned his head, eyed Luke, and the red tongue came out in a weak flick at Luke's cheek.

"Lie down, Dan," Luke said. As the dog lay down beside him, Luke closed his eyes, buried his head in the wet fur and wondered why all the muscles of his arms and legs began to jerk in a nervous reaction, now that it was all over. "Stay there, Dan," he said softly, and he went back to the path, got his clothes and came back beside Dan and put them on. "I think we'd better get away from this spot, Dan," he said. "Keep down, boy. Come on." And he crawled on through the tall grass till they were about seventy-five yards from the place where he had undressed. There they lay down together.

In a little while he heard his aunt's voice calling, "Luke. Oh, Luke! Come here, Luke!"

"Quiet, Dan," Luke whispered. A few minutes passed, and then Uncle Henry called, "Luke, Luke!" and he began to come down the path. They could see him standing there, massive and imposing, his hands on his hips as he looked down the path, then he turned and went back to the house.

As he watched the sunlight shine on the back of his uncle's neck, the exultation Luke had felt at knowing the collie was safe beside him turned to bewildered despair, for he knew that even if he should be forgiven for saving the dog when he saw it drowning, the fact was that his uncle had been thwarted. His mind was made up to get rid of Dan, and in a few days' time, in another way, he would get rid of him, as he got rid of anything around the mill that he believed to be useless or a waste of money.

As he lay back and looked up at the hardly moving clouds, he began to grow frightened. He couldn't go back to the house, nor could he take the collie into the woods and hide him and feed him there unless he tied him up. If he didn't tie him up, Dan would wander back to the house.

"I guess there's just no place to go, Dan," he whispered sadly. "Even if we start off

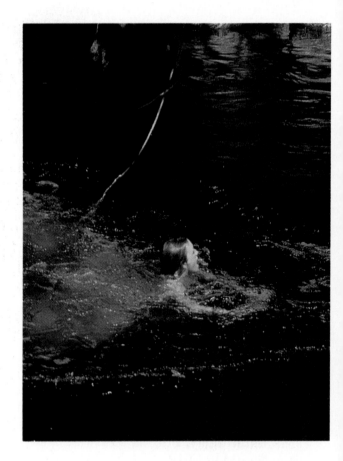

along the road, somebody is sure to see us."

But Dan was watching a butterfly that was circling crazily above them. Raising himself a little, Luke looked through the grass at the corner of the house, then he turned and looked the other way to the wide blue lake. With a sigh he lay down again, and for hours they lay there together, until there was no sound from the saws in the mill and the sun moved low in the western sky.

"Well, we can't stay here any longer, Dan," he said at last. "We'll just have to get as far away as we can. Keep down, old boy," and he began to crawl through the grass, going farther away from the house. When he could no longer be seen, he got up and began to trot across the field toward the gravel road leading to town.

On the road, the collie would turn from time to time as if wondering why Luke shuffled along, dragging his feet wearily, his head down. "I'm stumped, that's all Dan," Luke explained, "I can't seem to think of a place to take you."

When they were passing the Kemp place they saw the old man sitting on the veranda, and Luke stopped. All he could think of was that Mr. Kemp had liked them both and it had been a pleasure to help him get the cows in the evening. Dan had always been with them. Staring at the figure of the old man on the veranda, he said in a worried tone, "I wish I could be sure of him, Dan. I wish he was a dumb, stupid man who wouldn't know or care whether you were worth anything. . . . Well, come on." He opened the gate bravely, but he felt shy and unimportant.

"Hello, son. What's on your mind?" Mr. Kemp called from the veranda. He was a thin, wiry man in a tan-colored shirt. He had a gray, untidy mustache, his skin was wrinkled and leathery, but his eyes were always friendly and amused.

"Could I speak to you, Mr. Kemp?" Luke asked when they were close to the veranda.

"Sure. Go ahead."

"It's about Dan. He's a great dog, but I guess you know that as well as I do. I was wondering if you could keep him here for me."

"Why should I keep Dan here, son?"

"Well, it's like this," Luke said, fumbling the words awkwardly: "My uncle won't let me keep him any more . . . says he's too old." His mouth began to tremble, then he blurted out the story.

"I see, I see," Mr. Kemp said slowly, and he got up and came over to the steps and sat down and began to stroke the collie's head. "Of course, Dan's an old dog, son," he said quietly. "And sooner or later you've got to get

rid of an old dog. Your uncle knows that. Maybe it's true that Dan isn't worth his keep."

"He doesn't eat much, Mr. Kemp. Just one meal a day."

"I wouldn't want you to think your uncle was cruel and unfeeling, Luke," Mr. Kemp went on. "He's a fine man . . . maybe just a little bit too practical and straightforward."

"I guess that's right," Luke agreed, but he was really waiting and trusting the expression in the old man's eyes.

"Maybe you should make him a practical proposition."

"I—I don't know what you mean."

"Well, I sort of like the way you get the cows for me in the evenings," Mr. Kemp said, smiling to himself. "In fact, I don't think you need me to go along with you at all. Now, supposing I gave you seventy-five cents a week. Would you get the cows for me every night?"

"Sure I would, Mr. Kemp. I like doing it, anyway."

"All right, son. It's a deal. Now I'll tell you what to do. You go back to your uncle, and before he has a chance to open up on you, you say right out that you've come to him with a business proposition. Say it like a man, just like that. Offer to pay him the seventy-five cents a week for the dog's keep."

"But my uncle doesn't need seventy-five cents, Mr. Kemp," Luke said uneasily.

"Of course not," Mr. Kemp agreed. "It's the principle of the thing. Be confident. Remember that he's got nothing against the dog. Go to it, son. Let me know how you do," he added, with an amused smile. "If I know your uncle at all, I think it'll work."

"I'll try it, Mr. Kemp," Luke said. "Thanks very much." But he didn't have any confidence, for even though he knew that Mr. Kemp was a wise old man who would not deceive him, he couldn't believe that seventy-five cents a week would stop his uncle, who was an important man. "Come on, Dan," he called, and he went slowly and apprehensively back to the house.

When they were going up the path, his aunt cried from the open window, "Henry, Henry, in heaven's name, it's Luke with the dog!"

"Oh. Oh, I see," Uncle Henry said, and gradually the color came back to his face. "You fished him out, eh?" he asked, still looking at the dog uneasily. "Well, you shouldn't have done that. I told Sam Carter to get rid of the dog, you know."

"Just a minute, Uncle Henry," Luke said, trying not to falter. He gained confidence as Aunt Helen came out and stood beside her husband, for her eyes seemed to be gentle, and he went on bravely, "I want to make you a practical proposition, Uncle Henry."

"A what?" Uncle Henry asked, still feeling insecure, and wishing the boy and the dog weren't confronting him.

"A practical proposition," Luke blurted out quickly. "I know Dan isn't worth his keep to you. I guess he isn't worth anything to anybody but me. So I'll pay you seventy-five cents a week for his keep."

"What's this?" Uncle Henry asked, looking bewildered. "Where would you get seventy-five cents a week, Luke?"

"I'm going to get the cows every night for Mr. Kemp."

"Oh, for heaven's sake, Henry," Aunt Helen pleaded, looking distressed, "let him keep the dog!" and she fled into the house.

"None of that kind of talk!" Uncle Henry called after her. "We've got to be sensible about this!" But he was shaken himself, and overwhelmed with a distress that destroyed all his confidence. As he sat down slowly in the rocking chair and stroked the side of his big face, he wanted to say weakly, "All right, keep the dog," but he was ashamed of being so weak and sentimental. He stubbornly refused to yield to this emotion; he was trying desperately to turn his emotion into a bit of good, useful common sense, so he could justify his distress. So he rocked and pondered. At last he smiled. "You're a smart little shaver, Luke," he said slowly. "Imagine you working it out like this. I'm tempted to accept your proposition."

"Gee, thanks, Uncle Henry."

"I'm accepting it because I think you'll learn something out of this," he went on ponderously.

"Yes, Uncle Henry."

"You'll learn that useless luxuries cost the smartest of men hard-earned money."

"I don't mind."

"Well, it's a thing you'll have to learn sometime. I think you'll learn, too, because you certainly seem to have a practical streak in you. It's a streak I like to see in a boy. O.K., son," he said, and he smiled with relief and went into the house.

Turning to Dan, Luke whispered softly, "Well, what do you know about that?"

As he sat down on the step with the collie beside him and listened to Uncle Henry talking to his wife, he began to glow with exultation. Then gradually his exultation began to change to a vast wonder that Mr. Kemp should have had such a perfect understanding of Uncle Henry. He began to dream of someday being as wise as old Mr. Kemp and knowing exactly how to handle people. It was possible, too, that he had already learned some of the things about his uncle that his father had wanted him to learn.

Putting his head down on the dog's neck, he vowed to himself fervently that he would always have some money on hand, no matter what became of him, so that he would be able to protect all that was truly valuable from the practical people in the world.

THINKING ABOUT THE SELECTION

Recalling

1. Describe Luke's companion in his secret life at Uncle Henry's place.
2. When Uncle Henry decides to get rid of Dan, what promise does he make to Luke?
3. How does Luke ruin Uncle Henry's plan to destroy Dan?
4. What "business proposition" does Mr. Kemp suggest that Luke make to Uncle Henry?
5. What is Luke Baldwin's vow?

Interpreting

6. Early in the story, Uncle Henry advises Luke: "If you've got the facts, you know what's useful and what isn't useful. . ." What does this advice show about Uncle Henry?
7. Why does Uncle Henry agree to let Luke keep Dan?
8. Why does Luke make his vow?

Applying

9. Being practical is usually a good way to act. This story seems to suggest that sometimes people can be too practical. How can someone be too practical?

ANALYZING LITERATURE

Understanding Characterization

In "Luke Baldwin's Vow" Morley Callaghan uses both direct and indirect **characterization.** Sometimes he states directly what a character is like. Other times he shows the character's personality and traits through what the character says and does.

Tell whether the author is using direct or indirect characterization in each of the following passages from "Luke Baldwin's Vow."

1. "He looked like a powerful man, but his health was not good."
2. " 'None of that kind of talk!' Uncle Henry called

after her. 'We've got to be sensible about this!' "
3. "But Luke was frightened, for he knew what his uncle was like."

CRITICAL THINKING AND READING

Making Inferences About Character

An **inference** is a reasonable conclusion that you draw from information given. When an author uses indirect characterization, you must make inferences based on a character's words and actions.

The author is using indirect characterization in the following lines from "Luke Baldwin's Vow." What inference can you make about Uncle Henry from each passage?

1. " 'The plain fact is the old dog isn't worth his keep any more. It's time we got rid of him.' "
2. "As he sat down slowly in the rocking chair and stroked the side of his big face, he wanted to say weakly, 'All right, keep the dog,' but he was ashamed of being so weak and sentimental."
3. "At last he smiled. 'You're a smart little shaver, Luke,' he said slowly. 'Imagine you working it out like this. I'm tempted to accept your proposition.' "

THINKING AND WRITING

Writing About Characters

Often, people view the same object or person differently because of their own needs or concerns. In this story, Luke and Uncle Henry view Dan very differently. Make two columns on a sheet of paper. In one column write Luke's view of Dan and list his reasons for that view. In the other column, write Uncle Henry's view and his reasons. Then imagine that you want to explain these opposing views to Mr. Kemp. Write a description of the two views of the dog, and explain how the needs and concerns of Luke and his uncle determine how each one views Dan. When you revise be sure you have clearly presented the reasons for the different views.

Setting

EARLY SUMMER ON THE FARM
Karl Rodko
Three Lions

GUIDE FOR READING

All Summer in a Day

Ray Bradbury (1920–   ) was born in Waukegan, Illinois. As a boy, he was fascinated with magicians, circuses, and the stories of Edgar Allan Poe. These early interests influenced Bradbury's development as one of our best writers of fantasy and science fiction. His many honors and awards include membership in the National Institute of Arts and Letters. In "All Summer in a Day," you will enter Bradbury's world of gripping fantasy—a strange yet oddly believable world.

Setting

Setting is the time and place of a short story's action. In some stories, setting is little more than background, but in others it is of central importance. In "All Summer in a Day," for example, everything that happens depends on the setting: Venus, at a time when interplanetary travel is possible.

Look For

As you read the story, picture the strange world of Bradbury's Venus. Look for the details the author includes to make this place come alive for you. Imagine what it would be like to live and go to school there with the young people you are reading about. Would you like to live on Venus?

Writing

Imagine that you have traveled by rocket to Venus and, wearing a spacesuit, can explore the planet. What sights might you see? What might it feel like to be there? Freewrite about Venus as you imagine it.

Vocabulary

Knowing the following words will help you as you read "All Summer in a Day."

concussion (kən kush'ən) *n.*: Violent shaking (p. 107)

slackening (slak''n iŋ) *v.*: Becoming less active (p. 107)

surged (sʉrjd) *v.*: Moved in a violent swelling motion (p. 109)

immense (i mens') *adj.*: Vast (p. 109)

tumultuously (too mul'choo was lē) *adv.*: Noisy and violently (p. 110)

resilient (ri zil'yənt) *adj.*: Springing back into shape (p. 110)

savored (sā'vərd) *v.*: Enjoyed (p. 110)

All Summer in a Day

Ray Bradbury

"Ready?"

"Ready."

"Now?"

"Soon."

"Do the scientists really know? Will it happen today, will it?"

"Look, look; see for yourself!"

The children pressed to each other like so many roses, so many weeds, intermixed, peering out for a look at the hidden sun.

It rained.

It had been raining for seven years; thousands upon thousands of days compounded and filled from one end to the other with rain, with the drum and gush of water, with the sweet crystal fall of showers and the concussion of storms so heavy they were tidal waves come over the islands. A thousand forests had been crushed under the rain and grown up a thousand times to be crushed again. And this was the way life was forever on the planet Venus and this was the schoolroom of the children of the rocket men and women who had come to a raining world to set up civilization and live out their lives.

"It's stopping, it's stopping!"

"Yes, yes!"

Margot stood apart from them, from these children who could never remember a time when there wasn't rain and rain and rain. They were all nine years old, and if there had been a day, seven years ago, when the sun came out for an hour and showed its face to the stunned world, they could not recall. Sometimes, at night, she heard them stir, in remembrance, and she knew they were dreaming and remembering gold or a yellow crayon or a coin large enough to buy the world with. She knew they thought they remembered a warmness, like a blushing in the face, in the body, in the arms and legs and trembling hands. But then they always awoke to the tatting drum, the endless shaking down of clear bead necklaces upon the roof, the walk, the gardens, the forests, and their dreams were gone.

All day yesterday they had read in class about the sun. About how like a lemon it was, and how hot. And they had written small stories or essays or poems about it:

I think the sun is a flower,
That blooms for just one hour.

That was Margot's poem, read in a quiet voice in the still classroom while the rain was falling outside.

"Aw, you didn't write that!" protested one of the boys.

"I did," said Margot. "I *did*."

"William!" said the teacher.

But that was yesterday. Now the rain was slackening, and the children were crushed in the great thick windows.

"Where's teacher?"

"She'll be back."

"She'd better hurry, we'll miss it!"

They turned on themselves, like a feverish wheel, all fumbling spokes.

Margot stood alone. She was a very frail girl who looked as if she had been lost in the rain for years and the rain had washed out

SUNRISE IV
Arthur Dove
Hirshhorn Museum and Scupture Garden

the blue from her eyes and the red from her mouth and the yellow from her hair. She was an old photograph dusted from an album, whitened away, and if she spoke at all her voice would be a ghost. Now she stood, separate, staring at the rain and the loud wet world beyond the huge glass.

"What're *you* looking at?" said William.

Margot said nothing.

"Speak when you're spoken to." He gave her a shove. But she did not move; rather she let herself be moved only by him and nothing else.

They edged away from her, they would not look at her. She felt them go away. And this was because she would play no games with them in the echoing tunnels of the underground city. If they tagged her and ran, she stood blinking after them and did not follow. When the class sang songs about happiness and life and games

her lips barely moved. Only when they sang about the sun and the summer did her lips move as she watched the drenched windows.

And then, of course, the biggest crime of all was that she had come here only five years ago from Earth, and she remembered the sun and the way the sun was and the sky was when she was four in Ohio. And they, they had been on Venus all their lives, and they had been only two years old when last the sun came out and had long since forgotten the color and heat of it and the way it really was. But Margot remembered.

"It's like a penny," she said once, eyes closed.

"No, it's not!" the children cried.

"It's like a fire," she said, "in the stove."

"You're lying, you don't remember!" cried the children.

But she remembered and stood quietly

apart from all of them and watched the patterning windows. And once, a month ago, she had refused to shower in the school shower rooms, had clutched her hands to her ears and over her head, screaming the water mustn't touch her head. So after that, dimly, dimly, she sensed it, she was different and they knew her difference and kept away.

There was talk that her father and mother were taking her back to Earth next year; it seemed vital to her that they do so, though it would mean the loss of thousands of dollars to her family. And so, the children hated her for all these reasons of big and little consequence. They hated her pale snow face, her waiting silence, her thinness, and her possible future.

"Get away!" The boy gave her another push. "What're you waiting for?"

Then, for the first time, she turned and looked at him. And what she was waiting for was in her eyes.

"Well, don't wait around here!" cried the boy savagely. "You won't see nothing!"

Her lips moved.

"Nothing!" he cried. "It was all a joke, wasn't it?" He turned to the other children. "Nothing's happening today. *Is* it?"

They all blinked at him and then, understanding, laughed and shook their heads. "Nothing, nothing!"

"Oh, but," Margot whispered, her eyes helpless. "But this is the day, the scientists predict, they say, they *know*, the sun . . . "

"All a joke!" said the boy, and seized her roughly. "Hey, everyone, let's put her in a closet before teacher comes!"

"No," said Margot, falling back.

They surged about her, caught her up and bore her, protesting, and then pleading, and then crying, back into a tunnel, a room, a closet, where they slammed and locked the door. They stood looking at the door and saw it tremble from her beating and throwing herself against it. They heard her muffled cries. Then, smiling, they turned and went out and back down the tunnel, just as the teacher arrived.

"Ready, children?" She glanced at her watch.

"Yes!" said everyone.

"Are we all here?"

"Yes!"

The rain slackened still more.

They crowded to the huge door.

The rain stopped.

It was as if, in the midst of a film concerning an avalanche, a tornado, a hurricane, a volcanic eruption, something had, first, gone wrong with the sound apparatus, thus muffling and finally cutting off all noise, all of the blasts and repercussions and thunders, and then, second, ripped the film from the projector and inserted in its place a peaceful tropical slide which did not move or tremor. The world ground to a standstill. The silence was so immense and unbelievable that you felt your ears had been stuffed or you had lost your hearing altogether. The children put their hands to their ears. They stood apart. The door slid back and the smell of the silent, waiting world came in to them.

The sun came out.

It was the color of flaming bronze and it was very large. And the sky around it was a blazing blue tile color. And the jungle burned with sunlight as the children, released from their spell, rushed out, yelling, into the springtime.

"Now, don't go too far," called the teacher after them. "You've only two hours, you know. You wouldn't want to get caught out!"

But they were running and turning their faces up to the sky and feeling the sun on their cheeks like a warm iron; they were taking off their jackets and letting the sun burn their arms.

"Oh, it's better than the sun lamps, isn't it?"

"Much, much better!"

They stopped running and stood in the great jungle that covered Venus, that grew and never stopped growing, tumultuously, even as you watched it. It was a nest of octopi, clustering up great arms of fleshlike weed, wavering, flowering in this brief spring. It was the color of rubber and ash, this jungle, from the many years without sun. It was the color of stones and white cheeses and ink, and it was the color of the moon.

The children lay out, laughing, on the jungle mattress, and heard it sigh and squeak under them, resilient and alive. They ran among the trees, they slipped and fell, they pushed each other, they played hide-and-seek and tag, but most of all they squinted at the sun until tears ran down their faces, they put their hands up to that yellowness and that amazing blueness and they breathed of the fresh, fresh air and listened and listened to the silence which suspended them in a blessed sea of no sound and no motion. They looked at everything and savored everything. Then, wildly, like animals escaped from their caves, they ran and ran in shouting circles. They ran for an hour and did not stop running.

And then—

In the midst of their running one of the girls wailed.

Everyone stopped.

The girl, standing in the open, held out her hand.

"Oh, look, look," she said, trembling.

They came slowly to look at her opened palm.

In the center of it, cupped and huge, was a single raindrop.

She began to cry, looking at it.

They glanced quietly at the sky.

"Oh, Oh."

A few cold drops fell on their noses and their cheeks and their mouths. The sun faded behind a stir of mist. A wind blew cool around them. They turned and started to walk back toward the underground house, their hands at their sides, their smiles vanishing away.

A boom of thunder startled them and like leaves before a new hurricane, they tumbled upon each other and ran. Lightning struck ten miles away, five miles away, a mile, a half mile. The sky darkened into midnight in a flash.

They stood in the doorway of the underground for a moment until it was raining hard. Then they closed the door and heard the gigantic sound of the rain falling in tons and avalanches, everywhere and forever.

"Will it be seven more years?"

"Yes. Seven."

Then one of them gave a little cry.

"Margot!"

"What?"

"She's still in the closet where we locked her."

"Margot."

They stood as if someone had driven them, like so many stakes, into the floor. They looked at each other and then looked away. They glanced out at the world that was raining now and raining and raining steadily. They could not meet each other's glances. Their faces were solemn and pale. They looked at their hands and feet, their faces down.

"Margot."

One of the girls said, "Well . . .?"

No one moved.

"Go on," whispered the girl.

They walked slowly down the hall in the sound of cold rain. They turned through the doorway to the room in the sound of the storm and thunder, lightning on their faces, blue and terrible. They walked over to the closet door slowly and stood by it.

Behind the closet door was only silence.

They unlocked the door, even more slowly, and let Margot out.

THINKING ABOUT THE SELECTION

Recalling

1. At the start of the story, why are all the children excited?
2. In what way is Margot's experience of the sun different from the experience of all the other children on Venus?
3. How does this difference affect the way Margot gets along with her classmates?
4. What do the children do to Margot just before the rain stops?
5. What do the children do during the two hours that they are outdoors?.
6. What happens to Margot at the very end?

Interpreting

7. What point is made about Margot when the story says that the rain had washed the blue from her eyes and the red from her mouth and the yellow from her hair?
8. How do the children feel when they remember what they have done to Margot?
9. Having read the story, what do you think the title, "All Summer in a Day," means?

Applying

10. What does this story suggest about the problems individuals face if their backgrounds or experiences make them different from other people?

ANALYZING LITERATURE

Understanding Setting

The **setting** of a story is the time and place of the action. In "All Summer in a Day," Bradbury gives you many details that help you see what Venus is like. For example, in describing the constant rain he says that the children "always awoke to the tatting drum, the endless shaking down of clear bead necklaces upon the roof, the walk, the gardens, the forests . . . ."

1. Point out three other passages that give you a vivid impression of Venus.
2. What is the most significant feature of the setting?
3. Find at least two details that suggest that the time of the action is the future.

CRITICAL THINKING AND READING

Understanding the Effect of Setting

"All Summer in a Day" is a story in which the setting greatly affects the plot. Since the events occur only in a place where it rains almost constantly, this setting affects the way the characters behave.

1. What details of the setting make the story possible?
2. How is Margot affected by Venus?
3. How are the other children affected by it?

THINKING AND WRITING

Writing About Setting

Imagine that you have just arrived on Ray Bradbury's imagined Venus. After spending a day or so looking around, you decide to write a letter to a friend on Earth telling what Venus is like. First list on paper those sights and other details you will focus on. Then write a letter that will give your friend a clear picture of where you are. When you revise your writing, ask "Will my friend see what I am trying to convey? Is every sentence clear and specific?"

GUIDE FOR READING

The Trout

Sean O'Faolain (1900–   ) was born in Cork, Ireland. When he was fifteen, he saw a play about the lives of ordinary Irish people. This play inspired him to write. He has written stories about his country's struggle for independence from England and about life in the Irish countryside, with its pastures, bogs, mountains, and moody charm. In "The Trout" the spirit of rural Ireland is memorably captured.

Atmosphere

Atmosphere, or mood, is the feeling a place awakens in the reader. Such words as *gloomy, haunted, joyful, peaceful, restful, scary,* and *romantic* will give you some idea of the kinds of atmosphere frequently found in stories. The opening paragraphs of "The Trout," for example, present a place whose atmosphere might be described as pleasantly spooky.

Look For

As you read the story, look for the details that make the Laurel walk seem a pleasantly spooky place. Why does the author call it "The Dark Walk"?

Writing

What place have you visited that stands out clearly in your memory because of its beauty, peacefulness, scariness, or other quality of atmosphere? Freewrite about it. Try to describe it in a way that communicates its atmosphere.

Vocabulary

Knowing the following words will help you as you read "The Trout."

incredulous (in krej'oo ləs) *adj.*: unwilling or unable to believe (p. 113)

haughtily (hôt'ə lē) *adv.*: Showing pride in oneself and contempt for others (p. 113)

shrouded (shrou' d'd) *v.*: Hidden from view (p. 113)

resolutely (rez'ə lo͞ot'lē) *adv.*: In a determined way (p. 115)

superciliously (so͞o'pər sil'ē əs lē) *adv.*: Pridefully, scornfully (p. 116)

The Trout

Sean O'Faolain

One of the first places Julia always ran to when they arrived in G— was The Dark Walk. It is a laurel walk, very old; almost gone wild, a lofty midnight tunnel of smooth, sinewy branches. Underfoot the tough brown leaves are never dry enough to crackle: there is always a suggestion of damp and cool trickle.

She raced right into it. For the first few yards she always had the memory of the sun behind her, then she felt the dusk closing swiftly down on her so that she screamed with pleasure and raced on to reach the light at the far end; and it was always just a little too long in coming so that she emerged gasping, clasping her hands, laughing, drinking in the sun. When she was filled with the heat and glare she would turn and consider the ordeal again.

This year she had the extra joy of showing it to her small brother, and of terrifying him as well as herself. And for him the fear lasted longer because his legs were so short and she had gone out at the far end while he was still screaming and racing.

When they had done this many times they came back to the house to tell everybody that they had done it. He boasted. She mocked. They squabbled.

"Cry baby!"

"You were afraid yourself, so there!"

"I won't take you any more."

"You're a big pig."

"I hate you."

Tears were threatening so somebody said, "Did you see the well?" She opened her eyes at that and held up her long lovely neck suspiciously and decided to be incredulous. She was twelve and at that age little girls are beginning to suspect most stories: they have already found out too many, from Santa Claus to the Stork. How could there be a well! In The Dark Walk? That she had visited year after year? Haughtily she said, "Nonsense."

But she went back, pretending to be going somewhere else, and she found a hole scooped in the rock at the side of the walk, choked with damp leaves, so shrouded by ferns that she only uncovered it after much searching. At the back of this little cavern there was about a quart of water. In the water she suddenly perceived a panting trout. She rushed for Stephen and dragged him to see, and they were both so excited that they were no longer afraid of the darkness as they hunched down and peered in at the fish panting in his tiny prison, his silver stomach going up and down like an engine.

Nobody knew how the trout got there.

FOREST INTERIOR, 1882
Thomas Worthington Whittredge
© 1987 The Art Institute of Chicago

Even old Martin in the kitchen-garden laughed and refused to believe that it was there, or pretended not to believe, until she forced him to come down and see. Kneeling and pushing back his tattered old cap he peered in.

"Be cripes, you're right. How did that fella get there?"

She stared at him suspiciously.

"You knew?" she accused; but he said, "The divil a know"; and reached down to lift it out. Convinced she hauled him back. If she had found it then it was her trout.

Her mother suggested that a bird had carried the spawn. Her father thought that in the winter a small streamlet might have carried it down there as a baby, and it had been safe until the summer came and the water began to dry up. She said, "I see," and went back to look again and consider the matter in private. Her brother remained behind, wanting to hear the whole story of the trout, not really interested in the actual trout but much interested in the story which his mummy began to make up for him on the lines, of, "So one day Daddy Trout and Mammy Trout . . ." When he retailed[1] it to her she said, "Pooh."

It troubled her that the trout was always in the same position; he had no room to turn; all the time the silver belly went up and down; otherwise he was motionless. She wondered what he ate and in between visits to Joey Pony, and the boat and a bath to get cool, she thought of his hunger. She brought him down bits of dough; once she brought him a worm. He ignored the food. He just went on panting. Hunched over him she thought how, all the winter, while she was at school he had been in there. All the winter, in The Dark Walk, all day, all night,

floating around alone. She drew the leaf of her hat down around her ears and chin and stared. She was still thinking of it as she lay in bed.

It was late June, the longest days of the year. The sun had sat still for a week, burning up the world. Although it was after ten o'clock it was still bright and still hot. She lay on her back under a single sheet, with her long legs spread, trying to keep cool. She could see the D of the moon through the fir tree—they slept on the ground floor. Before they went to bed her mummy had told Stephen the story of the trout again, and she, in her bed, had resolutely presented her back to them and read her book. But she had kept one ear cocked.

"And so, in the end, this naughty fish who would not stay at home got bigger and bigger and bigger, and the water got smaller and smaller. . . "

Passionately she had whirled and cried, "Mummy, don't make it a horrible old moral story!" Her mummy had brought in a Fairy Godmother, then, who sent lots of rain, and filled the well, and a stream poured out and the trout floated away down to the river below. Staring at the moon she knew that there are no such things as Fairy Godmothers and that the trout, down in The Dark Walk, was panting like an engine. She heard somebody unwind a fishing reel. Would the *beasts* fish him out!

She sat up. Stephen was a hot lump of sleep, lazy thing. The Dark Walk would be full of little scraps of moon. She leaped up and looked out the window, and somehow it was not so lightsome now that she saw the dim mountains far away and the black firs against the breathing land and heard a dog say, bark-bark. Quietly she lifted the ewer[2] of

---

1. **retailed** (rē tāld') v.: In this case, it means "told."

2. **ewer** (yōō ər): A large water pitcher with a wide mouth.

water, and climbed out the window and scuttled along the cool but cruel gravel down to the maw[3] of the tunnel. Her pajamas were very short so that when she splashed water it wet her ankles. She peered into the tunnel. Something alive rustled inside there. She raced in, and up and down she raced, and flurried, and cried aloud, "Oh, Gosh, I can't find it," and then at last she did. Kneeling down in the damp she put her hand into the slimy hole. When the body lashed they were both mad with fright. But she gripped him and shoved him into the ewer and raced, with her teeth ground, out to the other end of the tunnel and down the steep paths to the river's edge.

All the time she could feel him lashing his tail against the side of the ewer. She was

---

3. maw (mô) *n.*: In this case, it means the opening or mouth of the tunnel. This word usually refers to the throat or jaws of an animal.

afraid he would jump right out. The gravel cut into her soles until she came to the cool ooze of the river's bank where the moon mice on the water crept into her feet. She poured out watching until he plopped. For a second he was visible in the water. She hoped he was not dizzy. Then all she saw was the glimmer of the moon in the silent-flowing river, the dark firs, the dim mountains, and the radiant pointed face laughing down at her out of the empty sky.

She scuttled up the hill, in the window, plonked down the ewer and flew through the air like a bird into bed. The dog said bark-bark. She heard the fishing reel whirring. She hugged herself and giggled. Like a river of joy her holiday spread before her.

In the morning Stephen rushed to her, shouting that "he" was gone, and asking "where" and "how." Lifting her nose in the air she said superciliously, "Fairy God-mother, I suppose?" and strolled away patting the palms of her hands.

THINKING ABOUT THE SELECTION

Recalling

1. Where does Julia find the trout?
2. What is Julia's mother's suggestion for how the trout got into the hole?
3. How does her father think the trout got there?
4. What troubles Julia about the position the trout is in?
5. Summarize the story about the trout that the mother makes up for Stephen.
6. What does Julia do to help the trout?

Interpreting

7. What do you learn about Julia's character from her going into a dark, scary place at night to help the trout?
8. What emotion do you think Julia is feeling in the last paragraph of the story?
9. What effect do you think the whole incident involving the trout has had on Julia?

Applying

10. Imagine Julia as an adult looking back on this incident. What importance to her life might she see in it?

ANALYZING LITERATURE

Understanding Atmosphere

Atmosphere may be thought of as the spirit, or personality, of a place. It is what makes The Dark Walk, for example, more than just a path shaded by trees.

1. Reread the paragraph that begins "It was late June, the longest days of the year" (page 115). How would you describe the atmosphere of Julia's room?
2. Describe the atmosphere of the river where Julia releases the trout.
3. Which three of the following adjectives could be used to describe the atmosphere created by the whole story: *joyful, mysterious, secretive, tense, comical, haunting, sad, peaceful, zany, tragic?*

CRITICAL THINKING AND READING

Identifying Details of Atmosphere

A skillful writer creates atmosphere by using specific details that allow you to "see" a place and feel its atmosphere. In the opening paragraph, for example, O'Faolain says of The Dark Walk, "It is a laurel walk, very old; almost gone wild, a lofty midnight tunnel of smooth, sinewy branches."

What specific details create atmosphere in the description of the river near the end of the story?

UNDERSTANDING LANGUAGE

Using the Adverb Suffix -ly

A **suffix** is one or more syllables added to the end of a word to form a new word. When the suffix -ly is added to an adjective, the adjective is changed into an adverb; for example, the adjective *slow* becomes the adverb *slowly.*

The following six adjectives are from "The Trout." Add the suffix -ly to make each one an adverb. Use the word in a sentence.

1. incredulous   3. mad
2. dim   4. radiant

THINKING AND WRITING

Extending a Story

Extend the story. Describe the river on the morning after Julia has freed the trout. First decide how the river looks. Then decide what atmosphere you wish to convey. Be sure to include specific details to give the reader both the look and the feel of the river as you imagine it. When you revise, concentrate on making your expression of atmosphere as vivid as you can.

GUIDE FOR READING

Caleb's Brother

James Baldwin (1924–1987) was born and raised in New York City. Though he had lived abroad, in Paris, for many years, much of his work was based on his youth in New York. *Go Tell It on the Mountain,* a novel that brought him early fame and recognition as a major black writer, tells of the adolescent experiences of a boy whose life is closely linked to the church in his Harlem neighborhood. In "Caleb's Brother," Baldwin again draws on his youthful experiences in the neighborhood where he grew up.

Atmosphere and Meaning

Atmosphere is the feeling a place awakens in the reader. In many short stories, the atmosphere may be an important part of the story's meaning. It gives you the feeling of what it is like to be in a particular place and helps you to understand the characters and situations you read about.

Look For

As you read "Caleb's Brother," look for the details that make the setting of the story cheerless and even threatening. Try to imagine how Leo's life and feelings are affected by his living in a world whose atmosphere is at times very dreary, and perhaps dangerous.

Writing

"Caleb's Brother" deals in part with a widespread situation, namely, that older boys and girls sometimes hurt the feelings of their younger brothers and sisters by ignoring them and their needs. List reasons why you think they behave this way.

Vocabulary

Knowing the following words will help you as you read "Caleb's Brother."

bravado (brə vä′dō) *n.*: Pretended courage (p. 119)
demeanor (di mēn′ ər) *n.*: Outward behavior, manner (p. 120)
indifferently (in dif′ər ənt lē) *adv.*: As if uninterested (p. 120)
distracted (dis trakt′ id) *adj.*: With the mind drawn away in another direction (p. 120)
decipher (di sī′fər) *v.*: To make out the meaning of (p. 120)

irrevocably (i rev′ ə kə blē) *adv.*: Unchangeably (p. 121)
susceptible (sə sep′tə b'l) *adj.*: Responsive (p. 121)
lethal (lē′thəl) *adj.*: Deadly (p. 121)
tempest (tem′pist) *n.*: A violent storm (p. 123)

Caleb's Brother

from *Tell Me How Long the Train's Been Gone*
James Baldwin

The hall was dark, smelling of cooking and of boiling diapers. We dropped down the stairs, Caleb going two at a time, pausing at each landing, briefly, to glance back up at me. I dropped down behind him as fast as I could. Sometimes Caleb was in a bad mood and then everything I did was wrong. But when Caleb was in a good mood, it didn't matter that everything I did was wrong. When I reached the street level, Caleb was already on the stoop, joking with some of his friends who were standing in the doorway—who seemed always to be in the doorway, no matter what hour one passed through. I didn't like Caleb's friends because I was afraid of them. I knew the only reason they didn't try to make life miserable for me the way they did for a lot of the other kids was because they were afraid of Caleb. I came through the door, passing between my brother and his friends, down to the sidewalk, feeling, as they looked briefly at me and then continued joking with Caleb, what they felt: that here was Caleb's round-eyed, frail and useless sissy of a little brother. They pitied Caleb for having to take me out. On the other hand, they also wanted to go to the show, but didn't have the money. Therefore, in silence, I could crow over them[1] even as they despised me. But this was always a terribly risky, touch-and-go business, for Caleb might always, at any moment, and with no warning, change his mind and drive me away, and, effectively, take their side against me. I always stood, those Saturday afternoons, in fear and trembling, holding on to the small shield of my bravado, while waiting for Caleb to come down the steps of the stoop, to come down the steps, away from his friends, to me. I prepared myself, always,

---

1. **crow over them:** To take great pleasure in their bad luck.

JIM, 1930
William H. Johnson
National Museum of American Art

for the moment when he would turn to me, saying, "Okay, kid. You run along. I'll see you later."

This meant that I would have to go to the movies by myself and hang around in front of the box office, waiting for some grown-up to take me in. I could not go back upstairs, for this would be informing my mother and father that Caleb had gone off somewhere—after promising to take me to the movies. Neither could I simply hang around the block, playing with the kids on the block. For one thing, my demeanor, as I came out of the house, those Saturdays, very clearly indicated that I had better things to do than play with *them*; for another, they were not terribly anxious to play with *me*; and, finally, my remaining on the block would have had exactly the same effect as my going upstairs. Someone would surely inform my father and mother, or they might simply look out of the window, or one of them would come downstairs to buy something they had forgotten while shopping, or my father would pass down the block on his way somewhere. In short, to remain on the block after Caleb's dismissal was to put myself at the mercy of the block and to put Caleb at the mercy of our parents.

So I prepared myself, those Saturdays, to respond with a cool, "Okay. See you later," and prepared myself then to turn indifferently away, and walk. This was surely the most terrible moment. The moment I turned away I was committed, I was trapped, and I then had miles to walk, so it seemed to me, before I would be out of sight, before the block ended and I could turn onto the avenue. I wanted to run out of that block, but I never did. I never looked back. I forced myself to walk very slowly, looking neither right nor left, trying to look neither up nor down—striving to seem at once distracted and offhand; concentrating on the cracks in the sidewalk, and stumbling over them, trying to

whistle, feeling every muscle in my body, from my pigeon toes[2] to my burning neck; feeling that all the block was watching me, and feeling—which was odd—that I deserved it. And then I reached the avenue, and turned, still not looking back, and was released from those eyes at least, but now faced other eyes, eyes coming toward me. These eyes were the eyes of children stronger than me, who would steal my movie money; these eyes were the eyes of cops, whom I feared; these eyes were the eyes of old folks who also thought I was a sissy and who might wonder what I was doing on this avenue by myself. And these eyes were the eyes of men and women standing on the corners, who certainly had no eyes for me, but who occupied the center of my bewildered attention because they seemed, at once, so abject and so free.

And then I got to the show. Sometimes, someone would take me in right away and sometimes I would have to wait. I looked at the posters which seemed magical indeed to me in those days. I was very struck, not altogether agreeably, by the colors. The faces of the movie stars were in red, in green, in blue, in purple, not at all like the colors of real faces and yet they looked more real than real. Or, rather, they looked like faces far from me, faces which I would never be able to decipher, faces which could be seen but never changed or touched, faces which existed only behind these doors. I don't know what I thought. Some great assault, certainly, was being made on my imagination, on my sense of reality. Caleb could draw, he was teaching me to draw, and I wondered if he could teach me to draw faces like these. I looked at the stills[3] from the show, seeing

---

2. pigeon toes: Toes or feet that turn inward.

3. stills (stilz) *n.*: Photographs made from single frames of a motion picture and used for advertising it.

people in attitudes of danger, in attitudes of love, in atittudes of sorrow and loss. They were not like any people I had ever seen and this made them, irrevocably, better. With one part of my mind, of course, I knew that here was James Cagney—holding his gun like a prize; and here was Clark Gable, all dimples, teeth, and eyes; here was Joan Crawford, gleaming with astonishment, and here was proud, quivering Katharine Hepburn, who could never be astonished, and here was poor, downtrodden Sylvia Sidney, weeping in the clutches of yet another gangster. But only the faces and the attitudes were real, more real than the lives we led, more real than our days and nights, and the names were merely brand-names, like Campbell's Baked Beans or Kellogg's Corn Flakes. We went to see James Cagney because we had grown accustomed to that taste, we knew that we would like it.

But, then, I would have to turn my attention from the faces and the stills and watch the faces coming to the box office. And this was not easy, since I didn't, after all, want everyone in the neighborhood to know that I was loitering outside the moviehouse waiting for someone to take me in, exactly like an orphan. Eventually, I would see a face which looked susceptible and which I did not know. I would rush up beside him or her—but it was usually a man, for they were less likely to be disapproving—and whisper, "Take me in," and give him my dime. Sometimes the man simply took the dime and disappeared into the movies, sometimes he gave my dime back to me and took me in, anyway. Sometimes I ended up wandering around the streets—but I couldn't wander into a strange neighborhood because I would be beaten up if I did—until I figured the show was out. It was dangerous to get home too early and, of course, it was practically lethal to arrive too late. If all went well, I could cover for Caleb, saying that I had left him

with some boys on the stoop. Then, if *he* came in too late and got a dressing down for it, it could not be considered my fault.

One time, it was raining and it was still too early for me to go home. I felt very, very low that day. It was one of the times that my tongue and my body refused to obey me—this happened often; when I was prey to my fantasies, or overwhelmed by my real condition; and I had not been able to work up the courage to ask anyone to take me into the show. I stood there, watching people go in, watching people come out. Every once in a while, when the doors opened, I caught a glimpse of the screen—huge, black and silver, moving all the time. The ticket-taker was watching me, or so I thought, with a hostile suspicion, as though he were thinking, You just *try* to get somebody to take you in. I dare you! Actually, it's very unlikely he was thinking at all, and certainly not of me. But I walked away from the show because I could no longer bear his eyes, or anybody's eyes.

I walked the long block east from the moviehouse. The street was empty, black, and glittering. The globes of the streetlamps, with the water slanting both behind them and before, told me how hard the rain was falling. The water soaked through my coat at the shoulders and water dripped down my neck from my cap. I began to be afraid. I could not stay out here in the rain because then my father and mother would know I had been wandering the streets. I would get a beating, and, though Caleb was too old to get a beating, he and my father would have a terrible fight and Caleb would blame it all on me and would not speak to me for days. I began to hate Caleb. I wondered where he was. If I had known where to find him, I would have gone to where he was and forced him, by screaming and crying even, to take me home or to take me wherever he was go-

HARLEM NOCTURNE
Alice Neel
Robert Miller Gallery

ing. And I wouldn't have cared if he hit me, or even if he called me a sissy. Then it occurred to me that he might be in the same trouble as myself, since if I couldn't go home without *him*, he, even more surely, couldn't go home without *me*. Perhaps he was also wandering around in the rain. If he was, then, I thought, it served him right: it would serve him right if he caught pneumonia and died; and I dwelt pleasantly on this possibility for the length of the block. But at the end of the block I realized that he was probably *not* wandering around in the rain—I was; and I, too, might catch pneumonia and die. I started in the direction of our house only because I did not know what else to do. Perhaps Caleb would be waiting for me on the stoop.

The avenue, too, was very long and silent. Somehow, it seemed old, like a picture in a book. It stretched straight before me, endless, and the streetlights did not so much illuminate it as prove how dark it was. The familiar buildings were now merely dark, silent shapes, great masses of wet rock; men stood against the walls or on the stoops, made faceless by the light in the hallway behind them. The rain was falling harder. Cars sloshed by, sending up sheets of water and bobbing like boats; from the bars I heard music faintly, and many voices. Straight ahead of me a woman walked, very fast, head down, carrying a shopping bag. I reached my corner and crossed the wide avenue. There was no one on my stoop.

Now, I was not even certain what time it was; and everything was so abnormally, wretchedly still that there was no way of guessing. But I knew it wasn't time yet for the show to be over. I walked into my hallway and wrung out my cap. I was sorry that I had not made someone take me into the show because now I did not know what to do. I *could* go upstairs and say that we had not liked the movie and had left early and that Caleb was with some boys on the stoop. But this would sound strange—I had never been known to dislike a movie; and if our father was home he might come downstairs to look for Caleb, who would not know what story I had told and who would, therefore, in any case, be greatly handicapped when he arrived. As far as Caleb knew, I was safely in the movies. That was our bargain, from which not even the rain released me. My nerve had failed me, but Caleb had no way of knowing that. I could not stay in my hallway because my father might not be at home and might come in. I could not go into the hallway of another building because if any of the kids who lived in the building found me they would have the right to beat me up. I could not go back out into the rain. I stood next to the big, cold radiator and I began to cry. But crying wasn't going to do me any good, either, especially as there was no one to hear me.

So I stepped out on my stoop again and looked carefully up and down the block. There was not a soul to be seen. The rain fell as hard as ever, with a whispering sound—like monstrous old gossips whispering together. The sky could not be seen. It was black. I stood there for a long time, wondering what to do. Then I thought of a condemned house, around the corner from us. We played there sometimes, though we were not supposed to, and it was very dangerous. The front door had been boarded up but the boards had been pried loose; and the basement windows had been broken and boys congregated in the basement and wandered through the rotting house. What possessed me to go there now I don't know, except that I could not think of another dry place in the whole world. I thought that I would just sit there, out of the rain, until I figured it was safe to come home. And I started running east, down our block. I turned two corners and I came to the house, with its black window sockets and garbage piled high around it and the rain moaning and whistling, clanging against the metal and drumming on the glass. The house stood by itself, for the house next to it had already been torn down. The house was completely dark. I had forgotten how afraid I was of the dark, but the rain was drenching me. I ran down the cellar steps and clambered into the house. I squatted there in a still, dry dread, in misery, not daring to look into the house but staring outward at the bright black area railing and the tempest beyond. I was holding my breath. I heard an endless scurrying in the darkness, a perpetual busy-ness, and I thought of rats, of their teeth and ferocity and fearful size and I began to cry again. If someone had come up then to murder me, I don't believe I could have moved or made any other sound.

I don't know how long I squatted there this way, or what was in my mind—I think there was nothing in my mind, I was as blank as a toothache. I listened to the rain and the rats. Then I was aware of another sound, I had been hearing it for awhile without realizing it. The sound came from the door which led to the backyard. I wanted to stand, but I crouched lower; wanted to run, but could not move. Sometimes the sound seemed to come closer and I knew that this meant my death; sometimes diminished or ceased altogether and then I knew that my assailant was looking for me. Oh, how I hated Caleb for bringing my life to an end so soon! How I wished I knew where to find him! I looked toward the backyard door and I seemed to see, silhouetted against the driving rain, a figure, half bent, moaning, leaning against the wall. I could not catch my breath to scream. Then I heard a laugh, a low, happy, wicked laugh, and the figure turned in my direction and seemed to start toward me. Then I screamed and stood straight up, bumping my head on the window frame and losing my cap, and scrambled up the cellar steps, into the rain. I ran head down, like a bull, away from that house and out of that block and it was my great good luck that no person and no vehicle were in my path. I ran up the steps of my stoop and bumped into Caleb.

"Where have you been? Hey! what's the matter with you?"

For I had jumped up on him, almost knocking him down, trembling and sobbing.

"You're *soaked*. Leo, what's the matter with you? Where's your cap?"

But I could not say anything. I held him around the neck with all my might, and I could not stop shaking.

"Come on, Leo," Caleb said, in a different tone, "tell me what's the matter. Don't carry on like this." He pried my arms loose and held me away from him so that he could look into my face. "Oh, little Leo. Little Leo. What's the matter, baby?" He looked as though he were about to cry himself and this

made me cry harder than ever. He took out his handkerchief and wiped my face and made me blow my nose. My sobs began to lessen, but I could not stop trembling. He thought that I was trembling from cold and he rubbed his hands roughly up and down my back and rubbed my hands between his. "What's the matter?"

I did not know how to tell him.

"Somebody try to beat you up?"

I shook my head. "No."

"What movie did you see?"

"I didn't go. I couldn't find nobody to take me in."

"And you just been wandering around in the rain all night?"

I shook my head. "Yes."

He looked at me and sat down on the hallway steps. "Oh, Leo." Then, "You mad at me?"

I said, "No, I was scared."

He nodded. "I reckon you were, man," he said. "I reckon you were." He wiped my face again. "You ready to go upstairs? It's getting late."

"Okay."

"How'd you lose your cap?"

"I went in a hallway to wring it out—and—I put it on the radiator and I heard some people coming—and—I ran away and I forgot it."

"We'll say you forgot it in the movies."

"Okay."

We started up the stairs.

"Leo," he said, "I'm sorry about tonight. I'm really sorry. I won't let it happen again. You believe me?"

"Sure, I believe you."

"Give us a smile, then."

I smiled up at him. He squatted down.

"Give us a kiss."

I kissed him.

"Okay. Climb up. I'll give you a ride—hold on, now."

He carried me piggyback up the stairs.

THINKING ABOUT THE SELECTION

Recalling

1. Why does Leo feel that he must prepare himself for Caleb's saying, "Okay, kid. You run along. I'll see you later"?
2. When Caleb goes off with his friends, why can't Leo go upstairs or stay on his block?
3. What does Leo fear when he reaches the avenue?
4. On the rainy day, why does Leo walk away from the movie theater and go to the condemned house?
5. Why does he run out of the house?
6. How does Caleb behave toward Leo at the end of the story?

Interpreting

7. For what reason does Caleb sometimes send Leo off on his own?
8. How does Leo show his concern for Caleb even when Caleb ignores him?
9. In what way is the title "Caleb's Brother" more appropriate than some other possible title, such as "Leo and Caleb"?

Applying

10. Explain why you think that Caleb is, or is not, a typical older brother.

ANALYZING LITERATURE

Understanding Atmosphere and Meaning

The **atmosphere** of a place can have an effect on the characters in a story. The very first sentence of "Caleb's Brother"—"The hall was dark, smelling of cooking and of boiling diapers"—begins to establish the atmosphere that young Leo must live with every day.

1. What are three of the places described in the story whose atmosphere affects Leo?
2. Could "Caleb's Brother" be the same story if it were set in a time and place with a different atmosphere, for example, a suburban town on a clear, sunny day? Why or why not?

CRITICAL THINKING AND READING

Identifying Details of Atmosphere

Atmosphere is created by specific details that enable you to see, hear, and feel a place as if you were there. Choose three details that help create the atmosphere of this story. Explain why you chose each detail. To what sense does each detail appeal?

UNDERSTANDING LANGUAGE

Choosing Meaning to Fit Context

Many words have more than one meaning. When you read, you must choose the meaning that fits the context. For example, the word *committed* has a number of meanings, but in the context of the sentence "The moment I turned away I was committed . . ." it means "bound" or "engaged."

Choose the meaning of the *italicized* word that best fits the context of each sentence.

1. Bill would not *stoop* to rudeness.
   a. a platform with steps
   b. bend forward
   c. lower or degrade oneself
   d. pounce on
2. From the *landing* I could see the doorway.
   a. the act of coming to shore
   b. the place where a ship is loaded
   c. the act of coming to the ground
   d. a platform at the end of a flight of stairs

THINKING AND WRITING

Writing About Atmosphere

Imagine you are writing for your school magazine. Compare and contrast the atmosphere of the condemned house in "Caleb's Brother" with the atmosphere of a place in one of the other short stories you have recently read. If you cannot think of a place you have read about, select a place you know first hand. First think of an adjective or two to describe the atmosphere created by each of the two places. Then list those details you would use to develop and support each description. When you revise your writing, make sure you have pointed out the similarities and differences.

GUIDE FOR READING

The Third Level

Jack Finney (1911–   ), who was born in Milwaukee, Wisconsin, now lives in Northern California. He is best known for *Invasion of the Body Snatchers,* a novel about aliens who come to Earth and inhabit human bodies. Escape from the harsh present to a peaceful past is a common idea in Finney's writing. It appears in his novel *Time and Again* and runs through *I Love Galesburg in the Springtime,* a collection of short stories. It is also at the heart of the unusual story you are about to read.

Time

Setting consists of both the place and the time of a story. Think of all the changes that occur over time. A person who lived in a city in the 1980's would probably know a very different place from someone who had lived in the same city in the 1890's. In "The Third Level," the main character lives in the present but longs to go back to the past.

Look For

As you read "The Third Level," notice the contrast that is established between life in the present and life in the past. What details make the modern world seem unpleasant? What details make the past seem pleasant?

Writing

List some of the ways in which you think that life in America today is different from life in America one hundred years ago.

Vocabulary

Knowing the following words will help you as you read "The Third Level."

refuge (ref′yooj) *n.*: A place of safety or shelter (p. 127)

arched (ärcht) *adj.*: curved (p. 127)

currency (kʉr′ən sē) *n.*: money (p. 129)

premium (prē′mē əm) *n.*: an additional charge (p. 129)

The Third Level

Jack Finney

The presidents of the New York Central and the New York, New Haven and Hartford railroads will swear on a stack of timetables that there are only two. But I say there are three, because I've *been* on the third level at Grand Central Station.[1] Yes, I've taken the obvious step: I talked to a psychiatrist friend of mine, among others. I told him about the third level at Grand Central Station, and he said it was a waking-dream wish fulfillment. He said I was unhappy. That made my wife kind of mad, but he explained that he meant the modern world is full of insecurity, fear, war, worry and all the rest of it, and that I just want to escape. Well, who doesn't? Everybody I know wants to escape, but they don't wander down into any third level at Grand Central Station.

But that's the reason, he said, and my friends all agreed. Everything points to it, they claimed. My stamp collecting, for example; that's a "temporary refuge from reality." Well, maybe, but my grandfather didn't need any refuge from reality; things were pretty nice and peaceful in his day, from all I hear, and he started my collection. It's a nice collection, too, blocks of four of practically every U.S. issue, first-day covers, and so on. President Roosevelt collected stamps, too, you know.

Anyway, here's what happened at Grand Central. One night last summer I worked late at the office. I was in a hurry to get uptown to my apartment so I decided to take the subway from Grand Central because it's faster than the bus.

Now, I don't know why this should have happened to me. I'm just an ordinary guy named Charley, thirty-one years old, and I was wearing a tan gabardine[2] suit and a straw hat with a fancy band; I passed a dozen men who looked just like me. And I wasn't trying to escape from anything; I just wanted to get home to Louisa, my wife.

I turned into Grand Central from Vanderbilt Avenue, and went down the steps to the first level, where you take trains like the Twentieth Century. Then I walked down another flight to the second level, where the suburban trains leave from, ducked into an arched doorway heading for the subway— and got lost. That's easy to do. I've been in and out of Grand Central hundreds of times, but I'm always bumping into new doorways and stairs and corridors. Once I got into a tunnel about a mile long and came out in the lobby of the Roosevelt Hotel. Another time I came up in an office building on Forty-sixth Street, three blocks away.

Sometimes I think Grand Central is

---

1. Grand Central Station: A large train station in New York City.

2. gabardine (gab′ ər dēn′): A cloth of wool, cotton, rayon, or other material used for suits and dresses.

growing like a tree, pushing out new corridors and staircases like roots. There's probably a long tunnel that nobody knows about feeling its way under the city right now, on its way to Times Square, and maybe another to Central Park. And maybe—because for so many people through the years Grand Central *has* been an exit, a way of escape— maybe that's how the tunnel I got into . . . But I never told my psychiatrist friend about that idea.

The corridor I was in began angling left and slanting downward and I thought that was wrong, but I kept on walking. All I could hear was the empty sound of my own foot-steps and I didn't pass a soul. Then I heard that sort of hollow roar ahead that means open space and people talking. The tunnel turned sharp left; I went down a short flight of stairs and came out on the third level at Grand Central Station. For just a moment I thought I was back on the second level, but I saw the room was smaller, there were fewer ticket windows and train gates, and the information booth in the center was wood and old-looking. And the man in the booth wore a green eyeshade and long black sleeve protectors. The lights were dim and sort of flickering. Then I saw why; they were open-flame gaslights.

There were brass spittoons[3] on the floor, and across the station a glint of light caught my eye; a man was pulling a gold watch from his vest pocket. He snapped open the cover, glanced at his watch, and frowned. He wore a derby hat,[4] a black four-button suit with tiny lapels, and he had a big, black, handlebar mustache. Then I looked around and saw that everyone in the station was dressed like eighteen-ninety-something; I never saw so many beards, sideburns and fancy mustaches in my life. A woman walked in through the train gate; she wore a dress with leg-of-mutton sleeves[5] and skirts to the top of her high-buttoned shoes. Back of her, out on the tracks, I caught a glimpse of a locomotive, a very small Currier & Ives[6] locomotive with a funnel-shaped stack. And then I knew.

To make sure, I walked over to a newsboy and glanced at the stack of papers at his feet. It was the *World;* and the *World* hasn't been published for years. The lead story said something about President Cleveland. I've found that front page since, in the Public Library files, and it was printed June 11, 1894.

I turned toward the ticket windows knowing that here—on the third level at Grand Central—I could buy tickets that would take Louisa and me anywhere in the United States we wanted to go. In the year 1894. And I wanted two tickets to Galesburg, Illinois.

Have you ever been there? It's a wonderful town still, with big old frame houses, huge lawns and tremendous trees whose branches meet overhead and roof the streets. And in 1894, summer evenings were twice as long, and people sat out on their lawns, the men smoking cigars and talking quietly, the women waving palm-leaf fans, with the fireflies all around, in a peaceful world. To be back there with the First World War still twenty years off, and World War II over forty years in the future . . . I wanted two tickets for that.

The clerk figured the fare—he glanced at my fancy hatband, but he figured the fare—and I had enough for two coach tickets, one way. But when I counted out the money and looked up, the clerk was staring at me. He nodded at the bills. "That ain't money, mister," he said, "and if you're trying to skin me[7] you won't get very far," and he glanced at the cash drawer beside him. Of course the money in his drawer was old-style bills, half again as big as the money we use nowadays, and different-looking. I turned away and got out fast. There's nothing nice about jail, even in 1894.

And that was that. I left the same way I came, I suppose. Next day, during lunch hour, I drew three hundred dollars out of the bank, nearly all we had, and bought old-style currency (that *really* worried my psychiatrist friend). You can buy old money at almost any coin dealer's, but you have to pay a premium. My three hundred dollars bought less than two hundred in old-style bills, but I didn't care; eggs were thirteen cents a dozen in 1894.

But I've never again found the corridor that leads to the third level at Grand Central Station, although I've tried often enough.

Louisa was pretty worried when I told her all this, and didn't want me to look for the third level any more, and after a while I

---

3. spittoons (spi to͞onz′): Jarlike containers into which people spit. Spitting in public was a more accepted habit in the past.

4. derby hat: A stiff felt hat with a round crown and curved brim.

5. leg-of-mutton sleeves: Sleeves that puff out toward the shoulder and resemble a leg of mutton (lamb or sheep).

6. Currier & Ives: These 19th-century American print makers became famous for their pictures of trains, yachts, horses, and scenes of nature.

7. skin me: An old-fashioned way of saying "cheat me."

stopped; I went back to my stamps. But now we're *both* looking, every weekend, because now we have proof that the third level is still there. My friend Sam Weiner disappeared! Nobody knew where, but I sort of suspected because Sam's a city boy, and I used to tell him about Galesburg—I went to school there—and he always said he liked the sound of the place. And that's where he is, all right. In 1894.

Because one night, fussing with my stamp collection, I found—well, do you know what a first-day cover is? When a new stamp is issued, stamp collectors buy some and use them to mail envelopes to themselves on the very first day of sale; and the postmark proves the date. The envelope is called a first-day cover. They're never opened; you just put blank paper in the envelope.

That night, among my oldest first-day covers, I found one that shouldn't have been there. But there it was. It was there because someone had mailed it to my grandfather at his home in Galesburg; that's what the address on the envelope said. And it had been there since July 18, 1894—the postmark showed that—yet I didn't remember it at all. The stamp was a six-cent, dull brown, with a picture of President Garfield. Naturally, when the envelope came to Granddad in the mail, it went right into his collection and stayed there—till I took it out and opened it.

The paper inside wasn't blank. It read:

> 941 Willard Street
> Galesburg, Illinois
> July 18, 1894

Charley:

I got to wishing that you were right. Then I got to believing you were right. And, Charley, it's true; I found the third level! I've been here two weeks, and right now, down the street at the Daly's, someone is playing a piano, and they're all out on the front porch singing, "Seeing Nellie home." And I'm invited over for lemonade. Come on back, Charley and Louisa. Keep looking till you find the third level! It's worth it, believe me!

The note was signed *Sam*.

At the stamp and coin store I go to, I found out that Sam bought eight hundred dollars' worth of old-style currency. That ought to set him up in a nice little hay, feed and grain business; he always said that's what he really wished he could do, and he certainly can't go back to his old business. Not in Galesburg, Illinois, in 1894. His old business? Why, Sam was my psychiatrist.

THINKING ABOUT THE SELECTION

Recalling

1. According to Charley's psychiatrist, why does Charley think he has been on the third level of Grand Central Station?
2. What is it about Grand Central Station that makes it easy for Charley to get lost there?
3. What is the first clue that he is in the Grand Central Station of the past?
4. Why is he unable to travel to Galesburg even after he gets currency that the ticket clerk will accept?
5. What proof does Charley get that the third level exists?

Interpreting

6. Describe the contrast the story presents between life in the modern world and life in Galesburg at the turn of the century.
7. What is the connection between this contrast and Charley's wanting to go to Galesburg?
8. As a psychiatrist, Sam must listen to the problems and fears of people living in the modern world. How might his work have led to his going to Galesburg?
9. What effect do you think Sam's letter has on Charley?

Applying

10. Many stories, novels, and films deal with escaping from the present into a more pleasant time, usually in the past. Do you think the idea of a past that is better than the present is, or is not, realistic? Explain why.

ANALYZING LITERATURE

Recognizing Time in a Setting

Time refers to the *when* of the action. Sometimes a story will shift from the present to the past.

Then you have to determine from clues when the action is taking place.

1. What is the first detail that hints Charley has entered in the Grand Central Station of 1894?
2. Identify at least three other details that show the third level is in the past.

CRITICAL THINKING AND READING

Understanding the Effects of Time

The time in which a story is set affects the characters. There is a close connection between how people live and when they live. As time changes, a society changes. For example, in "The Third Level" Charley's and Sam's unhappiness is linked to life in general in the modern world.

1. What view of modern life is given in the first paragraph of the story?
2. According to Sam, how has modern life affected Charley's mind?
3. What does Sam's letter to Charley say that suggests life in Galesburg in 1894 is better than life in modern-day New York?

THINKING AND WRITING

Writing a Time-Travel Story

Write a brief story in which a character—maybe yourself—steps into the past, experiences life as it was then lived, and suddenly returns to the present (perhaps changed by the strange experience). First select the time period for your story. List details about this period that you might use in your story, for example, 1890's—gas lights, long dresses, street cars. Figure out a way to get your character into the past and a way to return him or her to the present. You might also think about how the experience of the past will change the character's life in the future. Go over your writing to see whether you have managed to convey a vivid glimpse of the past time that you are presenting. Then share your story with your classmates.

GUIDE FOR READING

Rip Van Winkle

Washington Irving (1783–1859) was the first American author to achieve fame in both Europe and America. While living in England as a young man, he read old German folk tales in search of subjects he could use for stories of his own. One tale strongly appealed to him. He changed its setting from Europe to America, made other changes, and thus created "Rip Van Winkle." The magical quality of this story comes in part from its source—a strange old folk tale passed down from generation to generation of fascinated listeners.

Passage of Time

As a story moves forward in time, not only do characters and events change but the setting may change as well. How a place is described later in a story may be different from how it is described earlier. In "Rip Van Winkle," changes in the setting over time are especially important to the story as a whole.

Look For

As you read the story, try to picture the setting clearly. Look for the details that make the Catskill mountain region come vividly alive. How does the setting change as time passes?

Writing

Think of some place you know that has changed. It might be a piece of land, a house, a neighborhood, or another place. What did it look like before it changed? What did it look like after it changed? List details that would give a reader a clear picture of the "before" place. Then list the "after" details.

Vocabulary

Knowing the following words will help you as you read "Rip Van Winkle."

chivalrous (shiv''l rəs) *adj.:* Courteous (p. 134)

Martial (mär'shəl) *adj.:* Suitable for war (p. 134)

domestic (də mes'tik) *adj.:* Of the home and family (p. 134)

obliging (ə blī'jiŋ) *adj.:* Ready to do favors (p. 135)

keener (kēn' ər) *adj.:* Sharper and quicker (p. 136)

wistfully (wist'fəl lē) *adj.:* Showing vague yearnings (p. 137)

majestic (mə jes'tik) *adj.:* Grand, lofty (p. 137)

incomprehensible (in'käm pri hen'sə b'l) *adj.:* not able to be understood (p. 138)

evidently (ev'ə dənt lē) *adj.:* Obviously (p. 139)

melancholy (mel'ən käl'ē) *adj.:* Sad, gloomy (p. 139)

Rip Van Winkle

Washington Irving

RIP IN THE MOUNTAINS
Albertus Del Orient Brower
Shelburne Museum, Shelburne, Vermont

Whoever has made a voyage up the Hudson must remember the Catskill mountains. They are a branch of the great Appalachian family,[1] and are seen away to the west of the river, swelling up to a noble height, and lording it over the surrounding country. Every change of season, every change of weather, indeed every hour of the day, produces some change in the magical hues and shapes of these mountains, and they are regarded by all the good wives, far and near, as perfect barometers. When the weather is fair and settled, they are clothed in blue and purple, and print their bold outlines on the clear evening sky; but sometimes, when the rest of the landscape is cloudless, they will gather a hood of gray vapors about their summits,

---

1. Appalachian (ap'ə lā' c͡hən) **family:** A group of mountains extending from southern Quebec in Canada to northern Alabama.

which, in the last rays of the setting sun, will glow and light up like a crown of glory.

At the foot of these fairy mountains, the voyager may have seen the light smoke curling up from a village, whose shingle roofs gleam among the trees, just where the blue tints of the upland melt away into the fresh green of the nearer landscape. It is a little village, of great antiquity, having been founded by some of the Dutch colonists, in the early times of the province, just about the beginning of the government of the good Peter Stuyvesant,[2] (may he rest in peace!) and there were some of the houses of the original settlers standing within a few years,[3] built of small yellow bricks brought from Holland, having latticed windows and gable fronts,[4] surmounted with weathercocks.

In that same village, and in one of these very houses (which, to tell the precise truth, was sadly timeworn and weather-beaten), there lived many years since, while the country was yet a province of Great Britain, a simple good-natured fellow, of the name of Rip Van Winkle. He was a descendant of the Van Winkles who figured so gallantly in the chivalrous days of Peter Stuyvesant, and accompanied him to the siege of Fort Christina. He inherited, however, but little of the martial character of his ancestors. I have observed that he was a simple good-natured man; he was, moreover, a kind neighbor, and an obedient henpecked husband. Indeed, to the latter circumstance might be owing that meekness of spirit which gained him such universal popularity; for those men are most apt to be obsequious and conciliating abroad, who are under the discipline of shrews at home. Their tempers, doubtless, are rendered pliant and malleable in the fiery furnace of domestic tribulation which is worth all the sermons in the world for teaching the virtues of patience and long-suffering. A termagant[5] wife may, therefore, in some respects, be considered a tolerable blessing; and if so, Rip Van Winkle was thrice blessed.

Certain it is, that he was a great favorite among all the good wives of the village, who, as usual with the amiable sex, took his part in all family squabbles; and never failed, whenever they talked those matters over in their evening gossipings, to lay all the blame on Dame Van Winkle. The children of the village, too, would shout with joy whenever he approached. He assisted at their sports, made their playthings, taught them to fly kites and shoot marbles, and told them long stories of ghosts, witches, and Indians. Whenever he went dodging about the village, he was surrounded by a troop of them, hanging on his skirts, clambering on his back and playing a thousand tricks on him with impunity; and not a dog would bark at him throughout the neighborhood.

The great error in Rip's composition was an insuperable aversion to all kinds of profitable labor. It could not be from the want of perseverance; for he would sit on a wet rock, with a rod as long and heavy as a Tartar's lance,[6] and fish all day without a murmur, even though he should not be encouraged by a single nibble. He would carry a fowling piece[7] on his shoulder for hours together, trudging through woods and swamps, and up hill and down dale, to shoot

---

2. Peter Stuyvesant (stī′ və s'nt): The last governor of New Netherland, a Dutch colony, before it was taken over by the English in 1664 and renamed New York.
3. within a few years: Until recently. The story was written during the early part of the 19th century.
4. gable fronts: Triangular wall shapes where two roof slopes meet.

---

5. termagant (tər′ mə gənt) *adj.*: Scolding.
6. Tartar's (tär′ tərz) **lance:** The Tartars were a member of the Mongolian tribes that invaded Europe about 700 years ago; these warriors used lances, which are long and heavy spears.
7. fowling piece: A type of shotgun for hunting wild fowl or birds.

a few squirrels or wild pigeons. He would never refuse to assist a neighbor even in the roughest toil, and was a foremost man at all country frolics for husking Indian corn, or building stone fences; the women of the village, too, used to employ him to run their errands, and to do such little odd jobs as their less obliging husbands would not do for them. In a word, Rip was ready to attend to anybody's business but his own; but as to doing family duty, and keeping his farm in order, he found it impossible.

In fact, he declared it was of no use to work on his farm; it was the most pestilent[8] little piece of ground in the whole country; everything about it went wrong, and would go wrong, in spite of him. His fences were continually falling to pieces; his cow would either go astray, or get among the cabbages; weeds were sure to grow quicker in his fields than anywhere else; the rain always made a point of setting in just as he had some outdoor work to do; so that though his estate had dwindled away under his management, acre by acre, until there was little more left than a mere patch of Indian corn and potatoes, yet it was the worst conditioned farm in the neighborhood.

His children, too, were as ragged and wild as if they belonged to nobody. His son Rip, an urchin[9] begotten in his own likeness, promised to inherit the habits, with the old clothes of his father. He was generally seen trooping like a colt at his mother's heels, equipped in a pair of his father's cast-off galligaskins,[10] which he had much ado to hold up with one hand, as a fine lady does her train in bad weather.

Rip Van Winkle, however, was one of those happy mortals, of foolish, well-oiled dispositions, who take the world easy, eat white bread or brown, whichever can be got with least thought or trouble, and would rather starve on a penny than work for a pound.[11] If left to himself, he would have whistled life away in perfect contentment; but his wife kept continually dinning in his ears about his idleness, his carelessness, and the ruin he was bringing on his family. Morning, noon, and night, her tongue was incessantly going, and everything he said or did was sure to produce a torrent of household eloquence. Rip had but one way of replying to all lectures of the kind, and that, by frequent use, had grown into a habit. He shrugged his shoulders, shook his head, cast up his eyes, but said nothing. This, however, always provoked a fresh volley from his wife; so that he was fain[12] to draw off his forces, and take to the outside of the house—the only side which, in truth, belongs to a henpecked husband.

Rip's sole domestic adherent was his dog Wolf, who was as much henpecked as his master; for Dame Van Winkle regarded them as companions in idleness, and even looked upon Wolf with an evil eye, as the cause of his master's going so often astray. True it is, in all points of spirit befitting an honorable dog, he was as courageous an animal as ever scoured the woods—but what courage can withstand the ever-enduring and all-besetting terrors of a woman's tongue? The moment Wolf entered the house his crest fell, his tail drooped to the ground or curled between his legs, he sneaked about with a gallows air, casting many a sidelong glance at Dame Van Winkle, and at the least flourish of a broomstick or ladle, he would fly to the door with yelping precipitation.[13]

---

8. pestilent (pes′ t'l ənt) *adj.*: In this case, it means "annoying."

9. urchin (ər′ chin) *n.*: A mischievous boy.

10. galligaskins (gal′ i gas′ kinz) *n.*: Loosely fitting breeches worn in the 16th and 17th centuries.

11. pound (pound) *n.*: A British unit of money.

12. fain (fān) *adj.*: An old-fashioned word meaning "glad."

13. precipitation (pri sip′ ə tā′ shən) *n.*: Great speed.

Times grew worse and worse with Rip Van Winkle as years of matrimony rolled on; a tart temper never mellows with age, and a sharp tongue is the only edged tool that grows keener with constant use. For a long while he used to console himself, when driven from home, by frequenting a kind of perpetual club of the sages, philosophers, and other idle personages of the village; which held its sessions on a bench before a small inn, designated by a portrait of His Majesty George the Third. Here they used to sit in the shade through a long, lazy summer's day, talking listlessly over village gossip, or telling endless sleepy stories about nothing. But it would have been worth any statesman's money to have heard the profound discussions that sometimes took place when by chance an old newspaper fell into their hands from some passing traveler. How solemnly they would listen to the contents, as drawled out by Derrick Van Bummel, the schoolmaster, a dapper, learned little man, who was not to be daunted by the most gigantic word in the dictionary; and how sagely they would deliberate upon public events some months after they had taken place.

The opinions of this group were completely controlled by Nicholas Vedder, a patriarch of the village, and landlord of the inn, at the door of which he took his seat from morning till night, just moving sufficiently to avoid the sun and keep in the shade of a large tree; so that the neighbors could tell the hour by his movements as accurately as by a sundial. It is true, he was rarely heard to speak, but smoked his pipe incessantly. His adherents, however (for every great man has his adherents), perfectly understood

RIP AT THE INN
Albertus Del Orient Brower
Shelburne Museum, Shelburne, Vermont

him, and knew how to gather his opinions. When anything that was read or related displeased him, he was observed to smoke his pipe vehemently, and to send forth short, frequent, and angry puffs; but when pleased, he would inhale the smoke slowly and tranquilly, and emit it in light and placid clouds; and sometimes, taking the pipe from his mouth, and letting the fragrant vapor curl about his nose, would gravely nod his head in token of perfect approbation.

From even this stronghold the unlucky Rip was at length routed by his termagant wife, who would suddenly break in upon the tranquillity of the assemblage and call the members all to naught; nor was that august personage, Nicholas Vedder himself, sacred from the daring tongue of this terrible virago,[14] who charged him outright with encouraging her husband in habits of idleness.

Poor Rip was at last reduced almost to despair; and his only alternative, to escape from the labor of the farm and clamor of his wife, was to take gun in hand and stroll away into the woods. Here he would sometimes seat himself at the foot of a tree, and share the contents of his wallet[15] with Wolf, with whom he sympathized as a fellow-sufferer in persecution. "Poor Wolf," he would say, "thy mistress leads thee a dog's life of it; but never mind, my lad, whilst I live thou shalt never want a friend to stand by thee!" Wolf would wag his tail, look wistfully in his master's face, and if dogs can feel pity I verily believe he reciprocated the sentiment with all his heart.

In a long ramble of the kind on a fine autumnal day, Rip had unconsciously scrambled to one of the highest parts of the Catskill mountains. He was after his favorite sport of squirrel shooting, and the still solitudes had echoed and re-echoed with the reports of his gun. Panting and fatigued, he threw himself, late in the afternoon, on a green knoll, covered with mountain herbage, that crowned the brow of a precipice. From an opening between the trees he could overlook all the lower country for many a mile of rich woodland. He saw at a distance the lordly Hudson, far, far below him, moving on its silent but majestic course, with the reflection of a purple cloud, or the sail of a lagging bark,[16] here and there sleeping on its glassy bosom, and at last losing itself in the blue highlands.

On the other side he looked down into a deep mountain glen, wild, lonely, and shagged,[17] the bottom filled with fragments from the impending[18] cliffs, and scarcely lighted by the reflected rays of the setting sun. For some time Rip lay musing on this scene; evening was gradually advancing; the mountains began to throw their long blue shadows over the valleys; he saw that it would be dark long before he could reach the village, and he heaved a heavy sigh when he thought of encountering the terrors of Dame Van Winkle.

As he was about to descend, he heard a voice from a distance hallooing, "Rip Van Winkle! Rip Van Winkle!" He looked round, but could see nothing but a crow winging its solitary flight across the mountain. He thought his fancy[19] must have deceived him, and turned again to descend, when he heard the same cry ring through the still evening air: "Rip Van Winkle! Rip Van Winkle!"—at the same time Wolf bristled up his back, and giving a low growl, skulked to his master's

---

14. virago (vi rā′ gō) *n.*: A quarrelsome woman.
15. wallet (wôl′ it) *n.*: In this case, it means a bag for carrying provisions.

16. bark (bärk) *n.*: Any boat, especially a small sailing boat.
17. shagged (shagd) *adj.*: Shaggy or rough.
18. impending (im pend′ iŋ) *adj.*: An old-fashioned word for "overhanging."
19. fancy (fan′ sē) *n.*: An old-fashioned word for "imagination."

side, looking fearfully down into the glen. Rip now felt a vague apprehension stealing over him; he looked anxiously in the same direction, and perceived a strange figure slowly toiling up the rocks, and bending under the weight of something he carried on his back. He was surprised to see any human being in this lonely and unfrequented place, but supposing it to be some one of the neighborhood in need of his assistance, he hastened down to yield it. .

On nearer approach he was still more surprised at the singularity of the stranger's appearance. He was a short, square-built old fellow, with thick bushy hair, and a grizzled[20] beard. His dress was of the antique Dutch fashion—a cloth jerkin[21] strapped round the waist—several pairs of breeches, the outer one of ample volume, decorated with rows of buttons down the sides and bunches at the knees. He bore on his shoulder a stout keg, that seemed full of liquor, and made signs for Rip to approach and assist him with the load. Though rather shy and distrustful of this new acquaintance, Rip complied with his usual alacrity; and mutually relieving one another, they clambered up a narrow gully, apparently the dry bed of a mountain torrent. As they ascended, Rip every now and then heard long rolling peals, like distant thunder, that seemed to issue out of a deep ravine, or rather cleft, between lofty rocks, toward which their rugged path conducted. He paused for an instant, but supposing it to be the muttering of one of these transient thundershowers which often take place in mountain heights, he proceeded. Passing through the ravine, they came to a hollow, like a small amphitheater, surrounded by perpendicular precipices, over the brinks of which impending trees shot their branches, so that you only caught glimpses of the azure sky and the bright evening cloud. During the whole time, Rip and his companion had labored on in silence; for though the former marvelled greatly what could be the object of carrying a keg of liquor up this wild mountain, yet there was something strange and incomprehensible about the unknown that inspired awe and checked familiarity.

On entering the amphitheater, new objects of wonder presented themselves. On a level spot in the center was a company of odd-looking personages playing at ninepins. They were dressed in a quaint outlandish fashion; some wore short doublets,[22] others jerkins, with long knives in their belts, and most of them had enormous breeches, of similar style with that of the guide's. Their visages,[23] too, were peculiar; one had a large beard, broad face, and small piggish eyes; the face of another seemed to consist entirely of nose, and was surmounted by a white sugar-loaf hat,[24] set off with a little red cock's tail. They all had beards, of various shapes and colors. There was one who seemed to be the commander. He was a stout old gentleman, with a weather-beaten countenance,[25] he wore a laced doublet, broad belt and hanger,[26] high-crowned hat and feather, red stockings, and high-heeled shoes, with roses in them. The whole group reminded Rip of the figures in an old Flemish[27] painting, in the parlor of Dominie Van Shaick, the village parson, and which had been brought over from Holland at the time of the settlement.

22. doublets (dub′ lits) *n.*: Closefitting jackets.
23. visages (viz′ ij iz) *n.*: An old-fashioned word for "faces."
24. sugar-loaf hat: A hat shaped like a cone.
25. countenance (koun′ tə nəns) *n.*: An old-fashioned word for "face."
26. hanger (haŋ′ ər) *n.*: A short sword that hangs from the belt.
27. Flemish (flem′ ish) *adj.*: Referring to the former country of Flanders in northwest Europe.

20. grizzled (griz′ ′ld) *adj.*: An old-fashioned word for "gray."
21. jerkin (jər′ kin) *n.*: A short, closefitting jacket worn in the 16th and 17th centuries.

What seemed particularly odd to Rip was, that though these folks were evidently amusing themselves, yet they maintained the gravest face, the most mysterious silence, and were, withal, the most melancholy party of pleasure he had ever witnessed. Nothing interrupted the stillness of the scene but the noise of the balls, which, whenever they were rolled, echoed along the mountains like rumbling peals of thunder.

As Rip and his companion approached them, they suddenly desisted from their play, and stared at him with such fixed, statuelike gaze, and such strange, lackluster[28]

countenances, that his heart turned within him, and his knees smote together. His companion, now emptied the contents of the keg into large flagons,[29] and made signs to him to wait upon the company. He obeyed with fear and trembling; they quaffed[30] the liquor in profound silence, and then returned to their game.

By degrees Rip's awe and apprehension subsided. He even ventured, when no eye was fixed upon him, to taste the beverage, which he found had much of the flavor of ex-

---

28. lackluster (lak′ lus′ tər) *adj.*: Lacking brightness, dull.

29. flagons (flag′ ənz) *n.*: A container for liquids, with a handle, narrow neck, spout, and sometimes a lid.

30. quaffed (kwäft) *v.*: Drank in a thirsty way.

Rip Van Winkle   139

cellent Hollands.[31] He was naturally a thirsty soul, and was soon tempted to repeat the draft. One taste provoked another; and he reiterated his visits to the flagon so often that at length his senses were overpowered, his eyes swam in his head, his head gradually declined, and he fell into a deep sleep.

On waking, he found himself on the green knoll whence he had first seen the old man of the glen. He rubbed his eyes—it was a bright sunny morning. The birds were hopping and twittering among the bushes, and the eagle was wheeling aloft, and breasting the pure mountain breeze. "Surely," thought Rip, "I have not slept here all night." He recalled the occurrences before he fell asleep. The strange man with a keg of liquor—the mountain ravine—the wild retreat among the rocks—the woebegone party at ninepins—the flagon—"Oh! that flagon! that wicked flagon!" thought Rip—"what excuse shall I make to Dame Van Winkle?"

He looked round for his gun, but in place of the clean, well-oiled fowling piece, he found an old firelock lying by him, the barrel incrusted with rust,the lock falling of, and the stock worm-eaten. He now suspected that the grave roysters[32] of the mountain had put a trick upon him, and having dosed him with liquor, had robbed him of his gun. Wolf, too, had disappeared, but he might have strayed away after a squirrel or partridge. He whistled after him and shouted his name, but all in vain; the echoes repeated his whistle and shout, but no dog was to be seen.

He determined to revisit the scene of the last evening's gambol,[33] and if he met with any of the party, to demand his dog and gun. As he rose to walk, he found himself stiff in the joints, and wanting in his usual activity. "These mountain beds do not agree with me," thought Rip, "and if this frolic should lay me up with a fit of the rheumatism, I shall have a blessed time with Dame Van Winkle." With some difficulty he got down into the glen: he found the gully up which he and his companion had ascended the preceding evening; but to his astonishment a mountain stream was now foaming down it, leaping from rock to rock, and filling the glen with babbling murmurs. He, however, made shift to scramble up its sides, working his toilsome way through thickets of birch, sassafras, and witch hazel, and sometimes tripped up or entangled by the wild grapevines that twisted their coils or tendrils from tree to tree, and spread a kind of network in his path.

At length he reached to where the ravine had opened through the cliffs to the amphitheater; but no traces of such opening remained. The rocks presented a high impenetrable wall, over which the torrent came tumbling in a sheet of feathery foam, and fell into a broad deep basin, black from the shadows of the surrounding forest. Here, then, poor Rip was brought to a stand. He again called and whistled after his dog; he was only answered by the cawing of a flock of idle crows, sporting high in air about a dry tree that overhung a sunny precipice; and who, secure in their elevation, seemed to look down and scoff at the poor man's perplexities. What was to be done? The morning was passing away, and Rip felt famished for want of his breakfast. He grieved to give up his dog and gun; he dreaded to meet his wife; but it would not do to starve among the mountains. He shook his head, shouldered the rusty firelock, and with a heart full of trouble and anxiety, turned his steps homeward.

As he approached the village he met a number of people, but none whom he knew,

---

31. Hollands *n.*: Gin made in the Netherlands.
32. roysters (rois′ tərs) *n.*: An old-fashioned word for people who are having a good time at a party.
33. gambol (gam′ b'l) *v.*: Play, frolic.

which somewhat surprised him, for he had thought himself acquainted with everyone in the country round. Their dress, too, was of a different fashion from that to which he was accustomed. They all stared at him with equal marks of surprise, and whenever they cast their eyes upon him, invariably stroked their chins. The constant recurrence of this gesture induced Rip, involuntarily, to do the same, when, to his astonishment, he found his beard had grown a foot long!

He had now entered the outskirts of the village. A troop of strange children ran at his heels, hooting after him, and pointing at his gray beard. The dogs, too, not one of which he recognized for an old acquaintance, barked at him as he passed. The very village was altered; it was larger and more populous. There were rows of houses which he had never seen before, and those which had been his familiar haunts had disappeared. Strange names were over the doors—strange faces at the windows—every thing was strange. His mind now misgave him; he began to doubt whether both he and the world around him were not bewitched. Surely this was his native village, which he had left but the day before. There stood the Catskill mountains—there ran the silver Hudson at a distance—there was every hill and dale precisely as it had always been—Rip was sorely perplexed—"That flagon last night," thought he; "has addled[34] my poor head sadly!"

It was with some difficulty that he found the way to his own house, which he approached with silent awe, expecting every moment to hear the shrill voice of Dame Van Winkle. He found the house gone to decay—the roof fallen in, the windows shattered, and the doors off the hinges. A half-starved dog that looked like Wolf was skulking about it. Rip called him by name, but the cur snarled, showed his teeth, and passed on.

This was an unkind cut indeed—"My very dog," sighed poor Rip, "has forgotten me!"

He entered the house, which, to tell the truth, Dame Van Winkle had always kept in neat order. It was empty, forlorn, and apparently abandoned. This desolateness overcame all his fears—he called loudly for his wife and children—the lonely chambers rang for a moment with his voice, and then all again was silence.

He now hurried forth, and hastened to his old resort, the village inn—but it too was gone. A large rickety wooden building stood in its place, with great gaping windows, some of them broken and mended with old hats and petticoats, and over the door was painted, "The Union Hotel, by Jonathan Doolittle." Instead of the great tree that used to shelter the quiet little Dutch inn of yore, there now was reared a tall, naked pole, with something on the top that looked like a red nightcap,[35] and from it was fluttering a flag, on which was a singular assemblage of stars and stripes—all this was strange and incomprehensible. He recognized on the sign, however, the ruby face of King George, under which he had smoked so many a peaceful pipe; but even this was singularly metamorphosed.[36] The red coat was changed for one of blue and buff, a sword was held in the hand instead of a scepter, the head was decorated with a cocked hat, and underneath was painted in large characters, GENERAL WASHINGTON.

There was, as usual, a crowd of folk about the door, but none that Rip recollected. The very character of the people seemed changed. There was a busy, bustling, disputatious tone about it, instead of the accustomed drowsy tranquillity. He looked in vain for the sage Nicholas Vedder,

---

34. addled (ad'ld) v.: Muddled and confused.

35. red nightcap: A liberty cap, used by colonists to symbolize their freedom from Great Britain.
36. metamorphosed (met' ə môr' fōzd) v.: Changed.

with his broad face, double chin, and fair long pipe, uttering clouds of tobacco smoke instead of idle speeches; or Van Bummel, the school-master, doling forth the contents of an ancient newspaper. In places of these, a lean, bilious-looking[37] fellow, with his pockets full of handbills, was speaking vehemently about rights of citizens—elections— members of Congress—liberty—Bunker's Hill—heroes of seventy-six—and other words, which were a perfect Babylonish jargon[38] to the bewildered Van Winkle.

The appearance of Rip, with his long grizzled beard, his rusty fowling piece, his uncouth dress, and an army of women and children at his heels, soon attracted the attention of the tavern politicians. They crowded round him, eyeing him from head to foot with great curiosity. The orator bustled up to him, and, drawing him partly aside, inquired "on which side he voted?" Rip stared in vacant stupidity. Another short but busy little fellow pulled him by the arm, and, rising on tiptoe, inquired in his ear, "whether he was Federal or Democrat?"[39] Rip was equally at a loss to comprehend the question; when a knowing, self-important

---

37. bilious (bil′ yəs)**-looking** *adj.*: Looking cross or bad-tempered.

38. Babylonish (bab′ ə lō′ nish) **jargon:** A language he could not understand.

39. Federal or Democrat: Two political parties at that time.

RETURN OF RIP VAN WINKLE, 1829
John Quidor
National Gallery of Art, Washington

old gentleman in a sharp cocked hat made his way through the crowd, putting them to the right and left with his elbows as he passed, and planting himself before Van Winkle, with one arm akimbo,[40] the other resting on his cane, his keen eyes and sharp hat penetrating, as it were, into his very soul, demanded, in an austere tone, "what brought him to the election with a gun on his shoulder, and a mob at his heels, and whether he meant to breed a riot in the village?" "Alas! gentlemen," cried Rip, somewhat dismayed, "I am a poor, quiet man, a native of the place, and a loyal subject of the king, God bless him!"

Here a general shout burst from the bystanders—"A tory![41] a tory! a spy! a refugee! hustle him! away with him!" It was with great difficulty that the self-important man in the cocked hat restored order; and, having assumed a tenfold austerity of brow, demanded again of the unknown culprit, what he came there for, and whom he was seeking. The poor man humbly assured him that he meant no harm, but merely came there in search of some of his neighbors, who used to keep about the tavern.

"Well, who are they? Name them."

Rip bethought himself a moment, and inquired, "Where's Nicholas Vedder?"

There was a silence for a little while, when an old man replied, in a thin, piping voice, "Nicholas Vedder! why, he is dead and gone these eighteen years! There was a wooden tombstone in the churchyard that used to tell all about him, but that's rotten and gone too."

"Where's Brom Dutcher?"

"Oh, he went off to the army in the beginning of the war; some say he was killed at the storming of Stony Point[42]—others say he was drowned in a squall at the foot of Antony's Nose.[43] I don't know—he never came back again."

"Where's Van Bummel, the schoolmaster?"

"He went off to the wars, too, was a great militia general, and is now in Congress."

Rip's heart died away at hearing of these sad changes in his home and friends, and finding himself thus alone in the world. Every answer puzzled him too, by treating of such enormous lapses of time, and of matters which he could not understand; war—Congress—Stony Point—he had no courage to ask after any more friends, but cried out in despair, "Does nobody here know Rip Van Winkle?"

"Oh, Rip Van Winkle!" exclaimed two or three, "Oh, to be sure! that's Rip Van Winkle yonder, leaning against the tree."

Rip looked, and beheld a precise counterpart of himself, as he went up the mountain: apparently as lazy, and certainly as ragged. The poor fellow was now completely confounded. He doubted his own identity, and whether he was himself or another man. In the midst of his bewilderment, the man in the cocked hat demanded who he was, and what was his name.

"Goodness knows," exclaimed he, at his wit's end; "I'm not myself—I'm somebody else—that's me yonder—no—that's somebody else got into my shoes—I was myself last night, but I fell asleep on the mountain, and they've changed my gun, and everything's changed, and I'm changed, and I can't tell what's my name, or who I am!"

The bystanders began now to look at each other, nod, wink significantly, and tap

---

40. akimbo (ə kim′ bō) *adj.*: Hand on hip, with elbow pointing outward.

41. tory (tôr′ ē): A person who supported the British during the American Revolution.

42. Stony Point: A town on the Hudson River where a Revolutionary War battle was fought in 1779.

43. Antony's Nose: The name of a mountain on the Hudson River.

their fingers against their foreheads. There was a whisper, also, about securing the gun, and keeping the old fellow from doing mischief, at the very suggestion of which the self-important man in the cocked hat retired with some precipitation. At this critical moment a fresh, comely[44] women pressed through the throng to get a peep at the gray-bearded man. She had a chubby child in her arms, which, frightened at his looks, began to cry. "Hush, Rip," cried she, "hush, you little fool; the old man won't hurt you." The name of the child, the air of the mother, the tone of her voice, all awakened a train of recollections in his mind. "What is your name, my good woman?" asked he.

"Judith Gardenier."

"And your father's name?"

"Ah! poor man, Rip Van Winkle was his name, but it's twenty years since he went away from home with his gun and never has been heard of since—his dog came home without him; but whether he shot himself, or was carried away by the Indians, nobody can tell. I was then but a little girl."

Rip had but one question more to ask; but he put it with a faltering voice:

"Where's your mother?"

"Oh, she too had died but a short time since; she broke a blood vessel in a fit of passion at a New England peddler."

There was a drop of comfort, at least, in this intelligence.[45] The honest man could contain himself no longer. He caught his daughter and her child in his arms. "I am your father!" cried he—"Young Rip Van Winkle once—old Rip Van Winkle now! Does nobody know poor Rip Van Winkle?"

All stood amazed, until an old woman, tottering out from among the crowd, put her hand to her brow, and peering under it in his face for a moment, exclaimed, "Sure enough! it is Rip Van Winkle—it is himself! Welcome home again, old neighbor. Why, where have you been these twenty long years?"

Rip's story was soon told, for the whole twenty long years had been to him but as one night. The neighbors stared when they heard it; some were seen to wink at each other, and put their tongues in their cheeks; and the self-important man in the cocked hat, who, when the alarm was over, had returned to the field, screwed down the corners of his mouth, and shook his head—upon which there was a general shaking of the head throughout the assemblage.

It was determined, however, to take the opinion of old Peter Vanderdonk, who was seen slowly advancing up the road. He was a descendant of the historian of that name, who wrote one of the earliest accounts of the province. Peter was the most ancient inhabitant of the village, and well versed in all the wonderful events and traditions of the neighborhood. He recollected Rip at once, and corroborated his story in the most satisfactory manner. He assured the company that it was a fact, handed down from his ancestor the historian, that the Catskill mountains had always been haunted by strange beings. That it was affirmed that the great Henry Hudson, the first discoverer of the river and country,[46] kept a kind of vigil there every twenty years, with his crew of the *Half-Moon*; being permitted in this way to revisit the scenes of his enterprise, and keep a guardian eye upon the river, and the great city called by his name. That his father had once seen them in their old Dutch dresses playing at ninepins in a hollow of the mountain; and that he himself had heard, one

---

44. comely (kum′ lē) *adj.*: Attractive, pretty.
45. intelligence (in tel′ ə jəns) *n.*: In this case, it means "news."

---

46. country: The area around the Catskills.

summer afternoon, the sound of their balls, like distant peals of thunder.

To make a long story short, the company broke up, and returned to the more important concerns of the election. Rip's daughter took him home to live with her; she had a snug, well-furnished house, and a stout, cheery farmer for a husband, whom Rip recollected for one of the urchins that used to climb upon his back. As to Rip's son and heir, who was the ditto of himself, seen leaning against the tree, he was employed to work on the farm; but evinced an hereditary disposition to attend to anything else but his business.

Rip now resumed his old walks and habits; he soon found many of his former cronies, though all rather the worse for the wear and tear of time; and preferred making friends among the rising generation, with whom he soon grew into great favor.

Having nothing to do at home, and being arrived at that happy age when a man can be idle with impunity, he took his place once more on the bench at the inn door, and was reverenced as one of the patriarchs of the village, and a chronicle of the old times "before the war." It was some time before he could get into the regular track of gossip, or could be made to comprehend the strange events that had taken place during his torpor. How that there had been a revolutionary war—that the country had thrown off the yoke of old England—and that, instead of being a subject of his Majesty George the Third, he was now a free citizen of the United States.

Rip, in fact, was no politician; the changes of states and empires made but little impression on him; but there was one species of despotism under which he had long groaned, and that was—petticoat government. Happily that was at an end; he had got his neck out of the yoke of matrimony, and could go in and out whenever he pleased, without dreading the tyranny of Dame Van Winkle. Whenever her name was mentioned, however, he shook his head, shrugged his shoulders, and cast up his eyes; which might pass either for an expression of resignation to his fate, or joy at his deliverance.

He used to tell his story to every stranger that arrived at Mr. Doolittle's hotel. He was observed, at first, to vary on some points every time he told it, which was, doubtless, owing to his having so recently awaked. It at last settled down precisely to the tale I have related, and not a man, woman, or child in the neighborhood, but knew it by heart. Some always pretended to doubt the reality of it, and insisted that Rip had been out of his head, and that this was one point on which he always remained flighty. The old Dutch inhabitants, however, almost universally gave it full credit. Even to this day they never hear a thunderstorm of a summer afternoon about the Catskills, but they say Henry Hudson and his crew are at their game of ninepins; and it is a common wish of all henpecked husbands in the neighborhood, when life hangs heavy on their hands, that they might have a quieting draft out of Rip Van Winkle's flagon.

THINKING ABOUT THE SELECTION
Recalling

1. What problems does Rip Van Winkle have with his wife?
2. How do the people in the village feel about Rip?
3. Describe "the great error" in Rip's character.
4. What does Rip see when he enters the amphitheater with the strange man carrying the keg?
5. When Rip awakes, what is the first sign that he has been asleep a very long time?
6. What changes does Rip discover in the village?

Interpreting

7. A sentence in the story says that a quarrelsome wife may be considered a blessing. What does this mean?
8. How do Dame Van Winkle's personality and Rip's personality differ?
9. Compare and contrast Rip's life after his long sleep with his earlier life.

Applying

10. Imagine that you have fallen into a long sleep like Rip's. What changes in your neighborhood and country do you think you would discover when you awoke?

ANALYZING LITERATURE
Recognizing the Passage of Time

Changes in appearance indicate that time has passed. When Rip awakes, such changes show vividly the advance of time. They are also linked with other kinds of change.

1. What historical and political changes have occurred during Rip's long sleep?
2. What change has occurred that will make Rip's life at home different from what it was before his long sleep?

CRITICAL THINKING AND READING
Comparing and Contrasting Settings

When you **compare** and **contrast** a setting at different times, you note similarities, or comparisons, and differences, or contrasts.

1. When Rip looks around after he awakes, what features of the natural world does he see that have not changed at all?
2. What differences does he see in the mountain setting?
3. How has the village changed?
4. How is his home different from what it was?

UNDERSTANDING LANGUAGE
Looking Up Words in a Dictionary

A dictionary provides several different kinds of information about a word. It gives the word's spelling, pronunciation, part of speech, and meanings. Some dictionaries also provide information about its history. Look up the following words from "Rip Van Winkle" in a dictionary. Be able to tell each word's meanings, part of speech, and pronunciation.

1. barometer
2. lattice
3. obsequious
4. pliant
5. malleable
6. tribulation

THINKING AND WRITING
Describing a Place Then and Now

Look at the "before" and "after" details you listed before you read the story. Use these details to write a composition in which you contrast how a place looked before it changed and how it looked after. When you revise, make sure your description would be clear even to a reader who never saw the place you are writing about.

Theme

THE FOUR LEAF CLOVER
Winslow Homer
The Detroit Institute of Arts

GUIDE FOR READING

Utzel and His Daughter, Poverty

Isaac Bashevis Singer (1904–   ), who was born in Poland, writes primarily in Yiddish, a language spoken by East European Jews and some of their descendants. Singer came to the United States in 1935 and earned his living by writing for Yiddish newspapers. As his novels and short stories were translated into English, he became famous for his accounts of Jewish life in Eastern Europe. In 1978 he won the Nobel Prize for literature. In "Utzel and His Daughter, Poverty," Singer entertains and teaches at the same time.

Stated Theme

Theme is the general idea about life that is revealed through the story. In stories with a **stated theme**, the writer or one of the characters tells you this idea directly. "Utzel and His Daughter, Poverty" is a story with a stated theme.

Look For

As you read this humorous story, look for statements that indicate the theme. Pay special attention to the motto Utzel hangs on his wall at the end of the story. How is the theme supported by the events of the story?

Writing

In the story you are about to read, Utzel puts off tasks he does not enjoy doing. Have you ever known of someone who put off a job or a chore even though this person knew it would have to be done eventually? Freewrite about what happened as a result of the delay.

Vocabulary

Knowing the following words will help you as you read "Utzel and His Daughter, Poverty."

fitting (fit′ iŋ) *adj.*: Suitable; proper (p. 149)
reproached (ri prōcht′) *v.*: Blamed; scolded (p. 149)
consternation (kän′stər nā′ shən) *n.*: Sudden confusion and frustration (p. 150)

diligently (dil′ə jənt lē) *adv.*: With careful, steady effort (p. 152)
industrious (in dus′trē əs) *adj.*: Hard-working (p. 152)

Utzel and His Daughter, Poverty

Isaac Bashevis Singer

Once there was a man named Utzel. He was very poor and even more lazy. Whenever anyone wanted to give him a job to do, his answer was always the same: "Not today."

"Why not today?" he was asked. And he always replied, "Why not tomorrow?"

Utzel lived in a cottage that had been built by his great-grandfather. The thatched roof needed mending, and although the holes let the rain in, they did not let the smoke from the stove out. Toadstools grew on the crooked walls and the floor had rotted away. There had been a time when mice lived there, but now there weren't any because there was nothing for them to eat. Utzel's wife had starved to death, but before she died she had given birth to a baby girl. The name Utzel gave his daughter was very fitting. He called her Poverty.

Utzel loved to sleep and each night he went to bed with the chickens. In the morning he would complain that he was tired from so much sleeping and so he went to sleep again. When he was not sleeping, he lay on his broken-down cot, yawning and complaining. He would say to his daughter, "Other people are lucky. They have money without working. I am cursed."

Utzel was a small man, but as his daughter, Poverty, grew, she spread out in all directions. She was tall, broad, and heavy. At fifteen she had to lower her head to get through the doorway. Her feet were the size of a man's and puffy with fat. The villagers maintained that the lazier Utzel got, the more Poverty grew.

Utzel loved nobody, was jealous of everybody. He even spoke with envy of cats, dogs, rabbits, and all creatures who didn't have to work for a living. Yes, Utzel hated everybody and everything, but he adored his daughter. He daydreamed that a rich young man would fall in love with her, marry her, and provide for his wife and his father-in-law. But not a young man in the village showed the slightest interest in Poverty. When her father reproached the girl for not making friends and not going out with young men, Poverty would say, "How can I go out in rags and bare feet?"

One day Utzel learned that a certain charitable society in the village loaned poor people money, which they could pay back in small sums over a long period. Lazy as he was, he made a great effort—got up, dressed, and went to the office of the society. "I would like to borrow five gulden,"[1] he said to the official in charge.

"What do you intend to do with the

---

1. gulden (gool′dən) *n.*: A coin that was once used in Germany, Austria, and other countries.

money?" he was asked. "We lend money only for useful purposes."

"I want to have a pair of shoes made for my daughter," Utzel explained. "If Poverty has shoes, she will go out with the young people of the village and some wealthy young man will surely fall in love with her. When they get married, I will be able to pay back the five gulden."

The official thought it over. The chances of anyone falling in love with Poverty were very small. Utzel, however, looked so miserable that the official decided to give him the loan. He asked Utzel to sign a promissory note and gave him five gulden.

Utzel had tried to order a pair of shoes for his daughter a few months before. Sandler the shoemaker had gone so far as to take Poverty's measurements, but the shoemaker had wanted his money in advance. From the charitable society Utzel went directly to the shoemaker and asked whether he still had Poverty's measurements.

"And supposing I do?" Sandler replied. "My price is five gulden and I still want my money in advance."

Utzel took out the five gulden and handed them to Sandler. The shoemaker opened a drawer and after some searching brought out the order for Poverty's shoes. He promised to deliver the new shoes in a week, on Friday.

Utzel, who wanted to surprise his daughter, did not tell her about the shoes. The following Friday, as he lay on his cot yawning and complaining, there was a knock on the door and Sandler came in carrying the new shoes. When Poverty saw the shoemaker with a pair of shiny new shoes in his hand, she cried out in joy. The shoemaker handed her the shoes and told her to try them on. But, alas, she could not get them on her puffy feet. In the months since the measurements had been taken, Poverty's feet had be-

come even larger than they were before. Now the girl cried out in grief.

Utzel looked on in consternation. "How is it possible?" he asked. "I thought her feet stopped growing long ago."

For a while Sandler, too, stood there puzzled. Then he inquired, "Tell me, Utzel, where did you get the five gulden?" Utzel explained that he had borrowed the money from the charitable loan society and had given them a promissory note in return.

"So now you have a debt," exclaimed Sandler. "That makes you even poorer than you were a few months ago. Then you had nothing, but today you have five gulden less than nothing. And since you have grown

poorer, Poverty has grown bigger, and naturally her feet have grown with her. That is why the shoes don't fit. It is all clear to me now."

"What are we going to do?" Utzel asked in despair.

"There is only one way out for you," Sandler said. "Go to work. From borrowing one gets poorer and from work one gets richer. When you and your daughter work, she will have shoes that fit."

The idea of working did not appeal to either of them, but it was even worse to have new shoes and go around barefoot. Utzel and Poverty both decided that immediately after the Sabbath they would look for work.

Utzel got a job as a water carrier. Poverty became a maid. For the first time in their lives, they worked diligently. They were kept so busy that they did not even think of the new shoes, until one Sabbath morning Poverty decided she'd try them on again. Lo and behold, her feet slipped easily into them. The new shoes fit.

At last Utzel and Poverty understood that all a man possesses he gains through work, and not by lying in bed and being idle. Even animals were industrious. Bees make honey, spiders spin webs, birds build nests, moles dig holes in the earth, squirrels store food for the winter. Before long Utzel got a better job. He rebuilt his house and bought some furniture. Poverty lost more weight. She had new clothes made and dressed prettily like the other girls of the village. Her looks improved, too, and a young man began to court her. His name was Mahir and he was the son of a wealthy merchant. Utzel's dream of a rich son-in-law came true, but by then he no longer needed to be taken care of.

Love for his daughter had saved Utzel. In his later years he became so respected he was elected a warden of that same charitable loan society from which he had borrowed five gulden.

On the wall of his office there hung the string with which Sandler had once measured Poverty's feet, and above it the framed motto: *Whatever you can do today, don't put off till tomorrow.*

THINKING ABOUT THE SELECTION

Recalling

1. What is Utzel's daydream for his daughter?
2. Why does he want to buy shoes for Poverty?
3. Why are the shoes too small, even though Sandler the shoemaker took Poverty's measurements before making them?
4. What advice does Sandler give Utzel?
5. What does Utzel realize after he starts to work?

Interpreting

6. Why is it "fitting" that Utzel called his daughter Poverty?
7. The writer says that "the lazier Utzel got, the more Poverty grew." What could this statement indicate besides the fact that the girl grew physically larger?
8. What does the writer mean by saying, "Love for his daughter had saved Utzel"?

Applying

9. Why does a person become stronger by loving someone else?

ANALYZING LITERATURE

Identifying the Stated Theme

The **theme**, or central idea, of a story may be **stated** directly by the writer or one of the characters. In "Utzel and His Daughter, Poverty," there are several statements of the theme.

1. Find the place in the story where the character Sandler states the theme.
2. Find the place where the author, Isaac Bashevis Singer, states it.
3. How does the framed motto Utzel hangs on the wall also indicate the theme?

CRITICAL THINKING AND READING

Paraphrasing the Stated Theme

Paraphrasing a statement means putting it into your own words. By paraphrasing the stated theme, you will make sure that you really understand the story's point. You will gain more from your reading if you also think about this idea. It may turn out that you do not agree with what the writer is saying.

1. Paraphrase the stated theme of "Utzel and His Daughter, Poverty."
2. Explain why you agree or disagree with this idea.

SPEAKING AND LISTENING

Reading Dialogue in a Story

In a story, **dialogue** consists of the words characters say to each other. These words appear in quotation marks. To appreciate dialogue, you should try to imagine the way the different characters would talk. Sometimes a writer will tell you how a particular speech should sound by saying a character is "puzzled" or "happy" or "angry." However, you can also guess what characters sound like based on their personalities.

1. How do you imagine Utzel would speak through most of the story? Why?
2. With another person, read aloud the dialogue between Utzel and Sandler when Poverty first tries on her new shoes (page 150). Remember to use the writer's information about how these characters sound.

THINKING AND WRITING

Writing About a Motto

A **motto** is an expression that captures the goals or ideals of a person or group of people. At the end of the selection, Utzel chooses a motto for himself. Think about what this motto means and how it fits the way Utzel has changed. Draft a short essay explaining why you think it is or is not an appropriate motto for Utzel. Be sure to support your opinion with details from the story. Read over your essay, adding any details that would make your opinion more persuasive. Prepare a final draft and share it with your classmates.

GUIDE FOR READING

The Old Demon

Pearl Buck (1892–1973) was born in the United States, but her parents took her to China when she was still a baby. Altogether she lived in that country for nearly forty years and wrote about it in her stories, novels, plays, and essays. One of her novels about China, *The Good Earth,* was made into a successful motion picture. In 1938 Buck became the first American woman to win the Nobel Prize for literature. "The Old Demon" gives a picture of Chinese life in the late 1930's, when China was invaded and occupied by Japan.

Implied Theme

Stories often communicate important ideas about life, called **themes**. However, authors do not always state these ideas directly. Sometimes the theme of a story is **implied**, and you must figure it out for yourself. In "The Old Demon," for example, the theme is revealed through the actions of the major character, Mrs. Wang.

Look For

In this story the world that Mrs. Wang has known for many years vanishes before her eyes. As you read, try to determine the theme of the story by noticing how Mrs. Wang behaves and what she values during this time of crisis.

Writing

In "The Old Demon" the river changes forever the world that Mrs. Wang knows. Recall a time when you experienced, or saw a film about, a violent natural force like a flood or a storm. What effects did this force bring about? Freewrite about this time. In what way could it be called a demon?

Vocabulary

Knowing the following words will help you as you read "The Old Demon."

coarse (kôrs) *adj.:* Inferior; crude; common (p. 158)
wheedle (hwē′d'l) *v.:* Persuade a person by flattery or coaxing (p. 158)
inert (in urt′) *adj.:* Without power to move (p. 159)
somberly (säm′bər lē) *adv.:* Gloomily; dully (p. 160)
tentatively (ten′tə tiv lē) *adv.:* Hesitantly; uncertainly (p. 163)
impetuous (im pech′oo wəs) *adj.:* Moving with great force or violence (p. 164)
resolutely (rez′ə loot′lē) *adv.:* With a firm purpose (p. 164)

The Old Demon

Pearl S. Buck

Old Mrs. Wang knew, of course, that there was a war. Everybody had known for a long time that there was war going on and that Japanese were killing Chinese. But still it was not real and no more than hearsay since none of the Wangs had been killed. The Village of Three Mile Wangs on the flat banks of the Yellow River, which was old Mrs. Wang's clan village, had never seen a Japanese. This was how they came to be talking about Japanese at all.

It was evening and early summer, and after her supper Mrs. Wang had climbed the dike steps, as she did every day, to see how high the river had risen. She was much more afraid of the river than of the Japanese. She knew what the river would do. And one by one the villagers had followed her up the dike, and now they stood staring down at the malicious yellow water, curling along like a lot of snakes, and biting at the high dike banks.

"I never saw it as high as this so early," Mrs. Wang said. She sat down on a bamboo stool that her grandson, Little Pig, had brought for her, and spat into the water.

"It's worse than the Japanese, this old devil of a river," Little Pig said recklessly.

"Fool!" Mrs. Wang said quickly. "The river god will hear you. Talk about something else."

So they had gone on talking about the Japanese. . . . How, for instance, asked Wang, the baker, who was old Mrs. Wang's nephew twice removed, would they know the Japanese when they saw them?

Mrs. Wang at this point said positively, "You'll know them. I once saw a foreigner. He was taller than the eaves of my house and he had mud-colored hair and eyes the color of a fish's eyes. Anyone who does not look like us—that is a Japanese."

Then Little Pig spoke up in his disconcerting way. "You can't see them, Grandmother. They hide up in the sky in airplanes."

Mrs. Wang did not answer immediately. Once she would have said positively, "I shall not believe in an airplane until I see it." But so many things had been true which she had not believed—the Empress, for instance, whom she had not believed dead, was dead. The Republic,[1] again, she had not believed in because she did not know what it was. She still did not know, but they had said for a long time there had been one. So now she merely stared quietly about the dike where

---

1. The Republic: China became a republic, a state run by elected representatives, in 1912. Before that time, China had been ruled by emperors and empresses. When the Republic ended in 1949, China was taken over by communists.

they all sat around her. It was very pleasant and cool, and she felt nothing mattered if the river did not rise to flood.

"I don't believe in the Japanese," she said flatly.

They laughed at her a little, but no one spoke. Someone lit her pipe—it was Little Pig's wife, who was her favorite, and she smoked it.

"Sing, Little Pig!" someone called.

So Little Pig began to sing an old song in a high quavering voice, and old Mrs. Wang listened and forgot the Japanese. The evening was beautiful, the sky so clear and still that the willows overhanging the dike were reflected even in the muddy water. Everything was at peace. The thirty-odd houses which made up the village straggled along beneath them. Nothing could break this peace. After all, the Japanese were only human beings.

"I doubt those airplanes," she said mildly to Little Pig when he stopped singing.

But without answering her, he went on to another song.

Year in and year out she had spent the summer evenings like this on the dike. The first time she was seventeen and a bride, and her husband had shouted to her to come out of the house and up the dike, and she had come, blushing and twisting her hands together, to hide among the women while the men roared at her and made jokes about her. All the same, they had liked her. "A pretty piece of meat in your bowl," they had said to her husband. "Feet a trifle big," he had answered deprecatingly. But she could see he was pleased, and so gradually her shyness went away.

He, poor man, had been drowned in a flood when he was still young. And it had taken her years to get him prayed out of Buddhist purgatory.[2] Finally she had grown tired of it, what with the child and the land all on her back, and so when the priest said coaxingly, "Another ten pieces of silver and he'll be out entirely," she asked, "What's he got in there yet?"

"Only his right hand," the priest said, encouraging her.

Well, then, her patience broke. Ten dollars! It would feed them for the winter. Besides, she had had to hire labor for her share of repairing the dike, too, so there would be no more floods.

"If it's only one hand, he can pull himself out," she said firmly.

She often wondered if he had, poor silly fellow. As like as not, she had often thought gloomily in the night, he was still lying there, waiting for her to do something about it. That was the sort of man he was. Well, some day, perhaps, when Little Pig's wife had had the first baby safely and she had a little extra, she might go back to finish him out of purgatory. There was no real hurry, though. . . .

"Grandmother, you must go in," Little Pig's wife's soft voice said. "There is a mist rising from the river now that the sun is gone."

"Yes, I suppose I must," old Mrs. Wang agreed. She gazed at the river a moment. The river—it was full of good and evil together. It would water the fields when it was curbed and checked, but then if an inch were allowed it, it crashed through like a soaring dragon. That was how her husband had been swept away—careless, he was, about his bit of the dike. He was always go-

---

2. Buddhist purgatory (bood′ist pʉr′ gə tôr′ē): Buddhism is a religion popular in China and other Asian countries. Some Buddhists believe in purgatory, a place where the souls of certain dead people must stay until they can be freed.

ing to mend it, always going to pile more earth on top of it, and then in a night the river rose and broke through. He had run out of the house, and she had climbed on the roof with the child and had saved herself and it while he was drowned. Well, they had pushed the river back again behind its dikes, and it had stayed there this time. Every day she herself walked up and down the length of the dike for which the village was responsible and examined it. The men laughed and said, "If anything is wrong with the dikes, Granny will tell us."

It had never occurred to any of them to move the village away from the river. The Wangs had lived there for generations, and some had always escaped the floods and had fought the river more fiercely than ever afterward.

Little Pig suddenly stopped singing.

"The moon is coming up!" he cried. "That's not good. Airplanes come out on moonlight nights."

"Where do you learn all this about airplanes?" old Mrs. Wang exclaimed. "It is tiresome to me," she said, so severely that no one spoke. In this silence, leaning upon the arm of Little Pig's wife she descended slowly the earthen steps which led down into the village, using her long pipe in the other hand as a walking stick. Behind her the villagers came down, one by one, to bed. No one moved before she did, but none stayed long after her.

And in her own bed at last, behind the blue cotton mosquito curtains which Little Pig's wife fastened securely, she fell peacefully asleep. She had lain awake a little while thinking about the Japanese and wondering why they wanted to fight. Only very coarse persons wanted wars. In her mind she saw large coarse persons. If they came one must wheedle them, she thought, invite them to drink tea, and explain to them, reasonably—

only why should they come to a peaceful farming village . . . ?

So she was not in the least prepared for Little Pig's wife screaming at her that the Japanese had come. She sat up in bed muttering, "The tea bowls—the tea—"

"Grandmother, there's no time!" Little Pig's wife screamed. "They're here—they're here!"

"Where?" old Mrs. Wang cried, now awake.

"In the sky!" Little Pig's wife wailed.

They had all run out at that, into the clear early dawn, and gazed up. There, like wild geese flying in autumn, were great birdlike shapes.

"But what are they?" old Mrs. Wang cried.

And then, like a silver egg dropping, something drifted straight down and fell at the far end of the village in a field. A fountain of earth flew up, and they all ran to see it. There was a hole thirty feet across, as big as a pond. They were so astonished they could not speak, and then, before anyone could say anything, another and another egg began to fall and everybody was running, running . . .

Everybody, that is, but Mrs. Wang. When Little Pig's wife seized her hand to drag her along, old Mrs. Wang pulled away and sat down against the bank of the dike.

"I can't run," she remarked. "I haven't run in seventy years, since before my feet were bound. You go on. Where's Little Pig?" She looked around. Little Pig was already gone. "Like his grandfather," she remarked, "always the first to run."

But Little Pig's wife would not leave her, not, that is, until old Mrs. Wang reminded her that it was her duty.

"If Little Pig is dead," she said, "then it is necessary that his son be born alive." And when the girl still hesitated, she struck at her gently with her pipe. "Go on—go on," she exclaimed.

So unwillingly, because now they could scarcely hear each other speak for the roar of the dipping planes, Little Pig's wife went on with the others.

By now, although only a few minutes had passed, the village was in ruins and the straw roofs and wooden beams were blazing. Everybody was gone. As they passed they had shrieked at old Mrs. Wang to come on, and she had called back pleasantly:

"I'm coming—I'm coming!"

But she did not go. She sat quite alone watching now what was an extraordinary spectacle. For soon other planes came, from where she did not know, but they attacked the first ones. The sun came up over the fields of ripening wheat, and in the clear summery air the planes wheeled and darted and spat at each other. When this was over, she thought, she would go back into the village and see if anything was left. Here and there a wall stood, supporting a roof. She could not see her own house from here. But she was not unused to war. Once bandits had looted their village, and houses had been burned then, too. Well, now it had happened again. Burning houses one could see often, but not this darting silvery shining battle in the air. She understood none of it— not what those things were, nor how they stayed up in the sky. She simply sat, growing hungry, and watching.

"I'd like to see one close," she said aloud. And at that moment, as though in answer, one of them pointed suddenly downward, and, wheeling and twisting as though it were wounded, it fell head down in a field which Little Pig had ploughed only yesterday for soybeans. And in an instant the sky was empty again, and there was only this wounded thing on the ground and herself.

She hoisted herself carefully from the earth. At her age she need be afraid of nothing. She could, she decided, go and see what it was. So, leaning on her bamboo pipe, she made her way slowly across the fields. Behind her in the sudden stillness two or three village dogs appeared and followed, creeping close to her in their terror. When they drew near to the fallen plane, they barked furiously. Then she hit them with her pipe.

"Be quiet," she scolded, "there's already been noise enough to split my ears!"

She tapped the airplane.

"Metal," she told the dogs. "Silver, doubtless," she added. Melted up, it would make them all rich.

She walked around it, examining it closely. What made it fly? It seemed dead. Nothing moved or made a sound within it. Then, coming to the side to which it tipped, she saw a young man in it, slumped into a heap in a little seat. The dogs growled, but she struck at them again and they fell back.

"Are you dead?" she inquired politely.

The young man moved a little at her voice, but did not speak. She drew nearer and peered into the hole in which he sat. His side was bleeding.

"Wounded!" she exclaimed. She took his wrist. It was warm, but inert, and when she let it go, it dropped against the side of the hole. She stared at him. He had black hair and a dark skin like a Chinese and still he did not look like a Chinese.

"He must be a Southerner," she thought. Well, the chief thing was, he was alive.

"You had better come out," she remarked. "I'll put some herb plaster on your side."

The young man muttered something dully.

"What did you say?" she asked. But he did not say it again.

"I am still quite strong," she decided after a moment. So she reached in and seized him about the waist and pulled him out slowly, panting a good deal. Fortunately he was rather a little fellow and very light. When she had him on the ground, he seemed to find his feet; and he stood shakily and clung to her, and she held him up.

"Now if you can walk to my house," she said, "I'll see if it is there."

Then he said something, quite clearly. She listened and could not understand a word of it. She pulled away from him and stared.

"What's that?" she asked.

He pointed at the dogs. They were standing growling, their ruffs[3] up. Then he spoke again, and as he spoke he crumpled to the ground. The dogs fell on him, so that she had to beat them off with her hands.

"Get away!" she shouted. "Who told *you* to kill him?"

And then, when they had slunk back, she heaved him somehow onto her back; and, trembling, half carrying, half pulling him, she dragged him to the ruined village and laid him in the street while she went to find her house, taking the dogs with her.

Her house was quite gone. She found the place easily enough. This was where it should be, opposite the water gate into the dike. She had always watched that gate herself. Miraculously it was not injured now, nor was the dike broken. It would be easy enough to rebuild the house. Only, for the present, it was gone.

So she went back to the young man. He was lying as she had left him, propped against the dike, panting and very pale. He had opened his coat and he had a little bag from which he was taking out strips of cloth

and a bottle of something. And again he spoke, and again she understood nothing. Then he made signs and she saw it was water he wanted, so she took up a broken pot from one of many blown about the street, and, going up the dike, she filled it with river water and brought it down again and washed his wound, and she tore off the strips he made from the rolls of bandaging. He knew how to put the cloth over the gaping wound and he made signs to her, and she followed these signs. All the time he was trying to tell her something, but she could understand nothing.

"You must be from the South, sir," she said. It was easy to see that he had education. He looked very clever. "I have heard your language is different from ours." She laughed a little to put him at his ease, but he only stared at her somberly with dull eyes. So she said brightly, "Now if I could find something for us to eat, it would be nice."

He did not answer. Indeed he lay back, panting still more heavily, and stared into space as though she had not spoken.

---

3. ruffs (rufs) *n*.: Bands of fur around their necks.

"You would be better with food," she went on. "And so would I," she added. She was beginning to feel unbearably hungry.

It occurred to her that in Wang, the baker's, shop there might be some bread. Even if it were dusty with fallen mortar, it would still be bread. She would go and see. But before she went she moved the soldier a little so that he lay in the edge of shadow cast by a willow tree that grew in the bank of the dike. Then she went to the baker's shop. The dogs were gone.

The baker's shop was, like everything else, in ruins. No one was there. At first she saw nothing but the mass of crumpled earthen walls. But then she remembered that the oven was just inside the door, and the door frame still stood erect, supporting one end of the roof. She stood in this frame, and, running her hand in underneath the fallen roof inside, she felt the wooden cover of the iron caldron. Under this there might be steamed bread. She worked her arm delicately and carefully in. It took quite a long time, but, even so, clouds of lime and dust almost choked her. Nevertheless she was right. She squeezed her hand under the cover and felt the firm smooth skin of the big steamed bread rolls, and one by one she drew out four.

"It's hard to kill an old thing like me," she remarked cheerfully to no one, and she began to eat one of the rolls as she walked back. If she had a bit of garlic and a bowl of tea—but one couldn't have everything in these times.

It was at this moment that she heard voices. When she came in sight of the soldier, she saw surrounding him a crowd of other soldiers, who had apparently come from nowhere. They were staring down at the wounded soldier, whose eyes were now closed.

"Where did you get this Japanese, Old Mother?" they shouted at her.

"What Japanese?" she asked coming to them.

"This one!" they shouted.

"Is he a Japanese?" she cried in the greatest astonishment. "But he looks like us—his eyes are black, his skin—"

"Japanese!" one of them shouted at her.

"Well," she said quietly, "he dropped out of the sky."

"Give me that bread!" another shouted.

"Take it," she said, "all except this one for him."

"A Japanese monkey eat good bread?" the soldier shouted.

"I suppose he is hungry also," old Mrs. Wang replied. She began to dislike these men. But then, she had always disliked soldiers.

"I wish you would go away," she said. "What are you doing here? Our village has always been peaceful."

"It certainly looks very peaceful now," one of the men said, grinning, "as peaceful as a grave. Do you know who did that, Old Mother? The Japanese!"

"I suppose so," she agreed. Then she asked, "Why? That's what I don't understand."

"Why? Because they want our land, that's why!"

"Our land!" she repeated. "Why, they can't have our land!"

"Never!" they shouted.

But all this time while they were talking and chewing the bread they had divided among themselves, they were watching the eastern horizon.

"Why do you keep looking east?" old Mrs. Wang now asked.

"The Japanese are coming from there," the man replied who had taken the bread.

"Are you running away from them?" she asked, surprised.

"There are only a handful of us," he said apologetically. "We were left to guard a village—Pao An, in the county of—"

"I know that village," old Mrs. Wang interrupted. "You needn't tell me. I was a girl there. How is the old Pao who keeps the teashop in the main street? He's my brother."

"Everybody is dead there," the man replied. "The Japanese have taken it—a great army of men came with their foreign guns and tanks, so what could we do?"

"Of course, only run," she agreed. Nevertheless she felt dazed and sick. So he was dead, that one brother she had left! She was now the last of her father's family.

But the soldiers were straggling away again leaving her alone.

"They'll be coming, those little black dwarfs," they were saying. "We'd best go on."

Nevertheless, one lingered a moment, the one who had taken the bread, to stare down at the young wounded man, who lay with his eyes shut, not having moved at all.

"Is he dead?" he inquired. Then, before Mrs. Wang could answer, he pulled a short knife out of his belt. "Dead or not, I'll give him a punch or two with this—"

But old Mrs Wang pushed his arm away.

"No, you won't," she said with authority. "If he is dead, then there is no use in sending him into purgatory all in pieces. I am a good Buddhist myself."

The man laughed. "Oh well, he is dead," he answered; and then, seeing his comrades already at a distance, he ran after them.

A Japanese, was he? Old Mrs. Wang, left alone with this inert figure, looked at him tentatively. He was very young, she could see, now that his eyes were closed. His hand, limp in unconsciousness, looked like a boy's hand, unformed and still growing. She felt his wrist but could discern no pulse. She leaned over him and held to his lips the half of her roll which she had not eaten.

"Eat," she said very loudly and distinctly. "Bread!"

But there was no answer. Evidently he

was dead. He must have died while she was getting the bread out of the oven.

There was nothing to do then but to finish the bread herself. And when that was done, she wondered if she ought not to follow after Little Pig and his wife and all the villagers. The sun was mounting and it was growing hot. If she were going, she had better go. But first she would climb the dike and see what the direction was. They had gone straight west, and as far as eye could look westward was a great plain. She might even see a good-sized crowd miles away. Anyway, she could see the next village, and they might all be there.

So she climbed the dike slowly, getting very hot. There was a slight breeze on top of the dike and it felt good. She was shocked to see the river very near the top of the dike. Why, it had risen in the last hour!

"You old demon!" she said severely. Let the river god hear it if he liked. He was evil, that he was—so to threaten flood when there had been all this other trouble.

She stooped and bathed her cheeks and her wrists. The water was quite cold, as though with fresh rains somewhere. Then she stood up and gazed around her. To the west there was nothing except in the far distance the soldiers still half-running, and beyond them the blur of the next village, which stood on a long rise of ground. She had better set out for that village. Doubtless Little Pig and his wife were there waiting for her.

Just as she was about to climb down and start out, she saw something on the eastern horizon. It was at first only an immense cloud of dust. But, as she stared at it, very quickly it became a lot of black dots and shining spots. Then she saw what it was. It was a lot of men—an army. Instantly she knew what army.

"That's the Japanese," she thought. Yes,

above them were the buzzing silver planes. They circled about, seeming to search for someone.

"I don't know who you're looking for," she muttered, "unless it's me and Little Pig and his wife. We're the only ones left. You've already killed my brother Pao."

She had almost forgotten that Pao was dead. Now she remembered it acutely. He had such a nice shop—always clean, and the tea good and the best meat dumplings to be had and the price always the same. Pao was a good man. Besides, what about his wife and his seven children? Doubtless they were all killed, too. Now these Japanese were looking for her. It occurred to her that on the dike she could easily be seen. So she clambered hastily down.

It was when she was about halfway down that she thought of the water gate. This old river—it had been a curse to them since time began. Why should it not make up a little now for all the wickedness it had done? It was plotting wickedness again, trying to steal over its banks. Well, why not? She wavered a moment. It was a pity, of course, that the young dead Japanese would be swept into the flood. He was a nice-looking boy, and she had saved him from being stabbed. It was not quite the same as saving his life, of course, but still it was a little the same. If he had been alive, he would have been saved. She went over to him and tugged at him until he lay well under the top of the bank. Then she went down again.

She knew perfectly how to open the water gate. Any child knew how to open the sluice for crops. But she knew also how to swing open the whole gate. The question was, could she open it quickly enough to get out of the way?

"I'm only one old woman," she muttered. She hesitated a second more. Well, it would be a pity not to see what sort of a baby Little Pig's wife would have, but one could not see everything. She had seen a great deal in this life. There was an end to what one could see, anyway.

She glanced again to the east. There were the Japanese coming across the plain. They were a long clear line of black, dotted with thousands of glittering points. If she opened this gate, the impetuous water would roar toward them, rushing into the plains, rolling into a wide lake, drowning them, maybe. Certainly they could not keep on marching nearer and nearer to her, and to Little Pig and his wife who were waiting for her. Well, Little Pig and his wife—they would wonder about her—but they would never dream of this. It would make a good story— she would have enjoyed telling it.

She turned resolutely to the gate. Well, some people fought with airplanes and some with guns, but you could fight with a river, too, if it were a wicked one like this one. She wrenched out a huge wooden pin. It was slippery with silvery green moss. The rill of water burst into a strong jet. When she wrenched one more pin, the rest would give way themselves. She began pulling at it, and felt it slip a little from its hole.

"I might be able to get myself out of purgatory with this," she thought, "and maybe they'll let me have that old man of mine, too. What's a hand of his to all this? Then we'll—"

The pin slipped away suddenly, and the gate burst flat against her and knocked her breath away. She had only time to gasp, to the river:

"Come on, you old demon!"

Then she felt it seize her and lift her up to the sky. It was beneath her and around her. It rolled her joyfully hither and thither, and then, holding her close and enfolded, it went rushing against the enemy.

THINKING ABOUT THE SELECTION

Recalling

1. How did Mrs. Wang save herself and her child when her husband died?
2. What did she do for her husband after his death?
3. Why do the other people of her village run away?
4. How does she react when a soldier tries to kill the Japanese pilot?
5. How does she try to protect her land from the enemy?

Interpreting

6. In what ways is Mrs. Wang a person who protects and supports life?
7. In what ways does Mrs. Wang share some of the river's strength?
8. Explain the meaning of the story's title.

Applying

9. Although the Japanese pilot is an enemy, Mrs. Wang tries to help him. Do you think it is easier to fight an enemy you cannot see than one you can see? Explain your answer.

ANALYZING LITERATURE

Recognizing an Implied Theme

An **implied theme** is an idea about life that is suggested through a story. In "The Old Demon," the theme is suggested by the character of Mrs. Wang.

1. How does Mrs. Wang show that she values her family and her village?
2. What does her attempt to rescue the pilot reveal about her?
3. Which of the following statements best seems to express the implied theme of the story? Explain your answer.

a. Do not become involved with matters outside your family or community.
b. War is evil.
c. People should protect and care for each other.

4. How would you express the theme?

CRITICAL THINKING AND READING

Summarizing a Story

A **summary** of a story is a brief form of it containing the most important events in the order they occurred. By summarizing a story with many events like "The Old Demon," you can remember it more easily. Follow these steps in preparing a summary:

1. Reread the story
2. Decide which events are the most important
3. List these events in the order they occurred
4. Give a brief account of each one in your own words

Practice your summarizing skills on "The Old Demon."

1. Write a summary of the story.
2. When revising your summary, make sure it is brief but includes the key events.

THINKING AND WRITING

Responding to the Implied Theme

In "The Old Demon," the writer suggests that a person who protects and cares for others should be admired. List the reasons why you agree or disagree with this idea. Include examples to support your reasons. Then use your list to write a composition explaining your position. As you revise your work, check to see whether you have backed up your argument with good examples. Finally, share your composition with your classmates.

GUIDE FOR READING

Humaweepi, the Warrior Priest

Leslie Marmon Silko (1948–   ), who was born in Albuquerque, New Mexico, was raised as a Pueblo Indian. Though her background is not entirely Pueblo, she identifies strongly with this tradition. She has explored its meaning in her well-known novel *Ceremony* (1977). Silko once said about the Laguna Pueblo reservation: "This place I am from is everything I am as a writer and a human being." "Humaweepi, the Warrior Priest" communicates Silko's strong feeling for the Southwest and for American Indian ways.

Key to Theme: Character

The way a character in a story grows or changes is often a key to the theme. Sometimes characters grow because they are helped by others. In "Humaweepi, the Warrior Priest" a Pueblo boy's uncle helps him to become a warrior priest by teaching him about nature and tribal traditions. By focusing on the boy's development, you can understand the implied theme of the story.

Look For

As you read "Humaweepi, the Warrior Priest," look for each of the lessons the uncle teaches the boy. What do these lessons reveal about life in general?

Writing

List some of the important skills you have learned from your parents or other adults. You can include knowledge you have gained simply by observing the way someone behaves.

Vocabulary

Knowing the following words will help you as you read "Humaweepi, the Warrior Priest."

clan (klan) *n.*: A group of people, usually relatives (p. 167)
crevasses (kri vas′ əz) *n.*: Deep cracks (p. 168)
lacy (lā′sē) *adj.*: Having a delicate, open pattern, like lace (p. 168)
fragile (fraj′′l) *adj.*: Delicate; easily broken (p. 168)

derive (di rīv′) *v.*: To receive from someone or something (p. 169)
succulent (suk′yo͞o lənt) *adj.*: Juicy (p. 169)
triumphantly (trī um′fənt lē) *adv.*: Victoriously; successfully (p. 171)

from Humaweepi, the Warrior Priest

Leslie Marmon Silko

The old man didn't really teach him much; mostly they just lived. Occasionally Humaweepi would meet friends his own age who still lived with their families in the pueblo,[1] and they would ask him what he was doing; they seemed disappointed when he told them.

"That's nothing," they would say.

Once this had made Humaweepi sad and his uncle noticed. "Oh," he said when Humaweepi told him, "that shows you how little they know."

They returned to the pueblo for the ceremonials and special days. His uncle stayed in the kiva[2] with the other priests, and Humaweepi usually stayed with clan members because his mother and father had been very old when he was born and now they were gone. Sometimes during these stays, when the pueblo was full of the activity and excitement of the dances or the fiesta[3] when the Christians paraded out of the pueblo church carrying the saint, Humaweepi would wonder why he was living out in the hills with the old man. When he was twelve he thought he had it all figured out: the old man just wanted someone to live with him and help him with the goat and to chop wood and carry water. But it was peaceful in this place, and Humaweepi discovered that after all these years of sitting beside his uncle in the evenings, he knew the songs and chants for all the seasons, and he was beginning to learn the prayers for the trees and plants and animals. "Oh," Humaweepi said to himself, "I have been learning all this time and I didn't even know it."

Once the old man told Humaweepi to prepare for a long trip.

"Overnight?"

The old man nodded.

So Humaweepi got out a white cotton sack and started filling it with jerked venison,[4] piki bread,[5] and dried apples. But the old man shook his head sternly. It was late June then, so Humaweepi didn't bother to bring the blankets; he had learned to sleep on the ground like the old man did.

"Human beings are special," his uncle had told him once, "which means they can do anything. They can sleep on the ground like the doe and fawn."

And so Humaweepi had learned how to find the places in the scrub-oak thickets

---

1. pueblo (pweb′ lō) *n.*: A type of Native American village in the Southwest where families lived together in flat-roofed houses of stone or adobe.

2. kiva (kē′ və) *n.*: A large room in a pueblo dwelling used for religious or other purposes.

3. fiesta (fē eś tə) *n.*: A religious festival.

4. jerked venison: Deer meat that has been sliced into thin strips and dried in the sun to preserve it.

5. piki (pē′ kē) **bread:** Corn bread.

where the deer had slept, where the dry oak leaves were arranged into nests. This is where he and his uncle slept, even in the autumn when the nights were cold and Humaweepi could hear the leaves snap in the middle of the night and drift to the ground.

Sometimes they carried food from home, but often they went without food or blankets. When Humaweepi asked him what they would eat, the old man had waved his hand at the sky and earth around them. "I am a human being, Humaweepi," he said: "I eat anything." On these trips they had gathered grass roots and washed them in little sandstone basins made by the wind to catch rain water. The roots had a rich, mealy taste. Then they left the desert below and climbed into the mesa[6] country, and the old man had led Humaweepi to green leafy vines hanging from crevasses in the face of the sandstone cliffs. "Wild grapes," he said as he dropped some tiny dark-purple berries into Humaweepi's open palms. And in the high mountains there were wild iris roots and the bulbs from wild tulips which grew among the lacy ferns and green grass beside the mountain streams. They had gone out like this in each season. Summer and fall, and finally, spring and winter. "Winter isn't easy," the old man had said. "All the animals are hungry—not just you."

So this time, when his uncle shook his head at the food, Humaweepi left it behind as he had many times before. His uncle took the special leather pouch off the nail on the wall, and Humaweepi pulled his own buckskin bundle out from under his mattress. Inside he had a few objects of his own. A dried blossom. Fragile and yellow. A smooth pink

---

6. mesa (mā′ sə) *adj.*: Flat tableland with steep sides (usually a noun).

quartz crystal in the shape of a star. Tiny turquoise beads the color of a summer sky. And a black obsidian[7] arrowhead, shiny and sharp. They each had special meaning to him, and the old man had instructed him to assemble these things with special meaning. "Someday maybe you will derive strength from these things." That's what the old man had said.

They walked west toward the distant blue images of the mountain peaks. The water in the Rio Grande was still cold. Humaweepi was aware of the dampness on his feet; when he got back from the journey he decided he would make sandals for himself because it took hours for his boots to dry out again. His uncle wore old sandals woven from twisted yucca[8] fiber and they dried out almost immediately. The old man didn't approve of boots and shoes—bad for you, he said. In the winter he wore buckskin moccasins and in the warm months, these yucca sandals.

They walked all day, steadily, stopping occasionally when the old man found a flower or herb or stone that he wanted Humaweepi to see. And it seemed to Humaweepi that he had learned the names of everything, and he said so to his uncle.

The old man frowned and poked at a small blue flower with his walking stick. "That's what a priest must know," he said and walked rapidly then, pointing at stones and shrubs. "How old are you?" he demanded.

"Nineteen," Humaweepi answered.

"All your life," he said, "every day, I have been teaching you."

After that they walked along in silence, and Humaweepi began to feel anxious; all of a sudden he knew that something was going to happen on this journey. That night they reached the white sandstone cliffs at the foot of the mountain foothills. At the base of these cliffs were shallow overhangs with sandy floors. They slept in the sand under the rock overhang; in the night Humaweepi woke up to the call of a young owl; the sky was bright with stars and a half-moon. The smell of the night air made him shiver and he buried himself more deeply in the cliff sand.

In the morning they gathered tumbleweed sprouts that were succulent and tender. As they climbed the cliffs there were wild grapevines, and under the fallen leaves around the vine roots, the old man uncovered dried grapes shrunken into tiny sweet raisins. By noon they had reached the first of the mountain streams. There they washed and drank water and rested.

The old man frowned and pointed at Humaweepi's boots. "Take them off," he told Humaweepi; "leave them here until we come back."

So Humaweepi pulled off his cowboy boots and put them under a lichen-covered[9] boulder near a big oak tree where he could find them. Then Humaweepi relaxed, feeling the coolness of air on his bare feet. He watched his uncle, dozing in the sun with his back against a big pine. The old man's hair had been white and long ever since Humaweepi could remember; but the old face was changing, and Humaweepi could see the weariness there—a weariness not from their little journey but from a much longer time in this world. Someday he will die, Humaweepi was thinking. He will be gone and I will be by myself. I will have to do the things he did. I will have to take care of things.

Humaweepi had never seen the lake be-

---

7. obsidian (əb sid′ ē ən) *adj.*: Made of hard, black glass that comes from volcanoes (usually a noun).

8. yucca (yuk′ ə) *adj.*: Plants with stiff sword-shaped leaves and white flowers (usually a noun).

---

9. lichen (lī′ kən)**-covered:** Covered with small plants forming a crustlike growth.

fore. It appeared suddenly as they reached the top of a hill covered with aspen trees. Humaweepi looked at his uncle and was going to ask him about the lake, but the old man was singing and feeding corn pollen from his leather pouch to the mountain winds. Humaweepi stared at the lake and listened to the songs. The songs were snowstorms with sounds as soft and cold as snowflakes; the songs were spring rain and wild ducks returning. Humaweepi could hear this; he could hear his uncle's voice become the night wind—high-pitched and whining in the trees. Time was lost and there was only the space, the depth, the distance of the lake surrounded by the mountain peaks.

When Humaweepi looked up from the lake he noticed that the sun had moved down into the western part of the sky. He looked around to find his uncle. The old man was below him, kneeling on the edge of the lake, touching a big gray boulder and singing softly. Humaweepi made his way down the narrow rocky trail to the edge of the lake. The water was crystal and clear like air; Humaweepi could see the golden rainbow colors of the trout that lived there. Finally the old man motioned for Humaweepi to come to him. He pointed at the gray boulder that lay half in the lake and half on the shore. It was then that Humaweepi saw what it was. The bear. Magic creature of the mountains, powerful ally to men. Humaweepi unrolled his buckskin bundle and picked up the tiny beads—sky-blue turquoise and coral that was dark red. He sang the bear song and stepped into the icy, clear water to lay the beads on bear's head, gray granite rock, resting above the lake, facing west.

> "Bear
>
>   resting in the mountains
>   sleeping by the lake

> Bear
>
>   I come to you, a man,
>   to ask you:
> Stand beside us in our battles
>   walk with us in peace.
> Bear
>
>   I ask you for your power
>   I am the warrior priest
>   I ask you for your power
>   I am the warrior priest."

It wasn't until he had finished singing the song that Humaweepi realized what the words said. He turned his head toward the old man. He smiled at Humaweepi and nodded his head. Humaweepi nodded back.

Speaking to a friend, Humaweepi describes a trip he took with his uncle.

Humaweepi and his friend were silent for a long time. Finally Humaweepi said, "I'll tell you what my uncle told me, one winter, before he left. We took a trip to the mountain. It was early January, but the sun was warm and down here the snow was gone. We left early in the morning when the sky in the east was dark gray and the brightest star was still shining low in the western sky. I remember he didn't wear his ceremonial moccasins; he wore his old yucca sandals. I asked him about that.

"He said, 'Oh, you know the badger and the squirrel. Same shoes summer and winter,' but I think he was making that up, because when we got to the sandstone cliffs he buried the sandals in the sandy bottom of the cave where we slept and after that he walked on bare feet—up the cliff and along the mountain trail.

"There was snow on the shady side of the trees and big rocks, but the path we followed was in the sun and it was dry. I could hear melting snow—the icy water trickling down into the little streams and the little streams flowing into the big stream in the canyon where yellow bee flowers grow all summer. The sun felt warm on my body, touching me, but my breath still made steam in the cold mountain air.

" 'Aren't your feet cold?' I asked him.

"He stopped and looked at me for a long time, then shook his head. 'Look at these old feet,' he said. 'Do you see any corns or bunions?'

"I shook my head.

" 'That's right,' he said, 'my feet are beautiful. No one has feet like these. Especially you people who wear shoes and boots.' He walked on ahead before he said anything else. 'You have seen babies, haven't you?' he asked.

"I nodded, but I was wondering what this had to do with the old man's feet.

" 'Well, then you've noticed their grandmothers and their mothers, always worried about keeping the feet warm. But have you watched the babies? Do they care? No!' the old man said triumphantly, 'they do not care. They play outside on a cold winter day, no shoes, no jacket, because they aren't cold.' He hiked on, moving rapidly, excited by his own words; then he stopped at the stream. 'But human beings are what they are. It's not long before they are taught to be cold and they cry for their shoes.'

"The old man started digging around the edge of a stream, using a crooked, dry branch to poke through the melting snow. 'Here,' he said as he gave me a fat, round root, 'try this.'

"I squatted at the edge of the rushing, swirling water, full of mountain dirt, churning, and rolling—rich and brown and muddy with ice pieces flashing in the sun. I held the root motionless under the force of the stream water; the ice coldness of the water felt pure and clear as the ice that clung to the rocks in midstream. When I pulled my hand back it was stiff. I shook it and the root and lifted them high toward the sky.

"The old man laughed, and his mouth was full of the milky fibers of the root. He walked up the hill, away from the sound of the muddy stream surging through the snowbanks. At the top of the hill there was a grove of big aspens; it was colder, and the snow hadn't melted much.

" 'Your feet,' I said to him. 'They'll freeze.

"The snow was up to my ankles now. He was sitting on a fallen aspen, with his feet stretched out in front of him and his eyes half closed, facing into the sun.

" 'Does the wolf freeze his feet?' the old man asked me.

"I shook my head.

" 'Well then,' he said.

" 'But you aren't a wolf,' I started to say.

"The old man's eyes opened wide and then looked at me narrowly, sharply, squinting and shining. He gave a long, wailing, wolf cry with his head raised toward the winter sky.

"It was all white—pale white—the sky, the aspens bare white, smooth and white as the snow frozen on the ground. The wolf cry echoed off the rocky mountain slopes around us; in the distance, I thought I heard a wailing answer."

THINKING ABOUT THE SELECTION

Recalling

1. When Humaweepi was twelve, why did he think his uncle wanted them to live together?
2. What kinds of things has Humaweepi learned from his uncle through the years?
3. What does Humaweepi think after seeing the weariness in his uncle's face?
4. On one of their trips, how does his uncle respond when Humaweepi tells the barefoot old man that he isn't a wolf?

Interpreting

5. Why does Humaweepi's uncle take him on trips?
6. In his song Humaweepi asks the "Bear" for its "power." What kind of "power" do you think he wants?
7. Why do Humaweepi and his uncle nod at each other when the song is over?
8. Give three examples showing that Humaweepi's uncle feels close to nature.
9. At the beginning of the story, the author writes, "The old man didn't really teach him much; mostly they just lived." Do you think the author means you to take this statement at face value? Explain your answer.

Applying

10. Compare and contrast Humaweepi's education with the way most people learn in school.

ANALYZING LITERATURE

Understanding Theme

The way a character grows is often a good clue to the theme of a story. In "Humaweepi, the Warrior Priest," the boy realizes that "sitting beside his uncle," he had "been learning all this time and . . . didn't even know it."

1. Briefly describe what Humaweepi learns from his uncle.

2. What evidence is there that the old man wants Humaweepi to take his place after he dies?
3. Choose one of the following ideas and explain why it best expresses the story's theme:
   a. Tradition is less important than freedom of expression.
   b. Young people learn about traditions from their elders.
   c. It is harmful to live apart from other people.
4. How would you express the theme of this story?

CRITICAL THINKING AND READING

Recognizing the Writer's Purpose

In this story the writer teaches you about Native American traditions, while presenting insights into life. Just as Humaweepi learns from his uncle almost without knowing it, you also learn about the Pueblo heritage.

1. Find two examples that show that Native Americans have a deep understanding of plants or animals.
2. What evidence is there that Native Americans believe there is a living spirit in things that might not seem alive to others?
3. How is a "warrior priest" different from and similar to other teachers or religious leaders?

THINKING AND WRITING

Responding to Theme

Imagine that Humaweepi's uncle suddenly arrives at your door. He wants to take you and your best friend on one of his trips to the mountains. You want to go on the trip but your friend is not as enthusiastic. List the reasons that would convince your friend to support the decision to go on the trip. Then use the list to write a persuasive note to your friend. When you are finished, revise the note to make sure it will work.

GUIDE FOR READING

Home

Gwendolyn Brooks (1917–   ) was born in Topeka, Kansas, and grew up in Chicago, Illinois. In 1950 she won the Pulitzer Prize for poetry, and she has received other honors for her writing. She once remarked on her work by saying, "I like to vivify [give life to] the universal fact . . . but the universal wears contemporary clothing very well." What Brooks meant by this is illustrated in "Home." The universal fact of people's attachment to their home is vividly depicted in this brief story of a black American family faced with the loss of theirs.

Universal Theme

A **theme** is the central idea of a story, or the general idea about life that the story reveals. A **universal theme** is one that has meaning and importance for people all over the world. Usually such a theme will be implied rather than stated directly.

Look For

As you read "Home," ask yourself, "What does this home mean to the characters in this story? What universal truth does this story reveal about the importance of home to anyone, living anywhere?"

Writing

A house provides shelter, but a home provides much more. Freewrite about the meaning of the word *home.*

Vocabulary

Knowing the following words will help you as you read "Home."
obstinate (äb'stə nit) *adj.*: Stubborn (p. 175)
emphatic (im fat'ik) *adj.*: Felt with emphasis; forceful; definite (p. 175)
staccato (stə kät'ō) *adj.*: Made up of sharp separate little elements (p. 176)
emerged (i murj'd) *v.*: Became visible (p. 176)

Home

Gwendolyn Brooks

What had been wanted was this always, this always to last, the talking softly on this porch, with the snake plant in the jardiniere[1] in the southwest corner, and the obstinate slip from Aunt Eppie's magnificent Michigan fern at the left side of the friendly door. Mama, Maud Martha and Helen rocked slowly in their rocking chairs, and looked at the late afternoon light on the lawn, and at the emphatic iron of the fence and at the poplar tree.

These things might soon be theirs no longer. Those shafts and pools of light, the tree, the graceful iron, might soon be viewed possessively by different eyes.

Papa was to have gone that noon, during his lunch hour, to the office of the Home Owners' Loan. If he had not succeeded in getting another extension, they would be leaving this house in which they had lived for more than fourteen years. There was little hope. The Home Owners' Loan was hard. They sat, making their plans.

"We'll be moving into a nice flat[2] somewhere," said Mama. "Somewhere on South Park, or Michigan, or in Washington Park Court." Those flats, as the girls and Mama knew well, were burdens on wages twice the size of Papa's. This was not mentioned now.

"They're much prettier than this old house," said Helen. "I have friends I'd just as soon not bring here. And I have other friends that wouldn't come down this far for anything, unless they were in a taxi."

Yesterday, Maud Martha would have attacked her. Tomorrow she might. Today she said nothing. She merely gazed at a little hopping robin in the tree, her tree, and tried to keep the fronts of her eyes dry.

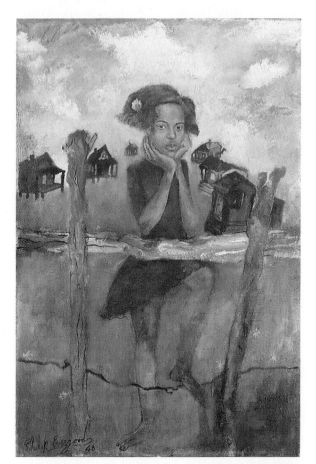

HER WORLD
Philip Evergood
The Metropolitan Museum of Art

---

1. jardiniere (jär'd'n ir') *n.*: An ornamental bowl, pot, or stand for flowers or plants.
2. flat (flat) *n.*: An apartment.

"Well, I do know," said Mama, turning her hands over and over, "that I've been getting tireder and tireder of doing that firing.[3] From October to April, there's firing to be done."

"But lately we've been helping, Harry and I," said Maud Martha. "And sometimes in March and April and in October, and even in November, we could build a little fire in the fireplace. Sometimes the weather was just right for that."

She knew, from the way they looked at her, that this had been a mistake. They did not want to cry.

But she felt that the little line of white, somewhat ridged with smoked purple, and all that cream-shot saffron,[4] would never drift across any western sky except that in back of this house. The rain would drum with as sweet a dullness nowhere but here. The birds on South Park were mechanical birds, no better than the poor caught canaries in those "rich" women's sun parlors.

"It's just going to kill Papa!" burst out Maud Martha. "He loves this house! He *lives* for this house!"

"He lives for us," said Helen. "It's us he loves. He wouldn't want the house, except for us."

"And he'll have us," added Mama, "wherever."

"You know," Helen sighed, "if you want to know the truth, this is a relief. If this hadn't come up, we would have gone on, just dragged on, hanging out here forever."

"It might," allowed Mama, "be an act of God. God may just have reached down, and picked up the reins."

"Yes," Maud Martha cracked in, "that's what you always say—that God knows best."

Her mother looked at her quickly, decided the statement was not suspect, looked away.

Helen saw Papa coming. "There's Papa," said Helen.

They could not tell a thing from the way Papa was walking. It was that same dear little staccato walk, one shoulder down, then the other, then repeat, and repeat. They watched his progress. He passed the Kennedys', he passed the vacant lot, he passed Mrs. Blakemore's. They wanted to hurl themselves over the fence, into the street, and shake the truth out of his collar. He opened his gate—the gate—and still his stride and face told them nothing.

"Hello," he said.

Mama got up and followed him through the front door. The girls knew better than to go in too.

Presently Mama's head emerged. Her eyes were lamps turned on.

"It's all right," she exclaimed. "He got it. It's all over. Everything is all right."

The door slammed shut. Mama's footsteps hurried away.

"I think," said Helen, rocking rapidly, "I think I'll give a party. I haven't given a party since I was eleven. I'd like some of my friends to just casually see that we're homeowners."

---

3. firing (fir´ iŋ) *n.*: Starting up and tending the fire in a stove or furnace.

4. saffron: (saf´ rən) An orange-yellow color.

THINKING ABOUT THE SELECTION

Recalling

1. What problem does the family face in "Home"?
2. What does Papa hope to do during his lunch hour to deal with this problem?
3. According to Helen, why does Papa want to keep the house?

Interpreting

4. How do Mama and the girls feel before Helen sees Papa returning?
5. How do Mama and the girls feel as they watch Papa approaching?
6. At the end Helen gets the idea of giving a party. What does this idea suggest about what she is feeling?

Applying

7. What are the conditions that would make moving to a new home a happy event?

ANALYZING LITERATURE

Understanding Universal Themes

A theme is **universal** when readers the world over can respond to it. "Home," for example, presents a black family living in Chicago sometime during this century. Yet the problem the family faces and the feelings these people have would be understood by people in China, South America, Italy, or anywhere else.

1. Find three passages in the story where love of home is revealed.
2. In your own words tell what idea the story suggests about love of home.
3. Why could people living anywhere respond to this idea?

CRITICAL THINKING AND READING

Reading Between the Lines

The expression *reading between the lines* means reading to grasp and understand what is not said directly. For example, consider this sentence from "Home": "The rain would drum with as sweet a dullness nowhere but here." In reality, the sound of rain is basically the same everywhere. But what is said "between the lines" is that Maud Martha is so attached to her home that she cannot imagine how another house can be as pleasant when it is raining. What can you read between the lines of the following sentences from "Home"?

1. "What had been wanted was this always, this always to last, the talking softly on this porch . . ."
2. "The birds on South Park were mechanical birds, no better than the poor caught canaries in those 'rich' women's sun parlors."

UNDERSTANDING LANGUAGE

Finding Synonyms

A **synonym** is a word that has the same or nearly the same meaning as another word. A dictionary or a thesaurus, which gives lists of synonyms for a word, can help you find synonyms. Using either of these books, find a synonym for each of the following words from "Home":

1. wages
2. gaze
3. hurl
4. stride
5. exclaim
6. presently

THINKING AND WRITING

Writing About Theme

One critic has identified a major theme in Gwendolyn Brooks's work as the need for stability, order, and beauty to keep life pleasant. Write a short composition explaining how "Home" reveals that these three qualities are necessary for a good life. Before you write your composition, take each one of these qualities and look for a passage in the story that suggests it is needed or wanted. (You may have to read between the lines to do this.) Then prepare your first draft. When you revise your composition, check that your statements all support your main point. Share your composition with your classmates.

GUIDE FOR READING

Hallucination

Isaac Asimov (1920–   ) was born in Russia and raised in Brooklyn, New York. He has written hundreds of books, many of which are science-fiction. Asimov's love of science fiction developed when he began reading the science-fiction magazines sold in his father's candy store. In a way this childhood reading can be considered the earliest inspiration for "Hallucination," a story in which Asimov probes the mysteries of communication between two worlds.

Theme in Science Fiction

The **theme** of a story is its central idea, or the general idea about life it reveals. In a science-fiction story, a science-fiction theme will often apply to life as we know it. Because the story is often set far away in space or time and the characters and events are strange and unusual, however, you are likely to see the theme in a new light—a way that makes it more vivid and memorable.

Look For

As you read "Hallucination," look for all that is said about the effects of fear on the human mind. Pay attention to how each character reacts to strange and unusual experiences. By keeping these details in mind and determining why Sam is able to communicate with the alien life form when others could not, you will come to understand the theme.

Writing

Fears may often prevent people from accomplishing goals or even from seeing situations as they really are. Think of four or five things that make people afraid. List them, and next to each one briefly tell how it gets in the way of doing or understanding something.

Vocabulary

Knowing the following words will help you as you read "Hallucination."

technology (tek näl′ə jē) *n.*: The ideas of science applied to practical problems (p. 179)

hexagonal (hek sag′ə n′l) *adj.*: Six-sided (p. 183)

concave (kän kāv′) *adj.*: Empty and curved like the inside of a hollow ball (p. 183)

billowed (bil′ōd) *v.*: Surged or swelled (p. 184)

tethered (teth′ ərd) *v.*: Fastened with a rope or chain (p. 185)

insolent (in′sə lənt) *adj.*: Disrespectful (p. 188)

opaque (ō pāk′) *adj.*: Not letting light pass through (p. 190)

Hallucination

Isaac Asimov

Sam Chase arrived on Energy Planet on his 15th birthday.

It was a great achievement, he had been told, to have been assigned there, but he wasn't at all sure he felt that at the moment.

It meant a three-year separation from Earth and from his family, while he continued a specialized education in the field, and that was a sobering thought. It was not the field of education in which he was interested, and he could not understand why Central Computer had assigned him to this project, and that was downright depressing.

He looked at the transparent Dome overhead. It was quite high, perhaps a thousand meters high, and it stretched in all directions farther than he could clearly see. He asked, "Is it true that this is the only dome on the planet, sir?"

Donald Gentry, to whom the question had been addressed, smiled. He was a large man, a little chubby, with dark brown, good-natured eyes, not much hair, and a short, graying beard.

He said, "The only one, Sam. It's quite large, though, and most of the housing facilities are underground, where you'll find no lack of space. Besides, once your basic training is done, you'll be spending most of your time in space. This is just our planetary base."

"I see, sir," said Sam, a little troubled.

Gentry said, "I am in charge of our basic trainees, so I have to study their records carefully. It seems to me that this assignment was not your first choice. Am I right?"

Sam hesitated, and then decided he didn't have much choice but to be honest about it. He said, "I'm not sure that I'll do as well as I would like to in gravitational engineering."

"Why not? Surely the Central Computer, which evaluated your scholastic record and your social and personal background, can be trusted in its judgments. And if you do well, it will be a great achievement for you; for right here, we are at the cutting edge of a new technology."

"I know that, sir," said Sam. "Back on Earth, everyone is very excited about it. No one before has ever tried to get close to a neutron star[1] and make use of its energy."

"Yes?" Gentry asked. "I haven't been on Earth for two years. What else do they say about it? I understand there's considerable opposition."

His eyes probed the boy.

Sam shifted uneasily, aware he was being tested. He said, "There are people on Earth who say it's all too dangerous and might be a waste of money."

"Do you believe that?"

"It might be so, but most new technologies have their dangers, and many are worth

---

1. neutron star: A collapsed star made up of many densely packed neutrons, or uncharged atomic particles.

doing despite that. This one is, I think."

"Very good. What else do they say on Earth?"

"They say the Commander isn't well and that the project might fail without him." When Gentry didn't respond, Sam added, hastily, "That's what they say."

Gentry acted as though he didn't hear. He put his hand on Sam's shoulder and said, "Come, I've got to show you to your Corridor, introduce you to your roommate and explain what your initial duties will be." As they walked toward the elevator that would take them downward, he said, "What was your first choice of assignment, Chase?"

"Neurophysiology,[2] sir."

"Not a bad choice. Even today, the human brain continues to be a mystery. We know more about neutron stars than we do about the brain—as we found out when this project first began."

"Oh?"

"Indeed! At the start, various people at the base—it was much smaller and more primitive then—reported having experienced hallucinations. It never had any bad effect, and after a while, there were no further reports. We never found out the cause."

Sam stopped, and looked up and about again. "Was that why the Dome was built, Dr. Gentry?"

"No, not at all. We needed a place with a completely Earth-like environment, but we haven't isolated ourselves. People can go outside freely. There are no hallucinations being reported now."

Sam said, "The information I was given about Energy Planet is that there is no life on it except for plants and insects, and that they're harmless."

"That's right, but they're also inedible.

So we grow our own vegetables, and keep some small animals, right here under the Dome. Still, we've found nothing hallucinogenic about the planetary life."

"Anything unusual about the atmosphere, sir?"

Gentry looked down from his only slightly greater height and said, "Not at all. People have camped in the open overnight on occasion, and nothing has happened. It is a pleasant world. There are streams but

---

2. neurophysiology (noor′ ō fiz′ ē äl′ ə jē) n.: The study of the brain and nervous system.

no fish, just algae[3] and water-insects. There is nothing to sting you or poison you. There are yellow berries that look delicious and taste terrible, but do no other harm. The weather's pretty nearly always good. There are frequent light rains, and it is sometimes windy, but there are no extremes of heat and cold."

"And no hallucinations anymore, Dr. Gentry?"

"You sound disappointed," said Gentry, smiling.

Sam took a chance. "Does the Commander's trouble have anything to do with the hallucinations, sir?"

The good nature vanished from Gentry's eyes. "What trouble do you refer to?"

Sam flushed, and they proceeded in silence.

---

3. algae (al′ jē) *n*.: Plants like seaweed that live in water or damp places.

Sam found few others in the Corridor he had been assigned to, but Gentry had explained it was a busy time at the forward station, where the power system was being built in a ring around the neutron star, the tiny object less than 10 miles across, that had all the mass of a normal star, and a magnetic field of incredible power.

It was a magnetic field that would be tapped. Energy would be led away in enormous amounts, and yet it would all be a pinprick, less than a pinprick to the star's rotational energy,[4] which was the ultimate source. It would take billions of years to bleed off all that energy, and in that time, dozens of populated planets, fed the energy through hyperspace, would have all they needed for an indefinite time.

Sharing Sam's room was Robert Gillette, a dark-haired, unhappy-looking young man. After cautious greetings had been exchanged, Robert revealed that he was 16 and had been "grounded" with a broken arm, though the break didn't show because it had been pinned internally.

Robert said, ruefully, "It takes a while before you learn to handle things in space. They may not have weight, but they have inertia,[5] and you have to allow for that."

Sam said, "They always teach you that . . ." He was going to say that it was taught in fourth-grade science, but realized that would be insulting, and stopped himself.

Robert caught the implication, however, and flushed. He said, "It's easy to know it in your head. It doesn't mean you get the ·proper reflexes till you've practiced quite a bit. You'll find out."

---

4. rotational energy: Energy that comes from the star's rotation, or turning.

5. inertia (in ʉr′ shə) *n.*: The tendency of an object to remain at rest if it is at rest, or to remain moving if it is moving—unless it is disturbed by an outside force.

Sam asked, "Is it very complicated to get to go outside?"

"No, but why do you want to go?"

"Have you ever been outside?"

"Sure."

Sam took a chance. He asked, very casually, "Did you ever see one of these hallucinations they talk about?"

Robert said, "*Who* talk about?"

Sam didn't answer directly. He said, "A lot of people used to see them—but they don't anymore. Or so they say."

"So *who* say?"

Sam took another chance. "Or if they see them, they keep quiet about them."

Robert said, gruffly, "Listen, don't get interested in these—whatever they are. If you start telling yourself you see—uh-something, you might be sent back. You'll lose your chance at a good education and an important career."

Sam shrugged and sat down on the unused bunk. "All right for this to be my bed?"

"It's the only other bed here," said Robert. He paused and then, as though to let bygones be bygones, said, "I'll show you around later."

"Thanks," said Sam. "What kind of a guy is the Commander?"

"He's aces. He knows more about hyperspatial technology than anyone, and he's got pull with the Space Agency, so we get the money and equipment we need."

Sam opened his trunk and, with his back to Robert, said, casually, "I hear he's not well."

"Things get him down. We're behind schedule, there are cost overruns, and like that."

"Depression, huh? Any connection, you suppose, with . . . ?"

Robert stirred impatiently in his seat. "Say, why are you so interested in all this?"

"Energy physics[6] isn't really my deal. Coming here. . . ."

"Well, here's where you are, mister, and you better make up your mind to it, or you'll get sent home, and then you won't be anywhere—I'm going to the library."

Sam remained in the room alone—with his thoughts.

It was not at all difficult for Sam to get permission to leave the Dome.

The Corridor-Master nodded. "Fair enough, but you only get three hours, you know. And don't wander out of sight of the Dome. If we have to look for you, we'll find you, because you'll be wearing this," and he held out a transmitter, which Sam knew had been tuned to his own personal wavelength, one which had been assigned him at birth. "But if we have to go to that trouble, you won't be allowed out again for a pretty long time. And it won't look good on your record, either."

It won't look good on your record. Any reasonable career these days had to include experience and education in space, so it was an effective warning. No wonder people might have stopped reporting hallucinations, even if they saw them.

Even so, Sam was going to have to take his chance. After all, the Central Computer *couldn't* have sent him here just to do energy physics.

As far as looks were concerned, the planet might have been Earth—some part of Earth anyway, someplace where there were a few trees and low bushes and lots of tall grass.

There were no paths, and with his every cautious step, the grass swayed, and flying creatures whirred upward with a soft, hissing noise of wings.

One of them landed on his finger, and Sam looked at it curiously. It was very small and, therefore, hard to see in detail, but it seemed hexagonal, bulging above and concave below. There were many short, small legs so that when it moved it almost seemed to do so on tiny wheels. There were no signs of wings till it suddenly took off, and then four tiny, feathery objects unfurled.

What made the planet different from Earth, though, was the smell. It wasn't unpleasant; it was just different. The plants must have an entirely different chemistry[7] from those on Earth.

The smell diminished with time, however, as it saturated his nostrils. He found an exposed bit of rocky ledge he could sit on and considered the prospect. The sky was filled with lines of clouds, and the sun was periodically obscured, but the temperature was pleasant, and there was only a light wind. The air felt a bit damp.

Sam had brought a small hamper with two sandwiches, water and a canned drink.

He chewed away and thought: Why should there be hallucinations?

Surely, those accepted for a job as important as that of taming a neutron star would have been selected for mental stability. It would be surprising to have even one hallucinating, let alone a number of them. Was it a matter of chemical influences on the brain?

They would surely have checked that out.

Sam plucked a leaf, tore it in two and squeezed. He then put the torn edge to his

---

6. energy physics (fiz′ iks): Physics is the science that deals with the properties of matter and energy; energy physics would be a branch of this science that studies energy especially.

7. chemistry (kem′ is trē) *n.*: The chemical makeup and reaction of substances.

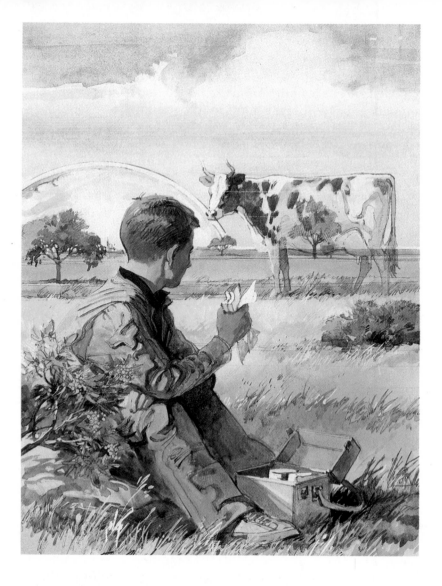

nose cautiously, and took it away again. A very acrid, unpleasant smell. He tried a blade of grass. Much the same.

Was the smell enough? It hadn't made him feel dizzy or in any way peculiar.

He used a bit of his water to rinse off the fingers that had held the plants, then finished his sandwiches slowly, trying to see if anything else might be considered unnatural.

All that greenery. There ought to be animals eating it, not just insects—or whatever those little things might be, with the gentle sighing of their tiny feathery wings and the very soft crackle of their munching of leaves and stalks.

What if there were a cow, a big, fat cow, doing the munching? And with the last mouthful of his second sandwich, Sam's munching stopped.

There was a kind of smoke in the air between himself and a line of hedges. It waved, billowed and altered, a very thin smoke. He blinked his eyes, then shook his head, but it was still there.

He swallowed hastily, closed his lunch box and slung it over his shoulder by its strap. He stood up.

He felt no fear. He was only excited—and curious.

The smoke was growing thicker, and taking on a shape. Vaguely, it looked like a cow, a smoky, insubstantial shape that he could see through. Was it a hallucination? A creation of his mind? He had just been thinking of a cow.

Hallucination or not, he was going to investigate.

With determination, he stepped toward the cow outlined in smoke on the strange, far planet on which his education and career were to be advanced.

He was convinced there was nothing wrong with his mind. It was the "hallucination" that Dr. Gentry had mentioned, but it was no hallucination. Even as he pushed his way through the tall, rank, grass-like greenery, he noted the silence, and knew not only that it was no hallucination, but what it really *was*.

The smoke seemed to condense and grow darker, outlining the cow more sharply. It was as though the cow were being painted in the air.

Sam laughed, and shouted, "Stop! Stop! Don't use me; I don't know a cow well enough. I've only seen pictures. You're getting it all wrong."

It looked more like a caricature than a real animal, and, as he cried out, the outline wavered and thinned. The smoke remained, but it was as though an unseen hand had passed across the air to erase what had been written.

Then a new shape began to take form. At first, Sam couldn't quite make out what it was intended to represent, but it changed and sharpened quickly. He stared in surprise, his mouth hanging open and his hamper bumping emptily against his side.

The smoke was forming a human being. There was no mistake about it. It was forming accurately, as though it had a model it could imitate, and of course it did have one, for Sam was standing there.

It was becoming Sam, clothes and all, even the outline of the hamper and the strap over his shoulder. It was another Sam Chase.

It was still a little vague, wavering a bit, insubstantial, but it firmed as though it were correcting itself, and then, finally, it was steady.

It never became entirely solid. Sam could see the vegetation dimly through it, and when a gust of wind caught it, it moved a bit as though it were a tethered balloon.

But it was real. It was no creation of his mind. Sam was sure of that.

But he couldn't just stand there, simply facing it. Diffidently, he said, "Hello, there."

Somehow, he expected the Other Sam to speak too, and, indeed, its mouth opened and closed, but no sound came out. It might just have been imitating the motion of Sam's mouth.

Sam said, again, "Hello. Can you speak?"

There was no sound but his own voice, and yet there was a tickling in his mind, a conviction that they could communicate.

Sam frowned. What made him so sure of that? The thought seemed to pop into his mind.

He asked, "Is that what has appeared to other people—human people—my kind—on this world?"

No answering sound, but he was quite sure what the answer to this question was. This had appeared to other people, not necessarily in their own shape, but *something*. And it hadn't worked.

What made him so sure of *that?* Where did these convictions come from in answer to his questions?

Yes, of course, they *were* the answers to his questions. The Other Sam was putting thoughts into his mind. It was adjusting the tiny electric currents in his brain cells so that the proper thoughts would arise.

He nodded thoughtfully at *that* thought, and the Other Sam must have caught the significance of the gesture, for it nodded too.

It had to be so. First a cow had formed, when Sam had thought of a cow, and then it had shifted when Sam had said the cow was imperfect. The Other Sam could grasp his thoughts somehow, and if it could grasp them, then it could modify them, too, perhaps.

Was this what telepathy[8] was like, then?

---

8. telepathy (tə lep′ ə thē) *n.*: Communication between minds by exchanging thoughts.

It was not like talking. It was having thoughts, except that the thoughts originated elsewhere and were not created entirely of one's own mental operations. But how could you tell your own thoughts from thoughts imposed from outside?

Sam knew the answer to that at once. Right now, he was unused to the process. He had never had practice. With time, as he grew more skilled at it, he would be able to tell one kind of thought from another without trouble.

In fact, he could do it now, if he thought about it. Wasn't he carrying on a conversation, in a way? He was wondering, and then knowing. The wondering was his own ques-

Roy Anderson

tion, the knowing was the Other Sam's answer. Of course it was.

There! The "of course it was," just now, was an answer.

"Not so fast, Other Sam," said Sam aloud. "Don't go too quickly. Give me a chance to sort things out, or I'll just get confused."

He sat down suddenly on the grass, which bent away from him in all directions.

The Other Sam slowly tried to sit down as well.

Sam laughed, "Your legs are bending in the wrong place."

That was corrected at once. The Other Sam sat down, but remained very stiff from the waist up.

"Relax," said Sam.

Slowly, the Other Sam slumped, flopping a bit to one side, then correcting that.

Sam was relieved. With the Other Sam so willing to follow his lead, he was sure goodwill was involved. It was! Exactly!

"No," said Sam. "I said, not so fast. Don't go by my thoughts. Let me speak out loud, even if you can't hear me. *Then* adjust my thoughts, so I'll know it's an adjustment. Do you understand?"

He waited a moment and was then sure the Other Sam understood.

Ah, the answer had come, but not right away. Good!

"Why do you appear to people?" asked Sam.

He stared earnestly at the Other Sam, and knew that the Other Sam wanted to communicate with people, but had not succeeded.

But then, no answer to that question had really been required. The answer was obvious. But, then, *why* had they failed?

He put it in words. "Why did you fail? You are successfully communicating with me."

Sam was beginning to learn how to understand the alien manifestation. It was as though his mind were adapting itself to a new technique of communication, just as it would adapt itself to a new language. Or was the Other Sam influencing Sam's mind and teaching him the method without Sam even knowing it was being done?

What Sam found himself doing was letting his mind empty itself of immediate thoughts. After he asked this question, he let his eyes focus on nothing and his eyelids droop, as though he were about to drop off to sleep, and then he knew the answer. There was a little clicking—or something—in his mind, a signal that something had been put in from outside.

He now knew, for instance, that the Other Sam's previous attempts at communication had failed because the people to whom it had appeared had been frightened. They had doubted their own sanity. And because they feared, their minds—tightened. Their minds would not receive. The attempts at communication diminished, though they had never entirely stopped.

"But you're communicating with me," said Sam.

Sam was different from all the rest. He had not been afraid.

"Couldn't you have made them not afraid first? Then talked to them?"

It wouldn't work. The fear-filled mind resisted all. An attempt to change might damage. It would be wrong to damage a thinking mind. There had been one such attempt, but it had not worked.

"What is it you are trying to communicate, Other Sam?"

A wish to be left alone. *Despair!*

Despair was more than a thought; it was an emotion; it was a frightening sensation. Sam felt despair wash over him intensely, heavily, and yet, it was not part of himself.

He felt despair on the surface of his mind, keenly, but underneath it, where his own mind was, he was free of it.

Sam said, wonderingly, "It seems to me as though you're giving up. Why? Are we interfering with you?"

Human beings had built the Dome, cleared a large area of all planetary life and substituted their own. And once the neutron star had its power station; once floods of energy moved outward through hyperspace to power-thirsty worlds; more power stations would be built and still more. Then what would happen to *Home?* (There must be a name for the planet that the Other Sam used, but the only thought Sam found in his mind was *Home* and, underneath that, the thought *ours—ours—ours.*)

This planet was the nearest convenient base to the neutron star. It would be flooded with more and more people, more and more Domes, and their home would be destroyed.

"But you could change our minds if you had to, even if you damaged a few, couldn't you?"

If they tried, people would find them dangerous. People would work out what was happening. Ships would approach, and from a distance, use weapons to destroy the life on Home, and then bring in People-life instead. This could be seen in the people's minds. People had a violent history; they would stop at nothing.

"But what can I do?" Sam asked. "I'm just an apprentice. I've just been here a few days. What can I do?"

Fear. Despair.

There were no thoughts that Sam could work out, just the numbing layer of fear and despair.

He felt moved. It was such a peaceful world. They threatened nobody. They didn't even hurt minds, although they had the ability to do so.

It wasn't their fault they were near a neutron star. It wasn't their fault they were in the way of expanding humanity.

He said, "Let me think."

He thought, and there was the feeling of another mind watching. Sometimes his thoughts skipped forward, and he recognized a suggestion from outside.

There came the beginning of hope, Sam felt it, but wasn't certain.

He looked at the time-strip on his wrist and jumped a little. Far more time had passed than he had realized. His three hours were nearly up. "I must go back now," he said.

He opened his lunch hamper and removed the small thermos of water, drank from it thirstily, and emptied it. He placed the empty thermos under one arm. He removed the wrapping of the sandwich and stuffed it in his pocket.

The Other Sam wavered and turned smoky. The smoke thinned, dispersed and was gone.

Sam closed the hamper, swung it over his shoulder and turned toward the Dome.

His heart was hammering. Would he have the courage to go through with his plan? And if he did, would it work?

When Sam entered the Dome, the Corridor-Master was waiting for him, and said, as he looked ostentatiously at his own time-strip, "You shaved it rather fine, didn't you?"

Sam's lips tightened, and he tried not to sound insolent. "I had three hours, sir."

"And you took two hours and 58 minutes."

"That's less than three hours, sir."

"Hmm," the Corridor-Master was cold and unfriendly. "Dr. Gentry would like to see you."

"Yes, sir. What for?"

"He didn't tell me. But I don't like you cutting it that fine your first time out,

Chase. And I don't like your attitude, either, and I don't like an officer of the Dome wanting to see you. I'm just going to tell you once, Chase: If you're a trouble-maker, I won't want you in this Corridor. Do you understand?"

"Yes, Sir. But what trouble have I made?"

"We'll find that out soon enough."

Sam had not seen Donald Gentry since their one and only meeting when the young apprentice had reached the Dome. Gentry still seemed good-natured and kindly, and there was nothing in his voice to indicate anything else. He sat in a chair behind his desk, and Sam stood before it, his hamper still bumping his side.

Gentry said, "How are you getting along, Sam? Having an interesting time?"

"Yes, sir," said Sam.

"Still feeling you'd rather be doing something else, working somewhere else?"

Sam said, earnestly, "No, sir. This is a good place for me."

"Because you're interested in hallucinations?"

"Yes, sir."

"You've been asking others about it, haven't you?"

"It's an interesting subject to me, sir."

"Because you want to study the human brain?"

"Any brain, sir."

"And you've been wandering about outside the Dome, haven't you?"

"I was told it was permitted, sir."

"It is. But few apprentices take advantage of that so soon. Did you see anything interesting?"

Sam hesitated, then said, "Yes, sir."

"A hallucination?"

"No, sir." He said it quite positively.

Gentry stared at him for a few moments, and there was a kind of speculative hardening of his eyes. "Would you care to tell me what you did see? Honestly."

Sam hesitated again. Then he said, "I saw and spoke to an inhabitant of this planet, sir."

"An intelligent inhabitant, young man?"

"Yes, sir."

Gentry said, "Sam, we had reason to wonder about you when you came. The Central Computer's report on you did not match our needs, though it was favorable in many ways, so I took the opportunity to study you that first day. We kept our collective eye on you, and when you left to wander about the planet on your own, we kept you under observation."

"Sir," said Sam, indignantly, "that violates my right of privacy."

"Yes, it does, but this is a most vital project, and we are sometimes driven to bend the rules a little. We saw you talking with considerable animation for a substantial period of time."

"I just told you I was, sir."

"Yes, but you were talking to nothing; to empty air. You were experiencing a hallucination, Sam!"

Sam was speechless. A hallucination? It couldn't be a hallucination.

Less than half an hour ago, he had been speaking to the Other Sam; had been experiencing the thoughts of the Other Sam. He knew exactly what had happened then, and he was still the same Sam Chase he had been during that conversation and before. He put his elbow over his lunch hamper as though it were a connection with the sandwiches he had been eating when the Other Sam had appeared.

He said, with what was almost a stammer. "Sir—Dr. Gentry—it wasn't a hallucination. It was real."

Gentry shook his head. "My boy, I saw you talking with animation to nothing at all. I didn't hear what you said, but you were talking. Nothing else was there except plants. Nor was I the only one. There were two other witnesses, and we have it all on record."

"On record?"

"On a television cassette. Why should we lie to you, young man? This has happened before. At the start, it happened rather frequently. Now it happens only very rarely. For one thing, we tell the new apprentices of the hallucinations at the start, as I told you, and they generally avoid the planet until they are more acclimated, and then it doesn't happen to them."

"You mean you scare them," blurted out Sam, "so that it's not likely to happen. And they don't tell you if it does happen—but I wasn't scared."

Gentry shook his head. "I'm sorry you weren't, if that was what it would have taken to keep you from seeing things."

"I wasn't seeing things. At least, not things that weren't there."

"How do you intend to argue with a television cassette, which will show you staring at nothing?"

"Sir, what I saw was not opaque. It was smoky, actually; foggy, if you know what I mean."

"Yes, I do. It looked as a hallucination might look, not as reality. But the television set would have seen even smoke."

"Maybe not, sir. My mind must have been focused to see it more clearly. It was probably less clear to the camera than to me."

"It focused your mind, did it?" Gentry stood up, and he sounded rather sad. "That's an admission of hallucination. I'm really sorry, Sam, because you are clearly intelligent, and the Central Computer rated you highly—but we can't use you."

"Will you be sending me home, sir?"

"Yes, but why should that matter? You didn't particularly want to come here."

"I want to stay here *now*."

"But I'm afraid you cannot."

"You can't just send me home. Don't I get a hearing?"

"You certainly can, if you insist, but in that case, the proceedings will be official and will go on your record, so that you won't get another apprenticeship anywhere. As it is, if you are sent back unofficially, as better suited to an apprenticeship in neurophysiology, you might get that, and be better off, actually, than you are now."

"I don't want that. I want a hearing— before the Commander."

"Oh, no, not the Commander. He can't be bothered with that."

"It *must* be the Commander," said Sam, with desperate force, "or this project will fail."

"Unless the Commander gives you a hearing? Why do you say that? Come, you are forcing me to think that you are unstable in ways other than those involved with hallucinations."

"Sir," the words were tumbling out of Sam's mouth now. "The Commander is ill— they know that even on Earth—and if he gets too ill to work, this project will fail. I did not see a hallucination, and the proof is that I know why he is ill and how he can be cured."

"You're not helping yourself," said Gentry.

"If you send me away, I tell you the project will fail. Can it hurt to let me see the Commander? All I ask is five minutes."

"Five minutes? What if he refuses?"

"Ask him, sir. Tell him that I say the same thing that caused his depression can remove it."

"No, I don't think I'll tell him that. But I'll ask him if he'll see you."

The Commander was a thin man, not

very tall. His eyes were a deep blue, and they looked tired.

His voice was very soft, a little low-pitched and definitely weary.

"You're the one who saw the hallucination?"

"It was not a hallucination, Commander, it was real. So was the one you saw, Commander." (If that did not get him thrown out, Sam thought, he might have a chance. He felt his elbow tightening on his hamper again. He still had it with him.)

The Commander seemed to wince. "The one *I* saw?"

"Yes, Commander. It said it had hurt one person. They had to try with you because you were the Commander, and they—did damage."

The Commander ignored that and said, "Did you ever have any mental problems before you came here?"

"No, Commander. You can consult my Central Computer record."

Sam thought: *He* must have had problems, but they let it go because he's a genius and they had to have him.

Then he thought: Was that my own idea? Or had it been put there?

The Commander was speaking. Sam had almost missed it. He said, "What you saw can't be real. There is no intelligent life-form on this planet."

"Yes, sir. There is."

"Oh? And no one ever discovered it till you came here and did the job?" The Commander smiled very briefly. "I'm afraid I have no choice but to . . ."

"Wait, Commander," said Sam, in a strangled voice. "We know about the intelligent life-form. It's the insects, the little flying things."

"You say the insects are intelligent?"

"Not an individual insect by itself, but they fit together when they want to, like little jigsaws. They can do it in any way they want.

And when they do, their nervous systems fit together too, and build up. A lot of them *together* are intelligent."

The Commander's eyebrows lifted. "That's an interesting idea, anyway. Almost crazy enough to be true. How did you come to that conclusion, young man?"

"By observation, sir. Everywhere I walked, I disturbed the insects in the grass, and they flew about in all directions. But once the cow started to form, and I walked toward it, there was nothing to see or hear. The insects were gone. They had gathered together in front of me, and they weren't in the grass anymore. That's how I knew."

"You talked with a cow?"

"It was a cow at first, because that's what I thought of. But they had it wrong, so they switched and came together to form a human being—*me.*"

"You?" And then, in a lower voice, "Well, that fits anyway."

"Did you see it that same way too, Commander?"

The Commander ignored that. "And when it shaped itself like you, it could talk as you did? Is that what you're telling me?"

"No, Commander. The talking was in my mind."

"Telepathy?"

"Sort of."

"And what did it say to you—or think to you?"

"It wanted us to refrain from disturbing this planet. It wanted us not to take it over." Sam was all but holding his breath. The interview had lasted more than five minutes already, and the Commander was making no move to put an end to it, to send him home.

"Quite impossible."

"Why, Commander?"

"Any other base will double and triple the expense. We're having enough trouble getting grants as it is. Fortunately, it is all a hallucination, young man, and the problem

does not arise." He closed his eyes, then opened them and looked at Sam without really focusing on him. "I'm sorry, young man. You will be sent back—officially."

Sam gambled again. "We can't afford to ignore the insects, Commander. They have a lot to give us."

The Commander had raised his hand partway, as though about to give a signal. He paused long enough to say, "Really? What do they have that they can give us?"

"The one thing more important than energy, Commander. An understanding of the brain."

"How do you know that?"

"I can demonstrate it. I have them here." Sam seized his hamper and swung it forward onto the desk.

"What's that?"

Sam did not answer in words. He opened the hamper, and a softly whirring, smoky cloud appeared.

The Commander rose suddenly and cried out. He lifted his hand high, and an alarm bell sounded.

Through the door came Gentry, others behind him. Sam felt himself seized by the arms, and then a kind of stunned and motionless silence prevailed in the room.

The smoke was condensing, wavering, taking on the shape of a head; a thin head, with high cheekbones, a smooth forehead and receding hairline. It had the appearance of the Commander.

"I'm seeing things," croaked the Commander.

Sam said, "We're all seeing the same thing, aren't we?" He wriggled and was released.

Gentry said in a low voice, "Mass hysteria."[9]

"No," said Sam, "it's real." He reached toward the Head in midair and brought back his finger with a tiny insect on it. He flicked it, and it could just barely be seen making its way back to its companions.

No one moved.

Sam said, "Head, do you see the problem with the Commander's mind?"

Sam had the brief vision of a snarl in an otherwise smooth curve, but it vanished and left nothing behind. It was not something that could be easily put into human thought. He hoped the others experienced that quick snarl. Yes, they had. He knew it.

The Commander said, "There is no problem . . ." and stopped.

Sam said, "Can you adjust it, Head?"

Of course, they could not. It was not right to invade a mind.

Sam said, "Commander, give permission."

The Commander put his hands to his eyes and muttered something Sam did not make out. Then he said, clearly, "It's a nightmare, but I've been in one since . . . Whatever must be done, I give permission."

Nothing happened.

Or nothing seemed to happen.

And then slowly, little by little, the Commander's face lit in a smile.

He said, just above a whisper. "Astonishing. I'm watching a sun rise. It's been cold night for so long, and now I feel the warmth again." His voice rose high. "I feel wonderful."

The Head deformed at that point, turned into a vague, pulsing fog, then formed a curving, narrowing arrow that sped into the hamper. Sam snapped it shut.

He asked, "Commander, have I your permission to restore these little insect-things to their own world?"

"Yes, yes," said the Commander, dismissing that with a wave of his hand. "Gentry, call a meeting. We've got to change all our plans."

---

9. mass hysteria (his ter′ ē ə): An outbreak of excited feeling in a group of people, sometimes causing them to see things that are not there.

Sam had been escorted outside the Dome by a solid guard and had then been confined to his quarters in the Corridor for the rest of the day.

It was late when Gentry entered, stared at him thoughtfully, and said, "That was an amazing demonstration of yours. The entire incident has been fed into the Central Computer, and we now have a double project, neutron star energy and neurophysiology. I doubt that there will be any question about pouring money into this project now. And we'll have a group of neurophysiologists arriving eventually. Until then you're going to be working with those little things, those insects, and you'll probably end up the most important person here."

Sam said, "But will we leave their world to them?"

Gentry said, "We'll have to if we expect to get anything out of them, won't we? The Commander thinks we're going to build elaborate settlements in orbit about this world and shift all operations to them except for a skeleton crew in this Dome to maintain direct contact with the insects—or whatever we'll decide to call them. It will cost a great deal of money, and take time and labor, but it's going to be worth it. No one will question that."

Sam said, "Good!"

Gentry stared at him again, longer and more thoughtfully than before.

"My boy," he said, "it seems that what happened came about because you did not fear the supposed hallucination. Your mind remained open, and that was the whole difference. Why was that? Why weren't you afraid?"

Sam flushed. "I'm not sure, sir. As I look back on it, though, it seemed to me I was puzzled as to why I was sent here. I had been doing my best to study neurophysiology through my computerized courses and I knew very little about astrophysics.[10] The Central Computer had my record, all of it, the full details of everything I had ever studied, and I couldn't imagine why I had been sent here.

"Then, when you first mentioned the hallucinations, I thought, 'That must be it. I was sent here to look into it.' I just made up my mind that was the thing I had to do. I had no *time* to be afraid, Dr. Gentry. I had a problem to solve, and I—I had faith in the Central Computer. It wouldn't have sent me here, if I weren't up to it."

Gentry shook his head. "I'm afraid I wouldn't have had that much faith in that machine. But they say faith can move mountains, and I guess it certainly did in this case."

---

10. astrophysics (as′ trō fiz′ iks) *n.*: The science of the physical properties of the stars, planets, and other heavenly bodies.

THINKING ABOUT THE SELECTION
Recalling

1. Why are Sam, Dr. Gentry, and the Commander on Energy Planet?
2. Describe the strange encounter Sam has when he leaves the Dome.
3. What message does the "Other Sam" communicate to Sam?
4. Why does Sam succeed in communicating with the life form when others could not?
5. How does Sam convince the Commander not to send him back to Earth?
6. What changes will be made in the project as a result of all that Sam has done?

Interpreting

7. How is the intelligence of the life form different from human intelligence?
8. What conclusions does Sam come to about how the alien life form is communicating with him?

Applying

9. Gentry says to Sam, "My boy, it seems that what happened came about because you did not fear the supposed hallucination. Your mind remained open, and that was the whole difference." What real-life examples of openmindedness and courage can you think of that have allowed people to gain knowledge that they otherwise could not have gained?

ANALYZING LITERATURE
Recognizing Theme in Science Fiction

The **theme** of a story is its central idea. In "Hallucination" the theme is revealed through what the main characters come to understand about the strange events taking place on an alien planet. The strangeness of the plot, of the aliens, and of the setting is what makes the theme stand out sharply.

1. Compare and contrast Sam's reaction to the alien life form he encounters with that of the Commander.
2. What does the story suggest about dealing with strange and unusual events?
3. What do you think is the theme of "Hallucination"?

CRITICAL THINKING AND READING
Looking at Reasoning

Reasoning is thinking logically. The part of the story in which Sam meets the alien life form reveals sound reasoning at work. Because of the way Sam reasons, events ultimately turn out favorably for him and the others assigned to Energy Planet.

1. Why does Sam reason that the reported hallucinations are highly unlikely?
2. When the cow appears before Sam, why does he reason that it is not a hallucination?
3. How does Sam figure out the way that the life form communicates?

THINKING AND WRITING
Writing Science Fiction

Imagine that you have been sent to Energy Planet shortly after the events presented in "Hallucination." Your duty is to send back to Earth reports on any strange or dangerous beings you meet outside the Dome. In your explorations you encounter one such being, and now you are writing a report about your adventure for an Information Committee on Earth made up of your classmates. Before you write the report, be sure you have assembled enough details to convey a full and clear picture of your experience. When you revise your work, keep in mind the question "Based on the information in my report, will people on Earth be able to visualize, or see, what I have seen?"

GUIDE FOR READING

A Season of Acceptance

C. J. Fosdick (1943–   ) was born and raised in Wisconsin and now lives in Minnesota, the setting of "A Season of Acceptance." Fosdick uses her own experiences as the basis for events in some of her short stories. For example, "A Season of Acceptance" centers on a young girl's reactions to an elderly grandfather and a young llama. Fosdick herself had a grandfather who was dear to her, and, although she did not have a llama, there were llamas on the farms in Minnesota and she *did* think of getting one.

Symbols

A **symbol** is something that stands for something other than itself. An object that serves as a symbol has its own meaning, but it also represents an idea, a belief, a value, or a group of feelings. For example, a dove is a symbol of peace and the American flag is a symbol of the United States and the American way of life. A sword may be a symbol of war and a red rose a symbol of love. Symbols can make ideas or feelings come alive in a vivid and concrete way.

Look For

Brewster, the pet llama in "A Season of Acceptance," is both a real animal and a symbol. Pay careful attention to what is said about him. Then form your own opinion about the ideas or feelings he represents.

Writing

Symbols such as the American flag have public, widely recognized meanings. But symbols may also have private and personal meanings, for example, a seashell kept for years may serve as a symbol of a happy family vacation at the shore. List three or four objects that have special meanings for you. Alongside each, write down the meaning—the memories—it holds for you.

Vocabulary

Knowing the following words will help you as you read "A Season of Acceptance."

astonished (ə stän′ isht) *v.*: Amazed (p. 198)

revoked (ri vōkt′) *v.*: Canceled, withdrawn (p. 198)

passive (pas′iv) *adj.*: Inactive (p. 199)

exuberance (ig zoo′bər əns) *n.*: High spirits (p. 200)

savoring (sā′vər iŋ) *v.*: Enjoying with appreciation (p. 201)

monogrammed (män′ə gram'd′) *n.*: Having a design made up of two or more letters (p. 202)

A Season of Acceptance

C. J. Fosdick

Christmas came early the year I turned sixteen. It was 1969, the year Neil Armstrong became the first man on the moon. For me, it was also a year of discovery and of gifts that didn't come wrapped in bright-colored paper. It all began on a rainy, wind-driven afternoon in April. I was in the barn, stoking up the wood stove to the obvious delight of our two milk cows, the Appaloosa,[1] two dogs, and a few barn cats. Listening to the chorus of the crackling fire and the lowing and purring of the animals, I had nearly forgotten the storm—until the door whistled open and Dad staggered in with a bundle I took to be a thirty-pound feed sack. He set it gently down. "It needs mothering," he said and winked.

Suddenly, the "bundle" rose on four spindly legs and squinted at me through milky-blue eyes. The wet, woolly gray creature with the scrawny neck and oversize lip was the ugliest animal I had ever seen. "Another rejected lamb, Dad?"

"A llama," Dad corrected. "There's a farmer in Rushford who raises them. He has his hands full with spring planting and worming his herd, but this little fella needed immediate care. I didn't think you'd mind helping out."

"Is he a keeper?" I asked, half afraid of the answer. Dad's territory was growing with his reputation as the best farm vet in Spring Valley, Minnesota. He often brought home sick animals to nurse back to health. Mom and I and sometimes even my ten-year-old brother, Ivan, were recruited as foster parents. Once in a while, as in the case of the cows, chickens, and our Irish setter, an animal became payment for services.

"He's yours if you'll have him, Hildy. Dry him off, and feed him some of the canned milk in the storeroom. I have another call to make yet today, so I'm depending on you to set up a nursing station." Dad bent to scratch the llama between his pointy ears. "How fragile life is," he mused, "if even an animal will reject her baby because it has blue eyes."

"Do you really think it was the eyes?" I asked.

Dad shrugged. "Llamas are usually brown-eyed."

The llama sucked eagerly from the bottle I fixed and fell into my lap, humming like a high-pitched harp. When I rubbed his wet fur with a towel, the soft hum faded into even sighs of slumber.

I could understand his problem: I was a brown-eyed child in a blue-eyed family. Everyone said I took after my grandparents on my mother's side. I barely remembered either of them. Mom's mother had died when I was two. My grandfather lived in St. Paul, a hundred miles north of Spring Valley. Mom visited him regularly, but children made him nervous, so Ivan and I stayed home. Rejected . . . like blue-eyed llamas.

I spent my entire spring break in the barn that year, sleeping on a cot, playing with the llama I'd named Brewster, bottle-feeding him like he was my own baby. On my first day back to school, Brewster staged a sit-in. He plunked himself down on my cot and refused to move or eat until I returned home. Even Dad was astonished.

When the weather improved, I let Brewster out to pasture with the horse and cows, but he quickly learned how to burrow under the fence. One morning, he actually followed me down the hill to the bus stop. Mom arrived in the truck and hauled Brewster back. "We'll have to get him a bell," she said, laughing. "Either that or a geometry book."

With three silver bells around his neck, my shadow jingled after me throughout the summer. Because he was such a novelty— and no bigger than a dog—on occasion he was even allowed inside the house. But Brewster's house privileges were revoked one muggy July day when Iván teased him and Brewster retaliated by spitting. This time, Mom wasn't amused. My room—and Ivan— had to be deodorized because of the foul-smelling saliva.

In November, Mom made her monthly trip to Grandfather's. When she called that night, she asked to speak to me. "Hildy, would you mind giving up your bedroom for a month or so? I'm bringing your grandfather home with me."

I was stunned. Give up my room to an old man who had no time for me?

"Your grandfather fell and broke his leg. He won't go to a nursing home and refuses live-in help. I can't leave him alone, so I'm kidnapping him."

"Mom, I can't bunk with Ivan the Terrible."

"You can for a month, Hildy Boardman. We'll be home for supper tomorrow." The receiver clicked off in my hand.

Like new recruits preparing for inspection, Dad, Ivan, and I spruced up for the new arrival. Even Dad was nervous about passing muster: Yesterday, he'd performed a tracheotomy[2] on a cat; tonight, peeling potatoes, he cut himself twice.

I had turned the temperature on the roaster down three times and was basting the vegetables with gravy when Mom and Grandfather arrived. "Say hello to your grandfather," Mom said, beaming, as she maneuvered the wheelchair toward our line of assembly. The old man was thin and pale, with a full head of white hair, a sparse beard, and a pencil-thin mustache that drooped like fangs from the corners of his mouth. His dark eyes snapped with the vitality of a man much younger than seventy-four, but the scowl aged him. A picture from my history book of Attila the Hun[3] flashed through my mind.

"Welcome, Grandfather," I said, feeling foolish because I dipped my knee in reflex.

For a fleeting moment, I thought I saw

---

2. tracheotomy (trā' kē ät' ə mē) n.: An operation in which the trachea, or windpipe, is cut to make an artificial breathing hole.

3. Attila the Hun: A feared military leader who lived in Europe about 1,500 years ago.

his face soften. "Too much makeup," he finally grunted before he shook hands with Dad and wheeled away as if he knew where he was going.

Dinner that first evening was tense. Grandfather sat stiffly, with his napkin tucked into his shirt, concentrating intently on his meal. He ate one thing at a time, advancing clockwise around his plate. At "eleven o'clock," he looked up and asked for a cup of black coffee, and Mom jumped up to pour.

"Hildy," she said, "isn't this Grandma's bread pudding recipe? How sweet of you to think of making it. Isn't that nice, Dad?"

"It needs more raisins," he muttered.

I excused myself and made it to the bathroom before the tears came. When I had scrubbed my face free of makeup, I ran to the barn and threw my arms around Brewster's woolly neck.

Later, Mom joined me on the cot with my history book and a lantern. "Honey, give it time," she said. "He's just not used to us."

"Was he ever?" I moaned.

"He was a good husband and a wonderful father. I try to remember the good times."

"What happened?"

Mom picked a few pieces of straw out of my hair. "People change. Some of us just don't age well. When Grandma died, something died in your grandfather, too."

"I'll never turn into a hateful old recluse!" I said. "Never!"

Mom chuckled. "Who knows, Hildy. At your age, you may have more in common with your grandfather than you think. Give him a chance. Loving people are loved people." She pointed to the illustration of Attila the Hun in my history book. "Someone probably even loved him," she said, and we both laughed.

I didn't have my mother's wisdom—or her thick skin—but I tried to humor the old man and in the next few weeks, there were more victories than defeats. Grandfather ate heartily at every meal, cleaning his plate in the same clockwork ritual of his first supper with us. He noticed when I anticipated him and poured his cup of black coffee precisely at eleven o'clock. Once or twice, I caught him beginning to smile.

Dad built a wheelchair ramp from the back door so Grandfather could come and go on his own. His leg was mending fast; the doctor at the clinic promised him a walking cast for Christmas. "I'll be going home for Christmas," Grandfather announced—almost daily.

"Not until your doctor's release," Mom reminded him cheerfully. "I want to see you skating first."

"Ice-skating!" he snorted. "Haven't done that since you were a little girl."

Mom turned to Ivan and me. "Your grandfather coached ice hockey many years ago. He taught Grandma and me how to play, and once in a while, I even subbed for a sick player."

"She was darn good, too," Grandfather said. "A real quick study." This time, he smiled broadly; his mustache looked as if it would take flight.

"Grandfather, will you teach me how to play?" Ivan asked.

The mustache drooped. "Won't be around long enough for that," he replied.

Only a few inches of snow fell in early December, but the almanac promised a white Christmas. Without being asked, Ivan kept the ramp and walk free of snow. He also gave us daily reports on the state of the duck pond. "Could almost drive a truck on there now," he'd say. Mom would wink at me over Grandfather's passive head.

In the beginning, Grandfather had kept to his room, whittling or reading until mealtime. Then Mom began to wheel him out, insisting she needed the company. When he didn't hold up his end of the conversation, she would flick on the TV and watch her favorite soap operas. "Great jumpin' bullfrogs, your mother used to watch that garbage. Real life ain't that twisted," he'd complain, pretending to be absorbed in a magazine or book.

He sat at the window for hours at a time, seeming to admire the icy laced trees and watching the birds and animals interact and respond to the changes in weather.

Once or twice, I felt his eyes on me, watching from the window when I played with Brewster. Brewster loved the cold, loved to run in the new snow. I was hitching him to a small sled, trying to teach him to pull when I heard the wheels crunching through the snow. "You can't teach an old goat anything," Grandfather said. He sat there with his plaster cast sticking out of the lap robe, hatless, gloveless, a scarf wound haphazardly around the lower part of his face.

"Better watch who you call an old goat, Grandfather," I said. "This is a llama."

"How's that?" He pulled the scarf free of one ear.

"A llama, more in the camel family. The Incas[4] used them as pack animals. Llamas are still used that way in the Andes.[5] In fact, I read they are still thought of there as worthy sacrifices to the Sun God."

Brewster padded over to the wheelchair for a sniff. "Get away from me, you old goat!" Grandfather yelled. When Grandfather batted him away, Brewster spit, and the smelly saliva ran down the old man's startled face and disappeared into the folds of his scarf.

With the greatest difficulty, I choked back my laughter and pushed the wheel-

---

4. Incas: A group of Indians who created an empire in South America hundreds of years ago.
5. Andes (an' dēz): A South American mountain range.

chair back to the house. Grandfather was cussing and waving the foul scarf when Mom met us at the door. "Get me a gun," he yelled, "I want to make a sacrifice to the Sun God!"

Grandfather didn't speak to me the rest of the week. He sat back from the window now, but I could tell by the flutter of curtain that he still watched me coaching Brewster on the sled. When Brewster had had enough, he staged a sit-down. In a way, Brewster and Grandfather were a lot alike. But their most obvious difference saddened me: Brewster loved people.

On Christmas Eve, Mom, Dad, Ivan, and I returned from an afternoon hike in the woods with a seven-foot fir tree. We all pretended not to notice Grandfather spying from the window. Ivan started throwing snowballs, and when Mom joined in, we chose up sides and started a snowball fight. We ended up building a giant snowman. Ivan found the scarf Brewster had ruined, and Dad tied it around Frosty's neck. We were going to dedicate our creation to Grandfather, but he was no longer at the window.

Instead, we brought the tree and our exuberance indoors, and with Christmas carols playing on the radio, we strung the tree with blinking lights and tinsel rope. Mom brought out her cherished box of dated ornaments: those she had kept since she was a child, those we had made for her of kindergarten clay, and those friends had given us each year—all of them carrying special meaning. We draped glittery yards of cotton snow beneath the tree, then added the row of little cardboard houses and trees that had come from Dad's grandmother.

That night after Dad read from the second chapter of Luke, Mom staggered in with boxes of gaily wrapped presents. There was hot wassail[6] to sip, cookies to munch, fresh shrimp and cheese, little meatballs, and the special holiday bread that Mom always complained was never as good as Grandma's.

We had gathered around Mom at the piano, singing *Silent Night*. I was the first to notice Grandfather, sitting there with four brown packages in his lap. I nudged Ivan, who nudged Dad, who then squeezed Mom on the shoulder. Caught staring at the tree with misty eyes, the old man fumbled for dignity. "How's a fellow supposed to nap with all this racket!" he roared.

"Merry Christmas, Dad." Mom kissed him in spite of his grimace, and when she handed him a gift, he could barely conceal his delight. He opened it slowly and stroked the soft beige muffler and the matching hat and suede gloves.

"The scarf is alpaca, Dad," Mom said. "The alpaca is related to the llama. I figured Brewster would have endorsed this gift."

He nodded toward the window. "I see my old scarf has found a colder neck to warm."

Shyly, Ivan gave Grandfather his gift, a can of mustache wax. The old man snorted. "I suppose this scraggly old thing could use a bit of sprucing up," he admitted. Ivan's face lit up.

Dad's gift to Grandfather was a block of cherry wood to carve and a book on bird-watching. "I don't know what to say. I don't deserve so many fine gifts." The old man sniffled. "Christmas is for kids . . ."

"No, it isn't," Mom interrupted. "Besides, wasn't it Mae West who said you're never too old to become younger?"

Grandfather actually laughed. "She was a fireball, that one. My favorite actress. Reminded me of your mother—not the build, of course, but there was something in her de-

livery." He sniffled again, this time swiping at his nose with a large blue hankie.

"There's more, Grandfather." I handed him my gift, and for the first time since Brewster spit at him, he looked me nose to eyeball and spoke my full name.

"Thank you, Hildegard." He opened it slowly, as if savoring the suspense.

The old man stared at the straw figure with the tiny silver bells around its neck. "I made it myself," I said, launching quickly into the little speech I had rehearsed all week. "It's supposed to be a llama. The bells are like Brewster's. I thought maybe if you put it on your chair, you and Brewster might become friends. You know, like people who speak the same language."

In the sudden stillness of the room, my lower lip began to tremble; I had offended him by the comparison. The tree lights blinked on and off, coloring his face red, blue, green, and gold. He hated my gift! When I tried to retrieve the llama, he caught my hand. "I have something for you, too," he said in an odd, deep voice.

I forced myself to open the brown paper package he offered and unfolded a white linen handkerchief edged in lace and embroidered with a faded silk *H*. The hankie formed a pocket for a silver locket also engraved with an *H*. Inside was a picture of a young couple.

Mom fastened the locket around my neck while Grandfather passed out his remaining gifts. "It was your grandmother's," she whispered. "You were named after her, you know." She studied the picture for a long time. "I didn't realize how much you favor her . . ."

I thanked the old man. "You can tear out the other picture," he said, watching my face intently.

"Not if that young man is you, Grandfather. I'd like to remember you smiling." Awk-

---

6. wassail (wäs' 'l) *n.*: A spiced drink used in celebrating.

wardly, I hugged him. When he hugged me back, my lower lip began to tremble again. But to my utter surprise, it was he who began to sob.

"She trusted me," he cried. "I promised her I wouldn't leave, but her pain—I ran all the way to the pharmacy." He slumped forward and seemed to shrink in the wheelchair. I offered him the hankie, but he only stared at it sadly. "She was gone when I got back. I prayed she was just asleep."

Tears brimming in her eyes, Mom knelt by the chair and wrapped her arms around the old man. "She *was* sleeping, Dad. She was waiting for you."

"She didn't want to die alone," he sobbed.

"No one wants to be alone," Mom held his flushed face between her hands. "That's why we're glad you're here. We missed you, Dad."

I sat beside my grandfather in church that Christmas Eve, my left hand gripping his, my right holding the wet monogrammed hankie of a well-loved woman. My grandparents, my family, and a bell-carrying llama named Brewster were never more special to me than on that night, a night of love and forgiveness and miracles great and small.

THINKING ABOUT THE SELECTION
Recalling

1. What is the similarity in the ways that Brewster and Grandfather come to stay with Hildy's family?
2. What explanation does Hildy's mother give for Grandfather's being so unpleasant?
3. What is Brewster's response when Grandfather drives him away?
4. What gifts do Hildy and Grandfather exchange on Christmas Eve?

Interpreting

5. Why does Hildy, early in the story, feel a kind of connection between herself and Brewster?
6. How does Hildy's Christmas gift to Grandfather suggest a connection between him and Brewster?
7. How does Grandfather's memory of his wife's death lead to his becoming more a part of the family?
8. What does Hildy mean when she says that 1969 was for her, "a year of discovery and of gifts that didn't come wrapped in bright-colored paper"?
9. Explain the title of the story.

Applying

10. At one point, Hildy's mother says, "Loving people are loved people." Do you think this is true of real life? Why or why not?

ANALYZING LITERATURE
Interpreting Symbols

An author may use a symbol to suggest the theme of a story. Usually, interpreting a symbol gives you a helpful clue to the theme.
1. How are Hildy and Brewster alike?
2. How are Grandfather and Brewster alike?
3. What does Brewster come to represent, or stand for?
4. Using the ideas that Brewster symbolizes, tell what you think the theme of the story is.

CRITICAL THINKING AND READING
Recognizing Symbols

A symbol is somewhat like a sign, but with a crucial difference. The meaning of a sign is usually simple and definite. For example, a red light means "Stop." The meaning of a symbol may be complex, and it may be different for different people. For example, the Statue of Liberty may mean political freedom to some, religious freedom to others, and economic opportunity to yet others. Moreover, it will arouse different feelings in different people.
1. Which of the following may be considered symbols, and which are signs?
   a. A flashing red light on a police car
   b. The Olympic torch
   c. A raised hand with two fingers forming a V
   d. The Liberty Bell in Philadelphia
   e. A candle in a window
   f. A red-and-white-striped barbershop pole
2. Choose one of the preceding objects that you identified as a symbol, and tell what feelings and ideas it suggests to you.

THINKING AND WRITING
Creating a Symbol

Imagine that you and a group of friends and acquaintances were stranded on a pleasant but uncharted island. Since you all expect to be there for a long time, the group has decided to draw up rules and laws for a society. You have been asked to create a symbol—a visual one—that will suggest what your society stands for, its goals, values, or ideals. First, think of the various things, living or nonliving, that might be appropriate symbols. Choose the best one. Write a paragraph that describes it, that explains its meaning and that tells why it is a good symbol for the island society. Revise your paper to make sure your reasoning is clear.

The Short Story

An active reader looks at the elements of the short story and considers how a writer uses them to make the story effective. By asking and answering questions about these elements, the reader gains a better appreciation of the story.

Plot

Plot is the sequence of events of the story. The events center on a conflict that may be external (outside the character) or internal (inside the character). The conflict reaches a climax that is finally resolved at the end, sometimes through a surprising turn of events.

Characters

Characters are the people—and sometimes the animals—in a story. The main character is the most important character in the story. The minor characters take part in the story's events but are not as important. Characters can be flat or round, depending on what the story reveals about them. A character's motivation, or reasons for acting, often sets the story moving in a certain direction.

Setting

Setting is the time and place in which the action of the story occurs. Time involves not only a historical period (past, present, future) but also the year, season, and time of day. Place involves not only the specific region or country, but also the city, town, or even type of neighborhood. Setting can be merely the backdrop for the story, or it can play a major role in the development of the plot and the characters.

Theme

Theme is the general idea about life that the story communicates. It is the central idea of the story, the idea to which all the elements—plot, characters, setting—add up. In some stories, the theme is stated directly. More often, however, it is implied, that is, suggested by the details of the story.

The comments in the margin of the story that follows review for you the elements of the short story. They also show questions an active reader might ask about these elements while reading.

After Twenty Years

O. Henry

Title: The title indicates a passage of time of twenty years. How will the characters have changed?

The policeman on the beat moved up the avenue impressively. The impressiveness was habitual and not for show, for spectators were few. The time was barely 10 o'clock at night, but chilly gusts of wind with a taste of rain in them had well nigh[1] depeopled the streets.

Setting: The story takes place on a city street at night. Will the facts that the street is empty and the time is night have any effect on the plot?

Trying doors as he went, twirling his club with many intricate and artful movements, turning now and then to cast his watchful eye adown the pacific thoroughfare,[2] the officer, with his stalwart form and slight swagger, made a fine picture of a guardian of the peace. The vicinity was one that kept early hours. Now and then you might see the lights of a cigar store or of an all-night lunch counter; but the majority of the doors belonged to business places that had long since been closed.

When about midway of a certain block the policeman suddenly slowed his walk. In the doorway of a darkened hardware store a man leaned, with an unlighted cigar in his mouth. As the policeman walked up to him the man spoke up quickly.

"It's all right, officer," he said, reassuringly. "I'm just waiting for a friend. It's an appointment made twenty years ago. Sounds a little funny to you, doesn't it? Well, I'll explain if you'd like to make certain it's all straight. About that long ago there used to be a restaurant where this store stands—'Big Joe' Brady's restaurant."

Plot: So this is the twenty years mentioned in the title! Why did the men agree to meet after twenty years? What will happen if the two men meet?

"Until five years ago," said the policeman. "It was torn down then."

The man in the doorway struck a match and lit his cigar. The light showed a pale, square-jawed face with keen eyes, and a little white scar near his right eyebrow. His scarfpin was a large diamond, oddly set.

Characters: The light from the match allows the policeman to clearly see the man in the doorway. Notice the scar and the diamond. Is this man honest?

"Twenty years ago tonight," said the man, "I dined here at 'Big Joe' Brady's with Jimmy Wells, my best chum, and the

---

1. **well nigh** (nī): Very nearly.
2. **pacific thoroughfare:** Calm street.

finest chap in the world. He and I were raised here in New York, just like two brothers, together. I was eighteen and Jimmy was twenty. The next morning I was to start for the West to make my fortune. You couldn't have dragged Jimmy out of New York; he thought it was the only place on earth. Well, we agreed that night that we would meet here again exactly twenty years from the date and time, no matter what our conditions might be or from what distance we might have to come. We figured that in twenty years each of us ought to have our destiny worked out and our fortunes made, whatever they were going to be."

"It sounds pretty interesting," said the policeman. "Rather a long time between meets, though, it seems to me. Haven't you heard from your friend since you left?"

"Well, yes, for a time we corresponded," said the other. "But after a year or two we lost track of each other. You see, the West is a pretty big proposition, and I kept hustling around over it pretty lively. But I know Jimmy will meet me here if he's alive, for he always was the truest, stanchest old chap in the world. He'll never forget. I came a thousand miles to stand in this door tonight, and it's worth it if my old partner turns up."

The waiting man pulled out a handsome watch, the lids of it set with small diamonds.

"Three minutes to ten," he announced. "It was exactly ten o'clock when we parted here at the restaurant door."

"Did pretty well out West, didn't you?" asked the policeman.

"You bet! I hope Jimmy has done half as well. He was a kind of plodder, though, good fellow as he was. I've had to compete with some of the sharpest wits going to get my pile. A man gets in a groove in New York. It takes the West to put a razor-edge on him."

The policeman twirled his club and took a step or two.

"I'll be on my way. Hope your friend comes around all right. Going to call time on him sharp?"

"I should say not!" said the other. "I'll give him half an hour at least. If Jimmy is alive on earth he'll be here by that time. So long, officer."

"Good night, sir," said the policeman, passing on along his beat, trying doors as he went.

There was now a fine, cold drizzle falling, and the wind

had risen from its uncertain puffs into a steady blow. The few foot passengers astir in that quarter hurried dismally and silently along with coat collars turned high and pocketed hands. And in the door of the hardware store the man who had come a thousand miles to fill an appointment, uncertain almost to absurdity, with the friend of his youth, smoked his cigar and waited.

About twenty minutes he waited, and then a tall man in a long overcoat, with collar turned up to his ears, hurried across from the opposite side of the street. He went directly to the waiting man.

"Is that you, Bob?" he asked, doubtfully.

"Is that you, Jimmy Wells?" cried the man in the door.

"Bless my heart!" exclaimed the new arrival, grasping both the other's hands with his own. "It's Bob, sure as fate. I was certain I'd find you here if you were still in existence. Well, well, well!—twenty years is a long time. The old restaurant's gone, Bob; I wish it had lasted, so we could have had another dinner there. How has the West treated you, old man?"

> **Setting and Characters:** The passage of twenty years has affected the setting, or place. Has it also affected the characters?

"Bully;[3] it has given me everything I asked it for. You've changed lots, Jimmy. I never thought you were so tall by two or three inches."

> **Plot:** This is odd! Why does Jimmy look so different?

"Oh, I grew a bit after I was twenty."

"Doing well in New York, Jimmy?"

"Moderately. I have a position in one of the city departments. Come on, Bob; we'll go around to a place I know of, and have a good long talk about old times."

The two men started up the street, arm in arm. The man from the West, his egotism enlarged by success, was beginning to outline the history of his career. The other, submerged in his overcoat, listened with interest.

At the corner stood a drug store, brilliant with electric lights. When they came into this glare each of them turned simultaneously to gaze upon the other's face.

The man from the West stopped suddenly and released his arm.

"You're not Jimmy Wells," he snapped. "Twenty years is a long time, but not long enough to change a man's nose from a Roman to a pug."

---

3. bully: Very well.

Theme: This statement appears to be important. What does it indicate about the theme of the story?

Plot: The policeman has the same last name as Jimmy. Could they be the same person?

Pulling It Together: Jimmy does turn out to be as honest as his friend thought he was, and he does keep his appointment. Have the two men changed? Why can't Jimmy arrest his friend? What clues paved the way for the surprise ending?

"It sometimes changes a good man into a bad one," said the tall man. "You've been under arrest for ten minutes, 'Silky' Bob. Chicago thinks you may have dropped over our way and wires us she wants to have a chat with you. Going quietly, are you? That's sensible. Now, before we go to the station here's a note I was asked to hand to you. You may read it here at the window. It's from Patrolman Wells."

The man from the West unfolded the little piece of paper handed him. His hand was steady when he began to read, but it trembled a little by the time he had finished. The note was rather short.

Bob: I was at the appointed place on time. When you struck the match to light your cigar I saw it was the face of the man wanted in Chicago. Somehow I couldn't do it myself, so I went around and got a plain-clothes man to do the job.

Jimmy

O. Henry (1862–1910) was born William Sidney Porter in Greensboro, North Carolina. Under the pen name of O. Henry, he wrote about ordinary people with warmth, humor, and a touch of romance. After spending time in prison for embezzlement (a crime for which he may not have been guilty), O. Henry moved to New York City, where he gathered material for his stories. His understanding of people on both sides of the law is evident in "After Twenty Years," as is his characteristic use of the surprise ending.

THINKING ABOUT THE SELECTION

Recalling

1. What promise did Bob and Jimmy make to each other twenty years ago?
2. What type of man does Bob believe Jimmy to be?
3. According to Bob, how does the West affect a person? In contrast, how does New York affect a person?
4. Why does Bob finally conclude that the man who pretends to be Jimmy Wells is in fact somebody else?
5. In fact, who is the man pretending to be Jimmy Wells and who is Bob?

Interpreting

6. What inference do you make about each man based on Bob's decision to go West and Jimmy's decision to remain in the East?
7. What do you infer about Bob when he says, "You see, the West is a pretty big proposition, and I kept hustling around over it pretty lively"?
8. What do you infer about Jimmy based on the information in his note to Bob?
9. Who has been more successful, Bob or Jimmy? Explain your answer.
10. What clues prepared you for the surprise ending?

Applying

11. Do you think people can be affected, or changed, by where they live? Do you think they can be affected by the passage of time? Explain your answers.

ANALYZING LITERATURE

Reviewing the Short Story

The elements of plot, characters, setting, and theme work together to create a total effect. Think of all these elements and apply them to "After Twenty Years."

1. Give a brief summary of the story.
2. Compare and contrast Bob and Jimmy.
3. What external conflict is present in the story? What internal conflict is present?
4. In what way does the setting play an important role in this story?
5. Find the sentence near the end of the story that suggests the theme. What is the theme?
6. What is the total effect of the story?

CRITICAL THINKING AND READING

Drawing Conclusions from Evidence

When people are presented with a fact or group of facts—evidence—it is natural for them to draw a conclusion. For example, in "After Twenty Years," Bob is presented with a fact: the shape of the nose of the man who claims to be Jimmy is different from the shape of the nose of the Jimmy he knew as a boy. From this fact, he draws the conclusion that the man who claims to be Jimmy Wells is lying.

1. What conclusion do you draw from the fact that both Bob and Jimmy keep their promise to meet after twenty years?
2. What conclusion do you draw from the fact that Jimmy has his old friend arrested?

THINKING AND WRITING

Writing an Addition to a Story

In this story, Bob tells briefly about the night he and Jimmy dined at "Big Joe" Brady's and promised to meet after twenty years. Picture this scene. What were Bob and Jimmy like at the time? What was the restaurant like? What was their conversation at dinner? Write the first draft of a story relating this event. When you revise your story, make sure your characters seem like younger versions of the characters in "After Twenty Years." Finally, edit your story, proofread it, and share it with your classmates.

Understanding Relationships

Reading a short story actively involves understanding the relationships that exist between events in the plot, setting, and characters. There are often clues in the story to help you see the connections. Understanding **time order, cause and effect,** and **comparison and contrast** relationships is important.

Time Order

Time order refers to the sequence of events in a story. Usually events are arranged chronologically so that one follows another. Writers often include signal words to help you see the sequence of events. Be aware of the following time-order signal words:

first	then	before	later	during	when
at last	next	after	earlier	finally	now

Activity

Read the following paragraph and jot down the time-order signal words. Then list the events in the order in which they occurred.

When Rikki-Tikki-Tavi first met Darzee, the tailorbird was miserable because Nag had eaten one of his babies. Before Darzee could tell Rikki who Nag was, Nag appeared. Then while Rikki was talking with the cobra, Nagaina tried to sneak up and attack Rikki. Luckily an earlier warning by Darzee prompted Rikki to jump as high in the air as he could, which saved him from the fatal cobra bite. Now he knew why the tailorbird so greatly feared the two snakes.

Cause and Effect

A **cause** is a reason for something happening. An **effect** is the result of some action or cause. The cause always occurs first and may produce many effects. The following signal words are often used to indicate a cause-and-effect relationship:

as	thus	therefore	consequently	so that
for	since	as a result	in order that	because

There were three cause-and-effect relationships in the preceding paragraph about Rikki-Tikki-Tavi.

Activity

Read the following sentences based on "Rikki-Tikki-Tavi."

Darzee was miserable because Nag had eaten his baby. Because the cobras had almost killed Rikki, the mongoose understood why the tailorbird greatly feared these snakes.

Note that the signal word *because* is used in each sentence to introduce the cause and that the cause can come at the beginning or end of the sentence.

Rewrite each sentence, using a different signal word and changing the order in which the cause-and-effect statements appear in the sentence. Then find the third cause-and-effect relationship in the paragraph and write it as a sentence.

Comparison and Contrast

Comparing involves finding ways that things are similar, while **contrasting** involves noting ways that they are different. By comparing and contrasting events, characters, themes, and other story elements, you gain greater insights and understanding. Words such as "both," "similar," and "just as much" indicate a comparison relationship. The following words are used to show contrasting relationships:

| but | although | in contrast | on the contrary | whereas |
| yet | however | nevertheless | on the other hand | while |

Activity

Make a chart to show how each of the animal characters in "Rikki-Tikki-Tavi" are alike and different. Write the following traits on the top of the chart: brave, shrewd, wicked, selfish, trustworthy, loving, fearful, sensible, curious, sly. Write the following names on the vertical side of the chart: Rikki, Darzee, Darzee's wife, Chuchundra, Nag, Nagaina, Karait. Make a checkerboard grid on the chart and check each box that applies to each character. Using the relationships that you noted in making the chart, write a paragraph comparing and contrasting the characters. Use the comparison and contrast signal words.

YOU THE WRITER

Assignment

1. The time and place where a story occurs is called the setting. Describe the setting of a short story you might write. Be sure this setting creates only a *single* overall impression.

Prewriting. Brainstorm, listing specific objects in this setting. From this list, select the ones that best create the desired impression.

Writing. Write the first draft of a description of the setting. Show the specific objects that help create impression. Be sure to show them in sharp detail.

Revising. When you revise, make sure you have created a vivid picture of the setting. Does your description create a unified impression?

Assignment

2. Authors make the characters in their stories seem real by showing (1) how they act, (2) how they speak, (3) how they look, and (4) how they think and feel. Write a character sketch of an imaginary character.

Prewriting. Make a list of several different kinds of personalities. Then take one of these personalities and make another list of the kinds of things a character with this personality might do and say and think.

Writing. Now write your character sketch. In the first sentence, tell what kind of person your imaginary character is. After you have done this, tell the kind of things this person does during the course of a day. Enter into this character's mind and show what he or she is thinking and feeling. Tell what he or she looks like and what he or she is wearing. Finally, let this person speak.

Revising. When you revise your composition, check to see that you have identified your character's main personality traits.

Assignment

3. Write a short story in which a character faces a problem and acts to resolve the problem. Try to make the ending a surprise.

Prewriting. Divide a sheet of paper into three columns. In the first column, make a list of problems a person might have. In the second column, list the solutions to these problems. In the third column, list the surprising ways in which these solutions might come about.

Writing. Using the lists you have made, write your story. Show your main character facing the problem you have chosen. Then show this person taking a series of actions to overcome this problem against some sort of opposition. Finally, show the character solving the problem in a surprising way.

Revising. When you revise your story, check to see that you have related events in chronological order.

YOU THE CRITIC

Assignment

1. The theme of coming of age is common in literature. Write an essay explaining how a character from a short story you have read comes of age.

    Prewriting. What does it mean to pass from childhood to maturity? Freewrite, exploring how one character does just that.

    Writing. Write the first draft of your essay. Relate events in chronological order. Remember to tell how the character is different at the end of the story.

    Revising. Make sure you have included enough details to prove that this character has truly come of age.

Assignment

2. The theme of a short story is the insight into life it reveals. Write an essay interpreting the theme of one of the short stories in this unit. Then support your opinion by referring to specific characters and incidents in the story.

    Prewriting. Freewrite about the short story and the characters. Ask yourself what these characters have learned during the course of the story. Then ask yourself what *you* have learned.

    Writing. Now write the first draft of your essay. In your opening paragraph, state the theme. In the body explain how the short story reveals this insight into life. In the last line of the essay, restate the theme, but add a little twist to it, something to end the essay with flair.

    Revising. As you revise your essay, check to see that you have fully interpreted the theme.

Assignment

3. Write an essay about how the author of one of the short stories in this unit prepares the reader in the early part of the story for things that will happen later.

    Prewriting. Before you write, examine the second half of the story first. Focus on the surprises that occur in this part, for it is these surprises that the author must prepare the reader for. After you have examined the surprises in the second half of the story, scan through the first half of the story to see how the author prepared you for them.

    Writing. Now write your essay. State your thesis or main idea in your introductory paragraph. In the body paragraphs, include a *brief* summary of the story, the surprises at the end, and the ways in which the author prepared you for these surprises.

    Revising. As you revise your essay, make sure you have arranged your information in a logical order.

PARADE CURTAIN AFTER PICASSO
© *David Hockney, 1980*

DRAMA

The word *drama* leaves a thrill in the air. Hear the word and you immediately think of the excitement of the theater with live actors on the stage and a live audience offering its applause. Or you recall the pleasure of drama brought into your home through television or radio or into the cinema through movies.

Since drama is meant to be performed, when you read it, you must imagine how it would appear on the stage or screen, or, if it is a radio play, how it would sound over the radio or on a tape cassette. The story of the drama is told mainly through dialogue, or conversation between characters. From what the characters say, you discover what they are feeling and what they are like. In addition, stage directions describe how the characters would move or act before an audience. The sets are the re-creation of settings on the stage; the props, the physical objects the characters use; the costumes, the clothes the characters wear; and the sound effects, the planned noise that accompanies the play. Each of these devices helps create the world of the play on the stage.

Just as a short story may be divided into episodes, a short play may be divided into scenes. Just as a novel is divided into chapters, a full-length play is divided into acts.

In this unit you will encounter plays on a variety of topics and for a variety of media. You will read a stage play, a radio play, a television play, and even a full-length play based on a famous book.

Drama

Drama is a story told in dialogue by performers before an audience. When we think of drama, we think of stage plays and the exciting world of the theater—actors, costumes, stage sets, and lights. But drama includes more than the theater; television plays and radio plays are drama too. Even movies are a form of drama. In all of these kinds of drama, actors make a world come alive before an audience.

Plays are meant to be performed, but it is possible just to read a play. When you read a play, you can make it come alive by staging it in your imagination. The play you are reading is a script. It contains not only the words that the actors speak but also the stage directions the playwright provides to indicate how to put on the play. Stage directions tell what the stage should look like, what the characters wear, how they speak their lines, and where they move.

Stage directions use a particular vocabulary. *Right, left, up, down,* and *center* refer to areas of the stage as the actors see it. To help you visualize what is meant when a stage direction tells an actor to move down left, for example, picture the stage like this:

THE STAGE

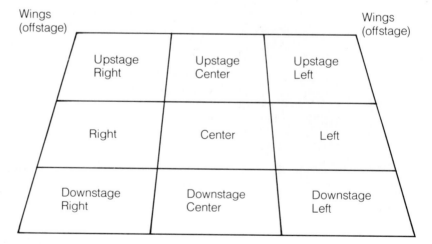

Upstage Right	Upstage Center	Upstage Left
Right	Center	Left
Downstage Right	Downstage Center	Downstage Left

Wings (offstage) — Wings (offstage)

Curtain

Television plays and film scripts have their own kinds of directions; these are camera directions. *Fade in, fade out, long shot, close up* should make sense to you. *Pan* means "to move the camera to follow a moving object or to create a panoramic scene." When you read these directions, you know what character or actions get emphasized.

Just as you read short stories actively, you should also read drama actively. Reading actively includes trying to see the play in your mind while you continually question the meaning of what the actors are saying and doing.

Use the following strategies to help you read drama actively. These strategies will help you to enjoy and appreciate the plays in this unit.

Visualize

Use the directions and information supplied by the playwright to picture the stage and the characters in action. Hear their voices. Go beyond the stated words and actions to create the scene in your mind.

Question

As you meet the characters, ask yourself what each character is like. What situation does each character face? What motives and traits does each character reveal by his or her words and actions?

Predict

Building on the play's conflict and the characters' words and actions, predict what you think will happen. How will the conflict be resolved? What will become of each character?

Clarify

If a character's words or actions are not clear to you, stop and try to make sense of them. Look for answers to your questions and check your predictions.

Summarize

Pause occasionally to review what has happened. Put the characters' actions and words together. What is the story being told?

Pull It Together

Pull together all of the elements of the play. What does the play mean? Is it purely entertainment or is there a message? What does it say to you?

Using these strategies when you read drama will help you to be a more effective reader. You will be better able to understand the conflict of the play and its resolution and to apply your understanding to your world.

Grandpa and the Statue

Arthur Miller (1915–   ) is one of America's most honored play-wrights. After graduating from the University of Michigan, he returned to New York City, where he was born, and wrote radio plays. Most of his work, though, has been for the stage. His play *Death of a Sales-man* is considered one of the greatest modern plays. Miller often writes about families, and the immigrant experience. The play you are about to read portrays a remarkable grandfather and shows the special meaning the Statue of Liberty comes to have for him.

Dialogue

Dialogue is talk between characters. In a play dialogue carries the plot forward and shows what the characters are like. In some plays it even establishes the setting: Characters can indicate by their words where they are and when something is happening. Because *Grandpa and the Statue* is a radio play, the dialogue is especially important.

Look For

Grandpa and the Statue was originally written to be presented on the radio. Since it is a radio play, as you read, pretend that you are only listening to it, not seeing it performed on the stage. Imagine the sound of the characters' voices. How would you read the lines? Notice the bracketed directions for music: They signal that the action is shifting from one place to another or from one time to another.

Writing

In this play the grandfather and grandson visit the Statue of Liberty. Think of a time you visited a special place that you had long looked forward to seeing. It might be a famous monument, a national park, a city, a professional-sports center, or any other place. Freewrite about what you expected before you made your trip and what you actually felt when you were there.

Vocabulary

Knowing the following words will help you as you read *Grandpa and the Statue*.

subscribed (səb skrībd′) *v.*: Supported (p. 221)
peeved (pēvd) *v.*: Irritated (p. 221)
register (rej′ is tər) *n.*: A record

containing a list of names (p. 222)
gleefully (glē′ fə lē) *adj.*: Merry (p. 223)

Grandpa and the Statue

Arthur Miller

CHARACTERS

Announcer	Grandfather Monaghan	Jack	Girl
August	Child Monaghan	Mike	Young Man
Young Monaghan	George	Joe	Megaphone Voice
Sheean	Charley	Alf	Veteran

[*Music: Theme*]

ANNOUNCER. The scene is the fourth floor of a giant army hospital overlooking New York Harbor. A young man sitting in a wheel chair is looking out a window; just looking. After a while another young man in another wheel chair rolls over to him and both look.

[*Music out*]

AUGUST. You want to play some checkers with me, Monaghan?

MONAGHAN. Not right now.

AUGUST. Okay. [*Slight pause*] You don't want to go feeling blue, Monaghan.

MONAGHAN. I'm not blue.

AUGUST. All you do most days is sit here looking out this window.

MONAGHAN. What do you want me to do, jump rope?

AUGUST. No, but what do you get out of it?

MONAGHAN. It's a beautiful view. Some companies make millions of dollars just printing that view on postcards.

AUGUST. Yeh, but nobody keeps looking at a postcard six, seven hours a day.

MONAGHAN. I come from around here, it reminds me of things. My young days.

AUGUST. That's right, you're Brooklyn, aren't you?

MONAGHAN. My house is only about a mile away.

AUGUST. That so. Tell me, are you looking at just the water all the time? I'm curious. I don't get a kick out of this view.

MONAGHAN. There's the Statue of Liberty out there. Don't you see it?

AUGUST. Oh, that's it. Yeh, that's nice to look at.

MONAGHAN. I like it. Reminds me of a lot of laughs.

AUGUST. Laughs? The Statue of Liberty?

MONAGHAN. Yeh, my grandfather. He got all twisted up with the Statue of Liberty.

AUGUST. [*Laughs a little*] That so? What happened?

PENNIES FOR THE PEDESTAL

OVER 1,000 PERSONS CONTRIBUTED YESTERDAY TO THE BARTHOLDI FUND.

A Great Day for Small Subscriptions—All the People Getting Ready to Give Something—Employees In Every Line of Business Responding to the "World's" Appeal—Each Day Bringing Redoubled Assurances of Success.

PENNIES FOR THE PEDESTAL
The World, *April 3, 1885*
Courtesy of the New York Historical Society, New York City

MONAGHAN. Well. My grandfather was the stingiest man in Brooklyn. "Mercyless" Monaghan, they used to call him. He even used to save umbrella handles.

AUGUST. What for?

MONAGHAN. Just couldn't stand seeing anything go to waste. After a big windstorm there'd be a lot of broken umbrellas laying around in the streets.

AUGUST. Yeh?

MONAGHAN. He'd go around picking them up. In our house the closets were always full of umbrella handles. My grandma used to say that he would go across the Brooklyn Bridge on the trolley just because he could come back on the same nickel. See, if you stayed on the trolley they'd let you come back for the same nickel.

AUGUST. What'd he do, just go over and come back?

MONAGHAN. Yeh, it made him feel good. Savin' money. Two and a half cents.

AUGUST. So how'd he get twisted up with the Statue of Liberty?

MONAGHAN. Well, way back in 1887 around there they were living on Butler Street. Butler Street, Brooklyn, practically runs right down to the river. One day he's sitting on the front porch, reading a paper he borrowed from the neighbors, when along comes this man Jack Sheean who lived up the block.

[*Music: Sneak into above speech, then bridge, then out*]

SHEEAN. [*Slight brogue*] A good afternoon to you, Monaghan.

MONAGHAN. How're you, Sheean, how're ya?

SHEEAN. Fair, fair. And how's Mrs. Monaghan these days?

MONAGHAN. Warm. Same as everybody else in summer.

SHEEAN. I've come to talk to you about the fund, Monaghan.

MONAGHAN. What fund is that?

SHEEAN. The Statue of Liberty fund.

MONAGHAN. Oh, that.

SHEEAN. It's time we come to grips with the subject, Monaghan.

MONAGHAN. I'm not interested, Sheean.

SHEEAN. Now hold up on that a minute. Let me tell you the facts. This here Frenchman has gone and built a fine statue of Liberty. It costs the Lord knows how many millions to build. All they're askin' us to do is contribute enough to put up a base for the statue to stand on.

MONAGHAN. I'm not . . . !

SHEEAN. Before you answer me. People all over the whole United States are puttin' in for it. Butler Street is doin' the same. We'd like to hand up a flag on the corner saying—"Butler Street, Brooklyn, is one hundred percent behind the Statue of Liberty." And Butler Street *is* a hundred percent subscribed except for you. Now will you give us a dime, Monaghan? One dime and we can put up the flag. Now what do you say to that?

MONAGHAN. I'm not throwin' me good money away for somethin' I don't even know exists.

SHEEAN. Now what do you mean by that?

MONAGHAN. Have you seen this statue?

SHEEAN. No, but it's in a warehouse. And as soon as we get the money to build the pedestal they'll take it and put it up on that island in the river, and all the boats comin' in from the old country will see it there and it'll raise the hearts of the poor immigrants to see such a fine sight on their first look at this country.

MONAGHAN. And how do I know it's in this here warehouse at all?

SHEEAN. You read your paper, don't you? It's been in all the papers for the past year.

MONAGHAN. Ha, the papers? Last year I read in the paper that they were about to pave Butler Street and take out all the holes. Turn around and look at Butler Street, Mr. Sheean.

SHEEAN. All right. I'll do this: I'll take you to the warehouse and show you the statue. Will you give me a dime then?

MONAGHAN. Well . . . I'm not sayin' I would, and I'm not sayin' I wouldn't. But I'd be more *likely* if I saw the thing large as life, I would.

SHEEAN. [*Peeved*] All right, then. Come along.

[*Music up and down and out*]
[*Footsteps, in a warehouse . . . echo . . . they come to halt*]

Now then. Do you see the Statue of Liberty or don't you see it?

MONAGHAN. I see it all right, but it's all broke!

SHEEAN. *Broke!* They brought it from France on a boat. They had to take it apart, didn't they?

MONAGHAN. You got a secondhand statute, that's what you got, and I'm not payin' for new when they've shipped us something that's all smashed to pieces.

SHEEAN. Now just a minute, just a minute. Visualize what I'm about to tell you, Monaghan, get the picture of it. When this statue is put together it's going to stand ten stories high. Could they get a thing ten stories high into a four-story building such as this is? Use your good sense, now, Monaghan.

MONAGHAN. What's that over there?

SHEEAN. Where?

MONAGHAN. That tablet there in her hand. What's it say? July Eye Vee [IV] MDCCLXXVI . . . what . . . what's all that?

SHEEAN. That means July 4, 1776. It's in Roman numbers. Very high class.

MONAGHAN. What's the good of it? If they're going to put a sign on her they ought to put it: Welcome All. That's it. Welcome All.

SHEEAN. They decided July 4, 1776, and July 4, 1776, it's going to be!

MONAGHAN. All right, then let them get their dime from somebody else!

SHEEAN. Monaghan!

MONAGHAN. No, sir! I'll tell you something. I didn't think there was a statue but there is. She's all broke, it's true, but she's here and maybe they can get her together. But even if they do, will you tell me what sort of a welcome to immigrants it'll be, to have a gigantic thing like that in the middle of the river and in her hand is July Eye Vee MCDVC . . . whatever it is?

SHEEAN. That's the date the country was made!

MONAGHAN. The divil with the date! A man comin' in from the sea wants a place to stay, not a date. When I come from the old country I git off at the dock and there's a feller says to me, "Would you care for a room for the night?" "I would that," I sez, and he sez, "All right then, follow me." He takes me to a rooming house. I no sooner sign me name on the register—which I was able to do even at that time—when I look around and the feller is gone clear away and took my valise in the bargain. A statue anyway can't move off so fast, but if she's going to welcome let her say welcome, not this MCDC. . . .

SHEEAN. All right, then, Monaghan. But all I can say is, you've laid a disgrace on the name of Butler Street. I'll put the dime in for ya.

MONAGHAN. Don't connect me with it! It's a swindle, is all it is. In the first place, it's

broke; in the second place, if they do put it up it'll come down with the first high wind that strikes it.

SHEEAN. The engineers say it'll last forever!

MONAGHAN. And I say it'll topple into the river in a high wind! Look at the inside of her. She's all hollow!

SHEEAN. I've heard everything now, Monaghan. Just about everything. Good-bye.

MONAGHAN. What do you mean, good-bye? How am I to get back to Butler Street from here?

SHEEAN. You've got legs to walk.

MONAGHAN. I'll remind you that I come on the trolley.

SHEEAN. And I'll remind you that I paid your fare and I'm not repeating the kindness.

MONAGHAN. Sheean? You've stranded me!

[*Music up and down*]

YOUNG MONAGHAN. That was grandpa. That's why I have to laugh every time I look at the statue now.

AUGUST. Did he ever put the dime in?

YOUNG MONAGHAN. Well—in a way. What happened was this: His daughters got married and finally my mom . . . put *me* out on Butler Street. I got to be pretty attached to grandpa. He'd even give me an umbrella handle and make a sword out of it for me. Naturally, I wasn't very old before he began working on me about the statue.

[*High wind*]

CHILD MONAGHAN. [*Softly, as though grandpa is in bed*] Grampa?

MONAGHAN. [*Awakened*] Heh? What are you doin' up?

CHILD MONAGHAN. Ssssh! Listen!

[*Wind rising up and fading. Rising higher and fading*]

MONAGHAN. [*Gleefully*] Aaaaaaaah! Yes, yes. This'll do it, boy. This'll do it! First thing in the morning we'll go down to the docks and I'll bet you me life that Mr. Sheean's statue is smashed down and layin' on the bottom of the bay. Go to sleep now, we'll have a look first thing.

[*Music up and down*]
[*Footsteps*]

CHILD MONAGHAN. If it fell down, all the people will get their dimes back, won't they, grampa? Slow down, I can't walk so fast.

MONAGHAN. Not only will they get their dimes back, but Mr. Sheean and the whole crew that engineered the collection are going to rot in jail. Now mark my words. Here, now, we'll take a short cut around this shed . . .

[*Footsteps continue a moment, then gradually . . . disappointedly they come to a halt*]

CHILD MONAGHAN. She's . . . she's still standing, grampa.

MONAGHAN. She is that. [*Uncomprehending*] I don't understand it. That was a terrible wind last night. Terrible.

CHILD MONAGHAN. Maybe she's weaker though. Heh?

MONAGHAN. Why . . . sure, that must be it. I'll wager she's hangin' by a thread. [*Realizing*] Of course! That's why they put her out there in the water so when she falls down she won't be flattening out a lot of poor innocent people. Hey—feel that?

CHILD MONAGHAN. The wind! It's starting to blow again!

MONAGHAN. Sure, and look at the sky blackening over!

[*Wind rising*]

Feel it comin' up! Take your last look at the statue, boy. If I don't mistake me eyes she's takin' a small list to Jersey already!

[*Music up and down*]

YOUNG MONAGHAN. It was getting embarrassing for me on the block. I kept promising the other kids that when the next wind came the statue would come down. We even had a game. Four or five kids would stand in a semicircle around one kid who was the statue. The statue kid had to stand on his heels and look right in our eyes. Then we'd all take a deep breath and blow in his face. He'd fall down like a stick of wood. They all believed me and grampa . . . until one day. We were standing around throwing rocks at an old milk can . . .

[*Banging of rocks against milk can*]

GEORGE. [*Kid*] What're you doin?

CHILD MONAGHAN. What do we look like we're doin?

GEORGE. I'm going someplace tomorrow.

CHARLEY. [*Kid*] I know, church. Watch out, I'm throwin'.

[*Can being hit*]

GEORGE. I mean after church.

JACK. Where?

GEORGE. My old man's going to take me out on the Statue of Liberty boat.

[*Banging against can abruptly stops*]

CHILD MONAGHAN. You're not going out on the statue, though, are you?

GEORGE. Sure, that's where we're going.

CHILD MONAGHAN. But you're liable to get killed. Supposing there's a high wind tomorrow?

GEORGE. My old man says that statue couldn't fall down if all the wind in the world and John L. Sullivan[1] hit it at the same time.

CHILD MONAGHAN. Is that so?

GEORGE. Yeh, that's so. My old man says that the only reason your grandfather's saying that it's going to fall down is that he's ashamed he didn't put a dime in for the pedestal.

CHILD MONAGHAN. Is that so?

GEORGE. Yeh, that's so.

CHILD MONAGHAN. Well, you tell your old man that if he gets killed tomorrow not to come around to my grandfather and say he didn't warn him!

JACK. Hey, George, would your father take me along?

GEORGE. I'll ask him, maybe he—

CHILD MONAGHAN. What, are you crazy, Jack?

MIKE. Ask him if he'd take me too, will ya, George?

CHILD MONAGHAN. Mike, what's the matter with you?

JOE. Me too, George, I'll ask my mother for money.

CHILD MONAGHAN. Joe! Didn't you hear what my grampa said?

JOE. Well . . . I don't really believe that any more.

CHILD MONAGHAN. You don't be . . .

MIKE. Me neither.

---

1. **John L. Sullivan:** A famous American boxer (1858–1918).

JACK. I don't really think your grampa knows what he's talkin' about.

CHILD MONAGHAN. He don't, heh? [*Ready to weep*] Okay . . . Okay. [*Bursting out*] I just hope that wind blows tomorrow, boy! I just hope that wind blows!

[*Music up and down*]
[*Creaking of a rocking chair*]

MONAGHAN. Huh?

CHILD MONAGHAN. Can you stop rocking for a minute?

[*Rocking stops*]

Can you put down your paper?

[*Rustle of paper*]

I—I read the weather report for tomorrow.

MONAGHAN. The weather report . . .

CHILD MONAGHAN. Yeh. It says fair and cool.

MONAGHAN. What of it?

CHILD MONAGHAN. I was wondering. Supposing you and me we went on a boat tomorrow. You know, I see the water every day when I go down to the docks to play, but I never sat on it. I mean in a boat.

MONAGHAN. Oh. Well, we might take the ferry on the Jersey side. We might do that.

CHILD MONAGHAN. Yeh, but there's nothing to see in Jersey.

MONAGHAN. You can't go to Europe tomorrow.

CHILD MONAGHAN. No, but couldn't we go toward the ocean? Just . . . *toward* it?

MONAGHAN. Toward it. What—what is it on your mind, boy? What is it now?

CHILD MONAGHAN. Well, I . . .

MONAGHAN. Oh, you want to take the Staten Island ferry. Sure, that's in the direction of the sea.

CHILD MONAGHAN. No, grampa, not the Staten Island ferry.

MONAGHAN. You don't mean—[*Breaks off*] Boy!

CHILD MONAGHAN. All the kids are going tomorrow with Georgie's old man.

MONAGHAN. You don't believe me any more.

CHILD MONAGHAN. I do, grampa, but . . .

MONAGHAN. You don't. If you did you'd stay clear of the Statue of Liberty for love of your life!

CHILD MONAGHAN. But, grampa, when is it going to fall down? All I do is wait and wait.

MONAGHAN. [*With some uncertainty*] You've got to have faith.

CHILD MONAGHAN. But every kid in my class went to see it and now the ones that didn't are going tomorrow. And they all keep talking about it and all I do . . . Well, I can't keep telling them it's a swindle. I—I wish we could see it, grampa. It don't cost so much to go.

MONAGHAN. As long as you put it that way I'll have to admit I'm a bit curious meself as to how it's managed to stand upright so long. Tell you what I'll do. Barrin' wind, we'll chance it tomorrow.

CHILD MONAGHAN. Oh, gramp!

MONAGHAN. But! If anyone should ask you where we went you'll say—Staten Island. Are y' on?

CHILD MONAGHAN. Okay, sure. Staten Island.

MONAGHAN. [*Secretively*] We'll take the early boat, then. Mum's the word, now. For if old man Sheean hears that I went out there I'll have no peace from the thief the rest of m' life.

[*Music up and down*]

[*Boat whistles*]

CHILD MONAGHAN. Gee, it's nice ridin' on a boat, ain't it, grampa?

MONAGHAN. Never said there was anything wrong with the boat. Boat's all right. You're sure now that Georgie's father is takin' the kids in the afternoon.

CHILD MONAGHAN. Yeh, that's when they're going. Gee, look at those two sea gulls. Wee!—look at them swoop! They caught a fish!

MONAGHAN. What I can't understand is what all these people see in that statue that they'll keep a boat like this full makin' the trip, year in year out. To hear the newspapers talk, if the statue was gone we'd be at war with the nation that stole her the followin' mornin' early. All it is is a big high pile of French copper.

CHILD MONAGHAN. The teachers says it shows us that we got liberty.

MONAGHAN. Bah! If you've got liberty you don't need a statue to tell you you got it; and if you haven't got liberty no statue's going to do you any good tellin' you you got it. It was a criminal waste of the people's money. [*Quietly*] And just to prove it to you I'll ask this feller sitting right over there what he sees in it. You'll see what a madness the whole thing was. Say, mister?

ALF. Hey?

MONAGHAN. I beg your pardon. I'm a little strange here, and curious. Could you tell me why you're going to the Statue of Liberty?

ALF. Me? Well, I tell ya. I always wanted to take an ocean voyage. This is a pretty big boat—bigger than the ferries—so on Sundays, sometimes, I take the trip. It's better than nothing.

THE WAKE OF THE FERRY II, 1907
John Sloan
The Phillips Collection

MONAGHAN. Thank you. [*To the kid*] So much for the great meaning of the statue, me boy. We'll talk to this lady standing at the rail. I just want you to understand why I didn't give Sheean me dime. Madam, would you be good enough to . . . Oh pardon me. [*To kid*] Better pass her by, she don't look so good. We'll ask that girl there. Young lady, if you'll pardon the curiosity of an old man . . . could you tell me in a few good words what it is about that statue that brings you out here?

GIRL. What statue?

MONAGHAN. Why, the Statue of Liberty up 'head. We're coming up to it.

GIRL. Statue of Liberty! Is this the Statue of Liberty boat?

MONAGHAN. Well, what'd you think it was?

GIRL. Oh, my! I'm supposed to be on the Staten Island ferry! Where's the ticket man? [*Going away*] Ticket man! Where's the ticket man?

CHILD MONAGHAN. Gee whiz, nobody seems to want to see the statue.

MONAGHAN. Just to prove it, let's see this fellow sitting on this bench here. Young man, say . . .

YOUNG MAN. I can tell you in one word. For four days I haven't had a minute's peace. My kids are screaming, my wife is yelling, upstairs they play the piano all day long. The only place I can find that's quiet is a statue. That statue is my sweetheart. Every Sunday I beat it out to the island and sit next to her, and she don't talk.

CHILD MONAGHAN. I guess you were right, grampa. Nobody seems to think it means anything.

MONAGHAN. Not only doesn't mean anything, but if they'd used the money to build an hon-est roomin' house on that island, the immigrants would have a place to spend the night, their valises wouldn't get robbed, and they—

MEGAPHONE VOICE. *Please keep your seats while the boat is docking. Statue of Liberty—all out in five minutes!*

CHILD MONAGHAN. Look down there, gramp! There's a peanut stand! Could I have some?

MONAGHAN. I feel the wind comin' up. I don't think we dare take the time.

[*Music up and down*]

CHILD MONAGHAN. Sssssseuuuuuww! Look how far you can see! Look at that ship way out in the ocean!

MONAGHAN. It is, it's quite a view. Don't let go of me hand now.

CHILD MONAGHAN. I betcha we could almost see California.

MONAGHAN. It's probably that grove of trees way out over there. They do say it's beyond Jersey.

CHILD MONAGHAN. Feels funny. We're standing right inside her head. Is that what you meant . . . July IV, MCD . . . ?

MONAGHAN. That's it. That tablet in her hand. Now shouldn't they have put Welcome All on it instead of that foreign language? Say! Do you feel her rockin'?

CHILD MONAGHAN. Yeah, she's moving a little bit. Listen, the wind!

[*Whistling of wind*]

MONAGHAN. We better get down, come on! This way!

CHILD MONAGHAN. No, the stairs are this way! Come on!

[*Running in echo. Then quick stop*]

MONAGHAN. No, I told you they're the other way! Come!

VETERAN. [*Calm, quiet voice*] Don't get excited, pop. She'll stand.

MONAGHAN. She's swayin' awful.

VETERAN. That's all right. I been up here thirty, forty times. She gives with the wind, flexible. Enjoy the view, go on.

MONAGHAN. Did you say you've been up here forty times?

VETERAN. About that many.

MONAGHAN. What do you find here that's so interesting?

VETERAN. It calms my nerves.

MONAGHAN. Ah. It seems to me it would make you more nervous than you were.

VETERAN. No, not me. It kinda means something to me.

MONAGHAN. Might I ask what?

VETERAN. Well . . . I was in the Philippine War[2] . . . back in '98. Left my brother back there.

MONAGHAN. Oh, yes. Sorry I am to hear it. Young man, I suppose, eh?

VETERAN. Yeh. We were both young. This is his birthday today.

MONAGHAN. Oh, I understand.

VETERAN. Yeh, this statue is about the only stone he's got. In my mind I feel it is anyway. This statue kinda looks like what we believe. You know what I mean?

MONAGHAN. Looks like what we believe . . . I . . . I never thought of it that way. I . . . I see what you mean. It does look that way. [*Angrily*] See now, boy? If Sheean had put it that way I'd a give him me dime. [*Hurt*] Now, why do you suppose he didn't tell me that? Come down now. I'm sorry, sir, we've got to get out of here.

[*Music up and down*]
[*Footsteps under*]

Hurry now, I want to get out of here. I feel terrible. I do, boy. That Sheean, that fool. Why didn't he tell me that? You'd think . . .

CHILD MONAGHAN. What does this say?

[*Footsteps halt*]

MONAGHAN. Why, it's just a tablet, I suppose. I'll try it with me spectacles, just a minute. Why, it's a poem, I believe . . . "Give me your tired, your poor, your huddled masses yearning to breathe free, the wretched refuse of your teeming shore. Send these, the homeless, tempest-tost to me, I lift . . . my lamp beside . . . the golden door!"[3] Oh, dear. [*Ready to weep*] It had Welcome All on it all the time. Why didn't Sheean tell me? I'd a given him a quarter! Boy . . . go over there and here's a nickel and buy yourself a bag of them peanuts.

CHILD MONAGHAN. [*Astonished*] Gramp!

MONAGHAN. Go on now, I want to study this a minute. And be sure the man gives you full count.

CHILD MONAGHAN. I'll be right back.

[*Footsteps running away*]

MONAGHAN. [*To himself*] "Give me your tired, your poor, your huddled masses . . . "

---

2. **Philippine War:** A brief conflict that took place between Spain and the United States in 1898 and is more frequently called the Spanish-American War.

3. **"Give me your tired . . .":** A quote from a poem about the statue written by the American poet Emma Lazarus (1849–1887) and engraved on the statue's pedestal.

THE UNVEILING OF THE STATUE OF LIBERTY
Edward Moran
Museum of the City of New York

[*Music swells from a sneak to full, then under to background*]

YOUNG MONAGHAN. [*Soldier*] I ran over and got my peanuts and stood there cracking them open, looking around. And I happened to glance over to grampa. He had his nose right up to that bronze tablet, reading it. And then he reached into his pocket and kinda spied around over his eyeglasses to see if anybody was looking, and then he took out a coin and stuck it in a crack of cement over the tablet.

[*Coin falling onto concrete*]

It fell out and before he could pick it up I got a look at it. It was a half a buck. He picked it up and pressed it into the crack so it stuck. And then he came over to me and we went home.

[*Music: Change to stronger, more forceful theme*]

That's why, when I look at her now through this window, I remember that time and that poem, and she really seems to say, Whoever you are, wherever you come from, Welcome All. Welcome Home.

[*Music: Flare up to finish*]

THINKING ABOUT THE SELECTION

Recalling

1. Why does Grandfather refuse Sheean's request?
2. What does Grandfather predict will happen to the Statue after it is put up?
3. What does the veteran tell Grandfather that changes his mind about the Statue of Liberty?

Interpreting

4. What does the veteran mean by the words "This statue kinda looks like what we believe"?
5. Near the end of the play, why does Grandfather put the half dollar into the crack above the tablet?

6. In what way do you think Monaghan's memories of his grandfather's relationship with the Statue of Liberty have affected him?

Applying

7. Why do monuments sometimes hold special significance for Americans?

ANALYZING LITERATURE

Reading Dialogue

Dialogue is talk between characters. When reading the dialogue in a play, pay attention to what is said that advances the plot or that provides background information. Through the dialogue you must form pictures in your mind of the movements and gestures of the characters and the details of the setting. Above all, as you read dialogue, you must imagine what the characters sound like as they speak. Put simply, you have to create a little theater in your own mind.

Reread the first twenty-two lines of dialogue between Sheean and Grandfather (pages 220–221).

1. What conflict is revealed through the dialogue?
2. What impression of Grandfather do you get from these lines?
3. Which of the following phrases describes how Grandfather probably sounds when he speaks in the play?
   a. meek, mild, and easily led by others
   b. stubborn, defensive, ready to argue
   c. consistently nasty and unpleasant

CRITICAL THINKING AND READING
Making Inferences About Characters

You can make inferences about characters by imagining how they utter their lines—their tone of voice, their facial expressions, and the gestures that go with their words. For example, when Grandfather and young Monaghan go to look at the Statue of Liberty on a windy morning, Grandfather says, "Sure, and look at the sky blackening over! Feel it comin' up! Take your last look at the statue, boy. . . ." His tone of voice as he speaks these words is probably one of pleased excitement. His eyes are wide. He is straining to see any sign that the Statue is about to collapse. By picturing all of this, you can infer something about Grandfather's feelings. He desperately wants to be proved right in his opposition to the Statue of Liberty fund.

From each of the following lines, what can you infer about Grandfather's feelings?

1. "Not only will they get their dimes back, but Mr. Sheean and the whole crew that engineered the collection are going to rot in jail."
2. "Looks like what we believe . . . I . . . I never

thought of it that way. I . . . I see what you mean. It does look that way. See now, boy? If Sheean had put it that way I'd a give him me dime."

UNDERSTANDING LANGUAGE
Recognizing Dialect

Dialect is the special kind of speech used by a particular group of people or found in a particular region of a country. Unusual, even nonstandard expressions and pronunciations are two signs of dialect. Sheean's remark, "This here Frenchman has gone and built a fine statue of Liberty" is an example of the dialect of the working-class Irish people who came to America in the late nineteenth and early twentieth centuries.

1. Reread the dialogue between Grandfather and Sheean near the beginning of the play (pp. 220–222). What other examples of dialect can you find?
2. Reread Grandfather's speech beginning "Why, it's just a tablet . . ." near the end of the play. Find examples of dialect here.

THINKING AND WRITING
Writing Dialogue

Imagine that you are visiting the place you wrote about before reading the play. Grandfather Monaghan walks up to you, informs you that he sees nothing interesting or important about the place, and asks you what it means to you. Write a dialogue between you and Grandfather modeled on the dialogue in the play. Grandfather should be just as he is in the play. He asks questions and makes comments just as Arthur Miller's character would. You reply as if you, too, were a character in a play. By the end of the dialogue, Grandfather should come to understand your point of view. After you have finished your first draft, revise your dialogue, making sure it contains enough details to make Grandfather come alive. Finally, with one of your classmates in the role of Grandfather, act out your dialogue before your class.

GUIDE FOR READING

The Dying Detective

Sir Arthur Conan Doyle (1859–1930) was born in Edinburgh, Scotland. While studying medicine there, he got to know Joseph Bell, a skillful surgeon who could diagnose a patient's occupation and character as well as disease. Bell was the model for Sherlock Holmes. Eventually, Doyle abandoned medicine to devote full time to writing. **Michael and Mollie Hardwick** are best-selling authors in England. Michael Hardwick is an expert on Sherlock Holmes and his creator. Mollie Hardwick has written numerous plays.

Staging

Staging a play means making it come to life on a stage. Staging includes acting, costumes, scenery, lighting, sound effects, and special effects. When you read a play, you should try your best to stage it in your imagination.

Look For

As you read *The Dying Detective,* read carefully the description at the start of each scene. Picture what you would see at a performance. Also, notice the stage directions. These statements in brackets will help you to picture the characters in action.

Writing

Think of a short story that you especially enjoyed and that you would make into a play. Make notes on how you would stage it. Your notes should answer these questions: In what place is the story set? What is the time of day? What objects should appear on stage, and how should they be arranged? What characters should be on stage at the start of the action? What do they look like? How are they dressed? What are they doing?

Vocabulary

Knowing the following words will help you as you read *The Dying Detective.*

masterful (mas' tər fəl) *adj.*: Able to force one's will on others (p. 235)

incubation (in' kyə bā' shən) *n.*: The phase in a disease between the infection and the first appearance of symptoms (p. 236)

pathological (path' ə läj' i k'l) *adj.*: Due to, concerned with, or involving disease (p. 236)

complaint (kəm plānt') *n.*: An illness (p. 236)

remonstrance (ri män' strəns) *n.*: The act of protesting or pleading (p. 236)

implore (im plôr') *v.*: Ask or beg earnestly (p. 238)

corroborate (kə räb' ə rāt') *v.*: Confirm, support (p. 243)

The Dying Detective

from a story by Sir Arthur Conan Doyle
Michael and Mollie Hardwick

CHARACTERS, IN ORDER OF APPEARANCE

Mrs. Hudson
Dr. Watson
Sherlock Holmes
Culverton Smith: "A great yellow face, coarse-grained and greasy, with heavy double chin, and two sullen, menacing gray eyes which glared at me from under tufted and sandy brows . . ."
Inspector Morton: Middle-aged, tough, dressed in plain clothes.

Scene 1: Sherlock Holmes's bedroom, *afternoon*
Scene 2: The same, *dusk*
Scene 3: The same, *evening*

Scene 1

[SHERLOCK HOLMES'S *bedroom at 221B Baker Street. The essential features are: a bed with a large wooden head, placed cross-wise on the stage, the head a foot or two from one side wall; a small table near the bed-head, on the audience's side, on which stand a carafe of water and a glass, and a tiny metal or ivory box; a window in the back wall, the curtains parted; and, under the window, a table or chest of drawers, on which stand a green wine bottle, some wine-glasses, a biscuit-barrel,[1] and a lamp. Of course, there may be further lamps and any amount of furnishing and clutter:* Holmes's bedroom was adorned with pictures of celebrated criminals and littered with everything from tobacco pipes to revolver cartridges.]

[*There is daylight outside the window.* SHERLOCK HOLMES *lies in the bed on his back, tucked up to the chin and evidently asleep. He is very pale.* MRS. HUDSON *enters followed by* DR. WATSON, *who is wearing his coat and hat and carrying his small medical bag.* MRS. HUDSON *pauses for a moment.*]

MRS. HUDSON. He's asleep, sir.

[*They approach the bed.* WATSON *comes round to the audience's side and looks down at* HOLMES *for a moment. He shakes his head gravely, then he and* MRS. HUDSON

---

1. **biscuit-barrel** (bis′ kit bar′ əl) *n.*: A British term for a container holding cookies or crackers.

move away beyond the foot of the bed. WAT-SON *takes off his hat and coat as they talk and she takes them from him.*]

WATSON. This is dreadful, Mrs. Hudson. He was perfectly hale and hearty when I went away only three days ago.

MRS. HUDSON. I know, sir. Oh, Dr. Watson, sir, I'm that glad you've come back. If anyone can save Mr. Holmes, I'm sure you can.

WATSON. I shall have to know what is the matter with him first. Mrs. Hudson, please tell me, as quickly as you can, how it all came about.

MRS. HUDSON. Yes, sir. Mr. Holmes has been working lately on some case down near the river—Rotherhithe,[2] I think.

WATSON. Yes, yes. I know.

MRS. HUDSON. Well, you know what he is for coming in at all hours. I was just taking my lamp to go to my bed on Wednesday night when I heard a faint knocking at the street door. I . . . I found Mr. Holmes there. He could hardly stand. Just muttered to me to help him up to his bed here, and he's barely spoken since.

WATSON. Dear me!

MRS. HUDSON. Won't take food or drink. Just lies there, sleeping or staring in a wild sort of way.

WATSON. But, goodness gracious, Mrs. Hudson, why did you not send for another doctor in my absence?

2. **Rotherhithe** (rä*th*′ ər hi*th*)

MRS. HUDSON. Oh, I told him straightaway I was going to do that, sir. But he got so agitated—almost shouted that he wouldn't allow any doctor on the premises. You know how masterful he is, Dr. Watson.

WATSON. Indeed. But you could have telegraphed for me.

[MRS. HUDSON *appears embarrassed.*]

MRS. HUDSON. Well, sir . . .

WATSON. But you didn't. Why, Mrs. Hudson?

MRS. HUDSON. Sir, I don't like to tell you, but . . . well, Mr. Holmes said he wouldn't even have you to see him.

WATSON. What? This is monstrous! I, his oldest friend, and . . .

[HOLMES *groans and stirs slightly.*]

Ssh! He's waking. You go along, Mrs. Hudson, and leave this to me. Whether he likes it or not, I shall ensure that everything possible is done.

MRS. HUDSON. Thank you, sir. You'll ring if I can be of help.

[*She exits with* WATSON's *things.* HOLMES *groans again and flings out an arm restlessly.* WATSON *comes to the audience's side of the bed and sits on it.*]

WATSON. Holmes? It's I—Watson.

HOLMES. [*Sighs*] Ahh! Well, Watson? We . . . we seem to have fallen on evil days.

WATSON. My dear fellow!

[*He moves to reach for* HOLMES's *pulse.*]

HOLMES. [*Urgently*] No, no! Keep back!

WATSON. Eh?

HOLMES. Mustn't come near.

WATSON. Now, look here, Holmes . . . !

HOLMES. If you come near . . . order you out of the house.

WATSON. [*Defiantly*] Hah!

HOLMES. For your own sake, Watson. Contracted . . . a disease—from Sumatra.[3] Very little known, except that most deadly. Contagious by touch. So . . . must keep away.

WATSON. Utter rubbish, Holmes! Mrs. Hudson tells me she helped you to your bed. There's nothing the matter with her.

HOLMES. Period of . . . incubation. Only dangerous after two or three days. Deadly by now.

WATSON. Good heavens, do you suppose such a consideration weighs with me? Even if I weren't a doctor, d'you think it would stop me doing my duty to an old friend? Now, let's have a good look at you. [*He moves forward again.*]

HOLMES. [*Harshly*] I tell you to keep back!

WATSON. See here, Holmes . . .

HOLMES. If you will stay where you are, I will talk to you. If you will not, you can get out.

WATSON. Holmes! [*Recovering*] Holmes, you aren't yourself. You're sick and as helpless as a child. Whether you like it or not, I'm going to examine you and treat you.

HOLMES. [*Sneering*] If I'm to be forced to have a doctor, let him at least be someone I've some confidence in.

WATSON. Oh! You . . . After all these years, Holmes, you haven't . . . confidence in me?

HOLMES. In your friendship, Watson—yes. But facts are facts. As a medical man you're a mere general practitioner, of limited experience and mediocre qualifications.

WATSON. Well. . . ! Well, really!

_____

3. **Sumatra** (sŏo mä′trə): A large island of Indonesia in the Pacific Ocean.

HOLMES. It is painful to say such things, but you leave me no choice.

WATSON. [*Coldly*] Thank you. I'll tell you this, Holmes. Such a remark, coming from you, merely serves to tell me what state your nerves are in. Still, if you insist that you have no confidence in me, I will not intrude my services. But what I shall do is to summon Sir Jasper Meek or Penrose Fisher, or any of the other best men in London.

HOLMES. [*Groans*] My . . . dear Watson. You mean well. But do you suppose they—any of them—know of the Tapanuli Fever?

WATSON. The Tap. . . ?

HOLMES. What do you yourself know of the Black Formosa Corruption?

WATSON. Tapanuli Fever? Black Formosa Corruption? I've never heard of either of 'em.

HOLMES. Nor have your colleagues. There are many problems of disease, many pathological possibilities, peculiar to the East. So I've learned during some of my recent researches. It was in the course of one of them that I contracted this complaint. I assure you, Watson, you can do nothing.

WATSON. Can't I? I happen to know, Holmes, that the greatest living authority on tropical disease, Dr. Ainstree, is in London just now.

HOLMES. [*Beseeching*] Watson!

WATSON. All remonstrance is useless. I am going this instant to fetch him.

[*He gets up.*]

HOLMES. [*A great cry*] No!

WATSON. Eh? Holmes . . . my dear fellow . . .

HOLMES. Watson, in the name of our old friendship, do as I ask.

WATSON. But . . .

HOLMES. You have only my own good at heart. Of course, I know that. You . . . you shall have your way. Only . . . give me time to . . . to collect my strength. What is the time now?

[WATSON *sits again and consults his watch.*]

WATSON. Four o'clock.

HOLMES. Then at six you can go.

WATSON. This is insanity!

HOLMES. Only two hours, Watson. I promise you may go then.

WATSON. Hang it, this is urgent, man!

HOLMES. I will see no one before six. I will not be examined. I shall resist!

WATSON. [*Sighing*] Oh, have it your own way, then. But I insist on staying with you in the meantime. You need an eye keeping on you, Holmes.

HOLMES. Very well, Watson. And now I must sleep. I feel exhausted. [*Drowsily*] I wonder how a battery feels when it pours electricity into a non-conductor?

WATSON. Eh?

HOLMES. [*Yawning*] At six, Watson, we resume our conversation. [*He lies back and closes his eyes.* WATSON *makes as though to move, but thinks better of it. He sits still, watching* HOLMES. *A slow black-out*]

Scene 2

[*The stage lights up again, though more dimly than before, to disclose the same scene. Twilight is apparent through the window.* HOLMES *lies motionless.* WATSON *sits as before, though with his head sagging, half asleep. His chin drops suddenly and he wakes with a jerk. He glances round, sees the twilight outside, and consults his watch. He yawns, flexes his arms,*

then proceeds to glance idly about him. His attention is caught by the little box on the bedside table. Stealthily, he reaches over and picks it up.]

HOLMES. [*Very loudly and urgently*] No! No, Watson, no!

WATSON. [*Startled*] Eh? What?

[HOLMES *starts up on to his elbow.*]

HOLMES. Put it down! Down this instant! Do as I say, Watson!

WATSON. Oh! All right, then. [*Putting the box down*]. Look here, Holmes, I really think . . .

HOLMES. I hate to have my things touched. You know perfectly well I do.

WATSON. Holmes . . . !

HOLMES. You fidget me beyond endurance. You, a doctor—you're enough to drive a patient into an asylum!

WATSON. Really!

HOLMES. Now, for heaven's sake, sit still, and let me have my rest.

WATSON. Holmes, it is almost six o'clock, and I refuse to delay another instant. [*He gets up determinedly.*]

HOLMES. Really? Watson, have you any change in your pocket?

WATSON. Yes.

HOLMES. Any silver?

WATSON. [*Fishing out his change*] A good deal.

HOLMES. How many half-crowns?

WATSON. Er, five.

HOLMES. [*Sighing*] Ah, too few, too few. However, such as they are, you can put them in your watch-pocket—and all the rest of your money in your left trouser-pocket. It will balance you so much better like that.

WATSON. Balance . . . ? Holmes, you're raving! This has gone too far . . . !

HOLMES. You will now light that lamp by the window, Watson, but you will be very careful that not for one instant shall it be more than at half flame.

WATSON. Oh, very well. [WATSON *goes to the lamp and strikes a match.*]

HOLMES. I implore you to be careful.

WATSON. [*As though humoring him*] Yes, Holmes.

[*He lights the lamp, carefully keeping the flame low. He moves to draw the curtains.*]

HOLMES. No, you need not draw the curtains.

[WATSON *leaves them and comes back round the bed.*]

So! Good. You may now go and fetch a specialist.

WATSON. Well, thank heaven for that.

HOLMES. His name is Mr. Culverton Smith, of 13 Lower Burke Street.

WATSON. [*Staring*] Eh?

HOLMES. Well, go on, man. You could hardly wait to fetch someone before.

WATSON. Yes, but . . . Culverton Smith? I've never heard the name!

HOLMES. Possibly not. It may surprise you to know that the one man who knows everything about this disease is not a medical man. He's a planter.

WATSON. A planter!

HOLMES. His plantation is far from medical aid. An outbreak of this disease there caused him to study it intensely. He's a very methodical man, and I asked you not to go before six because I knew you wouldn't find him in his study till then.

WATSON. Holmes, I . . . I never heard such a . . . !

HOLMES. You will tell him exactly how you have left me. A dying man.

WATSON. No, Holmes!

HOLMES. At any rate, delirious. Yes, not dying, delirious. [*Chuckles*] No, I really can't think why the whole ocean bed isn't one solid mass of oysters.

WATSON. Oysters?

HOLMES. They're so prolific, you know.

WATSON. Great Heavens! Now, Holmes, you just lie quiet, and . . .

HOLMES. Strange how the mind controls the brain. Er, what was I saying, Watson?

WATSON. You were . . .

HOLMES. Ah, I remember. Culverton Smith. My life depends on him, Watson. But you will have to plead with him to come. There is no good feeling between us. He has . . . a grudge. I rely on you to soften him. Beg, Watson. Pray. But get him here by any means.

WATSON. Very well. I'll bring him in a cab, if I have to carry him down to it.

HOLMES. You will do nothing of the sort. You will persuade him to come—and then return before him. [*Deliberately*] Make any excuse so as not to come with him. Don't forget that, Watson. You won't fail me. You never did fail me.

WATSON. That's all very well, Holmes, but . . .

HOLMES. [*Interrupting*] Then, shall the world be overrun by oysters? No doubt there are natural enemies which limit their increase. And yet . . . No, horrible, horrible!

WATSON. [*Grimly*] I'm going, Holmes. Say no more, I'm going!

[*He hurries out.* HOLMES *remains propped up for a moment, staring after* WATSON, *then sinks back into a sleeping posture as the stage blacks out.*]

Scene 3

[*The stage lights up on the same scene.* HOLMES *lies still. It is now quite dark outside. After a moment* WATSON *bustles in, pulling off his coat. He pauses to hand it to* MRS. HUDSON, *who is behind him.*]

WATSON. Thank you, Mrs. Hudson. A gentleman will be calling very shortly. Kindly show him up here immediately.

MRS. HUDSON. Yes, sir.

[*She exits.* WATSON *approaches the bed.*]

HOLMES. [*Drowsily*] Watson?

WATSON. Yes, Holmes. How are you feeling?

HOLMES. Much the same, I fear. Is Culverton Smith coming?

WATSON. Should be here any minute. It took me some minutes to find a cab, and I almost expected him to have got here first.

HOLMES. Well done, my dear Watson.

WATSON. I must say, Holmes, I'm only doing this to humor you. Frankly, I didn't take to your planter friend at all.

HOLMES. Oh? How So?

WATSON. Rudeness itself. He almost showed me the door before I could give him your message. It wasn't until I mentioned the name, Sherlock Holmes . . .

HOLMES. Ah!

WATSON. Quite changed him—but I wouldn't say it was for the better.

HOLMES. Tell me what he said.

WATSON. Said you'd had some business dealings together, and that he respected your character and talents. Described you as an amateur of crime, in the way that he regards himself as an amateur of disease.

HOLMES. Quite typical—and surely, quite fair?

WATSON. Quite fair—if he hadn't put such sarcasm into saying it. No, Holmes, you said he bears you some grudge. Mark my words, as soon as he has left this house I insist upon calling a recognized specialist.

HOLMES. My dear Watson, you are the best of messengers. Thank you again.

WATSON. Not at all. Holmes, Holmes—let me help you without any of this nonsense. The whole of Great Britain will condemn me otherwise. Why, my cabmen both inquired anxiously after you; and so did Inspector Morton . . .

HOLMES. Morton?

WATSON. Of the Yard. He was passing our door just now as I came in. Seemed extremely concerned.

HOLMES. Scotland Yard[4] concerned for me? How very touching! And now, Watson, you may disappear from the scene.

WATSON. Disappear! I shall do no such thing. I wish to be present when this Culverton Smith arrives. I wish to hear every word of this so-called medical expert's opinion.

HOLMES. [*Turning his head*] Yes, of course. Then I think you will just find room behind the head of the bed.

WATSON. What? Hide?

HOLMES. I have reason to suppose that his opinion will be much more frank and valuable if he imagines he is alone with me.

---

4. Scotland Yard: Headquarters of the London police, especially the detective bureau.

[*We hear the murmur of* MRS. HUDSON's *and* CULVERTON SMITH's *voices off-stage.*]

Listen! I hear him coming. Get behind the bed, Watson, and do not budge, whatever happens. *Whatever* happens, you understand?

WATSON. Oh, all right, Holmes. Anything to please you. But I don't like this. Not at all.

[*He goes behind the bed-head and conceals himself.* MRS. HUDSON *enters, looks round the room and then at* HOLMES. SMITH *enters behind her.*]

MRS. HUDSON. [*To* SMITH] Oh, Dr. Watson must have let himself out. No doubt he'll be back directly, sir.

SMITH. No matter, my good woman.

[MRS. HUDSON *bristles at this form of address.*]

You may leave me alone with your master.

MRS. HUDSON. As you wish—*sir.*

[*She sweeps out.* SMITH *advances slowly to the bed and stands at the foot, staring at the recumbent* HOLMES.]

SMITH. [*Almost to himself*] So, Holmes. It has come to this, then.

[HOLMES *stirs.* SMITH *chuckles and leans his arms on the bed-foot and his chin on them, continuing to watch* HOLMES.]

HOLMES. [*Weakly*] Watson? Who . . . ? Smith? Smith, is that you?

SMITH. [*Chuckles*]

HOLMES. I . . . I hardly dared hope you would come.

SMITH. I should imagine not. And yet, you see, I'm here. Coals of fire,[5] Holmes—coals of fire!

HOLMES. Noble of you . . .

SMITH. Yes, isn't it?

HOLMES. I appreciate your special knowledge.

SMITH. Then you're the only man in London who does. Do you know what is the matter with you?

HOLMES. The same as young Victor—your cousin.

SMITH. Ah, then you recognize the symptoms. Well, then, it's a bad look-out for you. Victor was a strong, hearty young fellow—but a dead man on the fourth day. As you said at the time, it *was* rather surprising that he should contract an out-of-the-way Asiatic disease in the heart of London—a disease of which I have made such a very special study. [*Chuckles*] And now, you, Holmes. Singular coincidence, eh? Or are you going to start making accusations once again—about cause and effect and so on.

HOLMES. I . . . I knew you caused Victor Savage's death.

[SMITH *comes round the bed.*]

SMITH. [*Snarling*] Did you? Well, proving it is a different matter, Holmes. But what sort of a game is this, then—spreading lying reports about me one moment, then crawling to me for help the next?

HOLMES. [*Gasping*] Give . . . give me water. For . . . pity's sake, Smith. Water!

[SMITH *hesitates momentarily, then goes to the table and pours a glass from the carafe.*]

---

5. Coals of fire: A reference to a Biblical passage, Proverbs 25:21-22, about revenging oneself on an enemy.

SMITH. You're precious near your end, my friend, but I don't want you to go till I've had a word with you.

[*He holds out the glass to* HOLMES *who struggles up feebly to take it and drinks.*]

HOLMES. [*Gulping water*] Ah! Thank . . . thank you. Please . . . do what you can for me. Only cure me, and I promise to forget.

SMITH. Forget what?

HOLMES. About Victor Savage's death. You as good as admitted just now that you had done it. I swear I will forget it.

SMITH. [*Laughs*] Forget it, remember it—do as you like. I don't see you in any witness-box, Holmes. Quite another shape of box, I assure you. But you must hear first how it came about.

HOLMES. Working amongst Chinese sailors. Down at the docks.

SMITH. Proud of your brains, aren't you? Think yourself smart? Well, you've met a smarter one this time.

[HOLMES *falls back, groaning loudly.*]

Getting painful, is it?

[HOLMES *cries out, writhing in agony.*]

SMITH. That's the way. Takes you as cramp, I fancy?

HOLMES. Cramp! Cramp!

SMITH. Well, you can still hear me. Now, can't you just remember any unusual incident— just about the time your symptoms began?

HOLMES. I . . . can't think. My mind is gone! Help me, Smith!

SMITH. Did nothing come to you through the post, for instance?

HOLMES. Post? Post?

SMITH. Yes. A little box, perhaps?

HOLMES. [*A shuddering groan*]

SMITH. [*Closer; deadly*] Listen! You *shall* hear me! Don't you remember a box—a little ivory box? [*He sees it on the table and holds it up.*] Yes, here it is on your bedside table. It came on Wednesday. You opened it—do you remember?

HOLMES. Box? Opened? Yes, yes! There was . . . sharp spring inside. Pricked my finger. Some sort of joke . . .

SMITH. It was no joke, Holmes. You fool! Who asked you to cross my path? If you'd only left me alone I would never have hurt you.

HOLMES. Box! Yes! Pricked finger. Poison!

SMITH. [*Triumphantly*] So you do remember.

Good, good! I'm glad indeed. Well, the box leaves this room in my pocket, and there's your last shred of evidence gone. [*He pockets it.*] But you have the truth now, Holmes. You can die knowing that I killed you. You knew too much about what happened to Victor Savage, so you must share his fate. Yes, Holmes, you are very near your end now. I think I shall sit here and watch you die. [*He sits on the bed.*]

HOLMES. [*Almost a whisper*] The . . . shadows . . . falling. Getting . . . so dark. I can't see. Smith! Smith, are you there? The light . . . for charity's sake, turn up the light!

[SMITH *laughs, gets up and goes to the light.*]

SMITH. Entering the valley of the shadow,[6] eh, Holmes? Yes, I'll turn up the light for you. I can watch your face more plainly, then. [*He turns the flame up full.*] There! Now, is there any *further* service I can render you?

HOLMES. [*In a clear, strong voice*] A match and my pipe, if you please.

[*He sits bolt upright.* SMITH *spins round to see him.*]

SMITH. Eh? What the devil's the meaning of this?

HOLMES. [*Cheerfully*] The best way of successfully acting a part is to *be* it. I give you my word that for three days I have neither tasted food nor drink until you were good enough to pour me out that glass of water. But it's the tobacco I find most irksome.

[*We hear the thud of footsteps running upstairs off-stage.*]

Hello, hello! Do I hear the step of a friend?

[INSPECTOR MORTON *hurries in.*]

---

6. valley of the shadow: A reference to death, based on Psalm 23 of the Bible, which mentions the "valley of the shadow of death."

MORTON. Mr. Holmes?

HOLMES. Inspector Morton, this is your man.

SMITH. What is the meaning of . . . ?

MORTON. Culverton Smith, I arrest you on the charge of the murder of one Victor Savage, and I must warn you that anything you say . . .

SMITH. You've got nothing on me? It's all a trick! A pack of lies!

[*He makes to escape.* MORTON *restrains him.*]

MORTON. Keep still, or you'll get yourself hurt!

SMITH. Get off me!

MORTON. Hold your hands out!

[*They struggle.* MORTON *gets out handcuffs and claps them on* SMITH's *wrists.*]

That'll do.

HOLMES. By the way, Inspector, you might add the attempted murder of one Sherlock Holmes to that charge. Oh, and you'll find a small box in the pocket of your prisoner's coat. Pray, leave it on the table, here. Handle it gingerly, though. It may play its part at his trial.

[MORTON *retrieves the box and places it on the table.*]

SMITH. Trial! You'll be the one in the dock,[7] Holmes. Inspector, he asked me to come here. He was ill, and I was sorry for him, so I came. Now he'll pretend I've said anything he cares to invent that will corroborate his insane suspicions. Well, you can lie as you like, Holmes. My word's as good as yours.

HOLMES. Good heavens! I'd completely forgotten him!

MORTON. Forgotten who, sir?

HOLMES. Watson, my dear fellow! Do come out!

[WATSON *emerges with cramped groans.*]

I owe you a thousand apologies. To think that I should have overlooked you!

WATSON. It's all right, Holmes. Would have come out before, only you said, whatever happened, I wasn't to budge.

SMITH. What's all this about?

HOLMES. I needn't introduce you to my witness, my friend Dr. Watson. I understand you met somewhat earlier in the evening.

SMITH. You . . . you mean you had all this planned?

HOLMES. Of course. To the last detail. I think I may say it worked very well—with your assistance, of course.

SMITH. Mine?

HOLMES. You saved an invalid trouble by giving my signal to Inspector Morton, waiting outside. You turned up the lamp.

[SMITH *and* WATSON *are equally flabbergasted.*]

MORTON. I'd better take him along now, sir. [*To* SMITH] Come on.

[*He bundles* SMITH *roughly toward the door.*]

We'll see you down at the Yard tomorrow, perhaps, Mr. Holmes?

HOLMES. Very well, Inspector. And many thanks.

WATSON. Goodbye, Inspector.

[MORTON *exits with* SMITH.]

[*Chuckles*] Well, Holmes?

HOLMES. Well, Watson, there's a bottle of claret over there—it is uncorked—and some biscuits in the barrel. If you'll be so kind, I'm badly in need of both.

[WATSON *goes to fetch them.*]

---

7. dock (däk) *n.:* The place where the accused sits or stands in court.

WATSON. Certainly. You know, Holmes, all this seems a pretty, well, elaborate way to go about catching that fellow. I mean, taking in Mrs. Hudson—*and me*—like that. Scared us half to death.

HOLMES. It was very essential that I should make Mrs. Hudson believe in my condition. She was to convey it to you, and you to him.

WATSON. Well . . .

HOLMES. Pray do not be offended, my good Watson. You must admit that among your *many* talents, dissimulation scarcely finds a place. If you'd shared my secret, you would never have been able to impress Smith with the urgent necessity of coming to me. It was the vital point of the whole scheme. I knew his vindictive nature, and I was certain he would come to gloat over his handiwork.

[WATSON *returns with the bottle, glasses and barrel.*]

WATSON. But . . . but your appearance, Holmes. Your face! You really do look ghastly.

HOLMES. Three days of absolute fast does not improve one's beauty, Watson. However, as you know, my habits are irregular, and such a feat means less to me than to most men. For the rest, there is nothing that a sponge won't cure. Vaseline to produce the glistening forehead; belladonna[8] for the watering of the eyes; rouge over the cheekbones and crust of beeswax round one's lips . . .

WATSON. [*Chuckling*] And that babbling about oysters! [*He begins pouring the wine.*]

HOLMES. Yes. I've sometimes thought of writing a monograph on the subject of malingering.[9]

WATSON. But why wouldn't you let me near you? There was no risk of infection.

HOLMES. Whatever I may have said to the contrary in the grip of delirium, do you imagine that I have no respect for your medical talents? Could I imagine that you would be deceived by a dying man with no rise of pulse or temperature? At four yards' distance I *could* deceive you.

[WATSON *reaches for the box.*]

WATSON. This box, then . . .

HOLMES. No, Watson. I wouldn't touch it. You can just see, if you look at it sideways, where the sharp spring emerges as you open it. I dare say it was by some such device that poor young Savage was done to death. He stood between that monster and an inheritance, you know.

WATSON. Then it's true, Holmes! You . . . you might have been killed, too!

HOLMES. As you know, my correspondence is a varied one. I am somewhat on my guard against any packages which reach me. But I saw that by pretending he had succeeded in his design I might be enabled to surprise a confession from him. That pretense I think I may claim to have carried out with the thoroughness of a true artist.

WATSON. [*Warmly*] You certainly did, Holmes. Er, a biscuit? [*He holds out the barrel.*]

HOLMES. On second thought, Watson, no thank you. Let us preserve our appetite. By the time I have shaved and dressed, I fancy it will just be nice time for something nutritious at our little place in the Strand.[10]

[*They raise their glasses to one another and drink. The curtain falls.*]

---

8. belladonna (bel′ ə dän′ ə) *n.*: A poisonous European plant.

9. monograph on . . . malingering: A study on the subject of pretending to be ill in order to avoid work.

---

10. the Strand: London's main shopping and entertainment district; also, the name of a specific street within this district.

THINKING ABOUT THE SELECTION

Recalling

1. What reasons does Sherlock Holmes give for not letting Dr. Watson treat him?
2. How does this deception fit in with Holmes's plan to bring Culverton Smith to justice?
3. What criminal doings does Holmes trick Smith into revealing?
4. What is the real reason that Holmes asks Culverton Smith to turn up the light?

Interpreting

5. Explain the importance of Watson's hiding place in Holmes's plot against Smith.
6. Why did Holmes not tell Watson of his plan for proving Smith a murderer?
7. Explain the purpose of each of the various steps in Holmes's plot to trap Smith.

Applying

8. Compare and contrast Sherlock Holmes with another fictional detective or a detective from television or movies. How are Holmes's personality and methods similar or different?

ANALYZING LITERATURE

Understanding Staging

Two important aspects of **staging** are sets and props. A **set** is the arrangement of physical objects that make up scenery. In *The Dying Detective* only one set is needed because the scenery remains the same from start to finish. **Props** are the objects that actors use, often to advance the plot or reveal character.

1. Describe the set of "The Dying Detective."
2. How are the bed and the window important to the plot?
3. How are the box and the lamp important to it?

CRITICAL THINKING AND READING

Relating Staging to Dramatic Purpose

In a detective play such as *The Dying Detective,* the creation of suspense is important to the plot.

1. The setting of the play is confined to a single room. How does this single-room setting add to the suspense?
2. Picture Watson in his hiding place behind the bed. How does this use of staging add to the suspense?

SPEAKING AND LISTENING

Presenting a Scene from the Play

With your classmates and yourself in the roles of the characters, read *The Dying Detective* aloud in class. When you rehearse the reading, discuss how each role should be played. Evaluate one another's performance, and make suggestions for improvement.

THINKING AND WRITING

Writing About Staging

Imagine that you are the director for the drama club in your school. The club will be presenting a dramatic adaptation of the short story you have selected. Using the notes you made before reading this play, write a memo to the drama coach in which you describe in detail the staging you want. Specify the sets and props. Revise your memo. Is the description clear? Is it complete? Is the staging appropriate for the story?

GUIDE FOR READING

The Monsters Are Due on Maple Street

Rod Serling (1924–1975) was born and raised in New York State. He is best known as the creator of the television series *The Twilight Zone*. In this series Serling often presented science-fiction plays that highlighted his views of life and society on this planet. *The Monsters Are Due on Maple Street* raises the question of whether the real monsters are up there or down here.

Conflict in Drama

Conflict, a struggle between opposing forces, is basic to drama. A play is usually based on one of the fundamental kinds of conflict. These include conflict between individuals, between an individual and society, between an individual and nature, and between an individual and himself or herself. Although one type of conflict will be central to a play, other types will often be present, too.

Look For

As you read this television play, notice the different kinds of conflict. Are characters in conflict with each other, with society, or with nature? Do certain characters seem torn apart, with one side of their personality warring against another side? Decide which type of conflict is the most important to the plot. Also, try to visualize how the various conflicts would appear when the play is broadcast on television.

Writing

The problems in this play start when strange happenings occur on Maple Street. Imagine that you and some friends are in a room in one of your homes. Strange things start to happen: Lights go on and off by themselves, chairs and tables move, weird noises are heard. Freewrite about the possible effects of such strange goings-on.

Vocabulary

Knowing the following words will help you as you read *The Monsters Are Due on Maple Street*.

flustered (flus′ tərd) *v.*: Made nervous (p. 249)

sluggishly (slug′ ish lē) *adv.*: As if lacking energy (p. 250)

assent (ə sent′) *n.*: Agreement (p. 250)

persistently (pər sist′ ənt lē) *adv.*: Firmly and steadily (p. 250)

defiant (di fi′ ənt) *adj.*: Boldly resisting (p. 251)

metamorphosis (met′ ə môr′ fə sis) *n.*: A change of form (p. 252)

scapegoat (skāp′ gōt′) *n.*: A person or group blamed for the mistakes or crimes of others (p. 256)

The Monsters Are Due on Maple Street

Rod Serling

CHARACTERS

Narrator
Figure One
Figure Two

Residents of Maple Street

Steve Brand	**Charlie's Wife**	**Mrs. Goodman**
Mrs. Brand	**Tommy**	**Woman**
Don Martin	**Sally,** Tommy's	**Man One**
Pete Van Horn	Mother	**Man Two**
Charlie	**Les Goodman**	

ACT I

[*Fade in on a shot of the night sky. The various nebulae and planet bodies stand out in sharp, sparkling relief, and the camera begins a slow pan across the Heavens.*]

NARRATOR'S VOICE. There is a fifth dimension beyond that which is known to man. It is a dimension as vast as space, and as timeless as infinity. It is the middle ground between light and shadow—between science and superstition. And it lies between the pit of man's fears and the summit of his knowledge. This is the dimension of imagination. It is an area which we call The Twilight Zone.

[*The camera has begun to pan down until it passes the horizon and is on a sign which reads "Maple Street." Pan down until we are shooting down at an angle toward the street below. It's a tree-lined, quiet residential American street, very typical of the small town. The houses have front porches on which people sit and swing on gliders, conversing across from house to house. Steve Brand polishes his car parked in front of his house. His neighbor, Don Martin, leans against the fender watching him. A Good Humor man rides a bicycle and is just in the process of stopping to sell some ice cream to a couple of kids. Two women gossip on the front lawn. Another man waters his lawn.*]

NARRATOR'S VOICE: Maple Street, U.S.A., late summer. A tree-lined little world of front porch gliders, hop scotch, the laughter of children, and the bell of an ice cream vendor.

[*There is a pause and the camera moves over to a shot of the Good Humor man and two small boys who are standing alongside, just buying ice cream.*]

NARRATOR'S VOICE. At the sound of the roar and the flash of light it will be precisely 6:43 P.M. on Maple Street.

[*At this moment one of the little boys, Tommy, looks up to listen to a sound of a tremendous screeching roar from overhead. A flash of light plays on both their faces and then it moves down the street past lawns and porches and rooftops and then disappears.*
   Various people leave their porches and stop what they're doing to stare up at the sky. Steve Brand, the man who's been pol-

ishing his car, now stands there transfixed, staring upwards. He looks at Don Martin, his neighbor from across the street.*]

STEVE. What was that? A meteor?

DON. [*Nods*] That's what it looked like. I didn't hear any crash though, did you?

STEVE. [*Shakes his head*] Nope. I didn't hear anything except a roar.

MRS. BRAND. [*From her porch*] Steve? What was that?

STEVE. [*Raising his voice and looking toward porch*] Guess it was a meteor, honey. Came awful close, didn't it?

MRS. BRAND. Too close for my money! Much too close.

[*The camera pans across the various por-*

ches to people who stand there watching and talking in low tones.]

NARRATOR'S VOICE. Maple Street. Six-forty-four P.M. on a late September evening. [*A pause*] Maple Street in the last calm and reflective moment . . . before the monsters came!

[The camera slowly pans across the porches again. We see a man screwing a light bulb on a front porch, then getting down off the stool to flick the switch and finding that nothing happens.

Another man is working on an electric power mower. He plugs in the plug, flicks on the switch of the power mower, off and on, with nothing happening.

Through the window of a front porch, we see a woman pushing her finger back and forth on the dial hook. Her voice is indistinct and distant, but intelligible and repetitive.]

WOMAN. Operator, operator, something's wrong on the phone, operator!

[Mrs. Brand comes out on the porch and calls to Steve.]

MRS. BRAND. [*Calling*] Steve, the power's off. I had the soup on the stove and the stove just stopped working.

WOMAN. Same thing over here. I can't get anybody on the phone either. The phone seems to be dead.

[We look down on the street as we hear the voices creep up from below, small, mildly disturbed voices highlighting these kinds of phrases:]

VOICES.
Electricity's off.
Phone won't work.
Can't get a thing on the radio.
My power mower won't move, won't work at all.

Radio's gone dead!

[Pete Van Horn, a tall, thin man, is seen standing in front of his house.]

VAN HORN. I'll cut through the back yard . . . See if the power's still on on Floral Street. I'll be right back!

[He walks past the side of his house and disappears into the back yard.

The camera pans down slowly until we're looking at ten or eleven people standing around the street and overflowing to the curb and sidewalk. In the background is Steve Brand's car.]

STEVE. Doesn't make sense. Why should the power go off all of a sudden, and the phone line?

DON. Maybe some sort of an electrical storm or something.

CHARLIE. That don't seem likely. Sky's just as blue as anything. Not a cloud. No lightning. No thunder. No nothing. How could it be a storm?

WOMAN. I can't get a thing on the radio. Not even the portable.

[The people again murmur softly in wonderment and question.]

CHARLIE. Well, why don't you go downtown and check with the police, though they'll probably think we're crazy or something. A little power failure and right away we get all flustered and everything.

STEVE. It isn't just the power failure, Charlie. If it was, we'd still be able to get a broadcast on the portable.

[There's a murmur of reaction to this. Steve looks from face to face and then over to his car.]

STEVE. I'll run downtown. We'll get this all straightened out.

[*He walks over to the car, gets in it, turns the key. Looking through the open car door, we see the crowd watching him from the other side. Steve starts the engine. It turns over sluggishly and then just stops dead. He tries it again and this time he can't get it to turn over. Then, very slowly and reflectively, he turns the key back to "off" and slowly gets out of the car.*

The people stare at Steve. He stands for a moment by the car, then walks toward the group.]

STEVE. I don't understand it. It was working fine before . . .

DON. Out of gas?

STEVE. [*Shakes his head*] I just had it filled up.

WOMAN. What's it mean?

CHARLIE. It's just as if . . . as if everything had stopped. [*Then he turns toward* STEVE.] We'd better walk downtown. [*Another murmur of assent at this.*]

STEVE. The two of us can go, Charlie. [*He turns to look back at the car.*] It couldn't be the meteor. A meteor couldn't do *this*.

[*He and Charlie exchange a look, then they start to walk away from the group.*

We see Tommy, a serious-faced fourteen-year-old in spectacles who stands a few feet away from the group. He is halfway between them and the two men, who start to walk down the sidewalk.]

TOMMY. Mr. Brand . . . you better not!

STEVE. Why not?

TOMMY. They don't want you to.

[*Steve and Charlie exchange a grin, and Steve looks back toward the boy.*]

STEVE. *Who* doesn't want us to?

TOMMY. [*Jerks his head in the general direction of the distant horizon*] Them!

STEVE. Them?

CHARLIE. Who are them?

TOMMY. [*Very intently*] Whoever was in that thing that came by overhead.

[*Steve knits his brows for a moment, cocking his head questioningly. His voice is intense.*]

STEVE. What?

TOMMY. Whoever was in that thing that came over. I don't think they want us to leave here.

[*Steve leaves Charlie and walks over to the boy. He kneels down in front of him. He forces his voice to remain gentle. He reaches out and holds the boy.*]

STEVE. What do you mean? What are you talking about?

TOMMY. They don't want us to leave. That's why they shut everything off.

STEVE. What makes you say that? Whatever gave you that idea?

WOMAN. [*From the crowd*] Now isn't that the craziest thing you ever heard?

TOMMY. [*Persistently but a little intimidated by the crowd*] It's always that way, in every story I ever read about a ship landing from outer space.

WOMAN. [*To the boy's mother, Sally, who stands on the fringe of the crowd*] From outer space, yet! Sally, you better get that boy of yours up to bed. He's been reading too many comic books or seeing too many movies or something.

SALLY. Tommy, come over here and stop that kind of talk.

STEVE. Go ahead, Tommy. We'll be right

back. And you'll see. That wasn't any ship or anything like it. That was just a . . . a meteor or something. Likely as not—[*He turns to the group, now trying to weight his words with an optimism he obviously doesn't feel but is desperately trying to instill in himself as well as the others.*] No doubt it did have something to do with all this power failure and the rest of it. Meteors can do some crazy things. Like sunspots.

DON. [*Picking up the cue*] Sure. That's the kind of thing—like sunspots. They raise Cain with[1] radio reception all over the world. And this thing being so close—why, there's no telling the sort of stuff it can do. [*He wets his lips, smiles nervously.*] Go ahead, Charlie. You and Steve go into town and see if that isn't what's causing it all.

[*Steve and Charlie again walk away from the group down the sidewalk. The people watch silently.*

Tommy stares at them, biting his lips, and finally calling out again.]

TOMMY. *Mr. Brand!*

[*The two men stop again. Tommy takes a step toward them.*]

TOMMY. Mr. Brand . . . please don't leave here.

[*Steve and Charlie stop once again and turn toward the boy. There's a murmur in the crowd, a murmur of irritation and concern as if the boy were bringing up fears that shouldn't be brought up; words which carried with them a strange kind of validity that came without logic but nonetheless registered and had meaning and effect. Again we hear a murmur of reaction from the crowd.*

Tommy is partly frightened and partly defiant as well.]

---

1. raise Cain with: Badly disturb.

TOMMY. You might not even be able to get to town. It was that way in the story. Nobody could leave. Nobody except—

STEVE. Except who?

TOMMY. Except the people they'd sent down ahead of them. They looked just like humans. And it wasn't until the ship landed that—

[*The boy suddenly stops again, conscious of the parents staring at them and of the sudden hush of the crowd.*]

SALLY. [*In a whisper, sensing the antagonism of the crowd*] Tommy, please son . . . honey, don't talk that way—

MAN ONE. That kid shouldn't talk that way . . . and we shouldn't stand here listening to him. Why this is the craziest thing I ever heard of. The kid tells us a comic book plot and here we stand listening—

[*Steve walks toward the camera, stops by the boy.*]

STEVE. Go ahead, Tommy. What kind of story was this? What about the people that they sent out ahead?

TOMMY. That was the way they prepared things for the landing. They sent four people. A mother and a father and two kids who looked just like humans . . . but they weren't.

[*There's another silence as Steve looks toward the crowd and then toward Tommy. He wears a tight grin.*]

STEVE. Well, I guess what we'd better do then is to run a check on the neighborhood and see which ones of us are really human.

[*There's laughter at this, but it's a laughter that comes from a desperate attempt to lighten the atmosphere. It's a release kind of laugh. The people look at one another in the middle of their laughter.*]

CHARLIE. There must be somethin' better to do than stand around makin' bum jokes about it. [*Rubs his jaw nervously*] I wonder if Floral Street's got the same deal we got. [*He looks past the houses.*] Where is Pete Van Horn anyway? Didn't he get back yet?

[*Suddenly there's the sound of a car's engine starting to turn over.*

We look across the street toward the driveway of Les Goodman's house. He's at the wheel trying to start the car.]

SALLY. Can you get it started, Les? [*He gets out of the car, shaking his head.*]

GOODMAN. No dice.

[*He walks toward the group. He stops suddenly as behind him, inexplicably and with a noise that inserts itself into the silence, the car engine starts up all by itself. Goodman whirls around to stare toward it.*

The car idles roughly, smoke coming from the exhaust, the frame shaking gently.

Goodman's eyes go wide, and he runs over to his car.

The people stare toward the car.]

MAN ONE. He got the car started somehow. He got his car started!

[*The camera pans along the faces of the people as they stare, somehow caught up by this revelation and somehow, illogically, wildly, frightened.*]

WOMAN. How come his car just up and started like that?

SALLY. All by itself. He wasn't anywheres near it. It started all by itself.

[*Don approaches the group, stops a few feet away to look toward Goodman's car and then back toward the group.*]

DON. And he never did come out to look at that thing that flew overhead. He wasn't even interested. [*He turns to the faces in the group, his face taut and serious.*] Why? Why didn't he come out with the rest of us to look?

CHARLIE. He always was an oddball. Him and his whole family. Real oddball.

DON. What do you say we ask him?

[*The group suddenly starts toward the house. In this brief fraction of a moment they take the first step toward performing a metamorphosis that changes people from a group into a mob. They begin to head purposefully across the street toward the house at the end. Steve stands in front of them. For a moment their fear almost turns their walk into a wild stampede, but Steve's voice, loud, incisive, and commanding, makes them stop.*]

STEVE. Wait a minute . . . wait a minute! Let's not be a mob!

[*The people stop as a group, seem to pause for a moment, and then much more quietly and slowly start to walk across the street. Goodman stands alone facing the people.*]

GOODMAN. I just don't understand it. I tried to start it and it wouldn't start. You saw me. All of you saw me.

[*And now, just as suddenly as the engine started, it stops and there's a long silence that is gradually intruded upon by the frightened murmuring of the people.*]

GOODMAN. I don't understand. I swear . . . I don't understand. What's happening?

DON. Maybe you better tell us. Nothing's working on this street. Nothing. No lights, no power, no radio. [*And then meaningfully*] Nothing except one car—yours!

[*The people pick this up and now their murmuring becomes a loud chant filling the air with accusations and demands for action. Two of the men pass Don and head toward Goodman, who backs away, backing into his car and now at bay.*]

GOODMAN. Wait a minute now. You keep your distance—all of you. So I've got a car that starts by itself—well, that's a freak thing, I admit it. But does that make me some kind of a criminal or something? I don't know why the car works—it just does!

[*This stops the crowd momentarily and now Goodman, still backing away, goes toward his front porch. He goes up the steps and then stops to stand facing the mob.*

We see a long shot of Steve as he comes through the crowd.]

STEVE. [*Quietly*] We're all on a monster kick, Les. Seems that the general impression holds that maybe one family isn't what we think they are. Monsters from outer space or something. Different than us. Fifth columnists[2] from the vast beyond. [*He chuckles.*] You know anybody that might fit that description around here on Maple Street?

GOODMAN. What is this, a gag or something? This a practical joke or something?

[*We see a close-up of the porch light as it suddenly goes out. There's a murmur from the group.*]

GOODMAN. Now I suppose that's supposed to incriminate me! The light goes on and off. That really does it, doesn't it?

[*He looks around the faces of the people.*] I just don't understand this—[*He wets his lips, looking from face to face.*] Look, you all know me. We've lived here five years. Right

---

2. Fifth columnists: People who help an invading enemy from within their own country.

in this house. We're no different from any of the rest of you! We're no different at all. Really . . . this whole thing is just . . . just weird—

WOMAN. Well, if that's the case, Les Goodman, explain why—[*She stops suddenly, clamping her mouth shut.*]

GOODMAN. [*Softly*] Explain what?

STEVE. [*Interjecting*] Look, let's forget this—

CHARLIE. [*Overlapping him*] Go ahead, let her talk. What about it? Explain what?

WOMAN. [*A little reluctantly*] Well . . . sometimes I go to bed late at night. A couple of times . . . a couple of times I'd come out on the porch and I'd see Mr. Goodman here in the wee hours of the morning standing out in front of his house . . . looking up at the sky. [*She looks around the circle of faces.*] That's right, looking up at the sky as if . . . as if he were waiting for something. [*A pause*] As if he were looking for something.

[*There's a murmur of reaction from the crowd again.*

We cut suddenly to a group shot. As Goodman starts toward them, they back away frightened.]

GOODMAN. You know really . . . this is for laughs. You know what I'm guilty of? [*He laughs.*] I'm guilty of insomnia. Now what's the penalty for insomnia? [*At this point the laugh, the humor, leaves his voice.*] Did you hear what I said? I said it was insomnia. [*A pause as he looks around, then shouts.*] I said it was insomnia! You fools. You scared, frightened rabbits, you. You're sick people, do you know that? You're sick people—all of you! And you don't even know what you're starting because let me tell you . . . let me tell you—this thing you're starting—that should frighten you. As God is my witness . . . you're letting something begin here that's a nightmare!

ACT II

[*We see a medium shot of the Goodman entry hall at night. On the side table rests an unlit candle. Mrs. Goodman walks into the scene, a glass of milk in hand. She sets the milk down on the table, lights the candle with a match from a box on the table, picks up the glass of milk, and starts out of scene.*

Mrs. Goodman comes through her porch door, glass of milk in hand. The entry hall, with table and lit candle, can be seen behind her.

Outside, the camera slowly pans down the sidewalk, taking in little knots of people who stand around talking in low voices. At the end of each conversation they look toward Les Goodman's house. From the various houses we can see candlelight but no electricity, and there's an all-pervading quiet that blankets the whole area, disturbed only by the almost whispered voices of the people as they stand around. The camera pans over to one group where Charlie stands. He stares across at Goodman's house.

We see a long shot of the house. Two men stand across the street in almost sentry-like poses. Then we see a medium shot of a group of people.]

SALLY. [*A little timorously*] It just doesn't seem right, though, keeping watch on them. Why . . . he was right when he said he was one of our neighbors. Why, I've known Ethel Goodman ever since they moved in. We've been good friends—

CHARLIE. That don't prove a thing. Any guy who'd spend his time lookin' up at the sky early in the morning—well, there's something wrong with that kind of person. There's something that ain't legitimate. Maybe under normal circumstances we could let it go by, but these aren't normal circumstances. Why, look at this street! Nothin' but candles. Why, it's like goin' back into the dark ages or somethin'!

[*Steve walks down the steps of his porch, walks down the street over to Les Goodman's house, and then stops at the foot of the steps. Goodman stands there, his wife behind him, very frightened.*]

GOODMAN. Just stay right where you are, Steve. We don't want any trouble, but this time if anybody sets foot on my porch, that's what they're going to get—trouble!

STEVE. Look, Les—

GOODMAN. I've already explained to you people. I don't sleep very well at night sometimes. I get up and I take a walk and I look up at the sky. I look at the stars!

MRS. GOODMAN. That's exactly what he does. Why this whole thing, it's . . . it's some kind of madness or something.

STEVE. [*Nods grimly*] That's exactly what it is—some kind of madness.

CHARLIE'S VOICE. [*Shrill, from across the street*] You best watch who you're seen with, Steve! Until we get this all straightened out, you ain't exactly above suspicion yourself.

STEVE. [*Whirling around toward him*] Or you, Charlie. Or any of us, it seems. From age eight on up!

WOMAN. What I'd like to know is—what are we gonna do? Just stand around here all night?

CHARLIE. There's nothin' else we can do! [*He turns back looking toward Steve and Good-*

man again.] One of 'em'll tip their hand. They got to.

STEVE. [*Raising his voice*] There's something you can do, Charlie. You could go home and keep your mouth shut. You could quit strutting around like a self-appointed hanging judge and just climb into bed and forget it.

CHARLIE. You sound real anxious to have that happen, Steve. I think we better keep our eye on you too!

DON. [*As if he were taking the bit in his teeth, takes a hesitant step to the front*] I think everything might as well come out now. [*He turns toward Steve.*] Your wife's

done plenty of talking, Steve, about how odd you are!

CHARLIE. [*Picking this up, his eyes widening*] Go ahead, tell us what she's said.

[*We see a long shot of Steve as he walks toward them from across the street.*]

STEVE. Go ahead, what's my wife said? Let's get it all out. Let's pick out every idiosyncrasy of every single man, woman, and child on the street. And then we might as well set up some kind of kangaroo court.[1] How about a firing squad at dawn, Charlie, so we can

---

1. kangaroo court: An unofficial court that does not follow normal rules.

get rid of all the suspects? Narrow them down. Make it easier for you.

DON. There's no need gettin' so upset, Steve. It's just that . . . well . . . Myra's talked about how there's been plenty of nights you spent hours down in your basement workin' on some kind of radio or something. Well, none of us have ever seen that radio—

[*By this time Steve has reached the group. He stands there defiantly close to them.*]

CHARLIE. Go ahead, Steve. What kind of "radio set" you workin' on? I never seen it. Neither has anyone else. Who you talk to on that radio set? And who talks to you?

STEVE. I'm surprised at you, Charlie. How come you're so dense all of a sudden? [*A pause*] Who do I talk to? I talk to monsters from outer space. I talk to three-headed green men who fly over here in what look like meteors.

[*Steve's wife steps down from the porch, bites her lip, calls out.*]

MRS. BRAND. Steve! Steve, please. [*Then looking around, frightened, she walks toward the group.*] It's just a ham radio set, that's all. I bought him a book on it myself. It's just a ham radio set. A lot of people have them. I can show it to you. It's right down in the basement.

STEVE. [*Whirls around toward her*] Show them nothing! If they want to look inside our house—let them get a search warrant.

CHARLIE. Look, buddy, you can't afford to—

STEVE. [*Interrupting*] Charlie, don't tell me what I can afford! And stop telling me who's dangerous and who isn't and who's safe and who's a menace. [*He turns to the group and shouts.*] And you're with him, too—all of you! You're standing here all set to crucify—all set to find a scapegoat—all desperate to point

some kind of a finger at a neighbor! Well now look, friends, the only thing that's gonna happen is that we'll eat each other up alive—

[*He stops abruptly as Charlie suddenly grabs his arm.*]

CHARLIE. [*In a hushed voice*] That's not the only thing that can happen to us.

[*Cut to a long shot looking down the street. A figure has suddenly materialized in the gloom and in the silence we can hear the clickety-clack of slow, measured footsteps on concrete as the figure walks slowly toward them. One of the women lets out a stifled cry. The young mother grabs her boy as do a couple of others.*]

TOMMY. [*Shouting, frightened*] It's the monster! It's the monster!

[*Another woman lets out a wail and the people fall back in a group, staring toward the darkness and the approaching figure.*

We see a medium group shot of the people as they stand in the shadows watching. Don Martin joins them, carrying a shotgun. He holds it up.]

DON. We may need this.

STEVE. A shotgun? [*He pulls it out of Don's hand.*] Good Lord—will anybody think a thought around here? Will you people wise up? What good would a shotgun do against—

[*Now Charlie pulls the gun from Steve's hand.*]

CHARLIE. No more talk, Steve. You're going to talk us into a grave! You'd let whatever's out there walk right over us, wouldn't yuh? Well, some of us won't!

[*He swings the gun around to point it toward the sidewalk.*

The dark figure continues to walk toward them.]

The group stands there, fearful, apprehensive, mothers clutching children, men standing in front of wives. Charlie slowly raises the gun. As the figure gets closer and closer he suddenly pulls the trigger. The sound of it explodes in the stillness. There is a long angle shot looking down at the figure, who suddenly lets out a small cry, stumbles forward onto his knees and then falls forward on his face. Don, Charlie, and Steve race forward over to him. Steve is there first and turns the man over. Now the crowd gathers around them.]

STEVE. [*Slowly looks up*] It's Pete Van Horn.

DON. [*In a hushed voice*] Pete Van Horn! He was just gonna go over to the next block to see if the power was on—

WOMAN. You killed him, Charlie. You shot him dead!

CHARLIE. [*Looks around at the circle of faces, his eyes frightened, his face contorted*] But . . . but I didn't know who he was. I certainly didn't know who he was. He comes walkin' out of the darkness—how am I supposed to know who he was? [*He grabs Steve.*] Steve—you know why I shot! How was I supposed to know he wasn't a monster or something? [*He grabs Don now.*] We're all scared of the same thing. I was just tryin' to . . . tryin' to protect my home, that's all! Look, all of you, that's all I was tryin' to do. [*He looks down wildly at the body.*] I didn't know it was somebody we knew! I didn't know—

[*There's a sudden hush and then an intake of breath. We see a medium shot of the living room window of Charlie's house. The window is not lit, but suddenly the house lights come on behind it.*]

WOMAN. [*In a very hushed voice*] Charlie . . . Charlie . . . the lights just went on in your house. Why did the lights just go on?

DON. What about it, Charlie? How come you're the only one with lights now?

GOODMAN. That's what I'd like to know.

[*A pause as they all stare toward Charlie.*]

GOODMAN. You were so quick to kill, Charlie, and you were so quick to tell us who we had to be careful of. Well, maybe you had to kill. Maybe Peter there was trying to tell us something. Maybe he'd found out something and came back to tell us who there was amongst us we should watch out for—

[*Charlie backs away from the group, his eyes wide with fright.*]

CHARLIE. No . . . no . . . it's nothing of the sort! I don't know why the lights are on. I swear I don't. Somebody's pulling a gag or something.

[*He bumps against Steve, who grabs him and whirls him around.*]

STEVE. A gag? A gag? Charlie, there's a dead man on the sidewalk and you killed him! Does this thing look like a gag to you?

[*Charlie breaks away and screams as he runs toward his house.*]

CHARLIE. No! No! Please!

[*A man breaks away from the crowd to chase Charlie.*

We see a long angle shot looking down as the man tackles Charlie and lands on top of him. The other people start to run toward them. Charlie is up on his feet, breaks away from the other man's grasp, lands a couple of desperate punches that push the man aside. Then he forces his way, fighting, through the crowd to once again break free, jumps up on his front porch. A rock thrown from the group smashes a window alongside of him, the broken glass flying past him. A couple of pieces cut him. He stands there perspiring, rumpled, blood running down from a cut on the cheek. His wife breaks away from the group to throw herself into his arms. He buries his face against her. We can see the crowd converging on the porch now.]

VOICES.
It must have been him.
He's the one.
We got to get Charlie.

[*Another rock lands on the porch. Now Charlie pushes his wife behind him, facing the group.*]

CHARLIE. Look, look I swear to you . . . it isn't me . . . but I do know who it is . . . I swear to you, I do know who it is. I know who the monster is here. I know who it is that doesn't belong. I swear to you I know.

GOODMAN. [*Shouting*] What are you waiting for?

WOMAN. [*Shouting*] Come on, Charlie, come on.

MAN ONE. [*Shouting*] Who is it, Charlie, tell us!

DON. [*Pushing his way to the front of the crowd*] All right, Charlie, let's hear it!

[*Charlie's eyes dart around wildly.*]

CHARLIE. It's . . . it's . . .

MAN TWO. [*Screaming*] Go ahead, Charlie, tell us.

CHARLIE. It's . . . it's the kid. It's Tommy. He's the one!

[*There's a gasp from the crowd as we cut to a shot of Sally holding her son Tommy. The boy at first doesn't understand and then, realizing the eyes are all on him, buries his face against his mother.*]

SALLY. [*Backs away*] That's crazy! That's crazy! He's a little boy.

WOMAN. But he knew! He was the only one who knew! He told us all about it. Well, how did he know? How *could* he have known?

[*The various people take this up and repeat the question aloud.*]

VOICES.
How could he know?
Who told him?
Make the kid answer.

DON. It was Charlie who killed old man Van Horn.

WOMAN. But it was the kid here who knew what was going to happen all the time. He was the one who knew!

[*We see a close-up of Steve.*]

STEVE. Are you all gone crazy? [*Pause as he looks about*] Stop.

[*A fist crashes at Steve's face, staggering him back out of the frame of the picture.*

There are several close camera shots suggesting the coming of violence. A hand fires a rifle. A fist clenches. A hand grabs the hammer from Van Horn's body, etc. Meanwhile, we hear the following lines.]

DON. Charlie has to be the one—Where's my rifle—

WOMAN. Les Goodman's the one. His car started! Let's wreck it.

MRS. GOODMAN. What about Steve's radio—He's the one that called them—

MR. GOODMAN. Smash the radio. Get me a hammer. Get me something.
STEVE. Stop—Stop—

CHARLIE. Where's that kid—Let's get him.

MAN ONE. Get Steve—Get Charlie—They're working together.

[*The crowd starts to converge around the mother, who grabs the child and starts to run with him. The crowd starts to follow, at first walking fast, and then running after him.*

We see a full shot of the street as suddenly Charlie's lights go off and the lights in another house go on. They stay on for a moment, then from across the street other lights go on and then off again.]

MAN ONE. [*Shouting*] It isn't the kid . . . it's Bob Weaver's house.

WOMAN. It isn't Bob Weaver's house, it's Don Martin's place.

CHARLIE. I tell you it's the kid.

DON. It's Charlie. He's the one.

[*We move into a series of close-ups of various people as they shout, accuse, scream, interspersing these shots with shots of houses as the lights go on and off, and then slowly in the middle of this nightmarish morass of sight and sound the camera starts to pull away, until once again we've reached the opening shot looking at the Maple Street sign from high above.*

The camera continues to move away until we dissolve to a shot looking toward the metal side of a space craft, which sits shrouded in darkness. An open door throws out a beam of light from the illuminated interior. Two figures silhouetted against the bright lights appear. We get only a vague feeling of form, but nothing more explicit than that.]

FIGURE ONE. Understand the procedure now? Just stop a few of their machines and radios and telephones and lawn mowers . . . throw them into darkness for a few hours, and then you just sit back and watch the pattern.

FIGURE TWO. And this pattern is always the same?

FIGURE ONE. With few variations. They pick the most dangerous enemy they can find . . . and it's themselves. And all we need do is sit back . . . and watch.

FIGURE TWO. Then I take it this place . . . this Maple Street . . . is not unique.

FIGURE ONE. [*Shaking his head*] By no means. Their world is full of Maple Streets. And we'll go from one to the other and let them destroy themselves. One to the other . . . one to the other . . . one to the other—

[*Now the camera pans up for a shot of the starry sky and over this we hear the Narrator's voice.*]

NARRATOR'S VOICE. The tools of conquest do not necessarily come with bombs and explosions and fallout. There are weapons that are simply thoughts, attitudes, prejudices— to be found only in the minds of men. For the record, prejudices can kill and suspicion can destroy and a thoughtless frightened search for a scapegoat has a fallout all its own for the children . . . and the children yet unborn. [*A pause*] And the pity of it is . . . that these things cannot be confined to . . . The Twilight Zone!

THINKING ABOUT THE SELECTION

Recalling

1. What are the first signs that something strange is happening on Maple Street?
2. What does Tommy think has happened?
3. Why do the people become suspicious of Les Goodman?
4. Why do they turn against Steve Brand?
5. Why does Charlie shoot Pete Van Horn?
6. What happens after the shooting?

7. What is the real cause of the strange occurrences on Maple Street?

Interpreting

8. Why does the group of friendly neighbors turn into a dangerous mob?
9. How does the appearance of the aliens at the end affect your view of the preceding action?
10. How do the events of the play prove the narrator's statement: "The tools of conquest do

not necessarily come with bombs and explosions and fallout"?

11. Who are the real "monsters"?

Applying

12. How do you think you would have responded if you were one of the residents of Maple Street?

ANALYZING LITERATURE
Recognizing Conflict in Drama

Conflict is a struggle between opposing forces. Understanding the different conflicts present will help you better understand the play.

1. How does Serling's play show conflict between individuals?
2. How does the play show conflict between individuals and society?
3. What other conflict occurs in the play?
4. What is the central conflict of the play?

CRITICAL THINKING AND READING
Identifying Invalid Conclusions

A **valid conclusion** is based on strong evidence or sound reasoning. For example, when Don Martin says that an electrical storm may have caused the loss of power on Maple Street, Charlie forms a valid conclusion. He says. "That don't seem likely. Sky's just as blue as anything. Not a cloud. No lightning. No thunder. . . ." His conclusion is valid because it is based on evidence.

An **invalid** conclusion is not well founded. It is based on little or no evidence, on faulty evidence, or on poor thinking. For example, when phones, portable radios, and lawn mowers stop working, Charlie concludes that an electrical-power failure has occurred. But if that were so, portable radios operating on batteries or transistors would be working—and they are not. Charlie's thinking is not sound and his conclusion is invalid.

1. Analyze the crowd's conclusion that Les

Goodman is guilty of something. Why is their conclusion invalid? (What is wrong with their evidence and thinking?)
2. Point out two other similar invalid conclusions made about characters in the play. Explain why each is invalid.

UNDERSTANDING LANGUAGE
Recognizing Colloquial English

Colloquial English is the relaxed, informal English that people use in conversation. Playwrights often use colloquial English in dialogue to make their characters sound realistic. Steve Brand, for example, is speaking colloquial English in the following lines: "We're all on a monster kick, Les. Seems that the general impression holds that maybe one family isn't what we think they are. Monsters from outer space or something." (p. 253) Slang expressions ("kick"), loose grammar ("Seems that . . ."), and incomplete sentences ("Monsters from outer space or something.") are characteristics of colloquial English.

1. Find two or three examples of colloquial English in the dialogue of the play.
2. Reread the narrator's speech at the very end of the play (p. 260). Tell why you think it is or is not an example of colloquial English.
3. Why do you suppose colloquial English is more acceptable in speech than in writing?

THINKING AND WRITING
Extending the Play

Imagine that the producers of *The Monsters Are Due on Maple Street* have asked you to write an additional scene for the play. It will fit in right after the dialogue between the two figures near the end and before the narrator's concluding words. The setting is Maple Street on the following morning. Write a scene that shows the new situation there. When you revise your scene, make sure it follows naturally from all that happens before. Finally proofread your scene and prepare a final draft.

GUIDE FOR READING

A Christmas Carol: Scrooge and Marley, Act I

Charles Dickens (1812–1870) was born in Portsmouth, England. He took upon himself the support of his family when he was twelve years old. For the rest of his life, he remembered what it was like to be poor. His sympathy for his fellow human beings is powerfully expressed in his story "A Christmas Carol." **Israel Horovitz** (1939–   ) has great respect for Dickens and this story. He has written, "I come to this work humbly, under the pressures of great respect for the Master: Charles Dickens."

Plot and Exposition

The **plot** of a play usually begins by introducing a conflict. The conflict rises to a climax, or high point of excitement or emotion. Then, as the play comes to a close, the excitement dies down, any unanswered questions about the story are answered, and the curtain falls.

Exposition is the revealing (exposing) of information needed to understand the action shown on stage. It often explains events that occurred before the start of the onstage events.

Look For

This play tells the story of a man who comes to learn sympathy for his fellow human beings. As you read Act I, notice how the plot develops in a way that makes you wonder what will happen to Scrooge. Also, notice the information given about events that occurred before Christmas 1843. How do these past events affect Scrooge?

Writing

Scrooge has become part of our everyday vocabulary. Brainstorm to list all the ideas that come to mind when you hear the word *Scrooge.*

Vocabulary

Knowing the following words will help you as you read *A Christmas Carol: Scrooge and Marley.*

implored (im plôrd') *v.*: Asked or begged earnestly (p. 265)

morose (mə rōs') *adj.*: Gloomy, ill-tempered (p. 266)

destitute (des' tə to͞ot') *adj.*: Living in complete poverty (p. 268)

misanthrope (mis' ən thrōp') *n.*: A person who hates or distrusts everyone (p. 270)

void (void) *n.*: Total emptiness (p. 270)

ponderous (pän' dər əs) *adj.*: Very heavy, bulky (p. 272)

A Christmas Carol: Scrooge and Marley

from *A Christmas Carol* by Charles Dickens

Israel Horovitz

THE PEOPLE OF THE PLAY

Jacob Marley, a specter
Ebenezer Scrooge, not yet
   dead, which is to say still alive
Bob Cratchit, Scrooge's clerk
Fred, Scrooge's nephew
Thin Do-Gooder
Portly Do-Gooder
Specters (Various), carrying money-
   boxes
The Ghost of Christmas Past
Four Jocund Travelers
A Band of Singers
A Band of Dancers
Little Boy Scrooge
Young Man Scrooge
Fan, Scrooge's little sister
The Schoolmaster
Schoolmates
Fezziwig, a fine and fair employer
Dick, young Scrooge's co-worker
Young Scrooge
A Fiddler
More Dancers
Scrooge's Lost Love
Scrooge's Lost Love's Daughter
Scrooge's Lost Love's Husband

The Ghost of Christmas
   Present
Some Bakers
Mrs. Cratchit, Bob Cratchit's wife
Belinda Cratchit, a daughter
Martha Cratchit, another
   daughter
Peter Cratchit, a son
Tiny Tim Cratchit, another son
Scrooge's Niece, Fred's wife
The Ghost of Christmas Fu-
   ture, a mute Phantom
Three Men of Business
Drunks, Scoundrels,
   Women of the Streets
A Charwoman
Mrs. Dilber
Joe, an old second-hand goods
   dealer
A Corpse, very like Scrooge
An Indebted Family
Adam, a young boy
A Poulterer
A Gentlewoman
Some More Men of Business

ACT I

Scene 1

[*Ghostly music in auditorium. A single spotlight on* JACOB MARLEY, D.C. *He is ancient; awful, dead-eyed. He speaks straight out to auditorium.*]

MARLEY. [*Cackle-voiced*] My name is Jacob Marley and I am dead. [*He laughs.*] Oh, no, there's no doubt that I am dead. The register of my burial was signed by the clergyman, the clerk, the undertaker . . . and by my chief mourner . . . Ebenezer Scrooge . . . [*Pause; remembers*] I am dead as a doornail.

[*A spotlight fades up, Stage Right, on* SCROOGE, *in his counting-house,[1] counting. Lettering on the window behind* SCROOGE *reads:* "SCROOGE AND MARLEY, LTD." *The spotlight is tight on* SCROOGE'S *head and shoulders. We shall not yet see into the offices and setting. Ghostly music continues, under.* MARLEY *looks across at* SCROOGE; *pitifully. After a moment's pause*]

I present him to you: Ebenezer Scrooge . . . England's most tightfisted hand at the grindstone, Scrooge! a squeezing, wrenching, grasping, scraping, clutching, covetous, old sinner! secret, and self-contained, and solitary as an oyster. The cold within him freezes his old features, nips his pointed nose, shrivels his cheek, stiffens his gait; makes his eyes red, his thin lips blue; and speaks out shrewdly in his grating voice. Look at him. Look at him . . .

[SCROOGE *counts and mumbles.*]

SCROOGE. They owe me money and I will collect. I will have them jailed, if I have to. They owe me money and I will collect what is due me.

[MARLEY *moves towards* SCROOGE; *two steps. The spotlight stays with him.*]

MARLEY. [*Disgusted*] He and I were partners for I don't know how many years. Scrooge was my sole executor, my sole administrator, my sole assign, my sole residuary legatee,[2] my sole friend and my sole mourner. But Scrooge was not so cut up by the sad event of my death, but that he was an excellent man of business on the very day of my funeral, and solemnized[3] it with an undoubted

---

1. counting house: An office for keeping financial records and writing business letters.

2. my sole executor (ig zek'yə tər), **my sole administrator, my sole assign** (ə sīn'), **my sole residuary legatee** (ri zij' oo wer' ē leg' ə tē'): All legal terms.

3. solemnized (säl' əm nīzd') v. : Honored or remembered; Marley is being ironic.

bargain. [*Pauses again in disgust*] He never painted out my name from the window. There it stands, on the window and above the warehouse door: Scrooge and Marley. Sometimes people new to our business call him Scrooge and sometimes they call him Marley. He answers to both names. It's all the same to him. And it's cheaper than painting in a new sign, isn't it? [*Pauses; moves closer to* SCROOGE] Nobody has ever stopped him in the street to say, with gladsome looks, "My dear Scrooge, how are you? When will you come to see me?" No beggars implored him to bestow a trifle, no children ever ask him what it is o'clock, no man or woman now, or ever in his life, not once, inquire the way to such and such a place. [MARLEY *stands next to* SCROOGE *now. They share, so it seems, a spotlight.*] But what does Scrooge care of any of this? It is the very thing he likes! To edge his way along the crowded paths of life, warning all human sympathy to keep its distance.

[*A ghostly bell rings in the distance.* MARLEY *moves away from* SCROOGE, *now, heading* D. *again. As he does, he "takes" the light:* SCROOGE *has disappeared into the black void beyond.* MARLEY *walks* D.C., *talking directly to the audience. Pauses*]

The bell tolls and I must take my leave. You must stay a while with Scrooge and watch him play out his scroogey life. It is now the story: the once-upon-a-time. Scrooge is busy in his counting-house. Where else? Christmas eve and Scrooge is busy in his counting-house. It is cold, bleak, biting weather outside: foggy withal: and, if you listen closely, you can hear the people in the court go wheezing up and down, beating their hands upon their breasts, and stamping their feet upon the pavement stones to warm them . . .

[*The clocks outside strike three.*]

Only three! and quite dark outside already: it has not been light all day this day.

[*This ghostly bell rings in the distance again.* MARLEY *looks about him. Music in.* MARLEY *flies away.*] (N.B. *Marley's comings and goings should, from time to time, induce the explosion of the odd flash-pot.* I.H.)

Scene 2

[*Christmas music in, sung by a live chorus, full. At conclusion of song, sound fades under and into the distance. Lights up in set: offices of Scrooge and Marley, Ltd.* SCROOGE *sits at his desk, at work. Near him is a tiny fire. His door is open and in his line of vision, we see* SCROOGE'S *clerk,* BOB CRATCHIT, *who sits in a dismal tank of a cubicle, copying letters. Near* CRATCHIT *is a fire so tiny as to barely cast a light: perhaps it is one pitifully glowing coal?* CRATCHIT *rubs his hands together, puts on a white comforter[4] and tries to heat his hands around his candle.* SCROOGE'S NEPHEW *enters, unseen.*]

SCROOGE. What are you doing, Cratchit? Acting cold, are you? Next, you'll be asking to replenish your coal from my coal-box, won't you? Well, save your breath, Cratchit! Unless you're prepared to find employ elsewhere!

NEPHEW. [*Cheerfully; surprising* SCROOGE] A merry Christmas to you, Uncle! God save you!

SCROOGE. Bah! Humbug![5]

---

4. comforter (kum′ fər tər) *n.*: A long, woolen scarf.
5. Humbug (hum′ bug′) *interj.*: Nonsense! (can also be used as a noun to mean nonsense or something done to cheat or deceive).

NEPHEW. Christmas a "humbug," Uncle? I'm sure you don't mean that.

SCROOGE. I do! Merry Christmas? What right do you have to be merry? What reason have you to be merry? You're poor enough!

NEPHEW. Come, then. What right have you to be dismal? What reason have you to be morose? You're rich enough.

SCROOGE. Bah! Humbug!

NEPHEW. Don't be cross, Uncle.

SCROOGE. What else can I be? Eh? When I live in a world of fools such as this? Merry Christmas? What's Christmastime to you but a time of paying bills without any money; a time for finding yourself a year older, but not an hour richer. If I could work my will, every idiot who goes about with "Merry Christmas" on his lips, should be boiled with his own pudding, and buried with a stake of holly through his heart. He should!

NEPHEW. Uncle!

SCROOGE. Nephew! You keep Christmas in your own way and let me keep it in mine.

NEPHEW. Keep it! But you don't keep it, Uncle.

SCROOGE. Let me leave it alone, then. Much good it has ever done you!

NEPHEW. There are many things from which I have derived good, by which I have not profited, I daresay. Christmas among the rest. But I am sure that I always thought of Christmas time, when it has come round— as a good time: the only time I know of, when men and women seem to open their shut-up hearts freely, and to think of people below them as if they really were fellow-passengers to the grave, and not another race of creatures bound on other journeys. And therefore, Uncle, though it has never put a scrap of gold or silver in my pocket, I believe that it *has* done me good, and that it *will* do me good; and I say, God bless it!

[*The* CLERK *in the tank applauds, looks at the furious* SCROOGE *and pokes out his tiny fire, as if in exchange for the moment of impropriety.* SCROOGE *yells at him.*]

SCROOGE. [*To the* CLERK] Let me hear another sound from *you* and you'll keep your Christmas by losing your situation. [*To the* NEPHEW] You're quite a powerful speaker, sir. I wonder you don't go into Parliament.[6]

NEPHEW. Don't be angry, Uncle. Come! Dine with us tomorrow.

SCROOGE. I'd rather see myself dead than see myself with your family!

NEPHEW. But, why? Why?

SCROOGE. Why did you get married?

NEPHEW. Because I fell in love.

SCROOGE. That, sir, is the only thing that you have said to me in your entire lifetime which is even more ridiculous than "Merry Christmas"! [*Turns from* NEPHEW] Good afternoon.

NEPHEW. Nay, Uncle, you never came to see me before I married either. Why give it as a reason for not coming now?

SCROOGE. Good afternoon, Nephew!

NEPHEW. I want nothing from you; I ask nothing of you; why cannot we be friends?

SCROOGE. Good afternoon!

NEPHEW. I am sorry with all my heart, to find you so resolute. But I have made the trial in homage to Christmas, and I'll keep my Christmas humor to the last. So A Merry Christmas, Uncle!

SCROOGE. Good afternoon!

NEPHEW. And A Happy New Year!

SCROOGE. Good afternoon!

NEPHEW. [*He stands facing* SCROOGE.] Uncle, you are the most . . . [*Pauses*] No, I shan't. My Christmas humor is intact . . . [*Pause*] God bless you, Uncle . . . [NEPHEW *turns and starts for the door; he stops at* CRATCHIT's *cage.*] Merry Christmas, Bob Cratchit . . .

CRATCHIT. Merry Christmas to you sir, and a very, very happy New Year . . .

SCROOGE. [*Calling across to them*] Oh, fine, a perfection, just fine . . . to see the perfect pair of you: husbands, with wives and children to support . . . my clerk there earning fifteen shillings a week . . . and the perfect pair of you, talking about a Merry Christmas! [*Pauses*] I'll retire to Bedlam![7]

NEPHEW. [*To* CRATCHIT] He's impossible!

CRATCHIT. Oh, mind him not, sir. He's getting on in years, and he's alone. He's noticed your visit. I'll wager your visit has warmed him.

NEPHEW. Him? Uncle Ebenezer Scrooge? *Warmed?* You are a better Christian than I am, sir.

CRATCHIT. [*Opening the door for* NEPHEW; *two* DO-GOODERS *will enter, as* NEPHEW *exits*] Good day to you, sir, and God bless.

NEPHEW. God bless . . . [*One man who enters is portly, the other is thin. Both are pleasant.*]

CRATCHIT. Can I help you, gentlemen?

---

6. Parliament (pär′ lə mənt): The national legislative body of Great Britain, in some ways like the American Congress.

7. Bedlam (bed′ ləm): A hospital in London for the mentally ill.

THIN MAN. [*Carrying papers and books; looks around* CRATCHIT *to* SCROOGE] Scrooge and Marley's, I believe. Have I the pleasure of addressing Mr. Scrooge, or Mr. Marley?

SCROOGE. Mr. Marley has been dead these seven years. He died seven years ago this very night.

PORTLY MAN. We have no doubt his liberality is well represented by his surviving partner . . . [*Offers his calling card*]

SCROOGE. [*Handing back the card; un-looked at*] . . . Good afternoon.

THIN MAN. This will take but a moment, sir . . .

PORTLY MAN. At this festive season of the year, Mr. Scrooge, it is more than usually desirable that we should make some slight provision for the poor and destitute, who suffer greatly at the present time. Many thousands are in want of common necessities; hundreds of thousands are in want of common comforts, sir.

SCROOGE. Are there no prisons?

PORTLY MAN. Plenty of prisons.

SCROOGE. And aren't the Union workhouses still in operation?

THIN MAN. They are. Still. I wish that I could say that they are not.

SCROOGE. The Treadmill[8] and the Poor Law[9] are in full vigor, then?

THIN MAN. Both very busy, sir.

---

8. the Treadmill (tred' mil'): A kind of mill wheel turned by the weight of persons treading steps arranged around it; this devise was used to punish prisoners in jails.

9. the Poor Law: A series of laws were passed in England from the 17th century on to help the poor; changes to the law in 1834 gave responsibility for this relief to the national government but did not provide much aid for the poor.

SCROOGE. Ohhh, I see. I was afraid, from what you said at first, that something had occurred to stop them from their useful course. [*Pauses*] I'm glad to hear it.

PORTLY MAN. Under the impression that they scarcely furnish Christian cheer of mind or body to the multitude, a few of us are endeavoring to raise a fund to buy the Poor some meat and drink, and means of warmth. We choose this time, because it is a time, of all others, when Want is keenly felt, and Abundance rejoices. [*Pen in hand; as well as notepad*] What shall I put you down for, sir?

SCROOGE. Nothing!

PORTLY MAN. You wish to be left anonymous?

SCROOGE. I wish to be left alone! [*Pauses; turns away; turns back to them*] Since you ask me what I wish, gentlemen, that is my answer. I help to support the establishments that I have mentioned: they cost enough: and those who are badly off must go there.

THIN MAN. Many can't go there; and many would rather die.

SCROOGE. If they would rather die, they had better do it, and decrease the surplus population. Besides—excuse me—I don't know that.

THIN MAN. But you might know it!

SCROOGE. It's not my business. It's enough for a man to understand his own business, and not to interfere with other people's. Mine occupies me constantly. Good afternoon, gentlemen! [*Scrooge turns his back on the gentlemen and returns to his desk.*]

PORTLY MAN. But, sir, Mr. Scrooge . . . think of the poor.

SCROOGE. [*Turns suddenly to them. Pauses*] Take your leave of my offices, sirs, while I am still smiling.

[*The* THIN MAN *looks at the* PORTLY MAN. *They are undone. They shrug. They move to door. Cratchit hops up to open it for them.*]

THIN MAN. Good day, sir . . . [*To* CRATCHIT] A merry Christmas to you, sir . . .

CRATCHIT. Yes. A Merry Christmas to both of you . . .

PORTLY MAN. Merry Christmas . . .

[CRATCHIT *silently squeezes something into the hand of the* THIN MAN.]

THIN MAN. What's this?

CRATCHIT. Shhhh . . .

[CRATCHIT *opens the door; wind and snow whistle into the room.*]

THIN MAN. Thank you, sir, thank you.

[CRATCHIT *closes the door and returns to his workplace.* SCROOGE *is at his own counting table. He talks to* CRATCHIT *without looking up.*]

SCROOGE. It's less of a time of year for being merry, and more a time of year for being loony . . . if you ask me.

CRATCHIT. Well, I don't know, sir . . .

[*The clock's bell strikes six o'clock.*]

Well, there it is, eh, six?

SCROOGE. Saved by six bells, are you?

CRATCHIT. I must be going home . . . [*He snuffs out his candle and puts on his hat.*] I hope you have a . . . very very lovely day tomorrow, sir . . .

SCROOGE. Hmmm. Oh, you'll be wanting the whole day tomorrow, I suppose?

CRATCHIT. If quite convenient, sir.

SCROOGE. It's not convenient, and it's not fair. If I was to stop half-a-crown for it, you'd think yourself ill-used, I'll be bound?

[CRATCHIT *smiles faintly.*]

CRATCHIT. I don't know, sir . . .

SCROOGE. And yet, you don't think me ill-used, when I pay a day's wages for no work . . .

CRATCHIT. It's only but once a year . . .

SCROOGE. A poor excuse for picking a man's pocket every 25th of December! But I suppose you must have the whole day. Be here all the earlier the next morning!

CRATCHIT. Oh, I will, sir. I will. I promise you. And, sir . . .

SCROOGE. Don't say it, Cratchit.

CRATCHIT. But let me wish you a . . .

SCROOGE. Don't say it, Cratchit. I warn you . . .

CRATCHIT. Sir!

SCROOGE. Cratchit!

[CRATCHIT *opens the door.*]

CRATCHIT. All right, then, sir . . . well . . . [*Suddenly*] Merry Christmas, Mr. Scrooge!

[*And he runs out the door, shutting same behind him.* SCROOGE *moves to his desk; gathering his coat, hat, etc. A* BOY *appears at his window. . . .*]

BOY. [*Singing*] "Away in a manger . . ."

[SCROOGE *seizes his ruler and whacks at the image of the* BOY *outside. The* BOY *leaves.*]

SCROOGE. Bah! Humbug! Christmas! Bah! Humbug! [*He shuts out the light.*]

A note on the crossover, following Scene 2:

[SCROOGE *will walk alone to his rooms from his offices. As he makes a long slow cross of the stage, the scenery should change. Christmas music will be heard, various people will cross by* SCROOGE, *often smiling happily.*

There will be occasional pleasant greetings tossed at him.

SCROOGE, *in contrast to all, will grump and mumble. He will snap at passing boys, as might a horrid old hound.*

In short, SCROOGE'*s sounds and movements will define him in contrast from all other people who cross the stage: he is the misanthrope, the malcontent, the miser. He is* SCROOGE.

This statement of SCROOGE'*s character, by contrast to all other characters, should seem comical to the audience.*

During SCROOGE'*s crossover to his rooms, snow should begin to fall. All passers-by will hold their faces to the sky, smiling, allowing snow to shower them lightly.* SCROOGE, *by contrast, will bat at the flakes with his walking-stick, as might an insomniac swat at a sleep-stopping, middle-of-the-night swarm of mosquitoes. He will comment on the blackness of the night, and, finally, reach his rooms and his encounter with the magical specter:* MARLEY, *his eternal mate.*]

Scene 3

SCROOGE. No light at all . . . no moon . . . *that* is what is at the center of a Christmas Eve: dead black: void . . .

[SCROOGE *puts his key in the door's keyhole. He has reached his rooms now. The door knocker changes and is now* MARLEY'*s face. A musical sound; quickly; ghostly.* MARLEY'*s image is not at all angry, but looks at* SCROOGE *as did the old* MARLEY *look at* SCROOGE. *The hair is curiously stirred; eyes wide open, dead: absent of focus.* SCROOGE *stares wordlessly here. The face, before his very eyes, does deliquesce.*[10] *It is a knocker again.* SCROOGE *opens the door and checks the back of same, probably for* MARLEY'S *pigtail. Seeing nothing but screws and nuts,* SCROOGE *refuses the memory.*]

Pooh, pooh!

[*The sound of the door closing resounds throughout the house as thunder. Every room echoes the sound.* SCROOGE *fastens the door and walks across the hall to the stairs, trimming his candle as he goes; and then he goes slowly up the staircase. He checks each room: sitting room, bedroom, lumber-room. He looks under the sofa, under the table: nobody there. He fixes his evening gruel on the hob,*[11] *changes his jacket.* SCROOGE *sits near the tiny low-flamed fire, sipping his gruel. There are various pictures on the walls: all of them now show likenesses of* MARLEY. SCROOGE *blinks his eyes.*]

Bah! Humbug!

[SCROOGE *walks in a circle about the room. The pictures change back into their natural images. He sits down at the table in front of the fire. A bell hangs overhead. It begins to ring, of its own accord. Slowly, surely, begins the ringing of every bell in the house. They continue ringing for nearly half a minute.* SCROOGE *is stunned by the phenomenon. The bells cease their ringing all at once. Deep below* SCROOGE, *in the basement of the house, there is the sound of clanking, of some enormous chain being dragged across the floors; and now up the stairs. We hear doors flying open.*]

---

10. deliquesce (del' ə kwes') *v.*: Melt away.
11. gruel (grōō' əl) **on the hob** (häb): A thin broth warming on a ledge at the back or side of the fireplace.

Bah still! Humbug still! This is not happening! I won't believe it!

[MARLEY'S GHOST *enters the room. He is horrible to look at: pigtail, vest, suit as usual, but he drags an enormous chain now, to which is fastened cash-boxes, keys, padlocks, ledgers, deeds, and heavy purses fashioned of steel. He is transparent.* MARLEY *stands opposite the stricken* SCROOGE.]

How now! What do you want of me?

MARLEY. Much!

SCROOGE. Who are you?

MARLEY. Ask me who I *was.*

SCROOGE. Who *were* you then?

MARLEY. In life, I was your business partner: Jacob Marley.

SCROOGE. I see . . . can you sit down?

MARLEY. I can.

SCROOGE. Do it then.

MARLEY. I shall. [MARLEY *sits opposite* SCROOGE, *in the chair across the table, at the front of the fireplace.*] You don't believe in me.

SCROOGE. I don't.

MARLEY. Why do you doubt your senses?

SCROOGE. Because every little thing affects them. A slight disorder of the stomach makes them cheat. You may be an undigested bit of beef, a blot of mustard, a crumb of cheese, a fragment of an underdone potato. There's more of gravy than of grave about you, whatever you are!

[*There is a silence between them.* SCROOGE *is made nervous by it. He picks up a toothpick.*]

Humbug! I tell you: humbug!

[MARLEY *opens his mouth and screams a ghosty, fearful scream. The scream echoes about each room of the house. Bats fly, cats screech, lightning flashes.* SCROOGE *stands and walks backwards against the wall.* MARLEY *stands and screams again. This time, he takes his head and lifts it from his shoulders. His head continues to scream.* MARLEY'S *face again appears on every picture in the room: all screaming.* SCROOGE, *on his knees before* MARLEY.]

Mercy! Dreadful apparition,[12] mercy! Why, O! why do you trouble me so?

MARLEY. Man of the worldly mind, do you believe in me, or not?

SCROOGE. I do. I must. But why do spirits such as you walk the earth? And why do they come to me?

MARLEY. It is required of every man that the spirit within him should walk abroad among his fellow-men, and travel far and wide; and if that spirit goes not forth in life, it is condemned to do so after death. [MARLEY *screams again; a tragic scream; from his ghosty bones.*] I wear the chain I forged in life. I made it link by link, and yard by yard. Is its pattern strange to *you?* Or would you know, you, Scrooge, the weight and length of the strong coil you bear yourself? It was full as heavy and long as this, seven Christmas Eves ago. You have labored on it, since. It is a ponderous chain.

[*Terrified that a chain will appear about his body,* SCROOGE *spins and waves the unwanted chain away. None, of course, appears. Sees* MARLEY *watching him dance about the room.* MARLEY *watches* SCROOGE; *silently.*]

SCROOGE. Jacob. Old Jacob Marley, tell me more. Speak comfort to me, Jacob . . .

---

12. apparition (ap′ ə rish′ ən) *n.*: Ghost.

MARLEY. I have none to give. Comfort comes from other regions, Ebenezer Scrooge, and is conveyed by other ministers, to other kinds of men. A very little more, is all that is permitted to me. I cannot rest, I cannot stay, I cannot linger anywhere . . . [*He moans again.*] my spirit never walked beyond our counting-house—mark me!—in life my spirit never roved beyond the narrow limits of our money-changing hole; and weary journeys lie before me!

SCROOGE. But you were always a good man of business, Jacob.

MARLEY. [*Screams word "business"; a flashpot explodes with him.*] BUSINESS!!! Mankind was my business. The common welfare was my business; charity, mercy, forbearance, benevolence, were, all, my business. [SCROOGE *is quaking.*] Hear me, Ebenezer Scrooge! My time is nearly gone.

SCROOGE. I will, but don't be hard upon me. And don't be flowery, Jacob! Pray!

MARLEY. How is it that I appear before you in a shape that you can see, I may not tell. I have sat invisible beside you many and many a day. That is no light part of my penance. I am here tonight to warn you that you have yet a chance and hope of escaping my fate. A chance and hope of my procuring, Ebenezer.

SCROOGE. You were always a good friend to me. Thank'ee!

MARLEY. You will be haunted by Three Spirits.

SCROOGE. Would that be the chance and hope you mentioned, Jacob?

MARLEY. It is.

SCROOGE. I think I'd rather not.

MARLEY. Without their visits, you cannot hope to shun the path I tread. Expect the first one tomorrow, when the bell tolls one.

SCROOGE. Couldn't I take 'em all at once, and get it over, Jacob?

MARLEY. Expect the second on the next night at the same hour. The third upon the next night when the last stroke of twelve has ceased to vibrate. Look to see me no more. Others may, but you may not. And look that, for your own sake, you remember what has passed between us!

[MARLEY *places his head back upon his shoulders. He approaches the window and beckons to* SCROOGE *to watch. Outside the window, specters[13] fly by, carrying money-boxes and chains. They make a confused sound of lamentation.* MARLEY, *after listening a moment, joins into their mournful dirge. He leans to the window and floats out into the bleak, dark night. He is gone.*]

SCROOGE. [*Rushing to the window*] Jacob! No, Jacob! Don't leave me! I'm frightened!

[*He sees that* MARLEY *has gone. He looks outside. He pulls the shutter closed, so that the scene is blocked from his view. All sound stops. After a pause, he re-opens the shutter and all is quiet, as it should be on Christmas Eve. Carolers carol out of doors, in the distance.* SCROOGE *closes the shutter and walks down the stairs. He examines the door by which* MARLEY *first entered.*]

No one here at all! Did I imagine all that? Humbug! [*He looks about the room.*] I did imagine it. It only happened in my foulest dream-mind, didn't it? An undigested bit of . . .

[*Thunder and lightning in the room; suddenly*]

Sorry! Sorry!

[*There is silence again. The lights fade out.*]

---

13. specters (spek′ tərz) *n.*: Ghosts.

Scene 4

[*Christmas music, choral, "Hark the Herald Angels Sing," sung by an onstage choir of children, spotlighted,* D.C. *Above,* SCROOGE *in his bed, dead to the world, asleep, in his darkened room. It should appear that the choir is singing somewhere outside of the house, of course, and a use of scrim[14] is thus suggested. When the singing is ended, the choir should fade out of view and* MARLEY *should fade into view, in their place.*]

MARLEY. [*Directly to audience*] From this point forth . . . I shall be quite visible to you, but invisible to him. [*Smiles*] He will feel my presence, nevertheless, for, unless my senses fail me completely, we are—you and I—witness to the changing of a miser: that one, my partner in life, in business, and in eternity: that one: Scrooge. [*Moves to staircase, below* SCROOGE] See him now. He endeavors to pierce the darkness with his ferret eyes.[15] [*To audience*] See him, now. He listens for the hour.

[*The bells toll.* SCROOGE *is awakened and quakes as the hour approaches one o'clock, but the bells stop their sound at the hour of twelve.*]

SCROOGE. [*Astonished*] Midnight! Why this isn't possible. It was past two when I went to bed. An icicle must have gotten into the clock's works! I couldn't have slept through the whole day and far into another night. It isn't possible that anything has happened to the sun, and this is twelve at noon! [*He runs to window; unshutters same; it is night.*] Night, still. Quiet, normal for the season, cold. It is certainly not noon. I cannot in any way afford to lose my days. Securities come

---

14. scrim (skrim) *n.*: A light, semi-transparent curtain.

15. ferret eyes: A ferret is a small, weasellike animal used for hunting rabbits; this expression means to look persistently, the way a ferret hunts.

due, promissory notes,[16] interest on investments: these are things that happen in the daylight! [*He returns to his bed.*] Was this a dream?

[MARLEY *appears in his room. He speaks to the audience.*]

MARLEY. You see? He does not, with faith, believe in me fully, even still! Whatever will it take to turn the faith of a miser from money to men?

SCROOGE. Another quarter and it'll be one and Marley's ghosty friends will come. [*Pauses; listens*] Where's the chime for one? [*Ding, dong*] A quarter *past* [*Repeats*] Half-past! [*Repeats*] A quarter to it! But where's the heavy bell of the hour one? This is a game in which I lose my senses! Perhaps, if I allowed myself another short doze . . .

MARLEY. . . . Doze, Ebenezer, doze.

[*A heavy bell thuds its one ring; dull and definitely one o'clock. There is a flash of light.* SCROOGE *sits up, in a sudden. A hand draws back the curtains by his bed. He sees it.*]

SCROOGE. A hand! Who owns it! Hello!

[*Ghosty music again, but of a new nature to the play. A strange figure stands before* SCROOGE—*like a child, yet at the same time like an old man: white hair, but unwrinkled skin, long, muscular arms, but delicate legs and feet. Wears white tunic; lustrous belt cinches waist. Branch of fresh green holly in its hand, but has its dress trimmed with fresh summer flowers. Clear jets of light spring from the crown of its head. Holds cap in hand. The Spirit is called* PAST.]

Are you the Spirit, sir, whose coming was foretold to me?

---

16. promissory (präm′ i sôr′ ē) **notes:** Written promises to pay someone a certain sum of money.

PAST. I am.

MARLEY. Does he take this to be a vision of his green grocer?

SCROOGE. Who, and what are you?

PAST. I am the Ghost of Christmas Past.

SCROOGE. Long past?

PAST. Your past.

SCROOGE. May I ask, please, sir, what business you have here with me?

PAST. Your welfare.

SCROOGE. Not to sound ungrateful, sir, and really, please do understand that I am plenty obliged for your concern, but, really, kind spirit, it would have done all the better for my welfare to have been left alone altogether, to have slept peacefully through this night.

PAST. Your reclamation, then. Take heed!

SCROOGE. My what?

PAST. [*Motioning to* SCROOGE *and taking his arm*] Rise! Fly with me! [*He leads* SCROOGE *to the window.*]

SCROOGE. [*Panicked*] Fly, but I am a mortal and cannot fly!

PAST. [*Pointing to his heart*] Bear but a touch of my hand *here* and you shall be upheld in more than this!

[SCROOGE *touches the* SPIRIT'S *heart and the lights dissolve into sparkly flickers. Lovely crystals of music are heard. The scene dissolves into another. Christmas music again*]

Scene 5

[SCROOGE *and the* GHOST OF CHRISTMAS PAST *walk together across an open stage. In the background, we see a field that is open; covered by a soft, downy snow: a country road.*]

SCROOGE. Good Heaven! I was bred in this place. I was a boy here!

[SCROOGE *freezes, staring at the field beyond.* MARLEY's *ghost appears beside him; takes* SCROOGE's *face in his hands, and turns his face to the audience.*]

MARLEY. You see this Scrooge: stricken by feeling. Conscious of a thousand odors floating in the air, each one connected with a thousand thoughts, and hopes, and joys, and care long, long forgotten. [*Pause*] This one—this Scrooge—before your very eyes, returns to life, among the living. [*To audience, sternly*] You'd best pay your most careful attention. I would suggest rapt.[17]

[*There is a small flash and puff of smoke and* MARLEY *is gone again.*]

---

17. rapt (rapt) *adj.*: Giving complete attention, totally carried away by something.

PAST. Your lip is trembling, Mr. Scrooge. And what is that upon your cheek?

SCROOGE. Upon my cheek? Nothing . . . a blemish on the skin from the eating of overmuch grease . . . nothing . . . [*Suddenly*] Kind Spirit of Christmas Past, lead me where you will, but *quickly!* To be stagnant in this place is, for me, *unbearable!*

PAST. You recollect the way?

SCROOGE. Remember it! I would know it blindfolded! My bridge, my church, my winding river! [*Staggers about, trying to see it all at once. He weeps again.*]

PAST. These are but shadows of things that have been. They have no consciousness of us.

[*Four jocund travelers enter, singing a Christmas song in four-part harmony—"God Rest Ye Merry Gentlemen."*]

SCROOGE. Listen! I know these men! I know them! I remember the beauty of their song!

PAST. But, why do you remember it so happily? It is Merry Christmas that they say to one another! What is Merry Christmas to you, Mr. Scrooge? Out upon Merry Christmas, right? What good has Merry Christmas ever done you, Mr. Scrooge? . . .

SCROOGE. [*After a long pause*] None. No good. None . . . [*He bows his head.*]

PAST. Look, you, sir, a school ahead. The schoolroom is not quite deserted. A solitary child, neglected by his friends, is left there still.

[SCROOGE *falls to the ground; sobbing as he sees, and we see, a small boy, the young* SCROOGE, *sitting and weeping, bravely, alone at his desk: alone in a vast space, a void.*]

SCROOGE. I cannot look on him!

PAST. You must, Mr. Scrooge, you must.

SCROOGE. It's me. [*Pauses; weeps*] Poor boy. He lived inside his head . . . alone . . . [*Pauses; weeps*] poor boy. [*Pauses; stops his weeping*] I wish . . . [*Dries his eyes on his cuff*] ah! it's too late!

PAST. What is the matter?

SCROOGE. There was a boy singing a Christmas Carol outside my door last night. I should like to have given him something: that's all.

PAST. [*Smiles; waves his hand to* SCROOGE] Come. Let us see another Christmas.

[*Lights out on little boy. A flash of light. A puff of smoke. Lights up on older boy*]

SCROOGE. Look! Me, again! Older now! [*Realizes*] Oh, yes . . . still alone.

[*The boy—a slightly older* SCROOGE—*sits alone in a chair, reading. The door to the room opens and a young girl enters. She is much, much younger than this slightly older* SCROOGE. *She is, say, six, and he is, say, twelve. Elder* SCROOGE *and the* GHOST OF CHRISTMAS PAST *stand watching the scene, unseen.*]

FAN. Dear, dear brother, I have come to bring you home.

BOY. Home, little Fan?

FAN. Yes! Home, for good and all! Father is so much kinder than he ever used to be, and home's like heaven! He spoke so gently to me one dear night when I was going to bed that I was not afraid to ask him once more if you might come home; and he said "yes" . . . you should; and sent me in a coach to bring you. And you're to be a man and are never to come back here, but first, we're to be together all the Christmas long, and have the merriest time in the world.

BOY. You are quite a woman, little Fan!

[*Laughing; she drags at* BOY, *causing him to stumble to the door with her. Suddenly we hear a mean and terrible voice in the hallway. Off. It is the* SCHOOLMASTER.]

SCHOOLMASTER. Bring down Master Scrooge's travel box at once! He is to travel!

FAN. Who is that, Ebenezer?

BOY. O! Quiet, Fan. It is the Schoolmaster, himself!

[*The door bursts open and into the room bursts with it the* SCHOOLMASTER.]

SCHOOLMASTER. Master Scrooge?

BOY. Oh, Schoolmaster. I'd like you to meet my little sister, Fan, sir . . .

[*Two boys struggle on with* SCROOGE'S *trunk.*]

FAN. Pleased, sir . . . [*She curtsies.*]

SCHOOLMASTER. You are to travel, Master Scrooge.

SCROOGE. Yes, sir. I know sir . . .

[*All start to exit, but* FAN *grabs the coattail of the mean old* SCHOOLMASTER.]

BOY. Fan!

SCHOOLMASTER. What's this?

FAN. Pardon, sir, but I believe that you've forgotten to say your goodbye to my brother, Ebenezer, who stands still now awaiting it . . . [*She smiles, curtsies, lowers her eyes.*] pardon, sir.

SCHOOLMASTER. [*Amazed*] I . . . uh . . . harumph . . . uhh . . . well, then . . . [*Outstretches hand*] Goodbye, Scrooge.

BOY. Uh, well, goodbye, Schoolmaster . . .

[*Lights fade out on all but* BOY *looking at* FAN; *and* SCROOGE *and* PAST *looking at them.*]

SCROOGE. Oh, my dear, dear little sister, Fan . . . how I loved her.

PAST. Always a delicate creature, whom a breath might have withered, but she had a large heart . . .

SCROOGE. So she had.

PAST. She died a woman, and had, as I think, children.

SCROOGE. One child.

PAST. True. Your nephew.

SCROOGE. Yes.

PAST. Fine, then. We move on, Mr. Scrooge. That warehouse, there? Do you know it?

SCROOGE. Know it? Wasn't I apprenticed[18] there?

---

18. apprenticed (ə pren' tist) *v.*: Receiving financial support and instruction in a trade in return for work.

PAST. We'll have a look.

[*They enter the warehouse. The lights crossfade with them, coming up on an old man in Welsh wig:* FEZZIWIG.]

SCROOGE. Why, it's old Fezziwig! Bless his heart; it's Fezziwig, alive again!

[FEZZIWIG *sits behind a large, high desk, counting. He lays down his pen; looks at the clock: seven bells sound.*]

Quittin' time . . .

FEZZIWIG. Quittin' time . . . [*He takes off his waistcoat and laughs; calls off*] Yo ho, Ebenezer! Dick!

[DICK WILKINS *and* EBENEZER SCROOGE—*a young man version—enter the room.* DICK *and* EBENEZER *are* FEZZIWIG'S *apprentices.*]

SCROOGE. Dick Wilkins, to be sure! My fellow-'prentice! Bless my soul, yes. There he is. He was very much attached to me, was Dick. Poor Dick! Dear, dear!

FEZZIWIG. Yo ho, my boys. No more work tonight. Christmas Eve, Dick. Christmas, Ebenezer!

[*They stand at attention in front of* FEZZIWIG; *laughing*]

Hilli-ho! Clear away, and let's have lots of room here! Hilli-ho, Dick! Chirrup, Ebenezer!

[*The young men clear the room, sweep the floor, straighten the pictures, trim the lamps, etc. The space is clear now. A fiddler enters, fiddling.*]

Hi-ho, Matthew! Fiddle away . . . where are my daughters?

[*The* FIDDLER *plays. Three young daughters of* FEZZIWIG *enter followed by six young male suitors. They are dancing to the music. All employees come in: workers, clerks, housemaids, cousins, the baker, etc.*]

All dance. Full number wanted here. Throughout the dance, food is brought into the feast. It is "eaten" in dance, by the dancers. EBENEZER *dances with all three of the daughters, as does* DICK. *They compete for the daughters, happily, in the dance.* FEZZIWIG *dances with his daughters.* FEZZIWIG *dances with* DICK *and* EBENZER. *The music changes:* MRS. FEZZIWIG *enters. She lovingly scolds her husband. They dance. She dances with* EBENEZER, *lifting him and throwing him about. She is enormously fat. When the dance is ended, they all dance off, floating away, as does the music.* SCROOGE *and the* GHOST OF CHRISTMAS PAST *stand alone now. The music is gone.*]

PAST. It was a small matter, that Fezziwig made those silly folks so full of gratitude.

SCROOGE. Small!

PAST. Shhh!

[*Lights up on* DICK *and* EBENEZER]

DICK. We are blessed, Ebenezer, truly, to have such a master as Mr. Fezziwig!

YOUNG SCROOGE. He is the best, best, the very and absolute best! If ever I own a firm of my own, I shall treat my apprentices with the same dignity and the same grace. We have learned a wonderful lesson from the master, Dick!

DICK. Ah, that's a fact, Ebenezer. That's a fact!

PAST. Was it not a small matter, really? He spent but a few pounds[19] of his mortal money on your small party. Three or four

---

19. pounds (pŏundz) *n.*: A common type of money used in Great Britain.

pounds, perhaps. Is that so much that he deserves such praise as you and Dick so lavish now?

SCROOGE. It isn't that! It isn't that, Spirit. Fezziwig had the power to make us happy or unhappy; to make our service light or burdensome; a pleasure or a toil. The happiness he gave is quite as great as if it cost him a fortune.

PAST. What is the matter?

SCROOGE. Nothing particular.

PAST. Something, I think.

SCROOGE. No, no. I should like to be able to say a word or two to my clerk just now! That's all!

[EBENEZER *enters the room and shuts down all the lamps. He stretches and yawns. The* GHOST OF CHRISTMAS PAST *turns to* SCROOGE; *all of a sudden.*]

PAST. My time grows short! Quick!

[*In a flash of light,* EBENEZER *is gone, and in his place stands an* OLDER SCROOGE, *this one a man in the prime of his life. Beside him stands a young woman in a mourning dress. She is crying. She speaks to the man, with hostility.*]

WOMAN. It matters little . . . to you, very little. Another idol has displaced me.

MAN. What idol has displaced you?

WOMAN. A golden one.

MAN. This is an even-handed dealing of the world. There is nothing on which it is so hard as poverty; and there is nothing it professes to condemn with such severity as the pursuit of wealth!

WOMAN. You fear the world too much. Have I not seen your nobler aspirations fall off one by one, until the master-passion, Gain, engrosses you? Have I not?

SCROOGE. No!

MAN. What then? Even if I have grown so much wiser, what then? Have I changed towards you?

WOMAN. No . . .

MAN. Am I?

WOMAN. Our contract is an old one. It was made when we were both poor and content to be so. You *are* changed. When it was made, you were another man.

MAN. I was not another man: I was a boy.

WOMAN. Your own feeling tells you that you were not what you are. I am. That which promised happiness when we were one in heart is fraught with misery now that we are two . . .

SCROOGE. No!

WOMAN. How often and how keenly I have thought of this, I will not say. It is enough that I *have* thought of it, and can release you . . .

SCROOGE. [*Quietly*] Don't release me, madame . . .

MAN. Have I ever sought release?

WOMAN. In words. No. Never.

MAN. In what then?

WOMAN. In a changed nature; in an altered spirit. In everything that made my love of any worth or value in your sight. If this has never been between us, tell me, would you seek me out and try to win me now? Ah, no!

SCROOGE. Ah, yes!

MAN. You think not?

WOMAN. I would gladly think otherwise if I could, heaven knows! But if you were free today, tomorrow, yesterday, can even I believe that you would choose a dowerless girl[20]—you who in your very confidence with her weigh everything by Gain; or, choosing her, do I not know that your repentance and regret would surely follow? I do; and I release you. With a full heart, for the love of him you once were.

SCROOGE. Please, I . . . I . . .

MAN. Please, I . . . I . . .

WOMAN. Please. You may—the memory of what is past half makes me hope you will—have pain in this. A very, very brief time, and you will dismiss the memory of it, as an unprofitable dream, from which it happened well that you awoke. May you be happy in the life that you have chosen for yourself . . .

SCROOGE. No!

WOMAN. Yourself . . . alone . . .

SCROOGE. No!

WOMAN. Goodbye, Ebenezer . . .

SCROOGE. Don't let her go!

MAN. Goodbye.

SCROOGE. No!

[*She exits.* SCROOGE *goes to younger man: himself.*]

You fool! Mindless loon! You fool!

MAN. [*To exited woman*] Fool. Mindless loon. Fool . . .

SCROOGE. Don't say that! Spirit, remove me from this place.

PAST. I have told you these were shadows of the things that have been. They are what they are. Do not blame me, Mr. Scrooge.

SCROOGE. Remove me! I cannot bear it!

[*The faces of all who appeared in this scene are now projected for a moment around the stage: enormous, flimsy, silent.*]

Leave me! Take me back! Haunt me no longer!

[*There is a sudden flash of light: a flare. The* GHOST OF CHRISTMAS PAST *is gone.* SCROOGE *is, for the moment, alone onstage. His bed is turned down, across the stage. A small candle burns now in* SCROOGE'S *hand. There is a child's cap in his other hand. He slowly crosses the stage to his bed, to sleep.* MARLEY *appears behind* SCROOGE, *who continues his long, elderly cross to bed.* MARLEY *speaks directly to the audience.*]

MARLEY. Scrooge must sleep now. He must surrender to the irresistible drowsiness caused by the recognition of what was. [*Pauses*] The cap he carries is from ten lives past: his boyhood cap . . . donned atop a hopeful hairy head . . . askew, perhaps, or at a rakish angle. Doffed now in honor of regret.[21] Perhaps even too heavy to carry in his present state of weak remorse . . .

[SCROOGE *drops the cap. He lies atop his bed. He sleeps. To audience*]

He sleeps. For him, there's even more trouble ahead. [*Smiles*] For you? The play house tells me there's hot cider, as should be your anticipation for the specter Christmas Present and Future, for I promise you both. [*Smiles again*] So, I pray you hurry back to your seats refreshed and ready for a miser—to turn his coat of gray into a blazen Christmas holly-red.

[*A flash of lightning. A clap of thunder. Bats fly. Ghosty music.* MARLEY *is gone.*]

---

20. a dowerless (dou´ ər ləs) **girl:** A girl without a dowery, the property or wealth a woman brought to her husband at marriage.

21. donned . . . regret: To *don* and *doff* a hat means to put it on and take it off; *askew* means "crooked," and *at a rakish angle* means "having a dashing or jaunty look."

THINKING ABOUT THE SELECTION

Recalling

1. What relationship did Scrooge and Marley have in the past?
2. For what purpose does scrooge's nephew come to see Scrooge?
3. What expression of Scrooge's sums up his attitude toward Christmas? Why?
4. How does Scrooge respond to the Thin Man and the Portly Man's request for money?
5. How does he respond to Cratchit's request for Christmas Day off?
6. What scenes of Scrooge's past life are revealed by the Ghost of Christmas Past?

Interpreting

7. How do the scenes of Scrooge's past reveal a change in him?
8. How does Scrooge react to each of these scenes?

Applying

9. Do you think people who are like Scrooge are ever really happy? Why or why not?

ANALYZING LITERATURE

Understanding Plot and Exposition

The **plot** of a play is the sequence of its incidents and events. The first part of the plot is called the **exposition**. Here the opening situation is established, major characters are introduced, and the central problem of the play is made clear. Also, here earlier events are revealed.

Once the opening situation is established, the plot of the play develops until the climax is reached. The part of the play that builds up to the climax is called the rising action.

1. Describe the situation established in Scene 1 of *A Christmas Carol: Scrooge and Marley.*
2. What earlier events are disclosed here?
3. What problem does Scrooge have?
4. As you were reading Act I, what thoughts or questions did you have about how the story would turn out?

CRITICAL THINKING AND READING

Recognizing Foreshadowing

Foreshadowing is the use of hints or clues to suggest future events. For example, in his speech at the end of Act I, Marley says of Scrooge: "For him, there's even more trouble ahead." When reading or viewing a play, you should be alert to such hints or clues.

1. Early in Scene 5, Scrooge says to the Ghost of Christmas Past, "There was a boy singing a Christmas Carol outside my door last night. I should like to have given him something . . ." How might this statement be a hint of a future development?
2. Find one other example of foreshadowing present in Act I.

UNDERSTANDING LANGUAGE

Understanding Latin Roots

A **root** is the part of a word that contains its basic meaning. Many words in English come from Latin roots. For example, when Marley describes Scrooge as "solitary as an oyster," he is using a word—*solitary*—that comes from the Latin root -*solus*-, meaning "alone." Look up the following words, which contain the same root, in a dictionary. Tell what each means.

1. solely
2. soliloquy
3. solitude
4. soloist

THINKING AND WRITING

Retelling *A Christmas Carol*

Imagine that you are going to entertain a group of young children by telling them the story of *A Christmas Carol,* Act I. Write a summary of the five scenes that you have just read so that if it were read aloud it would be a lively, easy-to-follow story that your young readers would understand and enjoy. Revise your summary to make sure it contains the important events.

GUIDE FOR READING

A Christmas Carol: Scrooge and Marley, Act II

A **character** in a play is portrayed, in part, by what he or she says in the dialogue. If the play is performed onstage, then the acting will greatly affect the portrayal. The actor's facial expressions, gestures, movements, speaking style, and so on, will make the character come alive. To understand a character when you are reading a play, therefore, imagine an actor performing the lines.

The **theme** of a play is its central idea, or insight into life. One way to arrive at the theme of a play is to notice how the main character changes. If you can explain why the main character changes for the better, or for the worse, you probably are very close to understanding the theme.

As you read Act II, notice how Scrooge reacts to the scenes presented by the Ghosts of Christmas Present and Christmas Future. In what way does he change? Why does he change? What does the change suggest about the theme of the play?

Write the heading What Makes People Change? on a piece of paper. Beneath it list six experiences that you think could lead to a big change in a person's life and behavior. Discuss your list with your classmates.

Knowing the following words will help you as you read Act II of *A Christmas Carol: Scrooge and Marley.*

astonish (ə stän′ ish) *v.*: Amaze (p. 283)

compulsion (kəm pul′ shən) *n.*: A driving, irresistible force (p. 285)

severe (sə vir′) *adj.*: Harsh (p. 285)

meager (mē′ gər) *adj.*: Of poor quality, small in amount (p. 286)

threadbare (thred′ ber) *adj.*: Worn, shabby (p. 287)

audible (ô′ də b'l) *adj.*: Loud enough to be heard (p. 291)

gnarled (närld) *adj.*: Knotty and twisted (p. 291)

dispelled (dis peld′) *v.*: Scattered and driven away, made to vanish (p. 297)

ACT II

Scene 1

[*Lights. Choral music is sung. Curtain.* SCROOGE, *in bed, sleeping, in spotlight. We cannot yet see the interior of his room.* MARLEY, *opposite, in spotlight equal to* SCROOGE'S. MARLEY *laughs. He tosses his hand in the air and a flame shoots from it, magically, into the air. There is a thunder clap, and then another; a lightning flash, and then another. Ghostly music plays under. Colors change.* MARLEY'S *spotlight has gone out and now reappears, with* MARLEY *in it, standing next to the bed and the sleeping* SCROOGE. MARLEY *addresses the audience directly.*]

MARLEY. Hear this snoring Scrooge! Sleeping to escape the nightmare that is his waking day. What shall I bring to him now? I'm afraid nothing would astonish old Scrooge now. Not after what he's seen. Not a baby boy, not a rhinoceros, nor anything in between would astonish Ebenezer Scrooge just now. I can think of nothing . . . [*Suddenly*] that's it! Nothing! [*He speaks confidentially.*] I'll have the clock strike one and, when he awakes expecting my second messenger, there will be no one . . . nothing. Then I'll have the bell strike twelve. And then one again . . . and then nothing. Nothing . . . [*Laughs*] nothing will . . . astonish him. I think it will work.

[*The bell tolls one.* SCROOGE *leaps awake.*]

SCROOGE. One! One! This is it: time! [*Looks about the room*] Nothing!

[*The bell tolls midnight.*]

Midnight! How can this be? I'm sleeping backwards.

[*One again*]

Good heavens! One again! I'm sleeping back and forth! [*A pause.* SCROOGE *looks about.*] Nothing! Absolutely nothing!

[*Suddenly, thunder and lightning.* MARLEY *laughs and disappears. The room shakes and glows. There is suddenly springlike music.* SCROOGE *makes a run for the door.*]

MARLEY. Scrooge!

SCROOGE. What?

MARLEY. Stay you put!

SCROOGE. Just checking to see if anyone is in here.

[*Lights and thunder again; more music.* MARLEY *is of a sudden gone. In his place sits the* GHOST OF CHRISTMAS PRESENT—*to be called in the stage directions of the play,* PRESENT—*center of room. Heaped up on the floor, to form a kind of throne, are turkeys, geese, game, poultry, brawn, great joints of meat, suckling pigs, long wreaths of sausages, mince-pies, plum puddings, barrels of oysters, red hot chestnuts, cherry-cheeked apples, juicy oranges, luscious pears, immense twelfth cakes, and seething bowls of punch, that make the chamber dim with their delicious steam. Upon this throne sits* PRESENT, *glorious to see. He bears a torch, shaped as a Horn of Plenty.[1]* SCROOGE *hops out of the door, and then peeks back again into his bedroom.* PRESENT *calls to* SCROOGE.]

PRESENT. Ebenezer Scrooge. Come in, come in! Come in and know me better!

SCROOGE. Hello. How should I call you?

PRESENT. I am the Ghost of Christmas Present. Look upon me.

---

1. Horn of Plenty: A horn overflowing with fruits, flowers, and grain, standing for wealth and abundance.

[PRESENT *is wearing a simple green robe. The walls around the room are now covered in greenery, as well. The room seems to be a perfect grove now: leaves of holly, mistletoe and ivy reflect the stage lights. Suddenly, there is a mighty roar of flame in the fireplace and now the hearth burns with a lavish, warming fire. There is an ancient scabbard girdling the* GHOST's *middle, but without sword. The sheath is gone to rust.*]

You have never seen the like of me before?

SCROOGE. Never.

PRESENT. You have never walked forth with younger members of my family; my elder brothers born on Christmases past.

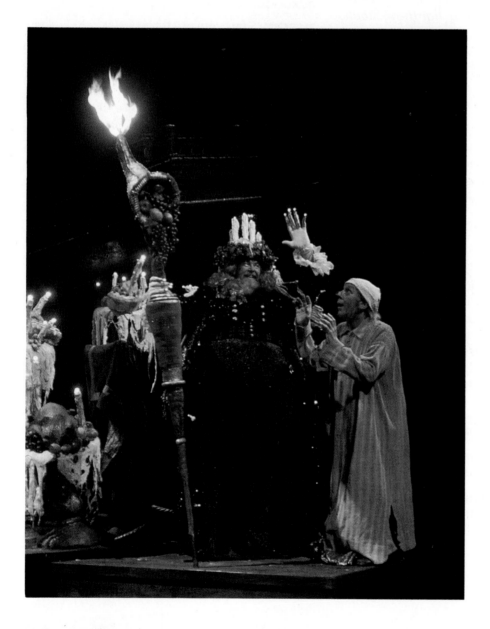

SCROOGE. I don't think I have. I'm afraid I've not. Have you had many brothers, Spirit?

PRESENT. More than eighteen hundred.

SCROOGE. A tremendous family to provide for! [PRESENT *stands*] Spirit, conduct me where you will. I went forth last night on compulsion, and learnt a lesson which is working now. Tonight, if you have aught to teach me, let me profit by it.

PRESENT. Touch my robe.

[SCROOGE *walks cautiously to* PRESENT *and touches his robe. When he does, lightning flashes, thunder claps, music plays. Blackout*]

Scene 2

[*PROLOGUE:* MARLEY *stands spotlit, L. He speaks directly to the audience.*]

MARLEY. My ghostly friend now leads my living partner through the city's streets.

[*Lights up on* SCROOGE *and* PRESENT]

See them there and hear the music people make when the weather is severe, as it is now.

[*Winter music. Choral group behind scrim, sings. When the song is done and the stage is re-set, the lights will fade up on a row of shops, behind the singers. The choral group will hum the song they have just completed now and mill about the streets,[2] carrying their dinners to the bakers' shops and restaurants. They will, perhaps, sing about being poor at Christmastime, whatever.*]

PRESENT. These revelers, Mr. Scrooge, carry their own dinners to their jobs, where they will work to bake the meals the rich men and women of this city will eat as their Christmas dinners. Generous people these . . . to care for the others, so . . .

[PRESENT *walks among the choral group and a sparkling incense[3] falls from his torch on to their baskets, as he pulls the covers off of the baskets. Some of the choral group become angry with each other.*]

MAN #1. Hey, you, watch where you're going.

MAN #2. Watch it yourself, mate!

[PRESENT *sprinkles them directly, they change.*]

MAN #1. I pray go in ahead of me. It's Christmas. You be first!

MAN #2. No, no, I must insist that YOU be first!

MAN #1. All right, I shall be, and gratefully so.

MAN #2. The pleasure is equally mine, for being able to watch you pass, smiling.

MAN #1. I would find it a shame to quarrel on Christmas Day . . .

MAN #2. As would I.

MAN #1. Merry Christmas then, friend!

MAN #2. And a Merry Christmas straight back to you!

[*Church bells toll. The choral group enter the buildings; the shops and restaurants; they exit the stage, shutting their doors closed behind them. All sound stops.* SCROOGE *and* PRESENT *are alone again.*]

SCROOGE. What is it you sprinkle from your torch?

PRESENT. Kindness.

---

2. mill about the streets: Walk around aimlessly.

3. incense (in′ sens) *n*.: Any of various substances that produce a pleasant odor when burned.

SCROOGE. Do you sprinkle your kindness on any particular people or on all people?

PRESENT. To any person kindly given. And to the very poor most of all.

SCROOGE. Why to the very poor most?

PRESENT. Because the very poor need it most. Touch my heart . . . here, Mr. Scrooge. We have another journey.

[SCROOGE *touches the* GHOST's *heart and music plays, lights change color, lightning flashes, thunder claps. A choral group appears on the street, singing Christmas carols.*]

Scene 3

[MARLEY *stands spotlit in front of a scrim on which is painted the exterior of* CRATCHIT's *four-roomed house. There is a flash and a clap and* MARLEY *is gone. The lights shift color again, the scrim flies away, and we are in the interior of the* CRATCHIT *family home.* SCROOGE *is there, with the* SPIRIT (PRESENT), *watching* MRS. CRATCHIT *set the table, with the help of* BELINDA CRATCHIT *and* PETER CRATCHIT, *a baby, pokes a fork into the mashed potatoes on his highchair's tray. He also chews on his shirt collar.*]

SCROOGE. What is this place, Spirit?

PRESENT. This is the home of your employee, Mr. Scrooge. Don't you know it?

SCROOGE. Do you mean Cratchit, Spirit? Do you mean this is Cratchit's home?

PRESENT. None other.

SCROOGE. These children are his?

PRESENT. There are more to come presently.

SCROOGE. On his meager earnings! What foolishness!

PRESENT. Foolishness, is it?

SCROOGE. Wouldn't you say so? Fifteen shillings[4] a week's what he gets!

PRESENT. I would say that he gets the pleasure of his family, fifteen times a week times the number of hours a day! Wait, Mr. Scrooge. Wait, listen and watch. You might actually learn something . . .

MRS. CRATCHIT. What has ever got your precious father then? And your brother, Tiny Tim? And Martha warn't as late last Christmas by half an hour!

[MARTHA *opens the door, speaking to her mother as she does.*]

MARTHA. Here's Martha, now, Mother! [*She laughs. The* CRATCHIT CHILDREN *squeal with delight.*]

BELINDA. It's Martha, Mother! Here's Martha!

PETER. Marthmama, Marthmama! Hullo!

BELINDA. Hurrah! Martha! Martha! There's such an enormous goose for us, Martha!

MRS. CRATCHIT. Why, bless your heart alive, my dear, how late you are!

MARTHA. We'd a great deal of work to finish up last night, and had to clear away this morning, Mother.

MRS. CRATCHIT. Well, never mind so long as you are come. Sit ye down before the fire, my dear, and have a warm, Lord bless ye!

BELINDA. No, no! There's Father coming. Hide, Martha, hide!

[MARTHA *giggles and hides herself.*]

MARTHA. Where? Here?

PETER. *Hide, hide!*

BELINDA. Not there! *THERE!*

---

4. fifteen shillings: A small amount of money for a week's work.

[MARTHA *is hidden.* BOB CRATCHIT *enters, carrying* TINY TIM *atop his shoulder. He wears a threadbare and fringeless comforter hanging down in front of him.* TINY TIM *carries small crutches and his small legs are bound in an iron frame brace.*]

BOB and **TINY TIM.** Merry Christmas.

BOB. Merry Christmas my love, Merry Christmas Peter, Merry Christmas Belinda. Why, where is Martha?

MRS. CRATCHIT. Not coming.

BOB. Not coming? Not coming upon Christmas Day?

MARTHA. [*Pokes head out*] Ohhh, poor Father. Don't be disappointed.

BOB. What's this?

MARTHA. 'Tis I!

BOB. Martha! [*They embrace.*]

TINY TIM. Martha! Martha!

MARTHA. Tiny Tim!

[TINY TIM *is placed in* MARTHA'S *arms.* BELINDA *and* PETER *rush him offstage.*]

BELINDA. Come, brother! You must come hear the pudding singing in the copper.

TINY TIM. The pudding? What flavor have we?

PETER. Plum! Plum!

TINY TIM! Oh, Mother! I love plum!

[*The children exit the stage, giggling.*]

MRS. CRATCHIT. And how did little Tim behave?

BOB. As good as gold, and even better. Somehow he gets thoughtful sitting by himself so much, and thinks the strangest things you ever heard. He told me, coming home, that he hoped people saw him in the church, be-cause he was a cripple, and it might be pleasant to them to remember upon Christmas Day, who made lame beggars walk and blind men see. [*Pauses*] He has the oddest ideas sometimes, but he seems all the while to be growing stronger and more hearty . . . one would never know. [*Hears* TIM'S *crutch on floor outside door*]

PETER. The goose has arrived to be eaten!

BELINDA. Oh, mama, mama, it's beautiful.

MARTHA. It's a perfect goose, Mother!

TINY TIM. To this Christmas goose, Mother and Father I say . . . [*Yells*] Hurrah! Hurrah!

OTHER CHILDREN. [*Copying* TIM] Hurrah! Hurrah!

[*The family sits round the table.* BOB *and* MRS. CRATCHIT *serve the trimmings, quickly. All sit; all bow heads; all pray.*]

BOB. Thank you, dear Lord, for your many gifts . . . our dear children; our wonderful meal; our love for one another; and the warmth of our small fire— [*Looks up at all*] A merry Christmas to us, my dear. God bless us!

ALL. [*Except* TIM] Merry Christmas! God bless us!

TINY TIM. [*In a short silence*] God bless us every one.

[*All freeze. Spotlight on* PRESENT *and* SCROOGE]

SCROOGE. Spirit, tell me if Tiny Tim will live.

PRESENT. I see a vacant seat . . . in the poor chimney corner, and a crutch without an owner, carefully preserved. If these shadows remain unaltered by the future, the child will die.

SCROOGE. No, no, kind Spirit! Say he will be spared!

PRESENT. If these shadows remain unaltered by the future, none other of my race will find him here. What then? If he be like to die, he had better do it, and decrease the surplus population.

[SCROOGE *bows his head. We hear* BOB's *voice speak* SCROOGE's *name.*]

BOB. Mr. Scrooge . . .

SCROOGE. Huh? What's that? Who calls?

BOB. [*His glass raised in a toast*] I'll give you Mr. Scrooge, the Founder of the Feast!

SCROOGE. Me, Bob? You toast *me*?

PRESENT. Save your breath, Mr. Scrooge. You can't be seen or heard.

MRS. CRATCHIT. The Founder of the Feast, indeed! I wish I had him here, that miser Scrooge. I'd give him a piece of my mind to feast upon, and I hope he'd have a good appetite for it!

BOB. My dear! Christmas Day!

MRS. CRATCHIT. It should be Christmas Day, I am sure, on which one drinks the health of such an odious, stingy, unfeeling man as Mr. Scrooge . . .

SCROOGE. Oh, Spirit, must I? . . .

MRS. CRATCHIT. You know he is, Robert! Nobody knows it better than you do, poor fellow!

BOB. This is Christmas Day, and I should like to drink to the health of the man who employs me and allows me to earn my living and our support and that man is Ebenezer Scrooge . . .

MRS. CRATCHIT. I'll drink to his health for your sake and the day's, but not for his sake . . . a Merry Christmas and a Happy New Year to you, Mr. Scrooge, wherever you may be this day!

SCROOGE. Just here, kind madam . . . out of sight, out of sight . . .

BOB. Thank you, my dear. Thank you.

SCROOGE. Thank *you*, Bob . . . and Mrs. Cratchit, too. No one else is toasting me, . . . not now . . . not ever. Of that I am sure . . .

BOB. Children . . .

ALL. Merry Christmas to Mr. Scrooge.

BOB. I'll pay you sixpence, Tim, for my favorite song.

TINY TIM. Oh, Father, I'd so love to sing it, but not for pay. This Christmas goose—this feast—you and Mother, my brother and sisters close with me: that's my pay—

BOB. Martha, will you play the notes on the lute,[5] for Tiny Tim's song.

BELINDA. May I sing, too, Father?

BOB. We'll all sing.

[*They sing a song about a tiny child lost in the snow—probably from Wordsworth's poem.* TIM *sings the lead vocal; all chime in for the chorus. Their song fades under, as* THE GHOST OF CHRISTMAS PRESENT *speaks.*]

---

5. lute (lo͞ot) *n.*: An old-fashioned stringed instrument like a guitar.

PRESENT. Mark my words, Ebenezer Scrooge. I do not present the Cratchits to you because they are a handsome, or brilliant family. They are not handsome. They are not brilliant. They are not well-dressed, or tasteful to the times. Their shoes are not even waterproofed by virtue of money or cleverness spent. So when the pavement is wet, so are the insides of their shoes and the tops of their toes. These are the Cratchits, Mr. Scrooge. They are not highly special. They are happy, grateful, pleased with one another, contented with the time and how it passes. They don't sing very well, do they? But, nonetheless, they do sing . . . [*Pauses*] think of that, Scrooge. Fifteen shillings a week and they do sing . . . hear their song until its end.

SCROOGE. I am listening.

[*The chorus sings full volume now, until . . . the song ends here.*]

Spirit, it must be time for us to take our leave. I feel in my heart that it is . . . that I must think on that which I have seen here . . .

PRESENT. Touch my robe again . . .

[SCROOGE *touches* PRESENT's *robe. The lights fade out on the* CRATCHITS, *who sit, frozen, at the table.* SCROOGE *and* PRESENT *in a spotlight now. Thunder, lightning, smoke. They are gone.*]

Scene 4

[MARLEY *appears D.L. in single spotlight. A storm brews. Thunder and lightning.* SCROOGE *and* PRESENT *"fly" past, U. The storm continues, furiously, and, now and again,* SCROOGE *and* PRESENT *will zip past in their travels.* MARLEY *will speak straight out to the audience.*]

MARLEY. The Ghost of Christmas Present, my co-worker in this attempt to turn a miser, flies about now with that very miser, Scrooge, from street to street, and he points out partygoers on their way to Christmas parties. If one were to judge from the numbers of people on their way to friendly gatherings, one might think that no one was left at home to give anyone welcome . . . but that's not the case, is it? Every home is expecting company and . . . [*He laughs.*] Scrooge is amazed.

[SCROOGE *and* PRESENT *zip past again. The lights fade up around them. We are in the* NEPHEW's *home, in the living room,* PRESENT *and* SCROOGE *stand watching the* NEPHEW: FRED *and his wife, fixing the fire.*]

SCROOGE. What is this place? We've moved from the mines!

PRESENT. You do not recognize them?

SCROOGE. It is my nephew! . . . and the one he married . . .

[MARLEY *waves his hand and there is a lightning flash. He disappears.*]

FRED. It strikes me as sooooo funny, to think of what he said `. . . that Christmas was a humbug, as I live! He believed it!

WIFE. More shame for him, Fred!

FRED. Well, he's a comical old fellow, that's the truth.

WIFE. I have no patience with him.

FRED. Oh, I have! I am sorry for him; I couldn't be angry with him if I tried. Who suffers by his ill whims? Himself, always . . .

SCROOGE. It's me they talk of, isn't it, Spirit?

FRED. Here, wife, consider this. Uncle Scrooge takes it into his head to dislike us,

and he won't come and dine with us. What's the consequence?

WIFE. Oh . . . you're sweet to say what I think you're about to say, too, Fred . . .

FRED. What's the consequence? He don't lose much of a dinner by it, I can tell you that!

WIFE. Ooooooo, Fred! Indeed, I think he loses a very good dinner . . . ask my sisters, or your bachelor friend, Topper . . . ask any of them. They'll tell you what old Scrooge, your uncle, missed: a dandy meal!

FRED. Well, that's something of a relief, wife. Glad to hear it! [*He hugs his wife. They laugh. They kiss.*] The truth is, he misses much yet. I mean to give him the same chance every year, whether he likes it or not, for I pity him. Nay, he is my only uncle and I feel for the old miser . . . but, I tell you, wife: I see my dear and perfect mother's face on his own wizened cheeks and brow: brother and sister they were, and I cannot erase that from each view of him I take . . .

WIFE. I understand what you say, Fred, and I am with you in your yearly asking. But he never will accept, you know. He never will.

FRED. Well, true, wife. Uncle may rail at Christmas till he dies. I think I shook him some with my visit yesterday . . . [*Laughing*] I refused to grow angry . . . no matter how nasty he became . . . [*Whoops*] It was HE who grew angry, wife! [*They both laugh now.*]

SCROOGE. What he says is true, Spirit . . .

FRED and **WIFE.** Bah, humbug!

FRED. [*Embracing his wife*] There is much laughter in our marriage, wife. It pleases me. You please me . . .

WIFE. And you please me, Fred. You are a good man . . . [*They embrace.*] Come now. We must have a look at the meal . . . our guests will soon arrive . . . my sisters, Topper . . .

FRED. A toast first . . . [*He hands her a glass.*] A toast to Uncle Scrooge . . . [*Fills their glasses*]

WIFE. A toast to him?

FRED. Uncle Scrooge has given us plenty of merriment. I am sure, and it would be ungrateful not to drink to his health. And I say . . . *Uncle Scrooge!*

WIFE. [*Laughing*] You're a proper loon,[6] Fred . . . and I'm a proper wife to you . . . [*She raises her glass.*] *Uncle Scrooge!* [*They drink. They embrace. They kiss.*]

SCROOGE. Spirit, please, make me visible! Make me audible! I want to talk with my nephew and my niece!

[*Calls out to them. The lights that light the room and* FRED *and wife fade out.* SCROOGE *and* PRESENT *are alone, spotlit.*]

PRESENT. These shadows are gone to you now, Mr. Scrooge. You may return to them later tonight in your dreams. [*Pauses*] My time grows short, Ebenezer Scrooge. Look you on me! Do you see how I've aged?

SCROOGE. Your hair has gone gray! Your skin, wrinkled! Are spirits' lives so short?

PRESENT. My stay upon this globe is very brief. It ends tonight.

SCROOGE. Tonight?

PRESENT. At midnight. The time is drawing near!

---

6. **a proper loon:** A silly person.

[*Clock strikes 11:45.*]

Hear those chimes? In a quarter hour, my life will have been spent! Look, Scrooge, man. Look you here.

[*Two gnarled baby dolls are taken from* PRESENT'S *skirts.*]

SCROOGE. Who are they?

PRESENT. They are Man's children, and they cling to me, appealing from their fathers. The boy is Ignorance; the girl is Want. Beware them both, and all of their degree, but most of all beware this boy, for I see that written on his brow which is doom, unless the writing be erased. [*He stretches out his arm. His voice is now amplified: loudly and oddly.*]

SCROOGE. Have they no refuge or resource?

PRESENT. Are there no prisons? Are there no workhouses? [*Twelve chimes*] Are there no prisons? Are there no workhouses?

[*A* PHANTOM, *hooded, appears in dim light, D., opposite.*]

Are there no prisons? Are there no workhouses?

[PRESENT *begins to deliquesce.* SCROOGE *calls after him.*]

SCROOGE. Spirit, I'm frightened! Don't leave me! Spirit!

PRESENT. Prisons? Workhouses? Prisons? Workhouses . . .

[*He is gone.* SCROOGE *is alone now with the* PHANTOM, *who is, of course, the* GHOST OF CHRISTMAS FUTURE. *The* PHANTOM *is shrouded in black. Only its outstretched hand is visible from under his ghostly garment.*]

SCROOGE. Who are you, Phantom? Oh, yes, I think I know you! You are, are you not, the Spirit of Christmas Yet to Come? [*No reply*] And you are about to show me the shadows of the things that have not yet happened, but will happen in time before us. Is that not so, Spirit?

[*The* PHANTOM *allows* SCROOGE *a look at his face. No other reply wanted here. A nervous giggle here*]

Oh, Ghost of the Future, I fear you more than any Specter I have seen! But, as I know that your purpose is to do me good and as I hope to live to be another man from what I was, I am prepared to bear you company.

[FUTURE *does not reply, but for a stiff arm, hand and finger set, pointing forward.*]

Lead on, then, lead on. The night is waning fast, and it is precious time to me. Lead on, Spirit!

[FUTURE *moves away from* SCROOGE *in the same rhythm and motion employed at its arrival.* SCROOGE *falls into the same pattern, a considerable space apart from the* SPIRIT. *In the space between them,* MARLEY *appears. He looks to* FUTURE *and then to* SCROOGE. *He claps his hands. Thunder and lightning. Three* BUSINESSMEN *appear, spotlighted singularly: One is D.L.; One is D.R.; One is U.C. Thus, six points of the stage should now be spotted in light.* MARLEY *will watch this scene from his position,* C. SCROOGE *and* FUTURE *are R. and L. of C.*]

FIRST BUSINESSMAN. Oh, no, I don't know much about it either way, I only know he's dead.

SECOND BUSINESSMAN. When did he die?

FIRST BUSINESSMAN. Last night, I believe.

SECOND BUSINESSMAN. Why, what was the matter with him? I thought he'd never die, really . . .

FIRST BUSINESSMAN. [*Yawning*] Goodness knows, goodness knows . . .

THIRD BUSINESSMAN. What has he done with his money?

SECOND BUSINESSMAN. I haven't heard. Have you?

FIRST BUSINESSMAN. Left it to his Company, perhaps. Money to money; you know the expression . . .

THIRD BUSINESSMAN. He hasn't left it to *me*. That's all I know . . .

FIRST BUSINESSMAN. [*Laughing*] Nor to me . . . [*Looks at* SECOND BUSINESSMAN] You, then? You got his money???

SECOND BUSINESSMAN. [*Laughing*] Me, me, his money? Nooooo! [*They all laugh.*]

THIRD BUSINESSMAN. It's likely to be a cheap funeral, for upon my life, I don't know of a living soul who'd care to venture to it. Suppose we make up a party and volunteer?

SECOND BUSINESSMAN. I don't mind going if a lunch is provided, but I must be fed, if I make one.

FIRST BUSINESSMAN. Well, I am the most disinterested among you, for I never wear black gloves, and I never eat lunch. But I'll offer to go, if anybody else will. When I come to think of it, I'm not all sure that I wasn't his most particular friend; for we used to stop and speak whenever we met. Well, then . . . bye, bye!

SECOND BUSINESSMAN. Bye, bye . . .

THIRD BUSINESSMAN. Bye, bye . . .

[*They glide offstage in three separate directions. Their lights follow them.*]

SCROOGE. Spirit, why did you show me this? Why do you show me businessmen from my streets as they take the death of Jacob Marley. That is a thing past. You are *future*!

[JACOB MARLEY *laughs a long, deep laugh. There is a thunder clap and lightning flash, and he is gone.* SCROOGE *faces* FUTURE, *alone on stage now.* FUTURE *wordlessly stretches out his arm-hand-and-finger-set, pointing into the distance, U. There, above them, Scoundrels "fly" by, half-dressed and slovenly. When this scene has passed, a woman enters the playing area. She is almost at once followed by a second woman; and then a man in faded black; and then, suddenly, an old man, who smokes a pipe. The old man scares the other three. They laugh, anxious.*]

FIRST WOMAN. Look here, old Joe, here's a chance! If we haven't all three met here without meaning it!

OLD JOE. You couldn't have met in a better place. Come into the parlor. You were made free of it long ago, you know; and the other two an't strangers [*He stands; shuts a door. Shrieking*] We're all suitable to our calling. We're well matched. Come into the parlor. Come into the parlor . . .

[*They follow him D.* SCROOGE *and* FUTURE *are now in their midst, watching; silent. A truck comes in on which is set a small wall with fireplace and a screen of rags, etc. All props for the scene.*]

Let me just rake this fire over a bit . . .

[*He does. He trims his lamp with the stem of his pipe. The* FIRST WOMAN *throws a large bundle on to the floor. She sits beside it, crosslegged; defiantly.*]

FIRST WOMAN. What odds then? What odds, Mrs. Dilber? Every person has a right to take care of themselves. HE always did!

MRS. DILBER. That's true indeed! No man more so!

FIRST WOMAN. Why, then, don't stand staring as if you was afraid, woman! Who's the wiser? We're not going to pick holes in each other's coats, I suppose?

MRS. DILBER. No, indeed! We should hope not!

FIRST WOMAN. Very well, then! That's enough. Who's the worse for the loss of a few things like these? Not a dead man, I suppose?

MRS. DILBER. [*Laughing*] No, indeed!

FIRST WOMAN. If he wanted to keep 'em after he was dead, the wicked old screw, why wasn't he natural in his lifetime? If he had been, he'd have had somebody to look after him when he was struck with Death, instead of lying gasping out his last there, alone by himself.

MRS. DILBER. It's the truest word that was ever spoke. It's a judgment on him.

FIRST WOMAN. I wish it were a heavier one, and it should have been, you may depend on it, if I could have laid my hands on anything else. Open that bundle, old Joe, and let me know the value of it. Speak out plain. I'm not afraid to be the first, nor afraid for them to see it. We knew pretty well that we were helping ourselves, before we met here, I believe. It's no sin. Open the bundle, Joe.

FIRST MAN. No, no, my dear! I won't think of letting you being the first to show what you've . . . earned . . . earned from this. I throw in mine. [*He takes a bundle from his shoulder, turns it upside down, and emp-*

ties its contents out on to the floor.] It's not very extensive, see . . . seals . . . a pencil case . . . sleeve buttons . . .

MRS. DILBER. Nice sleeve buttons, though . . .

FIRST MAN. Not bad, not bad . . . a brooch there . . .

OLD JOE. Not really valuable, I'm afraid . . .

FIRST MAN. How much, old Joe?

OLD JOE. [*Writing on the wall with chalk*] A pitiful lot, really. Ten and six and not a sixpence more!

FIRST MAN. You're not serious!

OLD JOE. That's your account and I wouldn't give another sixpence if I was to be boiled for not doing it. Who's next?

MRS. DILBER. Me! [*Dumps out contents of her bundle*] Sheets, towels, silver spoons, silver sugar-tongs . . . some boots . . .

OLD JOE. [*Writing on wall*] I always give too much to the ladies. It's a weakness of mine and that's the way I ruin myself. Here's your total comin' up . . . two pounds-ten . . . if you asked me for another penny, and made it an open question, I'd repent of being so liberal and knock off half-a-crown.

FIRST WOMAN. And now do MY bundle, Joe.

OLD JOE. [*Kneeling to open knots on her bundle*] So many knots, madam . . . [*He drags out large curtains; dark*] What do you call this? Bed curtains!

FIRST WOMAN. [*Laughing*] Ah, yes, bed curtains!

OLD JOE. You don't mean to say you took 'em down, rings and all, with him lying there?

FIRST WOMAN. Yes, I did, why not?

OLD JOE. You were born to make your fortune and you'll certainly do it.

FIRST WOMAN. I certainly shan't hold my hand, when I can get anything in it by reaching it out, for the sake of such a man as he was, I promise you, Joe. Don't drop that lamp oil on those blankets, now!

OLD JOE. His blankets?

FIRST WOMAN. Whose else's do you think? He isn't likely to catch cold without 'em, I daresay.

OLD JOE. I hope that he didn't die of anything catching? Eh?

FIRST WOMAN. Don't you be afraid of that. I ain't so fond of his company that I'd loiter about him for such things if he did. Ah! You may look through that shirt till your eyes ache, but you won't find a hole in it, nor a threadbare place. It's the best he had, and a fine one, too. They'd have wasted it, if it hadn't been for me.

OLD JOE. What do you mean "They'd have wasted it?"

FIRST WOMAN. Putting it on him to be buried in, to be sure. Somebody was fool enough to do it, but I took it off again . . . [*She laughs, as do they all, nervously.*] If calico[7] an't good enough for such a purpose, it isn't good enough then for anything. It's quite as becoming to the body. He can't look uglier than he did in that one!

SCROOGE. [*A low-pitched moan emits from his mouth; from the bones.*] [OOOOOOOoo oooOOOOOooooooOOOOOOOooooooOOOOO OooooooOO!

OLD JOE. One pound six for the lot. [*He produces a small flannel bag filled with*

---

7. **calico** (kal′ ə kō) *n.*: A coarse and cheap cloth.

money. *He divvies it out. He continues to pass around the money as he speaks. All are laughing.*] That's the end of it, you see! He frightened every one away from him while he was alive, to profit us when he was dead! Hah ha ha!

ALL. HAHAHAHAhahahahahahah!

SCROOGE. OOOoooOOOoooOOOoooOOOooo OOoooOOoooOOOooo! [*He screams at them.*] Obscene demons! Why not market the corpse itself, as sell its trimming??? [*Suddenly*] Oh, Spirit, I see it, I see it! This unhappy man—this stripped-bare corpse . . . could very well be my own. My life holds parallel! My life ends that way now!

[SCROOGE *backs into something in the dark behind his spotlight.* SCROOGE *looks at* FUTURE, *who points to the corpse.* SCROOGE *pulls back the blanket. The corpse is, of course,* SCROOGE, *who screams. He falls aside the bed; weeping.*]

Spirit, this is a fearful place. In leaving it, I shall not leave its lesson, trust me. Let us go!

[FUTURE *points to the corpse.*]

Spirit, let me see some tenderness connected with a death, or that dark chamber, which we just left now, Spirit, will be forever present to me.

[FUTURE *spreads his robes again. Thunder and lightning. Lights up, U., in the Cratchit home setting.* MRS. CRATCHIT *and her daughters, sewing*]

TINY TIM'S VOICE. [*Off*] And He took a child and set him in the midst of them.

SCROOGE. [*Looking about the room; to* FUTURE] Huh? Who spoke? Who said that?

MRS. CRATCHIT. [*Puts down her sewing*] The color hurts my eyes. [*Rubs her eyes*] That's

better. My eyes grow weak sewing by candlelight. I shouldn't want to show your father weak eyes when he comes home . . . not for the world! It must be near his time . . .

PETER. [*In corner, reading. Looks up from book*] Past it, rather. But I think he's been walking a bit slower than usual these last few evenings, Mother.

MRS. CRATCHIT. I have known him walk with . . . [*Pauses*] I have know him walk with Tiny Tim upon his shoulder and very fast indeed.

PETER. So have I, Mother! Often!

DAUGHTER. So have I.

MRS. CRATCHIT. But he was very light to carry and his father loved him so, that it was not trouble—no trouble.

[BOB, *at door*]

And there is your father at the door.

[BOB CRATCHIT *enters. He wears a comforter. He is cold, forlorn.*]

PETER. Father!

BOB. Hello, wife, children . . .

[*The daughter weeps; turns away from* CRATCHIT.]

Children! How good to see you all! And you, wife. And look at this sewing! I've no doubt, with all your industry, we'll have a quilt to set down upon our knees in church on Sunday!

MRS. CRATCHIT. You made the arrangements today, then, Robert, for the . . . service . . . to be on Sunday.

BOB. The funeral. Oh, well, yes, yes, I did. I wish you could have gone. It would have done you good to see how green a place it is. But you'll see it often, I promised him that I would walk there on Sunday, after the service. [*Suddenly*] My little, little child! My little child!

ALL CHILDREN. [*Hugging him*] Oh, Father . . .

BOB. [*He stands*] Forgive me. I saw Mr. Scrooge's nephew, who you know I'd just met once before, and he was so wonderful to me, wife . . . he is the most pleasant-spoken gentleman I've ever met . . . he said "I am heartily sorry for it and heartily sorry for your good wife. If I can be of service to you in any way, here's where I live." And he gave me this card.

PETER. Let me see it!

BOB. And he looked me straight in the eye, wife, and said, meaningfully, "I pray you'll come to me, Mr. Cratchit, if you need some help. I pray you do." Now it wasn't for the sake of anything that he might be able to do for us, so much as for his kind way. It seemed as if he had known our Tiny Tim and felt with us.

MRS. CRATCHIT. I'm sure that he's a good soul.

BOB. You would be surer of it, my dear, if you saw and spoke to him. I shouldn't be at all surprised, if he got Peter a situation.

MRS. CRATCHIT. Only hear that, Peter!

MARTHA. And then, Peter will be keeping company with someone and setting up for himself!

PETER. Get along with you!

BOB. It's just as likely as not, one of these days, though there's plenty of time for that, my dear. But however and whenever we part from one another, I am sure we shall none of us forget poor Tiny Tim—shall we?—or this first parting that was among us?

ALL CHILDREN. Never, Father, never!

BOB. And when we recollect how patient and mild he was, we shall not quarrel easily among ourselves, and forget poor Tiny Tim in doing it.

ALL CHILDREN. No, Father, never!

LITTLE BOB. I am very happy, I am, I am, I am very happy.

[BOB *kisses his little son, as does* MRS. CRATCHIT, *as do the other children. The family is set now in one sculptural embrace. The lighting fades to a gentle pool of light, tight on them.*]

SCROOGE. Specter, something informs me that our parting moment is at hand. I know it, but I know not how I know it.

[FUTURE *points to the other side of the stage. Lights out on Cratchits.* FUTURE *moves slowing, gliding.* SCROOGE *follows.* FUTURE *points opposite.* FUTURE *leads* SCROOGE *to a wall and a tombstone. He points to the stone.*]

Am *I* that man those ghoulish parasites[8] so gloated over? [*Pauses*] Before I draw nearer to that stone to which you point, answer me one question. Are these the shadows of things that will be, or the shadows of things that MAY be, only?

[FUTURE *points to the gravestone.* MARLEY *appears in light well U. He points to grave as well. Gravestone turns front and grows to ten feet high. Words upon it: EBENEZER SCROOGE. Much smoke billows now from the grave. Choral music here.* SCROOGE *stands looking up at gravestone.* FUTURE *does not at all reply in mortals' words, but*

---

8. ghoulish parasites (go͞ol' ish par' ə sits): The man and women who stole and divided Scrooge's goods after he died.

points once more to the gravestone. The stone undulates and glows. Music plays, beckoning SCROOGE. SCROOGE *reeling in terror*]

Oh, no. Spirit! Oh, no, no!

[FUTURE's *finger still pointing*]

Spirit! Hear me! I am not the man I was. I will not be the man I would have been but for this intercourse. Why show me this, if I am past all hope?

[FUTURE *considers* SCROOGE's *logic. His hand wavers.*]

Oh, Good Spirit, I see by your wavering hand that your good nature intercedes for me and pities me. Assure me that I yet may change these shadows that you have shown me by an altered life!

[FUTURE's *hand trembles; pointing has stopped.*]

I will honor Christmas in my heart and try to keep it all the year. I will live in the Past, the Present, and the Future. The Spirits of all Three shall strive within me. I will not shut out the lessons that they teach. Oh, tell me that I may sponge away the writing that is upon this stone!

[SCROOGE *makes a desperate stab at grabbing* FUTURE's *hand. He holds it firm for a moment, but* FUTURE, *stronger than* SCROOGE, *pulls away.* SCROOGE *is on his knees, praying.*]

Spirit, dear Spirit, I am praying before you. Give me a sign that all is possible. Give me a sign that all hope for me is not lost. Oh, Spirit, kind Spirit, I beseech thee: give me a sign . . .

[FUTURE *deliquesces, slowly, gently. The* PHANTOM's *hood and robe drop gracefully to the ground in a small heap. Music in. There is nothing in them. They are mortal cloth. The Spirit is elsewhere.* SCROOGE *has his sign.* SCROOGE *is alone. Tableau. The lights fade to black.*]

Scene 5

[*The end of it.* MARLEY, *spotlighted, opposite* SCROOGE, *in his bed, spotlighted.* MARLEY *speaks to audience, directly.*]

MARLEY. [*He smiles at* SCROOGE.] The firm of Scrooge and Marley is doubly blessed; two misers turned; one, alas, in Death, too late; but the other miser turned in Time's penultimate nick.[9] Look you on my friend, Ebenezer Scrooge . . .

SCROOGE. [*Scrambling out of bed; reeling in delight*] I will live in the Past, in the Present, and in the Future! The Spirits of all Three shall strive within me!

MARLEY. [*He points and moves closer to* SCROOGE's *bed.*] Yes, Ebenezer, the bedpost is your own. Believe it! Yes, Ebenezer, the room is your own. Believe it!

SCROOGE. Oh, Jacob Marley! Wherever you are, Jacob, know ye that I praise you for this! I praise you . . . and heaven . . . and Christmastime! [*Kneels facing away from* MARLEY] I say it to ye on my knees, old Jacob, on my knees! [*He touches his bed curtains.*] Not torn down. My bed curtains are not at all torn down! Rings and all, here they are! They are here: I am here: the shadows of things that would have been, may now be dispelled. They will be, Jacob! I know they will be! [*He chooses clothing for the day. He tries different pieces of clothing and settles,*

---

9. in Time's penultimate nick: Just at the last moment.

perhaps, on a dress suit, plus a cape of the bed clothing: something of color.] I am light as a feather, I am happy as an angel, I am as merry as a schoolboy. *[Yells out window and then out to audience]* Merry Christmas to everybody! Merry Christmas to everybody! A Happy New Year to all the world! Hallo here! Whoop! Whoop! Hallo! Hallo! I don't know what day of the month it is! I don't care! I don't know anything! I'm quite a baby! I don't care! I don't care a fig! I'd much rather be a baby than be an old wreck like me or Marley! (Sorry, Jacob, wherever ye be!) Hallo! Hallo there!

[*Church bells chime in Christmas Day. A small boy, named* ADAM, *is seen now D.R., as a light fades up on him.*]

Hey, you boy! What's today? What day of the year is it?

ADAM. Today, sir? Why, it's Christmas Day!

SCROOGE. It's Christmas Day, is it? Whoop! Well, I haven't missed it after all, have I? The Spirits did all they did in one night. They can do anything they like, right? Of course they can! Of course they can!

ADAM. Excuse me, sir?

SCROOGE. Huh? Oh, yes, of course, what's your name, lad?

[SCROOGE *and* ADAM *will play their scene from their own spotlights.*]

ADAM. Adam, sir.

SCROOGE. Adam! What a fine, strong name! Do you know the poulterer's[10] in the next street but one, at the corner?

ADAM. I certainly should hope I know him, sir!

SCROOGE. A remarkable boy! An intelligent boy! Do you know whether the poulterer's have sold the prize turkey that was hanging up there? I don't mean the little prize turkey, Adam, I mean the big one!

ADAM. What, do you mean the one they've got that's as big as me?

SCROOGE. I mean, the turkey the size of Adam: that's the bird!

ADAM. It's hanging there now, sir.

SCROOGE. It is? Go and buy it! No, no, I am absolutely in earnest. Go and buy it and tell 'em to bring it here, so that I may give them

---

10. poulterer's (pōl′ tər ərz) *n.*: A British word for a store that sells chickens, turkeys, and geese.

the directions to where I want it delivered, as a gift. Come back here with the man, Adam, and I'll give you a shilling. Come back here with him in less than five minutes, and I'll give you half-a-crown!

ADAM. Oh, my sir! Don't let my brother in on this.

[ADAM *runs offstage.* MARLEY *smiles.*]

MARLEY. An act of kindness is like the first green grape of summer: one leads to another and another and another. It would take a queer man indeed to not follow an act of kindness with an act of kindness. One simply whets the tongue for more . . . the taste of kindness is too too sweet. Gifts—goods—are lifeless. But the gift of goodness one feels in the giving is full of life. It . . . is . . . a . . . wonder.

[*Pauses; moves closer to* SCROOGE, *who is totally occupied with his dressing and arranging of his room and his day. He is making lists, etc.* MARLEY *reaches out to* SCROOGE.]

ADAM. [*Calling, off*] I'm here! I'm here!

[ADAM *runs on with a man, who carries an enormous turkey.*]

Here I am, sir. Three minutes flat! A world record! I've got the poultryman and he's got the poultry! [*He pants, out of breath.*] I have earned my prize, sir, if I live . . .

[*He holds his heart, playacting.* SCROOGE *goes to him and embraces him.*]

SCROOGE. You are truly a champion, Adam . . .

MAN. Here's the bird you ordered, sir . . .

SCROOGE. *Oh, my, MY!!!* Look at the size of that turkey, will you! He never could have stood upon his legs, that bird! He would have snapped them off in a minute, like sticks of sealingwax! Why you'll never be able to carry that bird to Camden-Town. I'll give you money for a cab . . .

MAN. Camden-Town's where it's goin', sir?

SCROOGE. Oh, I didn't tell you? Yes, I've written the precise address down just here on this . . . [*Hands paper to him*] Bob Cratchit's house. Now he's not to know who sends him this. Do you understand me? Not a word . . . [*Handing out money and chuckling*]

MAN. I understand, sir, not a word.

SCROOGE. Good. There you go then . . . this is for the turkey . . . [*Chuckle*] and this is for the taxi. [*Chuckle*] . . . and this is for your world-record run, Adam . . .

ADAM. But I don't have change for that, sir.

SCROOGE. Then keep it, my lad. It's Christmas!

ADAM. [*He kisses* SCROOGE's *cheek, quickly.*] Thank you, sir. Merry, Merry Christmas! [*He runs off.*]

MAN. And you've given me a bit overmuch here, too, sir . . .

SCROOGE. Of course I have, sir. It's Christmas!

MAN. Oh, well, thanking you, sir. I'll have this bird to Mr. Cratchit and his family in no time, sir. Don't you worry none about that. Merry Christmas to you, sir, and a very happy New Year, too . . .

[*The man exits.* SCROOGE *walks in a large circle about the stage, which is now gently lit. A chorus sings Christmas music far in the distance. Bells chime as well, far in the distance. A gentlewoman enters and passes.* SCROOGE *is on the streets now.*]

SCROOGE. Merry Christmas, madam . . .

WOMAN. Merry Christmas, sir . . .

[*The portly businessman from the first act enters.*]

SCROOGE. Merry Christmas, sir.

PORTLY MAN. Merry Christmas, sir.

SCROOGE. Oh, you! My dear sir! How do you do? I do hope that you succeeded yesterday! It was very kind of you. A Merry Christmas.

PORTLY MAN. Mr. Scrooge?

SCROOGE. Yes, Scrooge is my name though I'm afraid you may not find it very pleasant. Allow me to ask your pardon. And will you have the goodness to— [*He whispers into the man's ear.*]

PORTLY MAN. Lord bless me! My dear Mr. Scrooge, are you *serious!?!*

SCROOGE. If you please. Not a farthing[11] less. A great many back payments are included in it, I assure you. Will you do me that favor?

PORTLY MAN. My dear sir, I don't know what to say to such munifi—

SCROOGE. [*Cutting him off*] Don't say anything, please. Come and see me. Will you?

PORTLY MAN. I will! I will! Oh I will, Mr. Scrooge! It will be my pleasure!

SCROOGE. Thank'ee, I am much obliged to you. I thank you fifty times. Bless you!

[*Portly man passes offstage, perhaps by moving backwards.* SCROOGE *now comes to the room of his* NEPHEW *and* NIECE. *He stops at the door, begins to knock on it, loses his courage, tries again, loses his courage again, tries again, fails again, and then backs off and runs at the door, causing a tremendous bump against it. The* NEPHEW

---

11. farthing (fär' thiŋ) *n.:* A small British coin.

and NIECE *are startled.* SCROOGE, *poking head into room*]

Fred!

NEPHEW. Why, bless my soul! Who's that?

NEPHEW and **NIECE.** [*Together*] How now? Who goes?

SCROOGE. It's I. Your Uncle Scrooge.

NIECE. Dear heart alive!

SCROOGE. I have come to dinner. May I come in, Fred?

NEPHEW. *May you come in???!!!* With such pleasure for me you may, Uncle!!! What a treat!

NIECE. What a treat, Uncle Scrooge! Come in, come in!

[*They embrace a shocked and delighted* SCROOGE. FRED *calls into the other room.*]

NEPHEW. Come in here, everybody, and meet my Uncle Scrooge! He's come for our Christmas party!

[*Music in. Lighting here indicates that day has gone to night and gone to day again. It is early, early morning.* SCROOGE *walks alone from the party, exhausted, to his offices, opposite side of the stage. He opens his offices. The offices are as they were at the start of the play.* SCROOGE *seats himself with his door wide open so that he can see into the tank, as he awaits.* CRATCHIT, *who enters, head down, full of guilt.* CRATCHIT *starts writing almost before he sits.*]

SCROOGE. What do you mean by coming in here at this time of day, a full eighteen minutes late, Mr. Cratchit? Hallo, sir? Do you hear me?

BOB. I am very sorry, sir. I *am* behind my time.

SCROOGE. You are? Yes, I certainly think you are. Step this way, sir, if you please . . .

BOB. It's only but once a year, sir . . . it shall not be repeated. I was making rather merry yesterday and into the night . . .

SCROOGE. Now, I'll tell you what, Cratchit. I am not going to stand this sort of thing any longer. And therefore . . .

[*He stands and pokes his finger into* BOB's *chest.*]

I am . . . about . . . to . . . raise . . . your salary.

BOB. Oh, no, sir, I . . . [*Realizes*] what did you say, sir?

SCROOGE. A Merry Christmas, Bob . . . [*He claps* BOB's *back.*] A merrier Christmas, Bob, my good fellow! than I have given you for many a year. I'll raise your salary and endeavor to assist your struggling family and we will discuss your affairs this very afternoon over a bowl of smoking bishop.[12] Bob! Make up the fires and buy another coal scuttle before you dot another i, Bob. It's too cold in this place! We need warmth and cheer, Bob Cratchit! Do you hear me? DO . . . YOU . . . HEAR . . . ME?

[BOB CRATCHIT *stands, smiles at* SCROOGE. BOB CRATCHIT *faints. Blackout. As the main lights black out, a spotlight appears on* SCROOGE. C. *Another on* MARLEY. *He talks directly to the audience.*]

MARLEY. Scrooge was better than his word. He did it all and infinitely more; and to Tiny Tim, who did NOT die, he was a second father. He became as good a friend, as good a master, as good a man, as the good old city

---

12. smoking bishop: A hot, sweet, orange-flavored drink.

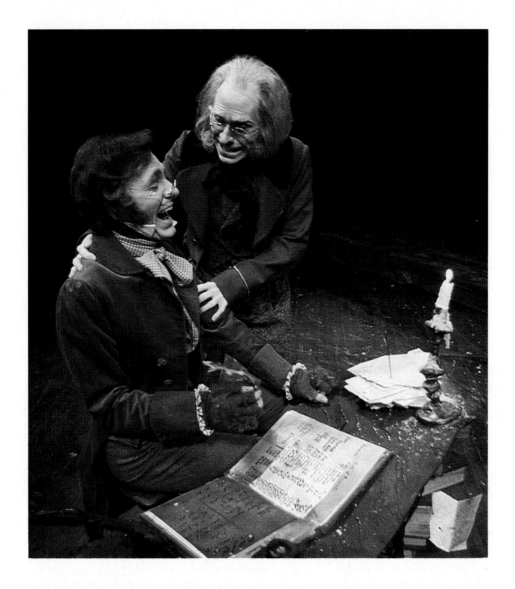

knew, or any other good old city, town, or borough in the good old world. And it was always said of him that he knew how to keep Christmas well, if any man alive possessed the knowledge. [*Pauses*] May that be truly said of us, and all of us. And so, as Tiny Tim observed . . .

TINY TIM. [*Atop* SCROOGE's *shoulder*] God Bless Us, Every One . . .

[*Lights up on chorus, singing final Christmas Song.* SCROOGE *and* MARLEY *and all spirits and other characters of the play join in. When the song is over, the lights fade to black.*]

THINKING ABOUT THE SELECTION

Recalling

1. What fate does the Ghost of Christmas Present foretell for Tiny Tim?
2. What does Scrooge ask of the Ghost of Christmas Present while observing Fred and his wife?
3. What promise does Scrooge make to the Ghost of Christmas Present at the end of Scene 4?
4. What four sights does the Ghost of Christmas Future show Scrooge?
5. How does Scrooge live up to his promise in the final scene?

Interpreting

6. Compare and contrast the attitudes of Cratchit and his wife toward Scrooge when they toast him.
7. What does this difference in attitudes indicate about each of these characters?
8. What does Scrooge mean when he says, "I will live in the Past, the Present, and the Future"?
9. The name Scrooge has come to stand for anyone who is miserly and heartless. Explain why the name as it is usually used would not fit Scrooge as he is at the end of the play.

Applying

10. Charles Dickens lived in the nineteenth century. Do you think the message of his play applies to our world today?

ANALYZING LITERATURE

Connecting Character and Theme

Theme is the central idea or insight about life revealed in a work of literature. Because the character of Scrooge is of central importance to the play, understanding why he changes will help you understand the theme.

1. Find three places in Act II where Scrooge's reactions show him changing for the better.
2. In general, why does Scrooge change for the better over the course of Act II?
3. Using your answer to the preceding question, write a brief statement of the theme.

CRITICAL THINKING AND READING

Supporting an Opinion of a Character

Although an opinion cannot be proven true or false, a sound opinion is one that is supported by facts or details. For instance, to support an opinion that Scrooge is willing to change, you could mention his statement to the Ghost of Christmas Present (early in Act II) "Tonight, if you have aught to teach me, let me profit by it."

1. In Act II, Scene 3, Scrooge observes the Cratchits at home. What does Scrooge say that could support the opinion that he is developing feelings of kindness or compassion?
2. Write a one-sentence description of Scrooge as he is at the end of the play. Support your statement with two details from the final scene.

THINKING AND WRITING

Writing a Review of a Play

A review of a play does two things. First, it gives the reader a clear idea of what the play is about. Second, it tells why the reviewer liked or did not like the play. Write a review of *A Christmas Carol: Scrooge and Marley*. To prepare for the writing, first list those details of the story you will use to give students who will read the play next an idea of what it is about. Then jot down your thoughts on why you liked or did not like the play. When you revise your first draft, make sure that your review would be fair and useful to someone who was considering whether or not to read the play.

Mapping

One good way to understand and remember what you read is to make a semantic map of the material. **Semantic mapping** is an easy method of organizing information in graphic form. It is an excellent study technique that helps you to see how things are related to one another and provides a graphic pattern that is easy to remember.

To make a semantic map, you first have to decide what is the important information in the material you read. What material do you want to organize? You may want to make a map that organizes the story elements such as plot, setting, and characters. You might choose to concentrate on plotting the character traits of one or more characters. After you have chosen your information, you need to determine what are the main ideas and pertinent details. Next decide what type of diagram is best suited to organizing this information. Now create your map. Once your map is constructed, begin filling it in with information you remember from your reading. First fill in all the information you can recall without referring back to the material. Then skim to find information you couldn't recall and to check your facts. After skimming, fill in any blanks.

To help you understand what a semantic map is like, look at the following map that was constructed to show how some of the story elements in *A Christmas Carol: Scrooge and Marley* relate to one another.

Notice that this map is very much like an outline because everything is organized into main ideas or headings and details or subheadings and everything is written as concisely as possible. "Who" refers to characters and includes only the major characters in the play. You could have expanded this map by listing two or three character traits under each character's name. "What" lists the main events in the plot, including those that occurred in the climax and conclusion. "Where" lists only the city in which the action takes place, but you could have included all of the various places Scrooge went.

Guidelines

- Select important information to organize.
- Identify the main ideas and pertinent details.
- Determine appropriate map shape.
- Construct map.
- Fill in map from memory.
- Fill in gaps by skimming material.

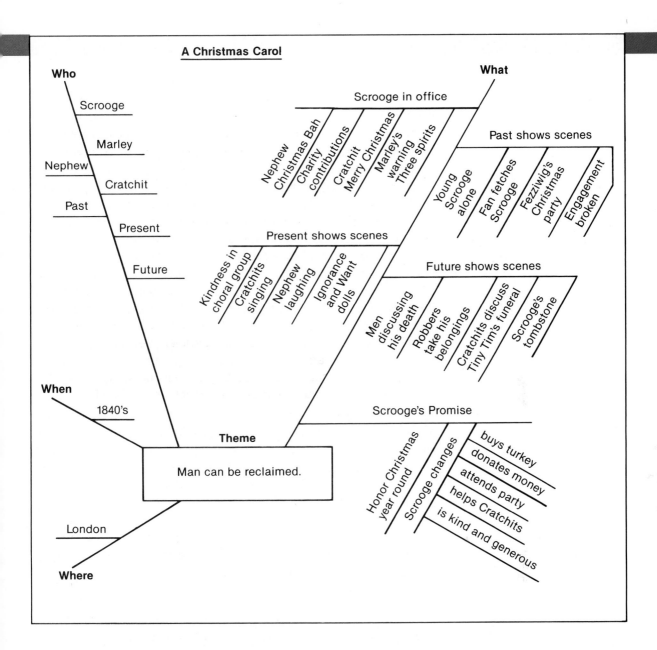

A Christmas Carol

Who
- Scrooge
- Marley
- Nephew
- Cratchit
- Past
- Present
- Future

What
Scrooge in office
- Nephew
- Christmas Bah
- Charity contributions
- Cratchit Merry Christmas
- Marley's warning
- Three spirits

Past shows scenes
- Young Scrooge alone
- Fan fetches Scrooge
- Fezziwig's Christmas party
- Engagement broken

Present shows scenes
- Kindness in choral group
- Cratchits singing
- Nephew laughing
- Ignorance and Want dolls

Future shows scenes
- Men discussing his death
- Robbers take his belongings
- Cratchits discuss Tiny Tim's funeral
- Scrooge's tombstone

Scrooge's Promise
- Honor Christmas year round
- Scrooge changes
  - buys turkey
  - donates money
  - attends party
  - helps Cratchits
  - is kind and generous

When
- 1840's

Theme
Man can be reclaimed.

Where
- London

Activity

Now you are going to create your own map. Brainstorm with your classmates to list the character traits that would apply to Scrooge in all the different periods in his life. Brainstorm some more to decide how you could organize these traits so that your map would show how he changed throughout the play. You will need to group the traits that refer to what he was like in the past in one group, in the present in another, and in the future in a third. Make your map. When you have created and filled in your map, compare it with those of your classmates.

YOU THE WRITER

Assignment

1. Among the most common types of conflict are (1) a conflict between two people, and (2) a conflict a person has within his or her own mind. Write a summary of a play which has both types of conflicts.

Prewriting. Before you write, think of the kinds of things that bring people into conflict. Then imagine a person coming into conflict with another person for one of these reasons. What might this person say and do? What might the other person say and do in response? Think of a surprising way in which he or she might resolve the problem.

Writing. As you write, tell something about the characters involved in the conflict. Show the two people confronting each other. Then show the main character taking action to resolve the problem.

Revising. When you revise, tighten up the plot by focusing on the way one person's actions cause the other person's response, and how this person's response causes the other person's next action.

Assignment

2. Write a brief scene that (1) introduces a conflict between two people, and (2) presents the basic facts about these people and the situation they are in—their relationship, ages, jobs, etc. Write this scene entirely in dialogue and stage directions.

Prewriting. Before you write, make an outline with the following categories: (1) how the conflict begins, (2) how it gets worse, (3) reasons for the conflict, (4) the personalities of the two characters.

Writing. Now write the scene. As you write, focus on the conflict between the two people. Show the characters bringing up the subject about which they have a conflict. Then show them getting more serious about it—perhaps after trying to avoid it for a while. Finally, show them confronting each other directly about it.

Revising. When you revise, check to see that the characters sound as if they're talking to each other.

Assignment

3. Write a composition explaining how you would show each of the following feelings in physical ways: anger, sorrow, grief, joy, weariness. Provide *two* physical expressions for each feeling.

Prewriting. Before you write, think of the ways different parts of the body might show each feeling. How can you show anger with your face? With your hands? With your feet? How can you show joy with your legs? With your fingers? With your entire body?

Writing. In your introductory paragraph, explain what you are about to do. In your body paragraphs, describe the feelings you are discussing one at a time. Then tell how you would express these feelings in physical ways.

Revising. Combine your sentences. Sentences that are combined in the right way have a mature ring to them.

YOU THE CRITIC

Assignment

1. Choose a character from one of the plays who has changed in some way. Write an essay in which you tell (1) what this character was like before the change, (2) what made this character change, and (3) the effect of his or her change.

Prewriting. As you scan the play, ask yourself what this character was like before the change, what made him or her change, and what effect his or her change had.

Writing. Start your essay by identifying the character who changes and the play in which this person appears. Tell what kind of change this person undergoes, what this person was like before the change, what made him or her change, and what effects his or her change had. Sum up what you have said and end with an interesting quotation.

Revising. When you revise, ask yourself these questions: Have I mentioned the names of the characters I wrote about? Have I described in enough detail the situations these characters are in? Have I connected my evidence so there are no logical gaps?

Assignment

2. A play review is an essay that briefly tells what a play is about and then indicates how the author of the review feels about the play. Write a review of one of the plays in this unit.

Prewriting. Before you write, make notes about your reactions to the characters and the plot.

Writing. Start by giving your overall opinion of the play. Then describe the plot and the characters (but don't tell the ending!). Next tell what you liked and disliked about the play. Cite specific characters and events and describe your reactions to them in specific terms. Conclude by telling whether you recommend this play.

Revising. When you revise, be sure your descriptions of the plot and characters and your reactions are as specific as possible.

Assignment

3. Write an essay in which you show that one of the characters learns something he or she didn't know before. Then show that this character's new way of looking at things led to a dramatic turnaround in the plot.

Prewriting. Select a play. Jot down notes about what a character learns.

Writing. Now write your essay. Describe the situation as it was before the character made the discovery. Then describe the discovery and how it came about. Next tell how the discovery led to a reversal in the plot. Finally, summarize.

Revising. When you revise, make sure you have shown both the discovery and the reversal.

RECLINING WOMAN, 1952
John Robinson

NONFICTION

Many people who love reading believe that the most interesting literature being written today is nonfiction. Nonfiction does not deal with imaginary people or events but with real life. The characters are real people and the events are actual happenings. If a work of nonfiction is concerned mainly with ideas or opinions, they are ideas or opinions taken from real life.

The world of nonfiction is a wide one. It includes true stories of people's lives and experiences. It includes thoughtful writings that instruct, persuade, or inform you. It includes diaries, speeches, letters, and magazine articles. Nonfiction is created by men and women who use words well. What they write has clarity, liveliness, interest, and style. When you read the nonfiction in this unit, try to notice these qualities. They contribute much to your reading enjoyment.

READING ACTIVELY

Nonfiction

Some people seem to gain more from their reading of nonfiction than others. Why? Most likely, they gain more because they read with an active mind. To read nonfiction successfully, you must interact with the information the author presents. Ask questions about this information and make predictions about where the information is leading. Pause to answer your questions and to check your predictions. At appropriate points, stop to summarize the information you have received so far.

Use the following strategies to help you read actively.

Question   Ask questions about the information the author presents. What does the author reveal about the topic? Determine whether the author's conclusions seem based on the information given. In addition, question the author's purpose for writing.

Predict   Think about what you already know about the topic. Make predictions about the conclusions you think the author will reach based on this information. As you read, you will find out whether your predictions are accurate.

Clarify   As you read, try to find the answers to your questions and check the accuracy of your predictions. In this way, you will monitor, or guide, your own reading and so gain the fullest understanding of the information presented.

Summarize   Every now and then, pause to summarize, or review, the information the author has presented so far. What important points has the author made? How has the author supported this information?

Pull It Together   Determine the main idea of the entire selection. What did you find out about the topic? How do you feel about the topic?

On the facing page is a model showing how an active reader might read an essay.

from In Search of Our Mothers' Gardens

Alice Walker

My mother made all the clothes we wore, even my brothers' overalls. She made all the towels and sheets we used. She spent the summers canning vegetables and fruits. She spent the winter evenings making quilts enough to cover all our beds.

During the "working" day, she labored beside—not behind—my father in the fields. Her day began before sunup, and did not end until late at night. There was never a moment for her to sit down, undisturbed, to unravel her own private thoughts; never a time free from interruption—by work or the noisy inquiries of her many children. And yet, it is to my mother—and all our mothers who were not famous—that I went in search of the secret of what has fed that muzzled[1] and often mutilated,[2] but vibrant,[3] creative spirit that the black woman has inherited, and that pops out in wild and unlikely places to this day.

But when, you will ask, did my overworked mother have time to know or care about feeding the creative spirit?

The answer is so simple that many of us have spent years discovering it. We have constantly looked high, when we should have looked high—and low.

For example: in the Smithsonian Institution[4] in Washington, D.C., there hangs a quilt unlike any other in the world. In fanciful,[5] inspired, and yet simple and identifiable figures,

---

1. muzzled (muz' 'ld) *adj.*: Prevented from expressing itself.
2. mutilated (myoot' 'l at' id) *adj.*: Damaged or injured.
3. vibrant (vī' brənt) *adj.*: Lively and energetic.
4. Smithsonian Institution: A group of museums with exhibits in the fields of science, art, and history.
5. fanciful (fan' si fəl) *adj.*: Playfully imaginative.

it portrays the story of the Crucifixion.[6] It is considered rare, beyond price. Though it follows no known pattern of quilt-making, and though it is made of bits and pieces of worthless rags, it is obviously the work of a person of powerful imagination and deep spiritual feeling. Below this quilt I saw a note that says it was made by "an anonymous[7] Black woman in Alabama, a hundred years ago."

Clarification: This anecdote explains why they should have looked low. Here an anonymous poor black woman has created a priceless quilt.

If we could locate this "anonymous" black woman from Alabama, she would turn out to be one of our grandmothers—an artist who left her mark in the only materials she could afford, and in the only medium her position in society allowed her to use.

Prediction: Walker will go on to explain how her mother has created works of art.

And so our mothers and grandmothers have, more often than not anonymously, handed on the creative spark, the seed of the flower they themselves never hoped to see: or like a sealed letter they could not plainly read.

And so it is, certainly, with my own mother. Unlike "Ma" Rainey's songs,[8] which retained their creator's name even while blasting forth from Bessie Smith's mouth,[9] no song or poem will bear my mother's name. Yet so many of the stories that I write, that we all write, are my mother's stories. Only recently did I fully realize this: that through years of listening to my mother's stories of her life, I have absorbed not only the stories themselves, but something of the manner in which she spoke, something of the urgency that involves the knowledge that her stories—like her life—must be recorded. It is probably for this reason that so much of what I have written is about characters whose counterparts in real life are so much older than I am.

But the telling of these stories, which came from my mother's lips as naturally as breathing, was not the only way my mother showed herself as an artist. For stories, too, were subject to being distracted, to dying without conclusion. Dinners must be started, and cotton must be gathered before the big rains. The artist that was and is my mother showed itself to me only after many years. This is what I finally noticed:

---

6. the Crucifixion (kroo′ sə fik′ shən): Jesus Christ's suffering and death on the cross.
7. anonymous (ə nän′ ə məs) adj.: With no name known.
8. "Ma" Rainey's songs: Gertrude ("Ma") Rainey, one of America's first blues singers, lived during the early years of this century.
9. Bessie Smith's mouth: Bessie Smith was a well-known blues singer (1898?–1937) who knew and learned from "Ma" Rainey.

Like Mem, a character in *The Third Life of Grange Copeland*,[10] my mother adorned with flowers whatever shabby house we were forced to live in. And not just your typical straggly[11] country stand of zinnias, either. She planted ambitious gardens—and still does—with over fifty different varieties of plants that bloom profusely from early March until late November. Before she left home for the fields, she watered her flowers, chopped up the grass, and laid out new beds. When she returned from the fields she might divide clumps of bulbs, dig a cold pit,[12] uproot and replant roses, or prune branches from her taller bushes or trees—until night came and it was too dark to see.

Question: Is this the garden mentioned in the title?

Whatever she planted grew as if by magic, and her fame as a grower of flowers spread over three counties. Because of her creativity with her flowers, even my memories of poverty are seen through a screen of blooms—sunflowers, petunias, roses, dahlias, forsythia, spirea, delphiniums, verbena . . . and on and on.

Clarification: This is why the garden is important. It screened the reality of poverty.

And I remember people coming to my mother's yard to be given cuttings from her flowers; I hear again the praise showered on her because whatever rocky soil she landed on, she

---

10. *The Third Life of Grange Copeland:* The title of a novel by Alice Walker.
11. straggly (strag′ lē) *adj.*: Spread out in an irregular way.
12. cold pit: A hole in which seedlings are planted at the beginning of the spring.

Summary: Walker's mother has displayed her artistry through the telling of stories and through the creation of her garden.

turned into a garden. A garden so brilliant with colors, so original in its design, so magnificent with life and creativity, that to this day people drive by our house in Georgia—perfect strangers and imperfect strangers—and ask to stand or walk among my mother's art.

I notice that it is only when my mother is working in her flowers that she is radiant, almost to the point of being invisible—except as Creator: hand and eye. She is involved in work her soul must have. Ordering the universe in the image of her personal conception of Beauty.

Clarification: Here is another reason the garden is important. It has taught Walker respect for the possibilities of life.

Her face, as she prepares the Art that is her gift, is a legacy[13] of respect she leaves to me, for all that illuminates and cherishes life. She has handed down respect for the possibilities—and the will to grasp them.

For her, so hindered and intruded upon in so many ways, being an artist has still been a daily part of her life. This ability to hold on, even in very simple ways, is work black women have done for a very long time.

This poem is not enough, but it is something, for the woman who literally covered the holes in our walls with sunflowers:

> *They were women then*
> *My mama's generation*
> *Husky of voice—Stout of*
> *Step*
> *With fists as well as*
> *Hands*
> *How they battered down*
> *Doors*
> *And ironed*
> *Starched white*
> *Shirts*
> *How they led*
> *Armies*
> *Headragged[14] Generals*
> *Across mined[15]*
> *Fields*

---

13. legacy (leg′ ə sē) *n.*: Something handed down by a parent or an ancestor.
14. headragged (hed′ rag′d) *adj.*: With head wrapped around by a rag or kerchief.
15. mined (mīnd) *adj.*: Filled with buried explosives that are set to go off when stepped on.

Booby-trapped[16]
Kitchens
To discover books
Desks
A place for us
How they knew what we
Must know
Without knowing a page
Of it
Themselves.

    Guided by my heritage of a love of beauty and a respect for strength—in search of my mother's garden, I found my own.

    And perhaps in Africa over two hundred years ago, there was just such a mother; perhaps she painted vivid and daring decorations in oranges and yellows and greens on the walls of her hut; perhaps she sang—in a voice like Roberta Flack's[17]—*sweetly* over the compounds of her village; perhaps she wove the most stunning mats or told the most ingenious[18] stories of all the village storytellers. Perhaps she was herself a poet—though only her daughter's name is signed to the poems that we know.

    Perhaps Phillis Wheatley's[19] mother was also an artist.

    Perhaps in more than Phillis Wheatley's biological life is her mother's signature made clear.

Question: What does Walker mean by this statement?

Pulling It Together: In searching for the secret of her mother's creative spirit, Walker has discovered her own wellspring of creativity.

---

16. booby-trapped (bo͞o′ bē trapt) *adj.*: With bombs or mines hidden and set to go off when someone touches or lifts an object.
17. Roberta Flack's: Roberta Flack is a contemporary black singer.
18. ingenious (in jēn′ yəs) *adj.*: Clever and inventive.
19. Phillis Wheatley's: Phillis Wheatley (1753?–1784) was a poet, considered the first important black writer in America.

Alice Walker (1944–   ), who was born in Eatonton, Georgia, is a black writer concerned with social injustice. A poet, novelist, biographer, and essayist, Walker has written widely about the experiences of women and black individuals and families. Her novel *The Color Purple*, which was made into a movie, was awarded a Pulitzer Prize in 1983. A major influence on Walker's life and writing has been her mother. She dedicated her novel *The Third Life of Grange Copeland* "for my mother, who made a way out of no way."

THINKING ABOUT THE SELECTION
Recalling

1. What does Walker set out to discover?
2. In what two ways did Walker's mother reveal herself as an artist?
3. What legacies, or gifts, has Walker's mother given her daughter?

Interpreting

4. What does Walker mean when she writes, "We have constantly looked high, when we should have looked high—and low"?
5. Do you think Walker's poem is a fitting tribute to her mother? Explain your answer.
6. Explain the following statement: "In search of my mother's garden, I found my own."
7. Why does Walker call this selection "In Search of *Our* Mothers' Gardens" instead of "In Search of *My* Mother's Garden"?

Applying

8. In what way are the signatures of our parents and grandparents made clear through us?

ANALYZING LITERATURE
Understanding Essays About People

An essay is a work of nonfiction. One common topic for the essay is a remembered person. Often an essay about a remembered person contains anecdotes, or little stories, that reveal what the person is like. However, such an essay presents not only a vivid portrait of the subject but also explains the subject's importance to the writer. In this way, the essay reveals both the subject and the writer.

1. In what way does Walker present her mother as a unique individual? In what way does she present her as representative of black women in general?
2. How would you describe Walker's attitude toward her mother?

CRITICAL THINKING AND READING
Understanding the Main Idea

The **main idea** is the most important idea the writer presents. In the essay the main idea is often expressed in a thesis statement near the beginning. The rest of the essay contains information that supports or clarifies the main idea.

1. Look again at the first two paragraphs. Which sentence expresses the main idea? Restate the main idea in your own words.
2. How does the anecdote of the quilt hanging in the Smithsonian Institute clarify the main idea?
3. Find one other detail that supports the main idea.
4. Find the sentence near the end of the selection that again expresses the main idea. Restate this sentence in your own words.

UNDERSTANDING LANGUAGE
Appreciating Vivid Adjectives

Essays about people often contain vivid adjectives. For example, in this essay, Walker describes her mother's creative spirit as "muzzled and often mutilated, but vibrant."

1. Why is *muzzled* an appropriate adjective to describe the creative spirit of black women?
2. Why is *mutilated* an appropriate word?
3. Why is *vibrant* appropriate?

THINKING AND WRITING
Writing About a Remembered Person

List people who have been important in your life. Choose the person you think you can describe most fully. Next, list everything you can remember about this person, such as appearance, traits, quirks. Select details you would include in an essay. Write a first draft telling your best friend why this person is significant to you. When you review your essay, make sure you have included enough details to support your main idea. Prepare a final draft and share it with your classmates.

Biographies and
Personal Accounts

SELF PORTRAIT, 1934
Malvin Johnson
National Museum of American Art

Eugenie Clark and the Sleeping Sharks

Margery Facklam (1927–   ) has been fascinated by the animal kingdom since she was a child. She pursued this interest by working as a volunteer at the Buffalo Zoo, in Buffalo, New York, and later she became the zoo's Educational Coordinator. She has also written a number of books about people involved with nature. In this biographical sketch, she tells about a scientist whose lifelong study of sharks has earned her the nickname of the "shark lady."

Biography

A **biography** is an account of a person's life written by someone else. Biographies often focus on the achievements of the people they describe. They also tell you about the difficulties these people had to overcome in order to reach their goals. An author usually chooses as the subject of the biography someone who has achieved something significant. Subjects of biographies may include baseball stars, political leaders, poets, kings and queens, generals, and scientists. "Eugenie Clark and the Sleeping Sharks," for example, is about a scientist with an unusual interest.

Look For

As you read, look for the facts about sharks and their behavior that Dr. Clark has discovered. What aspects of Clark's life make her a good subject for a biography?

Writing

Think about sharks you have seen on film or at an aquarium. Write about the way they looked and behaved and how you reacted to them.

Vocabulary

Knowing the following words will help you as you read "Eugenie Clark and the Sleeping Sharks."

assortment (ə sôrt′ mənt) *n.*: A group or collection of different kinds of things (p. 319)

repellent (ri pel′ ənt) *n.*: Something that pushes away (p. 319)

oozed ($\overline{oo}$zd) *v.*: Flowed or leaked slowly (p. 319)

commotion (kə mō′ shən) *n.*: Noisy reaction; confusion (p. 322)

elusive (i l$\overline{oo}$′ siv) *adj.*: Hard to find (p. 322)

diligently (dil′ ə jənt lē) *adv.*: With hard work; carefully (p. 325)

maneuver (mə n$\overline{oo}$′ vər) *n.*: A planned movement or procedure (p. 326)

Eugenie Clark
and the Sleeping Sharks

Margery Facklam

Sunlight sparkled on bright blue-green water as a small boat dropped anchor. Three divers wearing black wet suits adjusted their scuba gear. One diver leaned over the side of the boat and peered into the water. It was so clear he could see the rainbow assortment of fishes swimming around the coral reef.[1]

"Sharks below," he called.

"No problem," a second diver answered calmly. "Use this," she said, handing cans of shark repellent to the others.

When they had sprayed themselves all over with the repellent, the divers put on their masks and flipped backward out of the boat into the warm water. Two tiger sharks began to circle the divers. Silently they picked up speed to attack, but as they closed in on the swimmers, they slammed on invisible brakes. Suddenly their mouths seemed to be frozen open. They shook their heads as though trying to get rid of something. And the divers went about exploring the coral reef, unconcerned about the sharks.

So far, that scene is only make-believe. There is no shark repellent that really keeps sharks away, but there may be soon because Dr. Eugenie Clark was curious about a little fish called the Moses sole.

In 1960, Eugenie was netting fish in the Red Sea when she came across the fish known scientifically as *Pardachirus;* local fishermen called it the Moses sole. When she touched the fish, a milky substance oozed from the pores along its fins. It was slippery, and her fingers felt tingly and tight, the way they might feel if they fell asleep.

The Moses sole is a flatfish, like the flounder you buy at the market, and it got its name from a traditional story told in Israel. According to the legend, when Moses parted the Red Sea, this little fish was caught in the middle and split in half. Each half became a sole.

Eugenie is an ichthyologist,[2] a scientist who studies fish. She was working at the Marine Laboratory at the Hebrew University in Elat, Israel, when she decided to find out more about the sole's poison. A scientist had reported the poisonous substance in 1871, but no one had studied it further. When Eugenie tested it on sea urchins, starfish, and reef fishes, she found that small doses killed these creatures quickly. She began to wonder how it would work on larger fishes, especially sharks.

Three reef whitetip sharks lived in a tank at the laboratory, and they ate anything

---

1. **coral reef:** A ridge near the surface of the water made of countless skeletons of tiny ocean animals.

2. **ichthyologist** (ik′ thē äl′ ə jist)

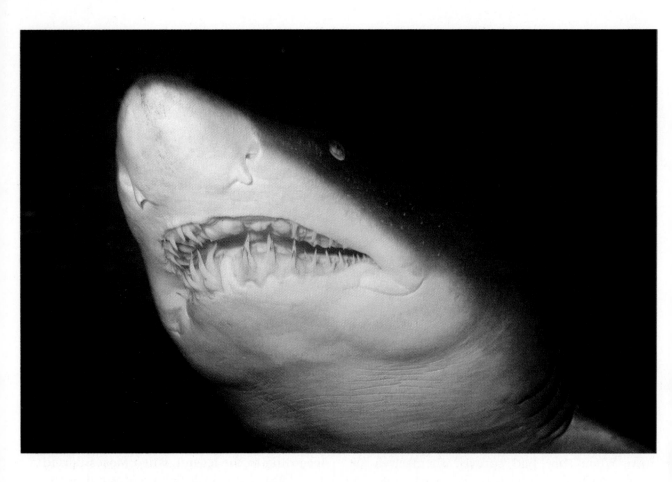

dropped into the water. One day as Eugenie was experimenting with the fish, she found one small Moses sole that had not been completely "milked" of its poison. She put a string through its gills, which did not hurt it, and lowered the fish into the shark's tank. The moment the sole touched the water, the sharks swept toward it with mouths open wide. But when they got within a few feet of the fish on the string, the sharks' jaws seemed to be frozen open. They dashed away, shaking their heads as though trying to get rid of something awful. For six hours Eugenie watched the sharks approach the sole, and the reactions were the same each time the sharks swam near the poisonous fish.

The use of this poison as a shark repellent was an exciting idea. So far everything invented to keep sharks away has not worked on all sharks all the time. Streams of air bubbles used as a barrier along beaches eventually attracted sharks, who seemed to enjoy the feeling of the bubbles as they swam through them. Different dyes that swimmers can release in the water only hide the swimmer from the shark temporarily but cannot keep a really hungry shark away. Lifeboats on ships and Navy planes are sometimes equipped with plastic bags large enough to hold a person. Stranded in the water, the person inflates the top ring and crawls into the tubelike bag. A shark cannot follow the scent of a human inside this bag, nor can it see kicking legs or blood from a wound. But such bags are not carried as regular equipment by swimmers at an ocean beach. A substance that can be sprayed on, the way mosquito repellent is, would be perfect.

But before Eugenie could experiment further on the Moses sole, she had to leave the Elat laboratory, and other work claimed her attention for many years. It wasn't until 1974 that she was able to collect some of the fish and test the shark-stopping poison. After dozens of experiments in tanks and in the sea, a final test was arranged to find out how free-swimming sharks reacted to the live Moses sole.

An eighty-foot shark line, with ten shorter lines dropping from it, was stretched close to the rocky Israeli coastline three feet underwater at a point where a ledge dropped off to a depth of one thousand feet. Each of the ten dropper lines was baited with parrot fish, groupers, nonpoisonous flatfish, and the Moses sole. As Eugenie, her fourteen-year-old son, and other assistants snorkeled[3] quietly along the underwater ledge and watched the sharks approach the bait at dawn or sunset, they saw the poison at work.

One by one the fish were gulped down by hungry sharks, but the Moses sole remained untouched. When Eugenie wiped the skin of a Moses sole with alcohol to remove the poison and tossed the fish into the water, a shark would instantly eat it. It was an excit-ing discovery—a substance that could really stop a shark. Further work is being done now to make a chemical compound like the poison of the Moses sole that can be used as a reliable commercial shark repellent.

Eugenie knew she wanted to be an ichthyologist long before she knew the word meant "someone who studies fish." Her father died when she was very small, and she lived in New York City with her mother. When her mother had to work on Saturdays, Eugenie went to the old aquarium in Battery Park at the tip of Manhattan. The hours went quickly for her as she watched the colorful reef fishes and the graceful sea turtles. It wasn't long before she had her own collection of guppies and swordtail platys, and she became the youngest member of the Queens County Aquarium Society. She learned to keep careful records of her fish and their scientific names.

All during elementary school and high school, her mother encouraged her in her new interest. When she went to Hunter College in New York for a degree in biology, Mrs. Clark, aware of the limited job possibilities for women, suggested that Eugenie add typing and shorthand to her studies. But Eugenie never had the time or interest to do it. When she graduated from Hunter College during World War II, there were not many jobs for biologists, so she worked for a while at the Celanese Corporation as a chemist and attended graduate school at night.

She wrote later on, "In the field of science, a Ph.D. degree is handy to have although not absolutely necessary. One of the most brilliant and accomplished ichthyologists in the country never went to college, although later he became a university professor. But a person without a formal education has a more difficult time proving his worth, especially when applying for a position. A Ph.D. among your qualifications helps start

---

3. snorkeled (snôr' k'ld) v.: Swam underwater using a snorkel, or breathing tube, that extends above the surface of the water.

things out on the right foot. I hoped to get this degree . . . my career had enough other disadvantages for a woman."

In 1947, the U.S. Fish and Wildlife Service was planning a survey of the Philippine Island area for possible fisheries. They needed a person who knew fish and chemistry. Eugenie was qualified. She applied for the job and got it.

"Several people were surprised that a girl had been hired for the job. Then it was called to someone's attention in Washington that I was the only female scientist on the program. Some commotion followed. I got as far as Hawaii, but my passport was mysteriously delayed because, they told me, the FBI had to check my Oriental [Eugenie's mother is Japanese] origin and connections. As far as I know they are still checking. They never did tell me I was cleared. After weeks of waiting, I accepted my fate and handed in my resignation to waiting hands. They hired a man in my place."

Being stranded in Hawaii was no hardship for Eugenie. For an ichthyologist, the freedom to dive among the fascinating fishes around the Hawaiian volcanic reefs[4] was as satisfying as being a cat free to roll in a meadow of catnip. But even that ended. She said later, "The longer you put off graduate studies, the harder it is to find the time and enthusiasm to go back to school." So she went back.

It takes years of study and research to complete a Ph.D. Very often the original research requires going into the field to learn about the subject firsthand.

"Women scientists have to buck some difficulties when it comes to field work," said Eugenie, "but I had one decided advantage. A man in my position often has a family to support and is not free to travel. I was independent and free to go anywhere and do anything I liked, and there was only my own neck to risk."

Eugenie went many places. She learned to dive while studying at Scripps Institute of Oceanography in California. She used her diving skills constantly in Micronesia in the Pacific Ocean, where she collected the *plectognaths* she was studying. These are small fish that live mostly in tropical waters near coral reefs. They include the triggerfish, porcupine fish, puffer, filefish, and boxfish.

One of her research fellowships took her to the Red Sea, where she found the Moses sole and collected the elusive garden eels that burrow in the ocean bottom. They are long, smooth fish that sway gently with the water currents as they feed upon small ocean creatures.

In Cairo, Egypt, Eugenie married a doctor she had met during her studies in the United States. When they returned to the States, Eugenie began the less glamorous part of being a scientist—sorting through notes and writing the scientific results of things she had found. And she began to raise a family.

In 1955, she was delighted to be asked to start a marine laboratory in Florida. Her husband was ready to open a medical office, and he agreed that Florida would be a good place to live. With their first two children, they moved to Florida's west coast, and Eugenie became the director of the Cape Haze Marine Laboratory. At first the laboratory was only a small wooden building, twelve by twenty feet, built on skids[5] so it could be moved if the first site did not work out. There was a dock and a boat for collecting.

---

4. volcanic reefs: Reefs built up on sunken volcanoes.

5. skids (skidz) *n.*: Planks or logs on which a heavy object can be slid.

Eugenie decided her first job should be to collect and identify all the local fishes.

The day after she arrived, she received a phone call from a doctor who needed shark livers for cancer research. She checked with the man who was going to handle the boat, and even before supplies were unpacked, they were in the shark-hunting business.

There are about 250 different sharks in the world, ranging in size from the 24-inch dogfish studied in biology classes to the 60-foot giant whale shark that eats plankton[6] and is so gentle that divers have hung onto its fins for a short ride. In between are the man-eaters we hear horror stories about. All the sharks belong to a group of fishes called cartilaginous. They have skeletons made not of bone but of cartilage, that bendable tissue our ears and noses are made of. And all the sharks are torpedo-shaped predators. They have many sets of razor-sharp teeth that they can fold back into a nonbiting position or thrust forward, ready to slice easily into prey. When a tooth is lost, another moves into place quite quickly.

The shark's always-staring eyes give it an evil appearance. It cannot blink or close its eyes for sleep, but it has a membrane that can cover the eye for protection.

Eugenie and her assistant began collecting some of the eighteen species of sharks found off the west coast of Florida. As she dissected hammerhead, nurse, lemon, and sand sharks on the dock, her children, neighbors, and children of visiting scientists watched. Sometimes she gave them jobs to do—measuring parts of the intestines, washing out a shark stomach, or hosing the dock after the dissection. Some of the sharks brought in on lines survived, and Eugenie wanted to know as much about the live animals as she knew about the organs she was weighing and measuring.

A stockaded pen, forty by seventy feet, was built next to the dock to hold the live sharks. A tiger shark, named Hazel, and a reddish color nurse shark, named Rosy, were two of the first guests in the pen, and a new problem arose. Nosy visitors, ignoring signs and fences, poked around and teased the animals. Eugenie was worried that both people and sharks would be hurt. When several of the sharks were killed by trespassers, Eugenie began to talk to groups in the community, especially at schools. She explained what sharks eat and how they live. Whenever people know about an animal, they fear it less. Soon the newspapers labeled her the "shark lady." It is a name that has stayed with her in spite of all her research with other sea creatures.

It wasn't long before Eugenie was involved in finding out how sharks learn. She enjoyed working with the live sharks day after day and getting to know the individual personalities of the animals.

When she set up experiments in which sharks would have to hit a target to receive the reward of food, one scientist warned her, "Don't be discouraged. It may take months." But he was wrong. The sharks learned quickly. When two lemon sharks learned that they could press an empty target and get food for it, Eugenie thought up harder problems for them to solve.

She trained them to swim to the end of the seventy-foot pen to pick up food after they pressed the target; and the female shark, who usually hung back and waited for the male to go first, quickly learned that if she circled the food drop area, she could pick up the male's reward while he was still at the target.

Eugenie stopped the tests during the winter months when the sharks lost interest

6. plankton (plaŋk' tən) *n.*: Very small animal and plant life that floats or drifts in the water.

in food, but she found that the sharks remembered everything they had learned when spring training began. She moved on to more complicated learning. She used targets of different sizes, shapes, and designs, and she found that sharks of the same species, like other animals, have great individual differences. Some are smarter than others.

Scientists from all over the world visited the Cape Haze laboratory, studying everything from parasites[7] on sharks to microscopic life on algae. By the time Eugenie had been the laboratory's director for ten years, she had four children who enjoyed diving and helping her underwater explorations.

When Eugenie heard that there were "sleeping" sharks a diver could swim right up to, she was determined to find out more about them. With her daughter, Aya, and some research assistants, she went to Mexico's beautiful Isla Mujeres[8] off the tip of the Yucatan Peninsula.[9] There, in the warm, clear underwater caves, she found the great, sleek sharks of the requiem[10] family—the notorious man-eaters. They were lying on the floor of the caves, looking half-asleep even though their open, staring eyes watched the divers swim toward them.

Ordinarily, these sharks must keep moving. They swim constantly in order to keep the oxygen-rich water flowing through their mouths and out over the gills. When they rest on the bottom, they must pump water over the gills, and that takes more energy than leisurely swimming. But in the caves the sharks were motionless. Even with di-

vers churning up water and sand, and even with the glare of photographers' lights, the sharks acted as though they were tranquilized.

Eugenie and her team measured the depth and temperature of the water in the cave. They mapped the water currents by dropping dyes in the water and following their paths. They took water and rock samples for chemical analysis. And they noticed

---

7. parasites (par′ ə sīts) *n.*: Animals that live on other organisms in order to get food, protection, or both. Often, parasites harm the organisms on which they live.
8. Isla Mujeres (ēs′ lä mōō her′ is)
9. Yucatán (yōō′ kä tän′) **Peninsula:** A projection of land, located mostly in southeast Mexico, that separates the Caribbean Sea from the Gulf of Mexico.
10. requiem (rek′ wē əm)

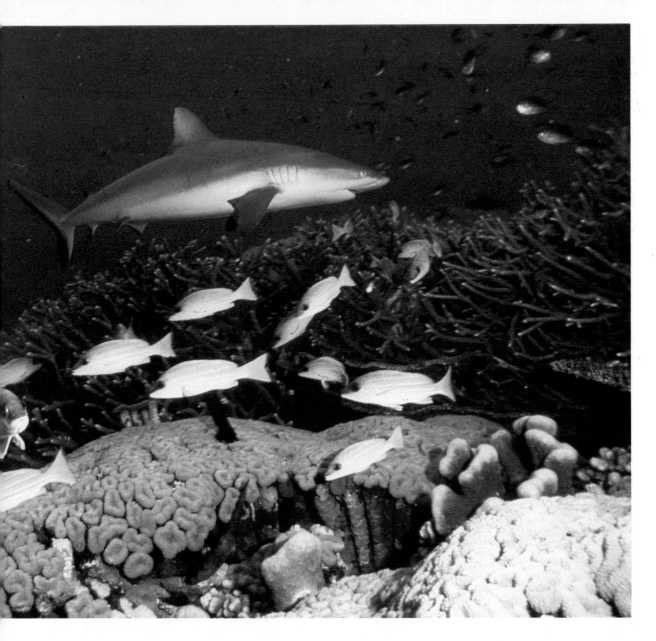

how clean the sharks looked compared to those caught by local fishermen. These cave sharks were not infested with the parasites found on most sharks.

They watched the "shark's faithful housekeeper," the small remora fish, as it worked around the eyes and mouths and into the gill slits of the resting sharks. The remora is a fish whose dorsal fin has evolved into a kind of suction disk on the top of its head. It can hitch a ride on a shark, sea turtle, whale, or even a ship by means of this suction disk. The remora picks up pieces of food dropped by its host. In the caves, however, these remoras worked diligently. Could it be that these "sleeping" sharks gathered in the caves for a health treatment? Were the caves cleaning stations?"

Eugenie discovered fresh water seeping into the caves, diluting the sea water. There was less salt in the caves than in the open ocean. She remembered that when she was a kid she would put her saltwater fish into fresh water for a little while so that the parasites would drop off. Perhaps the same thing was happening with the sharks. Maybe these eighteen-foot tiger and reef sharks were intelligent enough to seek comfort in the caves.

Eugenie had taught sharks to ring a bell and push targets for meals and to distinguish right from wrong targets at the Florida laboratory. "Surely," she said, "they are capable of learning that in water of below-normal salinity, a condition they apparently must sense, annoying parasites loosen their grip."

The sharks may not know the water is less salty, but they know it feels good, so they go there. There are three such caves known around Mexico. Recently, some underwater caves full of sharks were reported around Japan. So many divers swarmed into the caves, catching sharks by the hundreds for food, that by the time Eugenie got to Japan to see them, the sharks had learned it was not safe to go to that cleaning station. Another cave was discovered near Japan, but Eugenie and other scientists are keeping its location secret to protect the sharks.

When asked about her life as a scientist, Eugenie said, "Being a scientist and a woman has some advantages, some disadvantages. It balances out. It takes some time to prove yourself initially, but then you get more credit than a man when you do accomplish something. For example, I am a diver, and when I dive into a cave with sharks it seems to be much more amazing than when a man does it."

The "shark lady" publicity has followed Eugenie, and no matter what she does, people think of her as the spear-carrying shark hunter. But she said, "I get just as excited about the garden eels in the Red Sea. Perhaps the discovery that thrilled me the most was the first hermaphroditic vertebrate,[11] a fish that changes sex."

Looking for an excuse to go swimming one hot July day, Eugenie decided to take a census of the fish around a certain coral reef near the Cape Haze laboratory. She watched a tiny grouper fish, called *Serranus*. There were dozens of females swollen with eggs that would have to be laid and fertilized. But she could not find any males. No matter how long she followed some of these fish or what time of day she watched, no males appeared.

For a year she found no answers. But after many dives and long hours in the lab looking at fish under the microscope and watching live fish in lab tanks, she finally solved the mystery. *Serranus* is an hermaphrodite—an animal with both male and female parts. There are a few vertebrates that start life as one sex and turn into another, functioning as both in a lifetime, but never at the same time. *Serranus* turned out to be the first vertebrate found in which every individual could function at the same time as a male and female, able to fertilize itself. It seems, however, that this self-fertilization is used only in an emergency when a mate is not available. It was an exciting discovery that will probably lead to other investigations.

Eugenie Clark obviously loves what she does. "If from my research mankind gains some practical application or benefit, this is added delight and satisfaction to my work," she said. "But this is not what drives me to study late into the night or to watch a fish on the bottom making some strange maneuver until all the air in my scuba tank is gone and I hold my breath for those last few seconds."

---

11. vertebrate (vər′ tə brāt′): An animal with a backbone.

THINKING ABOUT THE SELECTION

Recalling

1. What two events led Dr. Clark to think that the poison from the Moses sole might be used as a shark repellent?
2. According to this article, what are three devices used to keep sharks away?
3. Describe the experiment Clark set up in 1974 to test the effectiveness of the poison from the Moses sole.
4. Find two ways in which Clark as a child displayed interest in the study of fish.
5. How did Clark's being a woman work against her goal to become a scientist? In what ways did it serve as an advantage?
6. What did Clark discover about the "sleeping" sharks?

Interpreting

7. What qualities of a good scientist does Clark display?
8. What does Clark's response to the killing of her sharks by trespassers reveal about her?

Applying

9. Clark said, "But a person without a formal education has a more difficult time proving his worth, especially when applying for a position." Why do you think this is so?

ANALYZING LITERATURE

Understanding Biography

A **biography** is an account of a person's life written by someone else.

1. Is Eugenie Clark a good subject for a biography? Why or why not?
2. How do you think the author wants you to feel about her subject—Dr. Clark?

CRITICAL THINKING AND READING

Learning About the Scientific Method

The term **scientific method** refers to the systematic way in which scientists try to solve a problem. The basic steps in this method are:

a. Stating the problem to be solved
b. Gathering information about the problem
c. Making a hypothesis, which is a possible explanation that can be tested
d. Performing experiments to test the hypothesis
e. Reaching a conclusion

With these steps in mind, look again at the passage on the "sleeping" sharks.

1. What problem was Dr. Clark trying to solve?
2. Show how she followed the second and third steps of the scientific method.
3. Think of an experiment that would test her hypothesis.

UNDERSTANDING LANGUAGE

Analyzing the Word Part -logy

The word *ichthyology* is made up of two parts: *ichthyo,* which comes from the Greek word for "fish," and *-logy,* which means a science or field of study. You will find the word part *-logy* in many scientific terms.

The following names of sciences all contain the word part *-logy.* Look up each one in a dictionary and use it in a sentence that explains the field of study.

1. seismology   2. geology   3. psychology

THINKING AND WRITING

Writing a Biography

Imagine that you want to make a television documentary about a person's life. You must convince the producers that your choice is a good one. Brainstorm to decide on a subject, and list some of the unusual or exciting events in this person's life. Then write a short biography of this person that will persuade the producers to use your idea. When you revise your biography, make sure you have included information about the difficulties that this person overcame.

No Gumption

Russell Baker (1925–   ) grew up in Virginia and New Jersey. When he was in the seventh grade, he decided to become a writer since "making up stories must surely be almost as much fun as reading them." As it turned out, he became a reporter rather than a fiction writer. He has won awards both for his newspaper column and for *Growing Up*, a book about his life. In this selection from his autobiography, you will learn about his failure in the business world—at a very young age!

Autobiography

An **autobiography** is a person's own account of his or her life. Like biographies, autobiographies often focus on conflicts and struggles. However, an autobiography can reveal more about its subject's thoughts and feelings because the writer and the subject are the same person.

Look For

As you read "No Gumption," try to understand the problems that Baker faced at this time in his childhood. Think about how he makes you see the humorous side of his childhood woes.

Writing

In this section from his autobiography, Russell Baker tells about how he once tried to sell newspapers. Perhaps like Baker you once tried to sell something. If not, imagine yourself in this type of situation— selling lemonade on the corner or raffle tickets door-to-door, for example. Freewrite about the experience, describing the product and telling whether or not you were successful. Try to capture the humorous aspects of the situation.

Vocabulary

Knowing the following words will help you as you read "No Gumption."

gumption (gump′ shən) *n.*: Courage and enterprise (p. 329)

appraisal (ə prā′ z′l) *n.*: Judgment of something's or someone's quality (p. 329)

paupers (pô′ pərz) *n.*: People who are very poor (p. 329)

interrogations (in ter′ ə gā′ shənz) *n.*: Situations where a person is formally questioned (p. 330)

crucial kroo′ shəl) *adj.*: Of great importance (p. 331)

accessible (ak ses′ ə b′l) *adj.*: Easy to get (p. 331)

aptitude (ap′ tə tood′) *n.*: Talent; ability (p. 332)

maxims (mak′ simz) *n.*: Wise sayings (p. 334)

No Gumption

Russell Baker

I began working in journalism when I was eight years old. It was my mother's idea. She wanted me to "make something" of myself and, after a level-headed appraisal of my strengths, decided I had better start young if I was to have any chance of keeping up with the competition.

The flaw in my character which she had already spotted was lack of "gumption." My idea of a perfect afternoon was lying in front of the radio rereading my favorite Big Little Book,[1] *Dick Tracy Meets Stooge Viller.* My mother despised inactivity. Seeing me having a good time in repose, she was powerless to hide her disgust. "You've got no more gumption than a bump on a log," she said. "Get out in the kitchen and help Doris do those dirty dishes."

My sister Doris, though two years younger than I, had enough gumption for a dozen people. She positively enjoyed washing dishes, making beds, and cleaning the house. When she was only seven she could carry a piece of short-weighted cheese back to the A&P, threaten the manager with legal action, and come back triumphantly with the full quarter-pound we'd paid for and a few ounces extra thrown in for forgiveness. Doris could have made something of herself if she hadn't been a girl. Because of this defect, however, the best she could hope for was a career as a nurse or schoolteacher, the only work that capable females were considered up to in those days.

This must have saddened my mother, this twist of fate that had allocated all the gumption to the daughter and left her with a son who was content with Dick Tracy and Stooge Viller. If disappointed, though, she wasted no energy on self-pity. She would make me make something of myself whether I wanted to or not. "The Lord helps those who help themselves," she said. That was the way her mind worked.

She was realistic about the difficulty. Having sized up the material the Lord had given her to mold, she didn't overestimate what she could do with it. She didn't insist that I grow up to be President of the United States.

Fifty years ago parents still asked boys if they wanted to grow up to be President, and asked it not jokingly but seriously. Many parents who were hardly more than paupers still believed their sons could do it. Abraham Lincoln had done it. We were only sixty-five years from Lincoln. Many a grandfather who walked among us could remember Lincoln's

1. Big Little Book: A small, inexpensive, illustrated book that often portrayed the adventures of comic strip heroes like Dick Tracy.

time. Men of grandfatherly age were the worst for asking if you wanted to grow up to be President. A surprising number of little boys said yes and meant it.

I was asked many times myself. No, I would say, I didn't want to grow up to be President. My mother was present during one of these interrogations. An elderly uncle, having posed the usual question and exposed my lack of interest in the Presidency, asked, "Well, what *do* you want to be when you grow up?"

I loved to pick through trash piles and collect empty bottles, tin cans with pretty labels, and discarded magazines. The most de-sirable job on earth sprang instantly to mind. "I want to be a garbage man," I said.

My uncle smiled, but my mother had seen the first distressing evidence of a bump budding on a log. "Have a little gumption, Russell," she said. Her calling me Russell was a signal of unhappiness. When she approved of me I was always "Buddy."

When I turned eight years old she decided that the job of starting me on the road toward making something of myself could no longer be safely delayed. "Buddy," she said one day, "I want you to come home right after school this afternoon. Somebody's coming and I want you to meet him."

When I burst in that afternoon she was in conference in the parlor with an executive of the Curtis Publishing Company. She introduced me. He bent low from the waist and shook my hand. Was it true as my mother had told him, he asked, that I longed for the opportunity to conquer the world of business?

My mother replied that I was blessed with a rare determination to make something of myself.

"That's right," I whispered.

"But have you got the grit, the character, the never-say-quit spirit it takes to succeed in business?"

My mother said I certainly did.

"That's right," I said.

He eyed me silently for a long pause, as though weighing whether I could be trusted to keep his confidence, then spoke man-to-man. Before taking a crucial step, he said, he wanted to advise me that working for the Curtis Publishing Company placed enormous responsibility on a young man. It was one of the great companies of America. Perhaps the greatest publishing house in the world. I had heard, no doubt, of the *Saturday Evening Post*?

Heard of it? My mother said that everyone in our house had heard of the *Saturday Post* and that I, in fact, read it with religious devotion.

Then doubtless, he said, we were also familiar with those two monthly pillars of the magazine world, the *Ladies Home Journal* and the *Country Gentleman.*

Indeed we were familiar with them, said my mother.

Representing the *Saturday Evening Post* was one of the weightiest honors that could be bestowed in the world of business, he said. He was personally proud of being a part of that great corporation.

My mother said he had every right to be.

Again he studied me as though debating whether I was worthy of a knighthood. Finally: "Are you trustworthy?"

My mother said I was the soul of honesty.

"That's right," I said.

The caller smiled for the first time. He told me I was a lucky young man. He admired my spunk. Too many young men thought life was all play. Those young men would not go far in this world. Only a young man willing to work and save and keep his face washed and his hair neatly combed could hope to come out on top in a world such as ours. Did I truly and sincerely believe that I was such a young man?

"He certainly does," said my mother.

"That's right," I said.

He said he had been so impressed by what he had seen of me that he was going to make me a representative of the Curtis Publishing Company. On the following Tuesday, he said, thirty freshly printed copies of the *Saturday Evening Post* would be delivered at our door. I would place these magazines, still damp with the ink of the presses, in a handsome canvas bag, sling it over my shoulder, and set forth through the streets to bring the best in journalism, fiction, and cartoons to the American public.

He had brought the canvas bag with him. He presented it with reverence fit for a chasuble.[2] He showed me how to drape the sling over my left shoulder and across the chest so that the pouch lay easily accessible to my right hand, allowing the best in journalism, fiction, and cartoons to be swiftly extracted and sold to a citizenry whose happiness and security depended upon us soldiers of the free press.

The following Tuesday I raced home from school, put the canvas bag over my

---

2. chasuble (chaz′ yoob′l) *n.:* A sleeveless outer garment worn by priests.

shoulder, dumped the magazines in, and, tilting to the left to balance their weight on my right hip, embarked on the highway of journalism.

We lived in Belleville, New Jersey, a commuter town at the northern fringe of Newark. It was 1932, the bleakest year of the Depression. My father had died two years before, leaving us with a few pieces of Sears, Roebuck furniture and not much else, and my mother had taken Doris and me to live with one of her younger brothers. This was my Uncle Allen. Uncle Allen had made something of himself by 1932. As salesman for a soft-drink bottler in Newark, he had an income of $30 a week; wore pearl-gray spats,[3] detachable collars, and a three-piece suit; was happily married; and took in threadbare relatives.

With my load of magazines I headed toward Belleville Avenue. That's where the people were. There were two filling stations at the intersection with Union Avenue, as well as an A&P, a fruit stand, a bakery, a barber shop, Zuccarelli's drugstore, and a diner shaped like a railroad car. For several hours I made myself highly visible, shifting position now and then from corner to corner, from shop window to shop window, to make sure everyone could see the heavy black lettering on the canvas bag that said *The Saturday Evening Post*. When the angle of the light indicated it was suppertime, I walked back to the house.

"How many did you sell, Buddy?" my mother asked.

"None,"

"Where did you go?"

"The corner of Belleville and Union Avenues."

"What did you do?"

"Stood on the corner waiting for somebody to buy a *Saturday Evening Post*."

"You just stood there?"

"Didn't sell a single one."

"For God's sake, Russell!"

Uncle Allen intervened. "I've been thinking about it for some time," he said, "and I've about decided to take the *Post* regularly. Put me down as a regular customer." I handed him a magazine and he paid me a nickel. It was the first nickel I earned.

Afterwards my mother instructed me in salesmanship. I would have to ring doorbells, address adults with charming self-confidence, and break down resistance with a sales talk pointing out that no one, no matter how poor, could afford to be without the *Saturday Evening Post* in the home.

I told my mother I'd changed my mind about wanting to succeed in the magazine business.

"If you think I'm going to raise a good-for-nothing," she replied, "you've got another think coming." She told me to hit the streets with the canvas bag and start ringing doorbells the instant school was out next day. When I objected that I didn't feel any aptitude for salesmanship, she asked how I'd like to lend her my leather belt so she could whack some sense into me. I bowed to superior will and entered journalism with a heavy heart.

My mother and I had fought this battle almost as long as I could remember. It probably started even before memory began, when I was a country child in northern Virginia and my mother, dissatisfied with my father's plain workman's life, determined that I would not grow up like him and his people, with calluses on their hands, overalls on their backs, and fourth-grade educations in their heads. She had fancier ideas of life's

---

3. spats (spats) *n.*: Pieces of cloth or leather that cover the upper part of the shoe or ankle.

possibilities. Introducing me to the *Saturday Evening Post*, she was trying to wean me as early as possible from my father's world where men left with lunch pails at sunup, worked with their hands until the grime ate into the pores, and died with a few sticks of mail-order furniture as their legacy. In my mother's vision of the better life there were desks and white collars, well-pressed suits, evenings of reading and lively talk, and perhaps—if a man were very, very lucky and hit the jackpot, really made something important of himself—perhaps there might be a fantastic salary of $5,000 a year to support a big house and a Buick with a rumble seat[4] and a vacation in Atlantic City.

And so I set forth with my sack of magazines. I was afraid of the dogs that snarled behind the doors of potential buyers. I was timid about ringing the doorbells of strangers, relieved when no one came to the door, and scared when someone did. Despite my mother's instructions, I could not deliver an engaging sales pitch. When a door opened I simply asked, "Want to buy a *Saturday Evening Post*?" In Belleville few persons did. It was a town of 30,000 people, and most weeks I rang a fair majority of its doorbells. But I rarely sold my thirty copies. Some weeks I canvassed the entire town for six days and still had four or five unsold magazines on Monday evening; then I dreaded the coming of Tuesday morning, when a batch of thirty fresh *Saturday Evening Posts* was due at the front door.

"Better get out there and sell the rest of those magazines tonight," my mother would say.

I usually posted myself then at a busy intersection where a traffic light controlled commuter flow from Newark. When the light turned red I stood on the curb and shouted my sales pitch at the motorists.

"Want to buy a *Saturday Evening Post*?"

One rainy night when car windows were sealed against me I came back soaked and with not a single sale to report. My mother beckoned to Doris.

"Go back down there with Buddy and show him how to sell these magazines," she said.

Brimming with zest, Doris, who was then seven years old, returned with me to the corner. She took a magazine from the bag, and when the light turned red she

---

4. rumble seat: In early automobiles, an open seat in the rear of the car that could be folded shut.

strode to the nearest car and banged her small fist against the closed window. The driver, probably startled at what he took to be a midget assaulting his car, lowered the window to stare, and Doris thrust a *Saturday Evening Post* at him.

"You need this magazine," she piped, "and it only costs a nickel."

Her salesmanship was irresistible. Before the light changed half a dozen times she disposed of the entire batch. I didn't feel humiliated. To the contrary. I was so happy I decided to give her a treat. Leading her to the vegetable store on Belleville Avenue, I bought three apples, which cost a nickel, and gave her one.

"You shouldn't waste money," she said.

"Eat your apple." I bit into mine.

"You shouldn't eat before supper," she said. "It'll spoil your appetite."

Back at the house that evening, she dutifully reported me for wasting a nickel. Instead of a scolding, I was rewarded with a pat on the back for having the good sense to buy fruit instead of candy. My mother reached into her bottomless supply of maxims and told Doris, "An apple a day keeps the doctor away."

By the time I was ten I had learned all my mother's maxims by heart. Asking to stay up past normal bedtime, I knew that a refusal would be explained with, "Early to bed and early to rise, makes a man healthy, wealthy, and wise." If I whimpered about having to get up early in the morning, I could depend on her to say, "The early bird gets the worm."

The one I most despised was, "If at first you don't succeed, try, try again." This was the battle cry with which she constantly sent me back into the hopeless struggle whenever I moaned that I had rung every doorbell in town and knew there wasn't a single potential buyer left in Belleville that week. After listening to my explanation, she handed me the canvas bag and said, "If at first you don't succeed . . ."

Three years in that job, which I would gladly have quit after the first day except for her insistence, produced at least one valuable result. My mother finally concluded that I would never make something of myself by pursuing a life in business and started considering careers that demanded less competitive zeal.

One evening when I was eleven I brought home a short "composition" on my summer vacation which the teacher had graded with an A. Reading it with her own schoolteacher's eye, my mother agreed that it was top-drawer seventh grade prose and complimented me. Nothing more was said about it immediately, but a new idea had taken life in her mind. Halfway through supper she suddenly interrupted the conversation.

"Buddy," she said, "maybe you could be a writer."

I clasped the idea to my heart. I had never met a writer, had shown no previous urge to write, and hadn't a notion how to become a writer, but I loved stories and thought that making up stories must surely be almost as much fun as reading them. Best of all, though, and what really gladdened my heart, was the ease of the writer's life. Writers did not have to trudge through the town peddling from canvas bags, defending themselves against angry dogs, being rejected by surly strangers. Writers did not have to ring doorbells. So far as I could make out, what writers did couldn't even be classified as work.

I was enchanted. Writers didn't have to have any gumption at all. I did not dare tell anybody for fear of being laughed at in the schoolyard, but secretly I decided that what I'd like to be when I grew up was a writer.

THINKING ABOUT THE SELECTION

Recalling

1. According to Russell's mother, what is the flaw in his character?
2. How does she try to repair this flaw when he is eight?
3. How does Russell feel about selling magazines?
4. What does his mother conclude after he has worked at his job for three years?
5. What is his mother's new plan for his career?

Interpreting

6. What qualities prevent him from being a good salesman? How might these same qualities help him in his chosen career?
7. How does Baker show a sense of humor in the way that he writes about this part of his life? Do you think he thought the situation humorous at the time the events were happening to him? Find evidence to support your answer.
8. How does Baker's sense of humor make you feel about him?

Applying

9. How does the description of Doris in the third paragraph show the different expectations people had for boys and for girls? Have these expectations changed since the time that this selection takes place? Support your answer.

ANALYZING LITERATURE

Understanding Autobiography

A person's account of his or her own life is called an **autobiography**. Such accounts include not only the facts of the writers' lives but their thoughts and feelings as well. In "No Gumption," Russell Baker gives you first-hand information about what happened when his mother tried to make him into a successful salesman at the age of eight.

1. What is the main problem that Baker faces during this part of his life?

2. Find a passage where he reveals his thoughts or feelings about this problem.
3. Would his account have been as humorous if he had written it as a boy? Why or why not?
4. Why is it that the passage of time can make events that seemed terrible when they happened now seem humorous?
5. How might the account of these events be different if Doris had written it?

CRITICAL THINKING AND READING

Comparing and Contrasting Characters

Comparing characters means seeing how they are similar. **Contrasting** them means finding how they are different. Although the main character of an autobiography is the writer, other characters will appear also. By comparing and contrasting these characters with the writer, you can gain a better idea of his or her personality.

1. How do Russell's and Doris's attitudes toward household chores differ?
2. Why was Doris better at selling magazines?
3. How does the incident where Russell buys an apple reveal a difference between them?
4. In what ways are both Doris and Russell admirable?

THINKING AND WRITING

Writing an Autobiographical Sketch

You have just started writing to a student your age in another country. Now that you have agreed to exchange letters, you want to tell this student something about your life. Think of a problem you faced when you were in kindergarten or first grade that now seems humorous to you. Before writing about this incident in a letter, list the most interesting and amusing parts of the story. Then turn this list into a humorous autobiographical sketch. When you revise your letter, make sure your description is clear and humorous. Then proofread your letter and prepare a final draft.

GUIDE FOR READING

from Barrio Boy

Ernesto Galarza (1905–1984) was born in the Mexican town of Jalcocotán. When his family resettled in California, they struggled to make ends meet. Ernesto was a good student. He eventually became a gifted teacher and writer. *Barrio Boy,* his most successful book, tells the story of his childhood in California. In this section from *Barrio Boy,* he tells of the frightening experience of attending school for the first time in a new country.

The Narrator in Autobiography

The **narrator** of a work is the person who tells the story. In an autobiography, the narrator is the writer telling you about his or her life. Ernesto Galarza, for example, is the narrator of *Barrio Boy.* Like most writers of autobiography, he refers to himself as "I" and tells you his thoughts and feelings about people and events.

Look For

As you read this section from *Barrio Boy,* put yourself in Ernesto's shoes. See the school, the students, and the teacher as they must have appeared to the young boy from Mexico. This will help you understand more fully his thoughts and feelings.

Writing

Everyone is a stranger at some time in life. Think about a time when you were a stranger. It could be when you moved to a new block, your first day at a new school, or your first day at a new camp, for example. Freewrite about your experiences.

Vocabulary

Knowing the following words will help you as you read this excerpt from *Barrio Boy.*

barrio (bär′ ē ō) *n.*: Part of a town or city where most of the people are Hispanic (p. 337)
menace (men′ is) *n.*: Danger; threat (p. 337)
formidable (fôr′ mə də b′l) *adj.*: Impressive (p. 338)
mobilized (mō′ bə līzd′) *v.*: Put into motion (p. 338)
interpreter (in tur′ prə tər) *n.*: Someone who translates from

one language into another (p. 338)
radiant (rā′ dē ənt) *adj.*: Shining brightly (p. 338)
consultations (kän′ s′l tā′ shənz) *n.*: Discussions (p. 338)
persistently (pər sis′ tənt lē) *adv.*: Constantly (p. 338)
grieving (grēv′ iŋ) *v.*: Feeling sorrow for a loss (p. 339)

from **Barrio Boy**

Ernesto Galarza

My mother and I walked south on Fifth Street one morning to the corner of Q Street and turned right. Half of the block was occupied by the Lincoln School. It was a three-story wooden building, with two wings that gave it the shape of a double-T connected by a central hall. It was a new building, painted yellow, with a shingled roof that was not like the red tile of the school in Mazatlán. I noticed other differences, none of them very reassuring.

We walked up the wide staircase hand in hand and through the door, which closed by itself. A mechanical contraption screwed to the top shut it behind us quietly.

Up to this point the adventure of enrolling me in the school had been carefully rehearsed. Mrs. Dodson had told us how to find it and we had circled it several times on our walks. Friends in the *barrio* explained that the director was called a principal, and that it was a lady and not a man. They assured us that there was always a person at the school who could speak Spanish.

Exactly as we had been told, there was a sign on the door in both Spanish and English: "Principal." We crossed the hall and entered the office of Miss Nettie Hopley.

Miss Hopley was at a roll-top desk to one side, sitting in a swivel chair that moved on wheels. There was a sofa against the opposite wall, flanked by two windows and a door that opened on a small balcony. Chairs were set around a table and framed pictures hung on the walls of a man with long white hair and another with a sad face and a black beard.

The principal half turned in the swivel chair to look at us over the pinch glasses crossed on the ridge of her nose. To do this she had to duck her head slightly as if she were about to step through a low doorway.

What Miss Hopley said to us we did not know but we saw in her eyes a warm welcome and when she took off her glasses and straightened up she smiled wholeheartedly, like Mrs. Dodson. We were, of course, saying nothing, only catching the friendliness of her voice and the sparkle in her eyes while she said words we did not understand. She signaled us to the table. Almost tiptoeing across the office, I maneuvered myself to keep my mother between me and the gringo lady. In a matter of seconds I had to decide whether she was a possible friend or a menace. We sat down.

Then Miss Hopley did a formidable thing. She stood up. Had she been standing when we entered she would have seemed tall. But rising from her chair she soared. And what she carried up and up with her was a buxom superstructure,[1] firm shoulders, a straight sharp nose, full cheeks slightly molded by a curved line along the nostrils, thin lips that moved like steel springs, and a high forehead topped by hair gathered in a bun. Miss Hopley was not a giant in body but when she mobilized it to a standing position she seemed a match for giants. I decided I liked her.

She strode to a door in the far corner of the office, opened it and called a name. A boy of about ten years appeared in the doorway. He sat down at one end of the table. He was brown like us, a plump kid with shiny black hair combed straight back, neat, cool, and faintly obnoxious.

Miss Hopley joined us with a large book and some papers in her hand. She, too, sat down and the questions and answers began by way of our interpreter. My name was Ernesto. My mother's name was Henriqueta. My birth certificate was in San Blas. Here was my last report card from the Escuela Municipal Numero 3 para Varones of Mazatlán,[2] and so forth. Miss Hopley put things down in the book and my mother signed a card.

As long as the questions continued, Doña[3] Henriqueta could stay and I was secure. Now that they were over, Miss Hopley saw her to the door, dismissed our interpreter and without further ado took me by the hand and strode down the hall to Miss Ryan's first grade.

Miss Ryan took me to a seat at the front of the room, into which I shrank—the better to survey her. She was, to skinny, somewhat runty me, of a withering height when she patrolled the class. And when I least expected it, there she was, crouching by my desk, her blond radiant face level with mine, her voice patiently maneuvering me over the awful idiocies of the English language.

During the next few weeks Miss Ryan overcame my fears of tall, energetic teachers as she bent over my desk to help me with a word in the pre-primer. Step by step, she loosened me and my classmates from the safe anchorage of the desks for recitations at the blackboard and consultations at her desk. Frequently she burst into happy announcements to the whole class. "Ito can read a sentence," and small Japanese Ito, squint-eyed and shy, slowly read aloud while the class listened in wonder: "Come, Skipper, come. Come and run." The Korean, Portuguese, Italian, and Polish first graders had similar moments of glory, no less shining than mine the day I conquered "butterfly," which I had been persistently pronouncing in standard Spanish as boo-ter-flee. "Children," Miss Ryan called for attention. "Ernesto has learned how to pronounce *butterfly!*" And I proved it with a perfect imitation of Miss Ryan. From that celebrated success, I was soon able to match Ito's progress as a sentence reader with "Come, butterfly, come fly with me."

Like Ito and several other first graders who did not know English, I received private lessons from Miss Ryan in the closet, a narrow hall off the classroom with a door at each end. Next to one of these doors Miss Ryan placed a large chair for herself and a small one for me. Keeping an eye on the class

---

1. buxom superstructure: Full figure.
2. Escuela Municipal Numero 3 para Varones of Mazatlán (es kwä lǝ mōō̄ nĕ sĕ päl nōō̄′me rŏ träs pärä vä rō′nas mä sät län′): Municipal School Number 3 for Boys of Mazatlán.
3. doña (dō′ nyä): A Spanish title of respect meaning "lady" or "madam".

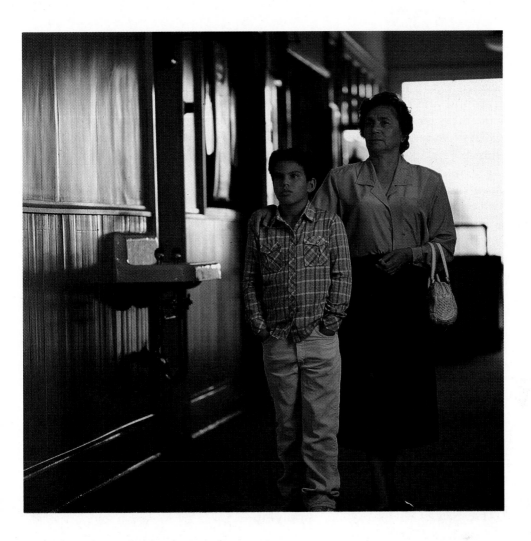

through the open door she read with me about sheep in the meadow and a frightened chicken going to see the king, coaching me out of my phonetic ruts in words like *pasture*, *bow-wow-wow*, *hay*, and *pretty*, which to my Mexican ear and eye had so many unnecessary sounds and letters. She made me watch her lips and then close my eyes as she repeated words I found hard to read. When we came to know each other better, I tried interrupting to tell Miss Ryan how we said it in Spanish. It didn't work. She only said "oh" and went on with *pasture*, *bow-wow-wow*, and *pretty*. It was as if in that closet

we were both discovering together the secrets of the English language and grieving together over the tragedies of Bo-Peep. The main reason I was graduated with honors from the first grade was that I had fallen in love with Miss Ryan. Her radiant, nononsense character made us either afraid not to love her or love her so we would not be afraid, I am not sure which. It was not only that we sensed she was with it, but also that she was with us.

Like the first grade, the rest of the Lincoln School was a sampling of the lower part of town where many races made their home.

My pals in the second grade were Kazushi, whose parents spoke only Japanese; Matti, a skinny Italian boy; and Manuel, a fat Portuguese who would never get into a fight but wrestled you to the ground and just sat on you. Our assortment of nationalities included Koreans, Yugoslavs, Poles, Irish, and home-grown Americans.

At Lincoln, making us into Americans did not mean scrubbing away what made us originally foreign. The teachers called us as our parents did, or as close as they could pronounce our names in Spanish or Japanese. No one was ever scolded or punished for speaking in his native tongue on the playground. Matti told the class about his mother's down quilt, which she had made in Italy with the fine feathers of a thousand geese. Encarnación acted out how boys learned to fish in the Philippines. I astounded the third grade with the story of my travels on a stagecoach, which nobody else in the class had seen except in the museum at Sutter's Fort. After a visit to the Crocker Art Gallery and its collection of heroic paintings of the golden age of California, someone showed a silk scroll with a Chinese painting. Miss Hopley herself had a way of expressing wonder over these matters before a class, her eyes wide open until they popped slightly. It was easy for me to feel that becoming a proud American, as she said we should, did not mean feeling ashamed of being a Mexican.

THINKING ABOUT THE SELECTION

Recalling

1. Why is Ernesto nervous at the start of this selection?
2. How does Miss Hopley reassure him?
3. Why is he afraid of Miss Ryan at first?
4. How does Miss Ryan make Ernesto and his classmates feel successful?

Interpreting

5. Explain the writer's statement that Miss Ryan was both "with it" and "with us."
6. What is the main problem that Ernesto faces during this part of his life?
7. What is the meaning of the title?

Applying

8. What qualities does a person need in order to make someone feel at home in a strange situation?
9. How would you make foreign students feel more at home in a school?

ANALYZING LITERATURE

Thinking About the Narrator

The **narrator** of a work is the person who tells the story. The narrator of an autobiography is the author. However, the narrator often tells about a different time in life. In this selection, the older, maturer Ernesto Galarza, tells about the young boy Ernesto.

Narrators of autobiographies, like Ernesto Galarza, refer to themselves as "I" and tell you their thoughts and feelings about the events of their lives. In this selection from *Barrio Boy,* Galarza focuses on the problems he faced and overcame as a new, Spanish-speaking student in an American school.

1. Find three places where Galarza refers to himself as "I."
2. Identify two passages where Galarza reports his thoughts or feelings.
3. Most readers probably feel glad when Galarza overcomes his problems. Why might readers be less involved if Galarza himself were not the narrator?
4. In what ways do you think the narrator Ernesto Galarza is different from the young boy Ernesto? Find evidence to support your answer.

CRITICAL THINKING AND READING
Understanding Stereotypes

A **stereotype** is a negative idea about the traits or behavior of a group of people. This idea does not let you see the individuals of that group for who they are. For example, Ernesto feels threatened by "tall, energetic teachers." Since Miss Ryan is a member of this group, he is afraid of her. However, as he begins to know her, he realizes that his stereotype was wrong.

1. Judging by Galarza's experience, what is the best way to overcome stereotypes?

2. Galarza comments that, "At Lincoln, making us into Americans did not mean scrubbing away what made us originally foreign." What does he mean by this statement?

UNDERSTANDING LANGUAGE
Learning Words from Spanish

Ernesto Galarza spoke Spanish before he learned English. In this selection, he uses a Spanish word that has become part of the English language. *Barrio* means "part of a town or city where most of the people are Hispanic."

Look up the following words in a dictionary and use each in a sentence.
1. rodeo   2. arroyo   3. lariat   4. taco

THINKING AND WRITING
Writing About a School Experience

Imagine that a young friend of yours is about to go to a new school. You want to encourage that person. To do so, write an account of your own first time in a strange situation. Look back at the writing assignment you did before reading this selection. Turn that description into an autobiographical sketch that your young friend will enjoy. When you revise the sketch, make sure you have used the word "I" when talking about yourself, just as Galarza does. Proofread your account and share it with your classmates.

GUIDE FOR READING

A Time of Beginnings

Jade Snow Wong (1922–   ) grew up in San Francisco's China-town. As a girl, she tried to learn American customs while her parents followed a traditional Chinese way of life. Wong tells about this period of her life in her popular autobiography *Fifth Chinese Daughter* (1950). In 1975, she published the story of her adult life in *No Chinese Stranger*. "A Time of Beginnings," which comes from that later book, describes how she fought against odds to become an artist and a businesswoman.

Third-Person Narrative in Autobiography

While in most autobiographies the writers refer to themselves as "I," Jade Snow Wong refers to herself by name or as "she." This method of writing is called **third-person narrative.** Wong explains this un-usual practice in the introduction to her autobiography, telling readers about the importance of modesty in the Chinese tradition. According to this tradition, it is "unnecessary to sign works of art and unbecom-ing to talk at length using 'I' or 'me.' "

Look For

As you read "A Time of Beginnings," look for the many problems that Wong must overcome to achieve success in her chosen field. What is it about Wong's character that helps her overcome these obstacles?

Writing

In this selection Jade Snow Wong explains how she succeeded as a potter. Think about something that you do well. It could be anything from building a model airplane to cooking a meal. How would you ex-plain what you do to someone else? List the important points you would include in your explanation.

Vocabulary

Knowing the following words will help you as you read "A Time of Be-ginnings."

ironically (ī rän' i k'l lē) *adv.*: In a way different from what is ex-pected (p. 343)

prevalent (prev' ə lənt) *adj.*: Widely accepted (p. 343)

utilizing (yōōt''l īz' iŋ) *v.*: Using (p. 343)

catastrophe (kə tas' trə fē) *n.*: Sudden disaster or misfortune (p. 345)

immeasurably (i mezh' ər əb' lē) *adv.*: Extremely; very (p. 345)

comparable (käm' pər ə b'l) *adj.*: Similar (p. 345)

liability (lī' ə bil' ə tē) *n.*: Disad-vantage (p. 345)

aesthetically (es thet' ik lē) *adv.*: From an artistic point of view (p. 347)

A Time of Beginnings

Jade Snow Wong

After Jade Snow began working in Mr. Fong's window, which confined her clay spatters, her activity revealed for the first time to Chinatown residents an art which had distinguished Chinese culture. Ironically, it was not until she was at college that she became fascinated with Tang and Sung Dynasty[1] achievements in clay, a thousand years ago.

Her ability to master pottery made her father happy, for Grandfather Wong believed that a person who could work with his hands would never starve. When Father Wong was young, Grandfather made him learn how to hand-pierce and stitch slipper soles, and how to knot Chinese button heads, both indispensable in clothing. But to Mother Wong, the merits of making pottery escaped her—to see her college-educated daughter up to her elbows in clay, and more clay flying around as she worked in public view, was strangely unladylike. As for Chinatown merchants, they laughed openly at her, "Here comes the girl who plays with mud. How many bowls could you sell today?" Probably they thought: Here is a college graduate foolish enough to dirty her hands.

It has been the traditional belief from Asia to the Middle East, with Japan the exception, that scholars do not soil their hands and that a person studied literature in order to escape hard work. (This attitude is still prevalent in most Asian countries outside of the People's Republic of China and Japan.)

From the first, the local Chinese were not Jade Snow's patrons. The thinness and whiteness of porcelains imported from China and ornate decorations which came into vogue during the late Ching Dynasty[2] satisfied their tastes. They could not understand why "silly Americans" paid dollars for a hand-thrown bowl[3] utilizing crude California colored clays, not much different from the inexpensive peasant ware of China. That the Jade Snow Wong bowl went back to an older tradition of understated beauty was not apparent. They could see only that she wouldn't apply a dragon or a hundred flowers.

Many years later when Jade Snow met another atypical artist, a scholar and calligrapher[4] born and educated in China, he was to say to her, "I shudder if the majority of people look at my brush work and say it is pretty, for then I know it is ordinary and I have failed. If they say they do not understand it, or even that it is ugly, I am happy, for I have succeeded."

---

1. Tang and Sung (soong) **Dynasty:** A dynasty is a succession of rulers who belong to the same family. The period of the Tang Dynasty was 618–906 and that of the Sung Dynasty 960–1279.

2. Ching Dynasty: This dynasty lasted from 1644 to 1912.

3. hand-thrown bowl: A bowl shaped by hand on a potter's wheel, which spins the clay around.

4. calligrapher (kə lig' rə fər) *n*.: Someone skilled in the art of beautiful handwriting.

However, there were enough numbers of the American public who bought Jade Snow's pottery to support her modestly. The store window was a temporary experiment which proved what she needed to know. In the meantime, her aging father, who was fearful that their home and factory might be in a redevelopment area, made a down payment with lifetime savings to purchase a small white wooden building with six rentable apartments at the perimeter of Chinatown. Jade Snow agreed to rent the two tiny empty ground-floor storefronts which he did not yet need, one for a display room, with supplies and packing center at its rear, the other for the potter's wheel, kiln,[5] glazing booth,[6] compressor,[7] and other equipment. Now, instead of paying Mr. Fong a commission on gross sales, she had bills to pay. Instead of sitting in a window, she worked with doors thrown open to the street.

Creativeness was 90 percent hard work and 10 percent inspiration. It was learning from errors, either from her lack of foresight or because of the errors of others. The first firing[8] in an unfamiliar new gas kiln brought crushing disappointment when the wares blew up into tiny pieces. In another firing,

---

5. kiln (kiln) *n.*: An oven to bake pottery.

6. glazing booth: A place to apply glaze, a glassy finish, to pottery.

7. compressor: (kəm pres' ər): A machine for compressing air or gas.

8. firing (fir' iŋ) *n.*: The application of heat to harden or glaze pottery.

glaze results were uneven black and dark green, for the chemical supply house had mistakenly labeled five pounds of black copper oxide as black iron oxide. One morning there was a personal catastrophe. Unaware of a slow leak all night from the partially opened gas cock, she lit a match at the kiln. An explosion injured both hands, which took weeks to heal.

The day-to-day work of potterymaking tested her deepest discipline. A "wedged" ball of clay (prepared by kneading) would be "thrown" (shaped) on the potter's wheel, then dried overnight and trimmed, sometimes decorated with Chinese brush or bamboo tools. It took about a hundred thoroughly dried pieces to fill a kiln for the first firing that transformed fragile mud walls into hard bisque ware.[9] Glazes, like clays the results of countless experiments, were then applied to each piece. A second twelve-hour firing followed, with the temperatures raised hour by hour up to the final maturing point of somewhere around 2,000 degrees Fahrenheit. Then the kiln was turned off for twenty-four hours of cooling. Breakage was a potential hazard at every stage; each step might measure short in technical and artistic accomplishment. A piece she worked on diligently could disappoint. Another made casually had been enhanced successively until it delighted. One piece in ten might be of exhibition quality, half might be salable, and the others would be flawed "seconds" she would discard.

Yet Jade Snow never wavered from her belief that if moments in time could result in a thing of beauty that others could share, those moments were immeasurably satisfying. She owned two perfect Sung tea bowls. Without copying, she tried to make her pottery "stand up" in strength and grace to that standard.

It became routine to work past midnight without days off. Hand work could not be rushed; failures had to be replaced, and a host of other unanticipated business chores suddenly manifested themselves. She had kept comparable hours when she worked all through college to meet her expenses. Again, the hope of reaching valued goals was her spur. If she should fail, then she could accept what tradition dictated for most Chinese daughters—to be a wife, daughter-in-law, and mother. But unlike her college, the American business world was not dedicated to helping her. Because she was pioneering in a new venture, her identity was a liability. Her brains and hands were her only assets. How could she convert that liability? How could she differ from other struggling potters?

To enlarge her production base, she experimented with enamels[10] on copper forms conceived in the fluid shapes of her pottery, layering jewel tones for brilliant effects. They differed from the earth tints of clay and attracted a new clientele. With another kiln and new equipment, she made functional forms, believing that fine things should become part of the user's everyday life. The best results were submitted to exhibitions. Some juries rejected them, some accepted, and others awarded prizes.

To reach a market larger than San Francisco, she wrote to store buyers around the country, and, encouraged, she called on them. Traveling to strange cities far across the United States, as a rare Oriental woman alone in hotel dining rooms, she developed strong nerves against curious stares. That trip produced orders. Stipulated delivery and

---

9. bisque (bisk) **ware:** Unglazed pottery.

10. enamels (i nam´´ls) *n.*: Glassy colored substances used as coatings on metal, glass, and pottery.

cancellation dates made it necessary to hire first one and then more helpers who had to be trained, checked, kept busy and happy.

The strains increased. So did the bills, and she borrowed in small amounts from her sympathetic father, who said, "A hundred dollars is easy to come by, but the first thousand is very, very tricky. Look at the ideograph[11] for hundred—solidly square. Look at it for thousand—pointed, slippery. The ancients knew this long ago." When hundreds were not enough, tactful Western friends offered help. Oldest Brother, noticing her worries and struggles, sniffed scornfully. "You'll be out of business in a year."

She had learned to accept family criticism in silence, but she was too deeply involved to give up. Money was a worry, but creating was exciting and satisfying. These were lonely years. Jade Snow's single-minded pursuit did not allow her pleasant interludes with friends. To start a kiln at dawn, then watch till its critical maturing moment, which could happen any time between early evening and midnight or later (when gas pressure was low, it took until the next dawn), kept her from social engagements.

Then, gradually, signs indicated that she was working in the right direction. The first was a letter from the Metropolitan Museum of Art in New York, where the Eleventh Ceramic National Syracuse Show had been sent. The curator wrote, "We think the green, gold and ivory enamel bowl a skillful piece of workmanship and are anxious to add it to our collections." They referred to a ten-inch shallow bowl which Jade Snow had made.

A reviewer in *Art Digest* wrote, "In plain enamels without applied design, Jade Snow

Wong of San Francisco seemed to this critic to top the list."

Recognition brought further recognition. National decorating magazines featured her enamels, and in the same year, 1947, the Museum of Modern Art installed an exhibit by Mies Van der Rohe[12] which displayed 100 objects of fine design costing less than $100. A note introducing this exhibit read, "Every so often the Museum of Modern Art selects and exhibits soundly designed objects available to American purchasers in the belief that this will encourage more people to use beautiful things in their everyday life. . . ."

---

11. ideograph (id′ē ə graf′) *n.*: A symbol that stands for a thing or idea without expressing the sounds that make up its name.

12. Mies Van der Rohe (mēz′ van dər rō′ə): Ludwig Mies Van der Rohe (1886–1969) was a German-born American architect.

Two of Jade Snow's enamels, a dinner plate in Chinese red and a dessert plate in grayish gold, were included in the exhibition, which subsequently went to Europe.

So it did not seem unusual to receive an interviewer from *Mademoiselle*, but it was indeed unexpected to receive one of the magazine's ten awards for 1948 to women outstanding in ten different fields. They invited Jade Snow to fly to New York to claim her silver medal.

The more deeply one delves into a field, the more one realizes limitations. When Bernard Leach, the famous English potter, accepted an invitation from Mills College to teach a special course, Jade Snow attended. Another summer, Charles Merritt came from Alfred University's staff to give a course in precise glaze chemistry. Again, she commuted to Oakland. She became friends with these two unusual teachers. Both agreed that in pottery making, one never found a final answer. A mass-produced bathtub may be a technical triumph; yet a chemically balanced glaze on a pot can be aesthetically dull. Some of the most pleasing glaze effects could never be duplicated, for they were the combination of scrapings from the glaze booth. Like the waves of the sea, no two pieces of pottery art can be identical.

After three years of downs, then ups, the business promised to survive. Debts had been cleared. A small staff could handle routine duties. A steady clientele of San Franciscans came to her out-of-the-way shop. A beginning had been made.

THINKING ABOUT THE SELECTION

Recalling

1. How did Wong's father and mother differ in their reactions to her work as a potter?
2. How did Wong defy traditional Chinese ways? How did she defy the traditional expectations of the time for women?
3. The ideograph for hundred is 百 and for thousand is 千 . According to Wong's father, what is the significance of these ideographs?

Interpreting

4. What do you infer about Wong from her success in reaching a market beyond San Francisco? What other incidents support this inference?
5. In what way was Wong's identity a liability? In what way were her brains and hands her only assets?
6. Explain the significance of the last line.

Applying

7. Jade Snow Wong says that her work did not allow her to spend much time with friends. Do you think it worth making such a sacrifice to reach a goal? Why or why not?
8. Another artist says to Wong, "I shudder if the majority of people look at my brush work and say it is pretty, for then I know it is ordinary and I have failed." What is the difference between an artistic success and a popular success? Can a person be both? Support your answer.

ANALYZING LITERATURE

Understanding Third-Person Narrative

This autobiography is unusual because Jade Snow Wong uses **third-person narrative,** referring to herself as "she" rather than "I." In keeping with the Chinese tradition of modesty, she records her struggles and successes as a potter as if she were talking about someone else.

1. Look at the paragraph beginning, "It became routine . . . ," on page 345. Reread it, changing every *she* to *I* and every *her* to *my*.
2. Compare and contrast your version of the paragraph with the original.
3. Wong uses third-person narrative so it will not seem that she is boasting. What else in her account shows her modesty?

CRITICAL THINKING AND READING

Distinguishing Details

Autobiographies contain both objective and subjective details. An **objective detail** is a description of an event or object in the world outside the writer's mind. For example, when Jade Snow Wong says that she received an award from *Mademoiselle* in 1948, this is an objective detail. A **subjective detail** is a description of the writer's thoughts or feelings or opinions and judgments. Wong's statement that "creating was exciting and satisfying" is a subjective detail.

Find three objective details Wong gives about herself. Find three subjective details.

THINKING AND WRITING

Writing a Third-Person Sketch

Imagine that you are doing the task you wrote about before reading this selection. Suddenly you have the power to actually leave your body and watch yourself at work. Write a description of the way you look from your new perspective. Include in this description not only what your hands and body are doing but also your ideas and feelings. To help you with your writing, use the list you made for the earlier writing assignment. When you revise what you have written, make sure you have referred to yourself by name or as "he" or "she," just as Jade Snow Wong does.

Essays for Enjoyment

ICED COFFEE
Fairfield Porter
Private Collection

GUIDE FOR READING

Cat on the Go

James Herriot (1916–   ) was born James Alfred Wight in Scotland. However, he uses the name Herriot when writing about his experiences as a veterinarian in Yorkshire, an English county. Herriot's books are famous for their lively descriptions of the characters he met, both animal and human. "Cat on the Go," which comes from his book *All Things Wise and Wonderful,* describes a cat that loves to go visiting.

Narrative Essay

An **essay** is a kind of musing, or thinking, upon a subject. It takes the form of a brief and personal discussion of any topic that a writer wants to consider. A **narrative essay** explores the subject by telling a true story. This type of essay may remind you of an autobiographical sketch. In an autobiography, however, the writer is always the central character, while a narrative essay may focus on a character other than the writer. The narrative essay "Cat on the Go," for instance, centers on the actions of Oscar, a friendly and restless cat.

Look For

As you read, pay close attention to the cat's personality. Look for how his personality gives you clues to the secret of his disappearances.

Writing

Oscar is a most unusual cat. Write about an animal you have known that stood out from others of its kind. What made this animal special?

Vocabulary

Knowing the following words will help you as you read "Cat on the Go."

grotesquely (grō tesk′ lē) *adv.*: In a strange or distorted way (p. 351)

emaciated (i mā′ shē āt′ əd) *adj.*: Extremely thin; starving (p. 351)

sieve (siv) *n.*: Utensil with many tiny openings; strainer (p. 353)

inevitable (in ev′ ə tə b'l) *adj.*: Certain to happen (p. 353)

sauntered (sôn′ tərd) *v.*: Strolled (p. 354)

distraught (dis trôt′) *adj.*: Extremely upset (p. 355)

despondent (di spän′ dənt) *adj.*: Lacking hope; depressed (p. 355)

intrigued (in trēgd′) *v.*: Fascinated (p. 356)

consolation (kän′ sə lā′ shən) *n.*: Comfort (p. 359)

surreptitiously (sur′ əp tish′ əs lē) *adv.*: Secretly (p. 360)

Cat on the Go

James Herriot

One winter evening Tristan shouted up the stairs from the passage far below.

"Jim! Jim!"

I went out and stuck my head over the bannisters. "What is it, Triss?"

"Sorry to bother you, Jim, but could you come down for a minute?" The upturned face had an anxious look.

I went down the long flights of steps two at a time and when I arrived slightly breathless on the ground floor Tristan beckoned me through to the consulting room at the back of the house. A teenage girl was standing by the table, her hand resting on a stained roll of blanket.

"It's a cat," Tristan said. He pulled back a fold of the blanket and I looked down at a large, deeply striped tabby. At least he would have been large if he had had any flesh on his bones, but ribs and pelvis stood out painfully through the fur and as I passed my hand over the motionless body I could feel only a thin covering of skin.

Tristan cleared his throat. "There's something else, Jim."

I looked at him curiously. For once he didn't seem to have a joke in him. I watched as he gently lifted one of the cat's hind legs and rolled the abdomen into view. There was a gash on the ventral surface[1] through which a coiled cluster of intestines spilled grotesquely onto the cloth. I was still shocked and staring when the girl spoke.

"I saw this cat sittin' in the dark, down Brown's yard. I thought 'e looked skinny, like, and a bit quiet and I bent down to give 'im a pat. Then I saw 'e was badly hurt and I went home for a blanket and brought 'im round to you."

"That was kind of you," I said. "Have you any idea who he belongs to?"

The girl shook her head. "No, he looks like a stray to me."

"He does indeed." I dragged my eyes away from the terrible wound. "You're Marjorie Simpson, aren't you?"

"Yes."

"I know your Dad well. He's our postman."

"That's right." She gave a half smile then her lips trembled.

"Well, I reckon I'd better leave 'im with you. You'll be going to put him out of his misery. There's nothing anybody can do about . . . about that?"

I shrugged and shook my head. The girl's eyes filled with tears, she stretched out a hand and touched the emaciated animal then turned and walked quickly to the door.

"Thanks again, Marjorie," I called after the retreating back. "And don't worry—we'll look after him."

In the silence that followed, Tristan and I looked down at the shattered animal. Under the surgery lamp it was all too easy to

---

1. **ventral** (ven′ trəl) **surface:** The surface near or on the belly.

see. He had almost been disemboweled[2] and the pile of intestines was covered in dirt and mud.

"What d'you think did this?" Tristan said at length. "Has he been run over?"

"Maybe," I replied. "Could be anything. An attack by a big dog or somebody could have kicked him or struck him." All things were possible with cats because some people seemed to regard them as fair game for any cruelty.

Tristan nodded. "Anyway, whatever happened, he must have been on the verge of starvation. He's a skeleton. I bet he's wandered miles from home."

"Ah well," I sighed. "There's only one thing to do. Those guts are perforated in several places. It's hopeless."

Tristan didn't say anything but he whistled under his breath and drew the tip of his forefinger again and again across the furry cheek. And, unbelievably, from somewhere in the scraggy chest a gentle purring arose.

The young man looked at me, round eyed. "My God, do you hear that?"

"Yes . . . amazing in that condition. He's a good-natured cat."

Tristan, head bowed, continued his stroking. I knew how he felt because, although he preserved a cheerfully hard-boiled attitude to our patients he couldn't kid me about one thing; he had a soft spot for cats. Even now, when we are both around the sixty mark, he often talks to me about the cat he has had for many years. It is a typical relationship—they tease each other unmercifully—but it is based on real affection.

"It's no good, Triss," I said gently. "It's got to be done." I reached for the syringe but

---

2. disemboweled (dis′ im bou′ əld) *v.*: Lost its intestines.

something in me rebelled against plunging a needle into that mutilated body. Instead I pulled a fold of the blanket over the cat's head.

"Pour a little ether onto the cloth," I said. "He'll just sleep away."

Wordlessly, Tristan unscrewed the cap of the ether bottle and poised it above the head. Then from under the shapeless heap of blanket we heard it again; the deep purring which increased in volume till it boomed in our ears like a distant motorcycle.

Tristan was like a man turned to stone, hand gripping the bottle rigidly, eyes staring down at the mound of cloth from which the purring rose in waves of warm friendly sound.

At last he looked up at me and gulped. "I don't fancy this much, Jim. Can't we do something?"

"You mean, put that lot back?"

"Yes."

"But the bowels are damaged—they're like a sieve in parts."

"We could stitch them, couldn't we?"

I lifted the blanket and looked again. "Honestly, Triss, I wouldn't know where to start. And the whole thing is filthy."

He didn't say anything, but continued to look at me steadily. And I didn't need much persuading. I had no more desire to pour ether onto that comradely purring than he had.

"Come on, then," I said. "We'll have a go."

With the oxygen bubbling and the cat's head in the anesthetic mask we washed the whole prolapse[3] with warm saline.[4] We did it again and again but it was impossible to remove every fragment of caked dirt. Then we started the painfully slow business of stitching the many holes in the tiny intestines,

and here I was glad of Tristan's nimble fingers which seemed better able to manipulate the small round-bodied needles than mine.

Two hours and yards of catgut[5] later, we dusted the patched up peritoneal[6] surface with sulfanilamide[7] and pushed the entire mass back into the abdomen. When I had sutured muscle layers and skin everything looked tidy but I had a nasty feeling of sweeping undesirable things under the carpet. The extensive damage, all that contamination—peritonitis[8] was inevitable.

"He's alive, anyway, Triss," I said as we began to wash the instruments. "We'll put him onto sulfapyridine and keep our fingers crossed." There were still no antibiotics at that time but the new drug was a big advance.

The door opened and Helen came in. "You've been a long time, Jim." She walked over to the table and looked down at the sleeping cat. "What a poor skinny little thing. He's all bones."

"You should have seen him when he came in." Tristan switched off the sterilizer and screwed shut the valve on the anesthetic machine. "He looks a lot better now."

She stroked the little animal for a moment. "Is he badly injured?"

"I'm afraid so, Helen," I said. "We've done our best for him but I honestly don't think he has much chance."

"What a shame. And he's pretty, too. Four white feet and all those unusual colors." With her finger she traced the faint bands of auburn and copper-gold among the gray and black.

---

3. prolapse (prō′ laps) *n.*: An internal organ—here, the intestines—that has fallen out of place.

4. saline (sā′ līn) *n.*: A salt solution.

5. catgut (kat′ gut′) *n.*: A tough string or thread used in surgery.

6. peritoneal (per′ it 'n ē′ əl) *adj.*: Having to do with the membrane that lines the abdomen.

7. sulfanilamide (sul′ fə nil′ ə mīd) *n.*: Sulfa drugs were used to treat infections before penicillin was discovered and other antibiotics were created.

8. peritonitis (per′ it 'n īt′ əs) *n.*: Inflammation of the abdominal lining.

Tristan laughed. "Yes, I think that chap has a ginger Tom somewhere in his ancestry."

Helen smiled, too, but absently, and I noticed a broody look about her. She hurried out to the stock room and returned with an empty box.

"Yes . . . yes . . ." she said thoughtfully. "I can make a bed in this box for him and he'll sleep in our room, Jim."

"He will?"

"Yes, he must be warm, mustn't he?"

"Of course."

Later, in the darkness of our bed-sitter,[9] I looked from my pillow at a cozy scene. Sam in his basket on one side of the flickering fire and the cat cushioned and blanketed in his box on the other.

As I floated off into sleep it was good to know that my patient was so comfortable, but I wondered if he would be alive in the morning. . . .

I knew he was alive at 7:30 a.m. because my wife was already up and talking to him. I trailed across the room in my pajamas and the cat and I looked at each other. I rubbed him under the chin and he opened his mouth in a rusty miaow. But he didn't try to move.

"Helen," I said. "This little thing is tied together inside with catgut. He'll have to live on fluids for a week and even then he probably won't make it. If he stays up here you'll be spooning milk into him umpteen times a day."

"Okay, okay." She had that broody look again.

It wasn't only milk she spooned into him over the next few days. Beef essence, strained broth and a succession of sophisticated baby foods found their way down his

throat at regular intervals. One lunch time I found Helen kneeling by the box.

"We shall call him Oscar," she said.

"You mean we're keeping him?"

"Yes."

I am fond of cats but we already had a dog in our cramped quarters and I could see difficulties. Still I decided to let it go.

"Why Oscar?"

"I don't know." Helen tipped a few drops of chop gravy onto the little red tongue and watched intently as he swallowed.

One of the things I like about women is their mystery, the unfathomable part of them, and I didn't press the matter further. But I was pleased at the way things were going. I had been giving the sulfapyridine every six hours and taking the temperature night and morning, expecting all the time to encounter the roaring fever, the vomiting and the tense abdomen of peritonitis. But it never happened.

It was as though Oscar's animal instinct told him he had to move as little as possible because he lay absolutely still day after day and looked up at us—and purred.

His purr became part of our lives and when he eventually left his bed, sauntered through to our kitchen and began to sample Sam's dinner of meat and biscuit it was a moment of triumph. And I didn't spoil it by wondering if he was ready for solid food; I felt he knew.

From then on it was sheer joy to watch the furry scarecrow fill out and grow strong, and as he ate and ate and the flesh spread over his bones the true beauty of his coat showed in the glossy medley of auburn, black and gold. We had a handsome cat on our hands.

Once Oscar had fully recovered, Tristan was a regular visitor.

He probably felt, and rightly, that he, more than I, had saved Oscar's life in the

_____

9. **bed-sitter:** A British term for a one-room apartment.

first place and he used to play with him for long periods. His favorite ploy was to push his leg round the corner of the table and withdraw it repeatedly just as the cat pawed at it.

Oscar was justifiably irritated by this teasing but showed his character by lying in wait for Tristan one night and biting him smartly[10] in the ankle before he could start his tricks.

From my own point of view Oscar added many things to our menage.[11] Sam was delighted with him and the two soon became firm friends, Helen adored him and each evening I thought afresh that a nice cat washing his face by the hearth gave extra comfort to a room.

Oscar had been established as one of the family for several weeks when I came in from a late call to find Helen waiting for me with a stricken face.

"What's happened?" I asked.

"It's Oscar—he's gone!"

"Gone? What do you mean?"

"Oh, Jim, I think he's run away."

I stared at her. "He wouldn't do that. He often goes down to the garden at night. Are you sure he isn't there?"

"Absolutely. I've searched right into the yard. I've even had a walk round the town. And remember." Her chin quivered. "He . . . he ran away from somewhere before."

I looked at my watch. "Ten o'clock. Yes, that is strange. He shouldn't be out at this time."

As I spoke the front door bell jangled. I galloped down the stairs and as I rounded the corner in the passage I could see Mrs. Heslington, the vicar's[12] wife, through the glass. I threw open the door. She was holding Oscar in her arms.

"I believe this is your cat, Mr. Herriot," she said.

"It is indeed, Mrs. Heslington. Where did you find him?"

She smiled. "Well it was rather odd. We were having a meeting of the Mothers' Union at the church house and we noticed the cat sitting there in the room."

"Just sitting . . .?"

"Yes, as though he were listening to what we were saying and enjoying it all. It was unusual. When the meeting ended I thought I'd better bring him along to you."

"I'm most grateful, Mrs. Heslington." I snatched Oscar and tucked him under my arm. "My wife is distraught—she thought he was lost."

It was a little mystery. Why should he suddenly take off like that? But since he showed no change in his manner over the ensuing week we put it out of our minds.

Then one evening a man brought in a dog for a distemper[13] inoculation and left the front door open. When I went up to our flat I found that Oscar had disappeared again. This time Helen and I scoured the marketplace and side alleys in vain and when we returned at half past nine we were both despondent. It was nearly eleven and we were thinking of bed when the doorbell rang.

It was Oscar again, this time resting on the ample stomach of Jack Newbould. Jack was a gardener at one of the big houses. He hiccuped gently and gave me a huge benevolent smile. "Brought your cat, Mr. Herriot."

"Gosh, thanks, Jack!" I said, scooping up Oscar gratefully. "Where the devil did you find him?"

"Well, s'matter o' fact 'e sort of found me."

"What do you mean?"

---

10. smartly (smärt′ lē) *adv*.: Sharply.

11. menage (mə näzh′) *n*.: Household.

12. vicar's (vik′ ərz) *n*.: A vicar is a parish priest.

---

13. distemper (dis tem′ pər) *n*.: An infectious virus disease of young dogs.

Jack closed his eyes for a few moments before articulating carefully. "Thish is a big night, tha knows, Mr. Herriot. Darts championship. Lots of t'lads round at t'Dog and Gun—lotsh and lotsh of 'em. Big gatherin'."

"And our cat was there?"

"Aye, he were there, all right. Sitting among t'lads. Shpent t'whole evenin' with us."

"Just sat there, eh?"

"That 'e did." Jack giggled reminiscently. "By gaw 'e enjoyed 'isself. Ah gave 'em a drop out of me own glass and once or twice ah thought 'e was going to have a go at chuckin' a dart. He's some cat." He laughed again.

As I bore Oscar upstairs I was deep in thought. What was going on here? These sudden desertions were upsetting Helen and I felt they could get on my nerves in time.

I didn't have long to wait till the next one. Three nights later he was missing again. This time Helen and I didn't bother to search—we just waited.

He was back earlier than usual. I heard the door bell at nine o'clock. It was the elderly Miss Simpson peering through the glass. And she wasn't holding Oscar—he was prowling on the mat waiting to come in.

Miss Simpson watched with interest as the cat stalked inside and made for the stairs. "Ah, good, I'm so glad he's come home safely. I knew he was your cat and I've been intrigued by his behavior all evening."

"Where . . . may I ask?"

"Oh, at the Women's Institute. He came in shortly after we started and stayed there till the end."

"Really? What exactly was your program, Miss Simpson?"

"Well, there was a bit of committee stuff, then a short talk with lantern slides by Mr. Walters from the water company and we finished with a cake-making competition."

"Yes . . . yes . . . and what did Oscar do?"

She laughed. "Mixed with the company, apparently enjoyed the slides and showed great interest in the cakes."

"I see. And you didn't bring him home?"

"No, he made his own way here. As you know, I have to pass your house and I merely rang your bell to make sure you knew he had arrived."

"I'm obliged to you, Miss Simpson. We were a little worried."

I mounted the stairs in record time. Helen was sitting with the cat on her knee and she looked up as I burst in.

"I know about Oscar now," I said.

"Know what?"

"Why he goes on these nightly outings. He's not running away—he's visiting."

"Visiting?"

"Yes," I said. "Don't you see? He likes getting around, he loves people, especially in groups, and he's interested in what they do. He's a natural mixer."

Helen looked down at the attractive mound of fur curled on her lap. "Of course . . . that's it . . . he's a socialite!"

"Exactly, a high stepper!"

"A cat-about-town!"

It all afforded us some innocent laughter and Oscar sat up and looked at us with evident pleasure, adding his own throbbing purr to the merriment. But for Helen and me there was a lot of relief behind it; ever since our cat had started his excursions there had been the gnawing fear that we would lose him, and now we felt secure.

From that night our delight in him increased. There was endless joy in watching this facet of his character unfolding. He did the social round meticulously, taking in most of the activities of the town. He became a familiar figure at whist drives,[14] jumble

---

14. whist (hwist) **drives:** Attempts to raise money for charities and other purposes by playing the card game whist.

sales,[15] school concerts and scout bazaars. Most of the time he was made welcome, but was twice ejected from meetings of the Rural District Council who did not seem to relish the idea of a cat sitting in on their deliberations.

At first I was apprehensive about his making his way through the streets but I watched him once or twice and saw that he looked both ways before tripping daintily across. Clearly he had excellent traffic sense and this made me feel that his original injury had not been caused by a car.

Taking it all in all, Helen and I felt that it was a kind stroke of fortune which had brought Oscar to us. He was a warm and cherished part of our home life. He added to our happiness.

When the blow fell it was totally unexpected.

I was finishing the evening surgery.[16] I looked round the door and saw only a man and two little boys.

"Next, please," I said.

The man stood up. He had no animal with him. He was middle-aged, with the rough weathered face of a farm worker. He twirled a cloth cap nervously in his hands.

"Mr. Herriot?" he said.

---

15. jumble sales: A British term for sales of contributed articles to raise money for charity.

16. surgery (sur′ jər ē) *n.:* A British term for "office hours."

"Yes, what can I do for you?"

He swallowed and looked me straight in the eyes. "Ah think you've got ma cat."

"What?"

"Ah lost ma cat a bit since." He cleared his throat. "We used to live at Missdon but ah got a job as plowman to Mr. Horne of Wederly. It was after we moved to Wederly that t'cat went missin'. Ah reckon he was tryin to find 'is way back to his old home."

"Wederly? That's on the other side of Brawton—over thirty miles away."

"Aye, ah knaw, but cats is funny things."

"But what makes you think I've got him?"

He twisted the cap around a bit more. "There's a cousin o' mine lives in Darrowby and ah heard tell from 'im about this cat that goes around to meetin's. I 'ad to come. We've been huntin' everywhere."

"Tell me," I said. "This cat you lost. What did he look like?"

"Gray and black and sort o' gingery. Right bonny[17] 'e was. And 'e was allus goin' out to gatherin's."

A cold hand clutched at my heart. "You'd better come upstairs. Bring the boys with you."

Helen was putting some coal on the fire of the bed-sitter.

"Helen," I said. "This is Mr.—er—I'm sorry, I don't know your name."

"Gibbons, Sep Gibbons. They called me Septimus because ah was the seventh in family and it looks like ah'm goin' t'same way 'cause we've got six already. These are our two youngest." The two boys, obvious twins of about eight, looked up at us solemnly.

I wished my heart would stop hammering. "Mr. Gibbons thinks Oscar is his. He lost his cat some time ago."

My wife put down her little shovel. "Oh . . . oh . . . I see." She stood very still for a moment then smiled faintly. "Do sit down. Oscar's in the kitchen, I'll bring him through."

She went out and reappeared with the cat in her arms. She hadn't got through the door before the little boys gave tongue.

"Tiger!" they cried. "Oh, Tiger, Tiger!"

The man's face seemed lit from within. He walked quickly across the floor and ran his big work-roughened hand along the fur.

"Hullo, awd lad," he said, and turned to me with a radiant smile. "It's 'im, Mr. Herriot. It's 'im awright, and don't 'e look well!"

"You call him Tiger, eh?" I said.

"Aye," he replied happily. "It's them gingery stripes. The kids called 'im that. They were brokenhearted when we lost 'im."

As the two little boys rolled on the floor our Oscar rolled with them, pawing playfully, purring with delight.

Sep Gibbons sat down again. "That's the way 'e allus went on wi' the family. They used to play with 'im for hours. By gaw we did miss 'im. He were a right favorite."

I looked at the broken nails on the edge of the cap, at the decent, honest, uncomplicated Yorkshire[18] face so like the many I had grown to like and respect. Farm men like him got thirty shillings a week in those days and it was reflected in the threadbare jacket, the cracked, shiny boots and the obvious hand-me-downs of the boys.

But all three were scrubbed and tidy, the man's face like a red beacon, the children's knees gleaming and their hair carefully slicked across their foreheads. They looked like nice people to me. I didn't know what to say.

Helen said it for me. "Well, Mr. Gibbons." Her tone had an unnatural brightness. "You'd better take him."

---

17. **bonny** (bän' ē) *adj.*: Pretty.

18. **Yorkshire:** A former county of northern England.

The man hesitated. "Now then, are ye sure, Missis Herriot?"

"Yes . . . yes, I'm sure. He was your cat first."

"Aye, but some folks 'ud say finders keepers or summat like that. Ah didn't come 'ere to demand 'im back or owt of t'sort."

"I know you didn't, Mr. Gibbons, but you've had him all those years and you've searched for him so hard. We couldn't possibly keep him from you."

He nodded quickly. "Well, that's right good of ye." He paused for a moment, his face serious, then he stooped and picked Oscar up. "We'll have to be off if we're goin' to catch the eight o'clock bus."

Helen reached forward, cupped the cat's head in her hands and looked at him steadily for a few seconds. Then she patted the boys' heads. "You'll take good care of him, won't you?"

"Aye, missis, thank ye, we will that." The two small faces looked up at her and smiled.

"I'll see you down the stairs, Mr. Gibbons," I said.

On the descent I tickled the furry cheek resting on the man's shoulder and heard for the last time the rich purring. On the front door step we shook hands and they set off down the street. As they rounded the corner of Trengate they stopped and waved, and I waved back at the man, the two children and the cat's head looking back at me over the shoulder.

It was my habit at that time in my life to mount the stairs two or three at a time but on this occasion I trailed upwards like an old man, slightly breathless, throat tight, eyes prickling.

I cursed myself for a sentimental fool but as I reached our door I found a flash of consolation. Helen had taken it remarkably well. She had nursed that cat and grown deeply attached to him, and I'd have thought an unforeseen calamity like this would have upset her terribly. But no, she had behaved calmly and rationally.

It was up to me to do as well. I adjusted my features into the semblance of a cheerful smile and marched into the room.

Helen had pulled a chair close to the table and was slumped face down against the wood. One arm cradled her head while the other was stretched in front of her as her body shook with an utterly abandoned weeping.

I had never seen her like this and I was appalled. I tried to say something comforting but nothing stemmed the flow of racking sobs.

Feeling helpless and inadequate I could only sit close to her and stroke the back of her head. Maybe I could have said something if I hadn't felt just about as bad myself.

You get over these things in time. After all, we told ourselves, it wasn't as though Oscar had died or got lost again—he had gone to a good family who would look after him. In fact he had really gone home.

And of course, we still had our much-loved Sam, although he didn't help in the early stages by sniffing disconsolately where Oscar's bed used to lie then collapsing on the rug with a long lugubrious sigh.

There was one other thing, too. I had a little notion forming in my mind, an idea which I would spring on Helen when the time was right. It was about a month after that shattering night and we were coming out of the cinema at Brawton at the end of our half day. I looked at my watch.

"Only eight o'clock," I said. "How about going to see Oscar?"

Helen looked at me in surprise. "You mean—drive on to Wederly?"

"Yes, it's only about five miles."

A smile crept slowly across her face. "That would be lovely. But do you think they would mind?"

"The Gibbons? No, I'm sure they wouldn't. Let's go."

Wederly was a big village and the plowman's cottage was at the far end a few yards beyond the Methodist chapel. I pushed open the garden gate and we walked down the path.

A busy-looking little woman answered my knock. She was drying her hands on a striped towel.

"Mrs. Gibbons?" I said.

"Aye, that's me."

"I'm James Herriot—and this is my wife."

Her eyes widened uncomprehendingly. Clearly the name meant nothing to her.

"We had your cat for a while," I added.

Suddenly she grinned and waved her towel at us. "Oh aye, ah remember now. Sep told me about you. Come in, come in!"

The big kitchen-living room was a tableau[19] of life with six children and thirty shillings a week. Battered furniture, rows of much-mended washing on a pulley, black cooking range and a general air of chaos.

Sep got up from his place by the fire, put down his newspaper, took off a pair of steel-rimmed spectacles and shook hands.

He waved Helen to a sagging armchair. "Well, it's right nice to see you. Ah've often spoke of ye to t'missis."

His wife hung up her towel. "Yes, and I'm glad to meet ye both. I'll get some tea in a minnit."

She laughed and dragged a bucket of muddy water into a corner. "I've been washin' football jerseys. Them lads just handed them to me tonight—as if I haven't enough to do."

As she ran the water into the kettle I peeped surreptitiously around me and I no-

ticed Helen doing the same. But we searched in vain. There was no sign of a cat. Surely he couldn't have run away again? With a growing feeling of dismay I realized that my little scheme could backfire devastatingly.

It wasn't until the tea had been made and poured that I dared to raise the subject.

"How—" I asked diffidently. "How is—er—Tiger?"

"Oh, he's grand," the little woman replied briskly. She glanced up at the clock on the mantelpiece. "He should be back any time now, then you'll be able to see 'im."

As she spoke, Sep raised a finger. "Ah think ah can hear 'im now."

He walked over and opened the door and our Oscar strode in with all his old grace and majesty. He took one look at Helen and leaped onto her lap. With a cry of delight she put down her cup and stroked the beautiful fur as the cat arched himself against her hand and the familiar purr echoed round the room.

"He knows me," she murmured. "He knows me."

Sep nodded and smiled. "He does that. You were good to 'im. He'll never forget ye, and we won't either, will we mother?"

"No, we won't, Mrs. Herriot," his wife said as she applied butter to a slice of gingerbread. "That was a kind thing ye did for us and I 'ope you'll come and see us all whenever you're near."

"Well, thank you," I said. "We'd love to—we're often in Brawton."

I went over and tickled Oscar's chin, then I turned again to Mrs. Gibbons. "By the way, it's after nine o'clock. Where has he been till now?"

She poised her butter knife and looked into space.

"Let's see, now," she said. "It's Thursday, isn't it? Ah yes, it's 'is night for the Yoga class."

---

19. tableau (tab′ lō) *n.*: A dramatic scene or picture.

THINKING ABOUT THE SELECTION

Recalling

1. What happens to the cat during one of its trips from the Gibbonses' home?
2. Explain how Herriot and his wife help the cat.
3. Where does the cat go each time it wanders off from the Herriots' apartment?
4. What do Herriot and his wife discover about the cat that makes them laugh?
5. Explain how the cat is reunited with his first owners.

Interpreting

6. What is the effect of the injured cat's purring on Herriot and Tristan?
7. Why does Helen decide to give the cat up rather than claim "finders keepers"?
8. What qualities make this cat special?

Applying

9. Why do you think that many people enjoy having pets?

ANALYZING LITERATURE

Understanding the Narrative Essay

An **essay** is a brief and personal discussion of any topic that a writer wants to consider. A **narrative essay** considers the topic by telling a true story. In "Cat on the Go," Herriot gives a strong personal flavor to his narrative by telling you his thoughts and feelings. He writes about the healing cat, for example, ". . . it was sheer joy to watch the furry scarecrow fill out. . . ."

1. What is the topic of this narrative essay? What is Herriot's attitude toward the topic?
2. Identify three passages where Herriot tells you his thoughts or feelings about the topic.
3. How does Herriot's enjoyment of the cat increase your interest in the essay?
4. Compare and contrast reading a narrative essay and hearing a friend tell a story.

CRITICAL THINKING AND READING

Considering Another Perspective

This story is told from the point of view of James Herriot. That is why the sequence of events begins when Herriot first hears about the injured cat from Tristan. If the story had been told by Septimus Gibbons, however, it would have had a different shape.

1. How might the story have begun if Mr. Gibbons were telling it?
2. Which events in Herriot's story might *not* have been included in Gibbons' story?
3. Would Gibbons' story have ended in the same way? Why?

UNDERSTANDING LANGUAGE

Recognizing British English

Although the English language is used in Great Britain and America, it is not exactly the same in both countries. For example, James Herriot, a British writer, refers to "jumble sales." Americans, however, would use the phrase *rummage sales* to describe "sales of contributed articles to raise money for charity." Other British terms that appear in the story are *bed-sitter* and *surgery* (see footnotes 9 and 16).

Look up the following British terms in a dictionary—the abbreviation *Brit.* usually appears next to the British meaning—and use each in a sentence.

1. petrol 2. lorry 3. bonnet

THINKING AND WRITING

Creating a Television Program

This essay has actually been made into a television program. Pretend that you were the writer hired to create this show. The producer has told you, however, that there is not enough time to include every episode. List the episodes that you think *must* appear in the program. Then write a memo to the producer defending your list. When you revise the memo, make sure it is convincing.

GUIDE FOR READING

The Night the Bed Fell

James Thurber (1894–1961) lost the vision in one eye due to a childhood accident; however, he did not allow this disability to slow him down. He worked as a newspaper reporter and later wrote humorous pieces for *The New Yorker,* a famous magazine. In addition to being a talented writer, Thurber was a cartoonist. His amusing line drawings often accompany his writing. "The Night the Bed Fell," like many of his essays, describes the funny goings-on in his family.

Humorous Essay

A **humorous essay** is a brief work of nonfiction that is meant to amuse you. Many of James Thurber's humorous essays, like "The Night the Bed Fell," are about his lovable but silly relatives. During the night that Thurber tells about in this essay, each family member, including Thurber himself, has a different and mistaken idea of what is going on. The result is total confusion for the characters and a great deal of fun for the reader.

Look For

As you read, look for Thurber's descriptions of the "crotchets," or peculiar ideas, of his relatives. Be aware of how Briggs's unusual notions, in particular, add to the confusion of the night's events. Think about how all these peculiarities work together to make you laugh.

Writing

Thurber tells how a simple event snowballs into an outrageous episode. Recall a time when you took part in an event with an amusing outcome. Describe the people who were involved, and make a list of the main things that happened. Make sure your description shows what made the event humorous.

Vocabulary

Knowing the following words will help you as you read "The Night the Bed Fell."

ominous (äm'ə nəs) *adj.*: Threatening (p. 363)

allay (ə lā') *v.*: Put to rest; calm (p. 363)

fortitude (fôr' tə tood') *n.*: Firm courage (p. 364)

perilous (per' əl əs) *adj.*: Dangerous (p. 364)

deluge (del' yooj) *n.*: A great flood or rush of anything (p. 365)

pungent (pun' jənt) *adj.*: Sharp-smelling (p. 365)

extricate (eks' trə kāt') *v.*: Set free; disentangle (p. 365)

culprit (kul' prit) *n.*: Guilty person (p. 366)

The Night the Bed Fell

James Thurber

I suppose that the high-water mark of my youth in Columbus, Ohio, was the night the bed fell on my father. It makes a better recitation (unless, as some friends of mine have said, one has heard it five or six times) than it does a piece of writing, for it is almost necessary to throw furniture around, shake doors, and bark like a dog, to lend the proper atmosphere and verisimilitude[1] to what is admittedly a somewhat incredible tale. Still, it did take place.

It happened, then, that my father had decided to sleep in the attic one night, to be away where he could think. My mother opposed the notion strongly because, she said, the old wooden bed up there was unsafe: it was wobbly and the heavy headboard would crash down on father's head in case the bed fell, and kill him. There was no dissuading him, however, and at a quarter past ten he closed the attic door behind him and went up the narrow twisting stairs. We later heard ominous creakings as he crawled into bed. Grandfather, who usually slept in the attic bed when he was with us, had disappeared some days before. On these occasions he was usually gone six or eight days and returned growling and out of temper, with the news that the Federal Union[2] was run by a passel of blockheads and that the Army of the Potomac[3] didn't have a chance.

We had visiting us at this time a nervous first cousin of mine named Briggs Beall, who believed that he was likely to cease breathing when he was asleep. It was his feeling that if he were not awakened every hour during the night, he might die of suffocation. He had been accustomed to setting an alarm clock to ring at intervals until morning, but I persuaded him to abandon this. He slept in my room and I told him that I was such a light sleeper that if anybody quit breathing in the same room with me, I would wake instantly. He tested me the first night—which I had suspected he would—by holding his breath after my regular breathing had convinced him I was asleep. I was not asleep, however, and called to him. This seemed to allay his fears a little, but he took the precaution of putting a glass of spirits of camphor[4] on a little table at the head of his bed. In case I didn't arouse him until he was almost gone, he said, he would sniff the camphor, a powerful reviver. Briggs was not the only member of his family who had his crotchets.[5] Old Aunt Melissa Beall (who could whistle like a man, with two fingers in her mouth) suffered under the premonition that she was destined to die on South High Street, because she had been born on South High Street and married on South High Street. Then there was Aunt Sarah Shoaf, who never went to bed at night without the

---

1. verisimilitude (ver′ ə si mil′ə tōōd′) *n.*: The appearance of being true or real.
2. Federal Union: The Northern side during the Civil War. He is under the illusion that the Civil War has not yet ended.
3. Army of the Potomac: One of the Northern armies during the Civil War.

4. spirits of camphor: A liquid with a powerful odor.
5. crotchets (kräch′ its) *n.*: Peculiar or stubborn ideas.

Copyright © 1933, 1961 James Thurber
From *My Life and Hard Times,*
published by Harper & Row

fear that a burglar was going to get in and blow chloroform[6] under her door through a tube. To avert this calamity—for she was in greater dread of anesthetics than of losing her household goods—she always piled her money, silverware, and other valuables in a neat stack just outside her bedroom, with a note reading: "This is all I have. Please take it and do not use your chloroform, as this is all I have." Aunt Gracie Shoaf also had a burglar phobia, but she met it with more fortitude. She was confident that burglars had been getting into her house every night for forty years. The fact that she never missed any thing was to her no proof to the contrary. She always claimed that she scared them off before they could take anything, by throwing shoes down the hallway. When she went to bed she piled, where she could get at them handily, all the shoes there were about her house. Five minutes after she had turned off the light, she would sit up in bed and say "Hark!" Her husband, who had learned to ignore the whole situation as long ago as 1903, would either be sound asleep or pretend to be sound asleep. In either case he would not respond to her tugging and pulling, so that presently she would arise, tiptoe to the door, open it slightly and heave a shoe down the hall in one direction, and its mate down the hall in the other direction. Some nights she threw them all, some nights only a couple of pair.

But I am straying from the remarkable incidents that took place during the night that the bed fell on father. By midnight we were all in bed. The layout of the rooms and the disposition[7] of their occupants is important to an understanding of what later occurred. In the front room upstairs (just under father's attic bedroom) were my mother and my brother Herman, who sometimes sang in his sleep, usually "Marching Through Georgia" or "Onward, Christian Soldiers." Briggs Beall and myself were in a room adjoining this one. My brother Roy was in a room across the hall from ours. Our bull terrier, Rex, slept in the hall.

My bed was an army cot, one of those affairs which are made wide enough to sleep on comfortably only by putting up, flat with the middle section, the two sides which ordinarily hang down like the sideboards of a drop-leaf table. When these sides are up, it is perilous to roll too far toward the edge, for

---

6. chloroform (klôr'ə fôrm') *n.*: A substance used at one time as an anesthetic, or pain-killer, during operations because it can cause a person to pass out.

7. disposition (dis' pə zish' ən) *n.*: Arrangement.

then the cot is likely to tip completely over, bringing the whole bed down on top of one, with a tremendous banging crash. This, in fact, is precisely what happened about two o'clock in the morning. (It was my mother who, in recalling the scene later, first referred to it as "the night the bed fell on your father.")

Always a deep sleeper, slow to arouse (I had lied to Briggs), I was at first unconscious of what had happened when the iron cot rolled me onto the floor and toppled over on me. It left me still warmly bundled up and unhurt, for the bed rested above me like a canopy. Hence I did not wake up, only reached the edge of consciousness and went back. The racket, however, instantly awakened my mother, in the next room, who came to the immediate conclusion that her worst dread was realized: the big wooden bed upstairs had fallen on father. She therefore screamed, "Let's go to your poor father!" It was this shout, rather than the noise of my cot falling, that awakened Herman, in the same room with her. He thought that mother had become, for no apparent reason, hysterical. "You're all right, Mamma!" he shouted, trying to calm her. They exchanged shout for shout for perhaps ten seconds:

"Let's go to your poor father!" and "You're all right!" That woke up Briggs. By this time I was conscious of what was going on, in a vague way, but did not yet realize that I was under my bed instead of on it. Briggs, awakening in the midst of loud shouts of fear and apprehension, came to the quick conclusion that he was suffocating and that we were all trying to "bring him out." With a low moan, he grasped the glass of camphor at the head of his bed and instead of sniffing it poured it over himself. The room reeked of camphor. "Ugf, ahfg," choked Briggs, like a drowning man, for he had almost succeeded in stopping his breath under the deluge of pungent spirits. He leaped out of bed and groped toward the open window, but he came up against one that was closed. With his hand, he beat out the glass, and I could hear it crash and tinkle on the alleyway below. It was at this juncture that I, in trying to get up, had the uncanny sensation of feeling my bed above me! Foggy with sleep, I now suspected, in my turn, that the whole uproar was being made in a frantic endeavor to extricate me from what must be an unheard-of and perilous situation. "Get me out of this!"

I bawled. "Get me out!" I think I had the nightmarish belief that I was entombed in a mine. "Gugh," gasped Briggs, floundering in his camphor.

By this time my mother, still shouting, pursued by Herman, still shouting, was trying to open the door to the attic, in order to go up and get my father's body out of the wreckage. The door was stuck, however, and wouldn't yield. Her frantic pulls on it only added to the general banging and confusion. Roy and the dog were now up, the one shouting questions, the other barking.

Father, farthest away and soundest sleeper of all, had by this time been awakened by the battering on the attic door. He decided that the house was on fire. "I'm coming, I'm coming!" he wailed in a slow, sleepy voice—it took him many minutes to regain full consciousness. My mother, still believing he was caught under the bed, detected in his "I'm coming!" the mournful, resigned note of one who is preparing to meet his Maker. "He's dying!" she shouted.

"I'm all right!" Briggs yelled to reassure her. "I'm all right!" He still believed that it was his own closeness to death that was worrying mother. I found at last the light switch in my room, unlocked the door, and Briggs and I joined the others at the attic door. The dog, who never did like Briggs, jumped for him—assuming that he was the culprit in whatever was going on—and Roy had to throw Rex and hold him. We could hear father crawling out of bed upstairs. Roy pulled the attic door open, with a mighty jerk, and father came down the stairs, sleepy and irritable but safe and sound. My mother began to weep when she saw him. Rex began to howl. "What in the name of heaven is going on here?" asked father.

The situation was finally put together like a gigantic jigsaw puzzle. Father caught a cold from prowling around in his bare feet but there were no other bad results. "I'm glad," said mother, who always looked on the bright side of things, "that your grandfather wasn't here."

THINKING ABOUT THE SELECTION

Recalling

1. How does a difference of opinion between Thurber's parents set the stage for the events of the night?
2. What is Briggs's crotchet, or peculiar idea?
3. Describe the layout of the rooms and their placement or grouping. Why is their placement important to the plot of the story?
4. In chronological, or time, order, list the actions that occur after Thurber's cot collapses.

Interpreting

5. Why does Thurber introduce the essay with a description of some of his relatives?
6. Identify the moment at which the events reach their climax.
7. What evidence is there that Thurber felt affection for his family?

Applying

8. Would you like to have known the Thurber family? Why or why not?

ANALYZING LITERATURE

Understanding the Humorous Essay

A **humorous essay** is a brief work of nonfiction that is meant to amuse you. In "The Night the Bed Fell" much of the humor comes from the contrast between what is really happening and what the characters think is happening. For example, Thurber's mother believes that her husband lies crushed in the wreckage of his bed when he is really safely asleep.

1. Contrast what actual happens when the bed falls and what each character thinks is happening.
2. Would the essay be as funny if you were as confused about what happened as the characters are? Why?
3. At the beginning of the essay, Thurber writes, "It makes a better recitation . . . than it does a piece of writing, for it is almost necessary to throw furniture around, shake doors, and bark like a dog, to lend the proper atmosphere and verisimilitude to what is admittedly a somewhat incredible tale." Do you think such theatrics would make this funny tale even funnier? Why or why not?

CRITICAL THINKING AND READING

Identifying Exaggeration

Writers of humorous essays often **exaggerate,** or enlarge, their descriptions to make them funnier. In "The Night the Bed Fell," for example, Thurber says that Briggs poured a "deluge of pungent spirits" on himself. Of course, we know that Briggs did not really *flood* himself with camphor. The contrast between what is really happening and the exaggerated description is humorous.

In each of the following passages, point out what is exaggerated and explain the contrast between the exaggeration and the reality.

1. " 'Get me out of this!' I bawled. 'Get me out!' I think I had the nightmarish belief that I was entombed in a mine."
2. ". . . Herman, still shouting, was trying to open the door to the attic, in order to go up and get my father's body out of the wreckage."

THINKING AND WRITING

Creating a Humorous Essay

Recall the amusing events that you listed before reading the essay. Use this list to tell the story aloud to different friends. Each time you tell it, try to make it funnier by exaggerating one of the events. When you have perfected your narrative, write a humorous essay based on it. In revising the essay, make sure you have included the exaggerations that worked best when you told the story aloud. You may include humorous drawings, as Thurber did. When you are finished, share your essay with your classmates.

GUIDE FOR READING

Rattlesnake Hunt

Marjorie Kinnan Rawlings (1896–1953) was born in Washington, D.C., but later moved to rural Florida, where "Rattlesnake Hunt" is set. There at Cross Creek she wrote about the world around her, and eventually, she became famous for her novels describing life in that part of the country. *The Yearling* (1938), for example, an American classic, was made into a successful film. Animals often play a major part in her work. As you will see, she was even fascinated by such creatures as rattlesnakes.

Description in an Essay

When writers describe people or scenes, they use language that appeals to your senses so that their descriptions come alive for you. For example, a writer describing a beach might tell about the surf that roars like an express train and the sand that feels powdery and warm. Good descriptions are just as important in essays as in other types of writing. You will be less likely to pay attention to what an essay writer says if you cannot see in your mind the people and places being discussed. In "Rattlesnake Hunt," Marjorie Kinnan Rawlings gives a vivid description of a desolate area in Florida where rattlesnakes live.

Look For

As you read "Rattlesnake Hunt," let the writer's skillful descriptions help you visualize the rattlers and their environment. To which of your senses do her descriptions appeal?

Writing

Have you ever seen a snake in the woods or watched one at the zoo or on a television program? Describe the snake's appearance and the reaction you had when you saw it.

Vocabulary

Knowing the following words will help you as you read "Rattlesnake Hunt."

data (dāt′ ə) *n.*: Information (p. 369)

desolate (des′ ə lit) *adj.*: Lonely; solitary (p. 369)

conventional (kən ven′ shən'l) *adj.*: Ordinary; usual (p. 370)

translucent (trans loo′ s'nt) *adj.*: Clear (p. 370)

arid (ar′ id) *adj.*: Dry and barren (p. 370)

mortality (môr tal′ ə tē) *n.*: Having to die someday (p. 371)

preferable (pref′ ər ə b'l) *adj.*: More desirable (p. 371)

camouflaged (kam′ ə fläzhd′) *v.*: Disguised (p. 371)

Rattlesnake Hunt

Marjorie Kinnan Rawlings

Ross Allen, a young Florida herpetologist,[1] invited me to join him on a hunt in the upper Everglades[2]—for rattlesnakes. Ross and I drove to Arcadia in his coupé[3] on a warm January day.

I said, "How will you bring back the rattlesnakes?"

"In the back of my car."

My courage was not adequate to inquire whether they were thrown in loose and might be expected to appear between our feet. Actually, a large portable box of heavy close-meshed wire made a safe cage. Ross wanted me to write an article about his work and on our way to the unhappy hunting grounds I took notes on a mass of data that he had accumulated in years of herpetological research. The scientific and dispassionate detachment of the material and the man made a desirable approach to rattlesnake territory. As I had discovered with the insects and varmints,[4] it is difficult to be afraid of anything about which enough is known, and Ross' facts were fresh from the laboratory.

The hunting ground was Big Prairie, south of Arcadia and west of the northern tip of Lake Okeechobee. Big Prairie is a deso-

late cattle country, half marsh, half pasture, with islands of palm trees and cypress and oaks. At that time of year the cattlemen and Indians were burning the country, on the theory that the young fresh wire grass that springs up from the roots after a fire is the best cattle forage. Ross planned to hunt his rattlers in the forefront of the fires. They lived in winter, he said, in gopher holes, coming out in the midday warmth to forage, and would move ahead of the flames and be easily taken. We joined forces with a big man named Will, his snake-hunting companion of the territory, and set out in early morning, after a long rough drive over deep-rutted roads into the open wilds.

I hope never in my life to be so frightened as I was in those first few hours. I kept on Ross' footsteps, I moved when he moved,

---

1. herpetologist (hʉr′ pə täl′ ə jist) *n*.: Someone who studies reptiles and amphibians.
2. Everglades: A large region of swampland in southern Florida, about 100 miles long and 50–75 miles wide.
3. coupé (ko͞o pā′) *n*.: A small, two-door automobile.
4. varmints (vär′ mənts) *n*.: Animals regarded as troublesome.

sometimes jolting into him when I thought he might leave me behind. He does not use the forked stick of conventional snake hunting, but a steel prong, shaped like an L, at the end of a long stout stick. He hunted casually, calling my attention to the varying vegetation, to hawks overhead, to a pair of the rare whooping cranes that flapped over us. In mid-morning he stopped short, dropped his stick, and brought up a five-foot rattlesnake draped limply over the steel L. It seemed to me that I should drop in my tracks.

"They're not active at this season," he said quietly. "A snake takes on the temperature of its surroundings. They can't stand too much heat for that reason, and when the weather is cool, as now, they're sluggish."

The sun was bright overhead, the sky a translucent blue, and it seemed to me that it was warm enough for any snake to do as it willed. The sweat poured down my back. Ross dropped the rattler in a crocus sack[5] and Will carried it. By noon, he had caught four. I felt faint and ill. We stopped by a pond and went swimming. The region was flat, the horizon limitless, and as I came out of the cool blue water I expected to find myself surrounded by a ring of rattlers. There were only Ross and Will, opening the lunch basket. I could not eat. Will went back and drove his truck closer, for Ross expected the hunting to be better in the afternoon. The hunting was much better. When we went back to the truck to deposit two more rattlers in the wire cage, there was a rattlesnake lying under the truck.

Ross said, "Whenever I leave my car or truck with snakes already in it, other rattlers always appear. I don't know whether this is because they scent or sense the presence of other snakes, or whether in this arid area

they come to the car for shade in the heat of the day."

The problem was scientific, but I had no interest.

That night Ross and Will and I camped out in the vast spaces of the Everglades prairies. We got water from an abandoned well and cooked supper under buttonwood bushes by a flowing stream. The camp fire blazed cheerfully under the stars and a new moon lifted in the sky. Will told tall tales of the cattlemen and the Indians and we were at peace.

Ross said, "We couldn't have a better night for catching water snakes."

After the rattlers, water snakes seemed innocuous enough. We worked along the edge of the stream and here Ross did not use his L-shaped steel. He reached under rocks and along the edge of the water and brought out harmless reptiles with his hands. I had said nothing to him of my fears, but he un-

---

5. crocus sack: A term used in the southern United States for a burlap bag.

one had come out or was still in the hole. Sometimes the two men dug the snake out. At times it was down so long and winding a tunnel that the digging was hopeless. Then they blocked the entrance and went on to other holes. In an hour or so they made the original rounds, unblocking the holes. The rattler in every case came out hurriedly, as though anything were preferable to being shut in. All the time Ross talked to me, telling me the scientific facts he had discovered about the habits of the rattlers.

"They pay no attention to a man standing perfectly still," he said, and proved it by letting Will unblock a hole while he stood at the entrance as the snake came out. It was exciting to watch the snake crawl slowly beside and past the man's legs. When it was at a safe distance he walked within its range of vision, which he had proved to be no higher than a man's knee, and the snake whirled and drew back in an attitude[7] of fighting defense. The rattler strikes only for paralyzing and killing its food, and for defense.

"It is a slow and heavy snake," Ross said. "It lies in wait on a small game trail and strikes the rat or rabbit passing by. It waits a few minutes, then follows along the trail, coming to the small animal, now dead or dying. It noses it from all sides, making sure that it is its own kill, and that it is dead and ready for swallowing."

A rattler will lie quietly without revealing itself if a man passes by and it thinks it is not seen. It slips away without fighting if given the chance. Only Ross' sharp eyes sometimes picked out the gray and yellow diamond pattern, camouflaged among the grasses. In the cool of the morning, chilled by the January air, the snakes showed no fight. They could be looped up limply over the steel L and dropped in a sack or up into

derstood them. He brought a small dark snake from under a willow root.

"Wouldn't you like to hold it?" he asked. "People think snakes are cold and clammy, but they aren't. Take it in your hands. You'll see that it is warm."

Again, because I was ashamed, I took the snake in my hands. It was not cold, it was not clammy, and it lay trustingly in my hands, a thing that lived and breathed and had mortality[6] like the rest of us. I felt an upsurgence of spirit.

The next day was magnificent. The air was crystal, the sky was aquamarine, and the far horizon of palms and oaks lay against the sky. I felt a new boldness and followed Ross bravely. He was making the rounds of the gopher holes. The rattlers came out in the mid-morning warmth and were never far away. He could tell by their trails whether

---

6. had mortality: Would die.

7. attitude: (at′ ə tōōd′) *n.*: In this case, a position or posture of the body.

the wire cage on the back of Will's truck. As the sun mounted in the sky and warmed the moist Everglades earth, the snakes were warmed too, and Ross warned that it was time to go more cautiously. Yet having learned that it was we who were the aggressors; that immobility meant complete safety; that the snakes, for all their lightning flash in striking, were inaccurate in their aim, with limited vision; having watched again and again the liquid grace of movement, the beauty of pattern, suddenly I understood that I was drinking in freely the magnificent sweep of the horizon, with no fear of what might be at the moment under my feet. I went off hunting by myself, and though I found no snakes, I should have known what to do.

The sun was dropping low in the west. Masses of white cloud hung above the flat marshy plain and seemed to be tangled in the tops of distant palms and cypresses. The sky turned orange, then saffron.[8] I walked leisurely back toward the truck. In the distance I could see Ross and Will making their way in too. The season was more advanced than at the Creek, two hundred miles to the north, and I noticed that spring flowers were blooming among the lumpy hummocks.[9] I leaned over to pick a white violet. There was a rattlesnake under the violet.

If this had happened the week before, if it had happened the day before, I think I should have lain down and died on top of the rattlesnake, with no need of being struck and poisoned. The snake did not coil, but lifted its head and whirred its rattles lightly. I stepped back slowly and put the violet in a buttonhole. I reached forward and laid the steel L across the snake's neck, just back of the blunt head. I called to Ross:

"I've got one."

He strolled toward me.

"Well, pick it up," he said.

I released it and slipped the L under the middle of the thick body.

"Go put it in the box."

He went ahead of me and lifted the top of the wire cage. I made the truck with the rattler, but when I reached up the six feet to drop it in the cage, it slipped off the stick and dropped on Ross' feet. It made no effort to strike.

"Pick it up again," he said. "If you'll pin it down lightly and reach just back of its head with your hand, as you've seen me do, you can drop it in more easily."

I pinned it and leaned over.

"I'm awfully sorry," I said, "but you're pushing me a little too fast."

He grinned. I lifted it on the stick and again as I had it at head height, it slipped off, down Ross' boots and on top of his feet. He stood as still as a stump. I dropped the snake on his feet for the third time. It seemed to me that the most patient of rattlers might in time resent being hauled up and down, and for all the man's quiet certainty that in standing motionless there was no danger, would strike at whatever was nearest, and that would be Ross.

I said, "I'm just not man enough to keep this up any longer," and he laughed and reached down with his smooth quickness and lifted the snake back of the head and dropped it in the cage. It slid in among its mates and settled in a corner. The hunt was over and we drove back over the uneven trail to Will's village and left him and went on to Arcadia and home. Our catch for the two days was thirty-two rattlers.

I said to Ross, "I believe that tomorrow I could have picked up that snake."

Back at the Creek, I felt a new lightness. I had done battle with a great fear, and the victory was mine.

---

8. saffron (saf′ rən) *adj.*: Orange-yellow.
9. hummocks (hum′ əks) *n.*: Areas of fertile, wooded land, higher than the surrounding swamp.

THINKING ABOUT THE SELECTION

Recalling

1. Why does Rawlings go on the rattlesnake hunt?
2. Describe the area to which she, Will, and Ross travel.
3. How does she show her fear of rattlesnakes?
4. Tell two facts she learns about rattlers.
5. How does she show that she has partly overcome her fear.

Interpreting

6. Why do Rawlings' feelings about snakes change when she holds one?
7. How do experience and knowledge influence her feelings about rattlers?
8. What reason can you suggest for rattlers having a "gray and yellow diamond pattern"?
9. At the end of the selection, why does Rawlings feel "a new lightness"? Is the victory truly hers?

Applying

10. Why does knowledge often drive away fear?

ANALYZING LITERATURE

Understanding Description in Essays

Descriptive passages include lively language and details that appeal to your senses. In this essay, for example, Rawlings writes: "Masses of white cloud . . . seemed to be tangled in the tops of distant palms and cypresses. The sky turned orange, then saffron." She helps you to see this scene by using many colors in her description: white, orange, and saffron. By using the verb "tangled," she gives you a vivid picture of the way the clouds look in the trees.

1. Find two other passages where Rawlings tells you the color of what she describes.
2. At the start of the essay, she writes: "In mid-morning he . . . brought up a five-foot rattlesnake draped limply over the steel L." Would this description have been better or worse if she had written "hanging" instead of "draped limply"? Why?

CRITICAL THINKING AND READING

Separating Fact from Opinion

A **fact** is something that can be proven, while an **opinion** is a person's belief or impression. Rawlings' statement that "The sweat poured down my back," is a fact. However, when she says, " 'I believe that tomorrow I could have picked up that snake,' " she is stating an opinion.

As you read essays, you should be able to separate fact from opinion. Indicate which of the following passages from this essay are facts and which are opinions.

1. "Our catch for the two days was thirty-two rattlers."
2. "It seemed to me that the most patient of rattlers might in time resent being hauled up and down. . . ."
3. "We stopped by a pond and went swimming."
4. "If this had happened the week before, . . . I think I should have lain down and died on top of the rattlesnake. . . ."

THINKING AND WRITING

Writing a Description

The year is 2020. A distant planet has just entered into radio communication with Earth. The people of this planet are eager to discover what kind of animals exist here. Choose a type of animal that you have often observed and list its important qualities. Then use your list to write a description of it that will satisfy the curiosity of these extraterrestrial creatures. In revising your work, make sure your description gives them a clear picture of the animal you have chosen.

GUIDE FOR READING

How to Enjoy Poetry

James Dickey (1923–   ) was born in Atlanta, Georgia, and attended Vanderbilt University. As a young man, he was a football player and a motorcycle enthusiast. Although these interests are not usually associated with poetry, Dickey is one of America's best-known poets. He is also famous for his novel *Deliverance* (1970), which was made into a film. In this selection, he demonstrates that poetry was not "invented as a school subject" and explains how to enjoy poetry as only a writer can.

Expository Essay

The purpose of an **expository essay** is to explain a subject or give information about it. You may have seen magazine articles with titles such as "How to Build Your Vocabulary" or "How to Operate a Computer." These articles explaining a process are expository essays. However, unlike many "How-to" articles, "How to Enjoy Poetry" does not give you rules that you *must* follow to achieve a goal. Instead, its purpose is to explain the value of poetry and offer suggestions for appreciating it.

Look For

Expository essays often contain key ideas. As you read "How to Enjoy Poetry," look for the **bold print** headings and use them as guideposts. The first sentence after each heading usually contains a key idea.

Writing

Dickey writes of the ice cube, "what more mysterious and beautiful *interior* of something has there ever been?" Look closely at an ice cube. Freewrite about what you see.

Vocabulary

Knowing the following words will help you as you read "How to Enjoy Poetry."

emblems (em′ bləmz) *n.*: Signs; symbols (p. 376)

encounter (in koun′ tər) *n.*: Meeting (p. 376)

compelling (kəm pel′ iŋ) *adj.*: Having a powerful effect (p. 377)

prose (prōz) *n.*: Nonpoetic language (p. 377)

definitive (di fin′ ə tiv) *adj.*: Final; the last word (p. 377)

inevitability (in ev′ ə tə b'l′ i tē) *n.*: Certainty (p. 377)

interacts (in′ tər akts′) *v.*: Affects and is affected by (p. 378)

vital (vīt′'l) *adj.*: Essential to life; living (p. 378)

How to Enjoy Poetry

James Dickey

What is poetry? And why has it been around so long? Many have suspected that it was invented as a school subject, because you have to take exams on it. But that is not what poetry is or why it is still around. That's not what it feels like, either. When you really feel it, a new part of you happens, or an old part is renewed, with surprise and delight at being what it is.

Where Poetry Is Coming From

From the beginning, people have known that words and things, words and actions, words and feelings, go together, and that they can go together in thousands of different ways, according to who is using them. Some ways go shallow, and some go deep.

Your Connection with Other Imaginations

The first thing to understand about poetry is that it comes to you from outside you, in books or in words, but that for it to live, something from within you must come to it and meet it and complete it. Your response with your own mind and body and memory and emotions gives the poem its ability to work its magic; if you give to it, it will give to you, and give plenty.

When you read, don't let the poet write down to you; read up to him. Reach for him from your gut out, and the heart and muscles will come into it, too.

Which Sun? Whose Stars?

The sun is new every day, the ancient philosopher Heraclitus[1] said. The sun of poetry is new every day, too, because it is seen in different ways by different people who have lived under it, lived with it, responded to it. Their lives are different from yours, but by means of the special spell that poetry brings to the *fact* of the sun—everybody's sun; yours, too—you can come into possession of many suns: as many as men and women have ever been able to imagine. Poetry makes possible the deepest kind of personal possession of the world.

The most beautiful constellation in the winter sky is Orion,[2] which ancient poets thought looked like a hunter, up there, moving across heaven with his dog Sirius.[3] What is this hunter made out of stars hunting for? What does he mean? Who owns him, if

---

1. Heraclitus (her' ə klīt' əs): A Greek philosopher who lived about 500 B.C.
2. Orion (ō rī' ən)
3. Sirius (sir' ē əs)

THE STARRY NIGHT, 1889
Vincent van Gogh
The Museum of Modern Art

anybody? The poet Aldous Huxley[4] felt that he did, and so, in Aldous Huxley's universe of personal emotion, he did.

> *Up from among the emblems of the*
> *wind into its heart of power,*
> *The Huntsman climbs, and all his*
> *living stars*
> *Are bright, and all are mine.*

---

4. **Aldous Huxley:** An English poet, essayist, and novelist (1894–1963).

Where to Start

The beginning of your true encounter with poetry should be simple. It should by-pass all classrooms, all textbooks, courses, examinations, and libraries and go straight to the things that make your own existence exist: to your body and nerves and blood and muscles. Find your own way—a secret way that just maybe you don't know yet—to open yourself as wide as you can and as deep as you can to the moment, the *now* of your own existence and the endless mystery of it, and perhaps at the same time to one other thing that is not you, but is out there: a handful of gravel is a good place to start. So is an ice cube—what more mysterious and beautiful *interior* of something has there ever been?

As for me, I like the sun, the source of all living things, and on certain days very good-feeling, too. "Start with the sun," D. H. Lawrence[5] said, "and everything will slowly, slowly happen." Good advice. And a lot *will* happen.

What is more fascinating than a rock, if you really feel it and *look* at it, or more interesting than a leaf?

> *Horses, I mean; butterflies, whales;*
> *Mosses, and stars; and gravelly*
> *Rivers, and fruit.*
>
> *Oceans, I mean; black valleys; corn;*
> *Brambles, and cliffs; rock, dirt, dust,*
> *ice . . .*

Go back and read this list—it is quite a list, Mark Van Doren's[6] list!—item by item. Slowly. Let each of these things call up an image out of your own life.

Think and feel. What moss do you see? Which horse? What field of corn? What brambles are *your* brambles? Which river is most yours?

The Poem's Way of Going

Part of the spell of poetry is in the rhythm of language, used by poets who understand how powerful a factor rhythm can be, how compelling and unforgettable. Almost anything put into rhythm and rhyme is more memorable than the same thing said in prose. Why this is, no one knows completely, though the answer is surely rooted far down in the biology by means of which we exist; in the circulation of the blood that goes forth from the heart and comes back, and in the repetition of breathing. Croesus[7] was a rich Greek king, back in the sixth century before Christ, but this tombstone was not his:

> *No Croesus lies in the grave you see;*
> *I was a poor laborer, and this suits*
> *me.*

That is plain-spoken and definitive. You believe it, and the rhyme helps you believe it and keep it.

Some Things You'll Find Out

Writing poetry is a lot like a contest with yourself, and if you like sports and games and competitions of all kinds, you might like to try writing some. Why not?

The possibilities of rhyme are great. Some of the best fun is in making up your own limericks.[8] There's no reason you can't invent limericks about anything that comes to your mind. No reason. Try it.

The problem is to find three words that rhyme and fit into a meaning. "There was a young man from . . ." *Where* was he from? What situation was he in? How can these things fit into the limerick form—a form everybody knows—so that the rhymes "pay off," and give that sense of completion and inevitability that is so deliciously memorable that nothing else is like it?

---

5. D. H. Lawrence: An English poet and novelist (1885–1930).
6. Mark Van Doren: An American poet, teacher, and critic (1894–1972).

7. Croesus (krē′ səs)
8. limericks (lim′ ər iks) *n*.: Nonsense poems of five lines.

SIMULTANEOUS CONTRASTS: SUN AND MOON, 1913
Robert Delaunay
The Museum of Modern Art

How It Goes with You

The more your encounter with poetry deepens, the more your experience of your own life will deepen, and you will begin to see things by means of words, and words by means of things.

You will come to understand the world as it interacts with words, as it can be re-created by words, by rhythms and by images.

You'll understand that this condition is one charged with vital possibilities. You will pick up meaning more quickly—and you will *create* meaning, too, for yourself and for others.

Connections between things will exist for you in ways that they never did before. They will shine with unexpectedness, wide-openness, and you will go toward them, on your own path. "Then . . ." as Dante[9] says, ". . . Then will your feet be filled with good desire." You will know this is happening the first time you say, of something you never would have noticed before, "Well, would you look at *that*! Who'd 'a thunk it?" (Pause, full of new light)

"*I* thunk it!"

---

9. Dante (dän' tä): An Italian poet (1265–1321) whose most famous work is *The Divine Comedy*.

THINKING ABOUT THE SELECTION
Recalling

1. According to James Dickey, how can you get the most from a poem?
2. How can poetry help you to own "many suns"?
3. Why are rhythm and rhyme important to poetry?
4. How is poetry "like a contest with yourself"?

Interpreting

5. What does Dickey mean when he writes, "when you read, don't let the poet write down to you; read up to him"? Why would reading this way increase your enjoyment?
6. Why do you think Dickey relates rhythm in poetry to biology?
7. What does he mean by asking you "to open yourself as wide as you can and as deep as you can to the moment. . . ."?

Applying

8. Dickey says you can enjoy poetry more by focusing on yourself and also on "one other thing that is not you." Which "other thing" would you choose? Why?

ANALYZING LITERATURE
Understanding the Expository Essay

The purpose of an **expository essay** is to explain a subject rather than present a story. In "How to Enjoy Poetry," James Dickey explains why poetry is valuable not as a school subject but as a response to life. He also offers suggestions for getting the most from poems.

1. What key idea does Dickey offer under the heading "Your connection with other imaginations"? What key idea does he offer under the heading "Which sun? Whose stars?"
2. Identify three suggestions that he offers for increasing your enjoyment of poetry.
3. Which suggestion do you find most helpful? Why?

CRITICAL THINKING AND READING
Experimenting with a Suggestion

In the section of this essay entitled "Where to Start," Dickey suggests reading a list of things in a poem and responding to each item.

1. Choose three items from the list in the poem.
2. Freewrite about the picture that each of these items calls up in you.
3. Has writing about these items given you a better appreciation of the lines from the poem? Why or why not?

UNDERSTANDING LANGUAGE
Recognizing the Latin Root *Vita-*

One of the words in this essay is *vital,* which means "living" or "essential to life." The Latin root *vita-,* which is the source of this word, means "life." This root is also part of other English words whose meaning is related to "life."

Write the meaning of each of the following *vita-* words or phrases. If you do not know what the word means, try to figure out the meaning and check your answer in a dictionary. Then use each word in a sentence.

1. vitality
2. vitamin
3. vitalize
4. vital signs

THINKING AND WRITING
Writing an Expository Essay

Imagine that a friend has moved to another city and you have told him or her about a new hobby you have taken up. This hobby can be anything you really like doing. Your friend wants to know about your hobby and to understand why you enjoy it so much. List the key aspects of your hobby and the reasons why it is fun. Then use this list to write a letter to your friend explaining what you do and why you enjoy it. In revising your letter, put yourself in your friend's place. Make sure that he or she will understand the value of what you do.

GUIDE FOR READING

Letter Writing

Andrew A. Rooney (1919–   ) received a bronze star for his service in the Air Force during World War II, and among his many books are *Air Gunner* and *The Fortunes of War*. He has also been a newspaper columnist for the *New York Herald Tribune*. Rooney, however, is probably best known for his work in television. He received television's highest award, the Emmy, and he appears often on the CBS show *60 Minutes*. In the essay "Letter Writing," he expresses himself as strongly in writing as he usually does on the air.

Persuasive Essay

A **persuasive essay** is a brief work of nonfiction in which a writer tries to convince you to accept a certain idea or view or to act a certain way. Writers usually offer arguments, or reasons, to support their position. In "Letter Writing," for example, Andrew A. Rooney states his opinion about personal letters at the start of his essay. Then he presents a variety of arguments to back up this idea.

Look For

Rooney states his main point in the first paragraph. React to this idea. Form an opinion of it. Then, as you read the essay, ask yourself whether Rooney's arguments are convincing and whether they cause you to agree with him.

Writing

Recall a time when you had to persuade someone that you were right. Tell what the discussion was about, how you tried to convince this person, and whether you were successful. If you were not, what might you have done to ensure your success?

Vocabulary

Knowing the following words will help you as you read "Letter Writing."

conspiring (kən spir′ iŋ) *v.*: Combining; working together (p. 381)
deteriorated (di tir′ ē ə rāt′ id) *v.*: Became worse (p. 381)
provisional (prə vizh′ ə n'l) *adj.*: Temporary, depending on future events (p. 381)

bias (bī′ əs) *n.*: Preference; learning; prejudice (p. 383)
retrospect (ret′ rə spekt′) *n.*: A looking back on the past (p. 383)

Letter Writing

Andrew A. Rooney

There ought to be a five-cent stamp for personal letters. Letter writing is one of the good things about a civilized society, and it should be encouraged. It's a shame that everything is conspiring against letter writing. Our whole postal system has deteriorated to the point where mail is no fun at all. The excitement we used to feel about the arrival of the mailman is gone.

It costs twenty-two cents for a regular stamp now. That's a terrible number, and you don't dare buy a roll of twenty-two-cent stamps because you know it's going to change before you get used to it and certainly before you use up a roll.

I object to the fact that it costs me more to send a letter to a friend than it costs some fly-by-night real estate operator to send me a phony brochure in the mail telling me I'm the provisional winner of a $10,000 sweepstakes. I don't like strangers knocking on my door trying to sell me something, and I don't want my mail cluttered with advertising. If anyone wants to accuse me of feeling that way because I make a living from the advertising found in newspapers and on television, go ahead and accuse me of it. It isn't true.

I don't get five good, genuine, personal letters a year. The time is coming when the letter written with pen and ink and sent as a personal message from one person to another will be as much of a rarity as the gold pocket watch carried on a chain. It's a shame.

There is something special about a personal letter. It's better than a phone call, no matter what the telephone company says. A phone call disappears into the air as soon as the receiver is put back on the hook. A good letter can last a lifetime.

Some of my most precious possessions are letters that have been written to me sometime in the past. I don't have a single memorable phone call stored in a box in my attic or basement. I've never thrown away a good letter and, like any real treasure, I don't even have to look at them to enjoy having them. I *know* I have them. The telephone calls come and go. They make no permanent impression on me and have no place in my memory.

A personal letter is a good thing because you say things you can't say in a crowd and might not even say to the person face to face. If you feel like it, a letter allows you to take yourself and your thoughts more seriously than you would dare take them in conversation. And you can say things without interruption.

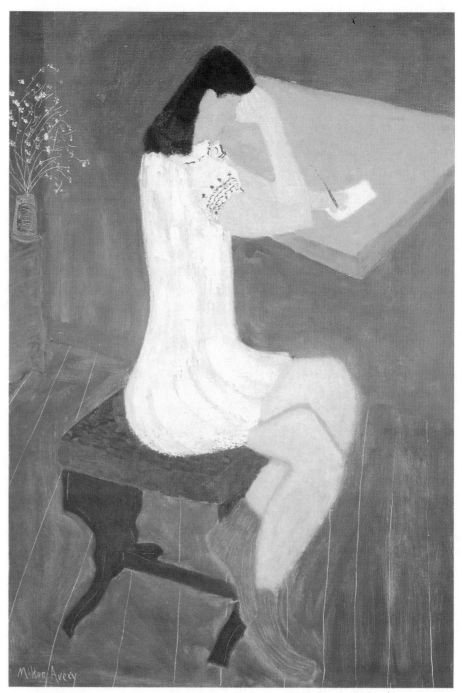

GIRL WRITING
Milton Avery
The Phillips Collection

A good letter is, in many ways, the exact opposite of a political speech. A politician addressing a crowd has to talk so broadly and generally about the issues in order not to offend any one of the thousands of people listening that he usually ends up saying nothing. A letter can be specific, and if the writer has some bias or prejudice, he can even reveal his true self by letting this show. Writing a friend, you shouldn't have to be careful. Abraham Lincoln's letter to his stepbrother telling him he wasn't going to loan him the eighty dollars he asked for tells you more about Abraham Lincoln than the Gettysburg Address does.

Some of our best history has come that way, from personal letters of famous people that scholars have dug up. You get a better idea of what someone is really like from a personal letter they weren't expecting you to read than you get from a carefully considered public statement they've made. We say real things in letters.

There are several reasons why we aren't writing many personal letters. We don't write letters with news of the family because we already have that by telephone; we don't write secrets because we're all so aware that they may fall into the wrong hands and end up in print; and we don't write awkward love letters much anymore because we're afraid of sounding silly. Love letters were almost always silly, but only in retrospect. The moment it is opened and read, a love letter is never silly. That's the other good thing about a personal letter. If you know each other well, it doesn't have to make absolute sense to anyone else.

Personal letters should go for a five-cent stamp.

Recalling

1. Rooney clearly states his thesis, or main idea, at the beginning of the essay. What is it?
2. Tell three of the arguments that Rooney uses to support this idea.
3. Explain why he thinks "A good letter is . . . the exact opposite of a political speech."
4. According to Rooney, why do people no longer write personal letters?

Interpreting

5. What does Rooney mean by saying that you can "take . . . your thoughts more seriously" in a letter than in a conversation? Do you agree with this? Why or why not?
6. What does he mean when he says that love letters are silly "only in retrospect" and not when received?

Applying

7. Would you rather get a letter or a phone call from a friend in a distant city. Why?

ANALYZING LITERATURE

Understanding the Persuasive Essay

A **persuasive essay** is a brief work of nonfiction in which a writer tries to convince you to accept a certain idea or view or to act a certain way. In "Letter Writing," for example, Andrew Rooney argues that personal letters should require only a five-cent stamp.

1. Why does he discuss the cost of personal letters at the start and end of the essay?
2. Identify two of his arguments that you think are especially persuasive.
3. Explain why the arguments you have chosen are convincing.

CRITICAL THINKING AND READING

Understanding Contrasts

Contrasting means showing differences. Writers often use this technique to indicate how an idea or approach they favor is better than others. For example, Andrew Rooney points up the value of personal letters by contrasting them with other types of communication. Explain how he uses each of the following contrasts to show that letters are superior.

1. Personal letters versus telephone calls
2. Personal letters versus political speeches

SPEAKING AND LISTENING

Debating a Premise

A **premise** is a statement that can be **debated,** meaning that reasons can be given for and against it. For example, the following statement from the essay can be taken as a premise for debate: . . . "a personal letter [is] better than a phone call. . . ."

Your teacher will divide you into two debating teams and a group that will judge the debate. One team will argue for the premise and the other against it.

Brainstorm for arguments. Then choose a speaker to present your case. If you are a judge, rate the two speakers on a scale of 1 (worst) to 5 (best) in the following categories: quality of evidence; organization; speaking skill.

THINKING AND WRITING

Writing a Persuasive Essay

Imagine that your school is running a contest. The prize is a free day to visit a park or a museum, see a sports event, or attend a concert. To win you must convince the panel of teachers that what you choose to do is educational. First select the activity that you would like to pursue. Then list the educational advantages of this activity. Use your list to write a persuasive essay that will win you a free day. In revising the essay, put yourself in the panel's place. Stress the arguments that will be the most convincing to them.

Essays in the Content Areas

THE LIBRARY
J. Lawrence
National Museum of American Art
The Smithsonian Institution

GUIDE FOR READING

Endlessness

Isaac Asimov (1920–   ) was born in Russia and grew up in Brooklyn. He has a Ph.D. in biochemistry, a subject he taught at Boston University from 1949 to 1958, when he turned to full-time writing. It is said that since 1969 he has written a book a month. His nonfiction works, such as the essay you are about to read, are admirable for making scientific and technological subjects understandable to the general reader. In this essay, he explores the subject of endlessness. What does it mean for something to be without end?

Outlining

Outlining means organizing the content of a piece of writing to show the main ideas and supporting details. An outline might look as follows:

    I. First main topic
        A. First subtopic
            1. First supporting idea or detail
            2. Second supporting idea or detail
        B. Second subtopic
    II. Second main topic {The outline continues in the same way.}

By dividing an essay into its main ideas and supporting details, you will understand and remember more of what you read.

Look For

As you read "Endlessness," pick out the main mathematical ideas of each of the four parts of the essay. Also, try to decide why other material is included—to explain, to illustrate, to clarify, or to achieve some other purpose.

Writing

Imagine a world without mathematics. Freewrite about the changes that would occur in your everyday life.

Vocabulary

Knowing the following words will help you as you read "Endlessness."

succession (sək sesh' ən) *n.*: The act of coming after another in order (p. 388)

clamoring (klam' ər iŋ) *v.*: Loudly demanding (p. 388)

expectantly (ik spek' tənt lē) *adv.*: In a way that shows eager waiting (p. 389)

conceivable (kən sē' və b'l) *adj.*: Imaginable (p. 389)

denumerable (di noo' mər ə b'l) *adj.*: Countable—said of a set whose elements can be put in one-to-one correspondence with the natural integers (p. 389)

Endlessness

Isaac Asimov

The "Not-a-Number"

Anyone thinking about numbers must come to the conclusion that there are a great many of them, and feel at a loss to express just how many. In poetry, one could make use of some simile: "as many as the sands of the sea"; "as numerous as the stars that shine and twinkle in the Milky Way."

To the mathematician, however, similes are of no use. To him, it merely seems that the integers are formed by beginning with one, adding one to that for the next number, and one to that for the next number, and so on. Since the mathematical rules do not set any limits to addition (*any* two numbers may be added) there can be no end to this process. After all, however large a number is named—*however* large—though it stretch in a line of small figures from here to the farthest star, it is always possible to say "that number plus one" and have a still higher number.

The series of integers, if written in order, 1, 2, 3 . . . is "infinite," a word coming from Latin words meaning "no end." Consequently, when we can write the series of numbers thus: 1, 2, 3. . . , we mean "1, 2, 3, and so on endlessly."

In the same way if we consider the negative numbers, -1, -2, -3, and so on, we can see that they too go on forever and can be written: -1, -2, -3 . . . Similarly, the series of positive imaginaries may be written as $+1i$, $+2i$, $+3i$ . . . , and the negative imaginaries as $-1i$, $-2i$, $-3i$ . . .

Now let's consider another kind of series of integers. Let's think of the even numbers: 2, 4, 6, 8, and so on. How many even numbers are there?

One way of arguing this question would be to say: Well, the integers can be divided into odd numbers and even numbers alternately, so that in the first ten numbers there are five odds and five evens, in the first hundred numbers there are fifty odds and fifty evens, and so on. This sort of thing would go on no matter how many integers are taken. Therefore, the total number of even integers is half the total number of all integers.

But this is not so. The number of integers is infinite, and one cannot talk of "a half of infinity."

Instead, consider the even integers this way. The series 2, 4, 6, 8 . . . can continue endlessly. There is no "largest even number" any more than there is a "largest number." For though you name an even number written in small numerals from here to the farthest star, it is always possible to say "that number plus two." Hence the series of even numbers should be written: 2, 4, 6 . . .

In the same way, odd numbers are 1, 3, 5 . . . ; the series of numbers, counting by fives , are 5, 10, 15 . . . ; and the series of numbers counting by millions are 1000000, 2000000, 3000000 . . . All these series of integers are endless and that is all that infinity (or an infinite number) means.

Counting Without Counting

But this may not satisfy you. Surely, you may be thinking, even though the series of even numbers is endless and the series of all integers is endless, the fact still remains that there are only half as many even numbers as there are all integers, and that there are only a millionth as many even-million numbers. It stands to reason!

(Never trust an argument *only* because it stands to reason. It stands to reason that if a man is facing north, his back is toward the south. However, if he's standing at the South Pole and is facing north, his back is also toward the north.)

Well, then, let's settle the matter by finding out how many even numbers there are compared with all the integers. How, if the quantity is endless? Why, we'll count.

Let's first see what we mean by counting. In the ordinary meaning of the word, we count objects by assigning each one a number in succession. This object is number one, that is number two, the other is number three, and so on. When we finish, if the last object was assigned number ten, then there are ten objects.

But can we count without numbers? So used are we to numbers for the purpose, that this sounds as though I were asking, Can we count without counting?—and yet we can.

Suppose you have a number of lollipops (you don't know how many) and a crowd of clamoring children (you don't know how many). You distribute the lollipops, one to a child, and when you are finished, all the children have lollipops and you still have additional lollipops in your hand. Obviously, then, even without counting in the ordinary fashion, you know there were more lollipops than children. If, on the other hand, you ran out of lollipops while some children still stood expectantly waiting, you would know there were more children than lollipops.

But if, at the conclusion of the distribution, each child had a lollipop, and there were no children left unsatisfied and no lollipops left in your hand, then you would know beyond the shadow of a doubt, and without ever having counted in the usual fashion, that the number of children was equal to the number of lollipops.

This way of counting, then, which consists of lining up two series (one of children and one of lollipops; or one of all integers and one of even numbers) will tell you whether the two series are equal or unequal; and, if unequal, which is the larger.

Suppose we line up the series of all integers and all even numbers, then, as follows:

$$1 \; 2 \; 3 \; 4 \; 5 \; 6 \; 7 \; 8 \; 9 \; 10 \; . \; . \; .$$
$$\updownarrow \; \updownarrow \; \updownarrow \; \updownarrow \; \updownarrow \; \updownarrow \; \updownarrow \; \updownarrow \; \updownarrow \; \updownarrow$$
$$2 \; 4 \; 6 \; 8 \; 10 \; 12 \; 14 \; 16 \; 18 \; 20 \; . \; . \; .$$

As you see there is an even number for every conceivable integer, and you can obtain the even number by simply doubling the integer. No matter how far you go, no integer need be omitted and no even number is missing. (Every child, in other words, is being satisfied with a lollipop.) At no point, no matter how far you go, will you find an integer for which you can't write an even number, and each integer (no matter how many you've gone through) has a different even number attached to it.

Does this mean that there are exactly as many even numbers as there are integers all together? Well, the phrase "as many" doesn't really have the usual everyday meaning when we're talking about things that are endless. Instead it is more proper to say that the series of even numbers is "in one-to-one corre-

spondence" with the series of all integers; meaning that the even numbers can be lined up systematically with the integers so that there is one of the first series for every one of the second and vice versa.

You can also set up a series of numbers counting by millions and compare it with the series of all integers in the same way. For every integer there's an even-million number obtained by multiplying the integer by a million. For 1 there's 1000000, for 6 there's 6000000, for 2873 there's 2873000000 and so on. So there are "as many" numbers counting by a million as there are integers altogether. Or, at least, the two series are in one-to-one correspondence. Any series of numbers that is in one-to-one correspondence with the series of integers is said to be "denumerable." And the set of integers is also called "denumerable."

The Infinite in a Nutshell

Of course, the "infinite" gives one a notion of vastness and foreverness. It may even seem to you to have no usefulness.

However, even if we concerned ourselves only with small numbers, notions of "infinity" would crop up. For instance, suppose we were to divide 1 by $\frac{1}{10}$. Remembering the reciprocal rule, this is the same as 1×10 and therefore $1 \div \frac{1}{10} = 10$. Similarly, $1 \div \frac{1}{100} = 100$, and $1 \div \frac{1}{1000} = 1000$.

In fact, the smaller you make your divisor, the larger your quotient becomes.

Indeed, when you divide 1 (or any number) by a series of numbers that grow smaller and smaller, then the quotient grows larger and larger, and as the divisor grows endlessly small, the answer grows endlessly large.

However, what, you may wonder, is meant by "endlessly small"? Surely smallness has an end at zero. Ah, but smallness may be expressed in the form of a fraction. Thus $\frac{1}{10}$ is a small number, $\frac{1}{100}$ is smaller, $\frac{1}{1000}$ is smaller still. There is no limit to the smallness as you increase the number of zeros to $\frac{1}{100000000000000000}$ . . . for no matter how far you increase it you never quite reach zero.

We may therefore also say: When you divide 1 (or any number) by a series of numbers that grows larger and larger, then the quotient grows smaller and smaller, and as the divisor grows endlessly large, the answer grows endlessly small.

Note, however, that we can never divide any number by 0. This operation is excluded from mathematics. And for a very good reason. What number, for instance, would be the quotient if we tried to divide 6, say, by 0? We would have $\frac{6}{0} = ?$ In other words, what number *times* zero comes out 6? There is no such number, since every number times 0 is 0. So we can never divide any number by 0.

The interval between any two numbers, say between 1 and 2, can be divided into any number of fractions by breaking it up into millionths, or trillionths, and each trillionth into trillionths and so on. This can be done for any smaller interval, such as that between $\frac{1}{4}$ and $\frac{1}{2}$ or between 0.0000000 and 0.0000001.

And yet mathematicians have managed to show that all conceivable fractions (that is, all rational numbers) can be arranged in such a way that a one-to-one correspondence can be set up with the series of integers. For every integer there will be a fraction, and vice versa, with no integers left out and no fractions left out. The series of all possible fractions is therefore denumerable.

Closer and Closer and Closer . . .

Consider a series of fractions like this: $\frac{1}{2}, \frac{1}{4}, \frac{1}{8}, \frac{1}{16}, \frac{1}{32}, \frac{1}{64}, \frac{1}{128}, \frac{1}{256}, \frac{1}{512},$ and so on endlessly.

Notice that each fraction is one-half the size of the preceding fraction, since the denominator doubles each time. (After all, if you take any of the fractions in the series, say $\frac{1}{128}$, and divide it by 2, that is the same as multiplying it by $\frac{1}{2}$, and $\frac{1}{128} \times \frac{1}{2} = \frac{1}{256}$, the denominator doubling.)

Although the fractions get continually smaller, the series can be considered endless because no matter how small the fractions get, it is always possible to multiply the denominator by 2 and get a still smaller fraction and the next in the series. Furthermore, the fractions never quite reach zero because the denominator can get larger endlessly and it is only if an end could be reached (which it can't) that the fraction could reach zero.

The question is, What is the sum of all those fractions? It might seem that the sum of an endless series of numbers must be endlessly large ("it stands to reason") but let's start adding, anyway.

First $\frac{1}{2}$ plus $\frac{1}{4}$ is $\frac{3}{4}$. Add $\frac{1}{8}$ and the sum is $\frac{7}{8}$; add $\frac{1}{16}$ and the sum is $\frac{15}{16}$; and $\frac{1}{32}$ and the sum is $\frac{31}{32}$, and so on.

Notice that after the first two terms of the series are added, the sum is $\frac{3}{4}$ which is only $\frac{1}{4}$ short of 1. Addition of the third term

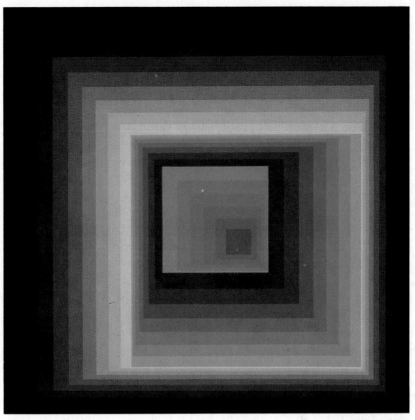

REYTEY, 1968
Victor Vasarely
Solomon R. Guggenheim Museum

gives a sum that is only $\frac{1}{8}$ short of 1. The next term gives a sum that is only $\frac{1}{16}$ short of 1, then $\frac{1}{32}$, $\frac{1}{64}$, and so on.

In other words, as you sum up more and more terms of that series of fractions, you get closer and closer to 1, as close as you want, to within a millionth of one, a trillionth of one, a trillionth of a trillionth of one. You get closer and closer and closer and closer to 1, but you *never quite reach 1.*

Mathematicians express this by saying that the sum of the endless series of fractions $\frac{1}{2}$, $\frac{1}{4}$, $\frac{1}{8}$ . . . "approaches 1 as a limit."

This is an example of a "converging series," that is, a series with an endless num-

ber of members but with a total sum that approaches an ordinary number (a "finite" number) as a limit.

The Greeks discovered such converging series but were so impressed with the endlessness of the terms of the series that they did not realize that the sum might not be endless. Consequently, a Greek named Zeno[1] set up a number of problems called "paradoxes"[2] which seemed to disprove things that were obviously true. He "disproved," for instance, that motion was possible. These paradoxes were famous for thousands of

---

1. Zeno (zē' no)
2. paradoxes (par' ə däks' iz) *n.*: Statements that seem to contain opposite meanings or to be unbelievable.

years, but all vanished as soon as the truth about converging series was realized.

Zeno's most famous paradox is called "Achilles[3] and the Tortoise." Achilles was a Homeric[4] hero renowned for his swiftness, and a tortoise is an animal renowned for its slowness. Nevertheless, Zeno set out to demonstrate that in a race in which the tortoise is given a head start, Achilles could never overtake the tortoise.

Suppose, for instance, that Achilles can run ten times as fast as the tortoise and that the tortoise is given a hundred-yard head start. In a few racing strides, Achilles wipes out that hundred-yard handicap, but in that time, the tortoise, traveling at one-tenth Achilles's speed (pretty darned fast for a tortoise), has moved on ten yards. Achilles next makes up that ten yards, but in that time the tortoise has moved one yard further. Achilles covers that one yard, and the tortoise has traveled an additional tenth of a yard. Achilles—

But you see how it is. Achilles keeps advancing, but so does the tortoise, and Achilles never catches up. Furthermore, since you could argue the same way, however small the tortoise's head start—one foot or one inch—Achilles could never make up any head start, however small. And this means that motion is impossible.

Of course, you know that Achilles *could* overtake the tortoise and motion *is* possible. Zeno's "proof" is therefore a paradox.

Now, then, what's wrong with Zeno's proof? Let's see. Suppose Achilles could run

ten yards per second and the tortoise one yard per second. Achilles makes up the original hundred-yard head start in 10 seconds during which time the tortoise travels ten yards. Achilles makes up the ten yards in 1 second, during which time the tortoise travels one yard. Achilles makes up the one yard in 0.1 second during which time the tortoise travels a tenth of a yard.

In other words, the time taken for Achilles to cover each of the successive head starts of the turtle forms a series that looks like this: 10, 1, 0.1, 0.01, 0.001, 0.0001, 0.00001, and so on.

How much time does it take for Achilles to make up all the head starts? Since there are an endless number of terms in this Zeno series, Zeno assumed the total sum was infinite. He did not realize that some series of endless numbers of terms "converge" and have a finite sum.

For instance, the sum of the first two terms in the Zeno series above is 11; the sum of the first three is 11.1; of the first four, 11.11; of the first five, 11.111 and so on. As you see, if you add up all the endless series of terms, you get an endless decimal as the sum; 11.11111111111111111 . . . and so on forever.

But if you work out the decimal equivalent of the number $11\frac{1}{9}$, you find that it also is the endlessly repeating decimal 11.1111111111111111111111111 . . . and so on forever.

The sum of the Zeno series is therefore $11\frac{1}{9}$ seconds and that is the time in which Achilles will overtake and pass the tortoise even though he has to work his way through an endless series of continually smaller head starts that the tortoise maintains. He *will* overtake the tortoise after all; motion *is* possible, and we can all relax.

---

3. Achilles (ə kil′ ēz): A legendary Greek hero who fought in the Trojan War, which the Greeks waged against the city of Troy in Asia Minor about 3,000 years ago.

4. Homeric (hō mer′ ik) *adj.*: The Greek poet Homer is said to have lived during the 8th century B.C. He wrote two epic poems, the *Iliad* and the *Odyssey*, about the Trojan War and the events that occurred afterward.

THINKING ABOUT THE SELECTION

Recalling

1. In mathematics, what does infinity mean?
2. What is a converging series?
3. What did Zeno's paradox seem to disprove?
4. How does Asimov disprove Zeno's paradox?

Interpreting

5. What does Asimov mean by "counting without counting"?
6. How does Asimov use fractions to demonstrate the concept of the "endlessly small"?

Applying

7. What new ideas about infinity do you now have as a result of reading "Endlessness"?

READING IN THE CONTENT AREAS

Outlining

Outlining means organizing the content of a piece of writing to show the main ideas and supporting details. For example, the following is an outline of the first part of "Endlessness."

I. Infinity
A. Poet—can use simile to show it
B. Mathematician—cannot use simile
1. No limits to addition
2. Any series of integers is infinite—can always be added to

Make an outline of the next part of the essay, headed "Counting Without Counting."

CRITICAL THINKING AND READING

Explaining Mathematics Inductively

Inductive reasoning means drawing a general conclusion from particular facts or cases. In "Endlessness," Asimov uses inductive reasoning to explain the general concepts with which his essay is concerned. For example, in the first part he wishes to explain the general concept that the total number of even integers is infinite, like the total number of all integers. He does so by reasoning from a particular case.

> The series 2, 4, 6, 8 . . . can continue endlessly . . . [because] it is always possible to say "that [even] number plus two."

1. How does Asimov use inductive reasoning to show that the series of fractions 1/2, 1/4, 1/8 . . . will never reach zero?
2. How does he use inductive reasoning to show that the sum total of all fractions in this series will never quite reach one.

UNDERSTANDING LANGUAGE

Understanding Mathematical Terms

Mathematical terms need to be understood exactly. When you come upon an unfamiliar term, try to figure out its meaning from the way it is used—from its context. When, for example, Asimov says that "the smaller you make your divisor, the larger your quotient becomes," the context helps to make clear what "divisor" and "quotient" mean. He says, "Similarly $1 \div 1/100 = 100$, and $1 \div 1/1000 = 1000$." This context clue suggests that a divisor is a number by which another number is divided and a quotient is the result obtained by the division. If, however, you cannot figure out from context what a math term means, you should consult a math book.

1. What is the difference between an integer and a number?
2. What is a paradox? What is an example of a paradox?

THINKING AND WRITING

Writing About Mathematics

Imagine that you are visiting a planet that has not discovered counting. Write an essay explaining the concept of counting to the people living on the planet. Revise your essay to make sure your explanation is clear.

GUIDE FOR READING

Winslow Homer: America's Greatest Painter

H. N. Levitt (1920–   ) was born and raised in New York City. During World War II he was a naval officer. After the war, he pursued a career as a playwright and college professor of drama. However, he has always loved the visual arts too. He learned how to paint with watercolors at a well-known art school, and he has written many magazine articles about painters. In this article he tells why he considers Winslow Homer "America's Greatest Painter."

Setting a Purpose for Reading

A **purpose** is a reason for doing something. You can learn more from any work of nonfiction if you set a purpose for your reading before you start. One strategy for setting a goal is to imagine that you are a newspaper reporter gathering information for a story. Reading "Winslow Homer: America's Greatest Painter" as a reporter, for instance, you would use the journalistic formula *who? what? when? where? why?* and *how?* You might wonder *who* Winslow Homer was, *what* he did, *when* and *where* he lived, *how* he worked, and *why* he is considered a great painter.

Your information about Homer will not be complete, however, unless you look at his paintings (pages 396 and 398). Glancing at them before you begin will give you a general sense of his art.

Look For

As you read look for answers to the questions *who? what? when? where?* and *why?* in regard to Winslow Homer.

Writing

Before starting, look at Homer's paintings on pages 396 and 398. Choose one. Study it carefully and freewrite about it. You might want to consider the subjects he paints, the colors he uses, and the feelings he communicates.

Vocabulary

Knowing the following words will help you as you read "Winslow Homer: America's Greatest Painter."

cantankerous (kan taŋ′ kər əs) *adj.*: Bad-tempered (p. 395)

subtle (sut′ 'l) *adj.*: Delicately skillful or clever (p. 395)

brutality (broo tal′ ə tē) *n.*: Violence; harshness (p. 396)

vanquished (vaŋ′ kwisht) *n.*: The person defeated (usually a verb) (p. 397)

serenity (sə ren′ ə tē) *n.*: Calmness (p. 397)

subservient (səb sʉr′ vē ənt) *adj.*: Inferior (p. 398)

Winslow Homer:
America's Greatest Painter

H. N. Levitt

His oil paintings and watercolors are in all major American museums and collections today. But even when Winslow Homer was alive, they called him America's greatest painter.

That wasn't all they said about him. They also called him crusty, bad-tempered, cantankerous, grouchy, sour as a crab, and surly as a bear. He was all those things, and more.

His brother's wife—and Winslow's only female friend—thought Homer the most courteous gentleman she ever knew. She said he knew what he wanted in life, and he went about getting it without any fuss or feathers.

When it came to painting, he took five lessons, decided that was enough, then went on to become a self-taught genius.

Homer was born into a middle-class family on Feb. 24, 1836. The family lived near the harbor in Boston, so Homer's earliest memories were of ships, sailors, fishermen and the sea.

When he was six, the family moved to Cambridge, directly across the street from Harvard College. Sometimes Winslow's dad would suggest that the boy consider attending Harvard someday. But it was no use. All young Winslow wanted to do was fish and draw.

After a while, the family realized there was something special about Winslow, because that's all he would do—fish and draw, day in and day out, all year long.

But even if Homer had wanted to go to college, there would have been no money for it. When Homer was 13, his dad sold all and left to make his fortune in the California gold rush. He came back a few years later empty-handed.

But the family remained close. And once they realized how important art was to Homer, they encouraged it. In fact, his brothers secretly bought up his paintings at early exhibitions so he wouldn't get discouraged if no one else bought them. Those two brothers remained his best friends all his life.

When the Civil War broke out in 1861, Homer was a young artist already on his way to fame. As a freelance illustrator for *Harper's Weekly*, America's most important news magazine, he was considered one of the country's finest wood-block engravers.

In those days, an artist would cut illustrations into a wood block, which was then inked in black and printed on sheets of paper. Techniques like subtle shadowing and distant perspective were hard to achieve, but Homer's illustrations were unusually lively and strong.

Harper's Weekly offered Homer a good

PRISONERS FROM THE FRONT, 1866
Winslow Homer
The Metropolitan Museum of Art

job, and he could have remained a weekly illustrator all his life. But he wanted to work for no one but himself, so he turned the offer down.

Homer left New York to paint the war. He joined Gen. George McClellan's Army of the Potomac[1] as a freelance artist-correspondent. He painted scenes at the siege of Yorktown[2] and did many drawings of Abraham Lincoln, the tall, gaunt, serious president who was desperately trying to keep the Union together.

In a few short years, Homer's Civil War paintings brought him fame at home and abroad. He painted war as no other artist ever had. He emphasized not brutality but rather scenes of loneliness, camp life, endless waiting, and even horseplay on the battlefield.

Homer was a Yankee,[3] but he showed equal concern for soldiers from both the North and South. His paintings did not glorify war; they seemed to cry out for it to end.

His *Prisoners from the Front* made a rep-

---

1. Gen. George McClellan's Army of the Potomac: McClellan served for a time as the general in chief of the Union Army during the Civil War. The Union Army in the East was known as the Army of the Potomac.

2. Yorktown: Yorktown, Virginia, which Gen. McClellan occupied on May 4, 1862.

3. Yankee: Here, a native or inhabitant of a Northern state.

utation overnight. This one painting, done in Homer's honest, realistic style, showed the common humanity that linked North and South, victor and vanquished, Americans all. Homer's war paintings give us the best record we have of how the Civil War soldier actually looked and acted.

After the war, railroads and new industries changed America from a rural to an industrial society almost overnight. But Homer paid no attention. He went back to painting the things he liked: country scenes, farmers, beautiful women in fashionable clothes, and kids at play.

He never painted kids with the gushy sentimentalism of other American painters. And he didn't look down on young people. His paintings showed what was then a typical American upbeat attitude marked by humor and innocence. The public loved it.

And then something strange happened. Homer stopped painting. For three years, his brushes sat idle. He left his studio for Europe, but avoided the art world in Paris. Instead, he went to Tynemouth, England, a small fishing port on the North Sea.

It was there, at Tynemouth, that Winslow Homer witnessed the fierce, day-to-day struggle of men and women against the sea. Their hard, bitter, dangerous lives made him think critically about his own life and work.

After that, women, children and country life appeared less often in his paintings. What replaced them was the harsh existence of men of the sea. These heroic people became, in his mind, the best examples of mankind. That's apparent in his famous painting *The Life Line*. To Homer, the sea had lost its serenity and had become a powerful force of nature.

Homer began painting larger pictures too, and his style became more bold and powerful. Some complained that his paintings now looked unfinished. But he didn't care. Nice finishing touches were no longer important.

Besides the sea and its people, Homer started painting scenes of the American wilderness. He did big, masculine pictures of hunting and fishing, canoeing the rapids, sitting around the campfire and trekking over rugged trails.

He painted large oils, but he also painted many watercolors. By the time he had hit his stride, he had become America's first great watercolor painter. It was he who developed the technique of using the white, unpainted paper as sparkling highlight.

Then, at 48, when he was selling just about everything he painted, he did another about-face.

He surprised his family, friends and fellow artists by turning his back on the city and the world of art. He packed up and left to spend the rest of his life—27 years—as a hermit on a rocky cliff overlooking the sea in Prouts Neck, Maine.

In typical, cantankerous, Yankee fashion, when asked how he could leave New York, the scene of his success, he said, "I left New York to escape jury duty."

In a more serious mood, he told his brother that his new, lonely life was the only setting in which he could do his work in peace, free from visitors and publicity seekers.

Winslow Homer finally came to love his life. It was at Prouts Neck that he finished one of his great masterpieces, *The Gulf Stream*, in 1899.

This painting showed a black man marooned in a broken-masted boat circled by sharks in the Gulf Stream.[4] It was an immediate sensation, but only one of a long series

---

4. Gulf Stream: The warm ocean current flowing from the Gulf of Mexico along the East Coast of the United States.

THE GULF STREAM, 1899
Winslow Homer
The Metropolitan Museum of Art

of oils and watercolors that Homer painted of American blacks. This was at a time when blacks were usually depicted as minstrel singers and servants, or in other subservient poses.

In his last years, Homer made another big change. Instead of painting scenes of men struggling against the sea and wilderness, he started painting the sea and wilderness alone.

Like a stubborn tree growing out of a rock, he stood on his lonely cliff and painted the sea, forever untamed and uncontrolled by man.

In 1910, just before he died, he wrote in a letter, "All is lovely outside my house and inside my house and myself." Winslow Homer was a simple, modest, unsentimental man—the kind of American we Americans like.

THINKING ABOUT THE SELECTION

Recalling

1. What scenes were part of Homer's first memories?
2. How did his family know there was "something special" about him?
3. In what way did the Civil War change Homer's life? What other turning points did he have in his life?
4. Why are Homer's Civil War paintings unusual? How did *Prisoners From the Front* affect his reputation?
5. How did his work change after he lived in Tynemouth, England?
6. Why did he leave New York City for Maine?

Interpreting

7. What do you think might have caused Homer to stop painting for three years?
8. How did Homer show his self-reliance and independent spirit throughout his life?
9. What does the author's last statement indicate about American values? Do you agree that these are values most Americans share? Support your answer.

Applying

10. Why do you think artists must have the ability to surprise the public?

READING IN THE CONTENT AREAS

Setting a Purpose for Reading

One way to set a purpose for reading is to pretend to be a reporter gathering information about a subject. After using this method with this essay about Winslow Homer, you should have the answers to the usual reporter's questions: Who? What? When? Where? Why? and How?

1. Who was Winslow Homer?
2. What did he do?
3. When and where did he work?
4. How did he work?
5. Why is he considered a great painter?

CRITICAL THINKING AND READING

Evaluating the Writer's Opinions

The writer, H. N. Levitt, comments specifically on the Homer paintings that accompany this essay. He says, for example, that *Prisoners From the Front* (page 396) is "honest" and "realistic," showing the "common humanity" of soldiers from both sides. You can evaluate the writer's opinions by looking carefully at the picture yourself.

1. Describe what is happening in the scene, identifying the soldiers from each side.
2. Consider whether the scene is "realistic." What leads you to think that Homer either changed it or painted it realistically?

UNDERSTANDING LANGUAGE

Learning About Art Terms

In discussing Winslow Homer and his work, the writer uses special words from the visual arts. Look up each of the following terms in the dictionary and explain how it relates to painting or drawing.

1. perspective
2. watercolor
3. shadowing
4. studio

THINKING AND WRITING

Writing About a Painting

Imagine that you are an editor putting together a book of Winslow Homer's paintings for junior high school students. You have been assigned to write several paragraphs to accompany *The Gulf Stream*. Before starting, review what H. N. Levitt said about Homer's career in general and this work in particular. Then look at the picture closely. List its important qualities. For instance, you might want to mention the drama of the scene, the portrayal of a black man, and the way Homer has painted the ocean. Consider whether the painting has a theme—an idea that it communicates. When revising, check your writing for clarity.

GUIDE FOR READING

The Mystery and Wonder of Words

Maxwell Nurnberg (1897–1984) was born in Poland but lived much of his life in New York City. He was a brilliant student of language and, afterward, a much-respected teacher of it. For thirty-six years, he taught English in a New York City high school. Later, he was a professor of English at New York University and a lecturer at Brooklyn College. The title of the following essay, "The Mystery and Wonder of Words," reflects Nurnberg's lifelong fascination with language.

Varying Rates of Reading

Vary your reading rate with the kind of material you are reading. Usually choose among three kinds of reading: slow intensive reading, rapid skimming, and rapid scanning. **Reading intensively** means reading carefully and slowly. It involves stopping after each paragraph or brief section and asking yourself, "What have I just read?" **Scanning** means running your eyes over a page rapidly until you find specific information you are looking for. **Skimming** means reading quickly to get a general idea of what a book or selection is about.

Look For

Skim Nurnberg's essay to get an overview of it. Then read it intensively, pausing frequently to question yourself on what you have read. When you are answering the questions that follow the selection, going back to the article and scanning it may prove helpful.

Writing

Like the author, have you, too, been fascinated by language? Think of a word or expression you may have heard at some time that caused you to stop and think about it. What was the word or expression? What struck you about it as odd or interesting? Write about the thoughts that occurred to you about it.

Vocabulary

Knowing the following words will help you as you read "The Mystery and Wonder of Words."

convey (kən vā') v.: Make known (p. 401)

aeons (ē' ənz) n.: Very long periods of time (p. 401)

equivalent (i kwiv' ə lənt) n.: A thing similar to another thing (p. 401)

distinctions (dis tiŋk' shənz) n.: Differences of meaning (p. 403)

unique (yo͞o nēk') adj.: Having no like or equal (p. 403)

amends (ə mendz') n.: Things given or done to make up for injury or loss (p. 404)

The Mystery and Wonder of Words

Maxwell Nurnberg

How long a time lies in one little word!
WILLIAM SHAKESPEARE: *King Richard II*

Millions of years ago, there were no words. There was no language. The first human beings, like animals, were probably able to make only those sounds that expressed the simplest feelings. They must have made sounds like the bark of a dog to convey excitement or like the purr of a cat to show contentment. Man was very much like Tennyson's

> *An infant crying in the night;*
> *An infant crying for the light,*
> *And with no language but a cry.*

These sounds and cries nature gave to man as she gave him hands. Man's hands, however, were not by themselves powerful enough to conquer the earth and get from it everything that was needed. Therefore, he had to invent tools made out of wood and stone to extend the power of his hands.

In the same way man had somehow to create or invent words, tools made from sounds, to extend his power of communication with others, to share with them some of the ideas that lay imprisoned in his brain.

One day, aeons ago, it is possible that an early ancestor of ours, running barefoot on the forest floor, suddenly happened to step on a sharp stone. Undoubtedly he uttered a startled, piercing cry of pain—the primitive equivalent of a word like *Ouch!* He was probably frightened by his outburst, yet somehow excited by it too.

Imagine him later that day back in his cave. Remembering the sharpness of the pain, he was eager to let the others know all about his experience. As he acted out his story for them with gestures, he came to his startled outcry. Having a sense of the dramatic, he pointed to the sole of his injured foot and, to make his story more vivid, let out the same piercing sound he had made at the time of his accident.

The story was an instant success. He was made to tell it over and over again, the others joining in when he came to the "sound effect." After frequent repetitions we can see how the sound became a word that they could now all use. And it probably had many meanings. Depending on the particular gesture that accompanied it, the word could mean "pain" or "wound" or "blood" or "sharp stone" or even "sole of a foot"!

How do we know all this? We don't. Through the years, students of language have developed many theories, pure guesses. This is my guess.

However, at this point science can step in to help us with part of the story of lan-

OWHI IN SAN PAO, 1951
Stuart Davis
The Whitney Museum of American Art

guage. For there is a theory which says, "Ontogeny[1] recapitulates phylogeny."[2] Simply stated, it tells us that the individual, especially in his earliest stages, goes through a development similar to those stages that the human race has gone through. If, therefore, we study how a little child's language devel-

ops, it may give us some idea of how language itself developed.

Let us take the case of Ellen. She was a big-city child, surrounded constantly by passing automobiles and trucks. Therefore, the first word she learned—it was really a sentence—was *It's a car.* She would call attention to each passing vehicle proudly with *It's a car.*

On her first day in the country, she saw an ant crawl by. Her pudgy little finger shot out and triumphantly she announced, "It's a

---

1. ontogeny (än täj′ ə nē) *n.*: The life cycle of a single organism or individual.
2. phylogeny (fī läj′ ə nē) *n.*: The development of a species or group.

car." For Ellen, anything that moved was a car. No distinctions or refinements were made. *It's-a-car* was a general word to describe any moving object.

In the same way, the *ouch* word of our earliest ancestors was a general word and often covered a lot of ground. Later, much later, more specific words were developed. *Ouch* remained the word for a cry of pain and other words were found for stone and sharp and pain and wound and blood and sole that had specific, unique meanings. Today, Webster's Third New International Dictionary contains 450,000 separate entries. And there exist in the world today about 2,500 languages!

In his play *Prometheus*[3] *Bound*, Robert Lowell[4] has Prometheus say:

"Before I made men talk and write with words, knowledge dropped like a dry stick into the fire of their memories, fed that fading blaze an instant, then died without leaving an ash behind."

It is written words that have made man's memories live on in others and have fed the flame of knowledge which lighted the avenues to all of man's serious thinking and his great achievements.

For example, you press a button and where there was darkness before there is now light. You press another button and you shoot up eighty floors, almost to the top of the Empire State Building. You turn a dial in your living room and you are present at an event taking place thousands of miles away. These miracles, which have taken millions of years to achieve, are taken for granted by all of us.

In the same way, we take for granted another miracle—the words we speak, read, and write so naturally and effortlessly. Let's take a very simple example. Every morning, wherever English is spoken, people sit down to what they call breakfast. Few of us ever think of the word as meaning more than merely some fruit juice, a cereal or egg, toast, and a hot drink. Yet if you look closely at the word, you see that it means that you are "breaking your fast," eating for the first time since the evening before.

You *don* (do on) your clothes before sitting down to breakfast and you may *doff* (do off) your hat when you say goodbye. But what are you saying when you say goodbye? In Shakespeare's plays you will find that characters, on leaving one another, sometimes say, "God be wi' ye!" (God be with you!) Now say *God be wi' ye* fast. Faster. Faster still. In a few seconds you have covered hundreds of years and you have arrived at the modern *goodbye*. Thus whenever you say goodbye you are really saying "God be with you."

In most modern languages of Western Europe the formal words of farewell have God in them. The French say *Adieu*[5]; so do the Germans and Austrians, though they pronounce it a little differently. The Spaniards say, *Adios*[6] and the Italians, *Addio*.[7] All of these words come from the Latin word for a god, *deus*,[8] which comes from the Greek *theos*,[9] which comes from—but that's another story.

You may eat breakfast with, or say goodbye to, a *companion*. Let's not take that word for granted. Let's look into it. *Compan-*

---

3. Prometheus (prə mē′ thē əs): In Greek mythology, a titan who stole fire from heaven for the benefit of mankind. To punish him, Zeus chained him to a rock, where a vulture attacked him each day.
4. Robert Lowell (1917–1977): American poet and dramatist.

5. Adieu: Pronounced ə dyo͞o′.
6. Adios: Pronounced a dē ōs′.
7. Addio: Pronounced a dē′ o.
8. deus: Pronounced dā oos.
9. theos: Pronounced thē′ əs.

THE PARIS BIT, 1959
Stuart Davis
The Whitney Museum of American Art

ion has the structure of most English words of three syllables or more: a prefix, *com;* a root, *pan;* a suffix, *ion*.

You have seen the prefix *com* in words like *combine, combat* (fight *with*), *compose* (put *together*), and you probably know that *com* is a prefix meaning "with" or "together." The suffix *ion* shows that the word is a noun.

But what does the all-important middle part *pan* mean? It comes from a Latin word *panis*, appearing in French as *pain* (pronounced "paa" with a nasal twist at the end), in Spanish as *pan*, and in Italian as *pane* (pronounced "pah-nay") and it means "bread." Is there a better way to describe a companion than to say that he is one with whom we share our bread?

You probably know that the word *alphabet* is made up of the first two Greek letters—*alpha* and *beta*. But do you know that the word atone really means "at one"? If you atone, if you make amends, for something you have done, you feel "at one" again with whomever you may have offended.

If all you know about a word is its spelling and its meaning, you sometimes don't know the half of it. As a matter of fact, you don't know the most interesting half of it. You don't know who its parents are, who its relatives are, what country it was born in, or what picture may be hidden somewhere within it. By the way, the word *infant* comes from Latin *in*, "not," plus *fant*, "speaking." Strictly speaking, therefore, you are no longer an infant when you begin to speak.

THINKING ABOUT THE SELECTION
Recalling

1. Why did human beings invent words?
2. Why is the word *breakfast* used for morning meals?
3. What earlier expression is the basis of the word *goodbye*?
4. When you look into the word parts (prefix, root, and suffix) that make up *companion,* what underlying meaning is revealed?

Interpreting

5. Explain the opening quotation from Shakespeare—"How long a time lies in one little word!" In what way could this quotation be considered a summary of the entire essay?
6. What is the similarity between the invention of words and the invention of tools?
7. What point does Nurnberg make by his analysis of such words as *breakfast, goodbye,* and *companion*?
8. According to Nurnberg, why are you "no longer an infant when you begin to speak"?

Applying

9. Henry Ward Beecher once wrote, "All words are pegs to hang ideas on." What is the meaning of this quotation? Do you think Nurnberg would agree with its main idea? Why or why not?

READING IN THE CONTENT AREAS
Varying Rates of Reading

Slow, careful, intensive reading, rapid skimming, and rapid scanning are three useful ways of reading depending on what you are reading and why you are reading it.

Think of all the different kinds of reading you do. Then answer the following questions.

1. For what kinds of reading can you appropriately use skimming?
2. What kinds of material would you scan?
3. What kinds of material would you read intensively?

CRITICAL THINKING AND READING
Distinguishing Fact from Speculation

A statement of **fact** is a statement that can be proved true or false. A **speculation** is a reasonable guess. For example, when Nurnberg says that a certain dictionary contains 450,000 separate entries, he is making a statement of fact. When he says that the first humans "must have made sounds like the bark of a dog to convey excitement," he is speculating.

Tell whether each of the following statements is a statement of fact or a speculation.

1. ". . . the *ouch* word of our earliest ancestors was a general word and often covered a lot of ground."
2. "All of these words [*Adieu, Adios, Addio*] come from the Latin word for a god, *deus.*"

THINKING AND WRITING
Speculating About Words

Early in his essay, Nurnberg tells a little story in which he speculates about how an interjection —a word that expresses sudden excitement or strong feeling—like *ouch* may have originated. Choose another injection—*aha, oops, psst, ugh,* or some other—and imagine the situation in which it might have first been used. Tell a brief story to express your speculation about how the word originated.

Before you write, take the time to imagine what was taking place that led someone to use the interjection. What other characters were there? What was the setting? When you revise, check that your story is a believable account of how your interjection was born.

GUIDE FOR READING

from Circle of the Seasons

Edwin Way Teale (1899–1980) was born and raised in Joliet, Illinois. Up to the age of sixteen, he spent his summers at his grandparents' farm in Indiana, close to Lake Michigan. Here he developed a fascination with plants and animals that lasted all his life. He became a naturalist and a Pulitzer Prize-winning author of nature books. The journal entries that follow are remarkable for their perceptiveness and thoughtfulness. They will show you how much nature can teach a sensitive observer.

Journal Writing

Journal writing is a way of recording events as they happen. Because a journal is personal, it usually includes a writer's thoughts, feelings, and insights as well as objective details. Many scientists keep journals as a record of observations and experiments. They can thereby keep track of their work. They can also use a journal to record information for future projects. Others, like Teale, treat journals as a place to do their best writing. Ultimately, such journals are published as books for the public.

Look For

As you read the excerpts from *Circle of the Seasons,* notice how Teale blends close and careful observations of nature with his own thoughts and scientific reflections.

Writing

Freewrite about your observations of a specific aspect of nature in or near your neighborhood. Include whatever thoughts, questions, or feelings occur to you as you write down your observations.

Vocabulary

Knowing the following words will help you as you read the excerpts from *Circle of the Seasons.*

susceptible (sə sep′ tə b'l) *adj.*: Easily affected by (p. 407)
apt (apt) *adj.*: Inclined; likely (p. 407)
invariable (in ver′ ē ə b'l) *adj.*: Not changing, uniform (p. 407)
opalescent (ō′ pə les′ 'nt) *adj.*: Showing a play of colors (p. 408)

from Circle of the Seasons

Edwin Way Teale

The following are excerpts from a journal that Edwin Way Teale kept for every day of a year. Scientists often use journals with dated entries as an ongoing record of their observations or experiments.

January 11

POISON IVY BERRIES. To the cedar woods at sunset. An overwintering catbird is feeding on the purple berries of the cat-briars and the gray berries of the poison ivy. Cows eat poison ivy leaves with immunity; birds eat the berries without ill effects. Only human beings, and only some human beings at that, are susceptible, through an allergy, to the torments of ivy poisoning. Yet those of us who fall victims, through this peculiarity in our own systems, are apt to bewail the presence of poison ivy in the world and to consider it an enemy lying in wait for our approach. Why was poison ivy put in the world?

The catbird, feeding in the quiet of this winter sunset, finding nourishment in the berries, supplies at least one of the answers. On the shifting sand of Fire Island,[1] there is another answer. There, the remarkably adaptive ivy, able to grow on barren sand as well as in swamps, anchors down the wind-blown earth. Each form of life, plant as well as animal, has its part to play. Whether the results delight or outrage man is no concern of nature's. Man plays, to be sure, a leading role in the drama of life. But he still is only a part of a cast that includes many, many actors.

January 24

THE WHITENESS OF THE SNOW. Looking across the white fields today, I am reminded that an invariable rule of nature is that nothing is invariable. "As like as two peas in a pod" is an exact statement of nature's way. For no two peas in a pod are ever exactly alike. Nature does not plagiarize herself, repeat herself. Her powers of innovation are boundless. No two hills or ants or oranges or sheep or snowflakes are identical. Ten thousand seem alike because we do not see them clearly enough, because our senses are too dull or inadequate or inaccurate to detect the differences.

And so it is with one of the oldest similes in the world: "As white as the snow." The whiteness of the snow is infinitely varied. In fact, its whiteness is produced by elements that are not white at all. The individual crystals that go into the make-up of a snowflake are transparent and colorless when they are created far up in the sky. They are like clear glass. It is when they are grouped together in flakes, when they lie in untold millions in a drift, that they appear white.

What is the explanation of this paradox? It is the same answer that explains how a transparent window pane when it is broken and powdered appears white while the intact pane is colorless. Both the infinite number of crystals that make up the snowdrift and

---

1. Fire Island: A long, narrow, sandy island off the south shore of Long Island, New York.

the vast number of particles that comprise the powdered glass have so many facets that they reflect all the rays of light in all directions. Put all the rays of the spectrum together and you have white just as when you take all the rays of the spectrum away you have black. It is the numberless crystals in the piled-up snow that turn it into a mound of the purest white.

Yet even this "purest white" has many subtle variations. The famous New York advertising photographer, H. I. Williams, once told me of his surprise in noting the differences in the whites recorded by his color camera. They all looked alike to his eyes. But the sensitive color film showed that some were tinged with blues or yellows or reds and some were pearly and opalescent. The white of a billiard ball, of a sheet of writing paper, of a dress shirt, of a tablecloth all were different. Probably no two tablecloths are exactly the same in whiteness, although our eyes are unable to detect the difference.

Similarly, it is likely that no two snowbanks are identical in the whiteness of their exterior. Their surroundings, the time of day, the conditions of the sky all contribute to their tinting. Even our eyes can note the blue in the shadows of trees stretching across the drifts and the pink glow of sunset spreading over an expanse of snow. But under the noonday sun, except when soot or mud has stained them or when old drifts have been discolored by deposits from the air, the whiteness of the snow remains all the same to our eyes—the purest white we know.

April 4

WORLD'S MOST VALUABLE ANIMAL. A long soaking rain before daybreak. And all along the way, when I walk for the morning papers, I find earthworms here and there stranded on the inhospitable cement of the sidewalk. Appearing naked and bewildered, they are in imminent danger of the early bird or of drying out in the sun-warmed air. This is the time of year when my morning walk is slowed by stops to put earthworms back on the ground where they belong. People probably wonder what treasure I am finding when they see me stoop so often!

And, in a way, I am dealing in treasure.

The pelt of a silver fox may sell for hundreds of dollars. The legs of a racehorse may be insured for a quarter of a million. Yet neither the silver fox nor the racehorse is the world's most valuable animal. This is the earthworm—a creature without fur and without legs; a creature that has neither paws nor eyes nor ears; a humble burrower, nature's plowman.

As frost has left the topsoil, earthworms have worked upward. They have begun once more their invaluable activity of plowing, pulverizing, aerating, fertilizing, leveling and thinning the soil. As many as 5,000 earthworms may plow through the earth of a single acre. During spring and summer and fall, they may bring as much as eighteen tons of new earth to the surface.

This labor is achieved with curious but effective equipment. Instead of legs, the earthworm employs hundreds of stiff bristles. Each body segment, except the first and last, is equipped with eight of these bristle-hooks. They are used to grip the soil on all sides and they explain the tugging of the robin when it seeks to drag an earthworm from the ground.

Underground, the earthworm pushes or literally eats its way through the soil. Its mouth, functioning like a suction pump, draws earth into its body. There it is pulverized and organic particles are digested. The rest is deposited as castings[2] at the mouth of the burrow. In its surface feeding, during

---

2. castings: (kas' tiηz) *n*.: Waste material.

the hours of darkness, the creature usually anchors its tail in its burrow and then, elongating its body, moves in a circle like a tethered calf in its search for bits of decayed leaves.

At such times, it is warned of danger by curious senses, amazingly keen. Although it has no eyes, its skin is so sensitive to light that it warns the worm when dawn is breaking. Although it has no ears, it is so sensitive to earth vibrations that it is alarmed by the footfall of even an approaching shrew.[3]

This is the earthworm, that humble and invaluable creature I see so frequently along my way this morning.

---

3. shrew: (shro͞o) *n.*: A small, slender, mouselike animal with soft, brown fur and a long pointed snout.

THINKING ABOUT THE SELECTION
Recalling

1. What are Teale's answers to the question "Why was poison ivy put in the world?"
2. Explain the different tintings of color in snow.

Interpreting

3. Why is the earthworm "nature's plowman"?
4. What is the meaning of Teale's remark that humans are only part of the drama of life?
5. How strong is his argument for the idea that the earthworm is the most valuable animal?

Applying

6. In the first entry, Teale points out the value of poison ivy. What are some other aspects of nature he might have written about in a similar way?

READING IN THE CONTENT AREAS
Journal Writing

Journal writing can be a way of learning. It can stimulate a writer's thinking so that he or she sees meaning in the events recorded.

1. What is the specific observation that begins the January 24th entry?
2. What rule of nature does this observation lead Teale to recall?

CRITICAL THINKING AND READING
Observing and Inferring

Observing is the act of noting and recording facts and events. For example, when Teal notes and records that poison ivy anchors down the windblown earth on Fire Island, he is making an observation. **Inferring** means drawing a conclusion—often from observations. For example, after observing that the catbird is nourished by poison-ivy berries and earth is anchored down by the ivy, Teale makes the inference that "Each form of life . . . has its part to play."

Tell why you think that the following statement is an observation or an inference: "Yet neither the silver fox nor the racehorse is the world's most valuable animal."

THINKING AND WRITING
Writing a Journal Entry

Using your freewriting as a starting point, write an entry modeled on any one of the three by Teale. Include any inferences or other thoughts that come to you. When you revise your entry, make sure your observation is presented in a way that will be clear to any reader. Compare your entry with those written by others in your class.

GUIDE FOR READING

from These Were the Sioux

Mari Sandoz (1901–1966) was born in Nebraska but learned English only when she entered school; her Swiss parents spoke German at home. Sandoz worked as a teacher and a proofreader in a newspaper office before she became a successful writer. Influenced by her childhood on a frontier farm, she wrote many books about the American West. She was especially fascinated by the history and customs of Native Americans. In this excerpt from *These Were the Sioux*, she describes the upbringing of Sioux children.

Taking Notes

Taking notes is an excellent technique for remembering the most important information from your reading. Before you even start to take notes, however, you will find it helpful to skim through the selection to gain a general idea of it. Then you can read the piece more slowly, listing the main points. It is not necessary to use complete sentences in your list. Also, you can make note-taking easier by eliminating articles (*a, an, the*) and using abbreviations. As you read, pay special attention to words that indicate main ideas—*in conclusion, most important, the causes of,* and similar phrases. Finally, you may want to review your notes after writing them so they stay in your memory.

Look For

Mari Sandoz knew about the Indian way of life from her own experience on the frontier. As you read her essay about the Sioux, pick out the main ideas she wants to convey.

Writing

Imagine that you have been given the responsibility of caring for a young friend or relative for a weekend. Tell what you would do to teach or entertain this child.

Vocabulary

Knowing the following words will help you as you read "These Were the Sioux."

favoritism (fā′ vər it iz′m) *n.*: Showing special kindness (p. 412)

rites (rīts) *n.*: Religious observances (p. 412)

usurped (yoo surpt′) *v.*: Took without right (p. 413)

tepid (tep′ id) *adj.*: Not warm or cold; lukewarm (p. 413)

enticing (in tīs′ iŋ) *adj.*: Tempting (p. 413)

regalia (ri gāl′ yə) *n.*: Splendid clothes and decorations (p. 414)

judicious (joo dish′ əs) *adj.*: Wise (p. 414)

latent (lāt′′nt) *adj.*: Hidden and not fully developed (p. 414)

from **These Were the Sioux**

Mari Sandoz

By the time I was seven or eight I had begun to sense a special kind of individual responsibility among the Sioux, not only for oneself but for the family, the band, the whole tribe. Then one morning I saw something of the start of this. A small girl from the camp across the road came tapping shyly at our door, motioning to me.

"Ahh, I have a brother too now," she whispered, her dark eyes on the baby astride my hip. "He is just born."

I pushed the oatmeal back on the stove, glanced toward the stable where Mother was milking our cow and hurried across the road as fast as I could, my brother bobbing on my side. I slowed up at the smoky old canvas tipi, shy, too, now, but I did peer into the dusky interior where an Indian woman bent over the new baby on her lap. At the noise of our excitement, the tiny red-brown face began to pucker up tighter, but the mother caught the little nose gently between her thumb and forefinger and with her palm over the mouth, stopped the crying. When the baby began to twist for breath, she let go a little, but only a little, and at the first sign of another cry, she shut off the air again, crooning a soft little song as she did this, a growing song of the Plains Indians, to make the boy straight-limbed and strong of body and heart as the grandson of Bad Arm must be.

I watched the mother enviously. Our babies always cried, and so I had to ride them on my hip, but I knew that none of our small Indian friends made more than a whimper at the greatest hurt, even falling from the high limb of a tree. Now I saw what an old woman had tried to explain to me. During the newborn minutes, that newborn hour, Indian children, boy and girl, were taught the first and greatest lesson of their lives: that no one could be permitted to endanger the people by even one cry to guide a roving enemy to the village or to spoil a hunt that could mean the loss of the winter meat for a whole band or even a small tribe. In return the child would soon discover that all the community felt an equal responsibility toward him. Every fire became like that of his parents, welcoming the exploring, the sleepy or injured toddler. Every pot would have a little extra for a hungry boy, and every ear was open to young sorrow, young joys and aspirations. I also knew that never, in the natural events of this small boy's life, would he be touched by a punishing adult hand. If he grew up like the Sioux of the old hunting days he would be made equal to the demands of his expanding world without any physical restriction beyond the confines of the cradleboard.[1] I still remember the closed, distant faces of the Sioux when I was whipped for staying out to watch the *heyoka*[2] in the thunderstorm, and at other whippings as well.

---

1. cradleboard (krā′ d'l bôrd) *n.*: A board for carrying a baby.
2. heyoka (hā ō′ kə) *n.*: An Indian who made others laugh by doing things backward, for example, wearing warm clothes in summer and hardly any clothes in winter; dreaming of thunder was one qualification for becoming a *heyoka*.

CHEE-A-KA-TCHEE, WIFE OF NOT-TO-WAY, 1830–39
George Catlin
National Museum of American Art
The Smithsonian Institution

In the old days our Sioux neighbors still had their traditional set of precautions against immaturities and resentments among their young people. They avoided overprotecting the young and saved the eldest son from the mother's favoritism that could destroy the parents as well as the boy. By custom every son and daughter, too, was provided with a second father and mother at birth—usually friends of the blood parents, or some relatives outside of the immediate family. The second father of a boy was often selected partly for excellence as hunter, war-rior, horse catcher, band historian, holy man who listened and advised, or medicine man—either healer or one learned in rites and ceremonials. Still earlier the man might have been a maker of arrows, spears or shields, an outstanding runner or gifted in decoying and snaring animals. His wife, the second mother, was preferably known as warmhearted, and fond of boys around the tipi, the lodge. Sometimes the youth showed a special and unexpected talent as he grew and then a third father might be selected, one gifted in this new bent. Or if the puberty dream was of thunder, a *heyoka* might be added as a sort of uncle.

The second mother took over much of the small boy's care so he would never shame his blood mother by trailing at her moccasin heel, never bring the scornful whisper, "Little husband! Little husband!" as he usurped another's place in her attention and affection. The Indians understood the anger and resentment that could grow up in the most tolerant, fortitudinous man if his wife preferred the son over the husband, used the boy against him, brought him humiliation in the village circle.

In the second mother's lodge the boy could tease and laugh in a way improper in his own home. He could talk freely, so long as it was respectful. And when a boy like Young One across the road went to war, whether in the old days against the Pawnees or the Crows, or later, to the Pacific or Korea,[3] the women of his second home could show emotion and cry out, "Be careful, our brother!" and "Be careful, our son!"

By the time Young One was six weeks old he was little trouble to anyone, either in the cradleboard propped against a tipi pole or riding a mother's back while she went about her work. He would be up there some of the time until he was a year old or more, out of harm's way, seeing all the world from the high place and unpossessed by the mother's eyes. Before Young One was two months old it was decided he must swim, "before he forget it," the older mother told us, by signs. I took my baby brother down to see this. The woman carried Young One into a quieter spot along the riverbank and with her hands under the chest and belly, she eased the boy into the shallow, tepid water until it came up

around him. Then, suddenly, his sturdy legs began to kick and his arms to flail out. The next time he lasted a little longer, and by the third or fourth time the woman could take her hands away for a bit while he held his head up and dog paddled for himself.

Winter babies, boys or girls, who couldn't be taught to swim early, were thrown into ponds or river holes in the spring by the father, the impact calculated to revive the fading urge to swim. Every Indian child had to keep himself afloat awhile if he slipped off into deep water, was caught in a cloudburst or in a river accident while the people were fleeing from enemies or a buffalo stampede.

The young Indian learned to make his own decisions, take the responsibility for his actions at an incredibly early age. When the baby began to crawl no one cried, "No, no!" and dragged him back from the enticing red of the tipi fire coals. Instead, his mother or anyone near watched only that he did not burn up. "One must learn from the bite of the fire to let it alone," he was told when he jerked his hand back, whimpering a little, and with tear-wet face brought his burnt finger to whoever was near for the soothing. The boy's eyes would not turn in anger toward the mother or other grownup who might have pulled him back, frustrated his natural desire to test, to explore. His anger was against the pretty coals, plainly the source of his pain. He would creep back another time but more warily, and soon he would discover where warmth became burning.

From birth the young Sioux was in the midst of the adult world. There was only one room in the lodge, and only one out-of-doors. Back when he was small his cradleboard often hung on a tipi pole or a meat rack, the wind swaying him drowsily, while the children played and raced and sang around him and one of his mothers or frequently several

---

3. the Pacific or Korea: World War II (1939–1945), fought on the Pacific Ocean and elsewhere, or the Korean War (1950–1953).

women worked nearby, busy with the meat or the hides or perhaps beading the regalia of the men.

But the little Sioux had to learn some use of his legs this summer. He spent more and more time on the ground, perhaps on a robe or soft grass but often alone, free to discover his body now and begin to get his discipline in the natural way, as he must be free to take his ideals and aspirations from the precepts and examples of those around him.

When the thrust of the boy's growing legs took on insistence, one of the fathers or perhaps an uncle lay on his back and held the baby erect for a short walk up his stomach and chest, laughing hard at the sturdy push of the legs, shouting that this was a warrior son, this was a great and powerful hunter. Perhaps the man was a young war chief, or, if older, just out of the evening council circle where any toddler could approach the headmen unhindered. He could see them smoking quietly, deliberating the common problems of today and tomorrow or planning ceremonials and hunts, perhaps selecting the warrior society to police the village for the next moon, and protect it from disturbances inside and out. The boy could hear the crier, always some old and very judicious and respected man, hurry through the camp with any news or with warnings of danger, or of a hunt coming up, perhaps carrying invitation sticks to a feast or a celebration, or proclaiming the council's decisions. And they were decisions, not orders, for no Sioux could tell anyone what to do. The only position a Sioux inherited was his membership in the tribe. He became a leader, a chief because some were willing to follow him and retained his position only as long as the following remained.

The young Sioux rode early. Sometimes before he could walk he was carried behind his father, clinging to the rawhide string of the man's breechclout.[4] He learned to climb up the foreleg of an old mare like a tree, mounting on the right side as the grown Indians all did, the man with the bow in his left hand when he leaped on, out of the way, and leaving the right hand free to draw the bowstring fast.

From back before he understood the words or the wisdom, the young Sioux heard the hero tales of his people told around the evening fires, but in his early years he learned most from the other children. They took joy in showing him all their knowledge, and in practicing the latent parent lying deep in everyone, eager to care for any small creature or being around. But he learned much, perhaps most, from the scorn and laughter of these peers, and from another boy's fist in his face. Eventually he discovered how to avoid some of the laughing, and the blows, or to fend them off.

When Bad Arm, the man who had once carried me home from the plum thicket, was asked if there wasn't injustice in this discipline by children he drew on his old pipe awhile. All life was injustice, he thought. Lightning found the good man and the bad; sickness carried no respect for virtue, and luck flitted around like the spring butterfly. "It is good to learn this in the days of the mother's milk. Discipline from the young comes as from the earth and is accepted like hunger and weariness and the bite of winter cold. Coming so, it hatches no anger against the grown-up ones, no anger and hatred to sit in the heart like an arrow pointed to shoot both ways."

So the young Sioux learned from his peers, learned from their companionship, their goodness and the power of their ridicule, the same ridicule he saw used against

---

4. breechclout (brĕch′ klout′) *n.*: A piece of cloth worn about the body at the hips.

those in highest position sometimes, for even great war leaders bowed in humiliation before concentrated laughter. And he saw men and women of his people walk in dignity through the village circle, the peaceful, orderly village where normally one heard no quarreling in tipi or outside.

"It is better to use ridicule early—to keep the young on the good road," Bad Arm and the *heyoka* agreed, telling me that in this, had I been a Sioux, I should have had a real place, for ridicule from the girls and the women stings like the yellow-striped hornet.

In the old buffalo days the very young Sioux learned to snare and track small animals, even the rabbit, with his trick of doubling back on his trail, teaching the hunter to use his eyes while other creatures taught him to sharpen his nose and his ears. As the boy grew he was drawn into the hunting games as he was those of the village: prairie ball, running and jumping contests, tag, snow snake in the winter, and always wrestling and horse racing, the boys riding sometimes so small they seemed like some four-footed creature clinging to the mane and back. Young One would have seen the men pile their wagers in goods at the betting stake before the horses were whipped home with dust and whooping. He would have learned to ride in a dead run while hanging to the far side of his pony with a moccasin toe over the back, a hand twisted into the mane, ready for war. He would have been along on raids against enemy horse herds as a young white man might study his father's methods of raiding a competitor's customers.

As the boy grew he ran with his village kind as young antelope run together. He teased the girls, grabbed bits of meat from the drying racks when he was hungry. He went to watch the older youths and young men stand in their courting blankets at this tipi or that one for a few words with the young daughter and could hardly wait until he, too, was a man. He imitated the warriors and ran their errands, hoping to be asked out on a raid, as was done for promising boys, particularly by the war society of a father or an uncle, much as a white youth would be eased toward his father's fraternity, and often with little more bloodshed. Except in a few tribal struggles for hunting grounds, Plains Indian fights were scarcely more dangerous than a hard-fought football game. The first-class coup—striking an enemy with the hand, the bow or the coup stick without harming him—was the highest war achievement, more important than any scalp.

Occasionally the boy was taken out on night guard of the village and the horse herds, or to scout the region for unauthorized war parties trying to slip away, endangering themselves and perhaps the village with avenging attacks. An Indian who gave up the right to cry at birth because it would bring enemies upon the people must not do the same thing by rash and foolish acts later.

Understanding of the regular ceremonials and rituals came gradually to the young Sioux. Eventually he realized what old Contrary told us through the interpretation of his teenage granddaughter, who cheerfully turned all the *heyoka* said around to its rightful meaning. The Sioux camp of any size was always set in a circle because all sacred things were round—the sun, the moon, the earth horizon, as one could plainly see. Even the tipis were round, and their openings as well as that of the whole camp always faced the east, to welcome and honor the light that brought the day and the springtime. But the simplest and perhaps the most profound ritual that the young Sioux saw was the most common. The first puff of the pipe at a smoking and the first morsel of food at a meal were always offered to the Great Powers—the earth, the sky and the four directions, which included everything that lay within their arms. All things were a part of these Powers, brothers in them, and anyone could understand what a brother was.

After his seventh birthday the Sioux boy never addressed his blood mother or sister directly again, speaking to them only through a third person. When he showed signs of coming manhood he was prepared for his puberty fasting by men close to the family, including some wise and holy one. There were also holy women among the Sioux, advising and officiating in many of the rites with both men and women but not for the puberty fasting, which was the youth's orientation into maleness. When he was ready the boy was escorted to some far barren hill and left there in breechclout and moccasins against the sun of day, the cold of night, without food or water. The ordeal was to strip away every superficiality, all the things of the flesh, to prepare for a dreaming, a vision from the Powers. Usually by the third or fourth day the youth had dreamed and was brought down, gaunt and weak. He was given a few drops of water at a time and some food, but slowly, and after he was restored a little, and bathed and feasted, his advisors and the holy man tried to interpret the vision that was to guide him in this manhood he was now entering.

THINKING ABOUT THE SELECTION

Recalling

1. What was "the first and greatest lesson" for the Sioux?
2. How did the Sioux feel about punishing children?
3. What custom protected children from favoritism?
4. How did the young learn from their peers?
5. How were boys trained to be warriors?
6. Why did young boys fast on a "far . . . hill"?

Interpreting

7. Why would a young Sioux learn to feel responsible for the whole tribe?
8. What can you infer from this essay about the qualities that the Sioux valued?

Applying

9. Explain whether or not the Sioux methods of child-rearing would work today, outside of the Sioux tribe.

READING IN THE CONTENT AREA

Taking Notes

Taking notes will help you to remember the important ideas in your reading. First you should skim through the piece. Then you should read it slowly, listing the main ideas and using words or phrases rather than complete sentences. The following notes, for example, cover the first four paragraphs.

At early age—senses Sioux have special feeling for family and tribe

Sioux mother stops baby's breathing to prevent crying—noise could bring enemies, chase away game

Benefits: children cared for by whole tribe, not physically punished

1. Skim through the rest of the essay and then take notes on it.
2. Compare your notes with the essay, making sure you have recorded the main ideas.

CRITICAL THINKING AND READING

Understanding Cause and Effect

A **cause** is what brings about a result, or **effect**. The writer of this essay tells you, for example, that a Sioux mother gently stops her baby's breathing when it cries. This action (cause) results in the baby's learning not to cry (effect).

On a separate piece of paper, write the missing cause.
1. *Cause*: ? *Effect*: The eldest son is protected from his mother's favoritism.
2. *Cause*: ? *Effect*: The Sioux are expert riders.

UNDERSTANDING LANGUAGE

Signaling Cause and Effect

The following words are among those that signal a cause-and-effect relationship: *because, since, therefore, consequently,* and *as a result.* For example, you can say, "The mother gently stopped her baby's breath when he cried; *consequently,* he learned not to cry." Or you can say, "The baby learned not to cry *because* his mother gently stopped his breath when he cried."

Connect the following statements with a word or phrase signaling cause and effect.
1. Every Indian knew how to swim. Indian babies were thrown into the water.
2. A child burned his hand on a hot coal. He crept back to the coal more carefully.

THINKING AND WRITING

Writing an Article About a Sioux Visitor

Imagine that a Sioux boy or girl from many years ago suddenly appears in your house. List some of the ways in which he or she would react to modern life. Then use the list to write a magazine article describing this miraculous visit. When revising your article, refer to "These Were the Sioux" to check that your portrait of a young Indian is accurate.

Nonfiction

Nonfiction is different from fiction in that it deals with real people and real events. Usually a nonfiction writer sets out with a certain purpose and intended audience in mind. A reader can gain a full appreciation of nonfiction by examining the techniques the writer uses to accomplish this purpose, the support the writer uses to back up or clarify the main idea, and the way the writer arranges this supporting information.

Purpose

Purpose is the author's reason for writing. A writer usually has both a general purpose and a specific purpose. The general purpose may be to explain or inform, to describe, or to persuade. The specific purpose is the main point the writer wants to make about the topic. Often this main point is stated in a thesis statement.

Techniques

Techniques are the tools the writer uses to accomplish the purpose. For example, the writer may use figurative language to vividly describe the subject or emotive language to arouse your feelings and so persuade you to do something.

Support

Support is the information the writer uses to back up or clarify the main idea. Support may take the form of facts and opinions or of reasons and examples. It may take the form of incidents or even of descriptive details.

Arrangement

The writer arranges the support material to best accomplish the purpose. The information may be arranged according to chronological order, spatial order, or order of importance.

On the following pages is an essay with annotations in the margin showing details an active reader might notice while reading.

Morning—
"The Bird Perched for Flight"

Anne Morrow Lindbergh

Purpose: The title provides a clue to the writer's main idea. What "bird" will this essay be about? What point will the author make about this "bird"?

We wake to the alarm at four thirty and leave our motel at five fifteen. The three astronauts must be already climbing into their seats at the top of their "thirty-six-story" rocket, poised for flight. The pilgrimage[1] of sightseers has started to the Cape.[2] Already the buses have left and lines of cars are on the roads. It is dark, a little chilly, with a sky full of stars. As we approach the Cape we see again the rocket and its launching tower from far off over the lagoon. It is still illumined with searchlights, but last night's vision has vanished. It is no longer tender or biological but simply a machine, the newest and most perfected creation of a scientific age—hard, weighty metal.

Purpose: The author's general purpose seems to be to describe an event. What is this event?

We watch the launching with some of the astronauts and their families, from a site near the Vehicle Assembly Building. Our cars are parked on a slight rise of ground. People get out, walk about restlessly, set up cameras and adjust their binoculars. The launch pad is about three miles away, near the beach. We look across Florida marsh grass and palmettos.[3] A cabbage palm[4] stands up black against a shadowy sky, just left of the rocket and its launching tower. As dawn flushes the horizon, an egret rises and lazily glides across the flats between us and the pad. It is a still morning. Ducks call from nearby inlets. Vapor trails of a high-flying plane turn pink in an almost cloudless sky. Stars pale in the blue.

Techniques: The author uses specific words and sensory details to create vivid word pictures. What specific words do you find? What details appeal to your senses?

---

1. pilgrimage (pil′ gram ij) *n.*: A long journey to a place of interest.
2. the Cape: Cape Canaveral, a sandy stretch of land that juts into the Atlantic Ocean from an island off the eastern coast of Florida. For many years, it has been an important site for rocket launchings. At the time this piece was written, it was called Cape Kennedy in honor of John F. Kennedy, 35th president of the United States (1961–1963).
3. palmettos (pal met′ ōz) *n.*: Palm trees with fan-shaped leaves.
4. cabbage palm (kab′ ij päm) *n.*: A palm tree with a bud that can be eaten as a vegetable.

With the morning light, Apollo 8[5] and its launching tower become clearer, harder, and more defined. One can see the details of installation. The dark sections on the smooth sides of the rocket, marking its stages, cut up the single fluid line. Vapor steams furiously off its side. No longer stark and simple, this morning the rocket is complicated, mechanical, earthbound. Too weighty for flight, one feels.

Arrangement: The details are arranged in chronological order. How does this arrangement help build suspense?

People stop talking, stand in front of their cars, and raise binoculars to their eyes. We peer nervously at the launch site and then at our wrist watches. Radio voices blare unnaturally loud from car windows. "Now only thirty minutes to launch time . . . fifteen minutes . . . six minutes . . . thirty seconds to go . . . twenty . . . T minus fifteen . . . fourteen . . . thirteen . . . twelve . . . eleven . . . ten . . . nine . . . Ignition!"

A jet of steam shoots from the pad below the rocket. "Ahhhh!" The crowd gasps, almost in unison. Now great flames spurt, leap, belch out across the horizon. Clouds of smoke billow up on either side of the rocket, completely hiding its base. From the midst of this holocaust,[6] the rocket begins to rise—slowly, as in a dream, so slowly it seems to hang suspended on the cloud of fire and smoke. It's impossible—it can't rise. Yes, it rises, but heavily, as if the giant weight is pulled by an invisible hand out of the atmosphere, like the lead on a plumb line[7] from the depths of the sea. Slowly it rises and—because of our distance—silently, as in a dream.

Techniques: Notice again the sensory details. Why do these details increase the suspense?

Suddenly the noise breaks, jumps across our three separating miles—a shattering roar of explosions, a trip hammer over one's head, under one's feet, through one's body. The earth shakes; cars rattle; vibrations beat in the chest. A roll of thunder, prolonged, prolonged, prolonged.

Purpose: We still do not know the author's specific purpose. Perhaps it has something to do with her feeling as if she is going to cry. Why would she feel this way?

I drop the binoculars and put my hands to my ears, holding my head to keep it steady. My throat tightens—am I going to cry?—my eyes are fixed on the rocket, mesmerized[8] by its slow ascent.

---

5. Apollo (ə päl′ ō) **8:** This spacecraft, carrying astronauts Frank Borman, William A. Anders, and James A. Lovell, Jr., orbited the moon 10 times. Apollo was the Greek god of music, prophecy, poetry, and medicine.

6. holocaust (häl′ ə kôst′) *n.:* In ancient times, an offering burned to the gods; the author is reminded of such offerings by the flames shooting from the rocket.

7. plumb (plum) **line:** A line weighted with lead at one end to measure the depth of water.

8. mesmerized (mez′ mər īzd′) *v.:* Hypnotized.

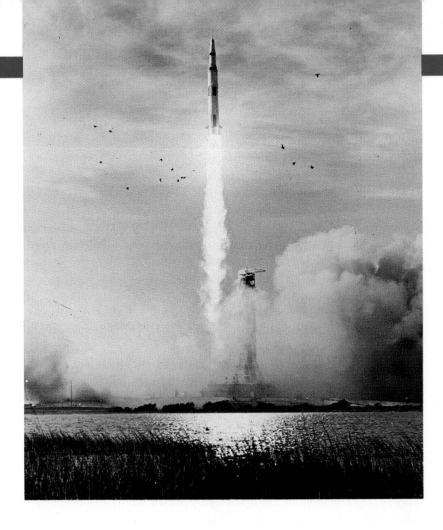

The foreground is now full of birds; a great flock of ducks, herons, small birds, rise pell-mell from the marshes at the noise. Fluttering in alarm and confusion, they scatter in all directions as if it were the end of the world. In the seconds I take to look at them, the rocket has left the tower.

It is up and away, a comet boring through the sky, no longer the vulnerable untried child, no longer the earth-bound machine, or the weight at the end of a line, but sheer terrifying force, blasting upward on its own titanic[9] power.

Techniques: Notice the contrast between the natural world and the world of rockets and machinery. How does this contrast make you feel about this takeoff?

It has gone miles into the sky. It is blurred by a cloud. No, it has made its own cloud—a huge vapor trail, which hides it. Out of the cloud something falls, cartwheeling down, smoking. "The first-stage cutoff," someone says. Where is the rocket itself?

---

9. titanic (tī tan′ ik) *adj.*: Having great size, strength, or power. In Greek mythology, the Titans were a race of giants who were defeated by the gods.

There, above the cloud now, reappears the rocket, only a very bright star, diminishing every second. Soon out of sight, off to lunar space.

One looks earthward again. It is curiously still and empty. A cloud of brown smoke hangs motionless on the horizon. Its long shadow reaches us across the grass. The launch pad is empty. The abandoned launching tower is being sprayed with jets of water to cool it down. It steams in the bright morning air. Still dazed, people stumble into cars and start the slow, jammed trek back to town. The monotone[10] of radio voices continues. One clings to this last thread of contact with something incredibly beautiful that has vanished.

Purpose and Support: Here the author states her specific purpose. What is it? Which details support her main idea?

"Where are they—where are they now?" In eleven minutes we get word. They are in earth orbit. They "look good" in the laconic[11] space talk that comes down from over a hundred miles above earth. And one realizes again that it is the men above all that matter, the individuals who man the machine, give it heart, sight, speech, intelligence, and direction; and the men on earth who are backing them up, monitoring[12] their every move, even to their heartbeats. This is not sheer power, it is power under control of man.

Pulling It Together: The author views the launching as a triumph for human beings. However, once the event is over, little trace of it is left in the natural world.

We drive slowly back to town. Above us the white vapor trail of the rocket is being scattered by wind into feathery shapes of herons' wings—the only mark in the sky of the morning's launching.

---

10. **monotone** (män′ ə tōn) *n.*: A single, unchanging tone.
11. **laconic** (lə kän′ ik) *adj.*: Using few words.
12. **monitoring** (män′ə tər′ iŋ) *v.*: Watching or keeping track of.

Anne Morrow Lindbergh (1906–   ) is especially well equipped to write about flight. The wife of Charles Lindbergh, the first pilot to fly solo across the Atlantic, she herself is also a licensed pilot. In fact, she accompanied her famous husband as a copilot on a 40,000-mile flight across five continents. Her many books and articles on flight have received wide praise. In this selection from *Earth Shine*, she describes the takeoff of Apollo 8.

THINKING ABOUT THE SELECTION

Recalling

1. Why does Lindbergh leave her motel room at five fifteen in the morning?
2. How does Apollo 8 look in the morning light? What does its appearance lead her to feel?
3. How do the people awaiting the launch lead her to feel?

Interpreting

4. Why does Lindbergh compare the rocket before blastoff to a "vulnerable untried child"?
5. Why does she call it "sheer terrifying force" immediately after takeoff?
6. When the rocket ascends, the birds scatter, "as if it were the end of the world." In what way does the rocket's takeoff signal the end of a world?

Applying

7. Do you consider the astronauts heroes? Explain your answer.

ANALYZING LITERATURE

Understanding an Essay

A common topic for an essay is a description of an event. Often this type of essay is written by a person who lived through the event, and so gives you first-hand information about it. Through the use of descriptive language, the author helps you visualize what has happened and imagine you are there experiencing the event for yourself. In most essays of this type, however, the author also shows you why this event is significant.

1. Find three descriptive details that give you an especially good picture of the sightseers. What impression do you form of the sightseers?
2. Find three descriptive details that give you an especially good picture of the site near the Vehicle Assembly Building. What impression do you form of the site?
3. Find three descriptive details that give you an especially good picture of the rocket. What impression do you form of the rocket?
4. What significance does Lindbergh see in the Apollo 8 takeoff?

CRITICAL THINKING AND READING

Separating Fact and Opinion

A **fact** can be proved true or false. For example, the following statement is a fact: Apollo 8 was launched in December 1968. An **opinion** expresses attitudes, evaluations, judgments, or even predicts the future. It cannot be proved true or false. For example, the following statement is an opinion: The rocket looked beautiful in the cold morning light. Writers will often include both facts and opinions in an essay describing an event.

Read the following sentences. Decide which contain facts and which contain opinions.

1. "[The rocket] is still illumined with searchlights. . . ."
2. "[The rocket] is no longer tender . . ."
3. "The launch pad is about three miles away, near the beach."
4. "And one realizes again that it is the men above all who matter, the individuals who man the machine . . ."

THINKING AND WRITING

Describing an Event

In this essay Lindbergh describes an historical event—the launching of Apollo 8. List all of the historical events you have lived through—for example, the election of a president, the disaster of the shuttle *Challenger*. From this list, select the event you would like to write about. Then freewrite about this event, exploring all your thoughts and feelings. Use your freewriting as a source of ideas for your first draft of an essay describing this event. When you revise your essay, make sure that your descriptions are clear and that you have shown the significance of the events. Prepare a final draft and share it with your classmates.

Understanding Persuasive Techniques

Authors often use **persuasive techniques** in nonfiction to try to convince readers to accept their opinions or to take some action. Understanding the persuasive techniques writers use will help you determine whether or not you should agree with the writer.

Stated Position

When reading persuasive writing, you must first identify the stated position that the writer wants you to accept. This position will be stated in the topic sentence and should be expressed simply and clearly so that it is easy to understand. Any terms that you may not know should be defined so that you have a clear idea of what the writer is proposing. This stated position is an opinion that the author holds and that can be debated. It is not a fact because there is nothing to debate about a fact.

Look at the following sentences:

Winslow Homer is a nineteenth-century American painter.
I like Winslow Homer's paintings.
Winslow Homer should be called America's greatest painter.

Neither the first nor second sentence would be an acceptable stated position. The first is a fact that cannot be disputed, while the second is merely an opinion that tells how someone feels. It cannot be debated. The third sentence, on the other hand, is a good topic sentence because it is stating an opinion that may or may not be accepted. Facts can be used to support or dispute it.

Major Points

Another effective persuasive technique is to restate the major points. Writers often restate their position at the conclusion of their essay. Therefore, looking for ideas that are repeated will help you locate the writer's stated position and major points.

To understand persuasive writing, you must identify the facts the author uses to back up his or her position. Evaluate them in terms of their quality and quantity. The following criteria will help you evaluate them. The supporting facts should be accurate, logical, and relevant to the argument. They should be introduced in an appropriate order. For instance, if you were trying to convince someone that Winslow Homer should be considered America's greatest painter, you probably would discuss the contributions that he made to painting in the order in which he made them, as this would be the easiest order to follow.

By using examples, descriptions, and comparisons to support facts, the writer makes the argument stronger. For example, a description of one of Homer's paintings could illustrate his techniques and accomplishments and thus clarify and strengthen the argument. A comparison of the types of scenes Homer and others painted of the Civil War would reveal the unique talent Homer possessed. Giving an example of people's reactions to Homer's work could also add weight to the argument.

Finally, the more facts a writer includes to support the stated position, the more convincing is the argument. Check that there are sufficient supporting facts or reasons to make a strong argument.

Guidelines

- Identify the writer's stated position. It should appear as the topic sentence and be an opinion that can be debated.
- Make sure you understand the stated position.
- Identify the major points that support the author's position.
- Evaluate these points insofar as they are
  accurate, logical, and relevant
  introduced in an appropriate order
  clarified through examples, descriptions, and the use of
    strong comparisons
  sufficient in number to make a strong argument

Activity

Reread "Letter Writing" by Andrew A. Rooney and use it to answer the following questions.

1. What is the stated position of the author? Is this position clearly expressed? Give reasons to support your answer.
2. Has the writer used repetition to emphasize his stated position? Where?
3. List the facts the author uses to back up his position.
4. Are these facts presented in an appropriate order? Explain your answer.
5. Are these facts accurate, logical, and relevant? Explain your answer.
6. Does the author use examples to back up his facts? If so, give examples.
7. Does the author use comparisons to clarify and make his supporting facts more convincing? If so, give examples.

YOU THE WRITER

Assignment

1. Write a personal narrative describing an incident. This incident may be funny, sad, exciting, scary, and so on.

Prewriting. Before you write, select an incident and freewrite about it.

Writing. Write your narrative. Tell what happened in chronological order. Try to give a sense of the place where this incident occurred. Was it quiet or noisy there? Was the weather hot or cold?

Revising. When you revise, check to see that your reader will understand the order in which events occurred. To help the reader, you might want to use time words like, "Later, . . ." or "Soon . . ."

Assignment

2. Write an essay about something you are interested in—a hobby, a sport, a favorite vacation spot. Include a description of your interest and your reactions.

Prewriting. Once you have chosen the subject, narrow it. For example, if you are going to write about baseball, narrow down your topic to hitting or playing second base. Then begin to cluster. Jot down ideas and feelings about the topic, connecting the ones that seem to go together.

Writing. Now write your essay. Follow your notes, but also pay attention to new ideas that come into your mind. Did you leave out any facts or impressions that you now want to include? If so, include them now—in the place where they fit most naturally. Explain any specialized terms you use.

Revising. Check to see that your ideas are in a reasonable order. Does one idea flow into the next one smoothly? You can make your ideas flow smoothly by using connecting expressions.

Assignment

3. Details are especially important in capturing the look, the spirit, the essence of a person. Write an essay in which you describe a person. Be sure to tell hard, sharp details about this person.

Prewriting. Jot down as many things about this person as you can think of: his or her appearance, gestures, activities, habits, way of speaking, ideas, and so on. Then cluster these details.

Writing. Now write your essay. Show your character *doing* something, maybe going about his or her daily routine. As he or she goes from one thing to another, insert your idea clusters in places where they fit naturally. For example, you might show how the character dresses as he or she leaves the house in the morning.

Revising. Make sure the images in your essay are clear by checking to see that the details are sharp and specific. Remember, good writing is the art of the particular.

Assignment

1. Choose an essay that you found especially interesting. Then write an essay in which you state the main idea of this essay and then show which devices the author used to support his or her main idea.

Prewriting. Write down the main idea the essay communicated. List the ways in which the author supported his or her ideas.

Writing. Now write your essay. State your main idea. In your body paragraphs, identify the ways in which the author supports the main idea, providing specific examples of each way you identify.

Revising. When you revise, check to see that your essay is well organized.

Assignment

2. Write an essay explaining what you can tell about the author of one of the essays based on his or her writing. Discuss the author's interests, personality, attitudes, beliefs, and so on.

Prewriting. Reread the essay you are going to write about. Read it for its explicit message, the points the author makes about the subject he or she is discussing. Read it also for its implicit message, the kinds of things the author is saying between the lines.

Writing. Write your first draft. Discuss the things you deduced about the author from the explicit message of the essay. Next discuss the things you deduced about the author from reading between the lines. Finally draw conclusions about the author.

Revising. Check to see that you have included enough information to give the reader a clear impression of the author. Also check to see that the evidence supports your conclusions.

Assignment

3. Write an essay about *two* essays, one that instructs more than it entertains and one that entertains more than it instructs. Explain what you learned in the instructional essay and what you found interesting in the entertaining essay.

Prewriting. Ask yourself which essay provided you with the most information about things you didn't know before. Ask yourself which essay you found the most entertaining. Now make a list of the things you have learned from the informative essay and a list of the things you found interesting in the entertaining essay.

Writing. Write your essay, organizing it in the following way: Start by stating your main idea. Then discuss the things you learned from the informative essay. Next discuss the things you found interesting in the entertaining essay. Finally sum up your major points.

Revising. When you revise, cut out unnecessary words and sentences, for these clutter up your essay and prevent your important ideas from shining through.

SPRINGTIME FANTASY
Adolphe Faugeron
Three Lions

POETRY

Poetry is language that says more than ordinary language and says it with fewer words and in less space. Poets use language in a special way. Like other writers, poets choose words for their sense, but they also choose words for what they hint at or suggest, for the way they sound, and for the word pictures they create. Ordinary language makes sense. Poetry makes sense—and sound, and rhythm and music, and vision.

Short stories, essays, newspaper articles, your schoolbooks, and so on, are written in prose. Poetry is usually written in verse. Verse is language with a definite rhythm, or beat. It is usually arranged in columns down the page. Sometimes these columns of lines are divided into units called stanzas. Lines of verse often (but not always) rhyme. Although you could say that poetry is what is written in verse, it is always more than rhythm and rhyme. Poetry, as a great poet said, is the most memorable kind of language.

Poetry

Reading poetry is an act of discovery. Active readers ask questions about the use of words and clarify the intended use of language. They listen for the music of the poem. They stop to summarize and to paraphrase the poem's meaning. Finally, they pull together all the elements of the poem and add to it themselves. Use the following strategies to help you read a poem actively.

Question

The poet Samuel Coleridge defined poetry as "the best words in the best order." As you read, ask questions about the effect of the words. Think about the vivid images, or word pictures. What do they make you see? What do they make you feel?

Clarify

Poems are often filled with figurative language—that is, language that says one thing but means another. As you read poetry, stop to clarify—to ask if the words mean exactly what they say. If the words suggest something beyond their basic literal meaning, perhaps the poet is using them figuratively or intends a more imaginative meaning.

Listen

Poetry has a musical quality. To fully enjoy it, listen to the music created by the use of rhythm and rhyme. Look for the effect of the repetition of sounds, words, and phrases. Also remember that the end of a sentence in poetry is not necessarily the end of a line. Let punctuation marks guide your reading.

Summarize

Some poems tell a story. When you read, stop at appropriate points in the story to summarize what has happened so far.

Paraphrase

Ask what the poem means, and then put this meaning into your own words. You do not truly own, or understand, a poem until you can express its meaning in your own words.

Pull It Together

A poem consists of words, images, rhythms, and meaning. However, as James Dickey says in "How to Enjoy Poetry" (page 375), "for a poem to live, something from within you must come to it and meet it and complete it." After you have read a poem, bring all the elements together. What did the poem say to you?

The Village Blacksmith

Henry Wadsworth Longfellow

Under a spreading chestnut tree
  The village smithy¹ stands;
The smith, a mighty man is he,
  With large and sinewy² hands;
5 And the muscles of his brawny arms
  Are strong as iron bands.

His hair is crisp,³ and black, and long,
  His face is like the tan;
His brow is wet with honest sweat,
10 He earns whate'er he can,
And looks the whole world in the face,
  For he owes not any man.

Week in, week out, from morn till night,
  You can hear his bellows⁴ blow;
15 You can hear him swing his heavy sledge,⁵
  With measured beat and slow,
Like a sexton⁶ ringing the village bell,
  When the evening sun is low.

And children coming home from school
20 Look in at the open door;
They love to see the flaming forge,
  And hear the bellows roar,
And catch the burning sparks that fly
  Like chaff from a threshing floor.

Question: What picture of the blacksmith do these words create? Which words are particularly effective? What feelings toward the blacksmith do the words arouse?

Clarify: The poet is using figurative language when he compares the blacksmith to a sexton.

Question: In what special way are the blacksmith and a sexton alike? What does this simile suggest about the blacksmith?

Listen: The poem has a slightly irregular rhythm. Read the lines aloud and tap out the pattern of stressed and unstressed syllables. The rhyme scheme is abcbdb. Which words rhyme?

---

1. smithy (smith′ ē) *n.*: The workshop of a blacksmith.
2. sinewy (sin′ yo͞o wē) *adj.*: Tough and strong.
3. crisp (krisp) *adj.*: In this case, it means closely curled and wiry.
4. bellows (bel′ ōz) *n.*: A device for quickening the fire by blowing air on it.
5. sledge (slej) *n.*: Sledgehammer, a long, heavy hammer, usually held with both hands.
6. sexton (seks′ tən) *n.*: A church official in charge of ringing the bells.

25 He goes on Sunday to the church,
       And sits among his boys;
   He hears the parson pray and preach,
       He hears his daughter's voice,
   Singing in the village choir,
30   And it makes his heart rejoice.

   It sounds to him like her mother's voice,
       Singing in Paradise!
   He needs must think of her once more,
       How in the grave she lies;
35 And with his hard, rough hand he wipes
       A tear out of his eyes.

   Toiling—rejoicing—sorrowing,
       Onward through life he goes;
   Each morning sees some task begin,
40   Each evening sees it close;
   Something attempted, something done,
       Has earned a night's repose.

   Thanks, thanks to thee, my worthy friend,
       For the lesson thou hast taught!
45 Thus at the flaming forge of life
       Our fortunes must be wrought;
   Thus on its sounding anvil shaped
       Each burning deed and thought.

Summarize: A hard-working blacksmith takes pleasure in hearing his daughter sing in the church choir, for her singing recalls to him his now-dead wife, and so brings a tear to his eye.

Listen: Three words end in *-ing*. What effect does this repetition create?

Paraphrase: The blacksmith's philosophy is that hard work has great value. The completion of a task earns one a good night's sleep.

Listen: Three words begin with the letter *f*. What effect does the repetition of this initial sound create?

Pull It Together: There is a lesson to be found in the blacksmith's life. The poet praises his ethic of hard work. However, he also points out that although the blacksmith has been hardened by life, his heart is still tender—he is kind to the village children and sheds a tear for his now-dead wife.

Henry Wadsworth Longfellow (1807–1882) was born in Maine. After graduating from Bowdoin College, he traveled in Europe, but returned to become a professor of languages at Bowdoin and later at Harvard. Longfellow is associated with a group of poets known as the Fireside Poets, since their work often attracted a family audience that would read the poems aloud while sitting around the fireplace. In many of his poems, Longfellow strove to portray the myths and values of the still-young nation. After the publication of his second book of poems, which included "The Village Blacksmith," he became recognized as one of the major poets in the United States.

THINKING ABOUT THE SELECTION
Recalling

1. Why is the blacksmith able to look the whole world in the face?
2. Why does his daughter's voice make his heart rejoice?
3. How does the blacksmith begin and end each day?

Interpreting

4. Which details tell you that the blacksmith is an honest, hard-working man?
5. What does the tear in his eye indicate about him?

Applying

6. President Theodore Roosevelt once said in a Labor Day address: "Far and away the best prize that life offers is the chance to work hard at work worth doing." Do you think the village blacksmith would agree or disagree with this sentiment? Explain your answer.

ANALYZING LITERATURE
Understanding Theme in Poetry

Theme is the insight into life revealed by the poem. Sometimes the theme is stated directly. To fully understand it, paraphrase it, or express it in your own words.
1. Which lines reveal the blacksmith's philosophy of life?
2. Paraphrase these lines.
3. Which details indicate that the poet agrees with the blacksmith's philosophy of life?

CRITICAL THINKING AND READING
Understanding the Poet's Purpose

When Longfellow wrote in the mid-nineteenth century, the United States was still a rather young country. One of his purposes for writing was to present myths for the new land and to portray the values of our native American culture.

1. Which details in the poem show the American culture during the nineteenth century valued independence?
2. Which details show that it valued sentiment, or tender feelings?
3. Which details show that it valued hard work?
4. Do you think views toward work in the later part of the twentieth century are different from those during Longfellow's time? Explain your answer.

UNDERSTANDING LANGUAGE
Interpreting Similes

A **simile** is a comparison between two basically unlike things. A simile makes its comparison by using the word *like* or *as*. By using a simile, a poet can make a point in a vivid way. For example: "And the muscles of his brawny arms/Are strong as iron bands." By comparing the muscles of the blacksmith's arms to iron bands, the poet emphasizes the muscles' strength.
1. What simile do you find in lines 15–18? What point does the poet make through the use of this simile?
2. What simile do you find in lines 23–24? What point does the poet make through the use of this simile?

THINKING AND WRITING
Writing About Work

Think of someone you know who enjoys his or her work. What does this person do? Why does this person take pleasure from the job? Write a short poem telling about a day in the work life of this person. Use similes to help you make your points. Revise your poem to make sure its meaning is clear. Prepare a final draft, and read it aloud to your classmates.

Narrative Poetry

THE BOY
Thomas Hart Benton
© *Three Lions*

The Highwayman

Alfred Noyes (1880–1958) was both a poet and critic. He was born in Staffordshire, England, although he lived for many years in the United States and taught at Princeton University. Noyes often wrote about legendary figures from English history, such as Robin Hood and Sir Francis Drake. He wrote "The Highwayman," his best-known poem, about an outlaw and his love, while visiting Bagshot Heath. The poem may have been inspired by the fact that this region of England had once been terrorized by outlaws.

Narrative Poetry

Narrative poetry is poetry that tells a story. Narrative poems have a special appeal. They present dramatic events in a vivid way, using some of the same elements as short stories: plot, characters, and dialogue, for example. Some narrative poems, like "The Highwayman," use words and phrases that are repeated throughout the work. These repetitions help to create a songlike rhythm and focus your attention on important details of the story.

Look For

While reading "The Highwayman," look for the words and phrases that are repeated. Decide why the poet might have wanted to emphasize these words and phrases. How does the repetition help create a romantic picture of the outlaw?

Writing

A highwayman was an outlaw who robbed travelers. Recall a famous outlaw you have heard or read about. List some of the details you remember about this outlaw's legend. Which of these details made the outlaw seem a romantic, or dashing figure?

Vocabulary

Knowing the following words will help you as you read "The Highwayman."

torrent (tôr′ ənt) *n.*: Flood (p. 437)

moor (moor) *n.*: Open, rolling land with swamps (p. 437)

breeches (brich′ iz) *n.*: Trousers that reach to or just below the knee (p. 437)

cascade (kas kād′) *n.*: Waterfall or anything tumbling like water (p. 439)

tawny (tô′ nē) *adj.*: Yellowish brown (p. 440)

strive (strīv) *v.*: Struggle (p. 441)

brandished (bran′ dishd) *v.*: Waved in a threatening way (p. 442)

The Highwayman

Alfred Noyes

Part One

The wind was a torrent of darkness among the gusty trees.
The moon was a ghostly galleon[1] tossed upon cloudy seas.
The road was a ribbon of moonlight over the purple moor,
And the highwayman came riding—
5   Riding—riding—
The highwayman came riding, up to the old inn door.

He'd a French cocked-hat on his forehead, a bunch of lace at
    his chin,
A coat of the claret velvet, and breeches of brown doeskin.
They fitted with never a wrinkle. His boots were up to the
    thigh.
10 And he rode with a jeweled twinkle,
        His pistol butts a-twinkle,
His rapier hilt[2] a-twinkle, under the jeweled sky.

Over the cobbles he clattered and clashed in the dark innyard.
He tapped with his whip on the shutters, but all was locked
    and barred.
15 He whistled a tune to the window, and who should be waiting
    there
But the landlord's black-eyed daughter,
        Bess, the landlord's daughter,
Plaiting[3] a dark red love knot into her long black hair.

And dark in the dark old innyard a stable wicket[4] creaked
20 Where Tim the ostler[5] listened. His face was white and peaked.
His eyes were hollows of madness, his hair like moldy hay,
But he loved the landlord's daughter,
        The landlord's red-lipped daughter.
Dumb as a dog he listened, and he heard the robber say—

---

1. galleon (gal′ ē ən) *n.*: A large Spanish sailing ship.
2. rapier (rā′ pē ər) **hilt:** The large cup-shaped handle of a rapier,
which is a type of sword.
3. plaiting (plāt′ iŋ) *n.*: Braiding.
4. stable wicket (stā′ b'l wik′ it): A small door or gate to a stable.
5. ostler (äs′ lər) *n.*: Someone who takes care of horses at an inn
or stable.

25 "One kiss, my bonny[6] sweetheart, I'm after a prize to-night,
But I shall be back with the yellow gold before the morning
    light;
Yet, if they press me sharply, and harry[7] me through the day,
Then look for me by moonlight,
      Watch for me by moonlight,
30 I'll come to thee by moonlight, though hell should bar the
    way."

He rose upright in the stirrups. He scarce could reach her
    hand,
But she loosened her hair in the casement.[8] His face burnt
    like a brand[9]
As the black cascade of perfume came tumbling over his
    breast;
And he kissed its waves in the moonlight,
35   (O, sweet black waves in the moonlight!)
Then he tugged at his rein in the moonlight, and galloped
    away to the west.

---

6. bonny (bän′ ē) *adj.*: Scottish for pretty.
7. harry (har′ ē) *v.*: To disturb by constant attacks.
8. casement (kās′ mənt) *n.*: A window frame that opens on hinges.
9. brand (brand) *n.*: A piece of burning wood.

Part Two

He did not come in the dawning. He did not come at noon;
And out of the tawny sunset, before the rise of the moon,
When the road was a gypsy's ribbon, looping the purple moor,
40 A redcoat troop came marching—
          Marching—marching—
King George's men[10] came marching, up to the old inn door.

They said no word to the landlord. They drank his ale instead.
But they gagged his daughter, and bound her, to the foot of
          her narrow bed.
45 Two of them knelt at her casement, with muskets at their
          side!
There was death at every window;
          And hell at one dark window;
For Bess could see, through her casement, the road that *he*
          would ride.

They had tied her up to attention, with many a sniggering
          jest.[11]
50 They had bound a musket beside her, with the muzzle
          beneath her breast!
"Now, keep good watch!" and they kissed her. She heard the
          doomed man say—
Look for me by moonlight;
          Watch for me by moonlight;
I'll come to thee by moonlight, though hell should bar the
          way!

55 She twisted her hands behind her; but all the knots held
          good!
She writhed her hands till her fingers were wet with sweat or
          blood!
They stretched and strained in the darkness, and the hours
          crawled by like years,
Till, now, on the stroke of midnight,
          Cold, on the stroke of midnight,
60 The tip of one finger touched it! The trigger at least was hers!

The tip of one finger touched it. She strove no more for the
          rest.

---

10. King George's men: Soldiers serving King George of England.
11. sniggering (snig′ ər iŋ) **jest:** Sly joke.

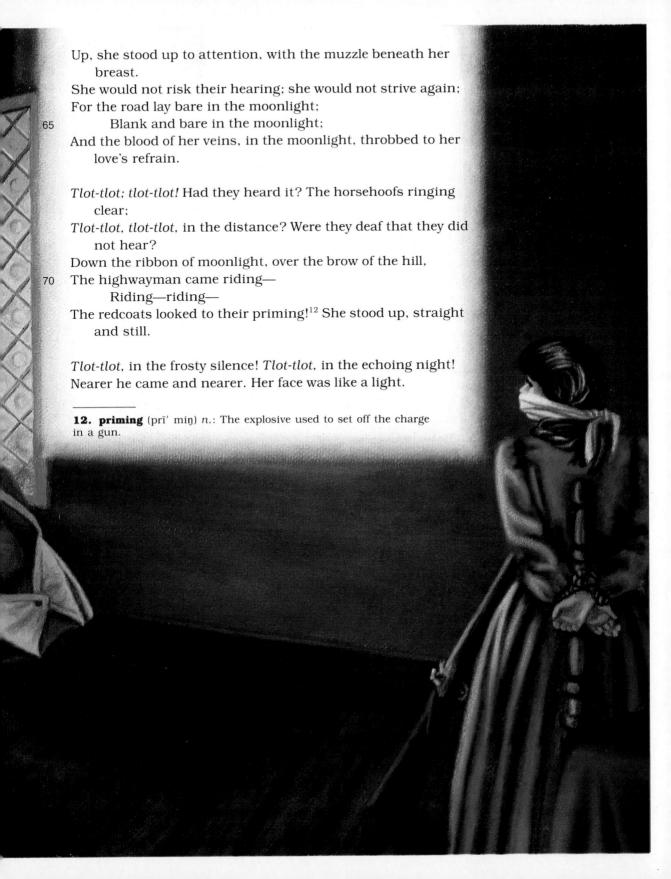

Up, she stood up to attention, with the muzzle beneath her
    breast.
She would not risk their hearing; she would not strive again;
For the road lay bare in the moonlight;
65   Blank and bare in the moonlight;
And the blood of her veins, in the moonlight, throbbed to her
    love's refrain.

Tlot-tlot; tlot-tlot! Had they heard it? The horsehoofs ringing
    clear;
Tlot-tlot, tlot-tlot, in the distance? Were they deaf that they did
    not hear?
Down the ribbon of moonlight, over the brow of the hill,
70   The highwayman came riding—
       Riding—riding—
The redcoats looked to their priming![12] She stood up, straight
    and still.

Tlot-tlot, in the frosty silence! *Tlot-tlot,* in the echoing night!
Nearer he came and nearer. Her face was like a light.

---

12. priming (prī' miŋ) *n.*: The explosive used to set off the charge
in a gun.

75 Her eyes grew wide for a moment; she drew one last deep
       breath,
   Then her finger moved in the moonlight,
           Her musket shattered the moonlight,
   Shattered her breast in the moonlight and warned him—with
       her death.

   He turned. He spurred to the west; he did not know who stood
80 Bowed, with her head o'er the musket, drenched with her own
       blood!
   Not till the dawn he heard it, and his face grew gray to hear
   How Bess, the landlord's daughter,
           The landlord's black-eyed daughter,
   Had watched for her love in the moonlight, and died in the
       darkness there.

85 Back, he spurred like a madman, shouting a curse to the sky,
   With the white road smoking behind him and his rapier
       brandished high.
   Blood-red were his spurs in the golden noon; wine-red was his
       velvet coat;
   When they shot him down on the highway,
           Down like a dog on the highway,
90 And he lay in his blood on the highway, with a bunch of lace
       at his throat.

   .   .   .   .

   And still of a winter's night, they say, when the wind is in
       the trees,
   When the moon is a ghostly galleon tossed upon cloudy
       seas,
   When the road is a ribbon of moonlight over the purple moor,
   A highwayman comes riding—
95   *Riding—riding—*
   A highwayman comes riding, up to the old inn door.

   Over the cobbles he clatters and clangs in the dark innyard.
   He taps with his whip on the shutters, but all is locked and
       barred.
   He whistles a tune to the window, and who should be
       waiting there
100 *But the landlord's black-eyed daughter,*
           Bess, the landlord's daughter,
   Plaiting a dark red love knot into her long black hair.

THINKING ABOUT THE SELECTION

Recalling

1. Explain the highwayman's plans. (Lines 25–30)
2. Describe the Redcoats' actions at the inn. (Lines 43–51)
3. How does Bess warn the highwayman of the soldier's presence? (Lines 75–80)
4. What happens to the highwayman when he returns the day after Bess's warning?

Interpreting

5. How do the soldiers learn of the highwayman's plans to return to the inn?
6. Find three details that make the highwayman appear a romantic, or dashing figure.
7. Find each mention of the color *red* in this poem. How does the repetition of this color add to the romantic quality of the poem?
8. How does the setting add to this quality?
9. Would this poem have been as effective if it had ended at line 90? Explain your answer.

Applying

10. What is it about outlaws that has made people romanticize them—or has made their lives seem romantic and glamorous?

ANALYZING LITERATURE

Understanding Narrative Poetry

Narrative poetry tells a story, using elements like plot, character, and setting. In "The Highwayman," for example, the two main characters are the outlaw and Bess. Using strong rhythm and repeated words, the poet tells how the love between Bess and the outlaw leads to their deaths.

1. Describe the two main characters.
2. How is the conflict resolved?
3. Where and when does most of the action take place?
4. How do the poem's rhythms and repetitions add to the drama of the story?

CRITICAL THINKING AND READING

Following the Sequence of Events

A storyteller creates an effect by the order in which he or she chooses to **sequence,** or arrange, the events. Noyes tells "The Highwayman" in **chronological sequence,** describing events in the order they occur.

1. List the important events of the poem in chronological sequence.
2. Would the poem be as effective if the sequence were changed and you knew right away what would happen? Why or why not?

SPEAKING AND LISTENING

Reading with Expression

Reading with expression means using your voice to bring out the meaning of a work. You can best practice this type of reading in small groups. Choose one of the following passages to read aloud: lines 1–18; lines 37–54; lines 91–102. Read your chosen passage several times to your group. Try varying the speed with which you say different words and phrases. Also, you may choose to say some phrases in a louder, or a softer, voice. In some places, you might want to stop at the end of a line, while in others you may want to continue smoothly from one line to the next.

THINKING AND WRITING

Summarizing a Narrative Poem

Summarizing a story means retelling it briefly in the correct order, giving only the essential details. Imagine that you are creating a movie based on this poem. In order to go ahead with your plans, you need a summary of the action. Look again at the list that you made of the poem's events. Turn this list into a summary of the story, adding only the most important details. In revising, make sure that your summary is brief but complete.

GUIDE FOR READING

The Cremation of Sam McGee

Robert Service (1874–1958) was a Canadian poet who grew up in Glasgow, Scotland. He moved to Canada at the age of twenty and was hired by a bank in 1905. When the bank transferred him to a branch in the Yukon, Service began to write lively poems about the trappers and prospectors he met there. These poems were an immediate success. Soon he was able to leave the bank and concentrate on writing. In "The Cremation of Sam McGee," Service creates a memorable character with an intense hatred of the cold.

Rhythm

Rhythm is the sound pattern created by combining stressed and unstressed syllables. In the following lines from "The Cremation of Sam McGee," for example, the stressed syllables (marked ´) receive more emphasis than the unstressed ones (marked ˘):

Aňd Ĭ looǩed ǎt iť, aňd Ĭ thoúght ǎ bít, aňd Ĭ looǩed ǎt mў frōzěn chūm;
Thěn "Hére," saǐd Í, with ǎ súdděn crý, "iš mў cré-mǎ-tór-ěuḿ."

The same general pattern of stressed and unstressed syllables continues throughout the poem. Other poems have different rhythms, and sometimes a poem's rhythm may change from line to line.

Look For

"The Cremation of Sam McGee" is a poem with a strong, thumping rhythm. Look for the drumbeat of the stressed syllables as you read. You may even want to tap out this rhythm with your fingers. What effect does the rhythm have on the poem?

Writing

A character in this poem, Sam McGee, does not like cold. Remember a time when, for one reason or another, you felt very cold. Write about the situation, telling how bitter cold it was.

Vocabulary

Knowing the following words will help you as you read "The Cremation of Sam McGee."

whimper (hwim' pər) v.: Make low, crying sounds; complain (p. 445)

cremated (krē' māt id) v.: Burned to ashes (p. 445)

ghastly (gast' lē) adj.: Ghost-like; frightful (p. 446)

brawn (brôn) n.: Physical strength (p. 446)

stern (sturn) adj.: Strict; unyielding (p. 446)

loathed (lōthd) v.: Hated (p. 446)

scowled (skould) v.: Frowned (p. 447)

grisly (griz' lē) adj.: Horrible (p. 447)

The Cremation of Sam McGee

Robert Service

There are strange things done in the midnight sun[1]
   By the men who moil[2] for gold;
The Arctic trails have their secret tales
   That would make your blood run cold;
5 *The Northern Lights have seen queer sights,*
   But the queerest they ever did see
Was that night on the marge[3] of Lake Lebarge
   I cremated Sam McGee.

Now Sam McGee was from Tennessee, where the cotton
   blooms and blows.
10 Why he left his home in the South to roam 'round the Pole,
   God only knows.
He was always cold, but the land of gold seemed to hold
   him like a spell;
Though he'd often say in his homely way that "he'd sooner
   live in hell."

On a Christmas Day we were mushing[4] our way over the
   Dawson trail.
Talk of your cold! through the parka's fold it stabbed like a
   driven nail.
15 If our eyes we'd close, then the lashes froze till sometimes
   we couldn't see;
It wasn't much fun, but the only one to whimper was Sam
   McGee.

And that very night, as we lay packed tight in our robes
   beneath the snow,
And the dogs were fed, and the stars o'erhead were dancing
   heel and toe,

---

1. the midnight sun: The sun visible at midnight in the arctic or
antarctic regions during the summer.
2. moil (moil) *v.*: To toil and slave.
3. marge (märj) *n.*: A poetic word for the shore of the lake.
4. mushing (mush' iŋ) *v.*: Traveling by foot over snow, usually with
a dog sled. "Mush" is a command to sled dogs to start or go faster.

He turned to me, and "Cap," says he, "I'll cash in[5] this trip,
   I guess;
20 And if I do, I'm asking that you won't refuse my last request."

Well, he seemed so low that I couldn't say no; then he says
   with a sort of moan:
"It's the cursèd cold, and it's got right hold till I'm chilled
   clean through to the bone.
Yet 'tain't being dead—it's my awful dread of the icy grave
   that pains;
So I want you to swear that, foul or fair, you'll cremate my
   last remains."
25 A pal's last need is a thing to heed, so I swore I would not
   fail;
And we started on at the streak of dawn; but God! he
   looked ghastly pale.
He crouched on the sleigh, and he raved all day of his home
   in Tennessee;
And before nightfall a corpse was all that was left of Sam
   McGee.

There wasn't a breath in that land of death, and I hurried,
   horror-driven,
30 With a corpse half hid that I couldn't get rid, because of a
   promise given;
It was lashed to the sleigh, and it seemed to say: "You may
   tax your brawn and brains,
But you promised true, and it's up to you to cremate those
   last remains."

Now a promise made is a debt unpaid, and the trail has its
   own stern code.
In the days to come, though my lips were dumb, in my
   heart how I cursed that load.
35 In the long, long night, by the lone firelight, while the
   huskies,[6] round in a ring,
Howled out their woes to the homeless snows—O God! how
   I loathed the thing.

And every day that quiet clay seemed to heavy and heavier
   grow;

---

5. cash in: A slang expression meaning "die."
6. huskies (hus' kēs) *n.*: Strong dogs used for pulling sleds over
the snow.

And on I went, though the dogs were spent and the grub
    was getting low;
The trail was bad, and I felt half mad, but I swore I would
    not give in;
40 And I'd often sing to the hateful thing, and it hearkened
    with a grin.

Till I came to the marge of Lake Lebarge, and a derelict[7]
    there lay;
It was jammed in the ice, but I saw in a trice it was called
    the "Alice May."
And I looked at it, and I thought a bit, and I looked at my
    frozen chum;
Then "Here," said I, with a sudden cry, "is my cre-ma-tor-
    eum."

45 Some planks I tore from the cabin floor, and I lit the boiler
    fire;
Some coal I found that was lying around, and I heaped the
    fuel higher;
The flames just soared, and the furnace roared—such a
    blaze you seldom see;
And I burrowed a hole in the glowing coal, and I stuffed in
    Sam McGee.

Then I made a hike, for I didn't like to hear him sizzle so;
50 And the heavens scowled, and the huskies howled, and the
    wind began to blow.
It was icy cold, but the hot sweat rolled down my cheeks,
    and I don't know why;
And the greasy smoke in an inky cloak went streaking
    down the sky.

I do not know how long in the snow I wrestled with grisly
    fear;
But the stars came out and they danced about ere again I
    ventured near;
55 I was sick with dread, but I bravely said: "I'll just take a
    peep inside.
I guess he's cooked, and it's time I looked"; . . . then the
    door I opened wide.

---

7. derelict (der′ ə likt′) n.: An abandoned ship.

And there sat Sam, looking cool and calm, in the heart of
    the furnace roar;
And he wore a smile you could see a mile, and he said:
    "Please close that door.
It's fine in here, but I greatly fear you'll let in the cold and
    storm—
60 Since I left Plumtree, down in Tennessee, it's the first time
    I've been warm."

There are strange things done in the midnight sun
    By the men who moil for gold;
The Arctic trails have their secret tales
    That would make your blood run cold;
65 *The Northern Lights have seen queer sights,*
    But the queerest they ever did see
Was that night on the marge of Lake Lebarge
    I cremated Sam McGee.

THINKING ABOUT THE SELECTION

Recalling

1. Where did Sam McGee come from? Why doesn't he go home? (Lines 8–11)
2. What does Sam ask the narrator to promise? (Lines 21–24)
3. Why does the narrator try to keep his promise, even though he curses the load? (Lines 29–36)
4. How is the narrator to keep his promise? (Lines 41–48)
5. Describe what the narrator finds when he opens the furnace door? (Lines 53–61)

Interpreting

6. Compare and contrast Sam and the narrator.
7. In what way is the ending of this poem an elaborate practical joke? Explain the details that suggest Sam was playing a trick on his pal in order to get warm.

Applying

8. Do you agree with the narrator that "a promise made is a debt unpaid"? Why or why not?

ANALYZING LITERATURE

Understanding Rhythm

Rhythm is the pattern of stressed and unstressed syllables in the lines of a poem. Many poems have the same rhythmic pattern in each line.

1. Tap out the pattern of stressed and unstressed syllables in line 43. Find three other lines with this exact same rhythm.
2. How does the rhythm of line 44 differ from that of line 43? Find three other lines with the exact same rhythm as line 44.
3. What conclusion do you draw about the rhythmic pattern of this poem?

CRITICAL THINKING AND READING

Evaluating the Effects of Rhythm

Like a drumbeat, the pattern of stressed syllables in poetry can produce different moods: excitement, peace, sadness, for example. In evaluating the effects of rhythm, compare a passage from a poem with a similar passage written as a paragraph.

1. Use your own words to summarize lines 57–60 of the poem in a paragraph.
2. Read your own words and the lines of poetry out loud.
3. Compare and contrast the mood of the poetry with that of your paragraph.

SPEAKING AND LISTENING

Practicing Choral Reading

Choral reading refers to the reading aloud of a poem by a group of people. Your teacher can divide the class in half and each group can prepare a choral reading of this poem for the other group. Remember that in a choral reading, some parts of the poem can be read by everyone. However, other parts, like Sam McGee's words, can be read by a single person.

Each group may also act as an audience for the other group. After hearing a choral reading, the audience can offer comments and suggestions for improvement.

THINKING AND WRITING

Patterning the Rhythm of a Poem

Imagine the narrator's reactions to Sam's trick. Freewrite about what you think the narrator said to Sam after he saw him looking cool and calm in the heart of the roaring furnace. Then use your freewriting as the basis for writing a new stanza for this poem. Using the same rhythmic pattern, write a stanza telling the narrator's reactions. Review your stanza, reading it aloud and tapping out the rhythm. Finally, prepare a proofread draft and read it to your classmates.

Sarah Cynthia Sylvia Stout
Would Not Take the Garbage Out

Shel Silverstein (1932–   ) was born in Chicago, Illinois, and grew up hoping to be a dancer or a baseball player someday. Instead, his artistic talents led him to become one of America's most popular writers and cartoonists. Illustrated with his own drawings, his poetry books, such as *Where the Sidewalk Ends,* are enjoyed by young and old alike. In the poem you are about to read, he humorously tells the outrageous results of Sarah Cynthia Sylvia Stout's refusal to take the garbage out.

Rhyme

Rhyme is the repetition of a sound in two or more words or phrases. The common type of rhyme that occurs at the end of lines is called **end rhyme**. However, rhyme can occur within a line as well. Some rhymes are **exact rhymes,** like *peas* and *cheese*. The sounds of these words are exactly alike, except for the consonants at the beginning. Other rhymes are **half rhymes**—words whose sounds are similar but not identical, like *pans* and *hams*.

Rhyme is important for several reasons. You soon begin to listen for it, and the expectation of hearing sounds repeated keeps you interested in a poem. Also, a poet can vary the **rhyme scheme,** or pattern of rhymes, to focus your attention on a particular passage.

Look For

Listen for the rhymes as you read this poem. Notice how the rhymes make the poem even more humorous.

Writing

This poem is about a chore that was left undone. Have you ever forgotten or put off doing a chore? Let your mind roam freely. Exaggerate the results of leaving the job undone.

Vocabulary

Knowing the following words will help you as you read "Sarah Cynthia Sylvia Stout Would Not Take the Garbage Out."

scour (skour) *v*.: To clean by rubbing vigorously (p. 451)

candy (kan' dē) *v*.: To coat with sugar (p. 451)

rinds (rīnds) *n*. Tough outer layers or skins (p. 451)

withered (with' ərd) *adj.*: Dried up (p. 451)

curdled (kur' d'ld) *adj.*: Thickened; clotted (p. 452)

rancid (ran' sid) *adj.*: Spoiled and bad-smelling (p. 452)

relate (ri lāt') *v*.: Tell (p. 452)

Sarah Cynthia Sylvia Stout Would Not Take the Garbage Out

Shel Silverstein

Sarah Cynthia Sylvia Stout
Would not take the garbage out!
She'd scour the pots and scrape the pans,
Candy the yams and spice the hams,
5 And though her daddy would scream and shout,
She simply would not take the garbage out.
And so it piled up to the ceilings:
Coffee grounds, potato peelings,
Brown bananas, rotten peas,
10 Chunks of sour cottage cheese.
It filled the can, it covered the floor,
It cracked the window and blocked the door
With bacon rinds and chicken bones,
Drippy ends of ice cream cones,
15 Prune pits, peach pits, orange peel,
Gloppy glumps of cold oatmeal,
Pizza crusts and withered greens,
Soggy beans and tangerines,
Crusts of black burned buttered toast,
20 Gristly bits of beefy roasts . . .
The garbage rolled on down the hall,
It raised the roof, it broke the wall . . .
Greasy napkins, cookie crumbs,
Globs of gooey bubblegum,
25 Cellophane from green baloney,
Rubbery blubbery macaroni,
Peanut butter, caked and dry,

Curdled milk and crusts of pie,
Moldy melons, dried up mustard,
30   Eggshells mixed with lemon custard,
Cold french fries and rancid meat,
Yellow lumps of Cream of Wheat.
At last the garbage reached so high
That finally it touched the sky.
35   And all the neighbors moved away,
And none of her friends would come to play.
And finally Sarah Cynthia Stout said,
"OK, I'll take the garbage out!"
But then, of course, it was too late
40   The garbage reached across the state,
From New York to the Golden Gate
And there, in the garbage she did hate,
Poor Sarah met an awful fate,
That I cannot right now relate
45   Because the hour is much too late.
But children, remember Sarah Stout
And always take the garbage out!

THINKING ABOUT THE SELECTION

Recalling

1. Name four chores that Sarah Cynthia Sylvia Stout does.
2. However, what chore does she absolutely refuse to do?
3. Find the lines that tell the reactions of her neighbors and friends. What do they do as a result of the situation?

Interpreting

4. At what point does the poem become unrealistic? What is the effect of the poet's use of exaggeration?

5. What reason might the poet have—besides the fact that it is "late"—for not telling you what happened to Sarah?
6. What do you think was Sarah's "awful fate"?
7. The poet parodies, or humorously imitates, the type of story told to teach a lesson. How do you know the poet does not mean for you to take this lesson seriously?

Applying

8. Shel Silverstein's poems are recognized for their ability to make people laugh. Discuss with your classmates what makes something funny.

ANALYZING LITERATURE
Understanding Rhyme

The repetition of sounds in two or more words, called **rhyme,** is a key element of poetry. In "Sarah Cynthia Sylvia Stout Would Not Take the Garbage Out," the poet uses rhymes that add humor as they seem to pile up just as the garbage does.

1. Are the rhymes at the end of lines 25 and 26 exact rhymes or half rhymes?
2. Find one example of a rhyme in the middle, rather than at the end, of a line.
3. How might the poem be different if most of the rhyming words did not come right after each other?

CRITICAL THINKING AND READING
Evaluating the Effect of Rhyme

Rhyme sets up an expectation that keeps you alert. The list of discarded items in this poem, for example, might become boring without the delightful rhymes. Also, a change in the rhyme scheme can be very dramatic, marking a turning point in the poem. Most of the pairs of lines in this poem have end rhymes, but the pattern is broken at one point.

1. Identify the two lines in the poem that do *not* rhyme.
2. What important event in the story occurs at this point?
3. What is the effect of the sudden lack of rhyme?
4. Why do you think that the poet used the same rhyme seven times in a row after the break in rhyme?

UNDERSTANDING LANGUAGE
Appreciating Specific Words

Specific words are words that appeal to the senses because they refer to particular things. For example, the word *animal* is not very specific, but the word *giraffe* is. Poets usually try to use specific words so that you can vividly picture what they are talking about.

1. Which of the following words from the poem are general and which are specific:
   a. bacon rinds   c. garbage
   b. chicken bones
2. Find at least ten other specific words.
3. What is the effect of having so many specific words in this poem?

THINKING AND WRITING
Writing a Rhymed Poem

Can you write a rhymed poem that will make your classmates laugh? Look again at your description of an undone job, and list the humorous aspects of the situation. Like Shel Silverstein, you may want to use exaggeration to increase the humor. Then turn your description and list into a funny, rhymed poem about the results of an undone job. After revising your poem, read it to some classmates to see whether they think it is amusing.

GUIDE FOR READING

Annabel Lee

Edgar Allan Poe (1809–1849) was born in Boston, the son of two actors who died before his third birthday. He was raised in the United States and England by John Allan, with whom he had a troubled relationship. Poe's adult life was difficult, too. He earned only a meager living from his writings. Still, during his short life he wrote poems and stories that have made him one of the best-known American authors. A critic has called his verse "easy but unforgettable," and "Annabel Lee" with its strange story and haunting melody is both.

Repetition in Poetry

Repetition is the use of a word or group of words more than once in a poem. Like rhyme, which is itself a form of repetition, this technique creates a variety of effects. In a quiet poem, for example, repetition creates a feeling of peacefulness, like the lapping waves of a calm sea. It can also create excitement and suspense in a poem with galloping rhythms, such as "The Highwayman." Still another use of repetition is to focus attention on important words and phrases. By employing several forms of repetition in "Annabel Lee," Poe creates a pattern of word-sounds very much like music.

Look For

While reading "Annabel Lee," look for repeated words and phrases and consider the effect they create. How do they help create a haunting melody?

Writing

In this poem Poe is haunted by the memory of "the beautiful Annabel Lee." Think of the most beautiful or handsome face that you have ever seen. It could be the face of a friend or of someone you saw in a movie, on television, or in a painting. Write a description of this face.

Vocabulary

Knowing the following words will help you as you read "Annabel Lee."
coveted (kuv' it əd) *v.*: Envied (p. 456)
sepulcher (sep' 'l kər) *n.*: Grave; tomb (p. 456)
demons (dē' mənz) *n.*: Evil spirits (p. 456)
beams (bēmz) *v.*: Shines brightly (p. 456)

Annabel Lee

Edgar Allan Poe

It was many and many a year ago,
    In a kingdom by the sea.
That a maiden there lived whom you may know
    By the name of Annabel Lee;—
5   And this maiden she lived with no other thought
    Than to love and be loved by me.

She was a child and *I* was a child,
    In this kingdom by the sea.

But we loved with a love that was more than love—
10   I and my Annabel Lee—
With a love that the wingèd seraphs[1] of Heaven
      Coveted her and me.

And this was the reason that, long ago,
      In this kingdom by the sea,
15 A wind blew out of a cloud by night
      Chilling my Annabel Lee;
So that her highborn kinsmen[2] came
      And bore her away from me,
To shut her up in a sepulcher
20   In this kingdom by the sea.

The angels, not half so happy in Heaven,
      Went envying her and me:—
Yes! that was the reason (as all men know,
      In this kingdom by the sea)
25 That the wind came out of a cloud, chilling
      And killing my Annabel Lee.

But our love it was stronger by far than the love
      Of those who were older than we—
      Of many far wiser than we—
30 And neither the angels in Heaven above
      Nor the demons down under the sea,
Can ever dissever[3] my soul from the soul
      Of the beautiful Annabel Lee:—

For the moon never beams without bringing me dreams
35 Of the beautiful Annabel Lee;
And the stars never rise but I see the bright eyes
      Of the beautiful Annabel Lee;
And so, all the nighttide,[4] I lie down by the side
Of my darling, my darling, my life and my bride,
40   In her sepulcher there by the sea—
      In her tomb by the side of the sea.

---

1. seraphs (ser′ əfs) *n.*: Angels.
2. highborn kinsmen: Relatives of noble birth.
3. dissever (di sev′ ər) *v.*: Separate.
4. nighttide (nīt′ tīd′) *n.*: An old-fashioned way of saying nighttime.

THINKING ABOUT THE SELECTION

Recalling

1. Where do the events in this poem take place?
2. At what stage of life was the narrator of the poem when he fell in love?
3. What caused Annabel Lee's death?
4. Why can neither the angels nor the demons separate the narrator's soul from that of Annabel Lee? (Lines 27–33)
5. What does the narrator do "all the nighttide"? (Lines 34–41)

Interpreting

6. How can a love be "more than love"? (Lines 9–10)
7. How would you describe the love between the narrator and Annabel Lee.
8. Describe the narrator's mood.

Applying

9. The poet Countee Cullen once wrote, "Never love with all your heart,/It only ends in aching." Do you think the narrator of Annabel Lee would agree? Why or why not?

ANALYZING LITERATURE

Understanding Repetition in Poetry

Poets sometimes use certain words and phrases over and over in the same poem. This technique, called **repetition,** can make a poem seem almost like a piece of music. Poe's "Annabel Lee," in particular, seems to be woven together from repeated word-sounds.

1. Not including the title, how many times does the name Annabel Lee appear in the poem?
2. What line in the first stanza is repeated, almost exactly, in the next three stanzas?.
3. Which adjective describing Annabel Lee is repeated three times in the poem?
4. How does the use of repetition help create a haunting melody?

CRITICAL THINKING AND READING

Evaluating the Effects of Repetition

A poet can use repetition for several reasons. It can help create a peaceful or disturbing rhythm in a poem. Also, by stressing certain words and phrases, it can show you that these are clues to the poem's meaning.

1. Is the rhythm created by the repetitions in this poem disturbing or restful? Give reasons for your answer.
2. Why do you think the writer repeats the name "Annabel Lee" so many times?
3. Why do you think he stresses the setting of the poem by repeating the word "sea"?

UNDERSTANDING LANGUAGE

Appreciating Old-Fashioned Words

Old-fashioned words are words that are no longer a part of everyday speech. Poets sometimes use them to create a mood. In "Annabel Lee," for example, Poe uses several old-fashioned words. Words like "seraph," "kinsman," and "nighttide" convey an old-time, romantic flavor.

Identify the old-fashioned word in each of the following pairs and look it up in a dictionary. Then use each word in a sentence.

1. galleon, ship
2. sky, firmament
3. horse, steed
4. garments, clothes

THINKING AND WRITING

Writing About a Narrative Poem

Write a letter to a friend explaining why you did or did not enjoy this poem. In your letter retell the story of the poem. Then explain the effect created by the use of repetition. As you revise your letter, make sure you have supported your opinion of the poem with details from it. Finally, proofread your letter and prepare a final draft.

GUIDE FOR READING

Oranges

Gary Soto (1952–   ) is a Mexican American, or Chicano, who grew up in the San Joaquin Valley in California. His first book of poetry, *The Elements of San Joaquin* (1977), describes the lives of migrant workers in that part of the country. Soto himself had worked in the fields as a migrant laborer, moving from farm to farm to harvest seasonal crops. One critic said that his poetry has "a lean, simple style." This description certainly is true of the poem "Oranges," a poem about the magic of an early love.

The Speaker in a Narrative Poem

When a narrative poem is told by a character in the story, we call that character the **speaker**. This speaker refers to himself or herself as "I." It is important to remember, however, that the "I" telling the story is not the poet. The speaker is an imaginary person whom the poet has invented, just like a first-person narrator in a short story. In "Oranges," for example, the speaker is a character remembering "The first time" he "walked/With a girl."

Look For

As you read "Oranges," look for details about the speaker. Decide what he is like and why the time he describes holds such magic memories for him.

Writing

Recall when you spent some time with someone you liked very much. Tell about the first moments of that experience. Or if you prefer, write a description of the first moments of an imaginary experience.

Vocabulary

Knowing the following words will help you as you read "Oranges."
rouge (ro͞ozh) *n.:* A reddish cosmetic used to color the cheeks (p. 459)
tiered (tird) *v.:* Stacked in rows (p. 459)
bleachers (blēch′ ərz) *n.:* Benches stacked in rows for spectators at sporting events (p. 459)
hissing (his′ iŋ) *v.:* Making a sound like a prolonged *s* (p. 459)

Oranges

Gary Soto

The first time I walked
With a girl, I was twelve,
Cold, and weighted down
With two oranges in my jacket.
5 December. Frost cracking
Beneath my steps, my breath
Before me, then gone,
As I walked toward
Her house, the one whose
10 Porchlight burned yellow
Night and day, in any weather.
A dog barked at me, until
She came out pulling
At her gloves, face bright
15 With rouge. I smiled,
Touched her shoulder, and led
Her down the street, across
A used car lot and a line
Of newly planted trees,
20 Until we were breathing
Before a drug store. We
Entered, the tiny bell
Bringing a saleslady
Down a narrow aisle of goods.
25 I turned to the candies
Tiered like bleachers,
And asked what she wanted—
Light in her eyes, a smile
Starting at the corners

30 Of her mouth. I fingered
A nickel in my pocket,
And when she lifted a chocolate
That cost a dime,
I didn't say anything.
35 I took the nickel from
My pocket, then an orange,
And set them quietly on
The counter. When I looked up,
The lady's eyes met mine,
40 And held them, knowing
Very well what it was all
About.

     Outside,
A few cars hissing past,
45 Fog hanging like old
Coats between the trees.
I took my girl's hand
In mine for two blocks,
Then released it to let
50 Her unwrap the chocolate.
I peeled my orange
That was so bright against
The gray of December
That, from some distance,
55 Someone might have thought
I was making a fire in my hands.

THINKING ABOUT THE SELECTION

Recalling

1. Describe the speaker of this poem at the time this event took place.
2. Describe the girl when she first comes out of her house.
3. Why does the speaker try to pay for the candy with a nickel and an orange?
4. What is the last action of the speaker in the poem?

Interpreting

5. How does the speaker feel about the girl? Give evidence to support your answer.
6. What does the speaker mean when he says the saleslady knew "Very well what it was all/About"?
7. Why does the narrator still have the orange at the end of the poem?
8. What has the orange come to represent, or stand for, to the speaker?
9. What does the speaker mean when he describes his orange as "so bright against/The gray of December"?

Applying

10. Why is a first date such an important event in a person's life?

ANALYZING LITERATURE

Understanding the Speaker

A narrative poem can be told by a **speaker** who takes part in the story and refers to himself or herself as "I." The speaker is an invented character, not the poet talking to you directly.

You can perform an experiment to see the difference between a narrative poem told by a speaker and one told by the poet. Read "Oranges" again, and every time you see "I" change it in your mind to "he." Also, each time you see "we," change it to "they." When you have made these changes, the poem will no longer have a speaker.

1. How is the poem different without a speaker?
2. Does the poem seem better to you with or without a speaker? Give reasons for your answer.

CRITICAL THINKING AND READING

Making Inferences About a Speaker

An **inference** is a reasonable conclusion you make based on stated information. In a poem like "Oranges," the poet does not tell you about the speaker directly. However, you can infer a great deal about the speaker from the way he talks, the details on which he focuses, and others' reactions to him. Your inferences will help you form an idea of his personality.

1. How does the saleslady act toward him?
2. How does his girlfriend act toward him?
3. The speaker seems to put special emphasis on the detail about the orange at the end of the poem. Why do you think this is so?
4. Does the speaker boast about this experience, or does he seem to be modest? Give reasons for your answer.
5. Based on all these clues, give a brief summary of the speaker's personality.

THINKING AND WRITING

Adding to a Narrative Poem

Every story involving two or more people has two or more different sides to it. Up to this point, we have heard only the boy's voice. How do you think the girl's side of the story would sound? Brainstorm to think of how she might talk differently from the boy. Which details of this story would she describe? Also, would she use short lines of poetry, as the boy does, or longer ones? Turn your ideas into another version of the story, using the girl as a speaker. When you revise your work, ask yourself whether the way you have written the poem is true to the girl's personality.

Figurative Language and Imagery

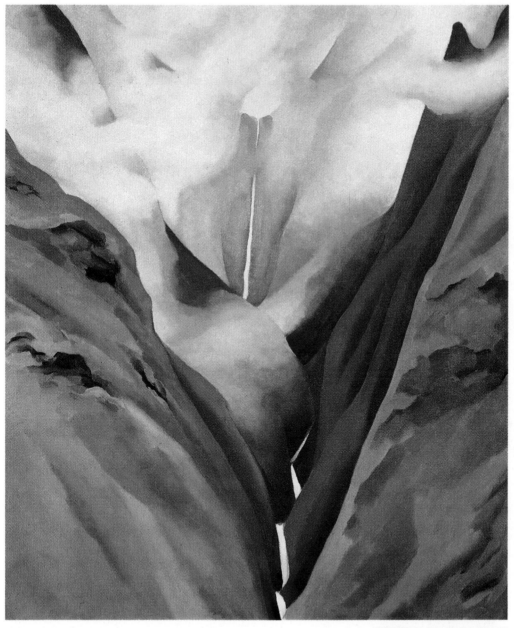

WATERFALL NO. III, IAO VALLEY
Georgia O'Keeffe, 1939
Art Resource

GUIDE FOR READING

Upon Mistress Susanna Southwell, Her Feet

Robert Herrick (1591–1674) was born in London and as a boy was apprenticed to a goldsmith there. He later became a minister, serving for more than thirty years at a remote country church. Herrick published just one book, a collection of 1,400 short poems, but these were good enough to establish Herrick as one of the finest English poets. In "Upon Mistress Susanna Southwell, Her Feet" he creates a vivid picture with a few skillfully chosen phrases.

The Pheasant

Robert P. Tristram Coffin (1892–1955) lived in New England, where his family had settled about 300 years earlier. Coffin wrote that he "grew up on a Maine saltwater farm . . . among lighthouses and barns and boats, tides and fogs and apples and hired men." He won many prizes for his poetry and wrote other types of books as well: biographies, novels, and collections of essays. Coffin's sharp eye for natural details brought him acclaim. He demonstrates his powers of observation in "The Pheasant."

Fog

Carl Sandburg (1878–1967) was born in Galesburg, Illinois, the son of Swedish immigrants. He was unique in winning the Pulitzer Prize for both poetry and history. Sandburg often wrote about the rough-and-tumble everyday world. By the time his first book appeared in 1916, Sandburg had been a farm worker, a stagehand, a railroad worker, a soldier, and a cook, among other things. He was working as a newspaper reporter when he wrote "Fog," a poem he jotted down one day while waiting to interview a Chicago judge.

Figurative language is language that is not meant literally, or exactly as the dictionary definition of the words would indicate. One important type of figurative language is simile. A **simile** uses the connecting words *like* or *as* to point up a similar quality in two generally unlike things. For example: The man's bright dinner jacket looks *like* an unfurled flag. The dinner jacket and the flag are unlike in many ways, but they are similar in being bright and showy.

A **metaphor** also indicates a similar quality in two generally unlike things. However, metaphors do not use the words *like* or *as*. The simplest way to create a metaphor is to say that two dissimilar things are the same. For example, you can turn the simile describing the dinner jacket into a metaphor by saying this: The man's bright dinner jacket is an unfurled flag. You can also create a metaphor by speaking about one thing in terms of another. For example: The crowd *floods* into the open area, *swirls* around, and *collects* in *small pools* of people. In this metaphor, the italicized words describe the crowd as if it were water.

An **extended metaphor** is a metaphor that continues past a single phrase or sentence. You might begin such a metaphor by saying, "The tornado is a dragon, gobbling up the houses." Then you could extend the metaphor by continuing to describe the tornado as a dragon.

Look For

As you read the following poems, look for similes, metaphors, and extended metaphors. How does the use of figurative language help create vivid word pictures?

Writing

The poems you are about to read use figurative language to create vivid word pictures. Recall the first time you met someone who later became your friend. Using similes or metaphors, create a vivid word picture of that person.

Vocabulary

Knowing the following words will help you as you read these poems.
scorn (skôrn) *n.*: Strong dislike for someone or something thought to be inferior (p. 466)
hymn (him) *n.*: A song of praise (p. 466)

meek (mēk) *adj.*: Patient and mild (p. 466)
haunches (hônch′ iz) *n.*: An animal's lower back and legs (p. 468)

Upon Mistress Susanna Southwell, Her Feet

Robert Herrick

Her pretty feet
Like snails did creep
A little out, and then,
As if they started at Bo-peep,[1]
5   Did soon draw in again.

---

1. started at Bo-peep: Were playing a game of Bo-peep, an old-fashioned name for peekaboo.

LITTLE GOODY TWO SHOES
John Newbery
New York Public Library

THINKING ABOUT THE SELECTION

Recalling

1. Without using figurative langauge, describe what Mistress Susanna Southwell's feet do in this poem.

Interpreting

2. Do you think it appropriate that the poet describes the feet as playing peekaboo? Why or why not?
3. How do you think the poet feels about Mistress Susanna Southwell? Find evidence to support your answer.

Applying

4. Use a simile to describe the way your own feet move.

ANALYZING LITERATURE

Understanding Simile

In a **simile,** a writer compares two apparently different things by using the connecting words *like* or *as*. Similes help you to see the world in a new way by suggesting surprising comparisons that you might not have made yourself.

1. How are Mistress Susanna Southwell's feet like snails?
2. Do you think this simile is an effective one? Why or why not?
3. How would the effect of this poem be different if the poet had compared Susanna's feet to tortoises?

The Pheasant

Robert P. Tristram Coffin

A pheasant cock sprang into view,
A living jewel, up he flew.

His wings laid hold on empty space,
Scorn bulged his eyeballs out with grace.

5   He was a hymn from tail to beak
With not a tender note or meek.

Then the gun let out its thunder,
The bird descended struck with wonder.

He ran a little, then, amazed,
10 Settled with his head upraised.

The fierceness flowed out of his eyes
And left them meek and large and wise.

Gentleness relaxed his head,
He lay in jeweled feathers, dead.

THINKING ABOUT THE SELECTION
Recalling

1. Summarize the action of this poem without using figurative language.

Interpreting

2. What is the meaning of lines 5–6?
3. What is the meaning of lines 7–8?
4. Compare and contrast the description of the bird in lines 1–6 with that in lines 9–14.
5. How do you think the poet wants you to feel about the event in this poem? Find evidence to support your answer.

Applying

6. Coffin describes the pheasant as "a hymn from tail to beak." What other creatures do you think fit this description? Explain your answer.

ANALYZING LITERATURE
Understanding Metaphor

Poets use **metaphors** to compare apparently unlike things. However, a metaphor identifies the two things being compared more closely than a

RING NECKED PHEASANT, 1977
Roger Tory Peterson
Courtesy of the artist and Mill Pond Press, Inc.

simile. For example, instead of saying that the pheasant is *like* a jewel, the poet simply calls it "a living jewel."

1. What quality or qualities do the pheasant and the jewel share?
2. Where is this metaphor of the pheasant as a jewel repeated later in the poem? Do you think this repetition adds to the effectiveness of the poem? Why or why not?
3. What other metaphor does the poet use to describe the pheasant?
4. In what essential way are a hymn and a jewel alike?

CRITICAL THINKING AND READING
Evaluating the Effect of a Metaphor

You can evaluate the effect of a metaphor by replacing it with a description that does not use figurative language and then comparing the two passages. Here, for example, are a metaphor from "The Pheasant" and a description expressing a similar idea:

Metaphor: "A living jewel, up he flew."
Description: Brightly colored, up he flew.

1. Compare and contrast these two lines.
2. Which do you find more effective? Explain your answer.

Fog

Carl Sandburg

The fog comes
on little cat feet.

It sits looking
over harbor and city
5 on silent haunches
and then moves on.

THINKING ABOUT THE SELECTION

Recalling

1. Being as specific as possible, describe the setting of this poem.
2. Describe the three things the fog does.

Interpreting

3. What impression does this poem create of the fog?
4. What is the effect of the writer's use of short lines?

Applying

5. Many poets have written poems about fog. What is it about this type of weather that makes it a good subject for a poem?

ANALYZING LITERATURE

Understanding Extended Metaphor

An **extended metaphor** develops beyond a single sentence or phrase. Once a poet has shown that two apparently unlike things are similar, it is fascinating to see how long the comparison can be continued. An extended metaphor can go on for several lines, or even many pages.

1. To what does the writer compare the fog?
2. What qualities of the fog does the writer emphasize with this comparison?
3. How would the poem have been different if the poet had compared the fog to a velvet blanket?

THINKING AND WRITING
Writing an Extended Metaphor

Sandburg created an effective poem by comparing the fog to a cat. Of what animal does the fog remind you? For example, does it remind you of a warm puppy or of a brown cow? Let your imagination roam freely. What qualities does the fog share with this animal? Using an extended metaphor, write a poem describing the fog. Read over your poem to make sure you have carried your metaphor through the poem. Prepare a final draft and place it on a bulletin board with your classmates' fog poems.

GUIDE FOR READING

The Bat

Theodore Roethke (1908–1963) was one of the best-known American poets writing after World War II. He won many awards for his work, including the Bollingen Prize, the Pulitzer Prize, and the National Book Award. In addition, he earned a reputation as a college teacher who challenged and inspired his students. Roethke was born and grew up in Saginaw, Michigan, where his father was a florist. As a boy, Roethke loved to play in and around the family greenhouse. These experiences gave him a feeling of kinship with nature that he never lost. In "The Bat" he writes with knowledge and humor about one of nature's more unusual creatures.

The Pasture

Robert Frost (1875–1963) is associated with New England, but he was born and spent his early years in San Francisco. When his father died, the family returned to its New England roots. Frost remained in that region for most of his life, making his living for a while as a farmer and part-time teacher. He was not well known as a writer until his first book of poetry, *A Boy's Will* (1913), appeared in Great Britain. Then, almost overnight, he became famous for his poems about New England people and landscapes. He won the Pulitzer Prize four times, more than any other poet. Frost used poetic forms that some writers thought old-fashioned. However, by combining these forms with the rhythms of everyday speech, he created highly original poems. "The Pasture" contains an invitation that makes you want to experience the joys of nature with the poet.

Images in Poetry

Images are the pictures that poets create with their words. As you read a poem, you can see these images in your mind's eye. Poets use lively and specific words so that you can see their images more clearly. In "The Pasture," for instance, Robert Frost says a small calf is so young that "It totters" when its mother "licks it with her tongue." By using the specific verb "totters," Frost paints a picture of the scene that is easy to visualize.

Look For

As you read "The Bat" and "The Pasture" look for the specific words the poets use to create vivid word pictures.

Writing

Picture an animal that fascinates you. It can be a pet, or an animal that you have seen in a zoo or on film. Freewrite about the qualities of this animal that interest you the most.

Vocabulary

Knowing the following words will help you as you read these poems.

amiss (ə mis') *adv.*: In a wrong way; improper (p. 472)

totters (tät' ərz) *v.*: Rocks or shakes as if about to fall; is unsteady (p. 473)

The Bat

Theodore Roethke

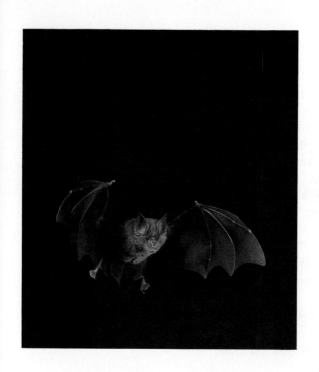

By day the bat is cousin to the mouse.
He likes the attic of an aging house.

His fingers make a hat about his head.
His pulse beat is so slow we think him dead.

5 He loops in crazy figures half the night
Among the trees that face the corner light.

But when he brushes up against a screen,
We are afraid of what our eyes have seen:

For something is amiss or out of place
10 When mice with wings can wear a human face

THINKING ABOUT THE SELECTION
Recalling

1. Where does the bat spend the daytime?
2. What does the bat do at night?

Interpreting

3. Contrast the description of the bat in lines 3 and 4 with that in lines 5 and 6.
4. What details make the picture that the poet paints in line 10 so strange?

Applying

5. What is it about animals like bats and snakes that makes people both curious and afraid?

ANALYZING LITERATURE
Understanding Images

Images are pictures in words. By choosing lively and specific language, poets invite you to see the world in a fresh and original way. In "The Bat," for example, Roethke creates a vivid picture when he says that this creature's "fingers make a hat about his head."

1. Describe the picture that Roethke paints in lines 5 and 6.
2. Why do you think Roethke saved the image in line 10 for the end of the poem?

THINKING AND WRITING
Writing a Poem About an Animal

Use your freewriting about a fascinating animal to write a brief poem. Organize the lines in groups of two, as Roethke does. When you revise your poem, replace general words with lively and specific ones. You might want to read your poem to several classmates when you are finished and ask them whether your images are clear. Then, based on your classmates' comments, prepare a final draft.

The Pasture

Robert Frost

I'm going out to clean the pasture spring;
I'll only stop to rake the leaves away
(And wait to watch the water clear, I may):
I shan't be gone long.—You come too.

5   I'm going out to fetch the little calf
That's standing by the mother. It's so young
It totters when she licks it with her tongue.
I shan't be gone long.—You come too.

THINKING ABOUT THE SELECTION

Recalling

1. What two chores is the speaker going to do?
2. What invitation does the speaker offer? What effect does this invitation have on you?

Interpreting

3. Although the speaker is going out to perform chores, he makes them sound attractive and inviting. What images make you feel like accompanying the speaker?

4. Why do you think the poet enclosed line 3 in parentheses?
5. Based on information in the poem, do you think the speaker is a grown man or a boy? Find evidence to support your answer.

Applying

6. An Indian holy book states: "What is work? and What is not work? are questions that perplex the wisest of men." Do you think the speaker in this poem considers the chores work? Find evidence to support your answer. How do you define work?

Seal

William Jay Smith (1918–   ) was born in Winnfield, Louisiana. He has led a busy life—teaching college, writing poetry and essays, translating Russian and French poetry, and even serving in the Vermont state legislature for three years. His most successful writing has been his poetry for young people. When you read "Seal," you will see why. Lively and amusing, it shows that poetry can be pure and simple fun.

Concrete Poetry

Concrete poetry is poetry that is meant to be seen on the page, as well as heard like an ordinary poem. In a concrete poem, the words are arranged into a shape, often one that looks like the subject. The term *concrete* refers to the shape's being a specific, or concrete, representation of something.

Look For

Look at the shape formed by the words in "Seal." Does it remind you of anything? When you have read the poem, see if you can explain how the shape added to your reading experience. What would be lost if "Seal" were written as a single straight column of words?

Writing

The activities the seal performs are described vividly in the poem you are about to read. Freewrite about some physical activity that you enjoy. It might be running, swimming, skating, or riding a bike. Try to describe the activity in a way that suggests the fun you get out of it.

Vocabulary

Knowing the following words will help you as you read "Seal."
feed (fēd) *n.*: The tiny particles that minnows feed on (p. 475)
swerve (swʉrv) *n.*: A curving motion (p. 475)
quicksilver (kwik′ sil′ vər) *n.*: Quick, changeable, unpredictable; like the chemical element mercury, which is silver-white and flows easily (p. 475)

Seal

William Jay Smith

See how he dives
    From the rocks with a zoom!
  See how he darts
    Through his watery room
  5 Past crabs and eels
    And green seaweed,
    Past fluffs of sandy
    Minnow feed!
  See how he swims
10 With a swerve and a twist,
  A flip of the flipper,
 A flick of the wrist!
Quicksilver-quick,
Softer than spray,
15 Down he plunges
And sweeps away;
Before you can think,
Before you can utter
Words like "Dill pickle"
20 Or "Apple butter,"
  Back up he swims
  Past Sting Ray and Shark,
  Out with a zoom,
  A whoop, a bark;
  25 Before you can say
    Whatever you wish,
    He plops at your side
    With a mouthful of fish!

THINKING ABOUT THE SELECTION

Recalling

1. In a sentence or two, summarize "Seal."

Interpreting

2. Describe the setting of the poem. Give evidence to support your answer.
3. How would you describe the spirit, or mood, of the poem? Find at least three words that help create this mood.

Applying

4. If you saw seals in an aquarium, how might this poem affect your response to them?

ANALYZING LITERATURE

Understanding Concrete Poetry

    Concrete poems are often lighthearted. When the words of a poem are arranged in a shape that imitates the subject or suggests something about it, the effect is usually playful.

1. How would the effect of "Seal" be changed if the poem did not have its unusual shape?
2. The lines of "Seal" are very short. What connection might there be between the shortness of the lines and the shape of the poem?
3. After reading the poem aloud, tell which of the following words or phrases best describes its rhythm: (a) slow and relaxed; (b) quick and lively; (c) powerful.

THINKING AND WRITING

Writing a Concrete Poem

    Use the freewriting you did as a starting point for writing a concrete poem. First decide on a suitable shape. It should be one that resembles, or suggests something about, your subject. Though you need not use rhyme, try to write lines that have a definite rhythm. When you revise, think of the effect you are trying to achieve. You should do your best to make everything about your poem contribute to that effect.

GUIDE FOR READING

Haiku

Taniguchi Buson (1715–1783) was a Japanese poet whose poems many Japanese of today know by heart. He was also a painter, and his sharp eye for detail no doubt helped him compose poems whose focus is on small things that express a great deal.

Otsuji (? –1772) wrote many essays about the art of writing haiku. He believed that a poet should view human life as part of the larger world of nature. He also felt that in the best haiku, emotions should be suggested, not expressed directly.

Kyorai (1651–1704) was the son of a physician to a royal Japanese family. He sought to write poems in which every word was necessary and none could be changed without destroying the poem's meaning.

Matsuo-Bashō (1644–1694) was born near Kyoto, Japan. In many of his haiku, he presents a scene in which a vivid or momentary feature stands out against an unchanging background. He can present a whole landscape or an entire season by describing just a few key details.

Haiku

Haiku is a form of poetry that originated in Japan. A haiku has three lines; the first and third lines have five syllables each; the second line has seven. A haiku usually depicts a scene in nature and often implies a strong feeling. In a good haiku, a mere handful of words will make you see an entire scene and will convey a universal feeling, such as fear, surprise, regret, hope, or mystery.

Look For

As you read and reread each of these little poems, try to put yourself in the poet's place. Try to see and hear what he saw and felt. Ask yourself, "What was the poet experiencing?" Remember that in a haiku every word counts.

Writing

Think of a simple scene in nature that is vivid in your memory. It should be one that is like a sharp, clear unforgettable snapshot. Describe in writing what this mental photograph shows. If you can make this brief description express a feeling without your saying directly what the feeling is, you will be writing the way haiku poets write.

Vocabulary

In haiku simple words are used to create vivid images. Although you may think you know the meaning of each word, pause over each one and think about what it implies.

Three Haiku

translated from the Japanese by Harry Behn

Deep in a windless
wood, not one leaf dares to move. . . .
Something is afraid.
Buson

Into a forest
I called. . . . The voice in reply
was no voice I knew.
Otsuji

I called to the wind,
"Who's there?" . . . Whoever it was
still knocks at my gate.
Kyorai

THINKING ABOUT THE SELECTION
Recalling

1. Describe the real-life scene or situation that is the basis of each haiku.

Interpreting

2. In the haiku by Buson, what might be the "something" that is afraid?
3. Whose voice do you think replies to the poet in the haiku by Otsuji?
4. In the haiku by Kyorai, how might the continual knocking at the gate be explained?

Applying

5. Tell why you would, or would not, use the haiku form if you wanted to write a poem expressing strong personal feelings about something.

ANALYZING LITERATURE
Understanding Haiku

A haiku has three lines. The first and third lines have five syllables each; the second line has seven. One reason that readers enjoy haiku is that a single poem can be interpreted in different ways, and it is interesting to compare and discuss different interpretations.

1. Review your classmates' answers to Question 2, under Thinking About the Selection. Which seem to you good answers, though different from yours?
2. What was the basis for your answer to Question 3, under Thinking About the Selection.
3. Some readers think that the haiku by Kyorai is meant to be humorous. What reasons might be given for this interpretation?

Three Haiku

Bashō

translated by Daniel C. Buchanan

On sweet plum blossoms
The sun rises suddenly.
Look, a mountain path!

Has spring come indeed?
On that nameless mountain lie
Thin layers of mist.

Temple bells die out.
The fragrant blossoms remain.
A perfect evening!

RAVENS IN MOONLIGHT, 1882
Gengyo
Omni Photo Communications

THINKING ABOUT THE SELECTION

Recalling

1. In your own words tell what the poet has noticed or observed in each haiku.

Interpreting

2. Why does the poet express surprise in the first haiku?
3. In the second haiku, why is he uncertain that spring has come?
4. In the third haiku, why do you think he feels that the evening is perfect?

Applying

5. Reread the biography of Bashō. Then decide which one of these three haiku best illustrates what is said there about his poetry. Why did you pick the poem you did rather than either of the other two?

THINKING AND WRITING

Writing a Haiku

Write a haiku based on the description you wrote before you read these haiku. Remember the correct form: the first and third lines have five syllables each; the second has seven. As you re-write and revise your haiku, be sure that every word counts. Let the scene or moment you describe suggest your feelings about it. When you are satisfied that you have said all you can in seventeen syllables, share your haiku with your classmates.

Lyric Poetry

YOUNG GIRLS AT THE PIANO
Pierre Auguste Renoir
Joslyn Art Museum

GUIDE FOR READING

Washed in Silver

James Stephens (1880–1950) was a poet and storyteller who grew up in a poor neighborhood of Dublin, Ireland. As a young man, he worked for a lawyer, but in his free time he read all he could about Irish legends and fairy tales. His books include *The Crock of Gold* (1912), which is an imaginative novel, and *Songs from the Clay* (1915), a volume of poems. Stephens had a wonderful speaking voice and gave many readings of his poetry. "Washed in Silver" captures the magical quality of Irish legends.

Feelings About Words

Mary O'Neill (1908–   ) began writing to entertain her family as she grew up in a small town near Cleveland, Ohio. She kept her interest in writing even while making a career in advertising. When her own children grew up, she published many stories and poems for young people. One of her best-loved books is *Words, Words, Words* (1966). Her fascination with words is clearly seen in her poem "Feelings About Words."

The Flower-Fed Buffaloes

Vachel Lindsay (1879–1931) believed that poetry was most exciting when it was heard. He often traveled through the countryside reading his poems aloud and receiving shelter and food in return. One of his books, in fact, is called *Rhymes to Be Traded for Bread* (1912). Lindsay used strong rhythms in his poetry and often wrote about popular figures like baseball players and movie stars. In "The Flower-Fed Buffaloes," repeated words and phrases add to both the rhythm and the meaning.

Lyric Poetry

A **lyric poem** is the expression of a poet's personal thoughts and feelings in vivid and musical language. In ancient times, lyric poetry was actually sung to the music of a stringed instrument known as a lyre. That is why such poetry was called *lyr*-ic and why we still refer to the words of songs as *lyrics*. While most lyric poems are no longer set to music, they still tend to be brief and melodic like songs.

Any subject that calls up a poet's thoughts and feelings is suitable for a lyric poem. James Stephens, for example, describes the "silvery radiance" of moonlight, while Vachel Lindsay imagines the mighty buffaloes that "trundle around the hills no more."

Lyric poetry can take many forms, with different patterns of rhyme and rhythm. Most lyric poems, however, include vivid language that is filled with energy. Such lively words help you remember a poet's thoughts and feelings.

Look For

As you read the following lyric poems, look for the vivid language that these poets use to express their thoughts and feelings. Listen for the musical quality of the poems. How does this musical quality help convey the meaning of the poems?

Writing

Think about the songs you like the best. What is it about the lyrics that makes you remember them? Brainstorm with your classmates to list the qualities of lyrics that make them memorable.

Vocabulary

Knowing the following words will help you as you read these poems.

squat (skwät) *adj.*: Short and heavy (p. 487)

glint (glint) *v.*: Gleam, flash, or glitter (p. 487)

saunter (sôn′ tər) *v.*: Walk about idly; stroll (p. 487)

preen (prēn) *v.*: Dress up; show pride in one's appearance (p. 487)

pomp (pämp) *n.*: An impressive show or display (p. 487)

trundle (trun′ d'l) *v.*: Move on wheels or as if on wheels (p. 488)

Washed in Silver

James Stephens

Gleaming in silver are the hills!
Blazing in silver is the sea!

And a silvery radiance spills
Where the moon drives royally!

5   Clad in silver tissue, I
March magnificently by!

THINKING ABOUT THE SELECTION

Recalling

1. Briefly describe what the poet sees.
2. What is the poet doing?

Interpreting

3. What does the poet mean by saying he is "Clad in silver tissue"?
4. Explain the poem's title.

Applying

5. Light is important in this lyric. How do different kinds of light affect people's moods?

ANALYZING LITERATURE

Understanding Lyric Poetry

A **lyric poem** expresses a poet's emotions and thoughts in language that is lively and musical. Most lyrics also contain vivid words that communicate the poet's feelings in a memorable way. As an example, at the end of "Washed in Silver," Stephens declares: ". . . I / March magnificently by!" With this bold phrase he communicates feelings of triumph and delight.

1. In songs, words and phrases are often repeated. How many times does the word *silver* appear in this poem? What effect does the repetition of this word have on the poem?
2. What picture does the vivid phrase "the moon drives royally" bring to your mind? Why do you think Stephens uses this phrase rather than "the moon shines in the sky"?
3. What feelings do you think the poet wants to communicate about the landscape bathed in moonlight?

DOMINANT CURVE, APRIL 1936
Wassily Kandinski
Solomon R. Guggenheim Museum

Feelings About Words

Mary O'Neill

Some words clink
As ice in drink.
Some move with grace
A dance, a lace.
5 Some sound thin:

Wail, scream and pin.
Some words are squat:
A mug, a pot,
And some are plump,
10 Fat, round and dump.
Some words are light:
Drift, lift and bright.
A few are small:
A, is and all.
15 And some are thick,
Glue, paste and brick.
Some words are sad:
"I never had . . ."
And others gay:
20 Joy, spin and play.
Some words are sick:
Stab, scratch and nick.
Some words are hot:
Fire, flame and shot.
25 Some words are sharp,
Sword, point and carp.
And some alert:
Glint, glance and flirt.
Some words are lazy:
30 Saunter, hazy.
And some words preen:
Pride, pomp and queen.
Some words are quick,
A jerk, a flick.
35 Some words are slow:
Lag, stop and grow,
While others poke
As ox with yoke.
Some words can fly—
40 There's wind, there's high;
And some words cry:
"Goodbye . . .
Goodbye . . ."

THINKING ABOUT THE SELECTION

Recalling

1. O'Neill calls some words "squat" and others "light." What examples does she give of each kind of word?
2. Name three other adjectives she uses to describe words. What examples does she give of each of these types of words?

Interpreting

3. Why is *flick* a good example of a quick word?
4. Why is *goodbye* a word that cries?
5. Why does O'Neill call this poem "Feelings About Words"? What are her feelings about words?

Applying

6. Look at the painting by Wassily Kandinski on page 486. In what way is a poet's love of words similar to an artist's love of color and form?

CRITICAL THINKING AND READING

Understanding Connotation

Connotation refers to the feelings and associations words stir up in us. O'Neill explores the connotations of different words. For example, she says that *saunter* gives her a lazy feeling. When you read *saunter,* you, like her, may picture someone who moves in a lazy fashion.

When people use words to persuade you to buy or do things, they often rely on connotation. A company selling a new kind of soap, for instance, will choose a name that suggests cleaniness—like Rainwater or Springtime.

1. O'Neill lists words that suggest grace to her. List four words that suggest grace to you.
2. List four words that suggest sadness to you.
3. List four words that suggest gaiety to you.
4. A car manufacturer once hired the poet Marianne Moore to think of names for its latest models. Do you think it was a good idea to choose a poet for this job? Why or why not?

The Flower-Fed Buffaloes

Vachel Lindsay

The flower-fed buffaloes of the spring
In the days of long ago,
Ranged where the locomotives sing
And the prairie flowers lie low:—
5   The tossing, blooming, perfumed grass
Is swept away by the wheat,
Wheels and wheels and wheels spin by
In the spring that still is sweet.
But the flower-fed buffaloes of the spring
10   Left us, long ago.
They gore no more, they bellow no more,
They trundle around the hills no more:—
With the Blackfeet, lying low,
With the Pawnees,[1] lying low,
15   Lying low.

---

1. Blackfeet, Pawnees: The names of groups of native Americans
who hunted buffalo.

THINKING ABOUT THE SELECTION
Recalling

1. According to the poem, in what ways has the prairie scene changed?
2. What has brought about this change?
3. With whom does Lindsay associate the buffaloes at the end of the poem? How are they alike?

Interpreting

4. Why does the poet describe the buffaloes as "flower-fed"? What is the effect of this image?

5. How does the repetition of the words "no more" in lines 11 and 12 emphasize the poem's meaning?
6. What is the implication of the words "lying low" in lines 13–15?
7. What does this poem suggest about progress?

Applying

8. The writer G. K. Chesterton defines progress as "leaving things behind us" and growth as "leaving things inside us." What do these definitions mean? What do you think is the difference between progress and growth?

UNDERSTANDING LANGUAGE
Appreciating Vivid Verbs

Poets and other writers use vivid, specific verbs to help you picture the actions they are describing. In "The Flower-Fed Buffaloes," Vachel Lindsay uses verbs like "bellow," and "trundle" to bring to life the vanished buffalo herds. Notice that the verb "trundle," for instance, is much more vivid and specific than the general verb *move*.

Replace the italicized word in each sentence with a more lively verb.

1. The lion *walked* through the jungle.
2. The airplane *traveled* down the runway.
3. The runner *went* around the track.

THINKING AND WRITING
Writing About a Lyric Poem

Imagine that your friend is going to give a public reading of "The Flower-Fed Buffaloes" and has asked for your help. List the important points that he or she should keep in mind while reading this poem aloud. Remember to consider where a reader's voice should be loud or soft. Also think about where a reader should pause or continue at the end of a line. Turn your list into a note to your friend that will help make the reading a success. When revising this note, make sure your friend will understand your instructions. Proofread your note and prepare a final draft.

The Courage That My Mother Had

Edna St. Vincent Millay (1892–1950) was born and raised in Rockland, Maine. Millay revealed her poetic talent very early, writing "Renascence," one of her most famous poems, when she was only nineteen years old. She published her first book of poetry while still only in her mid-20's and quickly became a well-known poet. In 1923, she won a Pulitzer Prize for three of her works. Millay had a special fondness for the sonnet, a fourteen-line poem with a regular rhythm and pattern of rhymes. She published a collection of her sonnets in 1941. In "The Courage That My Mother Had," as in many of her lyric poems, she expresses strong emotions and intense feelings.

My Mother Pieced Quilts

Teresa Palomo Acosta (1949–   ) grew up in Texas. She became a journalist after studying at the University of Texas and Columbia University. As a girl, Acosta listened to her grandfather's stories about his childhood in Mexico and his life as a cowboy. These stories inspired her to begin reading literature. She wrote "My Mother Pieced Quilts" as an assignment for a university class. This poem was later read at the University of Southern California, during the first national festival of Chicano literature and art (1973). In "My Mother Pieced Quilts," Acosta follows in her grandfather's and mother's footsteps as a recorder of family history.

Figurative language is language used with meaning beyond the usual dictionary definitions. It is the highly imaginative use of words. This type of language is often based on vivid comparisons that can help to change your usual way of seeing the world. By comparing a snowflake to a soldier, for instance, a writer can surprise you into looking at a snowstorm in a new way. Suddenly the bits of white may resemble an army retreating or attacking. This perception may lead you to see other aspects of a winter scene with fresh eyes.

Literal language refers to language that does not go beyond the dictionary definitions of the words. A literal description of a snowfall, for example, might include the ideas that each snowflake has six sides and that each falls at a certain rate of speed. Poets often weave literal and figurative language together in their work. This combination ensures that their poems will be both understandable and surprising.

Look For

As you read the following two poems, look for the ways these poets skillfully combine literal and figurative language to express their thoughts and emotions. Identify passages in each poem where the poet shifts from one kind of language to another.

Writing

The two poems you are about to read express strong positive feelings about courageous women. Freewrite about the meaning of courage.

Vocabulary

Knowing the following words will help you as you read these two poems.

quarried (kwôr′ ēd) *v.*: Carved out of the ground (p. 492)

brooch (brōch) *n.*: A large ornamental pin worn on a dress (p. 492)

somber (säm′ bər) *adj.*: Dark and solemn (p. 495)

mosaic (mō zā′ ik) *adj.*: Made of different pieces combined to form a whole (p. 495)

testimonies (tes′ tə mō′ nēz) *n.*: Statements or declarations (p. 495)

muslin (muz′ lin) *n.*: A plain, strong kind of cotton (p. 496)

The Courage That My Mother Had

Edna St. Vincent Millay

The courage that my mother had
Went with her, and is with her still:
Rock from New England quarried;
Now granite in a granite hill.

5   The golden brooch my mother wore
She left behind for me to wear;
I have no thing I treasure more:
Yet, it is something I could spare.

Oh, if instead she'd left to me
10 The thing she took into the grave!—
That courage like a rock, which she
Has no more need of, and I have.

THINKING ABOUT THE SELECTION

Recalling

1. What quality does the speaker wish for?
2. What would the speaker give up to have this quality?

Interpreting

3. Explain lines 3–4.
4. Why is a rock an effective metaphor for a courageous woman? How is courage also like granite?
5. What do lines 3–4 suggest about the importance of the mother's New England heritage?
6. In your own words, describe the feeling that the speaker expresses in this lyric poem.

Applying

7. The speaker implies that courage is a quality you either have or do not have. Do you think that a person could learn to be more courageous? Why or why not?

ANALYZING LITERATURE

Understanding Figurative Language

The poet uses both figurative language and literal language to express her strong feelings about her mother. For example, both literal and figurative language appear in the first stanza.

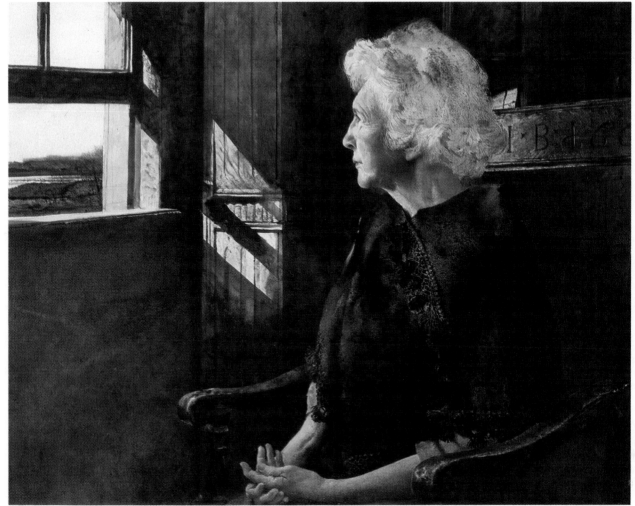

PORTRAIT OF HENRIETTE
Andrew Wyeth
Courtesy of the San Antonio Museum Association

1. Where in this stanza does the poet shift from a literal to a figurative description?
2. In which line of the third stanza does the poet start using figurative language again?
3. How would the poem be different if it were written entirely in literal language?

CRITICAL THINKING AND READING

Paraphrasing a Poem

   Paraphrasing a poem means briefly restating it in your own words. Often you can clarify a difficult poem by paraphrasing it. However, you should realize that a paraphrase does not include many of the qualities that make a poem exciting. The following is a paraphrase of the first stanza of "The Courage That My Mother Had."

   When my mother died, she took her courage with her. In its strength, that courage reminded me of New England granite. Now the granite of her courage is buried with her in the hill, just as real granite is buried.

1. Paraphrase the other two stanzas.
2. Why is the poem more exciting than the paraphrase?

My Mother Pieced Quilts

Teresa Palomo Acosta

they were just meant as covers
in winter
as weapons
against pounding january winds

5 but it was just that every morning I awoke to these
october ripened canvases
passed my hand across their cloth faces
and began to wonder how you pieced
all these together
10 these strips of gentle communion cotton and flannel
       nightgowns
wedding organdies[1]
dime store velvets

how you shaped patterns square and oblong and round
positioned
15 balanced
then cemented them
with your thread
a steel needle
a thimble

20 how the thread darted in and out
galloping along the frayed edges, tucking them in
as you did us at night
oh how you stretched and turned and re-arranged
your michigan spring faded curtain pieces
25 my father's santa fe[2] work shirt
the summer denims, the tweeds of fall

in the evening you sat at your canvas
—our cracked linoleum floor the drawing board

---

1. organdies (or′ gən dēz) *n*.: Thin, crisp cotton fabrics used for
items like dresses and curtains.
2. Santa Fe (san′ ta fā′): The capital of New Mexico.

me lounging on your arm
30 and you staking out the plan:
    whether to put the lilac purple of easter against the red
        plaid of winter-going
    into-spring
    whether to mix a yellow with blue and white and paint the
    corpus christi[3] noon when my father held your hand
35 whether to shape a five-point star from the
    somber black silk you wore to grandmother's funeral

    you were the river current
    carrying the roaring notes
    forming them into pictures of a little boy reclining
40 a swallow flying
    you were the caravan master at the reins
    driving your threaded needle artillery across the mosaic
        cloth bridges
    delivering yourself in separate testimonies.

---

3. Corpus Christi (kor′ pəs kris′ tē): A city in southeast Texas.

oh mother you plunged me sobbing and laughing
45 into our past
into the river crossing at five
into the spinach fields
into the plainview[4] cotton rows
into tuberculosis wards
50 into braids and muslin dresses
sewn hard and taut to withstand the thrashings of twenty-
five years

stretched out they lay
armed/ready/shouting/celebrating

knotted with love
55 the quilts sing on

---

4. Plainview: A town in Texas.

THINKING ABOUT THE SELECTION

Recalling

1. What were the quilts meant to do?
2. What kinds of materials went into the quilts?

Interpreting

3. Like the quilts themselves, the poem is "pieced . . . together" from literal and figurative language. In what way were the quilts weapons? What battles has the mother fought?
4. To what is the speaker comparing her mother by using the word *canvases* in line 6?
5. How do the quilts reflect family history?
6. The speaker wonders how her mother was able to shape and cement the pieces of cloth to form a quilt. Find evidence that shows she also wonders how her mother was able to shape and cement the family.

Applying

7. Compare the mother in this poem with the mother in Millay's poem.

UNDERSTANDING LANGUAGE

Appreciating Concrete Language

Concrete language is specific language. In "My Mother Pieced Quilts," the poet names many specific kinds of cloth rather than simply using a general term like *material*.

1. Identify two types of material named in the second stanza.
2. Find two types of fabric mentioned in the fourth stanza.
3. How does the poet relate a type of material to her family's history?

THINKING AND WRITING

Writing a Lyric Poem

Write a lyric poem about a courageous person. First brainstorm to list details that reveal this person's courage. Then shape these details into a poem expressing your feelings about this courageous person. Revise your poem to improve its musical quality. Prepare a final draft and share it with your classmates.

The Changing Seasons

BATCHEWANA WOOD, ALGOMA
J. E. H. MacDonald
Art Gallery of Ontario, Toronto

GUIDE FOR READING

In Just—

E. E. Cummings (1894–1962) was born in Cambridge, Massachusetts. Cummings graduated from Harvard University in 1915. He served in World War I as an ambulance driver. After the war, he worked as a painter and a poet. So successful a poet was he, that unlike many other poets, he was able to earn his living through his poetry. Individual liberty is a deeply rooted tradition in New England, and Cummings's life and writings are stamped with it. It is most clearly seen in the unusual way his poems are printed and in their strikingly original language. If you have not read any of Cummings's poems before, you will find "In just—" a unique reading experience, and probably a delightful one.

Winter

Nikki Giovanni (1943–   ) was born in Knoxville, Tennessee, and grew up in Cincinnati, Ohio. She has received numerous awards and honors, among them a National Book Award nomination and election to the Ohio Women's Hall of Fame. Much of her poetry expresses the feelings and experiences of the black-American community. She has also written about the joys and closeness of black family life. In "Winter," Giovanni writes about a universal subject, the first signs of the coming of winter.

Stopping by Woods on a Snowy Evening

Robert Frost (1875–1963) lived in rural New England for most of his life. As a result, Frost's poetry presents a full picture of nature and of country life in New Hampshire, Vermont, and other parts of New England. Frost won the Pulitzer Prize four times. His poems that describe and comment on a rural scene or event are among his most popular, and among these "Stopping by Woods on a Snowy Evening" is one of his best. If the poem seems to draw you into the scene described, it is partly because the scene is one that Frost knew well from real life.

Sensory Language

Sensory language is language that appeals to your senses. Poets as well as other writers frequently include details that appeal to your sense of sight, hearing, touch, taste, or smell.

To convey her impression of the heat of summer, the poet Hilda Doolittle (known as H. D.) wrote these lines in her poem "Garden":

> Fruit cannot drop
> Through this thick air;
> Fruit cannot fall into heat
> That presses up and blunts
> The points of pears,
> And rounds the grapes.

The sensory language here helps you almost see and feel the heavy, almost visible heat.

Look For

As you read the following poems, notice the clear word pictures they contain—the language that appeals to your sense of sight. Find examples of language that appeal to your sense of hearing and even to your sense of touch.

Writing

The poems you are about to read describe the changing seasons. Which one of the four seasons—spring, summer, fall, or winter—can you see most clearly in your imagination? Choose one, and list those sights, sounds, smells, and physical feelings that it brings to mind.

Vocabulary

Knowing the following words will help you as you read these poems.

wee (wē) *adj.*: Very small, tiny (p. 500)

burrow (bur′ ō) *v.*: To dig a hole or tunnel, especially for shelter (p. 502)

downy (doun′ ē) *adj.*: Soft and fluffy, like soft, fine feathers (p. 504)

In Just—
E. E. Cummings

in Just—
spring   when the world is mud-
luscious the little
lame balloonman

5   whistles   far   and wee

and eddieandbill come
running from marbles and
piracies and it's
spring

10   when the world is puddle-wonderful

the queer
old balloonman whistles
far   and   wee
and bettyandisbel come dancing

15   from hopscotch and jump rope and
it's
spring
and
    the

20   goat-footed[1]

balloonMan   whistles
far
and
wee

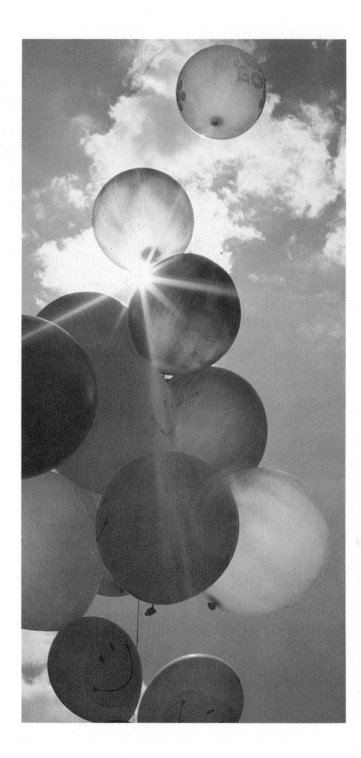

---

1. goat-footed: Like the Greek god Pan, who had the legs of a goat and was associated with fields, forests, and wild animals.

THINKING ABOUT THE SELECTION

Recalling

1. What event does this poem describe?

Interpreting

2. From whose point of view—a child's or adult's—is spring described? Which words seem especially appropriate for this group.
3. What is the effect of the poet's writing "eddieandbill" and "bettyandisbel" instead of "Eddie and Bill" and "Betty and Isbel"?
4. In what way does the arrangement of lines on the page mimic the way the people in the poem move?
5. Look at the adjectives used to describe the balloon man. How does the description of him change as the poem progresses?
6. The balloonman is associated with Pan, the goat-footed Greek god of woods and fields. What connection might there be between the balloonman's whistling and the children's running and dancing?

7. Why does the poet call this poem "In Just—," instead of "In Spring"?

Applying

8. What is it about spring that often makes us want to abandon our chores to play?

ANALYZING LITERATURE

Understanding Sensory Language

Sensory language is language that appeals to your senses. Poets frequently use such language to give you a vivid impression of the physical world. Cummings creates words that boldly appeal to your senses.

1. To which of your senses do the words "mud-luscious" and "puddle-wonderful" appeal?
2. The poet created these words by joining a noun and an adjective. In what way do these words capture the spirit of the poem?
3. Using the poet's technique of joining a noun and an adjective, create three words you think would be appropriate for describing spring.

Winter

Nikki Giovanni

Frogs burrow the mud
snails bury themselves
and I air my quilts
preparing for the cold

5   Dogs grow more hair
mothers make oatmeal
and little boys and girls
take Father John's Medicine[1]

Bears store fat
10   chipmunks gather nuts
and I collect books
For the coming winter

---

1. Father John's Medicine: An old-fashioned
cough syrup.

THINKING ABOUT THE SELECTION

Recalling

1. How does each animal mentioned prepare for winter?
2. What two things does the speaker do to prepare for winter?

Interpreting

3. In what way is the airing of quilts (line 3) a sign that winter is coming?

4. In what way does the collecting of books (line 11) suggest the approach of winter?
5. In what way does this poem suggest that people and animals are alike?

Applying

6. If you were asked to write an additional stanza for "Winter," what details might you include that fit in with those of the four stanzas Giovanni wrote?

THINKING AND WRITING

Writing a Poem

Write a poem in which you describe the activities you think of in connection with any one of the seasons where you live. Before writing, think about and then list the details that express your idea of the coming of the season you chose.

Although the details of your poem will be different from Giovanni's, follow the pattern she used. Write three four-line stanzas. Keep the lines short. Let some of the details be about nature and other people, and other details be about you.

Revise your poem and share it with your classmates.

Stopping by Woods on a Snowy Evening

Robert Frost

Whose woods these are I think I know.
His house is in the village, though;
He will not see me stopping here
To watch his woods fill up with snow.

5   My little horse must think it queer
To stop without a farmhouse near
Between the woods and frozen lake
The darkest evening of the year.

He gives his harness bells a shake
10 To ask if there is some mistake.
The only other sound's the sweep
Of easy wind and downy flake.

The woods are lovely, dark, and deep,
But I have promises to keep,
15 And miles to go before I sleep,
And miles to go before I sleep.

THINKING ABOUT THE SELECTION

Recalling

1. Describe the setting—both the time and the place—of the poem.
2. Why has the speaker stopped by the woods?
3. What is the horse's reaction to the pause in their journey?

Interpreting

4. What is the significance of the word *darkest* in line 8?

5. What does the speaker mean when he says that he has "promises to keep"?
6. What associations and feelings are stirred up by the word *sleep*? What might this word mean in this poem?

Applying

7. This is one of the most popular poems by one of America's best-loved poets. Why do you think it appeals to so many readers?

SPEAKING AND LISTENING

Reading a Lyric Poem

When you read a poem like "Stopping by Woods on a Snowy Evening"—a poem with rhythm and rhyme—you should be careful not to read it in a singsong way. For example, do not overemphasize the beat of the lines, and do not pause for the same length of time whenever you reach the end of a line.

The right way to read such a poem is to read the words with natural pronunciation and let the rhythm take care of itself. If there is no punctuation at the end of a line, read on, without a pause, to the first word of the next line. With these hints in mind, read Frost's poem aloud to your classmates.

THINKING AND WRITING

Writing About a Poem

"Stopping by Woods on a Snowy Evening," like most poems, can be understood on many levels. Write an explanation for your classmates of what you think the poem might mean. Start by making notes on why the speaker feels he must move on, where you think he might be going, and what promises he must keep. You might think of the situation as a mystery to be solved. Draft your ideas into a paragraph. End your paragraph with a summary statement about the meaning of the poem. Revise your draft, checking that what you have said is clear and sensible. Proofread it and prepare a final draft. Then share your interpretation of the poem with your classmates.

Season at the Shore

Phyllis McGinley (1905–1978) was born in Ontario, Oregon. She is most famous for her lighthearted, humorous poetry, for which she won a Pulitzer Prize in 1961. McGinley, who wrote with humor and affection about ordinary life, once summed up the viewpoint of her work by saying, "Cheerfulness was always breaking in." In "Season at the Shore," she takes her cheerfulness and humor to the beach for a romp on the sand.

When the Frost Is on the Punkin

James Whitcomb Riley (1849–1916) was born in Indiana. He wrote so many poems in the dialect, or country speech, of his native state that he has come to be known as "the Hoosier poet." He knew the land and the people of Indiana very well, and he used his knowledge to write poems that are still a source of local pride. "When the Frost Is on the Punkin" is both a colorful picture of an Indiana farm such as Riley would have known and a lively tune in the dialect that was for him a kind of music. Reading it aloud will add to your enjoyment of the language.

Sound devices are a poet's way of making language more expressive and musical. Two of the most frequently used of these devices are alliteration and onomatopoeia. **Alliteration** is the repetition of the same consonant sounds at the beginning of words. For example, in "Season at the Shore" McGinley writes, "*s*and in the *s*andwiches *s*pread for luncheon." Here the consonant sound *s* is repeated.

Onomatopoeia is the use of a word that imitates or suggests the sound of what the word refers to. For example, in "When the Frost Is on the Punkin" Riley writes, "And you hear the kyouck and gobble of the struttin' turkey-cock." Here "kyouck" and "gobble" suggest the sounds a turkey makes.

Look For

As you read "Season at the Shore," notice the frequent use of alliteration. What consonant sound occurs most often, and why do you think McGinley used this sound rather than another? What examples of onomatopoeia can you find in "When the Frost Is on the Punkin"? In what way does the use of onomatopoeia add to the poem's effectiveness?

Writing

Try using alliteration and onomatopoeia yourself. Imagine that you are visiting a zoo or animal preserve—or even traveling on foot through a jungle. Think of some of the animal sounds you might hear. Write down phrases you would use if you were going to describe these sounds in a report or magazine article. Use alliteration and onomatopoeia to make these descriptive phrases vivid and forceful. For example, the lion *r*oaring *r*egally, or Grrrr, roared the big cats.

Vocabulary

Knowing the following words will help you as you read "Season at the Shore" and "When the Frost Is on the Punkin."

adhesive (əd hē′ siv) *adj.*: Sticking (p. 508)

sibling (sib′ liŋ) *n.*: Brother or sister (p. 508)

odious (ō′ dē əs) *adj.*: Disgusting, offensive (p. 508)

gaiters (gāt′ ərz) *n.*: Coverings for the legs extending from the instep to the ankle or knee (p. 508)

stubble (stub′ 'l) *n.*: Short stumps of corn or grain (p. 513)

Season at the Shore

Phyllis McGinley

Oh, not by sun and not by cloud
And not by whippoorwill, crying loud,
And not by the pricking of my thumbs,
Do I know the way that the summer comes.
5   Yet here on this seagull-haunted strand,[1]
Here is an omen I understand—
Sand:

Sand on the beaches,
    Sand at the door,
10   Sand that screeches
    On the new-swept floor;
In the shower, sand for the foot to crunch on;
Sand in the sandwiches spread for luncheon;
Sand adhesive to son and sibling,
15   From wallet sifting, from pockets dribbling;
Sand by the beaker
    Nightly shed
From odious sneaker;
    Sand in bed;
20   Sahara[2] always in my seaside shanty
Like the sand in the voice
Of J. Durante.[3]

Winter is mittens, winter is gaiters
Steaming on various radiators.
25   Autumn is leaves that bog the broom.
Spring is mud in the living room
Or skates in places one scarcely planned.
But what is summer, her seal and hand?
Sand:

30   Sand in the closets,
    Sand on the stair,

---

1. **strand** (strand) n.: The ocean shore.
2. **Sahara** (sə har′ a): A large desert in North Africa.
3. **J. Durante** (də ran′ tē): Jimmy Durante (1893–1980), an American comedian with a husky, scraping voice.

Desert deposits
    In the parlor chair;
Sand in the halls like the halls of ocean;
35   Sand in the soap and the sun-tan lotion;
Stirred in the porridge, tossed in the greens,
Poured from the bottoms of rolled-up jeans;
    In the elmy street,
      On the lawny acre;
40   Glued to the seat
      Of the Studebaker;[4]
Wrapped in the folds of the *Wall Street Journal;*[5]
Damp sand, dry sand,
Sand eternal.
45   When I shake my garments at the Lord's command,
What will I scatter in the Promised Land?
Sand.

---

4. Studebaker: A car that is no longer made.
5. *Wall Street Journal*: A well-known financial newspaper.

THINKING ABOUT THE SELECTION

Recalling

1. What word is repeated more frequently than any other throughout the poem?
2. The poet thinks of sand as the "seal and hand" of summer. What things does she think of as standing for winter, autumn, and spring?

Interpreting

3. The poet includes a great number of images— word pictures—of sand in different places. What effect does the accumulation, or piling up, of details have on the poem? How is this effect reinforced by the repetition of the word *sand*?
4. To what senses does the poet appeal?
5. What is the poet's attitude toward sand?
6. Interpret, or explain the meaning of, the last three lines.
7. Why is "Season at the Shore" a better title for this poem than "Day at the Shore"?

Applying

8. What would you choose as the one thing that best represents summer? Why would this be your choice?

ANALYZING LITERATURE

Understanding Alliteration

Alliteration is the repetition of the same consonant sound at the beginning of words. This sound device can reinforce meaning as well as contribute to the "music" of a poem. The line "Sand adhesive to son and sibling," in which the s sound is repeated, is a more effective line in McGinley's poem than a line such as "Sand adhesive to daughter and brother" would have been. Why?

1. Find three or four other examples of alliteration in which the s sound is repeated.
2. Why is this sound especially appropriate to the poem?
3. Find an example of alliteration in which some other consonant sound is repeated.

THINKING AND WRITING

Writing a Poem with Alliteration

Write a four-line poem (it need not rhyme) in which you use alliteration. You may use one of the following subjects and the suggested consonant sound for alliteration, or you may choose another subject.

The winter wind (*w*, as in *wail, whoosh, wild*)
A snake (*s*, as in *slither, slimy, silent*)
A guitar (*p*, as in *pluck, play, pick*)
The rain (*d*, as in *downpour, damp, dreary*)

When you revise, first check that your poem says what you want to say about the subject. Then see if you can replace any words to add alliteration to your poem.

Read your poem to some of your classmates and listen to those they wrote.

When the Frost Is on the Punkin

James Whitcomb Riley

When the frost is on the punkin and the fodder's
    in the shock,[1]
And you hear the kyouck and gobble of the
    struttin' turkey-cock,
And the clackin' of the guineys,[2] and the cluckin' of
    the hens,
And the rooster's hallylooyer as he tiptoes on the
    fence;
5 O, it's then's the times a feller is a-feelin' at his
    best,
With the risin' sun to greet him from a night of
    peaceful rest,
As he leaves the house, bareheaded, and goes out
    to feed the stock,[3]
When the frost is on the punkin and the fodder's
    in the shock.

They's something kindo' harty-like about the
    atmusfere
10 When the heat of summer's over and the coolin' fall
    is here—
Of course we miss the flowers, and the blossums on
    the trees,
And the mumble of the hummin'-birds and buzzin'
    of the bees;
But the air's so appetizin'; and the landscape
    through the haze
Of a crisp and sunny morning of the airly[4] autumn
    days
15 Is a pictur' that no painter has the colorin' to mock[5]—

---

1. the fodder's in the shock: The corn or hay used to feed the
animals is stacked in piles, or shocks.
2. guineys (gin' ēs) guineas *n.*: Fowls with a featherless head,
rounded body, and dark feathers spotted with white.
3. stock (stäk) *n.*: Short for livestock, the domestic animals kept on
a farm.
4. airly (er' lē): Early.
5. mock (mäk) *v.*: Copy.

When the frost is on the punkin and the fodder's
        in the shock.

The husky, rusty russel of the tossels[6] of the corn,
And the raspin' of the tangled leaves, as golden as
        the morn;
The stubble in the furries[7]—kindo' lonesome-like,
        but still
20 A-preachin' sermuns to us of the barns they growed
        to fill;
The strawstack in the medder,[8] and the reaper in the
        shed;
The hosses in theyr stalls below—the clover
        overhead!—
O, it sets my hart a-clickin' like the tickin' of a
        clock,
When the frost is on the punkin and the fodder's
        in the shock!

25 Then your apples all is getherd, and the ones a
        feller keeps
Is poured around the celler-floor in red and yeller
        heaps;
And your cider-makin' 's over, and your wimmern-folks
        is through
With ther mince[9] and apple-butter, and theyr souse[10] and
        sausage, too! . . .
I don't know how to tell it—but ef sich a thing
        could be
30 As the Angels wantin' boardin', and they'd call
        around on *me*—
I'd want to 'commodate 'em[11]—all the whole-indurin'
        flock—
When the frost is on the punkin and the fodder's
        in the shock!

---

6. tossels: Tassels, which are silky, threadlike tufts at the tip of
an ear of corn.

7. furries (fŭr' ēs) *n.*: Furrows, which are narrow grooves cut in
the ground by a plow.

8. medder (med' ar): Meadow.

9. mince (mins) *n.*: Mincemeat, a mixture of chopped apples.
spices, and sometimes meat, used as a pie filling.

10. souse (sous) *n.*: A pickled food.

11. 'commodate (käm' ə dāt') **'em:** Accommodate them, or give
them food and a place to stay.

THINKING ABOUT THE SELECTION

Recalling

1. In the first stanza, what details suggest "the times a feller is a-feelin' at his best"?
2. In the second stanza, what does the speaker especially like about the atmosphere and landscape of fall?
3. Summarize in your own words what sets the speaker's heart "a-clickin' " in stanza three.

Interpreting

4. What is the meaning or point of the last four lines of the poem?
5. Summarize the speaker's feelings about fall, "when the frost is on the punkin."
6. What can you conclude about the speaker and his way of life?
7. This poem is written in dialect rather than standard English. Why might the poet have decided to write it this way?

Applying

8. Although this poem is set in rural Indiana, it has long appealed to readers all over the country. Why do you think its appeal is so widespread?

ANALYZING LITERATURE

Understanding Onomatopoeia

Onomatopoeia is the use of a word that imitates or suggests the sound of what the word refers to. The word "cluckin'," for example, in the phrase "the cluckin' of the hens," suggests the sound hens make. This device adds vividness to a poet's descriptions of sound.

1. Besides "kyouck," "gobble," and "cluckin'," what other examples of onomatopoeia can you find in the first stanza?
2. Find two examples in each of the next two stanzas.
3. Of the examples you found, which seems to you most effective?
4. To which of your senses do these uses of onomatopoeia appeal?
5. Why is onomatopoeia so effective in poetry?

THINKING AND WRITING

Writing a Travel Article

Write an article for your school newspaper or literary magazine about an imaginary trip you took to a zoo, an animal preserve, or a jungle. Using the phrases you wrote before reading these poems, describe the memorable sounds you heard. Use alliteration and onomatopoeia to make your descriptions vivid. When you revise your article, see if you can use more vivid words and phrases to make your description even more clear to someone who may never have heard the sounds you are writing about.

People in Their Variety

SNAPSHOT AT THE BEACH, 1891
Three Lions

Mother to Son

Langston Hughes (1902–1967) was born in Joplin, Missouri, and later lived in in different parts of the country. He is most associated with Harlem, an area in New York City. Many of his poems, including "Mother to Son," use the rhythms of black music, especially jazz and blues. These poems present memorable, and sometimes powerful, portraits of black life. Often, as in "Mother to Son," they center on a character with a distinctive and forceful voice.

A Song of Greatness

The **Chippewa Indians** lived at one time on the shores of Lake Superior. Today, about 30,000 Chippewa live on reservations in the Midwest and West. "A Song of Greatness" recalls the Chippewa past when battles were fought and heroes were made.

    Mary Austin (1868–1934) lived most of her life in the southwest, where she studied the ways of native Americans.

I'm Nobody

Emily Dickinson (1830–1886) hardly ever traveled outside Amherst, Massachusetts, where she was born. When she died, she had written about 1,175 poems, but only seven had been published—anonymously. "I'm Nobody" reflects her life. She was a private person. But it does not reflect her destiny. Today, her fame is worldwide and her admirers are without number.

Pete at the Zoo

Gwendolyn Brooks (1917–   ) became the first black American poet to win the Pulitzer Prize. She has said of her work, "I think that my poetry is related to life in the broad sense of the word, even though the subject relates closest to the Negro. . . . I hoped that people would recognize instantly that Negroes are just like other people; they have the same hates and loves and fears, the same tragedies and triumphs and deaths. . . . " In "Pete at the Zoo" the young black boy could be any child gazing at an elephant in wonder.

Tone

Tone in poetry is the poet's or speaker's attitude toward the subject, toward the reader, or toward himself or herself. It can often be described by such words as *serious, amused, sad, cheerful, proud,* or *mocking*. Tone comes from all the elements of a poem: the subject, what is said about it, the connotations of words, the rhythm, the figures of speech, and so on.

Look For

To understand the tone of a poem, read it as if you were the speaker uttering the words in real life. How you would describe your feelings as you were reading. Describe in a word or phrase the tone of each of the following poems.

Writing

Tone is the attitude shown through our words or our actions. Imagine that you are greeting the following people at a party: first, someone you have not seen in a very long time and are surprised and happy to see; second, someone you like who recently lost a much-loved pet; next, someone you dislike but wish to greet politely; and last, your best friend whom you see every day. Describe how you would greet each person. Do so in a way that shows the tone of your greetings. Include your words, the way you would speak the words, and any gestures you would use. For example, if you were greeting a widely respected public official visiting the school, you might describe your greeting this way: "Good morning, Senator," I said with a friendly smile and a slight bow of my head. "Thank you for visiting our school."

Vocabulary

Knowing the following words will help you as you read these poems.

esteemed (ə stēmd') *v.*: Respected, held in high regard (p. 520)

banish (ban' ish) *v.*: Send into exile (p. 521)

bog (bäg) *n.*: A small marsh or swamp (p. 521)

hunch (hunch) *v.*: Stand with one's back arched (p. 522)

Mother to Son

Langston Hughes

Well, son, I'll tell you:
Life for me ain't been no crystal stair.
It's had tacks in it,
And splinters,
5   And boards torn up,
And places with no carpet on the floor—
Bare.
But all the time
I'se been a-climbin' on,
10   And reachin' landin's,
And turnin' corners,
And sometimes goin' in the dark
Where there ain't been no light.
So boy, don't you turn back.
15   Don't you set down on the steps
'Cause you finds it's kinder hard.
Don't you fall now—
For I'se still goin', honey,
I'se still climbin',
20   And life for me ain't been no crystal stair.

THINKING ABOUT THE SELECTION

Recalling

1. What does the mother tell the boy her life has not been?
2. What advice does she give him?

Interpreting

3. The mother uses an extended metaphor to describe her life. What do the details in lines 3–7 suggest about this life?

4. What is the mother saying about her life in lines 8–13?
5. What is she telling her son in lines 14–17 about how to live?

Applying

6. Since our earliest days, Americans have valued stick-to-itiveness, or perseverance. What is it about our early history that would have made these traits desirable?

ORGANDY COLLAR, 1936
Edmund Archer
Whitney Museum of American Art

ANALYZING LITERATURE

Understanding Tone

Tone is the basic attitude expressed in a poem. It is like the emotional coloring you give your words in conversation by the way you use your voice. Just think, for example, of the different way you can say the one word *Hello*!

1. How would you describe the tone of the first sentence (lines 1–7) of the poem?

2. How is the tone different in the next sentence (lines 8–13)?

3. Which of the following descriptions best fits the tone of the entire poem? Give reasons for your choice.

   a. Exhausted and hopeless
   b. Weary, yet strong and determined
   c. Lively and humorous
   d. Sorrowful and gloomy

A Song of Greatness

Chippewa Traditional

Mary Austin

When I hear the old men
Telling of heroes,
Telling of great deeds
Of ancient days—
5 When I hear that telling,
Then I think within me
I, too, am one of these.

When I hear the people
Praising great ones,
10 Then I know that I too—
Shall be esteemed:
I, too, when my time comes
Shall do mightily.

THINKING ABOUT THE SELECTION

Recalling

1. To whom is the speaker referring when he says in line 7, "I, too, am one of these"?

Interpreting

2. Who might the "great ones" (line 9) be?
3. What is your impression of the speaker?
4. What makes the speaker think that he shall "be esteemed" and "do mightily"?

Applying

5. How does the attitude of young people today toward heroes of the past compare with the attitude of the speaker in this poem?

CRITICAL THINKING AND READING

Comparing and Contrasting Tone

Tone is the speaker's attitude toward his or her subject. For example, the tone may be sorrowful or pleased, angry or accepting. You will find it easier to grasp the tone of a poem by comparing and contrasting it with the tone of another poem, especially one with a similar subject or point of view.

1. Describe the tone of "A Song of Greatness."
2. If you have not already done so, read the preceding poem, "Mother to Son." How are the subjects of "Mother to Son" and "A Song of Greatness" similar?
3. Finally, compare and contrast the tone of "A Song of Greatness" with the tone of "Mother to Son."

I'm Nobody

Emily Dickinson

I'm Nobody! Who are you?
Are you—Nobody—too?
Then there's a pair of us!
Don't tell! they'd banish us—you know!

5   How dreary—to be—Somebody!
How public—like a Frog—
To tell your name—the livelong June—
To an admiring Bog!

THINKING ABOUT THE SELECTION

Recalling

1. What does the speaker believe will happen if it is discovered that they are "nobodies"?
2. What is it like to be a "Somebody"?

Interpreting

3. What does the word "Nobody" mean in this poem?
4. How does the speaker feel about discovering another nobody?
5. What does the word "public" suggest?
6. To what does the speaker compare being public?
7. What might the admiring bog stand for?

Applying

8. What is your opinion of the speaker's preference for being a nobody to being a somebody?

CRITICAL THINKING AND READING

Paraphrasing a Poem

Paraphrasing a poem means restating it in your own words. It is an excellent way of seeing through hard words, unusual sentence structures, and figurative language in order to come to a basic meaning of the poem.

The following lines are from a poem called "Solitude," by Alexander Pope. Notice how the paraphrase that follows them restates the meaning of the lines in simpler language.

> Happy the man whose wish and care
> A few paternal acres bound,
> Content to breathe his native air
>   In his own ground.

Paraphrase: A man is fortunate if everything he wants or worries about lies within the land he lives on. He is fortunate if he's happy at home and doesn't desire to travel.

Once you have paraphrased a poem, you can then reread it with greater understanding and enjoyment.

Write a paraphrase of "I'm Nobody." Be sure to restate the poem in your own words in a way that makes clear all that the poem is expressing.

Pete at the Zoo

Gwendolyn Brooks

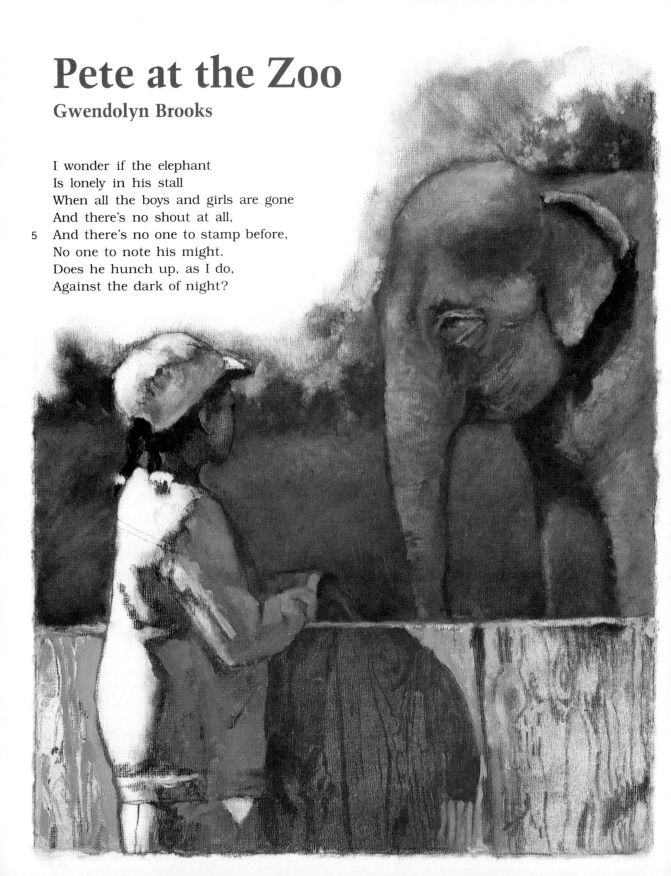

I wonder if the elephant
Is lonely in his stall
When all the boys and girls are gone
And there's no shout at all,
5 And there's no one to stamp before,
No one to note his might.
Does he hunch up, as I do,
Against the dark of night?

THINKING ABOUT THE SELECTION

Recalling

1. Who is the speaker in this poem?
2. What would he like to know about the elephant?

Interpreting

3. What impression of the speaker do you get from the poem?
4. How does the speaker feel about being alone? Find evidence to support your answer.
5. How does the speaker feel about the dark of night. Find evidence to support your answer.

Applying

6. What is it about the dark of night that stirs up fears and insecurities?

THINKING AND WRITING

Writing to Express Tone

Write a paragraph titled "Pete Speaks to the Elephant." Have Pete speak in a tone of voice suggested by Brooks's poem. What he says should be appropriate to the kind of boy you think Pete is. Before you write, think about other feelings, thoughts, or questions that might have passed through the mind of the boy in the poem. When you revise your paragraph, read it aloud to a friend or classmate and ask if your Pete sounds like the boy in the poem.

GUIDE FOR READING

Father William

Lewis Carroll (1832–1898) is the pen name of Charles Lutwidge Dodgson, who was born in Cheshire, England. Under his real name he wrote mathematical works, but as Lewis Carroll he wrote two of the most famous books for children of all time, *Alice in Wonderland* and *Through the Looking Glass*. His outward life was very quiet and uneventful, but in works like "Father William" he found escape from his serious work into a delightfully zany, topsy-turvy world that still amuses children old and young.

Humor

Humor in poetry can arise from a number of sources, such as surprise, exaggeration, or the bringing together of unrelated things. The majority of funny poems, however, have two things in common, rhythm and rhyme. These devices often make language more lively and sharp. This more spirited language makes humorous situations even more humorous. For example, here is a little poem by Ogden Nash called "The Porcupine."

> Any hound a porcupine nudges
> Can't be blamed for harboring grudges.
> I know one hound that laughed all winter
> At a porcupine that sat on a splinter.

Take away the rhythm and rhyme and the humor vanishes.

Look For

As you read "Father William," listen to the rhymes and catch the beat of the lines. By doing so you will find this funny poem even funnier. What do you feel is especially funny about it?

Writing

Imagine that you are interviewing a distinguished-looking adult about his or her career, interests, or way of life. For each question you ask, you get a reply that is absolutely ridiculous. Write down the questions you might ask and the zany replies that would follow.

Vocabulary

Knowing the following words will help you as you read "Father William."

incessantly (in ses′ 'nt lē) *adv.*: Without stopping (p. 525)
sage (sāj) *n.*: A very wise man (p. 526)
supple (sup′ 'l) *adj.*: Flexible (p. 526)

shilling (shil′ iŋ) *n.*: A British coin. In Carroll's day, a shilling had much more monetary value than it has today. (p. 526)

Father William

Lewis Carroll

"You are old, Father William," the young man said,
    "And your hair has become very white;
And yet you incessantly stand on your head—
    Do you think, at your age, it is right?"

5   "In my youth," Father William replied to his son,
    "I feared it might injure the brain;
But, now that I'm perfectly sure I have none,
    Why, I do it again and again."

"You are old," said the youth, "as I mentioned before.
10   And have grown most uncommonly[1] fat;
Yet you turned a back-somersault in at the door—
    Pray, what is the reason of that?"

YOU ARE OLD FATHER WILLIAM, 1865
Sir John Tenniel
The Granger Collection

"In my youth," said the sage, as he shook his gray locks,
    "I kept all my limbs very supple
15   By the use of this ointment—one shilling the box—
    Allow me to sell you a couple?"

"You are old," said the youth, "and your jaws are too weak
    For anything tougher than suet;[2]
Yet you finished the goose, with the bones and the beak—
20   Pray, how did you manage to do it?"

"In my youth," said his father, "I took to the law,
    And argued each case with my wife;
And the muscular strength, which it gave to my jaw
    Has lasted the rest of my life."

---

1. uncommonly (un käm′ ən lē) *adv.*: Remarkably.
2. suet (soo′ it) *n.*: Fat used in cooking.

YOU ARE OLD FATHER WILLIAM, 1865
Sir John Tenniel
The Granger Collection

25 "You are old," said the youth, "one would hardly suppose
        That your eye was as steady as ever;
    Yet you balanced an eel on the end of your nose—
        What made you so awfully clever?"

    "I have answered three questions, and that is enough,"
30   Said his father. "Don't give yourself airs!
    Do you think I can listen all day to such stuff?
        Be off, or I'll kick you downstairs!"

THINKING ABOUT THE SELECTION

Recalling

1. What reason does Father William give for incessantly standing on his head?
2. What enables him to do back-somersaults?
3. How did he develop jaws strong enough to devour a goose, including the bones and beak?
4. Why does he refuse to answer his son's question about balancing an eel on his nose?

Interpreting

5. What is it about Father William's physical condition that makes his behavior so absurd?
6. Which one of his zany activities struck you as the funniest? Explain.

Applying

7. Why do people like to laugh? Why do they enjoy telling utterly ridiculous stories?

ANALYZING LITERATURE

Understanding Humor in Poetry

Rhythm and rhyme are important aids to humorous poets, but they are not in themselves funny. The more common sources of humor include surprise, exaggeration, and bringing together unrelated things. For example, being elderly is not humorous, and neither (most of the time) is standing on one's head. But being elderly and standing on one's head is funny because we usually associate standing on one's head with children. Such humor is based on bringing together unrelated things.

1. First rewrite any one of the pairs of stanzas in which a question is asked and then answered. Remove the rhythm and rhyme, but do not change the meaning. How is the humor affected by the changes you made?
2. Next find in "Father William" an example of humor based on surprise or the unexpected.
3. Find an example of humor based on exaggeration.

THINKING AND WRITING

Writing a Humorous Poem

Using the questions and answers you wrote for your imaginary interview, write a humorous poem in dialogue with questions and replies. Your poem need not be as long as Carroll's, but it should be funny.

When you revise, read your poem to a friend to see if it is funny. Share your poem with your classmates.

GUIDE FOR READING

Two Limericks

Oliver Herford (1863–1935) was born in England but lived from childhood on in the United States. Once, passing a schoolhouse at night, he imagined the typical school day that lay ahead for the teacher and pupils. He entered the school and covered the chalkboard with drawings of animals. Next day, the teachers and pupils were as amused as they were surprised. This incident reveals two qualities of Herford's, his sense of humor and his fondness for animals as subjects. You will find both in his limericks.

Limericks

A **limerick** is a poem of five lines. The first, second, and fifth lines have three rhythmic beats and rhyme with one another. The third and fourth lines have two beats, and they also rhyme. Using letters to represent the different rhyme sounds, you can describe the rhyme pattern of a limeric as *aabba*. Limericks are always lighthearted, humorous poems.

Look For

As you read Herford's limericks, notice how they fit the pattern of rhythm and rhyme described above. Enjoy the humor more by reading these poems aloud.

Writing

To prepare for writing your own limericks, write the line *There once was a boy* (or *girl*) named . . . (supply a name). Then list a number of words that rhyme with the name and that could be used in funny statements about the boy or girl named. Since limericks have two rhyme sounds, make a second list of rhyme words.

Vocabulary

Knowing the following words will help you as you read Herford's two limericks.

dote (dōt) *v.*: To be extremely fond (p. 529)

scale (skāl) *n.*: A series of musical tones (p. 529)

quail (kwāl) *v.*: Draw back in fear (p. 529)

Two Limericks

Oliver Herford

Said the Lion: "On music I dote,
But something is wrong with my throat.
    When I practice a scale,
    The listeners quail,
And flee at the very first note!"

A puppy whose hair was so flowing
There really was no means of knowing
    Which end was his head,
    Once stopped me and said,
"Please, sir, am I coming or going?"

THINKING ABOUT THE SELECTION
Recalling

1. What activity does the lion say he performs?
2. How do his listeners respond?
3. Describe the puppy in the second limerick.

Interpreting

4. What is the lion really doing?
5. Why is the puppy's question funny?

Applying

6. Why do you think that the limerick form is never used for serious poetry?

ANALYZING LITERATURE
Understanding Limericks

A **limerick** has short lines, a swift, catchy rhythm, and heavily stressed rhymes. There are three beats in the first, second, and fifth lines, which rhyme, and two beats in the third and fourth lines, which also rhyme.

The following is a limerick about limericks. See if you can paraphrase it—restate it in your own words—to discover what it says about why limericks are amusing. (The word "conceits" in line 4 means "imaginative or clever ideas.")

Well, it's partly the shape of the thing
That gives the old limerick wing;
    These accordion pleats
    Full of airy conceits
Take it up like a kite on a string.

THINKING AND WRITING
Writing a Limerick

Using the opening line and the list of rhymes you have written, write a limerick of your own. When you revise, make sure that you did not damage the sense of your lines while getting them to rhyme. Also, check that your lines have the correct rhythm. Share your limerick with those of your classmates.

Poetry

Poetry is hard to categorize, although you probably know a poem when you see one. It can deal with any subject matter, take a variety of forms, use imagery and figurative language, and apply one or more of many sound devices. In addition, a poem often has a theme, or insight into life. To fully appreciate a poem, put the elements of it together.

Types of Poetry

There are several types of poetry. The most common are narrative poetry and lyric poetry. Narrative poetry tells a story. Lyric poetry expresses strong personal feelings about the subject.

Figurative Language

Figurative language consists of words used with meanings beyond their usual dictionary meanings. Three common types of figurative language are simile, metaphor, and extended metaphor. A simile is a comparison between two essentially unlike objects that uses the word *like* or *as* to make this comparison. A metaphor is like a simile, but it does not use the word like or as. An extended metaphor is carried through from the beginning to the end of the poem.

Imagery

Imagery is the use of vivid language to create word pictures. Usually these word pictures appeal to the senses and arouse strong feelings.

Sound Devices

The music of poetry is created by **sound devices.** Four common sound devices are rhythm, rhyme, alliteration, and onomatopoeia. Rhythm is the pattern of stressed and unstressed lines in a poem. Rhyme is the matching of sounds at the ends of words. Alliteration is the repetition of initial consonant sounds, and onomatopoeia is the creation of words to imitate sounds.

Theme

Many poems suggest an insight into life. As you read, ask yourself what general truth does the poem reveal to you.

GOOD FORTUNE, 1939
René Magritte
Museum Boymans-Van Beuningen, Rotterdam

Miracles

Walt Whitman

Theme: The title provides a clue to the theme. What does the title suggest about the theme of this poem?

Sound: This poem is written in free verse. It has no set pattern of stressed and unstressed syllables. Do the words at the end of lines rhyme? Are the lines of equal length? What effect is created by the use of free verse?

Why, who makes much of a miracle?
As to me I know of nothing else but miracles,
Whether I walk the streets of Manhattan,
Or dart my sight over the roofs of houses toward the sky,
5 Or wade with naked feet along the beach just in the edge of
   the water,

Or stand under trees in the woods,
Or talk by day with any one I love . . .
Or sit at table at dinner with the rest,
Or look at strangers opposite me riding in the car,
10 Or watch honeybees busy around the hive of a summer
        forenoon[1]
Or animals feeding in the fields,
Or birds, or the wonderfulness of insects in the air,
Or the wonderfulness of the sundown, or of stars shining
        so quiet and bright,
Or the exquisite[2] delicate thin curve of the new moon in
        spring;
15 These with the rest, one and all, are to me miracles,
The whole referring, yet each distinct[3] and in its place.

To me every hour of the light and dark is a miracle,
Every cubic inch of space is a miracle,
Every square yard of the surface of the earth is spread with
        the same,
20 Every foot of the interior swarms[4] with the same.

To me the sea is a continual miracle,
The fishes that swim—the rocks—the motion of the waves—
        the ships with men in them,
What stranger miracles are there?

Imagery: Notice the vivid imagery in these lines. Which words and phrases appeal to your senses?

Theme: These two lines provide a clue to the theme. In what way do all these details form a whole? In what way do they remain distinct.

Types of Poetry: This is a lyric poem. What strong feelings does the poem express?

Theme: The answer to the question provides a clue to the theme. What is the answer?

Pulling It Together: The poet sees miracles in the world around him. Both events in everyday life and in nature are so remarkable that they seem miraculous.

---

1. forenoon (fôr´ nōōn) *n.*: Morning.
2. exquisite (eks´ kwi zit) *adj.*: Very beautiful, especially in a delicate way.
3. distinct (dis tiŋkt´) *adj.*: Separate and different.
4. swarms (swôrmz) *v.*: Is filled or crowded.

Walt Whitman (1819–1892) was born on Long Island but lived most of his life in Brooklyn, New York. He worked at many occupations—printer, carpenter, teacher, newspaper reporter—and praised the value of the common person in many of his poems. Called the father of modern poetry, most of his poems are highly original, using free verse to capture the various rhythms and moods of American life. They are collected in *Leaves of Grass*.

THINKING ABOUT THE SELECTION

Recalling

1. What is a miracle? What is the first question the speaker asks about miracles?
2. Find at least ten events the speaker considers miracles.
3. What is the second question about miracles the speaker asks?

Interpreting

4. In what way is talking with a person you know a miracle?
5. In what way is the sea a continual miracle?
6. Think about the answer to the speaker's second question. How would you express the theme of the poem?

Applying

7. List at least five events you consider miracles.

ANALYZING LITERATURE

Understanding Free Verse

Free verse is poetry that has no regular rhythmic pattern and no regular rhyme scheme. Usually, free verse uses the sounds and rhythms of natural speech to create its own unique musical quality. One way free verse creates rhythm is by using a similar word-order pattern from line to line.

1. What do you notice about word order in lines 4–14?
2. What do you notice about word order in lines 17–22?
3. What effect is created by the similar structure of the lines?

CRITICAL THINKING AND READING

Categorizing

A category is a group of related items. When you form categories, you put things that are similar in the same group. For example, you might arrange the clothes in your closet into two groups: school clothes and play clothes. You might arrange the supplies you bring home into categories: for example, things that need to go directly into the refrigerator, canned goods, and cleaning supplies.

Arrange the events the speaker mentions in "Miracles" in groups.

1. Which events fit into the category "City Experiences"?
2. Which fit into the category "Wonders of the Natural World"?
3. Which fit into the category "Communicating with Others"?

UNDERSTANDING LANGUAGE

Building New Words

A miracle is so amazing that it causes you to wonder. The word *wonder* is at the root of many words that are probably already in your vocabulary. Define each of the words below based on the word *wonder*. Then use each word in a sentence.

1. wonderful
2. wonderment
3. wonderland
4. wonderworker
5. wondrous

THINKING AND WRITING

Writing a Poem About Miracles

Look over the list you created of things you consider miracles. Brainstorm with your classmates to add to this list. Then, using free verse, write a poem about miracles in everyday life. Revise your poem to be sure you have included enough details that appeal to the senses. Create a final draft, and share it with your classmates.

Making Inferences

Reading a poem requires careful reading and thinking because it is usually made up of very few words. Making inferences, or educated guesses, about what the poet is saying is often necessary to understand the poem. An **inference** is a conclusion based on evidence such as facts or clues provided by the author. Another form of evidence is the reader's background knowledge and experience. Both types of evidence must be carefully weighed to determine if they support the inference that is being made.

Setting

Inferences can help you understand the setting, characters, plot, words or phrases, and major ideas in a poem. Think about "The Highwayman." What is the setting at the beginning of this poem? The answer would be an extremely windy, cloudy, moonlit night in an area of the country that is desolate except for an old inn. How do you arrive at this conclusion? First, the words "torrent" and "gusty" indicate that the wind is blowing violently. "Ghostly" indicates that the moon is pale, while "cloudy seas" refer to the many clouds in the sky. Because a moor is considered a wasteland, this would indicate that the area was desolate except for the old inn.

Character

By making inferences, or "reading between the lines," you can gain insights into the characters. What can you infer about the highwayman? First you can infer that he makes a dashing, handsome, romantic figure because of the clothes he wears and his twinkling pistol butts and sword handle. Next you can infer that he is going to commit a robbery tonight because a highwayman is a robber and he says that he is "after a prize to-night." Then you can guess that he deeply loves Bess because he became so emotional when her hair cascaded over him that his face became fiery red, because his face grew gray when he learned of her plight, and because he is willing to risk his life for her. His actions as a robber and in seeking to avenge Bess's death indicate that he is daring and courageous.

Plot

Incidents in the plot become more understandable when you make inferences. For instance, how do you know who informed the soldiers that the highwayman would be returning to the inn? Look at the clues in the poem. Tim, who loved Bess himself, overheard the highwayman tell Bess he would return. Tim's eyes are described as "hollows of madness," which makes you think that he is crazy. Saying that he listened "dumb as a dog" suggests that he is not very intelligent. Your background knowledge would make you realize that someone who is dim-witted and mad would inform the authorities about the highwayman to get rid of a rival. Because there is no one else in the poem with a reason to inform on the highwayman, you can infer that Tim is the one who did it.

Activity

Read the following excerpt from Henry Wadsworth Longfellow's poem "The Building of the Ship." Then answer the questions.

Thou, too, sail on, O Ship of State!
Sail on, O Union, strong and great!
Humanity with all its fears,
With all its hopes of future years,
Is hanging breathless on thy fate!
We know what Master laid thy keel,
What Workmen wrought thy ribs of steel,
Who made each mast, and sail, and rope,
What anvils rang, what hammers beat,
In what a forge and what a heat
Were shaped the anchors of thy hope!
Fear not each sudden sound and shock,
'Tis of the wave and not the rock;
'Tis but the flapping of the sail,
And not a rent made by a gale!
In spite of rock and tempest's roar,
In spite of false lights on the shore,
Sail on, nor fear to breast the sea!
Our hearts, our hopes, are all with thee,
Our hearts, our hopes, our prayers, our tears,
Our faith, triumphant o'er our fears,

1. What is the "Ship of State"? Support your answer.
2. Why is humanity "hanging breathless" on the ship's fate? Give evidence to support your answer.
3. Why does the speaker say to "fear not each sudden sound and shock"? Give evidence to support your answer.
4. What might be the "rock and tempest's roar"?
5. What might be the "false lights on the shore"?
6. Why should the ship sail on? Support your answer.

Assignment

1. The ability to compare one thing to another is essential to the art of poetry. Write a short poem about a place you are familiar with—your room, the street you live on, a nearby woods or field, and so on. In your poem, compare five objects in this place to five other things.

Prewriting.   Choose carefully the place about which you are going to write. Be sure it contains lots of interesting objects, objects that suggest comparisons. Then picture it in your imagination. Letting your mind relax, scan it carefully, noting all the objects it contains. Jot down all the ideas that come into your mind.

Writing.   Now write your poem. Remember to include five vivid comparisons.

Revising.   When you revise, make sure your comparisons are original, fresh, and vivid.

Assignment

2. Write a poem about the people of a specific outdoors place—only these "people" will be *personified objects*. Have the objects in this place think, feel, talk, and act like people.

Prewriting.   Imagine an outdoors place close to home. What objects do you picture in this place? Pretend they are people. What would these objects be thinking, feeling, doing, and saying if they were human beings? How, for example, does the sand at the water's edge feel about being pounded all day by the ocean's "fist"? What do the rocks say when people aren't around?

Writing.   Now write about "The People in the _____."
Make one of these people cranky, another thoughtful, a third silly and loud. Let them talk to each other, each in his or her individual style.

Revising.   When you revise, examine the places where the "people" talk to each other to see that you have punctuated the dialogue correctly.

Assignment

3. Write a poem that creates a certain feeling or mood. Include objects associated with this mood.

Prewriting.   Before you write, decide on the mood you want to create. Jot down the feelings associated with this mood. Then connect the feelings that seem to go together. Look for physical things that "stand for" these feelings. Cobwebs, for example, "stand for" dusty and old. Fresh snow "stands for" winter and peace.

Writing.   Write your poem. Make the lines in your poem rhyme. Use comparisons—similes, metaphors, personification. Finally, use lots of images.

Revising.   When you revise, check to see that each of your objects really does help create the mood you want it to create. Prepare a final draft of your poem and share it with your classmates.

YOU THE CRITIC

Assignment

1. Some of the poems you have read are about specific characters. Choose two of these characters, each from a different poem, and then write an essay comparing and contrasting them.

Prewriting. Choose the two characters. Prepare a chart showing their similarities and their differences.

Writing. Now write your essay. Be sure to mention the names of the characters and the poems they are found in. Show how the two characters are similar and how they are different.

Revising. When you revise, make sure you have included a sufficient number of details from the poems to back up your points.

Assignment

2. A *central* image in a poem is one that dominates the poem, that is, ideas and feelings connected with this image are found in most of the lines of the poem. Write an essay about *two* poems with central images. Identify the central image in each and show how it helps the poet develop and clarify his or her feelings and ideas.

Prewriting. When you have selected two poems with central images, make notes about how these images are expressed throughout the poem.

Writing. Now write your essay. Treat each poem separately. For each poem (1) tell what the central image is, perhaps citing the line where it first appears. Then (2) show that words, ideas, and feelings connected with this image are found throughout the poem. Cite some of the lines that contain references to the central image.

Revising. When you revise, ask yourself these questions: (1) Did you identify the central image in each poem? (2) Did you show the ways in which the central image helps develop the meaning?

Assignment

3. An American poet has proclaimed as his motto: "No ideas except in things." By this he means that the best way for a poet to communicate his or her ideas is through concrete physical things. Choose *two* poems from this section and discuss the ways in which these poems follow the motto, "No ideas except in things."

Prewriting. Before you write, scan the poems in this section to find the two you intend to write about. Jot down lines that use concrete objects to portray ideas.

Writing. Now write your essay. Present your material one poem at a time. Cite several lines—or parts of lines—from each poem which express ideas through concrete things. Explain how each poem supports the motto.

Revising. When you revise, check to see that you have blended your citations from the poems smoothly into your essay.

FABLES, MYTHS, AND LEGENDS

Gods and goddesses, talking animals, strange and wondrous events—these are some of the subjects of fables, myths, and legends. All such stories are very old. They come to us from the distant past. Although different writers retell these stories in print, most of them originated long before reading and writing began. They have survived by being handed down by word of mouth from generation to generation. Taken together, fables, myths, and legends make up what is known as the oral tradition of literature.

Why have these old tales survived through the centuries? One reason is that they are about subjects that people love to read or hear about. Superhuman characters and marvelous events always make for entertaining stories. Another reason is that these tales say so much about human nature and the world. In fact, they represent some of the earliest efforts of the human race to explain the world. Reading fables, myths, and legends should be both a pleasurable and rewarding experience.

CLASSICAL FABLE, 1986
Thomas McKnight
Chalk & Vermilion

Fables, Myths, and Legends

Background

Fables, myths, legends, and folk tales are among the oldest forms of literature. Fables are short stories that teach moral lessons. The characters are usually animals who have human speech and characteristics. Usually associated with Greeks and Romans, myths are anonymous stories, usually involving gods and goddesses, that convey cultural ideals and beliefs, or explain natural occurrences such as lightning and volcanoes. Legends are also very old stories handed down through generations. Many are believed to have a historical basis. Although subjects of legends may have been actual people, the stories are fictitious and tend to emphasize traits admired by the cultures that created them. Folk tales are similar to myths but they are usually about ordinary people instead of gods. All cultures have their own traditions of such highly imaginative stories. They explain natural events, teach moral lessons, and emphasize behaviors, attitudes, and ideals admired by the people who create them.

Reading Strategies

As you read through this unit, you will find differences from other forms of literature that you should be aware of. For example, the characters in fables are animals, yet they speak and behave like humans. The myths, legends, and folktales contain names that you might have difficulty pronouncing and places you may never have heard of. Many of the events in myths are fantastic and even superhuman.

Have an open mind as you read the selections in this unit; accept what is presented and try to learn as much as you can about other people and cultures. You will find that, although the tales were created long ago and in different cultures, they convey ideas and attitudes common to people today. Finally, as you read, interact with the literature by using the active reading strategies: question, predict, clarify, summarize, and pull together.

Themes

You will encounter the following themes in the *Fables, Myths, and Legends* unit.
- The importance of conforming to the ideals and values of society
- The need to explain the unexplainable
- The strength and value of friendship and love
- The need for justice and truth
- The journey to personal fulfillment

CHARIOT OF THE MOON
Frederic E. Church
The Cooper-Hewitt Museum

Characters

Become familiar with the following characters before you read the *Fables, Myths, and Legends* unit.

Greek and Roman Myths
(In parentheses you will find the Roman form of the name.)

Zeus (Jupiter)—king of the gods
Hera (Juno)—queen of the gods
Poseidon (Neptune)—god of the sea
Hades (Pluto)—god of the underworld
Apollo (Apollo)—god of the sun
Athena (Minerva)—goddess of wisdom
Aphrodite (Venus)—goddess of love
Hermes (Mercury)—messenger of the gods
Demeter (Ceres)—goddess of agriculture
Persephone—daughter of Demeter and wife of Hades
Prometheus—a Titan who stole the secret of fire from the gods
Phaëthon—son of Apollo who tried, unsuccessfully, to drive his father's chariot
Baucis and Philemon—husband and wife who were rewarded by the gods for their hospitality to strangers
Icarus—son of Daedalus who refused to listen to his father
Daedalus—man who built wings for his son and himself to escape from prison
Narcissus—handsome youth who loved his own image too much
Echo—nymph who was punished by Hera for tricking her and who loved Narcissus

Myths, Legends, and Folktales from Around the World

Alida—daughter of an Indian chief who loved Taroo
Taroo—youth who fell in love with Alida, member of an enemy tribe
Ojeeg—great hunter who vanquished the Ice Man
The Ice Man (Peboan)—the spirit of winter
Popocatepetl—great warrior who loved Ixtlaccihuatl
Ixtlaccihuatl—daughter of the Emperor, who loved Popocatepetl
Anansi—a cunning and intelligent spider

Fables

THE BLUE HORSE
Franz Marc
© Three Lions

GUIDE FOR READING

The Town Mouse and the Country Mouse
The Fox and the Crow

Aesop (ē' śäp) (about 620–560 B.C.) was an ancient Greek whose name was associated with a collection of wise tales about animals. Little is known about him, except that he was a slave who was later freed by his master. Actually many of Aesop's tales or fables were based on tales told long before his birth. Many of them were also rewritten by others after his death. They are fun to read and contain good advice.

Fables

A **fable** is a brief tale, in prose or verse, that teaches a lesson called a **moral.** Often this moral appears as a wise saying at the end of the tale. In Aesop's fables, the characters are animals who act like human beings and often illustrate human failings and weaknesses. However, other writers use human characters in their fables or even plants and objects that talk and behave like humans.

Look For

As you read these entertaining fables, look for the ways in which the animals act like humans. Also, identify the human failings that some of the charaters illustrate. How does the way the characters act point to a moral?

Writing

Imagine that you are planning to write a fable in which pairs of animal characters will represent the following pairs of qualities: courage and cowardice, wisdom and foolishness, loyalty and faithlessness. Decide on an animal for each quality and briefly explain your choice.

Vocabulary

Knowing the following words will help you as you read these fables.
heartily (härt''l ē) *adv.*: Warmly; completely (p. 545)
fare (fer) *n.*: Food (p. 545)
glossy (glôs' ē) *adj.*: Smooth and shiny (p. 547)
surpass (sər pas') *v.*: Be superior to (p. 547)

flatterers (flat' ər ərz) *n.*: Those who praise a person insincerely in order to gain something for themselves (p. 547)

The Town Mouse and the Country Mouse

Aesop

Now you must know that a Town Mouse once upon a time went on a visit to his cousin in the country. He was rough and ready, this cousin, but he loved his town friend and made him heartily welcome. Beans and bacon, cheese and bread were all he had to offer, but he offered them freely. The Town Mouse rather turned up his long nose at this country fare, and said: "I cannot understand, Cousin, how you can put up with such poor food as this, but of course you cannot expect anything better in the country; come you with me and I will show you how to live. When you have been in town a week you will wonder how you could ever have stood a country life."

No sooner said than done: the two mice

set off for the town and arrived at the Town Mouse's residence late at night. "You will want some refreshment after our long journey," said the polite Town Mouse, and took his friend into the grand dining room. There they found the remains of a fine feast, and soon the two mice were eating up jellies and cakes and all that was nice. Suddenly they heard growling and barking.

"What is that?" said the Country Mouse.

"It is only the dogs of the house," answered the other.

"Only!" said the Country Mouse. "I do not like that music at my dinner."

Just at that moment the door flew open, in came two huge mastiffs,[1] and the two mice had to scamper down and run off.

"Good-by, Cousin," said the Country Mouse.

"What! going so soon?" said the other.

"Yes," he replied:

"Better beans and bacon in peace than cakes and ale in fear."

---

1. **mastiffs** (mas' tifs) *n.*: Large, powerful, smooth-coated dogs with hanging lips and drooping ears. They were used for hunting and as watchdogs.

THINKING ABOUT THE SELECTION
Recalling

1. What disturbs the Town Mouse about his meal in the country?
2. What disturbs the Country Mouse about his meal in town?

Interpreting

3. Compare and contrast the two mice. Explain what traits each mouse represents.
4. Which mouse do you feel more sympathy for? Explain your answer.

Applying

5. Why might a fable with animal characters teach a lesson better than a tale with human characters?

ANALYZING LITERATURE
Understanding Fables

A **fable** is a brief tale, in prose or verse, that teaches a lesson called a **moral**. In "The Town Mouse and the Country Mouse" each of the characters has a different approach to life. The moral suggests that the Country Mouse's point of view is better.

1. What is the moral of this fable?
2. Express the moral in your own words.
3. Explain why you agree or disagree with the moral.

THINKING AND WRITING
Writing a Fable

Write a fable with a moral that is the opposite of Aesop's lesson. The moral of your fable must be: *Better an interesting life with danger than a safe life that is dull.* Think of two contrasting animal characters for your fable. They can be animals of the same species, like the two mice, or different animals. Write a fable placing these characters in a modern setting. In revising your work, make sure that your tale really teaches the new moral. When you are finished, share your fable with your classmates.

The Fox and the Crow

Aesop

A Fox once saw a Crow fly off with a piece of cheese in its beak and settle on a branch of a tree. "That's for me, as I am a Fox," said Master Reynard,[1] and he walked up to the foot of the tree.

"Good day, Mistress Crow," he cried. "How well you are looking today: how glossy your feathers; how bright your eye. I feel sure your voice must surpass that of other birds, just as your figure does; let me hear but one song from you that I may greet you as the Queen of Birds."

The Crow lifted up her head and began to caw her best, but the moment she opened her mouth the piece of cheese fell to the ground, only to be snapped up by Master Fox. "That will do," said he. "That was all I wanted. In exchange for your cheese I will give you a piece of advice for the future—

"Do not trust flatterers."

---

1. Master Reynard (ren′ ərd): The fox in the medieval beast epic *Reynard the Fox*; therefore, a proper name for the fox in other stories.

THINKING ABOUT THE SELECTION

Recalling

1. How does the Crow lose the cheese?

Interpreting

2. What character traits do the Fox and the Crow represent?
3. How do the actions of these two animals support the moral?
4. The seventeenth-century Frenchman Jean La Fontaine rewrote many of Aesop's fables and stamped them with his own style. He expressed the moral of "The Fox and the Crow" as follows: Learn that every flatterer/Lives at the flattered listener's cost. Compare this version of the moral with Aesop's. How would you rewrite the moral to stamp it with your own style?

Applying

5. What is it about human nature that allows flattery to do its work?

The Fox and the Crow

James Thurber (1894–1961) admired the work of famous writers, but he was also influenced by comic strips and movies. In fact, a successful movie was made from his best-known short story, "The Secret Life of Walter Mitty." Thurber showed an awareness of human weaknesses in his stories, plays, and essays. However, he revealed these faults with humor and understanding. In "The Fox and the Crow," he rewrites an old fable to poke fun at a common flaw.

Satire

Satire is writing that uses laughter and wit to criticize or ridicule human weaknesses. This type of writing appears in various literary forms. In some cases, the humor of satire is bitter and harsh, while in others it is warm and affectionate. Thurber's satire in "The Fox and the Crow" is the more gentle type.

Look For

As you read Thurber's version of "The Fox and the Crow," look for the various ways in which Thurber has changed this traditional fable. Also, compare and contrast Thurber's moral with Aesop's. What does Thurber's moral tell you about the modern world?

Writing

Think of a foolish way of behaving that you have observed both in yourself and in others. This behavior should not be a serious fault, just a minor weakness that might seem amusing. Describe this behavior in a way that gently makes fun of it.

Vocabulary

Knowing the following words will help you as you read "The Fox and the Crow."

warblers (wôr′ blərz) *n.*: Songbirds (p. 549)

unique (yoo nēk′) *adj.*: Highly unusual or rare (p. 549)

cunning (kun′ iŋ) *adj.*: Sly; crafty (p. 550)

arrogantly (ar′ə gənt lē) *adv.*: Proudly; self-importantly (p. 550)

appeased (ə pēzd′) *v.*: Satisfied (p. 550)

forlornly (fər lôrn′ lē) *adv.*: Hopelessly; miserably (p. 550)

The Fox
and the Crow

James Thurber

Original art by James Thurber
© 1956 by James Thurber

A crow, perched in a tree with a piece of cheese in his beak, attracted the eye and nose of a fox. "If you can sing as prettily as you sit," said the fox, "then you are the prettiest singer within my scent and sight." The fox had read somewhere, and somewhere, and somewhere else, that praising the voice of a crow with a cheese in his beak would make him drop the cheese and sing. But this is not what happened to this particular crow in this particular case.

"They say you are sly and they say you are crazy," said the crow, having carefully removed the cheese from his beak with the claws of one foot, "but you must be nearsighted as well. Warblers wear gay hats and colored jackets and bright vests, and they are a dollar a hundred. I wear black and I am unique." He began nibbling the cheese, dropping not a single crumb.

"I am sure you are," said the fox, who was neither crazy nor nearsighted, but sly. "I recognize you, now that I look more closely, as the most famed and talented of all birds, and I fain[1] would hear you tell about yourself, but I am hungry and must go."

"Tarry[2] awhile," said the crow quicky, "and share my lunch with me." Whereupon he tossed the cunning fox the lion's share of the cheese, and began to tell about himself. "A ship that sails without a crow's nest[3] sails to doom," he said. "Bars may come and bars may go, but crow bars last forever. I am the pioneer of flight, I am the map maker. Last, but never least, my flight is known to scientists and engineers, geometrists and scholars, as the shortest distance between two points. Any two points," he concluded arrogantly.

"Oh, every two points, I am sure," said the fox. "And thank you for the lion's share of what I know you could not spare." And with this he trotted away into the woods, his appetite appeased, leaving the hungry crow perched forlornly in the tree.

MORAL: 'Twas true in Aesop's time, and La Fontaine's,[4] and now, no one else can praise thee quite so well as thou.

---

1. fain (fān) *adv.*: An old-fashioned way of saying "gladly."
2. tarry (tar′ ē) *v.*: An old-fashioned way of saying "wait."
3. crow's nest: A small, partly enclosed platform near the top of a ship's mast where the lookout stands.

4. La Fontaine (la′ fōn ten′): A French poet and writer of fables.

THINKING ABOUT THE SELECTION

Recalling

1. Why does the fox praise the crow's voice?
2. How does the crow answer the fox?
3. What does the fox say to make the crow share his lunch?

Interpreting

4. What evidence shows that the fox knows Aesop's fable about the fox and the crow?
5. How does the fox show the ability to solve new problems as they arise?
6. Explain the moral of this fable. How do the actions of these two animals support the moral?

Applying

7. Why are some people willing to give up valuable possessions just to have the opportunity to brag?

ANALYZING LITERATURE

Understanding Satire

Satire is writing that uses laughter and wit to criticize or ridicule human weaknesses. In "The Fox and the Crow" the animal characters of the fable stand for human beings. Thurber directs most of his satire at the type of person represented by the crow.

1. What weakness in human personality is Thurber satirizing?
2. How does the fox's rapid departure make the crow's long speech seem ridiculous?
3. What details suggest that Thurber's satire is more gentle than angry?

CRITICAL THINKING AND READING

Recognizing Satire in Foolish Boasts

In satire, writers include many details to point out the foolishness of the characters they are criticizing. One type of detail is a foolish boast. For in-stance, Thurber's crow brags to the fox, " 'I wear black and I am unique.' " You can picture him puffing himself up proudly as he speaks.

Find four other foolish boasts the crow makes. Explain each of these boasts.

UNDERSTANDING LANGUAGE

Finding Homophones

A **homophone** is a word that sounds like another word but has a different spelling and meaning from that word. For example, the words *piece* and *peace* are homophones. Some word-analogy tests require you to identify the first pair of words as homophones and complete the second pair with a homophone. For example:

pair : pear : : so :_____

The word *sew* completes the second pair.

The third word in each word analogy below is from "The Fox and the Crow." Complete each analogy with a homophone.

1. new : knew : : eye :_____
2. cash : cache : : claws :_____
3. not : knot : : scent :_____
4. there : their : : sail :_____
5. wood : would : : time :_____

THINKING AND WRITING

Comparing and Contrasting Fables

Comparing two things means showing how they are similar. **Contrasting** them means showing how they are different. List the ways in which Thurber's fable and Aesop's are similar and different. Consider the personalities of the fox and crow in each fable, the tricks that each fox uses, and the two morals. Then turn your list into a composition. Devote one paragraph to showing the similarities between the fables and one to showing the differences. When revising make sure you have shown how the two fables are both similar and different. Finally, share your writing with your classmates.

The Boy and the Wolf

Louis Untermeyer (1885–1977) read so many books as a teenager that he had three cards from his local library—two of them in the names of other family members. Untermeyer went on to produce books at almost the same speed that he read them. Besides writing poetry, fiction, and essays, he edited several well-known poetry anthologies. In 1956, he was awarded the Gold Medal of the Poetry Society of America. "The Boy and the Wolf" is his poetic version of a fable by Aesop.

A Fable and a Common Expression

"The Boy and the Wolf" is such a popular fable that it is the source of a commonly used expression: "Don't cry wolf!" The meaning of that expression will become clear to you as you read Untermeyer's version of the fable.

Look For

As you read "The Boy and the Wolf," look for the details that support the practical advice given in the lesson.

Writing

"The Boy and the Wolf" is about a boy who lies so much that people no longer trust him. Recall a book you have read or a television program you have seen in which one of the characters got into trouble for lying. Tell why this character lied and what happened to him or her as a result.

Vocabulary

Knowing the following words will help you as you read "The Boy and the Wolf."

despised (di spīzd') *v.*: Looked down on, disliked intensely (p. 553)

flock (fläk) *n.*: Group of sheep (p. 553)

heed (hēd) *n.*: Attention (p. 553)

The Boy and the Wolf
from the Greek of Aesop
Louis Untermeyer

A boy employed to guard the sheep
Despised his work. He liked to sleep.
And when a lamb was lost, he'd shout,
"Wolf! Wolf! The wolves are all about!"

The neighbors searched from noon till nine,
But of the beast there was no sign.
Yet "Wolf!" he cried next morning when
The villagers came out again.

One evening around six o'clock
A real wolf fell upon the flock.
"Wolf!" yelled the boy. "A wolf indeed!"
But no one paid him any heed.

Although he screamed to wake the dead,
"He's fooled us every time," they said,
And let the hungry wolf enjoy
His feast of mutton,[1] lamb—and boy.

THE MORAL'S this: The man who's wise
Does not defend himself with lies.
Liars are not believed, forsooth,[2]
Even when liars tell the truth.

---

1. **mutton** (mut' n) *n*.: Sheep.
2. **forsooth** (fər sooth′) *adv*.: No doubt.

THINKING ABOUT THE SELECTION

Recalling

1. What key fact do you learn about the boy in the first two lines?
2. Why did the people not come when a real wolf threatened the flock?

Interpreting

3. Why did the boy cry "Wolf!" whenever he lost a lamb?
4. Explain the last two lines of the poem?

Applying

5. A writer has compared trust among people to a plant that is watered by the truth but uprooted by lies. Explain what the writer meant by this observation.

ANALYZING LITERATURE

Understanding a Common Expression

"The Boy and the Wolf" is the source of a common expression in our language: "Don't cry wolf!" This fable shows you how a boy who did "cry wolf" once too often brought about his own downfall.

1. What do we mean by the expression, "Don't cry wolf"?
2. Describe a modern situation to which this expression could apply.

SPEAKING AND LISTENING

Reading a Fable Aloud

Since this fable is in poetic form, you can read it aloud the way you would read any poem. Do not pause at the end of a line unless there is a period or a comma. Pause briefly at a comma, and stop longer at a period. Above all, remember not to read in a singsong voice. A poem should sound as natural as ordinary speech.

1. Practice reading the fable aloud to one or two classmates.
2. Ask your classmates to comment on your reading, and use their suggestions to improve your presentation.

UNDERSTANDING LANGUAGE

Completing Word Analogies

Some word-analogy tests require you to identify whether the words in the first pair are synonyms or antonyms and to complete the second pair appropriately. For example:

employ : hire : : toil :_____

Since the first two words are synonyms, you should complete the second pair with a synonym: work.

awake : asleep : : truth :_____

Since the first two words are antonyms, you should complete the second pair with an antonym: lie.

Complete each of the word analogies below.

1. guard : watch : : despise :_____
2. lost : found : : morning :_____
3. real : false : : hungry :_____
4. fool : trick : : wise :_____

THINKING AND WRITING

Writing a Fable in Verse

You have thought about a modern situation to which this fable's moral would apply. Write a brief prose description of this situation. Then turn your description into a fable in verse, like Untermeyer's. However, you do not have to use rhymes or four-line stanzas. As you revise your poem, be sure you have included a moral at the end.

Greek and Roman Myths

HECTOR AND ANDROMACHE
Giorgio de Chirico
Scala/Art Resource

GUIDE FOR READING

Demeter and Persephone

The ancient Greeks often thought of **Demeter** (di mēt' ər) and her daughter **Persephone** (pər sef' ənē) as a pair, calling them the Two Goddesses. Farmers honored and worshiped Demeter during the planting and harvesting of corn, as important a crop in the ancient world as it is today. The Greek poet Homer described Demeter as "blonde," giving her the color of ripened corn.

Anne Terry White (1896–   ), the reteller of this myth, was a teacher and has written many books for young people.

Myth

A **myth** is an ancient story about gods or heroes created to express beliefs or explain natural events. Among the matters that myths explain are how the world began, why the sun travels across the sky, and how humans gained fire. Since myths are stories, these mythical explanations of nature are both lively and imaginative. Therefore, they have lasted for generations.

Greek and Roman myths have had the greatest influence on our own culture. For hundreds of years, writers have retold these stories in the English language. "Demeter and Persephone" has been especially popular because it explains the rhythms of nature in terms of human emotions.

Look For

Although the characters in this myth are gods and goddesses, they experience the same feelings as humans do. Look for these feelings and the events they cause.

Writing

Imagine that you come from a planet where the season is always winter. You are visiting the earth for the first time, just as the spring is beginning. Freewrite about your reaction to this new experience.

Vocabulary

Knowing the following words will help you as you read "Demeter and Persephone."

asunder (ə sun' dər) *adv.*: Into parts or pieces (p. 557)
realm (relm) *n.*: Kingdom (p. 557)
defies (di fīz') *v.*: Boldly opposes or resists (p. 557)
monarch (män' ərk) *n.*: Ruler; king or queen (p. 557)

dominions (də min' yənz) *n.*: Region over which he ruled (p. 558)
intervene (in' tər vēn') *v.*: Step into a situation (p. 558)
abode (ə bōd') *n.*: Home (p. 560)

Demeter and Persephone

Anne Terry White

Deep under Mt. Aetna, the gods had buried alive a number of fearful, fire-breathing giants. The monsters heaved and struggled to get free. And so mightily did they shake the earth that Pluto, the king of the underworld, was alarmed.

"They may tear the rocks asunder and leave the realm of the dead open to the light of day," he thought. And mounting his golden chariot, he went up to see what damage had been done.

Now the goddess of love and beauty, fair Aphrodite,[1] was sitting on a mountainside playing with her son, Eros.[2] She saw Pluto as he drove around with his coal-black horses and she said:

"My son, there is one who defies your power and mine. Quick! Take up your darts! Send an arrow into the breast of that dark monarch. Let him, too, feel the pangs of love. Why should he alone escape them?"

At his mother's words, Eros leaped lightly to his feet. He chose from his quiver[3] his sharpest and truest arrow, fitted it to his bow, drew the string, and shot straight into Pluto's heart.

The grim King had seen fair maids enough in the gloomy underworld over which he ruled. But never had his heart been touched. Now an unaccustomed warmth stole through his veins. His stern eyes softened. Before him was a blossoming valley, and along its edge a charming girl was gathering flowers. She was Persephone, daughter of Demeter, goddess of the harvest. She had strayed from her companions, and now that her basket overflowed with blossoms, she was filling her apron with lilies and violets. The god looked at Persephone

---

1. **Aphrodite** (af′ rə dīt′ ē)
2. **Eros** (er′ äs): In Greek mythology, the god of love, identified by the Romans with Cupid.
3. **quiver** (kwiv′ ər) *n.*: A case for arrows.

and loved her at once. With one sweep of his arm he caught her up and drove swiftly away.

"Mother!" she screamed, while the flowers fell from her apron and strewed the ground. "Mother!"

And she called on her companions by name. But already they were out of sight, so fast did Pluto urge the horses on. In a few moments they were at the River Cyane.[4] Persephone struggled, her loosened girdle[5] fell to the ground, but the god held her tight. He struck the bank with his trident.[6] The earth opened, and darkness swallowed them all— horses, chariot, Pluto, and weeping Persephone.

From end to end of the earth Demeter sought her daughter. But none could tell her where Persephone was. At last, worn out and despairing, the goddess returned to Sicily. She stood by the River Cyane, where Pluto had cleft[7] the earth and gone down into his own dominions.

Now a river nymph[8] had seen him carry off his prize. She wanted to tell Demeter where her daughter was, but fear of Pluto kept her dumb. Yet she had picked up the girdle Persephone had dropped, and this the nymph wafted[9] on the waves to the feet of Demeter.

The goddess knew then that her daughter was gone indeed, but she did not suspect Pluto of carrying her off. She laid the blame on the innocent land.

"Ungrateful soil!" she said. "I made you fertile. I clothed you in grass and nourishing grain, and this is how you reward me. No more shall you enjoy my favors!"

That year was the most cruel mankind had ever known. Nothing prospered, nothing grew. The cattle died, the seed would not come up, men and oxen toiled in vain. There was too much sun. There was too much rain. Thistles[10] and weeds were the only things that grew. It seemed that all mankind would die of hunger.

"This cannot go on," said mighty Zeus. "I see that I must intervene." And one by one he sent the gods and goddesses to plead with Demeter.

But she had the same answer for all: "Not till I see my daughter shall the earth bear fruit again."

Zeus, of course, knew well where Persephone was. He did not like to take from his brother the one joyful thing in his life, but he saw that he must if the race of man was to be preserved. So he called Hermes[11] to him and said:

"Descend to the underworld, my son. Bid Pluto release his bride. Provided she has not tasted food in the realm of the dead, she may return to her mother forever."

Down sped Hermes on his winged feet, and there in the dim palace of the king, he found Persephone by Pluto's side. She was pale and joyless. Not all the glittering treasures of the underworld could bring a smile to her lips.

"You have no flowers here," she would say to her husband when he pressed gems upon her. "Jewels have no fragrance. I do not want them."

When she saw Hermes and heard his message, her heart leaped within her. Her cheeks grew rosy and her eyes sparkled, for she knew that Pluto would not dare to disobey his brother's command. She sprang up,

---

4. River Cyane (sī' an): A river in Sicily, an island just south of Italy.

5. girdle (gər' d'l) n.: A belt or sash for the waist.

6. trident (trīd' 'nt) n.: A spear with three points.

7. cleft (kleft) v.: Split or opened.

8. river nymph (nimf): A goddess living in a river.

9. wafted (wäft' 'd) v.: Carried.

10. thistles (this' 'lz) n.: Stubborn, weedy plants with sharp leaves and usually purplish flowers.

11. Hermes (hur' mēz): A god who served as a messenger.

ready to go at once. Only one thing troubled her—that she could not leave the underworld forever. For she had accepted a pomegranate[12] from Pluto and sucked the sweet pulp from four of the seeds.

With a heavy heart Pluto made ready his golden car.[13] He helped Persephone in while Hermes took up the reins.

"Dear wife," said the King, and his voice trembled as he spoke, "think kindly of me, I pray you. For indeed I love you truly. It will be lonely here these eight months you are away. And if you think mine is a gloomy palace to return to, at least remember that your husband is great among the immortals. So fare you well—and get your fill of flowers!"

Straight to the temple of Demeter at Eleusis, Hermes drove the black horses. The goddess heard the chariot wheels and, as a deer bounds over the hills, she ran out swiftly to meet her daughter. Persephone flew to her mother's arms. And the sad tale of each turned into joy in the telling.

So it is to this day. One third of the year Persephone spends in the gloomy abode of Pluto—one month for each seed that she tasted. Then Nature dies, the leaves fall, the earth stops bringing forth. In spring Persephone returns, and with her come the flowers, followed by summer's fruitfulness and the rich harvest of fall.

---

12. pomegranate (päm′ gran′ it) n.: A round fruit with a red, leathery rind and many seeds.
13. car (kär) n.: chariot.

THINKING ABOUT THE SELECTION

Recalling

1. Who is Pluto? Who is Demeter? Who is Persephone?
2. What motivates Pluto to take Persephone to his kingdom?
3. What does Demeter think has happened to Persephone? Why does she make the earth infertile?
4. How is the situation saved?
5. Why is Persephone unable to leave the underworld forever?

6. How does nature change as Persephone moves between the earth and the underworld?

Interpreting

7. Why is Persephone unhappy in the underworld?
8. Why is Pluto referred to as "the grim King"? How do you know that he truly loves Persephone?
9. Evaluate the judgment of the gods in regard to Persephone's fate. Do you think it just? Why or why not?

Applying

10. Why do you think the return of spring would be so important to ancient Greeks and Romans?
11. Create a celebration in honor of the returning spring. Briefly describe what you would have people wear, say, and do.

ANALYZING LITERATURE
Appreciating Myth

A myth is an ancient story about gods or heroes created to express beliefs or explain natural events. Often in myths the explanation of natural events has its roots in the powerful emotions of the gods and goddesses involved. The story of "Demeter and Persephone," for example, explains why "the earth stops bringing forth" in the fall and winter but blooms again in the spring.

1. Identify the feelings that Pluto experiences during the course of the story.
2. What emotions do Persephone and Demeter experience in this myth?
3. How do the powerful emotions of these three characters account for the change in seasons?
4. Why do you think that the emotions expressed in this myth have touched people for thousands of years?

CRITICAL THINKING AND READING
Contrasting Science and Myth

Science and myth explain natural events in different ways. While a scientific explanation contains facts and theories, a myth offers a highly imaginative story as an explanation. For example, a scientific account of lightning would mention the discharge of electricity. A myth, however, might tell a story about an angry god hurling a spear.

1. In what way can myths reveal truths about life?
2. Which do you think reveals truths about life more vividly—myths or science? Which reveals truths more accurately?
3. Which explanations do you think make a greater impact on our hearts and minds? Explain your answer.

UNDERSTANDING LANGUAGE
Analyzing Words with the Root *mors*

A **prefix** is the part of a word that goes in front of its **root,** or core. The word *immortal,* which appears in "Demeter and Persephone," consists of the prefix *im-* ("not") and the root *mortal* ("a being that dies"). A god is immortal while a human being is mortal. Both of these words come from the Latin word *mors,* which means "death." The following words also contain this Latin root. Look up each in a dictionary and explain how it relates to the idea of death.

1. morgue   3. morbid   5. murder
2. mortician   4. mortuary

THINKING AND WRITING
Writing a Myth

Imagine a society that uses myth rather than science to explain dramatic and destructive earthquakes. Briefly outline the lively story about gods or heroes that this society might have devised. For instance, the story might involve giants battling under the earth, a god stamping with her foot, or anything you can imagine. Then, using your outline, write the myth in greater detail. In revising your myth, make sure the characters, like those in "Demeter and Persephone," express strong emotions. When you are finished, share your myth with your classmates.

GUIDE FOR READING

Prometheus the Fire-Bringer

Many ancient cultures have myths about gods or heroes who first taught humans to build fire or to plant crops. These stories show the importance that early people placed on this type of knowledge. It seemed so miraculous that it must have come from heaven! In Greek mythology **Prometheus** (prə mē′ thē əs) stole fire from the gods and taught humans to build fire.

    Jeremy Ingalls (1911–   ) has included her version of the Prometheus myth in her *Book of Legends*.

Conflict in Myth

A **conflict** is a struggle between opposing sides or forces. In "Prometheus the Fire-Bringer," there is a conflict between Zeus, the king of the gods, and the race of humans he has created. The Titan Prometheus makes this struggle more equal by taking the side of the humans.

Look For

Like people, the Greek gods can show many different character traits. As you read this myth, look for the contrast between the personalities of Zeus and his adviser Prometheus. How does this contrast lead to a serious conflict? What is the effect of this conflict?

Writing

If fire can seem mysterious today, it must have seemed even more mysterious to humans of long ago. Imagine that you have been transported back to those times. You are sitting near a campfire at night, staring into the dancing yellow and red flames. Freewrite about this experience.

Vocabulary

Knowing the following words will help you as you read "Prometheus the Fire-Bringer."

councilor (koun′ sə lər) *n.*: Adviser (p. 563)

ominous (äm′ ə nəs) *adj.*: Threatening (p. 564)

hearth (härth) *n.*: Stone or brick floor of a fireplace (p. 566)

deftly (deft′ lē) *adv.*: Skillfully (p. 568)

kindling (kin′ dliŋ) *n.*: Bits of dry wood for starting a fire (p. 568)

gravely (grāv′ lē) *adv.*: With great seriousness (p. 568)

Prometheus the Fire-Bringer

Jeremy Ingalls

Fire itself and the civilized life which fire makes possible—these were the gifts of Prometheus to the men of ancient times. Prometheus himself was not of the oldest race of men. He was not alive in the first age of mankind.

Ancient writers tell us there were three ages of men on earth before the fourth age in which we are now living. Each of the previous ages ended in terrible disasters which destroyed a large part of the human race. A raging fire ended the first age of the world. At the end of the second and of the third age, vast floods engulfed plains and mountains. According to the oldest poets these misfortunes were punishments the gods visited upon men for their wickedness and wrongdoing.

The story of Prometheus, remembered by the Greeks and set down in their books, tells of the days when Zeus[1] was king of the world and Prometheus was his chief councilor. From their ancestors they and their companions upon Mount Olympus had inherited the secrets of fire, of rain, of farming and metalworking. This knowledge gave them a power so great that they appeared as gods to the men who served them.

After the flood which destroyed many of the men of the second age, Zeus, with the help of Prometheus, had bred a new race of men in Arcadia.[2] But Zeus did not find life on earth so simple for men and gods as it had been in earlier times.

When Cronus,[3] the father of Zeus, had ruled the earth, summer had been the only season. Great land masses toward the north had barred all the icy winds. The age of Cronus was an age of contentment. No man

2. **Arcadia** (är kā′ dē ə): A beautiful region of ancient Greece.
3. **Cronus** (krō′ nəs)

1. **Zeus** (zoos)

had needed to work for food or clothes or a house to shelter him.

After the first flood, the land masses were broken. Winter winds blew upon countries which before had known only summer.

The race of gods did not suffer. They warmed their houses, having the secret of fire. And the women of the race were weavers of cloth, so that the gods were clothed and defended from the north wind.

But winter was a harsh season for the men and women who did not live on the gods' mountain. Without defense from the cold, they huddled with the animals. They complained against the gods, whom they must serve for what little comfort they might find of food and warmth. They scarcely believed the stories which their ancestors had handed down to them of a time when men had lived in endless summer weather, when men were friends and favorites of the gods.

Men became rebels and grumblers. For this reason Zeus, seeing winter coming on again, determined to destroy the people of Arcadia. Then Prometheus, his chief councilor, sought to save this third race of man from destruction.

"They quarrel among themselves," said Zeus angrily. "They start trouble in the fields. We must train up a new race of men who will learn more quickly what it means to serve the gods."

Zeus was walking across the bronze floor of his mountain palace. A tremendous, tall figure of a man he was, the king-god Zeus. But he who stood beside him, Prometheus of the family of Titans,[4] was even taller.

"Worthless," Zeus was saying as if to himself. "Worthless," he repeated again, "the whole race. They complain of the winters. They are too weak a race for the climate of these times. Why should we continue to struggle with them? Better to be rid of them, every man and woman of the troublesome tribe."

"And then?" inquired Prometheus. "What if you create a new race to provide manpower for the farms and the bigger buildings? That race, too, will rebel while they can see and envy our knowledge and our power."

"Even so, I will destroy these Arcadians," insisted Zeus stubbornly. "Men are our creatures. Let them learn to serve us, to do our will."

"Up here on your mountain," observed Prometheus thoughtfully, "you make men and destroy them. But what about the men themselves? How can they learn wisdom when, time after time, you visit them with destruction?"

"You have too much sympathy for them," answered Zeus in a sharp voice. "I believe you love these huddling, sheepish men."

"They have minds and hearts," replied Prometheus warmly, "and a courage that is worth admiring. They wish to live even as the gods wish to live. Don't we feed ourselves on nectar and ambrosia[5] every day to preserve our lives?"

Prometheus was speaking rapidly. His voice was deep. "This is your way," he went on. "You won't look ahead. You won't be patient. You won't give men a chance to learn how to live. Over and over again, with floods or with cracking red thunderbolts, you destroy them."

"I have let you live, Prometheus," said Zeus in an ominous tone, "to advise me when you can. You are my cousin. But I am not your child to be scolded." Zeus was smiling, but there was thunder behind the smile.

---

4. Titans (tīt′′nz): Giant gods who were defeated by the Olympian gods.

5. nectar (nek′ tər) **and ambrosia** (am brō′ zhə): The drink and food of the gods; by feeding on these substances, the gods were able to live forever.

Silently Prometheus turned away. Leaving the marble-columned hall, he went out among the gardens of Olympus, the gods' mountain. The last roses were fading before the time of winter winds and rain.

This was not the first time Prometheus had heard thunder in the voice of Zeus. Prometheus knew that someday Zeus would turn against him, betray him, and punish him. Prometheus the Titan had the gift of reading the future. He could foresee the fate hidden and waiting for him and for others and even for Zeus himself.

Climbing among the upper gardens, Prometheus stopped at last beside an ancient, twisted ash tree. Leaning against its trunk, he looked toward the south. Beyond the last canal, the last steep sea wall, he could see the ocean. He looked far out toward that last shining circle of water. Then, with his head bent, he sat down on the tree roots bulging in thick knots above the ground.

It would be hard to tell you all the thoughts in the mind of the Titan—thoughts that coiled and twined like a nest of dragons. In his mighty brain were long memories of the past and far-reaching prophecies of what was to come.

He thought most often of the future, but the talk with Zeus just now had brought the past before him once again. He remembered once more the terrible war in which Zeus had seized the kingship of the gods. He thought of the exile and imprisonment of Cronus, the father of Zeus. He remembered the Titans, his people, now chained in the black pit of Tartarus.[6]

The great god Cronus himself, who had given peace to gods and men, where was he now? And the mighty-headed Titans, the magnificent engineers, builders of bridges and temples, where were they? All of them fallen, helpless, as good as dead.

Zeus had triumphed. Of the Titans, only two now walked the upper earth—he, Prometheus, and Epimetheus,[7] his brother.

And now, even now, Zeus was not content. It was not enough for his glory, it seemed, to have dethroned his own father, not enough to have driven the race of Titans from the houses of the gods. Now Zeus was plotting to kill the race of men.

Prometheus had endured the war against the Titans, his own people. He had even given help to Zeus. Having seen what was to come, he had thought, "Since Zeus must win, I'll guide him. I'll control his fierce anger and his greed for power."

But Prometheus could not submit to this latest plot of Zeus. He would use all his wits to save the men of Arcadia from destruction.

Why were they to be destroyed? Because they were cold and full of fears, huddled together in caves like animals. It was well enough in the warm months. They worked willingly in the fields of the gods and reared the horses and bulls and guarded the sheep. But when the cold days came, they grumbled against Olympus. They grumbled because they must eat and hunt like the animals and had no hoof nor claw nor heavy fur for protection.

What did they need? What protection would be better than hoof or claw? Prometheus knew. It was fire they needed—fire to cook with, to warm them, to harden metal for weapons. With fire they could frighten the wolf and the bear and the mountain lion.

Why did they lack the gift of fire? Prometheus knew that too. He knew how jealously the gods sat guard about their flame.

More than once he had told Zeus the

---

6. Tartarus (tär′ tər əs): A dark pit beneath Hades (hā′ dēz), the home of the dead, which itself was under the earth.

---

7. Epimetheus (ə′ pi mē′ thē əs)

need men had of fire. He knew why Zeus would not consent to teach men this secret of the gods. The gift of fire to men would be a gift of power. Hardened in the fire, the spears which men might make to chase the mountain lion might also, in time, be hurled against the gods. With fire would come comfort and time to think while the flames leaped up the walls of hidden caves. Men who had time to think would have time to question the laws of the gods. Among men who asked questions disorder might breed, and rebellion stronger than any mere squabble in the fields.

"But men are worth the gift of fire," thought Prometheus, sitting against the roots of his favorite ash tree. He could see ahead dimly into that time to come when gods would lose their power. And he, Prometheus, through his love for men, must help to bring on that time.

Prometheus did not hesitate. By the fall of night his plans were accomplished. As the sun went down, his tall figure appeared upon a sea beach. Above the sands a hundred caves, long ago deserted by the waters of the ocean, sheltered families of Arcadians. To them the Titan was bringing this very night the secret of the gods.

He came along the pebble line of high water. In his hand he carried a yellow reed.

This curious yellow stalk was made of metal, the most precious of the metals of the gods. From it the metalworkers molded rare and delicate shapes. From it they made the reedlike and hollow stalks which carried in wisps of fennel[8] straw, coals from the gods' ever-burning fire. The gods who knew the sources of flame never built new fires in the sight of men. Going abroad on journeys, they took from their central hearth a smoldering coal.

Prometheus had left Olympus as one upon a journey. He alone knew he was not going to visit the home of Poseidon,[9] Zeus's brother, lord of the sea—nor going into India nor into the cold north. He was going only as far as the nearest sea beach.

He knew that, though he was going only to the sea beach, he was in truth starting upon a journey. He knew the hatred of Zeus would follow him. He knew that now he, Prometheus, could never return to the house of the gods. From this night he must live his life among the men he wished to save.

While the stars came out, bright as they are on nights when winter will soon come on, Prometheus gathered together a heap of driftwood. Opening the metal stalk, he set the flame of the gods in the waiting fuel.

Eating into the wood, the fire leaped up, fanned in the night breeze. Prometheus sat down beside the fire he had made. He was not long alone.

Shadowy figures appeared at the mouths of caves. One by one, men, women, and children crept toward the blaze. The night was

---

9. Poseidon (pō sī' d'n)

---

cold. North winds had blown that day. The winds had blown on the lands of men, even as they had blown on the head of Zeus in his palace above them. Now in the night they came, the people of men, to the warmth of the beckoning fire.

Hundreds there were of them now. Those nearest the tall fire-bringer, the Titan, were talking with him. They knew him well. It was not the first time Prometheus had come to talk with them. But never before had he come late, alone, and lighted a fire against the dark.

It was not the first time men had seen a fire or felt its warmth. More than once a god, walking the earth, had set a fire, lit from the coals he carried secretly. Men reverenced the slender magic wands with which, it seemed, the gods could call up flame. But never before had they stood so near a fire nor seen the firewand.

Now men might hold in their own hands the mysterious yellow rod. They said "Look" and "See" and, fingering the metal, "How wonderfully the gods can mold what is hard in the hands."

For a while Prometheus let them talk. He watched with pleasure the gleam of firelight in their shining eyes. Then quietly he took the metal stalk from the man who held it. With a swift gesture he threw it into the heap of burning wood.

The people groaned. The fire-wrought metal crumpled against the heat. The metal which carried well a single coal melted in the blazing fire.

The people murmured among themselves, "Hasn't he taken away the secret now? Hasn't he destroyed before our eyes the source of fire?"

Patiently, silently they waited. A few asked questions but got no answers. The cold wind cut them as the last of the burning driftwood grayed and blackened in the sand.

While the embers crumbled away, Prometheus rose, calling with him a few of the men who had asked him questions. Watching, they saw him scrape a hollow pit. Wondering, they followed his every movement, his hands holding a bronze knife, shaving chips of wood, taking from the fold of his cloak handfuls of bark and straw.

Next he set in his pit a chunk of ashwood, flat and firm, notched cleanly on one side. Beneath and around this notch he laid in bark and straw. Into the notch he set a pointed branch, slender, hard-tipped, and firm. Then slowly he swung the branch in his palms, twirled it in a steady rhythm, boring, drilling more and more rapidly with his skilled and powerful hands.

The wood grew warm. The dust ground from the ash block heated to smoldering. The straw caught. Light sputtered from the pit. Small sparks glowed, flew up, went out. Tugged by the night wind, smoke curled from the dry straw, from the bark, from the wood shavings fed gently from the heap Prometheus had made ready to his hand. At last, more suddenly than the eye could follow, out of the pit in the sand rose the living flame.

Deftly Prometheus removed the ash block, added heavier kindling. Last of all, the driftwood yielded to the strengthening fire. He knelt beside it a while, breathing upon it, guarding, urging the blaze. At last he rose, stood back, folded his arms. As if considering a thought, half sorrow, half pleasure, he looked up at the glare of fire invading the night sky.

Whispers and murmuring first, then cries, then shouting. Men ran to scoop new hollows in the sand. They begged Prometheus' knife. The children, running from the beach to the caves and fields, hurried back with fists crammed full of straw and withered leaves.

The people of the caves were breathless with excitement. Here was no secret. The fire-wand did not breed the fire as they had thought. No nameless power of the gods bred the flame.

The hard, pale ashwood passed from hand to hand as men struggled to light their own fires. They despaired at first. New sparks flew up and died. Or the hands were weak, too weak to drill the flame. But at last came triumph. A dozen fires sprang up. Women and children ran with laden arms to feed each growing blaze.

The gods, from their distant houses, saw the glow. There to the south it shone, fighting against the starlight, the glare in the sky. Was it the end of the world? Would the terrible fire consume the earth again?

Hermes,[10] the messenger, came at last with an answer to all their questions.

"Great Zeus," said Hermes gravely in the assembly of the gods, "Prometheus, your cousin, stands in the midst of those rising fires. He took coals from the central hearth as for a journey."

"So?" asked Zeus, nodding his head. Then, as if he were holding an argument with himself, he continued, saying, "But then? What then? The fire will die. It is not a crime for a god or for a Titan to light a fire for himself on a cold evening."

"But that fire will not die," interrupted Hermes. "That fire is not the fire of gods and Titans. Prometheus has taught men the source of fire. Those fires are their own, the fires of men. They've drilled flame out of hard wood with their own hands."

Then the gods knew the end of the world was not yet come upon them. But they knew, and Zeus most of all, that it might be their own great power that was burning away in the fires of men.

---

10. Hermes (hŭr′ mēz).

THINKING ABOUT THE SELECTION

Recalling

1. What was the earth like during the age of Cronus, the father of Zeus? How many ages of human beings has there been?
2. Why are humans unhappy under the rule of Zeus? How do they show their unhappiness?
3. How does Zeus want to solve the problem?
4. What does Prometheus say about this plan?
5. How will the gift of fire help humans?

Interpreting

6. In Greek, Prometheus means "forethought," or the ability to plan. Why is this a fitting name for the Titan?
7. Why does Prometheus feel "half sorrow, half pleasure" after building a fire for humans?
8. How will the gift of fire mark a change in the relationship between humans and gods?

Applying

9. Imagine that someone from a more advanced civilization could visit earth. We already know how to use fire, but what other important gift could this being bring to us?

ANALYZING LITERATURE

Understanding Conflict in Myth

A **conflict** is a struggle between opposing sides or forces. In this myth Prometheus opposes the plans of Zeus, who wants to destroy the human race.

1. Why is there a conflict between Zeus and human beings?
2. How is the conflict between Prometheus and Zeus resolved in this myth?
3. Do you think this resolution is final, or will the conflict continue? Explain.

CRITICAL THINKING AND READING

Evaluating the Reasons for a Conflict

Conflicts between gods seem more awesome than struggles between humans. However, gods oppose each other for many of the same reasons that humans do. Whether on Mount Olympus or earth, conflicts can result from differences in personality and background.

1. Compare and contrast the personalities of Zeus and Prometheus.
2. How might the fact that Prometheus is a Titan and not an Olympian god influence his attitude toward Zeus?
3. Show how their disagreement about humans arises from differences in their personalities and backgrounds.
4. Why do you think Prometheus disobeys Zeus?

UNDERSTANDING LANGUAGE

Interpreting the Adjective *Promethean*

As a result of this myth, the adjective *Promethean* has become part of our language. The general meaning of this word is "about or like Prometheus."

1. Recall what you know about Prometheus's personality and actions. Based on this knowledge, what kind of person or deed would you call Promethean?
2. Look up the word in a dictionary to see whether the definition you have arrived at is correct.

THINKING AND WRITING

Predicting the Outcome of a Conflict

Imagine that you have written a successful screenplay based on this version of the Prometheus myth. So many people have seen your movie that the producer wants to make a sequel called "Prometheus II." Briefly outline some of the events that would occur where this story leaves off. Would Zeus punish Prometheus? If so, what kind of punishment would he devise? How would the conflict be resolved? Use your outline to write a letter to the producer describing the plot of the new movie. As you revise this letter, make sure that moviegoers will be satisfied by the way you have resolved the conflict.

GUIDE FOR READING

Phaëthon, Son of Apollo

Apollo (ə päl′ ō) was the son of Zeus and Leto. He is portrayed in Greek art as a handsome and athletic young man. He was known as the god of poetry and music, and he was often shown carrying the ancient stringed instrument called a lyre. He was also associated with the life-giving power of the sun, as you will see in this myth.

Olivia E. Coolidge (1908–   ), the modern teller of this myth, has written many books for young people about history and ancient legends.

Character in Myth: Hubris

Hubris is a Greek word meaning excessive pride or arrogance. The ancient Greeks believed very strongly in the separation between mortal humans and immortal gods. A human being who boasted of god-like powers was guilty of hubris and would almost certainly be punished. In "Phaëthon, Son of Apollo," you will see what happens to a young man who reaches too high.

Look For

Phaëthon (fā′ ə thən) displays his hubris in many ways. Look for evidence of his excessive pride in both his words and deeds. Also, look for clues that hint at the outcome.

Writing

At the end of this myth, Phaëthon is taken on a wild ride as he tries to steer the chariot of the sun. Recall the most dangerous carnival ride that you have ever been on or seen and freewrite about it.

Vocabulary

Knowing the following words will help you as you read "Phaëthon, Son of Apollo."

mortal (môr′ t'l) *n.*: A being who must eventually die (p. 571)

rash (rash) *adj.*: Reckless (p. 571)

deference (def′ ər əns) *n.*: Respect (p. 571)

implored (im plôrd′) *v.*: Begged (p. 571)

dissuade (di swād′) *v.*: Advise someone against an action (p. 572)

anointed (ə noint′ əd) *v.*: Rubbed oil or ointment on (p. 573)

precipitous (pri sip′ ə təs) *adj.*: Very steep (p. 574)

amber (am′ bər) *n.*: A yellowish or brownish substance that comes from certain trees (p. 574)

Phaëthon, Son of Apollo

Olivia E. Coolidge

Though Apollo always honored the memory of Daphne she was not his only love. Another was a mortal, Clymene,[1] by whom he had a son named Phaëthon. Phaëthon grew up with his mother, who, since she was mortal, could not dwell in the halls of Olympus[2] or in the palace of the sun. She lived not far from the East in the land of Ethiopia, and as her son grew up, she would point to the place where Eos,[3] goddess of the dawn, lighted up the sky and tell him that there his father dwelt. Phaëthon loved to boast of his divine father as he saw the golden chariot riding high through the air. He would remind his comrades of other sons of gods and mortal women who, by virture of their great deeds, had themselves become gods at last. He must always be first in everything, and in most things this was easy, since he was in truth stronger, swifter, and more daring than the others. Even if he were not victorious, Phaëthon always claimed to be first in honor. He could never bear to be beaten, even if he must risk his life in some rash way to win.

Most of the princes of Ethiopia willingly paid Phaëthon honor, since they admired him greatly for his fire and beauty. There was one boy, however, Epaphos,[4] who was rumored to be a child of Zeus himself. Since this was not certainly proved, Phaëthon chose to disbelieve it and to demand from Epaphos the deference that he obtained from all others. Epaphos was proud too, and one day he lost his temper with Phaëthon and turned on him, saying, "You are a fool to believe all that your mother tells you. You are all swelled up with false ideas about your father."

Crimson with rage, the lad rushed home to his mother and demanded that she prove to him the truth of the story that she had often told. "Give me some proof," he implored her, "with which I can answer this insult of Epaphos. It is a matter of life and death to me, for if I cannot, I shall die of shame."

"I swear to you," replied his mother solemnly, "by the bright orb of the sun itself that you are his son. If I swear falsely, may I never look on the sun again, but die before the next time he mounts the heavens. More than this I cannot do, but you, my child, can go to the eastern palace of Phoebus[5] Apollo—it lies not far away—and there speak with the god himself."

The son of Clymene leaped up with joy at his mother's words. The palace of Apollo was indeed not far. It stood just below the eastern horizon, its tall pillars glistening with bronze and gold. Above these it was white with gleaming ivory, and the great doors were flashing silver, embossed with pictures of earth, sky, and sea, and the gods that

---

1. **Clymene** (klim′ ə nē)
2. **Olympus** (ō lim′ pas): A mountain in Northern Greece that was known as the home of the gods.
3. **Eos** (ē äs)
4. **Epaphos** (ep′ ə fəs)

---

5. **Phoebus** (fē′ bəs): Means "bright one" in Greek.

dwelt therein. Up the steep hill and the bright steps climbed Phaëthon, passing unafraid through the silver doors, and stood in the presence of the sun. Here at last he was forced to turn away his face, for Phoebus sat in state on his golden throne. It gleamed with emeralds and precious stones, while on the head of the god was a brilliant diamond crown upon which no eye could look undazzled.

Phaëthon hid his face, but the god had recognized his son, and he spoke kindly, asking him why he had come. Then Phaëthon plucked up courage and said, "I come to ask you if you are indeed my father. If you are so, I beg you to give me some proof of it so that all may recognize me as Phoebus' son."

The god smiled, being well pleased with his son's beauty and daring. He took off his crown so that Phaëthon could look at him, and coming down from his throne, he put his arms around the boy, and said, "You are indeed my son and Clymene's, and worthy to be called so. Ask of me whatever thing you wish to prove your origin to men, and you shall have it."

Phaëthon swayed for a moment and was dizzy with excitement at the touch of the god. His heart leaped; the blood rushed into his face. Now he felt that he was truly divine, unlike other men, and he did not wish to be counted with men any more. He looked up for a moment at his radiant father. "Let me drive the chariot of the sun across the heavens for one day," he said.

Apollo frowned and shook his head. "I cannot break my promise, but I will dissuade you if I can," he answered. "How can you drive my chariot, whose horses need a strong hand on the reins? The climb is too steep for you. The immense height will make you dizzy. The swift streams of air in the upper heaven will sweep you off your course.

Even the immortal gods could not drive my chariot. How then can you? Be wise and make some other choice."

The pride of Phaëthon was stubborn, for he thought the god was merely trying to frighten him. Besides, if he could guide the sun's chariot, would he not have proved his right to be divine rather than mortal? For that he would risk his life. Indeed, once he had seen Apollo's splendor, he did not wish to go back and live among men. Therefore, he insisted on his right until Apollo had to give way.

When the father saw that nothing else would satisfy the boy, he bade the Hours bring forth his chariot and yoke the horses. The chariot was of gold and had two gold-rimmed wheels with spokes of silver. In it there was room for one man to stand and hold the reins. Around the front and sides of it ran a rail, but the back was open. At the end of a long pole there were yokes for the four horses. The pole was of gold and shone with precious jewels: the golden topaz, the bright diamond, the green emerald, and the flashing ruby. While the Hours were yoking the swift, pawing horses, rosy-fingered Dawn hastened to the gates of heaven to draw them open. Meanwhile Apollo anointed his son's face with a magic ointment, that he might be able to bear the heat of the fire-breathing horses and the golden chariot. At last Phaëthon mounted the chariot and grasped the reins, the barriers were let down, and the horses shot up into the air.

At first the fiery horses sped forward up the accustomed trail, but behind them the chariot was too light without the weight of the immortal god. It bounded from side to side and was dashed up and down. Phaë-thon was too frightened and too dizzy to pull the reins, nor would he have known anyway whether he was on the usual path. As soon as the horses felt that there was no hand controlling them, they soared up, up with fiery speed into the heavens till the earth grew pale and cold beneath them. Phaëthon shut his eyes, trembling at the dizzy, precipitous height. Then the horses dropped down, more swiftly than a falling stone, flinging themselves madly from side to side in panic because they were masterless. Phaë-thon dropped the reins entirely and clung with all his might to the chariot rail. Mean-while as they came near the earth, it dried up and cracked apart. Meadows were reduced to white ashes, cornfields smoked and shriveled, cities perished in flame. Far and wide on the wooded mountains the forests were ablaze, and even the snowclad Alps were bare and dry. Rivers steamed and dried to dust. The great North African plain was scorched until it became the desert that it is today. Even the sea shrank back to pools and caves, until dried fishes were left baking upon the white-hot sands. At last the great earth mother called upon Zeus to save her from utter destruction, and Zeus hurled a mighty thunderbolt at the unhappy Phaë-thon, who was still crouched in the chariot, clinging desperately to the rail. The dart cast him out, and he fell flaming in a long trail through the air. The chariot broke in pieces at the mighty blow, and the maddened horses rushed snorting back to the stable of their master, Apollo.

Unhappy Clymene and her daughters wandered over the whole earth seeking the body of the boy they loved so well. When they found him, they took him and buried him. Over his grave they wept and could not be comforted. At last the gods in pity for their grief changed them into poplar trees, which weep with tears of amber in memory of Phaë-thon.

THINKING ABOUT THE SELECTION

Recalling

1. Why does Phaëthon go to Apollo's palace?
2. Why does Apollo urge Phaëthon to make a wish different from his first one?
3. What is Phaëthon's secret reason for his request?
4. What is the result of this request?
5. What natural features are explained in this myth?

Interpreting

6. Why do you think Phaëthon feels that he had to "always be first in everything"?
7. How does Phaëthon display his pride with his classmates? How does he display it with Apollo?
8. How might this story have been different if Phaëthon had resembled his father less?

Applying

9. Given Phaëthon's choice, tell what you would have requested from Apollo. Explain the reasons for your decision.

ANALYZING LITERATURE

Understanding Hubris

Hubris means excessive pride or arrogance. In this myth, Phaëthon shows hubris by wanting to become an immortal. However, his attempt to assume his father's godlike powers threatens the earth and causes his own death.

1. Why do you think Phaëthon could not stand to be an ordinary human being?
2. Was Phaëthon's hubris his own fault or was it the result of the fact that he *was* the son of a god? Explain.
3. Was the punishment that Phaëthon received too harsh? Why or why not?
4. What lesson does this myth suggest?

CRITICAL THINKING AND READING
Recognizing Clues to the Outcome

Throughout this myth there are clues that Phaëthon's behavior may lead to disaster. You can find these hints by looking for remarks he makes or feelings he experiences that seem exaggerated or too intense. These indicate how desperate he is to prove that he is immortal.

1. Find two examples where Phaëthon feels that he would risk his life to get his way.
2. Why is his reaction to Apollo's embrace a clue to the coming disaster?

UNDERSTANDING LANGUAGE
Understanding Word Histories

Olympus is the highest mountain in Greece. The ancient Greeks imagined that the gods lived on top of this mountain in a great palace surrounded by swirling clouds. As you learn in this myth, mortals "could not dwell in the halls of Olympus." The word *Olympian* has come to be used as an adjective meaning "majestic" or "celestial."

1. Aside from Mount Olympus and the Greek gods themselves, what kind of place or person would you describe with the adjective *Olympian*?
2. What were the Olympic games in ancient Greece?
3. What are they today?

THINKING AND WRITING
Creating a Modern Myth

You and your literary agent have decided that the story of Phaëthon would make a wonderful best-selling novel. However, readers will not buy your book unless the story is up to date. Brainstorm to gather ideas for putting this myth into a modern setting. Phaëthon's father, for instance, cannot be a god, but he could be the president of a billion-dollar company. In this modern setting, perhaps Phaëthon wants to fly his father's corporate jet. Present your best ideas in a letter to your agent explaining the modern situation and setting for your novel. Then revise the letter to make sure your agent will be convinced that the book will sell.

GUIDE FOR READING

Baucis and Philemon

Because myths have been retold so often, they exist in many different versions. One of the best known collections of myths is the *Metamorphoses,* by the Roman poet **Ovid** (äv′ id) (43 B.C.–A.D. 17). This long poem, whose title means "changes," contains many accounts of supernatural magical changes caused by the gods.

Edith Hamilton (1867–1963) used Ovid's poem as a source for her version of "Baucis and Philemon." She was famous for her books on ancient Greece and Rome.

Myths: Lessons in Living

Myths served many purposes. Although they tended to concentrate on explaining the origins of natural phenomena, often they also taught lessons. While stories about the gods and heroes explained such matters as how a certain flower or tree came to exist or how the sun traveled across the sky each day, myths also taught people how to live their lives. In "Baucis and Philemon," for instance, a devoted couple who treat guests kindly are rewarded by the gods for their behavior.

Look For

Look for the many ways in which Baucis (bô′ sis) and Philemon (fi lē′ mən) make their guests feel welcome. How do the gods show their appreciation?

Writing

Through the myths of a people, we learn what they value. The ancient Greeks and Romans valued hospitality. Recall an enjoyable visit you made to the home of a friend or relative. Tell how your host made you feel at ease.

Vocabulary

Knowing the following words will help you as you read "Baucis and Philemon."

immeasurable (i mezh′ ər ə b'l) *adj.*: So great it cannot be measured (p. 577)

pious (pī′ əs) *adj.*: Good; virtuous (p. 577)

shrewdest (shrood′ əst) *adj.*: Cleverest (p. 577)

insolently (in′ sə lənt lē) *adv.*: Rudely; disrespectfully (p. 577)

snug (snug) *adj.*: Cozy; comfortable (p. 577)

bustled (bus′′ ld) *v.*: Hurried (p. 577)

quavering (kwā′ vər iŋ) *adj.*: Shaking (p. 578)

despises (di spīz′ əz) *v.*: Looks down on with scorn (p. 578)

Baucis and Philemon

Edith Hamilton

In the Phrygian[1] hill-country there were once two trees which all the peasants near and far pointed out as a great marvel, and no wonder, for one was an oak and the other a linden, yet they grew from a single trunk. The story of how this came about is a proof of the immeasurable power of the gods, and also of the way they reward the humble and the pious.

Sometimes when Jupiter[2] was tired of eating ambrosia and drinking nectar[3] up in Olympus and even a little weary of listening to Apollo's lyre and watching the Graces[4] dance, he would come down to the earth, disguise himself as a mortal and go looking for adventures. His favorite companion on these tours was Mercury,[5] the most entertaining of all the gods, the shrewdest and the most resourceful. On this particular trip Jupiter had determined to find out how hospitable the people of Phrygia were. Hospitality was, of course, very important to him, since all guests, all who seek shelter in a strange land, were under his especial protection.

The two gods, accordingly, took on the appearance of poor wayfarers and wandered through the land, knocking at each lowly hut or great house they came to and asking for food and a place to rest in. Not one would admit them; every time they were dismissed insolently and the door barred against them. They made trial of hundreds; all treated them in the same way. At last they came upon a little hovel of the humblest sort, poorer than any they had yet found, with a roof made only of reeds. But here, when they knocked, the door was opened wide and a cheerful voice bade them enter. They had to stoop to pass through the low entrance, but once inside they found themselves in a snug and very clean room, where a kindly-faced old man and woman welcomed them in the friendliest fashion and bustled about to make them comfortable.

The old man set a bench near the fire and told them to stretch out on it and rest their tired limbs, and the old woman threw a soft covering over it. Her name was Baucis, she told the strangers, and her husband was called Philemon. They had lived in that cottage all their married life and had always been happy. "We are poor folk," she said, "but poverty isn't so bad when you're willing to own up to it, and a contented spirit is a great help, too." All the while she was talking, she was busy doing things for them. The coals under the ashes on the dark hearth she fanned to life until a cheerful fire was burning. Over this she hung a little kettle full of water and just as it began to boil her husband came in with a fine cabbage he

---

1. Phrygian (frij′ ē ən): Phrygia was an ancient country in Asia.
2. Jupiter (jo͞o′ pə tər): King of the gods in Roman Mythology, like Zeus in Greek Mythology.
3. ambrosia (am brō′ zhə) **. . . nectar:** The food and drink of the gods that enabled them to live forever.
4. the Graces: Three sister goddesses who were associated with pleasure, charm, and beauty.
5. Mercury (mʉr′ kyoo rē): The messenger of the gods in Roman Mythology, like Hermes in Greek Mythology.

had got from the garden. Into the kettle it went, with a piece of the pork which was hanging from one of the beams. While this cooked Baucis set the table with her trembling old hands. One table-leg was too short, but she propped it up with a bit of broken dish. On the board she placed olives and radishes and several eggs which she had roasted in the ashes. By this time the cabbage and bacon were done, and the old man pushed two rickety couches up to the table and bade his guests recline and eat.

Presently he brought them cups of beechwood and an earthenware mixing bowl which held some wine very like vinegar, plentifully diluted with water. Philemon, however, was clearly proud and happy at being able to add such cheer to the supper and he kept on the watch to refill each cup as soon as it was emptied. The two old folks were so pleased and excited by the success of their hospitality that only very slowly a strange thing dawned upon them. The mixing bowl kept full. No matter how many cups were poured out from it, the level of the wine stayed the same, up to the brim. As they saw this wonder each looked in terror at the other, and dropping their eyes they prayed silently. Then in quavering voices and trembling all over they begged their guests to pardon the poor refreshments they had offered. "We have a goose," the old man said, "which we ought to have given your lordships. But if you will only wait, it shall be done at once." To catch the goose, however, proved beyond their powers. They tried in vain until they were worn out, while Jupiter and Mercury watched them greatly entertained.

But when both Philemon and Baucis had had to give up the chase panting and exhausted, the gods felt that the time had come for them to take action. They were really very kind. "You have been hosts to

gods," they said, "and you shall have your reward. This wicked country which despises the poor stranger will be bitterly punished, but not you." They then escorted the two out of the hut and told them to look around them. To their amazement all they saw was water. The whole countryside had disappeared. A great lake surrounded them. Their neighbors had not been good to the old couple; nevertheless standing there they wept for them. But of a sudden their tears were dried by an overwhelming wonder. Before their eyes the tiny, lowly hut which had been their home for so long was turned into a stately pillared temple of whitest marble with a golden roof.

"Good people," Jupiter said, "ask whatever you want and you shall have your wish." The old people exchanged a hurried whisper, then Philemon spoke. "Let us be your priests, guarding this temple for you—and oh, since we have lived so long together, let neither of us ever have to live alone. Grant that we may die together."

The gods assented, well pleased with the two. A long time they served in that grand building, and the story does not say whether they ever missed their little cozy room with its cheerful hearth. But one day standing before the marble and golden magnificence they fell to talking about that former life, which had been so hard and yet so happy. By now both were in extreme old age. Suddenly, as they exchanged memories each saw the other putting forth leaves. Then bark was growing around them. They had time only to cry, "Farewell, dear companion." As the words passed their lips they became trees, but still they were together. The linden and the oak grew from one trunk.

From far and wide people came to admire the wonder, and always wreaths of flowers hung on the branches in honor of the pious and faithful pair.

THINKING ABOUT THE SELECTION

Recalling

1. What is special about the oak and linden mentioned in the opening paragraph?
2. Why does Jupiter disguise himself as a poor traveler to visit Phrygia?
3. How do most of the people greet him and Mercury? How do Baucis and Philemon treat them differently?
4. How do the gods reward Baucis and Philemon? How do they treat the other Phrygians?
5. What transformation, or changes, do Baucis and Philemon undergo?

Interpreting

6. Find two details that make the scene inside the little cottage come alive.
7. Why is it accurate to say that Baucis and Philemon are rewarded *twice* by the gods?

Applying

8. How would you make a guest feel comfortable in your home?

ANALYZING LITERATURE

Understanding Lessons in Myth

Myths were not only meant to entertain people or explain facts of nature. Sometimes these stories also contained lessons about the way to live. In this story, the gods reward Baucis and Philemon. You can therefore deduce what the myth is teaching by examining the couple's behavior and attitudes.

1. What does Baucis and Philemon's treatment of the two strangers reveal about them?
2. What do the two requests they make of the gods reveal about the couple?
3. What lessons is the myth teaching by holding up Baucis and Philemon as models of behavior?

CRITICAL THINKING AND READING

Learning About a Culture from Its Myths

You can learn what a culture values by examining its myths. The story of Baucis and Philemon indicates that the ancient Greeks and Romans valued hospitality.

1. How does Jupiter expect people to treat unexpected and unknown guests?
2. Why do you think hospitality was so important to the ancient Greeks and Romans?
3. Is hospitality as important in our society today? Why or why not?

UNDERSTANDING LANGUAGE

Analyzing Words with the Root *Phil*

The meaning of *Philemon* in Greek is "affectionate." This name contains the root *phil,* which means "love of." The Greek root *phil* (or *philo,* or *phile*) appears in many English words. Look up the following words in a dictionary, and write their meanings. Note how the definitions relate to the concept of love. Use each word in a sentence: 1. philosophy; 2. philanthrophy; 3. philharmonic; 4. Anglophile

THINKING AND WRITING

Writing Dialogue for a Myth

Dialogue is the words that characters speak to each other. Edith Hamilton includes only a few of the words that the characters would say. Imagine that you must make up more dialogue for a dramatized version of this myth to be presented before your classmates. Focus on the conversation that the characters have around the dinner table. Read the myth again to make sure you understand the sequence of events. Then write the dialogue. When revising this dialogue make sure it will not sound old-fashioned. Also, check to see that each character's words are in keeping with his or her personality.

GUIDE FOR READING

Icarus and Daedalus

The name Daedalus (ded' 'l əs) means "artful craftsman" in Greek, and Daedalus deserved his name. According to legend, he learned his craftsmanship from the gods themselves. Not only did he design buildings, machines, and weapons for various Greek kings, but he also made wonderful toys for their children. His son, Icarus (ik' ə rəs), is remembered for the fateful flight recounted in this myth.

Josephine Preston Peabody (1874–1922), who wrote this version of the myth, was best known for her poetry and plays.

Characters in Myth

Like people in real life or characters in fiction, the gods and heroes in myths have different ways of thinking and acting. Prometheus, for instance, is concerned about the results of his deeds, while Zeus is more stubborn and emotional. Hades is dark and forbidding, like his underworld kingdom, but Apollo loves the light.

You can understand the characters in myths by paying attention to what the storyteller says about them. You can also learn about them by observing what they say and do themselves. In "Icarus and Daedalus," you will meet a father and son who are quite different from each other.

Look For

In this myth, Daedalus invents wings that enable him and Icarus to fly. Look for the differences in the ways that these two characters respond to the experience of flight. What does this difference tell you about each character?

Writing

Have you ever wanted to fly—not in an airplane, but as a human being with wings? Imagine that you could drift in an updraft of air like a hawk or fly for great distances like a migrating bird. Describe the sensation of flying as you imagine it. For instance, what would you see and hear, and what would the wind feel like against your body?

Vocabulary

Knowing the following words will help you as you read "Icarus and Daedalus."

cunning (kun' iŋ) *adj.*: Skillful; clever (p. 581)

veered (vird) *v.*: Changed directions (p. 581)

fledgling (flej' liŋ) *n.*: Young bird (p. 581)

rash (rash) *adj.*: Reckless (p. 581)

vacancy (vā' kən sē) *n.*: Emptiness (p. 581)

sustained (sə stānd') *v.*: Supported (p. 582)

Icarus and Daedalus

Josephine Preston Peabody

Among all those mortals who grew so wise that they learned the secrets of the gods, none was more cunning than Daedalus.

He once built, for King Minos of Crete,[1] a wonderful Labyrinth[2] of winding ways so cunningly tangled up and twisted around that, once inside, you could never find your way out again without a magic clue. But the king's favor veered with the wind, and one day he had his master architect imprisoned in a tower. Daedalus managed to escape from his cell; but it seemed impossible to leave the island, since every ship that came or went was well guarded by order of the king.

At length, watching the sea-gulls in the air—the only creatures that were sure of liberty—he thought of a plan for himself and his young son Icarus, who was captive with him.

Little by little, he gathered a store of feathers great and small. He fastened these together with thread, moulded them in with wax, and so fashioned two great wings like those of a bird. When they were done, Daedalus fitted them to his own shoulders, and after one or two efforts, he found that by waving his arms he could winnow[3] the air

and cleave it, as a swimmer does the sea. He held himself aloft, wavered this way and that with the wind, and at last, like a great fledgling, he learned to fly.

Without delay, he fell to work on a pair of wings for the boy Icarus, and taught him carefully how to use them, bidding him beware of rash adventures among the stars. "Remember," said the father, "never to fly very low or very high, for the fogs about the earth would weigh you down, but the blaze of the sun will surely melt your feathers apart if you go too near."

For Icarus, these cautions went in at one ear and out by the other. Who could remember to be careful when he was to fly for the first time? Are birds careful? Not they! And not an idea remained in the boy's head but the one joy of escape.

The day came, and the fair wind that was to set them free. The father bird put on his wings, and, while the light urged them to be gone, he waited to see that all was well with Icarus, for the two could not fly hand in hand. Up they rose, the boy after his father. The hateful ground of Crete sank beneath them; and the country folk, who caught a glimpse of them when they were high above the treetops, took it for a vision of the gods—Apollo, perhaps, with Cupid after him.

At first there was a terror in the joy. The wide vacancy of the air dazed them—a glance downward made their brains reel. But when a great wind filled their wings, and Icarus

---

1. King Minos (mī′ nəs) **of Crete:** King Minos was a son of the god Zeus. Crete is a Greek island in the eastern Mediterranean sea, southeast of Greece.
2. Labyrinth (lab′ ə rinth′)
3. winnow (win′ ō) *v.*: Beat as with wings.

LANDSCAPE WITH THE FALL OF ICARUS (detail)
Pieter Breughel
Scala/Art Resource

felt himself sustained, like a halcyon bird[4] in the hollow of a wave, like a child uplifted by his mother, he forgot everything in the world but joy. He forgot Crete and the other islands that he had passed over: he saw but vaguely that wingèd thing in the distance before him that was his father Daedalus. He longed for one draft of flight to quench the thirst of his captivity: he stretched out his arms to the sky and made towards the highest heavens.

Alas for him! Warmer and warmer grew the air. Those arms, that had seemed to uphold him, relaxed. His wings wavered, drooped. He fluttered his young hands vainly—he was falling—and in that terror he remembered. The heat of the sun had melted the wax from his wings; the feathers were falling, one by one, like snowflakes; and there was none to help.

He fell like a leaf tossed down the wind, down, down, with one cry that overtook Daedalus far away. When he returned, and sought high and low for his poor boy, he saw nothing but the birdlike feathers afloat on the water, and he knew that Icarus was drowned.

The nearest island he named Icaria, in memory of the child; but he, in heavy grief, went to the temple of Apollo in Sicily, and there hung up his wings as an offering. Never again did he attempt to fly.

---

4. halcyon (hal′ sē ən) **bird** *n*.: A legendary bird, identified with the kingfisher, which could calm the sea by resting on it.

THINKING ABOUT THE SELECTION

Recalling

1. Why does Daedalus want to leave Crete?
2. How does Daedalus plan to escape?
3. Paraphrase the warning he gives to Icarus.
4. Why does Icarus fall from the sky?

Interpreting

5. Do you think that Daedalus was punished by the gods for daring an unusual deed? Explain.
6. Do you think Icarus was punished for disobeying his father? Explain.
7. What lesson does this myth teach?

Applying

8. Why do you think humans have always wanted to fly like birds?

ANALYZING CHARACTER

Understanding Characters in Myth

Like novels and short stories, myths present a variety of characters. In "Icarus and Daedalus," you learn about a famous father and son through what the storyteller says about them and what they do themselves.

1. Where does the storyteller inform you that Daedalus is "cunning"? In what ways does Daedalus display his cunning?
2. What does Daedalus reveal about himself in his words to his son?
3. At what point in the story does the storyteller hint that Icarus will disobey his father?
4. What does the boy's flying too close to the sun tell you about him?
5. Do you think Icarus's behavior is typical of that of most young people? Why or why not?

CRITICAL THINKING AND READING

Comparing and Contrasting Characters

Comparing means finding similarities. **Contrasting** means showing differences. By comparing and contrasting Icarus and Daedalus, you can learn even more about them.

1. Find evidence to show that the father and son both are eager to escape the island.
2. How are the two similar in their first reaction to the experience of flying?
3. How are they different in the ways they adapt to this new experience?
4. Explain whether the contrast between them results more from the difference in their ages or from their differing personalities.

SPEAKING AND LISTENING

Creating a Dramatic Monologue

A **dramatic monologue** is a poem in which a fictional character expresses his or her thoughts and feelings to an imaginary listener. Write a dramatic monologue in which Icarus tells about the escape. Include his thoughts and feelings about each important event. For instance, how did he feel as he saw his father making the wings, or what did he think when his father warned him about flight? The poem does not have to rhyme. After you have finished your peom, share it with classmates. Ask them to help you think about ways to revise your monologue so that it sounds like Icarus talking.

THINKING AND WRITING

Writing About Characters in Myth

Imagine that you are a reporter for an Athenian newspaper. You suddenly hear that an old man who just died on one of the Greek islands was Icarus. It turns out that he survived his fall into the sea and lived for many years, hiding his identity. Write a story for your newspaper with the following headline: The Secret Life of Icarus. In the story, tell what happened to Icarus after his fall. Explain such matters as how he survived the accident, whether he felt sorry for what he did, why he never contacted his father, and whether he married. As you revise your account, make sure it will be interesting enough to sell newspapers.

GUIDE FOR READING

Narcissus

The story of the handsome youth Narcissus (när sis′ əs) has been retold for hundreds of years. This popular Greek myth has also inspired many painters, who have shown Narcissus staring enchanted at his own reflection in the water.

   Jay MacPherson (1931–   ), the author of this version of the myth, has lived most of her life in Canada and is best known for her poetry.

Metamorphosis

Metamorphosis means change from one form into another. In the imaginative world of myths, both gods and mortals can experience this type of change. The sea-god Proteus, for example, has the power to transform himself into any shape he chooses. Also, the gods can change humans into other forms. At the end of "Phaëthon, Son of Apollo," the gods take pity on the grief of Clymene and her daughters and change them into poplar trees. In "Narcissus," you will read about another metamorphosis.

Look For

Identify the metamorphosis that occurs in this myth. Look for the resemblance between the character and the thing into which he changes.

Writing

Metamorphosis is not limited to myths. Many remarkable changes take place in the world around you. Have you ever watched a caterpillar develop into a butterfly, or a person grow from a small baby to a school-age child? Freewrite about an "everyday" metamorphosis that you have witnessed.

Vocabulary

Knowing the following words will help you as you read "Narcissus."

courted (kôrt′ əd) v.: Tried to win someone's love (p. 585)

marred (märd) v.: Disturbed (p. 585)

deluded (di lood′ əd) v.: Fooled; misled (p. 585)

disdained (dis dānd′) adj.: Scorned; regarded as unworthy (p. 585)

unrequited (un ri kwīt′ əd) adj.: Unreturned (p. 585)

haggard (hag′ ərd) adj.: Looking worn from grief or illness (p. 586)

lament (lə ment′) v.: Express deep sorrow for; mourn (p. 586)

Narcissus

Jay MacPherson

As beautiful as Adonis[1] was the ill-fated Narcissus, who from his childhood was loved by all who saw him but whose pride would let him love no one in return. At last one of those who had hopelessly courted him turned and cursed him, exclaiming: "May he suffer as we have suffered! May he too love in vain!" The avenging goddess Nemesis[2] heard and approved this prayer.

There was nearby a clear pool, with shining silvery waters. No shepherd had ever come there, nor beast nor bird nor falling branch marred its surface: the grass grew fresh and green around it, and the sheltering woods kept it always cool from the mid-day sun.

Here once came Narcissus, heated and tired from the chase, and lay down by the pool to drink. As he bent over the water, his eyes met the eyes of another young man, gazing up at him from the depth of the pool. Deluded by his reflection, Narcissus fell in love with the beauty that was his own. Without thought of food or rest he lay beside the pool addressing cries and pleas to the image, whose lips moved as he spoke but whose reply he could never catch. Echo came by, the most constant of his disdained lovers. She was a nymph who had once angered Hera, the wife of Zeus, by talking too much, and in consequence was deprived of the use of her tongue for ordinary conversation: all she could do was repeat the last words of others. Seeing Narcissus lying there, she pleaded with him in his own words. "I will die unless you pity me," cried Narcissus to his beloved. "Pity me," cried Echo as vainly to hers. Narcissus never raised his eyes to her at all, though she remained day after day beside him on the bank, pleading as well as she was able. At last she pined away, withering and wasting with unrequited love, till nothing was left of her but her voice, which the trav-

NARCISO ALLA FONTE
Caravaggio
Scala/Art Resource

---

1. Adonis (ə dän′is): A handsome young man loved by Aphrodite, the goddess of love.
2. Nemesis (nem′ ə sis)

eler still hears calling unexpectedly in woods and waste places.

As for the cruel Narcissus, he fared no better. The face that looked back at him from the water became pale, thin and haggard, till at last poor Echo caught and repeated his last "Farewell!" But when she came with the other nymphs to lament over his body, it was nowhere to be found. Instead, over the pool bent a new flower, white with a yellow center, which they called by his name. From this flower the Furies, the avengers of guilt, twist garlands to bind their hateful brows.

THINKING ABOUT THE SELECTION
Recalling

1. What does Narcissus do that causes him to be cursed?
2. How does Narcissus finally fall in love?
3. Why has Echo incurred the wrath of Hera? How does Hera get her revenge?
4. What does Echo do while Narcissus lies gazing at the object of his love?
5. How are Echo and Narcissus changed at the end of the myth?

Interpreting

6. How is what happens to Narcissus a fitting punishment for his pride?
7. What are two facts of nature explained by this myth?

Applying

8. Do you think there is a little bit of Narcissus in each of us? Explain.

ANALYZING LITERATURE
Understanding Metamorphosis

Metamorphosis refers to a change from one form to another. In this myth, Narcissus experiences such a change.

1. Why is it appropriate that Narcissus becomes a flower?
2. Explain how the story would be different if Narcissus simply died, without undergoing a magical change.

UNDERSTANDING LANGUAGE
Understanding Word Origins

The English word *narcissism,* which refers to a certain way of thinking and acting, is based on the name Narcissus. You can therefore infer that narcissism is related to the way that Narcissus thinks and behaves in this myth.

1. What do you think the word *narcissism* means?
2. Look up the word in a dictionary to check your answer.
3. Write a sentence using the word.

THINKING AND WRITING
Writing Sketches About Metamorphosis

Imagine that the American Mythological Society has offered a $150 award for the best article entitled Metamorphosis: The Inside Story. Most myths contain descriptions of metamorphosis from the outside. However, the Society wants you to describe what it actually feels like to undergo a magical change. Think of a transformation that you can describe. For instance, what would it be like to change into a flower, like Narcissus, or into a sportscar, a mountain, or anything else? Imagine that you are experiencing the metamorphosis and describe it in vivid terms. When revising your article make sure it is both unusual and convincing enough to win the award.

Myths, Legends, and Folktales from Around the World

THE SLEEPING GYPSY, 1897
Henri Rousseau
The Museum of Modern Art, New York

GUIDE FOR READING

The Legend of the Hummingbird

Puerto Rico (pwer′ tə rē′ kō) is a commonwealth of the United States located about 1,000 miles southeast of Florida. The earliest inhabitants of the island were the **Borinquen** Indians, from whom this legend comes. Some Puerto Ricans today can still trace their origins to this now vanished tribe.

Pura Belpre (pōō′ rä bel′ prā) (1899–1982), who retells this legend, was born in Puerto Rico and moved to New York City as a young woman. She wrote a number of books based on Puerto Rican folklore.

**Legend:
Universal Theme**

A **universal theme** is an idea or situation that has been common to many different groups throughout history. Such themes appear often in legends and folk tales. One repeated theme involves the problems that young people face when their love goes against the wishes of their families or society. In this legend, the daughter of an Indian chief invites danger by falling in love with a young man from an enemy tribe.

Look For

As you read, visualize the "small pool" where the two young Indians meet. Why do you think the story takes place there, rather than in a village or town? What happens to the two young lovers?

Writing

The two young Indians in this legend meet at a beautiful and secret pool "far up in the hills." Remember a secret place that you went to or heard about when you were a child. Describe this place and tell why it was special for you.

Vocabulary

Knowing the following word will help you as you read "The Legend of the Hummingbird."
dreaded (dred′ əd) *adj.*: Feared (p. 589)

The Legend of the Hummingbird

from **Puerto Rico**

Pura Belpré

Between the towns of Cayey and Cidra, far up in the hills, there was once a small pool fed by a waterfall that tumbled down the side of the mountain. The pool was surrounded by pomarosa trees, and the Indians used to call it Pomarosa Pool. It was the favorite place of Alida, the daughter of an Indian chief, a man of power and wealth among the people of the hills.

One day, when Alida had come to the pool to rest after a long walk, a young Indian came there to pick some fruit from the trees. Alida was surprised, for he was not of her tribe. Yet he said he was no stranger to the pool. This was where he had first seen Alida, and he had often returned since then to pick fruit, hoping to see her again.

He told her about himself to make her feel at home. He confessed, with honesty and frankness, that he was a member of the dreaded Carib tribe[1] that had so often attacked the island of Borinquen.[2] As a young boy, he had been left behind after one of those raids, and he had stayed on the island ever since.

Alida listened closely to his story, and the two became friends. They met again in the days that followed, and their friendship grew stronger. Alida admired the young man's courage in living among his enemies. She learned to call him by his Carib name, Taroo, and he called her Alida, just as her own people did. Before long, their friendship had turned into love.

Their meetings by the pool were always brief. Alida was afraid their secret might be discovered, and careful though she was, there came a day when someone saw them and told her father. Alida was forbidden to visit the Pomarosa Pool, and to put an end to her romance with the stranger, her father decided to marry her to a man of his own choosing. Preparations for the wedding started at once.

Alida was torn with grief, and one evening she cried out to her god: "O Yukiyú, help me! Kill me or do what you will with me, but do not let me marry this man whom I do not love!"

And the great god Yukiyú took pity on her and changed her into a delicate red flower.

Meanwhile Taroo, knowing nothing of Alida's sorrow, still waited for her by the Pomarosa Pool. Day after day he waited. Sometimes he stayed there until a mantle of stars was spread across the sky.

---

1. Carib (kar′ ib) **tribe:** Native Americans who formerly inhabited the Southwest Indies and the northern coast of South America.
2. Borinquen (bō′ rēn ken′): Puerto Rico.

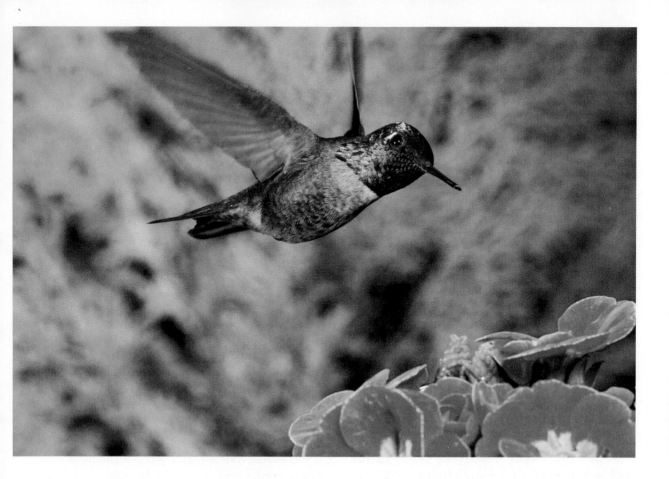

One night the moon took pity on him. "Taroo," she called from her place high above the stars. "O Taroo, wait no longer for Alida! Your secret was made known, and Alida was to be married to a man of her father's choosing. In her grief she called to her god, Yukiyú; he heard her plea for help and changed her into a red flower."

"Ahee, ahee!" cried Taroo. "O moon, what is the name of the red flower?"

"Only Yukiyú knows that," the moon replied.

Then Taroo called out: "O Yukiyú, god of my Alida, help me too! Help me to find her!"

And just as the great god had heard Alida's plea, he listened now to Taroo and decided to help him. There by the Pomarosa Pool, before the moon and the silent stars, the great god changed Taroo into a small many-colored bird.

"Fly, Colibrí, and find your love among the flowers," he said.

Off went the Colibrí, flying swiftly, and as he flew his wings made a sweet humming sound.

In the morning the Indians saw a new bird darting about among the flowers swift as an arrow and brilliant as a jewel. They heard the humming of its wings, and in amazement they saw it hover in the air over every blossom, kissing the petals of the flowers with its long slender bill. They liked the new bird with the music in its wings, and they called it Hummingbird.

Ever since then the little many-colored bird has hovered over every flower he finds, but returns most often to the flowers that are red. He is still looking, always looking, for the one red flower that will be his lost Alida. He has not found her yet.

THINKING ABOUT THE SELECTION

Recalling

1. Where does the stranger that Alida meets at the pool come from?
2. What relationship develops between Alida and the stranger?
3. How does Alida's father try to end it?
4. What happens to the two young lovers?

Interpreting

5. What does this legend tell you about the enduring quality of love?
6. Which facts of nature does this legend explain?

Applying

7. A proverb says: Love finds hidden paths. How does this legend prove the proverb?

ANALYZING LITERATURE

Understanding a Universal Theme

A **universal theme** is an idea or situation common to many different groups throughout history. Such themes appear often in literature and folklore. In *Romeo and Juliet,* for instance, William Shakespeare writes about the problems that young people face when they fall in love. "The Legend of the Hummingbird" deals with the same universal theme. Like Romeo and Juliet, Taroo and Alida encounter serious difficulties.

1. What problems might they have faced even if Alida's family accepted Taroo?
2. Why do you think that Alida's father did not approve of her romance?
3. Would the lovers have been happier if Yukiyú did not change them? Why or why not?

CRITICAL THINKING AND READING

Recognizing Clues to Outcomes

As you read this legend, you can find clues in the story to what will happen. You can become better at finding such clues by not only understanding events but also thinking where they might lead. For instance, the fact that Alida and Taroo become friends so quickly suggests that they may fall in love as well.

1. Find two clues indicating that Alida's father may not accept her romance.
2. How is the title a clue to what will happen when Alida becomes a flower?

UNDERSTANDING LANGUAGE

Completing Verbal Analogies

A **verbal analogy** is a comparison of relationships between words. For example, *wealth* is related to *riches* in the same way that *happiness* is related to *joy*. Each of the following word pairs consists of synonyms. In the following examples, choose the lettered pair of words that expresses the same relationship as that between the capitalized pair.

1. MANTLE:CAPE::
   a. pill:bottle
   b. arrow:target
   c. car:tire
   d. employee:worker

2. FEARED:DREADED::
   a. sold:bought
   b. helped:aided
   c. threw:caught
   d. sang:ate

THINKING AND WRITING

Writing a Legend

Many legends tell about real people but exaggerate their achievements. Imagine that you have been arguing with a friend about who is the greatest baseball player, television actor, or any other performer. List some of the accomplishments of the person you have chosen, and then exaggerate the items you have listed. Using one of the items on your list, write a legend about this person. Remember that a legend is in the form of a story. As you revise your legend, make sure it will persuade your friend that you are right.

GUIDE FOR READING

Ojeeg, the Hunter, and the Ice Man

This tale comes from the **Micmac** (mik' mak) Indians, who live in eastern Canada. Years ago, this tribe hunted, fished, and gathered clams for food. During the cold Canadian winter, they traveled by means of wooden toboggans and snowshoes. They kept themselves warm in tepees covered with birchbark or animal skins.

Dorothy de Wit (1916–1980) retells this Micmac tale in her book *The Talking Stone: An Anthology of Native American Tales and Legends* (1979).

Conflict in Legend

A **conflict** is a struggle between opposing sides or forces. Conflict plays an important role in legend, just as it does in short stories and novels. One difference, however, is that a legend may present a struggle between a hero with special powers and a supernatural being. In this Indian legend, the hero Ojeeg battles with old man Peboan, the powerful spirit of winter. Their weapons are not bows or guns, but the forces of ice and fire.

Look For

Look for the many details in this legend that re-create the warmth of a fire or the cold of a bitter winter. These details make the conflict between ice and fire seem even more vivid.

Writing

Imagine that you are designing a costume for a person who will represent the king or queen of the winter. Freewrite about this costume. Tell what colors, materials, and designs you would use to make this outfit represent the winter in an impressive way.

Vocabulary

Knowing the following words will help you as you read "Ojeeg, the Hunter, and the Ice Man."

vanquish (vaŋ' kwish) *v.*: Overcome (p. 593)

pummeled (pum'' ld) *v.*: Hit with repeated blows (p. 594)

extracted (ik strakt' əd) *v.*: Obtained by drawing out (p. 594)

rendered (ren' dərd) *v.*: Melted down (p. 594)

flaunted (flônt' əd) *v.*: Displayed; showed off (p. 594)

shuddered (shud' ərd) *v.*: Shook (p. 596)

grizzled (griz'' ld) *adj.*: Gray (p. 596)

flit (flit) *v.*: Fly lightly and rapidly (p. 596)

Ojeeg, the Hunter, and the Ice Man

from **the Micmac (Canada)**

Dorothy de Wit

On the shores of a large body of water, near the great evergreen forests of the north, there lived a hunter with his wife and young son. Their wigwam[1] stood by itself, far from the village, and they were very content, for Ojeeg was skilled with his arrows and brought as much game and furs to his wife as they had need of! The little boy would have been happy, indeed, if the snow had not been so deep or the winters so long. He did not miss companions to play with, for his father showed him the tracks of the grouse[2] and the squirrels. He pointed out the white coats of the rabbits and the weasel, and he trained him to use his bow carefully so that he would not waste his arrows.

But the cold grew more bitter as the long winter months dragged on. One day the boy saw a squirrel running around a stump, looking vainly for buried nuts, for the snow was too deep. Finally, the squirrel rested on his bushy tail, and as the boy came toward him, he said, "I am hungry, and there is no food to be found anywhere! Aren't you, too, tired of this ice and cold?"

"I am," said the hunter's son. "But what can we do against the power of the Ice Man? We are weak; he is cruel and strong!"

"You can cry! You can howl with hunger!" replied the squirrel. "Your father is a great hunter. He has strong power, and maybe he can vanquish the Ice Man if he sees your grief. Cry, cry, small brother! It may help!"

That night the young boy came into the wigwam, threw down his bow and arrows, and huddled beside the fire, sobbing. He would not answer his mother when she questioned him, and he would not stop crying. When his father came home, the boy's cries grew even louder, and nothing would make him stop, until at last the hunter asked, "Is it perhaps that you are lonely? That you do not like the snow and the cold?" At that the boy nodded his head. "Then," said the father, "I shall see if I have the power to change it."

He went out the next day on his snowshoes.[3] Long he traveled by the frozen water till he came to a narrow place that was

---

1. wigwam (wig′ wäm) *n.*: A shelter with a rounded top made by certain Native American groups.
2. grouse (grous) *n.*: A group of game birds.

3. snowshoes (snō′ shōōz′) *n.*: Racket-shaped pieces of wood crisscrossed with strips of leather, worn on the feet to prevent sinking in deep snow.

choked with huge blocks of ice. He took his sharp knife and a stone chisel, and he began to dig away at the chunks. Many hours he chipped and hacked and pummeled the ice, and in the end he heard the barricade crack! The ice began to move, and a part of it broke off and jostled and bumped around until more cracks appeared. The whole mass of ice began to float slowly away. The hunter rested and wiped the sweat from his face. Then he heard the voice of Peboan, the ice king, piercing the air: "You have won for now, my son! You are strong indeed, and your Manito power[4] is great! But I shall gain the final victory, for next year I will return, and I will bring even more snow! The North Wind will blow more fiercely, and the trees will break with the weight of the ice I will pile on their branches! The waters will freeze so that no matter how many warriors cross them, not a crack will appear. Then you will see, grandson, who is the master of winter!"

The hunter returned to his wigwam. The snows were melting, and green was returning to the earth. Sweet sap rose in the maple trees, and his little son shouted with joy! But the hunter remembered the threat which the ice king had made: "Next winter will be worse—much worse!"

So he set himself to cutting wood and piling it in great stacks; he gathered the resin[5] from the pine trees and formed it into great lumps. From the game which he brought home he extracted much fat, and this he rendered and stored in large oil pots. Baskets of evergreen cones and thick logs he stored up also. Then, when the maple and the oak flaunted their red and yellow ban-

ners at the dark hemlocks, he went somewhat apart from his own lodging and built a small, very tight new wigwam. He left his wife warm skins and food in quantity; then, with supplies for himself, he began stacking them, and the firewood, the resin lumps, the oil pots, and the baskets of cones, within his new lodging.

When the first snowfall whitened the ground, he bade his wife and son have courage and went to the new wigwam. He laced the skins tightly and closed the opening securely. With food and water at hand and warm furs to cover him, he built a very small

---

4. Manito (man' ə tō') **power:** Power that comes from nature spirits.
5. resin (rez' 'n) *n.:* A sticky brownish or yellowish substance that comes from evergreen trees.

fire in the center of the fire hole and sat down to wait for Peboan.

At first the frost was light, and the snow melted quickly. At night the wind did not rise much, and the hunter thought, "Perhaps I have frightened old Peboan away! He will see that it is not so easy to win over me!" But as the winter deepened, the tent poles rattled more, the skins shuddered a bit, and it took more fire to warm the wigwam. Still, Peboan did not come. The hunter heard the great owl swoop through the trees at night. He heard weasels and rabbits move through the snow, and once the heavy footfall of a moose crashed through the drifts. The cold became intense.

Then, suddenly one night, the skins across the door opening were torn away and a gust of North Wind almost blew the fire apart! Peboan stood there, grizzled and bent. His face was lined and cruel, and his long beard hung with icicles. "I have come as I said I would," he shouted.

The hunter rose swiftly, tied up the door skins, and put more wood on the fire. A chill ran through him—the ice king's power was very great! "Grandfather, be seated at my fire. You are my guest here!" he said. The old one sat far from the fire and watched him.

"My power is great! I blow my breath— the streams stand still; the waters are stiff and hard like rock crystal!"

The hunter shivered and put another log on the fire. "The snow covers the land when I shake my head; trees are without any leaves, and their branches break with the weight of my ice!"

The hunter added some cones, and the flames leaped up. "No birds fly now, for they have gone far away. Only the hardy ones flit around, and they are hungry."

The hunter added more wood to the fire, for the air in the wigwam was becoming bitter cold, and frost hung on his eyebrows and nose. "The animals hide away and sleep through the long cold." Peboan laughed grimly as he saw the man draw his fur closer around him.

"Even the hunters do not leave their lodges. The children curl deep into their blankets for warmth and cry with hunger."

Then Ojeeg pulled out the resin lumps; first one, then another he tossed into the coals, and they burned hotly. Peboan shook his white head and moved as far away from the heat as he could. When the hunter saw that, he added yet another clutch of pitch and more logs. Sweat began to roll down the wrinkled face; the ice king huddled close to the wall of the wigwam; his icy garments began to melt.

Ojeeg took up the pots of oil and poured them onto the fire. The flames burned orange and red and blue! They licked at the old man's long robe, at his ice-covered feet, at his snowy mantle, and the Ice Man cried out in pain, "Enough, enough! I have seen your power, Ojeeg! Take back your fire and heat! Stifle your flames!" But the hunter only built up the fire higher, and the Ice Man became smaller and smaller, till at last he melted into a pool of water which ran over the ground and out, under the wigwam opening. When he saw that, Ojeeg, the hunter, untied the skins and looked out. The Ice Man was gone completely! Beyond his doorway the ground was brown and soft with pine needles, he could hear running water, and birds flew through the treetops. How long had he been in his wigwam? The spring was at hand!

Ojeeg put out his fire and ran toward his wife and son, who had come out and stood waiting to welcome him! The ice king would not make so long a visit next year! Only the white flowers of the snowdrop, fragile and small, remained to mark where Peboan had left his footprints!

THINKING ABOUT THE SELECTION

Recalling

1. Why does the hunter decide to make the snow and cold go away?
2. Describe Peboan when he appears at the wigwam. What powers does he have?
3. Why does the ice king vanish?

Interpreting

4. How do you know that the hunter is a hero, with more power than an ordinary person?
5. How does Ojeeg influence the way that seasons change?
6. Why do you think the Micmacs thought of ice as having godlike powers?

Applying

7. Explain what you learn about the Micmac tribe from reading this legend.

ANALYZING LITERATURE

Understanding Conflict in a Legend

A **conflict** is a struggle between opposing sides or forces. Sometimes tales and legends present conflicts by giving a supernatural twist to a real situation. For instance, the Micmac had to fight against the cold in the northern woods. Their legend of Ojeeg and the Ice Man dramatizes that struggle by telling about a battle between a hero and a magical ice king.

1. How does Ojeeg win the first fight?
2. What is his plan to win again?
3. When does it seem that Ojeeg might lose?
4. What does he do to make Peboan retreat?
5. Is Ojeeg's victory total? Explain.

CRITICAL THINKING AND READING

Evaluating a Personification

A **personification** is a figure of speech that gives human qualities to an idea, an object, or an aspect of nature. In this legend, Peboan is a personification. Although he is magical, he represents the winter in human form. You can judge whether he is a suitable ice king by looking closely at his traits.

1. Why do you think he is personified as a grizzled old man rather than a boy or a young woman?
2. Why is his face "lined and cruel"?
3. Is Peboan a suitable personification of winter? Why or why not?
4. If you wanted to personify winter, what kind of person would you use?

SPEAKING AND LISTENING

Presenting a Readers Theater

A **readers theater** is a dramatic reading of a piece of literature. Work with your classmates to give a readers theater presentation of "Ojeeg, the Hunter, and the Ice Man." Some of the students in your class can speak the words the characters actually say, while others can narrate the rest of the story.

As you read, try to imitate the way your character would speak. If you have the part of the ice king, for example, remember that he is a "grizzled and bent" old man. You can also design costumes for the characters to make the presentation more effective.

THINKING AND WRITING

Creating a Personification

Imagine that an advertising agency is offering a prize for the best personification of winter. The agency will use the character created by the winner in a campaign to promote ski resorts. This character must therefore convey a positive image of the winter season. List the qualities that such a personification should have. Using your list, write a letter to the agency explaining your concept. As you revise your letter, make sure it will convince the agency, and you will win the prize.

GUIDE FOR READING

Popocatepetl and Ixtlaccihuatl

This folk legend comes to us from the **Aztec** Indians, who controlled a great empire in Mexico about 500 years ago. Some of their cities were even larger than European cities of that era. The Spanish destroyed this empire in 1521, but the influence of Aztec culture has continued in art, language, and food.

    Juliet Piggott (1924–   ), whose version of this tale appears in her book *Mexican Folk Tales,* has also written about Japanese history and folklore.

Motivation in Legend

The term **motivation** refers to the reasons that people act as they do. Like characters in fiction, those in legends have reasons or motives for their behavior. In "The Legend of the Hummingbird," for instance, Alida's motive for praying to her god is her wish to avoid marrying someone other than Taroo.

    A storyteller may reveal the characters' motives or let you figure them out for yourself. In "Popocatepetl and Ixtlaccihuatl" the storyteller uses both of these methods.

Look For

As you read this legend, look for the motives that influence the actions of each character. Often the storyteller will tell you directly what these motives are.

Writing

The two main characters in this legend are strongly motivated by love for each other. Freewrite about a story you have read or a film you have seen in which love was a key motivation. Tell how this motive affected the characters' actions.

Vocabulary

Knowing the following words will help you as you read "Popocatepetl and Ixtlaccihuatl."

besieged (bi sēj''d) *v.*: Surrounded (p. 601)

decreed (di krēd') *v.*: Officially ordered (p. 601)

relished (rel' isht) *v.*: Especially enjoyed (p. 601)

brandishing (bran' dish iŋ) *v.*: Waving in a menacing way (p. 602)

unanimous (yoo nan'ə məs) *adj.*: Based on complete agreement (p. 602)

refute (ri fyoot') *v.*: To prove someone wrong (p. 602)

routed (rout' əd) *v.*: Completely defeated (p. 604)

edifice (ed'ə fis) *n.*: Large structure (p. 604)

Popocatepetl and Ixtlaccihuatl

from **Mexico**

Juliet Piggott

Before the Spaniards came to Mexico and marched on the Aztec capital of Tenochtitlan[1] there were two volcanoes to the southeast of that city. The Spaniards destroyed much of Tenochtitlan and built another city in its place and called it Mexico City. It is known by that name still, and the pass through which the Spaniards came to the ancient Tenochtitlan is still there, as are the volcanoes on each side of that pass. Their names have not been changed. The one to the north is Ixtlaccihuatl[2] and the one on the south of the pass is Popocatepetl.[3] Both are snowcapped and beautiful, Popocatepetl being the taller of the two. That name means Smoking Mountain. In Aztec days it gushed forth smoke and, on occasion, it does so still. It erupted too in Aztec days and has done so again since the Spaniards came. Ixtlaccihuatl means The White Woman, for its peak was, and still is, white.

Perhaps Ixtlaccihuatl and Popocatepetl were there in the highest part of the Valley of Mexico in the days when the earth was very young, in the days when the new people were just learning to eat and grow corn. The Aztecs claimed the volcanoes as their own, for they possessed a legend about them and their creation, and they believed that legend to be true.

There was once an Aztec Emperor in Tenochtitlan. He was very powerful. Some thought he was wise as well, whilst others doubted his wisdom. He was both a ruler and a warrior and he kept at bay those tribes living in and beyond the mountains surrounding the Valley of Mexico, with its huge lake called Texcoco[4] in which Tenochtitlan was built. His power was absolute and the splendor in which he lived was very great.

It is not known for how many years the Emperor ruled in Tenochtitlan, but it is known that he lived to a great age. However, it was not until he was in his middle years that his wife gave him an heir, a girl. The Emperor and Empress loved the princess very much and she was their only child. She was a dutiful daughter and learned all she could from her father about the art of ruling, for she knew that when he died she would reign in his stead in Tenochtitlan.

Her name was Ixtlaccihuatl. Her parents

---

1. Tenochtitlan (te nôch′ tē tlän′): The Spanish conquered the Aztec capital in 1521.
2. Ixtlaccihuatl (ēs′ tä sē′ wät′l)
3. Popocatepetl (pō̆ pō̆′ kä tē′ pet′l)

4. Texcoco (tä skō′ kō)

ERUPTING VOLCANO, 1943
Dr. Atl (Gerardo Murillo)
Laurie Platt Winfrey, Inc.

and her friends called her Ixtla. She had a pleasant disposition and, as a result, she had many friends. The great palace where she lived with the Emperor and Empress rang with their laughter when they came to the parties her parents gave for her. As well as being a delightful companion Ixtla was also very pretty, even beautiful.

Her childhood was happy and she was content enough when she became a young woman. But by then she was fully aware of the great responsibilities which would be

hers when her father died and she became serious and studious and did not enjoy parties as much as she had done when younger.

Another reason for her being so serious was that she was in love. This in itself was a joyous thing, but the Emperor forbade her to marry. He wanted her to reign and rule alone when he died, for he trusted no one, not even his wife, to rule as he did except his much loved only child, Ixtla. This was why there were some who doubted the wisdom of the Emperor for, by not allowing his heiress to marry, he showed a selfishness and short-sightedness towards his daughter and his empire which many considered was not truly wise. An emperor, they felt, who was not truly wise could not also be truly great. Or even truly powerful.

The man with whom Ixtla was in love was also in love with her. Had they been allowed to marry their state could have been doubly joyous. His name was Popocatepetl and Ixtla and his friends all called him Popo. He was a warrior in the service of the Emperor, tall and strong, with a capacity for gentleness, and very brave. He and Ixtla loved each other very much and while they were content and even happy when they were together, true joy was not theirs because the Emperor continued to insist that Ixtla should not be married when the time came for her to take on her father's responsibilities.

This unfortunate but moderately happy relationship between Ixtla and Popo continued for several years, the couple pleading with the Emperor at regular intervals and the Emperor remaining constantly adamant. Popo loved Ixtla no less for her father's stubbornness and she loved him no less while she studied, as her father demanded she should do, the art of ruling in preparation for her reign.

When the Emperor became very old he also became ill. In his feebleness he channeled all his failing energies towards instructing Ixtla in statecraft, for he was no longer able to exercise that craft himself. So it was that his enemies, the tribes who lived in the mountains and beyond, realized that the great Emperor in Tenochtitlan was great no longer, for he was only teaching his daughter to rule and not ruling himself.

The tribesmen came nearer and nearer to Tenochtitlan until the city was besieged. At last the Emperor realized himself that he was great no longer, that his power was nearly gone and that his domain was in dire peril.

Warrior though he long had been, he was now too old and too ill to lead his fighting men into battle. At last he understood that, unless his enemies were frustrated in their efforts to enter and lay waste to Tenochtitlan, not only would he no longer be Emperor but his daughter would never be Empress.

Instead of appointing one of his warriors to lead the rest into battle on his behalf, he offered a bribe to all of them. Perhaps it was that his wisdom, if wisdom he had, had forsaken him, or perhaps he acted from fear. Or perhaps he simply changed his mind. But the bribe he offered to whichever warrior succeeded in lifting the siege of Tenochtitlan and defeating the enemies in and around the Valley of Mexico was both the hand of his daughter and the equal right to reign and rule, with her, in Tenochtitlan. Furthermore, he decreed that directly he learned that his enemies had been defeated he would instantly cease to be Emperor himself. Ixtla would not have to wait until her father died to become Empress and, if her father should die of his illness or old age before his enemies were vanquished, he further decreed that he who overcame the surrounding enemies should marry the princess whether he, the Emperor, lived or not.

Ixtla was fearful when she heard of her father's bribe to his warriors, for the only one whom she had any wish to marry was Popo and she wanted to marry him, and only him, very much indeed.

The warriors, however, were glad when they heard of the decree: there was not one of them who would not have been glad to have the princess as his wife and they all relished the chance of becoming Emperor.

And so the warriors went to war at their

ruler's behest, and each fought trebly[5] hard for each was fighting not only for the safety of Tenochtitlan and the surrounding valley, but for the delightful bride and for the right to be the Emperor himself.

Even though the warriors fought with great skill and even though each one exhibited a courage he did not know he possessed, the war was a long one. The Emperor's enemies were firmly entrenched around Lake Texcoco and Tenochtitlan by the time the warriors were sent to war, and as battle followed battle the final outcome was uncertain.

The warriors took a variety of weapons with them; wooden clubs edged with sharp blades of obsidian,[6] obsidian machetes,[7] javelins which they hurled at their enemies from troughed throwing boards, bows and arrows, slings and spears set with obsidian fragments, and lances, too. Many of them carried shields woven from wicker[8] and covered in tough hide and most wore armor made of thick quilted cotton soaked in brine.

The war was long and fierce. Most of the warriors fought together and in unison, but some fought alone. As time went on natural leaders emerged and, of these, undoubtedly Popo was the best. Finally it was he, brandishing his club and shield, who led the great charge of running warriors across the valley, with their enemies fleeing before them to the safety of the coastal plains and jungles beyond the mountains.

The warriors acclaimed Popo as the man most responsible for the victory and, weary though they all were, they set off for Tenochtitlan to report to the Emperor and for Popo to claim Ixtla as his wife at last.

But a few of those warriors were jealous of Popo. Since they knew none of them could rightly claim the victory for himself (the decision among the Emperor's fighting men that Popo was responsible for the victory had been unanimous), they wanted to spoil for him and for Ixtla the delights which the Emperor had promised.

These few men slipped away from the rest at night and made their way to Tenochtitlan ahead of all the others. They reached the capital two days later, having traveled without sleep all the way, and quickly let it be known that, although the Emperor's warriors had been successful against his enemies, the warrior Popo had been killed in battle.

It was a foolish and cruel lie which those warriors told their Emperor, and they told it for no reason other than that they were jealous of Popo.

When the Emperor heard this he demanded that Popo's body be brought to him so that he might arrange a fitting burial. He knew the man his daughter had loved would have died courageously. The jealous warriors looked at one another and said nothing. Then one of them told the Emperor that Popo had been killed on the edge of Lake Texcoco and that his body had fallen into the water and no man had been able to retrieve it. The Emperor was saddened to hear this.

After a little while he demanded to be told which of his warriors had been responsible for the victory but none of the fighting men before him dared claim the successful outcome of the war for himself, for each knew the others would refute him. So they were silent. This puzzled the Emperor and he decided to wait for the main body of his warriors to return and not to press the few

---

5. trebly (treʹ blē) *adv.*: Three times as much, triply.
6. obsidian (əb sidʹ ē ən) *n.*: A hard, usually dark-colored or black, volcanic glass.
7. machetes (mə shetʹ ēs) *n.*: Large, heavy-bladed knives.
8. wicker (wikʹ ər) *n.*: A thin, flexible twig.

QUETZALCOATL
Laurie Platt Winfrey, Inc.

who had brought the news of the victory and of Popo's death.

Then the Emperor sent for his wife and his daughter and told them their enemies had been overcome. The Empress was thoroughly excited and relieved at the news. Ixtla was only apprehensive. The Emperor, seeing her anxious face, told her quickly that Popo was dead. He went on to say that the warrior's body had been lost in the waters of Lake Texcoco, and again it was as though his wisdom had left him, for he spoke at some length of his not being able to tell Ixtla who her husband would be and who would become Emperor when the main body of warriors returned to Tenochtitlan.

But Ixtla heard nothing of what he told her, only that her beloved Popo was dead. She went to her room and lay down. Her mother followed her and saw at once she was very ill. Witch doctors were sent for, but they could not help the princess, and neither could her parents. Her illness had no name, unless it was the illness of a broken heart. Princess Ixtlaccihuatl did not wish to live if Popocatepetl was dead, and so she died herself.

The day after her death Popo returned to Tenochtitlan with all the other surviving warriors. They went straight to the palace and, with much cheering, told the Emperor that his enemies had been routed and that Popo was the undoubted victor of the conflict.

The Emperor praised his warriors and pronounced Popo to be the new Emperor in his place. When the young man asked first to see Ixtla, begging that they should be married at once before being jointly proclaimed Emperor and Empress, the Emperor had to tell Popo of Ixtla's death, and how it had happened.

Popo spoke not a word.

He gestured the assembled warriors to follow him and together they sought out the few jealous men who had given the false news of his death to the Emperor. With the army of warriors watching, Popo killed each one of them in single combat with his obsidian studded club. No one tried to stop him.

That task accomplished Popo returned to the palace and, still without speaking and still wearing his stiff cotton armor, went to Ixtla's room. He gently lifted her body and carried it out of the palace and out of the city, and no one tried to stop him doing that either. All the warriors followed him in silence.

When he had walked some miles he gestured to them again and they built a huge pile of stones in the shape of a pyramid. They all worked together and they worked fast while Popo stood and watched, holding the body of the princess in his arms. By sunset the mighty edifice was finished. Popo climbed it alone, carrying Ixtla's corpse with him. There, at the very top, under a heap of stones, he buried the young woman he had loved so well and for so long, and who had died for the love of him.

That night Popo slept alone at the top of the pyramid by Ixtla's grave. In the morning he came down and spoke for the first time since the Emperor had told him the princess was dead. He told the warriors to build another pyramid, a little to the southeast of the one which held Ixtla's body and to build it higher than the other.

He told them too to tell the Emperor on his behalf that he, Popocatepetl, would never reign and rule in Tenochtitlan. He would keep watch over the grave of the Princess Ixtlaccihuatl for the rest of his life.

The messages to the Emperor were the last words Popo ever spoke. Well before the evening the second mighty pile of stones was built. Popo climbed it and stood at the top, taking a torch of resinous pine wood with him.

And when he reached to top he lit the torch and the warriors below saw the white smoke rise against the blue sky, and they watched as the sun began to set and the smoke turned pink and then a deep red, the color of blood.

So Popocatepetl stood there, holding the torch in memory of Ixtlaccihuatl, for the rest of his days.

The snows came and, as the years went by, the pyramids of stone became high white-capped mountains. Even now the one called Popocatepetl emits smoke in memory of the princess whose body lies in the mountain which bears her name.

THINKING ABOUT THE SELECTION

Recalling

1. Why are Ixtla and Popo unable to marry?
2. How does the emperor show his selfishness? What effect does his selfishness have on the safety of his kingdom?
3. Why does the emperor offer Ixtla and his throne as a bribe to his warriors?
4. What leads to Ixtla's death at the end of the war?
5. Why does Popo refuse to rule in Tenochtitlan?

Interpreting

6. Is the emperor a wise man? Why or why not?
7. On the basis of this legend, what traits do you think the Aztecs admired?

Applying

8. What traits do you think are necessary in a leader?

ANALYZING LITERATURE

Understanding Motivation in Legend

The term **motivation** refers to the reasons people act as they do. In "Popocatepetl and Ixtlaccihuatl" the storyteller often explains the characters' **motives,** or reasons for acting.

1. Which event is caused by selfishness?
2. Which is caused by jealousy?
3. Which are caused by love?
4. What do you think this legend indicates about the power of love?

CRITICAL THINKING AND READING

Identifying Imaginative Details

Legends are traditional tales passed down over the generations. Often they are based on the lives of people who actually once lived. However, legends are not history. The events they tell about have been filtered through a people's imagination and enlarged upon.

1. Which events in this legend might have been based on historical events?
2. Which events are highly imaginative and probably not based on historical events?

UNDERSTANDING LANGUAGE

Using Synonyms as Context Clues

The **context** of a word means the words that surround it. You can often find clues to a word you do not know by looking for synonyms in the context. In "Popocatepetl and Ixtlaccihuatl" for instance, you learn that when Ixtla grew up "she became serious and studious." You can figure out the meaning of *studious* if you know the definition of its **synonym,** *serious*. (Both words can mean "thoughtful.")

Find the meaning of the following *italicized* words using clues in the context. Check your answers in a dictionary.

1. " . . . the Emperor remaining constantly *adamant*. Popo loved Ixtla no less for her father's stubbornness. . . . "
2. "Most of the warriors fought together and in *unison*."

THINKING AND WRITING

Writing About a Legend

Imagine you are either Ixtla, Popo, or one of the jealous soldiers. Tell this story from this character's point of view. First list the details you would emphasize in your retelling of the myth. Arrange these details in chronological order. Then write your first draft. Revise your tale, making sure you have stayed in character. Prepare a final draft and share it with your classmates.

GUIDE FOR READING

The Pointing Finger

Chinese literature is one of the great literatures of the world. Poems and tales have been produced in China for nearly 3,000 years. For most of China's history, literature, such as the folk tale you are about to read, has had an important place in people's lives.

Carol Kendall (1917–   ) has written two collections of Chinese tales. Translating Chinese is a special interest of hers. **Yao-wen Li** (1924–   ) was born and raised in pre-Communist China and now lives in Kansas.

Folk Tale

A **folk tale** is a story made up by the common people of a country. It is handed down by word of mouth for many generations. Folk tales are especially interesting for what they imply about the values and beliefs of the people who create them.

Look For

As you read "The Pointing Finger," think about why this tale has lasted so long. What have many generations of Chinese people found interesting and enjoyable about it?

Writing

Magical powers are used in this tale. If you were writing or telling a story about someone with such powers, which ones would you choose? List and briefly describe three or four of them. Then choose one and tell how your character would use it for some useful purpose.

Vocabulary

Knowing the following words will help you as you read "The Pointing Finger."

tedious (tē′ dē əs) *adj.*: Long and boring (p. 607)

taint (tānt) *n.*: A trace (p. 607)

avarice (av′ ər is) *n.*: Greed for riches (p. 607)

proffered (präf′ ərd) *v.*: Offered (p. 607)

cupidity (kyoo pid′ ə tē) *n.*: Strong desire for wealth (p. 607)

The Pointing Finger

from China

Carol Kendall and Yao-wen Li

Even P'eng-lai has its tedious days, and when time hung heavy over that fairy mountain isle in the Eastern Sea, the Eight Immortals who dwelt there remembered and talked of their previous existence as mortals on earth. Upon occasion they took disguises and transported themselves from P'eng-lai to their old world to nose about in human affairs in the hope of discovering improvements in human nature. On the whole, however, they found the mortals of today to have the same shortcomings and the same longcomings as those of yesterday.

It came about that one of the Immortals, on such a nosing-about expedition, was seeking an unselfish man. He vowed that when he found a man without the taint of greed in his heart, he would make of him an Immortal on the spot and transport him to P'eng-lai Mountain forthwith.[1]

His test for avarice was simple. Upon meeting a foot-traveler in lane or road, he would turn a pebble into gold by pointing his finger at it. He would then offer the golden pebble to the traveler.

The first person he met accepted the pebble eagerly, but then, turning it over and over between his fingers, his eyes beginning to gleam and glint, he said, "Can you do the same thing again? To those?" and he pointed at a small heap of stones at their feet.

The Immortal shook his head sadly and went on.

The second person looked at the proffered golden pebble long and thoughtfully. "Ah," he finally said, his eyes narrowed in calculation, "but this is a fine thing you would give me. It will feed my family for a year, and feed them well, but what then? Back to rice water and elm bark? That would be a cruelty. How could I face their tears and laments? Kind sir, as it is such an effortless task for you, perhaps you could turn your finger toward something a little larger, like, for example"—and he pointed at a boulder as big as himself beside the road—"that bit of stone?"

All along the way the story was the same, until the Immortal despaired of finding human beings whose cupidity did not outweigh their gratitude. After many a weary mile's walking, he came upon a man of middle years stumping along the lane and, greeting him, said, "I should like to make you a present." He pointed his finger at a stone, and it turned into gold before their eyes.

The man studied the gleaming chunk of stone, his head canted[2] to one side. "What sort of trick is that?" he asked with a frown.

---

1. forthwith (fôrth′ with′) *adv.*: At once.

2. canted (kant'd) *v.*: Tilted.

"No trick," said the Immortal. "Pick it up. Or would you prefer a larger stone?" He pointed his finger at a small rock, and it instantly blossomed gold. "Take it, brother. It is yours. I give it to you."

The man thought a while, then slowly shook his head. "No-o-o. Not that it's not a very clever trick, and a pretty sight to see."

With growing excitement the Immortal pointed at a larger rock and a larger, until their eyes were dazzled by the glint of gold all round them, but each time the man shook his head, and each time the shake became more decisive. Had he found his unselfish man at last? Should he transform him this instant into an Immortal and carry him back to P'eng-lai?

"But every human being desires *something*," the Immortal said, all but convinced that this was untrue. "Tell me what it is you want!"

"Your finger," said the man.

THINKING ABOUT THE SELECTION

Recalling

1. What is the Immortal seeking on earth?
2. What test does he use for this purpose?
3. What does the test reveal?

Interpreting

4. In what way does the third man seem at first different from the first two?
5. Why does the Immortal grow more and more excited as he speaks with the third man?
6. What is suggested by the very last sentence?

Applying

7. What does this story imply about the values or beliefs of the people who told it?

ANALYZING LITERATURE

Understanding a Folk Tale

Folk tales are part of our oral tradition. They are created by ordinary people and preserved by word of mouth. The tale is passed down from one generation to the next for many years, even centuries. Usually, if a folk tale is at last written down, it is because someone felt it ought to be preserved so that people of other lands can enjoy it.

1. In what way does "The Pointing Finger" remind you of other folk tales?
2. This folk tale is several hundred years old. Why do you think it has lasted so long?

CRITICAL THINKING AND READING

Evaluating Generalizations

A **generalization** is an idea or statement that covers a great many specific cases. For example, near the end of "The Pointing Finger" the Immortal says, "But every human being desires something." This is a generalization because the statement covers all human beings.

Generalizations need to be evaluated for their truth. To evaluate a generalization, look at the evidence. Does it indicate that the statement is solidly grounded in facts? Are there no exceptions—specific cases that do not fit the statement?

1. Evaluate the generalization that "every human being desires something."
2. Tell why it would or would not have been reasonable for the Immortal to make the generalization that all humans are greedy.

UNDERSTANDING LANGUAGE

Matching Meaning with Context

Many English words have more than one meaning. Often it is only the context that suggests which one of a word's meanings a writer intends. For example, the word *immortal* is frequently used to mean a person who has gained lasting fame. But in "The Pointing Finger," this word means an undying, godlike person.

What is the meaning in context of the italicized words below?

1. " 'Ah,' [the second person] finally said, his eyes narrowed in *calculation*."
2. "[The Immortal] came upon a man of *middle years* . . . "
3. "[The Immortals] found the mortals of today to have the same shortcomings and the same *longcomings* as those of yesterday."

THINKING AND WRITING

Summarizing a Folk Tale

Summarizing a folk tale means retelling it in shortened form. Summarize "The Pointing Finger." Before you write, think about the several events that make up the story. Think about the characters' motives and purposes. When you write your summary, make clear not only what happens but also why it happens. When you revise, check your summary against the folk tale. Did you cover all the main incidents? Did you make clear why things happen as they do?

GUIDE FOR READING

All Stories Are Anansi's

This folk tale comes from the **Ashanti** (ə shän′ tē), who ruled a large empire in West Africa during the 1700's and 1800's. Today, the Ashanti are an important people in the West African country of Ghana. They have made key contributions to farming, mining, and forestry. The Ashanti have also earned a reputation as skillful weavers.

    Harold Courlander (1908–   ) received a Guggenheim fellowship for work on African culture and has written versions of folk tales from many nations.

Folk Tales: The Trickster

Like fables, many folk tales contain animals that talk and behave like humans. One of the best-loved animal characters in folk tales is the **trickster,** who relies on brains rather than strength or speed. The trickster is usually able to outwit bigger and stronger animals. For many North American Indians, the coyote played the role of the shrewd trickster. In African folklore, however, the slyest creature is often Kwaku Anansi (kwä′ kōō ə nän′ sē), the spider.

Look For

As you read, look for the ways in which Anansi appeals to the fears or vanity of his victims in order to fool them.

Writing

Choose a type of animal that you think would make a good trickster. Write a description of this animal. In your description, explain the reasons for your choice.

Vocabulary

Knowing the following words will help you as you read "All Stories Are Anansi's."

yearned (yɵrnd) *v.*: Wanted very much (p. 611)

gourd (gôrd) *n.*: Fruit of a certain kind of plant; the dried, hollowed-shell of this fruit is used as a drinking cup or dipper (p. 611)

acknowledge (ək näl′ ij) *v.*: To recognize and admit (p. 612)

All Stories Are Anansi's

from the Ashanti (Ghana)
Harold Courlander

In the beginning, all tales and stories belonged to Nyame,[1] the Sky God. But Kwaku Anansi, the spider, yearned to be the owner of all the stories known in the world, and he went to Nyame and offered to buy them.

The Sky God said: "I am willing to sell the stories, but the price is high. Many people have come to me offering to buy, but the price was too high for them. Rich and powerful families have not been able to pay. Do you think you can do it?"

Anansi replied to the Sky God: "I can do it. What is the price?"

"My price is three things," the Sky God said. "I must first have Mmoboro,[2] the hornets. I must then have Onini,[3] the great python. I must then have Osebo,[4] the leopard. For these things I will sell you the right to tell all stories."

Anansi said: "I will bring them."

He went home and made his plans. He first cut a gourd from a vine and made a small hole in it. He took a large calabash[5] and filled it with water. He went to the tree where the hornets lived. He poured some of the water over himself, so that he was dripping. He threw some water over the hornets, so that they too were dripping. Then he put the calabash on his head, as though to protect himself from a storm, and called out to the hornets: "Are you foolish people? Why do you stay in the rain that is falling?"

The hornets answered: "Where shall we go?"

"Go here, in this dry gourd," Anansi told them.

The hornets thanked him and flew into the gourd through the small hole. When the last of them had entered, Anansi plugged the hole with a ball of grass, saying: "Oh, yes, but you are really foolish people!"

He took the gourd full of hornets to Nyame, the Sky God. The Sky God accepted them. He said: "There are two more things."

Anansi returned to the forest and cut a long bamboo pole and some strong vines. Then he walked toward the house of Onini, the python, talking to himself. He said: "My wife is stupid. I say he is longer and stronger. My wife says he is shorter and weaker. I give him more respect. She gives him less respect. Is she right or am I right? I am right, he is longer. I am right, he is stronger."

When Onini, the python, heard Anansi talking to himself, he said: "Why are you arguing this way with yourself?"

---

1. **Nyame** (nē ä′ mē)
2. **Mmoboro** (mō bô′ rō)
3. **Onini** (ō nē′ nē)
4. **Osebo** (ō sā′ bō)
5. **calabash** (kal′ ə bash′) *n.:* A large fruit that is dried and made into a bowl or cup.

"All Stories Are Anansi's" in *The Hat-Shaking Dance And Other Ashanti Tales from Ghana*, by Harold Courlander with Albert Kofi Prempeh. Harcourt Brace Jovanovich. Reprinted by permission of Harold Courlander. © 1957, 1985 by Harold Courlander.

The spider replied: "Ah, I have had a dispute with my wife. She says you are shorter and weaker than this bamboo pole. I say you are longer and stronger."

Onini said: "It's useless and silly to argue when you can find out the truth. Bring the pole and we will measure."

So Anansi laid the pole on the ground, and the python came and stretched himself out beside it.

"You seem a little short," Anansi said.

The python stretched further.

"A little more," Anansi said.

"I can stretch no more," Onini said.

"When you stretch at one end, you get shorter at the other end," Anansi said. "Let me tie you at the front so you don't slip."

He tied Onini's head to the pole. Then he went to the other end and tied the tail to the pole. He wrapped the vine all around Onini, until the python couldn't move.

"Onini," Anansi said, "it turns out that my wife was right and I was wrong. You are shorter than the pole and weaker. My opinion wasn't as good as my wife's. But you were even more foolish than I, and you are now my prisoner."

Anansi carried the python to Nyame, the Sky God, who said: "There is one thing more."

Osebo, the leopard, was next. Anansi went into the forest and dug a deep pit where the leopard was accustomed to walk. He covered it with small branches and leaves and put dust on it, so that it was impossible to tell where the pit was. Anansi went away and hid. When Osebo came prowling in the black of night, he stepped into the trap Anansi had prepared and fell to the bottom. Anansi heard the sound of the leopard falling, and he said: "Ah, Osebo, you are half-foolish!"

When morning came, Anansi went to the pit and saw the leopard there.

"Osebo," he asked, "what are you doing in this hole?"

"I have fallen into a trap," Osebo said. "Help me out."

"I would gladly help you," Anansi said. "But I'm sure that if I bring you out, I will have no thanks for it. You will get hungry, and later on you will be wanting to eat me and my children."

"I swear it won't happen!" Osebo said.

"Very well. Since you swear it, I will take you out." Anansi said.

He bent a tall green tree toward the ground, so that its top was over the pit, and he tied it that way. Then he tied a rope to the top of the tree and dropped the other end of it into the pit.

"Tie this to your tail," he said.

Osebo tied the rope to his tail.

"Is it well tied?" Anansi asked.

"Yes, it is well tied," the leopard said.

"In that case," Anansi said, "you are not merely half-foolish, you are all-foolish."

And he took his knife and cut the other rope, the one that held the tree bowed to the ground. The tree straightened up with a snap, pulling Osebo out of the hole. He hung in the air head downward, twisting and turning. And while he hung this way, Anansi killed him with his weapons.

Then he took the body of the leopard and carried it to Nyame, the Sky God, saying: "Here is the third thing. Now I have paid the price."

Nyame said to him: "Kwaku Anansi, great warriors and chiefs have tried, but they have been unable to do it. You have done it. Therefore, I will give you the stories. From this day onward, all stories belong to you. Whenever a man tells a story, he must acknowledge that it is Anansi's tale."

In this way Anansi, the spider, became the owner of all stories that are told. To Anansi all these tales belong.

THINKING ABOUT THE SELECTION

Recalling

1. What does Anansi want from Nyame? What is Nyame's price?
2. How does Anansi capture the hornets, the python, and the leopard?

Interpreting

3. Why do you think Anansi values so highly what Nyame owns?
4. What is Anansi's attitude toward the other animals?
5. Why is Anansi able to do what great warriors and chiefs have tried to do but have been unable to do?

Applying

6. Why do you think people enjoy folk tales in which animals behave like humans?

ANALYZING LITERATURE

Understanding the Trickster in Folklore

The trickster is a character in folklore, usually an animal, who relies on brains rather than strength or speed to accomplish his or her goals. In "All Stories Are Anansi's," the spider fools animals that could easily defeat him in a contest of strength.

1. What qualities does Anansi display?
2. How does each of these qualities help him succeed?
3. Why do you think the trickster has been such a popular character in folklore?
4. Modern versions of the trickster appear in literature and movies. For example, Captain Kirk of *Star Trek* displays many of the trickster's characteristics. What other figures can be considered tricksters? Explain your choices.

CRITICAL THINKING AND READING

Making Inferences About Characters

An **inference** is a conclusion based on evidence. You can make inferences about animal characters in folk tales just as you would about a character in a short story or novel. In "All Stories Are Anansi's," the trickster helps you to make inferences about the other animals by pointing up their weaknesses.

1. What can you infer about the hornets based on their response to Anansi's warning?
2. What do you infer about the python when he keeps stretching to make himself as long as the pole?
3. Why must a trickster be able to make inferences about other animals?

THINKING AND WRITING

Writing a Folk Tale

Write your own folk tale modeled on the Anansi story. You might start with the animal trickster you wrote about before reading this tale. Give him or her some goal to be achieved by trickery. Create three animal characters your trickster must deceive. When you revise your tale, try to increase the cleverness of the tricks. You might also try to make your tale convey an idea or teach a lesson. Share your folk tale with your classmates.

GUIDE FOR READING

The Little Lizard's Sorrow

Vietnam is a tropical country in Southeast Asia. The most popular form of literature in Vietnam is poetry, and poets are greatly respected there. This land also has a deeply rooted tradition of folk tales, of which "The Little Lizard's Sorrow" is an excellent example.

Mai Vo-Dinh (1933–   ), who translated the tale, was born in Vietnam. He came to live in the United States in 1960. He is not only a writer and translator of Vietnamese literature but also a painter and illustrator of books.

Symbols in Folk Tales

A **symbol** is an object that stands for an idea but also has its own existence. A dove, for example, is a symbol of peace. Symbols are frequently used in folk tales to express an idea in a concrete and memorable way.

Look For

As you read "The Little Lizard's Sorrow," look for those objects that seem to seem to have special meanings. Figure out what those special meanings might be.

Writing

Many interesting stories have been written in which games are of central importance. Make up a game in which a player can win or lose something that really matters. Describe the object of the game and its rules.

Vocabulary

Knowing the following words will help you as you read "The Little Lizard's Sorrow."

emitting (i mit′ iŋ) *v.*: Sending out or uttering (p. 615)

gaunt (gônt) *adj.*: Thin and bony (p. 615)

pauper (pô′ pər) *n.*: An extremely poor person (p. 615)

chortle (chor′ t'l) *v.*: Make an amused chuckling or snorting sound (p. 616)

domestic (də mes′ tik) *n.*: A servant for the home (p. 616)

harassed (hə rast′) *v.*: Troubled (p. 618)

The Little Lizard's Sorrow

from **Vietnam**

Translated by Mai Vo-Dinh

There is in Vietnam a certain species of small lizard only three inches long with webbed feet and a short, round head. They are often seen indoors, running swiftly upside down on the ceiling or along the walls, emitting little snapping cries that sound like "Tssst . . . tssst!" Suppose that you drop an egg on the kitchen floor; the kind of sound you would make then, with the tip of your tongue between your teeth, is like the cry of these harmless, funny little lizards. Sounds of mild sorrow, of genuine shock but somehow humorous regret that seem to say, "Oh, if only I had been . . . If only I had known . . . Oh, what a pity, what a pity . . . Tssst! Tssst!"

There was once a very rich man whose house was immense and filled with treasures. His land was so extensive that, as the Vietnamese say, "Cranes fly over it with outstretched wings," for cranes only do so over very long distances. Wealth breeding vanity, one of the rich man's greatest pleasures was beating other rich men at a game he himself had invented. One player would announce one of his rare possessions, the other would counter the challenge by saying that he, too—if he really did—owned such a treasure.

"A stable of fifty buffalos," one man would say. The other would reply, "Yes, I also have fifty of them." It was then his turn to announce, "I sleep in an all-teak[1] bed encrusted with mother-of-pearl."[2] The first player would lose if he slept on cherry planks![3]

One day, a stranger came to the rich man's house. Judging from his appearance, the gatekeeper did not doubt that the visitor was a madman. He wanted, he said, to play the famous game with the mansion's master. Yet dressed in clothes that looked as if they had been mended hundreds of times, and wearing broken straw sandals, the stranger appeared to be anything but a wealthy man. Moreover, his face was gaunt and pale as if he had not had a good meal in days. But there was such proud, quiet dignity to the stranger that the servant did not dare shut the gates in his face. Instead, he meekly went to inform his master of the unlikely visitor's presence. Intrigued, the man ordered that the pauper be ushered in.

Trying to conceal his curiosity and sur-

---

1. teak (tēk) *n.*: Yellowish-brown wood used for furniture.
2. mother-of-pearl *n.*: The hard, pearly inside of certain seashells.
3. cherry planks *n.*: Wood from a cherry tree.

prise, the rich man offered his visitor the very best chair and served him hot, perfumed tea.

"Well, stranger, is it true that you have deigned[4] to come here to play a game of riches with me?" he began inquiringly.

The visitor was apparently unimpressed by the rich surroundings, giving them only a passing, casual look. Perfectly at ease, sipping his tea from the rare porcelain cup, he answered in a quiet though self-assured voice, "Yes, sir, that is if you, too, so wish."

"Naturally, naturally," the rich man raised his hand in a sweeping motion. "But, may I ask, with your permission, where you reside and what is your honorable occupation?"

The stranger gave a little chortle, visibly amused. "Sir, would you gain any to know about these? I came here simply to play your game; only, I have two conditions, if you are so generous as to allow them."

"By all means! Pray, tell me what they are," the rich man readily inquired.

The visitor sat farther back on the brocaded chair, his voice soft and confidential. "Well, here they are. A game is no fun if the winner does not win anything and the loser does not lose anything. Therefore I would suggest that if I win I would take everything in your possession—your lands, your stables, your servants, your house and everything contained in it. But if you win—" Here the stranger paused, his eyes narrowed ever so slightly, full of humorous malice, "If you win, you would become the owner of everything that belongs to me." The stranger paused again. "And what belongs to me, sir, you will have no idea of. I am one of the most fortunate men alive, sir. . . . And besides that," he added with a knowing look, "I

would remain in this house to serve you as a domestic the rest of my life."

For a long moment, the rich man sat back in silence. Another long moment went by, then the rich man spoke: "That's agreed. But, please tell me your other condition."

Eyes dreamy, the stranger looked out of the window. "My second condition, sir, is not so much a condition as a request. I hope you would not mind giving me, a visitor, an edge over you. May I be allowed to ask the first question?"

The rich man thought for a long second, then said, "That is also agreed. Let's begin."

"Do I really understand that you have agreed to both my conditions?" the stranger asked thoughtfully.

Something in the visitor's manner and voice hurt the rich man's pride. He was ready to stake his very life on this game that he himself had created. There was no way out. "Yes," he said. "Yes, indeed I have. Now tell me, please, what do you have that I have not got?" The stranger smiled. Reaching to his feet, he took up his traveling bag, a coarse cotton square tied together by the

---

4. deigned (dānd) *v.*: Graciously agreed to do something beneath him.

four ends. Opening it slowly, ceremoniously, he took out an object and handed it to his host without a word. It was an empty half of a coconut shell, old and chipped, the kind poor people use as a container to drink water from.

"A coconut-shell cup!" the rich man exclaimed. One could not know whether he was merely amused or completely shattered.

"Yes, sir, a coconut-shell cup. A *chipped* shell cup. I use it to drink from on my wanderings. I am a wanderer," the visitor said quietly.

Holding the shell between his thumb and his forefinger and looking as if he had never seen such an object before, the rich man interrupted, "But, but you don't mean that I do not have a thing like this?"

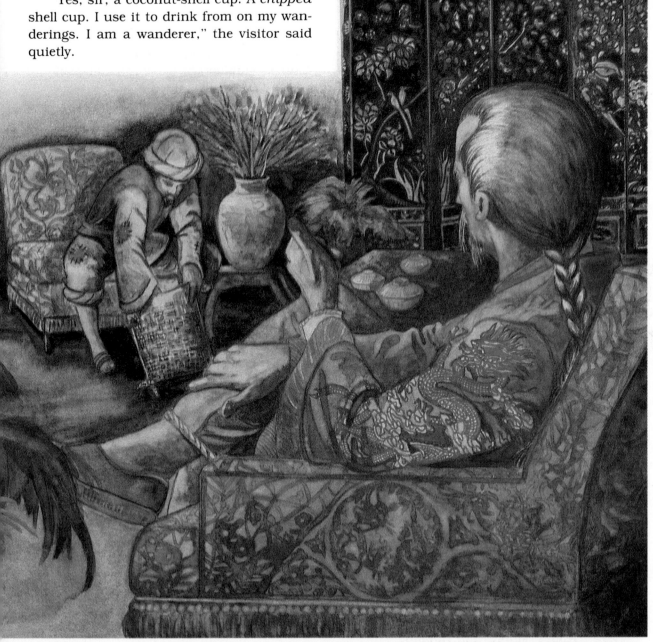

"No, sir, you have not. How could you?" the stranger replied.

Turning the residence upside down, the man and his servants discovered odds and ends of one thousand and one kinds, but they were unable to produce a drinking cup made from a coconut shell. In the servants' quarters, however, they found a few such utensils, but they were all brand new, not chipped. One could imagine that the servants of such a wealthy man would not deign to drink from a chipped cup. Even a beggar would throw it away. . . .

"You see, sir," the stranger said to the rich man once they were again seated across the tea table, "you see, I am a wanderer, as I have said. I am a free man. This cup here is several years old and my only possession besides these poor clothes I have on. If you do not think me too immodest, I would venture that I treasure it more than you do all of your collections of fine china. But, from this day, I am the owner and lone master of all that belongs to you. . . ."

Having taken possession of the rich man's land, houses, herds and all his other treasures, the stranger began to give them away to the poor and needy people. Then, one day, taking up his old cotton bag, he left the village and no one ever saw him again.

As for the dispossessed rich man, it is believed that he died of grief and regret and was transformed into this small lizard. Curiously, one sees him scurrying about only indoors. Running up and down the walls, crossing the ceiling, staring at people and furniture, he never stops his "Tssst, Tssst." Vietnamese children, in particular, are very fond of him for he looks so harassed, so funny.

But, oh, such sorrow, such regret, such self-pity.

THINKING ABOUT THE SELECTION

Recalling

1. Describe the game the rich man plays with other rich men.
2. Why does the servant not send the miserable-looking visitor away?
3. What two conditions for the game does the stranger request?
4. How does he defeat the rich man?
5. What does he do with his possessions?
6. What happens to the rich man at the end of the story?

Interpreting

7. Why does the stranger describe himself as one of the most fortunate men alive? Do you agree with this opinion? Why or why not?
8. Why does he treasure his coconut-shell cup more than the rich man treasures his china?
9. Why do you think the rich man is changed into a lizard rather than some other animal?
10. In what way does this folk tale teach a lesson in living?

Applying

11. J. Brotherton once wrote: "My riches consist not in the extent of my possessions but in the fewness of my wants." Would the stranger agree or disagree with him? Explain your answer.

ANALYZING LITERATURE

Understanding Symbols in Folk Tales

When some object—whether living or nonliving—seems to stand out as especially important in a folk tale, it is probably a **symbol**. In "The Little Lizard's Sorrow," the lizard and the coconut-shell cup are two such objects.

1. What human feelings are associated with the little lizard at the beginning and the end of the tale?
2. What, therefore, might the lizard symbolize?
3. What is said about the coconut-shell cup that suggests its importance to the stranger?
4. What might it symbolize?

UNDERSTANDING LANGUAGE

Recognizing the Root *mit*

Many English words are built on the Latin root *mit,* which is also spelled *miss*. It means "send." In the folk tale, the little lizard is described as "emitting little snapping cries . . ." Here "emitting" means "sending out." Recognizing this root and knowing what it means will help you to understand some unfamiliar words you may meet in your reading. Figure out what each of the following italicized words mean. Then check a dictionary to see if you were right.

1. Since I accidently paid too much for the game, the store *remitted* three dollars to me.
2. Try to *commit* these safety rules to memory.
3. The *transmission* of radio waves is often affected by weather conditions.

THINKING AND WRITING

Writing a Folk Tale with a Symbol

Using your description of the game you made up before reading this tale, write a folk tale modeled on "The Little Lizard's Sorrow." Include an object that symbolizes some important idea you wish to express. When you revise your work, check that your symbol fits in well with the rest of the story and helps to reveal its meaning. Share your folk tale with your classmates.

Making Generalizations

One way to increase your understanding of what you read and to get deeper meanings from it is to make generalizations. A generalization is a general statement or rule that is drawn from specific facts. It is a conclusion that is true for a number of different cases or situations.

Sound Generalizations

Louis Untermeyer in his adaptation of "The Boy and the Wolf" makes a sound generalization when he concludes that "Liars are not believed, forsooth, even when liars tell the truth." This is a generalization drawn from the facts that occurred in the fable. The boy had cried, "Wolf!" two different times when there really was no wolf about. The villagers had responded to his cry each time and searched for the wolf. However, when they realized none was around, they lost faith in the boy and considered him a liar. Therefore, when he cried wolf because there really was a wolf, none of the villagers would come. He was not believed because he had lied to them in the past. This is a sound generalization because the facts support it and it is generally true. People usually do not trust liars.

It is important to evaluate a generalization by determining if the facts do support it and if it applies to a number of other situations or cases besides the one you are considering. Be aware that a generalization does not have to apply to all cases.

Hasty Generalizations

Sometimes a generalization is drawn from insufficient facts or evidence. When this happens, it is called a **hasty generalization**. For instance, if you had drawn the conclusion that "Boys who watch sheep do not tell the truth" from "The Boy and the Wolf" fable, you would have made a hasty generalization. You have only one instance of a boy who watched sheep who did not tell the truth. There are insufficient facts to draw this conclusion.

Sometimes a hasty generalization is too broad for the facts it supports. For instance, the boy in the fable despised his work and liked to sleep. Therefore, when a lamb was lost, he shouted, "Wolf!" to get the villagers to come. If you had said, "All people who dislike their work lie," you would have drawn a generalization that is too broad. You do not have a sufficient number of cases to base this on; you have only one instance of a boy who disliked his work and lied. Avoid using words such as "all," "never," "must," and "definitely" because these kinds of words do not allow for any exceptions to the general rule.

Guidelines

- Make sure you understand the main idea and supporting details of the material.
- Make sure the conclusions you draw are adequately supported by facts or evidence.
- Make sure the generalization you draw applies to many different cases or situations.
- Make sure you do not use words such as "always" or "must," which do not allow for any exceptions and which make the generalization too broad.

Activity

Read each of the following statements. Identify whether each is a sound generalization or a hasty generalization.

1. The fables "The Fox and the Crow" and "The Town Mouse and the Country Mouse" were written by Aesop. Aesop is a Greek. Therefore, all fables were written by Greeks.
2. Liars never tell the truth.
3. People sometimes lie to get out of doing work.
4. Boys are not to be trusted with sheep.
5. Some fables were written by Greeks.

Activity

Read each set of statements below. Then make a generalization that is based on the set.

1. "The Fox and the Crow" is a fable about animals. "The Town Mouse and the Country Mouse" is a fable about animals. Aesop wrote many other fables about animals.
2. "Narcissus" is a myth that explains how the narcissus flower got its name. "Phaëthon, Son of Apollo" is a myth that explains how the North African plain became a desert and why the poplar trees weep tears of amber. "Popocatepetl and Ixtlaccihuatl" explains the existence of these two volcanoes.
3. "Popocatepetl and Ixtlaccihuatl" is a Mexican legend. "The Legend of the Hummingbird" is a Puerto Rican legend. "Ojeeg, the Hunter, and the Ice Man" is a Micmac legend.

YOU THE WRITER

Assignment

1. Write a fable that contains animals who act like human beings.

Prewriting. Make a list of morals, or clever sayings. You might work with a small group of students to create this list. Choose the moral about which you intend to write your fable. Choose an animal. Prepare a story chart in which you give the animal a problem, show it acting to solve the problem, and have it succeed or fail in solving the problem.

Writing. Now write your fable. Since showing is more dramatic than telling, show the characters in your story doing things: thinking, talking, acting. Bring them into conflict with each other. End your fable with your moral.

Revising. When you revise, check to see that you have followed the basics of good storytelling. Have you punctuated the speech of your characters accurately?

Assignment

2. Write a myth that explains one of the following: a. Why grass is green; b. Why there are stars in the sky; c. Why it must be cold in order for it to snow.

Prewriting. Relax and let your imagination roam. You may know the historical and scientific explanations for the topics listed above, but forget them and think up imaginative, mythical reasons for each. Remember, a good story is built around a conflict, so bring two people, or two giants, or two supernatural characters, or any mixture of the above, into conflict with each other.

Writing. When you write, focus on the conflict between the characters. Let the mythic explanation for your topic be revealed through the conflict.

Revising. When you revise, check to see that your story has a strong conflict and a surprising resolution. Also, is your explanation of the topic original, maybe even ingenious?

Assignment

3. Choose a person from American history, either someone from the past or someone still alive. Then write a legend about him or her.

Prewriting. Before you write, jot down information about the life of the character you intend to write about. Then confront your character with a problem. Freewrite about the outcome.

Writing. When narrating your legend, try to capture the oral style legends are told in. Make the hero's opponent and everything else in the story larger than life. Let the characters talk to each other, and be sure that what they say and the way they say it reflect the way they think.

Revising. Check to see that your hero's character and actions are consistent with the way he or she behaved.

YOU THE CRITIC

Assignment

1. Choose one fable from this section and write an essay in which you tell what lesson the fable teaches, cite words from the fable that tell what the lesson is, and indicate what made the fable effective.

    Prewriting. Before you read, freewrite about the moral of the fable you have chosen.

    Writing. Now write your essay. Start by stating your main idea. Then support your main idea by referring to specific characters and incidents in the fable.

    Revising. Make sure you have clearly stated the moral of the fable and shown why the fable was effective.

Assignment

2. Choose three selections from this section and write an essay explaining how they show that the peoples of the world are similar to modern citizens of the United States in some ways and different from us in other ways.

    Prewriting. Before you write, scan through the selections in this section. Draw up a list of similarities and differences.

    Writing. Using the list of similarities and differences you have drawn up, write your essay. After stating your main idea, tell about the similarities you have found, using specific references from the selections you have chosen and from life in the United States today. Next tell about the differences, again using specific references. Conclude your essay by restating the main-idea sentence.

    Revising. When you revise, make sure you have supported your main idea. Combine as many sentences as possible.

Assignment

3. Folk tales and legends often reflect the qualities that are admired by a certain society. For example, people who live in extremely cold climates might write about heroes who confront the Ice Demon and win. Select a legend or folk tale and write an essay discussing how it reflects qualities admired by the particular culture.

    Prewriting. Freewrite about the main character. Explore the qualities this character displayed.

    Writing. Write the first draft of an essay discussing the qualities the main character displayed. Speculate about why this culture may have admired these qualities. Be sure to use specific examples.

    Revising. Make sure you have provided adequate support for your main idea.

ON THE TRAIL
Winslow Homer
National Gallery of Art, Washington, D.C.

THE NOVEL

Like a short story, a novel is fiction. It is made up from an author's imagination, and it has the basic elements of fiction: plot, character, setting, and theme. The most obvious difference between a short story and a novel is length. A novel is longer—often much longer—than a short story. Because of its length, there are other differences, too. A novel often includes more characters than a short story. The plot may be more complicated. The setting may include a number of different places, and the time of the action may extend over months, years, and even decades. Most important, the total effect of a novel is different from that of a short story. A good short story makes a single, sharp impression on the reader. The effect of a novel, on the other hand, is like traveling to and getting to know a new part of the world. You get impression after impression, and you learn more and more about the people and their lives. At last, you feel that you have entered into that part of the world and that it has become part of you.

READING ACTIVELY

Background

This novel is set in the area of the country that the author, Wilson Rawls, knows best—the beautiful hills and river bottoms of the Ozark mountains in eastern Oklahoma. This land is characterized by its many streams and river valleys. The soil is very fertile, ideal for farming, and the wooded areas support a wide variety of animal life, including deer, opossums, raccoons, foxes, and squirrels. Rawls spent much of his time in these woods with the family hound dog. In fact, Rawls told his first stories to his dog.

Reading Strategies

As you read the novel, you will discover that it presents different advantages and problems from shorter works of fiction. Some advantages to the extended length of a novel are that the characters develop more fully and realistically, the plot can be more complex, more than one theme can be presented, and themes can be developed more fully than in shorter fiction. One of the problems is that unlike short stories, which are usually read in one sitting, the extended nature of a novel requires that it be read at intervals over a longer period of time. Because of this, readers sometimes forget portions of what they have read previously. It might help if you summarize what you have learned after you finish reading each portion of the novel. When you are ready to continue later, review the events and characters from the previous section. Finally, as you read, interact with the literature by using the active reading strategies: question, predict, clarify, summarize, and pull together.

Themes

You will encounter the following themes:
- The passage from youth to maturity
- The rewards of hard work and diligence
- The achievements gained through love and understanding
- The need to work together to achieve common goals

Characters

Become familiar with the following characters before you read:
Billy—the teenager who develops a close relationship with his two hound dogs
Papa—Billy's father, who is beginning to treat him like a man
Mama—Billy's mother, who tries to help him with all his problems
Grandpa—Billy's grandfather, who is Billy's good friend and advisor
Little Ann—Billy's female hound, the smaller and smarter dog
Old Dan—Billy's male hound, who is bigger and stronger

Where the Red Fern Grows

HUNTER IN THE ADIRONDACKS, 1892 (detail)
Winslow Homer
Courtesy of the Harvard University
Art Museums

GUIDE FOR READING

Where the Red Fern Grows, Chapters 1–7

Wilson Rawls (1913–   ) was born and raised in Oklahoma. He wrote stories throughout his life but felt that his lack of education prevented him from producing anything that was worthy of being published. It was not until 1959 that he, with the encouragement and help of his wife, rewrote a previously destroyed manuscript for his first novel, *Where the Red Fern Grows*. In this novel, Rawls draws upon his experiences as a youth exploring the hills and rivers around his home with his only companion at the time, an old hound dog.

Character

Characters are the people in a novel. As in a short story, characters have traits that make them seem like real people. However, because a novel is longer then a short story, characters may be developed more fully—they can change or grow over time. You can see how a character develops and grows as the novel progresses.

The main character in *Where the Red Fern Grows* is a boy named Billy. Billy is also the narrator of the story. You first meet him as a man, who then tells the story of his childhood. Because the story is told by Billy, you learn about the events as he sees them or makes them happen. Therefore, you learn about his qualities "from the inside out," that is, through what he says and what he does. You learn about the other characters only as they relate to Billy or as he thinks about them.

Look For

As you read Chapters 1–7, you will get to know the main character, Billy. What are the major traits of his character? What does he do or say that shows these traits?

Writing

In the opening chapters of *Where the Red Fern Grows,* Billy sets a goal for himself, which he works extremely hard to achieve. Have you ever set a goal that you had to plan for and work hard to achieve? Describe the steps you took to reach your goal.

Vocabulary

Knowing the following words will help you as you read Chapters 1–7 of *Where the Red Fern Grows*.

quavering (kwā′ vər iŋ) *v.*: Shaking or trembling (p. 641)

riffle (rif′ ′l) *n.*: A shallow area in a stream (p. 643)

winced (wins′ ′d) *v.*: Drew back slightly, twisting the face, as in pain or alarm (p. 644)

runt (runt) *n.*: The smallest animal of a litter (p. 651)

Where the Red Fern Grows

Wilson Rawls

Chapter 1

When I left my office that beautiful spring day, I had no idea what was in store for me. To begin with, everything was too perfect for anything unusual to happen. It was one of those days when a man feels good, feels like speaking to his neighbor, is glad to live in a country like ours, and proud of his government. You know what I mean, one of those rare days when everything is right and nothing is wrong.

I was walking along whistling when I heard the dogfight. At first I paid no attention to it. After all it wasn't anything to get excited about, just another dogfight in a residential section.

As the sound of the fight grew nearer, I could tell there were quite a few dogs mixed up in it. They boiled out of an alley, turned, and headed straight toward me. Not wanting to get bitten or run over, I moved over to the edge of the sidewalk.

I could see that all the dogs were fighting one. About twenty-five feet from me they caught him and down he went. I felt sorry for the unfortunate one. I knew if something wasn't done quickly the sanitation department would have to pick up a dead dog.

I was trying to make up my mind to help when I got a surprise. Up out of that snarling, growling, slashing mass reared an old redbone hound.[1] For a second I saw him. I caught my breath. I couldn't believe what I had seen.

Twisting and slashing, he fought his way through the pack and backed up under the low branches of a hedge. Growling and snarling, they formed a half-moon circle around him. A big bird dog, bolder than the others, darted in. The hedge shook as he tangled with the hound. He came out so fast he fell over backwards. I saw that his right ear was split wide open. It was too much for him and he took off down the street, squalling like a scalded cat.

A big ugly cur tried his luck. He didn't get off so easy. He came out with his left shoulder laid open to the bone. He sat down on his rear and let the world know that he had been hurt.

By this time, my fighting blood was boiling. It's hard for a man to stand and watch an old hound fight against such odds, especially if that man has memories in his heart like I had in mine. I had seen the time when an old hound like that had given his life so that I might live.

Taking off my coat, I waded in. My yelling and scolding didn't have much effect, but the swinging coat did. The dogs scattered and left.

Down on my knees, I peered back under the hedge. The hound was still mad. He growled at me and showed his teeth. I knew it wasn't his nature to fight a man.

In a soft voice, I started talking to him. "Come on, boy," I said. "It's all right. I'm your friend. Come on now."

---

1. **redbone hound:** A medium-sized, fast, dark red or red and tan hound used especially for hunting coon.

The fighting fire slowly left his eyes. He bowed his head and his long, red tail started thumping the ground. I kept coaxing. On his stomach, an inch at a time, he came to me and laid his head in my hand.

I almost cried at what I saw. His coat was dirty and mud-caked. His skin was stretched drum-tight over his bony frame. The knotty joints of his hips and shoulders stood out a good three inches from his body. I could tell he was starved.

I couldn't figure it out. He didn't belong in town. He was far out of place with the boxers, poodles, bird dogs, and other breeds of town dogs. He belonged in the country. He was a hunting hound.

I raised one of his paws. There I read the story. The pads were worn down slick as the rind on an apple. I knew he had come a long way, and no doubt had a long way to go. Around his neck was a crude collar. On closer inspection, I saw it had been made from a piece of check-line leather. Two holes had been punched in each end and the ends were laced together with bailing wire.

As I turned the collar with my finger, I saw something else. There, scratched deep in the tough leather, was the name "Buddie." I guessed that the crude, scribbly letters had probably been written by a little boy.

It's strange indeed how memories can lie dormant in a man's mind for so many years. Yet those memories can be awakened and brought forth fresh and new, just by something you've seen, or something you've heard, or the sight of an old familiar face.

What I saw in the warm gray eyes of the friendly old hound brought back wonderful memories. To show my gratitude, I took hold of his collar and said, "Come on, boy, let's go home and get something to eat."

He seemed to understand that he had found a friend. He came willingly.

I gave him a bath and rubbed all the soreness from his muscles. He drank quarts of warm milk and ate all the meat I had in the house. I hurried down to the store and bought more. He ate until he was satisfied.

He slept all that night and most of the next day. Late in the afternoon he grew restless. I told him I understood, and as soon as it was dark, he could be on his way. I figured he had a much better chance if he left town at night.

That evening, a little after sundown, I opened the back gate. He walked out, stopped, turned around, and looked at me. He thanked me by wagging his tail.

With tears in my eyes, I said, "You're more than welcome, old fellow. In fact, you could've stayed here as long as you wanted to."

He whined and licked my hand.

I was wondering which way he would go. With one final whimper he turned and headed east. I couldn't help smiling as I watched him trot down the alley. I noticed the way his hind quarters shifted over to the right, never in line with the front, yet always in perfect rhythm. His long ears flopped up and down, keeping time with the jogging motion of his body. Yes, they were all there, the unmistakable marks of a hunting hound.

Where the alley emptied into the street, he stopped and looked back. I waved my hand.

As I watched him disappear in the twilight shadows, I whispered these words: "Good-bye, old fellow. Good luck, and good hunting!"

I didn't have to let him go. I could have kept him in my back yard, but to pen up a dog like that is a sin. It would have broken his heart. The will to live would have slowly left his body.

I had no idea where he had come from or where he was going. Perhaps it wasn't too far, or maybe it was a long, long way. I tried to make myself believe that his home was in the Ozark Mountains somewhere in Missouri, or Oklahoma. It wasn't impossible even though it was a long way from the Snake River Valley in Idaho.

I figured something drastic must have happened in his life, as it is very unusual for a hound to be traveling all alone. Perhaps he had been stolen, or maybe he had been sold for some much-needed money. Whatever it was that had interrupted his life, he was trying to straighten it out. He was going home to the master he loved, and with the help of God, he would make it.

To him it made no difference how long the road, or how rough or rocky. His old red feet would keep jogging along, on and on, mile after mile. There would be no crying or giving up. When his feet grew tired and weary, he would curl up in the weeds and rest. Water from a rain puddle or a mountain stream would quench his thirst and cool his hot dry throat. Food found along the highway, or the offerings from a friendly hand would ease the pangs of hunger. Through the rains, the snows, or the desert heat, he would jog along, never looking back.

Some morning he would be found curled up on the front porch. The long journey would be over. He would be home. There would be a lot of tail-wagging and a few whimpering cries. His warm moist tongue would caress the hand of his master. All would be forgiven. Once again the lights would shine in his dog's world. His heart would be happy.

After my friend had disappeared in the darkness, I stood and stared at the empty alley. A strange feeling came over me. At first I thought I was lonely or sad, but I realized that wasn't it at all. The feeling was a wonderful one.

Although the old hound had no way of knowing it, he had stirred memories, and what priceless treasures they were. Memories of my boyhood days, an old K. C. Baking Powder can, and two little red hounds. Memories of a wonderful love, unselfish devotion, and death in its saddest form.

As I turned to enter my yard I started to lock the gate, and then I thought, "No, I'll leave it open. He might come back."

I was about halfway to the house when a cool breeze drifted down from the rugged Tetons.[2] It had a bite in it and goose pimples jumped out on my skin. I stopped at the woodshed and picked up several sticks of wood.

I didn't turn on any lights on entering the house. The dark, quiet atmosphere was a perfect setting for the mood I was in. I built a fire in the fireplace and pulled up my favorite rocker.

As I sat there in the silence, the fire grew larger. It crackled and popped. Firelight shadows began to shimmer and dance around the room. The warm, comfortable heat felt good.

I struck a match to light my pipe. As I did, two beautiful cups gleamed from the mantel. I held the match up so I could get a better look. There they were, sitting side by side. One was large with long, upright handles that stood out like wings on a mourning dove. The highly polished surface gleamed and glistened with a golden sheen. The other was smaller and made of silver. It was neat and trim, and sparkled like a white star in the heavens.

I got up and took them down. There was a story in those cups—a story that went back more than a half century.

As I caressed the smooth surfaces, my mind drifted back through the years, back to my boyhood days. How wonderful the memories were. Piece by piece the story unfolded.

Chapter 2

I suppose there's a time in practically every young boy's life when he's affected by that wonderful disease of puppy love. I don't mean the kind a boy has for the pretty little girl that lives down the road. I mean the real kind, the kind that has four small feet and a wiggly tail, and sharp little teeth that can gnaw on a boy's finger; the kind a boy can romp and play with, even eat and sleep with.

I was ten years old when I first became infected with this terrible disease. I'm sure no boy in the world had it worse than I did.

---

2. **Tetons** (tē′ tänz): A range of the Rocky Mountains in northwest Wyoming and southeast Idaho.

It's not easy for a young boy to want a dog and not be able to have one. It starts gnawing on his heart, and gets all mixed up in his dreams. It gets worse and worse, until finally it becomes almost unbearable.

If my dog-wanting had been that of an ordinary boy, I'm sure my mother and father would have gotten me a puppy, but my wants were different. I didn't want just one dog. I wanted two, and not just any kind of a dog. They had to be a special kind and a special breed.

I had to have some dogs. I went to my father and had a talk with him. He scratched his head and thought it over.

"Well, Billy," he said, "I heard that Old Man Hatfield's collie is going to have pups. I'm sure I can get one of them for you."

He may as well have poured cold water on me. "Papa," I said. "I don't want an old collie dog. I want hounds—coon hounds—and I want two of them."

I could tell by the look on his face that he wanted to help me, but couldn't.

He said, "Billy, those kind of dogs cost money, and that's something we don't have right now. Maybe some day when we can afford it, you can have them, but not right now."

I didn't give up. After my talk with Papa, I went to Mama. I fared no better there. Right off she said I was too young to be hunting with hounds. Besides, a hunter needed a gun, and that was one thing I couldn't have, not until I was twenty-one anyway.

I couldn't understand it. There I was sitting right in the middle of the finest hunting country in the world and I didn't even have a dog.

Our home was in a beautiful valley far back in the rugged Ozarks. The country was new and sparsely settled. The land we lived on was Cherokee land, allotted to my mother because of the Cherokee blood that flowed in her veins. It lay in a strip from the foothills of the mountains to the banks of the Illinois River in northeastern Oklahoma.

The land was rich, black, and fertile. Papa said it would grow hair on a crosscut saw. He was the first man to stick the cold steel point of a turning plow into the virgin soil.

Mama had picked the spot for our log house. It nestled at the edge of the foothills in the mouth of a small canyon, and was surrounded by a grove of huge red oaks. Behind our house one could see miles and miles of the mighty Ozarks. In the spring the aromatic scent of wild flowers, redbuds, papaws, and dogwoods, drifting on the wind currents, spread over the valley and around our home.

Below our fields, twisting and winding, ran the clear blue waters of the Illinois River. The banks were cool and shady. The rich bottom land near the river was studded with tall sycamores, birches, and box elders.

To a ten-year-old country boy it was the most beautiful place in the whole wide world, and I took advantage of it all. I roamed the hills and the river bottoms. I knew every game trail in the thick canebrakes,[3] and every animal track that was pressed in the mud along the riverbanks.

The ones that fascinated me the most were the baby-like tracks of a river coon. I'd lie for hours examining them. Before leaving, I'd take a switch and sweep them all away. These I called my "trail looks." The next day I'd hurry back, and sure enough, nine times out of ten, there in the clean-swept ground I would again find the tracks of a ringtail coon.

I knew he had passed over the trail during the night. I could close my eyes and almost see him, humped up and waddling

---

3. canebrakes (kān' brākz) *n*.: Dense growths of cane plants.

along, fishing under the banks with his delicate little paws for crawfish, frogs, and minnows.

I was a hunter from the time I could walk. I caught lizards on the rail fences, rats in the corn crib, and frogs in the little creek that ran through the fields. I was a young Daniel Boone.

As the days passed, the dog-wanting disease grew worse. I began to see dogs in my sleep. I went back to my father and mother. It was the same old story. Good hounds cost money, and they just didn't have it.

My dog-wanting became so bad I began to lose weight and my food didn't taste good any more. Mama noticed this and she had a talk with Papa.

"You're going to have to do something," she said. "I never saw a boy grieve like that. It's not right, not right at all."

"I know," said Papa, "and I feel just as badly as you do, but what can I do? You know we don't have that kind of money."

"I don't care," said Mama. "You've got to do something. I can't stand to see him cry like that. Besides he's getting to be a problem. I can't get my work done. He follows me around all day long begging for hounds."

"I offered to get him a dog," said Papa, "but he doesn't want just any kind of dog. He wants hounds, and they cost money. Do you know what the Parker boys paid for those two hounds they bought? Seventy-five dollars! If I had that much money, I'd buy another mule. I sure do need one."

I had overheard this conversation from another room. At first it made me feel pretty good. At least I was getting to be a problem. Then I didn't feel so good. I knew my mother and father were poor and didn't have any money. I began to feel sorry for them and myself.

After thinking it over, I figured out a way to help. Even though it was a great sacrifice,

I told Papa I had decided I didn't want two hounds. One would be enough. I saw the hurt in his eyes. It made me feel like someone was squeezing water out of my heart.

Papa set me on his lap and we had a good talk. He told me how hard times were, and that it looked like a man couldn't get a fair price for anything he raised. Some of the farmers had quit farming and were cutting railroad ties so they could feed their families. If things didn't get better, that's what he'd have to do. He said he'd give anything if he could get some good hounds for me, but there didn't seem to be any way he could right then.

I went off to bed with my heart all torn up in little pieces, and cried myself to sleep.

The next day Papa had to go to the store. Late that evening I saw him coming back. As fast as I could, I ran to meet him, expecting a sack of candy. Instead he handed me three small steel traps.

If Santa Claus himself had come down out of the mountains, reindeer and all, I would not have been more pleased. I jumped up and down, and cried a whole bucketful of tears. I hugged him and told him what a wonderful papa he was.

He showed me how to set them by mashing the spring down with my foot, and how to work the trigger. I took them to bed with me that night.

The next morning I started trapping around the barn. The first thing I caught was Samie, our house cat. If this didn't cause a commotion! I didn't intend to catch him. I was trying to catch a rat, but somehow he came nosing around and got in my trap.

My sisters started bawling and yelling for Mama. She came running, wanting to know what in the world was going on. None of us had to tell her. Samie told her with his spitting and squalling.

He was mad. He couldn't understand what that thing was that was biting his foot, and he was making an awful fuss about it. His tail was as big as a wet corncob and every hair on his small body was sticking straight up. He spit and yowled and dared anyone to get close to him.

My sisters yelled their fool heads off, all the time saying, "Poor Samie! Poor Samie!"

Mama shushed them up and told me to go get the forked stick from under the clothesline. I ran and got it.

Mama was the best helper a boy ever had. She put the forked end over Samie's neck and pinned him to the ground.

It was bad enough for the trap to be biting his foot, but to have his neck pinned down that way was too much. He threw a fit. I never heard such a racket in all my life.

It wasn't long until everything on the place was all spooked up. The chickens started cackling and flew way up on the hillside. Daisy, our milk cow, all but tore the barn lot up and refused to give any milk that night. Sloppy Ann, our hog, started running in circles, squealing and grunting.

Samie wiggled and twisted. He yowled and spit, but it didn't do him any good. Mama was good and stout. She held him down, tight to the ground. I ran in and put my foot on the trap spring, mashed it down, and released his foot. With one loud squall, he scooted under the barn.

After it was all over, Mama said, "I don't think you'll have any more trouble with that cat. I think he has learned his lesson."

How wrong Mama was. Samie was one of those nosy kind of cats. He would lie up on the red oak limbs and watch every move I made.

I found some slick little trails out in our garden down under some tall hollyhocks. Thinking they were game trails, and not knowing they were Samie's favorite hunting trails, I set my traps. Samie couldn't understand what I was doing out there, messing around his hunting territory. He went to investigate.

It wasn't long until I had him limping with all four feet. Every time Papa saw Samie lying around in the warm sun with his feet wrapped up in turpentine rags, he would laugh until big tears rolled down his cheeks.

Mama had another talk with Papa. She said he was going to have to say something to me, because if I caught that cat one more time, it would drive her out of her mind.

Papa told me to be a little more careful where I set my traps.

"Papa," I said, "I don't want to catch Samie, but he's the craziest cat I ever saw. He sees everything I do, and just has to go sniffing around."

Papa looked over at Samie. He was lying all sprawled out in the sunshine with all four paws bandaged and sticking straight up. His long tail was swishing this way and that.

"You see, Papa," I said, "he's watching me right now, just waiting for me to set my traps."

Papa walked off toward the barn. I heard him laughing fit to kill.

It finally got too tough for Samie. He left home. Oh, he came in once in a while, all long and lean looking, but he never was the same friendly cat any more. He was nervous and wouldn't let anyone pet him. He would gobble down his milk and then scoot for the timber.

Once I decided to make friends with him because I felt bad about catching him in my traps. I reached out my hand to rub his back. He swelled up like a sitting hen. His eyeballs got all green, and he growled way down deep. He spat at me, and drew back his paw like he was going to knock my head off. I decided I'd better leave him alone.

In no time at all I cleaned out the rats.

Then something bad happened. I caught one of Mama's prize hens. I got one of those "young man peach tree" switchings over that.

Papa told me to go down in the canebrakes back of our fields and trap. This opened up all kinds of new wonders. I caught opossums, skunks, rabbits, and squirrels.

Papa showed me how to skin my game. In neat little rows I tacked the hides on the smokehouse wall. I'd stand for hours and admire my magnificent trophies.

There was only one thing wrong. I didn't have a big coonskin to add to my collection. I couldn't trap old Mister Ringtail. He was too smart for me. He'd steal the bait from the traps, spring the triggers, and sometimes even turn them over.

Once I found a small stick standing upright in one of my traps. I showed it to Papa. He laughed and said the stick must have fallen from a tree. It made no difference what Papa said. I was firmly convinced that a smart old coon had deliberately poked that stick in my trap.

The traps helped my dog-wanting considerably, but like a new toy, the newness wore off and I was right back where I started from. Only this time it was worse, much worse. I had been exposed to the feel of wildlife.

I started pestering Mama again. She said, "Oh, no! Not that again. I thought you'd be satisfied with the traps. No, Billy, I don't want to hear any more about hounds."

I knew Mama meant what she said. This broke my heart. I decided I'd leave home. I sneaked out a quart jar of peaches, some cold corn bread, and a few onions, and started up the hollow back of our house. I had it all figured out. I'd go away off to some big town, get a hundred dogs, and bring them all back with me.

I made it all right until I heard a timber wolf howl. This stopped my home-leaving.

When the hunting season opened that fall, something happened that was almost more than I could stand. I was lying in bed one night trying to figure out a way I could get some dogs when I heard the deep baying of a coon hound. I got up and opened my window. It came again. The deep voice rang loud and clear in the frosty night. Now and then I could hear the hunter whooping to him.

The hound hunted all night. He quit when the roosters started crowing at daybreak. The hunter and the hound weren't the only ones awake that night. I stayed up and listened to them until the last tones of the hound's voice died away in the daylight hours.

That morning I was determined to have some hounds. I went again to Mama. This time I tried bribery. I told her if she'd get me a hunting dog, I'd save the money I earned from my furs, and buy her a new dress and a boxful of pretty hats.

That time I saw tears in her eyes. It made me feel all empty inside and I cried a little, too. By the time she was through kissing me and talking to me, I was sure I didn't need any dogs at all. I couldn't stand to see Mama cry.

The next night I heard the hound again. I tried to cover my head with a pillow to shut out the sound. It was no use. His voice seemed to bore its way through the pillow and ring in my ears. I had to get up and again go to the window. I'm sure if that coon hunter had known that he was slowly killing a ten-year-old boy, he would have put a muzzle on his hound.

Sleep was out of the question. Even on nights when I couldn't hear the hound, I couldn't sleep. I was afraid if I did, he would come and I would miss hearing him.

By the time hunting season was over, I was a nervous wreck. My eyes were red and bloodshot. I had lost weight and was as thin as a bean pole. Mama checked me over. She looked at my tongue and turned back one of my eyelids.

"If I didn't know better," she said, "I'd swear you weren't sleeping well. Are you?"

"Why, Mama," I said, "I go to bed, don't I? What does a boy go to bed for if it isn't to sleep?"

By the little wrinkles that bunched up on her forehead, I could tell that Mama wasn't satisfied. Papa came in during one of these inspections. Mama told him she was worried about my health.

"Aw," he said, "there's nothing wrong with him. It's just because he's been cooped up all winter. A boy needs sunshine, and exercise. He's almost eleven now, and I'm going to let him help me in the fields this summer. That will put the muscles back on him."

I thought this was wonderful. I'd finally grown up to be a man. I was going to help Papa with the farm.

Chapter 3

The dog-wanting disease never did leave me altogether. With the new work I was doing, helping Papa, it just kind of burned itself down and left a big sore on my heart. Every time I'd see a coon track down in our fields, or along the riverbanks, the old sore would get all festered up and start hurting again.

Just when I had given up all hope of ever owning a good hound, something wonderful happened. The good Lord figured I had hurt enough, and it was time to lend a helping hand.

It all started one day while I was hoeing corn down in our field close to the river.

Across the river, a party of fishermen had been camped for several days. I heard the old Maxwell car as it snorted and chugged its way out of the bottoms.[4] I knew they were leaving. Throwing down my hoe, I ran down to the river and waded across at a place called the Shannon Ford. I hurried to the camp ground.

It was always a pleasure to prowl where fishermen had camped. I usually could find things: a fish line, or a forgotten fish pole. On one occasion, I found a beautiful knife stuck in the bark of a sycamore tree, forgotten by a careless fisherman. But on that day, I found the greatest of treasures, a sportsman's magazine, discarded by the campers. It was a real treasure for a country boy. Because of that magazine, my entire life was changed.

I sat down on an old sycamore log, and started thumbing through the leaves. On the back pages of the magazine, I came to the "For Sale" section—"Dogs for Sale"—every kind of dog. I read on and on. They had dogs I had never heard of, names I couldn't make out. Far down in the right-hand corner, I found an ad that took my breath away. In small letters, it read: "Registered redbone coon hound pups—twenty-five dollars each."

The advertisement was from a kennel in Kentucky. I read it over and over. By the time I had memorized the ad, I was seeing dogs, hearing dogs, and even feeling them. The magazine was forgotten. I was lost in thought. The brain of an eleven-year-old boy can dream some fantastic dreams.

How wonderful it would be if I could have two of those pups. Every boy in the country but me had a good hound or two. But fifty dollars—how could I ever get fifty dollars? I

---

4. bottoms (bät' əmz) n.: Bottom land, or low land through which a river flows.

knew I couldn't expect help from Mama and Papa.

I remembered a passage from the Bible my mother had read to us: "God helps those who help themselves." I thought of the words. I mulled them over in my mind. I decided I'd ask God to help me. There on the banks of the Illinois River, in the cool shade of the tall white sycamores, I asked God to help me get two hound pups. It wasn't much of a prayer, but it did come right from the heart.

When I left the campground of the fishermen, it was late. As I walked along, I could feel the hard bulge of the magazine jammed deep in the pocket of my overalls. The beautiful silence that follows the setting sun had settled over the river bottoms. The coolness of the rich, black soil felt good to my bare feet.

It was the time of day when all furried things come to life. A big swamp rabbit hopped out on the trail, sat on his haunches, stared at me, and then scampered away. A mother gray squirrel ran out on the limb of a bur oak tree. She barked a warning to the four furry balls behind her. They melted from sight in the thick green. A silent gray shadow drifted down from the top of a tall sycamore. There was a squeal and a beating of wings. I heard the tinkle of a bell in the distance ahead. I knew it was Daisy, our milk cow. I'd have to start her on the way home.

I took the magazine from my pocket and again I read the ad. Slowly a plan began to form. I'd save the money. I could sell stuff to the fishermen: crawfish, minnows, and fresh vegetables. In berry season, I could sell all the berries I could pick at my grandfather's store. I could trap in the winter. The more I planned, the more real it became. There was the way to get those pups—save my money.

I could almost feel the pups in my hands.

I planned the little doghouse, and where to put it. Collars I could make myself. Then the thought came, "What could I name them?" I tried name after name, voicing them out loud. None seemed to fit. Well, there would be plenty of time for names.

Right now there was something more important—fifty dollars—a fabulous sum—a fortune—far more money than I had ever seen. Somehow, some way, I was determined to have it. I had twenty-three cents—a dime I had earned running errands for my grandpa, and thirteen cents a fisherman had given me for a can of worms.

The next morning I went to the trash pile behind the barn. I was looking for a can—my bank. I picked up several, but they didn't seem to be what I wanted. Then I saw it, an old K. C. Baking Powder can. It was perfect, long and slender, with a good tight lid. I took it down to the creek and scrubbed it with sand until it was bright and new-looking.

I dropped the twenty-three cents in the can. The coins looked so small lying there on the shiny bottom, but to me it was a good start. With my finger, I tried to measure how full it would be with fifty dollars in it.

Next, I went to the barn and up in the loft. Far back over the hay and up under the eaves, I hid my can. I had a start toward making my dreams come true—twenty-three cents. I had a good bank, safe from the rats and from the rain and snow.

All through that summer I worked like a beaver. In the small creek that wormed its way down through our fields, I caught crawfish with my bare hands. I trapped minnows with an old screen-wire trap I made myself, baited with yellow cornbread from my mother's kitchen. These were sold to the fishermen, along with fresh vegetables and roasting ears. I tore my way through the blackberry patches until my hands and feet were scratched raw and red from the thorns.

I tramped the hills seeking out the huckle-berry bushes. My grandfather paid me ten cents a bucket for my berries.

Once Grandpa asked me what I did with the money I earned. I told him I was saving it to buy some hunting dogs. I asked him if he would order them for me when I had saved enough. He said he would. I asked him not to say anything to my father. He promised me he wouldn't. I'm sure Grandpa paid little attention to my plans.

That winter I trapped harder than ever with the three little traps I owned. Grandpa sold my hides to fur buyers who came to his store all through the fur season. Prices were cheap: fifteen cents for a large opossum hide, twenty-five for a good skunk hide.

Little by little, the nickels and dimes added up. The old K. C. Baking Powder can grew heavy. I would heft its weight in the palm of my hand. With a straw, I'd measure from the lip of the can to the money. As the months went by, the straws grew shorter and shorter.

The next summer I followed the same routine.

"Would you like to buy some crawfish or minnows? Maybe you'd like some fresh vege-tables or roasting ears."

The fishermen were wonderful, as true sportsmen are. They seemed to sense the urgency in my voice and always bought my wares. However, many was the time I'd find my vegetables left in the abandoned camp.

There never was a set price. Anything they offered was good enough for me.

A year passed. I was twelve. I was over the halfway mark. I had twenty-seven dollars and forty-six cents. My spirits soared. I worked harder.

Another year crawled slowly by, and then the great day came. The long hard grind was over. I had it—my fifty dollars! I cried as I counted it over and over.

As I set the can back in the shadowy eaves of the barn, it seemed to glow with a radiant whiteness I had never seen before. Perhaps it was all imagination. I don't know.

Lying back in the soft hay, I folded my hands behind my head, closed my eyes, and let my mind wander back over the two long years. I thought of the fishermen, the blackberry patches, and the huckleberry hills. I thought of the prayer I had said when I asked God to help me get two hound pups. I knew He had surely helped, for He had given me the heart, courage, and determination.

Early the next morning, with the can jammed deep in the pocket of my overalls, I flew to the store. As I trotted along, I whistled and sang. I felt as big as the tallest mountain in the Ozarks.

Arriving at my destination, I saw two wagons were tied up at the hitching rack. I knew some farmers had come to the store, so I waited until they left. As I walked in, I saw my grandfather behind the counter. Tugging and pulling, I worked the can out of my pocket and dumped it out in front of him and looked up.

Grandpa was dumbfounded. He tried to say something, but it wouldn't come out. He looked at me, and he looked at the pile of coins. Finally, in a voice much louder than he ordinarily used, he asked, "Where did you get all this?"

"I told you, Grandpa," I said, "I was saving my money so I could buy two hound pups, and I did. You said you would order them for me. I've got the money and now I want you to order them."

Grandpa stared at me over his glasses, and then back at the money.

"How long have you been saving this?" he asked.

"A long time, Grandpa," I said.

"How long?" he asked.

I told him, "Two years."

His mouth flew open and in a loud voice he said, "Two years!"

I nodded my head.

The way my grandfather stared at me made me uneasy. I was on needles and pins. Taking his eyes from me, he glanced back at the money. He saw the faded yellow piece of paper sticking out from the coins. He worked it out, asking as he did, "What's this?"

I told him it was the ad, telling where to order my dogs.

He read it, turned it over, and glanced at the other side.

I saw the astonishment leave his eyes and the friendly-old-grandfather look come back. I felt much better.

Dropping the paper back on the money, he turned, picked up an old turkey-feather duster, and started dusting where there was no dust. He kept glancing at me out of the corner of his eye as he walked slowly down to the other end of the store, dusting here and there.

He put the duster down, came from behind the counter, and walked up to me. Laying a friendly old work-calloused hand on my head, he changed the conversation altogether, saying, "Son, you need a haircut."

I told him I didn't mind. I didn't like my

hair short; flies and mosquitoes bothered me.

He glanced down at my bare feet and asked, "How come your feet are cut and scratched like that?"

I told him it was pretty tough picking blackberries barefoot.

He nodded his head.

It was too much for my grandfather. He turned and walked away. I saw the glasses come off, and the old red handkerchief come out. I heard the good excuse of blowing his nose. He stood for several seconds with his back toward me. When he turned around, I noticed his eyes were moist.

In a quavering voice, he said, "Well, Son, it's your money. You worked for it, and you worked hard. You got it honestly, and you want some dogs. We're going to get those dogs."

He walked over and picked up the ad again, asking, "Is this two years old, too?"

I nodded.

"Well," he said, "the first thing we have to do is write this outfit. There may not even be a place like this in Kentucky any more. After all, a lot of things can happen in two years."

Seeing that I was worried, he said, "Now you go on home. I'll write to these kennels and I'll let you know when I get an answer. If we can't get the dogs there, we can get them someplace else. And I don't think, if I were you, I'd let my Pa know anything about this right now. I happen to know he wants to buy that red mule from Old Man Potter."

I told him I wouldn't, and turned to leave the store.

As I reached the door, my grandfather said in a loud voice, "Say, it's been a long time since you've had any candy, hasn't it?"

I nodded my head.

He asked, "How long?"

I told him, "A long time."

"Well," he said, "we'll have to do something about that."

Walking over behind the counter, he reached out and got a sack. I noticed it wasn't one of the nickel sacks. It was one of the quarter kind.

My eyes never left my grandfather's hand. Time after time, it dipped in and out of the candy counter: peppermint sticks, jawbreakers, horehound, and gumdrops. The sack bulged. So did my eyes.

Handing the sack to me, he said, "Here. First big coon you catch with those dogs, you can pay me back."

I told him I would.

On my way home, with a jawbreaker in one side of my mouth and a piece of horehound in the other, I skipped and hopped, making half an effort to try to whistle and sing, and couldn't for the candy. I had the finest grandpa in the world and I was the happiest boy in the world.

I wanted to share my happiness with my sisters but decided not to say anything about ordering the pups.

Arriving home, I dumped the sack of candy out on the bed. Six little hands helped themselves. I was well repaid by the love and adoration I saw in the wide blue eyes of my three little sisters.

Chapter 4

Day after day, I flew to the store. Grandpa would shake his head. Then on a Monday, as I entered the store, I sensed a change in him. He was in high spirits, talking and laughing with half a dozen farmers. Every time I caught his eye, he would smile and wink at me. I thought the farmers would never leave, but finally the store was empty.

Grandpa told me the letter had come. The kennels were still there, and they had dogs for sale. He said he had made the mail buggy wait while he made out the order. And, another thing, the dog market had gone downhill. The price of dogs had dropped five dollars. He handed me a ten-dollar bill.

"Now, there's still one stump in the way," he said. "The mail buggy can't carry things like dogs, so they'll come as far as the depot at Tahlequah,[5] but you'll get the notice here because I ordered them in your name."

I thanked my grandfather with all my heart and asked him how long I'd have to wait for the notice.

He said, "I don't know, but it shouldn't take more than a couple of weeks."

I asked how I was going to get my dogs out from Tahlequah.

"Well, there's always someone going in," he said, "and you could ride in with them."

That evening the silence of our supper was interrupted when I asked my father this question: "Papa, how far is it to Kentucky?"

I may as well have exploded a bomb. For an instant there was complete silence, and then my oldest sister giggled. The two little ones stared at me.

With a half-hearted laugh, my father said, "Well, now, I don't know, but it's a pretty good ways. What do you want to know for? Thinking of taking a trip to Kentucky?"

"No," I said. "I just wondered."

My youngest sister giggled and asked, "Can I go with you?"

I glared at her.

Mama broke into the conversation, "I declare, what kind of a question is that? How far is it to Kentucky? I don't know what's gotten into that mind of yours lately. You go around like you were lost, and you're losing weight. You're as skinny as a rail, and look

at that hair. Just last Sunday they had a haircutting over at Tom Rolland's place, but you couldn't go. You had to go prowling around the river and the woods."

I told Mama that I'd get a haircut next time they had a cutting. And I just heard some fellows talking about Kentucky up at the store, and wondered how far away it was. Much to my relief, the conversation was ended.

The days dragged by. A week passed and still no word about my dogs. Terrible thoughts ran through my mind. Maybe my dogs were lost; the train had a wreck; someone stole my money; or perhaps the mailman lost my order. Then, at the end of the second week, the notice came.

My grandfather told me that he had talked to Jim Hodges that day. He was going into town in about a week and I could ride in with him to pick up my dogs. Again I thanked my grandfather.

I started for home. Walking along in deep thought, I decided it was time to tell my father the whole story. I fully intended to tell him that evening. I tried several times, but somehow I couldn't. I wasn't scared of him, for he never whipped me. He was always kind and gentle, but for some reason, I don't know why, I just couldn't tell him.

That night, snuggled deep in the soft folds of a feather bed, I lay thinking. I had waited so long for my dogs, and I so desperately wanted to see them and hold them. I didn't want to wait a whole week.

In a flash I made up my mind. Very quietly I got up and put on my clothes. I sneaked into the kitchen and got one of Mama's precious flour sacks. In it I put six eggs, some leftover corn bread, a little salt, and a few matches. Next I went to the smokehouse and cut off a piece of salt pork. I stopped at the barn and picked up a gunny sack. I put the flour sack inside the gunny

---

5. Tahlequah (tal′ ə kwô): A town in eastern Oklahoma.

sack. This I rolled up and crammed length-wise in the bib of my overalls.

I was on my way. I was going after my dogs.

Tahlequah was a small country town with a population of about eight hundred. By the road it was thirty-two miles away, but as the crow flies, it was only twenty miles. I went as the crow flies, straight through the hills.

Although I had never been to town in my life, I knew what direction to take. Tah-lequah and the railroad lay on the other side of the river from our place. I had the Frisco Railroad on my right, and the Illinois River on my left. Not far from where the railroad crossed the river lay the town of Tahlequah. I knew if I bore to the right I would find the railroad, and if I bore to the left I had the river to guide me.

Sometime that night, I crossed the river on a riffle somewhere in the Dripping Springs country. Coming out of the river bottoms, I scatted up a long hogback ridge, and broke out on top in the flats. In a mile-eating trot, I moved along. I had the wind of a deer, the muscles of a country boy, a heart full of dog love, and a strong determination. I wasn't scared of the darkness, or the mountains, for I was raised in those moun-tains.

On and on, mile after mile, I moved along. I saw faint gray streaks appear in the east. I knew daylight was close. My bare feet were getting sore from the flint rocks and saw briers.[6] I stopped beside a mountain stream, soaked my feet in the cool water, rested for a spell, and then started on.

After leaving the mountain stream, my pace was much slower. The muscles of my legs were getting stiff. Feeling the pangs of hunger gnawing at my stomach, I decided I

would stop and eat at the next stream I found. Then I remembered I had forgotten to include a can in which to boil my eggs.

I stopped and built a small fire. Cutting off a nice thick slab of salt pork, I roasted it, and with a piece of cold corn bread made a sandwich. Putting out my fire, I was on my way again. I ate as I trotted along. I felt much better.

I came into Tahlequah from the north-east. At the outskirts of town, I hid my flour sack and provisions, keeping the gunny sack. I walked into town.

I was scared of Tahlequah and the peo-ple. I had never seen such a big town and so many people. There was store after store, some of them two stories high. The wagon yard had wagons on top of wagons; teams, buggies, and horses.

Two young ladies about my age stopped, stared at me, and then giggled. My blood boiled, but I could understand. After all, I had three sisters. I went on.

I saw a big man coming up the street. The bright shiny star on his vest looked as big as a bucket. I saw the long, black gun at his side and I froze in my tracks. I'd heard of sheriffs and marshals, but had never seen one. Stories repeated about them in the mountains told how fast they were with a gun, and how many men they had killed.

The closer he came, the more frightened I got. I knew it was the end for me. I could just see him aiming his big, black gun and shooting me between the eyes. It seemed like a miracle that he passed by, hardly glancing at me. Breathing a sigh, I walked on, seeing the wonders of the world.

Passing a large store window, I stopped and stared. There in the window was the most wonderful sight I had ever seen; every-thing under the sun; overalls, jackets, bolts of beautiful cloth, new harnesses, collars, bridles; and then my eyes did pop open.

---

6. saw briers (sô brī′ ərz) n.: Prickly plants.

There were several guns and one of them had two barrels. I couldn't believe it—two barrels. I had seen several guns, but never one with two barrels.

Then I saw something else. The sun was just right, and the plate glass was a perfect mirror. I saw the full reflection of myself for the first time in my life.

I could see that I did look a little odd. My straw-colored hair was long and shaggy, and was bushed out like a corn tassel that had been hit by a wind. I tried to smooth it down with my hands. This helped some but not much. What it needed was a good combing and I had no comb.

My overalls were patched and faded but they were clean. My shirt had pulled out. I tucked it back in.

I took one look at my bare feet and winced. They were as brown as dead sycamore leaves. The spider-web pattern of raw, red scratches looked odd in the saddle-brown skin. I thought, "Well, I won't have to pick any more blackberries and the scratches will soon go away."

I pumped up one of my arms and thought surely the muscle was going to pop right through my thin blue shirt. I stuck out my tongue. It was as red as pokeberry juice and anything that color was supposed to be healthy.

After making a few faces at myself, I put my thumbs in my ears and was making mule ears when two old women came by. They stopped and stared at me. I stared back. As they turned to go on their way, I heard one of them say something to the other. The words were hard to catch, but I did hear one word: "Wild."

As I turned to leave, my eyes again fell on the overalls and the bolts of cloth. I thought of my mother, father, and sisters. Here was an opportunity to make amends for leaving home without telling anyone.

I entered the store. I bought a pair of overalls for Papa. After telling the storekeeper how big my mother and sisters were, I bought several yards of cloth. I also bought a large sack of candy.

Glancing down at my bare feet, the storekeeper said, "I have some good shoes."

I told him I didn't need any shoes.

He asked if that would be all.

I nodded.

He added up the bill. I handed him my ten dollars. He gave me my change.

After wrapping up the bundles, he helped me put them in my sack. Lifting it to my shoulder, I turned and left the store.

Out on the street, I picked out a friendly-looking old man and asked him where the depot was. He told me to go down to the last street and turn right, go as far as I could, and I couldn't miss it. I thanked him and started on my way.

Leaving the main part of town, I started up a long street through the residential section. I had never seen so many beautiful houses, and they were all different colors. The lawns were neat and clean and looked like green carpets. I saw a man pushing some kind of a mowing machine. I stopped to watch the whirling blades. He gawked at me. I hurried on.

I heard a lot of shouting and laughing ahead of me. Not wanting to miss anything, I walked a little faster. I saw what was making the noise. More kids than I had ever seen were playing around a big red brick building. I thought some rich man lived there and was giving a party for his children. Walking up to the edge of the playground, I stopped to watch.

The boys and girls were about my age, and were as thick as flies around a sorghum mill. They were milling, running, and jumping. Teeter-totters and swings were loaded down with them. Everyone was laughing and having a big time.

Over against the building, a large blue

pipe ran up on an angle from the ground. A few feet from the top there was a bend in it. The pipe seemed to go into the building. Boys were crawling into its dark mouth. I counted nine of them. One boy stood about six feet from the opening with a stick in his hand.

Staring goggle-eyed, trying to figure out what they were doing, I got a surprise. Out of the hollow pipe spurted a boy. He sailed through the air and lit on his feet. The boy with the stick marked the ground where he landed. All nine of them came shooting out, one behind the other. As each boy landed, a new mark was scratched.

They ganged around looking at the lines. There was a lot of loud talking, pointing, and arguing. Then all lines were erased and a new scorekeeper was picked out. The others crawled back into the pipe.

I figured out how the game was played. After climbing to the top of the slide, the boys turned around and sat down. One at a time, they came flying down and out, feet first. The one that shot out the farthest was the winner. I thought how wonderful it would be if I could slide down just one time.

One boy, spying me standing on the corner, came over. Looking me up and down, he asked, "Do you go to school here?"

I said, "School?"

He said, "Sure. School. What did you think it was?"

"Oh. No, I don't go to school here."

"Do you go to Jefferson?"

"No. I don't go there either."

"Don't you go to school at all?"

"Sure I go to school."

"Where?"

"At home."

"You go to school at home?"

I nodded.

"What grade are you in?"

I said I wasn't in any grade.

Puzzled, he said, "You go to school at home, and don't know what grade you're in. Who teaches you?"

"My mother."

"What does she teach you?"

I said, "Reading, writing, and arithmetic, and I bet I'm just as good at it as you are."

He asked, "Don't you have any shoes?"

I said, "Sure, I have shoes."

"Why aren't you wearing them?"

"I don't wear shoes until it gets cold."

He laughed and asked where I lived.

I said, "Back in the hills."

He said, "Oh, you're a hillbilly."

He ran back to the mob. I saw him pointing at me and talking to several boys. They started my way, yelling, "Hillbilly, hillbilly."

Just before they reached me, a bell started ringing. Turning, they ran to the front of the building, lined up in two long lines, and marching like little tin soldiers disappeared inside the school.

The playground was silent. I was all alone, and felt lonely and sad.

I heard a noise on my right. I didn't have to turn around to recognize what it was. Someone was using a hoe. I'd know that sound if I heard it on a dark night. It was a little old white-headed woman working in a flower bed.

Looking again at the long, blue pipe, I thought, "There's no one around. Maybe I could have one slide anyway."

I eased over and looked up into the dark hollow. It looked scary, but I thought of all the other boys I had seen crawl into it. I could see the last mark on the ground, and thought, "I bet I can beat that."

Laying my sack down, I started climbing up. The farther I went, the darker and more scary it got. Just as I reached the top, my feet slipped. Down I sailed. All the way down I tried to grab on to something, but there was nothing to grab.

I'm sure some great champions had slid

out of that pipe, and no doubt more than one world record had been broken, but if someone had been there when I came out, I know the record I set would stand today in all its glory.

I came out just like I went in, feet first and belly down. My legs were spread out like a bean-shooter stalk. Arms flailing the air, I zoomed out and up. I seemed to hang suspended in air at the peak of my climb. I could see the hard-packed ground far below.

As I started down, I shut my eyes tight and gritted my teeth. This didn't seem to help. With a splattering sound, I landed. I felt the air whoosh out between my teeth. I tried to scream, but had no wind left to make a sound.

After bouncing a couple of times, I finally settled down to earth. I lay spread-eagled for a few seconds, and then slowly got to my knees.

Hearing loud laughter, I looked around. It was the little old lady with the hoe in her hand. She hollered and asked how I liked it. Without answering, I grabbed up my gunny sack and left. Far up the street, I looked back. The little old lady was sitting down, rocking with laughter.

I couldn't understand these town people. If they weren't staring at a fellow, they were laughing at him.

Chapter 5

On arriving at the depot, my nerve failed me. I was afraid to go in. I didn't know what I was scared of, but I was scared.

Before going around to the front, I peeked in a window. The stationmaster was in his office looking at some papers. He was wearing a funny little cap that had no top in it. He looked friendly enough but I still couldn't muster up enough courage to go in.

I cocked my ear to see if I could hear pup-pies crying, but could hear nothing. A bird started chirping. It was a yellow canary in a cage. The stationmaster walked over and gave it some water. I thought, "Anyone that is kind to birds surely wouldn't be mean to a boy."

With my courage built up I walked around to the front and eased myself past the office. He glanced at me and turned back to the papers. I walked clear around the depot and again walked slowly past the office. Glancing from the corner of my eye, I saw the stationmaster looking at me and smiling. He opened the door and came out on the platform. I stopped and leaned against the building.

Yawning and stretching his arms, he said, "It sure is hot today. It doesn't look like it's ever going to rain."

I looked up at the sky and said, "Yes, sir. It is hot and we sure could do with a good rain. We need one bad up where I come from."

He asked me where I lived.

I told him, "Up the river a ways."

"You know," he said, "I have some pup-pies in there for a boy that lives up on the river. His name is Billy Colman. I know his dad, but never have seen the boy. I figured he would be in after them today."

On hearing this remark, my heart jumped clear up in my throat. I thought surely it was going to hop right out on the depot platform. I looked up and tried to tell him who I was, but something went wrong. When the words finally came out they sounded like the squeaky old pulley on our well when Mama drew up a bucket of water.

I could see a twinkle in the stationmaster's eyes. He came over and laid his hand on my shoulder. In a friendly voice he said, "So you're Billy Colman. How is your dad?"

I told him Papa was fine and handed him the slip my grandpa had given me.

"They sure are fine-looking pups," he said. "You'll have to go around to the freight door."

I'm sure my feet never touched the ground as I flew around the building. He unlocked the door, and I stepped in, looking for my dogs. I couldn't see anything but boxes, barrels, old trunks, and some rolls of barbed wire.

The kindly stationmaster walked over to one of the boxes.

"Do you want box and all?" he asked.

I told him I didn't want the box. All I wanted was the dogs.

"How are you going to carry them?" he asked. "I think they're a little too young to follow."

I held out my gunny sack.

He looked at me and looked at the sack. Chuckling, he said, "Well, I guess dogs can be carried that way same as anything else, but we'll have to cut a couple of holes to stick their heads through so that they won't smother."

Getting a claw hammer, he started tearing off the top of the box. As nails gave way and boards splintered, I heard several puppy whimpers. I didn't walk over. I just stood and waited.

After what seemed like hours, the box was open. He reached in, lifted the pups out, and set them down on the floor.

"Well, there they are," he said. "What do you think of them?"

I didn't answer. I couldn't. All I could do was stare at them.

They seemed to be blinded by the light and kept blinking their eyes. One sat down on his little rear and started crying. The other one was waddling around and whimpering.

I wanted so much to step over and pick them up. Several times I tried to move my feet, but they seemed to be nailed to the floor. I knew the pups were mine, all mine, yet I couldn't move. My heart started acting like a drunk grasshopper. I tried to swallow and couldn't. My Adam's apple wouldn't work.

One pup started my way. I held my breath. On he came until I felt a scratchy little foot on mine. The other pup followed. A warm puppy tongue caressed my sore foot.

I heard the stationmaster say, "They already know you."

I knelt down and gathered them in my arms. I buried my face between their wiggling bodies and cried. The stationmaster, sensing something more than just two dogs and a boy, waited in silence.

Rising with the two pups held close to my chest, I asked if I owed anything.

He said, "There is a small feed bill but I'll take care of it. It's not much anyway."

Taking his knife he cut two slits in the sack. He put the pups in it and worked their heads through the holes. As he handed the sack to me, he said, "Well, there you are. Good-bye and good hunting!"

Walking down the street toward town, I thought, "Now, maybe the people won't stare at me when they see what I've got. After all, not every boy owns two good hounds."

Turning the corner onto the main street, I threw out my chest.

I hadn't gone far before I realized that the reception I got wasn't what I thought it would be. People began to stop and stare, some even snickered. I couldn't understand why they were staring. Surely it couldn't be at the two beautiful hound pups sticking out of the gunny sack.

Thinking that maybe I had a hole in the seat of my britches, I looked over to my reflection in a plate glass window. I craned my neck for a better view of my rear. I could see a patch there all right, and a few threadbare spots, but no whiteness was showing through. I figured that the people were just jealous because they didn't have two good hounds.

I hurried on, wanting to get away from the stares and the snickers.

It wouldn't have happened in a hundred years, but there they came. The same two old women I had met before. We stopped and had another glaring fight.

One said, "I declare."

The other one snorted, "Well, I never."

My face burned. I couldn't take any more. After all, a man can stand so much and no more. In a loud voice, I said, "You may have these people fooled with those expensive-looking feathers in your hats, but I know what they are. They're goose feathers painted with iodine."

One started to say something, but her words were drowned out by the roaring laughter from all around. Gathering up their long skirts, they swished on down the street.

All around me people began to shout questions and laugh. One wanted to know if I had the mother in the sack. Storekeepers stepped out and gawked. I could see the end of the street, but it looked as if it were a hundred miles away. My face was as red as a fox's tail. I ducked my head, tightened my grip on the sack, and walked on.

I don't know where they came from, but like chickens coming home to roost, they flocked around me. Most of them were about my age. Some were a little bigger, some smaller. They ganged around me, screaming and yelling. They started clapping their hands and chanting, "The dog boy has come to town. The dog boy has come to town."

My heart burst. Tears came rolling. The day I had waited for so long had turned black and ugly.

The leader of the gang was about my size. He had a dirty freckled face and his two front teeth were missing. I suppose he had lost them in a back alley fight. His shock of yellow sunburnt hair bobbed up and down as he skipped and jumped to the rhythm of the "dog boy" song. He wore a pair of cowboy boots. They were two sizes too big for him, no doubt handed down by an older brother.

He stomped on my right foot. I looked down and saw a drop of blood ooze out from under the broken nail. It hurt like the dickens but I gritted my teeth and walked on.

Freckle-face pulled the ear of my little girl pup. I heard her painful cry. That was too much. I hadn't worked two long hard years for my pups to have some freckle-face punk pull their ears.

Swinging the sack from my shoulder, I walked over and set it down in a doorway. As I turned around to face the mob, I doubled up my fist, and took a Jack Dempsey[7] stance.

Freckle-face said, "So you want to fight." He came in swinging.

I reached way back in Arkansas somewhere. By the time my fist had traveled all the way down to the Cherokee Strip, there was a lot of power behind it.

Smack on the end of Freck's nose it exploded. With a loud grunt he sat down in the dusty street. Grabbing his nose in both hands, he started rocking and moaning. I saw the blood squeeze out between his fingers.

Another one sailed in. He didn't want to fight. He wanted to wrestle. He stuck a finger in my mouth. I ground down. Shaking his hand and yelling like the hoot owls were after him, he ran across the street.

Another one bored in. I aimed for his eye, but my aim was a little low. It caught him in the Adam's apple. A sick look came over his face. Bending over, croaking like a bullfrog that had been caught by a water moccasin, he started going around in a circle.

But there were too many of them. By sheer weight and numbers, they pulled me down. I managed to twist over on my stomach and buried my face in my arms. I could feel them beating and kicking my body.

All at once the beating stopped. I heard loud cries from the gang. Turning over on my back, I was just in time to see the big marshal plant a number-twelve boot in the seat of the last kid. I just knew I was next. I wondered if he'd kick me while I was down.

I lay where I was. He started toward me. I closed my eyes. I felt a hand as big as an

---

7. **Jack Dempsey** (demp' sē): William Harrison ("Jack") Dempsey (1895–1983), an American heavyweight boxer.

anvil clamp on my shoulder. I thought, "He's going to stand me up, and then knock me down."

He raised me to a sitting position. His deep friendly voice said, "Are you all right, son?"

I opened my eyes. There was a smile on his wide rugged face. In a choking voice, I said, "Yes, sir. I'm all right."

He helped me to my feet. His big hands started brushing the dust from my clothes.

"Those kids are pretty tough, son," he said, "but they're really not bad. They'll grow up some day."

"Marshal," I said, "I wouldn't have fought them, but they pulled my pup's ears."

He looked over to my sack. One pup had worked its way almost out through the hole. The other one's head and two little paws were sticking out. Both of them were whimpering.

A smile spread all over the big marshal's face. "So that's what started the fight," he said.

Walking over, he knelt down and started petting the pups. "They're fine-looking dogs," he said. "Where did you get them?"

I told him I had ordered them from Kentucky.

"What did they cost you?" he asked.

"Forty dollars," I said.

He asked if my father had bought them for me.

"No," I said. "I bought them myself."

He asked me where I got the money.

"I worked and saved it," I said.

"It takes a long time to save forty dollars," he said.

"Yes," I said. "It took me two years."

"Two years!" he exclaimed.

I saw an outraged look come over the marshal's face. Reaching up, he pushed his hat back. He glanced up and down the street. I heard him mutter, "There's not a one in that bunch with that kind of grit."

Picking up my sack, I said, "Thanks for helping me out. I guess I'd better be heading for home."

He asked where I lived.

I said, "Up the river a way."

"Well, you've got time for a bottle of pop before you go, haven't you?"

I started to say "No," but looking at his big friendly smile, I smiled back and said, "I guess I have."

Walking into a general store, the marshal went over to a large red box and pulled back the lid. He asked what kind I wanted. I'd never had a bottle of pop in my life, and didn't know what to say.

Seeing my hesitation, he said, "This strawberry looks pretty good."

I said that would be fine.

The cool pop felt wonderful to my hot dry throat. My dark little world had brightened up again. I had my pups, and had found a wonderful friend. I knew that the stories I had heard about marshals weren't true. Never again would I be scared when I saw one.

Back out on the street, I shook hands with the marshal, saying as I did, "If you're ever up in my part of the country come over and see me. You can find our place by asking at my grandfather's store."

"Store?" he asked. "Why, the only store upriver is about thirty miles from here."

"Yes," I said, "that's my grandpa's place."

He asked if I was afoot.

"Yes," I said.

"You won't make it tonight," he said. "Will you?"

"No," I said. "I intend to camp out somewhere."

I saw he was bothered.

"I'll be all right," I said. "I'm not scared of the mountains."

He looked at me and at my pups. Taking

off his hat, he scratched his head. Chuckling deep down in his barrel-like chest, he said, "Yes, I guess you will be all right. Well, good-bye and good luck! If you're ever in town again look me up."

From far down the street, I looked back. The marshal was still standing where I had left him. He waved his hand. I waved back.

On the outskirts of town, I stopped and picked up a can and my provisions.

I hadn't gone far before I realized that I had undertaken a tough job. The sack became heavier and heavier.

For a while my pups cried and whimpered. They had long since pulled their heads back in the sack. I would peek in at them every once in a while. They were doing all right. Curled up into two little round balls on my bundles, they were fast asleep.

Deep in the heart of the Sparrow Hawk Mountains, night overtook me. There, in a cave with a stream close by, I put up for the night.

Taking my pups and bundles from the gunny sack, I used it to gather leaves to make us a bed. My pups followed me on every trip, whimpering and crying, tumbling and falling over sticks and rocks.

After the bed was made I built a fire. In a can of water from the mountain stream, I boiled three eggs. Next, I boiled half of the remaining salt pork. Cutting the meat up in small pieces, I fed it to my pups. Each of us had a piece of candy for dessert. My pups enjoyed the candy. With their needle-sharp teeth, they gnawed and worried with it until it was melted away.

While they were busy playing, I dragged up several large timbers and built a fire which would last for hours. In a short time the cave grew warm and comfortable from the heat. The leaves were soft, and felt good to my tired body and sore feet. As I lay stretched out, my pups crawled all over me.

I played with them. They would waddle up to the front of the cave, look at the fire, and come scampering back to roll and play in the soft leaves.

I noticed the boy dog was much larger than the girl dog. He was a deeper red in color. His chest was broad and solid. His puppy muscles knotted and rippled under the velvety skin. He was different in every way. He would go closer to the fire. I saw right away he was bold and aggressive.

Once he went around the fire and ventured out into the darkness. I waited to see if he would come back. He came wobbling to the mouth of the cave, but hesitated there. He made several attempts to come back, but the flames were leaping higher by the minute. The space between the fire and the wall of the cave was much hotter than when he had ventured out. Whimpering and crying, he kept trying to get around the fire. I said not a word; just watched.

Puppy though he was, he did something which brought a smile to my face. Getting as close as he could to the side of the cave, he turned his rear to the fire. Hopping sideways, yipping at every jump, he made it through the heat and sailed into the pile of leaves. He had had enough. Curling up in a ball close to me, he went to sleep.

The girl pup was small and timid. Her legs and body were short. Her head was small and delicate. She must have been a runt in the litter. I didn't have to look twice to see that what she lacked in power, she made up in brains. She was a much smarter dog than the boy dog, more sure of herself, more cautious. I knew when the trail became tough, she would be the one to unravel it.

I knew I had a wonderful combination. In my dogs, I had not only the power, but the brains along with it.

I was a tired boy. My legs were stiff, and my feet sore and throbbing. My shoulders were red and raw from the weight of the sack. I covered my pups up in the leaves and moved my body as close to them as I could. I knew as night wore on, and the fire died down, the chill would come. Tired but happy, I fell asleep.

Along in the silent hours of night, I was awakened. I opened my eyes, but didn't move. I lay and listened, trying to figure out what it was that had aroused me. At first I thought one of my pups had awakened me by moving and whimpering. I discarded this thought for I could see that they were both fast asleep. I decided it was my imagination working.

My fire had burned down, leaving only a glowing red body of coals. The cave was dark and silent. Chill from the night had crept in. I was on the point of getting up to rebuild my fire, when I heard what had awakened me. At first I thought it was a woman screaming. I listened. My heart began to pound. I could feel the strain all over my body as nerves grew tighter and tighter.

It came again, closer this time. The high pitch of the scream shattered the silence of the quiet night. The sound seemed to be all around us. It screamed its way into the cave and rang like a blacksmith's anvil against the rock walls. The blood froze in my veins. I was terrified. Although I had never heard one, I knew what it was. It was the scream of a mountain lion.

The big cat screamed again. Leaves boiled and stirred where my pups were. In the reflection of the glowing coals, I could see that one was sitting up. It was the boy dog. A leaf had become entangled in the fuzzy hair of a floppy ear. The ear flicked. The leaf dropped.

Again the fiendish scream rang out over the mountains. Leaves flew as my pup left the bed. I jumped up and tried to call him back.

Reaching the mouth of the cave, he stopped. Raising his small red head high in the air, he bawled his challenge to the devil cat. The bawl must have scared him as much as it had startled me. He came tearing back. The tiny hairs on his back were standing on end.

My father had told me lions were scared of fire. I started throwing on more wood. I was glad I'd dragged up a good supply while making camp.

Hearing a noise from the bed, I looked back. The girl pup, hearing the commotion, had gotten up and joined the boy dog. They were sitting side by side with their bodies stiff and rigid. Their beady little eyes bored into the darkness beyond the cave. The moist tips of their little black noses wiggled and twisted as if trying to catch a scent.

What I saw in my pups gave me courage. My knees quit shaking and my heart stopped pounding.

I figured the lion had scented my pups. The more I thought about anything harming them, the madder I got. I was ready to die for my dogs.

Every time the big cat screamed, the boy dog would run to the mouth of the cave and bawl back at him. I started whooping and throwing rocks down the mountainside, hoping to scare the lion away. Through the long hours of the night, I kept this up.

The lion prowled around us, screaming and growling; first on the right, and then on the left, and above and below. In the wee hours of morning, he gave up and left to stalk other parts of the mountains. I'm sure he thought he didn't stand a chance against two vicious hounds and a big hunter.

Chapter 6

After the terrifying night, the bright morning sun was a welcome sight. I fixed breakfast and soon we were on our way. I tried to get the pups to follow me, so as to lighten my load. They would for a way, and then, sitting down on their rears, they would cry and whimper. Back in the sack they would go, with their heads sticking out of the holes and their long ears flopping. I moved on.

About midday I entered country I knew. I wasn't far from home. I dropped down out of the mountains into the bottoms far above the place I had crossed the river on my way to town.

Staying on the left of the river, I followed its course past several campgrounds, but didn't stop until I came to the one where I had found the magazine. Here I took the pups out of the sack and sat down in the warm sand.

As the afternoon wore on, I sat there deep in thought. I was trying to think what I was going to tell my mother and father. I could think of nothing. Finally I decided I would just tell them the truth, and with the help of the new overalls, cloth, and candy, I would weather the storm.

My pups were having a big time playing. With their little front paws locked around each other, they were growling, rolling, and chewing on one another. They looked so cute, I laughed out loud.

While I was watching their romping, the thought came, "I haven't named them."

I went over the list of names. For him, I tried "Red," "Bugle," "Lead," name after name as before. For her, I tried "Susie," "Mabel," "Queen," all kinds of girl names. None seemed to fit.

Still mumbling names over and over, I glanced up. There, carved in the white bark of a sycamore tree, was a large heart. In the center of the heart were two names, "Dan" and "Ann." The name Dan was a little larger than Ann. It was wide and bold. The scar stood out more. The name Ann was small, neat, and even. I stared unbelieving—for there were my names. They were perfect.

I walked over and picked up my pups. Looking at him, I said, "Your name is Dan. I'll call you Old Dan." Looking at her, I said, "Your name, little girl, is Ann. I'll call you Little Ann."

It was then I realized it was all too perfect. Here in this fishermen's camp, I had found the magazine and the ad. I looked over at the old sycamore log. There I had asked God to help me get two hound pups. There were the pups, rolling and playing in the warm sand. I thought of the old K. C. Baking Powder can, and the fishermen. How freely they had given their nickels and dimes.

I looked up again to the names carved in the tree. Yes, it was all there like a large puzzle. Piece by piece, each fit perfectly until the puzzle was complete. It could not have happened without the help of an unseen power.

I stayed at the campground until dark. I knew I had to go home but I put it off as long as I could. The crying of the pups, telling me they were hungry, made up my mind for me. I knew the time had come for me to face my mother and father.

I sacked up my dogs and waded the river. As I came out of the bottoms, I could see the lamplight glow from the windows of our home. One of the small yellow squares darkened for an instant. Someone had walked across the floor. I wondered who it was. I heard Daisy, our milk cow, moo. I was thinking so hard of what I would say, it startled me for a second.

Reaching the gate to our house, I stopped. I had never thought our home very pretty, but that night it looked different. It looked clean and neat and peaceful, nestled there in the foothills of the Ozarks. Yes, on that night I was proud of our home.

My bare feet made no noise as I crossed the porch. With my free hand, I reached and pulled the leather that worked the latch. Slowly the door swung inward.

I couldn't see my father or sisters. They

were too far to the right of me, but my mother was directly in front of the door, sitting in her old cane-bottom rocker, knitting.

She looked up. I saw all the worry and grief leave her eyes. Her head bowed down. The knitting in her hands came up to cover her face. I stepped inside the room. I wanted to run to her and comfort her and tell her how sorry I was for all the worry and grief I had caused her.

The booming voice of my father shook me from my trance.

He said, "Well, what have you got there?"

Laughing, he got up from his chair and came over to me. He reached and took the sack from my shoulder.

"When we started looking for you," he said, "I went to the store and your grandpa told me all about it. It wasn't too hard to figure out what you had done, but you should have told us."

I ran to my mother and, dropping to my knees, I buried my face in her lap.

As Mama patted my head, I heard her say in a quavering voice, "Oh, why didn't you tell us? Why?"

I couldn't answer.

Between sobs, I heard the squeals of delight from my sisters as they fondled my pups.

I heard my father say, "What's this other stuff you've got?"

Without raising my head from my mother's lap, in a choking voice I said, "One is for you, one is for Mama, and the other is for the girls."

I heard the snapping of string and the rattle of paper. The oh's and ah's from my sisters were wonderful to hear.

Papa came over to Mama. Laying the cloth on the arm of her chair, he said, "Well, you've been wanting a new dress. Here is enough cloth to make half a dozen dresses."

Realizing that everything was forgiven, I stood up and dried my eyes. Papa was pleased with his new overalls. My sisters forgot the pups for the candy. The light that was shining from my mother's eyes, as she fingered the cheap cotton cloth, was something I will never forget.

Mama warmed some milk for the pups. They drank until their little tummies were tight and round.

As I ate, Papa sat down at the table and started talking man-talk to me. He asked, "How are things in town?"

I told him it was boiling with people. The wagon yard was full of wagons and teams.

He asked if I had seen anyone I knew.

I told him I hadn't, but the stationmaster had asked about him.

He asked me where I had spent the night.

I told him about the cave in the Sparrow Hawk Mountains.

He said that must have been the one called "Robber's Cave."

My youngest sister piped up, "Did you stay all night with some robbers?"

My oldest sister said, "Silly, that was a long time ago. There aren't any robbers there now."

The other one put her nickel's worth in, "Weren't you scared?"

"No," I said, "I wasn't scared of staying in the cave, but I heard a mountain lion scream and it scared me half to death."

"Aw, they won't bother you," Papa said. "You had a fire, didn't you?"

I said, "Yes."

He said, "They'll never bother you unless they are wounded or cornered, but if they are, you had better look out."

Papa asked me how I liked town.

I said I didn't like it at all, and wouldn't live there even if they gave it to me.

With a querying look on his face, he said, "I'm afraid I don't understand. I thought you always wanted to go to town."

"I did," I said, "but I don't any more. I don't like the people there and couldn't understand them."

"What was wrong with them?" he asked.

I told him how they had stared at me, and had even laughed and made fun of me.

He said, "Aw, I don't think they were making fun of you, were they?"

"Yes, they were," I said, "and to beat it all, the boys jumped on me and knocked me down in the dirt. If it hadn't been for the marshal, I would have taken a beating."

Papa said, "So you met the marshal. What did you think of him?"

I told him he was a nice man. He had bought me a bottle of soda pop.

At the mention of soda pop, the blue eyes of my sisters opened wide. They started firing questions at me, wanting to know what color it was, and what it tasted like. I told them it was strawberry and it bubbled and tickled when I drank it, and it made me burp.

The eager questions of my three little sisters had had an effect on my father and mother.

Papa said, "Billy, I don't want you to feel badly about the people in town. I don't think they were poking fun at you, anyway not like you think they were."

"Maybe they weren't," I said, "but I still don't want to ever live in town. It's too crowded and you couldn't get a breath of fresh air."

In a sober voice my father said, "Some day you may have to live in town. Your mother and I don't intend to live in these hills all our lives. It's no place to raise a family. A man's children should have an education. They should get out and see the world and meet people."

"I don't see why we have to move to town to get an education," I said. "Hasn't Mama taught us how to read and write?"

"There's more to an education than just reading and writing," Papa said. "Much more."

I asked him when he thought we'd be moving to town.

"Well, it'll be some time yet," he said. "We don't have the money now, but I'm hoping some day we will."

From the stove where she was heating salt water for my feet, Mama said in a low voice, "I'll pray every day and night for that day to come. I don't want you children to grow up without an education, not even knowing what a bottle of soda pop is, or ever seeing the inside of a schoolhouse. I don't think I could stand that. I'll just keep praying and some day the good Lord may answer my prayer."

I told my mother I had seen the schoolhouse in town. Again I had to answer a thousand questions for my sisters. I told them it was made of red brick and was bigger than Grandpa's store, a lot bigger. There must have been at least a thousand kids going to school there.

I told all about the teeter-totters, the swings made out of log chains, the funny-looking pipe that ran up the side of the building, and how I had climbed up in it and slid out like the other kids. I didn't tell them how I came out.

"I think that was a fire escape," Papa said.

"Fire escape!" I said. "It looked like a slide to me."

"Did you notice where it made that bend up at the top?" he asked.

I nodded my head.

"Well, inside the school there's a door," he said. "If the school gets on fire, they open the door. The children jump in the pipe and slide out to safety."

"Boy, that's a keen way of getting out of a fire," I said.

"Well, it's getting late," Papa said. "We'll talk about this some other time. We'd better get to bed as we have a lot of work to do tomorrow."

My pups were put in the corncrib for the night. I covered them with shucks and kissed them good night.

The next day was a busy one for me. With the hampering help of my sisters I made the little doghouse.

Papa cut the ends off his check lines and gave them to me for collars. With painstaking care, deep in the tough leather I scratched the name "Old Dan" on one and "Little Ann" on the other. With a nail and a rock two holes were punched in each end of the straps. I put them around their small necks and laced the ends together with baling wire.

That evening I had a talk with my mother. I told her about praying for the two pups, about the magazine and the plans I had made. I told her how hard I had tried to find names for them and how strange it was finding them carved in the bark of a sycamore tree.

With a smile on her face, she asked, "Do you believe God heard your prayer and helped you?"

"Yes, Mama," I said. "I know He did and I'll always be thankful."

Chapter 7

It seems that the worries and wants of a young boy never cease. Now that I had my pups another obstacle had cropped up. This one looked absolutely impossible. I had to have a coonskin so I could train them.

With my three little traps and a bull-dogged determination, I set out to trap Mister Ringtail. For three solid weeks I practically lived on the river. I tried every trick I knew. It was no use. I just couldn't catch the wily old coons.

In desperation I went to my grandfather. He smiled as he listened to my tale of woe.

"Well, we'll have to do something about that," he said. "To train those dogs right, you'll need that coon hide, that's for sure. Now you watch the store while I go over to my tool shed. I'll be right back."

After what seemed like an eternity, I saw him coming. He was carrying a brace and bit,[8] that was all.

With a mischievous little smile on his face, he said, "You wouldn't think a fellow could catch a coon with this brace and bit, would you?"

I thought he was kidding me and it made me feel bad. "Why, Grandpa," I said, "you couldn't catch a coon in a jillion years with that thing. You just don't have any idea how smart they are."

"Yes, you can," he said. "You bet your boots you can. Why, when I was a boy I caught coons on top of coons with one of these things."

I saw Grandpa was serious and I got interested.

He laid the brace down on the counter, picked up a small paper sack, and filled it about half-full of horseshoe nails.

"Now you do everything exactly as I tell you," he said, "and you'll catch that coon."

"Yes, sir, Grandpa," I said, "I will. I'll do anything to catch one of them."

"Now the first thing you'll need is some bright objects," he said. "The best thing is bright shiny tin. Cut out some little round pieces, a little smaller than this bit. Do you understand?"

I nodded my head.

"Now," he said, "you go down along the river where there are a lot of coon tracks. Find a good solid log close by and bore a hole down about six inches. Drop one of the

---

8. brace and bit *n.*: A tool for boring, consisting of a drill (bit) turned by cranking a handle (brace).

bright pieces of tin down in the hole, and be sure it's laying right on the bottom."

I was all ears. I didn't want to miss one word my grandfather said. Now and then I would glance at him to see if he was kidding me.

In a serious voice, he went on talking. "Now pay close attention," he said, "because this is the main part of the trap."

With eyes as big as a hoot owl's, I looked and listened.

He took four of the horseshoe nails from the sack. With the thumb and forefinger of his left hand he made a small "o" about the size of the bit, which was an inch and a half in diameter.

"Now, we'll say this is the hole you bored in the log," he said. "About an inch apart, drive these nails in on a slant opposite each other."

Holding one of the nails in his right hand, he showed me the right angle.

"The ends of the nails will enter the hole about halfway between the top and the piece of tin," he continued. "Leave an opening between the sharp points big enough for a coon to get his paw through."

He asked me if I understood.

Again I nodded my head and moved a little closer to him.

"How is that going to catch a coon, Grandpa?" I asked.

"It'll catch him all right," he said, "and it won't fail. You see a coon is a curious little animal. Anything that is bright and shiny attracts him. He will reach in and pick it up. When his paw closes on the bright object it balls up, and when he starts to pull it from the hole, the sharp ends of the nails will gouge into his paw and he's caught."

He looked over at me.

"Well, what do you think of it?" he asked.

I closed my eyes and in my mind I could see the funnel-like entrance of the hole, and the sharp slanting points of the nails. I could see the coon reaching in for the shiny piece of metal. Naturally his paw would be much larger when closed than it was when he reached in. It would be impossible for it to pass the sharp nails.

It was all looking pretty good to me and I was on the point of saying so, when it hit me. Why, all the coon had to do was open his paw, drop the object, and he was free. It all blew up then and there. I just knew my grandfather was playing a joke on me.

I stepped back and almost cried as I said, "Grandpa, you're kidding me. That kind of a trap couldn't catch a coon. Why all he'd have to do is open his paw, drop the piece of tin, and he could pull it from the hole."

Grandpa started roaring with laughter. This did make me feel bad. With tears in my eyes, I started for the door.

"Wait a minute," Grandpa said. "I'm not kidding you. Oh, I know I like to have my jokes, same as any man, but I meant every word I said."

I turned around and looked at him. He had stopped laughing and there was a hurt expression on his face.

"I wasn't laughing at you," he said. "I was laughing more at myself than you. I just wanted to see if you were smart enough to see that there was a way the coon could free himself."

"A fellow wouldn't have to be very smart to see that," I said.

Grandpa started talking seriously again. "You know," he said, "a coon has more than one peculiarity about him. When I was a boy I had a pet coon. By watching him, I saw and learned a lot of things.

"He had a den in an old hollow tree in our front yard. I don't know the number of times I'd have to climb that tree and get my mother's scissors, buttons, needles, and thimble from his den. Why, he'd even carry out our knives, forks, and spoons. Anything that was bright and shiny, he took to his den."

Grandpa stopped talking for a few minutes. I could see a faraway look in his eyes. Once again he was living in those long-ago days. I waited in silence for him to go on with his story.

"One of the most peculiar things about that coon," he said, "was his front feet. Once he wrapped those little paws around something he would never let go.

"My mother had an old churn. It was one of those kinds with a small hole in the lid for the dasher. When she would get through churning, she would take the dasher out to wash it. That crazy coon would climb up on top of the churn, poke his little front paw through the hole, and get a fistful of butter. The hole was small, and when he closed his paw, he couldn't get it back out. All he had to do was open it, drop the butter, and he would be free, but do you think he would? No, sir. He would carry that churn lid all over the house, squalling and growling. Why, it took everyone in the house to free him. I'd have to wrap him up in a gunny sack or an old coat and pry his claws loose from the butter. Seeing this time after time is what gave me the idea for this trap. Once he reaches in and gets hold of that tin, he's caught, because he will never open his paw."

With my confidence restored, it all sounded pretty good to me and I was anxious to try out this wonderful plan. I thanked him and, taking the brace and nails, I left the store.

By the time I reached home it was too late in the day to start making my traps. That night I talked the idea over with Papa.

"I've heard of coons being caught that way," he said, "but I never paid much attention to it. Your grandfather should know, though, for he was quite a coon hunter when he was a boy."

"From what he told me," I said, "it never fails."

Papa asked if I wanted him to help make my traps.

"No," I said, "I think I can do it myself."

I didn't sleep too well that night. I bored holes, drove nails, and fought coons practically all night.

Early the next morning I went to the trash pile. As I stirred around in the rusty old cans, I thought of another time I had searched for a can. Finally I found the one I wanted. It was bright and shiny.

Everything was going along just fine until Mama caught me cutting out the circles of tin with her scissors. I always swore she could find the biggest switches of any woman in the Ozarks. That time she overdid it. I was almost to the river before the stinging stopped.

It wasn't hard to find places for my traps. All along the river large sycamore logs lay partly submerged in the clear blue water. On one where I could see the muddy little tracks of the ringtails, I bored a hole, dropped in a piece of tin, and drove my nails.

On down the river I went, making my traps. I stopped when I ran out of nails. Altogether I had fourteen traps.

That night Papa asked me how I was making out.

"Oh, all right," I said. "I've got fourteen of them made."

He laughed and said, "Well, you can't ever tell. You may catch one."

The next morning I was up with the chickens. I took my pups with me as I just knew I'd have a big ringtail trapped and I wanted them to see it. I was a disappointed boy when I peeked out of a canebrake at my last trap and didn't see a coon. All the way home I tried to figure out what I had done wrong.

I went to Papa. He put his thinking cap on and thought the situation over. "Maybe you left too much scent around when you made those traps," he said. "If you did, it'll take a while for it to go away. Now I wouldn't get too impatient. I'm pretty sure you'll catch one sooner or later."

Papa's words perked me up just like air does a deflated inner tube. He was right. I had simply left too much scent around my traps. All I had to do was wait until it disappeared and I'd have my coon hide.

Morning after morning it was the same old disappointment; no coon. When a week had gone by and still no results from my traps, I gave up. What little patience I had was completely gone. I was firmly convinced that coons didn't walk on sycamore logs any more, and bright shiny objects had about as much effect on them as a coon hound would.

One morning I didn't get up to run my trap line. I stayed in bed. What was the use? It was just a waste of time.

When the family sat down to breakfast, I heard my oldest sister say, "Mama, isn't Billy going to get up for breakfast?"

"Why, is he in his room?" Mama asked. "I didn't know. I thought he was down looking at his traps."

I heard Papa say, "I'll go wake him up."

He came to the door and said, "You'd better get up, Billy. Breakfast is ready."

"I don't want any breakfast," I said. "I'm not hungry."

Papa took one look at me and saw I had a bad case of the ringtail blues. He came over and sat down on the bed.

"What's the matter?" he asked. "You having coon trouble?"

"Grandpa lied to me, Papa," I said. "I should've known better. Who ever heard of anyone catching a coon with a brace and bit and a few horseshoe nails."

"I wouldn't say that," Papa said. "I don't think your grandpa deliberately lied to you. Besides, I've heard of coons being caught that way."

"Well, I don't think I've done anything wrong," I said. "I've done everything exactly as he said, and I haven't caught one yet."

"I still think it's that scent," Papa said. "You know, someone told me, or I read it somewhere, that it takes about a week for scent to die away. How long has it been since you made those traps?"

"It's been over a week," I said.

"Well, the way I figure, it's about time for you to catch one. Yes, sir, I wouldn't be surprised if you came in with one any day now."

After Papa had left the room I lay thinking of what he had said. "Any day now." I got up and hurried into my clothes.

As soon as I was finished with breakfast, I called my pups and lit out for the river.

The first trap was empty. So was the second one. That old feeling of doubt came over me again. I thought, "It's no use. I'll never catch one and I so need the skin to train my pups."

On the way to my third trap I had to walk through a thick stand of wild cane. It was tough going and my pups started whimpering. I stopped and picked them up.

"We'll be out of this in a few minutes," I said, "and then you'll be all right."

I came plowing out of the matted mass and was right on the trap before I realized it. I was met by a loud squall. I was so surprised I dropped the pups. There he was, my first coon.

He was humped up on the sycamore log, growling and showing his teeth. He kept jerking his front paw, which was jammed deep in the hole I had bored. He was trapped by his own curiosity.

I couldn't move and I felt like my wind had been cut off. I kept hearing a noise but couldn't make out what it was. The movement of the boy pup shook me from my trance. The unidentified sound was his bawling. He was trying to climb up on the log and get to the coon.

I yelled at him and darted in to get hold of his collar. On seeing my movement, the coon let out another squall. It scared me half to death. I froze in my tracks and started yelling again at my pup.

The girl pup worked around behind the coon and climbed up on the log. I screamed at her. She paid no attention to me.

Digging his sharp little claws in the bark, the boy pup made it to the top. He didn't hesitate. Straight down that sycamore log he charged. With teeth bared, the coon waited. When my pup was about two feet from him, he made a lunge. The coon just seemed to pull my pup up under his stomach and went to work with tooth and claw.

The girl pup saved him. Like a cat in a corncrib, she sneaked in from behind and sank her needle-sharp teeth in the coon's back.

It was too much for Old Ringy. He turned the boy pup loose, turned around, and slapped her clear off the log. She came running to me, yelping her head off. I grabbed her up in my arms and looked for the boy pup. When the coon had turned him loose, he too had fallen off the log. He was trying to get back to the coon. I darted in and grabbed him by the hind leg.

With a pup under each arm and running as fast as I could, I lit out for the house. Coming out of the bottoms into a fresh-plowed field I set my pups down so I could get a little more speed. I started yelling as soon as I came in sight of the house.

Mama came flying out with my sisters right behind her. Papa was out by the barn harnessing his team. Mama yelled something to him about a snake. He dropped the harness, jumped over the rail fence, and in a long lope started for me.

Mama reached me first. She grabbed me and shouted, "Where did it bite you?"

"Bite me?" I said. "Why Mama, I'm not bit. I've got him, Mama. I've got him."

"Got what?" Mama asked.

"A big coon," I said. "The biggest one in the river bottoms. He's this big, Mama." I made a circle with my arms as big as a twenty-gallon keg.

Mama just groaned way down deep and covered her face with her hands. Some big tears squeezed out between her fingers. Almost in a whisper, I heard her say, "Thank God; I thought you were snake-bitten."

My sisters, seeing Mama crying, puckered up and started bawling.

"He needs a whipping," the oldest one said, "that's what he needs, scaring Mama that way."

Something busted loose inside me and I cried a little, too.

"I didn't mean to scare Mama," I sniffed. "I just wanted everyone to know I caught a coon."

Up until this time Papa hadn't said a word. He just stood looking on.

"Here now," he said, "let's have none of this crying. He didn't mean to scare anyone."

Taking his handkerchief from his pocket, he stepped over to Mama, put his arm around her, and started drying her eyes.

Mama poked her head around him and glared at me. "Billy Colman," she shouted, "if you ever scare me like that again, I'll take a switch and wear you to a frazzle."

This hurt my feelings and I really did get tuned up. "Everyone's mad at me," I said, "and I haven't done anything but catch the biggest coon on the river."

Mama came over. "I'm sorry," she said. "I didn't mean to be cross, but you did scare me. I thought a rattlesnake had bitten you."

"Now that that's all settled," Papa said, "we had better go get that coon." Looking at Mama, he said, "Why don't you and the girls go with us. I don't think it'll take long."

Mama looked at me, smiled, and turned to the girls. "Would you like to go?" she asked.

Their only answer was a lot of squealing and jumping up and down.

On the way, Mama noticed some blood on my shirt. She stopped me and started looking me over.

"Where did that come from?" she asked. "Did that coon bite you?"

"No, Mama," I said. "I didn't get close enough for him to bite me."

With a worried look on her face, she jerked out my shirt. "You don't seem to be scratched anywhere," she said.

"Maybe this is where it came from," Papa said.

He reached down and picked up my boy pup. His little black nose was split wide open and was bleeding.

I saw a relieved look come over Mama's face.

Looking at me, she started shaking her head. "I don't know," she said. "I just don't know."

"Did that coon get hold of this pup?" Papa asked.

"He sure did, Papa," I said, "but it wasn't the coon's fault. If it hadn't been for Little Ann, he'd have eaten him up."

I told how my dogs had tied into the coon.

Papa laughed as he fondled my pup. "This dog is going to be a coon hound," he said, " and I mean a good one."

The coon started squalling as soon as we came in sight.

"My goodness," Mama said, "you wouldn't think anything so small would be so vicious."

Papa picked up a club. "Now everybody stand back out of the way," he said. "This won't take long."

My pups were wanting to get to the coon so badly that they were hard to hold. I had to squeeze them up tight to keep them from jumping right out of my arms.

My sisters, with eyes as big as blue marbles, got behind Mama and peeked around her.

Papa whacked the coon a good one across the head. He let out a loud squall, growled, and showed his teeth. He tried hard to get to Papa but the trap held him.

The girls buried their faces in Mama's dress and started bawling. Mama turned her back on the fight. I heard her say, "I wish we hadn't come. Poor thing."

Papa whacked him again and it was all over.

It was too much for Mama and the girls. They left. I heard the tall cane rattling as they ran for the house.

After the coon was killed, I walked over. Papa was trying to get the coon's paw from the trap. He couldn't do it. Taking a pair of pliers from his pocket, he said, "It's a good thing I had these along or we would have had to cut his foot off."

After Papa had pulled the nails, he lifted the coon's paw from the hole. There, clamped firmly in it, was the bright piece of tin.

In a low voice Papa said, "Well, I'll be darned. All he had to do was open it up and

he was free, but he wouldn't do it. Your grandfather was right."

A sorrowful look came over Papa's face as he ran his fingers through the soft, yellow hair. "Billy," he said, "I want you to take a hammer and pull the nails from every one of those traps. It's summertime now and their fur isn't any good. Besides, I don't think this is very sportsmanlike. The coon doesn't have a chance. It's all right this time. You needed this one, but from now on I want you to catch them with your dogs. That way they have a fifty-fifty chance."

"I will, Papa," I said. "That's what I intended to do."

While we were skinning the coon, Papa asked me when I was going to start training my dogs.

"I don't know," I said. "Do you think they're too young?"

"No, I·don't think so," he said. "I've heard that the younger they are the better it is."

"Well, in that case," I said, "I'll start tomorrow."

With the help of my oldest sister, we started giving my pups their first lessons. She would hold their collars while I made trails with the hide for them to follow.

I'd climb trees that leaned out over the river, jump out into the water, swim to the other side, and make trails up and down the bank. With a long pole and wire, I'd drag the hide on top of rail fences, swing it through the air, and let it touch the ground twenty or thirty feet away. I did everything with that hide a coon would do and probably a lot of things a coon couldn't do.

It was a beautiful sight to see my pups work those trails. At first they were awkward and didn't know what to do, but they would never quit trying.

Old Dan would get so eager and excited, he would overrun a trail. Where it twisted or turned, he would run straight on, bawling up a storm. It didn't take him long to realize that a smart old coon didn't always run in a straight line.

Little Ann never overran a trail. She would wiggle and twist, cry and whine, and pretty soon she would figure it out.

At first they were afraid of water. I never would admit it even to myself. I always said that they just didn't like to get wet. They would follow the trail to the stream and stop. Sitting down on their rears, they would cry and beg for help. With a pup under each arm, I'd wade out into the stream and set them down in the cool water. Nine times out of ten, one pup would swim one way and the other one would go just the opposite way. I had a time with this part of their training, but my persistence had no bounds.

It wasn't long until they loved the water. Old Dan would jump as far out as he could and practically knock the river dry. Little Ann would ease herself in and swim like a muskrat for the opposite shore.

I taught my dogs every trick I knew and any new ones I heard about. I taught them how to split up on a riverbank to search for the hidden trail, because it was impossible to tell where a coon would come out of the water. Sometimes he might swim downstream and other times he might swim upstream. Maybe he would come back to the bank he had just left, or he would cross over to the other side. Perhaps he would stop in the middle of the stream on an old drift.

Sometimes he would come out of the water by catching the dangling limbs of a leaning birch and climbing up, never touching the bank. Or he could come out on the same trail he used to go in, and backtrack. He would sometimes crawl up under an undermined bank or into an old muskrat den.

One of the favorite tricks of a smart old ringtail is the treebarking trick. This he accomplished by running far up on the side of a tree and using his stout legs for leverage,

springing twenty or thirty feet away before touching the ground. Dumb hounds trail up to the tree and start bawling treed. I taught my dogs to circle for a good hundred yards to be sure he was still in the tree before bawling.

In order to learn more about coon hunting, I'd hang around my grandfather's store and listen to the stories told by the coon hunters. Some of the tales I heard were long and tall, but I believed them all.

I could always tell when Grandpa was kidding me by the twinkle in his eyes. He told me how a coon could climb right up the fog and disappear in the stars, and how he could leap on a horse's back and run him over your dogs. I didn't care, for I loved to hear the tall tales. Anything that had a coon hair in it I believed completely.

All through that summer and into the late fall the training went on. Although I was worn down to a frazzle, I was a happy boy. I figured I was ready for the ringtails.

Late one evening, tired and exhausted, I sat down by a big sycamore and called my dogs to me. "It's all over," I said. "There'll be no more lessons. I've worked hard and I've done my best. From now on it's all up to you. Hunting season is just a few days away and I'm going to let you rest for I want you to be in good shape the night it opens."

It was wonderful indeed how I could have heart-to-heart talks with my dogs and they always seemed to understand. Each question I asked was answered in their own doggish way.

Although they couldn't talk in my terms, they had a language of their own that was easy to understand. Sometimes I would see the answer in their eyes, and again it would be in the friendly wagging of their tails. Other times I could hear the answer in a low whine or feel it in the soft caress of a warm flicking tongue. In some way, they would always answer.

THINKING ABOUT THE SELECTION

Recalling

1. Describe Billy's home and family.
2. In what ways does Billy attempt to get the dogs he wants?
3. Describe three incidents that occur on Billy's trip to and from Tahlequah.
4. What steps does Billy take to train his dogs?

Interpreting

5. How do the events in Chapter 1 bring back the memories of the narrator's childhood?
6. Why are dogs so important to Billy?
7. How does Billy feel about working in the fields with his father for the first time?
8. Describe Billy's relationship with his grandfather.
9. Contrast the ways that Billy's mother and father treat him, particularly when he returns from his trip to get his dogs.

Applying

10. When Billy is in town, some people stare and laugh at him, and others try to beat him up. Why do people often act negatively toward those who seem different?

ANALYZING LITERATURE

Understanding Character

You find out about Billy's character and the characters of others by what Billy sees, thinks, or does and by what others say to him.

1. Name two of Billy's character traits.
2. What does Billy's decision to walk twenty miles to Tahlequah rather than wait a week for his dogs reveal about his character?
3. Why do Grandfather and the sheriff react as they do when Billy tells them what he did to get the dogs?

CRITICAL THINKING AND READING

Making Inferences About Characters

An **inference** is a conclusion that you draw from stated information. In a novel, a writer pre-sents a character's actions, words, and thoughts. From this given information, you can make infer-ences about the characters. For example, Billy works hard and saves his money for two years. You can infer from these actions that he is very persistent and highly motivated.

1. What statements made by other characters support this inference?
2. What can you infer about Billy's character from his actions toward his family when he returns home from Tahlequah?

UNDERSTANDING LANGUAGE

Discovering Word Origins

American English contains thousands of words that have interesting origins. Many of these words are borrowed from other languages, includ-ing the languages of the Native Americans. For example, the origin of the proper noun *Oklahoma* is two words from the Choctaw Indian language: *okla,* meaning "people," and *homma,* meaning "red."

Look up in a dictionary the following proper nouns from the novel. Find the language from which each word comes and its original meaning.

1. Missouri
2. Cherokee
3. Kentucky
4. Ozark
5. Arkansas

THINKING AND WRITING

Writing About Character

Imagine that you are Billy's grandfather and you are writing a letter to a friend describing your grandson. Tell your friend about the time that Billy came into the store with a can of money and asked you to help him get the dogs. First make a list of character traits that describe Billy as Grand-father sees him. Then write the letter, including examples of Billy's actions that show his charac-ter traits.

As you revise, be sure you have given specific examples.

GUIDE FOR READING

Where the Red Fern Grows, Chapters 8–11

Plot in a Novel

Plot is the sequence of related events in a story or novel. These events develop around a conflict, which is a struggle between opposing sides. The plot usually develops in a pattern, in which the events rise to a climax, or point of highest interest. The conflict is then resolved.

In a novel, the plot develops over a longer period of time, often through episodes. An **episode** is a narrative incident complete in itself, including its own conflict, climax, and resolution. For example, the incident in which Billy travels into town and returns with his puppies is one episode. The separate plot episodes are unified by common characters and a common theme.

Look For

There are four episodes in Chapters 8–11. Look for them as you read. Each episode has its own conflict. What problem must Billy overcome to resolve the conflict in each episode?

Writing

In this novel, Billy encounters many problems, which he always manages to solve. Think of a time when you worked, alone or with a friend, to solve a difficult problem. Write down your problem-solving approach. Review the cause of the problem and the steps you took to solve it. What were the results of your efforts?

Vocabulary

Knowing the following words will help you as you read Chapters 8–11 of *Where the Red Fern Grows*.

baying (bā′ iŋ) *v.*: Long, deep barking (p. 668)

momentum (mō men′ təm) *n.*: The increasing force of a moving object (p. 681)

nonchalantly (nän′ shə länt′ lē) *adv.*: In a casual way (p. 683)

belligerent (bə lij′ ər ənt) *adj.*: Showing a readiness to fight (p. 685)

slough (slou) *n.*: A swamp, bog, or marsh that is part of an inlet or backwater (p. 687)

Chapter 8

The day hunting season opened, I was as nervous as Samie, our house cat. Part of that seemingly endless day was spent getting things ready for the coming night.

I cleaned my lantern and filled it full of oil. With hog lard I greased my boots until they were as soft as a hummingbird's nest. I was grinding my ax when Papa came around.

He smiled as he said, "This is the big night, isn't it?"

"It sure is, Papa," I said, "and I've waited a long time for it."

"Yes, I know," he said. "I've been thinking—there's not too much to do around here during the hunting season. I'm pretty sure I can take care of things, so you just go ahead and hunt all you want to."

"Thanks, Papa," I said. "I guess I'll be out pretty late at night, and I'll probably have to do a lot of sleeping in the daytime."

Papa started frowning. "You know," he said, "your mother doesn't like this hunting of yours very much. She's worried about you being out all by yourself."

"I can't see why Mama has to worry," I said. "Haven't I been roaming the woods ever since I was big enough to walk, and I'm almost fourteen now."

"I know," said Papa. "It's all right with me, but women are a little different than men. They worry more."

"Now just to be on the safe side, I think it would be a good idea for you to tell us where you'll be hunting. Then if anything happens, we'll know where to look."

I told him I would, but I didn't think anything was going to happen.

After Papa had left, I started thinking. "He doesn't even talk to me like I was a boy any more. He talks to me like I was a man." These wonderful thoughts made me feel just about as big as our old red mule.

I had a good talk with my dogs. "I've waited almost three years for this night," I said, "and it hasn't been easy. I've taught you everything I know and I want you to do your best."

Little Ann acted like she understood. She whined and saved me a wash job on my face. Old Dan may have, but he didn't act like it. He just lay there in the sunshine, all stretched out and limber as a rag.

During supper Mama asked me where I was going to hunt.

"I'm not going far," I said, "just down on the river."

I could tell Mama was worried and it didn't make me feel too good.

"Billy," she said, "I don't approve of this hunting, but it looks like I can't say no; not after all you've been through, getting your dogs, and all that training."

"Aw, he'll be all right," Papa said. "Besides, he's getting to be a good-size man now."

"Man!" Mama exclaimed. "Why, he's still just a little boy."

"You can't keep him a little boy always," Papa said. "He's got to grow up some day."

"I know," Mama said, "but I don't like it, not at all, and I can't help worrying."

"Mama, please don't worry about me," I said. "I'll be all right. Why, I've been all over these hills, you know that."

"I know," she said, "but that was in the daytime. I never worried too much when it was daylight, but at night, that's different. It'll be dark and anything could happen."

"There won't be anything happening," I said. "I promise I'll be careful."

Mama got up from the table saying, "Well, it's like I said, I can't say no and I can't help worrying. I'll pray every night you're out."

The way Mama had me feeling, I didn't know whether to go hunting or not. Papa must have sensed how I felt. "It's dark now," he said, "and I understand those coons start stirring pretty early. You had better be going, hadn't you?"

While Mama was bundling me up, Papa lit my lantern. He handed it to me, saying, "I'd like to see a big coonskin on the smokehouse wall in the morning."

The whole family followed me out on the porch. There we all got a surprise. My dogs were sitting on the steps, waiting for me.

I heard Papa laugh. "Why, they know you're going hunting," he said, "know it as well as anything."

"Well, I never," said Mama. "Do you really think they do? It does look like they do. Why, just look at them."

Little Ann started wiggling and twisting. Old Dan trotted out to the gate, stopped, turned around, and looked at me.

"Sure they know Billy's going hunting," piped the little one, "and I know why."

"How do you know so much, silly?" asked the oldest one.

"Because I told Little Ann, that's why," she said, "and she told Old Dan. That's how they know."

We all had to laugh at her.

The last thing I heard as I left the house was the voice of my mother. "Be careful, Billy," she said, "and don't stay out late."

It was a beautiful night, still and frosty. A big grinning Ozark moon had the countryside bathed in a soft yellow glow. The starlit heaven reminded me of a large blue umbrella, outspread and with the handle broken off.

Just before I reached the timber, I called my dogs to me. "Now the trail will be a little different tonight," I whispered. "It won't be a hide dragged on the ground. It'll be the real thing, so remember everything I taught you and I'm depending on you. Just put one up a tree and I'll do the rest."

I turned them loose, saying, "Go get 'em."

They streaked for the timber.

By the time I had reached the river, every nerve in my body was drawn up as tight as a fiddlestring. Big-eyed and with ears open, I walked on, stopping now and then to listen. The way I was slipping along anyone would have thought I was trying to slip up on a coon myself.

I had never seen a night so peaceful and still. All around me tall sycamores gleamed like white streamers in the moonlight. A prowling skunk came wobbling up the riverbank. He stopped when he saw me. I smiled at the fox-fire glow of his small, beady, red eyes. He turned and disappeared in the underbrush. I heard a sharp snap and a feathery rustle in some brush close by. A small rodent started squealing in agony. A night hawk had found his supper.

Across the river and from far back in the rugged mountains I heard the baying of a hound. I wondered if it was the same one I had heard from my window on those nights so long ago.

Although my eyes were seeing the wonders of the night, my ears were ever alert, listening for the sound of my hounds telling me they had found a trail.

I was expecting one of them to bawl, but when it came it startled me. The deep tones of Old Dan's voice jarred the silence around me. I dropped my ax and almost dropped my lantern. A strange feeling came over me. I took a deep breath and threw back my head to give the call of the hunter, but something went wrong. My throat felt like it had been tied in a knot. I swallowed a couple of times and the knot disappeared.

As loud as I could, I whooped, "Who-e-e-e. Get him, Dan. Get him."

Little Ann came in. The bell-like tones of her voice made shivers run up and down my spine. I whooped to her. "Who-e-e-e. Tell it to him, little girl. Tell it to him."

This was what I had prayed for, worked and sweated for, my own little hounds bawling on the trail of a river coon. I don't know why I cried, but I did. While the tears rolled, I whooped again and again.

They straightened the trail out and headed down river. I took off after them as fast as I could run.

A mile downstream the coon pulled his first trick. I could tell by my dogs' voices that they had lost the trail. When I came to them they were out on an old drift, sniffing around.

The coon had pulled a simple trick. He had run out on the drift, leaped into the water, and crossed the river. To an experienced coon hound, the crude trick would have been nothing at all, but my dogs were just big, awkward pups, trailing their first live coon.

I stood and watched, wondering if they

would remember the training I had given them. Now and then I would whoop, urging them on.

Old Dan was having a fit. He whined and he bawled. He whimpered and cried. He came to me and reared up, begging for help.

"I'm not going to help you," I scolded, "and you're not going to find him out on that drift. If you would just remember some of the training I gave you, you could find the trail. Now go find that coon."

He ran back out on the drift and started searching.

Little Ann came to me. I could see the pleading in her warm gray eyes. "I'm ashamed of you, little girl," I said. "I thought you had more sense than this. If you let him fool you this easily, you'll never be a coon dog."

She whined, turned, and trotted downstream to search again for the lost trail.

I couldn't understand. Had all the training I had given them been useless? I knew if I waded the river they would follow me. Once on the other side, it would be easy for them to find the trail. I didn't want it that way. I wanted them to figure it out by themselves. The more I thought about it, the more disgusted I became. I sat down and buried my face in my arms.

Out on the drift, Old Dan started whining. It made me angry and I got up to scold him again.

I couldn't understand his actions. He was running along the edge of the drift, whimpering and staring downriver. I looked that way. I could see something swimming for the opposite shore. At first I thought it was a muskrat. In the middle of the stream, where the moonlight was the brightest, I got a good look. It was Little Ann.

With a loud whoop, I told her how proud I was. My little girl had remembered her training.

She came out on a gravel bar, shook the water from her body, and disappeared in the thick timber. Minutes later, she let me know she had found the trail. Before the tones of her voice had died away, Old Dan plowed into the water. He was so eager to join her I could hear him whining as he swam.

As soon as his feet touched bottom in the shallows, he started bawling and lunging. White sheets of water, knocked high in the moonlight by his churning feet, gleamed like thousands of tiny white stars.

He came out of the river onto a sand bar. In his eagerness, his feet slipped in the loose sand and down he went. He came out of his roll, running and bawling. Ahead of him was a log jam. He sailed over it and disappeared down the riverbank. Seconds later I heard his deep voice blend with the sharp cries of Little Ann.

At that moment no boy in the world could have been more proud of his dogs than I was. Never again would I doubt them.

I was hurrying along, looking for a shallow riffle so I could wade across, when the voices of my dogs stopped. I waited and listened. They opened again on my side of the stream. The coon had crossed back over.

I couldn't help smiling. I knew that never again would a ringtail fool them by swimming the river.

The next trick the old fellow pulled was dandy. He climbed a large water oak standing about ten feet from the river and simply disappeared.

I got there in time to see my dogs swimming for the opposite shore. For half an hour they worked that bank. Not finding the trail, they swam back. I stood and watched them. They practically tore the riverbank to pieces looking for the trail.

Old Dan knew the coon had climbed the water oak. He went back, reared up on it, and bawled a few times.

"There's no use in doing that, boy," I said. "I know he climbed it, but he's not there now. Maybe it's like Grandpa said, he just climbed right on out through the top and disappeared in the stars."

My dogs didn't know it, but I was pretty well convinced that that was what the coon had done.

They wouldn't give up. Once again they crossed over to the other shore. It was no use. The coon hadn't touched that bank. They came back. Old Dan went up the river and Little Ann worked downstream.

An hour and a half later they gave up and came to me begging for help. I knelt down between their wet bodies. While I scratched and petted them, I let them know that I still loved them.

"I'm not mad," I said. "I know you did your best. If that coon can fool both of us, then we're just beat. We'll go someplace else to hunt. He's not the only coon in these bottoms."

Just as I picked up my ax and lantern, Little Ann let out a bawl and tore out down the riverbank. Old Dan, with a bewildered look on his face, stood for a moment looking after her. Then, raising his head high in the air, he made my eardrums ring with his deep voice. I could hear the underbrush popping as he ran to join her.

I couldn't figure out what had taken place. Surely Little Ann had heard or seen something. I could tell by their voices that whatever it was they were after, they were close enough to see it and were probably running by sight.

The animal left the bottoms and headed for the mountains. Whatever it was, it must have realized my dogs were crowding it too closely. At the edge of the foothills it turned and came back toward the river.

I was still trying to figure out what was going on, when I realized that on striking the river the animal had again turned and was coming straight toward me. I set my lantern down and tightened my grip on the ax.

I was standing my ground quite well when visions of bears, lions, and all kinds of other animals started flashing across my mind. I jumped behind a big sycamore and was trying hard to press my body into the tree when a big coon came tearing by. Twenty-five yards behind him came my dogs, running side by side. I saw them clearly when they passed me, bawling every time their feet touched the ground.

After seeing that there was nothing to be scared of, once again I was the fearless hunter, screaming and yelling as loud as I could, "Get him, boy, get him."

I tore out after them. The trails I knew so well were forgotten. I took off straight through the brush. I was tearing my way through some elders when the voices of my dogs stopped.

Holding my breath, I stood still and waited. Then it came, the long-drawn-out bawl of the tree bark. My little hounds had done it. They had treed their first coon.

When I came to them and saw what they had done I was speechless. I groaned and closed my eyes. I didn't want to believe it. There were a lot of big sycamores in the bottoms but the one in which my dogs had treed was the giant of them all.

While prowling the woods, I had seen the big tree many times. I had always stopped and admired it. Like a king in his own domain, it towered far above the smaller trees.

It had taken me quite a while to find a name suitable for the big sycamore. For a while I had called it "the chicken tree." In some ways it had reminded me of a mother hen hovering over her young in a rainstorm. Its huge limbs spread out over the small birch, ash, box elder, and water oak as if it alone were their protector.

Next, I named it "the giant." That name didn't last long. Mama told us children a story about a big giant that lived in the mountains and ate little children that were lost. Right away I started looking for another name.

One day, while lying in the warm sun staring at its magnificent beauty, I found the perfect name. From that day on, it was called "the big tree." I named the bottoms around it "the big tree bottoms."

Walking around it, and using the moon as a light, I started looking for the coon. High up in the top I saw a hollow in the end of a broken limb. I figured that that was the coon's den.

I could climb almost any tree I had ever seen but I knew I could never climb the big sycamore and it would take days to chop it down.

There had been very little hope from the beginning, but on seeing the hollow I gave up. "Come on," I said to my dogs. "There's nothing I can do. We'll go someplace else and find another coon."

I turned to walk away. My hounds made no move to follow. They started whining. Old Dan reared up, placed his front paws on the trunk, and started bawling.

"I know he's there," I said, "but there's nothing I can do. I can't climb it. Why it's sixty feet up to the first limb and it would take me a month to cut it down."

Again I turned and started on my way.

Little Ann came to me. She reared up and started licking my hands. Swallowing the knot in my throat, I said, "I'm sorry, little girl. I want him just as badly as you do, but there's no way I can get him."

She ran back to the tree and started digging in the soft ground close to the roots.

"Come on now," I said in a gruff voice. "You're both acting silly. You know I'd get the coon for you if I could but I can't."

With a whipped-dog look on her face and with her tail between her legs, Little Ann came over. She wouldn't even look at me. Old Dan walked slowly around behind the tree and hid himself. He peeped around the big trunk and looked at me. The message I read in his friendly eyes tore at my heart. He seemed to be saying, "You told us to put one in a tree and you would do the rest."

With tears in my eyes, I looked again at the big sycamore. A wave of anger came over me. Gritting my teeth, I said, "I don't care how big you are, I'm not going to let my dogs down. I told them if they put a coon in a tree I would do the rest and I'm going to. I'm going to cut you down. I don't care if it takes me a whole year."

I walked over and sank my ax as deep as I could in the smooth white bark. My dogs threw a fit. Little Ann started turning in circles. I could hear her pleased whimpering cry. Old Dan bawled and started gnawing on the big tree's trunk.

At first it was easy. My ax was sharp and the chips flew. Two hours later things were different. My arms felt like two dead grapevines, and my back felt like someone had pulled a plug out of one end of it and drained all the sap out.

While taking a breather, I saw I was making more progress than I thought I would. The cut I had started was a foot deep, but I still had a long way to go.

Sitting on their rears, my dogs waited and watched. I smiled at the look on their faces. Every time I stopped chopping they would come over. While Little Ann washed the sweat from my face, Old Dan would inspect my work. He seemed to be pleased with what he saw for he always wagged his tail.

Along about daylight I got my second wind and I really did make the chips fly. This burst of energy cost me dearly. By sunup I was so stiff I could hardly move. My hands and arms were numb. My back screamed with pain. I could go no further. Sitting down, I leaned back against the big tree and fell asleep.

Little Ann woke me up by washing my face. I groaned with the torture of getting to my feet. Every muscle in my body seemed to be tied in a knot. I was thinking of going down to the river to wash my face in the cool water when I heard a loud whoop. I recognized my father's voice. I whooped to let him know where I was.

Papa was riding our red mule. After he rode up, he just sat there and looked me over. He glanced at my dogs and at the big sycamore. I saw the worry leave his face. He straightened his shoulders, pursed his lips, and blew out a little air. He reminded me of someone who had just dropped a heavy load.

In a slow, calm voice, he asked, "Are you all right, Billy?"

"Yes, Papa," I said. "Oh, I'm a little tired and sleepy, otherwise I'm fine."

He slid from the mule's back and came over. "Your mother's worried" he said. "When you didn't come in, we didn't know what had happened. You should've come home."

I didn't know what to say. I bowed my head and looked at the ground. I was trying hard to choke back the tears when I felt his hand on my shoulder.

"I'm not scolding," he said. "We just thought maybe you had an accident or something."

I looked up and saw a smile on his face.

He turned and looked again at the tree. "Say," he said, "this is the sycamore you call 'the big tree,' isn't it?"

I nodded my head.

"Is there a coon in it?" he asked.

"There sure is, Papa," I said. "He's in that hollow limb. See—that one way up there. That's why I couldn't come home. I was afraid he'd get away."

"Maybe you just think he's there," Papa said. "I believe I'd make sure before I'd cut down a tree that big."

"Oh, he's there all right," I said. "My dogs weren't ten feet behind him when he went up it."

"Why are you so determined to get this coon?" Papa asked. "Couldn't you go somewhere else and tree one? Maybe the tree would be a smaller one."

"I thought about that, Papa," I said, "but I made a bargain with my dogs. I told them that if they would put one in a tree, I'd do the rest. Well, they fulfilled their part of the bargain. Now it's up to me to do my part, and I'm going to, Papa. I'm going to cut it down. I don't care if it takes me a year."

Papa laughed and said, "Oh, I don't think it'll take that long, but it will take a while. I tell you what I'll do. You take the mule and go get some breakfast. I'll chop on it until you get back."

"No, Papa," I said. "I don't want any help. I want to cut it down all by myself. You see, if someone helps me, I wouldn't feel like I kept my part of the agreement."

An astonished look came over my father's face. "Why, Billy," he said, "you can't stay down here without anything to eat and no sleep. Besides, it'll take at least two days to cut that tree down and that's hard work."

"Please, Papa," I begged, "don't make me quit. I just have to get that coon. If I don't, my dogs won't ever believe in me again."

Papa didn't know what to tell me. He scratched his head, looked over to my dogs and back at me. He started walking around. I waited for him to make up his mind. He finally reached a decision.

"Well, all right," he said. "If that's the way you want it, I'm for it even if it is only an agreement between you and your dogs. If a man's word isn't any good, he's no good himself.

"Now I have to get back and tell your mother that you're all right. It's a cinch that you can't do that kind of work on an empty stomach, so I'll send your oldest sister down with a lunch bucket."

With tears in my eyes, I said, "Tell Mama I'm sorry for not coming home last night."

"Don't you worry about your mother," he said, as he climbed on the mule's back. "I'll take care of her. Another thing, I have to make a trip to the store today and I'll talk this over with your grandfather. He may be able to help some way."

After Papa left, things were a little different. The tree didn't look as big, and my ax wasn't as heavy. I even managed to sing a little as I chopped away.

When my sister came with the lunch bucket, I could have kissed her, but I didn't. She took one look at the big tree and her blue eyes got as big as a guinea's egg.

"You're crazy," she gasped, "absolutely crazy. Why, it'll take a month to cut that tree down, and all for an old coon."

I was so busy with the fresh side pork, fried eggs, and hot biscuits, I didn't pay much attention to her. After all, she was a girl, and girls don't think like boys do.

She raved on. "You can't possibly cut it down today, and what are you going to do when it gets dark?"

"I'm going to keep right on chopping," I said. "I stayed with it last night, didn't I? Well, I'll stay till it's cut down. I don't care how long it takes."

My sister got upset. She looked at me, threw back her small head, and looked up to the top of the big sycamore. "You're as crazy as a bedbug," she said. "Why, I never heard of such a thing."

She stepped over in front of me and very seriously asked if she could look in my eyes.

"Look in my eyes?" I said. "What do you want to do that for? I'm not sick."

"Yes, you are, Billy," she said, "very sick. Mama said when Old Man Johnson went crazy, his eyes turned green. I want to see if yours have."

This was too much. "If you don't get out of here," I shouted, "you're going to be red instead of green, and I mean that."

I grabbed up a stick and started toward her. Of course, I wouldn't have hit her for anything.

This scared her and she started for the house. I heard her saying something about an old coon as she disappeared in the underbrush.

Down in the bottom of my lunch bucket I found a neat little package of scraps for my dogs. While they were eating I walked down to a spring and filled the bucket with cool water.

The food did wonders for me. My strength came back. I spit on my hands and, whistling a coon hunter's tune, I started making the chips fly.

The cut grew so big I could have laid down in it. I moved over to another side and started a new one. Once while I was taking a rest, Old Dan came over to inspect my work. He hopped up in the cut and sniffed around.

"You had better get out of there," I said. "If that tree takes a notion to fall, it'll mash you flatter than a tadpole's tail."

With a "no care" look on his friendly face, he gave me a hurry-up signal with a wag of his tail.

Little Ann had dug a bed in a pile of dead leaves. She looked as if she were asleep but I knew she wasn't. Every time I stopped swinging the ax, she would raise her head and look at me.

Chapter 9

By late evening the happy tune I had been whistling was forgotten. My back throbbed like a stone bruise. The muscles in my legs and arms started quivering and jerking. I couldn't gulp enough air to cool the burning heat in my lungs. My strength was gone. I could go no further.

I sat down and called my dogs to me.

With tears in my eyes, I told them that I just couldn't cut the big tree down.

I was trying hard to make them understand when I heard someone coming. It was Grandpa in his buggy.

I'm sure no one in the world can understand a young boy like his grandfather can. He drove up with a twinkle in his eyes and a smile on his whiskery old face.

"Hello! How are you gettin' along?" he boomed.

"Not so good, Grandpa," I said. "I don't think I can cut it down. It's just too big. I guess I'll have to give up."

"Give up!" Grandpa barked. "Now I don't want to hear you say that. No, sir, that's the last thing I want to hear. Don't ever start anything you can't finish."

"I don't want to give up, Grandpa," I said, "but it's just too big and my strength's gone. I'm give out."

"Course you are," he said. "You've been going at it wrong. To do work like that a fellow needs plenty of rest and food in his stomach."

"How am I going to get that, Grandpa?" I asked. "I can't leave the tree. If I do, the coon will get away."

"No, he won't," Grandpa said. "That's what I came down here for. I'll show you how to keep that coon in the tree."

He walked around the big sycamore, looking up. He whistled and said, "Boy, this is a big one all right."

"Yes, it is, Grandpa," I said. "It's the biggest one in the river bottoms."

Grandpa started chuckling. "That's all right," he said. "The bigger they are the harder they fall."

"How are you going to make the coon stay in the tree, Grandpa?" I asked.

With a proud look on his face, he said, "That's another one of my coon-hunting tricks; learned it when I was a boy. We'll keep him there all right. Oh, I don't mean we can

keep him there for always, but he'll stay for four or five days. That is, until he gets so hungry he just has to come down."

"I don't need that much time," I said. "I'm pretty sure I can have it down by tomorrow night."

Grandpa looked at the cut. "I don't know," he said. "Even though it is halfway down, you must remember you've been cutting on it half of one night and one day. You might make it, but it's going to take a lot of chopping."

"If I get a good night's sleep," I said, "and a couple of meals under my belt, I can do a lot of chopping."

Grandpa laughed. "Speaking of meals," he said, "your ma is having chicken and dumplings for supper. Now we don't want to miss that, so let's get busy."

"What do you want me to do, Grandpa?" I asked.

"Well, let's see," he said. "First thing we'll need is some sticks about five feet long. Take your ax, go over in that canebrake, and get us six of them."

I hurried to do what Grandpa wanted, all the time wondering what in the world he was going to do. How could he keep the coon in the tree?

When I came back, he was taking some old clothes from the buggy. "Take this stocking cap," he said. "Fill it about half-full of grass and leaves."

While I was doing this, Grandpa walked over and started looking up in the tree. "You're pretty sure he's in that hollow limb, are you?" he asked.

"He's there all right, Grandpa," I said. "There's no other place he could be. I've looked all over it and there's no other hollow anywhere."

"Well, in that case," Grandpa said, "we'd better put our man along about here."

"What man, Grandpa?" I asked in surprise.

"The one we're going to make," he said. "To us it'll be a scarecrow, but to that coon it'll be a man."

Knowing too well how smart coons were, right away I began to lose confidence. "I don't see how anything like that can keep a coon in a tree," I said.

"It'll keep him there all right," Grandpa said. "Like I told you before, they're curious little devils. He'll poke his head out of that hole, see this man standing here, and he won't dare come down. It'll take him four or five days to figure out that it isn't a real honest-to-goodness man. By that time it'll be too late. You'll have his hide tacked on the smokehouse wall."

The more I thought about it, the more I believed it, and then there was that serious look on Grandpa's face. That was all it took. I was firmly convinced.

I started laughing. The more I thought about it, the funnier it got. Great big laughing tears rolled down my cheek.

"What's so funny?" Grandpa asked. "Don't you believe it'll work?"

"Sure it'll work, Grandpa," I said. "I know it will. I was just thinking—those coons aren't half as smart as they think they are, are they?"

We both had a good laugh at this.

With the sticks and some baling wire, Grandpa made a frame that looked almost like a gingerbread man. On this he put an old pair of pants and a red sweater. We stuffed the loose flabby clothes with grass and leaves. He wired the stocking-cap head in place and stepped back to inspect his work.

"Well, what do you think of it?" he asked.

"If it had a face," I said, "you couldn't tell it from a real man."

"We can fix that," Grandpa chuckled.

He took a stick and dug some black grease from one of the hub caps on the buggy. I stood and watched while he applied his artistic touch. In the stocking-cap head he made two mean-looking eyes, a crooked nose, and the ugliest mouth I had ever seen.

"Well, what do you think of that?" he asked. "Looks pretty good, huh?"

Laughing fit to kill, and talking all at the same time, I told him that I wouldn't blame the coon if he stayed in the tree until Gabriel blew his horn.

"He won't stay that long," Grandpa chuckled, "but he'll stay long enough for you to cut that tree down."

"That's all I want," I said.

"We'd better be going," Grandpa said. "It's getting late and we don't want to miss that supper."

I was so stiff and sore he had to help me to the buggy seat.

I called to my dogs. Little Ann came, but not willingly. Old Dan refused to leave the tree.

"Come on, boy," I coaxed. "Let's go home and get something to eat. We'll come back tomorrow."

He bowed his head and looked the other way.

"Come on," I scolded, "we can't sit here all night."

This hurt his feelings. He walked around behind the big sycamore and hid.

"Well, I'll be darned," Grandpa said as he

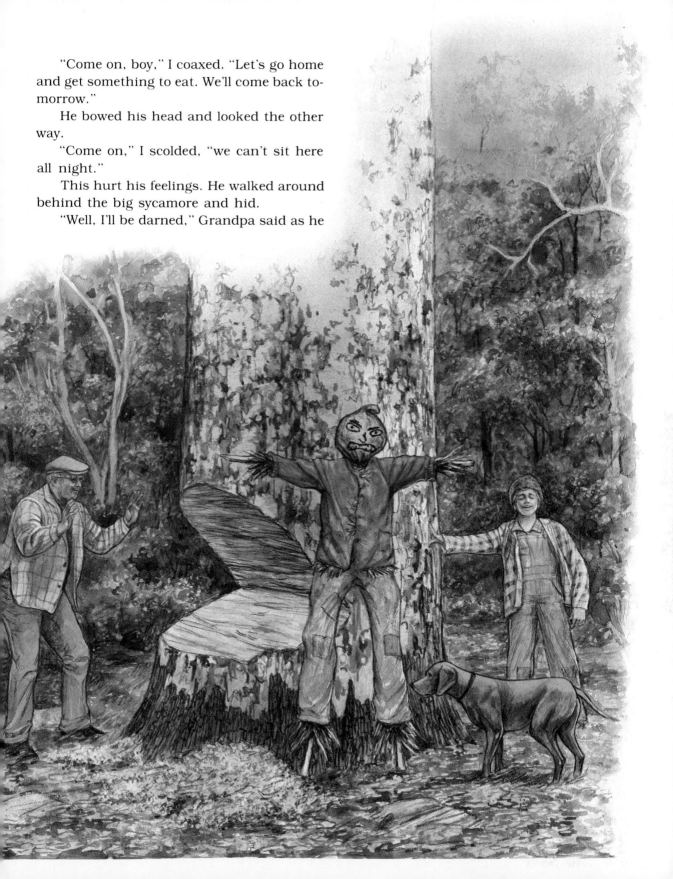

jumped down from the buggy. "He knows that coon's there and he doesn't want to leave it. You've got a coon hound there and I mean a good one."

He picked Old Dan up in his arms and set him in the buggy.

All the way home I had to hold on to his collar to keep him from jumping out and going back to the tree.

As our buggy wound its way up through the bottoms, Grandpa started talking. "You know, Billy," he said, "about this tree-chopping of yours, I think it's all right. In fact, I think it would be a good thing if all young boys had to cut down a big tree like that once in their life. It does something for them. It gives them determination and will-power. That's a good thing for a man to have. It goes a long way in his life. The American people have a lot of it. They have proved that, all down through history, but they could do with a lot more of it."

I couldn't see this determination and will-power that Grandpa was talking about very clearly. All I could see was a big sycamore tree, a lot of chopping, and the hide of a ringtail coon that I was determined to have.

As we reached the house, Mama came out. Right away she started checking me over. "Are you all right?" she asked.

"Sure, Mama," I said. "What makes you think something's wrong with me?"

"Well, I didn't know," she said. "The way you acted when you got down from the buggy, I thought maybe you were hurt."

"Aw, he's just a little sore and stiff from all that chopping," Grandpa said, "but he'll be all right. That'll soon go away."

After Mama saw that there were no broken bones, or legs choppped off, she smiled and said, "I never know anymore. I guess I'll just have to get used to it."

Papa hollered from the porch, "Come on in. We've been waiting supper on you."

"We're having chicken and dumplings," Mama beamed, "and I cooked them especially for you."

During the meal I told Grandpa I didn't think that the coon in the big tree was the same one my dogs had been trailing at first.

"What makes you think that?" he asked.

I told how the coon had fooled us and how Little Ann had seen or heard this other coon. I figured he had just walked up on my dogs before he realized it.

A smile spread all over Grandpa's face. Chuckling, he said, "It does look that way, but it wasn't. No, Billy, it was the same coon. They're much too smart to ever walk up on a hound like that. He pulled a trick and it was a good one. In fact, it'll fool nine out of ten dogs."

"Well, what did he do, Grandpa?" I asked. "I'm pretty sure he didn't cross the river, so how did he work it?"

Grandpa pushed the dishes back and, using his fork as a pencil, he drew an imaginary line on the tablecloth. "It's called the backtracking trick," he said. "Here's how he worked it. He climbed that water oak but he only went up about fifteen or twenty feet. He then turned around and came down in his same tracks. He backtracked on his original trail for a way. When he heard your dogs coming he leaped far up on the side of the nearest tree and climbed up. He was in that tree all the time your dogs were searching for the lost trail. After everything had quieted down, he figured that they had given up. That's when he came down and that's when Little Ann either heard or saw him."

Pointing the fork at me, Grandpa said very seriously, "You mark my word, Billy, in no time at all that Little Ann will know every trick a coon can pull."

"You know, Grandpa," I said, "she wouldn't bark treed at the water oak like Old Dan did."

"Course she wouldn't," he said. "She knew he wasn't there."

"Why, I never heard of such a thing," Mama said. "I'd no idea coons were that smart. Why, for all anyone knows he may not be in the big tree at all. Maybe he pulled another trick. It'd be a shame if Billy cut it down and found there was no coon in it."

"Oh, he's there, Mama," I hastily replied. "I know he is. They were right on his tail when he went up. Besides, Little Ann was bawling her head off when I came to them."

"Of course he's there," Grandpa said. "They were crowding him too closely. He didn't have time to pull another trick."

Grandpa left soon after supper, saying to me, "I'll be back down in a few days and I want to see that coon hide."

I thanked him for helping me and walked out to the buggy with him.

"Oh, I almost forgot," he said. "I heard there was a fad back in the New England states. Seems like everyone is going crazy over coonskin coats. Now if this is true, I look for the price of coon hides to take a jump."

I was happy to hear this and told my father what Grandpa had said. Papa laughed and said, "Well, if you can keep the coons out of those big sycamores, you might make a little money."

Before I went to bed, Mama made me take a hot bath. Then she rubbed me all over with some liniment that burned like fire and smelled like a civet cat.

It seemed like I had barely closed my eyes when Mama woke me up. "Breakfast is about ready, Billy," she said.

I was so stiff and sore I had trouble putting my clothes on. Mama helped me.

"Maybe you'd better let that coon go," she said. "I don't think he's worth all of this."

"I can't do that, Mama," I said. "I've gone too far now."

Papa came in from the barn. "What's the matter?" he asked. "You a little stiff?"

"A little stiff!" Mama exclaimed. "Why he could hardly put his clothes on."

"Aw, he'll be all right," Papa said. "If I know anything about swinging an ax, it won't be long before he's as limber as a rag."

Mama just shook her head and started putting our breakfast on the table.

While we were eating, Papa said, "You know I woke up several times last night and each time I was sure I heard a hound bawling. It sounded like Old Dan."

I quit the table on the run and headed for my doghouse. I didn't have to go all the way. Little Ann met me on the porch. I asked her where Old Dan was and called his name. He was nowhere around.

Little Ann started acting strangely. She whined and stared toward the river bottoms. She ran out to the gate, came back, and reared up on me.

Mama and Papa came out on the porch.

"He's not here," I said. "I think he has gone back to the tree."

"I don't think he'd do that, would he?" Mama said. "Maybe he's around someplace. Have you looked in the doghouse?"

I ran and looked. He wasn't there.

"Everybody be quiet and listen," I said.

I walked out beyond the gate a little ways and whooped as loud as I could. My voice rang like a bell in the still, frosty morning. Before the echo had died away the deep "Ou-u-u-u" of Old Dan rolled out of the river bottoms.

"He's there," I said. "He wanted to make sure the coon stayed in the tree. You see, Mama, why I have to get that coon. I can't let him down."

"Well, I never in all my life," she said. "I had no idea a dog loved to hunt that much. Yes, Billy, I can see now, and I want you to get him. I don't care if you have to cut down every tree in those bottoms. I want you to get that coon for those dogs."

"I'm going to get him, Mama," I said,

"and I'm going to get him today if I possibly can."

Papa laughed and said, "Looks like there wasn't any use in building that scarecrow. All you had to do was tell Old Dan to stay and watch the tree."

I left the house in a run. Now and then I would stop and whoop. Each time I was answered by the deep voice of Old Dan.

Little Ann ran ahead of me. By the time I reached the big tree, their voices were making the bottoms ring.

When I came tearing out of the underbrush, Old Dan threw a fit. He tried to climb the sycamore. He would back way off, then, bawling and running as fast as he could, he would claw his way far up on its side.

Little Ann, not to be outdone, reared up and placed her small front paws on the smooth white bark. She told the ringtail coon that she knew he was there.

After they had quieted down, I called Old Dan to me. "I'm proud of you, boy," I said. "It takes a good dog to stay with a tree all night, but there wasn't any need in you coming back. The coon wouldn't have gotten away. That's why we built the scarecrow."

Little Ann came over and started rolling in the leaves. The way I was feeling toward her, I couldn't even smile at her playful mood. "Of course you feel good," I said in an irritated voice, "and it's no wonder, you had a good night's sleep in a nice warm doghouse, but Old Dan didn't. He was down here in the cold all by himself, watching the tree. The way you're acting, I don't believe you care if the coon gets away or not."

I would have said more but just then I noticed something. I walked over for a better look. There, scratched deep in the soft leaves were two little beds. One was smaller than the other. Looking at Little Ann, I read the answer in her warm gray eyes.

Old Dan hadn't been alone when he had gone back to the tree. She too had gone

along. There was no doubt that in the early morning she had come home to get me.

There was a lump in my throat as I said, "I'm sorry, little girl, I should've known."

The first half-hour was torture. At each swing of the ax my arms felt like they were being torn from their sockets. I gritted my teeth and kept hacking away. My body felt like it did the time my sister rolled me down the hill in a barrel.

As Papa had said, in a little while the warm heat from the hard work limbered me up. I remembered what my father did when he was swinging an ax. At the completion of each swing, he always said, "Ha!" I tried it. Ker-wham. "Ha!" Ker-wham. "Ha!" I don't know if it helped or not, but I was willing to try anything if it would hurry the job.

Several times before noon I had to stop and rake my chips out of the way. I noticed that they weren't the big, even, solid chips like my father made when he was chopping. They were small and seemed to crumble up and come all to pieces. Neither were the cuts neat and even. They were ragged and looked more like the work of beavers. But I wasn't interested in any beautiful tree-chopping. All I wanted was to hear the big sycamore start popping.

Along in the middle of the afternoon, I felt a stinging in one of my hands. When I saw it was a blister I almost cried. At first there was only one. Then two. One after another they rose up on my hands like small white marbles. They filled up and turned a pale pinkish color. When one would burst, it was all I could do to keep from screaming. I tore my handkerchief in half and wrapped my hands. This helped for a while, but when the cloth began to stick to the raw flesh I knew it was the end.

Crying my heart out, I called my dogs to me and showed them my hands. "I can't do it," I said. "I've tried, but I just can't cut it down. I can't hold the ax any longer."

Little Ann whined and started licking my sore hands. Old Dan seemed to understand. He showed his sympathy by nuzzling me with his head.

Brokenhearted, I started for home. As I turned, from the corner of my eye I saw Grandpa's scarecrow. It seemed to be laughing at me. I looked over to the big sycamore. It lacked so little being cut down. A small wedge of solid wood was all that was holding it up. I let my eyes follow the smooth white trunk up to the huge spreading limbs.

Sobbing, I said, "You think you have won, but you haven't. Although I can't get the coon, neither can you live, because I have cut off your breath of life." And then I thought, "Why kill the big tree and not accomplish anything?" I began to feel bad.

Kneeling down between my dogs, I cried and prayed. "Please God, give me the strength to finish the job. I don't want to leave the big tree like that. Please help me finish the job."

I was trying to rewrap my hands so I could go back to work when I heard a low droning sound. I stood up and looked around. I could still hear the noise but couldn't locate it. I looked up. High in the top of the big sycamore a breeze had started the limbs to swaying. A shudder ran through the huge trunk.

I looked over to my right at a big black gum tree. Not one limb was moving. On its branches a few dead leaves hung silent and still. One dropped and floated lazily toward the ground.

Over on my left stood a large hackberry. I looked up to its top. It was as still as a fence post.

Another gust of wind caught in the top of the big tree. It started popping and snapping. I knew it was going to fall. Grabbing my dogs by their collars, I backed off to safety.

I held my breath. The top of the big syca-more rocked and swayed. There was a loud crack that seemed to come from deep inside the heavy trunk. Fascinated, I stood and watched the giant of the bottoms. It seemed to be fighting so hard to keep standing. Several times I thought it would fall, but in a miraculous way it would pull itself back into perfect balance.

The wind itself seemed to be angry at the big tree's stubborn resistance. It growled and moaned as it pushed harder against the wavering top. With one final grinding, creaking sigh, the big sycamore started down. It picked up momentum as the heavy weight of the overbalanced top dove for the ground. A small ash was smothered by its huge bulk. There was a lightning-like crack as its trunk snapped.

In its downward plunge, the huge limbs stripped the branches from the smaller trees. A log-sized one knifed through the top of a water oak. Splintered limbs flew skyward and rained out over the bottoms. With a cyclone roar, the big tree crashed to the ground, and then silence settled over the bottoms.

Out of the broken, twisted, tangled mass streaked a brown furry ball. I turned my dogs loose and started screaming at the top of my voice, "Get him, Dan, get him."

In his eagerness, Old Dan ran head on into a bur oak tree. He sat down and with his deep voice told the river bottoms that he had been hurt.

It was Little Ann who caught the coon. I heard the ringtail squall when she grabbed him. Scared half to death, I snatched up a club and ran to help her.

The coon was all over her. He climbed up on her head, growling, slashing, ripping, and tearing. Yelping with pain, she shook him off and he streaked for the river. I thought surely he was going to get away. At the very edge of the river's bank, she caught him again.

I was trying hard to get in a lick with my club but couldn't for fear of hitting Little Ann. Through the tears in my eyes I saw the red blurry form of Old Dan sail into the fight. He was a mad hound. His anger at the bur oak tree was taken out on the coon.

They stretched Old Ringy out between them and pinned him to the ground. It was savage and brutal. I could hear the dying squalls of the coon and the deep growls of Old Dan. In a short time it was all over.

With sorrow in my heart, I stood and watched while my dogs worried the lifeless body. Little Ann was satisfied first. I had to scold Old Dan to make him stop.

Carrying the coon by a hind leg, I walked back to the big tree for my ax. Before leaving for home, I stood and looked at the fallen sycamore. I should have felt proud over the job I had done, but for some reason I couldn't. I knew I would miss the giant of the bottoms, for it had played a wonderful part in my life. I thought of the hours I had whiled away staring at its beauty and how hard it had been finding the right name for it.

"I'm sorry," I said. "I didn't want to cut you down, but I had to. I hope you can understand."

I was a proud boy as I walked along in the twilight of the evening. I felt so good even my sore hands had stopped hurting. What boy wouldn't have been proud? Hadn't my little hounds treed and killed their first coon? Along about then I decided I was a full-fledged coon hunter.

Nearing our house, I saw the whole family had come out on the porch. My sisters came running, staring wide-eyed at the dead coon.

Laughing, Papa said, "Well, I see you got him."

"I sure did, Papa," I said. I held the coon up for all to see. Mama took one look at the lifeless body and winced.

"Billy," she said, "when I heard that big tree fall, it scared me half to death. I didn't know but what it had fallen on you."

"Aw, Mama," I said, "I was safe. Why, I backed way off to one side. It couldn't have fallen on me."

Mama just shook her head. "I don't know," she said. "Sometimes I wonder if all mothers have to go through this."

"Come on," Papa said, "I'll help you skin it."

While we were tacking the hide on the smokehouse wall, I asked Papa if he had noticed any wind blowing that evening.

He thought a bit and said, "No, I don't believe I did. I've been out all day and I'm pretty sure I haven't noticed any wind. Why did you ask?"

"Oh, I don't know, Papa," I said, "but I thought something strange happened down in the bottoms this afternoon."

"I'm afraid I don't understand," said Papa. "What do you mean, 'something strange happened'?"

I told him about how my hands had gotten so sore I couldn't chop any more, and how I had asked for strength to finish the job.

"Well, what's so strange about that?" he asked.

"I don't know," I said, "but I didn't chop the big tree down. The wind blew it over."

"Why that's nothing," Papa said. "I've seen that happen a lot of times."

"It wasn't just the wind," I said. "It was the way it blew. It didn't touch another tree in the bottoms. I know because I looked around. The big tree was the only one touched by the wind. Do you think God heard my prayer? Do you think He helped me?"

Papa looked at the ground and scratched his head. In a sober voice, he said, "I don't know, Billy. I'm afraid I can't answer that. You must remember the big sycamore was the tallest tree in the bottoms. Maybe it was up there high enough to catch the wind where the others couldn't. No, I'm afraid I can't help you there. You'll have to decide for yourself."

It wasn't hard for me to decide. I was firmly convinced that I had been helped.

Chapter 10

Mama made me a cap out of my first coon hide. I was as proud of it as Papa would've been if someone had given him a dozen Missouri mules. Mama said afterwards that she wished she hadn't made it for me because, in some way, wearing that cap must've affected my mind. I went coon crazy.

I was out after the ringtails every night. About the only time I didn't go hunting was when the weather was bad, and even then Mama all but had to hog-tie me.

What wonderful nights they were, running like a deer through the thick timber of the bottoms, tearing my way through stands of wild cane, climbing over drifts, and jumping logs, running, screaming, and yelling, "Who-e-e-e, get him, boy, get him," following the voices of my little hounds.

It wasn't too hard for a smart old coon to fool Old Dan, but there were none that prowled the riverbanks that could fool my Little Ann.

As Grandpa had predicted, the price of coonskins jumped sky-high. A good-size hide was worth from four to ten dollars, depending on the grade and quality.

I kept the side of our smokehouse plastered with hides. Of course I would spread them out a little to cover more space. I always stretched them on the side facing the road, never on the back side. I wanted everyone in the country to see them.

The money earned from my furs was turned over to my father. I didn't care about it. I had what I wanted—my dogs. I supposed that Papa was saving it for something because I never saw anything new turn up around our home, but, like any young boy, I wasn't bothered by it and I asked no questions.

My whole life was wrapped up in my dogs. Everywhere I went they went along. There was only one place I didn't want them to go with me and that was to Grandpa's store. Other dogs were always there, and it seemed as if they all wanted to jump on Old Dan.

It got so about the only time I went to see my grandfather was when I had a bundle of fur to take to the store. This was always a problem. In every way I could, I would try to slip away from my dogs. Sometimes I swore that they could read my mind. It made no difference what I tried; I couldn't fool them.

One time I was sure I had outsmarted them. The day before I was to make one of my trips I took my furs out to the barn and hid them. The next morning I hung around the house for a while, and then nonchalantly whistled my way out to the barn. I climbed up in the loft and peeked through a crack. I could see them lying in front of their doghouse. They weren't even looking my way.

Taking my furs, I sneaked out through a back door and, walking like a tomcat, I made it to the timber. I climbed a small dogwood tree and looked back. They were still there and didn't seem to know what I'd done.

Feeling just about as smart as Sherlock Holmes, I headed for the store. I was walking along singing my lungs out when they came tearing out of the underbrush, wiggling and twisting, and tickled to death to be with me. At first I was mad but one look at dancing Little Ann and all was forgiven. I sat down on my bundle of fur and laughed till I hurt all over. I could scold them a little, but I could no more have whipped one of them than I could have kissed a girl. After all, a boy just doesn't whip his dogs.

Grandpa always counted my furs carefully and marked something down on a piece of paper. I'd never seen him do this with other hunters and it got the best of my curiosity. One day while he was writing I asked him, "Why do you do that, Grandpa?" He looked at me over his glasses and said kind of sharp, "Never mind. I have my reasons."

When Grandpa talked to me like that I didn't push things any further. Besides, it didn't make any difference to me if he marked on every piece of paper in the store.

I always managed to make my trips on Saturdays as that was "coon hunters'" day. I didn't have to stand around on the outside of the circle any more and listen to the coon hunters. I'd get right up in the middle and say my piece with the rest of them.

I didn't have to tell any whoppers for some of the things my dogs did were almost unbelievable anyhow. Oh, I guess I did make things a little bigger than they actually were but I never did figure a coon hunter told honest-to-goodness lies. He just kind of stretched things a little.

I could hold those coon hunters spellbound with some of my hunting tales. Grandpa would never say anything while I was telling my stories. He just puttered around the store with a silly little grin on his face. Once in a while when I got too far off the beaten path, he would come around and cram a bar of soap in my pocket. My face would get all red, I'd cut my story short, fly out the door, and head for home.

The coon hunters were always kidding me about my dogs. Some of the remarks I heard made me fighting mad. "I never saw hounds so small, but I guess they are hounds, at least they look like it." "I don't believe Little Ann is half as smart as he says she is. She's so little those old coons think she's a rabbit. I bet she sneaks right up on them before they realize she's a dog." "Some of these nights a big old coon is going to carry her off to his den and raise some little coon puppies."

I always took their kidding with a smile on my face, but it made my blood boil like the water in Mama's teakettle. I had one way of shutting them up. "Let's all go in the store," I'd say, "and see who has the most hides in there."

It was true that my dogs were small, especially Little Ann. She could walk under an ordinary hound; in fact, she was a regular midget. If it had not been for her long ears, no one could have told that she was a hound. Her actions weren't those of a hunting hound. She was constantly playing. She would play with our chickens and young calves, with a piece of paper or a corncob. What my little girl lacked in size, she made up in sweetness. She could make friends with a tomcat.

Old Dan was just the opposite. He strutted around with a belligerent and tough attitude. Although he wasn't a tall dog, he was heavy. His body was long and his chest broad and thick. His legs were short, big, and solid. The muscles in his body were hard and knotty. When he walked, they would twist and jerk under the skin.

He was a friendly dog. There were no strangers to him. He loved everyone. Yet he was a strange dog. He would not hunt with another hound, other than Little Ann, or another hunter, not even my father. The strangest thing about Old Dan was that he would not hunt, even with me, unless Little Ann was with him. I found this out the first night I tried it.

Little Ann had cut the pad of her right foot on a sharp, jagged flint rock. It was a nasty cut. I made a little boot of leather and put it on her wounded foot. To keep her from following me, I locked her in the corncrib.

Two nights later I decided to take Old Dan hunting for a while. He followed me down to the river bottoms and disappeared in the thick timber. I waited and waited for him to strike a trail. Nothing happened. After about two hours, I called to him. He didn't come. I called and called. Disgusted, I gave up and went home.

Coming up through the barn lot, I saw him rolled up in a ball on the ground in front of the corncrib. I immediately understood. I walked over and opened the door. He jumped up in the crib, smelled Little Ann's foot, twisted around in the shucks, and lay down by her side. As he looked at me, I read this message in his friendly gray eyes, "You could've done this a long time ago."

I never did know if Little Ann would hunt by herself or not. I am sure she would have, for she was a smart and understanding dog, but I never tried to find out.

Little Ann was my sisters' pet. They rubbed and scratched and petted her. They would take her down to the creek and give her baths. She loved it all.

If Mama wanted a chicken caught, she would call Little Ann. She would run the chicken down and hold it with her paws until Mama came. Not one feather would be harmed. Mama tried Old Dan once. Before she got the chicken, there wasn't much left but the feathers.

By some strange twist of nature, Little Ann was destined to go through life without being a mother. Perhaps it was because she was stunted in growth, or maybe because she was the runt in a large litter. That may have had something to do with it.

During the fur season, November through February, I was given complete freedom from work. Many times when I came home, the sun was high in the sky. After each hunt, I always took care of my dogs. The flint rocks and saw briers were hard on their feet. With a bottle of peroxide and a can of salve I would doctor their wounds.

I never knew what to expect from Old Dan. I never saw a coon hound so determined or one that could get into so many predicaments. More than one time, it would have been the death of him if it hadn't been for smart Little Ann.

One night, not long after I had entered the bottoms, my dogs struck the trail of an old boar coon. He was a smart old fellow and had a sackful of tricks. He crossed the river time after time. Finally, swimming to the middle and staying in the swift current, he swam downstream.

Knowing he would have to come out somewhere, my dogs split up. Old Dan took the right side. Little Ann worked the other side. I came out of the bottoms onto a gravel bar and stood and watched them in the moonlight.

Little Ann worked downriver, and then she came up. I saw her when she passed me going up the bank, sniffing and searching for the trail. She came back to me. I patted her head, scratched her ears, and talked to her. She kept staring across the river to where Old Dan was searching for the trail.

She waded in and swam across to help him. I knew that the coon had not come out of the river on her side. If he had, she would have found the trail. I walked up to a riffle, pulled off my shoes, and waded across.

My dogs worked the riverbank, up and down. They circled far out into the bottoms. I could hear the loud snuffing of Old Dan. He was bewildered and mad. I was getting a thrill from it all, as I had never seen them fooled like this.

Old Dan gave up on his side, piled into the river, and swam across to the side Little Ann had worked. I knew that it was useless for him to do that.

I was on the point of giving up, calling them to me, and going elsewhere to hunt, when I heard the bawl of Little Ann. I couldn't believe what I heard. She wasn't bawling on a trail. She was sounding the tree bark. I hurried down the bank.

There was a loud splash. I saw Old Dan swimming back. By this time, Little Ann was really singing a song. In the bright moonlight, I could see Old Dan clearly. His powerful front legs were churning the water.

Then I saw a sight that makes a hunter's heart swell with pride. Still swimming, Old Dan raised his head high out of the water and bawled. He couldn't wait until he reached the bank to tell Little Ann he was coming. From far out in the river he told her.

Reaching the shallows, he plowed out of the river onto a sand bar. Not even taking time to shake the water from his body, again he raised his head and bawled, and tore out down the bank.

In a trot, I followed, whooping to let them know I was coming. Before I reached the tree, Old Dan's deep voice was making the timber shake.

The tree was a large birch, standing right on the bank of the river. The swift current had eaten away at the footing, causing it to lean. The lower branches of the tree dangled in the water.

I saw how the smart old coon had pulled his trick. Coming in toward the bank from midstream, he had caught the dangling limbs and climbed up. Exhausted from the long swim, he stayed there in the birch thinking he had outsmarted my dogs. I couldn't understand how Little Ann had found him.

It was impossible to fall the tree toward the bottoms. It was too much off balance. I did the next best thing. I cut a long elder switch. Unbuckling one of my suspenders, I tied it to the end and climbed the tree.

The coon was sitting in a fork of a limb. Taking my switch, I whopped him a good one and out he came. He sailed out over the river. With a loud splash, he hit the water and swam for the other side. My dogs jumped off the bank after him. They were no match against his expert swimming. On reaching the other bank, he ran downriver.

Climbing down out of the tree, I picked up my ax and lantern, and trotted down to another riffle and waded across. I could tell by the bawling of my dogs, they were close to the coon. He would have to climb a tree, or be caught on the ground.

All at once their voices stopped. I stood still and waited for them to bawl treed. Nothing happened. Thinking the coon had taken to the river again, I waited to give them time to reach the opposite bank. I waited and waited. I could hear nothing. By then I knew he had not crossed over. I thought perhaps they had caught him on the ground. I hurried on.

I came to a point where a slough of crystal-clear water ran into the river. On the other side was a bluff. I could hear one of my dogs over there. As I watched and waited, I heard a dog jump in the water. It was Little Ann. She swam across and came up to me. Staying with me for just a second, she jumped in the slough and swam back to the other side.

I could hear her sniffing and whining. I couldn't figure out where Old Dan was. By squatting down and holding the lantern high over my head, I could dimly see the op-posite bank. Little Ann was running up and down. I noticed she always stayed in one place of about twenty-five yards, never leaving that small area.

She ran down to the water's edge and stared out into the slough. The horrible thought came that Old Dan had drowned. I knew a big coon was capable of drowning a dog in water by climbing on his head and forcing him under.

As fast as I could run, I circled the slough, climbed up over the bluff, and came down to where Little Ann was. She was hysterical, running up and down the bank and whining.

I tied my lantern on a long pole, held it out over the water, and looked for Old Dan's body. I could see clearly in the clear spring waters, but I couldn't see my dog anywhere. I sat down on the bank, buried my face in my hands, and cried. I was sure he was gone.

Several minutes passed, and all that time Little Ann had never stopped. Running here and there along the bank, she kept sniffing and whining.

I heard when she started digging. I looked around. She was ten feet from the water's edge. I got up and went over to her. She was digging in a small hole about the size of a big apple. It was the air hole for a muskrat den.

I pulled Little Ann away from the hole, knelt down, and put my ear to it. I could hear something, and feel a vibration in the ground. It was an eerie sound and seemed to be coming from far away. I listened. Finally I understood what the noise was.

It was the voice of Old Dan. Little Ann had opened the hole up enough with her digging so his voice could be heard faintly. In some way he had gotten into that old muskrat den.

I knew that down under the bank, in the

water, the entrance to the den could be found. Rolling up my sleeve, I tried to find it with my hand. I had no luck. It was too far down.

There was only one thing to do. Leaving my ax and lantern, I ran for home. Picking up a long-handled shovel, I hurried back.

The sun was high in the sky before I had dug Old Dan out. He was a sight to see, nothing but mud from the tip of his nose to the end of his tail. I held on to his collar and led him down to the river to wash him off. The water there was much warmer than the cold spring water of the slough.

After washing him, I turned him loose. Right back to the hole he ran. Little Ann was already digging. I knew the coon was still there. Working together, we dug him out.

After the coon was killed, I saw what had made him so smart. His right front foot was twisted and shriveled. At one time he must have been caught in a trap and had pulled himself free. He was an old coon. His face was almost white. He was big and heavy and had beautiful fur.

Tired, muddy, wet, and hungry, I started for home.

I've often wondered how Old Dan got into that old muskrat den. Perhaps there was another entrance I had overlooked. I'll never know.

One night, far back in the mountains, in a place called "The Cyclone Timber," Old Dan really pulled a good one.

Many years before my time, a terrible cyclone had ripped its way through the mountains, leaving its scar in the form of fallen timber, twisted and snarled. The path of the cyclone was several miles wide and several miles long. It was a wonderful place to hunt as it abounded with game.

My dogs had struck the trail of a coon about an hour before. They had really been warming him up. I knew it was about time

for him to take up a tree, and sure enough, I heard the deep voice of Old Dan telling the world he had a coon up a tree.

I was trotting along, going to them, when his voice stopped. I could hear Little Ann, but not Old Dan. I wondered why, and was a little scared, for I just knew something had happened. Then I heard his voice. It seemed louder than it had been before. I felt much better.

When I came up to the tree I thought Little Ann had treed Old Dan. She was sitting on her haunches staring up and bawling the tree bark. There, a good fifteen feet from the ground, with his hind legs planted firmly in the center of a big limb, and his front feet against the trunk of the tree, stood Old Dan, bawling for all he was worth.

Above him some eight or nine feet was a baby coon. I was glad it was a young one, for if it had been an old one, he would have jumped out. Old Dan would have followed, and he surely would have broken all of his legs.

From where I was standing, I could see it was impossible for Old Dan to have climbed the tree. It was dead and more of an old snag than a tree, with limbs that were crooked and twisted. The bark had rotted away and fallen off, leaving the trunk bare and slick as glass. It was a good ten feet up to the first limb. I couldn't figure out how Old Dan had climbed that tree. There had to be a solution somewhere.

Walking around to the other side, I saw how he had accomplished his feat. There in the bottom was a large hole. The old tree was hollow. Stepping back, I looked up and could see another hole, which had been hidden from me because of Old Dan's body.

He had simply crawled into the hole at the bottom, climbed up the hollow of the tree, and worked his way out on the limb. In some way he had turned around and reared up, placing his front feet against the trunk.

There he was. I didn't know what to do. I couldn't cut the tree down and I was afraid to climb it for fear I would scare the coon into jumping out. If he did, Old Dan would jump, too, and break his legs.

I ran plan after plan around in my mind. None would work. I finally came to the conclusion that I had to climb the tree and get ahold of that crazy dog. I blew out my lantern, pulled off my shoes and socks, and started shinnying up the tree. I prayed that the coon wouldn't jump out.

Inching along, being as quiet as I could, I made it up to Old Dan and grabbed his collar. I sat down on the limb, and held him tight. He would bawl now and then, and all but burst my eardrums. I couldn't drop him to the ground, and I couldn't climb down with him. I couldn't sit there on that limb and hold him all night. I would be no better off when daylight came.

Glancing at the hole by my side gave me the solution to my problem. I thought, "If he came out of this hole, he can go back in it."

That was the way I got my dog down from the tree. This had its problems, too. In the first place, Old Dan didn't want to be put in the hole head first. By scolding, pushing, shoving, and squeezing, I finally got him started on his way.

Like a fool, I sat there on the limb, waiting to see him come out at the bottom, and come out he did. Turning around, bawling as he did, right back in the hole he went. There was nothing I could do but sit and wait. I understood why his voice had stopped for a while. He just took time out to climb a tree.

Putting my ear to the hole, I could hear him coming. Grunting and clawing, up he came. I helped him out of the hole, turned him around, and crammed him back in. That time I wasn't too gentle with my work. I was tired of sitting on the limb, and my bare feet were getting cold.

I started down the same time he did. He beat me down. Looking over my shoulder, I saw him turn around and head back for the hole. I wasn't far from the ground so I let go. The flint rocks didn't feel too good to my feet when I landed.

I jumped to the hole just in time to see the tip end of his long tail disappearing. I grabbed it. Holding on with one hand, I worked his legs down with my other, and pulled him out. I stopped his tree-climbing by cramming rocks and chunks into the hole.

How the coon stayed in the tree, I'll never know, but stay he did. With a well-aimed rock, I scared him out. Old Dan satisfied his lust to kill.

I started for home. I'd had all the hunting I wanted for that night.

Chapter 11

I had often wondered what Old Dan would do if Little Ann got into some kind of a predicament. One night I got my answer.

For several days a northern blizzard had been blowing. It was a bad one. The temperature dropped down to ten below. The storm started with a slow cold drizzle and then sleet. When the wind started blowing, everything froze, leaving the ground as slick as glass.

Trapped indoors, I was as nervous as a fish out of water. I told Mama I guessed it was just going to storm all winter.

She laughed and said, "I don't think it will, but it does look like it will last for a while."

She ruffled up my hair and kissed me between the eyes. This did rile me up. I didn't like to be kissed like that. It seemed that I could practically rub my skin off and still feel it, all wet and sticky, and kind of burning.

Sometime on the fifth night, the storm blew itself out and it snowed about three inches. The next morning I went out to my doghouse. Scraping the snow away from the two-way door, I stuck my head in. It was as warm as an oven. I got my face washed all over by Little Ann. Old Dan's tail thumped out a tune on the wall.

I told them to be ready because we were going hunting that night. I knew the old ringtails would be hungry and stirring for they had been denned up during the storm.

That evening as I was leaving the house, Papa said, "Billy, be careful tonight. It's slick down under the snow, and it would be easy to twist an ankle or break a leg."

I told him I would and that I wasn't going far, just down back of our fields in the bottoms.

"Well, anyway," he said, "be careful. There'll be no moon tonight and you're going to see some fog next to the river."

Walking through our fields I saw my father was right about it being slick and dark. Several times I slipped and sat down. I couldn't see anything beyond the glow of my lantern, but I wasn't worried. My light was a good one, and Mama had insisted that I make two little leather pouches to cover the blades of my ax.

Just before I reached the timber, Old Dan shook the snow from the underbrush with his deep voice. I stopped and listened. He bawled again. The deep bass tones rolled around under the tall sycamores, tore their way out of the thick timber, traveled out over the fields, and slammed up against the foothills. There they seemed to break up and die away in the mountains.

Old Dan was working the trail slowly and I knew why. He would never line out until Little Ann was running by his side. I thought she would never get there. When she did, her beautiful voice made the blood pound in my temples. I felt the excitement of the hunt as it ate its way into my body. Taking a deep breath, I reared back and whooped as loud as I could.

The coon ran upriver for a way and then,

cutting out of the bottoms, he headed for the mountains. I stood and listened until their voices went out of hearing. Slipping and sliding, I started in the direction I had last heard them. About halfway to the foothills I heard them coming back.

Somewhere in the rugged mountains, the coon had turned and headed toward the river. It was about time for him to play out a few tricks and I was wondering what he would do. I knew it would be hard for him to hide his trail with snow on the ground, and I realized later that the smart old coon knew this, too.

As the voices of my dogs grew louder, I could tell that they were coming straight toward me. Once I started to blow out my lantern, thinking that maybe I could see them when they crossed our field, but I realized I didn't stand a chance of seeing the race in the skunk-black night.

Down out of the mountains they brought him, singing a hound-dog song on his heels. The coon must have scented me, or seen my lantern. He cut to my right and ran between our house and me. I heard screaming and yelling from my sisters. My father started whooping.

I knew my whole family was out on the porch listening to the beautiful voices of my little red hounds. I felt as tall as the tallest sycamore on the riverbank. I yelled as loud as I could. Again I heard the squealing of my sisters and the shouts of my father.

The deep "Ou-ou-ou's" of Old Dan and the sharp "Aw-aw-aw-aw's" of Little Ann bored a hole in the inky-black night. The vibrations rolled and quivered in the icy silence.

The coon was heading for the river. I could tell my dogs were crowding him, and wondered if he'd make it to the water. I was hoping he wouldn't, for I didn't want to wade the cold water unless I had to do it.

I figured the smart old coon had a reason

for turning and coming back to the river and wondered what trick he had in mind. I remembered something my grandfather had told me. He said, "Never underestimate the cunning of an old river coon. When the nights are dark and the ground is frozen and slick, they can pull some mean tricks on a hound. Sometimes the tricks can be fatal."

I was halfway through the fog-covered bottoms when the voices of my dogs stopped. I stood still, waited, and listened. A cold silence settled over the bottoms. I could hear the snap and crack of sap-frozen limbs. From far back in the flinty hills, the long, lonesome howl of a timber wolf floated down in the silent night. Across the river I heard a cow moo. I knew the sound was coming from the Lowery place.

Not being able to hear the voices of my dogs gave me an uncomfortable feeling. I whooped and waited for one of them to bawl. As I stood waiting I realized something was different in the bottoms. Something was missing.

I wasn't worried about my dogs. I figured that the coon had pulled some trick and sooner or later they would unravel the trail. But the feeling that something was just not right had me worried.

I whooped several times but still could get no answer. Stumbling, slipping, and sliding, I started on. Reaching the river, I saw it was frozen over. I realized what my strange uneasy feeling was. I had not been able to hear the sound of the water.

As I stood listening I heard a gurgling out in the middle of the stream. The river wasn't frozen all the way across. The still eddy waters next to the banks had frozen, but out in the middle, where the current was swift, the water was running, leaving a trough in the ice pack. The gurgling sound I had heard was the swift current as it sucked its way through the channel.

The last time I had heard my dogs they were downstream from me. I walked on, listening.

I hadn't gone far when I heard Old Dan. What I heard froze the blood in my veins. He wasn't bawling on a trail or giving the tree bark. It was one, long, continuous cry. In his deep voice there seemed to be a pleading cry for help. Scared, worried, and with my heart beating like a churn dasher, I started toward the sound.

I almost passed him but with another cry he let me know where he was. He was out on the ice pack. I couldn't see him for the fog. I called to him and he answered with a low whine. Again I called his name. This time he came to me.

He wasn't the same dog. His tail was between his legs and his head was bowed down. He stopped about seven feet from me. Sitting down on the ice, he raised his head and howled the most mournful cry I had ever heard. Turning around, he trotted back out on the ice and disappeared in the fog.

I knew something had happened to Little Ann. I called her name. She answered with a pleading cry. Although I couldn't see her, I guessed what had happened. The coon had led them to the river. Running out on the ice, he had leaped across the trough. My dogs, hot on the trail, had followed. Old Dan, a more powerful dog than Little Ann, had made his leap. Little Ann had not made it. Her small feet had probably slipped on the slick ice and she had fallen into the icy waters. Old Dan, seeing the fate of his little friend, had quit the chase and come back to help her. The smart old coon had pulled his trick, and a deadly one it was.

I had to do something. She would never be able to get out by herself. It was only a matter of time until her body would be paralyzed by the freezing water.

Laying my ax down, I held my lantern

out in front of me and stepped out on the ice. It started cracking and popping. I jumped back to the bank. Although it was thick enough to hold the light weight of my dogs, it would never hold me.

Little Ann started whining and begging for help. I went all to pieces and started crying. Something had to be done and done quickly or my little dog was lost. I thought of running home for a rope or for my father, but I knew she couldn't last until I got back. I was desperate. It was impossible for me to swim in the freezing water. I wouldn't last for a minute. She cried again, begging for the one thing I couldn't give her, help.

I thought, "If only I could see her maybe I could figure out some way I could help."

Looking at my lantern gave me an idea. I ran up the bank about thirty feet, turned, and looked back. I could see the light, not well, but enough for what I had in mind. I grabbed my lantern and ax and ran for the bottoms.

I was looking for a stand of wild cane. After what seemed like ages, I found it. With the longest one I could find, I hurried back. After it was trimmed and the limber end cut off, I hung the lantern by the handle on the end of it and started easing it out on the ice.

I saw Old Dan first. He was sitting close to the edge of the trough, looking down. Then I saw her. I groaned at her plight. All I could see was her head and her small front paws. Her claws were spread out and digging into the ice. She knew if she ever lost that hold she was gone.

Old Dan raised his head and howled. Hound though he was, he knew it was the end of the trail for his little pal.

I wanted to get my light as close to Little Ann as I could, but my pole was a good eight feet short. Setting the lantern down, I eased the pole from under the handle. I thought, "I'm no better off than I was before. In fact I'm worse off. Now I can see when the end comes."

Little Ann cried again. I saw her claws slip on the ice. Her body settled lower in the water. Old Dan howled and started fidgeting. He knew the end was close.

I didn't exactly know when I started out toward my dog. I had taken only two steps when the ice broke. I twisted my body and fell toward the bank. Just as my hand closed on a root I thought my feet touched bottom, but I wasn't sure. As I pulled myself out I felt the numbing cold creep over my legs.

It looked so hopeless. There didn't seem to be any way I could save her.

At the edge of the water stood a large sycamore. I got behind it, anything to blot out that heartbreaking scene. Little Ann, thinking I had deserted her, started crying. I couldn't stand it.

I opened my mouth to call Old Dan. I wanted to tell him to come on and we'd go home as there was nothing we could do. The words just wouldn't come out. I couldn't utter a sound. I lay my face against the icy cold bark of the sycamore. I thought of the prayer I had said when I had asked God to help me get two hound pups. I knelt down and sobbed out a prayer. I asked for a miracle which would save the life of my little dog. I promised all the things that a young boy could if only He would help me.

Still saying my prayer and making promises, I heard a sharp metallic sound. I jumped up and stepped away from the tree. I was sure the noise I heard was made by a rattling chain on the front end of a boat.

I shouted as loud as I could. "Over here. I need help. My dog is drowning."

I waited for an answer. All I could hear were the cries of Little Ann.

Again I hollered. "Over here. Over on the bank. Can you see my light? I need help. Please hurry."

I held my breath waiting for an answer-ing shout. I shivered from the freezing cold of my wet shoes and overalls. A straining si-lence settled over the river. A feathery rustle swished by in the blackness. A flock of low-flying ducks had been disturbed by my loud shouts. I strained my ears for some sound. Now and then I could hear the lapping slap of the ice-cold water as it swirled its way through the trough.

I glanced to Little Ann. She was still holding on but I saw her paws were almost at the edge. I knew her time was short.

I couldn't figure out what I had heard. The sound was made by metal striking metal, but what was it? What could have caused it?

I looked at my ax. It couldn't have made the sound as it was too close to me. The noise had come from out in the river.

When I looked at my lantern I knew that it had made the strange sound. I had left the handle standing straight up when I had taken the pole away. Now it was down. For some unknown reason the stiff wire handle had twisted in the sockets and dropped. As it had fallen it had struck the metal frame, making the sharp metallic sound I had heard.

As I stared at the yellow glow of my light, the last bit of hope faded away. I closed my eyes, intending to pray again for the help I so desperately needed. Then like a blinding red flash the message of the lantern bored its way into my brain. There was my miracle. There was the way to save my little dog. In the metallic sound I had heard were my instructions. They were so plain I couldn't help but understand them. The bright yellow flame started flickering and dancing. It seemed to be saying, "Hurry. You know what to do."

Faster than I had ever moved in my life I went to work. With a stick I measured the water in the hole where my feet had broken through the ice. I was right. My foot had touched bottom. Eighteen inches down I felt the soft mud.

With my pole I fished the lantern back to the bank. I took the handle off, straightened it out, and bent a hook in one end. With one of my shoelaces I tied the wire to the end of the cane pole. I left the hook sticking out about six inches beyond the end of it.

I started shouting encouragement to Little Ann. I told her to hang on and not to give up for I was going to save her. She answered with a low cry.

With the hook stuck in one of the ventilating holes in the top of my light, I lifted it back out on the ice and set it down. After a little wiggling and pushing, I worked the hook loose and laid the pole down.

I took off my clothes, picked up my ax, and stepped down into the hole in the icy water. It came to my knees. Step by step, breaking the ice with my ax, I waded out.

The water came up to my hips, and then to my waist. The cold bite of it took my breath away. I felt my body grow numb. I couldn't feel my feet at all but I knew they were moving. When the water reached my armpits I stopped and worked my pole toward Little Ann. Stretching my arms as far out as I could, I saw I was still a foot short. Closing my eyes and gritting my teeth, I moved on. The water reached my chin.

I was close enough. I started hooking at the collar of Little Ann. Time after time I felt the hook almost catch. I saw I was fishing on a wrong angle. She had settled so low in the water I couldn't reach her collar. Raising my arms above my head so the pole would be on a slant I kept hooking and praying. The seconds ticked by. I strained for one more inch. The muscles in my arms grew numb from the weight of the pole.

Little Ann's claws slipped again. I thought she was gone. At the very edge of the ice, she caught again. All I could see now were her small red paws and her nose and eyes.

By Old Dan's actions I could tell he understood and wanted to help. He ran over close to my pole and started digging at the ice. I whopped him with the cane. That was the only time in my life I ever hit my dog. I had to get him out of the way so I could see what I was doing.

Just when I thought my task was impossible, I felt the hook slide under the tough leather. It was none too soon.

As gently as I could I dragged her over the rim of the ice. At first I thought she was dead. She didn't move. Old Dan started whining and licking her face and ears. She moved her head. I started talking to her. She made an effort to stand but couldn't. Her muscles were paralyzed and the blood had long since ceased to flow.

At the movement of Little Ann, Old Dan threw a fit. He started barking and jumping. His long red tail fanned the air.

Still holding onto my pole, I tried to take a step backward. My feet wouldn't move. A cold gripping fear came over me. I thought my legs were frozen. I made another effort to lift my leg. It moved. I realized that my feet were stuck in the soft muddy bottom.

I started backing out, dragging the body of my little dog. I couldn't feel the pole in my hands. When my feet touched the icy bank, I couldn't feel that either. All the feeling in my body was gone.

I wrapped Little Ann in my coat and hurried into my clothes. With the pole I fished my light back.

Close by was a large drift. I climbed up on top of it and dug a hole down through the ice and snow until I reached the dry limbs. I poured half of the oil in my lantern down into the hole and dropped in a match. In no time I had a roaring fire.

I laid Little Ann close to the warm heat and went to work. Old Dan washed her head with his warm red tongue while I massaged and rubbed her body.

I could tell by her cries when the blood started circulating. Little by little her strength came back. I stood her on her feet and started walking her. She was weak and wobbly but I knew she would live. I felt much better and breathed a sigh of relief.

After drying myself out the best I could, I took the lantern handle from the pole, bent it back to its original position, and put it back on the lantern. Holding the light out in front of me, I looked at it. The bright metal gleamed in the firelight glow.

I started talking to it. I said, "Thanks, old lantern, more than you'll ever know. I'll always take care of you. Your globe will always be clean and there'll never be any rust or dirt on your frame."

I knew if it had not been for the miracle of the lantern, my little dog would have met her death on that night. Her grave would have been the cold icy waters of the Illinois River.

Out in the river I could hear the cold water gurgling in the icy trough. It seemed to be angry. It hissed and growled as it tore its way through the channel. I shuddered to think of what could have happened.

Before I left for home, I walked back to the sycamore tree. Once again I said a prayer, but this time the words were different. I didn't ask for a miracle. In every way a young boy could, I said "thanks." My second prayer wasn't said with just words. All of my heart and soul were in it.

On my way home I decided not to say anything to my mother and father about Little Ann's accident. I knew it would scare Mama and she might stop my hunting.

Reaching our house, I didn't hang the lantern in its usual place. I took it to my room and set it in a corner with the handle standing up.

The next morning I started sneezing and came down with a terrible cold. I told Mama I had gotten my feet wet. She scolded me a little and started doctoring me.

For three days and nights I stayed home. All this time I kept checking the handle of the lantern. My sisters shook the house from the roof to the floor with their playing and romping, but the handle never did fall.

I went to my mother and asked her if God answered prayers every time one was said. She smiled and said, "No, Billy, not every time. He only answers the ones that are said from the heart. You have to be sincere and believe in Him."

She wanted to know why I had asked.

I said, "Oh, I just wondered, and wanted to know."

She came over and straightened my suspenders, saying, "That was a very nice question for my little Daniel Boone to ask."

Bending over, she started kissing me. I finally squirmed away from her, feeling as wet as a dirt dauber's nest. My mother never could kiss me like a fellow should be kissed. Before she was done I was kissed all over. It always made me feel silly and baby-like. I tried to tell her that a coon hunter wasn't supposed to be kissed that way, but Mama never could understand things like that.

I stomped out of the house to see how my dogs were.

THINKING ABOUT THE SELECTION

Recalling

1. What commitment does Billy make to his dogs just before the first hunt?
2. Describe Billy's feelings as his dogs are chasing the first raccoon.
3. How does Old Dan react when Billy takes him hunting without Little Ann?
4. Describe what occurs during a typical hunt.

Interpreting

5. In Chapter 8 Billy realizes that his father, "doesn't even talk to me like I was a boy any more. He talks to me like I was a man." Why does this realization make Billy so happy? Why have Father's reactions to Billy changed?
6. Why does Billy insist on cutting down the big sycamore and doing it by himself? How does this action make his family feel about him?
7. Give three examples of the bond of love and faithfulness between Billy and the dogs.
8. Compare and contrast the hunting skills of Old Dan and Little Ann. How do they complement each other?

Applying

9. Billy decides that he must cut down a tree that he has enjoyed for years to fulfill a promise he made to his dogs. Why is it important for people to keep promises?

ANALYZING LITERATURE

Understanding Plot Development

The sequence of events in a novel is the plot. In *Where the Red Fern Grows*, the events occur in **episodes,** separate incidents that together make up the plot. Each episode has a conflict that reaches a climax and is resolved.

1. Briefly describe two episodes that occur while Billy and the dogs are hunting.
2. What is the climax of each episode?
3. How is each episode resolved?

CRITICAL THINKING AND READING

Solving Problems

Like the characters in novels, you may face problems that are difficult to resolve. Here is a problem-solving strategy that you can apply in many situations. First, define the problem clearly. Then consider possible solutions and compare the possible outcomes to each solution. Finally, decide on the best solution, supporting your choice with reasons.

Billy uses this strategy when Little Ann is about to slip into the icy river. He quickly goes over the problem: she fell through the ice and must be rescued. Then, he considers several possible solutions: he could run back to the house for help or he could swim out to get her. He decides that neither of these solutions is practical. Finally, he realizes that the best solution is to reach Little Ann with the lantern handle attached to a cane pole.

1. Review the process Billy went through in Chapters 2–5 to solve the problem of getting hunting dogs.
2. Using the problem-solving strategy described here, devise a way that Billy can use to prevent his dogs from following him to Grandfather's store.

THINKING AND WRITING

Writing a News Article

Imagine that you are a reporter for the local newspaper in Billy's county. You are in Grandfather's store one day, and you hear about Billy and his dogs. Write a news article about an episode in the plot. A news article answers the questions *Who? What? When? Where? Why?* and *How?* Include the answers to these questions in your report. When you revise, be sure you have included specific details about the episode. Add an eye-catching headline that will make people want to read your article.

Where the Red Fern Grows, Chapters 12–15

Setting in a Novel

The **setting** of a novel is the place and the time of the events. Setting is often closely related to other elements in the story. *Where the Red Fern Grows* is set in the farm country and river bottoms of the Illinois River in the Ozark Mountains during the early 1900's. This setting is reflected in the character's manner of living, and therefore, in the events in the novel.

Look For

You have already been introduced to the setting in this novel. As you continue reading, look for how the details of the setting affect the characters and the plot. Would this story have been the same if it had occurred anywhere else? Why or why not?

Writing

Think about the region where you live and how it affects your life. Write about how your setting affects your thoughts and your actions, as well as how it affects others around you. Consider how your life would be different if you lived anywhere else.

Vocabulary

Knowing the following words will help you as you read Chapters 12–15 of *Where the Red Fern Grows*.

leering (lir′ iŋ) *v.*: Looking with harmful intent (p. 699)
jubilant (jōō′b′l ənt) *adj.*: Joyful and triumphant (p. 718)

gloated (glōt′′d) *v.*: Gazed or grinned in scornful triumph (p. 720)

Chapter 12

The fame of my dogs spread all over our part of the Ozarks. They were the best in the country. No coon hunter came into my grandfather's store with as many pelts as I did. Grandpa never overlooked an opportunity to brag. He told everyone the story of my dogs, and the part he had played in getting them.

Many was the time some farmer, coming to our home, would say, "Your Grandpa was telling me you got three big coons over in Pea Vine Hollow the other night." I would listen, knowing I only got one, or maybe none, but Grandpa was my pal. If he said I caught ten in one tree, it was just that way.

Because of my grandfather's bragging, and his firm belief in my dogs and me, a terrible thing happened.

One morning, while having breakfast, Mama said to Papa, "I'm almost out of corn meal. Do you think you can go to the mill today?"

Papa said, "I intended to butcher a hog. We're about out of meat." Looking at me, he said, "Shell a sack of corn. Take one of the mules and go to the mill for your mother."

With the help of my sisters, we shelled the corn. Throwing it over our mule's back, I started for the store.

On arriving at the millhouse, I tied my mule to the hitching post, took my corn, and set it by the door. I walked over to the store and told Grandpa I wanted to get some corn ground.

He said, "I'll be with you in just a minute."

As I was waiting, I heard a horse coming. Looking out, I saw who it was and didn't like what I saw. It was the two youngest Pritchard boys. I had run into them on several occasions during pie suppers and dances.

The Pritchards were a large family that lived upriver about five miles. As in most small country communities, there is one family that no one likes. The Pritchards were it. Tales were told that they were bootleggers, thieves, and just all-around "no-accounts." The story had gone round that Old Man Pritchard had killed a man somewhere in Missouri before moving to our part of the country.

Rubin was two years older than I, big and husky for his age. He never had much to say. He had mean-looking eyes that were set far back in his rugged face. They were smoky-hued and unblinking, as if the eyelids were paralyzed. I had heard that once he had cut a boy with a knife in a fight over at the saw-mill.

Rainie was the youngest, about my age. He had the meanest disposition of any boy I had ever known. Because of this he was disliked by young and old. Wherever Rainie went, trouble seemed to follow. He was always wanting to bet, and would bet on anything. He was nervous, and could never seem to stand still.

Once at my grandfather's store, I had given him a piece of candy. Snatching it out of my hand, he ate it and then sneered at me and said it wasn't any good. During a pie supper one night, he wanted to bet a dime that he could whip me.

My mother told me always to be kind of Rainie, that he couldn't help being the way he was. I asked, "Why?" She said it was because his brothers were always picking on him and beating him.

On entering the store, they stopped and glared at me. Rubin walked over to the counter. Rainie came over to me.

Leering at me, he said, "I'd like to make a bet with you."

I told him I didn't want to bet.

He asked if I was scared.

"No. I just don't want to bet," I said.

His neck and ears looked as though they hadn't been washed in months. His ferret-like eyes kept darting here and there. Glancing down to his hands, I saw the back of his right sleeve was stiff and starchy from the constant wiping of his nose.

He saw I was looking him over, and asked if I liked what I saw.

I started to say, "No," but didn't, turned, and walked away a few steps.

Rubin ordered some chewing tobacco.

"Aren't you a little young to be chewing?" Grandpa asked.

"Ain't for me. It's for my dad," Rubin growled.

Grandpa handed two plugs to him. He paid for it, turned around, and handed one plug to Rainie. Holding the other up in front of him, he looked it over. Looking at Grandpa, he gnawed at one corner of it.

Grandpa mumbled something about how kids were brought up these days. He came from behind the counter, saying to me, "Let's go grind that corn."

The Pritchard boys made no move to follow us out of the store.

"Come on," Grandpa said. "I'm going to lock up till I get this corn ground."

"We'll just stay here. I want to look at some of the shirts," said Rubin.

"No, you won't," said Grandpa. "Come on, I'm going to lock up."

Begrudgingly, they walked out.

I helped Grandpa start the mill and we proceeded to grind the corn. The Pritchard boys had followed us and were standing looking on.

Rainie walked over to me. "I hear you have some good hounds," he said.

I told him I had the best in the country. If he didn't believe me, he could just ask my grandfather.

He just leered at me. "I don't think they're half as good as you say they are," he said. "Bet our old blue tick hound can out-hunt both of them."

I laughed, "Ask Grandpa who brings in the most hides."

"I wouldn't believe him. He's crooked," he said.

I let him know right quick that my grandfather wasn't crooked.

"He's a storekeeper, ain't he?" he said.

I glanced over at Grandpa. He had heard the remark made by Rainie. His friendly old face was as red as a turkey gobbler's wattle.

The last of my corn was just going through the grinding stones. Grandpa pushed a lever to one side, shutting off the power. He came over and said to Rainie, "What do you do? Just go around looking for trouble. What do you want, a fight?"

Rubin sidled over. "This ain't none of your business," he said. "Besides, Rainie's not looking for a fight. We just want to make a bet with him."

Grandpa glared at Rubin. "Any bet you would make sure would be a good one all right. What kind of a bet?"

Rubin spat a mouthful of tobacco juice on the clean floor. He said, "Well, we've heard so much about them hounds of his, we just think it's a lot of talk and lies. We'd like to make a little bet; say about two dollars."

I had never seen my old grandfather so mad. The red had left his face. In its place was a sickly, paste-gray color. The kind old eyes behind the glasses burned with a fire I had never seen.

In a loud voice, he asked, "Bet on what?"

Rubin spat again. Grandpa's eyes followed the brown stain in its arch until it landed on the clean floor and splattered.

With a leering grin on his ugly, dirty face, Rubin said, "Well, we got an old coon up in our part of the country that's been there a long time. Ain't no dog yet ever been smart enough to tree him, and I—"

Rainie broke into the conversation. "He ain't just an ordinary coon. He's an old-timer. Folks call him the 'ghost coon.' Believe me, he is a ghost. He just runs hounds long enough to get them all warmed up, then climbs a tree and disappears. Our old blue hound has treed him more times than—"

Rubin told Rainie to shut up and let him do the talking. Looking over at me, he said, "What do you say? Want to bet two dollars your hounds can tree him?"

I looked at my grandfather, but he didn't help me.

I told Rubin I didn't want to bet, but I was pretty sure my dogs could tree the ghost coon.

Rainie butted in again, "What's the matter? You 'yellow'?"

I felt the hot blood rush into my face. My stomach felt like something alive was crawling in it. I doubled up my right fist and was on the point of hitting Rainie in one of his eyes when I felt my grandfather's hand on my shoulder.

I looked up. His eyes flashed as he looked at me. A strange little smile was tugging at the corner of his mouth. The big artery in his neck was pounding out and in. It reminded me of a young bird that had fallen out of a nest and lay dying on the ground.

Still looking at me, he reached back and took his billfold from his pocket, saying, "Let's call that bet." Turning to Rubin, he said, "I'm going to let him call your bet, but now you listen. If you boys take him up there to hunt the ghost coon, and jump on him and beat him up, you're sure going to hear from me. I don't mean maybe. I'll have both of you taken to Tahlequah and put in jail. You had better believe that."

Rubin saw he had pushed my grandfather far enough. Backing up a couple of steps, he said, "We're not going to jump on him. All we want to do is make a bet."

Grandpa handed me two one-dollar bills, saying to Rubin, "You hold your money and he can hold his. If you lose, you had better pay off." Looking back to me, he said, "Son, if you lose, pay off."

I nodded my head.

I asked Rubin when he wanted me to come up for the hunt.

He thought a minute. "You know where that old log slide comes out from the hills onto the road?" he asked.

I nodded.

"We'll meet you there tomorrow night about dark," he said.

It was fine with me, I said, but I told him not to bring his hounds because mine wouldn't hunt with other dogs.

He said he wouldn't.

I agreed to bring my ax and lantern.

As they turned to leave, Rainie smirked. "Sucker!" he said.

I made no reply.

After the Pritchard boys had gone, my grandfather looked at me and said, "Son, I have never asked another man for much, but I sure want you to catch the ghost coon."

I told him if the ghost coon made one track in the river bottoms, my dogs would get him.

Grandpa laughed.

"You'd better be getting home. It's getting late and your mother is waiting for the corn meal," he said.

I could hear him chuckling as he walked toward his store. I thought to myself, "There goes the best grandpa a boy ever had."

Lifting the sack of meal to the back of my old mule, I started for home. All the way, I kept thinking of Old Dan, Little Ann, ghost coons, and the two ugly, dirty Pritchard boys. I decided not to tell my mother and father anything about the hunt for I knew Mama wouldn't approve of anything I had to do with the Pritchards.

The following evening I arrived at the designated spot early. I sat down by a red oak tree to wait. I called Little Ann over to me and had a good talk with her. I told her how much I loved her, scratched her back, and looked at the pads of her feet.

"Sweetheart," I said, "you must do something for me tonight. I want you to tree the ghost coon for it means so much to Grandpa and me."

She seemed to understand and answered by washing my face and hands.

I tried to talk to Old Dan, but I may as well have talked to a stump for all the attention he paid to me. He kept walking around sniffing here and there. He couldn't understand why we were waiting. He was wanting to hunt.

Rubin and Rainie showed up just at dark. Both had sneers on their faces.

"Are you ready?" Rubin asked.

"Yes," I said, and asked him which way was the best to go.

"Let's go downriver a way and work up," he said. "We're sure to strike him coming upriver, and that way we've got the wind in our favor."

"Are these the hounds that we've been hearing so much about?" Ranie asked.

I nodded.

"They look too little to be any good," he said.

I told him dynamite came in little packages.

He asked me if I had my two dollars.

"Yes," I said.

He wanted to see my money. I showed it to him. Rubin, not to be outdone, showed me his.

We crossed an old field and entered the river bottoms. By this time it was quite dark. I lit my lantern and asked which one wanted to carry my ax.

"It's yours," Rainie said. "You carry it."

Not wanting to argue, I carried both the lantern and the ax.

Rainie started telling me how stingy and crooked my grandfather was. I told him I hadn't come to have any trouble or to fight. All I wanted to do was to hunt the ghost coon. If there was going to be any trouble, I would just call my dogs and go home.

Rubin had a nickel's worth of sense, but Rainie had none at all. Rubin told him if he didn't shut up, he was going to bloody his nose. That shut Rainie up.

Old Dan opened up first. It was a beautiful thing to hear. The deep tones of his voice rolled in the silent night.

A bird in a canebrake on our right started chirping. A big swamp rabbit came running down the riverbank as if all hell was close to his heels. A bunch of mallards, feeding in the shallows across the river, took flight with frightened quacks. A feeling that only a hunter knows slowly crept over my body. I whooped to my dogs, urging them on.

Little Ann came in. Her bell-like tones blended with Old Dan's, in perfect rhythm. We stood and listened to the beautiful music, the deep-throated notes of hunting hounds on the hot-scented trail of a river coon.

Rubin said, "If he crosses the river up at the Buck Ford, it's the ghost coon, as that's the way he always runs."

We stood and listened. Sure enough, the voices of my dogs were silent for a few minutes. Old Dan, a more powerful swimmer than Little Ann, was the first to open up after crossing over. She was close behind him.

Rubin said, "That's him, all right. That's the ghost coon."

They crossed the river again.

We waited.

Rainie said, "You may as well get your money out now."

I told him just to wait a while, and I'd show him the ghost coon's hide.

This brought a loud laugh from Rainie, which sounded like someone had dropped an empty bucket on a gravel bar and then had kicked it.

The wily old coon crossed the river several times, but couldn't shake my dogs from his trail. He cut out from the bottoms, walked a rail fence, and jumped from it into a thick canebrake. He piled into an old slough. Where it emptied into the river, he swam to the middle. Doing opposite to what most coons do, which is swim downstream, he swam upstream. He stopped at an old drift in the middle of it.

Little Ann found him. When she jumped him from the drift, Old Dan was far downriver searching for the trail. If he could have gotten there in time, it would have been the last of the ghost coon, but Little Ann couldn't do much by herself in the water. He fought his way free from her, swam to our side, and ran upstream.

I could hear Old Dan coming through the bottoms on the other side, bawling at every jump. I could feel the driving power in his voice. We heard him when he hit the water to cross over. It sounded like a cow had jumped in.

Little Ann was warming up the ghost coon. I could tell by her voice that she was close to him.

Reaching our side, Old Dan tore out after her. He was a mad hound. His deep voice was telling her he was coming.

We were trotting along, following my dogs, when I heard Little Ann's bawling stop.

"Wait a minute," I said. "I think she has treed him. Let's give her time to circle the tree to make sure he's there."

Old Dan opened up bawling treed. Rubin started on.

"Something's wrong," I said. "I can't hear Little Ann."

Rainie spoke up, "Maybe the ghost coon ate her up."

I glared at him.

Hurrying on, we came to my dogs. Old Dan was bawling at a hole in a large syca-more that had fallen into the river.

At that spot, the bank was a good ten feet above the water level. As the big tree had fallen, the roots had been torn and twisted from the ground. The jagged roots, acting as a drag, had stopped it from falling all the way into the stream. The trunk lay on a steep slant from the top of the bank to the water. Looking down, I could see the broken tangled mass of the top. Debris from floods had caught in the limbs, forming a drift.

Old Dan was trying to dig and gnaw his way into the log. Pulling him from the hole, I held my lantern up and looked down into the dark hollow. I knew that somewhere down below the surface there had to be an-other hole in the trunk, as water had filled the hollow to the river level.

Rubin, looking over my shoulder, said, "That coon couldn't be in there. If he was, he'd be drowned."

I agreed.

Rainie spoke up. "You ready to pay off?" he asked. "I told you, them hounds couldn't tree the ghost coon."

I told him the show wasn't over.

Little Ann had never bawled treed, and I knew she wouldn't until she knew exactly where the coon was. Working the bank up and down, and not finding the trail, she swam across the river and worked the other side. For a good half-hour she searched that side before she came back across to where Old Dan was. She sniffed around the hollow log.

"We might as well get away from here," Rainie said. "They ain't going to find the ghost coon."

"It sure looks that way," Rubin said.

I told them I wasn't giving up until my dogs did.

"You just want to be stubborn," Rubin said. "I'm ready for my money now."

I asked him to wait a few minutes.

"Ain't no use," he said. "No hound yet ever treed that ghost coon."

Hearing a whine, I turned around. Little Ann had crawled up on the log and was inch-ing her way down the slick trunk toward the water. I held my lantern up so I could see better. Spraddle-legged, claws digging into the bark, she was easing her way down.

"You'd better get her out of there," Rubin said. "If she gets down in that old tree top, she'll drown."

Rubin didn't know my Little Ann.

Once her feet slipped. I saw her hind quarters fall off to one side. She didn't get scared. Slowly she eased her legs back up on the log.

I made no reply. I just watched and waited.

Little Ann eased herself into the water. Swimming to the drift, she started sniffing around. In places it was thin and her legs would break through. Climbing, clawing, and swimming, she searched the drift over, looking for the lost trail.

I saw when she stopped searching. With her body half in the water, and her front feet curved over a piece of driftwood, she turned her head and looked toward the shore. I could see her head twisting from side to side. I could tell by her actions that she had gotten the scent. With a low whine, she started back.

I told Rubin, "I think she smells something."

Slowly and carefully she worked her way through the tangled mass. I lost sight of her when she came close to the undermined bank. She wormed her way under the overhang. I could hear her clawing and wallowing around, and then out from under the bank came the biggest coon I had ever seen, the ghost coon.

He came out right over Little Ann. She caught him in the old treetop. I knew she was no match for him in that tangled mass of limbs and logs. He fought his way free and swam for the opposite bank. She was right behind him.

Old Dan didn't wait, look, or listen. He piled off the ten-foot bank and disappeared from sight. I looked for him. I knew he was tangled in the debris under the surface. I started to take off my overalls, but stopped when I saw his red head shoot up out of the water. Bawling and clawing his way free of the limbs and logs, he was on his way.

On reaching midstream, the ghost coon headed downriver with Little Ann still on his tail.

We ran down the riverbank. I could see my dogs clearly in the moonlight. The ghost coon was about fifteen feet ahead of Little Ann. About twenty-five yards behind them came Old Dan, trying so hard to catch up. I whooped to them.

Rubin grabbed a pole, saying, "He may come out on this side."

Knowing the ghost coon was desperate, I wondered what he would do. Reaching a gravel bar below the high bank, we ran out on it to the water's edge. Then the ghost coon did something that I never expected. Coming even with us, he turned from midstream and came straight for us.

I heard Rubin yell, "Here he comes!"

He churned his way through the shallows and ran right between us. Rubin swung his pole, missed the coon, and almost hit Little Ann. The coon headed for the river bottoms with her right on his heels.

The bawling of Little Ann and our screaming and hollering made so much noise, I didn't hear Old Dan coming. He tore out of the river, plowed into me, and knocked me down.

We ran through the bottoms, following my dogs. I thought the ghost coon was going back to the sycamore log but he didn't. He ran upriver.

While hurrying after them, I looked over at Rainie. For once in his life, I think he was excited. He was whooping and screaming, and falling over logs and limbs.

I felt good all over.

Glancing over at me, Rainie said, "They ain't got him yet."

The ghost coon crossed the river time after time. Seeing that he couldn't shake Old Dan and Little Ann from his trail, he cut through the river bottoms and ran out into an old field.

At this maneuver, Rubin said to Rainie, "He's heading for that tree."

"What tree?" I asked.

"You'll see," Rainie said. "When he gets tired, he always heads for that tree. That's where he gets his name, the ghost coon. He just disappears."

"If he disappears, my dogs will disappear with him," I said.

Rainie laughed.

I had to admit one thing. The Pritchard boys knew the habits of the ghost coon. I knew he couldn't run all night. He had already far surpassed any coon I had ever chased.

"They're just about there," Rubin said.

Just then I heard Old Dan bark treed. I waited for Little Ann's voice. I didn't hear her. I wondered what it could be this time.

"He's there all right," Rubin said. "He's in that tree."

"Well, come on," I said. "I want to see that tree."

"You might as well get your money out," Rainie said.

I told him he had said that once before, back on the riverbank.

Chapter 13

Coming up to the tree, I could see it was a huge bur oak. It wasn't tall. It was just the opposite, rather low and squatty. The top was a thick mass of large limbs, and it hadn't shed all of its leaves yet.

It stood by itself in an old field. There were no other trees within fifty yards of it. About fifteen feet to the left were the remains of a barbed-wire fence. An old gate hung by one rusty hinge from a large corner post. I could tell that at one time a house had stood close by.

Rubin saw me looking around. "A long time ago some Indians lived here and farmed these fields," he said.

I walked around the tree looking for the coon, but could see very little in the dark shadows.

"Ain't no use to look," Rubin said. "He won't be there."

Rainie spoke up. "This ain't the first time we've been to this tree," he said.

Rubin told Rainie to shut up. "You talk too much," he said.

In a whining voice, Rainie said, "Rubin, you know the coon ain't in that tree. Make him pay off and let's go home. I'm getting tired."

I told Rubin I was going to climb the tree.

"Go ahead," he said. "It won't do you any good."

The tree was easy to climb. I looked all over it, on each limb, and in every dark place. I looked for a hollow. The ghost coon wasn't there. I climbed back down, scolded Old Dan to stop his loud bawling, and looked for Little Ann.

I saw her far up the old fence row, sniffing and running here and there. I knew the ghost coon had pulled a real trick, but I couldn't figure out what it was. Little Ann had never yet barked treed. I knew if the coon was in the tree she wouldn't still be searching for a trail.

Old Dan started working again.

My dogs covered the field. They circled and circled. They ran up and down the barbed-wire fence on both sides.

I knew the coon hadn't walked the barbed wire. Ghost or no ghost, he couldn't do that. I walked over to the old gate and looked around. I sat down and stared up into the tree. Little Ann came to me.

Old Dan, giving up his search, came back to the tree and bawled a couple of times. I scolded him again.

Rubin came over. Leering at me, he said, "You give up?"

I didn't answer.

Little Ann once again started searching for the lost trail. Old Dan went to help her.

Rainie said, "I told you that you couldn't tree the ghost coon. Why don't you pay off so we can go home?"

I told him I hadn't given up. My dogs were still hunting. When they gave up, I would, too.

Rubin said, "Well, we're not going to stay here all night."

Looking back to the tree, I thought perhaps I had overlooked something. I told Rubin I was going to climb it again.

He laughed, "Go ahead. Won't do any good. You climbed it once. Ain't you satisfied?"

"No, I'm not satisfied," I said. "I just don't believe in ghost coons."

Rubin said, "I don't believe in ghosts either, but facts are facts. To tell you the truth, I've climbed that tree a dozen times and there just ain't no place in it for a coon to hide."

Rainie spoke up. "Our old blue hound has treed the ghost coon in this tree more times than one. Maybe you two don't believe in ghosts, but I do. Why don't you pay off so we can get away from here?"

"I'll climb it one more time," I said. "If I can't find him, I'll pay off."

Climbing up again, I searched and searched. When I got through, I knew the ghost coon wasn't in that tree. When I came down, I saw my dogs had given up. That took the last resistance out of me. I knew if they couldn't find the ghost coon, I couldn't.

Digging the two one-dollar bills out of my pocket, I walked over to Rubin. Little Ann was by my side. I handed my money over, saying, "Well, you won it fair and square."

With a grin on his face, Rubin took my money. He said, "I bet this will break your old grandpa's heart."

I didn't reply.

Reaching down, I caught Little Ann's head in my hands. Looking into her warm friendly eyes, I said, "It's all right, little girl, we haven't given up yet. We'll come back. We may never catch the ghost coon, but we'll run him until he leaves the country."

She licked my hands and whined.

A small breeze began to stir. Glancing up into the tree, I saw some leaves shaking. I said to Rubin, "Looks like the wind is coming up. It may blow up a storm. We'd better be heading for home."

Just as I turned, I saw Little Ann throw up her head and whine. Her body grew stiff and taut. I watched her. She was testing the wind. I knew she had scented something in the breeze. Stiff-legged, head high in the air, she started walking toward the tree. Almost there, she turned back and stopped. I knew she had caught the scent but could only catch it when a breeze came.

Looking at Rubin, I said, "I haven't lost that two dollars yet."

Another breeze drifted out of the river bottoms. Little Ann caught the scent again. Slowly she walked straight to the large gatepost, reared up on it with her front feet, and bawled the most beautiful tree bark I ever heard in my life.

Old Dan, not understanding why Little Ann was bawling, stood and looked. He walked over to the post, reared up on it, and sniffed. Then, raising his head, he shook the dead leaves in the bur oak tree with his deep voice.

I looked at Rainie. Laughing, I said, "There's your ghost coon. Now what do you think of my dogs?"

For once he made no reply.

Going over to the post, I saw it was a large black locust put there many years ago to hang the gate. Looking up at the tree, I saw how the ghost coon had pulled his trick. One large long limb ran out and hung directly over the gate. It was a drop of a good twelve feet from the branch to the top of the gatepost, but I knew we weren't after an ordinary coon. This was the ghost coon.

I said to Rubin, "Boost me up and I'll see if the post is hollow."

After breaking off a long jimpson weed to use as a prod, I got up on Rubin's shoulder, and he raised me up. The post was hollow. Not knowing how far down the hole went, I started the switch down. About halfway, I felt something soft. I gave it a hard jab.

I heard him coming. He boiled out right in my face. I let go of everything. Hitting the ground, I rolled over on my back and looked up.

For a split second, the ghost coon stayed on top of the post, and then he jumped. My dogs were on him the instant he hit the ground. The fight was on.

I knew the coon didn't have a chance as he wasn't in the waters of the river. He didn't give up easily even though he was on dry land. He was fighting for his life and a good account he gave. He fought his way to freedom, and made it back to the bur oak tree. He was a good six feet up the side when Old Dan, leaping high in the air, caught him and pulled him back down.

At the foot of the tree, the fight went on. Again the ghost coon fought his way free. This time he made it and disappeared in the dark shadows of the tree. Old Dan was furious. Never before had I seen a coon get away from him.

I told Rubin I would climb up and run him out. As I started climbing, I saw Little Ann go to one side and Old Dan to the other. My dogs would never stay together when they had treed a coon, so that any way he left a tree, he was met by one of them.

About halfway up, far out on a limb, I found the ghost coon. As I started toward him, my dogs stopped bawling. I heard something I had heard many times. The sound was like the cry of a small baby. It was the cry of a ringtail coon when he knows it is the end of the trail. I never liked to hear this cry, but it was all in the game, the hunter and the hunted.

As I sat there on the limb, looking at the old fellow, he cried again. Something came over me. I didn't want to kill him.

I hollered down and told Rubin I didn't want to kill the ghost coon.

He hollered back, "Are you crazy?"

I told him I wasn't crazy. I just didn't want to kill him.

I climbed down.

Rubin was mad. He said, "What's the matter with you?"

"Nothing," I told him. "I just don't have the heart to kill the coon."

I told him there were plenty more; why kill him? He had lived here a long time, and more than one hunter had listened to the voices of his hounds bawling on his trail.

Rainie said, "He's chicken-livered, that's what it is."

I didn't like that but, not wanting to argue, I didn't say anything.

Rubin said, "I'll go up and run him out."

"I won't let my dogs kill him," I said.

Rubin glared at me. "I'm going up and run that coon out," he said. "If you stop your dogs, I'm going to beat you half to death."

"Do it anyway, Rubin," Rainie said.

"I've a good mind to," said Rubin.

Just as Rubin started to climb the tree, Old Dan growled. He was staring into the darkness. Something was coming.

"What's that?" I asked.

"I don't know," Rubin said. "Don't sound like anything I ever heard."

"It's ghosts," Rainie said. "Let's get away from here."

An animal was coming out of the darkness. It was walking slowly in an odd way, as if it were walking sideways. The hair on the back of my neck stood straight out.

As the animal came closer, Rainie said, "Why, it's Old Blue. How did he get loose?"

It was a big blue tick hound. Around his neck was a piece of rope about three feet long. One could see that the rope had been gnawed in two. The frayed end had become entangled in a fair-sized dead limb. Dragging the limb was what made the dog look so odd. I felt much better when I found out what it was.

The blue tick hound was like the Pritchards, mean and ugly. He was a big dog, tall and heavy. His chest was thick and solid. He came up growling. The hair on his back was standing straight up. He walked stiff-legged around Old Dan, showing his teeth.

I told Rainie he had better get hold of his dog, or there was sure to be a fight.

"You better get hold of your dog," he said. "I'm not worried about Old Blue. He can take care of himself."

I said no more.

"Don't make no difference now whether you kill the ghost coon or not," Rubin said. "Old Blue will take care of him."

I knew the killing of the coon was out of my control, but I didn't want to see him die. I said to Rubin, "Just give back my two dollars and I'll go home. I can't keep you from killing him, but I don't have to stay and see it."

"Rubin, don't give him the money," Rainie said. "He ain't killed the ghost coon."

"That's right," Rubin said. "You ain't, and I wouldn't let you now, even if you wanted to."

I told them my dogs had treed the ghost coon and that was the bet, to tree the ghost coon.

"No, it wasn't," Rubin said. "You said you would kill him."

"It was no such thing," I said. "I've done all I said I would."

Rubin walked up in front of me. He said, "I ain't going to give you the money. You didn't win it fair. Now what are you going to do about it?"

I looked into his mean eyes. I started to make some reply, but decided against it.

He saw my hesitation, and said, "You better get your dogs and get out of here before you get whipped."

In a loud voice, Rainie said, "Bloody his nose, Rubin."

I was scared. I couldn't whip Rubin. He was too big for me. I started to turn and leave when I thought of what my grandfather had told them.

"You had better remember what my grandpa said," I reminded them. "He'll do just what he said he would."

Rubin didn't hit me. He just grabbed me and with his brute strength threw me down on the ground. He had me on my back with my arms outspread. He had a knee on each arm. I made no effort to fight back. I was scared.

"If you say one word to your grandpa about this," Rubin said, "I'll catch you hunting some night and take my knife to you."

Looking up into his ugly face, I knew he would do just what he said. I told him to let me up and I would go and not say anything to anyone.

"Don't let him up, Rubin," Rainie said. "Beat him, or hold him and let me do it."

Just then I heard growling, and a commotion off to one side. The blue hound had finally gotten a fight out of Old Dan. Turning my head sideways, I could see them standing on their hind legs, tearing and slashing at each other. The weight of the big hound pushed Old Dan over.

I told Rubin to let me up so we could stop the fight.

He laughed, "While my dog is whipping yours, I think I'll just work you over a little." So saying, he jerked my cap off, and started whipping me in the face with it.

I heard Rainie yell, "Rubin, they're killing Old Blue."

Rubin jumped up off me.

I clambered up and looked over to the fight. What I saw thrilled me. Faithful Little Ann had gone to the assistance of Old Dan.

I knew my dogs were very close to each other. Everything they did was done as a combination, but I never expected this. It is a very rare occasion for a female dog to fight another dog, but fight she did.

I could see that Little Ann's jaws were glued to the throat of the big hound. She would never loosen that deadly hold until the last breath of life was gone.

Old Dan was tearing and slashing at the soft belly. I knew the destruction his long sharp teeth were causing.

Again Rainie yelled, "Rubin, they're killing him. They're killing Old Blue. Do something quick."

Rubin darted over to one side, grabbed my ax from the ground, and said in a loud voice, "I'll kill them hounds."

At the thought of what he was going to do with the ax, I screamed and ran for my dogs. Rubin was about ten feet ahead of me, bent over, running with the ax held out in front of him. I knew I could never get to them in time.

I was screaming, "No, Rubin, no!"

I saw the small stick when it whipped up from the ground. As if it were alive, it caught between Rubin's legs. I saw him fall. I ran on by.

Reaching the dogfight, I saw the big hound was almost gone. He had long since ceased fighting. His body lay stretched full-length on the ground. I grabbed Old Dan's collar and pulled him back. It was different with Little Ann. Pull as I might, she wouldn't let go of the hound's throat. Her jaws were locked.

I turned Old Dan loose and, getting astraddle of Little Ann, I pried her jaws apart with my hands. Old Dan had darted back in. Grabbing his collar again, I pulled them off to one side.

The blue hound lay where he was. I thought perhaps he was already dead, and then I saw him move a little.

Still holding my dogs by their collars, I looked back. I couldn't understand what I saw. Rubin was laying where he had fallen. His back was toward me, and his body was bent in a "U" shape. Rainie was standing on the other side of him, staring down.

I hollered and asked Rainie, "What's the matter?"

He didn't answer. He just stood as though in a trance, staring down at Rubin.

I hollered again. He still didn't answer. I didn't know what to do. I couldn't turn my dogs loose. They would go for the hound again.

Again I hollered at Rainie, asking him to come and help me. He neither moved nor answered. I had to do something.

Looking around, my glance fell on the old barbed-wire fence. I led my dogs to it. Holding onto their collars with one hand, I worked a rusty barbed wire backwards and forwards against a staple until it broke. Running the end of it under their collars, I tied them up. They made two or three lunges toward the hound, but the wire held.

I walked over and stopped at Rainie's side. I again asked, "What's the matter?"

He said not a word.

I could see that Rainie was paralyzed with fright. His mouth and eyes were opened wide, and his face was as white as chalk. I laid my hand on his shoulder. At the touch of my hand, he jumped and screamed. Still screaming, he turned and started running. I watched him until he disappeared in the darkness.

Looking down at Rubin, I saw what had paralyzed Rainie. When Rubin had tripped, he had fallen on the ax.

Turning my back to the horrible sight, I closed my eyes. The muscles in my stomach knotted and jerked. A nauseating sickness spread over my body. I couldn't look at him.

Seeing a movement from Rubin, I thought he was going to get up. He fell back to the ground. I knew he was dead.

Scared, not knowing what to do, I called for Rainie. I got no answer. I called his name again and again. I could get no reply. My voice echoed in the darkness of the silent night. A cold chill ran over my body.

I suppose it is natural at a time like that for a boy to think of his mother. I thought of mine. I wanted to get home.

Going over to my dogs, I glanced to where the blue hound was. He was trying to get up. I was glad he wasn't dead.

Picking up my lantern, I thought of my ax. I left it. I didn't care if I never saw it again.

Knowing I couldn't turn my dogs loose, I broke off enough of the wire to lead them. As I passed under the branches of the bur oak tree, I looked up into the dark foliage. I could see the bright eyes of the ghost coon. Everything that had happened on this terrible night was because of his very existence, but it wasn't his fault.

I also knew he was a silent witness to the horrible scene. Behind me lay the still body of a young boy. On my left a blue tick hound lay torn and bleeding. Even after all that had happened, I could feel no hatred for the ghost coon and was not sorry I had let him live.

Arriving home, I awakened my mother and father. Starting at my grandfather's mill, I told everything that had happened. I left nothing out. My mother had started crying long before I had completed my story. Papa said nothing, just sat and listened. When I had finished, he kept staring down at the floor in deep thought. I could hear the sobbing of my mother in the silence. I walked over to her. She put her arms around me and said, "My poor little boy."

Getting to his feet, Papa reached for his coat and hat. Mama asked him where he was going.

"Well, I'll have to go up there," he said. "I'm going to get Grandpa, for he is the only man in the country that has authority to move the body."

Looking at me, he said, "You go across the river and get Old Man Lowery, and you may as well go on up and tell the Bufords, too. Tell them to meet us at your grandfather's place."

I hurried to carry the sad message.

The following day was a nasty one. A slow, cold drizzle had set in. Feeling trapped indoors, I prowled from room to room. I couldn't understand why my father hadn't come back from the Pritchards'. I sat by the window and watched the road.

Understanding my feelings, Mama said, "Billy, I wouldn't worry. He'll be back before long. It takes time for things like that."

"I know," I said, "but you would think he would've been back by now."

Time dragged slowly by. Late in the afternoon, I saw Papa coming. Our old mule was jogging along. Water was shooting out from under his feet in small squirts at every step.

Papa had tied the halter rope around the mule's neck. He was sitting humped over, with his hands jammed deep in the pockets of his patched and worn mackinaw. I felt sorry for him. He was soaking wet, tired, sleepy, and hungry.

Telling Mama, "Here he is," I grabbed my jumper and cap, and ran out to the gate and waited.

I was going to ask him what had happened at the Pritchards' but on seeing his tired face and wet clothes, I said, "Papa, you had better go in to the fire. I'll take care of the mule, and do the feeding and milking."

"That would be fine," he said.

After doing the chores, I hurried to the house. I couldn't wait any longer. I had to find out what had happened.

Walking into the front room, I saw my father had changed clothes. He was standing in front of the fireplace, drinking coffee.

"Boy, that's bad weather, isn't it?" he said.

I said it was, and asked him about Rubin.

"We went to the old tree and got Rubin's body," Papa said. "We were on our way back to the Pritchards' when we met them. They were just this side of their place. They had started to look for him. Rainie had been so dazed when he got home, they couldn't make out what he was trying to tell them, but they knew it must have been something bad. They wanted to know what had happened. I did my best to explain the accident. It hit Old Man Pritchard pretty hard. I felt sorry for him."

Mama asked how Mrs. Pritchard was taking it.

Papa said he didn't know as he never did get to see any of the womenfolks. He said they were the funniest bunch he had ever seen. He couldn't understand them. There wasn't one tear shed that he could see. All of the men had stayed out at the barn. They never had been invited in for a cup of coffee or anything.

Mama asked when they were to have the funeral.

"They have their own graveyard right there on the place," Papa said. "Old Man Pritchard said they would take care of everything, and didn't want to bother people. He said it was too far for anyone to come, and it was bad weather, too."

Mama said she couldn't help feeling sorry for Mrs. Pritchard, and wished they were more friendly.

I asked Papa about Rainie.

Papa said, "According to what Old Man Pritchard said, Rainie just couldn't seem to get over the shock. They were figuring on taking him into town to see the doctor."

In a stern voice, Papa said, "Billy, I don't want you fooling around with the Pritchards any more. You have plenty of country around here so you don't have to go there to hunt."

I said I wouldn't.

I felt bad about the death of Rubin. I didn't feel like hunting and kept having bad dreams. I couldn't forget the way he had looked at me just before he died. I moped and wandered around in a daze. I wanted to do something but didn't know what it was.

I explained my feelings to my mother. She said, "Billy, I feel the same way and would like to do something to help, but I guess there's nothing we can do. There are people like the Pritchards all through the hills. They live in little worlds of their own and are all alone. They don't like to have outsiders interfere."

I told my mother I had been thinking about how dangerous it was to carry an ax while hunting, and I had decided I'd save a few coon hides and get a good gun. Boy, I just shouldn't have mentioned getting a gun. My mother got "sitting-hen" mad.

"You're not getting a gun," she said. "I won't have that at all. I told you a long time ago you could have one when you are twenty-one years old, and I mean just that. I worry enough with you out there in the hills all hours of the night, running and jumping, but I couldn't stand it if I knew you had a gun with you. No, sir. You can just forget about a gun."

"Yes, Mama," I said, and sulked off to my room.

Lying on my bed, still trying to figure out what I could do to help, I glanced over to the wall. There, tied in a small bundle, was just what I needed.

Some time back my sisters had made some flowers for Decoration Day.[1] They had given me a small bouquet for my room. Taking them down, I could see they had faded a little, and looked rather old, but they were still pretty. I blew the dust off and straightened the crinkled petals. Putting them inside my shirt, I left the house.

I hadn't gone far when I heard something behind me. It was my dogs. I tried to tell them I wasn't going hunting. I just had a little business to attend to, and if they would go back, I'd take them out that night. It was no use. They couldn't understand.

Circling around through the flats, I came to the hollow above the Pritchards' place. Down below me, I could see the graveyard, and the fresh mound of dirt. As quietly as I could, I started easing myself down the mountainside.

Old Dan loosened a rock. The farther it bounced, the louder it got. It slammed up against a post oak tree and sounded like a gunshot. I held my breath and watched the house. No one came out.

I glared at Old Dan. He wagged his tail, and just to show off, he sat down on his rear and started digging at a flea with his hind leg. The way his leg was thumping in the leaves, anyone could have heard it for a mile. I waited until he quit thumping before starting on.

Reaching the bottom, I had about twenty yards of clearing to cross, but the grass and bushes were pretty thick. Laying down on my stomach, with my heart beating like a triphammer, I wiggled my way to Rubin's

---

1. Decoration Day: Memorial Day.

grave. I laid the flowers on the fresh mound of earth, and then turned around and scooted for the timber.

Just as we reached the mountaintop, my foot slipped and I kicked loose a large rock. Down the side of the mountain it rolled. This time the blue tick hound heard the noise. He came out from under the house bawling. I heard a door slam and Mrs. Pritchard came out. She stood looking this way and that way.

The hound ran up to the graveyard and started sniffing and bawling. Mrs. Pritchard followed him. Seeing the flowers on Rubin's grave, she picked them up and looked at them. She scolded the hound, and then looked up at the hillside. I knew she couldn't see me because the timber was too thick, but I felt uncomfortable anyway.

Scolding the hound again, she knelt down and arranged the flowers on the grave. Taking one more look at the hillside, she started back. Halfway to the house, I saw her reach down and gather the long cotton skirt in her hand and dab at her eyes.

I felt much better after paying my respects to Rubin. Everything looked brighter, and I didn't have that funny feeling any more.

All the way home my dogs kept running out in front of me. They would stop, turn around, and look at me. I had to smile, for I knew what they wanted. I stopped and petted them a little and told them that as soon as I got home and had my supper, we would go hunting.

Chapter 14

A few days later, on his way back from the mill, one of the Hatfield boys stopped at our place. He told me my grandfather wanted to see me. It was unusual for Grandpa to send for me and it had me worried. I figured that he wanted to talk to me about the death of Rubin Pritchard. I always enjoyed talking to my grandpa but I didn't want to talk about Rubin's death. Every time I thought of him, I lived the horrible tragedy all over again.

After a practically sleepless night, the next morning I started for the store. I was walking along deep in thought when Little Ann zipped by me. She was as happy as a young gray squirrel. She wiggled and twisted and once she barked at me. I looked behind me. There was Old Dan trotting along. He stopped when I turned around. Little Ann came up to me. I scolded them and tried to explain that I wasn't going hunting. I was just going up to the store to see what my grandpa wanted. They couldn't, or didn't, want to understand.

I picked up a small stick and slapped my leg with it. In a deep voice I said, "Now you go home, or I'm going to wear you out."

This hurt their feelings. With their tails between their legs and trotting side by side, they started back. Every little way they would stop and look back at me. It was too much. I couldn't stand it. I began to feel bad all over.

"Well, all right," I said. "Come on, you can go, but, Dan, if there are any dogs around the store, and you get in a fight, I won't take you hunting for a whole year, and I mean that," although I knew I didn't.

They came running, tickled to death. Little Ann took one of her silly spells. She started nipping at the long red tail of Old Dan. Not getting any reaction from him, she jumped over him. She barked at him. He wouldn't even look at her. She ran around in front of him and laid down in the trail, acting like a cat ready to spring. Stiff-legged, he walked up close to her, stopped, and showed his teeth. I laughed out loud. I knew he wouldn't bite her any more than he would bite me. He was just acting tough because he was a boy dog.

After several attempts to get him to play,

Little Ann gave up. Together they started sniffing around in the underbrush.

As I walked up in front of the store, Grandpa hollered at me from the barn. I went over to him. Right away he wanted to know all about Rubin's accident. He listened while I told the story over again.

After I had had my say, Grandpa stood looking down at the ground. There was a deep frown on his face, and a hurt look in his eyes. His quietness made me feel uneasy. He finally raised his head and looked at me. What I could see in his friendly old face tore at my heart. It seemed that there were more wrinkles than I had ever seen before. His un-combed, iron-gray hair looked almost white. I noticed that his wrinkled old hand trembled as he rubbed the wire-stiff stubble on his chin.

In a low voice that quivered as he talked, he said, "Billy, I'm sorry about all this. Truly sorry. I can't help but feel that in a way it was my fault."

"No, Grandpa," I said, "it wasn't your fault. It wasn't anyone's fault. It just happened and no one could help it."

"I know," he said, "but if I hadn't called Rubin's bet, nothing would have happened. I guess when a man gets old he doesn't think straight. I shouldn't have let those boys get under my skin."

"Grandpa," I said, "Rubin and Rainie could get under anybody's skin. You couldn't help that. Why, they get under everyone's skin that gets close to them."

"Yes, I know," he said, "but still I acted like a fool. Billy, I had no idea things were going to turn out like they did, or I wouldn't have called that bet."

Wanting to change the conversation, I said, "Grandpa, we won that bet fair and square, but they took my money anyway."

I saw the fire come back to his eyes. This made me feel better. He was more like the Grandpa I loved.

"That's all right," he said. "We'll just forget the whole thing."

He stepped over and laid his hand on my shoulder. In a solemn voice, he said, "We won't talk about this again. Now, I want you to forget it ever happened because it wasn't your fault. Oh, I know it's hard for a boy to ever completely forget something like that. All through your life you'll think of it now and then, but try not to let it bother you, and don't ever feel guilty about it. It's not good for a young boy to feel that way."

I nodded my head, thinking if people would just stop questioning me about Rubin's death, maybe I could forget.

Grandpa said, "Well, the accident wasn't the only thing I wanted to talk to you about. I've got something else—something I think will help us both forget a lot of things."

The twinkle in Grandpa's eyes reminded me of what my father had said: "Seems like that old man can cook up more deals than anyone in the country."

I didn't care how many deals Grandpa cooked up. He was still the best grandpa in the whole wide world.

"What have you got?" I asked.

"Come over to the store," he said, "and I'll show you."

On our way over, I heard him mutter, "I hope this doesn't turn out like the ghost-coon hunt."

On entering the store, Grandpa walked to the post office department, and came back with a newspaper in his hand. He spread it out on the counter.

Pointing with his finger, he said in a loud voice, "Look, there!"

I looked. The large black letters read: CHAMPIONSHIP COON HUNT TO BE HELD. My eyes popped open. Again I read the words.

Grandpa was chuckling.

I said, "Boy, if that isn't something. A championship coon hunt." Wide-eyed, I asked, "Where are they having this hunt, and what does it have to do with us?"

Grandpa was getting excited. Off came his glasses and out came the old red handkerchief. He blew his breath on the lens and polished them. He snorted a time or two, reared back, and almost shouted, "Do with us? Why it has everything to do with us. All my life I've wanted to go to one of these big coon hunts. Why I've even dreamed about it. And now the opportunity has come. Yes, sir, now I can go." He paused. "That is, if it's all right with you."

I was dumbfounded. I said, "All right with me? Why, Grandpa, you know it's all right with me, but what have I got to do with it?"

Grandpa was so excited I thought he was going to burst a blood vessel.

Talking excitedly, he said, "I've got it all fixed, Billy. We can enter Old Dan and Little Ann in this championship hunt."

I was so surprised at what Grandpa had said I couldn't utter a word. At first I was scared and then a wonderful feeling came over me. I felt the excitement of the big hunt as it burned its way into my body. I started breathing like I had been running for a hundred miles. After several attempts, I croaked, "Can just any dog be in this hunt?"

Grandpa almost jumped as he answered, "No, sir, not just any hound can be entered. They have to be the best, and they have to be registered, too."

He started talking with his hands. Pointing to a chair, he said, "Sit down and I'll tell you all about it."

Grandpa calmed down a little and started talking in a serious voice. "Billy," he said, "it takes some doing to have a set of dogs entered in this hunt. I've been working on this for months. I've written letters on top of letters. I've even had several good friends in town helping me. You see, I've kept a record of all the coons your dogs have caught, and believe me, their catch is up there with the best of them. Now, I have already paid the entry fee and everything is fixed. All we have to do is go."

"Entry fee? How much did it cost?" I asked.

"You let me worry about that," he said. "Now what do you say? Want to give it a whirl? I understand the winner receives a gold cup, and you never can tell, we might come home with it. We have as good a chance as anyone else."

Grandpa had me so worked up by this time, I didn't think anyone else had any good hounds but me.

I reared back and blurted, "It's all right with me, Grandpa. Just tell me what to do."

Grandpa flew out of gear like a Model-T Ford. He slapped the counter with his hand. In a pent-up voice, he said, "That's the boy! That's the way I like to hear a coon hunter talk."

With a questioning look on his face, he asked, "Didn't I see your dogs with you when you came up?"

"Yes, they followed me," I said. "They're outside."

"Well, call them in," he said. "I've got something for them."

I called to them. Little Ann came in the store, walking like she was scared. Old Dan came to the door and stopped. I tried to coax him in. It was no use. My dogs, never being allowed in the house, were scared to come in.

Grandpa walked over to a hoop of cheese and cut off two chunks about the size of my fist. He walked to the door, talking to Old Dan. "What's the matter, boy?" he said. "You scared to come in? Well, that shows you're a good dog."

He handed him a piece of the cheese. I heard it rattle in his throat as he gulped it down.

Grandpa came back and set Little Ann up on the counter. He chuckled as he broke the cheese up in small pieces and fed her.

"Yes, sir," he said, "I think we have the best darn coon hounds in these Ozark Mountains, and just as sure as shootin', we're going to win that gold cup."

Grandpa didn't have to say that. The way I was feeling, I already had the cup. All I had to do was go and get it.

Finished with his feeding of Little Ann, Grandpa said, "Now, let's see. The hunt starts on the twenty-third. That's about—well, let's see—this is the seventeenth." Counting on his fingers he finally figured it out. "That's six days from now," he said in a jubilant voice.

I nodded my head.

"We can leave here early on the morning of the twenty-second," he said, "and barring accidents, we should make the campground in plenty of time for the grand opening."

I asked how we were going.

"We'll go in my buggy," he said. "I'll load the tent and everything the night before."

I asked him what he wanted me to bring.

"Nothing," he said, "but these two little hounds, and you be here early; and I believe I'd let these dogs rest, 'cause we want them in tiptop shape when we get there."

I saw the thinking wrinkles bunch up on Grandpa's forehead.

"You reckon your daddy would like to go?" he asked. "As late in the fall as it is, I don't think he's too busy, is he?"

"No, our crops are all gathered," I said. "We've been clearing some of the bottom land, but that's almost done now."

"Well, ask him," he said. "Tell him I'd like to have him go."

"I'll ask him," I said, "but you know how Papa is. The farm comes first with him."

"I know," Grandpa said, "but you ask him anyway, and tell him what I said. Now it's getting late and you had better be heading for home."

I was almost to the door when Grandpa said, "Wait a minute."

He walked over behind the candy counter and shook out one of the quarter sacks. He filled it up to the brim, bounced it on the counter a few times, and dropped in a few more gumdrops.

With a twinkle in his eye, and a smile on his face, he handed it to me saying, "Save some for your sisters."

I was so choked up I couldn't say anything. I took it and flew out the door, calling to my dogs.

On my way home I didn't walk on the ground. I was way up in the clouds just skipping along. With a song, I told the sycamore trees and the popeyed gray squirrels how happy I was.

Little Ann sensed my happiness. She pranced along on the trail. With a doggish grin on her face, she begged for a piece of candy, which I so gladly gave.

Even Old Dan felt the pleasant atmosphere. His long red tail fanned the air. Once he raised his head and bawled. I stood still and listened to the droning tones of his deep voice. The sound seemed to be trapped for an instant in the thick timber. It rolled around under the tall white sycamores, beat its way through the wild cane, and found freedom out over the clear blue waters of the river. The sound, following the river's course, rolled like the beat of a jungle drum.

As the echo died away in the distance, silence settled over the bottoms. The gray squirrels stopped their chattering. The wild birds quit their singing. I stood still. No sound could be heard. It seemed that all the creatures of the wild were holding their breath. I gazed up to the towering heights of the tall trees. No leaf was stirring. The silence seemed strained and expectant, like a young boy waiting for a firecracker to explode.

I looked at Old Dan. He was standing perfectly still, with his right front foot raised and his long ears fanned open. He seemed to be listening, and challenging any living creature to make a noise.

The silence was broken by the "Whee-e-e-e" of a red-tailed hawk. This seemed to be a signal. All around me the happy atmosphere resumed its natural state.

I heard the "Bam, bam, bam" of a woodpecker high in the top of a box elder snag. The cry of a kingfisher and the scream of a bluejay blended perfectly with the drumlike beat. A barking red squirrel, glued to the side of a hackberry tree, kept time to the music with the beat of his tail.

Each noise I heard and each sight I saw was very familiar to me but I never grew tired of listening and watching. They were a God-sent gift and I enjoyed them all.

As I skipped along, it was hard for me to realize all the wonderful things that had happened to me in such a few short years. I had two of the finest little hounds that ever bawled on the trail of a ringtail coon. I had a wonderful mother and father and three little sisters. I had the best grandpa a boy ever had, and to top it all, I was going on a championship coon hunt. It was no wonder that my heart was bursting with happiness. Wasn't I the luckiest boy in the world?

Everyone was just sitting down to supper when I got home. My sisters quit the table for the candy. I told them to divide it equally. The oldest one asked if I wanted any of it.

"No," I said. "I brought it all for you." Of course, I didn't tell them about the four pieces I had in my pocket.

They thanked me with their clear blue eyes.

I guess it's pretty hard for a young boy to fool his mama. She took one look at me and called me over. She ruffled up my hair, kissed me, and said, "If my little boy's eyes get any bigger they're going to pop right out of his head. Now tell me, what are you so happy about?"

Before I could say anything, Papa chuckled and asked, "What's going on between you and your grandpa? What are you and that old man cooking up now?"

As fast as I could talk I started telling about the big coon hunt. I told how hard Grandpa had been working to have my dogs entered, and how he had already paid my entry fee.

Catching my breath and looking at Papa, I said, "We're going in his buggy and he wants you to go."

I waited in silence for his reply. Papa sat there staring off into space, sipping his coffee and saying nothing. I knew he was thinking.

In the silence I was sure I could hear my heart thumping.

I said, "Papa, please go. We'll have a lot of fun and besides the winner receives a big golden cup."

He scratched his head and said, "Billy, I'd sure like to go, but I don't see how I can with all this work around here."

I was beginning to think that Papa wasn't going to go. Then Mama started talking.

"Work?" she said. "Why, all the work is practically done. I don't know of one thing you couldn't put off for a few days. Why don't you go? You haven't been anywhere since I don't know when."

Papa spoke up. "It's sure going to be a big hunt," he said. "I heard something about it up at the store one day."

"Grandpa said there would be hunters there from everywhere," I said, "and some of the best coon hounds in the country."

"Do you think you have a chance to win the cup?" Papa asked.

I started to answer him when the little one piped up. "They can't beat Old Dan and Little Ann," she said. "I just bet they can't."

Everyone laughed at her serious remark. I would have kissed her but she had candy, corn bread, and molasses all over her face.

I told Papa I didn't know how good those dogs were, but there was one thing I did know. If they beat mine, they would have to hunt harder than they ever had before.

After I had had my say about the dogs, a silence settled over the dining room. Everyone was looking at Papa and waiting for his answer.

I saw a pleased smile spread over his face. He stood up. "All right, I'll go," he said, "and, by golly, we'll bring that gold cup back, too."

My sisters started clapping their hands and squealing with delight. A satisfied smile spread over my mother's face.

At that moment I'm sure no boy in the world could have been happier than I. Tears of happiness rolled down my cheeks. Mama wiped them away with her apron.

In the midst of all the excitement, my little sister, saying not a word, climbed down from her chair. No one said anything. We just watched her.

Still clutching a spoon in her small hand, she came around the table and walked up to me. Looking down at the floor, in a bashful voice, she asked. "Can I have the gold cup?"

Putting my finger under her sticky little chin, I tilted her head up. I smiled as I looked into her clear blue eyes. I said, "Honey, if I win it, I'll give it to no one but you."

I had to cross my heart and hope to die several times before she was satisfied.

Back in her chair she gloated over the others. "You just wait and see," she said. "It'll be all mine, nobody's but mine, and I'll put my banty eggs in it."

"Silly, you don't put banty eggs in a gold cup," the oldest one said. "They're just made to look at."

That night I dreamed about gold cups, little red hounds, and coons as big as rain barrels. Once I woke myself up whooping to my dogs.

The next few days were busy ones for me. Knowing that Papa and I would be gone for several days, I did everything I could to make things convenient for Mama. I chopped a large pile of wood and stacked it close to the kitchen door. To make it easy for her to feed our stock, I cut some poles from the hillside and boxed up one of the stalls in the barn. I filled it full of hay so she wouldn't have to climb the ladder to the loft.

Papa laid down the law to my sisters about being good and helping Mama while we were gone.

The day before we were to leave, I was as nervous as a June bug in a henhouse. The day seemed endless. A few of the miserable hours were spent talking to my dogs. I told them all about the big hunt and how important it was.

"Now if you don't win the golden cup," I said, "I won't be mad because I know you will do your best."

Old Dan wouldn't even look at me, and paid no attention to what I said. He was sulking because I hadn't been taking him hunting. When I talked to Little Ann, it was different. She listened and seemed to understand everything I said.

I dreaded to go to bed that night. I thought sleep would be impossible. I must have been more tired than I thought I was. I fell asleep almost immediately. Old Red, our rooster, woke me at daybreak, crowing his fool head off.

It was a beautiful morning, clear and frosty.

After a good breakfast, we kissed Mama good-bye and started for the store.

I'm sure there were a lot of coon hunters in the Ozarks, but on that morning none could have felt as big and important as I. Walking along by the side of my father, I threw out my chest and tried hard to keep pace with his long strides. He noticed and laughed.

"You'll have to grow a little bit," he said, "before you can take steps that long."

I didn't say anything, I just smiled.

Hearing a noise overhead, I looked up. The gray ones were winging their way southward. I listened to their talking and wondered what they were saying.

Looking to the mountains around us, I saw that the mysterious artist who comes at night had paid us a visit. I wondered how he could paint so many different colors in one night: red, wine, yellow, and rust.

My dogs were trotting along in front of us. I smiled at the way their hind quarters shifted to the right. Little Ann would jump and bounce and try to get Old Dan to play, but the solemn old boy just jogged along, heedless of everything.

"You know," Papa said, "she doesn't even act like a hound. She is bouncing and playing all the time. Why, she acts more like a little pup than a hound."

"Yes, I know," I said. "I've noticed that myself, but you know one thing, Papa, she's the smartest dog I've ever seen. Why, some of the things she does are almost unbelievable."

"Yes, I know," said Papa, "but still it's strange, very strange."

"There's only one thing wrong with her, Papa," I said.

"Yes, what's that?" he asked.

"You won't believe it," I said, "but she's gun-shy."

"Gun-shy? How do you know she's gun-shy?" Papa asked.

"I didn't know for a long time," I said, "until one day when I was hoeing corn down in the field by the old slough. She and Old Dan were digging in a bank after a ground hog. Across the river some fishermen started shooting a gun. It scared Little Ann, and she came running to me, shaking all over."

"Aw," Papa said, "maybe you just thought she was scared."

"No, I didn't, Papa," I said. "It happened again up at the store one day. Grandpa shot a chicken hawk. When the gun went off, it scared her half to death. No, she's gun-shy all right."

"Aw, well," Papa said, "that doesn't mean anything. A lot of dogs are afraid of guns."

"I know," I said, "but you wouldn't think she would be that way. I believe if I had a gun of my own I could break her of being gun-shy."

Papa looked at me. He said, "From what your mother says, you won't be getting a gun for some time yet."

"Yes, I know," I said.

When we reached the store we saw the team was already hitched to the buggy and was standing in front of the store. Grandpa had loaded the tent and several boxes of groceries.

I had never seen him in such high spirits. He slapped Papa on the back, saying, "I'm sure glad you could go with us. It'll do you good to get out once in a while."

Papa laughed and said, "It looked like I had to go or have everyone in the family mad at me."

Looking in the buggy I saw my ax. I didn't think I ever wanted to see it again, but for some reason it didn't look like I thought it would. There was no blood on it and it looked harmless enough laying there all clean and bright.

Grandpa saw me looking at it. He came over.

"I kept it a few days," he said, "just in case the marshal wanted to ask some questions. Everything seems to be all right now, and we may need a good ax on this hunt."

Grandpa sensed how I felt about the ax.

He waited in silence for my answer.

The excitement of the hunt was so strong in me, even the sight of the ax brought back only a fleeting remembrance of Rubin's accident.

I said, "Yes, we will need one. Besides, it's a good one and there's no use in throwing it away."

Grandpa laughed, reached over, and screwed my cap around on my head, saying, "That's the boy, that's what I wanted you to say. Now, you better go to the barn and get some hay and make a bed in the buggy box for your dogs."

"Aw, Grandpa," I said, "they can walk. They don't ever get tired; besides, they're used to walking."

"Walk!" Grandpa almost shouted. "They're not going to walk. No, sir, not if I can help it. You want them to be footsore when we get there?"

Papa chuckled and said, "We can't win a gold cup with two sore-footed hounds, can we?"

"Of course not," Grandpa said. "Now, you go and get that hay like I said."

As I turned to go to the barn I couldn't help but smile. It made me feel good to have my papa and grandpa so concerned about my dogs.

Just when I thought we were ready to leave, Grandma came bustling out. She handed Grandpa a pair of long-handle underwear and a scarf, saying, "I knew you'd forget something."

Grandpa snorted but knew there was no use arguing with her.

She started picking around in the groceries, asking about salt, pepper, and matches.

"Nannie, we've got everything," he said. "You must think I'm a baby and don't know how to pack a grub box."

"A baby," Grandma snorted. "Why, you're worse than a baby. At least they have a little sense. You don't have any at all. An old codger like you out chasing a coon all over the hills."

At her biting remark, I thought Grandpa was going to blow up. He snorted like Daisy, our milk cow, when she had seen a booger.

I crawled up in the buggy box with my dogs and hung my feet out.

Grandma came over and asked me about warm clothes. I told her I had plenty.

She kissed me good-bye and we were on our way.

Chapter 15

Over a dim rocky road, in a northeasterly direction, our buggy moved on.

I noticed that the road stayed at the edge of the foothills, but always in sight of the river.

About the middle of the afternoon we stopped at a small stream to water the team. Papa asked Grandpa if he intended to go all the way to the campground before stopping.

"No," he said, "I figure to put up for the night when we reach Bluebird Creek. With a good early start in the morning we can make the campgrounds in plenty of time to pitch our tent and set up camp."

Late that evening we reached Bluebird Creek. We didn't set up our tent. With a tarp we made a lean-to and built a large fire out in front of it.

While Grandpa fed and watered the team, Papa and I carried our bedding to the shelter and made down our beds.

Grandpa said, "While we're cooking supper, you see to your dogs. Feed them and fix them a warm bed."

"I figure to cook them some corn-meal mush," I said. "That's what they're used to eating."

"Mush!" Grandpa growled. "They're not going to have mush, not if I can help it."

He walked over to a grocery box, mumbling as he did, "Mush! A hound can't hunt on a bellyful of that stuff."

He came back and handed me two large cans of corned-beef hash, saying, "Here. Reckon they'll eat this."

I wanted to hug my old grandpa's neck. "Sure, Grandpa," I said, "They'll love that."

Opening one of the cans, I dumped it out on a piece of bark in front of Old Dan. He sniffed at it and refused to eat. I laughed, for I knew why. While I was opening the other can, Grandpa came over.

"What's the matter," he asked. "Won't he eat it?"

"Sure, Grandpa," I said, "he'll eat, but not before Little Ann gets her share."

With the second can opened, I fed her on another piece of bark. Both of them started eating at the same time.

With an astonished look on his face, Grandpa exclaimed, "Well, I'll be darned. I never saw anything like that. Why, I never saw a hound that wouldn't eat. Did you train them to do that?"

"No, Grandpa," I said. "They've always been that way. They won't take anything away from each other, and everything they do, they do it as one."

Papa had overheard our conversation. He said, "You think that's strange. You should have seen what I saw one day.

"One of the girls threw two cold biscuits out in the back yard to Old Dan. He stood and looked at them for a bit, then, picking both of them up in his mouth, he trotted around the house. I followed just to see what he was going to do. He walked up in front of the doghouse, laid them down, and growled; not like he was mad. It was a strange kind of a growl. Little Ann came out of the doghouse and each of them ate a biscuit. Now, I saw

this with my own eyes. Believe me, those dogs are close to each other—real close."

After Papa had stopped talking, silence settled over the camp.

Grandpa stood staring at my dogs. In a slow voice, as if he were picking his words, he said, "You know, I've always felt like there was something strange about those dogs. I don't know just what it is, and I can't exactly put my finger on it, yet I can feel it. Maybe it's just my imagination. I don't rightly know."

Turning to my father, he said, "Did you ever notice the way they watch this boy? They see every move he makes."

Papa said, "Yes, I've noticed a lot of things they have done. In fact, I could tell you of a few that you would never believe, but right now here's something you had better believe. Supper is ready."

While I was helping myself to hot dutch-oven corn bread, fried potatoes, and fresh side meat, Grandpa poured the coffee. Instead of the two cups I expected to see, he set out three and filled them to the brim with the strong black liquid.

I had never been allowed to drink coffee at home and didn't exactly know what to do. I glanced at Papa. He seemed too busy with his eating to pay any attention to me. Taking the bull by the horns, I reached over and ran my finger through the cup's handle. I held my breath as I walked over and sat down by a post oak stump. Nothing was said. Grandpa and Papa paid no attention to what I did. My head swelled up as big as a number-four washtub. I thought, "I'm not only big enough to help Papa with the farm. Now I'm big enough to drink coffee."

With supper over and the dishes washed, Grandpa said, "Well, we had better turn in as I want to get an early start in the morning."

Long after Grandpa and Papa had fallen

asleep, I lay thinking of the big hunt. My thoughts were interrupted when the wonders of night life began to stir in the silence around us.

From a ridge on our right a red fox started barking. He was curious and, in his small way, challenging the intruders that had dared to stop in his wild domain. From far back in the flinty hills, the monotonous calls of a hoot owl floated down in the silent night. It was the mating call and was answered from a distant mountain.

I could hear the stamping feet of our horses, and the grinding, crunching noise made by their strong teeth as they ate the hard, yellow kernels of corn in their feed boxes. A night hawk screamed as he winged his way through the starlit night. An eerie screech from a tree close by made shivers run up and down my spine. It was a screech owl.

I didn't like to hear the small owl, for there was a superstition in the mountains concerning them. It was said that if you heard one owl it meant nothing at all, but if you heard more than one, it meant bad luck.

I lay and listened to the eerie twittering sound. It was coming from the left of our camp. The creepy noise stopped, and for several moments there was silence. When next I heard the cry, it was coming from the right. I sat up in alarm. Had I heard two owls?

My movement had awakened Grandpa. In a sleepy voice, he asked, "What's the matter? Can't you sleep? What are you sitting up like that for?"

"Grandpa, I heard two screech owls," I said.

Grunting and mumbling, he sat up. Rubbing the sleep from his eyes, he said, "You heard two screech owls. Why, that's nothing. I've heard two—oh, I see. You're thinking of the bad-luck superstition. There's nothing to that; nothing at all. Now

you lie down and go to sleep. Tomorrow is going to be a big day."

I tried hard to fall asleep, but couldn't. I couldn't get the owls out of my mind. Had I really heard two? Were we going to have bad luck? Surely nothing bad could happen. Not on such a wonderful hunt.

I found peace in my mind by telling myself that the owl had changed trees. Yes, that was it. He had simply flown out of one tree to another.

The next morning, while having breakfast, Grandpa started kidding me about the screech owls.

"I wish you could have caught one of those owls last night," he said. "We could have boiled him in our coffee pot. I've heard there is nothing like strong hoot-owl coffee."

"It wasn't a hoot owl, Grandpa," I said. "It was a screech owl. I don't know for sure if I heard one or two. It could have been just one." Pointing to a small red oak, I said, "I think the first time I heard him, he was over there. The next time, it was over in that direction. Maybe he changed trees. I sure hope so."

Grandpa saw I was bothered. "You don't believe that hogwash superstition, do you? Bad luck! Baw, there's nothing to it."

Papa laughed, and said, "These mountains are full of that jinx stuff. If a man believed it all, he'd go crazy."

The encouraging words from Papa and Grandpa helped some, but there was still some doubt. It's hard for a young boy to completely forget things like that.

Breakfast over, and our gear stowed back in the buggy, we left Bluebird Creek.

On that day Grandpa drove a little faster than he had on the previous one. I was glad of this, for I was anxious to reach the campground.

About noon he stopped the team. I heard him ask Papa, "Is this Black Fox Hollow?"

"No," Papa said. "This is Waterfall. Black Fox is the next one over. Why?"

"Well," Grandpa said, "there's supposed to be a white flag in the mouth of Black Fox. That's where we leave the road. The camp is in the river bottoms."

By this time I was so excited, I stood up in the buggy box so I could get a better view.

"Maybe you ought to step them up a little, Grandpa," I said. "It's getting pretty late."

Papa joined in with his loud laughter. "You just take it easy," he said. "We'll get there in plenty of time. Besides, these mares can't fly."

I saw the flag first. "There it is, Grandpa," I shouted.

"Where?" he asked.

"Over there. See, tied on that grapevine."

As we left the main road, I heard Papa say, "Boy, look at all those tracks. Sure has been a lot of traveling on this road."

"That smoke over there must be coming from the camps," Grandpa said.

When we came in sight of the camp, I couldn't believe what I saw. I stared in amazement. I had never seen so many people at one gathering. Tents were spread out over an acre and a half of ground; all colors, shapes, and sizes. There were odd-looking cars, buggies, wagons, and saddle horses.

I heard Grandpa say almost in a whisper, "I knew there would be a lot of people here but I never expected so many."

I saw the astonished look on my father's face.

Off to one side of the camp, under a large black gum tree, we set up our tent. I tied my dogs to the buggy, and fixed a nice bed for them under it. After everything was taken care of, I asked if I could look around the camp.

"Sure," Grandpa said. "Go any place you want to go, only don't get in anyone's way."

I started walking through the large camp. Everyone was friendly. Once I heard a voice say, "That's the boy who owns the two little red hounds. I've heard they're pretty good."

If my head had gotten any bigger, I know it would have burst.

I walked on, as straight as a canebrake cane.

I looked at the hounds. They were tied in pairs here and there. I had seen many coon hounds but none that could equal these. There were redbones, blue ticks, walkers, and bloodhounds. I marveled at their beauty. All were spotlessly clean with slick and glossy coats. I saw the beautiful leather leashes and brass-studded collars.

I thought of my dogs. They were tied with small cotton ropes, and had collars made from old checkline leather.

As I passed from one set of dogs to another, I couldn't help but wonder if I had a chance to win. I knew that in the veins of these hounds flowed the purest of breeded blood. No finer coon hounds could be found anywhere. They came from the Smoky Mountains of Tennessee, the bayou country of Louisiana, the Red River bottoms of Texas, and the flinty hills of the Ozarks.

Walking back through the camp, I could feel the cold fingers of doubt squeezing my heart. One look at my dogs drove all doubt away. In the eyes of Little Ann it seemed I could read this message: "Don't worry. Just wait. We'll show them."

That night, Grandpa said, "Tomorrow they'll have a contest for the best-looking hound. Which one are you going to enter?"

I told him I didn't think I'd enter either one of my dogs. They were so little. I didn't think they had a chance.

Grandpa got all huffed up. He said, "It doesn't make any difference how little they are. They're coon hounds, aren't they?"

I asked him if he had seen any of the other hounds.

He said, "Yes, I've seen them all. Sure they're big and good dogs, too, but it makes no difference. I don't care if your dogs are no bigger than a snuff can. They still have a chance. Now, which one are you going to enter?"

I couldn't decide. I said, "I'll think it over tonight and let you know tomorrow."

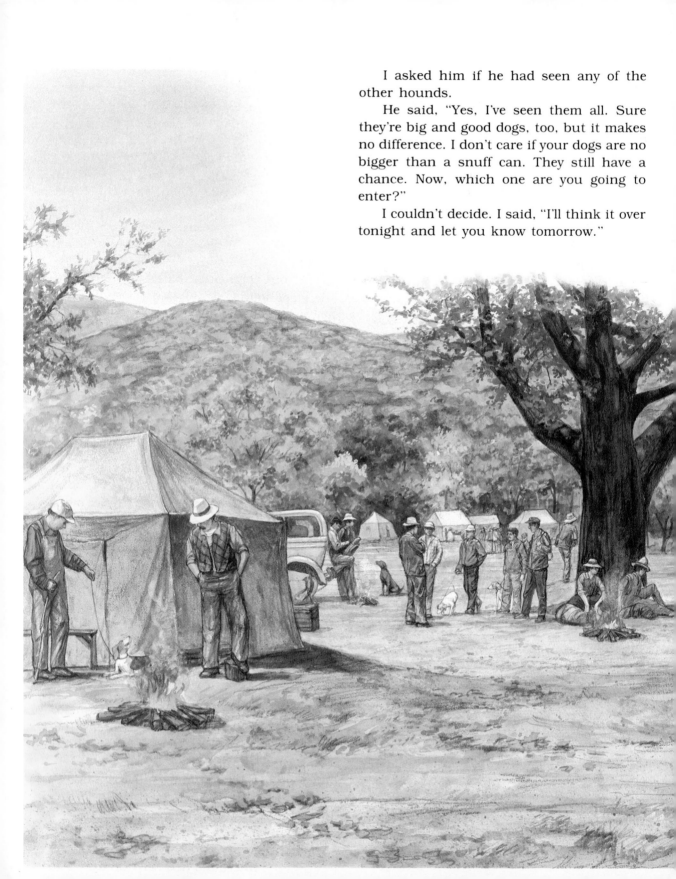

The next morning when I stepped outside the tent I saw the men everywhere. They were combing and brushing their dogs, and getting them pruned for the beauty contest. Beautiful combs and brushes were used to brush expensive oils into their glossy hair.

Going over to my dogs, I stood and looked at them. I started to untie Old Dan but, taking a closer look at him, I could see he could never win a beauty contest. His face and ears were a mass of old scars, caused from the many fights with tough old coons and bobcats. I held his head in my hands

and felt sorry for him, but loved him that much more.

I looked Little Ann over and couldn't see any scars. I laughed because I knew why. She was too smart to walk right up in the face of a fight. She would wait until Old Dan took hold and then dart in.

I untied her rope and walked her over to our tent.

My father and grandfather were gone. No doubt they were in some tent visiting old friends and making new ones.

Looking around to find something I could use to groom my dog, I saw Grandpa's open suitcase. There, right on top, was the very thing I needed, his beautiful bone-handled hairbrush and his ivory comb. Picking them up, I turned them over and over in my hand.

Little Ann stood looking at me. Impulsively I reached down and raked her from shoulder to hip with the brush. She seemed to like it. I knew I shouldn't do it, but I decided to use them.

Knowing I had no oils, I got some butter from our grocery box. With the homemade butter and Grandpa's hair set, I brushed her until she shone. All the time I was grooming her, she tried to lick the butter from my hands.

The job completed, I stepped back and inspected her. I was surprised at the change. Her short red hair glistened and every one was in perfect place.

Shaking my finger at her, I said, "If you lay down and roll, I'll wear you out," although I knew I wouldn't.

Hearing a lot of movement outside, I looked out. Men were setting their dogs on a long table which had been built in the center of the campground. Leading Little Ann to it, I picked her up and set her on the table, too.

I told her to act like a lady. She wagged

her tail as though she understood. I untied the rope and stepped back.

After the dogs were all lined up, the judging started. Four judges walked around and around the table, looking at them from all angles. When one of them would point at a hound, he was taken down and eliminated from the contest. Dog after dog was disqualified. Little Ann was still on the table.

My eyes were wide, my throat dry, and my heart thumping. One judge stopped in front of Little Ann. My heart stopped, too. Reaching over, he patted her on the head.

Turning to me, he asked, "Is this your dog?"

I couldn't speak. I just nodded my head.

He said, "She's a beautiful hound."

He walked on down the line. My heart started beating again.

There were eight dogs left. Little Ann was still holding her own. Then there were four. I was ready to cry. Two more were taken down. Little Ann and a big walker hound owned by a Mr. Kyle were the only ones left. The judges couldn't seem to make up their minds.

Everyone started shouting, "Walk them! Walk them!"

I didn't know what they meant.

Mr. Kyle and I were told to go to one end of the table. Our dogs were placed at the other end. Mr. Kyle snapped his fingers and called to his dog.

The big hound started walking toward his master. What a beautiful sight it was. He walked like a king. His body was stiff and straight, his head high in the air, his large muscles quivered and jerked under his glossy coat, but something went wrong. Just before he reached the end, he broke his stride, turned, and jumped down from the table.

A low murmur ran through the crowd.

It was my turn. Three times I tried to call to Little Ann. Words just wouldn't come out. My throat was too dry. The vocal cords refused to work, but I could snap my fingers. That was all I needed. She started toward me. I held my breath. There was silence all around me.

As graceful as any queen, with her head high in the air, and her long red tail arched in a perfect rainbow, my little dog walked down the table. With her warm gray eyes staring straight at me, on she came. Walking up to me, she laid her head on my shoulder. As I put my arms around her, the crowd exploded.

During the commotion I felt hands slapping me on the back, and heard the word "congratulations" time after time. The head judge came over and made a speech. Handing me a small silver cup, he said, "Congratulations, son. It was justly won."

The tears came rolling. I gathered my dog up in my arms and walked to our tent. Grandpa followed, proudly carrying the cup.

That evening the head judge stepped up on the table. He had a small box in his hand. He shouted, "Over here, men! I have some announcements to make."

We all gathered around.

In a loud voice, he said, "Gentlemen, the contest will start tonight. I'm sure most of you men have been in these hunts before. For those of you who haven't, I will explain the rules. Each night five sets of dogs will be taken out to hunt. A judge will go along with each pair of hounds. Every morning, the judges will turn in that night's catch. The two hounds that tree the most coons will qualify for the championship runoff. The other four sets will be eliminated from the hunt. Of course, if there is a tie, both sets will qualify. On the following nights, only those hounds tying the first night's score, or getting more, will be in the runoff.

"Now, gentlemen, this hunt must be carried out in a sportsmanlike way. If the coon is treed where he can't be caught, such as in a bluff, it will not be counted. You must catch the coon, skin it, and turn the hide over to your judge.

"You are allowed to take an ax, a lantern, and a gun with bird shot, which you can use to get a coon out of a tree.

"Twenty-five sets of hounds have been entered in the hunt. In this box, I have twenty-five cards. Everyone in the contest will now line up for the drawing. The card you draw will tell you what night your hounds are to hunt."

Walking along in the line, I noticed the beautiful red coats, the caps, and the soft leather boots worn by the other hunters. I felt out of place in my faded blue overalls, old sheepskin coat, and scuffed and worn shoes, but to the wonderful men it made no difference. They treated me like a man, and even talked to me like a man.

When it came my time to draw, my hand was shaking so hard I could hardly get it in the box. Pulling the card out, I saw I had drawn the fourth night.

After the hunters had left, we stood around our campfires sipping strong black coffee and listening to the baying of the hounds. Time after time, we heard the tree bark.

Once two hounds came close to the camp, hot on a trail. We listened to their steady bawling. All at once they stopped.

After several minutes of waiting, a hunter said, "You know what? That old coon took to the river and in some way has fooled those dogs."

Another one said, "Yes, sir, he sure has."

A friendly hunter looked at me and asked, "Do you think he could have fooled your dogs?"

Thinking his question over, I said, "You know, sometimes when I am hunting, away back in the mountains or down on the river, I sing a little song I made up myself. One of the verses goes like this:

> *You can swim the river, Old Mister Ringtail,*
> *And play your tricks out one by one.*
> *It won't do any good, Old Mister Ringtail,*
> *My Little Ann knows every one.*

The hunters roared with laughter. Some slapped me on the back.

Tired and sleepy, but with a smile on my face, I went off to bed.

The next morning two blue tick hounds, from the Smoky Mountains of Tennessee, came out in the lead with three big coons to their credit. The other four sets were eliminated.

The following morning all five sets of dogs were eliminated. None had even tied the blue ticks, although two sets had gotten two coons, and one of these had treed a third one in a bluff.

That day, while eating dinner, my grandfather asked me if my dogs had ever treed three coons in one night.

I said, "Yes, four different times, but that's all."

"Where do you think we should hunt on our night?" Papa asked.

I told him if we could get our judge to go with us in the buggy, we would be better off if we could go far downriver and get out of the range where other dogs had hunted.

He said, "That's a good idea. I'll go to see the judges about it."

While I was washing the dishes, Grandpa said, "I think I'll shave."

I should've left the tent then, but I wasn't done with my dish-washing.

With a pin, Grandpa hung a small mirror on the tent wall. After much snorting, mumbling, and screwing of his face this way and that, the job was completed. Dabbing a little water on his iron-gray hair, he reached for his brush and comb.

From the corner of my eye I watched him. I had tried to clean the beautiful brush but hadn't been able to get all the short red hair from it.

With two fingers, Grandpa pulled some of the hair from the bristles. Holding it in front of him, he looked it over carefully. Then, bending over close to the mirror, peeking over his glasses, he inspected his head. Straightening up, he looked at the brush again. Turning around quickly, he looked straight at me and said, "Say, young—"

Not waiting for anything more, I scooted for the door. Crawling under the buggy, I lay down between my dogs. I knew he wouldn't be mad at me, but it would be best to stay away for a while.

The third night, the blue ticks were tied by two black and tan hounds from the bayou country of Louisiana.

All that day I was restless. I prowled through the camp. Every little while I would go and see how Old Dan and Little Ann were. Once I took two weenies from our groceries. I heated them and gave them to my dogs for a treat. Old Dan swallowed his down in one gulp, and looked at me as if to say, "Is that all?" Little Ann ate hers in a ladylike way. I could have sworn I saw a small grin on her face.

Grandpa was hopping around like a grasshopper, going here and there. Once, passing a tent, I heard his voice. I knew he was bragging about my dogs. I smiled to myself.

Another hunter stopped me and asked, "Is it true that your hounds have treed six coons in one night, three up in one tree, or is that old man just blowing off steam?"

I told him my grandfather had a little steam, but he was the best grandpa a boy ever had.

He patted me on the head, turned, and walked away laughing.

THINKING ABOUT THE SELECTION
Recalling

1. Describe the Pritchard boys.
2. Why does Grandfather call Rainie's bet?
3. What happens when Billy finally corners the ghost coon in the tree?
4. How does the hunt for the ghost coon end?
5. What are Grandfather's reasons for arranging the trip for Billy, Papa and himself to the Championship Coon Hunt?

Interpreting

6. Compare and contrast Billy and the Pritchards.

7. Why do Billy and the Pritchards want to catch the ghost coon so badly?
8. What are Billy's feelings after the death of Rubin? How do you think he will change as a result of Rubin's death?
9. Why is it important to Billy that he is treated as an equal by the men at the Championship Coon Hunt? Do you think he deserves to be treated this way? Why or why not?

Applying

10. Throughout the novel, Billy has experiences that contribute to his maturing. Discuss some of Billy's responsibilities and experiences and compare them to your own.

ANALYZING LITERATURE

Appreciating Setting in a Novel

Setting is the physical background and time period in which a novel takes place. In *Where the Red Fern Grows,* the setting has an important influence on the characters and the plot of the story.

1. Describe the features of the river bottoms as Billy sees them.
2. What aspects of the setting make coon hunting challenging?
3. How has the setting helped to shape Billy's character?

CRITICAL THINKING AND READING

Inferring the Effect of Setting

The setting in *Where the Red Fern Grows* affects other aspects of the novel. You can make inferences about its effect on the plot and the characters. For example, Billy would not have walked all the way to Tahlequah if the events took place in today's world of cars and buses.

1. How does the setting of Tahlequah make the characters living there different from Billy?
2. How do the surroundings noted on page 718 affect Billy's mood?
3. How would the events of the story differ if Billy's family lived in Tahlequah?

UNDERSTANDING LANGUAGE

Using Synonyms

Synonyms are words that have similar meanings. However, most synonyms are not exactly alike. In this novel, Wilson Rawls uses a number of synonyms to describe the dogs' cries in different situations. The dogs *whimper* and *cry* when they get confused. They *whine* in anticipation when they catch the scent of a raccoon. Big Dan *howls* in despair when Little Ann falls into the icy river.

Following are four synonyms. Use a dictionary to find their differences in meaning. Complete each sentence with the synonym that best fits the meaning of the sentence. Use each word only

  dark dim murky gloomy

1. The cave was so _____ that he couldn't see two inches in front of his face.
2. The fog from the ocean made it difficult to see through the _____ air.
3. The _____ atmosphere of the forest gave me the creeps.
4. Obscured by the clouds, the sun was so _____ that it gave off little warmth.

THINKING AND WRITING

Writing About Setting

Imagine that you have a friend in another country who is going to visit you for the first time. Write your friend a letter describing where you live. As you plan your letter, refer to the description of your region that you wrote before reading these chapters. Keep in mind that this person is completely unfamiliar with your country. As you review your letter, be sure you have included the effect of your surroundings on your thoughts, actions, and appearance.

GUIDE FOR READING

Where the Red Fern Grows, Chapters 16–20

Theme in a Novel

A **theme** is a general idea about life presented through the characters and their actions in a novel. In your reading to this point, you have seen a deepening relationship between Billy and his dogs. With his dogs, Billy has experienced many emotions, including joy, fear, and contentment. Billy's feelings and his relationship with his dogs point out a theme.

Look For

As you read these last chapters, take note of how the bond of love between the dogs and Billy is expressed. What general statement about life is Wilson Rawls making through Billy and his dogs?

Writing

Many people experience a relationship with their animals similar to the one Billy has with his dogs. Write about the feelings involved in a relationship you have had or have with a pet. If you do not have any experiences with animals, write about someone you know who does, or write about Billy's relationship with his dogs.

Vocabulary

Knowing the following words will help you as you read Chapters 16–20 of *Where the Red Fern Grows*.

haggard (hag′ ərd) *adj.*: Having a worn look from sleeplessness (p. 746)

predatory (pred′ə tôr′ē) *adj.*: Living by capturing and feeding on other animals (p. 753)

sinews (sin′ yoos) *n.*: Tendons (p. 754)

berserk (bər surk′) *adj.*: Into a violent or destructive rage (p. 754)

lithe (līth) *adj.*: Flexible and supple (p. 754)

disembowel (dis′ im bou′ əl) *v.*: Take out the inner organs (p. 755)

scourge (skurj) *n.*: The cause of serious trouble (p. 756)

entrails (en′ trālz) *n.*: The inner organs of animals (p. 757)

Chapter 16

In the afternoon our judge came over and introduced himself. He told us he'd be going with us that night.

About sundown we piled in our buggy and drove a few miles downriver. I noticed other hunters doing the same thing. Everyone was trying to get away from the already-hunted territory.

It was dark by the time Grandpa stopped. I untied the ropes from my dogs. Little Ann reared up on me and whined. Old Dan walked off a few yards, stretched his body, and dragged his claws through the soft bottom soil. Opening his mouth, he let out one loud bawl, and then disappeared in the thick timber. Little Ann was right on his heels.

We took off after them.

Grandpa got nervous. He said to me, "Don't you think you ought to whoop to them?"

I told him to wait a little while. There would be plenty of time for whooping.

He snorted and said he thought a hunter always whooped to his dogs.

"I do, Grandpa," I said, "but not before they strike a trail."

We walked on. Every now and then we would stop and listen. I could hear the loud snuffing of Old Dan. Once we caught a glimpse of Little Ann as she darted across an opening that was bathed in moonlight. She was as silent as a ghost and as quick as a flitting shadow.

Papa said, "It sure is a beautiful night for hunting."

The judge said, "You can't beat these Ozark Mountain nights for beauty. I don't care where you go."

Grandpa started to say something. His voice was drowned out by the bell-like cry of Little Ann.

In a whisper, I said, "Come on, Dan. Hurry and help her."

As if in answer to my words, his deep voice hammered its way up through the river bottoms. I felt the blood tingling in my veins. That wonderful feeling that only a hunter knows crept over my body.

Looking over at Grandpa, I said, "Now you can whoop."

Jerking off his hat and throwing back his head, he let out a yell. It wasn't a whoop, or a screech, it was about halfway in between. Everyone laughed.

The coon was running upriver toward our campground. We turned and followed. I could tell by the dogs' voices that they were running side by side, and were hot on the trail. Closing my eyes, I could almost see them running, bodies stretched to their fullest length, legs pounding up and down, white steam rolling from their hot breath in the frosty night.

Grandpa got tangled up in some underbrush, and lost his hat and spectacles. It took us a while to find the glasses. Papa said something about getting them wired on with baling wire. Grandpa snorted. The judge laughed.

The coon crossed the river and ran on upstream. Soon my dogs were out of hearing distance. I told Papa we had better stay on our side of the river and keep going until we could hear them again.

Twenty minutes later we heard them coming back. We stopped.

"I think they have crossed back to our side," I said.

All at once the voices of my dogs were drowned out by a loud roar.

"What in the world was that?" Grandpa said.

"I don't know," the judge said. "Reckon it was wind or thunder?"

About that time we heard it again.

The judge started laughing. "I know now what it is," he said. "Those hounds have run that coon right back by our camp. The noise we heard was the other hunters whooping to them."

Everyone laughed.

A few minutes later I heard my dogs bawling treed. On reaching the tree, Papa ran his hand back under his coat. He pulled out Grandpa's gun.

"That's a funny-looking gun," the judge said. "It's a 410-gauge pistol, isn't it?"

"It's the very thing for this kind of work," Papa said. "You couldn't kill a coon with it if you tried, especially if you're using bird shot. All it will do is sting his hide a little."

At the crack of the gun, the coon gave a loud squall and jumped. My dogs lost no time in killing him.

We skinned the coon, and soon were on our way again.

The next time my dogs treed, they were across the river from us. Finding a riffle, we pulled off our shoes and started across.

Grandpa very gingerly started picking his way. His tender old feet moved from one smooth rock to another. Everything was fine until we reached midstream, where the current was much swifter. He stepped on a loose round rock. It rolled and down he went.

As the cold river water touched his body, he let out a yell that could have been heard for miles. He looked so funny we couldn't keep from laughing.

Papa and the judge helped him to his feet. Laughing every step of the way, we finally reached the other side. Grandpa kept going in his wet clothes until we reached the tree where the dogs were.

After killing the coon, we built a large fire so Grandpa could dry his clothes. He'd get up as close to the fire as he could, and turn this way and that. He looked so funny standing there with his long underwear steaming. I started rolling with laughter.

He looked over at me and snapped, "What's so funny?"

I said, "Nothing."

"Well, why are you laughing?" he said.

At this remark, Papa and the judge laughed until their eyes watered.

Mumbling and grumbling, Grandpa said, "If you fellows were as cold as I am, you wouldn't be laughing."

We knew we shouldn't be laughing, but we couldn't help ourselves.

The judge looked at his watch. "It's after three o'clock," he said. "Do you think they'll tree another one?"

As if to throw the words back in the judge's face, Old Dan opened up. I stood up and whooped. "Whoo-e-e! Get him, Dan! Get him! Put him up a little tree."

There was a mad scramble. Grandpa tried to put his britches on backwards. The judge and Papa ran over to help him with his shoes. Each one tried to put a shoe on the wrong foot. I was laughing so hard I could do nothing.

A hundred yards from the fire, I realized we had forgotten the coonskins. I ran back for them.

My dogs had jumped the coon in swampland. He tore out for the river bottoms. I could tell they were close to him by their fast bawling. All at once their baying stopped. We stood still and listened. Old Dan bawled treed a few more times and then stopped.

Grandpa asked, "What's happened?"

I told him the coon had probably pulled some kind of trick.

Coming up to my dogs, we saw they were working up and down an old rail fence. We stood and watched. Every now and then, Old Dan would rear up on a large hackberry tree that was standing about seven feet from the fence and bawl treed.

As yet Little Ann had not bawled the tree bark. We watched her. She was working everywhere. She climbed up on the rail fence and followed its zigzag course until she disappeared in the darkness.

I told Papa I was sure the coon had walked the rail fence and in some way had fooled my dogs.

Old Dan would keep coming back to the hackberry tree. He would rear up on it and bawl treed. We walked up to him. Looking the tree over, we could see that the coon wasn't in it.

The judge said, "It looks like he has them fooled."

"Maybe you had better call them off," Grandpa said. "We can go someplace else and hunt. We've got to get one more coon, even if I have to tree it myself."

For some reason, no one laughed at his remark.

"It's almost daylight," Papa said.

"Yes, that's what has me worried," I said. "We don't have time to do any more hunting. If we lose this one, we're beat."

Hearing the word beat, Grandpa began to fidget. He asked me, "What do you think happened? How did that coon fool them?"

"I don't know for sure," I said. "He walked that rail fence. The hackberry tree has something to do with his trick, but I don't know what."

"Son," the judge said, "I wouldn't feel too badly if I were you. I've seen some of the very best hounds fooled by a smart old coon."

Regardless of all the discouraging talk, the love and belief I had in my little red hounds never faltered. I could see them now and then, leaping over old logs, tearing through the underbrush, sniffing and searching for the lost trail. My heart swelled with pride. I whooped, urging them on.

In a low voice, the judge said, "I'll say one thing. They don't give up easily."

Birds began to chirp all around us. The sky took on a light gray color. Tiny dim stars were blinking the night away.

"It looks like we're beat," Papa said. "It's getting daylight."

At that moment, the loud clear voice of a redbone hound, bawling treed, rang through the river bottoms. It was the voice of Little Ann.

Sucking in a mouthful of air, I held it. I could feel my heart pounding against my ribs. I closed my eyes tight and gritted my teeth to keep the tears from coming.

"Let's go to them," Grandpa said.

"No, wait a minute," I said.

"Why?" he asked.

'Wait till Old Dan gets there," I said. "It's daylight now, and if we walk up to the tree, the coon will jump out. It's hard to keep a coon in a tree after daylight. Let's wait until Old Dan gets there. Then if he jumps, he won't have a chance to get away."

"The boy's right," the judge said. "It's hard to keep a coon in a tree after daybreak."

Just then we heard Old Dan. His deep voice shattered the morning silence. Searching for the lost trail, he had crossed the fence and worked his way out into an old field. Turning around, we saw him coming. He was a red blur in the gray morning shadows. Coming to the trail fence, and without breaking his stride, he raised his body into the air. About halfway over and while still in the air he bawled.

Hitting the ground with a loud grunt, he ran past us. Everyone whooped to him. Ahead was a deep washout about ten feet wide. On the other side was a canebrake. His long red body, stretched to its fullest length, seemed to float in the air as he sailed over it. We could hear the tall stalks rattling as he plowed his way through them. A bunch of sleepy snow birds rose from the thick cane, flitted over, and settled in a row on the old rail fence.

Nearing the tree, we could see it was a tall sycamore, and there high in the top was the coon.

Grandpa threw a fit. He hopped around whooping and hollering. He threw his old hat down on the ground and jumped up and down on it. Then he ran over and kissed Little Ann right on the head.

After we killed and skinned the coon, the judge said, "Let's walk back to that old fence. I think I know how the old fellow pulled his trick."

Back at the fence, the judge stood and looked around for a few minutes. Smiling, he said, "Yes, that's how he did it."

"How?" Grandpa asked.

Still smiling, the judge said, "That old coon walked this rail fence. Coming even with the hackberry tree, he leaped up on its side, and climbed up. Notice how thick the timber is around here. See that limb way up there in the top, the one that runs over and almost touches the sycamore?"

We saw what he meant.

"The coon walked out on that limb," he said, "leaped over, and caught the sycamore limb. Repeating this over and over, from tree to tree, he worked his way far out into the river bottoms. What I can't figure out is how that hound found him."

Gazing at Little Ann, he shook his head and said, "I've been hunting coons and judging coon hunts for forty years, but I've never seen anything like that.

He looked at me. "Well, son," he said, "you have tied the leading teams. There's only one more night of eliminations. Even if some of them get more than three coons, you will still be in the runoff, and from what I've seen here tonight, you have a good chance of winning the cup."

I knew that Little Ann had scented the coon in the air, the same as she had the ghost coon. I walked over and knelt down by her side. The things I wanted to say to her I couldn't, for the knot in my throat, but I'm sure she understood.

As we came into the campground, the hunters came out of their tents and gathered around us. The judge held up the three big coon hides. There was a roar from the crowd.

One man said, "That was the most beautiful sight I've ever seen."

"What was a beautiful sight?" Grandpa asked.

"Last night those little red hounds brought that coon right through camp."

The judge said, "We figured they did when we heard the noise."

Laughing, the man said, "We heard them when they ran up the other side of the river. Way up above here they crossed over. We could tell they were coming back so we doused all the fires and, sure enough, they came right through camp. Those two little hounds weren't fifty yards behind the coon, running side by side. Boy, they were picking them up and laying them down, and bawling every time their feet touched the ground. I'll tell you, it was the prettiest sight I ever saw."

When the judge started telling about the last coon Little Ann had treed I took my dogs over to our tent and fed and watered them. After they had had their fill, I gave them a good rubdown with a piece of gunny sack. Taking them out to the buggy, I tied them up. I stood and watched while they twisted around in the hay making their bed.

That day I tried to get some sleep in our tent, but the soaking Grandpa had taken in the river had given him a cold, causing him to snore. I never heard such a racket in all my life. I'd have sworn he rattled the paper sacks in our grocery boxes. Taking a blanket, I went out to my dogs. Little Ann had wiggled up as close to Old Dan as she could. Prying them apart, I lay down between them and fell asleep.

The last night of the eliminations turned out like the second night. None of the judges turned in more than two hides.

That day, about noon, the owners of the other winning teams and I were called for a conference with the head judge. He said, "Gentlemen, the eliminations are over. Only three sets of hounds are left for the runoff. The winner of tonight's hunt will receive the gold cup. If there is a tie for the championship, naturally there will be another runoff."

He shook hands with each of us and wished us good luck.

Tension began to build up in the camp. Here and there hunters were standing in small groups, talking. Others could be seen going in and out of tents with rolls of money in their hands. Grandpa was the busiest one of all. His voice could be heard all over the camp. Men were looking at me, and talking in low tones. I strutted like a turkey gobbler.

That evening, while we were having supper, a hunter dropped by. He had a small box in his hand. Smiling, he said, "Everyone has agreed that we should have a jackpot for the winner. I've been picked to do the collecting."

Grandpa said, "You may as well leave it here now."

Looking at me, the hunter said, "Son, I think almost every man in this camp is hoping you win it, but it's not going to be easy. You're going up against four of the finest hounds there are." Turning to my father, he said, "Did you know the two big walker hounds have won four gold cups?"

Very seriously, Papa said, "You know I have two mules down on my place. One is almost as big as a barn. The other one isn't much bigger than a jack rabbit, but that little mule can outpull the big one every time."

Smiling, the hunter turned to leave. He said, "You could be right."

Papa asked me again where I thought we should start hunting.

I had been thinking about this all day. I said, "You remember where we jumped the last coon in the swamp?"

Papa said, "Yes."

"Well, the way I figure, more than one coon lives in that swamp," I said. "It's a good place for them as there are lots of crawfish and minnows in those potholes. If a hound jumps one there, he has a good chance to tree him."

Papa asked, "Why?"

"It's a long way back to the river, and about the same distance to the mountains," I said. "Either way he runs, a dog can get pretty close to him, and so he would have to take to a tree."

That evening we climbed into Grandpa's buggy and headed for the swamp. It was dark by the time we reached it.

Grandpa handed Papa his gun, saying, "You're getting to be a pretty good shot with this thing."

"I hope I get to shoot it a lot tonight," Papa said.

Under my breath, I said, "I do, too."

After untying the ropes from my dogs, I held onto their collars for a minute. Pulling them up close, I knelt down and whispered, "This is the last night. I know you'll do your best."

They seemed to understand and tugged at their collars. When I turned them loose, they started for the timber. Just as they reached the dark shadows, they stopped, turned around, and stared straight at me for an instant.

The judge saw their strange actions. Laying a hand on my shoulder, he asked, "What did they say, son?"

I said, "Nothing that anyone could understand, but I can feel that they know this hunt is important. They know it just as well as you or I."

It was Little Ann who found the trail. Before the echo of her sharp cry had died away, Old Dan's deep voice floated out of the swamp.

"Well, let's go," Papa said eagerly.

"No, let's wait a minute," I said.

"Wait? Why?" Grandpa asked.

"To see which way he's going to run," I said.

The coon broke out of the swamp and headed for the river. Listening to my dogs, I could tell they were close to him. I said to Papa, "I don't think he'll ever make it to the river. They're right on his heels now."

By the time we had circled the swamp, they were bawling treed.

The judge said, "Boy, that was fast."

I felt my father's hand on my shoulder. Looking at me, he smiled and nodded his head. Papa and I knew I had judged the coon perfectly. He didn't have time to reach the river or the mountains.

My dogs had treed the coon in a tall ash which stood about fifty yards from the river. I knew the fifty yards had saved us a good hour, because he could have pulled trick after trick if he had gotten in the water.

We spied the coon in the topmost branches. At the crack of the gun, he ran far out on a limb and jumped. He landed in an old fallen treetop. He scooted through it. Coming out on the other side, he ran for the river. The tangled mass of limbs slowed my dogs and they all but tore the treetop apart getting out of it. The coon was just one step ahead of them as they reached the river. We heard them hit the water.

Running over, we stood and watched the fight. The coon was at home in the river. He crawled up on Old Dan's head, trying to force him under. Before he could do it, Little Ann reached up and pulled him off.

In a scared voice, Papa said, "That water looks deep to me."

"Maybe you had better call them off," said the judge. "That's a big coon and he could drown one of them easily in that deep water."

"Call them off?" I said. "Why, you couldn't whip them off with a stick. There's no use for anyone to get scared. They know exactly what they're doing. I've seen this more times than one."

Grandpa was scared and excited. He was jumping up and down, whooping and hollering.

Papa raised the gun to aim.

I jumped and grabbed his arm. "Don't do that," I yelled. "You're sure to hit one of my dogs."

Round and round in the deep water the fight went on. The coon climbed on Old Dan's head and sank his teeth in one of his long tender ears. Old Dan bawled with pain. Little Ann swam in and caught one of the coon's hind legs in her mouth. She tried hard to pull him off. All three disappeared under the water.

I held my breath.

The water churned and boiled. All three came to the top about the same time. The coon was between the bank we were standing on and my dogs. He swam toward us. They caught him again just as he reached shore. He fought his way free and ran for a large sycamore. Old Dan caught him just as he started up. I knew that was the end of the fight.

After it was all over and the coon had been skinned, Grandpa said, "I hope we don't have to go through that again tonight. For a while I sure thought your dogs were goners."

The judge said, "Well, have you ever seen that? Look over there!"

Old Dan was standing perfectly still, with eyes closed and head hanging down. Little Ann was licking at his cut and bleeding ears.

"She always does that," I said. "If you'll watch, when she gets done with him, he'll do the same for her."

We stood and watched until they had finished doctoring each other. Then, trotting side by side, they disappeared in the darkness.

We followed along, stopping now and then to listen.

Chapter 17

Looking up the sky, Papa said, "That doesn't look good up there. I think we are in for a storm."

The sky had turned a dark gray. Fast-moving clouds were rolling through the heavens.

Grandpa said, "Looks like we're going to get some wind, too."

Scared and thinking everyone might want to stop hunting because of a few clouds, I said, "If a storm is brewing, it's a good night to hunt. All game stirs just before a storm."

Thirty minutes later, Papa said, "Listen."

We stood still. A low moaning sound could be heard in the tops of the tall sycamores.

Grandpa said, "I was afraid of that. We're going to get some wind."

We heard a rattling in the leaves and underbrush. It was beginning to sleet. The air turned cold and chilly.

From far downriver, we heard the deep baying of a hound on a trail. It was Old Dan. Seconds later, the rhythmic crying of Little Ann could be heard. Swallowing the lump that had jumped up in my throat, I whooped as loud as I could.

The ground was turning white with sleet. The storm had really set in. We hurried along.

I said to Papa, "If this keeps up that old coon won't run long. He'll head for his den."

"If it gets much worse," Grandpa said, "I know some coon hunters that won't be running very long. They'll be frozen too stiff to run."

The judge asked if there was any danger of getting lost.

"I don't know," Papa said. "It's all strange country to me."

My dogs' voices sounded far away. I knew they were much closer than they sounded as they were downwind from us. Finding three large sycamores growing close together, we stopped on the leeward[1] side.

Papa shouted above the wind, "I don't

know if we can take much more of this."

"It is bad," Grandpa replied, "and it looks like it's going to get worse."

"You can't see over fifteen feet now," the judge said. "Do you think we can find the buggy?"

"I think we can find the buggy all right," Papa said.

I could no longer hear the voices of my dogs. This had me worried. I didn't want to leave them out in the storm.

"Can anyone hear the hounds?" Grandpa asked.

"I can't," Papa said.

The judge spoke up. "Fellows, I think we'd better go in," he said. "There's no telling where they are. They may have crossed the river."

Scared and knowing I had to do something, I said, "They're closer than you think, probably treed by now. You can't hear them for this wind." I begged, "Let's go a little farther."

There was no reply and no one made a move to leave the shelter of the trees.

Taking a few steps, I said, "I'll take the lead. Just follow me."

"Billy, we couldn't find them," Papa said. "You can't see or hear a thing. We had better start back for camp."

"I think so, too," the judge said.

At this remark, I cried, "I've been out in storms like this before, all by myself. I've never left my dogs in the woods, and I'm not going to now, even if I have to look for them by myself."

No one answered.

"Please go just a little farther," I begged. "I just know we'll hear them."

Still no one spoke or made a move to go on.

Stepping over to my father, I buried my faces in his old mackinaw coat. Sobbing, I pleaded with him not to turn back.

He patted my head. "Billy," he said, "a

---

1. leeward (lē′ wərd) *adj.*: Sheltered from the wind.

man could freeze to death in this storm, and besides, your dogs will give up and come in."

"That's what has me worried," I cried. "They won't come in. They won't, Papa. Little Ann might, but not Old Dan. He'd die before he'd leave a coon in a tree."

Papa was undecided. Making up his mind, he stepped away from the tree and said to the others, "I'm going on with him. You fellows coming, or going back?"

He turned and followed me. Grandpa and the judge fell in behind him.

By this time the ground was covered with a thin white layer of sleet. We kept slipping and falling. I could hear Grandpa mumbling and grumbling. The wind-driven sleet stung our skin like thousands of pricking needles. Strong gusts of wind growled and moaned through the tops of the tall timber.

Once during a momentary lull of the storm, I thought I heard the baying of a hound. I told my father I thought I had heard Old Dan.

"From which direction?" he asked.

"From that way," I said, pointing to our left.

We started on. A few minutes later Papa stopped. He shouted to my grandfather, "Did you hear anything?"

"No," Grandpa shouted back. "I can't hear anything in this storm."

"I thought I did, but I'm not sure," the judge said.

"Where was it coming from?" Papa asked.

"Over that way," the judge said, pointing to our right.

"That's the way it sounded to me," Papa said.

At that moment, all of us heard the deep voice of Old Dan.

"It sounds as if they're close," Grandpa said.

"Let's split up," said the judge. "Maybe one of us can find them."

"No," Papa said, "it'd be easy to get lost in the storm."

"I think they're more to the right of us," I said.

"I do, too," Papa said.

We trudged on. Old Dan bawled again. The sound of his voice seemed to be all around us.

"The way that wind is whipping the sound through this timber," the judge said, "we'd be lucky if we ever found them."

Papa shouted over the roar of the wind, "We can't take much more of this. We'll freeze to death."

The men were giving up. I felt the knot again as it crawled up in my throat. Salt water froze on my eyelashes. Kneeling down, I put my ear close to the icy ground in hopes I could hear my dogs, but I couldn't hear anything above the roar of the blizzard.

Standing up, I peered this way and that. All I could see was a white wall of whirling sleet. I closed my eyes and said a silent prayer and hoped for a miracle.

We heard a sharp crack and a loud crashing noise. A large limb, torn from a tree by the strong wind, fell to the ground. The sharp crack of the limb gave me the idea. Shouting to my father, I said, "Shoot the gun. If my dogs are close enough to hear it, maybe Little Ann will come to us."

Papa didn't hesitate. Pointing the gun high over his head, he pulled the trigger. The sharp crack rang out into the teeth of the storm.

We waited.

Just when I had given up all hope and had sunk to the lowest depth of despair, out of the white wall of driving sleet, my little dog came to me. I knelt down and gathered her in my arms.

Taking one of the lead ropes from my pocket, I tied it to her collar. I said, "Find him, little girl. Please find Old Dan."

Right then I didn't care about coons,

gold cups, or anything. All I wanted was my dogs.

I don't know how she did it. Straight into the face of the storm she led us. Time after time she would stop and turn her head this way and that. I knew she couldn't scent or see anything. Instinct alone was guiding her. Over a winding and twisting trail, we followed.

Coming out of the bottoms, she led us into a thick canebrake. The tall stalks sheltered us from the storm. The roaring of the wind didn't seem as loud. Like ghostly figures, large trees loomed out of the almost solid mass. Falling and stumbling, we kept pushing on.

Grandpa shouted, "Hold up a minute. I'm just about all in."

We stopped.

"Do you think that hound knows what she's doing?" the judge asked. "Maybe we're just running around in circles."

Looking at me, Papa said, "I hope she does. Some of these canebrakes cover miles. If we get lost in here, we'll be in bad shape."

Grandpa said, "I think we've gone too far. The last time I heard Old Dan, he sounded quite close."

"That was because the wind carried the sound," I said.

The judge spoke up, "Fellows, no dog is worth the lives of three men. Now let's do the smart thing and get out of here while we can. Our clothes are wet. If we keep on wandering around in this jungle, we'll freeze to death. It doesn't look like this blizzard is ever going to let up."

I could hear the roar of the blizzard back in the thick timber of the bottoms. Two large limbs being rubbed together by the strong wind made a grinding creaking sound. The tall slender cane around us rattled and swayed.

I could feel the silence closing in. I knew the judge's cold logic had had its effect on my father and grandfather. The men had given up. There was no hope left for me.

Kneeling down, I put my arms around Little Ann. I felt the warm heat from her moist tongue caressing my ear. Closing my eyes, I said, "Please, Dan, bawl one more time, just one more time."

I waited for my plea to be answered.

With its loud roaring, the north wind seemed to be laughing at us. All around, tall stalks of cane were weaving and dancing to the rattling rhythm of their knife-edged blades.

My father tried to talk above the wind, but his words were lost in the storm. Just before another blast, clear as a foghorn on a stormy sea, Old Dan's voice rang loud and clear. It seemed louder than the roar of the wind or the skeleton-like rustling of the tall swaying cane.

I jumped to my feet. My heart did a complete flip-flop. The knot in my throat felt as big as an apple. I tried to whoop, but it was no use. Little Ann bawled and tugged on the rope.

There was no mistaking the direction. We knew that Little Ann had been right all along. Straight as an arrow, she had led us to him.

Old Dan was treed down in a deep gully. I slid off the bank and ran to him. His back was covered with a layer of frozen sleet. His frost-covered whiskers stood out straight as porcupine quills.

I worked the wedges of ice from between his toes, and scraped the sleet from his body with my hands. Little Ann came over and tried to wash his face. He didn't like it. Jerking loose from me, he ran over to the tree, reared up on it, and started bawling.

Hearing shouting from the bank above me, I looked up. I could dimly see Papa and the judge through the driving sleet. At first I thought they were shouting to me, but on peering closer I could see that they had their backs to me. Catching hold of some long stalks of cane that were hanging down from the steep bank, I pulled myself up.

Papa shouted in my ear, "Something has happened to your grandfather."

Turning to the judge, he said, "He was behind you. When was the last time you saw him?"

"I don't know for sure," the judge said. "I guess it was back there when we heard the hound bawl."

"Didn't you hear anything?" Papa asked.

"Hear anything?" the judge exclaimed. "How could I hear anything in all that noise? I thought he was behind me all the time, and didn't miss him until we got here."

I couldn't hold back the tears. My grandfather was lost and wandering in that white jungle of cane. Screaming for him, I started back.

Papa caught me. He shouted, "Don't do that."

I tried to tear away from him but his grip on my arm was firm.

"Shoot the gun," the judge said.

Papa shot time after time. It was useless. We got no answer.

Little Ann came up out of the washout. She stood and stared at me. Turning, she disappeared quickly in the thick cane. Minutes later we heard her. It was a long, mournful cry.

The only times I had ever heard my little dog bawl like that were when she was baying at a bright Ozark moon, or when someone played a French harp or a fiddle close to her ear. She didn't stop until we reached her.

Grandpa lay as he had fallen, face down in the icy sleet. His right foot was wedged in the fork of a broken box elder limb. When the ankle had twisted, the searing pain must have made him unconscious.

Papa worked Grandpa's foot free and turned him over. I sat down and placed his head in my lap. While Papa and the judge massaged his arms and legs, I wiped the frozen sleet from his eyes and face.

Burying my face in the iron-gray hair, I cried and begged God not to let my grandfather die.

"I think he's gone," the judge said.

"I don't think so," Papa said. "He took a

bad fall when that limb tripped him, but he hasn't been lying here long enough to be frozen. I think he's just unconscious."

Papa lifted him to a sitting position and told the judge to start slapping his face. Grandpa moaned and moved his head.

"He's coming around," Papa said.

I asked Papa if we could get him back to the gully where Old Dan was. I had noticed there was very little wind there and we could build a fire.

"That's the very place," he said. "We'll build a good fire and one of us can go for help."

Papa and the judge made a seat by catching each other's wrists. They eased Grandpa between them.

By the time we reached the washout, Grandpa was fully conscious again, and was mumbling and grumbling. He couldn't see why they had to carry him like a baby.

After easing him over the bank and down into the gully, we built a large fire. Papa took his knife and cut the boot from Grandpa's swollen foot. Grandpa grunted and groaned from the pain. I felt sorry for him but there was nothing I could do but look on.

Papa examined the foot. Shaking his head, he said, "Boy, that's a bad one. It's either broken or badly sprained. I'll go for some help."

Grandpa said, "Now wait just a minute. I'm not going to let you go out in that blizzard by yourself. What if something happens to you? No one would know."

"What time is it?" he asked.

The judge looked at his watch. "It's almost five o'clock," he said.

"It's not long till daylight," Grandpa said. "Then if you want to go, you can see where you're going. Now help me get propped up against this bank. I'll be all right. It doesn't hurt any more. It's numb now."

"He's right," the judge said.

"Think you can stand it?" Papa asked.

Grandpa roared like a bear. "Sure I can stand it. It's nothing but a sprained ankle. I'm not going to die. Build that fire up a little more."

While Papa and the judge made Grandpa comfortable, I carried wood for the fire.

"There's no use standing around gawking at me," Grandpa said. "I'm all right. Get the coon out of that tree. That's what we came for, isn't it?"

Up until then, the coon-hunting had practically been forgotten.

The tree was about thirty feet from our fire. We walked over and took a good look at it for the first time. My dogs, seeing we were finally going to pay some attention to them, started bawling and running around the tree.

Papa said, "It's not much of a tree, just an old box elder snag. There's not a limb on it."

"I can't see any coon," said the judge. "It must be hollow."

Papa beat on its side with the ax. It gave forth a loud booming sound. He said, "It's hollow all right."

He stepped back a few steps, scraped his feet on the slick ground for a good footing, and said, "Stand back, and hold those hounds. I'm going to cut it down. We need some wood for our fire anyway."

Squatting down between my dogs, I held onto their collars.

Papa notched the old snag so it would fall away from our fire. As the heavy ax chewed its way into the tree, it began to lean and crack. Papa stopped chopping. He said to the judge, "Come on and help me. I think we can push it over now."

After much grunting and pushing, snapping and popping, it fell.

I turned my dogs loose.

On hitting the ground, the snag split

and broke up. Goggle-eyed, I stood rooted in my tracks and watched three big coons roll out of the busted old trunk.

One started up the washout, running between us and the fire. Old Dan caught him and the fight was on. The second coon headed down the washout. Little Ann caught him.

Hearing a loud yell from Grandpa, I looked that way. Old Dan and the coon were fighting close to his feet. He was yelling and beating at them with his hat. The judge and Papa ran to help.

The third coon started climbing up the steep bank close to me. Just before reaching the top, his claws slipped in the icy mud. Tumbling end over end, down he came. I grabbed up a stick and threw it at him. Growling and showing his teeth, he started for me. I threw the fight to him then and there. Some ten yards away I looked back. He was climbing the bank. That time he made it and disappeared in the thick cane.

Hearing a squall of pain from Little Ann, I turned. The coon was really working her over. He had climbed up on her back and was tearing and slashing. She couldn't shake him off. Grabbing a club from the ground, I ran to help her.

Before we had killed our coon, Old Dan came tearing in. We stood and watched the fight. When the coon was dead, Papa picked it up and we walked back to the fire.

"How many coons were in that old snag?" Papa asked.

"I saw three," I said. "The one that got away climbed out over there." I pointed in the direction the coon had taken.

I never should have pointed. My dogs turned as one, and started bawling and clawing their way up the steep bank. I shouted and scolded, but to no avail. They disappeared in the rattling cane.

We stood still, listening to their voices.

The sound died away in the roaring storm. Sitting down close to the fire, I buried my face in my arms and cried.

I heard the judge say to my father, "This beats anything I have ever seen. Why, those dogs can read that boy's mind. He just pointed at that bank and away they went. I never saw anything like it. I can't understand some of the things they have done tonight. Hounds usually aren't that smart. If they were collies, or some other breed of dog, it would be different, but they're just redbone hounds, hunting dogs."

Papa said, "Yes, I know what you mean. I've seen them do things that I couldn't understand. I'd never heard of hounds that ever had any affection for anyone, but these dogs are different. Did you know they won't hunt with anyone but him, not even me?"

Hearing my grandfather call my name, I went over and sat down by his side. Putting his arm around me, he said, "Now, I wouldn't worry about those dogs. They'll be all right. It's not long till daylight. Then you can go to them."

I said, "Yes, but what if the coon crosses the river? My dogs will follow him. If they get wet they could freeze to death."

"We'll just have to wait and hope for the best," he said. "Now straighten up and quit that sniffling. Act like a coon hunter. You don't see me bawling, and this old foot is paining me something awful."

I felt better after my talk with Grandpa.

"Come on, let's skin these coons," Papa said.

I got up to help him.

After the skins were peeled from the carcasses, I had an idea. Holding one up close to the fire until it was warm, I took it over and wrapped it around Grandpa's foot. Chuckling, he said, "Boy, that feels good. Heat another skin the same way."

I kept it up for the rest of the night.

Chapter 18

Just before dawn, the storm blew itself out with one last angry roar. It started snowing. A frozen silence settled over the canebrake.

Back in the thick timber of the river bottoms, the sharp snapping of frozen limbs could be heard. The tall stalks of wild cane looked exhausted from the hellish night. They were drooping and bending from the weight of the frozen sleet.

I climbed out of the deep gully and listened for my dogs. I couldn't hear them. Just as I started back down the bank, I heard something. I listened. Again I heard the sound.

Papa was watching me. "Can you hear the dogs?" he asked.

"No, not the dogs," I said, "but I can hear something else."

"What does it sound like?" he asked.

"Like someone whooping," I said.

Papa and the judge hurried up the bank. We heard the sound again. It was coming from a different direction.

"The first time I heard it," I said, "it was over that way."

"It's the men from camp," the judge said. "They're searching for us."

We started whooping. The searchers answered. Their voices came from all directions. The first one to reach us was Mr. Kyle. He looked haggard and tired. He asked if everything was all right.

"Yes, we're all right," Papa said, "but the old man has a bad ankle. It looks like we'll have to carry him out."

"Your team broke loose and came back to camp about midnight," Mr. Kyle said. "This really spooked us. We were sure something bad had happened. Twenty-five of us have been searching since then."

Several men climbed down the bank and went over to Grandpa. They looked at his an-

kle. One said, "I don't think it's broken, but it sure is a bad sprain."

"You're in luck," another one said. "We have one of the best doctors in the state of Texas in our camp, Dr. Charley Lathman. He'll have you fixed up in no time."

"Yes," another said, "and if I know Charley, he's probably got a small hospital with him."

Back in the crowd, I heard another man say, "You mean that Lathman fellow, who owns those black and tan hounds, is a doctor?"

"Sure is," another said. "One of the best."

Mr. Kyle asked where my dogs were. I told him that they were treed somewhere.

"What do you mean, treed somewhere?" he asked.

Papa explained what had happened.

With a wide-eyed look on his face, he said, "Do you mean to tell me those hounds stayed with the tree in that blizzard?"

I nodded.

Looking at me, he said, "Son, I hope they have that coon treed, because you need that one to win the cup. Those two walker hounds caught three before the storm came up. When it got bad, all the hunters came in."

The judge spoke up. "I'll always believe that those hounds knew that boy needed another coon to win," he said. "If you fellows had seen some of the things those dogs have done, you'd believe it, too."

One hunter walked over to the broken snag. "Three out of one tree," he said. "No wonder, look here! That old snag was half-full of leaves and grass. Why, it was a regular old den tree."

Several of the men walked over. I heard one say, "I've seen this happen before. Remember that big hunt in the Red River bottoms, when the two little beagle hounds treed four coons in an old hollow snag? They won the championship, too."

"I wasn't there but I remember reading about it," one said.

"Say, I don't see Benson," Mr. Kyle said.

The men started looking at each other.

"He was searching farther downriver than the rest of us," one fellow said. "Maybe he didn't hear us shouting."

Some of the men climbed out of the gully. They started whooping. From a distance we heard an answering shout.

"He hears us," someone said. "He's coming."

Everyone looked relieved.

Mr. Benson struck the washout a little way above us. He was breathing hard, as if he'd been running. He started talking as soon as he was within hearing distance.

"It scared me when I first saw them," he said. "I didn't know what they were. They looked like white ghosts. I'd never seen anything like it."

A hunter grabbed Mr. Benson by the shoulder, shaking him. "Get ahold of yourself, man," he said. "What are you talking about?"

Mr. Benson took a deep breath to control himself, and started again in a much calmer voice. "Those two hounds," he said. "I found them. They're frozen solid. They're nothing but white ice from the tips of their noses to the ends of their tails."

Hearing Mr. Benson's words, I screamed and ran to my father. Everything started whirling around and around. I felt light as a feather. My knees buckled. I knew no more.

Regaining consciousness, I opened my eyes and could dimly see the blurry images of the men around me. A hand was shaking me. I could hear my father's voice but I couldn't understand his words. Little by little the blackness faded away. My throat was dry and I was terribly thirsty. I asked for some water.

Mr. Benson came over. He said, "Son,

I'm sorry, truly sorry. I didn't mean it that way. Your dogs are alive. I guess I was excited. I'm very sorry."

I heard a deep voice say, "That's a hell of a thing to do. Come running in here saying the dogs are frozen solid."

Mr. Benson said, "I didn't mean it to sound that way. I said I'm sorry. What more do you want me to do?"

The deep voice growled again. "I still think it was a hell of a thing for a man to do."

Mr. Kyle took over. "Now let's not have any more of this," he said. "We have work to do. We've been standing here acting like a bunch of schoolkids. All this time that old man has been lying there suffering. A couple of you men cut two poles and make a stretcher to carry him."

While the men were getting the poles, Papa heated the coonskins again and rewrapped Grandpa's foot.

With belts and long leather laces from their boots, the hunters made a stretcher. Very gently they put Grandpa on it.

Again Mr. Kyle took command. "Part of us will start for camp with him," he said. "The others will go after the dogs."

"Here, take this gun," Papa said. "I'll go with him."

Looking at me, Mr. Kyle said, "Come on, son. I want to see your hounds."

Mr. Benson led the way. "As soon as we get out of this cane," he said, "we may be able to hear them. They have the coon treed in a big black gum tree. You're going to see a sight. Now I mean a sight. They've walked a ring around that tree clear down through the ice and snow. You can see the bare ground."

"Wonder why they did that?" someone asked.

"I don't know," Mr. Benson replied, "unless they ran in that circle to keep from freezing to death, or to keep the coon in the tree."

I figured I knew why my dogs were covered with ice. The coon had probably crossed the river, maybe several times. Old Dan and Little Ann would have followed him. They had come out of the river with their coats dripping wet, and the freezing blast of the blizzard had done the rest.

Nearing the tree, we stopped and stared.

"Did you ever see anything like that?" Mr. Benson asked. "When I first saw them, I thought they were white wolves."

My dogs hadn't seen us when we came up. They were trotting round and round. Just as Mr. Benson had said, we could see the path they had worn down through the ice and snow till the bare black earth was visible. Like ghostly white shadows, around and around they trotted.

In a low voice, someone said, "They know that if they stop they'll freeze to death."

"It's unbelievable," said Mr. Kyle. "Come on. We must do something quick."

With a choking sob, I ran for my dogs.

On hearing our approach, they sat down and started bawling treed. I noticed their voices didn't have that solid ring. Their ice-covered tails made a rattling sound as they switched this way and that on the icy ground.

A large fire was built. Standing my dogs close to the warm heat, the gentle hands of the hunters went to work. With handkerchiefs and scarves heated steaming hot, little by little the ice was thawed from their bodies.

"If they had ever lain down," someone said. "they would've frozen to death."

"They knew it," another said. "That's why they kept running in that circle."

"What I can't understand is why they stayed with the tree," Mr. Benson said. "I've seen hounds stay with a tree for a while, but not in a northern blizzard."

"Men," said Mr. Kyle, "people have been trying to understand dogs ever since the be-ginning of time. One never knows what they'll do. You can read every day where a dog saved the life of a drowning child, or lay down his life for his master. Some people call this loyalty. I don't. I may be wrong, but I call it love—the deepest kind of love."

After these words were spoken, a thoughtful silence settled over the men. The mood was broken by the deep growling voice I had heard back in the washout.

"It's a shame that people all over the world can't have that kind of love in their hearts," he said. "There would be no wars, slaughter, or murder; no greed or selfishness. It would be the kind of world that God wants us to have—a wonderful world."

After all the ice was thawed from my dogs and their coats were dried out, I could see they were all right. I was happy again and felt good all over.

One of the hunters said, "Do you think those hounds are thawed out enough to fight a coon?"

"Sure, just run him out of that tree," I said.

At the crack of the gun, the coon ran far out on a big limb and stopped. Again the hunter sprinkled him with bird shot. This time he jumped. Hitting the ground, he crouched down.

Old Dan made a lunge. Just as he reached him, the coon sprang straight up and came down on his head. Holding on with his claws, the coon sank his teeth in a long tender ear. Old Dan was furious. He started turning in a circle, bawling with pain.

Little Ann was trying hard to get ahold of the coon but she couldn't. Because of his fast circling, Old Dan's feet flew out from under him and he fell. This gave Little Ann a chance. Darting in, her jaws closed on the back of the coon's neck. I knew the fight was over.

Arriving back at camp, I saw that all the

tents had been taken down but ours. A hunter said, "Everyone was in a hurry to get out before another blizzard sets in."

Papa told me to take my dogs into the tent as Grandpa wanted to see them.

I saw tears in my grandfather's eyes as he talked to them. His ankle was wrapped in bandages. His foot and toes were swollen to twice their normal size. They had turned a greenish-yellow color. Placing my hand on his foot, I could feel the feverish heat.

Dr. Lathman came over. "Are you ready to go now?" he asked.

Snorting and growling, Grandpa said, "I told you I wasn't going anywhere till I see the gold cup handed to this boy."

Turning to face the crowd, Dr. Lathman said, "Men, let's get this over. I want to get this man to town. That's one of the meanest sprains I've ever seen and it should be in a cast, but I don't have any plaster of Paris with me."

The hunter who had come by our tent collecting the jackpot money came up to me. Handing me the box, he said, "Here you are, son. There's over three hundred dollars in this box. It's all yours."

Turning to the crowd, he said, "Fellows, I can always say this. On this hunt I've seen two of the finest little coon hounds I ever hope to see."

There was a roar of approval from the crowd.

Looking down, I saw the box was almost full of money. I was shaking all over. I tried to say "Thanks," but it was only a whisper. Turning, I handed the box to my father. As his rough old hands closed around it, I saw a strange look come over his face. He turned and looked at my dogs.

Some of the men started shouting, "Here it is!"

The crowd parted and the judge walked through. I saw the gleaming metal of the gold cup in his hand. After a short speech,

he handed it to me, saying, "Son, this makes me very proud. It's a great honor to present you with this championship cup."

The crowd exploded. The hunters' shouts were deafening.

I don't know from where the two silly old tears came. They just squeezed their way out. I felt them as they rolled down my cheeks. One dropped on the smooth surface of the cup and splattered. I wiped it away with my sleeve.

Turning to my dogs, I knelt down and showed the cup to them. Little Ann licked it. Old Dan sniffed one time, and then turned his head away.

The judge said, "Son, there's a place on the cup to engrave the names of your dogs. I can take it into Oklahoma City and have it done, or you can have it done yourself. The engraving charge has already been paid by the association."

Looking at the cup, it seemed that far down in the gleaming shadows I could see two wide blue eyes glued to a windowpane. I knew that my little sister was watching the road and waiting for our return. Looking back at the judge, I said, "If you don't mind, I'll take it with me. My grandfather can send it in for me."

Laughing, he said, "That's all right." Handing me a slip of paper, he said, "This is the address where you should send it."

Grandpa said, "Now that that's settled, I'm ready to go to town." Turning to Papa, he said, "You'll have to bring the buggy, and I wish you'd look after my stock. I know Grandma will want to go in with us and there'll be no one there to feed them. Tell Bill Lowery to come up and take care of the store. You'll find the keys in the usual place."

"We'll take care of everything," Papa said. "Don't worry about a thing. I don't intend to stop until we get back, because it looks like we're in for some more bad weather."

I went over and kissed Grandpa goodbye. He pinched my cheek, and whispered, "We'll teach these city slickers that they can't come up here and beat our dogs."

I smiled.

Grandpa was carried out and made comfortable in the back seat of Dr. Lathman's car. I stood and watched as it wheezed and bounced its way out of sight.

"While I'm harnessing the team," Papa said, "you take the tent down and pack our gear."

On the back seat of the buggy, I made a bed out of our bed-clothes. Down on the floor boards, I fixed a nice place for my dogs.

All through the night, the creaking wheels of our buggy moved on. Several times I woke up. My father had wrapped a tarp around himself. Reaching down, I could feel my dogs. They were warm and comfortable.

Early the next morning, we stopped for breakfast. While Papa tended to the team, I turned my dogs loose and let them stretch.

"We made good time last night," Papa said. "If everything goes right, we'll be home long before dark."

Reaching Grandpa's store in the middle of the afternoon, Papa said, "I'll put the team in the barn and feed the stock while you unload the buggy."

Coming back from the barn, he said, "In the morning, I'll go over and tell Bill Lowery to come up and open the store."

Looking around, he said, "It snowed more here than it did where we were hunting."

Feeling big and important, I said, "I don't like the looks of this weather. We'd better be scooting for home."

Papa laughed. "Sure you're not in a

hurry to get home to show off the gold cup?" he asked.

A smile was my only answer.

Two hundred yards this side of our home, the road made a turn around a low foothill shutting our house off from view.

Papa said, "You're going to see a scramble as soon as we round that bend."

It was more of a stampede than a scramble. The little one came out first, and all but tore the screen door from its hinges. The older girls passed her just beyond the gate. In her hurry, she slipped and fell face down in the snow. She started crying.

The older girls ran up asking for the cup.

Holding it high over my head, I said, "Now wait a minute. I've got another one for you two." I held the small silver cup out to them.

While they were fighting over it, I ran to the little one. Picking her up, I brushed the snow from her long, braided hair and her tear-stained face. I told her there was no use to cry. I had brought the gold cup to her, and no one else was going to get it.

Reaching for the cup, she wrapped her small arms around it. Squeezing it up tight, she ran for the house to show it to Mama.

Mama came out on the porch. She was just as excited as the girls were. She held out her arms. I ran to her. She hugged me and kissed me.

"It's good to have you home again," she said.

"Look what I have, Mama," the little one cried, "and it's all mine."

She held the golden cup out in her two small hands.

As Mama took the beautiful cup, she looked at me. She started to say something but was interrupted by the cries from the other girls.

"We have one, too, Mama," they cried, "and it's just as pretty as that one."

"It's not either," the little one piped in a defiant voice. "It's not even as big as mine."

"Two cups!" Mama exclaimed. "Did you win two!"

"Yes, Mama," I said. "Little Ann won that one all by herself."

The awed expression on my mother's face was wonderful to see. Holding a cup in each hand, she held them out in front of her.

"Two," she said. "A gold one and a silver one. Who would have thought anything so wonderful could have happened to us. I'm so proud; so very proud."

Handing the cups back to the girls, she walked over to Papa. After kissing him, she said, "I just can't believe everything that has happened. I'm so glad you went along. Did you enjoy yourself?"

With a smile on his face, Papa almost shouted, "Enjoy myself? Why, I never had such a time in my life."

His voice trailed off to a low calm, "That is, except for one thing. Grandpa had a bad accident."

"Yes, I know," Mama said. "One of Tom Logan's boys was at the store when they arrived. He came by and told us all about it. The doctor said it wasn't as bad as it looked, and he was pretty sure Grandpa would be home in a few days."

I was happy to hear this news, and could tell by the pleased look on my father's face, he was glad to hear it, too.

On entering the house, Papa said, "Oh, I almost forgot." He handed the box of money to Mama.

"What's this?" she asked.

"Oh, it's just a little gift from Old Dan and Little Ann," Papa said.

Mama opened the box. I saw the color drain from her face. Her hands started trembling. Turning her back to us, she walked over and set it on the mantel. A peaceful silence settled over the room. I could hear the clock ticking away. The fire in the fireplace crackled and popped.

Turning from the mantel, Mama looked straight at us. Her lips were tightly pressed together to keep them from quivering. Walking slowly to Papa, she buried her face in his chest. I heard her say, "Thank God, my prayers have been answered."

There was a celebration in our home that night. To me it was like a second Christmas.

Mama opened a jar of huckleberries and made a large cobbler. Papa went to the smokehouse and came back with a hickory-cured ham. We sat down to a feast of the ham, huge plates of fried potatoes, ham gravy, hot corn bread, fresh butter, and wild bee honey.

During the course of the meal, the entire story of the championship hunt was told, some by Papa but mostly by me.

Just when everything was so perfect and peaceful, an argument sprang up between the two oldest girls. It seemed that each wanted to claim the silver cup. Just when they were on the verge of sawing it in two, so each would have her allotted share, Papa settled the squabble by giving the oldest one a silver dollar. Once again peace and harmony was restored.

That night as I was preparing for bed, a light flashed by my window. Puzzled, I tiptoed over and peeked through the pane. It was Mama. Carrying my lantern and two large plates heaped high with food, she was heading for the doghouse. Setting the light down on the ground in front of it, she called to my dogs. While they were eating, Mama did something I couldn't understand. She knelt down on her knees in prayer.

After they had eaten their food, Mama started petting them. I could hear her voice but couldn't make out her words. Whatever she was saying must have pleased them. Little Ann wiggled and twisted. Even Old Dan wagged his long red tail, which was very unusual.

Papa came out. I saw him put his arm around Mama. Side by side they stood for several minutes looking at my dogs. When they turned to enter the house, I saw Mama dab at her eyes with her apron.

Lying in bed, staring into the darkness, I tried hard to figure out the strange actions of my parents. Why had Mama knelt in prayer in front of my dogs? Why had she wept?

I was running all the why's around in my mind when I heard them talking.

"I know," Papa said, "but I think there's a way. I'm going to have a talk with Grandpa. I don't think that old foot of his is ever going to be the same again. He's going to need some help around the store."

I knew they were talking about me, but I couldn't understand what they meant. Then I thought, "Why, that's it. They want me to help Grandpa." That would be all right with me. I could still hunt every night.

Feeling smart for figuring out their conversation, I turned over and fell asleep.

Chapter 19

Although the winning of the cups and the money was a big event in my life, it didn't change my hunting any. I was out after the ringtails every night.

I had been hunting the river bottoms hard for about three weeks. On that night, I decided to go back to the Cyclone Timber country. I had barely reached the hunting ground when my dogs struck a trail. Old Dan opened up first.

They struck the trail on a ridge and then dropped down into a deep canyon, up the other side, and broke out into some flats. I could tell that the scent was hot from their steady bawling. Three times they treed the animal.

Every time I came close to the tree, the animal would jump, and the race would be on. After a while, I knew it wasn't a coon. I decided it was a bobcat.

I didn't like to have my dogs tree the big cats, for their fur wasn't any good, and all I could expect was two cut-up hounds.

They could kill the largest bobcat in the hills, and had on several occasions, but to me it was useless. The only good I could see in killing one was getting rid of a vicious predatory animal.

The fourth time they treed, they were on top of a mountain. After the long chase, I figured the animal was winded and would stay in the tree. In a trot I started to them.

As I neared the tree, Little Ann came to me, reared up, and whined. By her actions, I knew something was wrong. I stopped. In the moonlight, I could see Old Dan sitting on his haunches, staring up at the tree and bawling.

The tree had lots of dead leaves on it. I knew it was a large white oak because it is one of the last trees in the mountains to lose its leaves.

Old Dan kept bawling. Then he did something he had never done before. For seconds his deep voice was still, and silence settled over the mountains. My eyes wandered from the tree to him. His lips were curled back and he snarled as he stared into the dark foliage of the tree. His teeth gleamed white in the moonlight. The hair on his neck and along his back stood on end. A low, deep, rumbling growl rolled from his throat.

I was scared and I called to him. I wanted to get away from there. Again I called, but it was no use. He wouldn't leave the tree, for in his veins flowed the breeded blood of a hunting hound. In his fighting heart, there was no fear.

I set the lantern down and tightened my grip on the handle of the ax. Slowly I started walking toward him. I thought, "If I can get close enough to him, I can grab his collar." I kept my eyes on the tree as I edged forward. Little Ann stayed by my side. She, too, was watching the tree.

Then I saw them—two burning, yellow eyes—staring at me from the shadowy foliage of the tree. I stopped, petrified with fear.

The deep baying of Old Dan stopped and again the silence closed in.

I stared back at the unblinking eyes.

I could make out the bulk of a large animal, crouched on a huge branch, close to the trunk of the big tree. Then it moved. I heard the scratch of razor-sharp claws on the bark. It stood up and moved out of the shadows on to the limb. I saw it clearly as it passed between the moon and me. I knew what it was. It was the devil cat of the Ozarks, the mountain lion.

The silence was shattered by one long, loud bawl from Old Dan. I'd never heard my dog bawl like that. It was different. His voice rang out over the mountains, loud and clear. The vibration of the deep tones rolled in the silence of the frosty night, on and on, out over the flats, down in the canyons, and died away in the rimrocks, like the cry of a lost soul. Old Dan had voiced his challenge to the devil cat.

There was a low cough and a deep growl from the lion. I saw him crouch. I knew what was coming. My hands felt hot and sweaty on the smooth ash handle of the ax. With a blood-curdling scream he sprang from the tree with claws outspread and long, yellow fangs bared.

Old Dan didn't wait. Rearing up on his hind legs, he met the lion in the air. The heavy weight bowled him over and over. He wound up in a fallen treetop.

The impact of the two bodies threw the lion off balance. Little Ann darted in. Her aim was true. I heard the snap of her steel-trap jaws as they closed on his throat.

With a squall of pain and rage, the big cat rolled over on his side, dragging Little

Ann with him. His right paw reached out and curved over her shoulder. Sinews tightened and razor-sharp claws dug inward. With a cry of pain, she loosened her hold. I saw the blood squirting from the deep wound in her shoulder. She ignored it and bored back into the fight.

Old Dan, stunned for an instant from the impact of the lion's body, fought his way from the treetop. Bawling the cry of the damned, he charged back in.

I went berserk, and charged into the fight.

There in the flinty hills of the Ozarks, I fought for the lives of my dogs. I fought with the only weapon I had, the sharp cutting blade of a double-bitted ax.

Screaming like a madman, with tears running down my face, I hacked and chopped at the big snarling mountain cat.

Once, feeling the bite of the sharp blade, the devil cat turned on me. His yellow slitted eyes burned with hate. The long, lithe body dipped low to the ground. The shoulder muscles knotted and bulged. I tried to jump back but my foot slipped and I dropped to my knees. I knew I was trapped. With a terrifying scream he sprang.

I never saw my dogs when they got between the lion and me, but they were there. Side by side, they rose up from the ground as one. They sailed straight into those jaws of death, their small, red bodies taking the ripping, slashing claws meant for me.

I screamed and charged back into the fight, swinging my ax, but I was careful not to hit one of my dogs.

The battle raged on and on, down the side of the mountain, over huckleberry bushes, fallen logs, and rocks. It was a rolling, tumbling mass of fighting fury. I was in the middle of it all, falling, screaming, crying and backing away at every opportunity.

I had cut the big cat several times. Blood showed red on the bit of the ax, but as yet I had not gotten in the fatal lick. I knew it had to be soon for my dogs were no match against the razor-sharp claws and the long, yellow fangs.

The screams of the big cat and the deep bellowing voices of my dogs echoed through the mountains. Down the side of the mountain, the terrible fight went on, down to the very bottom of the canyon.

The big cat had Old Dan by the throat. I knew he was seeking to cut the all-important vein, the jugular. At the pitiful bawl of Old Dan, Little Ann, throwing caution to the wind, ran in and sank her teeth in the lion's tough neck.

With her claws digging into the moun-

tain soil, she braced herself, and started pulling. The muscles in her small legs knotted and quivered. She was trying hard to pull the devil cat's fangs from the throat of Old Dan.

In the rays of a bright Ozark moon, I could see clearly. For an instant I saw the broad back of the big cat. I saw the knotty bulge of steel-bound muscle, the piston-like jerk of the deadly hind claws, trying for the downward stroke that could disembowel a dog.

Raising the ax high over my head, I brought it down with all the strength in my body. My aim was true. Behind the shoulders, in the broad muscular back, the heavy blade sank with a sickening sound. The keen edge cleaved through the tough skin. It seemed to hiss as it sliced its way through bone and gristle.

I left the ax where it was, sunk to the eye in the back of the devil cat.

He loosened his hold on the throat of Old Dan. With a scream of pain, he reared up on his hind legs and started pawing the air. Little Ann dangled from his neck, still holding on. Her eyes were shut tight and her small feet were digging and clawing at the body.

Old Dan, spewing blood from a dozen wounds, leaped high in the air. His long, red body sailed in between the outspread paws of the lion. I heard the snap of his powerful jaws as they closed on the throat.

The big cat screamed again. Blood gurgled and sprayed. In a bright red mist, it rained out over the underbrush and rattled like sleet on the white oak leaves. In a boxer's stance, he stood and clawed the air. His slitted eyes turned green with hate. He seemed to be unaware of the two hounds hanging from his body, and kept staring at me. I stood in a trance and stared back at the ghastly scene.

The breath of life was slowly leaving him.

He was dying on his feet but refusing to go down. My ax handle stuck straight out from his back. Blood, gushing from the mortal wound, glistened in the moonlight. A shudder ran through his body. He tried once again to scream. Blood gurgled in his throat.

It was the end of the trail for the scourge of the mountains. No more would he scream his challenge from the rimrocks to the valley below. The small, harmless calves and the young colts would be safe from his silent stalk.

He fell toward me. It seemed that with his last effort he was still trying to get at me.

As his heavy body struck the ground, something exploded in my head. I knew no more.

When I came to, I was sitting down. It was silent and still. A bird, disturbed by the fight, started chirping far up on the side of the mountain. A small winter breeze rustled some dead leaves in the deep canyon. A cold, crawling chill crept over my body.

I looked over at the lion. My dogs were still glued to his lifeless body. In his dying convulsions the ax had become dislodged from the wound. It lay there in the moonlight, covered with blood.

My numb brain started working. I thought of another time the ax had been covered with blood. I don't know why I thought of Rubin Pritchard at that time, or why I thought of these words I had often heard: "There is a little good in all evil."

I got to my feet and went over to my dogs. I knew I had to inspect them to see how badly they were hurt. It wasn't too hard to get Little Ann to loosen her hold. I examined her body. She was cut in several places, but nothing fatal. The only bad wound she had was in her shoulder. It was nine inches long and down to the clean, white bone. She started licking it immediately.

It was different with Old Dan. Try as I might, he wouldn't turn loose. Maybe he could remember the night in the cave when he was a pup. How the big cat had screamed and how he had bawled back at him.

I took hold of his hind legs and tried to pull him loose. It was no use. He knew that the hold he had was a deadly one and he wasn't going to let go. I tried to tell him it was all over, that the lion was dead, to turn loose as I wanted to see how badly he was hurt. He couldn't understand and wouldn't even open his eyes. He was determined to hold on until the body turned cold and stiff.

With my ax handle, I pried apart his locked jaws. Holding on to his collar, I led him off to one side. I couldn't turn him loose as I knew if I did, he would go back to the lion.

With one hand I started examining him. I ran my fingers through the short, red hair. I could feel the quivering muscles and the hot, sweaty skin. He was a bloody mess. His long, velvety ears were shredded. His entire body was a mass of deep, raw, red wounds. On both sides of his rib carriage, the sharp claws had laid the flesh open to the bone.

His friendly old face was pitiful to see. A razor-sharp claw had ripped down on an angle across his right eye. It was swollen shut. I wondered if he would ever see from that eye again.

Blood dripped from his wounds and fell on the white-oak leaves. I saw he was bleeding to death. With tears running down my cheeks, I did the only thing a hunter could do. I raked the leaves away and let his blood drip on the black mountain soil. Mixing it into a mud, I worked it into his wounds to stop the flow of blood.

With my ax in one hand and holding onto his collar with the other, we climbed out of the canyon. I knew if I could get him far enough away from the lion he wouldn't go back.

On reaching the top, I saw the yellow glow of my lantern. I turned Old Dan loose and walked over and picked it up.

Not knowing exactly where I was, I looked down out of the mountains to get my bearings. Beyond the foothills and fields I could see the long, white, crooked line of steam, marking the river's course. Following the snakelike pattern with my eyes, in no time I knew exactly where I was, for I knew every bend in the river.

Anxious to get home so I could take care of my dogs, I turned to call to them. Little Ann was close by. She was sitting down, licking at the wound in her shoulder. I saw the shadowy form of Old Dan sniffing around the tree where the lion had been treed.

As I stood and watched him in the moonlight, my heart swelled with pride. Wounded though he was, he wanted to make sure there were no more lions around.

I called to him. In a stiff-legged trot he came to me. I caught hold of his collar and gave him another inspection. In the lantern light I could see the mudcaked wounds clearly. The bleeding had almost stopped. I felt much better.

Little Ann came over. I knelt down and put my arms around them. I knew that if it hadn't been for their loyalty and unselfish courage I would have probably been killed by the slashing claws of the devil cat.

"I don't know how I'll ever pay you back for what you've done," I said, "but I'll never forget it."

Getting up, I said, "Come on, let's go home so I can take care of those wounds."

I hadn't gone far when I heard a cry. At first I thought it was a bird, or a night hawk. I stood still and listened. I glanced at Little Ann. She was looking behind me. I turned around and looked for Old Dan. He was nowhere in sight.

The cry came again, low and pitiful. Instantly Little Ann started back the way we had come. I followed as fast as I could run.

I found Old Dan lying on his side, pleading for help. What I saw was almost more than I could stand. There, tangled in the low branches of a huckleberry bush, were the entrails of my dog. With a gasping cry I knelt down by his side.

I knew what had happened. Far back in the soft belly, the slashing, razor-sharp claws of the lion had cut into the hollow. In my inspections I had overlooked the wound. His entrails had worked out and had become entangled in the bush. The forward motion of his body had done the rest.

He whimpered as I laid my hand on his head. A warm, red tongue flicked out at it. With tears in my eyes, I started talking to him. "Hang on, boy," I said. "Everything will be all right. I'll take care of you."

With trembling hands, I unwound the entrails from the bush. With my handkerchief I wiped away the gravel, leaves, and pine needles. With fingers that shook, I worked the entrails back into the wound.

Knowing that I couldn't carry him and the ax and lantern, I stuck the ax deep in the side of a white oak tree. I blew out the lantern and hung the handle over the other blade. I wrapped my dog in my old sheepskin coat and hurried for home.

Arriving home, I awakened my mother and father. Together we doctored my dogs. Old Dan was taken care of first. Very gently Mama worked the entrails out and in a pan of warm soapy water, washed them clean of the pine needles, leaves, and grit.

"If I only knew what I was doing," Mama said, as she worked, "I'd feel better."

With gentle hands, she worked the entrails back through the opening. The wound was sewn up and bandaged with a clean white cloth.

Little Ann wasn't hard to doctor. I held her head while Mama cleaned her wounds with peroxide. Feeling the bite of the strong liquid, she whined and licked at my hands.

"It's all right, little girl," I said. "You'll be well in no time."

I opened the door and watched her as she limped off to the doghouse.

Hearing a whimper, I turned around. There in the doorway to the room stood my sisters. I could tell by the looks on their faces that they had been watching for some time. They looked pitiful standing there in their long white gowns. I felt sorry for them.

"Will Little Ann be all right?" my oldest sister asked.

"Yes," I said, "she'll be all right. She only had one bad wound and we've taken care of that."

"Old Dan's hurt bad, isn't he?" she said.

I nodded my head.

"How bad is it?" she asked.

"It's bad," I said. "He was cut wide open."

They all started crying.

"Now here," Mama said, going over, "you girls get back in bed. You'll take a death of cold being up like this in your bare feet."

"Mommie," the little one said. "God won't let Old Dan die, will He?"

"I don't think so, honey," Mama said. "Now off to bed."

They turned and walked slowly back to their room.

"The way your dogs are cut up," Papa said, "it must have been a terrible fight."

"It was, Papa," I said. "I never saw anything like it. Little Ann wouldn't have fought the lion if it hadn't been for Old Dan. All she was doing was helping him. He wouldn't quit. He just stayed right in there till the end. I even had to pry his jaws loose from the lion's throat after the lion was dead."

Glancing at Old Dan, Papa said, "It's in his blood, Billy. He's a hunting hound, and the best one I ever saw. He only has two loves—you and hunting. That's all he knows."

"If it hadn't been for them, Papa," I said, "I probably wouldn't be here now."

"What do you mean," Mama said, "you wouldn't be here now?"

I told them how the lion had leaped at me and how my dogs had gotten between him and me.

"They were so close together," I said, "when they came up off the ground they looked just like one."

There was a moaning sigh from Mama. She covered her face with her hands and started crying.

"I don't know," she sobbed, "I just don't know. To think how close you came to being killed. I don't think I can stand any more."

"Now, now," Papa said, as he walked over and put his arms around her. "Don't go all to pieces. It's all over. Let's be thankful and do our best for Old Dan."

"Do you think he'll die, Papa?" I asked.

"I don't know, Billy," Papa said, shaking his head. "He's lost an awful lot of blood and he's a mighty sick dog. All we can do now is wait and see."

Our wait wasn't long. My dog's breathing grew faster and faster, and there was a terrible rattling in his throat. I knelt down and laid his head in my lap.

Old Dan must have known he was dying. Just before he drew one last sigh, and a feeble thump of his tail, his friendly gray eyes closed forever.

At first I couldn't believe my dog was dead. I started talking to him. "Please don't die, Dan," I said. "Don't leave me now."

I looked to Mama for help. Her face was as white as the bark on a sycamore tree and the hurt in her eyes tore at my heart. She opened her mouth to say something but words wouldn't come out.

Feeling as cold as an arctic wind, I got up and stumbled to a chair. Mama came over and said something. Her words were only a murmur in my ears.

Very gently Papa picked Old Dan up in his arms and carried him out on the porch. When he came back in the house, he said, "Well, we did all we could do, but I guess it wasn't enough."

I had never seen my father and mother look so tired and weary as they did on that night. I knew they wanted to comfort me, but didn't know what to say.

Papa tried. "Billy," he said, "I wouldn't think too much about this if I were you. It's not good to hurt like that. I believe I'd just try to forget it. Besides, you still have Little Ann."

I wasn't even thinking about Little Ann at that moment. I knew she was all right.

"I'm thankful that I still have her," I said, "but how can I forget Old Dan? He gave his life for me, that's what he did—just laid down his life for me. How can I ever forget something like that?"

Mama said, "It's been a terrible night for all of us. Let's go to bed and try to get some rest. Maybe we'll all feel better tomorrow."

"No, Mama," I said. "You and Papa go on to bed. I think I'll stay up for a while. I couldn't sleep anyway."

Mama started to protest, but Papa shook his head. Arm in arm they walked from the room.

Long after my mother and father had retired, I sat by the fire trying to think and couldn't. I felt numb all over. I knew my dog was dead, but I couldn't believe it. I didn't want to. One day they were both alive and happy. Then that night, just like that, one of them was dead.

I didn't know how long I had been sitting there when I heard a noise out on the porch. I got up, walked over to the door, and lis-tened. It came again, a low whimper and a scratchy sound.

I could think of only one thing that could have made the noise. It had to be my dog. He wasn't dead. He had come back to life. With a pounding heart, I opened the door and stepped out on the porch.

What I saw was more than I could stand. The noise I had heard had been made by Little Ann. All her life she had slept by Old Dan's side. And although he was dead, she had left the doghouse, had come back to the porch, and snuggled up close to his side.

She looked up at me and whimpered. I couldn't stand it. I didn't know I was running until I tripped and fell. I got to my feet and ran on and on, down through our fields of shocked corn, until I fell face down on the river's bank. There in the gray shadows of a breaking dawn, I cried until I could cry no more.

The churring of gray squirrels in the bright morning sun told me it was daylight. I got to my feet and walked back to the house.

Coming up through our barn lot, I saw my father feeding our stock. He came over and said, "Breakfast is about ready."

"I don't want any breakfast, Papa," I said. "I'm not hungry and I have a job to do. I'll have to bury my dog."

"I tell you what," he said. "I'm not going to be very busy today, so let's have a good breakfast and then I'll help you."

"No, Papa," I said. "I'll take care of it. You go and eat breakfast. Tell Mama I'm not hungry."

I saw a hurt look in my father's eyes. Shaking his head, he turned and walked away.

From rough pine slabs, I made a box for my dog. It was a crude box but it was the best I could do. With strips of burlap and corn shucks, I padded the inside.

Up on the hillside, at the foot of a beautiful red oak tree, I dug his grave. There where the wild mountain flowers would grow in the spring, I laid him away.

I had a purpose in burying my dog up there on the hillside. It was a beautiful spot. From there one could see the country for miles, the long white crooked line of the river, the tall thick timber of the bottoms, the sycamore, birch, and box elder. I thought perhaps that on moonlight nights Old Dan would be able to hear the deep voices of the hounds as they rolled out of the river bottoms on the frosty air.

After the last shovel of dirt was patted in place, I sat down and let my mind drift back through the years. I thought of the old K. C. Baking Powder can, and the first time I saw my pups in the box at the depot. I thought of the fifty dollars, the nickels and dimes, and the fishermen and blackberry patches.

I looked at his grave and, with tears in my eyes, I voiced these words: "You were worth it, old friend, and a thousand times over."

In my heart I knew that there in the grave lay a man's best friend.

Two days later, when I came in from the bottoms where my father and I were clearing land, my mother said, "Billy, you had better look after your dog. She won't eat."

I started looking for her. I went to the barn, the corncrib, and looked under the porch. I called her name. It was no use.

I rounded up my sisters and asked if they had seen Little Ann. The youngest one said she had seen her go down into the garden. I went there, calling her name. She wouldn't answer my call.

I was about to give up, and then I saw her. She had wiggled her way far back under the thorny limbs of a blackberry bush in the corner of the garden. I talked to her and tried to coax her out. She wouldn't budge. I

got down on my knees and crawled back to her. As I did, she raised her head and looked at me.

Her eyes told the story. They weren't the soft gray eyes I had looked into so many times. They were dull and cloudy. There was no fire, no life. I couldn't understand.

I carried her back to the house. I offered her food and water. She wouldn't touch it. I noticed how lifeless she was. I thought perhaps she had a wound I had overlooked. I felt and probed with my fingers. I could find nothing.

My father came and looked at her. He shook his head and said, "Billy, it's no use. The life has gone out of her. She has no will to live."

He turned and walked away.

I couldn't believe it. I couldn't.

With eggs and rich cream, I made a liquid. I pried her mouth open and poured it down. She responded to nothing I did. I carried her to the porch, and laid her in the same place I had laid the body of Old Dan. I covered her with gunny sacks.

All through the night I would get up and check on her. Next morning I took warm fresh milk and again I opened her mouth and fed her. It was a miserable day for me. At noon it was the same. My dog had just given up. There was no will to live.

That evening when I came in from the fields, she was gone. I hurried to my mother. Mama told me she had seen her go up the hollow from the house, so weak she could hardly stand. Mama had watched her until she had disappeared in the timber.

I hurried up the hollow, calling her name. I called and called. I went up to the head of it, still calling her name and praying she would come to me. I climbed out onto the flats; looking, searching, and calling. It was no use. My dog was gone.

I had a thought, a ray of hope. I just knew I'd find her at the grave of Old Dan. I hurried there.

I found her lying on her stomach, her hind legs stretched out straight, and her front feet folded back under her chest. She had laid her head on his grave. I saw the trail where she had dragged herself through the leaves. The way she lay there, I thought she was alive. I called her name. She made no movement. With the last ounce of strength in her body, she had dragged herself to the grave of Old Dan.

Kneeling down by her side, I reached out and touched her. There was no response, no whimpering cry or friendly wag of her tail. My little dog was dead.

I laid her head in my lap and with tear-filled eyes gazed up into the heavens. In a choking voice, I asked, "Why did they have to die? Why must I hurt so? What have I done wrong?"

I heard a noise behind me. It was my mother. She sat down and put her arm around me.

"You've done no wrong, Billy," she said. "I know this seems terrible and I know how it hurts, but at one time or another, everyone suffers. Even the Good Lord suffered while He was here on earth."

"I know, Mama," I said, "but I can't understand. It was bad enough when Old Dan died. Now Little Ann is gone. Both of them gone, just like that."

"Billy, you haven't lost your dogs altogether," Mama said. "You'll always have their memory. Besides, you can have some more dogs."

I rebelled at this. "I don't want any more dogs," I said. "I won't ever want another dog. They wouldn't be like Old Dan and Little Ann."

"We all feel that way, Billy," she said. "I do especially. They've fulfilled a prayer that I thought would never be answered."

"I don't believe in prayers any more," I said. "I prayed for my dogs, and now look, both of them are dead."

Mama was silent for a moment; then, in a gentle voice, she said, "Billy, sometimes it's hard to believe that things like this can happen, but there's always an answer. When you're older, you'll understand better."

"No, I won't," I said. "I don't care if I'm a hundred years old, I'll never understand why my dogs had to die."

As if she were talking to someone far away, I heard her say in a low voice, "I don't know what to say. I can't seem to find the right words."

Looking up to her face, I saw that her eyes were flooded with tears.

"Mama, please don't cry," I said. "I didn't mean what I said."

"I know you didn't," she said, as she squeezed me up tight. "It's just your way of fighting back."

I heard the voice of my father calling to us from the house.

"Come now," Mama said. "I have supper ready and your father wants to talk to you. I think when you've heard what he has to say, you'll feel better."

"I can't leave Little Ann like this, Mama," I said. "It'll be cold tonight. I think I'll carry her back to the house."

"No, I don't think you should do that," Mama said. "Your sisters would go all to pieces. Let's make her comfortable here."

Raking some dead leaves into a pile, she picked Little Ann up and laid her in them. Taking off my coat, I spread it over her body. I dreaded to think of what I had to do on the morrow.

My father and sisters were waiting for us on the porch. Mama told them the sad story.

My sisters broke down and started crying. They ran to Mama and buried their faces in her long cotton dress.

Papa came over and laid his hand on my shoulder. "Billy," he said, "there are times in a boy's life when he has to stand up like a man. This is one of those times. I know what you're going through and how it hurts, but there's always an answer. The Good Lord has a reason for everything He does."

"There couldn't be any reason for my dogs to die, Papa," I said. "There just couldn't. They hadn't done anything wrong."

Papa glanced at Mama. Getting no help from her, he said, "It's getting cold out here. Let's go in the house. I have something to show you."

"Guess what we're having for supper," Mama said, as we turned to enter the house. "Your favorite, Billy, sweet potato pie. You'll like that, won't you?"

I nodded my head, but my heart wasn't in it.

Papa didn't follow us into the kitchen. He turned and entered his bedroom.

When he came into the room, he had a small shoe box in his hand. I recognized the box by the bright blue ribbon tied around it. Mama kept her valuables in it.

A silence settled over the room. Walking to the head of the table, Papa set the box down and started untying the ribbon. His hands were trembling as he fumbled with the knot. With the lid off, he reached in and started lifting out bundles of money.

After stacking them in a neat pile, he raised his head and looked straight at me. "Billy," he said, "you know how your mother has prayed that some day we'd have enough money to move out of these hills and into town so that you children could get an education."

I nodded my head.

"Well," he said, in a low voice, "because of your dogs, her prayers have been answered. This is the money earned by Old Dan and Little Ann. I've managed to make the farm feed us and clothe us and I've saved every cent your furs brought in. We now have enough."

"Isn't it wonderful," Mama said. "It's just like a miracle."

"I think it is a miracle," Papa said. "Remember, Billy said a prayer when he asked for his pups and then there were your prayers. Billy got his pups. Through those dogs your prayers were answered. Yes, I'm sure it is a miracle."

"If he gave them to me, then why did he take them away?" I asked.

"I think there's an answer for that, too," Papa said. "You see, Billy, your mother and I had decided not to separate you from your dogs. We knew how much you loved them. We decided that when we moved to town we'd leave you here with your grandpa for a while. He needs help anyway. But I guess the Good Lord didn't want that to happen. He doesn't like to see families split up. That's why they were taken away."

I knew my father was a firm believer in fate. To him everything that happened was the will of God, and in his Bible he could always find the answers.

Papa could see that his talk had had very little effect on me. With a sorrowful look on his face, he sat down and said, "Now let us give thanks for our food and for all the wonderful things God has done for us. I'll say a special prayer and ask Him to help Billy."

I barely heard what Papa had to say.

During the meal, I could tell that no one was enjoying the food. As soon as it was over, I went to my room and lay down on the bed.

Mama came in. "Why don't you go to

bed," she said, "and get a good night's sleep. You'll feel better tomorrow."

"No, I won't, Mama," I said. "I'll have to bury Little Ann tomorrow."

"I know," she said, as she turned my covers down. "I'll help if you want me to."

"No, Mama," I said, "I don't want anyone to help. I'd rather do it all by myself."

"Billy, you're always doing things by yourself," Mama said. "That's not right. Everyone needs help some time in his life."

"I know, Mama," I said, "but, please, not this time. Ever since my dogs were puppies, we've always been together—just us three. We hunted together and played together. We even went swimming together.

"Did you know, Mama, that Little Ann used to come every night and peek in my window just to see if I was all right? I guess that's why I want to be by myself when I bury her."

"Now say your prayers and go to sleep. I'm sure you'll feel better in the morning."

I didn't feel like saying any prayers that night. I was hurting too much. Long after the rest of the family had gone to bed, I lay staring into the darkness, trying to think and not able to.

Some time in the night I got up, tiptoed to my window, and looked out at my doghouse. It looked so lonely and empty sitting there in the moonlight. I could see that the door was slightly ajar. I thought of the many times I had lain in my bed and listened to the squeaking of the door as my dogs went in and out. I didn't know I was crying until I felt the tears roll down my cheeks.

Mama must have heard me get up. She came in and put her arms around me. "Billy," she said, in a quavering voice, "you'll just have to stop this. You're going to make yourself sick and I don't think I can stand any more of it."

"I can't, Mama," I said. "It hurts so much, I just can't. I don't want you to feel bad just because I do."

"I can't help it, Billy," she said. "Come now and get back in bed. I'm afraid you'll catch cold."

After she had tucked me in, she sat on the bed for a while. As if she were talking to the darkness, I heard her say, "If only there were some way I could help—something I could do."

"No one can help, Mama," I said. "No one can bring my dogs back."

"I know," she said, as she got up to leave the room, "but there must be something— there just has to be."

After Mama had left the room, I buried my face in my pillow and cried myself to sleep.

The next morning I made another box. It was smaller than the first one. Each nail I drove in the rough pine boards caused the knot in my throat to get bigger and bigger.

My sisters came to help. They stood it for a while, then with tears streaming, they ran for the house.

I buried Little Ann by the side of Old Dan. I knew that was where she wanted to be. I also buried a part of my life along with my dog.

Remembering a sandstone ledge I had seen while prowling the woods, I went there. I picked out a nice stone and carried it back to the graves. Then, with painstaking care, I carved their names deep in its red surface.

As I stood looking at the two graves, I tried hard to understand some of the things my father had told me, but I couldn't—I was still hurting and still had that empty feeling.

I went to Mama and had a talk with her.

"Mama," I asked, "do you think God made a heaven for all good dogs?"

"Yes," she said, "I'm sure He did."

"Do you think He made a place for dogs to hunt? You know—just like we have here on our place—with mountains and sycamore trees, rivers and cornfields, and old rail fences? Do you think He did?"

"From what I've read in the Good Book, Billy," she said, "He put far more things up there than we have here. Yes, I'm sure He did."

I was thinking this over when Mama came up to me and started tucking my shirt in. "Do you feel better now?" she asked.

"It still hurts, Mama," I said, as I buried my face in her dress, "but I do feel a little better."

"I'm glad," she said, as she patted my head. "I don't like to see my little boy hurt like this."

Chapter 20

The following spring we left the Ozarks. The day we moved I thought everyone would be sad, but it was just the opposite. Mama seemed to be the happiest one of all. I could hear her laughing and joking with my sisters as they packed things. She had a glow in her eyes I had never seen before and it made me feel good.

I even noticed a change in Papa. He didn't have that whipped look on his face any more. He was in high spirits as we carried the furniture out to our wagon.

After the last item was stored in the wagon, Papa helped Mama to the spring seat and we were ready to go.

"Papa, would you mind waiting a few minutes?" I asked, "I'd like to say good-bye to my dogs."

"Sure," he said, smiling. "We have plenty of time. Go right ahead."

Nearing the graves, I saw something different. It looked like a wild bush had grown up and practically covered the two little mounds. It made me angry to think that an old bush would dare grow so close to the graves. I took out my knife, intending to cut it down.

When I walked up close enough to see what it was, I sucked in a mouthful of air and stopped. I couldn't believe what I was seeing. There between the graves, a beautiful red fern had sprung up from the rich mountain soil. It was fully two feet tall and its long red leaves had reached out in rainbow arches curved over the graves of my dogs.

I had heard the old Indian legend about the red fern. How a little Indian boy and girl were lost in a blizzard and had frozen to death. In the spring, when they were found, a beautiful red fern had grown up between their two bodies. The story went on to say that only an angel could plant the seeds of a red fern, and that they never died; where one grew, that spot was sacred.

Remembering the meaning of the legend, I turned and started hollering for Mama.

"Mama! Mama!" I shouted. "Come here! And hurry! You won't believe it."

In a frightened voice, she shouted back, "What is it, Billy? Are you all right?"

"I'm all right, Mama," I shouted, "but hurry. You just won't believe it."

Holding her long skirt in her hand and with a frightened look on her face, Mama came puffing up the hillside. Close behind her came Papa and my sisters.

"What is it, Billy?" Mama asked, in a scared voice. "Are you all right?"

"Look!" I said, pointing at the red fern.

Staring wide-eyed, Mama gasped and covered her mouth with her hand. I heard her say, almost in a whisper, "Oh-h-h-h, it's a red fern—a sacred red fern."

She walked over and very tenderly started fingering the long red leaves. In an awed voice, she said, "All my life I've wanted to see one. Now I have. It's almost unbelievable.

"Don't touch it, Mama," my oldest sister whispered. "It was planted by an angel."

Mama smiled and asked, "Have you heard the legend?"

"Yes, Mama," my sister said. "Grandma told me the story, and I believe it, too."

With a serious look on his face, Papa said, "These hills are full of legends. Up until now I've never paid much attention to them, but now I don't know. Perhaps there is something to the legend of the red fern. Maybe this is God's way of helping Billy understand why his dogs died."

"I'm sure it is, Papa," I said, "and I do understand. I feel different now, and I don't hurt any more."

"Come," Mama said, "let's go back to the wagon. Billy wants to be alone with his dogs for a while."

Just as they turned to leave, I heard Papa murmur in a low voice, "Wonderful indeed is the work of our Lord."

As I stood looking at the two graves, I noticed things I hadn't seen before. Wild violets, rooster heads, and mountain daisies had completely covered the two little mounds. A summer breeze gushed down from the rugged hills. I felt its warm caress as it fanned my face. It hummed a tune in the underbrush and rustled the leaves on the huge red oak. The red fern wavered and danced to the music of the hills.

Taking off my cap, I bowed my head. In a choking voice, I said, "Good-bye, Old Dan and Little Ann. I'll never forget you; and this I know—if God made room in heaven for all good dogs, I know He made a special place for you."

With a heavy heart, I turned and walked away. I knew that as long as I lived I'd never forget the two little graves and the sacred red fern.

Not far from our home, the road wound its way up and over a hill. At the top Papa stopped the team. We all stood up and looked back. It was a beautiful sight, one I'll never forget.

As I stood and looked at the home of my birth, it looked sad and lonely. There was no spiral of lazy blue smoke twisting from the rock chimney, no white leghorn hen chasing a June bug, no horse or cow standing with head down and tail switching.

I saw I had left the door to the barn loft open. A tuft of hay hung out. It wavered gently in the warm summer breeze.

Something scurried across the vacant yard and disappeared under the barn. It was Samie, our house cat. I heard my little sister say in a choking voice, "Mommie, we forgot Samie."

There was no answer.

To the left, I could see our fields and the zigzag lines of rail fences. Farther down, I could see the shimmering whiteness of the tall sycamores. My vision blurred as tears came to my eyes.

The sorrowful silence was broken by my mother's voice. She asked, "Billy, can you see it?"

"See what, Mama?" I asked.

"The red fern," she said.

My oldest sister spoke up. "I can see it," she said.

Rubbing my eyes, I looked to the hillside above our home. There it stood in all its wild beauty, a waving red banner in a carpet of green. It seemed to be saying, "Good-bye, and don't worry, for I'll be here always."

Hearing a sniffling, I turned around. My three little sisters had started crying. Mama said something to Papa. I heard the jingle of the trace chains as they tightened in the singletrees.

Our wagon moved on.

I have never been back to the Ozarks. All I have left are my dreams and memories, but if God is willing, some day I'd like to go back—back to those beautiful hills. I'd like to walk again on trails I walked in my boyhood days.

Once again I'd like to face a mountain breeze and smell the wonderful scent of the redbuds, and papaws, and the dogwoods. With my hands I'd like to caress the cool white bark of a sycamore.

I'd like to take a walk far back in the flinty hills and search for a souvenir, an old double-bitted ax stuck deep in the side of a white oak tree. I know the handle has long since rotted away with time. Perhaps the rusty frame of a coal-oil lantern still hangs there on the blade.

I'd like to see the old home place, the barn and the rail fences. I'd like to pause under the beautiful red oaks where my sisters and I played in our childhood. I'd like to walk up the hillside to the graves of my dogs.

I'm sure the red fern has grown and has completely covered the two little mounds. I know it is still there, hiding its secret beneath those long, red leaves, but it wouldn't be hidden from me for part of my life is buried there, too.

Yes, I know it is still there, for in my heart I believe the legend of the sacred red fern.

THINKING ABOUT THE SELECTION

Recalling

1. In what ways is Billy the leader of his group during the championship hunt?
2. How do the dogs save Billy from the mountain lion?
3. What is the result of the fight with the mountain lion?
4. Describe Billy's reaction to the deaths of his dogs.
5. What is the legend of the Red Fern?

Interpreting

6. Why do Billy and Little Ann risk their lives to help Old Dan as he is fighting the lion?
7. Why does Little Ann die?
8. What is the meaning of the novel's title?

Analyzing

9. Why is it so difficult to accept the loss of someone or something you care for?

ANALYZING LITERATURE

Understanding Theme

A **theme,** or general idea about life, is revealed through the events of a novel. In the various episodes of this novel, Billy has developed a strong and loving relationship with his dogs.

1. What theme is Wilson Rawls presenting through this relationship?
2. What episodes in the story support the theme that hard work is very rewarding?

CRITICAL THINKING AND READING

Evaluating a Novel

Evaluating a novel means judging carefully how good it is. You comment on its strengths and weaknesses, using your knowledge of literary elements. It is important to remember that when you evaluate, your judgment must be supported by evidence in the novel, not by personal likes and dislikes. For example, if you think the characters in a novel are unrealistic, then by supporting your judgment with details, you could conclude that the work was unsuccessful.

Answer the following questions about *Where the Red Fern Grows*. Support your answers with details from the novel.

1. Do the characters seem like real people? Why or why not?
2. Do the conflicts in the plot hold your interest?
3. Is the setting described realistically?

UNDERSTANDING LANGUAGE

Understanding Derived Words

By adding prefixes or suffixes to a word, you can form new words. For example, you can derive several words from the verb *believe*. If you add the suffix *-able,* you create the adjective *believable*. If you then add the prefix *un-,* the word has the opposite meaning: *unbelievable*. Other words from *believe* are *believability* and *believably*.

Create derived words from the following words.

1. appear	3. tangle	5. settle
2. touch	4. forgive	6. play

THINKING AND WRITING

Writing a Book Review

A **book review** is a discussion and evaluation of ideas in a book. Write a book review of *Where the Red Fern Grows*. Begin with an introduction that identifies the author and the title of the book and gives a brief, one- or two-sentence description of the events. In the body of the review, evaluate one of the elements you studied in the four sections of the novel: character, plot, setting, or theme. You might review your answers to the questions in the **Critical Thinking and Reading** activity, Evaluating a Novel. End with a concluding sentence that provides your judgment of the book. As you revise, be sure you have supported your comments with specific examples.

Distinguishing Facts from Opinions

Most material that you read contains statements of fact and opinion. By determining which statements are facts and which are opinions, you will gain a greater understanding of what the author is saying and whether or not you agree with it. You will be able to evaluate the material.

Facts

A **fact** is a statement that can be checked to see if it is true or false. Look at the following sentences:

Wilson Rawls wrote *Where the Red Fern Grows*.
Grandpa wrote a letter to a place in Arkansas to get Billy two hunting dogs.

Both sentences are factual because the facts they contain can be checked. However, the first sentence is true, whereas the second is false because the place Grandpa wrote to was in Kentucky. You could check these facts by referring back to the book. Often you will have to use reference books and articles to prove facts.

Opinions

An **opinion** differs from a fact because it cannot be checked. It is someone's belief, judgment, or feeling. Carefully read the following sentences to find the differences between them:

Where the Red Fern Grows is the best book Wilson Rawls ever wrote.
"*Where the Red Fern Grows,* written by Wilson Rawls, is the best book in our library.

The word *best* makes the first sentence a statement of opinion or judgment. Someone else may think one of the other books Wilson Rawls authored was his best. The second sentence, on the other hand, contains both facts and opinions. It is a fact that the novel was written by Wilson Rawls; however, the word *best* indicates an opinion.

Signals

Distinguishing between facts and opinions can be difficult because sentences may contain both and some sentences that seem to be facts may prove to be opinions. Looking for signal words can help you accurately identify facts and opinions.

Watch for words such as "I (we) think," and "I (we) feel," for they signal a statement of belief or opinion. Positive judgments are indicated by words such as "best," "fantastic," or "helpful"; whereas negative judgments are suggested by words such as "awful," "offensive," or "harmful." Words like "never" and "always" often signal an exaggerated statement of opinion. And "must," "should," and "have to" clearly indicate a command or suggestion and thus show that the statement is expressing someone's feeling or opinion.

Guidelines

- If the statement can be proven to be true or false, it is a fact.
- If the statement expresses a belief or a judgment of feeling, it is an opinion.
- If the statement contains words such as "think," "great," "horrible," "never," or "must," it is usually an opinion.

Activity

Read each of the following statements. Identify whether each is a fact (F), an opinion (O), or a mixture of both (BOTH).
1. The marshal bought Billy a bottle of soda pop.
2. Old Dan and Little Ann were the best hunting dogs in the Ozarks.
3. Billy had three adorable little sisters.
4. Billy saved fifty dollars, which was a tremendous amount of money for a young boy to accumulate.

Activity

Read this passage and answer the questions that follow.

Where the Red Fern Grows is the story of a young boy's growing-up years in the Ozarks. It is told by Billy Coleman, now a grown man, who is reminiscing about his youth. He recalls the training of Old Dan and Little Ann, the nighttime coon hunts, and the tremendous love that developed between a boy and his dogs. His dogs became the finest hunting team in his part of the Ozarks. This story is always exciting and everyone loves it. You must read the book.

1. Identify two statements of fact.
2. Identify two statements of opinion.
3. Identify one mixed statement.
4. Identify the signal words that indicate an opinion.

YOU THE WRITER

Assignment

1. Imagine that you are going to write a novel. Since you want to get to know one of the characters in the novel better—from the inside out—have this person write a diary entry.

    Prewriting. Jot down facts about this character as they come to you: name, age, school, the names of parents, sisters, brothers. Describe this character's attitudes. Ask and answer questions.

    Writing. Organize your material in chronological order. Try to include at least one encounter with another person. Include some dialogue.

    Revising. Evaluate your composition. Ask yourself this question: Have I created a real person, one with a clear identity? Have I included the specific details that will make my character jump off the page?

Assignment

2. Plan a novel about two characters with contrasting personalities who come into conflict. Write an essay in which you describe the different personalities and the conflict.

    Prewriting. Look around you at people you know who have contrasting personalities. Jot down notes comparing and contrasting them.

    Writing. In your thesis sentence, tell the reader in a general way what each of the characters is like. Then indicate that one day they came into conflict with each other. Finally, trace the chain of events leading to the crisis that brings them into conflict.

    Revising. Check to see that you have told your "story" in a step-by-step way. Also check to see that you have described the personalities of the characters.

Assignment

3. Some novels are told through an exchange of letters. Write *two* letters, one from character A to character B, and one from character B to character A. In the letters, have the characters discuss a problem they have with a third character.

    Prewriting. Before you write, establish the personalities of each of the three characters. In fact, try to make the two characters writing the letters opposites.

    Writing. Now write your letters. Tell the story of the problem the letter writers have with the third person in chronological order. Let the first letter tell the first part of the story and the second letter tell the rest.

    Revising. Check to see that your sentences are smooth. Tie your thoughts together more tightly by combining sentences.

YOU THE CRITIC

Assignment

1. Identify a character in the novel you have read who changes in an important way. Then write an essay in which you show (1) the character's personality before the change, (2) the event or sequence of events that changed him or her, (3) the change itself, and (4) the effect the character's change had on the story.

Prewriting. Make a brief outline. Fill in the outline, telling (1) what the character was like before the change, (2) what caused him or her to change, (3) what he or she was like after the change, and (4) how the character's change affected the story.

Writing. Now write your essay. Start by identifying the character you are going to write about and indicating that he or she underwent a change that affected the story. In your body paragraphs, cover each of the four topics. Include a citation from the novel.

Revising. When you revise, check to see that you have answered the question fully. Have you covered all four of the sections?

Assignment

2. Identify two minor characters in the novel you read. Then write an essay in which you (1) describe their personalities, (2) tell what motivates them to take the actions they do, and (3) show that the actions they take play a role in moving the story along.

Prewriting. Before you write, divide a sheet of paper into two columns. In the left-hand column, list the major characters. In the right-hand column, list the minor characters. Then choose two characters from the right-hand column and jot down notes about them.

Writing. Write your essay. In the opening paragraph, state your thesis, or main idea. Divide the body into three paragraphs, one for each section of the question. Conclude by summing up the points.

Revising. When you revise, make sure you have followed each of the three steps in the assignment.

Assignment

3. Write an essay about a person in the novel whom you like or admire. Explain why you like or admire this person.

Prewriting. Look over the novel again and examine your reactions to each of the characters. Which ones do you like or admire? Which ones don't you like? Choose one character and freewrite.

Writing. Now write your essay. First identify the character you like or admire. Then, in your thesis statement, indicate the qualities and actions that make this character sympathetic. In your body paragraphs, discuss these qualities and actions in detail. Refer to specific things this person says and does in the novel.

Revising. When you revise, tighten the connections between your ideas by using transitional words and phrases.

HANDBOOK OF WRITING ABOUT LITERATURE

SECTION 1: UNDERSTANDING THE WRITING PROCESS

Lesson 1: Prewriting

Writing is a process that involves several stages:

1. *Prewriting:* planning your writing
2. *Drafting:* creating a first version, or draft, of your writing
3. *Revising:* making improvements in your draft
4. *Proofreading:* checking for errors in grammar and usage, spelling, punctuation, capitalization, and manuscript form
5. *Publishing,* or *Sharing:* letting others read what you have written

This lesson will teach you the steps of prewriting.

STEP 1: ANALYZE THE SITUATION

To *analyze* something is to divide it into parts, or elements, and then to study these parts. Before writing, you should always analyze the elements of the writing situation in which you find yourself. To do so, ask yourself the following questions:

1. *Topic* (the subject you will be writing about): What exactly are you going to write about? Can you state your subject in a sentence? Is your subject too broad or too narrow?
2. *Purpose* (what you want your writing to accomplish): Do you want your writing to explain? to describe? to persuade? to tell a story? to entertain? What do you want your audience to learn or to understand?
3. *Audience* (the people who will read or listen to your writing): Who is your audience? What might they already know about your subject? What basic facts will you have to provide for them?

4. *Voice* (the way your writing will sound to your reader): What impression do you want to make? Do you want to sound formal or informal? Should you sound cool and reasoned or full of emotion?
5. *Content* (the subject and all the information you will provide about it): How much do you already know about this subject? What else do you need to find out? What libraries can you consult for newspapers, books, magazines, and other resources? Are there people you can ask for information?
6. *Form* (the shape that your writing will take, including its length and its organization): How do you picture your finished work? How long will it be? Will it be one paragraph or several? Will you use a special form like a verse or a drama? In what order will you present your information?

When you begin your prewriting, try to answer these questions. Doing so will help you to clarify your goals. If you are writing a paper for school, your teacher may give you a topic or may ask that the writing take a specific form. However, many decisions about the writing will still be up to you.

STEP 2: MAKE A PLAN

After thinking about the writing situation, you may find that you need more information. If so, you must decide how to gather this information. On the other hand, you may find that you already have too much information—that your topic is too broad. If this is the case, then you must decide how to narrow your topic. If you have the right amount of information but don't know how to present it clearly, you will have to choose a way to organize your information.

STEP 3: GATHER INFORMATION

There are many ways to gather information, to narrow a topic, and to organize ideas. You must find ways that work well for you. The following are some ways that you can try:

1. *Brainstorming:* Discuss the topic with a group of people. Follow these rules in your discussion: Try to generate as many ideas as possible. Do not pause to evaluate your ideas. This can be done later. Do not allow any member of the group to make negative comments about what another member says.
2. *Freewriting:* Write down everything that comes to your mind about the topic. Don't worry about spelling or about writing complete, grammatical sentences. Simply write nonstop for one to five minutes. Then read your freewriting and look for ideas you can use in your first draft.
3. *Clustering:* Write your topic in the middle of a piece of paper and circle it. Then write all the ideas you can think of that relate to your topic in circles around the main topic. Connect your circles with lines that show how your ideas, or subtopics, branch out from your main topic. You may even think of some ideas that branch off from your subtopics. If you need to narrow your topic, you might select one of your subtopics as a new main topic.
4. *Analyzing:* Divide your topic into parts that you can consider separately. Make notes about each part. Then study how the parts are related both to each other and to the main topic.
5. *Questioning:* Make a list of questions about the topic. Begin your questions with words like *who, what, where, when, why,* and *how.* Then answer the questions by doing research to find the information you need.
6. *Using Outside Sources:* Talk to other people about your topic. Conduct formal interviews. Read relevant books, pamphlets, newspapers, magazines, and reference works. Watch movies or television shows or listen to radio programs that deal with your topic.
7. *Making Charts* or *Lists:* Make a list or chart of relevant information. Possibilities include a time line, an ordered list of events, a pros-and-cons chart, a list of reasons, or a list of parts.

Any of these methods for finding information can also be used to identify a topic in the first place.

STEP 4: ORGANIZE YOUR NOTES

Once you have gathered enough information, you will have to organize it. Careful organization will make your writing easy to read and understand. The following methods of organization are common:

1. *Time Order,* or *Chronological Order:* organization in order of occurence (from earliest to latest, for example)
2. *Spatial Order:* organization by position in space (from left to right, for example)
3. *Degree Order:* organization by size, amount, or intensity (from coldest to warmest, for example)
4. *Priority Order:* organization by importance, value, usefulness, or familiarity (from worst to best, for example)

CASE STUDY: PREWRITING

Pilar's English teacher asked the students in her class to write single paragraphs about their hobbies. Pilar chose to write about reading. Here are her preliminary notes for her paragraph:

- Topic: reading as a hobby
- Purpose: to inform
- Audience: my classmates and teacher
- Voice: informal and probably with some feelings
- Content: not sure. I have so many thoughts and feelings about reading, I don't know what to say.
- Form: single paragraph

Pilar reviewed her notes and decided that she needed to define her purpose more clearly. She decided to try freewriting:

> I really enjoy reading—especially about kids my age and families. Some of my friends share my interests, but others prefer fantasy or adventure or travel reading—other friends don't read much. Too bad—they're missing something special. . . .

Pilar read her freewriting and realized that her purpose could be to persuade non-reading classmates that reading is fun. Pilar decided to gather more ideas and information by using the questioning technique:

> What kinds of books do I enjoy? Where do I read? Why do I read? How do I read? When do I read? Whose books do I enjoy?
>
> I love stories about kids like me. I usually read on the floor or all cozy in bed. I read for lots of reasons: to find out what other kids' lives are like (seeing how they manage things), for privacy, for company, because a friend has suggested the book, to get out of a grouchy mood, and also because I've liked other things by the writer. I read with or without a snack, with lots of noise or in silence. I usually read before bedtime to relax. I enjoy just about any books about kids.

Pilar looked over her notes and decided that in her paragraph she would first introduce the topic, Why reading is a pleasurable hobby. Then she would give reasons why she enjoys reading, choosing three reasons and organizing them by degree, from least to most important.

ACTIVITIES AND ASSIGNMENTS

A. Answer the following questions about the case study.

1. Find the section of Pilar's notes in which she analyzed the writing situation. Which parts of her earliest notes needed to be expanded? Which were sufficient?
2. Why did Pilar freewrite? Why did she list questions and answer them?

B. Choose one of the following topics or one of your own: *sports, travel, pets,* or *outer space.* Prepare to write a paragraph about your topic. Follow these steps:

1. Make notes about the topic, purpose, audience, voice, content, and form of your paragraph.
2. Review your notes. Decide on a plan of action. To analyze the writing situation and to gather ideas, use prewriting techniques such as freewriting, clustering, analyzing, questioning, consulting outside sources, and making charts or lists.
3. Organize your notes, then make a rough outline for your paragraph. Your outline should include your main topic and two or three subtopics, or parts of the main topic. Under each subtopic, list specific details that you will include in your writing. Save your prewriting notes in a folder.

Lesson 2: Drafting and Revising

WRITING A DRAFT

Drafting follows prewriting and is the second stage in the writing process. When drafting, you simply write down ideas and information in sentence form. The following are important points to remember about drafting:

1. Write your rough draft slowly or quickly— whichever way works for you. Some writers like to work from detailed, thorough outlines and to write very slowly, correcting and polishing as they go. Other writers prefer to jot down brief outlines, write their rough drafts very quickly, and then go back to make corrections and revisions. Each of these methods is perfectly OK. Only you can decide which approach works best for you.

2. Do not try to make your rough draft a finished product. The main point of a draft is to get your ideas down on paper. Once this is done, you can go back and make improvements. Save concern over spelling, punctuation, and so on for the revision and proofreading stages of the writing process.

3. Refer to your prewriting notes as you draft. Do not ramble on about unrelated subjects—stick to your main topic.

4. Keep your audience and purpose in mind as you write. Try not to speak above or below the heads of your audience. Make sure that the ideas and information that you include are consistent with your purpose.

5. Be flexible. Don't be afraid to set aside earlier ideas if later ones work better. If you have already written part of a draft and a more interesting aspect of your topic comes to mind, use it! Remember, too, that you can always do more prewriting activities to gather more information or to focus your thinking.

6. Write as many rough drafts as you need. After you have written one draft, you might review it and realize that you need to add more information, to change your purpose, or to narrow your focus. If this happens, try some more prewriting activities and then write another draft. When you have a draft you are satisfied with, you are ready to go on to the next stage of the writing process—revising.

REVISING YOUR DRAFT

Revising is the process of reworking what you have written to make it as good as it can be. As you revise, use the Checklist for Revision on the next page. If you answer "no" to any of the questions on the checklist, then you will have to change, or revise, your draft accordingly.

EDITORIAL SYMBOLS

When you revise a rough draft, use the standard editorial symbols in the chart on the next page.

CASE STUDY: DRAFTING AND REVISING

Pilar used her prewriting notes from the last lesson to begin drafting her paragraph. Here is the beginning of her first rough draft:

> I love reading stories about kids like me for many reasons, and I think you should too. I like the privacy and also because a friend has suggested the book. I especially like to find out about other kids. How they handle their lives.

Pilar stopped writing and looked at her draft. She had given the three reasons she enjoyed reading and now had nothing more to say. She realized that her paragraph would never con-

CHECKLIST FOR REVISION

Topic and Purpose
☐ Is my topic clear?
☐ Does the writing have a specific purpose?
☐ Does the writing achieve its purpose?

Audience
☐ Will everything that I have written be clear to my audience?
☐ Will my audience find the writing interesting?
☐ Will my audience respond in the way I would like?

Voice, Word Choice
☐ Is the impression that my writing conveys the one that I intended it to convey?
☐ Is my language appropriately formal or informal?
☐ Have I avoided vague, undefined terms?
☐ Have I used vivid, specific nouns, verbs, and adjectives?
☐ Have I avoided jargon that my audience will not understand?
☐ Have I avoided clichés?
☐ Have I avoided slang, odd connotations, euphemisms, and gobbledygook (except for novelty or humor)?

Content/Development
☐ Have I avoided including unnecessary or unrelated ideas?
☐ Have I developed my topic completely?
☐ Have I supplied examples or details that support the statements that I have made?
☐ Are my sources of information unbiased, up-to-date, and authoritative?
☐ Are any quotations that I have used verbatim, or word-for-word?

Form
☐ Have I followed a logical method of organization?
☐ Have I used transitions, or connecting words, to make the organization clear?
☐ Does the writing have a clear introduction, body, and conclusion?

SYMBOL	MEANING	EXAMPLE
	move text	She wants / to go also
	delete	Meghan is quite / very happy.
∧	insert	*that* of book
⌒	close up; no space	dish washer
⊙	insert period	was free
	insert comma	pencils, books / and pens
	add apostrophe	childrens books
	add quotation marks	The Raven
∿	transpose	to quickly run
	begin paragraph	book. If
/	make lower case	the President
≡	capitalize	president Adams

vince someone that reading was an interesting and fun hobby. Pilar set two goals for her next draft:

1. To keep her purpose more clearly in mind as she wrote
2. To give more reasons for her argument, with details to make the reasons persuasive.

Pilar wrote several more drafts of her paragraph. Here is her revised final draft:

Have you considered reading as a hobby?

When you have a free hour alone to relax ~~by~~

~~yourself you might~~ try reading a good book.

Ask freinds ~~who know you~~ to reccommend

good books they think you'll like, or read

something ~~or other~~ by a Writer you enjoyed in

Find a comfortabel place to read and

school. ~~Get comfy,~~ see what happens.

Here's what happens for me.

Reading gives me both privacy and ~~I like the~~

company at the same time. When I'm involved

in a book I'm away from my every day world. I

can discover places, people, and information I

Most of all,

might never otherwise have known. I especially

like finding out about how other ~~kids~~ live their

situations I might find myself in

lifes. I actually learn about ~~real life.~~ And see

ways I might handle my own life. Maybe you'll

for

enjoy reading ~~because of~~ some of the same

reasons I do. Its a pleasure.

ACTIVITIES AND ASSIGNMENTS

A. Answer the following questions about the revised final draft in the case study:

1. Has Pilar corrected all the errors in her draft? Why isn't it necessary for all the errors to be corrected in the revision stage?
2. Why did Pilar delete material in the second and third sentences?
3. Why did Pilar add the sentence "Here's what happens for me"?
4. Why did Pilar delete the phrase "I like the" before the word "company"?
5. Why did Pilar take out the word "kids" in the third from the last sentence?
6. What transitional words did Pilar add to indicate that she was about to give the last reason why she enjoys reading?
7. Why did Pilar replace the words "real life" with other words?
8. What other revisions did Pilar make? Why did she make them?

B. Using your prewriting notes from the last lesson, write the rough draft of a paragraph on your topic. Then revise the draft until you are pleased with it.

Follow these steps for drafting and revising your paragraph:

1. Introduce your topic in a sentence or two.
2. Write the body of your paragraph, referring as necessary to your rough outline and to your prewriting notes. Do not spend time worrying about spelling and mechanics at this stage.
3. Write a conclusion of one or two sentences. In the conclusion, sum up the main idea of your paragraph.
4. Revise your draft, using the Checklist for Revision. Be sure that you can answer "yes" to every question. If not, use editorial symbols to make the necessary corrections.

Lesson 3: Proofreading and Publishing

PROOFREADING YOUR FINAL DRAFT

Once you have finished revising your rough draft, the next step is to make a clean copy and then proofread it. When you *proofread,* you check for errors in grammar and usage, spelling, punctuation, capitalization, and manuscript form. Use the checklist at right when proofreading.

If your answer to any of the questions in the checklist, is "no," use editorial symbols to make the necessary corrections on your final draft. Refer to a dictionary, writing textbook, or handbook of style as necessary.

PUBLISHING, OR SHARING YOUR WORK

After proofreading your final, revised draft, you are ready for the final step in the writing process—sharing your work with others. Much of the writing that you do for school will be handed in to your teachers. However, you can share your writing with other people as well. These are some of the many ways in which you can share your work:

1. Share your writing in a small group by reading it aloud or by passing it around for others to read.
2. Read your work aloud to the class.
3. Make copies of your writing for members of your family or for your friends.
4. Display your work on a classroom bulletin board.
5. Save your writing in a folder for later publication. At the end of the year, choose the best pieces from your folder and bind them together. Share the collection with your relatives and friends.
6. Submit your writing to the school literary magazine, or start a literary magazine for your school or for your class.
7. Submit your writing to your school or community newspaper.

CHECKLIST FOR PROOFREADING

Grammar and Usage
- ☐ Are all of my sentences complete? That is, have I avoided sentence fragments?
- ☐ Do all of my sentences express only one complete thought? That is, have I avoided run-on sentences?
- ☐ Do the verbs I have used agree with their subjects?
- ☐ Have all the words in my paper been used correctly? Am I sure about the meanings of all of these words?
- ☐ Is the thing being referred to by each pronoun (*I, me, this, each,* etc.) clear?
- ☐ Have I used adjectives and adverbs correctly?

Punctuation
- ☐ Does every sentence end with a punctuation mark?
- ☐ Have I used commas, semicolons, colons, hyphens, dashes, parentheses, quotation marks, and apostrophes correctly?

Spelling
- ☐ Am I absolutely sure that each word has been spelled correctly?

Capitalization
- ☐ Have I capitalized any words that should not be capitalized?
- ☐ Should I capitalize any words that I have not capitalized?

Manuscript Form
- ☐ Have I indented the first line(s) of my paragraph(s)?
- ☐ Have I written my name and the page number in the top, right-hand corner of each page?
- ☐ Have I double spaced the manuscript?
- ☐ Is my manuscript neat and legible?

---

8. Enter your writing in literary contests for student writers.
9. Submit your writing to a magazine that publishes work by young people.

CASE STUDY: PROOFREADING AND PUBLISHING

After revising her final draft, Pilar made a fresh, clean copy. Then she was ready for the proofreading stage. She read the Checklist for Proofreading on the previous page and applied each question to her revised draft. She found several errors. Pilar's paragraph with the proofreading corrections that she made is in the right-hand column.

Pilar made a clean final copy of her paragraph. Then she shared her paragraph with other students in a small-group discussion.

ACTIVITIES AND ASSIGNMENTS

A. Answer the following questions about the case study:

1. What errors in spelling did Pilar correct during proofreading?
2. What capitalization error did Pilar correct?
3. What run-on sentence did she correct? How did she do this?
4. What punctuation errors did Pilar correct?
5. What error in manuscript form did she correct?
6. Are there any changes that you think should still be made in Pilar's paragraph?

Proofreading to correct any errors in your draft. Share the final copy of your paragraph with your family, your teacher, and your classmates.

B. Make a clean copy of your revised draft from the last lesson. Then use the Checklist for

¶ Have you considered reading as a hobby? When you have a free hour alone to relax, try reading a good book. Ask friends to recommend good books they think you'll like, or read something by a Writer you enjoyed in school. Find a comfortable place to read, and see what happens. Here's what happens for me: Reading gives me both privacy and company at the same time. When I'm involved in a book, I'm away from my everyday world. I can discover places, people, and information I might never otherwise have known. Most of all, I especially like finding out about how others live their lifes. I actually learn about situations I might find myself in and see ways I might handle my own life. Maybe you'll enjoy reading for some of the same reasons I do. Its a pleasure.

SECTION 2: UNDERSTANDING THE PARTS OF A LITERARY WORK: ANALYSIS AND INTERPRETATION

Lesson 4: Writing About Images

WHAT IS AN IMAGE?

An *image* is a portrayal, in words, of a sight, sound, touch, taste, or smell. This haiku contains images of sight:

> The snake slid away,
> But the eyes that glared at me,
>   Remained in the grass.
>   —Kyoshi (trans. R. H. Blyth)

The following lines contain images of touch:

> Ah grief and sadness!
> The fishing line trembles
>   In the autumn breeze.
>   —Buson (trans. R. H. Blyth)

These lines contain images of sound:

> The silence!
> The voice of the cicada
>   Penetrates the rocks.
>   —Bashō (trans. R. H. Blyth)

WHY DO WRITERS USE IMAGES?

Writers use images for two purposes:
1. To create pictures, in words, of people, places, and things, and
2. To create feelings, or moods.

Consider the use of images in the following poem:

THE RUNNER

Walt Whitman

> On a flat road runs the well-trained runner,
> He is lean and sinewy with muscular legs.
> He is thinly clothed, he leans forward as he runs,
> With lightly closed fists and arms partially rais'd.

The images in this poem
1. Create a picture of a lean, swift runner, and
2. Create a mood of intense concentration.

CASE STUDY: WRITING ABOUT IMAGES

Prewriting

Roberto's English teacher asked the class to write an analysis of a favorite poem. Roberto chose to write about the use of images in the following poem:

OLD FLORIST

Theodore Roethke

> That hump of a man bunching chrysanthemums
> Or pinching-back asters, or planting azaleas,
> Tamping and stamping dirt into pots,—
> How he could flick and pick
> Rotten leaves or yellowy petals,
> Or scoop out a weed close to flourishing roots,
> Or make the dust buzz with a light spray,
> Or drown a bug in one spit of tobacco juice,
> Or fan life into wilted sweet-peas with his hat,
> Or stand all night watering roses, his feet blue in rubber boots.

Roberto began by looking up the words he didn't know in a dictionary. He made a list of their definitions:

- chrysanthemums: plants with colorful, showy flowers

- asters: plants with daisylike flowers of various colors

- azaleas: shrubs with flowers of various colors

- tamping: packing down tightly

Roberto reread the poem with these definitions in mind. Next Roberto made a chart in his notes of the images in the poem:

- Images of sight: every line includes visual images of the "hump of a man" who actively, busily tends to his colorful flowers

- Images of sound:
  "tamping and stamping dirt"
  "make the dust buzz with a light spray"
  "drown a bug in one spit of tobacco juice"

- Images of touch:
  "tamping and stamping dirt into pots"
  "flick and pick rotten leaves or yellow petals"
  "fan life into wilted sweet-peas with his hat"

- Images of taste:
  none

- Images of smell:
  none directly, but flowers and earth suggest fragrances

Roberto decided to write about how Roethke uses images to create a vivid picture of the florist carefully tending to his plants. He made the following rough outline for his writing:

- Topic sentence:
  tell what poem I'm writing about.
  state my purpose—to show how Roethke uses images to create a vivid picture of the florist.

- Body:
  describe the images of sight, sound, and touch in the poem.

- Conclusion:
  suggest that the images contribute to the mood of the poem—reader feels the florist's loving, attentive attitude toward his plants.

Drafting and Revising

Using his outline and his prewriting notes, Roberto wrote a draft of his analysis. Then he read what he had written and decided that it could be made much clearer. Some of his sentences were not really related to his topic. Roberto revised his draft, making his writing clearer and more focused.

Proofreading and Publishing

Roberto made a clean copy of his revised draft. He used the Checklist for Proofreading, on page 780, to help him to correct errors in grammar and usage, spelling, punctuation, capitalization, and manuscript form. Then Roberto made a clean final copy of his paper and shared it with a small group of classmates. First he read the Roethke poem aloud to them. Then he read his analysis of the poem. He and his classmates each discussed their thoughts about the poem and learned quite a bit from one another.

ACTIVITIES AND ASSIGNMENTS

A. Write a paragraph such as Roberto might have written, based on prewriting notes in the case study. Follow these steps when writing, revising, proofreading, and publishing your draft:

1. Reread "Old Florist." As you read, ask yourself whether there are any images not mentioned in Roberto's notes that you would like to include in your paragraph. If there are, add them to your own prewriting notes.

2. Write a topic sentence that tells what your paragraph will be about.

3. In the body of your paragraph, describe the images in the poem, and tell to what senses these images appeal.

4. Write a conclusion of one or two sentences that sums up the feeling that the images create in the reader.

5. Revise your rough draft to make sure that your paragraph is clear and well organized. Also make sure that your writing accomplishes its purpose and does not stray from your topic.

6. Make a clean copy of your revised draft, and proofread this copy for errors in grammar and usage, spelling, punctuation, capitalization, and manuscript form.

7. Share your final, proofread draft with friends and with your teacher.

B. Choose one of these poems and write a paragraph about its images: "The Village Blacksmith," on page 431; "The Highwayman," on page 437; "The Pheasant," on page 466; "The Bat," on page 472; "Seal," on page 475; one of the haiku on pages 478 and 479; "Washed in Silver," on page 484; "The Flower-Fed Buffaloes," on page 488; "My Mother Pieced Quilts," on page 494; "In Just—," on page 500; or "Stopping by Woods on a Snowy Evening," on page 504. Follow these steps when planning and writing your paragraph:

1. Read the poem carefully several times. Look up any words that you don't know in a dictionary.

2. In your prewriting notes, make a chart with columns labeled *sight, sound, touch, taste,* and *smell.* Fill it in with the images used in the poem.

3. Make notes telling what picture or pictures are created by the images. Also tell what mood you feel is created by the images.

4. Write a topic sentence that tells the name of the poem and that summarizes the main point you plan to make about its images.

5. Write several body sentences that present the images used in the poem.

6. Write a concluding sentence or two to sum up your paragraph. You might want to conclude by telling how the images in the poem create a certain mood or feeling.

7. Revise your paragraph carefully. Add any important details that you left out. Make sure that you have made all your ideas clear to the reader. Check to see that your writing is well organized and that it doesn't stray from the topic.

8. Proofread your paragraph, using the Checklist for Proofreading on page 780.

9. Share your proofread paragraph with your classmates and with your teacher.

Lesson 5: Writing About Sound

SOUND AND MEANING

When you hear written words read aloud, you may discover that they have another dimension of meaning. Read the following haiku aloud, and listen to the sounds of the words:

As lightning flashes . . .
Zig-zag screeches of the heron
    Flying in the dark
        —Bashō

The way the poem sounds gives the reader a richer sense of the way its subjects—the lightning and the heron—sound. The words *flashes, zig-zag,* and *screeches* all sound like what they mean. In both prose and poetry, the sounds and the meanings of words often go hand in hand.

TECHNIQUES INVOLVING SOUND

Writers can use many literary devices to add a dimension of sound to their writing. The following devices of sound are commonly used in literature.

Read the entries in the Handbook of Literary Terms, on page 832, for more detailed explanations of the terms listed in the chart. Then read the following case study.

CASE STUDY: WRITING ABOUT SOUND

André's English class was studying the use of devices of sound in poetry. For a writing assignment about sound, André chose the following poem:

BROADWAY, TWILIGHT

Tom Prideaux

Roaring, clanking,
Sirens screaming
In confusion;
Pink and yellow,
Shifting, gleaming
In profusion.

Above the deepening blue
The stars blink calmly through.

SOUND DEVICES

Onomatopoeia: words that sound like what they mean, like *bleep, crunch,* and *chirp.*

Euphony: pleasant sounds, like those used by Langston Hughes in the following lines from "Harlem Night Song":
    Come,
    Let us roam the night together
    Singing

Cacophony: harsh, jarring sounds, as in "twisted, crushed, junked automobiles"

Alliteration: repetition of initial consonant sounds, as in "*w*inding *w*ay"

Consonance: repetition of internal consonant sounds, as in "The spo*tt*ed ki*tt*en slep*t* quie*t*ly on ma*tt*ed fur"

Assonance: repetition of vowel sounds, as in "y*ou*ng, f*u*zzy p*u*ppy"

Meter: words with a regular rhythm as in "The sún is shíning bríghtly nów."

Parallelism: repetition of grammatical patterns, as in *"through the door* and *up the stairs"*

Repetition: the repeated use of a sound, word, phrase, sentence, rhythmical pattern, or grammatical pattern. Forms of repetition include alliteration, consonance, assonance, meter, parallelism, and rhyme.

Prewriting

First André read Prideaux's poem aloud several times, listening carefully to its sounds. Then, to gather information for his writing, he made a copy of the poem and marked it as follows:

1. He underlined examples of onomatopoeia.
2. He circled all the rhyming words.
3. He underlined, twice, all the repeated sounds he could find.
4. In the margins he noted examples of alliteration, consonance, assonance, and parallelism.
5. He also marked the stresses, or beats, in each line of the poem to show meter.

Here is André's marked copy of the poem:

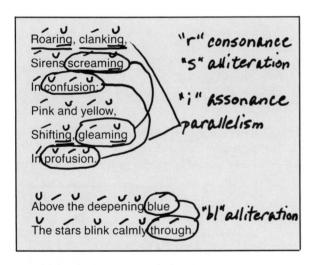

Next André made a detailed list in his notes of the sound devices used in the poem:

- Onomatopoeia: "Roaring," "clanking," and "screaming" all sound like what they describe.

- Cacophony: The first stanza has many harsh-sounding words that describe the "confusion."

- Euphony: The second stanza is melodious compared to the first.

- Meter: pounding beat in the first stanza— almost every word has stressed first syllable. The second stanza flows peacefully, quietly.

- Rhyme: screaming/gleaming; confusion/ profusion; pink/blink; blue/through.

- Repetition:
    Alliteration: "Sirens screaming," "blue . . . blink"
    Consonance: "Roaring . . . Sirens screaming"
    Assonance: "Pink . . . Shifting . . . In"
    Parallelism: "Roaring, clanking"/ "Shifting, gleaming"; "In confusion"/"In profusion."

André reviewed the poem and his notes. He made an observation about the poem as a whole that he thought he could use in the introduction to his paragraph. He added this observation to his notes:

> title foreshadows contrast between the sounds, colors, and movement of a busy street (Broadway) and the calm beauty of the overhead twilight sky

André wanted to make a rough outline before he began writing. He considered two possible ways to organize his paragraph. He could organize sequentially—line by line in the order of the poem—or he could use a topic organization and discuss each sound device in turn. He decided to use the topic organization.

Drafting and Revising

Using his prewriting notes and his rough outline, André wrote a rough draft. This is the beginning of his rough draft:

> In his poem "Broadway: Twilight, Tom Prideaux uses a whole lot of sound devices, to show what broadway looks and sounds like, specially in contrast to the calm, darkning twilight sky. First of all, the otomatopia really lets the reader hear the street noises "Roaring, clanking,/Sirens screaming," the first two lines,

start things off with a bang. Second of all, Mr. Prideaux uses lot of repetition devices. The short *i* sound is assonance in every single one of the first six lines: "roaring, clanking," "screaming/in confusion;/Pink", "shifting, gleaming/In profusion." For consonance the *r* sound repeats three times in the first six words. The *ing* sound too occurs five times in the first stanza. In line 2 the alliteration of "Sirens screaming" repeats the *s* sound.

André finished his draft, revised it, and copied it over.

Proofreading and Publishing

André carefully proofread his revised draft for errors in grammar and usage, spelling, punctuation, capitalization, and manuscript form. Then he shared his paper with a small group of classmates before giving it to his teacher.

ACTIVITIES AND ASSIGNMENTS

A. Finish André's rough draft, using information from André's prewriting notes. Then revise and proofread the rough draft. Make sure that you correct all of André's errors in spelling and mechanics. Share your final, proofread draft with your classmates.

B. Write a two-paragraph composition on the use of sound in one of the following poems: "The Highwayman," on page 437; "Feelings About Words," on page 486; "The Flower-Fed Buffaloes," on page 488; or "In Just—," on page 500. Follow these steps when writing your paper:

1. Read the poem aloud several times, and listen carefully to its sounds.
2. Make a copy of the poem. If it is an especially long poem, you may decide to write about only one or two stanzas.
3. Mark your copy of the poem as follows:
   a. Underline examples of onomatopoeia once.
   b. Circle rhyming words.
   c. Underline repeated sounds twice.
   d. In the margins, note examples of alliteration, consonance, assonance, parallelism, and repeated words.
4. Read the section on Meter in the Handbook of Literary Terms and Techniques, on page 839. Then choose one stanza of your poem, and mark its feet and stresses, as follows:

There was an old man with a beard,
Who said, "It is just as I feared!—
Two Owls and a Hen, four Larks and a Wren,
Have all built their nests in my beard!

5. Organize your notes. Write a rough outline for your paper.
6. Use your prewriting notes and your outline to write a rough draft. In your first paragraph, be sure that you inform your readers about the following:
   a. the title and author of the poem you are writing about
   b. the topic of your paper—the poet's use of sound devices and
   c. the meter and rhyme scheme of the poem.
      In the second paragraph of your draft, discuss the remaining devices of sound used in the poem.
7. Revise your rough draft. Then make a clean copy of your revised draft, and proofread it for errors in grammar and usage, spelling, punctuation, capitalization, and manuscript form.
8. Share your proofread draft with your classmates before handing it in.

Lesson 6: Writing About Figures of Speech

WHAT IS A FIGURE OF SPEECH?

A *figure of speech* is language that is not meant to be taken literally. Consider these lines from a novel by Zora Neale Hurston:

> Phoeby's hungry listening helped Janie to tell her story. So she went on thinking back to her young years and explaining them to her friend in soft, easy phrases while all round the house, the night time put on flesh and blackness.

Listening can't literally be "hungry," nor can night "put on flesh and blackness." The reader understands that these ideas are meant to be interpreted figuratively—that the writer is using figures of speech.

The following figures of speech are often used in literature:

```
┌─────────────────────────────────────────┐
│            FIGURES OF SPEECH             │
├─────────────────────────────────────────┤
│                                          │
│ Hyperbole: exaggeration for emphasis:    │
│                                          │
│ "I'm so tired I could sleep for a month  │
│ and a half."                             │
│                                          │
│ Personification: speaking or writing     │
│ about a subject that isn't human as      │
│ though it were:                          │
│                                          │
│ "The sky wore her fanciest, most         │
│ colorful dress."                         │
│                                          │
│ Simile: a comparison between two         │
│ subjects, using like or as:              │
│                                          │
│ "The lines on his face were like ditches │
│ on a well-traveled road."                │
│                                          │
│ Metaphor: a comparison of two subjects   │
│ that does not use like or as:            │
│                                          │
│ "His room is a pigsty."                  │
│                                          │
└─────────────────────────────────────────┘
```

WHY WRITERS USE FIGURES OF SPEECH

Writers use figures of speech to express their ideas vividly. Consider the difference between the following passages.

Without figures of speech:
"I enjoyed the rhythm of the rain falling on my rainhat."

With figures of speech:
"The rain tapped a tune on my rainhat, and my brain danced with delight."

The figures of speech in the second passage convey a fuller, more vivid sense of the experience.

HOW WRITERS CREATE FIGURES OF SPEECH

Hyperbole is a relatively simple figure of speech. To create a hyperbole, a writer first thinks of a subject and of a quality or characteristic of the subject:

Subject: myself
Quality: tiredness

Next the writer creates a sentence exaggerating the quality:

I'm so tired I could sleep for a month and a half.

Simile and metaphor are more complex. As with hyperbole, the writer thinks of a subject and of a quality or characteristic of the subject. For example, the subject might be a room, and the characteristic might be its messiness. Then the writer thinks of some other subject that has the same characteristic, such as a pigsty. Then the writer can put the two together, using *like* or *as*, to form a simile:

His room is like a pigsty.

If the writer makes the comparison without using *like* or *as,* the result is a metaphor:

His room is a pigsty.

Personification works just like metaphor. The only difference is that one of the two subjects is human and the other is not. The nonhuman subject is described as having some human characteristics.

CASE STUDY: WRITING ABOUT FIGURES OF SPEECH

Verlinda's English teacher asked the class to write a paragraph about the figures of speech used in a poem. Verlinda decided to write about the following poem:

CONSTRUCTION
Patricia Hubbell

The house frames hang like spider webs
Dangling in the sun,
While up and down the wooden strands
The spider workers run.
They balance on the two-by-fours,
They creep across the beams,
While down below, the heap of wood,
A spider-stockpile, gleams.
The spider-workers spin the web
And tack it tight with nails.
They ready it against the night
　When all work ends.

Verlinda studied the poem carefully and decided that the figure of speech most important to it was metaphor. The speaker of the poem was comparing the work of the men to the work of spiders. Verlinda made the following notes:

- Poem: "Construction," by Patricia Hubbell

- Figure of speech used: metaphor

- Two subjects being compared: men working at a construction site and spiders working on a web

- Similarities between the two subjects:
　"house frames hang like spider webs"
　Workers move like spiders, running "up

and down," sometimes creeping.
Materials gleam in sun like a spider's materials.
Both building a structure that must be well fastened before night comes.

Verlinda reviewed her prewriting and organized her information in a rough outline.

Drafting and Revising

Verlinda used her prewriting notes to write a rough draft of her paragraph. Here is that draft, with Verlinda's corrections and revisions:

In her poem "Construction" the poet Patricia Hubbell uses metaphor to create a vivid, unusual portrait of an ordinary scene. Just as People stop to admire spiders at work, the reader of this poem stops to admire construction workers building a house. In fact, The central metaphor of the poem compares construction workers to spiders and an unfinished house to a web. By using the metaphor of the spiders Hubbell gives her readers a new look at the construction worker's job delicate grace and even magic of art. Hubbell describes the "spider workers as skilfully moving about, running, balancing and creeping across the wooden strands. The house itself having frames that "hang like spider webs" Furthermore, The materials in the workers stock pile look like a spiders stock pile. They Finally, like spiders, gleem in the sun. The workers must make sure that the structure they are is well fastened before night comes.

Proofreading and Publishing

Verlinda made a clean final copy of her paragraph for her teacher, who displayed it on the bulletin board.

ACTIVITIES AND ASSIGNMENTS

A. Answer the following questions about the revised draft in the case study.

1. Why do you think Verlinda moved the sentence that begins "By using the metaphor" to the end of her paragraph?
2. What sentences did Verlinda combine? Why do you think she did so?
3. What transitional words, or transitions, did Verlinda add?
4. What specific details and evidence from the poem did Verlinda add?
5. What errors in spelling and punctuation did Verlinda catch during revision? What errors in punctuation and spelling remain in her draft?

B. Write a paragraph on figures of speech in one of the following poems: "Upon Mistress Susanna Southwell, Her Feet," on page 464; "The Pheasant," on page 466; "Fog," on page 468; "Washed in Silver," on page 484; "My Mother Pieced Quilts," on page 494; or "Mother to Son," on page 518. Follow these steps:

1. Read the poem several times. Then copy the poem by hand onto a sheet of paper. Writing out the poem in this way lets you become familiar with the author's exact words.
2. On the copy, underline all the figures of speech that you can find. List them on a separate sheet of paper under the following headings: Hyperbole, Personification, Simile, and Metaphor.
3. Decide which figure of speech you think is the most important to the meaning of the poem as a whole. Make prewriting notes about this figure of speech, explaining how it works and how it contributes to the poem as a whole.
4. Use your prewriting notes to develop your paragraph. Begin with a topic sentence. In the body of your paragraph, cite evidence from the poem. Conclude with a sentence that briefly summarizes the main idea of your paragraph.
5. Revise your paragraph. Then make a clean final copy and proofread it. Use the Checklist for Proofreading on page 780. Finally, share the proofread copy with your family and friends before giving it to your teacher.

Lesson 7: Writing About Setting

WHAT IS SETTING?

The *setting* of a story, novel, poem, or play is the time and place in which the action occurs. However, when creating a setting, a writer tells more than the date and the location. The writer also reveals details about elements of the environment such as weather, scenery, rooms, local customs, clothing, and dialects.

The second chapter of Wilson Rawls's novel *Where the Red Fern Grows,* on page 629, contains a detailed description of setting. The author includes sensory images and details about the landscape, local customs, and the time of year:

> Our home was in a beautiful valley far back in the rugged Ozarks. The country was new and sparsely settled. The land we lived on was Cherokee land, allotted to my mother because of the Cherokee blood that flowed in her veins. It lay in a strip from the foothills of the mountains to the banks of the Illinois River in northeastern Oklahoma.... Mama had picked the spot for our log house. It nestled at the edge of the foothills in the mouth of a small canyon, and was surrounded by a grove of huge red oaks. Behind our house one could see miles and miles of the mighty Ozarks. In the spring the aromatic scent of wild flowers, redbuds, papaws, and dogwoods, drifting on the wind currents, spread over the valley and around our home.

WHY DO WRITERS CREATE SETTINGS?

Writers create settings to serve various functions, or purposes, as shown in the chart, Uses of Setting.

CASE STUDY: WRITING ABOUT SETTING

Kyra read James Baldwin's "Caleb's Brother," on page 119. She thought that the

---

USES OF SETTING

To create a mood, or atmosphere: For example, a description of a log cabin nestled in a beautiful mountain canyon creates a peaceful, happy mood. On the other hand, details about a wet, dark tunnel might create a scary mood.

To inform readers about different ways of life: Through such details as customs, clothing, and speech patterns, a reader can get a sense of what it would be like to grow up in the backwoods of the Ozarks or to be a small boy living in a big city.

To make the action of a literary work seem more real: The vivid details of a setting can take readers to imaginary or faraway times and places.

To contribute to the conflict, or struggle, in a work: For example, a work set in the Arctic Circle might involve a character's struggle to survive extremely cold weather.

To symbolize, or stand for, some idea that the writer wants to emphasize: For example, if a story opens in the Ozarks in the springtime, its setting might symbolize hopeful beginnings and growth. A winter setting, on the other hand, might symbolize death.

---

setting was important to the story, so she decided to write a composition about the setting in "Caleb's Brother" for her English class.

Prewriting

Kyra reread "Caleb's Brother," paying careful attention to the setting. She narrowed the topic of her composition to the setting in one particular scene in the story, the scene in which Leo, wet and lonely, walks home in the rain and finds no one on his stoop.

To gather information, Kyra made the following chart in her prewriting notes:

SETTING	DETAILS
long avenue	"stretched straight before me, endless"
familiar buildings	"dark, silent shapes, great masses of wet rock"
men on stoops	"stood against the walls or against the stoops, made faceless by the light in the hallway behind them"
rain and splashing	"rain was falling harder"; "cars sloshed by, sending up sheets of water"
music and voices in the distance	"heard music faintly, and many voices"
woman ahead	"walked, very fast, head down"

Kyra looked over her prewriting chart and made notes about the function of the setting in the scene:

- *Function of setting:*
    To provide a backdrop for the story
    To emphasize the mood of emptiness and loneliness
    To symbolize Leo's struggle with loneliness
    To make the story realistic

Kyra decided that the two most important functions of the setting were to create a mood and to symbolize Leo's conflict with loneliness.

She wrote a topic sentence and made a rough outline for her paper.

Drafting and Revising

Kyra used her prewriting notes and her outline to write the following draft of her composition:

An important use of setting in James Baldwins "Caleb's Brother is the scene when Leo walks home alone in the dark, cold, rain. This setting does more than provide a backdrop for the action of the story, it emphasizes little Leo's feelings of isolation, and it symbolizes Leo's conflict. Leo's big brother is suppose to take him to the movies every saturday. His brother, however, is usually busy with his friends, though, so that he sends Leo off alone. Because of his youth, Leo must ask at the theater until he finds someone to take him in. This also makes him feel badly. On this rainy day, Leo does'nt ask anyone to take him in, and no body offers. Feeling lousy, Leo heads home. Specific details about the setting that create the mood of loneliness include the men who seem to have no faces. Faces are the physical part of people that we relate to, so Leo has no way of relating to these men. Music and voices remind the reader and perhaps Leo too that others are not lonelie. The weather adds to Leo's pain. The pouring rain and the splashing cars emphasize the wet, cold elements that punch at Leo's spirit. A woman, almost running, her head down, seems to be in the act of fleeing away from Leo she is another person rejecting him. His very own building stoop is empty. Nobody is there for him at home. The whole setting underlines Leo's feelings of painful loneliness and rejection. These are the feelings Leo battles each week when his brother sends him off alone.

Kyra revised her composition to cut out details that didn't relate to setting and to make it more clearly organized. She also added some direct quotations from the story to make her writing more interesting.

Proofreading and Publishing

Kyra made a fresh copy of her revised draft and proofread it carefully. Then she made a clean final copy and shared it with her parents and with her English teacher.

ACTIVITIES AND ASSIGNMENTS

A. Rewrite the draft in the case study, adding some direct quotations from the story "Caleb's Brother." Use the quotations from Kyra's prewriting chart or any others that you think are helpful or interesting. Then revise the draft so that it is well organized and clear. Make a fresh copy of the revised draft, and proofread this copy for errors in grammar and usage, spelling, punctuation, capitalization, and manuscript form. Share your final copy with your classmates and with your teacher.

B. Choose one of the following works for a composition on setting: "All Summer in a Day," on page 107; "The Trout," on page 113; "The Third Level," on page 127; "Rip Van Winkle," on page 133; "The Highwayman," on page 437; "The Cremation of Sam McGee," on page 445; or "Annabel Lee," on page 455. Follow these steps when planning and writing your paper:

1. Read your chosen work once. Ask yourself what the setting is, and whether setting is more important in particular scenes in the work. You may want to select one setting to write about if the work has several different settings. Then read the work again, paying careful attention to the details that help to create the setting.

2. Write a topic sentence for your composition. Make a chart in your prewriting notes like the one in the case study, listing specific examples from the work to support your topic sentence.

3. Decide what the most important function of the setting is. Is the most important function to create a mood? to show a particular lifestyle? to make the story realistic? to create a conflict? to symbolize an important idea? Your topic sentence should reflect what this most important function is. Now make a rough outline for your composition.

4. Write a draft of your paper based on your notes and your outline. Revise the draft using the Checklist for Revision on page 778.

5. Make a clean copy of your draft for proofreading. Proofread your writing, using the Checklist for Proofreading on page 780. Make a final copy of your composition, and share it with your classmates and with your teacher.

Lesson 8: Writing About Plot

WHAT IS PLOT?

Plot is the sequence of events—what happens and how it happens—in a short story, a novel, a play, or a narrative poem. To enjoy and interpret any work that tells a story, you must understand its plot.

WHAT ARE THE PARTS OF A PLOT?

To analyze a plot, you can group the events of a story into parts. Here is an example of plot that can be divided into parts:

A girl wants a racing bicycle. She works for eight months after school and weekends in a supermarket to earn the money to buy it. When she has just saved enough money to buy the bicycle, the money is stolen from her house. The girl then works another six months in the bicycle shop. She finally is able to buy the bicycle, and she becomes a state champion bicycle racer.

Major sections of a plot include the following:

1. *The inciting incident:* This is an event that creates the *central conflict,* or struggle. In the example, the inciting incident occurs when the girl decides that she wants an expensive racing bicycle but realizes that she has no money to buy it.
2. *The development:* This is the part of the story in which the struggle takes place. In the example the development takes place when the girl is working in the supermarket.
3. *The climax:* This is the high point of interest and suspense in the story. In the example, the climax occurs when the girl's money is stolen.
4. *The resolution:* This is the point at which the central conflict is ended, or resolved. In the example the resolution occurs when the girl finally gets her new bicycle.

Not all plots have this exact structure. For example, in some stories the inciting incident takes place before the beginning of the work. In the example, if the girl were already working in the supermarket at the opening of the story, the inciting incident would have occurred before the story began.

In some stories the climax and the resolution are the same event. If, in the example, the girl had decided she no longer wanted a bicycle when she discovered that her money had been stolen, then the climax and the resolution would have occurred at the same time.

Some stories have a section before the inciting incident. This section, called the *exposition,* introduces the reader to the setting and the characters. Other stories have a section that follows the resolution, called the *denouement.* The denouement gives the writer the chance to answer any questions that might remain in the reader's mind.

WHAT ARE SOME SPECIAL TECHNIQUES OF PLOT?

There are a number of special techniques writers use to make their plots more interesting. The following are some of the most common:

1. *Suspense:* This is the feeling of excitement or tension the reader experiences as the action of the plot unfolds. A writer creates suspense by raising questions in the reader's mind. In the example the writer might add suspense by creating stumbling blocks for the girl that keep the reader wondering, "Will she get the bicycle?"
2. *Foreshadowing:* This is a hint or clue about an event that will occur later in the story. In the example the writer could use foreshadowing

by having the girl's brother warn her that she shouldn't leave a large amount of money in the house.

3. *Flashback:* This is a section in a story where the action is interrupted to tell about an earlier event. In the example, when the girl discovers that her money has been stolen, the writer might insert a flashback in which the girl remembers how hard she had worked to earn that money. After the flashback ended, the narrative would return to the present action.

4. *Surprise ending:* This is an ending that catches the reader off guard with an unexpected turn of events. In the example there would be a surprise ending if the girl found out that her money hadn't been stolen after all.

WHAT IS CONFLICT?

Conflict is a struggle between opposing forces. Without some sort of conflict, there would be no basis for a plot. The central conflict of a story occurs when the main character must fight against some force or make an important decision. There may also be minor conflicts taking place in a story at the same time as the central conflict.

Conflicts are either external or internal. An *external conflict* takes place when a person or group struggles against another person or group or against a nonhuman force such as a storm or a car that won't start.

An *internal conflict* takes place within a person's mind. For example, a character in a story might be torn between risking his life to save someone else and not taking the chance.

CASE STUDY: WRITING ABOUT PLOT

Maria's English class learned how plot is used in literary works. Then her teacher asked the class to choose a short story and analyze its plot. Maria selected Ernest Hemingway's "A Day's Wait," on page 33.

Prewriting

Maria read the short story twice. She thought about what the central conflict was, and she decided that it was an internal conflict—the boy struggling against his fear of dying. Then Maria used freewriting to list the events in the story. She grouped the events into parts of the plot, as follows:

- Inciting incident: The boy looks sick and feverish, so his father sends him to bed and calls a doctor. The doctor says that the boy has a fever of one hundred and two.

- Development: The boy continues to look worse and starts to act strange. His father can't understand what is bothering him so much.

- Climax: After the boy's father has taken his temperature, the boy asks how long it will be before he dies. Suddenly Papa—and the reader—realize that the boy has expected to die all along.

- Resolution: Papa discovers that the boy, who only knows about French thermometers, thinks that his 102-degree fever will kill him. He explains the difference between American and European thermometers, and the boy realizes that he is not going to die.

Maria also made notes about the conflict and about special plot devices used in the short story:

- Conflict: At first it appears to be external—the boy against his illness. At the climax of the story, however, the reader discovers that the conflict is really internal—the boy struggling to be brave in the face of death.

- Suspense: Throughout the development, the reader wonders what is wrong with the boy and what is going to happen to him.

Maria made a rough outline for her composition. Her outline showed how she would organize the information from her prewriting notes.

Drafting and Revising

Maria wrote the first draft of her composition very quickly. Then she went back and carefully revised what she had written. She made sure everything she said in her paper was closely related to her topic—the plot of "A Day's Wait."

Proofreading and Publishing

Maria made a fresh copy of her paper and proofread it carefully. She shared her final copy with her class by reading it aloud to them.

ACTIVITIES AND ASSIGNMENTS

A. Read the short story "A Day's Wait," on page 33. Then use Maria's prewriting notes from the case study to write a paragraph about the plot of the story. Follow these steps:

1. Write a topic sentence that tells what your paragraph will be about. Do not begin your sentence with the words *This paragraph will be about.* You might start off with the words *The fascinating plot of Ernest Hemingway's "A Day's Wait"* . . .

2. Write the body of your paragraph. Explain the parts of the plot and include quotations from the story to support your main points.

3. Write a concluding sentence for your paragraph. In this concluding sentence, tell how Hemingway's handling of the plot, especially the news revealed in the climax, makes the story enjoyable to read.

4. Revise and proofread your paragraph. Share it with your classmates in a small-group discussion.

B. Choose one of the following works for a paragraph on plot: "Rikki-tikki-tavi," on page 13; "The Confidence Game," on page 25; "A Boy and a Man," on page 37; "A Secret for Two," on page 45; "Zoo," on page 51; "The Highwayman," on page 437; or "Oranges," on page 459. Follow these steps when planning and writing your paragraph:

1. Read the work once. Ask yourself what the central conflict in the work is, and write this conflict in your notes. Then read the work a second time, paying careful attention to the parts of the plot and to special plot devices.

2. Make a chart in your prewriting notes with spaces for *Exposition, Inciting incident, Development, Climax, Resolution, Denouement, Suspense, Foreshadowing, Flashback,* and *Surprise ending.* Fill in the chart with information from the story or poem. Bear in mind that some stories do not contain all these parts.

3. Write a topic sentence that tells what the main idea of your paragraph will be.

4. Write the body of your paragraph, describing the parts of the plot. Include evidence, such as quotations from the work, to support your ideas.

5. Write a concluding sentence that sums up your paragraph by telling how the plot makes the work interesting to read.

6. Revise your paragraph, making sure all of your ideas are clear. Then proofread your paragraph for errors in grammar and usage, spelling, punctuation, capitalization, and manuscript form. Share your paragraph with your classmates and with your teacher.

Lesson 9: Writing About Character

TYPES OF CHARACTER

A *character* is a person or animal who takes part in the action of a short story, novel, poem, or play. The main character is called the *protagonist*. What happens to the protagonist is usually the focus of the literary work. Other characters in the work may be *major characters*—characters who play important roles—or *minor characters*—characters who play less important roles. In some works the protagonist struggles against another major character who is called the *antagonist*.

CHARACTERIZATION

Characterization is a process of showing what a character is really like. Writers use many techniques to characterize the people and animals in their works. In *direct characterization* the writer simply tells the reader what a character is like. A statement such as "Danny felt lonely and frightened" is a direct characterization.

In *indirect characterization* the writer shows what a character is like by describing what the character says or does, how a character looks, or what other characters say about him or her.

ELEMENTS OF CHARACTER

A well-developed character—just like a real person—has many different *traits,* or characteristics. The following are some traits that help a reader understand a character fully:

1. *Appearance:* What does the character look like? What does the character wear? What can you learn about the character from his or her appearance?
2. *Personality:* Does the character tend to be emotional or rational? shy or outgoing? tal- ented or clumsy? happy or sad? caring or cold? a leader or a follower? honest or dishonest?
3. *Background:* Where did the character grow up? What experiences has he or she had? What is the character's social status? occupation? How much schooling has the character had? What are his or her hobbies or skills?
4. *Motivation:* What makes the character do what he or she does? What does the character like or dislike? What are the character's wishes, goals, desires, dreams, and needs?
5. *Relationships:* How is the character related to other characters in the work? How does the character interact with other characters? Does the character have many friends or many enemies?
6. *Conflict:* Is the character involved in some struggle? If so, is this an internal conflict—one that takes place within the character's mind— or an external conflict—a struggle between the character and some outside force? Is the conflict ever resolved? If so, how?
7. *Change:* Does the character change in the course of the work? Does he or she learn or grow? That is, is the character static (unchanging) or dynamic (changing)?

When planning a paper about a character, follow these steps:

1. Determine what character you are dealing with—the main character, another major character, or a minor character.
2. As you read the work, pay close attention to details that show what the character is like. Note what the narrator says about the character, what other characters say about the character, and what the character says and does.
3. Answer the questions from the lesson about appearance, personality, background, motivation, relationships, conflict, and change. Find

evidence in the work to support your answers.

4. Choose one aspect of the character to focus on in your paper. Write a topic sentence about this aspect of the character.

5. Find evidence from your prewriting notes to support your topic sentence.

CASE STUDY: WRITING ABOUT CHARACTER

Marc's English teacher asked the class to choose a main character from a short story and to write a composition about that character. Marc decided to write about the character Colin in Paul Annixter's "Last Cover," on page 57.

Prewriting

Marc read the story once. To gather information for his paper, he did some freewriting. He imagined that he was describing Colin to someone who knew nothing about him, and he wrote down everything he knew and felt about Colin.

Marc then reread the story to gather more evidence about the characterization of Colin. He made the chart displayed in the right-hand column as part of his prewriting notes.

Marc added several more details to his chart so that he would have plenty of evidence to support his topic sentence.

Next, Marc reviewed his notes to decide which aspect of Annixter's characterization of Colin would be the focus of his paper. He wrote the following topic sentence for his composition:

> Although Colin may appear to be weak, he is really very strong inside.

Marc made a rough outline for his composition to organize his information.

Drafting and Revising

Marc used his prewriting notes and his outline to write a draft of his composition. Here is his unrevised first draft:

> The main character of Paul Annixter's short story, "Last Cover," an eleven-year-old boy

TRAIT AND SPECIFIC EXAMPLE	WHAT THE EXAMPLE SAYS ABOUT COLIN
Appearance: "small for his age, delicate and blond, his hair much lighter and softer than mine, his eyes deep and wide and blue"	frail, probably quiet and thoughtful, not a "typical" eleven-year-old boy
Relationships: "the fox became Colin's whole life"; father gives him a hard time, scorns his art: "'white-livered' interpretation of nature through pen and pencil instead of rod and rifle"	devoted to a wild animal—maybe even more than to humans; in conflict with father over art
Interests: "growing love of wild things"; "threatened to break the family tradition with his leaning toward art"	loner; independent thinker; mind of his own

with soft, light hair. He's often sick. From his appearance, he looks frail. He's not a "typical" country boy all day outside and can't wait to go hunting with the men. He's really good at drawing. Colin's dad hates the interest in art. He wants Colin to be an outdoorsman. He gives Colin a hard time. Colin doesn't give in though. Although Colin may appear to be weak, he is really very strong inside.

Colin's real love is the wild fox he found as a kit and raised that is named Bandit. Bandit has grown up and returned to the wild. Now the fox and his wife, unafraid of people, have become experts at raiding neighborhood farms. Bandit must be killed. Colin turns out to be really tuff. He hides out with the fox the day the farmers hunt for it. But he seems to understand and except that Bandit must be killed. Hes not a crybaby this time. The fox gets killed that night, and colin really shows strength and matureness. He uses drawing to help himself deal with his grief. When Colin's father sees it, even he is proud of his son. You would be too. Colin's strength is nice.

Marc read his first draft and realized that it needed major revisions. He revised the draft, adding more specific details and making his sentences clearer.

Proofreading and Publishing

Marc made a clean copy of his draft and proofread it carefully. Then he shared his final copy with his teacher, who displayed it on the class bulletin board.

ACTIVITIES AND ASSIGNMENTS

A. Revise and proofread the draft from the case study. Follow these steps:

1. Read "Last Cover," on page 57. Then read Marc's rough draft, noting how it is organized. What is the topic sentence? Is the rest of the composition directly related to the topic sentence? Is there enough evidence to support the topic sentence? If you answered "no" to either of the last two questions, revise Marc's draft accordingly.
2. Use the Checklist for Revision on page 778 to finish revising the draft.

3. Make a clean copy of the revised draft, and proofread this copy for errors in grammar and usage, spelling, punctuation, capitalization, and manuscript form. Share your final copy with a small group of your classmates.

B. Choose one of the following short stories for a paragraph about character: "The Sneaker Crisis," on page 67; "The Luckiest Time of All," on page 75; "Amigo Brothers," on page 79; "Stolen Day," on page 89; "Luke Baldwin's Vow," on page 95; or "Caleb's Brother," on page 119. Follow these steps:

1. Read the story and choose a main character to write about. Freewrite about the character as though you were describing him or her to a friend.
2. Reread the story to find details to support your description of the character. List your information in a chart like the one Marc made in the case study.
3. Choose one aspect of your character that you think is especially interesting. Write a topic sentence to indicate you are going to write about this aspect. Then make a rough outline for your paragraph that shows how you will organize your information when you write.
4. Write a draft of your paragraph according to your outline. Then revise it to make it clear and specific.
5. Proofread your draft using the Checklist for Proofreading on page 780. Make a clean final copy of your paragraph.
6. Share your paragraph with your classmates in a small group-discussion. Then share it with your teacher.

Lesson 10: Writing About Narration and Point of View

WHAT IS NARRATION?

Narration is the act of telling a story, or *narrative.* Narratives include short stories, novels, dramas, nonfictional narrative essays, and narrative poems. The voice that tells the story is called the *narrator.* The type of narrator a work has determines the point of view.

WHAT IS POINT OF VIEW?

Point of view refers to the narrative voice, the voice that tells a story. Imagine a grandmother telling you a story about when she was young. She will use many first-person pronouns (*I, me, us, our,* and so on) because she is a character in her own story. Now imagine that the grandmother is telling a fairy tale to a small child. She will no longer refer to herself or use first-person pronouns. Instead, the grandmother will use many third-person pronouns such as *she, his,* and *them* to talk about the characters because she is telling the story from outside the action.

To determine the point of view of a particular story, you must first ask whether the narrator is a character in the story. If the narrator does take part in the action, then the story is told from the *first-person point of view.* If the narrator is outside the action, then the story is told from the *third-person point of view.*

In addition to deciding whether the writer has used a first-person or third-person point of view, you must decide how much the narrator knows about what each of the characters thinks and feels. A narrator who can tell about the thoughts and feelings of all the characters is *omniscient,* or "all-knowing." A narrator who knows only what goes on in the mind of one major or minor character is *limited.* If the narrator does not discuss the thoughts or feelings of any of the characters but reports only what they do, then the story has an *objective narrator.*

CASE STUDY: WRITING ABOUT NARRATION AND POINT OF VIEW

Linda's English class was given an assignment to write a composition describing the point of view in a short story. Linda decided to write about point of view in Jack Finney's "The Third Level," on page 127.

Prewriting

Linda read the short story quickly and noticed that the narrator referred to himself as "I" throughout the narrative and that he participated in the action of the story. She then knew that the story was told from the first-person point of view.

Next she asked herself whether the narrator was omniscient, limited, or objective. The narrator, Charley, had expressed his own thoughts and feelings, so Linda knew that the voice was not objective. She reread the story and looked for clues that would help her to determine whether the point of view was omniscient or limited. She realized that the narrator did not view the events of the story through several characters' eyes, so she concluded that "The Third Level" was told from the first-person limited point of view.

Linda needed a plan of action for gathering information for her composition. She decided to try the questioning method. She listed the following questions in her prewriting notes:

> What do I know about the narrator, and how do I know it?
> How would the story be different if it were told by a different narrator? (Consider one or two possibilities.)

What advantages are there to the story's being told from this point of view?

Why do I think the author chose this point of view?

Linda answered the questions, using specific examples and details from the story. Then she looked at the information she had gathered and made a rough outline for her composition.

Drafting and Revising

Linda used her prewriting notes and her outline to write a first draft of her composition. Then she revised her paper, using standard editorial symbols to mark her changes. Linda's revised draft appears in the right-hand column.

Proofreading and Publishing

Linda made a fresh copy of her composition. She proofread it carefully. Then she shared it with a friend in her class who had also enjoyed "The Third Level."

ACTIVITIES AND ASSIGNMENTS

A. Answer the following questions based on the case study:

1. What error in manuscript form did Linda correct at the beginning of her composition?
2. Why did Linda eliminate the sentence *I think this because of what he says?*
3. Why did Linda change *the train station* to *Grand Central Station* and *another century* to *the nineteenth century?*
4. What other changes did Linda make? Why did she make them?

B. Choose one of the following short stories for a one- or two-paragraph composition about point of view: "A Day's Wait," on page 33; "A Secret for Two," on page 45; "Last Cover," on page 57; "Amigo Brothers," on page 79; "Luke Baldwin's Vow," on page 95; "Caleb's Brother,"

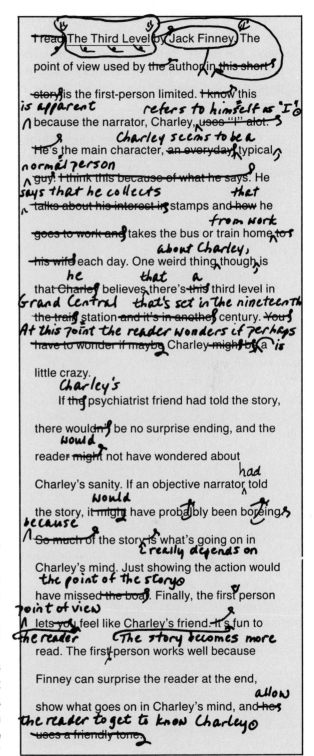

on page 119; or "Hallucination," on page 179. Follow these steps:

1. Read the story carefully. Determine what point of view is used in the story. Is it first person or third person? omniscient, limited, or objective?

2. In your prewriting notes, write the answers to the questions that Linda asked herself in the case study. Read the story a second time, noting any important details about the point of view.

3. Make a rough outline that shows how you will organize your information when you write your paper.

4. Write a topic sentence that states the title, author, and point of view of your chosen story.

5. Write the rest of your composition from your outline and your prewriting notes.

6. Revise your paper and then proofread it carefully. Make a clean final copy and share it with your classmates and with your teacher.

Lesson 11: Writing About Theme

WHAT IS THEME?

The *theme* of a literary work is its central message, or insight into life. Theme is more than a statement of what a work is about—it is a statement of what the work means. For example, the story "A Secret for Two," on page 45, is about what happens to a man and his horse, but this subject is not the story's theme. The theme is that a relationship can be so strong that one member of the pair can't go on without the other.

Not every literary work has a theme, or "something to say." A wonderful ghost story or a good mystery, for example, might simply be entertaining.

HOW WRITERS PRESENT THEMES

A theme may be stated directly or it may be implied. For example, in "Utzel and His Daughter, Poverty," on page 149, one of the characters states the theme directly. Also the framed motto Utzel hangs on the wall indicates the theme.

Often the writer of a literary work does not state his or her theme directly. Instead, the reader must decide what the message of the work is, based on other elements of the work such as the outcome of the plot. Such a theme is implied.

To understand the theme of a work, you often must think carefully about the work and read it several times.

STATING THE THEME

Consider the theme of this poem:

SONG FORM

Amiri Baraka

(Leroi Jones)

Morning uptown, quiet on the street,
no matter the distinctions that can be
made, quiet, very quiet, on the street.
Sun's not even up, just some kid and me,
skating, both of us, at the early sun, and
amazed there is grace for us, without our
having to smile too tough, or be very pleasant
even to each other. Merely to be merely to be

The poem is about how the speaker and "some kid" find themselves both skating on a quiet street at sunrise. The two are surprised because at this quiet hour they can go about their ways peacefully, just being themselves.

Here is one way of stating the theme: "The quiet of early morning can be magical." Here's another way: "Tensions between people let up when people can just be themselves." Different readers will state the theme, or significance of the poem, in different ways.

CASE STUDY: WRITING ABOUT THEME

Zoraida's English class was given an assignment to write one or two paragraphs about the theme of a short story. Zoraida decided to write about the theme of Pat Carr's "The Confidence Game," on page 25.

Prewriting

Zoraida read the story once straight through. Then she wrote down what she thought the theme might be.

- *Possible themes:*
    Positive thinking can help you succeed.
    Doing your best is more important than being the best.
    Hating someone who's better at something than you are can make you act and feel bad, but being kind to the person can make you act and feel good.

Zoraida thought her third statement of the theme best captured the meaning of the story. She reread the story with that theme in mind, and she decided the story in fact supported that theme. She did some freewriting about the theme of the story, then, using ideas from her freewriting and referring to the story for details, Zoraida made a chart of events in the story that communicate its theme. This is her chart:

Theme: Hating someone who's better at something than you are can make you act and feel bad, but being kind to the person can make you act and feel good.

Tobi becomes a poor sport	does not let Angela pass, even though her "conscience" tells her "to move over"; starts showing up late to workouts
Tobi stops being nice to others	ignores someone's shout and just hops on her bike and peddles away
Tobi feels bad	"I was miserable."
Tobi cheats and feels bad about doing this	walks on bottom to gain speed; later regrets having done so
Tobi's poor attitude affects her swimming skills	coach says, "your attitude is hurting your performance."
Tobi changes	sees Angela upset, "sitting with her back against the wall alone," after doing poorly in a heat, and realizes that "There's no worse anger than the kind you feel toward yourself when you've ruined something you care about."
Tobi shares her "confidence game" with Angela	"I think about all the good things I've done in my previous races . . . picturing myself the perfect swimmer"
Tobi becomes good sport again	she manages to give Angela "a congratulatory hug" when Angela wins

---

Drafting and Revising

Zoraida used her prewriting notes to make a rough outline. She began her rough draft with an introduction stating the title of the story, its author, and its theme. As she wrote, she kept her purpose in mind—to show how the story supported her statement of the theme. In the body of her paper she cited examples from the story and gave reasons for her interpretation of the theme. Finally, Zoraida concluded by restating the theme and commenting on it. When she finished her draft, Zoraida revised it carefully, paying attention to whether she had supported her topic sentence.

Proofreading and Publishing

Zoraida proofread her revised draft for errors. Then she made two copies, one for her English teacher and another for her writing folder.

ACTIVITIES AND ASSIGNMENTS

A. If you haven't already done so, read "The Confidence Game," on page 25. Then, using Zoraida's prewriting notes from the case study, write a one- or two-paragraph composition about the theme of the story. Follow these steps:

1. Add to Zoraida's notes any important details that were omitted.
2. Write a topic sentence that states the theme of "The Confidence Game."
3. Use Zoraida's prewriting notes and your additions to write your composition. Remember to refer to the story for details to support your topic sentence.
4. Write a concluding sentence that restates the theme; comment on the theme.
5. Revise your composition, using the Checklist for Revision on page 778. Then proofread for errors in spelling and mechanics, using the Checklist for Proofreading on page 780. Share your work with a classmate before giving it to your English teacher.

B. Choose one of the stories from the Theme section of your text, and write a paragraph or two about its themes. In your composition, explain how the story suggests that theme. Your purpose is to convince your reader that the story does, in fact, have the theme you think it has. Follow these steps:

1. Read the short story once. Write down possible themes. Remember to use a full sentence to state each theme. Think about your themes. Ask yourself which version of the theme best describes the significance of the story.
2. Reread the story. Then freewrite about the theme, asking yourself these questions: What do I mean by my statement of theme? What reasons in the story support my statement of the theme?
3. Make a chart of evidence from the story, supporting your statement of its theme.
4. Write a topic sentence that gives the name and author of the work and that states its theme.
5. Write several body sentences supporting your view of the theme by giving evidence from the story.
6. Write a concluding sentence that sums up and comments on the theme.
7. Revise your composition carefully. Add any important details you may have left out. Delete unnecessary or repeated words. Then copy over your revised composition and carefully proofread it.
8. Make a clean final copy. Share this copy with a classmate before giving it to your English teacher.

SECTION 3: UNDERSTANDING THE WORK AS A WHOLE: INTERPRETATION AND SYNTHESIS

Lesson 12: Writing About a Short Story

To write about a work as a whole, you must understand it thoroughly. You must consider each of its parts separately before you can interpret the meaning of the entire work. Here is a list of questions about the parts of a short story. After you have read a short story carefully, ask yourself the following questions:

1. *Author:* Who is the author of the story?
2. *Title:* What is the story's title? Does the title suggest the story's subject or theme?
3. *Setting:* What are the time and place of the story? What mood is created by the setting? Does the setting determine the action or conflict of the story?
4. *Point of view:* Is the story written from the first-person or third-person point of view? Is the narrator limited or omniscient?
5. *Central conflict:* What is the central conflict, or struggle, of the story? Is this conflict internal or external? If the conflict is external, is it a conflict between two people, between a person and nature, between a person and society, or between a person and a supernatural force?
6. *Plot:* What are the major events of the story? What happens in the introduction? What is the inciting incident? What happens during the development? What is the climax of the story? How is the central conflict resolved, or ended? What, if anything, happens after the resolution? That is, does the story have a denouement?

   What special plot devices are used in the story? Does the story make use of foreshad-

owing or flashbacks? Is the story suspenseful? If so, what expectations on the part of the reader create this suspense? Does the story have a surprise ending?

7. *Characterization:* Who is the main character, or protagonist? Who are the other major and minor characters? What is revealed in the story about each character's appearance, personality, background, motivations, and relationships? What conflicts do these characters face? Which of these characters change in the course of the story and in what ways? What roles do the minor characters play in advancing the action of the story?
8. *Devices of sound and figures of speech:* Does the story make use of special devices of sound such as onomatopoeia or parallelism? of figures of speech such as metaphor or hyperbole?
9. *Theme:* What is the theme, or message, of the story? How is this theme revealed?

In this lesson you will learn how to write a composition of several paragraphs that explains your interpretation of a short story. Your composition will have three main parts: an introduction, a body, and a conclusion. The introduction will include a thesis statement—a sentence that makes an important general point about the story. The body will give specific examples from the story that support the thesis statement. Your answers to the questions in the preceding list will provide these examples. Finally, the conclusion will restate the thesis statement and sum up the main point of your composition.

CASE STUDY: WRITING ABOUT A SHORT STORY

Dewayne's English teacher asked the class to write a three- or four-paragraph composition about a favorite short story. The composition was supposed to state the theme of the story and explain how other aspects of the story work to reveal the theme. Dewayne decided to write about Gwendolyn Brooks's "Home," on page 175.

Prewriting

To gather information for his composition, Dewayne answered the questions in the list. Here are his prewriting notes:

- Author: Gwendolyn Brooks

- Title: "Home." The title suggests the subject of the story.

- Setting: The time is the late afternoon. The place is the front porch of the characters' home. The mood created by the setting is one of comfort and familiarity. The setting does determine the conflict of the story—the members of the family do not want to leave their home.

- Point of view: third-person omniscient

- Central conflict: The three women struggle to hide their true feelings about moving from their home. The conflicts are internal.

- Plot:
  Introduction—The setting is described and the mood is established.
  Inciting incident—Papa is faced with getting an extension on his homeowner's loan (This event takes place before the opening scene of the story).
  Development—During the course of the conversation between Mama and the girls, their feelings about their home are revealed, and the reader realizes how important it is that Papa get the extension.
  Climax—Papa returns home, and he and Mama go inside to discuss what happened with the loan.
  Resolution—Mama comes back onto the porch and tells the girls that everything is fine.
  Denouement—Helen, relieved, says proudly that she wants to give a party so that her friends can see that her family owns a house.
  Special devices—Suspense is created by the reader's wondering whether the family will have to leave their home.

- Characterization: There are three main characters—Mama, Maud Martha, and Helen. Papa is a minor character. Mama and Helen are alike in their trying to act cheerful about the prospect of moving to a city flat. Maud Martha is less successful at hiding the way she really feels.

- Theme: The theme of the story is that people often try to hide painful feelings by saying things they don't mean.

Drafting and Revising

Dewayne used his prewriting notes and his rough outline to write a draft of his composition. Then he revised it carefully. His revised draft was clear and well organized.

Dewayne used his notes to make a rough outline of his composition:

- Introduction (paragraph 1): Include author, title, setting, and thesis statement. Thesis statement: "The theme of Gwendolyn Brooks's 'Home' is that people often deal with painful emotions by saying things they don't really mean."

- Body (paragraph 2): Explain how plot reveals theme. The plot revolves around the conversation on the porch. Thus the characterizations of Mama, Maud Martha, and

Helen through dialogue are essential to the story.

- Body (paragraph 3): Explain how point of view reveals theme. The narrator is omniscient and can describe the thoughts of the characters. Thus the narrator can reveal the contrast between the characters' words and their true feelings.

- Conclusion (paragraph 4): Restate thesis statement and sum up the main point(s) of the composition. Say that story has an important message that applies to real life.

Proofreading and Publishing

Dewayne made a clean copy of his revised draft. Then he proofread it for errors in grammar and usage, spelling, punctuation, capitalization, and manuscript form. When he was sure that he had corrected all his errors, he made a clean final copy of his composition and shared it with his classmates and with his teacher.

ACTIVITIES AND ASSIGNMENTS

A. Write a draft of a four-paragraph composition from the notes and the rough outline in the case study. Revise the draft, and then proofread it. Make a clean final copy of the composition and share it with a small group of your classmates.

B. Choose one of the following short stories for a three- or four-paragraph composition analy-sis: "The Confidence Game," on page 25; "A Boy and a Man," on page 37; "Amigo Brothers," on page 79; "All Summer in a Day," on page 107; "Utzel and His Daughter, Poverty," on page 149; or "A Season of Acceptance," on page 197. Follow these steps when planning and writing your composition:

1. Read the story carefully. In your prewriting notes, answer the questions listed in this lesson.
2. Write a thesis statement that tells the theme of the story.
3. Decide what important elements of the story—setting, point of view, conflict, plot, characterization, devices of sound, or figures of speech—support your thesis statement. Choose one or two of these elements to discuss in the body of your composition.
4. Make a rough outline showing how you will organize the information from your notes in the paragraphs of your composition.
5. Write a draft of your composition based on your outline. Be sure to include quotations from the story to support your points. Also make sure that your writing does not stray from its purpose, which is to support your thesis statement with evidence from the story.
6. Revise your draft using the Checklist for Revision on page 778. Then make a clean copy of the draft and proofread it. Make a final copy of your composition and share it with your classmates and with your teacher.

Lesson 13: Writing About a Poem

Before writing about a poem, you must understand it thoroughly. Poetry is often very compact—that is, it uses few words to express many ideas. Therefore, you must understand the meaning and significance of each word and phrase before you can write about the poem as a whole. Here is a list of steps you should follow when planning a composition about a poem:

1. Read the poem once, silently, and note any words you do not know. Look up these words in a dictionary and write down their definitions. Reread the poem with the definitions in mind.
2. Read the poem aloud, listening for any special devices of sound such as rhythm, rhyme, onomatopoeia, and alliteration.
3. Read the poem again, silently. This time pay close attention to the images and to the figures of speech in the poem.
4. Paraphrase the poem. That is, restate each sentence of the poem in your own words. As you do so, think not only about what is stated directly in the poem but also about what is suggested or implied.

   In your prewriting notes, answer the following questions about the poem:

1. *Author:* Who is the poem's author?
2. *Title:* What is the title of the poem? Does the title suggest the poem's subject or theme?
3. *Genre:* What is the poem's genre, or type? Is it a *lyric poem*—a highly musical work that expresses emotion? Is it a *narrative poem*—one that tells a story? Is it a *dramatic poem*—one that contains characters who speak dialogue? Is it a *concrete poem*—one with a shape that suggests its meaning?
4. *Stanza form:* Is the poem divided into stanzas? If so, how many lines does each stanza have? Is the poem written in some standard stanza form such as couplets, quatrains, sonnet form, haiku form, or limerick form? Does each stanza function as a separate unit of meaning, like a paragraph in a composition?
5. *Devices of sound:* Is the poem in free verse or in some regular meter? If the poem has a regular meter, how many feet are in an average line? What kind of foot is most common in the poem?

   Does the poem have a regular rhyme scheme, or pattern of rhyming words? If so, what is this rhyme scheme?

   Does the poem make use of onomatopoeia? alliteration? consonance? assonance? internal rhyme? euphony? cacophony? parallelism? repetition? Does it have a refrain? What examples can you find of these devices?
6. *Imagery:* Does the poem contain images of sight? of sound? of taste? of touch? of smell? What effects do these images have?
7. *Figures of speech:* Does the poem contain examples of metaphor? of simile? of personification? of hyperbole? Does the poet make use of symbols? allusions? irony? What effect is created by the figures of speech in the poem?
8. *Other literary devices:* What is the poem's general mood? Does this mood change in the course of the poem?

   What is the poem's setting? How is the setting related to the poem's mood? to the action of the poem?

   What seems to be the poem's central message, or theme? What do you think the writer's purpose was?

   Is the poem written in complete sentences?

Does the poem use punctuation, capitalization, or spacing in special ways? Are there any words not in the dictionary that the poet has created for some purpose?

Does the poem invite the reader to contrast two or more things?

9. *Questions about lyric poems:* What can you infer about the poem's speaker? Does the poem give you any hints about the speaker's background, situation, personality, emotional state, or views?

Is the speaker of the poem addressing anyone in particular? If so, whom? What can you infer about the relationship between the speaker and the speaker's audience?

10. *Questions about narrative and dramatic poems:* What can you infer about the main speaker of the poem? Is the poem told from the first-person or the third-person point of view?

How many characters appear in the poem? What can you infer about these characters? about the relationships between or among them?

Does this poem tell a story? If so, does this story involve a conflict? What is the plot of the poem?

If you have questions about any of the terms in the preceding list, refer to the Handbook of Literary Terms and Techniques on page 832.

CASE STUDY: WRITING ABOUT A POEM

Bob's English teacher asked the class to write a three- or four-paragraph composition about a poem. The composition was supposed to do two things:

1. state an important idea about the poem, and
2. give evidence from the poem that shows how the idea was expressed by the poet.

Bob decided to write about Vachel Lindsay's "The Flower-Fed Buffaloes," on page 488.

Prewriting

Bob knew that his first task was to understand the poem thoroughly. He began by reading the poem to himself. He then looked up the word *trundle* in a dictionary and found that it meant "to roll along."

Next Bob read the poem aloud and listened carefully for any devices of sound. Then he looked for examples of imagery and figurative language. He asked himself what the poem meant and *paraphrased,* or restated, the poem in his prewriting notes. Finally, he answered the questions from the lesson and added this information to his notes. Here is a section from Bob's notes:

- Author: Vachel Lindsay

- Title: "The Flower-Fed Buffaloes." The title suggests the subject and theme of the poem: Buffaloes were beautiful creatures, fed on flowers.

- Devices of sound: The poem is written in a regular meter. There are many rhyming words at the ends of lines—spring/sing, ago/low, and wheat/sweet.

   There are several examples of alliteration: "wheels *s*pin by/In the *s*pring that *s*till is *s*weet" and "*L*eft us, *l*ong ago . . . /*l*ying *l*ow." The alliteration of *l* sounds and the euphony throughout the poem create the effect of a lullaby—perhaps a gentle goodnight song to the buffaloes. The phrases *no more* and *lying low* are repeated for effect near the end of the poem.

- Images:
   Sight—buffaloes roaming about the prairie, grazing amidst flowers, grasses, and wheat fields.
   Sound—locomotive singing, buffaloes bellowing.
   Taste—none (What does a flower taste like?)
   Touch—grass tossing, wheels spinning, buffaloes trundling.
   Smell—"perfumed grass," "sweet" spring.

- Figures of speech: The poet describes locomotives as singing and prairie flowers as lying low. These personifications suggest that even the scenery "feels" the happy mood of the first part of the poem.

- Mood: The mood shifts from happy and carefree in the first part of the poem to sad in the last part. The setting—the prairie in springtime—helps to convey the joyful atmosphere in the first eight lines.

- Theme: The poet's purpose seems to be to express sadness over the fact that the buffaloes have disappeared from the prairie. He wants to keep the buffaloes from disappearing from people's memories as well.

Bob made the following rough outline from his prewriting notes.

- Introductory paragraph: Tell what poem I'm writing about—author and title. Include thesis statement: "The poem shows the sadness of the buffaloes' disappearance but allows the buffaloes to live on in people's memories."

- Body paragraph 1: Describe how devices of sound help to create moods of happiness and then sadness.

- Body paragraph 2: Describe how the images in the poem contribute to the contrasting moods in the poem.

- Concluding paragraph: Sum up mood of poem. Restate thesis statement in light of what I've written in the body paragraphs.

Drafting and Revising

Bob wrote a draft of his composition from his prewriting notes and his outline. Then he revised his work, adding more quotations from the poem to support his ideas.

Proofreading and Publishing

Bob made a fresh copy of his composition.

He proofread it for errors in spelling and mechanics. Then he made a clean final copy of his paper and read it aloud to the class.

ACTIVITIES AND ASSIGNMENTS

A. Using the notes and the rough outline from the case study, write a draft of Bob's composition. Feel free to add any important ideas that are missing from Bob's prewriting notes. Revise and proofread the composition. Then share it with your classmates and with your teacher.

B. Choose one of the following poems for a three- or four-paragraph composition: "Oranges," on page 459; "The Pheasant," on page 466; "The Pasture," on page 473; "The Courage That My Mother Had," on page 492; "In Just—," on page 500; "Season at the Shore," on page 508; "Mother to Son," on page 518; or "Father William," on page 525. Follow these steps in planning and writing your paper.

1. Follow the steps in this lesson for reading and thinking about the poem. List your questions and answers about the poem in your prewriting notes. Then look over your notes and decide what important point about the poem will be the main idea of your composition.

2. Make a rough outline showing how you will organize your information into three or four paragraphs.

3. Write a thesis statement that tells the main point of your composition. Include this thesis statement in the first paragraph, or introduction, of your rough draft.

4. Finish your draft according to your outline.

5. Revise your draft using the Checklist for Revision on page 778.

6. Make a clean copy of your revised draft, and proofread this copy for errors in grammar and usage, spelling, punctuation, capitalization, and manuscript form. Then make a final copy of your composition and share it with your friends and with your teacher.

Lesson 14: Writing About Drama

In many respects drama is like other forms of literature. Dramas have plots, conflicts, settings, and characters, as do short stories, novels, and narrative poems. They also express themes and make use of special literary devices such as imagery, sound, and figurative language. Therefore, when writing about dramas, you will use many of the same methods discussed in previous sections of this handbook.

However, drama differs from other types of literature in one very important respect. Dramas are intended to be performed before an audience, not merely to be read. When you read a drama, you should constantly imagine what it would be like to watch actors and actresses perform the drama. The characters should come alive in your mind as you imagine how they would move and speak on stage.

In its printed form, drama reflects the fact that it has been written to be performed. It is made up of dialogue and stage directions. Each line of *dialogue*—the words to be spoken by the actors—follows the name of the character who will speak it. When specific instructions are needed about how the play is to be performed, the writer gives *stage directions*. Stage directions give information about how the actors will move and speak; how the stage should look to the audience; what properties, or movable pieces, should be used by the actors; and what special effects of sound and lighting should be used during the production.

When writing about a drama, you can write about it solely as a work of literature, or you can write about it as a performance. The following are some possible approaches to writing about drama.

The Drama as Literature:
1. Choose a character who intrigues you, and write about how that character changes during the course of the drama.
2. Write an analysis of the plot of the drama. Explain the parts of the plot, including the introduction, the inciting incident, the development, the climax, the resolution, and the denouement.
3. Explain the theme of the drama, and relate this theme to other elements of the work that reveal the theme.

The Drama as Performance:
1. Choose a character who intrigues you, and write about how that character should be portrayed in an actual production.
2. Choose a scene from the drama, and write a description of a stage setting for that scene as it would be viewed from the audience.
3. Write a review of an actual performance of the drama. Comment on the quality of the acting, the set, the costumes, the lighting, and the sound.

CASE STUDY: WRITING ABOUT DRAMA

Kenneth's English class was asked to write a composition about a drama. Kenneth chose a play that he especially liked, *The Dying Detective,* on page 233.

Prewriting

To find a topic for his composition, Kenneth decided to do some freewriting:

> Reading this play was fun because I kept trying to figure out how or if Holmes was going to live. As literature, the play has wonderful suspense and a surprise ending. As performance, the setting might make the drama even better by adding to the suspense. Actually seeing Holmes pale and near death, getting sicker instead of healthier, adds to the already strong drama.

Kenneth read over his prewriting and found an interesting idea for his composition. He realized that he could write about how the visual elements of the performance—the stage set and what Holmes looks like—contribute to the effectiveness of the play.

Kenneth's next step was to draft a topic sentence. He wanted his topic sentence to express the main idea of his composition and to guide him in gathering more information for his writing. Here is the first draft of Kenneth's topic sentence:

> When I read *The Dying Detective,* by Michael and Mollie Hardwick based on a story by Sir Arthur Conan Doyle, I especially enjoyed the suspense and Sherlock Holmes's pale face and what the set looked like.

Kenneth read his topic sentence and realized that it would need to be revised for several reasons. First, the sentence was confusing. It wasn't at all clear whether he had actually seen the play or had merely read it. Second, the sentence was too specific—details such as "Holmes's pale face" should be saved for the body of the composition.

Kenneth decided that his main idea would best be stated in two sentences. He therefore wrote two introductory sentences, as follows:

> In *The Dying Detective,* by Michael and Mollie Hardwick from a story by Sir Arthur Conan Doyle, the literary and performance elements work well together. Suspense is created by the plot and reinforced by the setting and by Holmes's physical appearance.

Kenneth needed a plan of action for gathering information. First, he decided to do more freewriting about the plot. He wrote about all the major events in the plot and commented on those moments when the suspense was greatest. Second, he made a chart of information about the setting and about Holmes's physical appearance. In the first column he listed specific details from the drama about the setting and

about Holmes's appearance. In the second column he listed the impact each detail had on the reader or on the audience.

The last step in Kenneth's prewriting activities was to make a rough outline for his composition. Here is Kenneth's rough outline:

- Introductory paragraph: Tell what I'm going to write about in general. Include topic sentence.

- Body paragraph 1: Describe how the plot creates suspense.

- Body paragraph 2: Describe how the visual elements—the set and Holmes's appearance—add to the suspense created by the plot.

- Concluding paragraph: Sum up what I've written. Say that the drama is well worth reading or watching.

Drafting and Revising

Kenneth wrote a draft of his composition according to his outline. He included many specific details from the drama to support the points he wanted to make. Then he revised his draft so that it was clear and easy to read.

Proofreading and Publishing

Kenneth made a fresh copy of his revised draft and proofread it carefully. Then he made a final copy of his composition and read it aloud to a small group of his classmates before turning it in to his teacher.

ACTIVITIES AND ASSIGNMENTS

A. Using Kenneth's prewriting from the case study, write a composition about some aspect of *The Dying Detective,* on page 233. Follow these steps:

1. Read the drama carefully. Review Kenneth's introductory sentences and outline. You may decide to use these or you may decide to

choose a new topic and to develop your own notes, topic sentence, and outline. In either case, do some freewriting about the play to gather ideas for your composition.

2. Write a draft of your composition. Make sure that it has a clear introduction, body, and conclusion.

3. Revise your rough draft carefully, using the Checklist for Revision on page 778. Then make a clean copy and proofread it for errors in grammar and usage, spelling, punctuation, capitalization, and manuscript form. Refer to the Checklist for Proofreading on page 780.

4. Make a final copy of your composition, and share this copy with a small group of your classmates.

B. Write a three- or four-paragraph composition about *Grandpa and the Statue,* on page 219, or *The Monsters Are Due on Maple Street,* on page 247. Follow these steps when planning and writing your composition:

1. Read carefully the drama you have chosen. Review the possible approaches to writing about drama explained in this lesson. Then freewrite to find a specific topic for your composition.

2. Write a topic sentence that tells what your composition will be about. Do not include details from the drama in this sentence—keep the sentence general.

3. Do some more prewriting activities, such as charting or clustering, to gather ideas and information. Then make a rough outline that tells what information you will include in each paragraph of your composition.

4. Write a draft of your composition. Revise the draft using the Checklist for Revision on page 778. Make a clean copy of your revised draft and proofread it using the Checklist for Proofreading on page 780. Share the final copy of your composition with your classmates and with your teacher.

SECTION 4: JUDGING A LITERARY WORK: EVALUATION
Lesson 15: Evaluating a Literary Work

WHAT IS EVALUATION?

Imagine that your older brother, who knows that you have just finished reading Quentin Reynold's "A Secret for Two," on page 45, asks you what you thought of the story. If you merely reply, "I liked it," he will probably ask you, "Well, *why* did you like it?" Then you might say something like, "I thought the theme of the story was important. Also, the characters really came alive. I could relate to the way Pierre felt about his horse because of the way I feel about our dog." This is an *evaluation* of, or a judgment about, the short story.

An evaluation tells what you think is good—or bad—about a literary work. It is an opinion about the quality of the work, not a fact about it. A statement such as "This story is about a man and a horse" is a fact. The statement "This story's main character is easy to relate to" is an evaluation.

CRITERIA FOR EVALUATION

In the preceding example, "A Secret for Two" was evaluated according to two *criteria,* or standards: the importance of the theme and the characterization of Pierre. The following are some common criteria for evaluating literary works:

1. *Originality or inventiveness:* One quality often found in great literature is originality. Originality means dealing with a topic that has never been written about before or exploring a topic in a new and imaginative way. A work that lacks originality is trite or a cliché and probably will not get a favorable evaluation.

2. *Consistency or completeness of effect:* A literary work is usually aimed at creating a certain effect. For example, in "The Sneaker Crisis," on page 67, Shirley Jackson tries to create the effect of humor. The authors of *The Dying Detective,* on page 233, have tried to create the effect of suspense. Literature is often evaluated according to how well the author has achieved an effect. Consider the following haiku:

   1.   A dog walks up and
        Quickly licks a young boy's face
             And then disappears.

   2.   Bounding mass of fur
        Pink tongue on astonished cheek
             Grateful little boy

   Each of these poems describes the same incident involving a boy and a dog. However, in the first poem, the effect is spoiled by the word *walks,* which is vague and inappropriate. The word *bounding,* in the second poem, is more appropriate and contributes to the effect of the poem as a whole.

3. *Importance:* Some literary works are judged to be better than others because they deal with matters of greater importance. For example, Walt Whitman's poem "Miracles," on page 531, might be considered a greater work than either of the haiku in the previous example because it deals with a more serious topic—the wonder to be found in every aspect of life on earth.

4. *Moral or ethical message:* Sometimes literary works are evaluated according to the moral or ethical messages they convey. How a work will be evaluated depends on whether the

person evaluating the work agrees or disagrees with the message in the work. For example, a person who agrees with the statement "People shouldn't expect life to be easy" would probably have good things to say about Langston Hughes's poem "Mother to Son," on page 518.

5. *Clarity:* No matter what ideas an author wants to convey in a literary work, the work will not be evaluated favorably unless the author expresses them clearly. Clarity does not mean easiness—a work may be difficult without being unclear. However, an author cannot be careless when expressing ideas and still write great literature.

CASE STUDY: EVALUATING A LITERARY WORK

Janet's English teacher asked the class for advice in selecting the literature for next year's seventh-grade students. The teacher asked each student to select a work from the text and to write an evaluation of that work, telling why it should be included in next year's reading. Janet chose Shel Silverstein's poem "Sarah Cynthia Sylvia Stout Would Not Take the Garbage Out," on page 451.

Prewriting

To gather ideas for her evaluation, Janet tried freewriting about why she liked the poem. Here is Janet's freewriting:

> I love it! This is me! I hate to take the trash out, and my parents nag me all the time. This poet is the first one to make a joke out of something so usually grown-up serious as taking out the garbage. You can almost smell and feel the yucky junky accumulating garbage....

Janet now had a general idea of why she liked the poem. She was ready to choose some criteria for her evaluation. She looked at the list of criteria in this lesson and made the following addition to her prewriting notes:

- Originality: This is the first poem I've ever seen that deals with not taking the garbage out.

- Effect: The humorous effect is definitely achieved! Silverstein does this in three ways. First, the vivid images of the items in Sarah's trash make garbage seem funny and reminds the reader of his or her own messy garbage. Second, the poet uses hyperbole to exaggerate what might happen if one didn't take the garbage out for a really long time. Third, the poem has many instances of alliteration, which make the descriptions seem even funnier.

Next Janet made a chart listing specific examples from the poem to support her evaluation. Here is the first part of that chart.

LITERARY DEVICE AND EXAMPLES	EFFECT
Alliteration: b sounds throughout poem; "*black burned buttered toast*"	makes poem slide, just like oozing, creeping pile of garbage; descriptions seem even sillier
Images: "brown bananas"; "gloppy glumps of cold oatmeal"; "pizza crusts"; "greasy napkins"	reader can really imagine how the garbage looks, smells, and feels

Janet finished her chart and then made a rough outline for her evaluation.

Drafting and Revising

Janet wrote the first draft of her evaluation. First she wrote a topic sentence that introduced the title and author of the poem and the purpose of her writing—to explain why the poem should be used in next year's seventh-grade classes. Then she wrote the specific reasons why she thought the poem was a good one, giving examples from the poem to support her reasons. Finally, she wrote a concluding sentence that summed up the main point of her evaluation. She revised her draft carefully, making sure that all of her points were clear.

Proofreading and Publishing

Janet made a clean copy of her revised draft and proofread it. Then she shared the final copy of her evaluation with her class discussion group and with her teacher.

ACTIVITIES AND ASSIGNMENTS

A. Read "Sarah Cynthia Sylvia Stout Would Not Take the Garbage Out," on page 451. Then write an evaluation of the poem, using the prewriting notes in the case study. If you do not agree with any of Janet's main points, write your own reaction to the poem. Be sure that you can support your ideas with specific examples. Revise and proofread your draft, and share the final copy of your evaluation with a small group of your classmates.

B. Write an evaluation of one of the following works: "Zoo," on page 51; "The Sneaker Crisis," on page 67; "All Summer in a Day," on page 107; "Home," on page 175; *The Monsters Are Due on Maple Street,* on page 247; "A Time of Beginnings," on page 343; "The Night the Bed Fell," on page 363; "Endlessness," on page 387; "Annabel Lee," on page 455; "Fog," on page 468; "Feelings About Words," on page 486; "Stopping by Woods on a Snowy Evening," on page 504; or "I'm Nobody," on page 521. Follow these steps:

1. Read the work carefully. Then freewrite about why you liked or did not like the work. If there are elements that you like and others that you dislike in the work, write about both.
2. Ask yourself what criteria—originality, effect, importance, moral or ethical message, or clarity—could be applied to your chosen work. Then write in your notes whether the work fulfills each criterion.
3. Gather examples from the work to support your judgments. List these in a chart in your prewriting notes.
4. Make a rough outline for your paper. Then write a first draft of your evaluation.
5. Revise your draft, making sure that all of your main points are clear and that you have included specific examples from the work to support your statements.
6. Proofread your evaluation carefully. Then make a clean final copy of your paper, and share this copy with your classmates and with your teacher.

Lesson 16: Writing a Comparative Evaluation

WHAT IS A COMPARATIVE EVALUATION?

Imagine that a classmate of yours shows you two poems. After you have read the poems, your classmate asks you, "Which did you like better?" When you answer that question, supporting your opinion with evidence from the two poems, you are giving a *comparative evaluation.* You are evaluating both poems according to certain criteria, and you are making a judgment about which poem does a better job of meeting each criterion.

When choosing literary works to compare, you should not select two that are completely unlike each other. For example, you would probably not try to compare Shel Silverstein's poem "Sarah Cynthia Sylvia Stout Would Not Take the Garbage Out," on page 451, to James Baldwin's short story "Caleb's Brother," on page 119. One is a humorous poem, while the other is a serious short story. It is better to compare two works that have something in common, such as the same author, the same subject, the same form, or the same theme.

STEPS IN WRITING A COMPARATIVE EVALUATION

Your first step is to select two works to compare and to decide what feature of the works you will be comparing. List these in your notes as follows:

- Works to be compared: Quentin Reynold's short story "A Secret for Two," on page 45, and Paul Annixter's short story "Last Cover," on page 57.

- Feature to be compared: how a relationship between a human being and an animal is shown

The next step is to study each work and to make notes about the feature you are comparing. Decide which writer has done a better job of handling the feature, and list reasons why you think this is true.

When you write your composition, begin by explaining your topic and purpose in your introductory paragraph. Then write one paragraph about each of the works you are comparing. Finally, write a concluding paragraph that summarizes your reasons for believing one work is better than the other.

CASE STUDY: WRITING A COMPARATIVE EVALUATION

Eddie's English teacher asked the class to write a comparative evaluation of two poems by Robert Frost: "The Pasture," on page 473, and "Stopping by Woods on a Snowy Evening," on page 504.

Prewriting

Eddie began by reading both poems carefully. He read them silently and then aloud. Next he did some freewriting to gather ideas about why he liked one poem better than the other. Here is Eddie's freewriting:

> I like "The Pasture" better, I think—I like the way it invites me to join in the poem. I can picture the calf and the spring when the speaker says what he's going to do. The "Woods" poem is nice, too, but it's cold and lonely. Nature in that poem is silent and dark, not lively and inviting as in "The Pasture."

Next Eddie needed to gather information. He made the chart on page 819 to compare the literary elements in each poem.

LITERARY ELEMENT	"THE PASTURE"	"STOPPING BY WOODS ON A SNOWY EVENING"
Point of view	first person—speaking directly to reader	first person—addressed to no one in particular
Character	farmer	a person who enjoys nature
Setting	farm; farmer is about to do chores: clean spring, fetch newborn calf—farmer invites reader along	deep in the woods on a dark, snowy winter night; nobody around except speaker and his horse
Images	"watch the water clear"; touch images of mother cow licking calf and calf's tottering	tinkle of harness bells; sound of snowflakes falling; darkness; woods filling with snow
Subject	speaker describes how he enjoys nature and invites the reader to enjoy it with him	speaker tells about his own enjoyment of nature
Theme	nature is worth seeing and it's a thing to be shared	nature is lovely
Figures of speech	none	personification of horse "thinking"
Sound	repetition of last line of each stanza; lines 2 and 3 rhyme in each 2-line stanza; meter regular except for last line of each stanza	last line repeated twice; lines 1, 2, and 4 rhyme in each stanza except in last; line 3 rhymes with lines 1, 2, and 4 of next stanza; meter regular

Eddie needed to decide on two or three literary elements to serve as the criteria for his evaluation. Eddie knew that another student writing about the same two poems could evaluate them completely differently and say that "Stopping by Woods on a Snowy Evening" was the better poem. Therefore, he wanted to be sure that he could back up his judgment with plenty of facts about both poems. He chose the three elements he thought would best support his evaluation: subject, images, and setting.

Eddie made the following rough outline for his composition:

• Introductory paragraph:
  Give titles and authors of works to be compared.
  Tell what opinion about the works will be supported.
  Tell what criteria will be used.
• First body paragraph:
  Discuss "Stopping by Woods on a Snowy Evening":

Subject
Images
Setting
Give evaluation based on criteria.

- Second body paragraph:
  Discuss "The Pasture";
  Subject
  Images
  Setting
  Give evaluation based on criteria.

- Concluding paragraph:
  Sum up evaluation, say that "The Pasture" has a more friendly tone and is therefore more fun to read and easier to relate to.

Drafting and Revising

Eddie used his prewriting notes and his outline to write the first draft of his composition. Then he revised it several times, making sure that all of his main points were clear and were backed up with evidence from the poems.

Proofreading and Publishing

Eddie proofread his revised draft and made a clean final copy of his evaluation. He read his paper aloud to the class, and he and his classmates discussed their opinions of the two poems he had evaluated.

ACTIVITIES AND ASSIGNMENTS

A. Read "The Pasture," on page 473, and "Stopping by Woods on a Snowy Evening," on page 504. Then, using the prewriting notes and the rough outline in the case study, write a draft of Eddie's evaluation. Revise and proofread your paper carefully, and discuss the evaluation with a small group of your classmates. In your discussion, give reasons why you agree or disagree with Eddie's judgment.

B. Write a comparative evaluation based on one of the following pairs of literary works: "The Bat," on page 472, and "Seal," on page 475; "The Courage That My Mother Had," on page 492, and "Mother to Son," on page 518; or "All Summer in a Day," on page 107, and "The Third Level," on page 127. Follow these steps:

1. Read the works carefully. Then freewrite about why you liked one better than the other.
2. Set up a comparison chart like the one in the case study, and fill in this chart with specific information from the two works.
3. Sum up your opinion about the works in a sentence or two, stating why you like one better than the other. Then choose two or three criteria you think best support your opinion.
4. Make an outline for your composition like the one in the case study. Then write a draft of your evaluation, including many specific examples from the works to support your main points.
5. Revise your draft, making sure that all of your ideas are expressed clearly. Then proofread your composition for errors in spelling and mechanics.
6. Share the final copy of your evaluation with a small group of your classmates who wrote about the same two works that you did. Discuss the reasons why your evaluations were similar or different. Then share your evaluation with your teacher.

SECTION 5: WRITING CREATIVELY
Lesson 17: Writing a Short Story

FINDING A STORY IDEA

Short stories contain many elements, such as setting, conflict, plot, character, point of view, and theme. Brainstorming about any of these elements can lead to an idea for a story. The following are some ways to find an interesting idea for a short story:

1. Think of a time and a place that interest you. The place might be a real one—a place you have visited or would like to visit—or it might be an imaginary one, such as an Earth colony on another planet in the distant future.

2. Think of a conflict that interests you. You might pick an external conflict, such as an argument between two people, or an internal conflict, such as one person's struggle to make an important decision.

3. Think of an interesting person whom you know. Create a character who is like this person in some way.

4. Think of an important idea or belief that you would like others to think about. Make this idea the theme of your short story, and try to think of a situation in which the idea might be tested or shown to be true. This situation will be the basis of the plot of your short story.

DEVELOPING YOUR IDEA

Once you have an idea for one part of your story, you must develop the other parts. To do this, answer the following questions:

1. *Setting:* When does the action of the story occur? Where does the story take place? What images of sight, sound, touch, taste, and smell can I use to describe this place?

2. *Character:* Who is the main character in the story? What is the character's name? How does this character look, act, and talk? What is this character's personality like? What kind of background does this character have? What is this character's relationship to other characters? What does this character love and hate? Will the character change in the course of the story? Will there be one major character with whom this character is in conflict? Will there be other major and minor characters in the story? What will each of these characters be like? What roles will they play in the story? How will they be related to the main character?

3. *Conflict:* What will be the central conflict that the main character is involved in? Will this conflict be within the character's own mind? Will it be a conflict between the character and some outside force, such as nature, another person, or society?

4. *Plot.* What events will occur in the story, and in what order?

    Introduction: What background information will you need to supply about the setting? about the characters?

    Inciting incident: What event will introduce the central conflict of the story?

    Development: What events will occur as a result of the central conflict? How will this conflict develop?

    Climax: What will be the high point of interest or suspense in the story?

    Resolution: What event will resolve, or end, the conflict?

    Denouement: What, if anything, will happen after the conflict is resolved?

5. *Theme:* What will be the central point, or insight, of the story? How will the insightful idea be revealed?

6. *Point of view:* Will the story be told by one of the characters or by an outside narrator? That is, will it be told from the first-person or the third-person point of view? Will the narrator be limited or omniscient?

DRAFTING YOUR STORY

Use your answers to the preceding questions to write your story. Begin with an introduction that grabs the attention of the reader. Then describe the events of the story in the order in which they happen. Be sure to use lots of specific details to keep the story interesting. Develop suspense by keeping the reader wondering what will happen next. If you like, you may use special literary techniques such as foreshadowing, flashbacks, and a surprise ending.

CASE STUDY: WRITING A SHORT STORY

Todd's English teacher asked the class to write a short story. Todd decided to try brainstorming in order to come up with an idea for his story. Here is a section from his prewriting notes:

- Setting: the beach in summer; my living room; the school playground; this year; a sunny day; far in the future; the planet Venus

- Conflict: don't want to leave the beach but my parents say I have to; bored to death and don't know what to do; competing to make the softball team; aliens are attacking the planet

- Character: myself; my little sister; Rudy, my best friend; Cesar, my next-door neighbor; a kid from Venus; a pro basketball player; a race car driver

Todd looked over his brainstorming notes and decided to set his story in his living room

because this setting was familiar to him. He decided to create an internal conflict in which his main character struggles against boredom on a rainy afternoon. There would be two major characters in the story, one based on himself and the other based on his best friend, Rudy. He named these characters Jeremy and Raoul. One minor character in Todd's story would be Jeremy's mother.

Todd made the following notes about the events that would take place in his story:

- Inciting incident: Jeremy and Raoul have nothing to do. It's winter, cold and wet outside, so they want to stay indoors and find something to do in Jeremy's living room.

- Conflict: The conflict is really internal. Both boys want to think of something fun and interesting to do. They are both irritable, though, and blame each other for not coming up with any good ideas.

- Development: The boys discuss various ideas but can't agree on anything. They are growing more and more annoyed with each other.

- Climax: Jeremy and Raoul have a big argument about how the other one never has any good ideas for anything to do. They wrestle on the floor of the living room, almost knocking over one of Jeremy's mother's favorite vases. Jeremy's mother comes into the room and says that if the boys do not settle down, Raoul will have to go home. They decide to read the newspaper to see if anything interesting is going on in the rest of the world.

- Resolution: The boys start talking about how much fun it would be to work on a newspaper. One of them suggests that they start their own newspaper to report about life in their school and in their town. Their problem is solved, and they begin making plans excitedly.

Drafting and Revising

Todd used his prewriting notes to write a draft of his short story. Then he revised his story, adding more dialogue and specific details to make it more interesting and vivid.

Proofreading and Publishing

Todd made a fresh copy of his story and proofread it for errors in spelling and mechanics. He made two final copies and submitted one to his English teacher and the other to his school literary magazine.

ACTIVITIES AND ASSIGNMENTS

A. Use Todd's prewriting notes in the case study to write the short story that he planned. Revise the story, adding more specific details where necessary. Then proofread the story and share your final copy with your classmates and your teacher.

B. Write an original short story. Follow these steps:

1. Use the guidelines for brainstorming in this lesson to find an interesting idea for your story. When you have decided on an idea for one part of your story, develop the other parts by answering the questions listed in this lesson.

2. Use your notes to write a rough draft of your story. Begin with a brief introduction of the setting and the characters. Then tell the events of the plot in the order in which they happen. Make sure that by the end of your story the central conflict has been resolved.

3. Revise your draft, adding details and dialogue where necessary to make your story more interesting and fun to read.

4. Proofread your story for errors in grammar and usage, spelling, punctuation, capitalization, and manuscript form. Then share the final copy of your story with your classmates and with your teacher.

Lesson 18: Writing a Poem

There are many kinds of poems and many ways to go about writing them. In this lesson you will learn about three simple verse forms. Then you will have the chance to write some verses of your own.

THREE VERSE FORMS

1. *Haiku:* The haiku is a form of verse that originated in Japan. The purpose of a haiku is to capture a brief moment and to describe it vividly to the reader. A haiku usually contains images of sight, sound, touch, taste, or smell that help the reader to experience the subject of the poem.

   A haiku consists of three unrhymed lines. The first and third lines have five syllables and the second line has seven syllables. The following is an example of haiku:

> The falling flower
> I saw drift back to the branch
> Was a butterfly.
> —Moritake

Notice how the author has used the visual image of a falling flower to describe the movement of a fluttering butterfly. As you read the poem, count the syllables in each line. You will see that this haiku follows the 5–7–5 pattern.

2. *Concrete poems:* A concrete poem is one whose words are arranged on the page to form a visual picture. The shape of a concrete poem often is related to the poem's subject. William Jay Smith's poem "Seal," on page 475, is a concrete poem. Its shape reminds the reader of the slippery, fluid motion of a seal.

3. *Couplets:* A couplet is a pair of rhymed lines. The lines in a couplet usually have the same number of beats, or stresses, and usually have a similar rhythm. Many poems are made up of couplets. For example, Robert P. Tristam Coffin's "The Pheasant," on page 466, is composed of couplets:

> A pheasant cock sprang into view,
> A living jewel, up he flew.

Notice the rhyming words at the end of the lines in the couplet. Read the lines aloud and listen for the rhythmical pattern in each line. You will hear the patterns are similar for each of the lines in the couplet.

CASE STUDY: WRITING A POEM

Joel's English teacher asked the class to write a poem in one of the verse forms they had studied in this lesson.

Prewriting

Joel needed to think of a topic for his poem. He brainstormed for five minutes, writing all the ideas he could think of on a piece of paper. Then he selected the idea he liked best: *Games My Dad and I Used to Play.* Joel remembered that his father used to help him to fall asleep by making him laugh. He decided that the topic of his poem would be the game he called "Mr. Pillow-Head." He then wrote details in his prewriting notes about how the game was played.

Next Joel needed to decide what form of verse he would use for his poem. He knew that he could not describe the game in only three lines, so he would not write a haiku. He considered writing a concrete poem, but he did not think that arranging the poem in the shape of a pillow would add much to its meaning. He decided that he would write a poem in couplets.

Drafting and Revising

Joel wrote the following first draft of his poem:

> There were times when I was small
> When I couldn't sleep at all.
> I'd lie awake in bed
> 'Til Dad came in and said,
> "Why can't you get to sleep?
> Have you tried counting sheep?"
> "Yes, Dad," I'd say, and then
> It was that time again.
> He'd take my pillow, turn away,
> Then reappear, and next he'd say
> As I was laughing 'til I was red,
> "Hello! I'm Mr. Pillow-Head."
> When that was done, he'd tuck me in
> And I'd fall asleep, my face in a grin.

Joel read his poem aloud, listening to the rhythmical pattern of the lines. Then he revised his poem, changing some words to make it flow more easily. He also added more vivid adjectives and verbs.

Proofreading and Publishing

Joel made a clean copy of his poem and proofread it for errors in spelling and punctuation. Then he made two final copies of his poem, one for his father and one for his teacher.

ACTIVITIES AND ASSIGNMENTS

A. Revise Joel's poem, making any necessary changes to smooth the rhythm. Also add some more vivid adjectives and verbs to describe the action of the poem. Make a clean copy of the poem and proofread it carefully. Then share your final copy with a small group of your classmates, and discuss the changes that they made in Joel's poem.

B. Write a poem of your own. Decide what verse form you would like to use, then follow one of the following sets of directions.

Haiku:

1. Choose a scene or an event you would like to describe in a haiku. Make a list of images related to that scene or event in your prewriting notes.
2. Make a list of vivid adjectives and verbs that describe the subject of your haiku. If you would like to use a figure of speech—a simile, metaphor, personification, or hyperbole— write down ideas for these in your notes also.
3. Write several versions of each line of the haiku. Make sure that the syllable count is 5–7–5.
4. Select the version of each line that is the most descriptive and that goes best with the other lines of the haiku.

Concrete poem:

1. Choose a subject that could easily be represented by a simple shape.
2. Make a list of images that describe the subject of your poem.
3. Write a description of your subject using the images from your list.
4. Arrange the words of your description on a page to form a picture of your subject.

Couplets:

1. Choose a subject that you can describe in a few short lines.
2. Describe your subject in one to three sentences.
3. Choose a few sets of rhyming words that will fit into your description.
4. Rewrite your sentences in verse form, inserting your rhyming words so that they fall at the ends of the lines in your poem.
5. Rewrite your lines as necessary so that both lines in each couplet contain the same number of beats, or stresses.

When you have finished drafting your poem, read it aloud and listen to how it sounds. Revise it as necessary to make it sound the way you would like it to. Proofread your poem and share your final copy with your classmates and with your teacher.

Lesson 19: Writing a Short Dramatic Sketch

A *dramatic sketch* is a short scene that makes a single point. The purpose of the scene may be to convey an important message or merely to make the audience laugh; that is, a dramatic sketch may be serious or comic.

ELEMENTS OF A DRAMATIC SKETCH

A dramatic sketch is written in the same form as a full-length drama. It is made up of dialogue and stage directions. *Dialogue,* or the words spoken by each character in the sketch, follows the names of the characters who speak it. The characters' names are written in capital letters. The following is a line of dialogue from *A Christmas Carol: Scrooge and Marley:*

> SCROOGE. Remember it! I would know it blind-folded! My bridge, my church, my winding river!

Stage directions are notes that tell important details such as what the setting of the sketch should look like, what special effects of lighting or sound should be used, and how the characters should move and speak. They appear in square brackets or parentheses and are itali-cized or underlined. Note the stage directions in this passage from *The Dying Detective:*

> HOLMES. [*Cheerfully.*] The best way of success-fully acting a part is to *be* it. I give you my word that for three days I have neither tasted food nor drink until you were good enough to pour me out that glass of water. But it's the tobacco I find most irksome.
>
> [*We hear the thud of footsteps running upstairs off-stage.*]
>
> Hello, hello! Do I hear the step of a friend?

[INSPECTOR MORTON *hurries in.*]

PLANNING A DRAMATIC SKETCH

Before you begin writing a dramatic sketch, you need to decide whether your sketch will be serious or comic, what its setting will be, what characters will be involved, and what events will take place.

When you plan your setting, keep in mind the fact that when the sketch is performed, the set will have to be constructed on a stage. It is easier to build a set that looks like a living room than to build one that looks like the view from a mountain peak! In your prewriting notes, list the time and place where your sketch will occur. Then write down important details about the setting that will be essential to the action of the sketch.

Next, make a list of the characters that will participate in the action of your sketch, and describe each of them briefly. Make note of the way you want each character to look, move, and speak.

Finally, make a list of the events that will occur in your sketch. Make sure that the sketch has a definite beginning, middle, and end.

WRITING THE SKETCH

Begin your sketch with a title and a list of characters. Then use stage directions to de-scribe, briefly, the setting of the sketch. After these stage directions, begin the dialogue of the characters.

As you write the dialogue, insert stage direc-tions wherever necessary to tell how the charac-ters should move or speak. You don't need to describe every single action in detail or tell how every line should be spoken. Include stage directions only when they are necessary to understand the action of the sketch. However, it is important always to indicate when characters enter and exit the stage.

When writing dialogue, it is a good idea to stop from time to time and read the lines aloud. Make sure that your dialogue sounds natural and believable.

CASE STUDY: WRITING A SHORT DRAMATIC SKETCH

Laura's English teacher asked the class to write a short dramatic sketch based on one of Aesop's fables. Laura decided to use "The Fox and the Crow," on page 547.

Prewriting

Laura read the fable several times and tried to imagine seeing it performed on stage. To gather information about what each character would be like, she made the following prewriting notes:

FOX:

- Appearance: red fur; wears black and yellow plaid pants, black high-top sneakers, black suspenders; smiles a lot, showing gleaming white teeth

- Personality: sly; sneaky; a smooth talker; smart

- Speech: an enthusiastic speaker; strong, smooth voice

CROW:

- Appearance: shiny black feathers; wears a yellow bonnet

- Personality: flirtatious; vain

- Speech: speaks slowly and carefully; uses formal language

Next Laura made a chart to list details about the setting of her sketch:

- Time: a fall day

- Place: a country road

- Lighting: afternoon sun

- Other details: The action occurs at a large oak tree on which the crow is perched.

- Properties: cheese

In her prewriting notes, Laura listed, in order, the events that would take place in her sketch. She organized the events into a beginning, a middle, and an end, as follows:

- Beginning:
  The fox strolls down a country road, wondering how he can get something to eat.
  The fox spots the crow in the tree with cheese in her beak.
  The fox gets an idea.

- Middle:
  The fox flatters the crow and asks her to sing.
  The crow starts to sing and drops the cheese on the ground.
  The fox grabs the cheese and eats it happily.

- End:
  The fox tells the crow, "Do not trust flatterers."

Drafting and Revising

Laura wrote the title of her sketch at the top of her page, and below it she listed the cast of characters with a brief description of each. Then she wrote a description of the setting in brackets and underlined it.

Next, Laura wrote the dialogue of her sketch, adding stage directions wherever she wanted to describe particular movements or ways of speaking by the characters. When she had finished her draft, she read the dialogue aloud and revised it to make it sound more natural.

Proofreading and Publishing

Finally, Laura proofread her dramatic sketch and made a clean final copy of it. This she shared with her teacher, who suggested that Laura plan a performance of the sketch for the class.

ACTIVITIES AND ASSIGNMENTS

A. Using the prewriting notes from the case study, write a short dramatic sketch based on "The Fox and the Crow." Follow the same steps that Laura did in the case study. When you have finished the first draft of the sketch, revise and proofread it carefully. Then make a clean final copy of your sketch, and share this copy with your classmates and with your teacher.

B. Write your own short dramatic sketch based on one of the following works: "The Town Mouse and the Country Mouse," on page 545; "The Boy and the Wolf," on page 553; "Prometheus, the Fire-Bringer," on page 563; "Baucis and Philemon," on page 577; or "Narcissus," on page 585. Follow these steps:

1. Select one of the works and read it carefully. Try to imagine what it would be like to see the story acted out on a stage.

2. Make a chart in your prewriting notes to gather information about the characters in your sketch. Fill in the chart with details about how each character should look, act, and speak.

3. List in your notes the important details about the setting of your sketch. Be sure to include a list of the properties, or movable objects, that will appear on stage.

4. List the events that will take place in the sketch. Make sure that your sketch has a beginning, a middle, and an end.

5. Write the title and the list of characters at the top of your page. Then use stage directions to describe the setting of the sketch.

6. Write the dialogue of your sketch. Include stage directions whenever you want to indicate a special effect of lighting or sound or to tell how a character should move or speak.

7. Revise your draft, making sure that all of the dialogue sounds natural. Then proofread your revised draft for errors in grammar and usage, spelling, punctuation, and capitalization.

8. Make a clean final copy of your dramatic sketch, and share this copy with your teacher. If you wish to do so, you could suggest that the sketch be performed for the class.

Lesson 20: Writing a Personal Essay

The purpose of a *personal essay* is to share your thoughts and experiences with others. Writing a personal essay is similar to writing a composition about literature in several ways. First, you use the writing process—prewriting, drafting, revising, proofreading, and publishing. Second, you have a main idea that you support with evidence. Third, your essay has an introduction, a body, and a conclusion.

However, a personal essay differs from the compositions that you have written in other parts of this handbook in one very important way. The evidence that you use to support your main idea does not come from literary works but from your own experiences and ideas. A personal essay allows you to share a part of your life with your readers. The topic of such an essay should be something especially important or meaningful to you.

Once you have decided on a topic for your essay, you must decide what your purpose in writing about that topic will be. You might want to tell a story, to describe something, to explain something, or to persuade people to believe or to do something. Your purpose will determine what techniques you will use when writing your essay.

When you know the topic and the purpose of your essay, you should write a thesis statement that tells both of these. The following are examples of thesis statements for different types of essays:

1. *Narrative essay:* Last Thanksgiving I had a very funny experience at my grandmother's house.
2. *Descriptive essay:* The mountains of Vermont are among the most beautiful in the world.
3. *Expository essay:* Learning how to perform tricks with a yo-yo can be easy if you know the proper technique.

4. *Persuasive essay:* The school cafeteria should not raise the price of milk for students.

To gather information to support your thesis statement, use techniques such as freewriting, clustering, questioning, and making lists or charts. In some cases it is helpful to conduct interviews. If you are writing a narrative essay, you could make a time line of the events you will write about. If you are writing a descriptive essay, you could list all the images of sight, sound, touch, taste, and smell that describe your subject. For an expository essay, try listing all the steps or parts of the thing that you are explaining. To gather evidence for a persuasive essay, make a chart listing the pros and cons of the idea that you are trying to convince your readers to accept.

CASE STUDY: WRITING A PERSONAL ESSAY

Adam was asked by his English teacher to write a personal essay about a place that was especially meaningful to him.

Prewriting

Adam needed to think of a place to write about. To gather ideas for topics, he listed all the familiar places he could think of:

Grandma's living room
my bedroom
the alley behind my house
the school baseball diamond
the local swimming pool
the public library
the amusement park we visited last summer

Adam decided to write about his own room. The purpose of his essay would be to describe his room. To collect ideas about why his room was special to him, he used the questioning technique. He listed the following questions in his prewriting notes:

> What people do I associate with my room?
> What does my room look like?
> What events do I associate with my room?
> What objects do I associate with my room?

Then Adam answered the questions:

> I think of having friends visit—we play Monopoly or write stories or just talk. I love the desk in the corner against my wall. I especially think of the bottom drawer in my chest where I keep all my letters from friends—they're nice to reread when I feel lonely. I like to look out the window at the lawn of the library next door—in different seasons I see different things. Sometimes I just do nothing—stretch out on my bed. When I close my door, nobody can enter without knocking—privacy!

Next Adam wrote several possible topic statements for his essay. Here are the sentences that he considered:

> I like my room a lot.
> I'm happy in my room.
> My room is important to me because there I feel a wonderful sense of privacy.

Adam was pleased with his third topic sentence because it told the main idea of his essay. The evidence he had collected in his prewriting would support this main idea.

Adam's next step was to make a rough outline. He wanted to organize his information into an introduction, a body, and a conclusion for his essay. Here is Adam's rough outline:

- Introduction: State place and briefly tell what it means.
- Body: Provide specific examples to show the reader what the place means.
- Conclusion: Restate main idea and say something interesting about it.

Drafting and Revising

Adam used his notes and his outline to write a draft of his essay. Then he revised the draft. Here is Adam's draft with his revisions marked in standard editorial symbols:

Proofreading and Publishing

Adam made a clean copy of his essay and proofread it for errors in spelling and mechanics. Then he shared his essay with his friends and with his teacher.

ACTIVITIES AND ASSIGNMENTS

A. Answer the following questions about the case study:

1. What changes did Adam make in his topic sentence? How did these changes make it a better topic sentence?
2. What run-on sentence did Adam correct when he revised his essay? What sentence fragment?
3. Where did Adam change a sentence in which the language was too informal?
4. What spelling errors did Adam correct?
5. Where did Adam combine sentences to make his writing smoother?
6. What other changes did Adam make? Why did he make them?

B. Write your own personal essay about a place that is important to you. Your purpose will be to describe the place and to show why it is significant to you. Follow these steps when planning and writing your essay:

1. Think of a place that is special to you. Try brainstorming to gather possible ideas.
2. To gather information about the place you have chosen to write about, try any of the following prewriting techniques: freewriting, clustering, analyzing, questioning, or making charts or lists.
3. Write a topic sentence that tells the main idea of your essay. Make sure that the information you have gathered during prewriting supports this main idea.
4. Make a rough outline for the rest of your essay. Organize your information under three headings: introduction, body, and conclusion.
5. Write a draft of your essay according to your outline.
6. Revise your essay. Make sure that all your ideas are clear and are supported by specific information about your special place.
7. Proofread your essay using the Checklist for Proofreading on page 780. Then make a clean final copy, and share this copy with your classmates and with your teacher.

HANDBOOK OF LITERARY TERMS AND TECHNIQUES

ALLITERATION *Alliteration* is the repetition of initial consonant sounds. Writers use alliteration to create musical effects and to draw attention to certain words or ideas. Shel Silverstein uses alliteration for humorous effect in the title of his poem "*Sarah Cynthia Sylvia Stout*," on page 451. In the following lines from "Who Has Seen the Wind," Christina Rossetti uses alliteration to imitate the sound of the wind:

> *Who h*as seen the wind
> Neither you nor I:
> But *wh*en the trees bow down their heads
> The *w*ind is passing by.

In "The Highwayman," on page 437, Alfred Noyes uses alliteration to imitate the sound of horseshoes on a stone pavement:

> Over the *c*obbles he *c*lattered and
>   *c*lashed in the dark innyard.

ALLUSION An *allusion* is a reference to a well-known person, place, event, literary work, or work of art. Understanding what a writer is saying often depends on recognizing allusions. E.E. Cummings's "goat-footed balloonman" in the poem "In Just—," on page 500, is an allusion to Greek myths about the god Pan. Pan was a goat-footed god associated with spring.

ANAPEST See *Meter.*

ANECDOTE An *anecdote* is a brief story about an interesting, amusing, or strange event. Writers tell anecdotes for specific reasons. For example, in "Cat on the Go," on page 351, James Herriot tells several anecdotes about the character named Oscar. Herriot tells these anecdotes to amuse the reader and to reveal Oscar's unusual personality.

ANTAGONIST An *antagonist* is a character or force in conflict with a main character, or protagonist. In "Rikki-tikki-tavi," on page 13, there are two antagonists, the cobras Nag and Nagaina. The protagonist is the mongoose, Rikki.
See *Conflict* and *Protagonist.*

ATMOSPHERE See *Mood.*

AUTOBIOGRAPHY *Autobiography* is a form of nonfiction in which a person tells his or her own life story. This text contains several excerpts from autobiographies, including the selections from Ernesto Galarza's *Barrio Boy,* on page 337, and from Jade Snow Wong's *Fifth Chinese Daughter,* "A Time of Beginnings," on page 343.

Because autobiographies are about real people and events, they are a form of nonfiction. The best autobiographies contain many elements of short stories, including plots, settings, and characters. Most autobiographies, including *Barrio Boy,* are written in the first person. However, a few autobiographies, like *Fifth Chinese Daughter,* are written in the third person.
See *Biography, Nonfiction,* and *Point of View.*

BALLAD A *ballad* is a songlike poem that tells a story, often one dealing with adventure and romance. Most ballads are written in four- to six-line stanzas and have regular rhythms and rhyme schemes. A ballad often features a refrain—a regularly repeated line or group of lines.

The following stanza is from the traditional English ballad "Willie O'Winsbury":

> The king has called on his merry men all,
> By thirty and by three,
> Saying, "Fetch me this Willie O'Winsbury,
> For hanging he shall be."

Originally, ballads were not written down. They were composed orally and then sung. As these early *folk ballads* passed from singer to singer, they often changed dramatically. As a result, folk ballads usually exist in many different forms.

Many writers of the modern era have used the ballad form to create *literary ballads*—written imitations of folk ballads. The influence of the ballad tradition can be seen in Alfred Noyes's "The Highwayman," on page 437. While Noyes's poem is not written in typical ballad form, it does tell a story of adventure in rhyming stanzas.

See *Oral Tradition* and *Refrain.*

BIOGRAPHY   *Biography* is a form of nonfiction in which a writer tells the life story of another person. Examples from the text include "Eugenie Clark and the Sleeping Sharks," on page 319, and "Winslow Homer: America's Greatest Painter," on page 395. Because biographies deal with real people and real events, they are classified as nonfiction.

See *Autobiography* and *Nonfiction.*

BLANK VERSE   *Blank verse* is poetry written in unrhymed iambic pentameter lines. The following lines from Robert Frost's "Birches" are written in blank verse:

When I see birches bend to
   left and right
Across the lines of straighter
   darker trees,
I like to think some boy's
   been swinging them.

See *Meter.*

CHARACTER   A *character* is a person or animal who takes part in the action of a literary work. The *main character* is the most important character in a story, poem, or play. A *minor character* is one who takes part in the action but who is not the focus of attention. In Pearl Buck's "The Old Demon," on page 155, the main character is Mrs. Wang. Her grandson and his wife are minor characters.

Characters are sometimes classified as flat or round. A *flat character* is one-sided and often stereotypical. A *round character,* on the other hand, is fully developed and exhibits many traits—often both faults and virtues. In O. Henry's "After Twenty Years," on page 205, both Patrolman Wells and "Silky" Bob are flat characters. In Pat Carr's "The Confidence Game," on page 25, Tobi, the main character, is round, or fully developed.

Characters can also be classified as dynamic or static. A *dynamic character* is one who changes in the course of the work. A *static character* is one who does not change. Tobi is a dynamic character. Patrolman Wells and "Silky" Bob are static characters.

See *Characterization, Hero/Heroine,* and *Motivation.*

CHARACTERIZATION   *Characterization* is the act of creating and developing a character. Writers use two major methods of characterization—direct and indirect.

When describing a character *directly,* a writer simply states the character's traits, or characteristics. In "A Secret for Two," on page 45, Quentin Reynolds describes Jacques directly, saying, "Jacques was a kind man."

When describing a character *indirectly,* a writer depends on the reader to draw conclusions about the character's traits. Sometimes the writer describes the character's appearance, actions, or speech. At other times the writer tells what other participants in the story say and think about the character. The reader then draws his or her own conclusions.

See *Character* and *Motivation.*

CINQUAIN   See *Stanza.*

CLIMAX   See *Plot.*

CONCRETE POEM   A *concrete poem* is one with a shape that suggests its subject. The poet arranges the letters, punctuation, and lines to create an image, or picture, on the page. William Jay Smith's "Seal," on page 475, is a concrete poem. Its swirling shape suggests the form of a seal's body and the way the seal moves.

CONFLICT   A *conflict* is a struggle between opposing forces. Conflict is one of the most important elements of stories, novels, and plays because it causes the action.

There are two kinds of conflict: external and internal. An *external conflict* is one in which a character struggles against some outside force. For example, in "A Boy and a Man," on page 37, the character Rudi struggles against nature to save the life of a man who has fallen into a crevasse.

An *internal conflict* is one that takes place within the mind of a character. The character struggles to make a decision, take an action, or overcome a feeling. For example, in "The Confidence Game," on page 25, the character Tobi struggles with her feelings of anger and jealousy toward her rival, Angela.
See *Plot.*

COUPLET   See *Stanza.*

DACTYL   See *Meter.*

DENOUEMENT   See *Plot.*

DESCRIPTION   A *description* is a portrait, in words, of a person, place, or object. Descriptive writing uses images that appeal to the five senses—sight, hearing, touch, taste, and smell. See *Image.*

DEVELOPMENT   See *Plot.*

DIALECT   A *dialect* is the form of a language spoken by people in a particular region or group. The English language is divided into many dialects. British English differs from American English. The English spoken in Boston differs from that spoken in Charleston, Chicago, Houston, or San Francisco. This variety adds richness to the language. Dialects differ in pronunciation, grammar, and word choice.

Writers use dialects to make their characters seem realistic. In the following selection from Lucille Clifton's "The Luckiest Time of All," on page 75, the character speaking uses a dialect from the rural Southern United States:

It was just this time, spring of the year, and me and my best friend Ovella Wilson, who is now gone, was goin to join the Silas Greene. Usta be a kinda show went all through the South, called it the Silas Greene show. Somethin like the circus. Me and Ovella wanted to join that thing and see the world. Nothin wrong at home or nothin, we just wanted to travel and see new things and have high times. Didn't say nothin to nobody but one another. Just up and decided to do it.

DIALOGUE   A *dialogue* is a conversation between characters. In poems, novels, and short stories, dialogue is usually set off by quotation marks:

"And you just been wandering around in the rain all night?"
I shook my head. "Yes."
   —James Baldwin, "Caleb's Brother"

In a play, dialogue follows the names of the characters, and no quotation marks are used:

MONAGHAN: I see it all right, but it's all broke!
SHEEAN: *Broke!* They brought it from France on a boat. They had to take it apart, didn't they?
   —Arthur Miller, *Grandpa and the Statue*

See *Drama.*

DIMETER   See *Meter.*

DRAMA A *drama* is a story written to be performed by actors. Although a drama is meant to be performed, one can also read the *script,* or written version, and imagine the action. The script of a drama is made up of dialogue and stage directions. The *dialogue* is the words spoken by the actors. The *stage directions,* usually printed in italics, tell how the actors should look, move, and speak. They also describe the setting and effects of sound and lighting.

Dramas are often divided into parts called *acts.* The acts are often divided into smaller parts called *scenes. The Dying Detective,* on page 233, is a one-act drama. All of its action takes place in one act that has three scenes.

DRAMATIC IRONY See *Irony.*

DYNAMIC CHARACTER See *Character.*

ESSAY An *essay* is a short, nonfiction work about a particular subject. Most essays have a single major focus and a clear introduction, body, and conclusion.

There are many types of essays. A *narrative essay,* like "Rattlesnake Hunt," on page 369, tells a story about a real-life experience. An *expository essay,* like the excerpt from *These Were the Sioux,* on page 411, relates information or provides explanations. A *persuasive essay,* like "Letter Writing," on page 381, presents and supports an opinion. Most essays contain passages that describe people, places, or objects. However, there are very few purely descriptive essays.
See *Description, Exposition, Narration,* and *Persuasion.*

EXPOSITION *Exposition* is writing or speech that explains, informs, or presents information. This Handbook of Literary Terms is an example of exposition. So are the introductions to the selections in this text.

In the plot of a story or drama, the *exposition,* or introduction, is the part of the work that introduces the characters, setting, and basic situation.
See *Plot.*

EXTENDED METAPHOR In an *extended metaphor,* as in a regular metaphor, a subject is spoken or written of as though it were something else. However, extended metaphor differs from regular metaphor in that several comparisons are made. Carl Sandburg uses extended metaphor in his poem "Fog," on page 468. The poem points out a number of similarities between fog and a cat. Like a cat, the fog is silent and moves stealthily.
See *Metaphor.*

FABLE A *fable* is a brief story, usually with animal characters, that teaches a lesson, or moral. The moral is usually stated at the end of the fable.

The fable is an ancient literary form found in many cultures. The fables written by Aesop, a Greek slave who lived in the sixth century B.C., are still popular with children today. Many familiar expressions, such as "crying wolf," "sour grapes," and "crying over spilt milk," come from Aesop's fables. Other famous writers of fables include La Fontaine, the seventeenth-century French poet, and James Thurber, the twentieth-century American humorist. Thurber called his works fables for our time. Many of Thurber's fables have surprise endings. See the fables by Aesop and Thurber on pages 545, 547, and 549.
See *Irony* and *Moral.*

FANTASY *Fantasy* is highly imaginative writing that contains elements not found in real life. Joan Aiken's "The Third Wish," on page 3, is a fantasy. The story contains such unreal, fantastic elements as a talking animal, magic wishes, and a swan that changes into a woman and back again. Many science fiction stories, such as Isaac Asimov's "Hallucination," on page 179, contain elements of fantasy.

See *Science Fiction.*

FICTION   *Fiction* is prose writing that tells about imaginary characters and events. Short stories and novels are works of fiction. Some writers base their fiction on actual events and people, to which they add invented characters, dialogue, settings, and plots. Other writers of fiction rely on imagination alone to provide their materials.

See *Narration, Nonfiction,* and *Prose.*

FIGURATIVE LANGUAGE   *Figurative language* is writing or speech that is not meant to be taken literally. The many types of figurative language are known as *figures of speech.* Common figures of speech include hyperbole, metaphor, personification, and simile.

Writers use figurative language to state ideas in vivid and imaginative ways. For example, in "The River," by Javier Héraud, the speaker uses figurative language to express his own wildness:

I am a river,
I flow each moment more
  furiously,
more violently

The speaker does not mean, literally, that he is a river. However, by using figurative language to compare himself to a river, the speaker conveys the idea of his wildness vividly and imaginatively.

See *Metaphor, Personification, Simile,* and *Symbol.*

FIGURE OF SPEECH   See *Figurative Language.*

FLASHBACK   A *flashback* is a section of a literary work that interrupts the sequence of events to relate an event from an earlier time. Arthur Miller uses this technique extensively in his play *Grandpa and the Statue,* on page 219. The play's action shifts from the present, when Monaghan is an adult in an army hospital, to the past, when Monaghan is a child in Brooklyn.

FLAT CHARACTER   See *Character.*

FOLK BALLAD   See *Ballad.*

FOLK TALE   A *folk tale* is a story composed orally and then passed from person to person by word of mouth. Folk tales originated among people who could neither read nor write. These people entertained one another by telling stories aloud, often ones dealing with heroes, adventure, magic, or romance. Eventually, modern scholars like Wilhelm and Jakob Grimm began collecting these stories and writing them down. In this way folk tales have survived into the present day. The Brothers Grimm collected many European folk tales and published these as *Grimm's Fairy Tales.* The Grimm's tales include such famous stories as "Cinderella," "Rapunzel," and "The Bremen Town Musicians." In the United States, scholars have also collected folk tales. These tales deal with such fanciful heroes as Pecos Bill, Paul Bunyan, Mike Fink, and Davy Crockett. "The Little Lizard's Sorrow," on page 615, is a retelling of a Vietnamese folk tale.

See *Fable, Legend, Myth,* and *Oral Tradition.*

FOOT   See *Meter.*

FORESHADOWING   *Foreshadowing* is the use, in a literary work, of clues that suggest events that have yet to occur. Writers use foreshadowing to build their readers' expectations and to create suspense. For example, at the beginning of *The Monsters Are Due on Maple Street,* on page 247, the narrator makes the following statement:

NARRATOR'S VOICE. Maple Street. Six-forty-four P.M. on a late September evening. [*A pause*] Maple Street in the last calm and reflective moment...before the monsters came!

The narrator's comment foreshadows, or predicts, what will happen later in the play. It leads the reader or audience to feel suspense and to expect the arrival of monsters. Later the reader or audience is surprised to find out who the monsters really are.

FREE VERSE *Free verse* is poetry not written in a regular rhythmical pattern, or meter. Walt Whitman's "Miracles," on page 531, is written in free verse. So are the traditional Chippewa Indian song, "A Song of Greatness" on page 520, and Langston Hughes's "Mother to Son" on page 518.

In a free verse poem the poet is free to write lines of any length or with any number of strong stresses, or beats. Free verse is therefore less constraining than *metrical verse,* in which every line must have a certain length and a certain number of stresses.
See *Meter.*

GENRE A *genre* is a division or type of literature. Literature is commonly divided into three major genres: poetry, prose, and drama. Each major genre is in turn divided into lesser genres, as follows:
1. *Poetry:* lyric poetry, concrete poetry, dramatic poetry, narrative poetry, epic poetry
2. *Prose:* fiction (novels and short stories) and nonfiction (biography, autobiography, letters, essays, and reports)
3. *Drama:* serious drama and tragedy, comic drama, melodrama, and farce
See *Drama, Poetry,* and *Prose.*

HAIKU *Haiku* is a three-line Japanese verse form. The first and third lines of a haiku have five syllables. The second line has seven syllables. A writer of haiku uses images to create a single, vivid picture, generally of a scene from nature. See the examples of haiku on pages 478 and 479.

HEPTAMETER See *Meter.*

HEPTASTICH See *Stanza.*

HERO/HEROINE A *hero* or *heroine* is a character whose actions are inspiring or noble. Often heroes and heroines struggle mightily to overcome foes or to escape difficulties. This is true, for example, of Demeter in "Demeter and Persephone," on page 557, and of Prometheus in "Prometheus the Fire-Bringer," on page 563. The most obvious examples of heroes and heroines are the larger-than-life characters in myths and legends. However, characters who are more ordinary than Demeter and Prometheus can also act heroically. For example, in Alfred Noyes's poem on page 437, the landlord's daughter, Bess, sacrifices her own life to save that of the highwayman. This is a heroic deed, and Bess is therefore a heroine.

Note that the term *hero* was originally used only for male characters and the term *heroine* for female characters. However, it is now acceptable to use *hero* to refer to females as well as to males.

HEXAMETER See *Meter.*

HUBRIS *Hubris* is the fault of excessive pride. In "Narcissus," on page 585, and in "Phaëthon, Son of Apollo," on page 571, the central characters are guilty of hubris.

IAMB See *Meter.*

IMAGE An *image* is a word or phrase that appeals to one or more of the five senses. Writers use images to describe how their subjects look, sound, feel, taste, and smell. In the following lines from the poem "Kansas Land," Gordon

Parks uses images of sight, sound, and smell to re-create the natural wonders of life in Kansas:

Cloud tufts billowing across the round
blue sky.
Butterflies to chase through grass high
as the chin.
Junebugs, swallowtails, red robin and
bobolink,
Nights filled with soft laughter, fire
flies and restless stars,
The winding sound of crickets rubbing
dampness from their wings.
Silver September rain, orange-red-brown
Octobers and white Decembers with
hungry
Smells of hams and pork butts curing in
the smokehouse.

IMAGERY   See *Image.*

INCITING INCIDENT   See *Plot.*

IRONY   *Irony* is the general name given to literary techniques that involve surprising, interesting, or amusing contradictions. In *verbal irony,* words are used to suggest the opposite of their usual meaning. In *dramatic irony,* there is a contradiction between what a character thinks and what the reader or audience knows to be true. In *irony of situation,* an event occurs that directly contradicts the expectations of the characters, the reader, or the audience. O. Henry uses irony in his short story "After Twenty Years," on page 205. In this story a seemingly respectable and successful man waits on a street corner for a reunion with an old friend. In an ironic twist at the end of the story, the reader learns that the man is really a criminal and that the friend for whom he is waiting is a policeman.

IRONY OF SITUATION   See *Irony.*

LEGEND   A *legend* is a widely told story about the past, one that may or may not have a foundation in fact. Every culture has its own legends— its familiar, traditional stories. Examples of leg-

ends in the text include "Ojeeg, the Hunter, and the Ice Man," on page 593, and "Popocatepetl and Ixtlaccihuatl," on page 599. The former is a legend from the Micmac Indians of Canada. The latter is a legend from the Aztec Indians of Mexico.
See *Oral Tradition.*

LIMERICK   A *limerick* is a humorous, rhyming, five-line poem with a specific meter and rhyme scheme. Most limericks have three strong stresses in lines 1, 2, and 5 and two strong stresses in lines 3 and 4. Most follow the rhyme scheme *aabba.* See the limericks by Oliver Herford on page 529.

LYRIC POEM   A *lyric poem* is a highly musical verse that expresses the observations and feelings of a single speaker. Examples of lyric poems in the text include "My Mother Pieced Quilts," on page 494, and "I'm Nobody," on page 521.

MAIN CHARACTER   See *Character.*

METAMORPHOSIS   A *metamorphosis* is a change in shape, or form. Many ancient Greek and Roman myths involve characters who undergo dramatic changes. One famous collection of these myths, by the Roman poet Ovid, is called *Metamorphoses.*

In the myth of "Narcissus," on page 585, a conceited young man who loves to gaze at his own reflection in a pool is transformed into a flower. In this same myth a talkative young woman named Echo is changed into a bodiless voice that can only repeat what is said to her. These metamorphoses are inflicted on Narcissus and Echo as punishments for their misdeeds.
See *Myth.*

METAPHOR   A *metaphor* is a figure of speech in which something is described as though it were something else. A metaphor, like a simile, works by pointing out a similarity between two unlike things. In "A Far Cry From Africa," the West Indian poet Derek Walcott uses the following metaphor:

A wind is ruffling the tawny pelt
  Of Africa.

A "tawny pelt" is a brownish-yellow animal hide. By comparing Africa to a tawny pelt, Walcott suggests two similarities. First, the African grasslands are like a tawny pelt because they are brownish-yellow in color. Second, Africa itself is like that proud, strong animal that wears a tawny pelt—the lion.
See *Extended Metaphor* and *Simile.*

METER   The *meter* of a poem is its rhythmical pattern. This pattern is determined by the number and types of stresses, or beats, in each line. To describe the meter of a poem, you must *scan* its lines. *Scanning* involves marking the stressed and unstressed syllables, as follows:

The life | I lead | I want | to be

As you can see, each strong stress is marked with a slanted line (´) and each weak stress with a horseshoe symbol (˘). The weak and strong stresses are then divided by vertical lines (|) into groups called *feet.*

The following types of feet are common in English poetry:

1. *Iamb:* a foot with one weak stress followed by one strong stress, as in the word "begin"

2. *Trochee:* a foot with one strong stress followed by one weak stress, as in the word "people"

3. *Anapest:* a foot with two weak stresses followed by one strong stress, as in the phrase "on the sea"

4. *Dactyl:* a foot with one strong stress followed by two weak stresses, as in the word "happiness"

5. *Spondee:* a foot with two strong stresses, as in the word "downtown"

6. *Pyrrhic:* a foot with two weak stresses, as in the last foot of the word "unev|enly"

7. *Amphibrach:* a foot with a weak syllable, one strong syllable, and another weak syllable, as in "the shimmer|ing sunlight"

8. *Amphimacer:* a foot with a strong syllable, one weak syllable, and another strong syllable, as in "Jack and Jill"

Depending on the type of foot that is most common in them, lines of poetry are described as *iambic, trochaic, anapestic,* or *dactylic.*

Lines are also described in terms of the number of feet that occur in them, as follows:

1. *Monometer:* verse written in one-foot lines

Thus I
Pass by
And die

    —Robert Herrick, "Upon His Departure"

2. *Dimeter:* verse written in two-foot lines

There was | a woman
Who lived | on a hill.
If she's | not gone,
She lives | there still.

    —Anonymous

3. *Trimeter:* verse written in three-foot lines

Where dips | the rock|y highland
Of Sleuth | Wood in | the lake,
There lies | a leaf|y island
Where flapp|ing her|ons wake

The drows|y wat|er rats;

    —W.B. Yeats, "The Stolen Child"

4. *Tetrameter:* verse written in four-foot lines

When wear|y with | the long | day's care,
   And earth|ly change | from pain | to pain,
And lost, | and read|y to | despair,
   Thy kind | voice calls | me back | again

    —Emily Brontë, "To Imagination"

5. *Pentameter:* verse written in five-foot lines

Amidst | these scenes, | O Pil|grim, seek'st|
   thou Rome?
Vain is | thy search|—the pomp | of Rome | is
   fled

    —Francisco de Quevedo, "Rome in Her Ruins"

A six-foot line is called a *hexameter.* A line with seven feet is a *heptameter.*

A complete description of the meter of a line tells both how many feet there are in the line and what kind of foot is most common. Thus the lines from Quevedo's poem would be described as *iambic pentameter,* with one variation, a trochee, in the second line. *Blank verse* is poetry written in unrhymed iambic pentameter. Poetry that does not have a regular meter is called *free verse.*
See *Blank Verse* and *Free Verse.*

MINOR CHARACTER   See *Character.*

MONOMETER   See *Meter.*

MOOD   *Mood,* or *atmosphere,* is the feeling created in the reader by a literary work or passage. Writers use many devices to create mood, including images, dialogue, setting, and plot. Often a writer creates a mood at the beginning of a work and then sustains this mood throughout. Sometimes, however, the mood of the work changes dramatically. For example, the mood of most of "A Boy and a Man," on page 37, is tense and suspenseful. This mood changes after the man is rescued from the crevasse.

MORAL   A *moral* is a lesson taught by a literary work. A fable usually ends with a moral that is directly stated. For example, Aesop's fable "The Fox and the Crow," on page 547, ends with the moral "Do not trust flatterers." A poem, novel, short story, or essay often suggests a moral that is not directly stated. The moral must be drawn by the reader, based on other elements in the work.
See *Fable.*

MOTIVATION   A *motivation* is a reason that explains or partially explains a character's thoughts, feelings, actions, or speech. Writers try to make their characters' motivations, or motives, as clear as possible. If the motives of a main character are not clear, then the character will not be believable.

Characters are often motivated by needs such as hunger or comfort. They are also motivated by feelings such as fear, love, and pride. In "Last Cover," on page 57, Colin's fierce, protective love for his pet fox motivates him to go into the woods each day and to create a beautiful drawing. In turn, admiration for Colin's drawing motivates Father to support Colin's plan to become an artist.

MYTH   A *myth* is a fictional tale that explains the actions of gods or heroes or the origins of elements of nature. Myths are part of the oral tradition. They are composed orally and then passed from generation to generation by word of mouth. Every ancient culture has its own mythology, or collection of myths. The stories on pages 557–585 of your text are retellings, in writing, of myths from ancient Greece and Rome. These Greek and Roman myths, known collectively as *classical mythology,* tell about such gods and

heroes as Zeus, Demeter, Apollo, and Prometheus. Some, such as the myths of "Narcissus," on page 585, and of "Baucis and Philemon," on page 577, explain the origins of items in nature such as narcissus flowers, echoes, linden trees, and oaks.
See *Oral Tradition.*

NARRATION   *Narration* is writing that tells a story. The act of telling a story is also called *narration.* Fictional works such as novels and short stories are examples of narration. So are poems that tell stories, such as "The Cremation of Sam McGee," on page 445. Narration can also be found in many kinds of nonfiction, including autobiographies, biographies, and newspaper reports. A story told in fiction, nonfiction, poetry, or even in drama is called a *narrative.*
See *Narrative Poem* and *Narrator.*

NARRATIVE   See *Narration.*

NARRATIVE POEM   A *narrative poem* is a story told in verse. Narrative poems often have all the elements of short stories, including characters, setting, conflict, and plot. Examples of narrative poems include "The Highwayman," on page 437, and "Annabel Lee," on page 455.

NARRATOR   A *narrator* is a speaker or character who tells a story. A *third-person narrator* is one who stands outside the action and speaks about it. A *first-person narrator* is one who tells a story *and* participates in its action.

In some dramas, like *The Monsters Are Due on Maple Street,* on page 247, there is a separate character called "The Narrator" who introduces, comments on, and concludes the play.
See *Point of View.*

NONFICTION   *Nonfiction* is prose writing that presents and explains ideas or that tells about real people, places, objects, or events. Autobiographies, biographies, essays, reports, letters, memos, and newspaper articles are all types of nonfiction.
See *Fiction.*

NOVEL   A *novel* is a long work of fiction. Novels contain all of the elements of short stories, including characters, plot, conflict, and setting. However, novels are much longer than short stories. The writer of novels, or novelist, can therefore develop these elements more fully than a writer of short stories can. In addition to its main plot, a novel may contain one or more subplots, or independent, related stories. A novel may also have several themes. This text contains one full-length novel, *Where the Red Fern Grows,* by Wilson Rawls, on page 629.
See *Fiction.*

OCTAVE   See *Stanza.*

ONOMATOPOEIA   *Onomatopoeia* is the use of words that imitate sounds. *Crash, buzz, screech, hiss, neigh, jingle,* and *cluck* are examples of onomatopoeia. *Chickadee, towhee,* and *whippoorwill* are onomatopoeic names of birds.

In her poem "Onomatopoeia," Eve Merriam uses words to re-create the sounds of water splashing from a faucet:

> The rusty spigot
> sputters,
> utters
> a splutter,
> spatters a smattering of drops,
> gashes wider;
> slash,
> splatters,
> scatters,
> spurts,
> finally stops sputtering
> and plash!
> gushes rushes splashes
> clear water dashes.

ORAL TRADITION   The *oral tradition* is the passing of songs, stories, and poems from generation to generation by word of mouth. Folk songs, folk tales, legends, and myths all come from the oral tradition. No one knows who first created these stories and poems. They are *anonymous.*

Here is an anonymous poem from the oral tradition:

Monday's child is fair of face,
Tuesday's child is full of grace,
Wednesday's child is full of woe,
Thursday's child has far to go,
Friday's child is loving and giving,
Saturday's child works hard for its
living,
And a child that is born on the Sabbath
day
Is fair and wise and good and gay.

See *Folk Tale, Legend,* and *Myth.*

PARALLELISM   See *Repetition.*

PENTAMETER   See *Meter.*

PERSONIFICATION   *Personification* is a type of figurative language in which a nonhuman subject is given human characteristics. In "Feelings About Words," on page 486, Mary O'Neil personifies words, describing some as "lazy" and some as full of "pride" and "pomp." In the following lines from the poem "Minor Elegy," Henriqueta Lisboa personifies death:

How do you recognize death?
Maybe she looks gray.
Does she give out calling cards, with
her name correctly embossed?
Will she waylay us in the hall?

PERSUASION   *Persuasion* is writing or speech that attempts to convince the reader to adopt a particular opinion or course of action. Newspaper editorials and letters to the editor are examples of persuasion. So are advertisements and campaign speeches given by political candidates. In "How to Enjoy Poetry," on page 375,

James Dickey attempts to persuade the reader to start reading poetry.

PLOT   *Plot* is the sequence of events in a literary work. In most novels, dramas, short stories, and narrative poems, the plot involves both characters and a central conflict. The plot usually begins with an *exposition* that introduces the setting, the characters, and the basic situation. This is followed by the *inciting incident,* which introduces the central conflict. The conflict then increases during the *development* until it reaches a high point of interest or suspense, the *climax.* The climax is followed by the end, or *resolution,* of the central conflict. Any events that occur after the resolution make up the *denouement.*

Some plots do not have all of these parts. Some stories begin with the inciting incident and end with the resolution. In some the inciting incident has occurred before the opening of the story.
See *Conflict.*

POETRY   *Poetry* is one of the three major types of literature, the others being prose and drama. Defining *poetry* more precisely isn't easy, for there is no single, unique characteristic that all poems share. Poems are often divided into lines and stanzas and often employ regular rhythmical patterns, or meters. However, some poems are written out just like prose, and some are written in free verse. Most poems make use of highly concise, musical, and emotionally charged language. Many also make use of imagery, figurative language, and special devices of sound such as rhyme.

Major types of poetry include lyric poetry, narrative poetry, and concrete poetry. E.E. Cummings's "In Just—," on page 500, and Teresa Palomo Acosta's "My Mother Pieced Quilts," on page 494, are both lyric poems. Alfred Noyes's "The Highwayman" on page 437, is a narrative poem. William Jay Smith's "Seal," on page 475, is a concrete poem.

Other forms of poetry include *dramatic poetry,* in which characters speak in their own voices, and *epic poetry,* in which the poet tells a long, involved tale about gods or heroes.
See *Concrete Poem, Genre, Lyric Poetry,* and *Narrative Poetry.*

POINT OF VIEW   *Point of view* is the perspective, or vantage point, from which a story is told. Three commonly used points of view are first person, omniscient third person, and limited third person.

In stories told from the *first-person point of view,* the narrator is a character in the story and refers to himself or herself with the first-person pronoun *I.* The "Confidence Game," on page 25, is told by a first-person narrator—the story's main character, Toby.

The two kinds of third-person point of view, limited and omniscient, are called "third person" because the narrator uses third-person pronouns such as *he* and *she* to refer to the characters. There is no *I* telling the story.

In stories told from the *omniscient third-person point of view,* the narrator knows and tells about what each character feels and thinks. "Rikki-tikki-tavi," on page 13, is written from the omniscient third-person point of view.

In stories told from the *limited third-person point of view,* the narrator relates the inner thoughts and feelings of only one character, and everything is viewed from this character's perspective. "A Boy and a Man," on page 37, is written from the limited third-person point of view.
See *Narrator.*

PROSE   *Prose* is the ordinary form of written language. Most writing that is not poetry, drama, or song is considered prose. Prose is one of the major genres of literature and occurs in two forms: fiction and nonfiction.
See *Fiction, Genre,* and *Nonfiction.*

PROTAGONIST   The *protagonist* is the main character in a literary work. In "Rikki-tikki-tavi," on page 13, the protagonist, or main character, is Rikki, the mongoose.
See *Antagonist* and *Character.*

PYRRHIC   See *Meter.*

QUATRAIN   See *Stanza.*

REFRAIN   A *refrain* is a regularly repeated line or group of lines in a poem or song. In the following lines from a traditional Eskimo poem, the refrain has been italicized:

> I wonder what the dear south wind
>   has on its mind
>   *as it blows past?*
> Does it think about the small people
>   who live north of us?
> Does it think of them,
>   *as it blows past?*

REPETITION   *Repetition* is the use, more than once, of any element of language—a sound, word, phrase, clause, or sentence. Repetition is used in both prose and poetry. In prose a situation or character may be repeated with some variations. A subplot, for example, may repeat, with variations, the circumstances presented in the main plot. Poets make use of many varieties of repetition. *Rhyme, alliteration,* and *rhythm* are all repetitions of sounds or sound patterns. A *refrain* is a repeated line. Patterns of rhythm and rhyme may be repeated throughout a long poem, as in "The Cremation of Sam McGee," by Robert Service, on page 445.

The following poem makes use of a type of repetition called *parallelism.* In parallelism a grammatical pattern is repeated but the words are changed.

Grandfather sings, I dance.
Grandfather speaks, I listen.
Now I sing, who will dance?
I speak, who will listen?

Grandfather hunts, I learn.
Grandfather fishes, I clean.
Now I hunt, who will learn?
I fish, who will clean?

Grandfather dies, I weep.
Grandfather buried, I am left alone.
When I am dead, who will cry?
When I am buried, who will be alone?
   —Shirley Crawford, "Grandfather"

See *Alliteration, Meter, Plot, Rhyme,* and *Rhyme Scheme.*

RESOLUTION   See *Plot.*

RHYME   *Rhyme* is the repetition of sounds at the end of words. Poets use rhyme to lend a songlike quality to their verses and to emphasize certain words and ideas. Many traditional poems contain *end rhymes,* or rhyming words at the ends of lines. See, for example, the end rhymes in Robert Frost's "The Pasture," on page 473. Another common device is the use of *internal rhymes,* or rhyming words within lines. Notice, for example, the internal rhymes in the following passage from Edgar Allan Poe's "Annabel Lee," on page 455:

> For the moon never *beams* without
>   bringing me *dreams*
> Of the beautiful Annabel Lee;
> And the stars never *rise* but I see
>   the bright *eyes*
> Of the beautiful Annabel Lee

See *Rhyme Scheme.*

RHYME SCHEME   A *rhyme scheme* is a regular pattern of rhyming words in a poem. To indicate the rhyme scheme of a poem, one uses lower case letters. Each rhyme is assigned a different letter, as follows:

Under a spreading chestnut *tree*	a
The village smithy *stands;*	b
The smith, a mighty man is *he,*	a
With large and sinewy *hands;*	b
And the muscles of his brawny *arms*	c
Are strong as iron *bands.*	b

   —Henry Wadsworth Longfellow, "The
    Village Blacksmith"

The rhyme scheme of these lines is thus *ababcb.*

RHYTHM   *Rhythm* is the pattern of beats, or stresses, in spoken or written language.
See *Meter.*

ROUND CHARACTER   See *Character.*

SCAN/SCANNING   See *Meter.*

SCENE   See *Drama.*

SCIENCE FICTION   *Science fiction* is writing that tells about imaginary events that involve science or technology. Many science fiction stories are set in the future. "All Summer in a Day," on page 107, is a science fiction story. In this story Ray Bradbury describes events that take place in the future on the planet Venus. *The Monsters Are Due on Maple Street,* on page 247, is a science fiction drama.

SENSORY LANGUAGE   *Sensory language* is writing or speech that appeals to one or more of the five senses.
See *Image.*

SESTET   See *Stanza.*

SETTING   The *setting* of a literary work is the time and place of the action. The time includes not only the historical period—the past, present, or future—but also the year, the season, the time of day, and even the weather. The place may be a specific country, state, region, community, neighborhood, building, institution, or home. Details such as dialects, clothing, customs, and modes of transportation are often used to establish setting.

In most stories the setting serves as a backdrop—a context in which the characters interact. In some stories the setting is crucial to the plot. For example, the weather on the planet Venus is central to the plot of Ray Bradbury's story "All Summer in a Day," on page 107. Setting can also help to create a mood, or feeling. In "The Third Level," on page 127, the writer's description of a summer evening in a small Illinois town creates a mood of peace and innocence:

> It's a wonderful town still, with big old frame houses, huge lawns and tremendous trees whose branches meet overhead and roof the streets. And in 1894, summer evenings were twice as long, and people sat out on their lawns, the men smoking cigars and talking quietly, the women waving palm-leaf fans, with the fireflies all around, in a peaceful world. To be back there with the First World War still twenty years off, and World War II over forty years in the future . . . I wanted two tickets for that.

See *Mood.*

SHORT STORY   A *short story* is a brief work of fiction. Like a novel, a short story presents a sequence of events, or plot. The plot usually deals with a central conflict faced by a main character, or protagonist. Like a lyric poem, a short story is concise and creates a single effect, or dominant impression, on its reader. The events in a short story usually communicate a message about life or human nature. This message, or central idea, is the story's *theme.*
See *Conflict, Plot,* and *Theme.*

SIMILE   A *simile* is a figure of speech that makes a direct comparison between two unlike subjects using either *like* or *as.* Everday speech often contains similes such as "pale as a ghost,"

"good as gold," "spread like wildfire," and "clever as a fox."

Writers use similes to describe people, places, and things vividly. Poets, especially, create similes to point out new and interesting ways of viewing the world. In the following poem, Maxine Kumin uses a simile that compares the wings of moths beating against a screen to the end of a piece of film hitting the spool of a movie projector:

> Once he puts out the light
> moth wings on the window screen slow
> and drop away *like film lapping the spool*
> *after the home movie runs out.*
> —Maxine Kumin, "The Hermit Has a
>   Visitor"

SPEAKER   The *speaker* is the imaginary voice assumed by the writer of a poem. In other words, the speaker is the character who tells the poem. This character, or voice, often is not identified by name. The speaker in the following lines, by poet Sylvia Plath, is a mirror:

> I am silver and exact. I have no
>   preconceptions.
> Whatever I see I swallow immediately
> Just as it is, unmisted by love or dislike.
> I am not cruel, only truthful—
>   —Sylvia Plath, "Mirror"

See *Narrator.*

SPONDEE   See *Meter.*

STAGE DIRECTIONS   *Stage directions* are notes included in a drama to describe how the work is to be performed or staged. Stage directions are usually printed in italics and enclosed within parentheses or brackets. Some stage directions describe the movements, costumes, emotional states, and ways of speaking of the characters. For example, these stage directions from *The Dying Detective,* on page 233, tell how the characters should move:

(*She exits with* WATSON's *things.* HOLMES *groans again and flings out an arm restlessly.* WATSON *comes to the audience's side of the bed and sits on it.*)

The following stage directions, from the same play, tell how the actor playing Holmes should sound:

HOLMES (*Urgently*). No, no! Keep back!

Stage directions may also describe special effects of lighting or sound, as follows:

(*We hear the thud of footsteps running upstairs offstage.*)

See *Drama.*

STANZA   A *stanza* is a group of lines in a poem, considered as a unit. Many poems are divided into stanzas that are separated by spaces. Stanzas often function just like paragraphs in prose. Each stanza states and develops a single main idea.

Stanzas are commonly named according to the number of lines found in them, as follows:
1. *Couplet:* a two-line stanza
2. *Tercet:* a three-line stanza
3. *Quatrain:* a four-line stanza
4. *Cinquain:* a five-line stanza
5. *Sestet:* a six-line stanza
6. *Heptastich:* a seven-line stanza
7. *Octave:* an eight-line stanza

Robert P. Tristam Coffin's "The Pheasant," on page 466, is written in couplets:

The fierceness flowed out of his eyes
And left them meek and large and wise.

Gentleness relaxed his head,
He lay in jeweled feathers, dead.

Robert Frost's "Stopping by Woods on a Snowy Evening," on page 504, is written in quatrains:

Whose woods these are I think I know.
His house is in the village, though;

He will not see me stopping here
To watch his woods fill up with snow.

My little horse must think it queer
To stop without a farmhouse near
Between the woods and frozen lake
The darkest evening of the year.

Division into stanzas is common in traditional poetry and is often accompanied by rhyme. Notice, for example, that in each of the stanzas from the Frost poem, the first, second, and fourth lines rhyme. That is, each stanza follows the rhyme scheme *aaba*. However, some rhyming poems are not divided into stanzas, and some poems divided into stanzas do not contain rhyme. See, for example, Nikki Giovanni's "Winter," on page 502, which is divided into unrhymed quatrains.

STATIC CHARACTER   See *Character.*

SUBPLOT   See *Novel.*

SURPRISE ENDING   A *surprise ending* is a conclusion that is unexpected. Sometimes a surprise ending follows a false resolution. The reader thinks that the conflict has already been resolved but then is confronted with a new twist that changes the outcome of the plot. Often a surprise ending is *foreshadowed,* or subtly hinted at, in the course of the work. Writer O. Henry was a master of the surprise ending. See the surprise ending of his story "After Twenty Years," on page 205.
See *Foreshadowing* and *Plot.*

SUSPENSE   *Suspense* is a feeling of anxious uncertainty about the outcome of events in a literary work. Writers create suspense by raising questions in the minds of their readers. For example, in "A Day's Wait," on page 33, Ernest Hemingway raises questions about why the boy is acting so strangely and whether the boy will recover from his illness. In "A Boy and a Man," on page 37, James Ullman makes the reader wonder whether the character Rudi will succeed in saving the life of the explorer trapped in the crevasse.

SYMBOL   A *symbol* is anything that stands for or represents something else. Symbols are common in everyday life. A dove with an olive branch in its mouth is a symbol of peace. A blindfolded woman holding a balanced scale is a symbol of justice. A crown is a symbol of a king's status and authority.

TERCET   See *Stanza.*

TETRAMETER   See *Meter.*

THEME   A *theme* is a central message, concern, or purpose in a literary work. A theme can usually be expressed as a generalization, or general statement, about human beings or about life. The theme of a work is not a summary of its plot. The theme is the central idea that the writer communicates.

A theme may be stated directly by the writer, although this is unusual. In "Utzel and His Daughter, Poverty," on page 149, Isaac Bashevis Singer states his theme directly: "all a man possesses he gains through work, and not by lying in bed and being idle." This statement is a generalization that applies to all human beings. Singer illustrates this theme by telling the story of what happens to Utzel and his daughter.

Most themes are not directly stated but are implied. When the theme is implied, the reader must figure out what the theme is by looking carefully at what the work reveals about people or about life.

TRIMETER   See *Meter.*

TROCHEE   See *Meter.*

VERBAL IRONY   See *Irony.*

HANDBOOK OF CRITICAL THINKING AND READING TERMS

ABSTRACT *adj.* Anything that is not concrete or definite is *abstract.* Examples of abstract words include *truth, beauty, justice, goodness,* and *freedom.* A writer can express an abstract idea clearly by using concrete examples or details. Suppose that a writer wants to describe a beautiful summer day. A good writer will avoid writing a sentence like "It was a beautiful day" because the word *beautiful* is too abstract. Instead, the writer will use description to create concrete images of a beautiful day. For instance, the writer might describe sunlight shining through green leaves or clouds drifting in a clear blue sky. These details make make the abstract idea of beauty quite clear.

ANALOGY *n.* An *analogy* is a comparison of two unlike subjects. In the following passage, an analogy is drawn between atoms and the solar system:

> An atom is like a little solar system. Where the sun would be is the nucleus of the atom made up of neutrons and protons. Circling the nucleus, like planets, are electrons. Most of the area of the atom, like most of the solar system, is empty space.

For an analogy to work, the two subjects being compared must have one or more characteristics in common. An analogy can be expressed using a variety of literary techniques, such as simile, metaphor, and extended metaphor. See the entries for these terms in the Handbook of Literary Terms.

ANALYSIS *n.* *Analysis* is the process of studying the parts of a whole. Analyzing something is like taking a machine apart to see how it works. These are the steps you should take when conducting an analysis:

1. Break the whole down into its parts.
2. Study the characteristics of each part.
3. Notice how the parts are related to one another and to the whole.

The study of literature involves analysis. Suppose, for example, that you wish to study a short story. To do so, you must look carefully at each of its parts—setting, characters, plot, and theme. Then you must think about how the parts are related to one another.

ARGUMENT *n.* An *argument* is a set of reasons for accepting some conclusion. Andrew A. Rooney's essay "Letter Writing," on page 381, presents an argument supporting the conclusion that "there ought to be a five-cent stamp for personal letters." Rooney states this conclusion in his first paragraph and then provides reasons to support this conclusion in the rest of his essay.

Whenever you write about a literary work in a paper or in an essay test, you must present an argument. That is, you must present a set of reasons for accepting a conclusion about the work. Suppose, for example, that you are writing about the character called Uncle Henry in the short story "Luke Baldwin's Vow," on page 95. You might decide to argue that Uncle Henry is overly practical. If so, you would state this conclusion. Then you would support it by giving reasons, or evidence, from the story. For instance, Uncle Henry decides that the collie Dan is not worth his keep because Dan is too old, almost blind, and no longer a good watchdog. Uncle Henry allows Luke to keep Dan because Luke's business proposition will teach Luke something, not because Luke loves Dan.

Short essays or summaries of literary works are also called *arguments*. Thus, if you wrote a summary of the plot of "Luke Baldwin's Vow," you would be presenting the argument of the story.

See *Conclusion, Deduction, Evidence, Induction,* and *Inference.*

BANDWAGON/SNOB APPEAL See *Propaganda Techniques.*

CATEGORIZATION *n.* *Categorization* is the process of placing objects or ideas into groups or classes. When you categorize something, you follow these steps:

1. List the object's characteristics.
2. Place the object into a group with other things that have the same characteristics or qualities.
3. Find or create a name for the group. For example, the selection from Ernesto Galarza's book *Barrio Boy,* on page 337, belongs to the category of literature called "nonfiction." Nonfiction is based on real-life experiences.

CAUSE AND EFFECT *n. phrase* When one event precedes and brings about another event, the first is said to be a *cause* and the second an *effect.* For example, in "The Third Wish," on page 3, Leita grows thin and pale because she is unhappy being human. Unhappiness is the cause; thinness and paleness are the effects.

Without cause and effect, works of literature would have no plots. Literary plots rely on a series of causes and effects to advance the story.

CIRCULAR REASONING/BEGGING THE QUESTION See *Logical fallacy.*

COMPARISON *n.* *Comparison* is the process of observing and pointing out similarities. If you were to write a comparison of Angela and Tobi,

the main characters in "The Confidence Game," on page 25, you might say that both are strong swimmers, leaders, and outgoing girls. You might also mention that both conquer their pre-race jitters and learn the value of working together.

See *Contrast.*

CONCLUSION *n.* A *conclusion* is an idea that follows reasonably from another idea or group of ideas. In his essay "Letter Writing," on page 381, Andrew A. Rooney's conclusion that "there ought to be a five-cent stamp for personal letters" follows from the evidence presented: a telephone call cannot take the place of a letter because it cannot be saved or re-read, and the rising cost of stamps discourages letter writing.

CONTRAST *n.* *Contrast* is the process of observing and pointing out differences.

See *Comparison.*

DEDUCTION *n.* *Deduction* is a form of argument in which the conclusion has to be true if the premises are true. Consider, for example, the following argument:

Premise: Peter Jennings is a newscaster.
Premise: Peter Jennings hosts *World News Tonight.*
Premise: *World News Tonight* is a television show.
Conclusion: Peter Jennings is on television.

This argument is a deduction because if you agree that the premises are true, then you must also agree that the conclusion is true.

See *Generalization* and *Inference.*

DEFINITION *n.* *Definition* is the process of explaining the meaning of a word or a phrase. The following are some types of definitions:

1. *Ostensive definition:* the actual naming of an object. If a child points to a ball and says

"ball," she has given an ostensive definition of the word *ball*.

2. *Lexical definition:* the definition found in the dictionary. There are different kinds of lexical definitions, including definition by synonym, definition by antonym, definition by examples, and genus and differentia definition.

   a. *Definition by synonym* uses a word or phrase that has the same meaning as the word being defined:

   A house is a "dwelling."

   b. *Definition by antonym* uses a word or phrase that has the opposite meaning from the word being defined:

   Scrooge is *penurious.* That is, he is not generous.

   c. *Definition by example* uses a list of related terms, or examples, to which the word being defined applies:

   The Empire State Building and the Sears Tower are both *skyscrapers.*

   d. In a definition by *genus and differentia,* the object being defined is placed in a large group and is then defined by how it differs from the other objects in the group:

   To be defined: *licorice whip*
   Genus, or group: candy
   Differentia: thin, string-shaped
   red or black color
   Definition: A *licorice whip* is a thin, string-shaped piece of red or black candy.

Lexical definitions should be used to define key terms when writing about literature.

EITHER/OR FALLACY   See *Logical Fallacy.*

EVALUATION *n.*   *Evaluation* is the process of making judgments about the quality or value of something. When you evaluate a literary work, you analyze and interpret it. You can judge the work once you have taken the time to under-stand it. If you do not understand the work, then you will not be able to support your evaluation with facts. If you judge a work to be boring but do not support your evaluation by citing passages where the description is too long or where the writer uses too many words to get an idea across, then your evaluation is vague. To convince your reader to agree with you, you will have to cite specific examples from the work. See *Opinion* and *Judgment.*

EVIDENCE *n.*   *Evidence* is factual information presented to support an argument. When you write an evaluation, you must present evidence from the work to support your claims. For example, in "Luke Baldwin's Vow," on page 95, Morley Callaghan says that "the first thing Luke learned about Uncle Henry was that everyone had great respect for him." Callaghan supports this claim by pointing out the Luke observed the behavior of Uncle Henry's employees—they were always polite and attentive to him. He also adds that Uncle Henry's wife, Aunt Helen, never argued with him. If Callaghan did not provide this information, you, the reader, would have no way of knowing how Luke arrived at his conclusion. You would not know if Luke was right or if he was merely expressing an unsubstantiated opinion.
See *Fact, Reason,* and *Support.*

FACT *n.*   A *fact* is a statement that is true by definition or that can be proved by observation. Some facts are known by definition: A bicycle has two wheels. Others can be proved through observation: The sun rises in the east and sets in the west.

Writers use facts as evidence to support their conclusions or opinions. Facts are also used to tell the reader about the characters or the setting of the work. Whenever you speak or write, you should present facts to support any opinions that you express.
See *Opinion.*

FALSE ANALOGY   See *Logical Fallacy.*

GENERALIZATION *n.*   A *generalization* is a broad statement, one that applies to more than one thing. You will know that a generalization is false if you can find contrary examples. For example, suppose you feel that your teenage brother is a good driver, and then you hear someone say that all teenagers are bad drivers. You will know that this generalization is false because your brother is a teenager and a good driver. Therefore, *all* teenagers are not bad drivers.

Generalizations are often used in arguments. The following is a *deductive argument* beginning with a generalization:

Premise: (generalization) Luke loves all dogs.
Conclusion: Luke loves his collie, Dan.

Inductive arguments often end with a generalization:

Premise: Maple trees lose their leaves in the fall.
Premise: Oak trees lose their leaves in the fall.
Conclusion: (generalization) Many trees lose their leaves in the fall.

Always avoid overgeneralizations in your writing. To do so, use *qualifiers,* words that limit statements. Such words include *many, some, a couple, almost,* and *nearly.* For example, a qualifier transforms the overgeneralization that all teenagers are bad drivers into a true generalization: Some teenagers are bad drivers.
See *Conclusion* and *Stereotype.*

INDUCTION *n.*   *Induction* is a form of argument in which the conclusion is probably but not necessarily true. The conclusion of an inductive argument is usually a generalization, as in the following example:

My house is red.
My aunt's house is red.

My best friend's house is red.
My neighbor's house is red.
Conclusion: Many houses are red.

Inductive arguments can be disproved by finding counter examples—ones that contradict the conclusion. For example, if the conclusion of the preceding argument were that *all* houses are red, it would be easy to find an example that would disprove this conclusion.
See *Generalization* and *Inference.*

INFERENCE *n.*   An *inference* is any logical or reasonable conclusion. The conclusions of inductive and deductive arguments are inferences. Whenever you read someone's work or have a conversation with someone, you must make inferences. For example, if a writer tells you that a character is smiling and laughing, you can infer that the character is happy. Likewise, if someone tells you in a telephone conversation that she has a fever and is coughing, you can infer that she is sick. The number of conclusions that you can draw is limited only by your thoughtfulness and by the information that you can gather. Whenever you read or listen, think about the language and draw conclusions, or inferences, from it.
See *Conclusion, Deduction,* and *Induction.*

INTERPRETATION *n.*   *Interpretation* is the process of determining the meaning or significance of speech, writing, art, music, or actions. The following steps should be taken when interpreting a literary work:
1. Read the work carefully and actively by questioning, predicting, clarifying, summarizing, and pulling it all together.
2. Break the work down into its parts for analysis. Study the characteristics of and relationships between these parts.
3. Draw conclusions about the meaning of the work from your analysis. Support your general conclusion with specific facts.

An interpretation of a work is often a statement of its central message, or theme. The interpretation must be supported by facts drawn from careful reading and analysis of the work. For example, if you were to interpret the story "Hallucination," on page 179, you might say: "The theme of Isaac Asimov's story 'Hallucination' is that fear closes the mind and prevents a person from being receptive to new ideas." You would then use examples from the story as evidence to support your general interpretation. See *Analysis.*

JUDGMENT *n.* A *judgment* is a statement about the quality or value of something. Personal opinions are judgments, not facts. Judgments are not facts because they are subjective. However, sound judgments are ones that are supported by facts.
See *Evaluation* and *Opinion.*

LOADED WORDS See *Propaganda Techniques.*

LOGICAL FALLACY *n. phrase* A *logical fallacy* is a flaw in reasoning. The following logical fallacies are all quite common:
1. *Overgeneralization:* This fallacy occurs when a conclusion goes far beyond what the evidence can support. "All teenagers love rock music" is an example of overgeneralization.
2. *Post hoc, ergo propter hoc:* (Latin, literally, "After this, therefore because of this"). This fallacy occurs when someone falsely concludes that one event caused a second event to occur simply because the event occurred before the second event. Suppose, for example, that you get sick while hiking and conclude that the mountain air caused your sickness. If you then find out that your sickness is due to food poisoning, you will realize that your first explanation was an example of the *post hoc* fallacy.

3. *The either/or fallacy:* This fallacy occurs when one reduces the alternatives or possibilities to only two when in fact there are more. Often, one of the alternatives is completely unacceptable, leaving only one choice. The statement "Either you learn to love camping, or you will never appreciate nature" is an example of the either/or fallacy.
4. *Circular reasoning/begging the question:* This fallacy occurs when one fails to provide any logical support for an opinion. This fallacy is known as *begging the question* because the writer or speaker is asking his or her audience to accept an opinion without sufficient proof. The statement "San Francisco is a more beautiful city than New York because it is more scenic" is an example of circular reasoning and begging the question.
5. *False analogy:* This fallacy occurs when superficial similarities are used to support a major conclusion. One cannot assume that just because two things are similar in some ways they will be similar in all ways. Frequently, writers and speakers try to compare their opinion or position to another that is more familiar and accepted. Because the two views have surface similarities, they hope that acceptance of one will encourage acceptance of the other. For example, the statement "Workers are like machines and can therefore be disposed of when they wear out" is an example of false analogy.

MAIN IDEA *n. phrase* The *main idea* is the central point a speaker or writer wants to communicate. Main ideas in essays are usually stated at the beginning, in the thesis statement, or at the end, in the conclusion. In some literary works the main idea is not stated directly but is implied by statements in the work or by the work as a whole.
See *Purpose.*

OBJECTIVE *adj.* Something is *objective* if it has an existence independent of any particular

person's attitudes, ideas, or beliefs. An objective statement is a fact that can be verified, or proved, by anyone. For example, the statement "Arthur Miller wrote the play *Grandpa and the Statue*" is objective because anyone can check to see whether the statement is true. However, the statement "Miller's play is lighthearted and frivolous" is subjective. This statement expresses one person's attitude toward the play after seeing or reading it. Other people might reasonably disagree with this opinion.
See *Subjective.*

OPINION *n.* An *opinion* is a statement that cannot be proved true or false. Often it can be supported by facts but is not itself a fact. There are different kinds of opinions. *Judgments* are opinions about the value or quality of things. The statement "'When the Frost is on the Punkin' is a wonderful poem" is a judgment. A *prediction* is an opinion about the future. "Cars will eventually run on electricity" is a prediction. A *statement of obligation* is an opinion about what people should or should not do. "If you see someone cheating on a test, you should tell the teacher" is a statement of obligation.

When you express an opinion in writing or in conversation, you should be able to support your opinion with facts. If you cannot, others can dismiss it as being unsound or merely personal. If you can support your opinion with facts, others can use your facts to decide whether to agree or disagree with your opinion.
See *Facts, Judgment,* and *Prediction.*

OVERGENERALIZATION See *Logical Fallacy.*

PARAPHRASE *n.* A *paraphrase* is a restatement in different words. Paraphrasing is a helpful technique to use when you want to make sure you understand what someone is saying. It is particularly helpful when you are interpreting a literary work. Putting the writer's meaning into your own words can help you to understand the work.

Paraphrasing is also helpful when you want to quote someone else's thoughts or ideas but don't want to quote his or her exact words. Remember that paraphrases, like word-for-word quotations, must be credited to their sources.

POST HOC, ERGO PROPTER HOC See *Logical Fallacy.*

PREDICTION *n.* *Prediction* is the act of making statements about the future. Writers use the technique of foreshadowing to give readers clues or hints about what will happen next. Readers do not always have to rely on clues from writers, however. Frequently readers can predict what will happen because they have read stories with similar plots or because they know how certain types of people, and thus characters, would act in a given situation.

A prediction leads a reader to have certain expectations. If a reader predicts that the hero will walk into the villain's trap, the reader will experience suspense until this event occurs or fails to occur. Writers create expectations to heighten the reader's involvement.
See *Opinion.*

PROBLEM SOLVING *n. phrase* *Problem solving* is the process by which a person comes up with an answer to some question or a way out of some difficulty. Problem solving is something that everyone does every day. The process of solving a problem often involves the following steps:

1. Define the problem.
2. Examine the circumstances surrounding the problem.
3. Decide what the result or goal should be once the problem is solved.
4. Take action to reach the desired outcome or goal.

If a problem is particularly difficult, it is helpful to try the following problem-solving strategies:

1. Break the problem down into parts and solve the parts separately.
2. Think of a simpler problem of the same type that you have solved before. Apply part or all of your previous solution to your current difficult problem.
3. Restate the problem in your own words.
4. Ask someone to help you with parts of the problem that are especially difficult.
5. Ask "What if" questions to come up with possible solutions. Test each of these solutions.
6. Define the key terms or concepts involved in the problem.
7. Try diagramming, freewriting, and other techniques for generating ideas.
8. Use means/ends analysis. That is, at each step in the solution, compare where you are to where you want to be.

See *Analysis.*

PROPAGANDA TECHNIQUE *n. phrase* A *propaganda technique* is used by a writer or speaker to mislead an audience by appealing to its emotions. Several common propaganda techniques follow:

1. *Bandwagon* is the technique of pressuring people to accept some belief or to take some action merely because other people are doing so.
2. *Loaded words* are those that have strong positive or negative connotations. Loaded words with positive connotations are called *purr words.* Such words include *natural, intelligent,* and *strong, Snarl words,* on the other hand, have negative connotations. Such words include *unnatural, dumb,* and *weak.*
3. *Transfer* is the technique of attempting to get people to associate their positive feelings about one thing with another, unrelated thing. An advertiser who uses red, white, and blue banners may be attempting to get people to associate patriotism with buying particular products.

4. *Unreliable testimonial* is a personal endorsement made by someone who is not qualified to make the endorsement. The following advertisement provides an example: "As a professional athlete, I care about what I eat. So I choose Crunchy Flakes because they are nutritious. If you care about your health like me, you'll buy Crunchy Flakes."

PURPOSE *n.* The *purpose* is the goal or aim of a literary work. A work may serve any of a number of different purposes. Sometimes writers or speakers try to persuade their audiences to accept certain points of view. At other times a writer or speaker may attempt to explain a concept, tell a story, describe an event, or merely entertain. A single work may have more than one purpose. For example, "The Mystery and Wonder of Words" on page 401 entertains the reader, conveys knowledge about the origins of words, and instills curiosity about language.
See *Main Idea.*

REALISTIC DETAILS/FANTASTIC DETAILS *n. phrases* A *realistic detail* is one that is drawn from actual or possible experience. A *fantastic detail* is one that is not based on actual experience but is improbable or imaginary. Realistic details lend believability to fiction, poetry, and drama. The reader feels that he or she is reading about real people, places, and events. The use of fantastic details heightens the reader's interest and forces him or her to think imaginatively. Some stories use both realistic and fantastic details. For example, in "Hallucination," on page 179, Isaac Asimov uses realistic details such as grass, insects, and human beings to make his story believable. He also uses fantastic details such as another planet, a time in the future, and thinking insects.

REASON *n.* A *reason* is a statement given in support of some conclusion. As a verb, *to reason* refers to the human ability to think logically and rationally.

See *Argument* and *Conclusion.*

SOURCE *n.* A *source* is anything from which ideas and information are obtained. Libraries are filled with sources. Works of fiction, newspapers, dictionaries, and reference books are all sources. Television shows, computerized information services, and movies are sources, too. Even your own experiences and those of other people are sources. Writers use various sources of information to support their ideas.

As a writer, you must be sure to credit the sources that you use either in the text of your writing or in footnotes or end notes. Failing to attribute statements or facts to their proper sources tricks the reader into believing that what is really someone else's thought or idea is your own. Such plagiarism should be avoided at all costs.

Some sources are better than others. Sources that are current and unbiased are best. *Firsthand,* eyewitness accounts are excellent sources. These are preferable to *secondhand* sources. Secondhand sources usually get their information from firsthand sources and then retell it. "Winslow Homer: America's Greatest Painter," on page 395, is H.N. Levitt's secondhand account of Winslow Homer's life and work. Levitt used various sources of information and then wrote this article based on his analysis of the information. "These Were the Sioux," on page 411, is a firsthand account in which Mari Sandoz recounts her own experiences with the Sioux Indians.

STEREOTYPE *n.* A *stereotype* is a generalization applied to a whole group of people. It is a fixed or conventional notion or characterization. Some common stereotypes are the mad scientist and the absent-minded professor. Most stereotypes are misleading and false. For instance, children who have no brothers or sisters are often stereotyped as being spoiled, always getting their way, and manipulating adults into doing what they want them to do. However, these things are not true of all such children, and the stereotype leads to unfair or absurd conclusions. Therefore, you should avoid using stereotypes in your work.

Writers of short stories often resort to stereotyping because they have very little space in which to develop complete, rounded characters. However, even when used in works of fiction, stereotypes can lead to unwarranted overgeneralizations about groups of people.

See *Generalization.*

SUBJECTIVE *adj.* Something is *subjective* if it has to do with personal experience rather than some objective reality. People's feelings about literary works are subjective because they are internal experiences. When you evaluate a literary work, you state your subjective impressions of it. However, your statements must be supported by objective, factual evidence.

See *Objective.*

SUMMARIZE *v.* To *summarize* something is to restate it briefly in different words. For example, a brief summary of *A Christmas Carol: Scrooge and Marley* might read as follows:

Scrooge is a very stingy businessman whose partner, Marley, was equally, if not stingier than Scrooge. After Marley dies, Scrooge continues his stingy ways. Then, one Christmas Eve, Marley's ghost visits Scrooge and tells him that three visions will appear to him that night: the Ghost of Christmas Past, the Ghost of Christmas Present, and the Ghost of Christmas Yet-to-Come. At first Scrooge is disbelieving, but eventually he becomes receptive to the lessons being taught to him. By morning, Scrooge is a changed person.

SUPPORT *v.* To *support* a statement is to provide evidence for it.

See *Evidence.*

TIME ORDER *n. phrase*   *Time order* is organization by order of occurrence. Events are told in time order in most novels, plays, short stories, and narrative poems. Many types of nonfiction, including autobiographies, biographies, and histories, also use time order. Time order is some- times called *chronological order.*

TRANSFER   See *Propaganda Technique.*

UNRELIABLE TESTIMONIAL   See *Propaganda Technique.*

GLOSSARY

READING THE GLOSSARY ENTRIES

The words in this glossary are from selections appearing in your textbook. Each entry in the glossary contains the following parts:

1. Entry Word. This word appears at the beginning of the entry, in boldface type.

2. Pronunciation. The symbols in parentheses tell how the entry word is pronounced. If a word has more than one possible pronunciation, the most common of these pronunciations is given first.

3. Part of Speech. Appearing after the pronunciation, in italics, is an abbreviation that tells the part of speech of the entry word. The following abbreviations have been used:

n. noun   **p.** pronoun   **v.** verb
adj. adjective **adv.** adverb **conj.** conjunction

4. Definition. This part of the entry follows the part-of-speech abbreviation and gives the meaning of the entry word as used in the selection in which it appears.

KEY TO PRONUNCIATION SYMBOLS USED IN THE GLOSSARY

The following symbols are used in the pronunciations that follow the entry words:

Symbol	Key Words	Symbol	Key Words
a	asp, fat, parrot	b	bed, fable, dub
ā	ape, date, play	d	dip, beadle, had
ä	ah, car, father	f	fall, after, off
		g	get, haggle, dog
e	elf, ten, berry	h	he, ahead, hotel
ē	even, meet, money	j	joy, agile, badge
		k	kill, tackle, bake
i	is, hit, mirror	l	let, yellow, ball
ī	ice, bite, high	m	met, camel, trim
		n	not, flannel, ton
ō	open, tone, go	p	put, apple, tap
ô	all, horn, law	r	red, port, dear
o͞o	ooze, tool, crew	s	sell, castle, pass
oo	look, pull, moor	t	top, cattle, hat
yo͞o	use, cute, few	v	vat, hovel, have
yoo	united, cure, globule	w	will, always, swear
oi	oil, point, toy	y	yet, onion, yard
ou	out, crowd, plow	z	zebra, dazzle, haze
u	up, cut, color	ch	chin, catcher, arch
ʉr	urn, fur, deter	sh	she, cushion, dash
		th	thin, nothing, truth
ə	a in ago	th	then, father, lathe
	e in agent	zh	azure, leisure
	i in sanity	ŋ	ring, anger, drink
	o in comply	'	[see explanatory note below and also *Foreign sounds* below]
	u in focus		
ər	perhaps, murder		

This pronunciation key is from *Webster's New World Dictionary*, Second College Edition. Copyright © 1986 by Simon & Schuster. Used by permission.

---

abet (ə bet') *v.* To help or encourage
abode (ə bōd') *n.* Home
accessible (ak ses' ə b'l) *adj.* Easy to get
acknowledge (ək näl' ij) *v.* To recognize and admit

adamant (ad' ə mənt) *adj.* Unyielding; inflexible
addled (ad' 'ld) *adj.* Muddled and confused
adhesive (əd hē' siv) *adj.* Sticking
aeon (ē' än) *n.* A very long period of time
aesthetic (es thet' ik) *adj.* From an artistic point of view
akimbo (ə kim' bō) *adv.* Hands on hips, with elbows pointing outward
algae (al' jē) *n.* Plants like seaweed that live in water or damp places
allay (ə lā') *v.* To put to rest; calm
amber (am' bər) *n.* A brownish-yellow substance; *adj.* of a brownish-yellow color
ambulance (am' byə ləns) *n.* A specially equipped vehicle for carrying the sick or wounded
amends (ə mendz') *n.* Things given or done to make up for injury or loss
amiss (ə mis') *adv.* In a wrong way; improper
Anglophile (aŋ' glə fīl) *n.* A person who is strongly devoted to England, its people, customs, or influence
anoint (ə noint') *v.* To rub oil or ointment on
anonymous (ə nän' ə məs) *adj.* With no name known
apparition (ap' ə rish' ən) *n.* Ghost
appease (ə pēz') *v.* To satisfy
appraisal (ə prā' z'l) *n.* Judgment of something's or someone's quality
apprehensive (ap'rə hen' siv) *adj.* Anxious; fearful
apprentice (ə pren' tis) *v.* To receiving financial support and instruction in a trade in return for work
apt (apt) *adj.* Inclined; likely
aptitude (ap' tə to͞od') *n.* Talent; ability
arched (ärchd) *adj.* Curved
arid (ar' id) *adj.* Dry and barren
Arkansas (är' k'n sô') [<Fr.<Siouan tribal name; ? "downstream people"] State of the south central United States
arrogant (ar' ə gənt) *adj.* Proud; self-important
arroyo (ə roi' ō) *n.* A dry gully or ravine
assent (ə sent') *n.* Agreement
assortment (ə sôrt' mənt) *n.* A group or collection of different kinds of things
astonish (ə stän' ish) *v.* To amaze
astrophysics (as' trō fiz' iks) *n.* The science of the physical properties of the stars, planets, and other heavenly bodies
asunder (ə sun' dər) *adv.* Into parts or pieces
audible (ô' də b'l) *adj.* Loud enough to be heard
avarice (av' ər is) *n.* Greed for riches
awe (ô) *n.* A mixed feeling of fear and wonder

banish (ban' ish) *v.* To send into exile
bantam (ban' təm) *n.* A small chicken
bark (bärk) *n.* Any boat, especially a small sailing boat
barometer (bə räm' ə tər) *n.* An instrument for measuring atmospheric pressure
barrage (bə räzh') *n.* A heavy attack

barrio (bär′ ē ō)   *n.* Part of a town or city where most of the people are Hispanic

bay (bā′)   *v.* To bark with deep, prolonged tones

beam (bēm)   *v.* To shine brightly

belligerent (bə lij′ ər ənt)   *adj.* Showing a readiness to fight

bellow (bel′ ō)   *v.* To roar with a powerful, reverberating sound

bellows (bel′ ōz)   *v.* A device for quickening the fire by blowing air on it

berserk (bər sʉrk′)   *adj.* Into a violent or destructive rage

besiege (bi sēj′)   *v.* To surround

bias (bī′ əs)   *n.* Preference; leaning; prejudice

bilious (bil′ yəs)   *adj.* Bad-tempered; cross

billow (bil′ ō)   *v.* To surge or swell

bleachers (blēch′ ərz)   *n.* Benches stacked in rows for spectators at sporting events

blemish (blem′ ish)   *n.* A defect or scar

bog (bäg)   *n.* A small marsh or swamp

bonnet (bän′ it)   *n.* [Brit.] An automobile hood

brandish (bran′ dish)   *v.* To wave in a threatening way

bravado (brə vä′ dō)   *n.* Pretended courage

brawn (brôn)   *n.* Physical strength

breeches (brich′ iz)   *n.* Trousers that reach to or just below the knee

brooch (brōch)   *n.* A large ornamental pin worn on a dress

brutality (brōō tal′ ə tē)   *n.* Violence; harshness

buffet (bə fā′)   *n.* A piece of furniture with drawers and cupboards for dishes, table linen, and so on

burly (bʉr′ lē)   *adj.* Heavy and muscular

burrow (bʉr′ o)   *v.* To dig a hole or tunnel, especially for shelter

bustle (bus′ 'l)   *v.* To hurry

calabash (kal′ ə bash′)   *n.* A large fruit that is dried and made into a bowl or cup

calico (kal′ ə kō)   *n.* A coarse and cheap cloth

calligrapher (kə lig′ rə fər)   *n.* Someone skilled in the art of beautiful handwriting

camouflage (kam′ ə fläzh′)   *v.* Disguise

candy (kan′ dē)   *v.* To coat with sugar

canebrake (kān′ brāk)   *n.* A dense growth of cane plants

cant (kant)   *v.* To tilt

cantankerous (kan taŋ′ kər əs)   *adj.* Bad-tempered

cantonment (kan tän′ mənt)   *n.* Temporary quarters assigned to troops

canvas (kan′ vəs)   *n.* Closely woven cloth used for tents and sails

carp (kärp)   *n.* A fresh-water fish living in a pond or other quiet water

cascade (kas kād′)   *n.* A waterfall or anything tumbling like water

casement (kās′ mənt)   *n.* A window frame that opens on hinges

castings (kas′ tiŋz)   *n.* Waste material

cataract (kat′ ə rakt′)   *n.* An eye disease in which the lens becomes clouded over, causing partial or total blindness

catastrophe (kə tas′ trə fē)   *n.* A sudden disaster or misfortune

catgut (kat′ gut′)   *n.* A tough string or thread used in surgery

chemistry (kem′ is trē)   *n.* The chemical makeup and reaction of substances

Cherokee (cher′ ə kē′)   *n.* [<tribal name *Tsárăgĭ*, prob.< Choctaw *chiluk-ki*, "cave people"] A member of a tribe of Iroquoian Indians most of whom were moved from the southeast United States to Oklahoma

chivalrous (shiv′ 'l rəs)   *adj.* Courteous

chloroform (klôr′ ə fôrm′)   *n.* A substance used at one time as an anesthetic

chortle (chôr′ t'l)   *v.* To make an amused chuckling or snorting sound

clamor (klam′ər)   *v.* To cry out; to demand loudly

clan (klan)   *n.* A group of people, often relatives

claret (klar′ it)   *adj.* Purplish-red

cleft (kleft)   *v.* Split or opened

coarse (kôrs)   *adj.* Inferior; crude; common

comely (kum′ lē)   *adj.* Attractive; pretty

comforter (kum′ fər tər)   *n.* A long, woolen scarf

commence (kə mens′)   *v.* To begin

commit (kə mit′)   *v.* To deliver for safekeeping; entrust;
commit to memory to learn by heart

commotion (kə mō′ shən)   *n.* Noisy reaction; confusion

comparable (käm′ pər ə b'l)   *adj.* Similar

compel (kəm pel′)   *adj.* To have a powerful effect

competent (käm′ pə tənt)   *adj.* Capable

complaint (kəm plānt′)   *n.* An illness

compulsion (kəm pul′ shən)   *n.* A driving force

concave (kän kāv′)   *adj.* Hollow and curved like the inside of an empty ball

conceivable (kən sē′ və b'l)   *adj.* Imaginable

concussion (kən kush′ ən)   *n.* Violent shaking

confound (kən found′)   *v.* To confuse

consolation (kän′ sə lā′ shən)   *n.* Something that makes one feel better

conspire (kən spīr′)   *v.* To combine; to work together

consternation (kän′ stər nā′ shən)   *n.* Sudden confusion and frustration

consultation (kän′ s'l tā′ shən)   *n.* Discussion

conventional (kən ven′ shən 'l)   *adj.* Ordinary; usual

convey (kən vā′)   *v.* To make known

corroborate (kə räb′ ə rāt′)   *v.* Confirm; support

councilor (koun′ sə lər)   *n.* Adviser

countenance (koun′ tə nəns)   *n.* Face

coupe (kōō pā′) *n.* A small, two-door automobile

court (kôrt)   *v.* To try to win someone's love

covet (kuv′ it)   *v.* To envy

covey (kuv′ ē)   *n.* A small flock of birds

crafty (kraf′ tē)   *adj.* Sly; cunning

cremate (krē′ māt)   *v.* To burn to ashes

crevasse (kri vas′)   *n.* Deep crack

crotchet (kräch′ it)   *n.* A peculiar or stubborn idea

crucial (krōō′ shəl)   *adj.* Of great importance

cul-de-sac (kul′ də sak′)   *n.* A blind alley; a deadend street

culprit (kul′ prit)   *n.* Guilty person

cunning (kun′ iŋ)   *adj.* Skillful; clever

cupidity (kyōō pid′ ə tē)   *n.* Strong desire for wealth

curdle (kʉr′ d'l)   *v.* To thicken; clot

currency (kʉr′ən sē)   *n.* Money

dabbling (dab′ 'liŋ)   *n.* The act of dipping lightly in water

dark (därk)   *adj.* Entirely or partly without light

data (dāt′ə)   *n.* Information

decipher (di sī′ fər) *v.* To make out the meaning of

decreed (di crēd′) *v.* Officially ordered

deference (def′ ər əns) *n.* Respect

defiant (di fī′ ənt) *adj.* Boldly resisting

definitive (di fin′ ə tive) *adj.* Final; the last word

deft (deft′) *adj.* Skillful

defy (di fī′) *v.* To boldly oppose or resist

deign (dān) *v.* To graciously agree to do something beneath one

delude (di lōōd′) *v.* To fool; to mislead

deluge (del′ yōōj) *n.* A great flood or rush of anything

demeanor (di mēn′ər) *n.* Outward behavior; manner

democracy (di mäk′ rə sē) *n.* Government in which the people hold the ruling power

democrat (dem′ ə krat) *n.* A person who believes in and upholds government by the people

demon (dē′ mən) *n.* Evil spirit

denumerable (di nōō′ mər ə b'l) *adj.* Countable; said of a set whose elements can be put in a one-to-one correspondence with the natural integers

derelict (der′ ə likt′) *v.* An abandoned ship

derive (di rīv′) *n.* To receive from someone or something

desolate (des′ ə lit) *adj.* Lonely; solitary

despair (di sper′) *n.* Loss of hope

despise (di spīz′) *v.* Look down on with scorn

despondent (di spän′ dənt) *adj.* Lacking hope; depressed

destitute (des′ tə tōōt′) *adj.* Living in complete poverty

deteriorate (di tir′ ē ə rāt) *v.* To become worse

dignitary (dig′ nə ter′ ē) *n.* Person holding a high position or office

diligent (dil′ə jənt) *adj.* Careful, steady effort

dim (dim) *adj.* Not bright; somewhat dark; not clearly seen

disdain (dis dān′) *v.* To scorn; regard as unworthy

disembowel (dis′ im bou′ əl) *v.* To take out the inner organs

dispel (dis pel′) *v.* To scatter and drive away

disposition (dis′ pə zish′ ən) *n.* Arrangement

dissever (di sev′ ər) *v.* To separate

dissuade (di swād′) *v.* To advise someone against an action

distemper (dis tem′ pər) *v.* An infectious virus disease of young dogs

distinct (dis tiŋkt′) *adj.* Separate and different

distinction (dis tiŋk′ shən) *n.* Difference of meaning

distracted (dis trakt′ id) *adj.* With the mind drawn away in another direction

distraught (dis′ trôt′) *adj.* Extremely upset

divisor (də vī′ zər) *n.* The number or quantity by which the dividend is divided to produce the quotient

domestic (də mes′ tik) *adj.* Of the home and family

dominion (də min′ yən) *n.* Region over which one rules

dote (dōt) *v.* To be extremely fond

downy (doun′ ē) *adj.* Soft and fluffy, like soft, fine feathers

draggled (drag′ 'ld) *adj.* Wet and dirty

dreaded (dred′ ad) *adj.* Feared

ecstatic (ik stat′ ik) *adj.* Delighted

edifice (ed′ ə fis) *n.* Large structure

elusive (i lōō′ siv) *adj.* Hard to find

emaciated (i mā′ shē āt′əd) *adj.* Extremely thin, starving

emblem (em′ bləm) *n.* Sign; symbol

emerge (i murj′) *v.* To become visible

emit (i mit′) *v.* To send out or utter

emphatic (im fat′ ik) *adj.* Felt with emphasis; forceful; definite

enamel (i nam′ 'l) *n.* Glassy colored substance used as coating on metal, glass, and pottery

encounter (in koun′ tər) *n.* Meeting

entice (in tīs′) *v.* To tempt

entrails (en′ trālz) *n.* The inner organs of animals

epidemic (ep′ə dem′ ik) *n.* Outbreak of a contagious disease

equivalent (i kwiv′ ə lənt) *n.* A thing similar to another thing

esteem (ə stēm′) *v.* To respect; to hold in high regard

evident (ev′ ə dent) *adj.* Obvious

ewer (yōō′ ər) *n.* A large water pitcher with a wide mouth

exclaim (iks klām′) *v.* To cry out; speak or say suddenly and vehemently

expectant (ik spek′ tənt) *adj.* Showing eager waiting

exquisite (eks′ kwi zit) *adj.* Very beautiful, especially in a delicate way

extract (ik strakt′) *v.* To draw out

extricate (eks′ trə kāt) *v.* To set free; disentangle

exuberance (ig zōō′ bər əns) *n.* High spirits

exultation (eg′ zəl tā′ shən) *n.* Rejoicing

falter (fôl′ tər) *v.* To show uncertainty; act hesitantly

fanciful (fan′ si fəl) *adj.* Playfully imaginative

fantasia (fan tā′ zhə) *n.* A musical composition of no fixed form, with a structure determined by the composer's fancy

fantasize (fan′ tə sīz) *v.* To have daydreams; indulge in fantasies

fare (fer) *n.* Food

favoritism (fā′ vər it iz'm) *n.* Showing special kindness

feed (fēd) *n.* The tiny particles that minnows feed on

feint (fānt) *v.* To pretend to make an attack

fennel (fen′ 'l) *n.* A tall herb

file (fīl) *v.* To move in line

firing (fir′ iŋ) *n.* The application of heat to harden or glaze pottery

firmament (fur′ mə mənt) *v.* The sky, viewed poetically as a solid arch or vault

fitting (fit′ iŋ) *adj.* Suitable; proper

flagon (flag′ ən) *n.* A container for liquids with a handle, narrow neck, spout, and sometimes a lid

flat (flat) *n.* An apartment

flatterer (flat′ ər ər) *n.* One who praises a person insincerely in order to gain something for oneself

flaunt (flônt) *v.* To display; to show off

fledgling (flej′ liŋ) *n.* A young bird

flinch (flinch) *v.* To move back, as if away from a blow

flit (flit) *v.* To fly lightly and rapidly

flock (fläk) *n.* Group of sheep

flush (flush) *v.* To drive from hiding

fluster (flus′ tər) *v.* To make nervous

forlorn (fər lôrn′) *adj.* Hopeless; miserable

formidable (fôr′ mə də b'l) *adj.* Impressive

forthwith (fôrth′ with′) *adv.* At once

fortitude (fôr′ tə tōōd′) *n.* Firm courage

fragile   (fraj' 'l)   *adj.* Delicate; easily broken

free-lance   (frē' lans')   *adj.* Working independently by selling services to individual buyers

gabardine   (gab' ər dēn')   *n.* A cloth of wool, cotton, rayon, or other material, used for suits and dresses

gaiter   (gāt' ər)   *n.* Covering for the leg extending from the instep to the ankle or knee

galleon   (gal' ē ən)   *n.* A large Spanish ship of the 15th and 16th centuries, used as both a warship and a trader

gambol   (gam' b'l)   *n.* Play; frolic

garment   (gär' mənt)   *n.* An article of clothing; costume

gaunt   (gônt)   *adj.* Thin and bony

gaze   (gāz)   *v.* To look intently and steadily

geology   (jē äl' ə jē)   The science dealing with the physical nature and history of the earth

ghastly   (gast' lē)   *adj.* Ghostlike; frightful

girdle   (gər' d'l)   *n.* A belt or sash for the waist

glacier   (glā' shər)   *n.* Large mass of ice and snow

gleeful   (glē' fəl)   *adj.* Merry

glint   (glint)   *v.* To gleam, flash, or glitter

gloat   (glōt)   *v.* To gaze or grin in scornful triumph

gloomy   (gloom' ē)   *adj.* Causing gloom; dismal; depressing

glossy   (glôs' ē)   *adj.* Smooth and shiny

gnarled   (närld)   *adj.* Knotty and twisted

gnawing   (nô' iŋ)   *adj.* Tormenting; bothering

gourd   (gôrd)   *n.* The fruit of a certain kind of plant: the dried, hollowed shell of this fruit used as a drinking cup or dipper

gout   (gout)   *n.* A disease characterized by swelling and pain in the hands and feet

grave   (grāv)   *adj.* Serious

grieve   (grēv')   *v.* To feel sorrow for a loss

grisly   (griz' lē)   *adj.* Horrible

grizzled   (griz''ld)   *adj.* Gray

grotesque   (grō tesk')   *n.* A strange or distorted character

grouse   (grous)   *n.* A group of game birds

gumption   (gump' shən)   *n.* Courage and enterprise

haggard   (hag' ərd)   *adj.* Looking worn from grief or illness

harass   (hə ras')   *v.* To trouble or worry

haughty   (hôt' ə)   *adj.* Showing pride in oneself and contempt for others

haunch   (hônch)   *n.* An animal's lower back; hip

hearth   (härth)   *n.* The stone or brick floor of a fireplace

heartily   (härt' 'l ē)   *adv.* Warmly; completely

heed   (hēd)   *v.* Attention

henceforth   (hens fôrth')   *adv.* From this time on

herpetologist   (hur' pə täl' ə jist)   *n.* Someone who studies reptiles and amphibians

hexagonal   (hek sag' ə n'l)   *n.* Six-sided

hissing   (his' iŋ)   *v.* Making a sound like a prolonged *s*

holocaust   (häl' ə kôst')   *n.* In ancient times an offering burned to the gods

hummock   (hum' ək)   *n.* Area of fertile, wooded land, higher than the surrounding swamp

hunch   (hunch)   *v.* To stand with one's back bent

hurl   (hurl)   *v.* To throw with force or violence

Husky   (hus' kē)   *n.* A strong dog used for pulling a sled over the snow

hymn   (him)   *n.* A song of praise

idiograph   (id' ē ə graf')   *n.* A symbol that stands for a hing or idea without expressing the sounds that make up its name

immeasurable   (i mezh' ər ə b'l)   *adj.* So great that it cannot be measured

immense   (i mens')   *adj.* Vast

impetuous   (im pech' oo wəs)   *adj.* Moving with great force or violence

implore   (im plôr')   *v.* To beg

impressive   (im pres' iv)   *adj.* Having a strong effect on the mind or emotions

improvise   (im' prə vīz')   *v.* To make with the tools and materials at hand, usually to fill an unforeseen and immediate need

incense   (in' sens)   *n.* Any of various substances that produce a pleasant odor when burned

incessant   (in ses' 'nt)   *adj.* Without stopping

incomprehensible   (in'käm pri hen' seb'l)   *adj.* Not able to be understood

incredulous   (in krej' oo ləs)   *adj.* Unwilling or unable to believe

incubation   (in' kyə bā' shən)   *n.* The phase in a disease between the infection and the first appearance of symptoms

indifferent   (in dif' ər ənt)   *adj.* Uninterested

industrious   (in dus' trē əs)   *adj.* Hard-working

inert   (in urt')   *adj.* Without power to move

inertia   (in ur' shə)   *n.* The tendency of an object to remain at rest if it is at rest, or to remain moving if it is moving—unless it is disturbed by an outside force

inevitable   (in ev' ə tə b'l)   *adj.* Certain to happen

inflammatory   (in flam' ə tôr'ē)   *adj.* Characterized by pain and swelling

ingenious   (in jēn' yəs)   *adj.* Clever and inventive

insolent   (in' sə lənt)   *adj.* Disrespectful

integer   (in' tə jər)   *n.* Any positive or negative whole number

interact   (in' tər akt')   *v.* To affect and be affected by

interplanetary   (in' tər plan' ə ter' ē)   *adj.* Between planets

interpreter   (in tur' prə tər)   *n.* Someone who translates from one language to another

interrogation   (in ter' ə gā' shən)   *n.* Situation where people are formally questioned

intervene   (in' tər vēn')   *v.* To step into a situation

interwoven   (in'tər wō' vən)   *adj.* Mixed together

intrigue   (in trēg)   *v.* To fascinate

invariable   (in ver' ē ə b'l)   *adj.* Not changing; uniform

ironical   (ī rän' i k'l)   *adj.* In a different way from what is expected

irrevocable   (i rev' ə kə b'l)   *adj.* Unchangeable

jubilant   (joo' b'l ənt)   *adj.* Joyful and triumphant

judicious   (joo dish' əs)   *adj.* Wise

keener   (kēn' ər)   *adj.* Sharper and quicker

Kentucky   (kən tuk' ē)   [<Iroquoian (Wyandot), level land, plain] Eastern central state of the United States

kiln   (kiln)   *n.* An oven to bake pottery

kilometer   (ki läm' ə tər)   *n.* 1,000 meters or about 5/8 of a mile

kindling   (kin' dliŋ)   *n.* Bits of dry wood for starting a fire

lackluster (lak′ lus′ tər) *adj.* Lacking brightness; dull

laconic (lə kän′ ik) *adj.* Using few words

lacy (lā′ sē) *adj.* Having a delicate, open pattern, like lace

lament (lə ment′) *v.* To express deep sorrow for; mourn

lariat (lar′ ē it) *n.* A rope for tethering grazing horses; lasso

latent (lāt′ ′nt) *adj.* Hidden and not fully developed

lattice (lat′ is) *n.* An openwork structure of crossed strips or bars of wood, metal, and the like

leer (lir′) *v.* To look with harmful intent

leeward (lē′ wərd) *adj.* Sheltered from the wind

legacy (leg′ ə sē) *n.* Something handed down by a parent or an ancestor

lethal (lē′ thəl) *adj.* Deadly

liability (lī ə bil′ ə tē) *n.* A disadvantage

lichen (lī′ kən) *n.* Any of a large group of small plants

limerick (lim′ ər ik) *n.* A nonsense poem of five lines

lithe (līth) *adj.* Flexible and supple

loathe (lōth) *v.* To hate

lollop (läl′ əp) *v.* To move in a clumsy or relaxed way, bobbing up and down or from side to side

lorry (lôr′ ē) *n.* [Brit.] A motor truck

lute (lōōt) *n.* An old-fashioned stringed instrument like a guitar

machete (mə shet′ ē) *n.* Large, heavy-bladed knife

madly (mad′ lē) *adv.* Insanely; wildly or furiously; foolishly; extremely

majestic (mə jes′ tik) *adj.* Grand; lofty

malleable (mal′ ē ə b′l) *adj.* Able to be hammered, pounded, or pressed into various shapes without breaking

maneuver (mə nōō′ vər) *n.* A planned movement or procedure

mantle (man′ t′l) *n.* A loose, sleeveless cloak or cape

marred (märd) *v.* Disturbed

martial (mär′ shəl) *adj.* Suitable for war

masterful (mas′ tər fəl) *adj.* Able to force one's will on others

mastiff (mas′ tif) *n.* A large, powerful, smooth-coated dog with hanging lip and drooping ears

maxim (mak′ sim) *n.* Wise saying

meager (mē′ gər) *adj.* Of poor quality; small in amount

meek (mēk) *adj.* Patient and mild

melancholy (mel′ ən käl′ ē) *adj.* Sad, gloomy

menace (men′ is) *n.* Danger, threat

menage (mə näzh′) *n.* Household

mesa (mā′ sə) *n.* A flat tableland with steep sides

mesmerize (mez′ mər īz′) *v.* To hypnotize

metamorphose (met′ ə môr′ fōz) *v.* To change

metamorphosis (met′ ə môr′ fə sis) *n.* A change of form

milling (mil′ iŋ) *v.* Moving in a circular or random motion

mined (mīnd) *adj.* Filled with buried explosives that are set to go off when stepped on

miracle (mir′ ə k′l) *n.* An event or action that apparently contradicts known scientific laws and is hence thought to be due to supernatural causes

misanthrope (mis′ ən thrōp′) A person who hates or mistrusts everyone

Missouri (mi zoor′ ē) [<Algonquian, literally, people of the big canoes] Middle Western state of the central United States

mobilize (mō′ bə līz′) *v.* To put into motion

mock (mäk) *v.* To copy

moil (moil) *v.* To toil and slave

momentum (mō men′ təm) *n.* The increasing force of a moving object

monarch (män′ ərk) *n.* A ruler; king or queen

monitoring (män′ ə tər iŋ) *v.* Watching or keeping track of

monogrammed (män′ ə gramd′) *adj.* Having a design made up of two or more letters

monotone (män′ ə tōn) *v.* A single, unchanging tone

moor (moor) *n.* Rolling land with swamps

morbid (môr′ bid) *adj.* Of, having, or caused by disease; unhealthy

morgue (môrg) *n.* A place where the bodies of dead persons are kept to be examined or identified before burial

morose (mə rōs′) *adj.* Gloomy; ill-tempered

mortal (môr′ t′l) *n.* A being who must eventually die

mortality (môr tal′ ə tē) *n.* Having to die someday

mortician (môr tish′ ən) *n.* An undertaker; funeral director

mortuary (mor′ chōō wer′ ē) *n.* A place where dead bodies are kept before burial or cremation, such as a morgue or funeral home

mosaic (mō zā′ ik) *adj.* Made of different pieces combined to form a whole

mourning (môr′ niŋ) *v.* Feeling sorrow for the death of a loved one

murder (mur′ dər) *v.* To kill unlawfully and with malice

murky (mur′ kē) *adj.* Heavy and obscure with smoke or mist

mush (mush) *v.* To travel by foot over snow, usually with a dog sled

muslin (muz′ lin) *n.* A plain, strong kind of cotton cloth

mustache (mus′ tash) *n.* The hair on the upper lip of men

mutilated (myōōt′ ′l āt′ əd) *adj.* Damaged or injured

mutton (mut′ ′n) *n.* Sheep

muzzled (muz′ ′ld) *adj.* Prevented from talking or expressing an opinion

narcissism (när′ sə siz′m) *n.* Self-love; excessive interest in one's own appearance, comfort, importance, or abilities

neurophysiology (noor′ ō fiz′ ē äl′ ə jē) *n.* The study of the brain and nervous system

nimble (nim′ b′l) *adj.* Moving quickly and lightly

nonchalant (nän′ shə länt′) *adj.* Casual

obliging (ə blīj′ iŋ) *adj.* Ready to do favors

obsequious (əb sē′ kwē əs) *adj.* Much too willing to serve or obey; overly submissive

obsidian (əb sid′ ē ən) *n.* A hard, usually dark-colored or black, volcanic glass

obstinate (äb′ stə nit) *adj.* Stubborn

odious (ō′ dē əs) *adj.* Disgusting; offensive

oil painting (oil′ pānt′ iŋ) *n.* A picture painted in oil colors

ominous (äm′ ə nəs) *adj.* Threatening

ontogeny (än täj′ ə nē) *n.* The life cycle of a simple organism or individual

ooze (ōōz) *v.* To flow or leak slowly

opalescent (ō′ pə les′ 'nt)   *adj.* Showing a play of colors like an opal

opaque (ō pāk′)   *adj.* Not letting light pass through

organdy (or′ gən dē)   *n.* Thin, crisp cotton fabric used for items like dresses and curtains

ostler (äs′ lər)   *n.* Someone who takes care of horses at an inn or stable

outskirts (out′ skurts)   *n.* Part or district remote from the center or midst

Ozark (ō′ zärk)   **Mountains** [<Fr. *aux Arcs,* to the (region of the) Arc (Arkansa) Indians] Highland region in N.W. Arkansas, SW Missouri, and NE Oklahoma

pandemic (pan dem′ ik)   *adj.* Prevalent over a whole area; universal

paradox (par′ ə däks′)   *n.* A statement that seems contradictory, unbelievable, or absurd but that may actually be true in fact

parasite (par′ ə sīt)   *n.* An animal that lives on another organism in order to get food, protection, or both

passive (pas′ iv)   *adj.* Inactive

pathological (path′ə läj′ i k'l)   *adj.* Due to or involving disease

pauper (pô′ pər)   *n.* An extremely poor person

peeved (pēvd)   *adj.* Irritated

perilous (per′ əl əs)   *adj.* Dangerous

perpetual (pər pech′ oo wəl)   *adj.* Never stopping

persistent (pər sis′ tənt)   *adj.* Constantly recurring

perspective (pər spek′ tiv)   *n.* The appearance of objects or scenes as determined by their relative distance and positions; a specific point of view

pestilent (pes′ t'l ənt)   *adj.* Deadly; annoying

petrol (pet′ rəl)   *n.* [Brit.] Gasoline

phantasmagoria (fan taz′ mə gôr′ ē ə)   *n.* An early type of magic-lantern show consisting of various optical illusions

phantom (fan′ təm)   *n.* Something that seems to appear to the sight but has no physical existence

philanthropy (fi lan′ thrə pē)   *n.* A desire to help mankind; benevolence

philharmonic (fil′ här män′ ik)   *adj.* Loving or devoted to music

philosophy (fi läs′ ə fē)   *n.* Originally, love of, or the search for wisdom or knowledge

phylogeny (fī läj′ ə nē)   *n.* The development of a species or group

pilgrimage (pil′ grəm ij)   *n.* A long journey to a place of interest

pious (pī′ əs)   *adj.* Good; virtuous

plaiting (plāt′ iŋ)   *n.* Braiding

plankton (plaŋk′ tən)   *n.* Very small animal and plant life that floats or drifts in the water

pliant (plī′ ənt)   *adj.* Easily bent; adaptable

poise (poiz)   *v.* To balance

pomegranate (päm′ gran′ it)   *n.* A round fruit with a red, leathery rind and many seeds

pomp (pämp)   *n.* Impressive show or display

ponderous (pän′ dər əs)   *adj.* Very heavy, bulky

posting (pōs′ tiŋ)   Notice of the racing time of each swimmer

pound (pound)   *n.* A unit of money used by the British

precipitation (pri sip′ ə tā′ shən)   *n.* Great speed

precipitous (pri sip′ ə təs)   *adj.* Very steep

predatory (pred′ ə tôr′ ē)   *adj.* Living by capturing and feeding on other animals

predestined (prē des′ tind)   *adj.* In this case, marked to die early

preen (prēn)   *v.* To dress up; show pride in one's appearance

preening (prēn′ iŋ)   *n.* The act of cleaning and trimming feathers with a beak

preferable (pref′ ər ə b'l)   *adj.* More desirable

premium (prē′ mē əm)   *n.* An additional charge

prescribed (pri skrīb′'d)   *adj.* Advised as a medicine by a doctor

presently (prez′ 'nt lē)   *adv.* In a little while

presumptuous (pri zump′ choo wəs)   *n.* Overstepping ordinary bounds of courtesy

prevalent (prev′ ə lənt)   *adj.* Widely accepted

priming (prī′ miŋ)   *n.* The explosive used to set off the charge in a gun

proffer (präf′ ər)   *v.* To offer

prolapse (prō′ laps)   *n.* An internal organ that has fallen out of place

Promethean (prə mē′ thē ən)   *adj.* Life-bringing, creative, or courageously original

promissory (präm′ i sôr′ ē)   **notes** *n.* Written promises to pay someone a certain sum of money

prone (prōn)   *adj.* Lying face downward

prose (prōz)   *n.* Nonpoetic language

providence (präv′ ə dəns)   *n.* A godsend; a valuable gift

provisional (prə vizh′ ən 'l)   *adj.* Temporary; depending on future events

psychology (sī käl′ ə jē)   *n.* The science dealing with the mind

pummel (pum′ 'l)   *v.* To hit with repeated blows

pungent (pun′ jənt)   *adj.* Sharp-smelling

quaff (kwäf)   *v.* To drink in a thirsty way

quail (kwāl)   *v.* To draw back in fear

quarry (kwôr′ ē)   *v.* To carve out of the ground

quaver (kwā′ vər)   *v.* To shake or tremble

quicksilver (kwik′ sil′ vər)   *adj.* Quick; changeable; unpredictable; like the chemical element mercury, which is silver-white and flows easily

quip (kwip)   *v.* To make a witty remark

quiver (kwiv′ ər)   *n.* A case for arrows

radiant (rā′ dē ənt)   *adj.* Shining brightly

rancid (ran′ sid)   *adj.* Spoiled and bad smelling

rapt (rapt)   *adj.* Giving complete attention; totally carried away by something

rash (rash)   *adj.* Reckless

realm (relm)   *n.* A kingdom

reconnoiter (rē′ kə noit′ ər)   *v.* To look around

refuge (ref′ yōōj)   *n.* A place of safety or shelter

refute (ri fyōōt′)   *v.* To prove someone wrong

regalia (ri gāl′ yə)   *n.* Splendid clothes and decorations

register (rej′ is tər)   *n.* A record containing a list of names

relate (ri lāt′)   *v.* To tell

relish (rel′ ish)   *v.* To especially enjoy

remit (ri mit′)   *v.* To forgive or pardon; put back

remonstrance (ri män′ strəns)   *n.* The act of protesting or pleading

render (ren′ dər)   *v.* To melt down

repellent (ri pel′ ənt)   *n.* Something that pushes away
reproach (ri prōch′)   *v.* To blame; scold
resigned (ri zīn′ 'd)   *adj.* In a yielding and uncomplaining manner
resilient (ri zil′ yənt)   *adj.* Springing back into shape
resin (rez′ 'n)   *n.* A sticky brownish or yellowish substance that comes from evergreen trees
resolute (rez′ ə lōōt′)   *adj.* Of firm purpose
resourceful (ri sôrs′ fəl)   *adj.* Able to deal effectively with problems
retrospect (ret′ rə spekt′)   *n.* A looking back on the past
revoke (ri vōk′)   *v.* To cancel, withdraw
rheumatism (rōō′ mə tiz'm)   *n.* Pain and stiffness of the joints and muscles
riffle (rif′ 'l)   *n.* A shallow area in a stream
rigorous (rig′ ər əs)   *adj.* Strict; thorough
rind (rīnd)   *n.* Tough outer layer or skin
rite (rīt)   *n.* Religious observance
rodeo (rō′ dē ō′)   *n.* A public exhibition or competition of the skills of cowboys
rouge (rōōzh)   *n.* A reddish cosmetic used to color the cheeks
rout (rout′)   *v.* To completely defeat
ruff (ruf)   *n.* A band of fur around the necks of animals or birds
runt (runt)   *n.* The smallest animal of a litter

saffron (saf′ rən)   *n.* An orange-yellow color
sage (sāj)   *n.* A very wise man
saline (sā′ līn)   *n.* A salt solution
sanction (saŋk′ shən)   *n.* Support
sanctuary (saŋk′ choo wer′ ē)   *n.* A place of protection
saunter (sôn′ tər)   *v.* To walk about idly; stroll
savor (sā′ vər)   *v.* To enjoy
scale (skāl)   *n.* A series of musical tones
scapegoat (skāp′ gōt′)   *n.* A person or group blamed for the mistakes or crimes of others
scorn (skôrn)   *n.* A strong dislike for someone or something thought to be inferior
scour (skour)   *v.* To clean by rubbing vigorously
scourge (skurj)   *n.* The cause of serious trouble
scowl (skoul)   *v.* To frown
scrim (skrim)   *n.* A light, semi-transparent curtain
scrooge (skrōōj)   *n.* A hard, misery misanthrope
scurry (skur′ ē)   *v.* To run hastily; scamper
scuttle (skut′ 'l)   *v.* To run or move quickly; scurry
seismology (sīz mäl′ ə jē)   *n.* A geophysical science dealing with earthquakes and related phenomena
sentimental (sen′ tə men′ t'l)   *adj.* Acting from feeling rather than from practical motives
sepulcher (sep′ 'l kər)   *n.* Grave; tomb
seraph (ser′ əf)   *n.* Angel
serenity (sə ren′ ə tē)   *n.* Calmness
severe (sə vir′)   *adj.* Harsh
sexton (seks′ tən)   *n.* A church official in charge of ringing the bells
shadowing (shad′ ō iŋ)   *v.* Shading an area in a picture or painting
sheen (shēn)   *n.* Brightness; shininess
shilling (shil′ iŋ)   *n.* A British coin worth five pennies
shrew (shrōō)   *n.* A small, slender, mouselike animal with soft, brown fur and a long, pointed snout

shrewdest (shrōōd′ əst)   *adj.* Cleverest
shrouded (shroud′ əd)   *adj.* Hidden from view
shudder (shud′ ər)   *v.* To shake
sibling (sib′ liŋ)   *n.* A brother or sister
sieve (siv)   *n.* A utensil with many tiny openings; strainer
sinew (sin′ yōō)   *n.* Tendon
sinewy (sin′ yōō wē)   *adj.* Tough and strong
skids (skidz)   *n.* Planks or logs on which a heavy object can be slid
slacken (slak′ 'n)   *v.* To become less active
slither (slith′ ər)   *v.* To slide
slough (slōō)   *n.* A swamp, bog, or marsh that is part of an inlet or backwater
sluggish (slug′ ish)   *adj.* Lacking energy
sluice (slōōs)   *n.* An artificial channel or passage for water, having a gate or valve at its head to regulate the flow
smartly (smärt′ lē)   *adv.* Sharply
snorkel (snôr′ k'l)   *v.* To swim underwater using a snorkel, or breathing tube, that extends above the surface of the water
snowshoes (snō′ shōōz′)   *n.* Racket-shaped pieces of wood crisscrossed with strips of leather, worn on the feet to prevent sinking in deep snow
snug (snug)   *adj.* Cozy; comfortable
solemn (säl′ əm)   *adj.* Serious; somber
solemnize (säl′ əm nīz)   *v.* To honor
somber (säm′ bər)   *adj.* Dark and solemn
spectacle (spek′ tə k'l)   *n.* Something to look at; unusual display
spectacles (spek′ tə k'lz)   *n.* A pair of eyeglasses
spectator (spek′ tāt ər)   *n.* A person who sees or watches something without taking an active part
specter (spek′ tər)   *n.* A ghost or ghostlike appearance
spectral (spek′ trəl)   *adj.* Like a specter; phantom; ghostly
spectroscope (spek′ trə skōp′)   *n.* An optical instrument used for forming spectra for study
spittoon (spi tōōn′)   *n.* A jarlike container into which people spit
squat (skwät)   *adj.* Short and heavy
stable (stā′ b'l)   *n.* A building in which horses or cattle are sheltered and fed
staccato (stə kät′ ō)   *adj.* Made up of sharp, separate little elements
stalk (stôk)   *v.* To walk slowly and stiffly
steed (stēd)   *n.* A high-spirited riding horse
stern (sturn)   *adj.* Strict; unyielding
still (stil)   *n.* A photograph made from a single frame of a motion picture and used for advertising it
straggly (strag′ lē)   *adj.* Spread out
straightforward (strāt′ fôr′ wərd)   *adj.* Direct; frank; honest
strand (strand)   *n.* The ocean shore
stride (strīd)   *v.* To walk with long steps, especially in a vigorous manner
strive (strīv)   *v.* To struggle
stubble (stub′ 'l)   *n.* Short stumps of corn or grain
studio (stōō′ dē ō′)   A room or rooms where an artist or photographer works
subscribe (səb skrīb′)   *v.* To support
subservient (səb sur′ vē ənt)   *adj.* Inferior
subtle (sut′ 'l)   *adj.* Delicately skillful or clever

succession   (sǝk sesh' ǝn)   *n.* The act of coming after another in order

succulent   (suk' yoo lent)   *adj.* Juicy

supercilious   (soo' pǝr sil' ē ǝs)   *adj.* Proud; scornful

supple   (sup' 'l)   *adj.* Flexible

surge   (sᴇrj')   *v.* To move in a violent swelling motion

surpass   (sǝr pas')   *v.* To be superior to

surreptitious   (sᴇr' ǝp tish' ǝs)   *adj.* Secret

susceptible   (sǝ sep' tǝ b'l)   *adj.* Responsive

sustain   (sǝ stān')   *v.* To support

swarm   (swôrm)   *v.* To be filled or crowded

swerve   (swᴇrv)   *n.* A curving motion

tableau   (tab' lō)   *n.* A dramatic scene or picture

taco   (tä' kō)   *n.* A Mexican dish consisting of a fried, folded tortilla filled with chopped meat, shredded lettuce, and the like

taint   (tānt)   *n.* A trace

taut   (tôt)   *adj.* Tightly stretched

tawny   (tô' nē)   *adj.* Yellowish-brown

teak   (tēk)   *n.* Yellowish-brown wood

technology   (tek näl' ǝ jē)   *n.* The ideas of science applied to practical problems

tedious   (tē' dē ǝs)   *adj.* Long and boring

tempest   (tem' pist)   *n.* A violent storm

tentative   (ten' tǝ tiv)   *adj.* Hesitant; uncertain

tepid   (tep' id)   *adj.* Not warm or cold; lukewarm

termagant   (tᴇr' mǝ gǝnt)   *adj.* Scolding

testimony   (tes' ti mō' nē)   *n.* Statement or declaration

tether   (teth' ǝr)   *v.* To fasten with a rope or chain

thistle   (this' 'l)   *n.* A stubborn, weedy plant with sharp leaves and usually purplish flowers

threadbare   (thred' ber')   *adj.* Worn, shabby

tiered   (tird)   *adj.* Stacked in rows

titanic   (tī tan' ik)   *adj.* Having great size, strength, or power

torrent   (tôr' ǝnt)   *n.* A flood

totter   (tät' ǝr)   *v.* To rock or shake as if about to fall; to be unsteady

tracheotomy   (trā' kē ät' ǝ mē)   *n.* An operation in which the trachea, or windpipe, is cut to make an artificial breathing hole

translucent   (trans loo' s'nt)   *adj.* Clear

transmission   (trans mish' ǝn)   *n.* The passage of radio waves through space between the transmitting station and the receiving station

trebly   (tre' blē)   *adv.* Three times as much; triply

tribulation   (trib' yǝ lā' shǝn)   *n.* Great misery or distress

trident   (trīd' 'nt)   *n.* A spear with three points

trifle   (trī' f'l)   *n.* Something of little value or importance

triumphant   (trī um' fǝnt)   *adj.* Rejoicing for victory; exulting in success

trundle   (trun' d'l)   *v.* To move on wheels or as if on wheels

tumultuous   (too mul' choo wǝs)   *adj.* Noisy and violent

unanimous   (yoo nan' ǝ mǝs)   *adj.* Based on complete agreement

unique   (yoo nēk')   *adj.* Highly unusual or rare

unison   (yoo' nǝ sǝn)   *n.* Complete agreement; harmony

unrequited   (un' ri kwī' t'd)   *adj.* Unreturned

urchin   (ᴇr' chin)   *n.* A mischievous boy

usurp   (yoo sᴇrp')   *v.* To take without right

utilize   (yoot' 'l īz')   *v.* To make useful

vacancy   (vā' kǝn sē)   *n.* Emptiness

vanquish   (van' kwish)   *v.* To overcome

varmint   (vär' mǝnt)   *n.* An animal regarded as troublesome

veer   (vir)   *v.* To change direction

verge   (vᴇrj)   *n.* The edge or brink

verisimilitude   (ver' ǝ si mil' ǝ tood')   *n.* The appearance of being true or real

vertebrate   (vᴇr' tǝ brāt')   *n.* An animal with a backbone

vibrant   (vī' brǝnt)   *adj.* Throbbing with life and activity; lively; energetic

vicar   (vik' ǝr)   *n.* A parish priest in the Anglican Church

virago   (vi rā' gō)   *n.* A quarrelsome woman

visage   (viz' ij)   *n.* Face

vital   (vīt' 'l)   *adj.* Essential to life; living

vitality   (vī tal' ǝ tē)   *n.* The power to live or go on living

vitalize   (vīt' 'l īz')   *n.* To make vital; give life to

vital signs   (vīt' 'l sīnz')   *n.* Indicators of the efficient functioning of the body; especially pulse, temperature, and respiration

vitamin   (vīt' ǝ min)   *n.* Any of a number of complex organic substances found in most foods

vixen   (vik' s'n)   *n.* A female fox

void   (void)   *n.* Emptiness

waft   (wâft)   *v.* Carry

wages   (wāj' ǝz)   *n.* Money paid to an employee for work done

warbler   (wôr' blǝr)   *n.* Songbird

wassail   (wäs' 'l)   *n.* A spiced drink used in celebrating

watercolor   (wôt' ǝr kul' ǝr)   *n.* A pigment or coloring matter that is mixed with water for use as a paint; a painting done with such paints

wee   (wē)   *adj.* Very small, tiny

wheedle   (hwē' d'l)   *v.* To persuade a person by flattery or coaxing

whimper   (hwim' pǝr)   *v.* To make low, crying sounds; complain

wicker   (wik' ǝr)   *n.* A thin, flexible twig

wigwam   (wig' wäm)   *n.* A shelter with a rounded top made by certain Native American groups

wily   (wī' lē)   *adj.* Sly

wince   (wins' d)   *v.* Draw back

winnow   (win' ō)   *v.* To beat as with wings

wistfully   (wist' fǝl lē)   *adj.* Showing vague yearnings

wither   (with' ǝr)   *v.* Dry up

wonderful   (wun' dǝr fǝl)   *adj.* That causes wonder; marvelous; amazing

wonderland   (wun' dǝr land')   *n.* An imaginary land full of wonders

wonderment   (wun' dǝr mǝnt)   *n.* Astonishment

wonderworker   (wun' dǝr wᴇrk' ǝr)   *n.* One who performs miracles or wonders

wondrous   (wun' drǝs)   *adj.* Wonderful; extraordinary

yearn   (yᴇrn)   *v.* Want very much

yucca   (yuk' ǝ)   *adj.* Plants with stiff sword-shaped leaves and white flowers

INDEX OF FINE ART

INDEX OF SKILLS

CRITICAL THINKING AND READING

READING IN THE CONTENT AREAS

SPEAKING AND LISTENING

STUDY AND RESEARCH

THINKING AND WRITING

UNDERSTANDING LANGUAGE

INDEX OF TITLES BY THEMES

A TIME FOR COURAGE

FANTASY AND THE UNEXPLAINED

THE ENVIRONMENT AND THE TOUCHED AND UNTOUCHED EARTH

LAUGHTER AND SORROW

INDEX OF AUTHORS AND TITLES

Page numbers in italics refer to biographical information.

ACKNOWLEDGMENTS (continued)

Delacorte Press
"The Luckiest Time of All" excerpted from the book *The Lucky Stone* by Lucille Clifton. Copyright © 1979 by Lucille Clifton. Reprinted by permission of Delacorte Press.

Delacorte Press/Seymour Lawrence
"Seal" excerpted from the book *Laughing Time* by William Jay Smith. Copyright © 1953, 1955, 1956, 1957, 1959, 1968, 1974, 1977, 1980 by William Jay Smith. Reprinted by permission of Delacorte Press/Seymour Lawrence.

Devin-Adair Publishers
"The Trout" from *The Man Who Invented Sin and Other Stories* by Sean O'Faolain. The Devin-Adair Company, 1948, renewed in 1976.

Adriaan de Wit
"Ojeeg, the Hunter, and the Ice Man" retold by Dorothy de Wit in *The Talking Stone*, edited by Dorothy de Wit. Copyright © 1979 by Dorothy de Wit.

Dodd, Mead & Company, Inc.
"The Cremation of Sam McGee" by Robert Service. Reprinted by permission of Dodd, Mead & Company, Inc. from *The Collected Poems of Robert Service*. Reprinted by permission of Dodd, Mead & Company, Inc. from *Circle of the Seasons* by Edwin Way Teale. Copyright 1953 by Edwin Way Teale. Copyright renewed 1981 by Nellie D. Teale.

Doubleday, a division of Bantam, Doubleday, Dell Publishing Group, Inc.
"The Third Wish" by Joan Aiken first appeared in *All and More* copyright © 1974 by Joan Aiken from, *Not What You Expected*. Excerpts from *Tell Me How Long the Train's Been Gone* by James Baldwin. Copyright © 1968 by James Baldwin. "After Twenty Years" by O. Henry from *The Complete Works of O. Henry*. "Broadway, Twilight" by Tom Prideaux from *Creative Youth* edited by Hughes Mearns. Copyright 1925 by Doubleday & Company, Inc. Text of *Where the Red Fern Grows* by Woodrow Wilson Rawls. Copyright © 1961 by Woodrow Wilson Rawls and copyright © 1961 by the Curtis Publishing Company. "The Bat" copyright 1938 by Theodore Roethke from *The Collected Poems of Theodore Roethke*. "Old Florist" by Theodore Roethke, copyright 1946 by Harper & Brothers from *The Collected Poems of Theodore Roethke*. Reprinted by permission of Doubleday.

E. P. Dutton, a division of New American Library
"The Flower-Fed Buffaloes" from *Going-to-the-Stars* by Vachel Lindsay. Copyright 1926 by D. Appleton & Co., renewed 1954 by Elizabeth C. Lindsay. A Hawthorn book. Reprinted by permission of E. P. Dutton, a division of New American Library.

Farrar, Straus and Giroux, Inc.
Excerpt titled "The Sneaker Crisis" from *Raising Demons* by Shirley Jackson. Copyright 1953, 1954, 1956, 1957 by Shirley Jackson. Copyright renewed © 1985 by Laurence Hyman, Barry Hyman, and Sarah Hyman Elias. "Utzel and His Daughter, Poverty" from *Stories for Children* by Isaac Bashevis Singer. Copyright © 1962, 1967, 1968, 1970, 1972, 1973, 1974, 1975, 1976, 1979, 1980, 1984 by Isaac Bashevis Singer. Excerpt from "A Far Cry From Africa" from *Collected Poems 1948–1984* by Derek Walcott. Copyright © 1962, 1963, 1964 and 1986 by Derek Walcott. Reprinted by permission of Farrar, Straus and Giroux, Inc.

C. J. Fosdick and Triangle Communications Inc.
"A Season of Acceptance" by C. J. Fosdick, reprinted from *Seventeen* Magazine, December 1985. Copyright © 1985 by Triangle Communications, Inc. All rights reserved. Reprinted by permission of the author.

Gruner + Jahr U.S.A. Publishers, Inc.
"The Confidence Game" by Pat Carr. From *Young Miss*, © 1977. Parents' Magazine Enterprises, Inc. Reprinted by permission of Gruner + Jahr U.S.A. Publishers, Inc.

Harcourt Brace Jovanovich, Inc.
"Eugenie Clark and the Sleeping Sharks" from *Wild Animals, Gentle Women*, copyright © 1978 by Margery Facklam. "Morning—'The Bird Perched for Flight' " from "The Heron and the Astronaut" in *Earth Shine*, copyright © 1969 by Anne Morrow Lindbergh. "Fog" from *Chicago Poems* by Carl Sandburg, copyright 1916 by Holt, Rinehart and Winston, Inc.; renewed 1944 by Carl Sandburg. "The Boy and the Wolf" from *The Magic Circle* by Louis Untermeyer, copyright 1952 by Harcourt Brace Jovanovich, Inc.; renewed 1980 by Bryna Ivens Untermeyer, Lawrence S. Untermeyer, and John F. Moore. From "In Search of Our Mothers' Gardens" copyright © 1974 by Alice Walker. Reprinted from her volume *In Search of Our Mothers' Gardens*. "Women" copyright © 1970 by Alice Walker. Reprinted from her volume *Revolutionary Petunias & Other Poems*. Reprinted by permission of Harcourt Brace Jovanovich, Inc.

Harcourt Brace Jovanovich, Inc., the author's literary estate, and The Hogarth Press Ltd.
From *A Room of One's Own* by Virginia Woolf, copyright 1929 by Harcourt Brace Jovanovich, Inc.; renewed 1957 by Leonard Woolf.

Harper & Row, Publishers, Inc.
"Rikki-tikki-tavi" from *The Jungle Book* by Rudyard Kipling. Haiku, "The Falling Flower" by Moritake from *Poetry Handbook: A Dictionary of Terms*, 4th edition by Babette Deutsch (Thomas Y. Crowell). Copyright © 1957, 1962, 1969, 1974 by Babette Deutsch. "The Highwayman" from *Collected Poems* by Alfred Noyes (J. B. Lippincott). Chapter 2, "A Boy and a Man" from *Banner in the Sky* by James Ramsey Ullman (J. B. Lippincott). Copyright 1954 by James Ramsey Ullman. Reprinted by permission of Harper & Row, Publishers, Inc.

Harper & Row, Publishers, Inc. and Olwyn Hughes
First four lines from "Mirror" from *The Collected Poems of Sylvia Plath* edited by Ted Hughes. Copyright © 1963 by Ted Hughes. Published in London by Faber and Faber Ltd., copyright Ted Hughes 1971 and 1981. Reprinted by permission.

Harvard University Press and the Trustees of Amherst College
"I'm Nobody! Who are you?" Reprinted by permission of the publishers and the Trustees of Amherst College from *The Poems of Emily Dickinson*, edited by Thomas H. Johnson, Cambridge, Mass.: The Belknap Press of Harvard University Press, Copyright 1951, © 1955, 1979, 1983 by The President and Fellows of Harvard College.

Lawrence Hill and Company
''Last Cover'' reprinted from *The Best Nature Stories of Paul Annixter* by Jane and Paul Annixter by permission of Lawrence Hill and Company. Copyright 1974.

Edward D. Hoch
''Zoo'' by Edward D. Hoch, © 1958 by King-Size Publications, Inc.; © renewed 1986 by Edward D. Hoch. Reprinted by permission of the author.

The Hokuseido Press
Haiku poems (''The silence!'' by Bashō; ''Ah, grief and sadness!'' by Buson; and ''The snake slid away'' by Kyoshi) from *Haiku*, translated by R. H. Blyth, The Hokuseido Press, 1971. Reprinted by permission of The Hokuseido Press.

Henry Holt and Company, Inc.
Lines from ''Birches'' copyright © 1969 by Holt, Rinehart and Winston, Inc; copyright © 1962 by Robert Frost; copyright © 1975 by Lesley Frost Ballantine; ''The Pasture'' copyright 1939, © 1967, 1969 by Holt, Rinehart and Winston, Inc.; and ''Stopping by Woods on a Snowy Evening'' copyright 1923, © 1969 by Holt, Rinehart and Winston, Inc.; copyright 1951 by Robert Frost. From *The Poetry of Robert Frost* edited by Edward Connery Lathem. Reprinted by permission of Henry Holt and Company, Inc.

Houghton Mifflin Company
''Endlessness'' from *Realm of Numbers* by Isaac Asimov. Copyright © 1959 by Isaac Asimov. ''A Song of Greatness'' from *The Children Sing in the Far West* by Mary Austin. Copyright 1928 by Mary Austin. Copyright © renewed 1956 by Kenneth M. Chapman and Mary C. Wheelwright. ''Phaëthon, Son of Apollo'' from *Greek Myths* by Olivia Coolidge. Copyright 1949 and copyright © renewed 1977 by Olivia Coolidge. ''The Village Blacksmith'' from *The Poetical Works of Longfellow*, Cambridge Edition, 1975. Lines from ''Patterns'' from *The Complete Poetical Works of Amy Lowell*. Copyright © 1955 by Hougton Mifflin Company; copyright © renewed 1983 by Houghton Mifflin Company, Brinton P. Roberts, Esquire, and G. D'Andelot Belin, Esquire. ''Icarus and Daedalus'' from *Old Greek Folk Stories Told Anew* by Josephine Preston Peabody. The Riverside Press. Reprinted by permission of Houghton Mifflin Company.

Jeremy Ingalls
''Prometheus the Fire-Bringer,'' one of her fifteen stories in her *A Book of Legends* initially published by Harcourt Brace and Company in 1941. Copyright purchased by author in 1950. Copyright © 1950, 1968 by Jeremy Ingalls.

International Creative Management, Inc.
Grandpa and the Statue by Arthur Miller. Copyright © 1945, 1973 by Arthur Miller. ''Feelings About Words'' from *Words, Words, Words* by Mary O'Neill. Copyright © 1966 by Mary O'Neill. *The Monsters Are Due on Maple Street* by Rod Serling. Copyright © 1960 by Rod Serling. Reprinted by permission of International Creative Management, Inc.

International Paper Company
''How to Enjoy Poetry'' by James Dickey from the Power of the Printed Word Program. Reprinted by permission of International Paper Company.

Japan Publications, Inc.
''On sweet plum blossoms,'' ''Has spring come indeed?'' and ''Temple bells die out'' by Bashō. Reprinted from *One Hundred Famous Haiku* by Daniel C. Buchanan, with permission from Japan Publications ©1973.

Johns Hopkins University Press
Lines from ''Rome in Her Ruins'' by Francisco de Quevedo, translated by Felicia D. Hemans. Reprinted from *Ten Centuries of Spanish Poetry: An Anthology in English Verse with Original Texts* edited by Eleanor L. Turnbull. Copyright 1955 by The Johns Hopkins Press. Reprinted by permission.

Alfred A. Knopf, Inc.
''Amigo Brothers'' adapted by permission of Alfred A. Knopf, Inc. from *Stories from El Barrio* by Piri Thomas. Copyright © 1978 by Piri Thomas. ''Mother to Son'' copyright 1926 by Alfred A. Knopf, Inc., and renewed 1954 by Langston Hughes. Reprinted from *Selected Poems of Langston Hughes*, by permission of the publisher. Lines from ''Harlem Night Song'' copyright 1926 and renewed 1954 by Langston Hughes. Reprinted from *Selected Poems of Langston Hughes*, by permission of the publisher. ''Annabel Lee'' from *The Complete Poems and Stories of Edgar Allan Poe, with Selections from His Writings*, edited by Arthur Hobson Quinn. Lines from ''The Puritan's Ballad'' from *Collected Poems of Elinor Wylie* by Elinor Wylie; copyright 1928 by Alfred A. Knopf, Inc. and renewed 1965 by Edwina C. Rubinstein, by permission of Alfred A. Knopf, Inc.

H. N. Levitt
''Winslow Homer: America's Greatest Painter'' by H. N. Levitt from *Boy's Life*, September 1986. Copyrighted H. N. Levitt 1986. Reprinted by permission of the author.

Little, Brown and Company
''Baucis and Philemon'' from *Mythology* by Edith Hamilton. Copyright 1942 by Edith Hamilton; copyright © renewed 1969 by Dorian Fielding Reid and Doris Fielding Reid. ''The Porcupine'' from *Verses from 1929 On* by Ogden Nash. Copyright 1944 by Ogden Nash. First appeared in *The Saturday Evening Post*. By permission of Little, Brown and Company.

Liveright Publishing Corporation
''In Just—'' is reprinted from *Tulips & Chimneys* by E. E. Cummings by permission of Liveright Publishing Corporation. Copyright 1923, 1925 and renewed 1951, 1953 by E. E. Cummings. Copyright © 1973, 1976 by the Trustees for the E. E. Cummings Trust. Copyright © 1973, 1976 by George James Firmage.

Sterling Lord Literistic, Inc.
''Song Form'' from *Black Magic Poetry 1961–1967* by Amiri Baraka (LeRoi Jones). Copyright © 1969 by Amiri Baraka (LeRoi Jones). Reprinted by permission of Sterling Lord Literistic, Inc.

Macmillan of Canada, a division of Canada Publishing Corporation
''Narcissus'' from *Four Ages of Man: The Classical Myths* ©1962 by Jay MacPherson. Reprinted by permission of Macmillan of Canada, a division of Canada Publishing Corporation.

Macmillan Publishing Company
"The Pheasant" from *Collected Poems* by Robert P. Tristram Coffin. Copyright 1935 by Macmillan Publishing Company, renewed 1963 by Margaret Coffin Halvosa. "The Town Mouse and the Country Mouse" and "The Fox and the Crow" from *The Fables of Aesop: Selected, Told Anew and Their History Traced* by Joseph Jacobs. Copyright © 1964 by Macmillan Publishing Company. "When the Frost is on the Punkin" from *The Complete Works of James Whitcomb Riley*, Vol. 2 (Indianapolis: Bobbs-Merrill, 1913). Reprinted with permission of Macmillan Publishing Company.

Macmillan Publishing Company and The Society of Authors on behalf of the copyright owner, Mrs. Iris Wise
"Washed in Silver" from *Collected Poems* by James Stephens. Copyright 1915 by Macmillan Publishing Company, renewed 1943 by James Stephens. Reprinted with permission.

Macmillan Publishing Company and A. P. Watt Ltd. on behalf of Michael B. Yeats and Macmillan London Ltd.
Lines from "The Stolen Child" reprinted with permission from *Collected Poems of W.B. Yeats* (New York: Macmillan, 1956).

McIntosh and Otis, Inc.
From *These Were the Sioux* by Mari Sandoz. Copyright © 1961 by Mari Sandoz. Reprinted by permission of McIntosh and Otis, Inc.

William Morrow & Company, Inc.
"Winter" from *Cotton Candy on a Rainy Day* by Nikki Giovanni. Copyright © 1978 by Nikki Giovanni. By permission of William Morrow & Company, Inc.

John Murray (Publishers) Ltd.
"The Dying Detective" from *The Game's Afoot* by Michael and Mollie Hardwick. Copyright © Michael & Mollie Hardwick 1969.

New American Library
"Miracles" from *Leaves of Grass* by Walt Whitman.

New Directions Publishing Corporation
Lines from "Garden" by H.D., *Collected Poems 1912–1944*. Copyright © 1982 by the Estate of Hilda Doolittle. Reprinted by permission of New Directions Publishing Corporation.

Harold Ober Associates Inc.
"Stolen Day" by Sherwood Anderson, originally published in *This Week* Magazine. Copyright 1941 by United Newspapers Magazine Corp. Copyright renewed 1968 by Eleanor Copenhaver Anderson. "The Old Demon" by Pearl S. Buck, originally published in *Cosmopolitan*. Copyright 1939 by Pearl S. Buck. Copyright © renewed 1966 by Pearl S. Buck. Reprinted by permission of Harold Ober Associates Inc.

The Peter Pauper Press
Haiku, "As lightning flashes . . ." by Bashō from *Cherry-Blossoms: Japanese Haiku*, Series III. Copyright © 1960 by The Peter Pauper Press. Reprinted by permission of the Peter Pauper Press, White Plains, NY.

Prentice-Hall, Inc.
"The Mystery and Wonder of Words" from the book *Wonder in Words* by Maxwell Nurnberg, © 1968. Used by permission of the publisher, Prentice-Hall, Inc., Englewood Cliffs, NJ.

The Putnam Publishing Group
"Rip Van Winkle" from *A Legend of the Kaatskill Mountains* by Washington Irving. G. P. Putnam & Sons, 1871.

Random House, Inc.
"Father William" from *The Complete Works of Lewis Carroll* by Lewis Carroll. Lines from "Minor Elegy" by Henriqueta Lisboa, translated by Willis Barnstone and Nelson Cerqueira. Reprinted from *A Book of Women Poets from Antiquity to Now* edited by Aliki Barnstone and Willis Barnstone, Schocken Books.

Marian Reiner
Haiku by Buson, Otsuji, and Ryorai from *More Cricket Songs: Japanese Haiku* translated by Harry Behn. Copyright © 1971 by Harry Behn. All rights reserved. Reprinted by permission of Marian Reiner.

Marian Reiner for Eve Merriam
"Onomatopoeia" from *It Doesn't Always Have to Rhyme* by Eve Merriam. Copyright © 1964 by Eve Merriam. All Rights Reserved. Reprinted by permission of Marian Reiner for the author.

Estate of Quentin Reynolds
"A Secret for Two" by Quentin Reynolds. Copyright 1936 Crowell-Collier Publishing Co. Reprinted by permission.

St. Martin's Press, Inc. and Harold Ober Associates Inc.
"Cat on the Go" from *All Things Wise and Wonderful* by James Herriot. Copyright © 1976, 1977 by James Herriot.

Charles Scribner's Sons, an imprint of Macmillan Publishing Co.
Ernerst Hemingway, "A Day's Wait" from *Winner Take Nothing*. Copyright 1933 Charles Scribner's Sons; copyright renewed © 1961 Mary Hemingway. Marjorie Kinnan Rawlings, "Rattlesnake Hunt" from *Cross Creek*. Copyright 1942 Marjorie Kinnan Rawlings; copyright renewed © 1970 Norton Baskin. Reprinted with the permission of Charles Scribner's Sons, an imprint of Macmillan Publishing Co.

Charles Scribner's Sons and Juliet Wood
Juliet Piggott, "Popocatepetl and Ixtlaccihuatl" from *Mexican Folk Tales*. Copyright © 1973 Juliet Piggott. Reprinted with permission.

Leslie Marmon Silko
From "Humaweepi, the Warrior Priest" by Leslie Marmon Silko. Reprinted by permission of the author.

Simon & Schuster, Inc.
Pronunciation key from *Webster's New World Dictionary—Second College Edition*. Copyright © 1984 by Simon & Schuster, Inc. Reprinted by permission.

Gary Soto and Poetry
"Oranges" by Gary Soto. First appeared in *Poetry*, copyright © 1983 by The Modern Poetry Association.

Rosemary A. Thurber
"The Fox and the Crow" by James Thurber. Copyright © 1950 James Thurber. Copyright © 1978 Helen Thurber. From *Further Fables for Our Time*, published by Simon & Schuster, Inc.

TriQuarterly
Lines from "The River" by Javier Héraud, translated by Paul Blackburn. From *TriQuarterly*, No. 13–14, Fall/Winter issue, 1969. Copyright © 1969 by *TriQuarterly*, Evanston, IL. Reprinted by permission of the publisher.

University of Notre Dame Press
From *Barrio Boy* by Ernesto Galarza. © 1971 by University of Notre Dame Press. Reprinted by permission.

University of Pittsburgh Press
Lines from "A Forgotten Man's Song about the Winds" (Tatilgak traditional) reprinted from *Eskimo Poems from Canada and Greenland* by Tom Lowenstein, by permission of the University of Pittsburgh Press. © 1973 by Tom Lowenstein.

Viking Penguin Inc.
"The Legend of the Hummingbird" from *Once in Puerto Rico* by Pura Belpré. Copyright © 1973 by Pura Belpré. Lines from "The Hermit Has a Visitor" from *Our Ground Time Here Will Be Brief* by Maxine Kumin. Copyright © 1972 by Maxine Kumin. "Season at the Shore" from *Times Three* by Phyllis McGinley. Copyright 1954 by Phyllis McGinley, renewed © 1982 by Phyllis Hayden Blake. Originally published in *The New Yorker*. Reprinted by permission of Viking Penguin Inc.

Mai Vo-Dinh
"The Little Lizard's Sorrow" from *The Toad Is the Emperor's Uncle, Animal Folktales from Viet-Nam*, told and illustrated by Vo-Dinh. Copyright © 1970 by Mai Vo-Dinh.

Western Publishing Company, Inc.
"The Bride of Pluto" (retitled "Demeter and Persephone") adapted from *Golden Treasury of Myths and Legends* by Anne Terry White, © 1959 Western Publishing Company, Inc. Reprinted by permission.

Jade Snow Wong and Curtis Brown, Ltd.
From "A Time of Beginnings" in *No Chinese Stranger* by Jade Snow Wong. Copyright © 1975 by Jade Snow Wong. Reprinted by permission of the author and Curtis Brown, Ltd.

Writers & Artists Agency
A Christmas Carol: Scrooge and Marley adapted from Charles Dickens by Israel Horovitz. Reprinted by permission.

Note: Every effort has been made to locate the copyright owner of material reprinted in this book. Omissions brought to our attention will be corrected in subsequent editions.

ART CREDITS

Cover and Title Page: Frank Weston Benson, *Rainy Day*, 1906, oil on canvas, 63/5 × 76.2 cm, Friends of American Art 1910.314, © 1987, The Art Institute of Chicago, all rights reserved; **p. 1:** *The Boating Party*, 1893/1894, Mary Cassatt, The National Gallery of Art, Washington, Chester Dale Collection; **p. 5:** *Bouquet with Flying Lovers*, c. 1934–47, Marc Chagall, The Tate Gallery, London; **p. 8:** Glass mosaic wall mural: Landscape—Base and Fountain, c. 1905–15 (detail), Tiffany Studios, The Metropolitan Museum of Art, Gift of Lillian Nassau, 1976, and Gift of Mrs. L. Groves Geer, 1978; **p. 11:** Ufer, Walter (1876–1936), 1984-66, *The Callers*, oil on canvas, executed ca. 1926, 50½ × 50½", National Museum of American Art, Smithsonian Institution, Gift of Mr. and Mrs. Crosby Kemper, Jr.; **p. 12:** *Rudyard Kipling* (detail), 1899, P. Burne-Jones, National Portrait Gallery, London; **p. 55:** *Four Girls,* August Macke, Three Lions; **p. 75:** Johnson, William H., *Mom and Dad* (or) *Portrait of a Lady with Kittens,* 1944, National Museum of American Art, Smithsonian Institution, Gift of the Harmon Foundation; **p. 89:** *A Country Lad,* Winslow Homer, Cooper-Hewitt Museum, Smithsonian Institution; **p. 91:** *Young Fisherman,* 1889, Louis Michel Eilshemius, Hirshhorn Museum and Sculpture Garden, Smithsonian Institution, Gift of Joseph H. Hirshhorn, 1966; **p. 105:** *Early Summer on the Farm,* Karl Rodko, Three Lions; **p. 108:** Sunrise IV, 1937, Arthur Dove, Hirshhorn Museum and Sculpture Garden, Smithsonian Institution; **p. 114:** Thomas Worthington Whittredge, *Forest Interior,* 1882, oil on canvas, 69.9 × 69.9 cm, Roger McCormick Fund, 1981.643, © 1987 The Art Institute of Chicago. All rights reserved. **p. 119:** Johnson, William H., *Jim,* 1930, National Museum of American Art, Smithsonian Institution, Gift of the Harmon Foundation; **p. 122:** *Harlem Nocturne,* 1952, Alice Neel, Courtesy Robert Miller Gallery, New York: **p. 132:** *Washington Irving* (detail), Daniel Huntington, National Portrait Gallery, Smithsonian Institution; **p. 133:** *Rip in the Mountains,* Albertus Del Orient Brower, Shelburne Museum, Shelburne, Vermont; **p. 136:** *Rip at the Inn,* Albertus Del Orient Brower, Shelburne Museum, Shelburne, Vermont; **p. 139:** *Rip Van Winkle Asleep,* Albertus Del Orient Brower, Shelburne Museum, Shelburne, Vermont; **p. 142:** *Return of Rip Van Winkle,* 1829, John Quidor, National Gallery of Art, Washington, Laurie Platt Winfrey, Inc.; **p. 147:** Winslow Homer, American, 1836–1910, *The Four Leaf Clover,* 1873, oil on canvas, 14¼" × 20-3/8", 70.150, © 1987 The Detroit Institute of Arts, Bequest of Robert H. Tannahill; **p. 154:** *Pearl S. Buck* (detail), Vita P. Solomon, National Portrait Gallery, Smithsonian Institution, Gift of the Pearl S. Buck Foundation; **p. 175:** Evergood, Philip, *Her World,* 1948, The Metropolitan Museum of Art, Arthur Hoppock Hearn Fund, 1950. Copyright © 1986 by The Metropolitan Museum of Art; **p. 214:** *Parade Curtain After Picasso,* 1980, oil on canvas, 48 × 60", © David Hockney, 1980; **p. 220:** Pennies for the Pedestal, *The World,* April 3, 1885, courtesy of the New York Historical Society, New York City; **p. 226:** *Wake of the Ferry II,* 1907, Joan Sloan, The Phillips Collection, Washington, D.C.; **p. 229:** *The Unveiling of the Statue of Liberty,* 1880, Edward Moran, Museum of the City of New York; **p. 232:** *Sir Arthur Conan Doyle* (detail), 1927, H. L. Gates, National Portrait Gallery, London; **p. 308:** *Reclining Woman,* 1952, John Robinson, Private Collection, Courtesy of the artist; **p. 317:** Johnson, Malvin Gray, *Self Portrait,* 1934, National Museum of American Art, Smithsonian Institution, Gift of the Harmon Foundation; **p. 349:** Fairfield Porter, *Iced Coffee,* Courtesy Private Collection, Brookline, Massachusetts; **pp. 364, 365, 366:** Copyright © 1933, 1961, James Thurber, from *My Life and Hard Times,* published by Harper & Row; **p. 376:** van Gogh, Vincent, *The Starry Night* (1889), oil on canvas, 29 × 36¼", Collection, The Museum of Modern Art, New York, Acquired through the Lillie P. Bliss Bequest; **p. 378:** Delaunay, Robert, *Simultaneous Contrasts: Sun and Moon* (1913. Dated on painting 1912), oil on canvas, 53" diameter, Collection, The Museum of Modern Art, New York, Mrs. Simon Guggenheim Fund; **p. 382:** *Girl Writing,* 1941, Milton Avery, The Phillips Collection, Washington, D.C.; **p. 385:** Lawrence, Jacob, *The Library,* 1960, National Museum of American Art, Smithsonian Institution, Gift of S. D. Johnson & Son, Inc.; **p. 391:** Victor Vasarely, *Reytey,* 1968, Collection, Solomon R. Guggenheim Museum, New York, Photo: Carmelo

Guadagno; **p. 396:** Homer, Winslow, *Prisoners from the Front,* The Metropolitan Museum of Art, Gift of Mrs. Frank B. Porter, 1922 (22.207), Copyright © 1980 by the Metropolitan Museum of Art; **p. 398:** Homer, Winslow, *The Gulf Stream,* Copyright © 1980 by the Metropolitan Museum of Art, The Metropolitan Museum of Art, Wolfe Fund, 1906; Catherine Lorillard Wolfe Collection; **p. 402:** Stuart Davis, *Owh! in San Pao,* 1951, oil on canvas, 52¼ × 41¾″, Collection of Whitney Museum of American Art, Purchase, Acq. #52.2; **p. 404:** Stuart Davis, *The Paris Bit,* 1959, oil on canvas, 46 × 60″, Collection of Whitney Museum of American Art, Purchase, with funds from the Friends of the Whitney Museum of American Art, Acq. #59.38; **p. 410:** *Mari Sandoz* (detail) by Louise Austen, University Archives, Love Library, University of Nebraska; **p. 412:** Catlin, George, *Chee-A-Ka-Tchee, Wife of Not-To-Way,* 1835–1836, National Museum of American Art, Smithsonian Institution, Gift of Mrs. Joseph Harrison, Jr.; **p. 415:** *Sioux Encampment,* Jules Tavernier, c. 1874–1884, oil on canvas, 171.5 × 99 cm, The Oakland Museum, Oakland, CA, The Kahn Collection, Laurie Platt Winfrey, Inc.; **p. 428:** *Springtime Fantasy,* Adolphe Faugeron, Three Lions; **p. 433:** *Henry Wadsworth Longfellow* (detail), Thomas B. Read, National Portrait Gallery, Smithsonian Institution; **p. 435:** *The Boy,* Thomas Hart Benton, Three Lions; **p. 455:** MacDonald, J. E. H., *Belgium,* 1915, oil on cardboard, 52.7 × 74.9 cm (20¾″ × 29½″), Art Gallery of Ontario, Toronto, Purchase, 1963, 62/21, Photo, Larry Ostrom, Art Gallery of Ontario; **p. 451:** *Waterfall No. III, Iao Valley,* Georgia O'Keeffe, 1939, Art Resource; **p. 462:** *Carl Sandburg* (detail), 1951, Emerson C. Burkhart, National Portrait Gallery, Smithsonian Institution; **p. 464:** John Newbery, ''Little Goody-Two-Shoes,'' 1766 ed., from *Illustrators of Children's Books, 1744–1945,* by Bertha Mahoney, Boston, Hornbook, 1947, The New York Public Library, Astor, Lenox and Tilden Foundations; **p. 467:** *Ring-Necked Pheasant,* 1977, © 1977 Roger Tory Peterson, Courtesy of the artist and Mill Pond Press, Inc., Venice, FL 33495; **p. 476** (detail) and **p. 479:** *Ravens in Moonlight,,* 1882, Gengyo, Omni Photo Communications, © LEA; **p. 481:** *Young Girls at the Piano,* Pierre Auguste Renoir, Joslyn Art Museum, Omaha, Nebraska; **p. 482:** James Stephens (detail), Sir William Rothenstein, The Tate Gallery, London; **p. 486:** *Dominant Curve,* April 1936, Wassily Kandinski, Solomon R. Guggenheim Museum, New York, Photo, David Heald; **p. 489:** *The Buffalo Trail,* 1867–68, Albert Bierstadt, American, 1830–1902, oil on canvas, 32 × 48 in. (81.3 × 122.0 cm), Gift of Mrs. Maxim Karolik for the Karolik Collection of American Paintings, 1815–1865, Courtesy, Museum of Fine Arts, Boston; **p. 490:** *Edna St. Vincent Millay* (detail), 1934, Charles Ellis, National Portrait Gallery, Smithsonian Institution; **p. 493:** *Portrait of Henriette,* Andrew Wyeth, Courtesy of the San Antonio Museum Association, San Antonio, TX; **p. 497:** MacDonald, J. E. H., Canadian, 1873–1932, *Mist Fantasy,* 1922, oil on canvas, 93.7 × 66.7 cm, Art Gallery of Ontario, Toronto, Gift of Mrs. S. J. Williams in memory of F. Elinor Williams, 1927; **p. 498:** *Edward Estlin Cummings* (detail), 1958, Self Portrait, National Portrait Gallery, Smithsonian Institution; **p. 506:** *John Singer Sargent* (detail), James Whitcomb Riley, Indianapolis Museum of Art; **p. 515:** *Snapshot at the Beach,* 1891, 19th Century, Three Lions; **p. 516:** *Langston Hughes* (detail) by Winold Reiss, c. 1925, National Portrait Gallery, Smithsonian Institution, Gift of W. Tjark Reiss in memory of his father, Winold Reiss; **p. 519:** Edmund Archer, *Organdy Collar* (1936), oil on canvas, 19 × 16″, Collection of Whitney Museum of American Art, Purchase, Acq. #38.49; **pp. 525, 526:** *You Are*

Old Father William, 1865, Sir John Tenniel, The Granger Collection 931.11; **p. 531:** *Good Fortune,* René Magritte, Museum Boymans-Van Beuningen, Rotterdam; **p. 538:** *Classical Fable,* © 1986 Thomas McKnight, Chalk & Vermilion; **p. 541:** *Chariot of the Moon,* Frederic E. Church, Courtesy of The Cooper-Hewitt Museum, Smithsonian Institution; **p. 543:** *The Blue Horse,* Franz Marc, Three Lions; **p. 549:** Original art by James Thurber, © 1956 by James Thurber; **p. 555:** *Hector and Andromache,* Giorgio De Chirico, Scala/Art Resource; **p. 576:** *Philemon and Baucis* (detail), 1658, Rembrandt van Rijn, National Gallery of Art, Washington, Widener Collection; **p. 580:** (detail) and **582:** *Landscape with the Fall of Icarus* (detail), Peter Breughel, Scala/Art Resource; **p. 584:** Claude: *Landscape* (detail), *Narcissus,* 1644, The Granger Collection, C. 19; **p. 585:** *Narciso Alla Fonte,* Caravaggio, Scala/Art Resource; **p. 587:** Rousseau, Henri, *The Sleeping Gypsy,* 1897, oil on canvas, 51″ × 6'7″, Collection, The Museum of Modern Art, New York, Gift of Mrs. Simon Guggenheim; **pp. 598** (detail) and **600:** *Erupting Volcano,* 1943, Dr. Atl (Gerardo Murillo), Laurie Platt Winfrey; **p. 603:** *Quetzalcoatl,* from Codex Borbonicus (copy), Mixtec, ca. A.D. 1500, M.N.A.H., Biblioteca, Laurie Platt Winfrey, Inc.; **p. 610:** *Spider,* 1887, Odilon Redon, Lithograph printed in black sheet, 11 × 8-9/16″ (28 × 21.7 cm), Collection, the Museum of Modern Art, New York, Mrs. Bertram Smith Fund; *On the Trail,* Winslow Homer, National Gallery of Art, Washington, Gift of Ruth K. Henschel in memory of her husband, Charles R. Henschel; **p. 627:** *Hunter in the Adirondacks,* 1892 (detail), Winslow Homer, Courtesy of the Harvard University Art Museums (Fogg Art Museum), Anonymous gift

PHOTOGRAPH CREDITS

p. 13: Candice Bauer/Bruce Coleman; **p. 15:** Alan Blank/Bruce Coleman; **p. 19:** D. Lyons/Bruce Coleman; **p. 21:** Norman Morris/Bruce Coleman; **p. 24:** Duane Carr; **p. 26:** Chad Slattery/After Image; **p. 28:** Steven E. Sutton/Duomo; **p. 30:** Ken Karp; **p. 32:** Larry Burrows © Time, Inc., 1959; **p. 36:** AP/Wide World World Photos; **p. 38:** Keith Gunnar/Bruce Coleman; **p. 44:** AP/Wide World Photo; **p. 50:** Patricia M. Hoch; **p. 56:** New York Public Library Picture Collection; **p. 66:** AP/Wide World Photo; **p. 74:** Rollie McKenna; **p. 88:** UPI/Bettmann Newsphotos; **p. 94:** AP/Wide World Photo; **pp. 96–97:** Julie Habel/West Light; **p. 98:** Barbara Hanson; **p. 110:** Burk Uzzle/Archive Pictures; **p. 106:** Thomas Victor; **p. 112:** Godfrey Graham, Little Brown & Co.; **p. 118:** Thomas Victor; **p. 128:** Culver Pictures; **p. 130:** Illinois State Historical Society; **p. 148:** Thomas Victor; **p. 166:** Thomas Victor; **p. 168:** Peter Menzel/Wheeler Pictures; **p. 171:** Ralph Loony/Shostal #401, 518; **p. 172:** Gary Meszaros/Bruce Coleman; **p. 174:** Mark Leighton, UPI/Bettmann News Photos; **p. 178:** Thomas Victor; **p. 208:** UPI/Bettmann News Photos; **p. 218:** Thomas Victor; **p. 246:** International Creative Management; **p. 248:** Frank Wing/Stock Boston; **p. 255:** Jean-Pierre Pieuchot/The Image Bank; **p. 259:** D. Carroll/The Image Bank; **p. 262:** The Granger Collection; **p. 265, 269, 275, 278, 284, 288, 298, 302:** The Guthrie Theatre; **p. 313:** Harvey Lloyd/The Stock Market; **p. 315:** Thomas Victor; **p. 318:** Dave Gannan; **p. 320:** Norman Owen Tomalin/Bruce Coleman; **pp. 324–25:** Ron and Valerie Taylor/Bruce Coleman; **p. 328:** Thomas Victor; **p. 330:** Russell Baker; **p. 333:** Russell Baker; **p. 336:** Mae Galorza; **p. 339:** Rodney Jones; **p. 342:** Courtesy of the author; **pp. 344, 346–47:** Jade Snow-Wong; **p. 350:** John Wyand; **p. 352:** Mike Mazzaschi/Stock Boston; **p. 357:** Louis Panuse/DPI; **p. 362**

UPI/Bettmann News Photo; **p. 368:** AP/Wide World Photo; **p. 369:** M. P. Kahl/Bruce Coleman; **pp. 370–71:** Wendell Metzen/Bruce Coleman; **p. 374:** Thomas Victor; **p. 380:** AP/Wide World Photo; **p. 386:** Thomas Victor; **p. 394:** John Kleinhans; **p. 406:** AP/Wide World Photo; **p. 421:** NASA 68-HC-853; **p. 422:** Bettmann Archives; **p. 436:** New York Public Library Picture Collection; **p. 444:** AP/Wide World Photo; **p. 450:** AP/Wide World Photo; **p. 454:** UPI/Bettmann News Photos; **p. 458:** Dianne Trejo; **p. 462:** (top) New York Public Library Picture Collection; (middle) AP/Wide World Photo; **pp. 468–69:** Andrei Lloyd/The Stock Market; **p. 470:** (top) AP/Wide World; (bottom) Dmitri Kessel, *Life* magazine, © Time, Inc.; **p. 472:** S. C. Bisserot/Bruce Coleman; **p. 474:** Sonja H. Smith; **p. 482:** (middle) John Gannon; (bottom) The Bettmann Archives; **pp. 484–85:** Harald Sund; **p. 495:** Photography, Rod Hansen/Collection of the Yakima Valley Museum and Historical Assoc.; **p. 498:** (bottom) Dmitri Kessel, *Life* magazine © Time, Inc.; **p. 500:** David Herman/Shostal 508–529; **p. 503:** Gordon R. Gainer/Stock Market; **p. 505:** D. S. Henderson/The Image Bank; **p. 506:** (top) AP/Wide World ; **p. 509:** Jerry Simions/Shostal Assoc. 502–945; **p. 513:** David Barnes/Stock Market; **p. 516:** (second down) Courtesy of the Huntington Library; (third down) Granger Collection; (bottom) Mark Leighton/UPI/Bettmann Archives; **p. 524:** New York Public Library Picture Collection; **p. 528:** New York Public Library Picture Collection; **p. 532:** UPI/Bettmann News Photo; **p. 548:** UPI/Bettmann News Photo; **p. 588:** Lois and George Cox/Bruce Coleman; **p. 590:** Bob and Clara Calhoun/Bruce Coleman; **p. 628:** Courtesy Doubleday and Co.

ILLUSTRATION CREDITS

pp: 46, 51, 52 ,57, 60, 63, 67, 72, 80, 84, 151, 156, 161, 181, 184, 186, 192, 196, 197, 202, 234, 241, 432, 438-39, 441, 448, 522, 545, 553, 557, 559, 563, 567, 572, 595, 608, 617-18, 630-31, 639, 648, 655, 661, 669, 677, 684, 689, 694, 703, 709, 716-17, 726-27, 735, 743, 750, 754-55, 765: The Art Source